CANADIAN
OXFORD
WORLD
ATLAS

4TH EDITION

QUENTIN H. STANFORD
GENERAL EDITOR

OXFORD
UNIVERSITY PRESS

2 Contents

Understanding topographic maps 4
Map Projections 5
Latitude, longitude, and scale 6
Direction and satellite imagery 7

Maps that show general features of regions, countries or continents are called **topographic maps.** These maps are shown with a light band of colour in the contents list.

For example:

Central Canada

Canada

Canada 8·9
Pleistocene glaciation 9
Relief profile 9
Geology 10
Glacial effect on landforms 10
Landforms 11
Wetlands 11
Climate: 12·15
    Isotherms 12
    Temperature range 12
    Heating the Earth 12
    Mean annual precipitation 13
    Mean annual snowfall 13
    Thunderstorms/tornadoes 13
    Air masses and winds 13
    Contribution of
      greenhouse gases
      to global warming 13
    January wind chill 14
    Growing season 14
    Humidex
      (effective temperature) 14
    Sunshine 14
    Canadian weather records 14
    Climate regions 15
    Climate graphs 15
Natural vegetation, forestry 16
Ecozones 17
Fishing: 17
    Pacific Coast 17
    Atlantic Coast 17
Soils and agriculture 18
Soil capability by province 18
Agriculture: 19
    Agricultural lands 19
    Wheat production
      and export 19
Endangered species
    and protected land 20
Water resources, electrical power 21
Great Lakes pollution 21
Electricity trade 21
Nonfuel minerals 22
Mineral reserves 22
Fuel minerals 23
Petroleum transfers/production
    and consumption 23
Manufacturing (value added) 24
Trade 25
Population distribution, 1996 26
Population distribution, 1901 26
Census Metropolitan Areas 26
First language/cultural origin 27
Migration 27
Population by age and sex 27
Native peoples 28
Eastern exploration 29
Arctic and Western exploration 30
Territorial evolution 1667-1912 31
Political divisions 32·33
Area of land and water 32
Distance chart 33

A map of the whole of Canada can be found on pages 8 and 9

British Columbia 34·35
Southwestern BC 34
Western Canada satellite images 36
Alberta 37
Saskatchewan 38
Manitoba 39
Ontario 40·41
Central Canada 42·43
The St. Lawrence Seaway 43
Central Ontario 44
Eastern Canada satellite images 45
Québec 46·47
Atlantic provinces 48·49
Nova Scotia and
    Prince Edward Island 49

Northern Canada
Vancouver; Toronto
Montréal; Ottawa; Halifax
Edmonton; Calgary; Winnipeg

North America

Physical relief
Political
Population and communications
Build/mineral deposits
Land use, energy, minerals, ind
Climate

United States of America
USA political
Northeast USA
New York
California
Mexico, Central America,
    and the Caribbean
Trinidad
Barbados
Jamaica

Contents 3

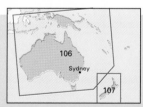

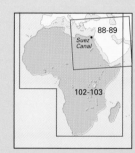
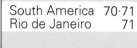

4 Understanding Topographic Maps

Topographic maps (physical-political) show the main features of the physical and human landscape. There are small differences in the symbols and colours used for the maps of Canada and those for the rest of the World.

Canadian Maps

Boundaries

international

province, territory

region, county, district, regional municipality

national park/ provincial park

Communications

expressway/other multilane highway

other highway

winter road

railway

canal

⊕ major airport

✈ other airport

Cities and towns

◁ built-up areas

■ over 1 million inhabitants

● more than 100 000 inhabitants

• smaller urban places

+ historic sites

Physical features

marsh

ice cap

Scale 1:5 000 000

0   50   100 km

Scale is shown by a representative fraction and a scale line.

Non-Canadian maps

Boundaries

international

disputed

internal

national park

Communications

expressway

other major road

track

railway

canal

✈ major airport

Cities and towns

◁ built-up areas

■ over 1 million inhabitants

● more than 100 000 inhabitants

• smaller towns

+ historic sites

Physical features

seasonal river/lake

marsh

salt pan

ice cap

sand dunes

coral reef

Place names
Local spellings are used. Anglicised and other common spellings are shown in brackets.

e.g. **Roma** (Rome)

This atlas has been designed for English speaking readers and so all places have been named using the Roman alphabet. Compare this extract of the map of Southern Asia with the same map printed in Bengali.

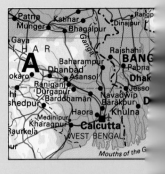

Type style
Contrasting type styles are used to show the difference between physical features, settlements, and administrative areas. Physical features (except for peaks) are shown in italics.

e.g. *Hautes Fagnes*   *Maas*

Peaks are shown in condensed type.

e.g. Hohe Acht 746

Settlement names are shown in upper and lower case.

e.g. Valkenswaard

Administrative areas are shown in capital letters.

e.g. LIÈGE

The importance of places is shown by the size of the type and whether the type face is **bold,** medium or light.

e.g. Malmédy   Bergheim   Duisburg

Land height
Colours on topographic maps refer only to the height of the land. They do not give information about land use or other aspects of the environment.

Sea ice
White stipple patterns over the sea colour show the seasonal extent of sea ice.

Sea Ice

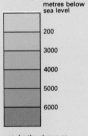

unnavigable

pack ice - average fall minimum

pack ice - average spring max.

Sea depth

metres below sea level

200

3000

4000

5000

6000

sea depths shown as minus numbers

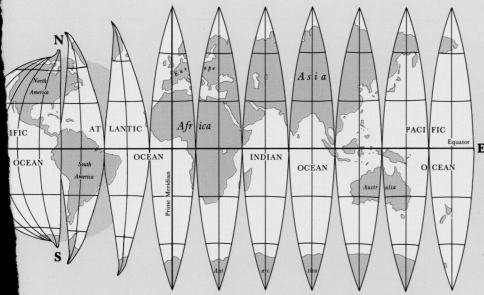

The most accurate way of looking at the earth's land and sea areas is to use a globe. For obvious reasons maps are more convenient to use than globes. One method of changing the surface of the globe into a map is to unpeel strips or gores from the globe's surface, but such a method has obvious drawbacks. Since it is impossible to flatten the curved surface of the earth without stretching or cutting part of it, it is necessary to employ other methods in order to produce an orderly system of parallels and meridians on which a map can be drawn. Such systems are referred to as **map projections**.

There are two main types of projections: **equal area projections,** where the area of any territory is shown in correct size proportion to other areas, and **conformal projections,** where the emphasis is on showing shape correctly. No map can be both equal area and conformal, though some projections are designed to minimize distortions in both area and shape.

Oblique Aitoff projection
... area. The arrangement ... nd masses allows a ... iew of routes in the ... ern hemisphere. The ... ion of North America and ... on either side of the ... ic is shown clearly.

Mercator's projection is a conformal projection and was initially designed (1569) to be used for navigation. Any straight line on the map is a line of constant compass bearing. Straight lines are not the shortest routes, however. Shape is accurate on a Mercator projection but the size of the land masses is distorted. Land is shown larger the further away it is from the equator. (For example, Alaska is shown four times larger than its actual size.)

——— Line of constant compass bearing

- - - - Shortest route

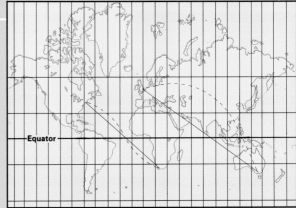

Navigation Chart. Mercator's projection.

Peters' projection is an equal area projection. The land masses are the correct size in relation to each other, but there is considerable distortion in shape. This projection has been used to emphasize the size of the poor countries of the South compared with the rich countries of the North.

——— Brandt Line

▨ Rich North

▨ Poor South.

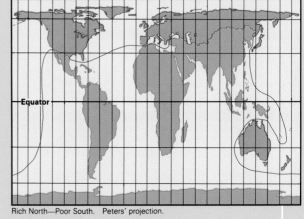

Rich North—Poor South. Peters' projection.

Gall's projection
compromises between equal area and conformal. A modified version is used in this atlas as a general world map. This map shows states which have gained their independence since 1945.

▨ States independent since 1945.

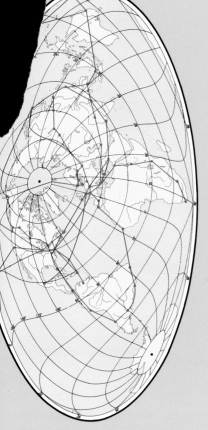

Major air routes. Oblique Aitoff projection.

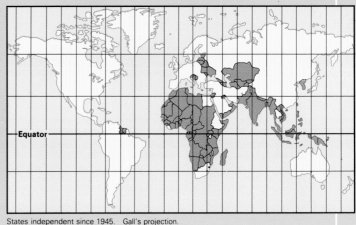

States independent since 1945. Gall's projection.

6 Latitude, Longitude, and Scale

The Earth is a small, blue planet.
Seen from space it has no right way up.

Latitude
Parallels of latitude are concentric circles that diminish in diameter from the Equator to the Poles. They are used to determine locations either north or south in relation to the Equator. North of the Equator parallels are designated north (N), while those south of the Equator are labelled south (S). The Equator is at latitude 0°. The Poles are at latitudes 90°N and 90°S.

Longitude
Meridians of longitude pass through both Poles intersecting all parallels of latitude at right angles. The meridian through Greenwich, England was chosen in 1884 as the Prime Meridian and given the value 0°. Meridians determine locations east (E) or west (W) of the Prime Meridian. The 180° meridian of longitude was designated the International Date Line and has a special role in the operation of Standard Time.

The Equator divides the E into halves : the Northern Hemisphere and the Sou Hemisphere. The Prime Meridian and the 180° m together also divide the into halves : the Wester Hemisphere and the Ea Hemisphere.

An imaginary grid is used to pinpoint the position of any place on Earth.
The grid consists of two sets of lines. Those running east and west are called parallels of latitude and those extending north and south are called meridians of longitude. Both are measured in degrees.

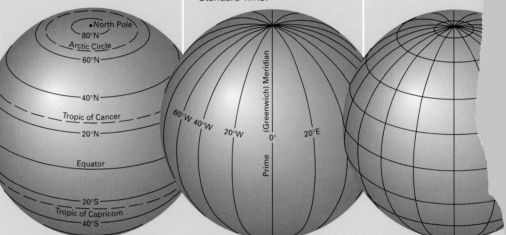

Scale
Maps or globes are devices used to represent all or part of the surface of the Earth. Every map has a scale to indicate how much the area on the map has been reduced from its actual size on the Earth's surface. Thus the map scale indicates the proportion (or ratio) between a distance on a map and the corresponding distance on the Earth's surface.

Scale can be shown in three ways :

| The scale statement | 1 cm to 5 km | which means 1 centimetre on the map represents five kilometres on the Earth's surface. |

| The representative fraction (RF) | 1 : 500 000 | which means 1 centimetre on the map represents 500 000 centimetres on the Earth's surface, or one of any unit of measurement represents 500 000 of the same units. |

The linear scale   0   5   10   15 km

When used together, lines latitude and longitude form The position of places on surface of the Earth can i located accurately using

To locate places really acc each degree of latitude an longitude can be divided in 60 minutes and each minut into 60 seconds. A location specified in degrees, minute and seconds (for example, 44° 25' 14" N, 80° 45' 36" W) will describe a location accurat. to within a few metres.

It is important to understand the **relationship between scale and area**. In this atlas Canada is shown mainly on maps that have a larger scale than the rest of the World.

For example:
All of northern Africa appears on two pages at a scale of 1: 19 000 000, while British Columbia, also on two pages, has a scale of 1: 5 000 000. We know from the scale that the African map shows a greater area, but how much greater?

The table shows that as the scale doubles, the area it represents increases four times. Thus a square centimetre on the Africa map represents an area more than fourteen times larger than a square centimetre on the British Columbia map.

Scale	Scale statement	Area of 1 km²
1: 10 000	1 cm to 0.1 km	0.01 km²
1: 20 000	1 cm to 0.2 km	0.04 km²
1: 100 000	1 cm to 1 km	1 km²
1: 200 000	1 cm to 2 km	4 km²
1: 5 000 000	1 cm to 50 km	2500 km²
1: 10 000 000	1 cm to 100 km	10 000 km²
1: 20 000 000	1 cm to 200 km	40 000 km²

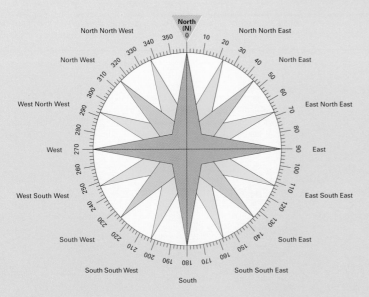

Direction

The magnetic compass is the most common way of determining direction.

A direction can be expressed either in terms of north, east, south, and west and various intermediate positions as shown on the diagram of the compass rose, or in degrees as a bearing. Direction by bearing ranges from 0° (north) to 359° (one degree west of north).

In the atlas, the cardinal points (north, east, south, and west) can be determined from the parallels and meridians. Thus all parallels run north and south, and meridians east and west. Intermediate directions require the application of the compass rose or the use of bearings. Direction using bearings can be accomplished using a protractor.

Satellite imagery

Satellite images are found on a number of pages throughout this atlas. These images are taken by satellites orbiting the Earth at high altitudes. For example, most of the images in this atlas were produced by Landsat satellites which orbit the Earth 14.5 times each day at an altitude of approximately 900 km. As a satellite travels, it is continuously scanning an area 185 km wide. In order to be visible, objects on the Earth must be at least 30 m^2 in size.

Most cameras are sensors that operate only in the "visible" part of the electromagnetic spectrum and thus produce a record of what the eye can see. The images that are normally described as satellite images are produced by instruments that use a multi spectral scanning system to record reflected energy from different parts of the electromagnetic spectrum from microwaves, through infrared, and visible light to the near ultraviolet sections. The scanner sends the radiation received in specifically designated bands to a set of detectors on the satellite. The signal is digitized and then transmitted back to Earth. It is then transformed into images such as the ones shown in this atlas.

The various objects that make up the Earth's surface such as rocks, soil, vegetation, crops, and building materials such as concrete or asphalt absorb and reflect radiation differently (each has its own spectral signature) and so can be easily recognized on satellite images. Even within any surface category there are different spectral signatures; thus, one crop can be distinguished from another and different types of wetland can be recognized. Because these surfaces reflect one part of the electromagnetic spectrum better than others, the colours we see on the images are false colours. For example, green vegetation reflects better in the red than the blue-green, urban areas are blue-grey, and bare soil will show as black to green to white depending on its moisture, and organic content.

Satellite image of the area around Winnipeg, Manitoba.

0   15   30 km

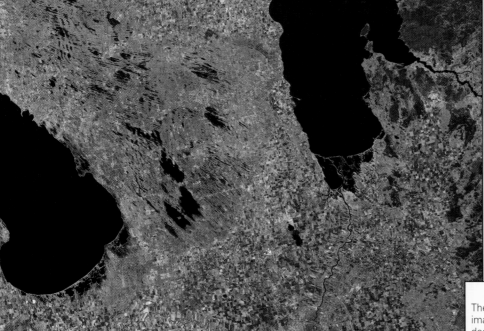

The number of uses that have been developed for satellite imagery is very great and beyond the scope of this brief description. Some of the non-military applications include : weather prediction, land-use planning, crop and forest inventories, changes in sea ice, surveillance of fishing fleets, and monitoring air pollution.
New uses are continually being found.

© Oxford University Press
LANDSAT data received by the Canada Centre for Remote Sensing.
Provided courtesy of RADARSAT International.

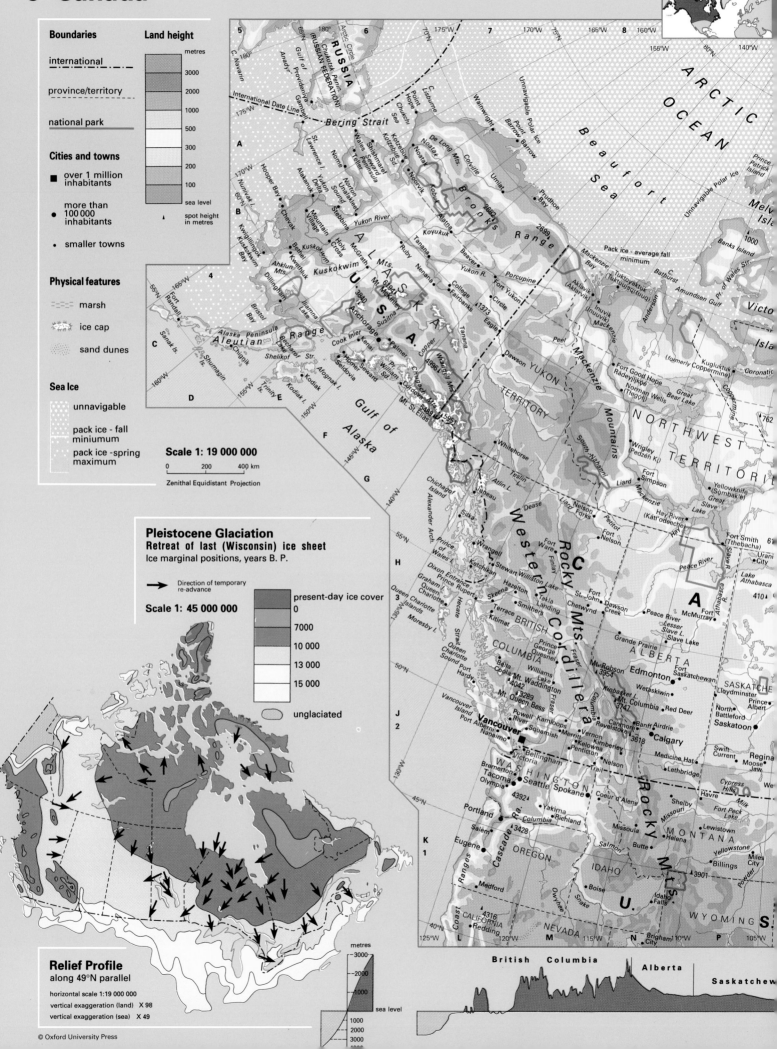

Canada

Land Area: 9 215 430km²
Total Area: 9 970 610km²

Census Population

1871	3 689 257
1891	4 833 239
1911	7 206 643
1931	10 376 786
1951	14 009 429
1961	18 238 247
1971	21 568 310
1981	24 343 181
1991	27 296 859
1996	28 846 761
Urban	77.9%
Rural	22.1%

Census Metropolitan Areas, 1996 (over 500 000)

Toronto	4 263 757
Montréal	3 326 510
Vancouver	1 831 665
Ottawa-Hull	1 010 498
Edmonton	862 597
Calgary	821 628
Quebec	671 889
Winnipeg	667 209
Hamilton	624 360

Gross Domestic Product
(1995 $542.3 billion)

goods producing	%
Agriculture	2.1
Logging	0.5
Fishing & Trapping	0.2
Mining	4.4
Manufacturing	18.9
Construction	5.1
Other Utilities	3.1
service producing	%
Transport & Communications	8.7
Wholesale & Retail	12.2
Finance, Insurance, & Real Estate	15.8
Services	22.4
Government Services	6.0

Glacial effect on landforms

- existing glaciers
- areas of glacial erosion and deposition
- generally unglaciated areas
- areas once covered by seas
- areas once covered by lakes

international ----
province/territory ----

Scale 1:90 000 000
Zenithal Equidistant Projection

ice cap

Cenozoic

- 1 — Pleistocene and Recent — Alluvium, glacial drift. (All Canada was affected by Pleistocene glaciation).
  - Paleocene, Eocene, Oligocene — Sedimentary rocks (sandstone, shale, conglomerate, coal measures).
- T — Tertiary — Volcanic rocks (basalt, andesite) associated with sedimentary rocks (sandstone, shale, conglomerate, coal measures).

Mesozoic

- K — Cretaceous — Mainly sedimentary rocks (sandstone, shale, conglomerate), oil and natural gas, coal, tar sand, bentonite.
- J — Jurassic — Sedimentary and volcanic rocks (argillite, greywacke, sandstone, andesite, volcanic breccia, tuff), oil.
- T̅R̅ — Triassic — Sedimentary and volcanic rocks (argillite, quartzite, limestone, andesite, volcanic breccia, tuff), may include oil and natural gas.
- 2 — undivided

Paleozoic

- C — Carboniferous and Permian — Mainly sedimentary rocks (sandstone, limestone, shale, conglomerate), some volcanic rocks; coal measures, oil and natural gas, gypsum.
- D — Devonian — Sedimentary and volcanic rocks (shale, limestone, dolomite, conglomerate, sandstone; volcanic rocks), salt; oil and natural gas.
- S — Silurian — Mainly sedimentary rocks (sandstone, shale, limestone, conglomerate, dolomite), some volcanic rocks; gypsum, salt; oil and natural gas.
- O — Ordovician — Sedimentary rocks (limestone, dolomite, shale, argillite, sandstone, quartzite, grit); oil and natural gas.
- Є — Cambrian — Sedimentary rocks (dolomite, limestone, shale, chert, quartzite, sandstone, conglomerate).
- 3 — undivided

Pre Cambrian

- 4 — Proterozoic — Mainly sedimentary and volcanic rocks and derived metamorphic rocks (shale, argillite, slate, chert, limestone, dolomite, sandstone, quartzite, arkose, greywacke, conglomerate; schists, gneiss, greenstone, andesite, basalt, trachyte; tuff, volcanic breccia; iron formation).
- 5 — Archean — Mainly sedimentary and derived metamorphic rocks (argillite, slate, arkose, quartzite, greywacke, conglomerate, sedimentary gneiss and schist). Associated with areas mainly volcanic and derived metamorphic rocks (andesite, dacite, basalt; rhyolite, trachyte, volcanic breccia and tuff; greenstone schist, hornblende gneiss; iron formation).

Intrusive rocks

Paleozoic, Mesozoic and Cenozoic
- A — Mainly acid rocks (granodiorite, quartz monzonite, quartz diorite, granite, syenite). Some areas of basic and ultrabasic rocks (gabbro, pyroxenite, serpentine).

Pre Cambrian (Proterozoic and Archean)
- B — Mainly acid rocks (granodiorite, granite, quartz diorite, granite gneiss), including some granitized sedimentary and volcanic rock. Some areas of basic and ultrabasic rocks (anorthosite, gabbro, diabase sills and dykes).

Earthquakes
- · with a magnitude greater than 5.5 on the Richter scale

Boundaries
- international ---·---

Scale 1:24 000 000
Zenithal Equidistant Projection

Geological time scale (to nearest million years)

present	63	135	180	230	345	405 425	500	600	over 4.4 billion
Pleistocene and Recent	Cretaceous	Jurassic	Triassic	Carboniferous and Permian	Devonian	Silurian	Ordovician	Cambrian	Pre Cambrian

Paleocene, Eocene, Oligocene, Tertiary

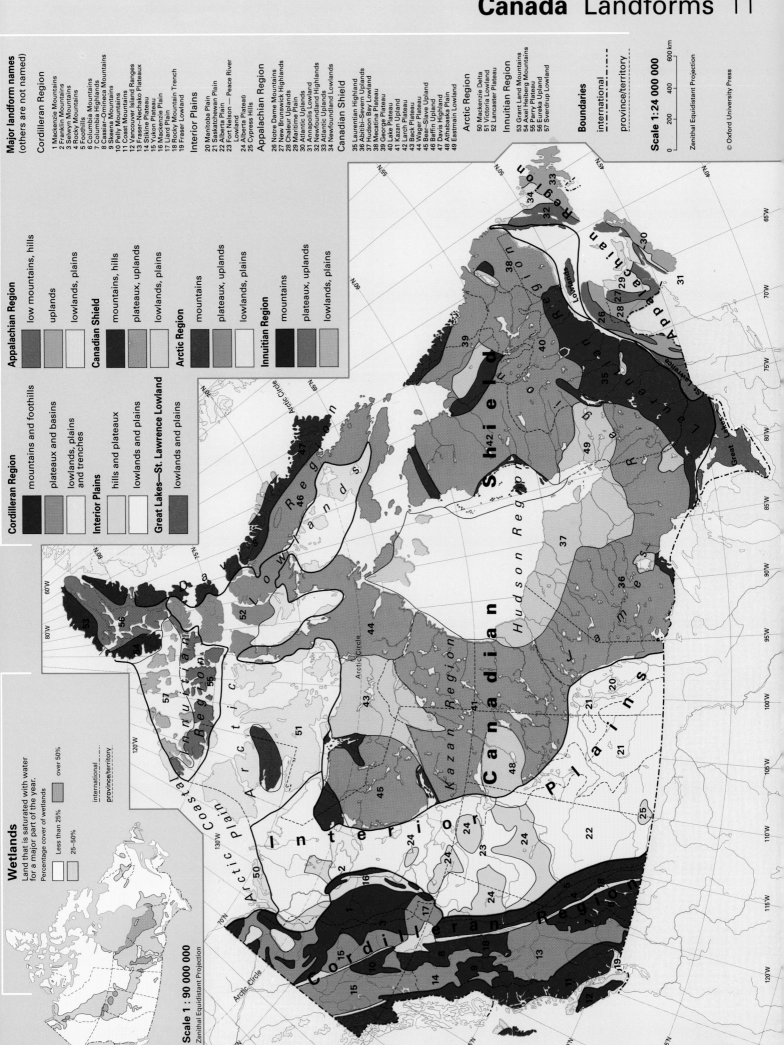

Major landform names
(others are not named)

Cordilleran Region
1 Mackenzie Mountains
2 Franklin Mountains
3 Selwyn Mountains
4 Rocky Mountains
5 Foothills
6 Columbia Mountains
7 Columbia Highlands
8 Cassiar–Omineca Mountains
9 Skeena Mountains
10 Pelly Mountains
11 Coast Mountains
12 Vancouver Island Ranges
13 Fraser–Nechako Plateaux
14 Stikine Plateau
15 Yukon Plateau
16 Mackenzie Plain
17 Liard Plain
18 Rocky Mountain Trench
19 Fraser Lowland

Interior Plains
20 Manitoba Plain
21 Saskatchewan Plain
22 Alberta Plain
23 Fort Nelson — Peace River
   Lowland
24 Alberta Plateau
25 Cypress Hills

Appalachian Region
26 Notre Dame Mountains
27 New Brunswick Highlands
28 Chaleur Uplands
29 Maritime Plain
30 Atlantic Uplands
31 Annapolis Lowland
32 Newfoundland Highlands
33 Atlantic Uplands
34 Newfoundland Lowlands

Canadian Shield
35 Laurentian Highland
36 Abitibi–Severn Uplands
37 Hudson Bay Lowland
38 Mecatina Plateau
39 George Plateau
40 Lake Plateau
41 Kazan Plateau
42 Larch Plateau
43 Back Plateau
44 Wager Plateau
45 Bear–Slave Upland
46 Baffin Upland
47 Davis Highland
48 Athabaska Plain
49 Eastmain Lowland

Arctic Region
50 Mackenzie Delta
51 Victoria Lowland
52 Lancaster Plateau

Innuitian Region
53 Grant Land Mountains
54 Axel Heiberg Mountains
55 Parry Plateau
56 Eureka Upland
57 Sverdrup Lowland

Boundaries
international -·-·-·-
province/territory ----

Scale 1:24 000 000
0 200 400 600 km

Zenithal Equidistant Projection

© Oxford University Press

Cordilleran Region
mountains and foothills
plateaux and basins
lowlands, plains and trenches

Interior Plains
hills and plateaux
lowlands and plains

Great Lakes–St. Lawrence Lowland
lowlands and plains

Appalachian Region
low mountains, hills
uplands
lowlands, plains

Canadian Shield
mountains, hills
plateaux, uplands
lowlands, plains

Arctic Region
mountains
plateaux, uplands
lowlands, plains

Innuitian Region
mountains
plateaux, uplands
lowlands, plains

Wetlands
Land that is saturated with water
for a major part of the year.
Percentage cover of wetlands

Less than 25%
25–50%
over 50%

international ----
province/territory ----

Scale 1 : 90 000 000
Zenithal Equidistant Projection

Heating the Earth
The Greenhouse Effect

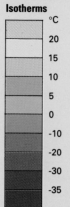

Incoming Solar Radiation

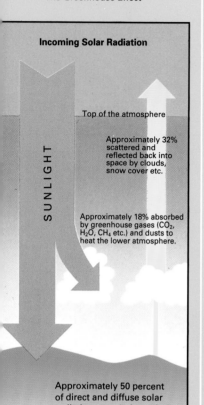

Top of the atmosphere

Approximately 32% scattered and reflected back into space by clouds, snow cover etc.

Approximately 18% absorbed by greenhouse gases (CO_2, H_2O, CH_4 etc.) and dusts to heat the lower atmosphere.

Approximately 50 percent of direct and diffuse solar radiation passes through the atmosphere to heat the Earth

Outgoing Earth Radiation

Top of the atmosphere

Eventually all heat energy received is lost to space

Earth radiation window

Radiation from land and water (also latent heat of condensation and conduction) absorbed by greenhouse gases* (CO_2, H_2O, CH_4 etc.) and dusts to heat the lower atmosphere.

Counter radiation

Absorbed solar radiation converts to heat (warms the air, evaporates water, melts snow and ice) used in photosynthesis, is released into the atmosphere and ultimately is lost to space

Global warming is occurring because additions to greenhouse gases (see p126) resulting from human activity.

Temperature
Isotherms

°C
- 20
- 15
- 10
- 5
- 0
- -10
- -20
- -30
- -35

Permafrost

The state of the ground (soil or rock) that remains below 0°C for more than a year

approximate southern limit of:

— continuous permafrost 90-100% underlain by permafrost

- - - discontinuous permafrost 10-90% underlain by permafrost

data for Alaska not available

Growing degree days

Number of degrees above 5°C added together for all the days of the growing season

— 1000
— 1500
---- 2000

Boundaries

international

province/territory

Scale 1: 44 000 000

0   500 km

Further information on this topic is located in the Canada Statistics section which begins on page 185.

Temperature range

The difference between the average daily mean temperature in January and July

- 0°C
- 10
- 20
- 30
- 40
- 50

Boundaries

international

province/territory

Scale 1: 44 000 000

0   500 km

Zenithal Equidistant Projection

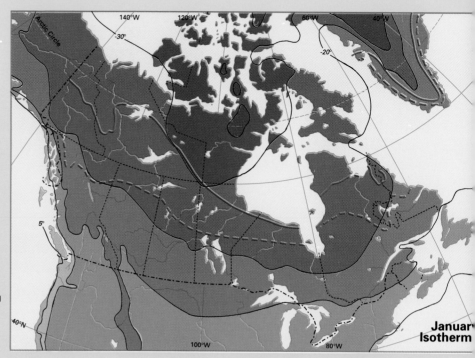

January Isotherms

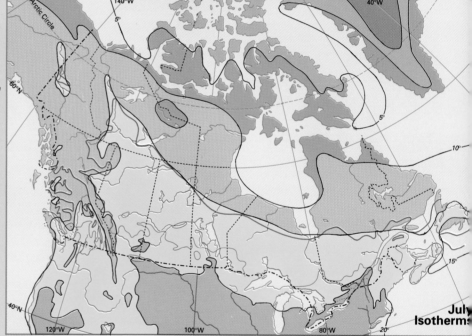

July Isotherms

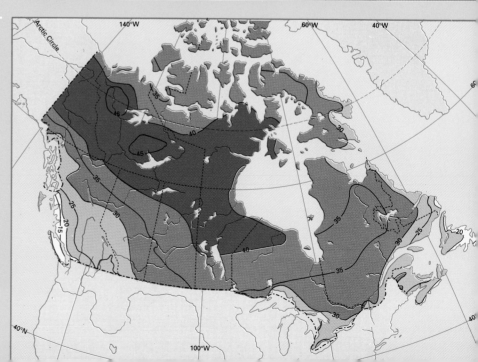

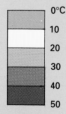

Mean annual precipitation

mm

- over 2000
- 1000-2000
- 600-1000
- 400-600
- 200-400
- under 200

Boundaries

international

province/
territory

Scale 1: 44 000 000

0   500 km

Mean annual snowfall

cm

- more than 400
- 300-400
- 200-300
- 100-200
- less than 100

Boundaries

international

province/
territory

Scale 1: 44 000 000

0   500 km

Thunderstorms

Average annual number of days with thunderstorms

- 5
- 10
- 20

Tornadoes

Average annual frequency of tornadoes per 10 000 km²

- more than 2.0
- 1.2-2.0
- 0.8-1.2

Scale 1: 44 000 000

0   500 km

Zenithal Equidistant Projection

Winter

maritime arctic

Aleutian Low L

maritime polar

continental arctic

Icelandic Low L

maritime arctic

maritime polar

North Pacific High H

maritime tropical

maritime tropical

Azores-Bermuda High H

Summer

maritime polar

maritime arctic

maritime polar

North Pacific High H

maritime tropical

maritime tropical

Azores-Bermuda High H

Air masses and winds

→ prevailing winds

▸▸ polar jet stream (average position)

H high
L low } semi-permanent pressure

Scale 1: 108 000 000

Oblique Mercator Projection

Relative contribution of greenhouse gases to global warming during the past decade

| carbon dioxide 55% | CFC's 11 and 12 17% | methane 14.5% | other CFC's 7% | nitrous oxide 6.5% |

In 1991 Canada ranked third amongst all the countries of the world (after Iraq and the USA) in per capita greenhouse gas emissions.

© Oxford University Press

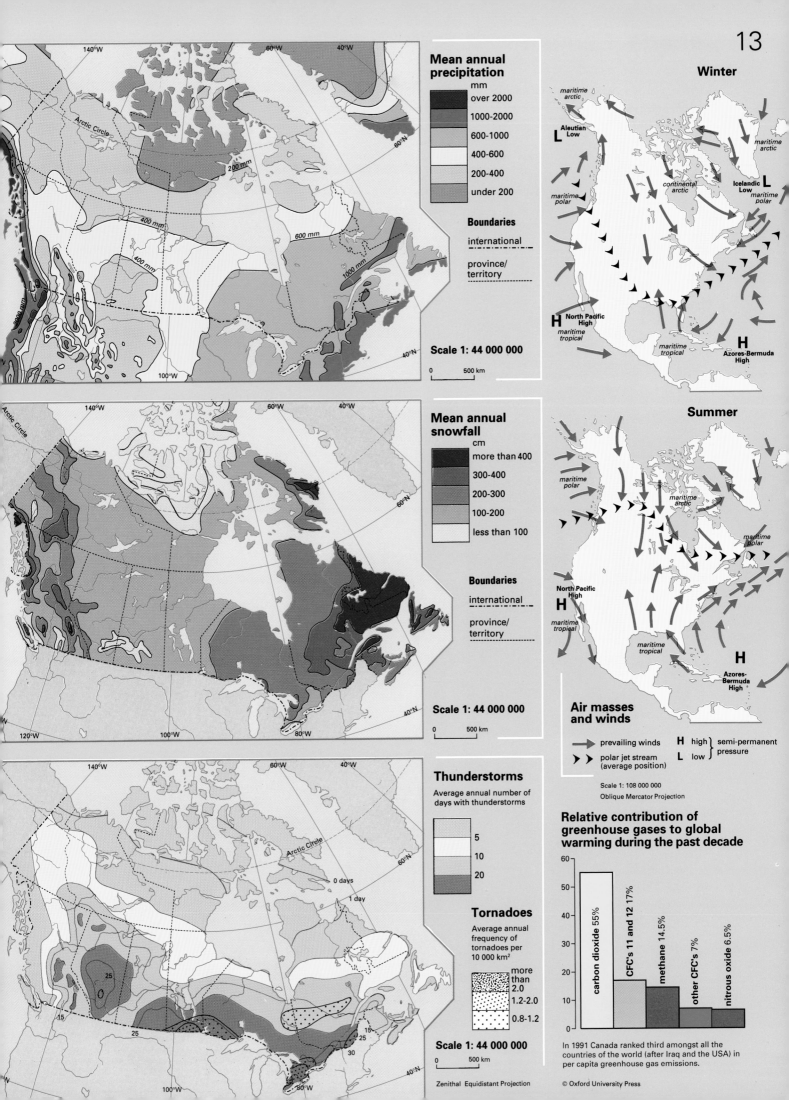

Wind Chill

a measure of the wind's cooling effect, as felt on exposed flesh, expressed either as the **wind chill equivalent temperature** (in °C) or as **heat loss** (in watts/m²)

Wind chill equivalent temperature

referenced to a base wind speed of 8 km per hour

Temperature (°C)	wind speed in km per hour					
	10	**20**	**30**	**40**	**50**	**60**
5	4	-2	-5	-7	-8	-9
0	-2	-8	-11	-14	-16	-17
-5	-7	-14	-18	-21	-23	-24
-10	-12	-20	-25	-28	-30	-32
-15	-18	-26	-32	-35	-38	-39
-20	-23	-32	-38	-42	-45	-47
-25	-28	-39	-45	-49	-52	-54
-30	-33	-45	-52	-56	-60	-62
-35	-39	-51	-59	-64	-67	-69
-40	-44	-57	-65	-71	-74	-77

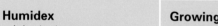

Humidex

an index showing temperature measures that allow for the added stress that results from high humidities - referred to as **effective temperature**

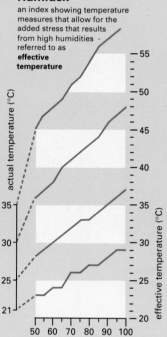

actual temperature (°C)

effective temperature (°C)

humidity (%)

Canadian weather records

highest air temperature	45°C Midale and Yellow Grass, Sask. July 5, 1937
lowest air temperature	-63°C Snag, Y.T. February 3, 1947
coldest month	-47.9°C Eureka, N.W.T February, 1979
highest sea-level pressure	107.96 kPa Dawson, Y.T. February 2, 1989
lowest sea-level pressure	94.02 kPa St.Anthony, New foundland January 20, 1977
greatest precipitation in 24 hours	489.2 mm Ucluelet Brynnor Mines, B.C. October 6, 1967
greatest precipitation in one month	2235.5 mm Swanson Bay, B.C. November 1917
greatest precipitation in one year	8122.6 mm Henderson Lake, B.C. 1931
greatest average annual precipitation	6655 mm Henderson Lake, B.C.
least annual precipitation	12,7 mm Arctic Bay, N.W.T. 1949
highest average annual number of thunderstorm days	34 days London, Ontario

January wind chill

The values on the map indicate the maximum wind chill; there is a 5% chance of having a wind chill value worse than the value shown

Wind chill equivalent temperature

°C	heat loss watts /m²
-70	2755
-60	2488
-50	2220
-40	1953
-30	1685
-20	1418

Boundaries

international

province/territory

Scale 1: 44 000 000

0   500   1000 km

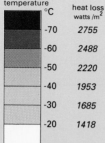

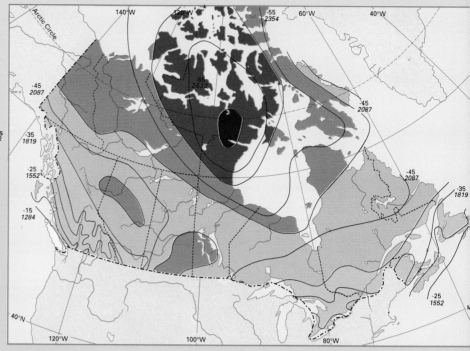

Growing season

Average number of days with an average temperature over 5 °C

	days
	under 60
	60-100
	100-140
	140-180
	180-220
	220-260
	over 260

Boundaries

international

province/territory

Scale 1: 44 000 000

0   500   1000 km

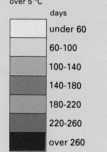

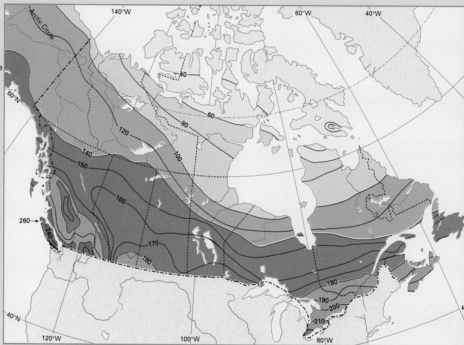

Sunshine

Average annual hours

	1200
	1600
	2000

253   number of days with some sun

Boundaries

international

province/territory

Scale 1: 44 000 000

0   500   1000 km

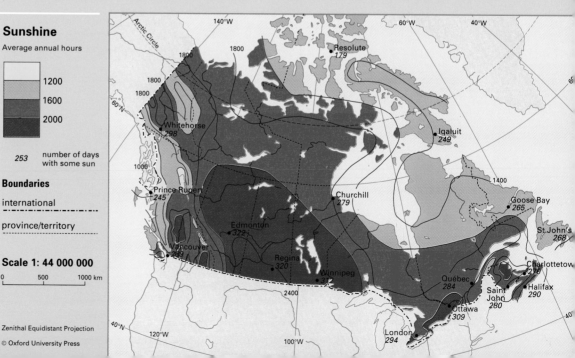

Zenithal Equidistant Projection

© Oxford University Press

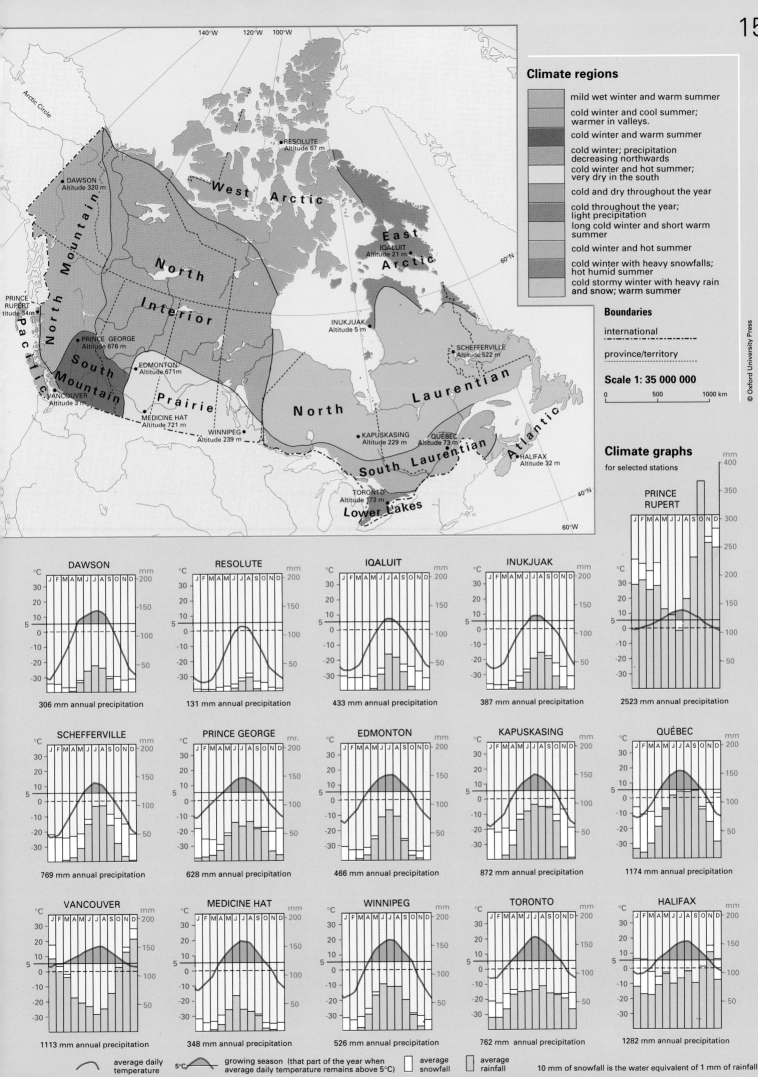

Climate regions

- mild wet winter and warm summer
- cold winter and cool summer; warmer in valleys.
- cold winter and warm summer
- cold winter; precipitation decreasing northwards
- cold winter and hot summer; very dry in the south
- cold and dry throughout the year
- cold throughout the year; light precipitation
- long cold winter and short warm summer
- cold winter and hot summer
- cold winter with heavy snowfalls; hot humid summer
- cold stormy winter with heavy rain and snow; warm summer

Boundaries

international

province/territory

Scale 1: 35 000 000

0   500   1000 km

© Oxford University Press

Climate graphs

for selected stations

DAWSON — 306 mm annual precipitation

RESOLUTE — 131 mm annual precipitation

IQALUIT — 433 mm annual precipitation

INUKJUAK — 387 mm annual precipitation

PRINCE RUPERT — 2523 mm annual precipitation

SCHEFFERVILLE — 769 mm annual precipitation

PRINCE GEORGE — 628 mm annual precipitation

EDMONTON — 466 mm annual precipitation

KAPUSKASING — 872 mm annual precipitation

QUÉBEC — 1174 mm annual precipitation

VANCOUVER — 1113 mm annual precipitation

MEDICINE HAT — 348 mm annual precipitation

WINNIPEG — 526 mm annual precipitation

TORONTO — 762 mm annual precipitation

HALIFAX — 1282 mm annual precipitation

average daily temperature

growing season (that part of the year when average daily temperature remains above 5°C)

average snowfall

average rainfall

10 mm of snowfall is the water equivalent of 1 mm of rainfall

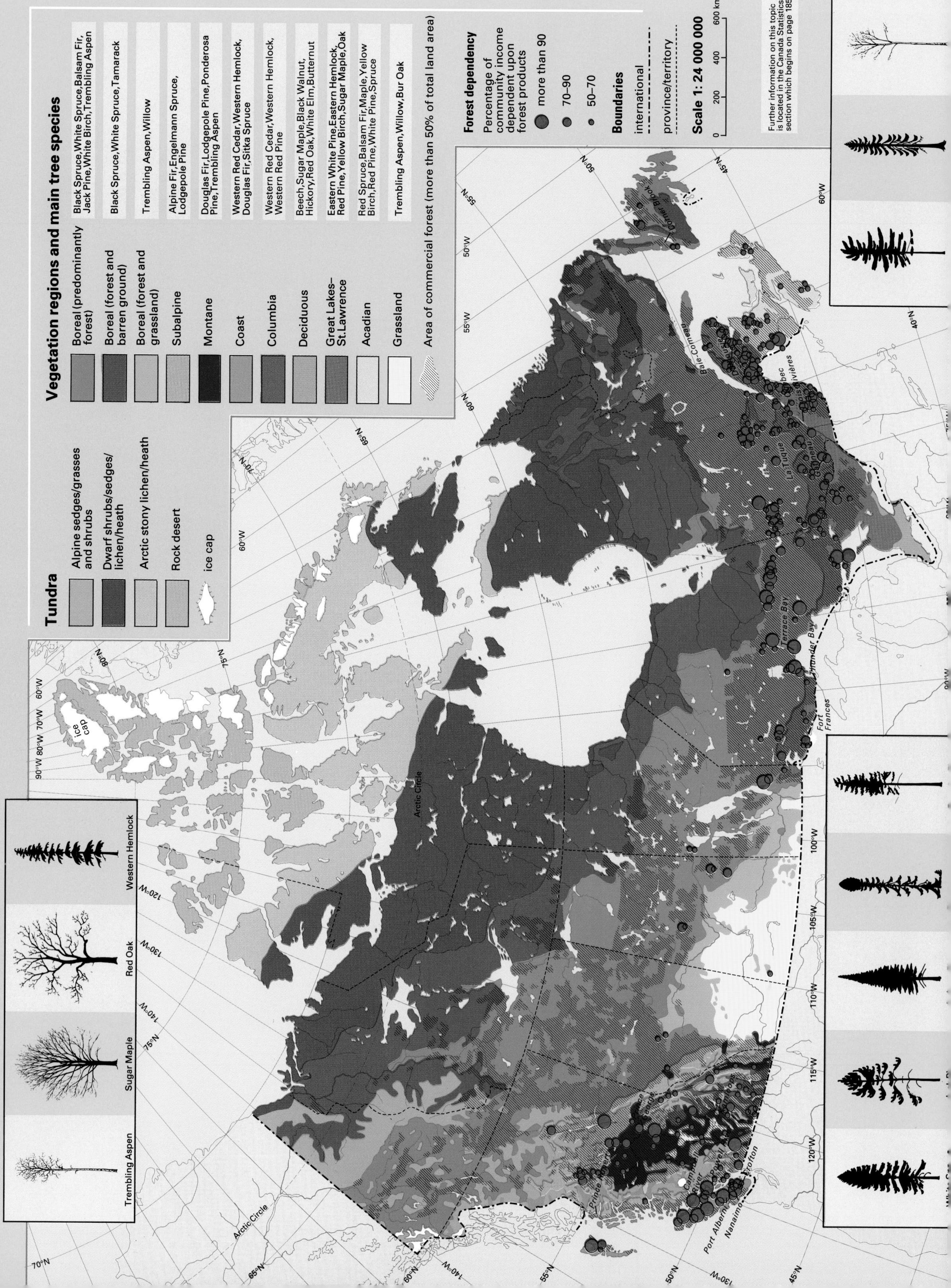

Vegetation regions and main tree species

- Boreal (predominantly forest): Black Spruce, White Spruce, Balsam Fir, Jack Pine, White Birch, Trembling Aspen
- Boreal (forest and barren ground): Black Spruce, White Spruce, Tamarack
- Boreal (forest and grassland): Trembling Aspen, Willow
- Subalpine: Alpine Fir, Engelmann Spruce, Lodgepole Pine
- Montane: Douglas Fir, Lodgepole Pine, Ponderosa Pine, Trembling Aspen
- Coast: Western Red Cedar, Western Hemlock, Douglas Fir, Sitka Spruce
- Columbia: Western Red Cedar, Western Hemlock, Western Red Pine
- Deciduous: Beech, Sugar Maple, Black Walnut, Hickory, Red Oak, White Elm, Butternut
- Great Lakes–St. Lawrence: Eastern White Pine, Eastern Hemlock, Red Pine, Yellow Birch, Sugar Maple, Oak
- Acadian: Red Spruce, Balsam Fir, Maple, Yellow Birch, Red Pine, White Pine, Spruce
- Grassland: Trembling Aspen, Willow, Bur Oak

Area of commercial forest (more than 50% of total land area)

Tundra

- Alpine sedges/grasses and shrubs
- Dwarf shrubs/sedges/lichen/heath
- Arctic stony lichen/heath
- Rock desert
- ice cap

Forest dependency

Percentage of community income dependent upon forest products
- more than 90
- 70–90
- 50–70

Boundaries

- international
- province/territory

Scale 1 : 24 000 000

0   200   400   600 km

Further information on this topic is located in the Canada Statistics section which begins on page 185.

Zenithal Equidistant Projection   © Oxford University Press

Trembling Aspen

Sugar Maple

Red Oak

Western Hemlock

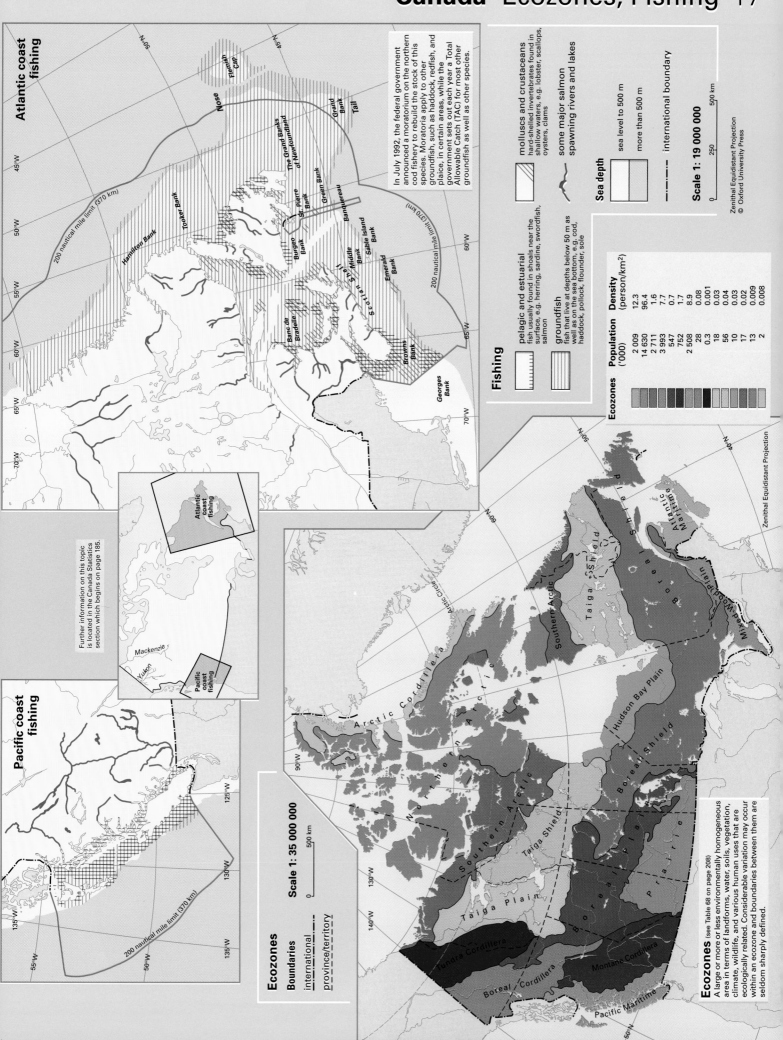

Atlantic coast fishing

Flemish Cap

Nose

Grand Bank

Tail

The Grand Banks of Newfoundland

Hamilton Bank

Tooker Bank

St. Pierre Bank

Green Bank

Burgeo Bank

Banquereau

Banc de Bradelle

St. Pierre Middle Bank

Sable Island Bank

Emerald Bank

Browns Bank

Georges Bank

200 nautical mile limit (370 km)

200 nautical mile limit (370 km)

In July 1992, the federal government announced a moratorium on the northern cod fishery to rebuild the stock of this species. Moratoria apply to other groundfish, such as haddock, redfish, and plaice, in certain areas, while the government sets out each year a Total Allowable Catch (TAC) for most other groundfish as well as other species.

Pacific coast fishing

Mackenzie

Yukon

200 nautical mile limit (370 km)

Further information on this topic is located in the Canada Statistics section which begins on page 185.

Atlantic coast fishing

Pacific coast fishing

Ecozones

Boundaries

international

province/territory

Scale 1: 35 000 000

0   500 km

Fishing

	pelagic and estuarial fish usually found in shoals near the surface, e.g. herring, sardine, swordfish, salmon
	groundfish fish that live at depths below 50 m as well as on the sea bottom, e.g. cod, haddock, pollock, flounder, sole
	molluscs and crustaceans hard-shelled invertebrates found in shallow waters, e.g. lobster, scallops, oysters, clams
	some major salmon spawning rivers and lakes

Sea depth

| | sea level to 500 m |
| | more than 500 m |

— · — · — international boundary

Scale 1: 19 000 000

0   250   500 km

Zenithal Equidistant Projection
© Oxford University Press

Ecozones	Population ('000)	Density (person/km²)
	2 009	12.3
	14 630	96.4
	2 711	1.6
	3 993	7.7
	547	0.7
	752	1.7
	2 508	8.9
	28	0.08
	0.3	0.001
	18	0.03
	56	0.04
	10	0.03
	17	0.02
	13	0.009
	2	0.008

Arctic Cordillera

Northern Arctic

Southern Arctic

Taiga Shield

Boreal Shield

Arctic Circle

Hudson Bay Plain

Taiga Plain

Taiga Shield

Boreal Plain

Boreal Shield

Prairie

Atlantic Maritime

Mixed Wood Plain

Tundra Cordillera

Boreal Cordillera

Montane Cordillera

Pacific Maritime

Zenithal Equidistant Projection

Ecozones

(see Table 68 on page 208)

A large or more or less environmentally homogeneous area in terms of landforms, water, soils, vegetation, climate, wildlife, and various human uses that are ecologically related. Considerable variation may occur within an ecozone and boundaries between them are seldom sharply defined.

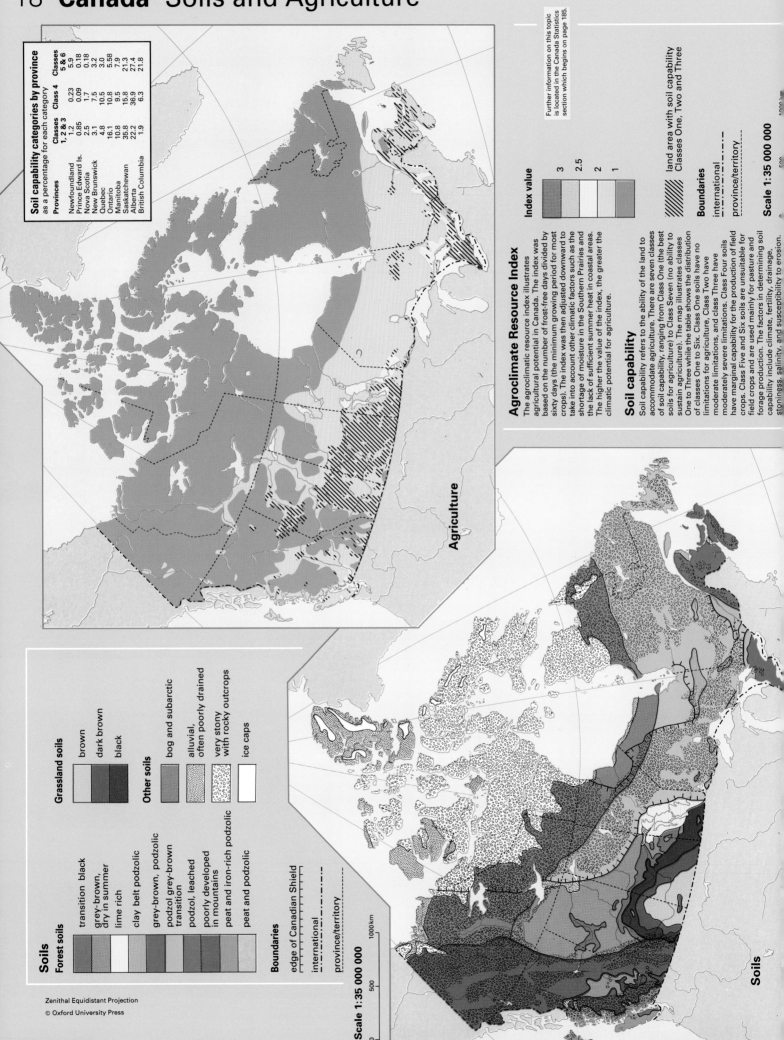

Soil capability categories by province
as a percentage for each category

Provinces	Classes 1, 2 & 3	Class 4	Classes 5 & 6
Newfoundland	1.2	0.23	5.9
Prince Edward Is.	0.85	0.09	0.18
Nova Scotia	2.5	1.7	0.18
New Brunswick	3.1	7.5	3.2
Quebec	4.8	10.5	3.0
Ontario	16.1	10.8	5.58
Manitoba	10.8	9.5	7.9
Saskatchewan	35.8	15.8	21.3
Alberta	22.2	36.9	27.4
British Columbia	1.9	6.3	21.8

Further information on this topic is located in the Canada Statistics section which begins on page 185.

Agroclimatic Resource Index

The agroclimatic resource index illustrates agricultural potential in Canada. The index was based on the number of frost-free days divided by sixty days (the minimum growing period for most crops). The index was then adjusted downward to take into account other climatic factors such as the shortage of moisture in the Southern Prairies and the lack of sufficient summer heat in coastal areas. The higher the value of the index, the greater the climatic potential for agriculture.

Soil capability

Soil capability refers to the ability of the land to accommodate agriculture. There are seven classes of soil capability, ranging from Class One (the best soils for agriculture) to Class Seven (no ability to sustain agriculture). The map illustrates classes One to Three while the table shows the distribution of classes One to Six. Class One soils have no limitations for agriculture, Class Two have moderate limitations, and class Three have moderately severe limitations. Class Four soils have marginal capability for the production of field crops. Class Five and Six soils are unsuitable for field crops and are used mainly for pasture and forage production. The factors in determining soil capability include climate, fertility, drainage, stoniness, salinity, and susceptibility to erosion.

Index value

	3
	2.5
	2
	1

land area with soil capability Classes One, Two and Three

Boundaries

international

province/territory

Scale 1:35 000 000

Agriculture

Soils

Forest soils

	transition black
	grey-brown, dry in summer
	lime rich
	clay belt podzolic
	grey-brown, podzolic
	podzol grey-brown transition
	podzol, leached
	poorly developed in mountains
	peat and iron-rich podzolic
	peat and podzolic

Grassland soils

	brown
	dark brown
	black

Other soils

	bog and subarctic
	alluvial, often poorly drained
	very stony with rocky outcrops
	ice caps

Boundaries

edge of Canadian Shield

international

province/territory

Scale 1:35 000 000

Zenithal Equidistant Projection

© Oxford University Press

Soils

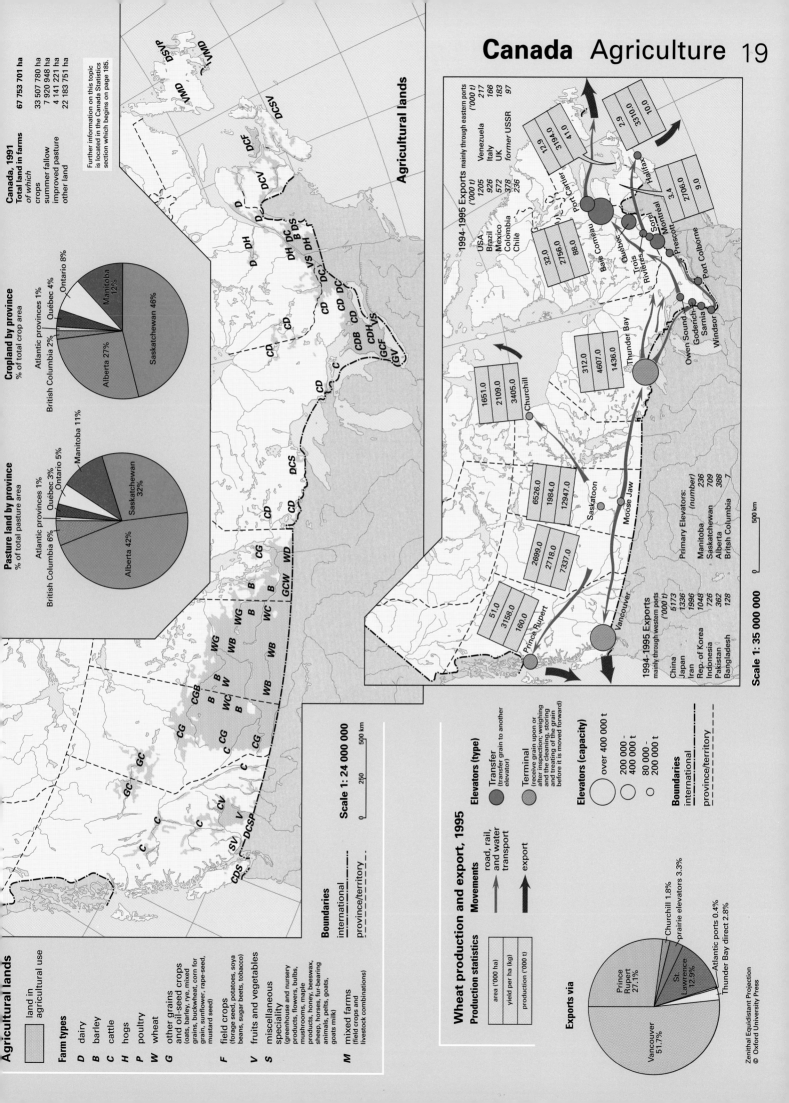

Agricultural lands

land in agricultural use

Farm types

- **D** dairy
- **B** barley
- **C** cattle
- **H** hogs
- **P** poultry
- **W** wheat
- **G** other grains and oil-seed crops
  (oats, barley, rye, mixed grains, buckwheat, corn for grain, sunflower, rape-seed, mustard seed)
- **F** field crops
  (forage seed, potatoes, soya beans, sugar beets, tobacco)
- **V** fruits and vegetables
- **S** miscellaneous speciality
  (greenhouse and nursery products, flowers, bulbs, mushrooms, maple products, honey, beeswax, sheep, horses, fur-bearing animals, pelts, goats, goats milk)
- **M** mixed farms
  (field crops and livestock combinations)

Boundaries

international
province/territory

Scale 1: 24 000 000

0   250   500 km

Agricultural lands

Canada, 1991

Total land in farms   67 753 701 ha

of which

crops	33 507 780 ha
summer fallow	7 920 948 ha
improved pasture	4 141 221 ha
other land	22 183 751 ha

Further information on this topic is located in the Canada Statistics section which begins on page 185.

Cropland by province
% of total crop area

- Atlantic provinces 1%
- Québec 4%
- Ontario 8%
- Manitoba 12%
- Saskatchewan 46%
- Alberta 27%
- British Columbia 2%

Pasture land by province
% of total pasture area

- Atlantic provinces 6%
- British Columbia 1%
- Québec 3%
- Ontario 5%
- Manitoba 11%
- Saskatchewan 32%
- Alberta 42%

Wheat production and export, 1995

Production statistics

- area ('000 ha)
- yield per ha (kg)
- production ('000 t)

Movements

- road, rail, and water transport
- export

Elevators (type)

- **Transfer** (transfer grain to another elevator)
- **Terminal** (receive grain upon or after inspection; weighing and the cleaning, storing and treating of the grain before it is moved forward)

Elevators (capacity)

- over 400 000 t
- 200 000 - 400 000 t
- 80 000 - 200 000 t

Boundaries

international
province/territory

Scale 1: 35 000 000

0   500 km

1994-1995 Exports mainly through eastern ports

	('000 t)
USA	1205
Brazil	926
Mexico	572
Colombia	378
Chile	236
Venezuela	217
Italy	166
UK	183
former USSR	97

1994-1995 Exports mainly through western ports

	('000 t)
China	5173
Japan	1336
Iran	1996
Rep. of Korea	1048
Indonesia	726
Pakistan	362
Bangladesh	128

Primary Elevators *(number)*

Manitoba	236
Saskatchewan	709
Alberta	388
British Columbia	7

Exports via

- Prince Rupert 27.1%
- Vancouver 51.7%
- Thunder Bay direct 2.8%
- St. Lawrence 12.9%
- Churchill 1.8%
- prairie elevators 3.3%
- Atlantic ports 0.4%

Port locations: Port Cartier, Baie Comeau, Québec, Trois Rivières, Sorel, Montréal, Prescott, Halifax, Port Colborne, Owen Sound, Goderich, Sarnia, Windsor, Thunder Bay, Churchill, Saskatoon, Moose Jaw, Prince Rupert, Vancouver

Zenithal Equidistant Projection
© Oxford University Press

Endangered species

There are five classifications of endangered species:

Extinct means that a species no longer exists anywhere.

Extirpated means that a species no longer exists in a particular region or country but does still exist somewhere.

Endangered refers to those species with population numbers so low that they face extinction or extirpation.

Threatened means that a species is likely to become endangered if current negative factors continue.

Vulnerable refers to a species that is at risk because of its declining numbers.

In 1994 in Canada, there were 256 species of mammals, birds, reptiles and amphibians, fish, and plants listed in these five categories. Some of the birds and mammals are shown on the map.

EX   extinct
EXT   extirpated
E   endangered
T   threatened
R   rare (vulnerable)

Protected lands

- National Parks (Reserves)
- selected Provincial/Territorial Parks
- Bird/Game Sanctuaries and other Federal designations
- ☆ World Heritage Sites
- + selected Ecological Reserves
- — Heritage River

National Parks

area square kilometres
n/a not available

1.	Wood Buffalo	44 802
2.	Ivvavik	10 168
3.	Pacific Rim	500
4.	Glacier	1 349
5.	Mount	
6.	Revelstoke	260
	Kootenay	1 406
7.	Yoho	1 313
8.	Jasper	10 878
9.	Banff	6 641
10.	Elk Island	194
11.	Waterton Lakes	505
12.	Grasslands	906
13.	Prince Albert	3 874
14.	Riding Mountain	2 973
15.	Pukaskwa	1 878
16.	Fathom Five National Marine Park (part of item 17.)	
17.	Bruce Peninsula	154
18.	Georgian Bay Islands	25
19.	Point Pelee	15
20.	St. Lawrence Is.	8
21.	Parc national de la Mauricie	536
22.	Parc national de la Forillon	240
23.	Kouchibouguac	239
24.	Fundy	206
25.	Cape Breton Islands	948
26.	Kejimkujik	404
27.	Prince Edward I.	22
28.	Gros Morne	1 805
29.	Terra Nova	400
30.	Vuntut	4345
31.	Aulavik	12 200
32.	Tuktut Nogait	16 340
33.	North Baffin	n/a
34.	Wapusk	11 475

National Park Reserves

area square kilometres

35.	Ellesmere Is.	37 775
36.	Kluane	22 013
37.	Nahanni	4 765
38.	Auyuittuq	21 469
39.	Gwaii Haanas	1 495
40.	Mingan Archipelago	151

Habitat region

- Marine coastal
- Pacific/mountain
- Arctic
- Boreal
- Prairie
- Great Lake/St. Lawrence
- Atlantic Maritime

Boundaries

- international
- province/territory

Scale 1: 24 000 000

0   200   400   600 km

Further information on this topic is located in the Canada Statistics section which begins on page 185.

Zenithal Equidistant Projection

Three major goals of conservation

- Maintaining essential ecological processes and life support systems.
- Preserving genetic diversity.
- Ensuring the sustainable use of species and ecosystems.

Human activity causes 95% of all extinctions as a result of
- The fragmentation, degradation, and loss of habitat.
- Hunting and harvesting (e.g. clear-cut logging).
- Pollution.
- The introduction of foreign species.

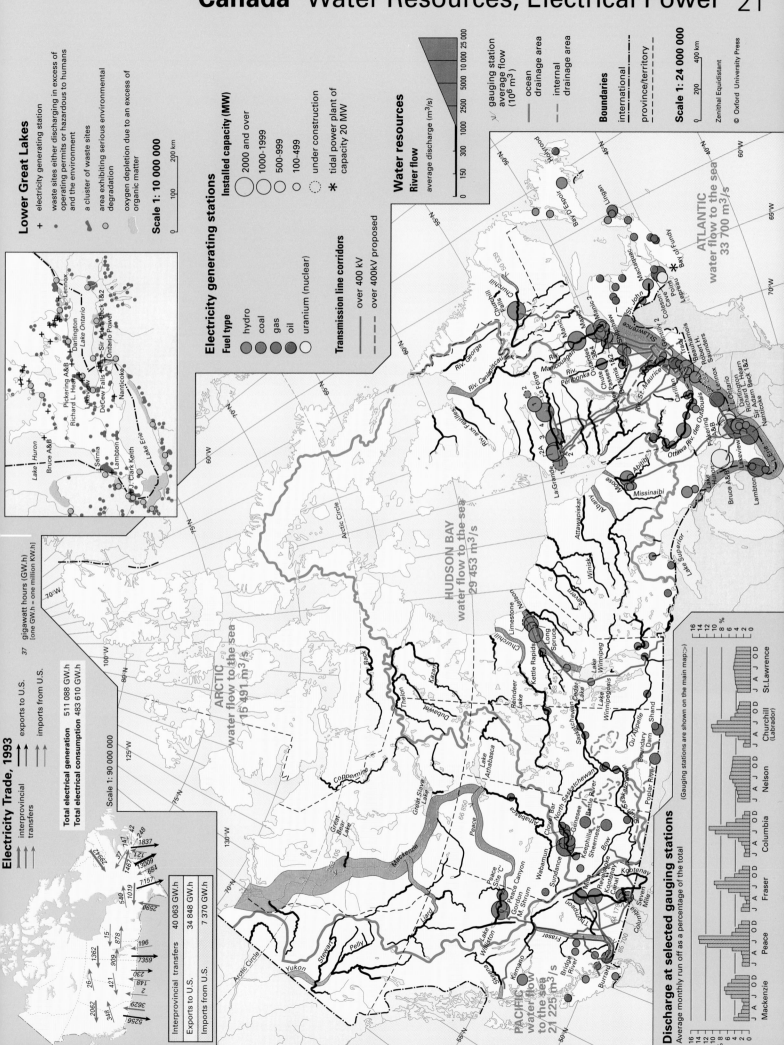

Minerals

Fe	iron ore
Cu	copper
Ni	nickel
Au	gold
Ag	silver
Mo	molybdenum
Pb	lead
Zn	zinc
Co	cobalt
Pt	platinum
Mg	magnesium
Ti	titanium
Al	aluminum
KOH	potash
S	sulphur (from natural gas processing, oil sands plants, and oil refineries)
NaCl	salt
Gy	gypsum
Asb	asbestos

Mining centres

◆ major
◆ minor
+ mine under development

Processing plants

● smelter/refinery
▲ pig iron plant
● reduced iron plant
▽ ferroalloy plant
* iron ore agglomerate plant

Geological Provinces

Continental Shelf
Cordilleran Orogen
Interior Platform
Innuitian Orogen
Arctic Platform
Canadian Shield
Hudson Platform
St. Lawrence Platform
Appalachian Orogen

Orogen refers to an area affected by mountain building (tectonic activity) while *platform* refers to an area largely unaffected.

Boundaries

international
province/territory

Scale 1: 24 000 000

0 200 400 600 km

Zenithal Equidistant Projection

© Oxford University Press

Relative abundance of selected Canadian and World mineral reserves, 1994

reserve life in years

	World / Canada
Natural gas	
Uranium	2
Asbestos	15
Nickel	13
Crude oil	1
Copper	4
Gold	4
Lead	10
Zinc	15
Silver	13

24 = 24 Canadian reserve as a percentage of world reserve

World ☐   Canada ☐

The World and Canadian figures for coal are 232 and 93, and iron ore are 178 and 171 respectively.

Geological Provinces

- Continental Shelf
- Cordilleran Orogen
- Interior Platform
- Innuitian Orogen
- Arctic Platform
- Canadian Shield
- Hudson Platform
- St. Lawrence Platform
- Appalachian Orogen

Orogen refers to an area affected by mountain building (tectonic activity) while platform refers to an area largely unaffected.

Oil and Gas

- oil field
- oil sands deposits (surface and non-surface)
- oil pipeline
- gas field
- gas pipeline

Oil refineries (capacity)

- more than 100 000 barrels/day
- 25 000 – 100 000
- 5 000 – 25 000

Coal (1995)

- producing mines of over 1 000 000 t per annum
- coal exports (% of production)
- coal imports

Uranium mines

- major
- other
- * processing plant

Boundaries

- international
- province/territory

Scale 1 : 24 000 000

0   200   400   600 km

Zenithal Equidistant Projection

© Oxford University Press

Petroleum transfers

- interprovincial
- export
- import

2.8 thousand cubic metres per day

Production and consumption, 1996 (000 m³ per day)

- crude oil production
- refinery production
- consumption of petroleum products

Losses, adjustments and storage mean that these figures do not add up exactly.

North Sea 51%
Western Hemisphere 13%
Middle East 13%
Other 23%

Scale 1 : 90 000 000

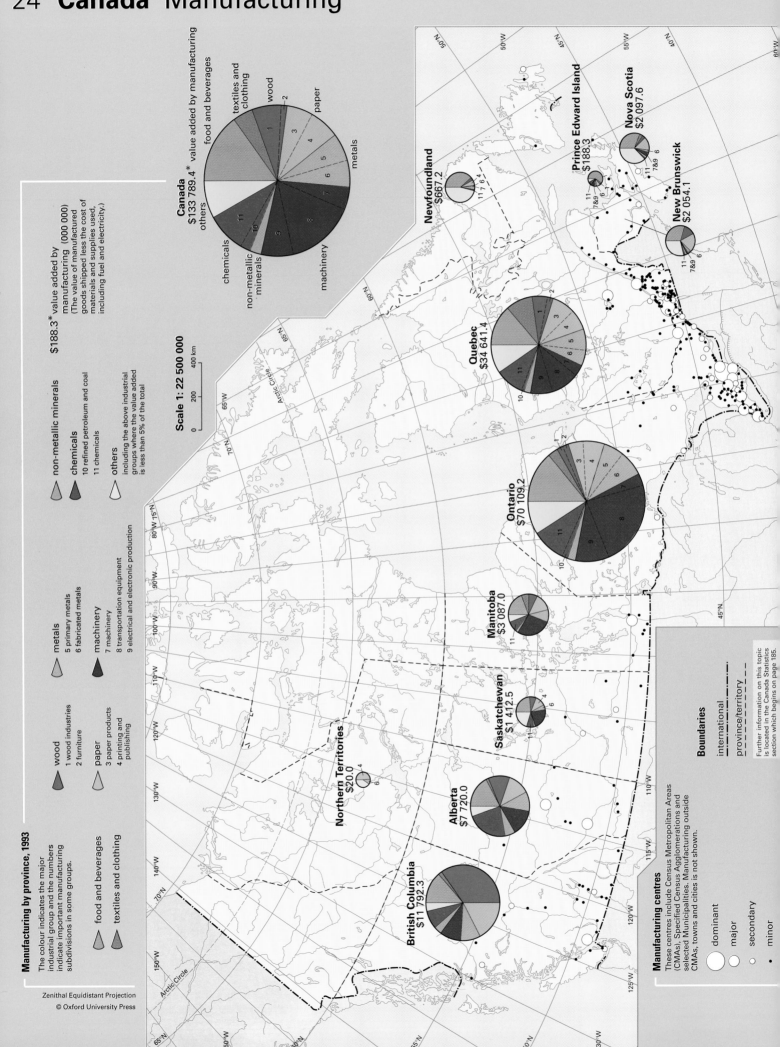

Manufacturing by province, 1993

The colour indicates the major industrial group and the numbers indicate important manufacturing subdivisions in some groups.

$188.3* value added by manufacturing

metals
- 5 primary metals
- 6 fabricated metals

machinery
- 7 machinery
- 8 transportation equipment
- 9 electrical and electronic production

wood
- 1 wood industries
- 2 furniture

paper
- 3 paper products
- 4 printing and publishing

food and beverages

textiles and clothing

non-metallic minerals

chemicals
- 10 refined petroleum and coal
- 11 chemicals

others

including the above industrial groups where the value added is less than 5% of the total

Zenithal Equidistant Projection

© Oxford University Press

Canada
$133 789.4* value added by manufacturing (000 000)
(The value of manufactured goods shipped less the cost of materials and supplies used, including fuel and electricity.)

textiles and clothing
wood
paper
metals
food and beverages
machinery
non-metallic minerals
chemicals
others

Scale 1: 22 500 000

0   200   400 km

Newfoundland
$667.2

Prince Edward Island
$188.3

Nova Scotia
$2 097.6

New Brunswick
$2 054.1

Quebec
$34 641.4

Ontario
$70 109.2

Manitoba
$3 087.0

Saskatchewan
$1 412.5

Northern Territories
$20.0

Alberta
$7 720.0

British Columbia
$11 792.3

Manufacturing centres

These centres include Census Metropolitan Areas (CMAs), Specified Census Agglomerations and selected Municipalities. Manufacturing outside CMAs, towns and cities is not shown.

dominant
major
secondary
minor

Boundaries

international

province/territory

Further information on this topic is located in the Canada Statistics section which begins on page 185.

Arctic Circle

Trade with the United States
Top sixteen exports, 1995

	$ millions
vehicles	56 631
mineral fuels	20 550
machinery	18 381
paper products	12 611
wood products	10 162
electrical equipment	9 543
iron and steel products	6 207
aluminum products	5 438
plastics	5 321
wood pulp	4 571
furniture	3 600
rubber products	2 338
precious stones and metals	2 306
aircraft, spacecraft, and parts	2 151
chemicals	2 051
copper	2 013

Total exports, 1995
$245 703 441 000

Further information on this topic is located in the Canada Statistics section which begins on page 185.

Trade with the United States
Top sixteen imports, 1995

	$ millions
vehicles	34 671
machinery	29 091
electrical equipment	17 151
plastics	5 824
iron and steel products	5 166
optical and photo equipment	4 946
paper products	3 335
printed materials	2 494
rubber products	2 469
furniture	2 275
aluminum products	2 230
chemicals	2 074
aircraft, spacecraft, and parts	1 888
mineral fuels	1 844
wood products	1 707
textiles and clothing	1 497

Total imports, 1995
$225 493 245 000

Value of exports, 1995
by country of destination

$ million

196 160 (USA only)	
more than 3 000	
1 000 - 3 000	
200 - 1 000	
50 - 200	
less than 50	

Value of imports, 1995
by country of source

$ million

150 705 (USA only)	
more than 3000	
1 000 - 3 000	
200 - 1 000	
50 - 200	
less than 50	

Equatorial scale 1 : 190 000 000

All exports and imports exceeding $200 million in value are listed and indicated in bold (with their value in $ million shown).
The others listed have a value between $50 and $200 million.
Because of space limitations, all of the exports and imports in the second category are not shown.
This is especially true for the United States and Canada's other large trading partners.

The United States dominates Canada's trade, receiving 79% of Canada's exports and sending 67% of Canada's imports. The top sixteen exports and imports are listed in separate tables.

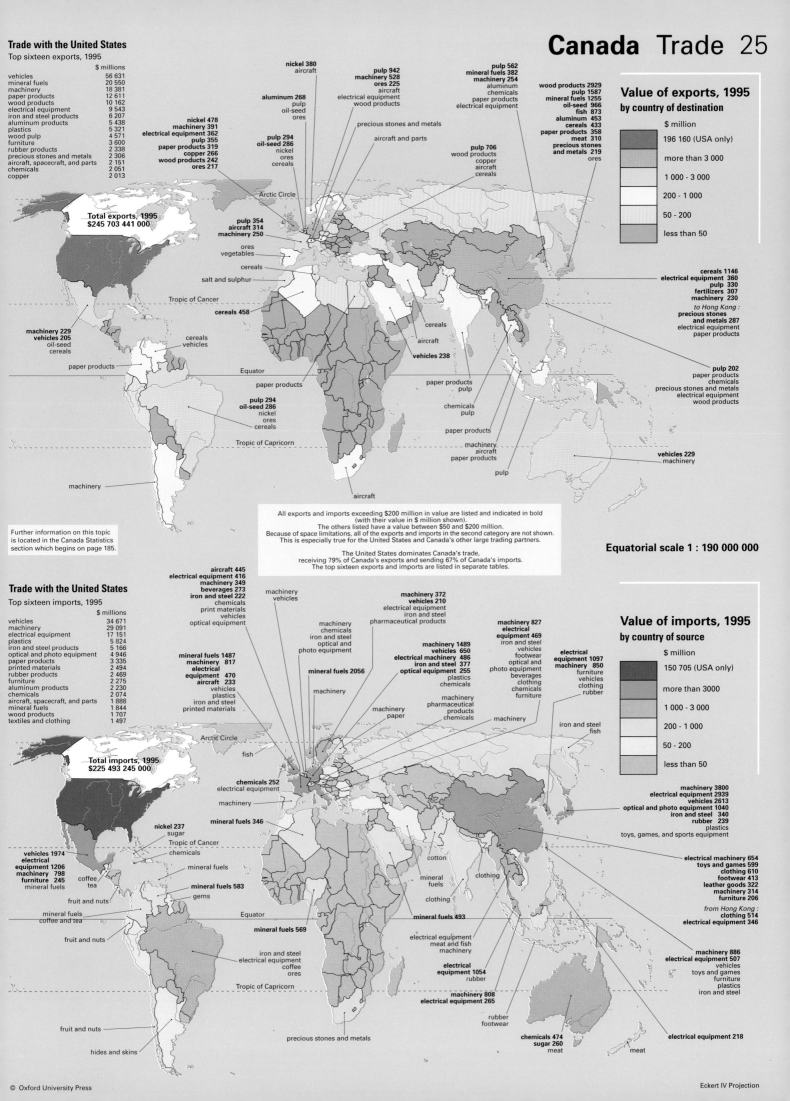

© Oxford University Press

Eckert IV Projection

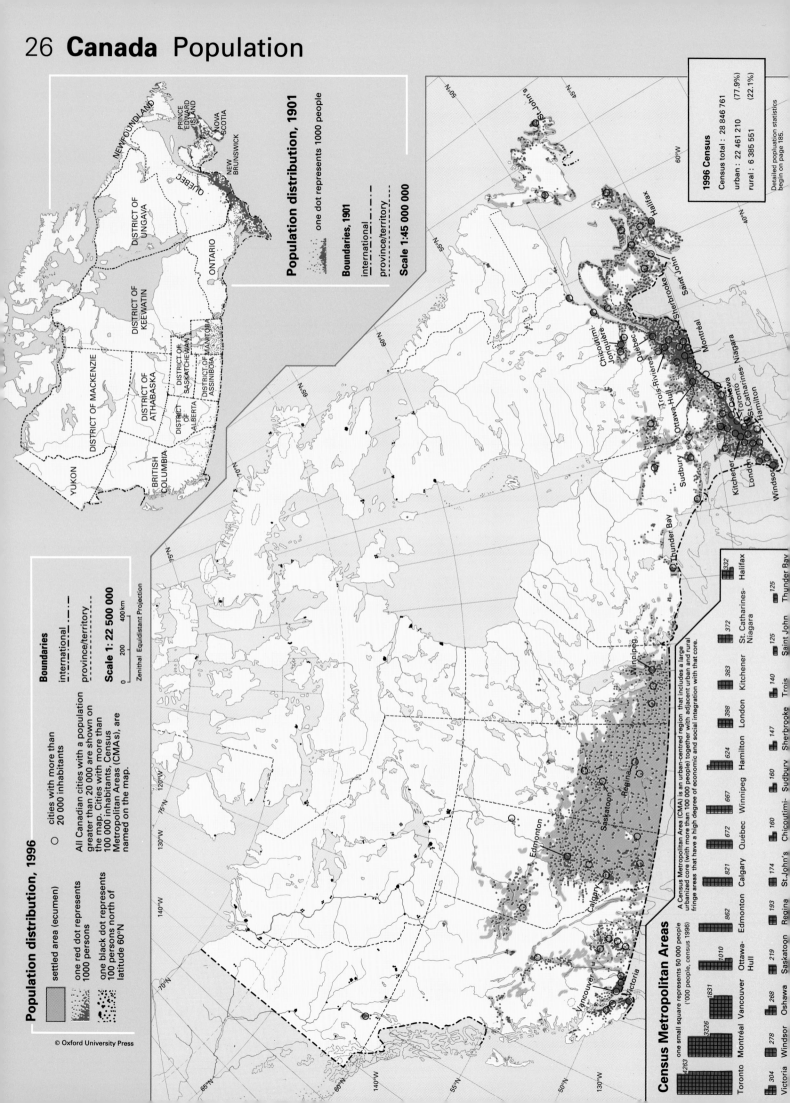

Population distribution, 1901

one dot represents 1000 people

Boundaries, 1901

international

province/territory

Scale 1:45 000 000

1996 Census

Census total : 28 846 761

urban : 22 461 210 (77.9%)

rural : 6 385 551 (22.1%)

Detailed population statistics begin on page 185.

NEWFOUNDLAND

PRINCE EDWARD ISLAND

NOVA SCOTIA

NEW BRUNSWICK

QUÉBEC

DISTRICT OF UNGAVA

ONTARIO

DISTRICT OF KEEWATIN

DISTRICT OF MACKENZIE

DISTRICT OF ATHABASKA

DISTRICT OF SASKATCHEWAN

DISTRICT OF MANITOBA

DISTRICT OF ALBERTA

DISTRICT OF ASSINIBOIA

YUKON

BRITISH COLUMBIA

Population distribution, 1996

settled area (ecumen)

one red dot represents 1000 persons

one black dot represents 100 persons north of latitude 60°N

Boundaries

international

province/territory

Scale 1 : 22 500 000

0   200   400 km

Zenithal Equidistant Projection

○ cities with more than 20 000 inhabitants

All Canadian cities with a population greater than 20 000 are shown on the map. Cities with more than 100 000 inhabitants, Census Metropolitan Areas (CMAs), are named on the map.

© Oxford University Press

St. John's

Halifax

Chicoutimi-Jonquière

Québec

Trois-Rivières

Montréal

Ottawa-Hull

Sherbrooke

Saint John

Niagara

Oshawa

Toronto

St. Catharines

Hamilton

Sudbury

Kitchener

London

Windsor

Thunder Bay

Winnipeg

Regina

Saskatoon

Edmonton

Calgary

Vancouver

Victoria

Census Metropolitan Areas

one small square represents 50 000 people
('000 people, census 1996)

A Census Metropolitan Area (CMA) is an urban-centred region that includes a large urbanized core (with more than 100 000 people) together with adjacent urban and rural fringe areas that have a high degree of economic and social integration with that core.

3326 Toronto	1010 Ottawa-Hull	332 Halifax
3326	862 Edmonton	372 St. Catharines-Niagara
1831 Montréal	821 Calgary	383 Kitchener
1263	672 Québec	398 London
	667 Winnipeg	624 Hamilton
1010 Vancouver	219 Saskatoon	125 Saint John
	193 Regina	125 Thunder Bay
	174 St. John's	140 Trois-Rivières
	268 Oshawa	147 Sherbrooke
	278 Windsor	160 Chicoutimi-Jonquière
	304 Victoria	160 Sudbury

xford University Press
thal Equidistant Projection

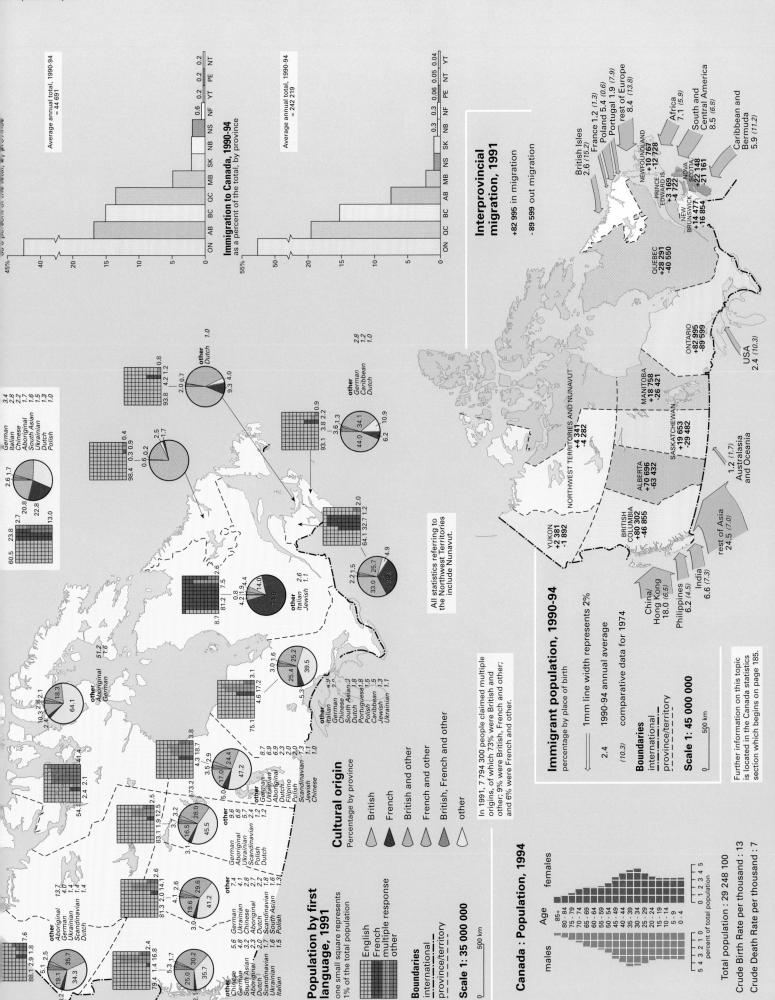

Native peoples

Indian/non-status Indian

■	more than 5000 people
□	1000-5000
●	500-1000 people
○	100-500 people
·	50-100 people

Inuit

□	1000-5000
●	500-1000 people
○	100-500 people
·	50-100 people

Linguistic groups at the time of European contact

Algonquian · Athapaskan · Eskimo-Aleut · Haida · Iroquoian · Kootenayan · Salishan · Siouan · Tlingit · Tsimshian · Wakashan · Sahaptin-nez Perce · Caddoan · Uto-Aztecan · Beothukan

Canadian Aboriginal languages grouped by families

Family	Member languages	Estimated number of speakers
Algonquian	Abenak, Blackfoot, Cree, Delaware, Malecite, Micmac, Montagnais-Naskapi, Ojibwa, Potawatomi	100 000
Athapaskan	Beaver, Carrier, Chilcotin, Chipewyan, Han, Dogrib, Hare, Kasha, Kutchin, Sarcee, Sekani, Save, Tagish, Tahltan, Tuchone	17 000
Eskimo-Aleut	Inuktitut	16 000
Haida	Haida	150
Iroquoian	Cayuga, Mohawk, Oneida, Onondaga, Seneca, Tuscarora	2700
Kootenayan	Kutenai (or Kootenay)	30-40
Salishan	Bella Coola, Comox, Halkomelem, Lillooet, Okanagan, Schelt, Shuswap, Squamish, Straita, Thompson	3 000
Siouan	Dakota	5 000
Tlingit	Inland Tlingit	100
Tsimshian	Coast Tsimshian, Southern Tsimshian, Nass-Gitksan	2 300
Wakashan	Haisla, Heiktsuk, Kvakiutl, Nuu-chah-nulth (also known as Nootka) Nitinat	3 400

Beothuk were a small group of native people (500-1000) who lived in Newfoundland probably from prehistoric times. Contact with Europeans led to slaughter and disease; the last survivor died in 1829.

Further information on this topic is located in the Canada Statistics section which begins on page 185.

Number of native people, 1991
as a percentage by province

Native Indian **783 980**

Ontario · British Columbia · Québec · Alberta · Manitoba · Saskatchewan · Nova Scotia · New Brunswick · Northwest Territories · Yukon Territories · Newfoundland · Prince Edward I.

Métis **212 650**
Inuit **49 225**

0 10 20 30 40 50 60 70 80 90 100%

Boundaries, 1997
international
province/territory

Scale 1: 24 000 000
0 200 400 km

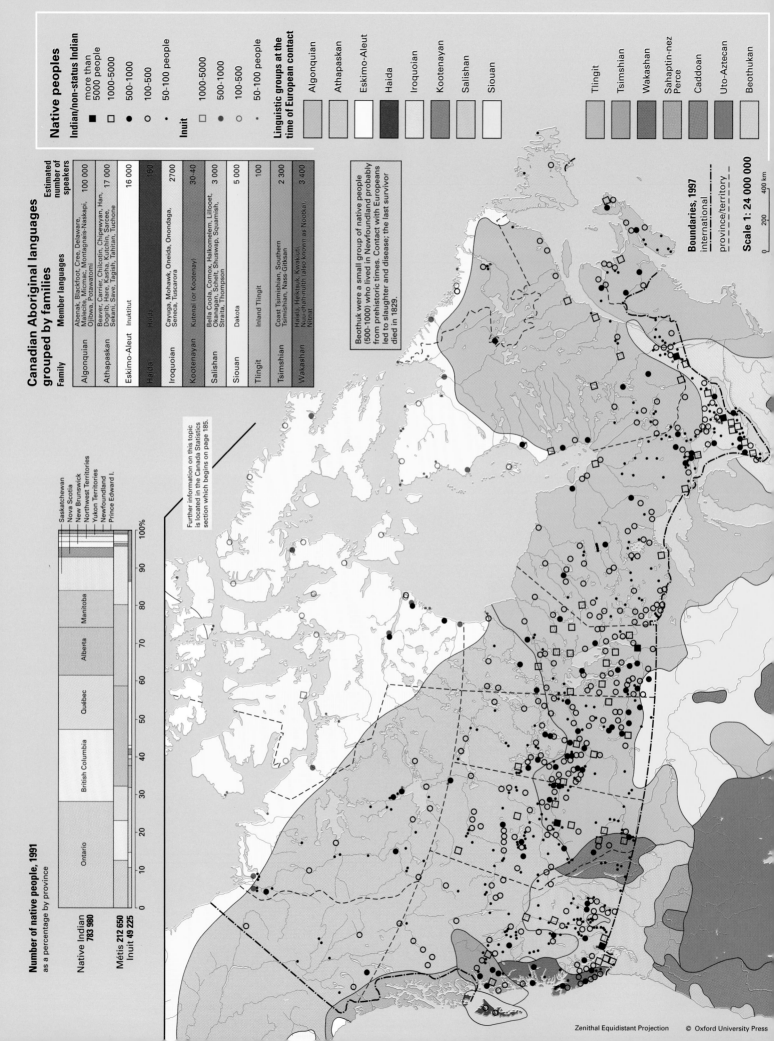

Zenithal Equidistant Projection   © Oxford University Press

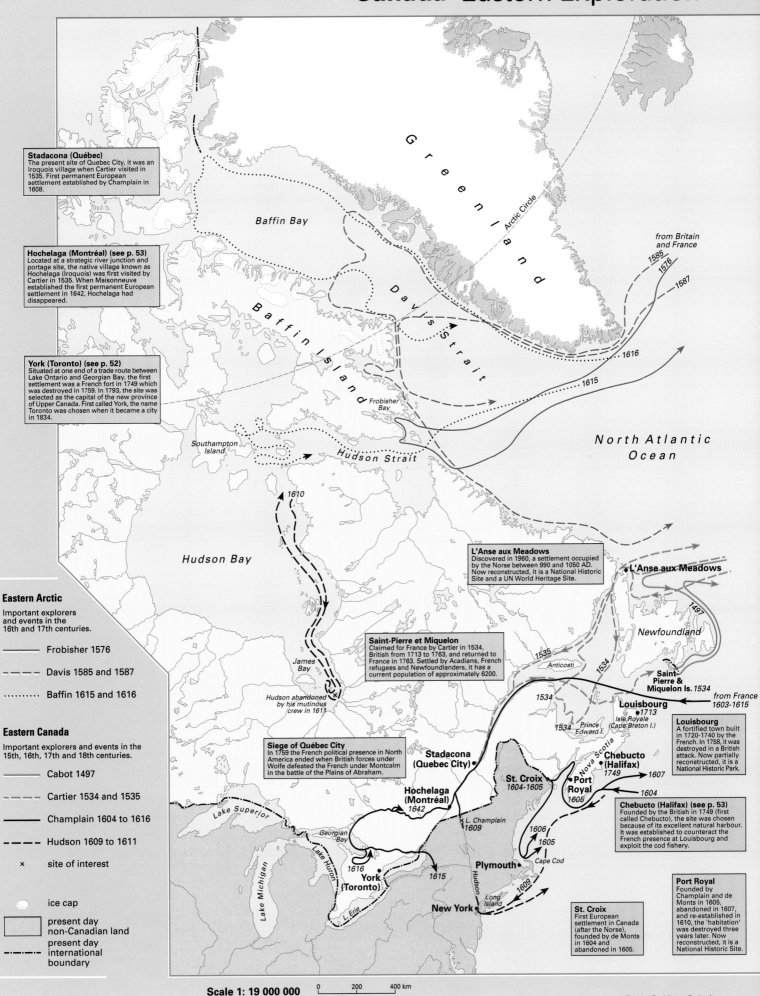

Stadacona (Québec)
The present site of Quebec City, it was an Iroquois village when Cartier visited in 1535. First permanent European settlement established by Champlain in 1608.

Hochelaga (Montréal) (see p. 53)
Located at a strategic river junction and portage site, the native village known as Hochelaga (Iroquois) was first visited by Cartier in 1535. When Maisonneuve established the first permanent European settlement in 1642, Hochelaga had disappeared.

York (Toronto) (see p. 52)
Situated at one end of a trade route between Lake Ontario and Georgian Bay, the first settlement was a French fort in 1749 which was destroyed in 1759. In 1793, the site was selected as the capital of the new province of Upper Canada. First called York, the name Toronto was chosen when it became a city in 1834.

Eastern Arctic
Important explorers and events in the 16th and 17th centuries.

— Frobisher 1576

– – – Davis 1585 and 1587

· · · · · Baffin 1615 and 1616

Eastern Canada
Important explorers and events in the 15th, 16th, 17th and 18th centuries.

— Cabot 1497

– – – Cartier 1534 and 1535

—·— Champlain 1604 to 1616

– – Hudson 1609 to 1611

× site of interest

ice cap

present day non-Canadian land

–··– present day international boundary

L'Anse aux Meadows
Discovered in 1960, a settlement occupied by the Norse between 990 and 1050 AD. Now reconstructed, it is a National Historic Site and a UN World Heritage Site.

Saint-Pierre et Miquelon
Claimed for France by Cartier in 1534, British from 1713 to 1763, and returned to France in 1763. Settled by Acadians, French refugees and Newfoundlanders, it has a current population of approximately 6200.

Siege of Québec City
In 1759 the French political presence in North America ended when British forces under Wolfe defeated the French under Montcalm in the battle of the Plains of Abraham.

Louisbourg
A fortified town built in 1720-1740 by the French. In 1758, it was destroyed in a British attack. Now partially reconstructed, it is a National Historic Park.

Chebucto (Halifax) (see p. 53)
Founded by the British in 1749 (first called Chebucto), the site was chosen because of its excellent natural harbour. It was established to counteract the French presence at Louisbourg and exploit the cod fishery.

Port Royal
Founded by Champlain and de Monts in 1605, abandoned in 1607, and re-established in 1610, the 'habitation' was destroyed three years later. Now reconstructed, it is a National Historic Site.

St. Croix
First European settlement in Canada (after the Norse), founded by de Monts in 1604 and abandoned in 1605.

Greenland

Baffin Bay

Davis Strait

Arctic Circle

from Britain and France

1585
1576
1587
1616
1615

Baffin Island

North Atlantic Ocean

Frobisher Bay

Southampton Island

Hudson Strait

1610

Hudson Bay

James Bay

Hudson abandoned by his mutinous crew in 1611

L'Anse aux Meadows

1497

Newfoundland

Saint-Pierre & Miquelon Is. 1534

1535
1534
1534
1534
1534

Anticosti

from France 1603-1615

Louisbourg
1713
Isle Royale (Cape Breton I.)

Prince Edward I.

Nova Scotia

Stadacona (Quebec City)

St. Croix 1604-1605

Chebucto (Halifax) 1749

1607
1604

Port Royal 1605

Hochelaga (Montréal) 1642

Lake Superior

L. Champlain 1609

1606
1605

Cape Cod

Georgian Bay

Lake Huron

Lake Michigan

1616

York (Toronto)

1615

Plymouth

Hudson

New York

Long Island

1609

L. Erie

Scale 1: 19 000 000

0   200   400 km

Zenithal Equidistant Projection

© Oxford University Press

Arctic Important explorers and events in the 19th and early 20th centuries.

———— Parry 1819 to 1823
– – – Franklin 1845 to 1847
········· M'Clure 1850 to 1854
–·–·– M'Clintock 1853 and 1859
———— Amundsen 1903 to 1906

× site of interest
✳ ice cap

present day non-Canadian land
present day international boundary

The Northwest Passage
Finding the Northwest Passage, a route through the Arctic to the Pacific, challenged many explorers from the 16th to the 20th centuries. The actual route was proven to exist by M'Clure in 1854 but it wasn't until the 1903-06 voyage of Roald Amundsen that the first transit was achieved.

On his third voyage to search for the Northwest Passage, Sir John Franklin (1845-1847) in his ships Erebus and Terror were frozen in the ice west of King William Island. Franklin and entire crew perished.

Arctic Ocean

G r e e n l a n d

Melville Island
Bathurst Island
Cornwallis Island
Devon Island
Lancaster Sound

Banks Island

Amundsen Gulf

Somerset Island
Prince of Wales Island

B a f f i n   B a y

B a f f i n   I s l a n d

Baffin Bay

Richardson 1826

Victoria Island

site of Franklin's death June 1847 ×

King William Island

Boothia Peninsula

Melville Peninsula

Arctic Circle

Mackenzie

Fort Good Hope

Great Bear Lake

Fort Norman

Coppermine

1821

Southampton Island

Hudson Strait

Fort Simpson
Fort Liard

Fort Providence

Great Slave Lake

Chesterfield Inlet

Fort Resolution

Lake Athabasca
Fond du Lac

H u d s o n   B a y

Fort St. John
Fort Vermillion
Fort Chipewyan

Peace

Athabasca

Reindeer Lake

Prince of Wales Fort (Churchill)

Fort Rupert

Fort St. James
Fort Fraser

Churchill

1785

York Factory

Nelson

Oxford House

Fort Portage

P a c i f i c   O c e a n

Jasper House
Fort Edmonton

North Saskatchewan

Cumberland House

Norway House

Rocky Mountain House

Fort Carlton

1790

South Branch House

Lake Winnipeg

Fort Langley
Fort Kamloops

Kootenay House

South Saskatchewan

1810

Assiniboine

1741

Fort Victoria

Chesterfield House

Brandon House

Fort Gibraltar

1811

Columbia

Lewis' return route 1806

Missouri

1738

Red

Fort Garry

Lake of the Woods

1731

Fort William

1805

Snake

1805

Yellowstone

Clark's return route 1806

Powder

1742-43

1804

Lake Superior

from St. Louis

Fraser

Western Canada

Important explorers and events in the 18th and 19th centuries.

– – – La Vérendrye 1731 to 1743
········· Hearne 1770 to 1772
–·–·– Cook 1778
———— Mackenzie 1789 and 1793
▬▬▬ Thompson 1785 to 1811
········· Vancouver 1792 to 1794
–·–·– Fraser 1806 to 1809
– – – Franklin 1819 and 1827
········· Lewis and Clark 1804 to 1806

Some important fur trading posts

■ Hudson's Bay Company
● North West Company

Rupert's Land
Palliser's Triangle

Scale 1: 19 000 000
0   200   400 km

Zenithal Equidistant Projection
© Oxford University Press

The Dominion of Canada was formed in 1867 and included the provinces of Nova Scotia, New Brunswick, Québec and Ontario. The North-Western Territory, Rupert's Land, and Manitoba were added in 1870; British Columbia in 1871; Prince Edward Island in 1873; Saskatchewan and Alberta in 1905; and Newfoundland in 1949. With some exceptions, the present day boundaries were in place by 1912.

1667

RUPERT'S LAND

NEW FRANCE

French

ENGLISH COLONIES

NEW SPAIN

1667–1867

English

French

disputed

Spanish

American

unclaimed land

P.E.I. Prince Edward Island

Boundaries

.... colonial/territorial

.... undefined

———— district

– – – – province

–··–··– international

Scale 1 : 78 000 000

0   500   1000 km

1763

GREENLAND (Denmark)

NEWFOUNDLAND

RUPERT'S LAND

INDIAN COUNTRY

QUÉBEC

NOVA SCOTIA

French

LOUISIANA

BRITISH COLONIES

1791

GREENLAND (Denmark)

RUPERT'S LAND

NEWFOUNDLAND

French

UPPER CANADA

LOWER CANADA

CAPE BRETON I.

ST. JOHNS I.

NEW BRUNSWICK

LOUISIANA

U.S.A.

1867

ALASKA (U.S.A)

THE NORTH-WESTERN TERRITORY

GREENLAND (Denmark)

BRITISH COLUMBIA

RUPERT'S LAND

NEWFOUNDLAND

ONTARIO

QUÉBEC

P.E.I

St.-P. & M.

NOVA SCOTIA

NEW BRUNSWICK

UNITED STATES OF AMERICA

1873

ALASKA (U.S.A)

GREENLAND (Denmark)

BRITISH COLUMBIA

THE NORTH-WEST TERRITORIES

NEWFOUNDLAND

QUÉBEC

MANITOBA

ONTARIO

P.E.I

St-Pierre & Miquelon (Fr.)

NOVA SCOTIA

NEW BRUNSWICK

UNITED STATES OF AMERICA

1889

ALASKA (U.S.A)

NORTH-WEST TERRITORIES

GREENLAND (Denmark)

BRITISH COLUMBIA

District of Athabasca

District of Alberta

District of Saskatchewan

District of Assiniboia

District of Keewatin

NORTH-WEST TERRITORIES

NEWFOUNDLAND

MANITOBA

ONTARIO

QUÉBEC

P.E.I

St-Pierre & Miquelon (Fr.)

NOVA SCOTIA

NEW BRUNSWICK

UNITED STATES OF AMERICA

1905

ALASKA (U.S.A)

YUKON TERRITORY

NORTHWEST TERRITORIES

District of Franklin

GREENLAND (Denmark)

District of Mackenzie

BRITISH COLUMBIA

ALBERTA

SASKATCHEWAN

District of Keewatin

District of Ungava

NEWFOUNDLAND

QUÉBEC

MANITOBA

ONTARIO

P.E.I

St.-Pierre & Miquelon (Fr.)

NOVA SCOTIA

NEW BRUNSWICK

UNITED STATES OF AMERICA

1912

ALASKA (U.S.A)

YUKON TERRITORY

NORTHWEST TERRITORIES

District of Franklin

GREENLAND (Denmark)

District of Mackenzie

BRITISH COLUMBIA

ALBERTA

SASKATCHEWAN

District of Keewatin

NEWFOUNDLAND

MANITOBA

ONTARIO

QUÉBEC

P.E.I

St.-P. & M.

NOVA SCOTIA

NEW BRUNSWICK

UNITED STATES OF AMERICA

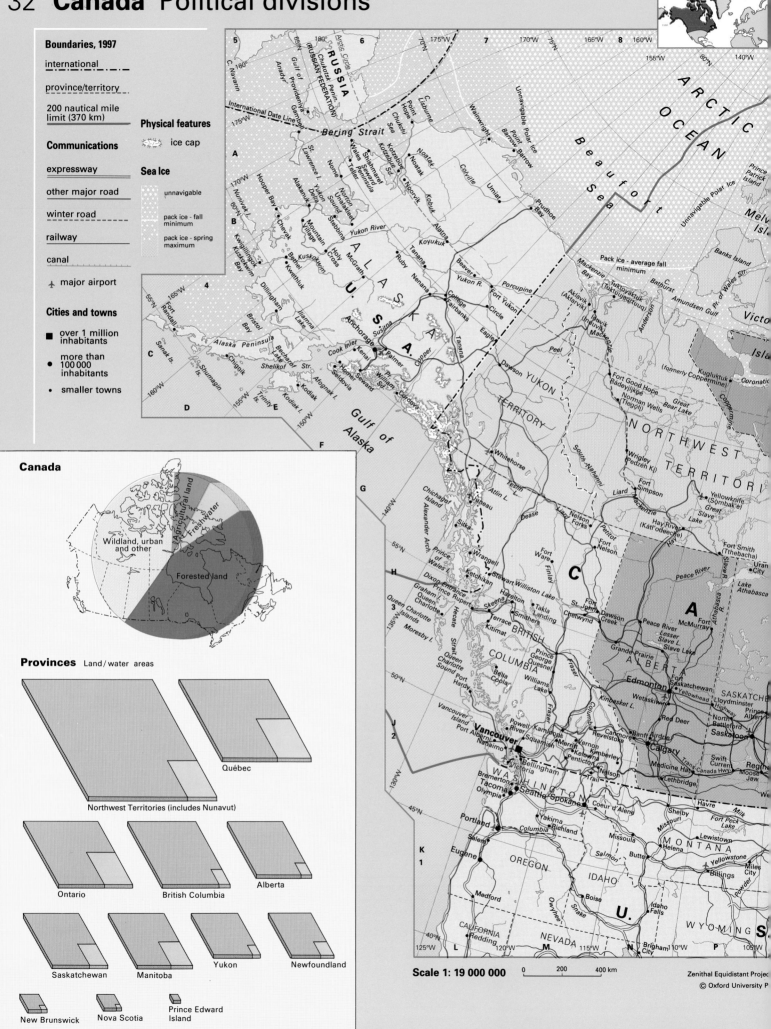

Boundaries, 1997

international

province/territory

200 nautical mile limit (370 km)

Physical features

ice cap

Communications

expressway

other major road

winter road

railway

canal

✈ major airport

Sea Ice

unnavigable

pack ice - fall minimum

pack ice - spring maximum

Cities and towns

■ over 1 million inhabitants

● more than 100 000 inhabitants

• smaller towns

Canada

Wildland, urban and other

Agricultural land

Freshwater

Forested land

Provinces Land / water areas

Québec

Northwest Territories (includes Nunavut)

Ontario

British Columbia

Alberta

Saskatchewan

Manitoba

Yukon

Newfoundland

New Brunswick

Nova Scotia

Prince Edward Island

Scale 1: 19 000 000

0 200 400 km

Zenithal Equidistant Projec

© Oxford University P

Distance chart
official highway distances, in kilometres

	Calgary	Charlottetown	Edmonton	Fredericton	Halifax	Montréal	Ottawa	Québec	Regina	St. John's	Saskatoon	Thunder Bay	Toronto	Vancouver	Victoria	Whitehorse	Winnipeg	Yellowknife	
•	4917	299	4558	5042	3743	3553	4014	764	6183	620	2050	3434	1057	1123	2385	1336	1811	**Calgary**
	•	4949	359	232	1184	1374	945	4163	1294	4421	2878	1724	5985	6051	7034	3592	6460	**Charlottetown**
		•	4598	5082	3764	3574	4035	785	6212	528	2071	3455	1244	1310	2086	1357	1511	**Edmonton**
			•	346	834	1024	586	3813	1622	4070	2527	1373	5634	5700	6684	3241	6109	**Fredericton**
				•	1318	1508	912	4297	1349	4554	3011	1857	6119	6185	7168	3726	6593	**Halifax**
					•	190	270	2979	2448	3236	1693	539	4801	4867	5850	2408	5275	**Montréal**
						•	460	2789	2638	3046	1503	399	4611	4677	5660	2218	5086	**Ottawa**
							•	3249	2208	3507	1963	810	5071	5137	6120	2678	5546	**Québec**
								•	5427	257	1286	2670	1822	1888	2871	571	2297	**Regina**
									•	5684	4141	2987	7248	7314	8298	4855	7723	**St. John's**
										•	1543	2927	1677	1743	2614	829	2039	**Saskatoon**
											•	1384	3108	3174	4157	715	3582	**Thunder Bay**
												•	4492	4558	5528	2099	4966	**Toronto**
													•	66	2697	2232	2411	**Vancouver**
														•	2763	2298	2477	**Victoria**
															•	3524	2704	**Whitehorse**
																•	2868	**Winnipeg**
																	•	**Yellowknife**

Boundaries

international
province, territory
national park/
provincial park

Communications

multilane highway
other highway
railway
ferry
West Coast Trail
✈ major airport
✈ other airport

Physical features

marsh
ice cap

Land height

metres
2000
1000
500
300
200
100
sea level
▲ spot height
in metres

Cities and towns

built-up areas
● more than 100 000
inhabitants
· smaller
urban places
+ historic site

Scale 1:5 000 000
0   50   100 km

Southwestern BC

Scale 1:2 000 000
0   25   50 km

PACIFIC

OCEAN

PACIFIC
RIM

NATIONAL

PARK

Vancouver Island

STRATHCONA
PROV.
PARK

COAST MOUNTAINS

BRITISH COLUMBIA

GARIBALDI
PROVINCIAL
PARK

Vancouver

Victoria

WASHINGTON

U.S.A.

ALASKA
U.S.A.

GLACIER BAY

NATIONAL PARK

ATLIN
PROV.
PARK

Alexander

Archipelago

YUKON

TERRITORY

Dixon Entrance

Queen
Charlotte
Islands

GWAII HAANAS
NATIONAL PARK
RESERVE

Hecate Strait

CASCADE
RANGE

MANNING
PROV. PARK

NORTH
CASCADES
NATIONAL
PARK

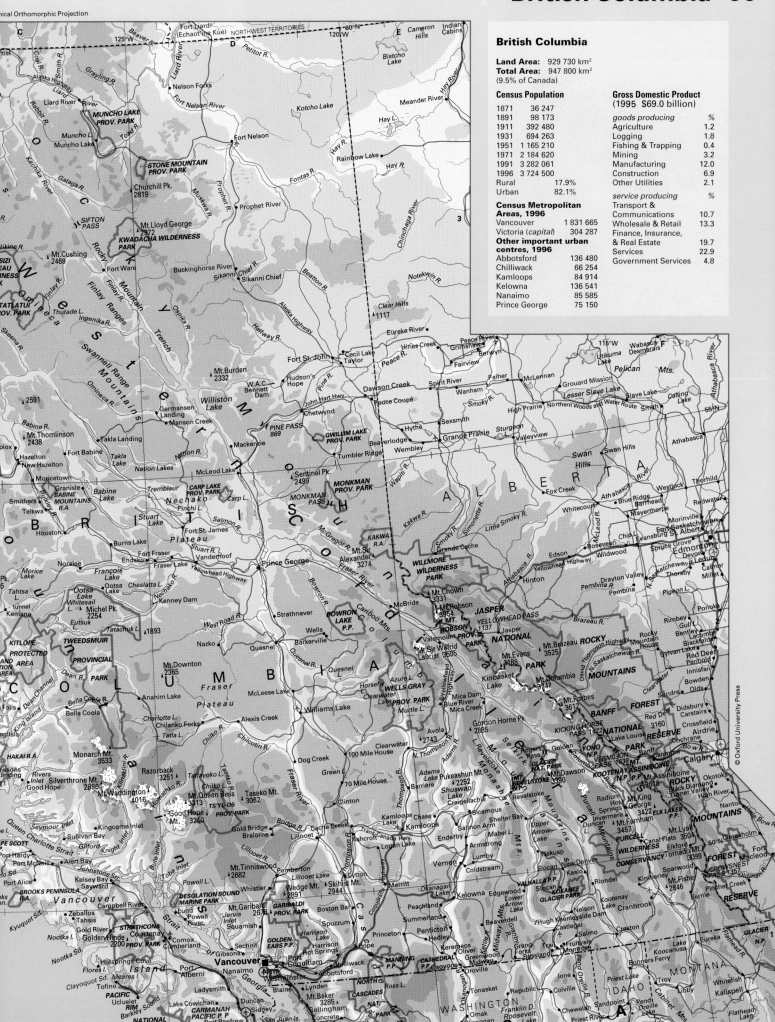

nical Orthomorphic Projection

British Columbia

Land Area: 929 730 km²
Total Area: 947 800 km²
(9.5% of Canada)

Census Population	
1871	36 247
1891	98 173
1911	392 480
1931	694 263
1951	1 165 210
1971	2 184 620
1991	3 282 061
1996	3 724 500
Rural	17.9%
Urban	82.1%

Census Metropolitan Areas, 1996
Vancouver	1 831 665
Victoria (*capital*)	304 287

Other important urban centres, 1996
Abbotsford	136 480
Chilliwack	66 254
Kamloops	84 914
Kelowna	136 541
Nanaimo	85 585
Prince George	75 150

Gross Domestic Product
(1995 $69.0 billion)

goods producing	%
Agriculture	1.2
Logging	1.8
Fishing & Trapping	0.4
Mining	3.2
Manufacturing	12.0
Construction	6.9
Other Utilities	2.1

service producing	%
Transport & Communications	10.7
Wholesale & Retail	13.3
Finance, Insurance, & Real Estate	19.7
Services	22.9
Government Services	4.8

© Oxford University Press

Satellite images of Calgary, and
Vancouver and the Fraser Delta
can be found on page 55.

The Mackenzie Delta, Northwest Territories,
showing the retreat of the winter ice from
both land and sea.

0   15   30 km

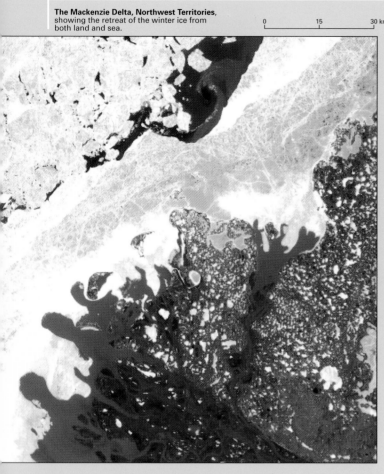

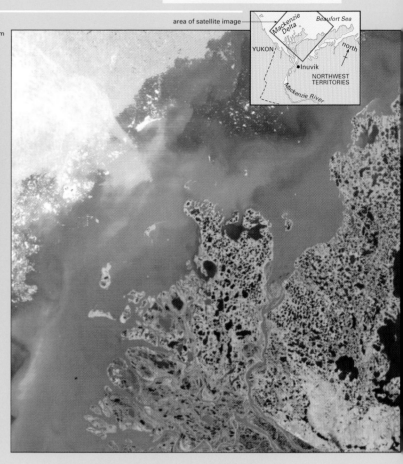

area of satellite image

Beaufort Sea

Mackenzie Delta

YUKON

north

•Inuvik

NORTHWEST
TERRITORIES

Mackenzie River

LANDSAT data received by the Canada Centre for Remote Sensing.
Provided courtesy of RADARSAT International.

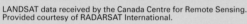

area of satellite image

North Saskatchewan

Prince Albert

north

Saskatchewan

•Saskatoon

South

Lake
Diefenbaker

•Moose
Jaw

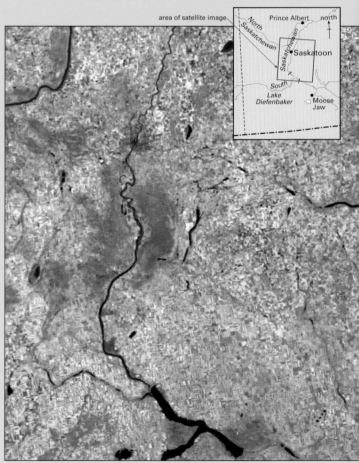

north

Fraser River

Vernon
Okanagan
Lake
•Kelowna

Vancouver

Okanagan River

area of satellite image

The Okanagan River valley, British Columbia.
Kelowna can be seen in the centre of the image,
on the shore of Okanagan Lake. The settlements
of Vernon and Coldstream are clearly visible at
the top of the image.

0   5   10   15 km

The area around Saskatoon, Southern Saskatchewan.
From Lake Diefenbaker in the south, the South Saskatchewan
River runs north through the centre of the image.
Saskatoon lies on the banks of this river, just north of centre.

0   15   30 km

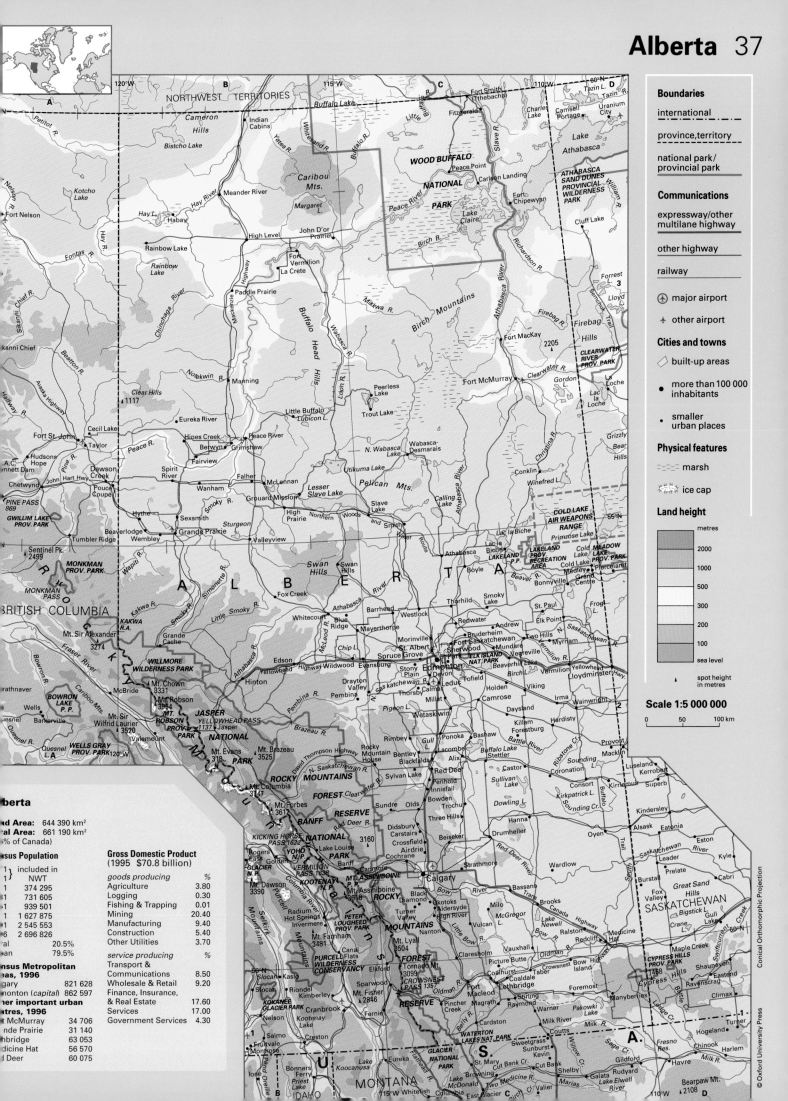

Boundaries
international
province, territory
national park/provincial park

Communications
expressway/other multilane highway
other highway
railway
✈ major airport
✈ other airport

Cities and towns
built-up areas
• more than 100 000 inhabitants
• smaller urban places

Physical features
marsh
ice cap

Land height
metres
2000
1000
500
300
200
100
sea level
▲ spot height in metres

Scale 1:5 000 000
0   50   100 km

...berta

...d Area: 644 390 km²
...al Area: 661 190 km²
...% of Canada)

...sus Population
...1   included in
...1   NWT
...1   374 295
...1   731 605
...1   939 501
...1   1 627 875
...6   2 545 553
...6   2 696 826
...al   20.5%
...an   79.5%

...sus Metropolitan ...as, 1996
...gary   821 628
...onton (capital)   862 597

...er important urban ...tres, 1996
...t McMurray   34 706
...nde Prairie   31 140
...hbridge   63 053
...dicine Hat   56 570
...Deer   60 075

Gross Domestic Product (1995 $70.8 billion)

goods producing	%
Agriculture	3.80
Logging	0.30
Fishing & Trapping	0.01
Mining	20.40
Manufacturing	9.40
Construction	5.40
Other Utilities	3.70

service producing	%
Transport & Communications	8.50
Wholesale & Retail	9.20
Finance, Insurance, & Real Estate	17.60
Services	17.00
Government Services	4.30

Conical Orthomorphic Projection

© Oxford University Press

Boundaries

international

province, territory

national park/
provincial park

Communications

expressway/other
multilane highway

other highway

railway

⊕ major airport

✦ other airport

Cities and towns

⬦ built-up areas

● more than 100 000
inhabitants

• smaller
urban places

Physical features

〜〜〜 marsh

Land height

metres

1000

500

300

200

100

sea level

▲ spot height
in metres

+ historic sites

Scale 1:5 000 000

0   50   100 km

Saskatchewan

Land Area: 570 700 km²
Total Area: 652 330 km²
(6.5% of Canada)

Census Population

1871 }	included in
1891	NWT
1911	492 432
1931	921 785
1951	831 728
1971	826 240
1991	988 928
1996	990 237
Rural	36.7%
Urban	63.3%

**Census Metropolitan
Areas, 1996**

Regina (*capital*)	193 652
Saskatoon	219 056

**Other important urban
centres, 1996**

Lloydminster (Sask.-Alb.)	18 953
Moose Jaw	34 829
Prince Albert	41 706

Gross Domestic Product
(1995 $18.1 billion)

goods producing	%
Agriculture	10.30
Logging	0.30
Fishing & Trapping	0.03
Mining	13.00
Manufacturing	6.00
Construction	5.30
Other Utilities	2.90

service producing	%
Transport & Communications	10.30
Wholesale & Retail	10.60
Finance, Insurance, & Real Estate	15.50
Services	18.70
Government Services	6.00

© Oxford University Press

Conical Orthomorphic Projection

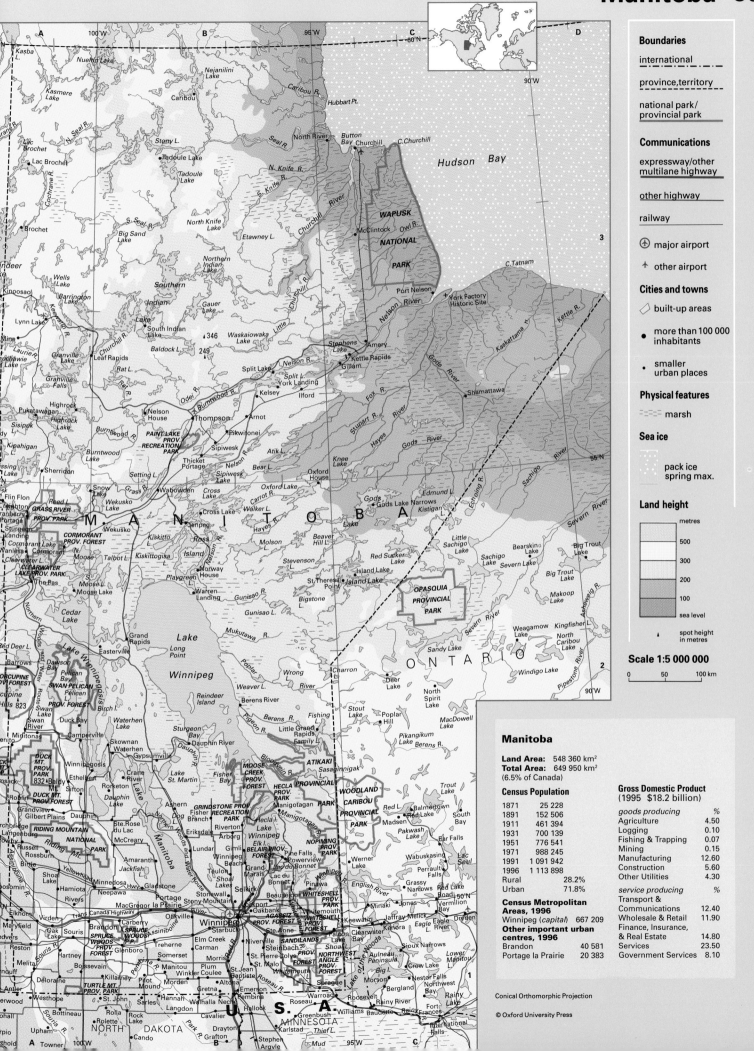

Conical Orthomorphic Projection

© Oxford University Press

Boundaries

international

province, territory

national park/
provincial park

Communications

expressway/other
multilane highway

other highway

railway

⊕ major airport

✈ other airport

Cities and towns

◇ built-up areas

● more than 100 000
inhabitants

• smaller
urban places

Physical features

marsh

Sea ice

pack ice
spring max.

Land height

metres
500
300
200
100
sea level

▲ spot height
in metres

Scale 1:5 000 000

0   50   100 km

Manitoba

Land Area: 548 360 km²
Total Area: 649 950 km²
(6.5% of Canada)

Census Population

1871	25 228
1891	152 506
1911	461 394
1931	700 139
1951	776 541
1971	988 245
1991	1 091 942
1996	1 113 898
Rural	28.2%
Urban	71.8%

Census Metropolitan Areas, 1996

Winnipeg (capital) 667 209

Other important urban centres, 1996

Brandon	40 581
Portage la Prairie	20 383

Gross Domestic Product
(1995 $18.2 billion)

goods producing	%
Agriculture	4.50
Logging	0.10
Fishing & Trapping	0.07
Mining	0.15
Manufacturing	12.60
Construction	5.60
Other Utilities	4.30

service producing	%
Transport & Communications	12.40
Wholesale & Retail	11.90
Finance, Insurance, & Real Estate	14.80
Services	23.50
Government Services	8.10

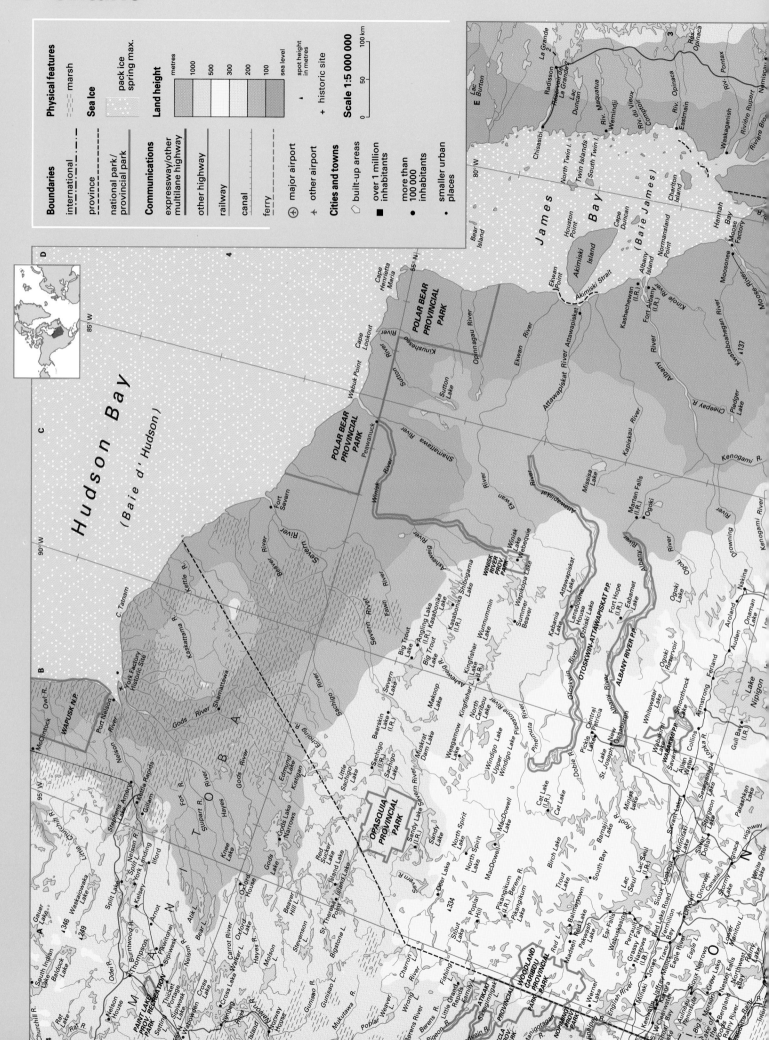

Physical features

--- marsh

Sea Ice

- - - pack ice
spring max.

Land height

metres
1000
500
300
200
100
sea level

▲ spot height
in metres
+ historic site

Boundaries

--- international

--- province

national park/
provincial park

Communications

expressway/other
multilane highway

other highway

railway

canal

ferry

⊕ major airport

+ other airport

Cities and towns

◇ built-up areas

over 1 million
inhabitants

■ more than
100 000
inhabitants

● smaller urban
places

Scale 1:5 000 000

0   50   100 km

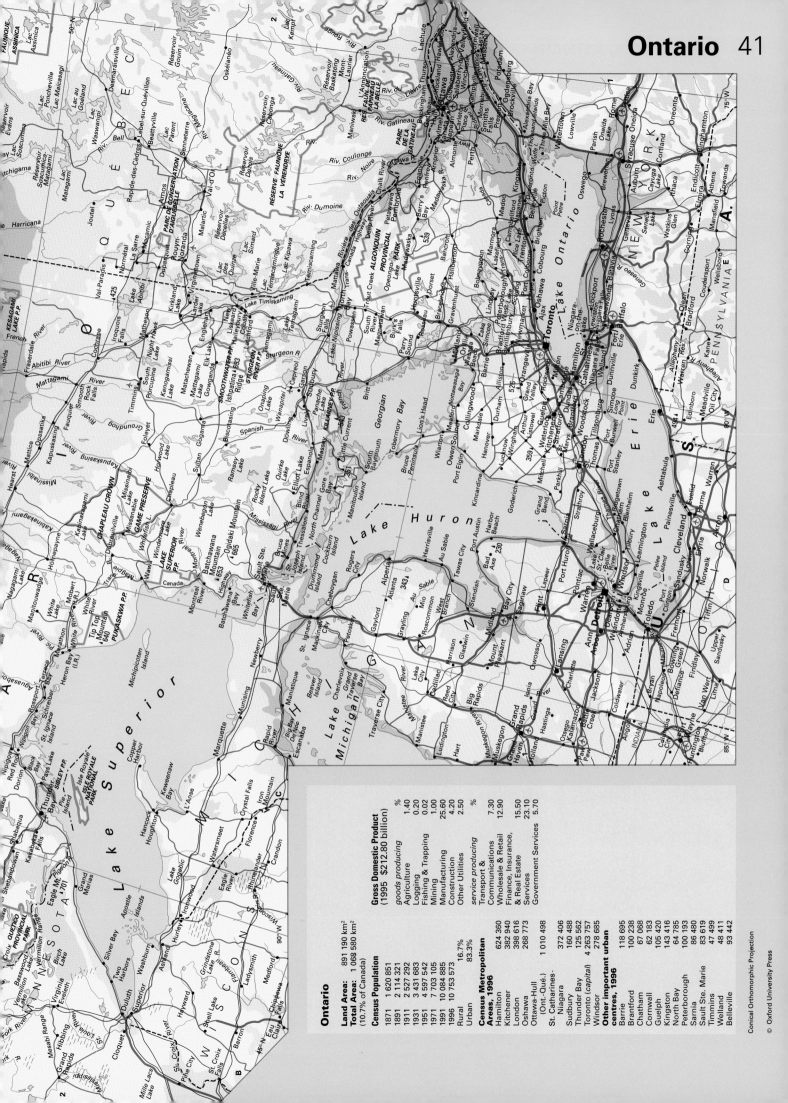

Ontario

Land Area: 891 190 km²
Total Area: 1 068 580 km²
(10.7% of Canada)

Census Population

Year	Population
1871	1 620 851
1891	2 114 321
1911	2 527 292
1931	3 431 683
1951	4 597 542
1971	7 703 105
1991	10 084 885
1996	10 753 573
Rural	16.7%
Urban	83.3%

Census Metropolitan Areas, 1996

Hamilton	624 360
Kitchener	382 940
London	398 616
Oshawa	268 773
Ottawa-Hull (Ont.-Que.)	1 010 498
St. Catharines-Niagara	372 406
Sudbury	160 488
Thunder Bay	125 562
Toronto (capital)	4 263 757
Windsor	278 685

Other important urban centres, 1996

Barrie	118 695
Brantford	100 238
Chatham	67 068
Cornwall	62 183
Guelph	105 420
Kingston	143 416
North Bay	64 785
Peterborough	100 193
Sarnia	86 480
Sault Ste. Marie	83 619
Timmins	47 499
Welland	48 411
Belleville	93 442

Gross Domestic Product (1995 $212.80 billion)

	%
goods producing	
Agriculture	1.40
Logging	0.20
Fishing & Trapping	0.02
Mining	1.00
Manufacturing	25.60
Construction	4.20
Other Utilities	2.50
service producing	%
Transport & Communications	7.30
Wholesale & Retail	12.90
Finance, Insurance, & Real Estate	15.50
Services	23.10
Government Services	5.70

Conical Orthomorphic Projection

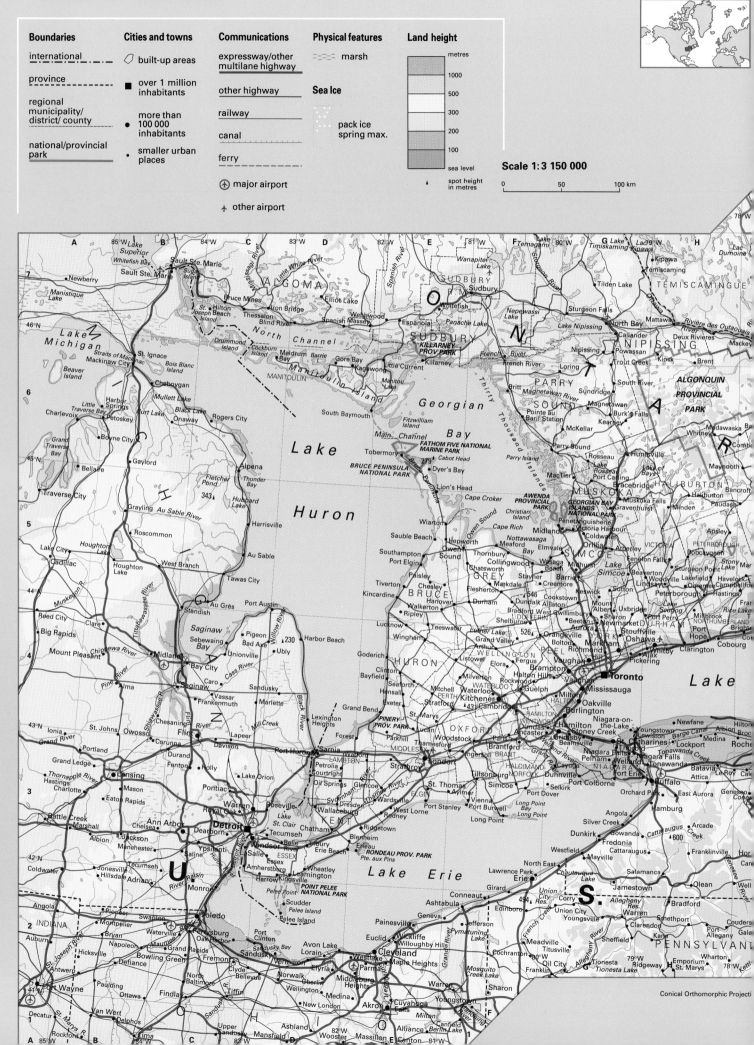

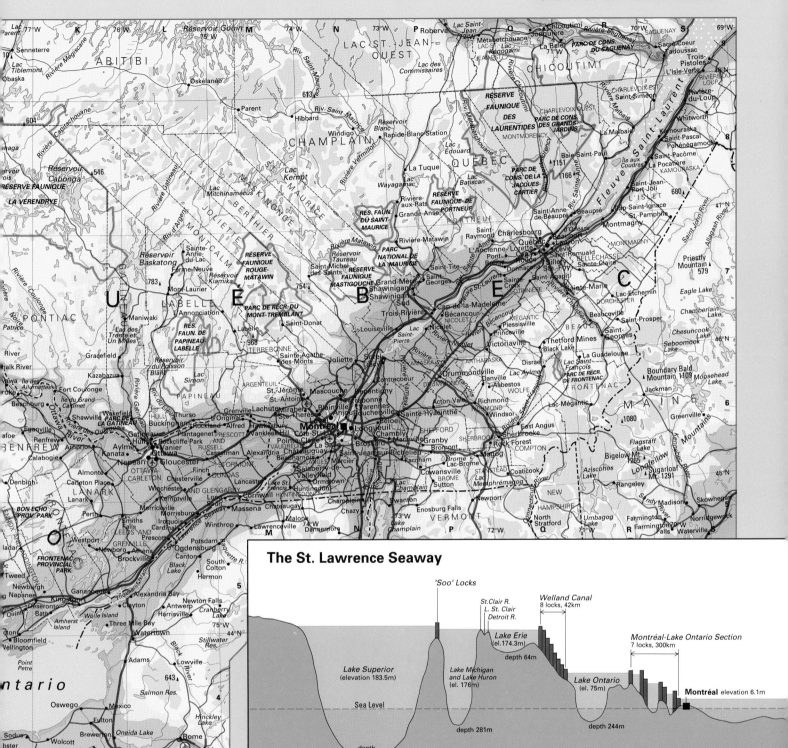

The St. Lawrence Seaway

'Soo' Locks

St.Clair R.
L. St. Clair
Detroit R.

Welland Canal
8 locks, 42km

Lake Erie
(el.174.3m)

depth 64m

Montréal-Lake Ontario Section
7 locks, 300km

Lake Superior
(elevation 183.5m)

Lake Michigan
and Lake Huron
(el. 176m)

Lake Ontario
(el. 75m)

Montréal elevation 6.1m

Sea Level

depth 281m

depth 244m

depth
405m

The St. Lawrence Seaway Authority was established in 1951 for the purpose of constructing, operating, and maintaining a deep waterway between the Port of Montréal and Lake Erie, replacing an earlier network of shallow draught canals. Two of the seven seaway locks along the St. Lawrence River, in the United States, are operated by the U.S. St. Lawrence Seaway Development Corporation.

The St. Lawrence Seaway was officially opened in 1959. It allows navigation by ships not exceeding 222.5 m in length, 23.2 m in width, and loaded to a maximum draught of 7.9 m in a minimum water depth of 8.2 m.

Beginning at Montréal, the Seaway naturally divides into four sections:

1. The Lachine Section required the construction of the 33 km South Shore Canal, to by-pass the Lachine Rapids.

The St. Lambert and Côte Ste. Catherine locks provide a lift 13.7 m to Lake St. Louis.

2. The Soulanges Section contains the two Beauharnois locks, by-passing the Beauharnois hydro-electric plant to reach Lac Saint-François.

3. The Lac Saint-François Section extends to a point just east of Cornwall, Ontario.

4. The International Rapids Section was developed simultaneously for hydro-electric power generation and navigation. Ontario and the State of New York jointly built the Moses-Saunders Power Dam, the Long Sault and Iroquois control dams, and undertook the flooding of the river above the power dam to form Lake St. Lawrence, the 'head pond' of the generating station.

The Wiley-Dondero Canal and the Snell and Eisenhower locks allow ships to by-pass the Moses-Saunders power station. The Iroquois lock and adjacent control dam are used to adjust the level of Lake St. Lawrence to that of Lake Ontario.

The Welland Canal joins lakes Ontario and Erie and allows ships to by-pass Niagara Falls by means of eight locks. The present Welland Canal, completed in 1932, was later deepened to ensure 7.9 m draught navigation throughout the Seaway.

The final section consists of four parallel locks, the 'Soo' locks, on the St. Mary's River and connects Lake Superior to Lake Huron. This section is not part of the St. Lawrence Seaway Authority.

Oxford University Press

Conical Orthomorphic Proje
© Oxford University

Boundaries
international
county (Ontario only)
national park/provincial park

Cities and towns
⌀ built-up areas
● more than 100 000 inhabitants
• smaller urban places

Communications
expressway/other multilane highway
other highway
railway
canal
✈ major airport
✈ other airport

Physical features
- - - marsh
Niagara Escarpment

Land height
metres
500
300
200
100
sea level
▲ spot height in metres

Scale 1:1 250 000

0   25 km

Satellite images of Toronto and Central Ontario, and Montréal and the St. Lawrence River can be found on page 55.

Eastern Canada Satellite Images 45

area around Happy Valley-Goose Bay, Labrador, Newfoundland.
Churchill River is visible at the base of the image, as it flows into
ose Bay and then on to Lake Melville (only partly visible).
nd Lake is the long narrow shape across the top of the image.

5   10   15 km

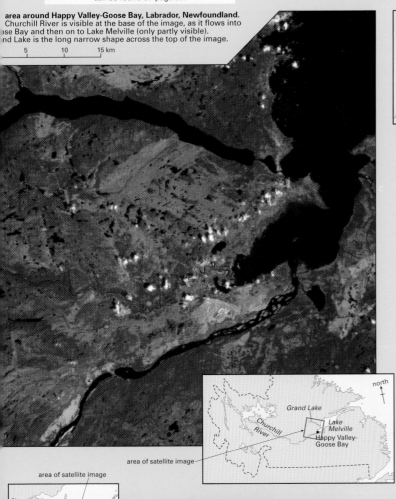

north

Grand Lake

Churchill River

Lake Melville

Happy Valley-Goose Bay

area of satellite image

QUÉBEC

Fleuve Saint Laurent

Péninsule de la Gaspésie

Île d'Anticosti

area of satellite image

Baie des Chaleurs

NEW BRUNSWICK

PRINCE EDWARD ISLAND

north

Gaspé Peninsula, Québec.
To the south the Baie des Chaleurs,
to the north the St. Lawrence River.

0   15   30 km

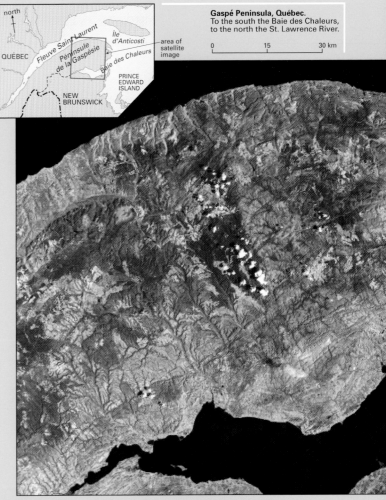

area of satellite image

NEW BRUNSWICK

PRINCE EDWARD ISLAND

Northumberland St.

Moncton

Chignecto Bay

Bay of Fundy

north

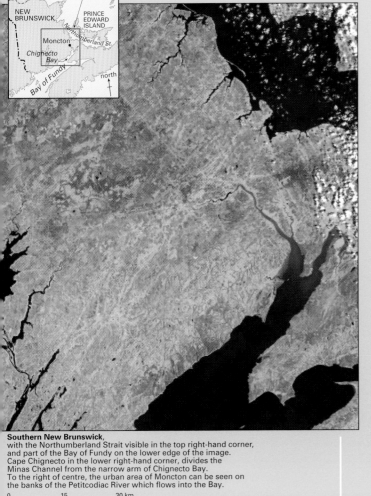

LANDSAT data received by the Canada Centre for Remote Sensing.
Provided courtesy of RADARSAT International.

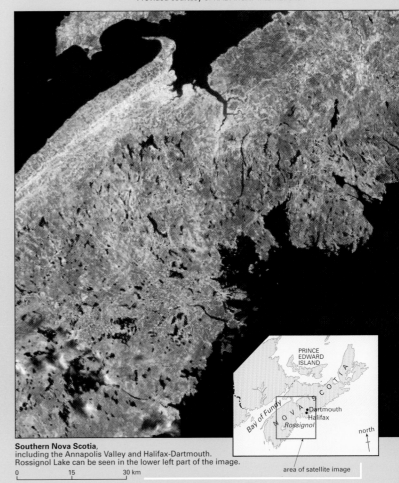

Southern New Brunswick,
with the Northumberland Strait visible in the top right-hand corner,
and part of the Bay of Fundy on the lower edge of the image.
Cape Chignecto in the lower right-hand corner, divides the
Minas Channel from the narrow arm of Chignecto Bay.
To the right of centre, the urban area of Moncton can be seen on
the banks of the Petitcodiac River which flows into the Bay.

0   15   30 km

Southern Nova Scotia,
including the Annapolis Valley and Halifax-Dartmouth.
Rossignol Lake can be seen in the lower left part of the image.

0   15   30 km

PRINCE EDWARD ISLAND

NOVA SCOTIA

Bay of Fundy

Dartmouth

Halifax

Rossignol

north

area of satellite image

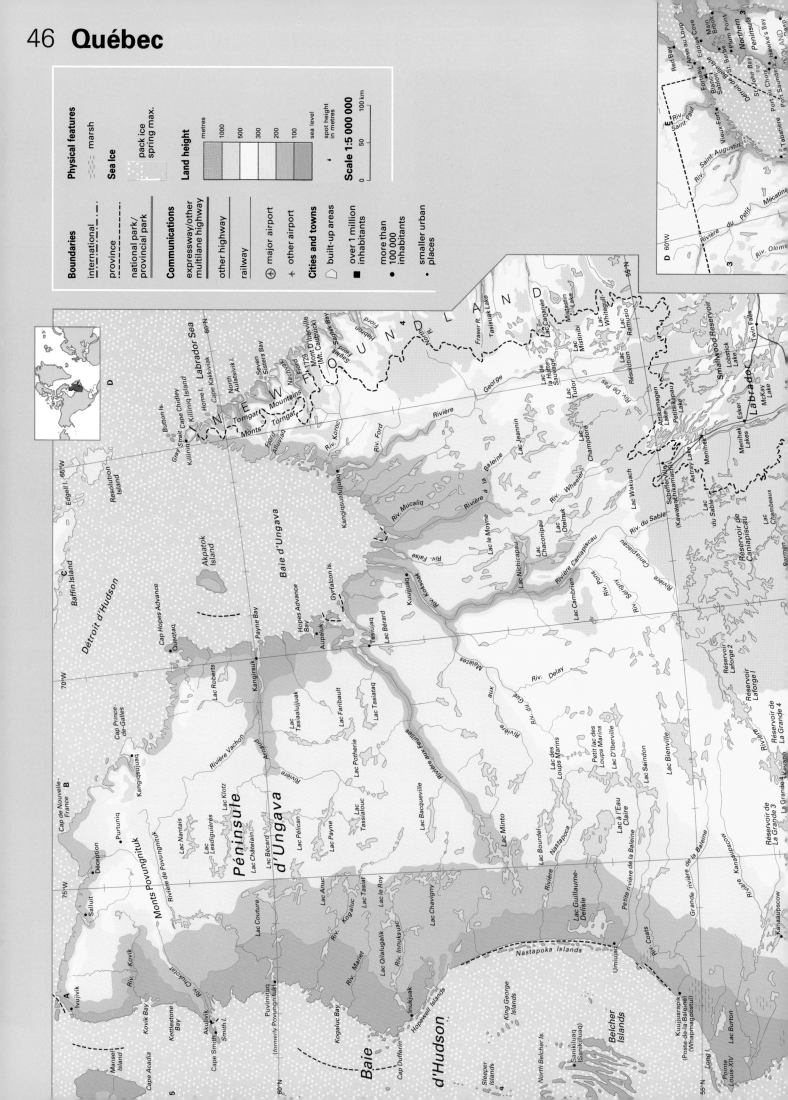

Québec

Land Area: 1 356 790 km²
Total Area: 1 540 680 km²
(15.5% of Canada)

Census Population

1871	1 191 516
1891	1 488 535
1911	2 005 776
1931	2 874 662
1951	4 055 681
1971	6 027 765
1996	7 138 795
Rural	21.6%
Urban	78.4%

Census Metropolitan Areas, 1996

Chicoutimi–Jonquière	160 454
Montréal	3 326 510
Québec *(capital)*	671 889
Sherbrooke	147 384
Trois-Rivières	139 950
Ottawa-Hull (Ont.-Qué.)	1 010 498

Other important urban centres, 1996

Saint-Jean-sur-Richelieu	76 461
Shawinigan	59 851
Drummondville	65 119
Granby	58 872
Saint-Hyacinthe	50 027
Rimouski	48 104

Gross Domestic Product
(1995 $118.9 billion)

	%
goods producing	
Agriculture	1.70
Logging	0.50
Fishing & Trapping	0.05
Mining	1.00
Manufacturing	21.70
Construction	5.00
Other Utilities	4.00
service producing	%
Transport & Communications	8.30
Wholesale & Retail	12.40
Finance, Insurance, & Real Estate	13.40
Services	24.40
Government Services	6.50

Conical Orthomorphic Projection

© Oxford University Press

Boundaries
- international
- province, territory
- county
- national/provincial park/sanctuary

Communications
- expressway/other multilane highway
- other highway
- winter road
- railway
- canal
- ferry
- ⊕ major airport
- ✈ other airport

Cities and towns
- ◇ built-up areas
- ● more than 100 000 inhabitants
- ● smaller urban places
- • smaller urban places

Physical features
- marsh
- pack ice spring max.
- Sea ice

Land height

metres
1000
500
300
200
100
sea level

▲ spot height in metres

Scale 1:5 000 000
0 ___ 100 km

Newfoundland

Land Area: 371 690 km²
Total Area: 405 720 km²
(4.1% of Canada)

Census Population†

1871	152 500
1891	202 040
1911	242 619
1931	281 500
1951	361 416
1971	522 105
1991	568 474
1996	551 792
Rural	43.1%
Urban	56.9%

†Newfoundland became a province of Canada in 1949

Census Metropolitan Areas, 1996

St. John's (capital)	174 051

Other important urban areas, 1996

Corner Brook	27 945

Gross Domestic Product (1995 $6.6 billion)

	%
goods producing	
Agriculture	0.4
Logging	0.8
Fishing & Trapping	1.2
Mining	4.4
Manufacturing	7.0
Construction	7.5
Other Utilities	5.1
service producing	%
Transport & Communications	10.4
Wholesale & Retail	10.4
Finance, Insurance, & Real Estate	15.4
Services	25.4
Government Services	10.9

Nova Scotia

Land Area: 52 840 km²
Total Area: 55 490 km²
(0.6% of Canada)

Census Population

1871	387 800
1891	450 396
1911	492 338
1931	512 846
1951	642 584
1971	788 960
1991	899 942
1996	909 282
Rural	45.2%
Urban	54.8%

Census Metropolitan Areas, 1996

Halifax (capital)	332 518

Other important urban areas, 1996

Cape Breton (Sydney, Glace Bay, etc.)	117 849
Truro	44 102

Gross Domestic Product (1995 $13.2 billion)

	%
goods producing	
Agriculture	1.2
Logging	0.8
Fishing & Trapping	1.6
Mining	1.6
Manufacturing	11.9
Construction	5.6
Other Utilities	2.5
service producing	%
Transport & Communications	9.8
Wholesale & Retail	12.2
Finance, Insurance, & Real Estate	16.8
Services	23.9
Government Services	10.8

New Brunswick

Land Area: 72 090 km²
Total Area: 73 440 km²
(0.7% of Canada)

Census Population

1871	285 594
1891	321 236
1911	351 889
1931	408 219
1951	515 697
1971	634 556
1991	723 900
1996	738 133
Rural	51.2%
Urban	48.8%

Census Metropolitan Areas, 1996

Saint John	125 705

Other important urban areas, 1996

Fredericton (capital)	78 950
Moncton	113 491

Gross Domestic Product (1995 $10.6 billion)

	%
goods producing	
Agriculture	1.2
Logging	1.8
Fishing & Trapping	1.0
Mining	1.8
Manufacturing	14.0
Construction	6.6
Other Utilities	4.6
service producing	%
Transport & Communications	10.7
Wholesale & Retail	11.3
Finance, Insurance, & Real Estate	14.1
Services	22.5
Government Services	9.4

Prince Edward Island

Land Area: 5 660 km²
Total Area: 5 660 km²
(0.05% of Canada)

Census Population

1871	94 621
1891	109 078
1911	93 728
1931	88 038
1951	98 429
1971	110 640
1991	129 765
1996	134 557
Rural	55.8%
Urban	44.2%

Important urban centres, 1996

Charlottetown (capital)	57 224
Summerside	16 001

Gross Domestic Product (1995 $1.8 billion)

	%
goods producing	
Agriculture	9.2
Logging	0.4
Fishing & Trapping	2.0
Mining	—
Manufacturing	8.7
Construction	7.2
Other Utilities	3.1
service producing	%
Transport & Communications	8.0
Wholesale & Retail	11.4
Finance, Insurance, & Real Estate	14.8
Services	23.5
Government Services	10.8

Pack ice - average spring maximum

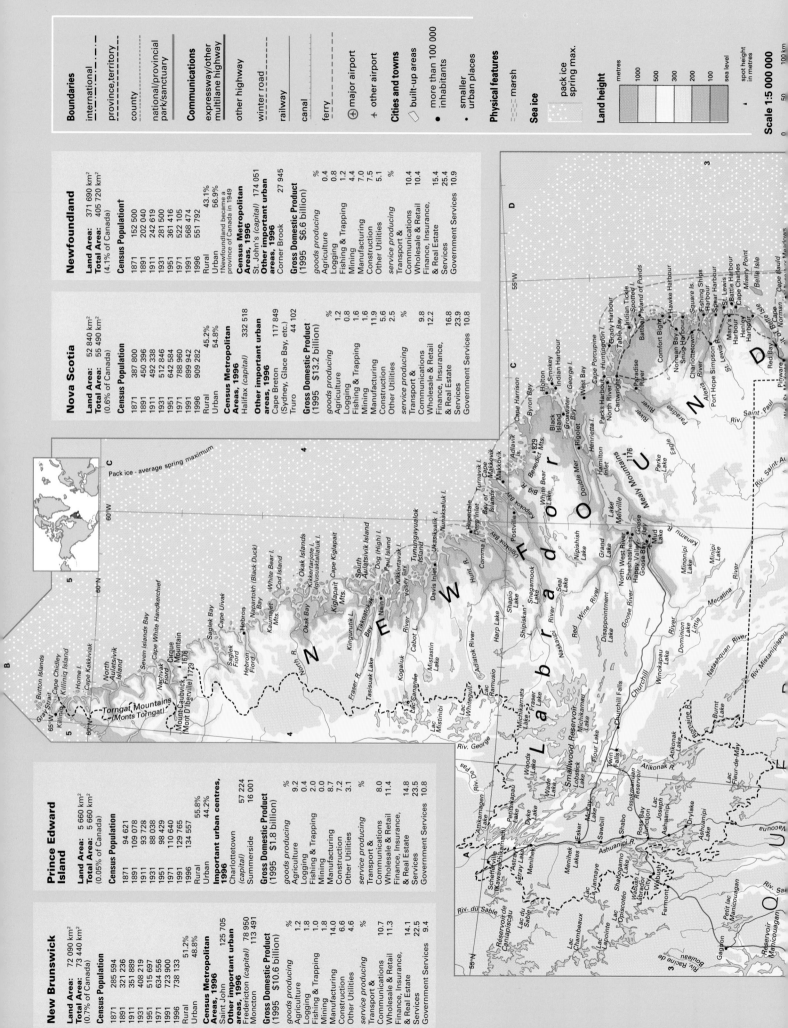

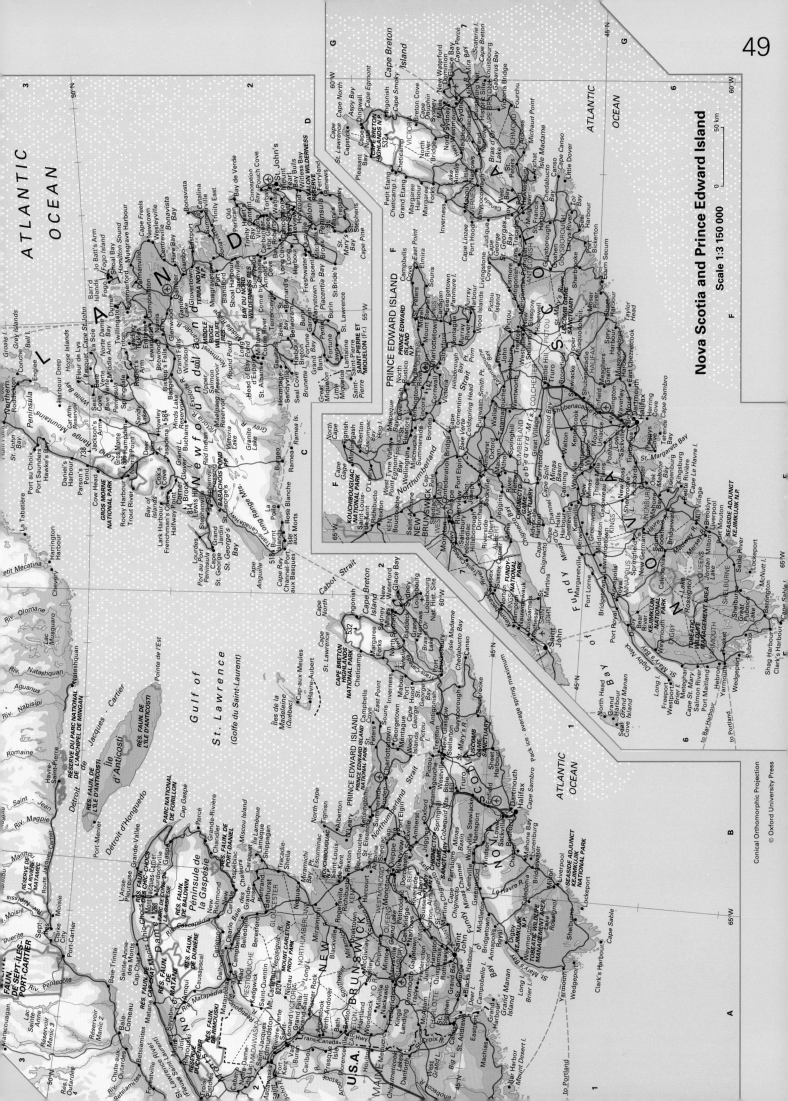

Nova Scotia and Prince Edward Island

Scale 1:3 150 000

0   50 km

Conical Orthomorphic Projection

© Oxford University Press

ATLANTIC OCEAN

NEWFOUNDLAND

PRINCE EDWARD ISLAND

NOVA SCOTIA

NEW BRUNSWICK

Gulf of St. Lawrence
(Golfe du Saint-Laurent)

Île d'Anticosti

Îles de la Madeleine (Québec)

Cabot Strait

Northumberland Strait

Bay of Fundy

U.S.A.

MAINE

Boundaries

international

province/territory

national/provincial park/sanctuary

Communications

other road

winter road

railway

⊕ major airport

✦ other airport

Towns

● more than 1000 inhabitants

○ less than 1000 inhabitants

+ historic sites

Physical features

marsh

ice cap

Sea ice

unnavigable

pack ice fall minimum

pack ice spring max.

Land height

metres

2000
1000
500
300
200
100
sea level

▲ spot height in metres

Scale 1:12 000 000

0   200km

N

active layer   1–2m   2–3m

45m   1–2m

permafrost

400m   unfrozen ground

CONTINUOUS PERMAFROST   DISCONTINUOUS PERMAFROST

Cross-section showing a typical permafrost distribution in Northern Canada

Limits of continuous and discontinuous permafrost are shown on the map below.

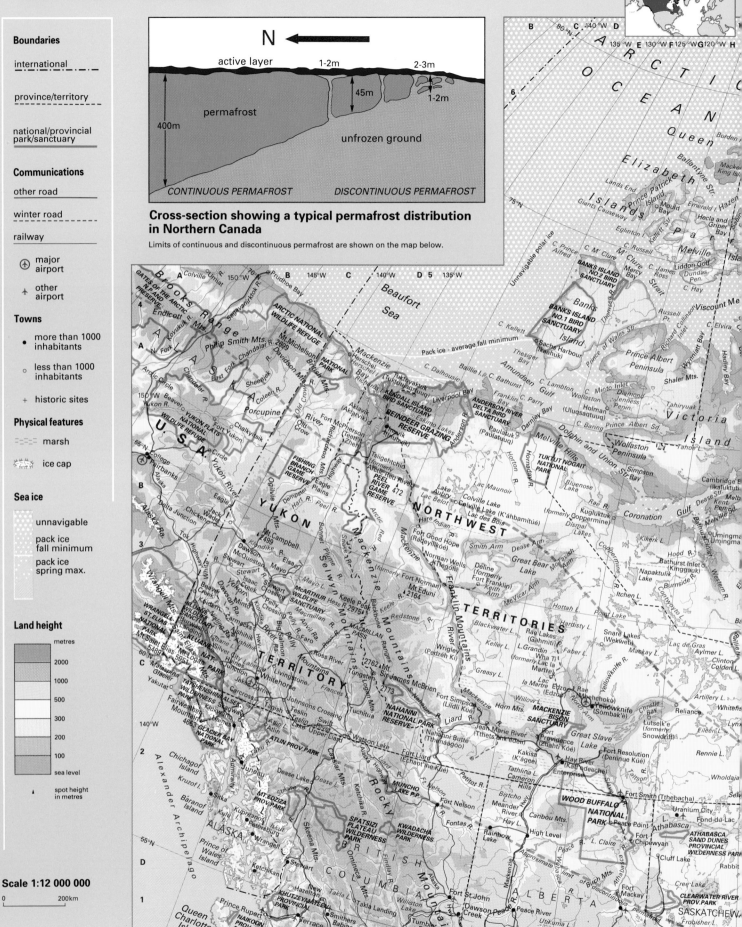

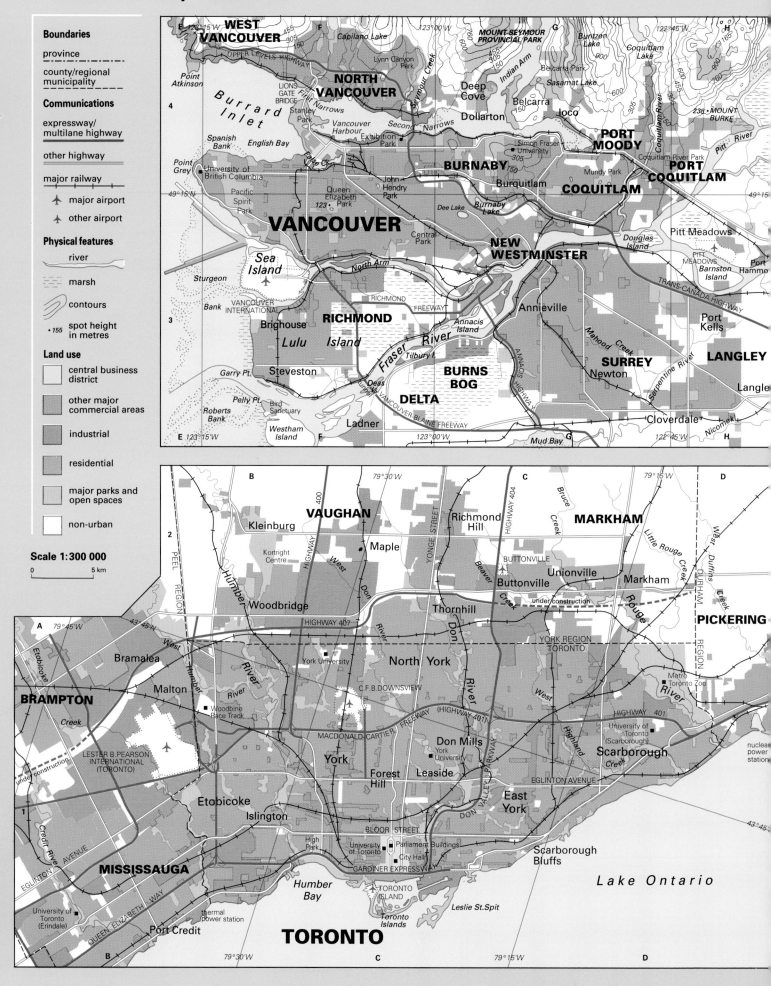

Boundaries

province

county/regional municipality

Communications

expressway/ multilane highway

other highway

major railway

✈ major airport

✈ other airport

Physical features

river

marsh

contours

·155 spot height in metres

Land use

central business district

other major commercial areas

industrial

residential

major parks and open spaces

non-urban

Scale 1:300 000

0   5 km

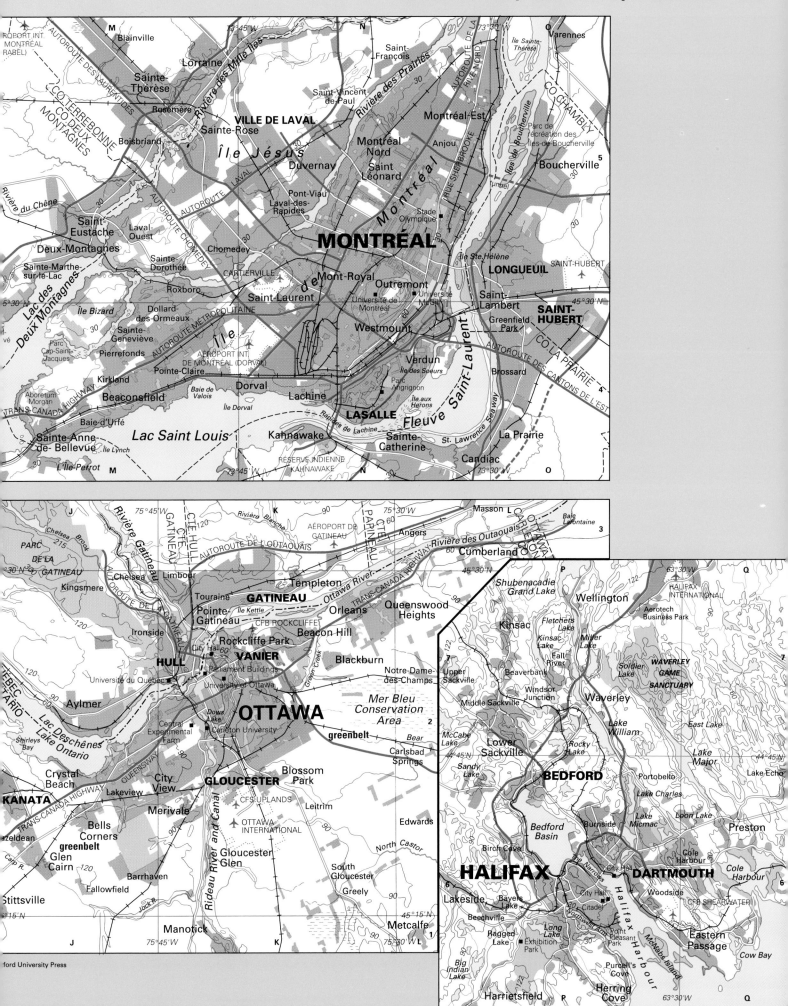

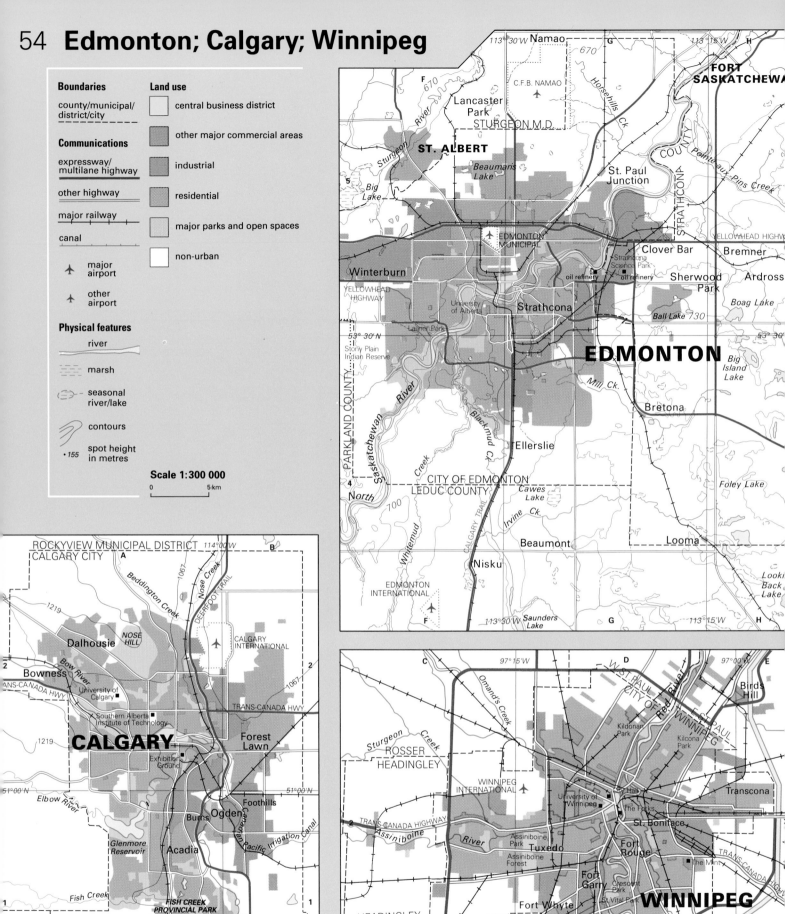

Boundaries

county/municipal/
district/city

Communications

expressway/
multilane highway

other highway

major railway

canal

✈ major airport

✦ other airport

Physical features

river

marsh

seasonal
river/lake

contours

•155 spot height
in metres

Scale 1:300 000

0   5km

Land use

central business district

other major commercial areas

industrial

residential

major parks and open spaces

non-urban

© Oxford University Press

A satellite image of Winnipeg can be found on page 7.

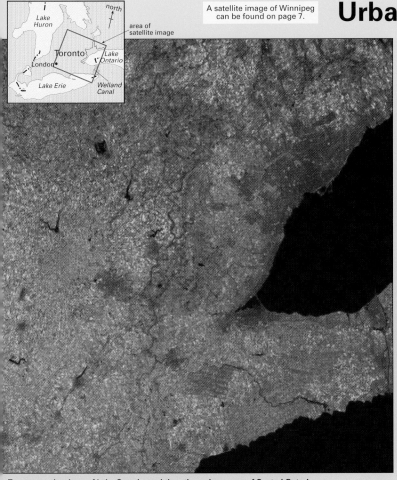

Toronto on the shore of Lake Ontario, and the other urban areas of Central Ontario.
The city of London is visible in the lower left-hand corner. The Welland Canal and St. Catharines can be seen on the extreme right-hand edge of the image.

0   15   30 km

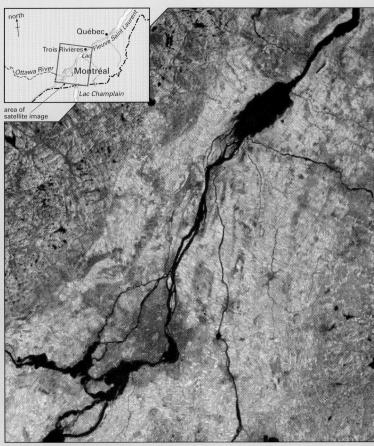

Montréal and the valley of the St. Lawrence River
as far as Trois Rivières and Lac Saint Pierre, Québec

0   15   30 km

Vancouver and the Fraser River Delta, British Columbia.
The Fraser River is seen down the right-hand edge of the image turning eventually westwards as it flows into the delta on which Vancouver is built. The Lillooet River is shown flowing from Lake Lillooet in the centre top of the image, through Harrison Lake to join the Fraser River.

0   15   30 km

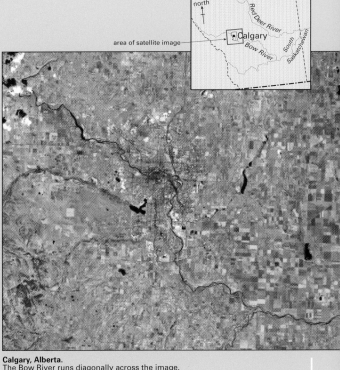

Calgary, Alberta.
The Bow River runs diagonally across the image.
Calgary lies on the banks of the river, in the centre of the image, with the distinctive shape of the Glenmore Reservoir, on the Elbow River, situated within its urban area.

0   5   10   15 km

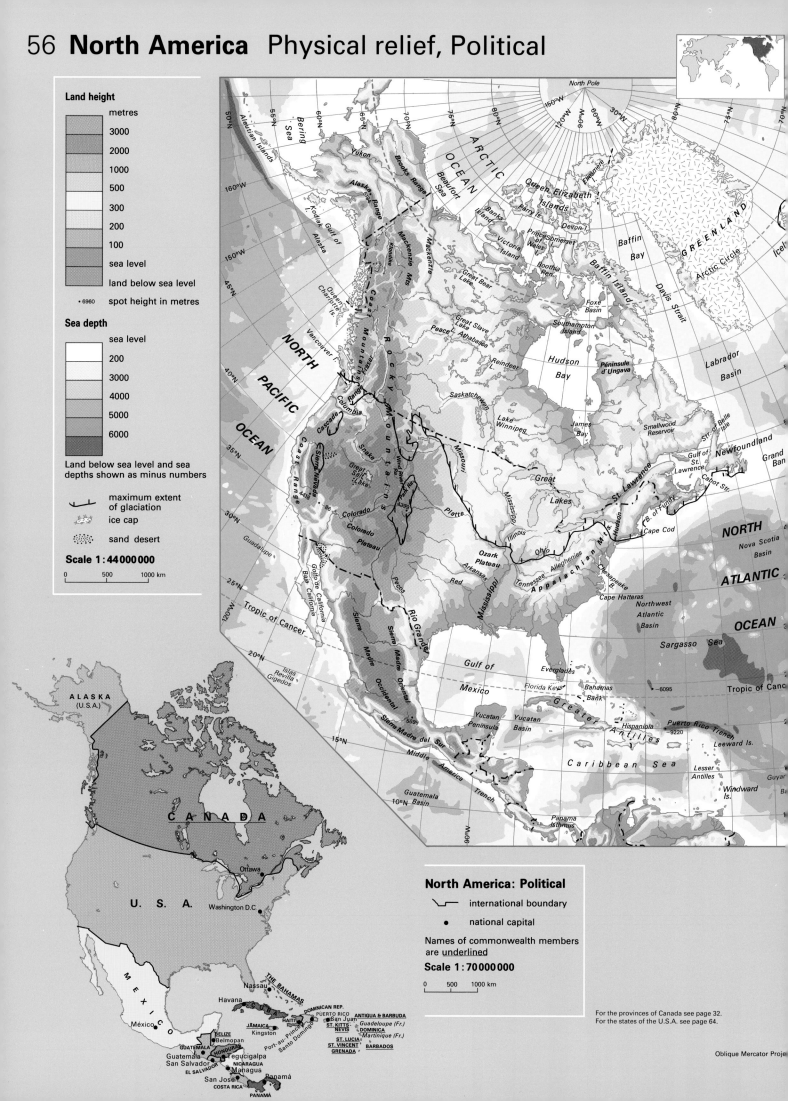

Land height

metres

3000
2000
1000
500
300
200
100
sea level
land below sea level

• 6960   spot height in metres

Sea depth

sea level
200
3000
4000
5000
6000

Land below sea level and sea depths shown as minus numbers

⌐ maximum extent of glaciation

ice cap

sand desert

Scale 1 : 44 000 000

0   500   1000 km

North America: Political

international boundary

• national capital

Names of commonwealth members are underlined

Scale 1 : 70 000 000

0   500   1000 km

For the provinces of Canada see page 32.
For the states of the U.S.A. see page 64.

Oblique Mercator Proje

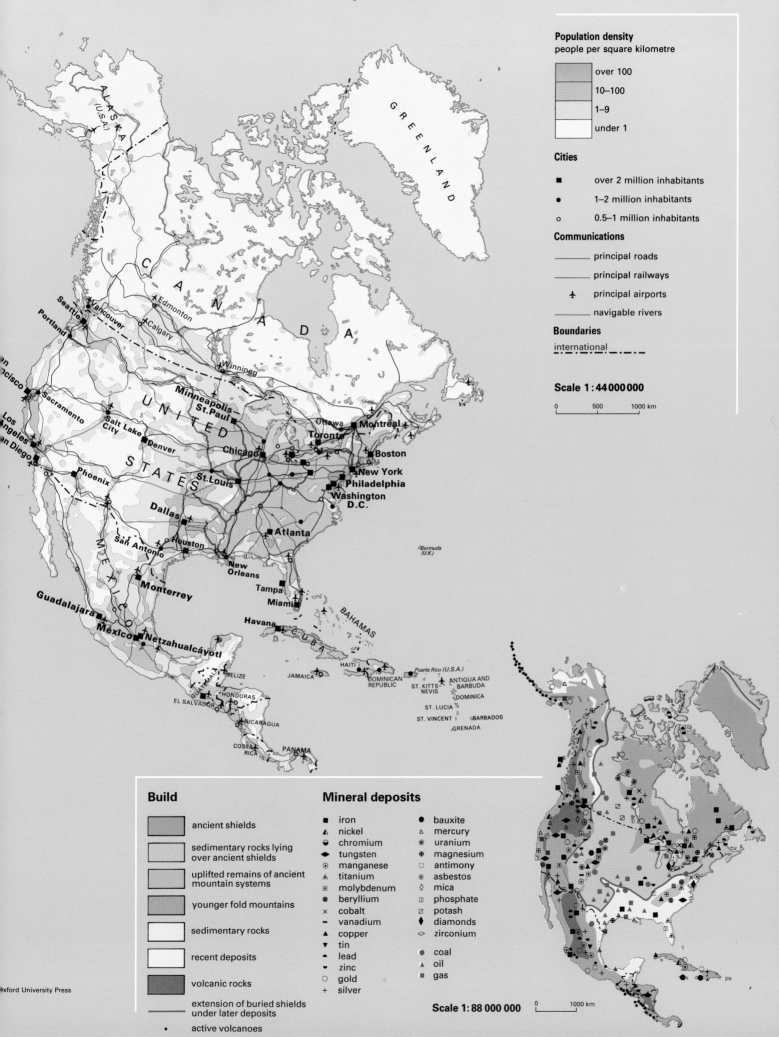

Population density
people per square kilometre

over 100
10–100
1–9
under 1

Cities

■ over 2 million inhabitants

● 1–2 million inhabitants

○ 0.5–1 million inhabitants

Communications

—— principal roads

—— principal railways

✈ principal airports

—— navigable rivers

Boundaries

international

Scale 1 : 44 000 000

0   500   1000 km

Build

ancient shields

sedimentary rocks lying over ancient shields

uplifted remains of ancient mountain systems

younger fold mountains

sedimentary rocks

recent deposits

volcanic rocks

extension of buried shields under later deposits

● active volcanoes

Mineral deposits

■ iron
▲ nickel
◒ chromium
◆ tungsten
⊙ manganese
▲ titanium
⊡ molybdenum
⊗ beryllium
× cobalt
− vanadium
⌐ copper
▼ tin
⊢ lead
⊣ zinc
○ gold
+ silver

● bauxite
△ mercury
⊛ uranium
⊕ magnesium
□ antimony
⊞ asbestos
◇ mica
⊟ phosphate
⊠ potash
◆ diamonds
◇ zirconium

● coal
▲ oil
■ gas

Scale 1 : 88 000 000

0   1000 km

Oxford University Press

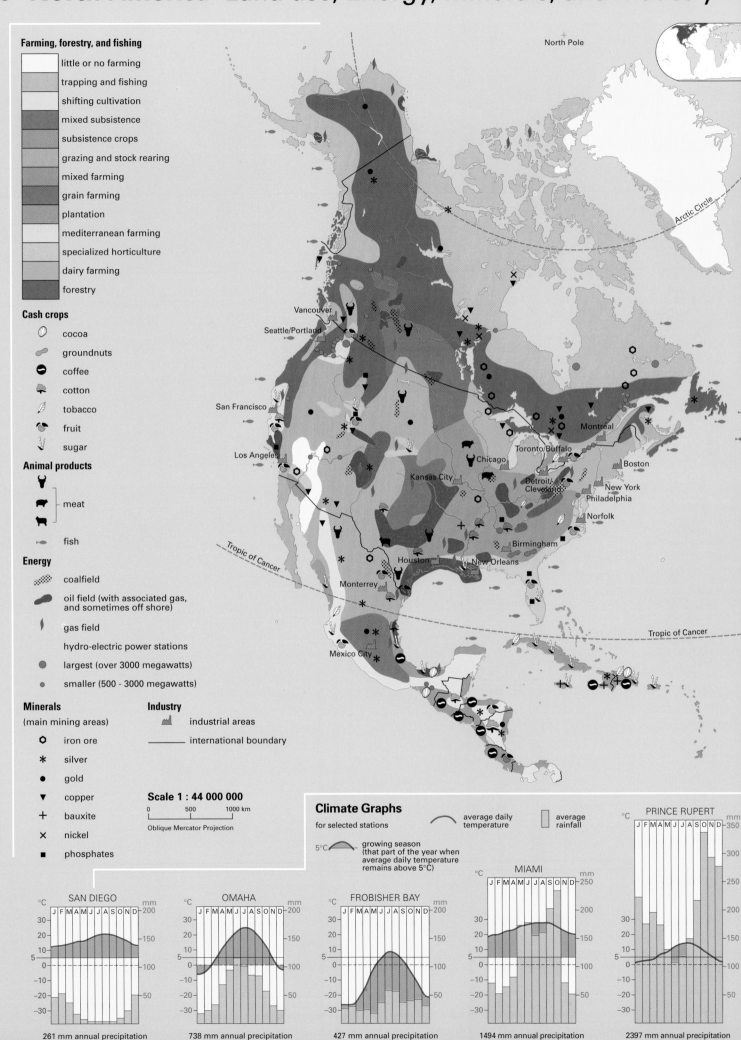

Farming, forestry, and fishing

- little or no farming
- trapping and fishing
- shifting cultivation
- mixed subsistence
- subsistence crops
- grazing and stock rearing
- mixed farming
- grain farming
- plantation
- mediterranean farming
- specialized horticulture
- dairy farming
- forestry

Cash crops

- cocoa
- groundnuts
- coffee
- cotton
- tobacco
- fruit
- sugar

Animal products

- meat
- fish

Energy

- coalfield
- oil field (with associated gas, and sometimes off shore)
- gas field
- hydro-electric power stations
- largest (over 3000 megawatts)
- smaller (500 - 3000 megawatts)

Minerals
(main mining areas)

- iron ore
- * silver
- gold
- ▼ copper
- + bauxite
- × nickel
- ■ phosphates

Industry

- industrial areas
- international boundary

Scale 1 : 44 000 000

0   500   1000 km

Oblique Mercator Projection

North Pole

Arctic Circle

Vancouver
Seattle/Portland
San Francisco
Los Angeles
Montreal
Toronto/Buffalo
Boston
Chicago
Kansas City
Detroit/Cleveland
New York
Philadelphia
Norfolk
Birmingham
Houston
New Orleans
Monterrey
Mexico City

Tropic of Cancer

Tropic of Cancer

© Oxford University Press

Climate Graphs
for selected stations

average daily temperature

average rainfall

5°C growing season
(that part of the year when average daily temperature remains above 5°C)

SAN DIEGO
261 mm annual precipitation

OMAHA
738 mm annual precipitation

FROBISHER BAY
427 mm annual precipitation

MIAMI
1494 mm annual precipitation

PRINCE RUPERT
2397 mm annual precipitation

Actual surface temperature

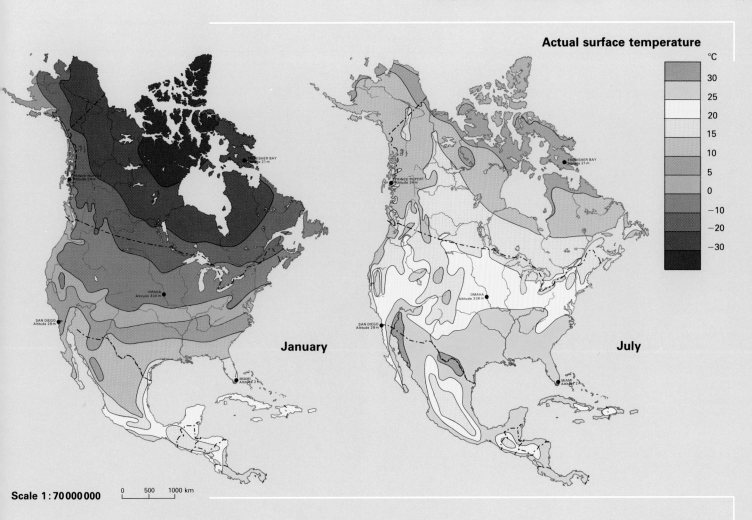

°C
30
25
20
15
10
5
0
−10
−20
−30

January

July

Scale 1 : 70 000 000

0   500   1000 km

Precipitation

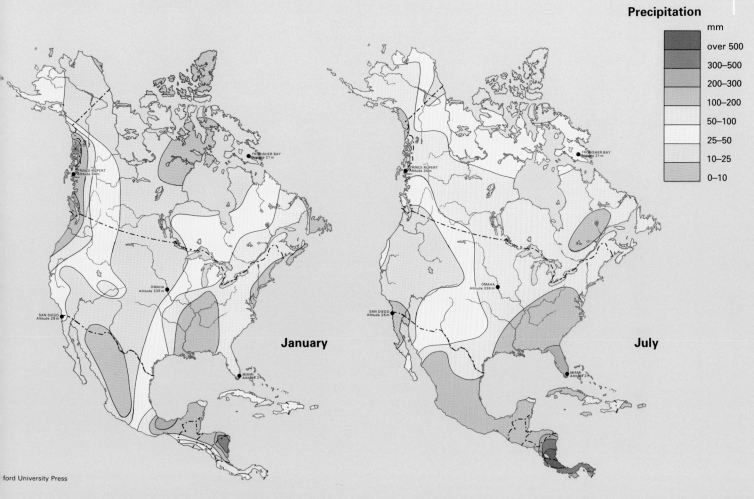

mm
over 500
300–500
200–300
100–200
50–100
25–50
10–25
0–10

January

July

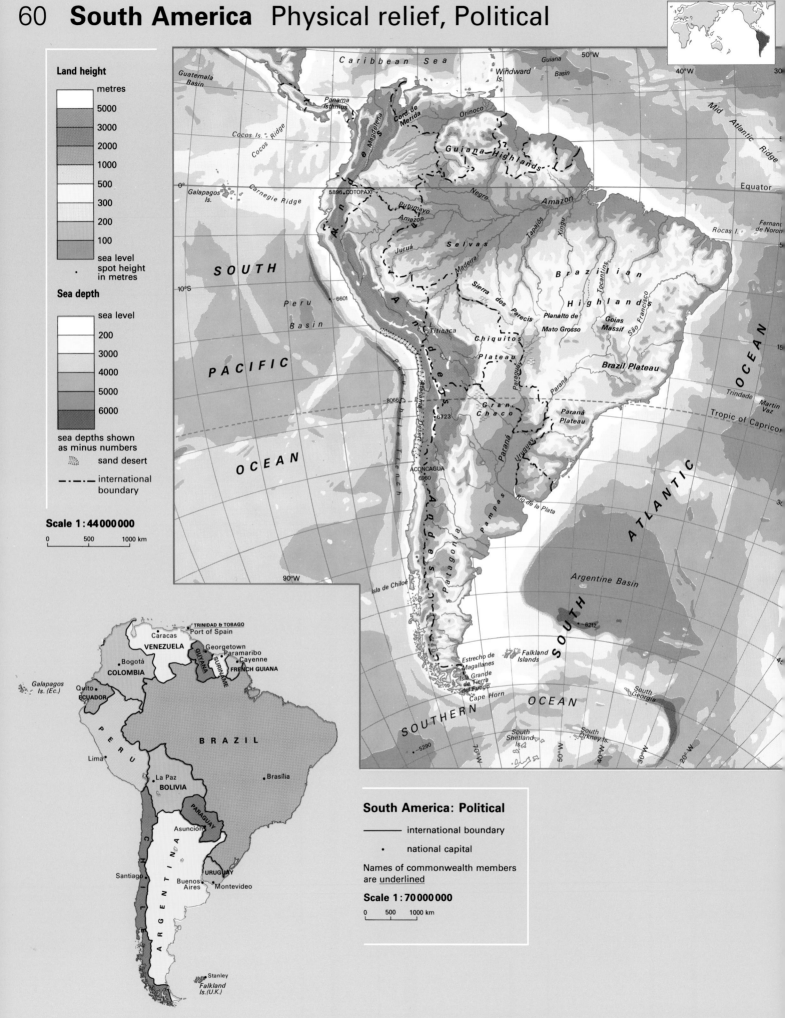

Land height

Land height
metres
5000
3000
2000
1000
500
300
200
100
sea level
· spot height
in metres

Sea depth

sea level
200
3000
4000
5000
6000

sea depths shown
as minus numbers

sand desert

–·–·– international
boundary

Scale 1:44 000 000

0   500   1000 km

South America: Political

——— international boundary

· national capital

Names of commonwealth members
are underlined

Scale 1:70 000 000

0   500   1000 km

Oblique Mercator Proje

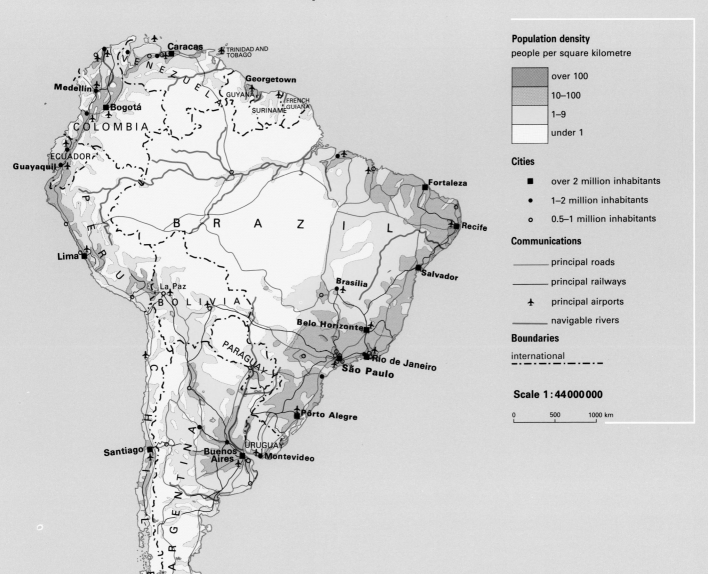

Population density
people per square kilometre

	over 100
	10–100
	1–9
	under 1

Cities

- ■ over 2 million inhabitants
- ● 1–2 million inhabitants
- ○ 0.5–1 million inhabitants

Communications

———— principal roads

———— principal railways

✈ principal airports

———— navigable rivers

Boundaries

international —·—·—·—·—

Scale 1 : 44 000 000

0   500   1000 km

Build

	ancient shields
	sedimentary rocks lying over ancient shields
	uplifted remains of ancient mountain systems
	younger fold mountains
	sedimentary rocks
	recent deposits
	volcanic rocks

——— extension of buried shields under later deposits

● active volcanoes

Mineral deposits

■	iron	●	bauxite
▲	nickel	△	mercury
◓	chromium	⊛	uranium
◆	tungsten	⊕	magnesium
⊙	manganese	□	antimony
⬚	titanium	⊞	asbestos
⊡	molybdenum	◇	mica
✪	beryllium	⊟	phosphate
×	cobalt	⬓	potash
–	vanadium	◆	diamonds
▲	copper	◇	zirconium
▾	tin		
▬	lead	●	coal
▾	zinc	▲	oil
○	gold	■	gas
+	silver		

Scale 1 : 88 000 000

0   1000 km

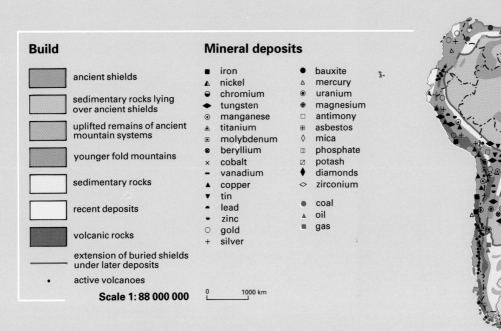

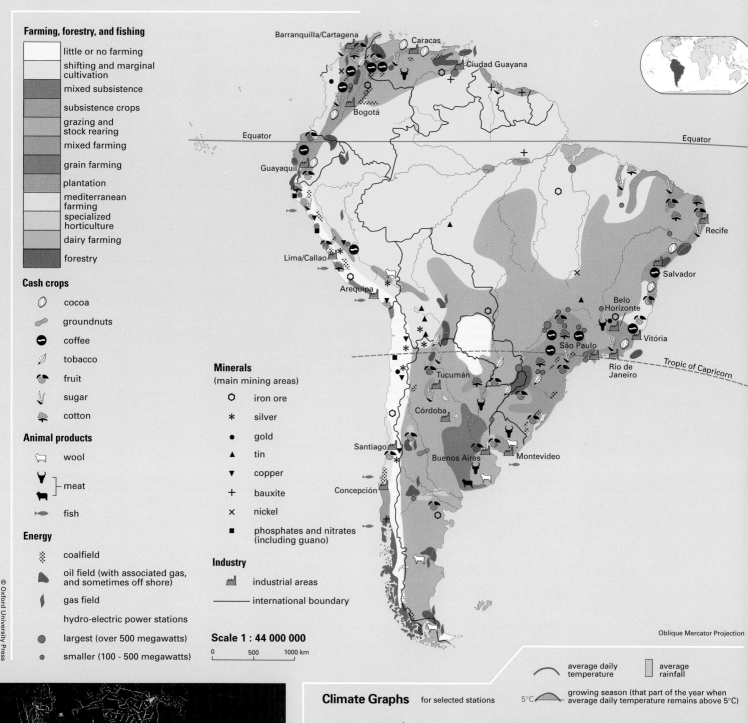

Farming, forestry, and fishing

- little or no farming
- shifting and marginal cultivation
- mixed subsistence
- subsistence crops
- grazing and stock rearing
- mixed farming
- grain farming
- plantation
- mediterranean farming
- specialized horticulture
- dairy farming
- forestry

Cash crops

- cocoa
- groundnuts
- coffee
- tobacco
- fruit
- sugar
- cotton

Animal products

- wool
- meat
- fish

Energy

- coalfield
- oil field (with associated gas, and sometimes off shore)
- gas field
- hydro-electric power stations
  - largest (over 500 megawatts)
  - smaller (100 - 500 megawatts)

Minerals
(main mining areas)

- iron ore
- silver
- gold
- tin
- copper
- bauxite
- nickel
- phosphates and nitrates (including guano)

Industry

- industrial areas
- international boundary

Scale 1 : 44 000 000

0   500   1000 km

Oblique Mercator Projection

© Oxford University Press

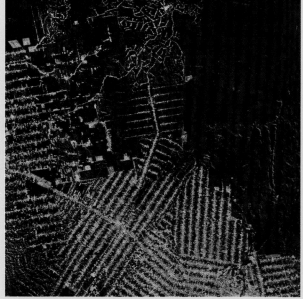

Deforestation in Brazil.
Satellite image processed to give approximately natural colour.
Dark green : natural forest.
Pale green and pink : areas of forest loss.

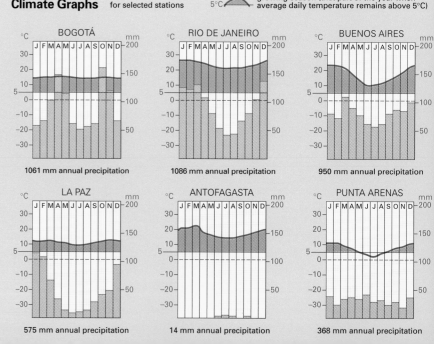

Climate Graphs   for selected stations

- average daily temperature
- average rainfall
- growing season (that part of the year when average daily temperature remains above 5°C)

BOGOTÁ
1061 mm annual precipitation

RIO DE JANEIRO
1086 mm annual precipitation

BUENOS AIRES
950 mm annual precipitation

LA PAZ
575 mm annual precipitation

ANTOFAGASTA
14 mm annual precipitation

PUNTA ARENAS
368 mm annual precipitation

Actual surface temperature

°C
25
20
15
10
5
0

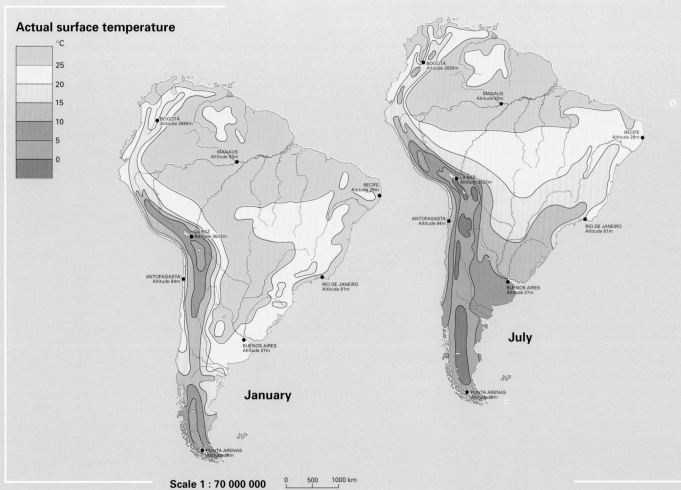

January

July

Scale 1 : 70 000 000

0   500   1000 km

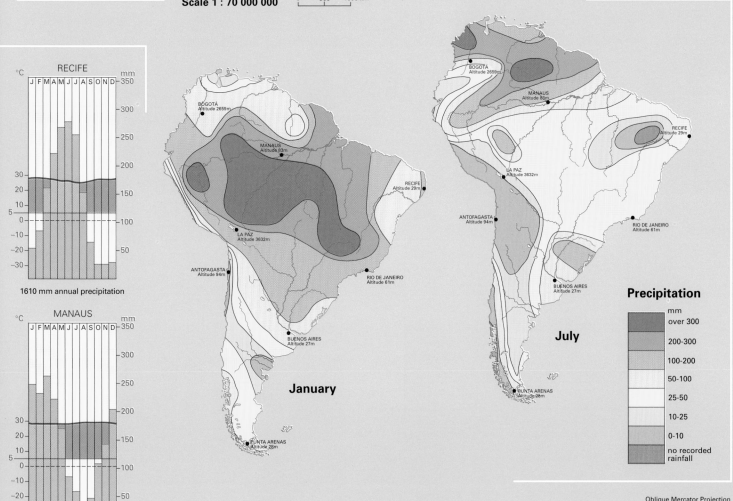

January

July

RECIFE

°C | JFMAMJJASOND | mm

1610 mm annual precipitation

MANAUS

°C | JFMAMJJASOND | mm

1811 mm annual precipitation

Precipitation

mm
over 300
200-300
100-200
50-100
25-50
10-25
0-10
no recorded rainfall

Oblique Mercator Projection

© Oxford University Press

Boundaries

international

internal

national park

Communications

expressway

major road

railway

canal

✈ major airport

Cities and towns

■ over 1 million inhabitants

● more than 100 000 inhabitants

• smaller towns

Physical features

seasonal river/lake

marsh

salt pan

ice cap

sand dunes

Land height

metres
3000
2000
1000
500
300
200
100
sea level

Sea Ice

pack ice spring maximum

▲ spot height in metres

Scale 1: 12 500 000

0   125   250 km

PACIFIC OCEAN

BRITISH COLUMBIA

ALBERTA

SASKATCHEWAN

CANADA

WASHINGTON

OREGON

IDAHO

MONTANA

WYOMING

NEVADA

UTAH

COLORADO

CALIFORNIA

ARIZONA

NEW MEXICO

NEBRASKA

NORTH DAKOTA

SOUTH DAKOTA

TEXAS

R O C K Y   M O U N T A I N S

U.S.A.

MEXICO

SONORA

CHIHUAHUA

COAHUILA

NUEVO LEON

DURANGO

SINALOA

BAJA CALIFORNIA NORTE

BAJA CALIFORNIA SUR

Golfo de California

ALASKA (U.S.A.)

1

States of USA

1 Alaska	18 New York	35 Maryland
2 Washington	19 Vermont	36 New Jersey
3 Montana	20 New Hampshire	37 Delaware
4 North Dakota	21 Maine	38 Arizona
5 South Dakota	22 Massachusetts	39 New Mexico
6 Minnesota	23 Connecticut	40 Oklahoma
7 Wisconsin	24 Rhode Island	41 Arkansas
8 Michigan	25 California	42 Tennessee
9 Oregon	26 Nevada	43 North Carolina
10 Idaho	27 Utah	44 South Carolina
11 Wyoming	28 Colorado	45 Texas
12 Nebraska	29 Kansas	46 Louisiana
13 Iowa	30 Missouri	47 Mississippi
14 Illinois	31 Kentucky	48 Alabama
15 Indiana	32 West Virginia	49 Georgia
16 Ohio	33 Virginia	50 Florida
17 Pennsylvania	34 District of Columbia	

Hawaii is also a state of USA but is not shown on the map.
A map of the Hawaiian Islands can be found on page 111.

USA: Political

⌐ international boundary

● national capital

Scale 1: 70 000 000

0   500   1000 km

Oblique Mercator Projection

Conical Orthomorphic Projection

© Oxford University

Northeast USA Scale 1 : 2 000 000

Conical Orthomorphic Projection

0   25   50 km

Boundaries

state

county

Physical features

river

marsh

contours

•155 spot height in metres

Communications

expressway

other major road

major railway

canal

✈ major airport

✈ other airport

Land use

central business district

other major commercial areas

industrial

residential

major parks and open spaces

non-urban

Scale 1 : 300 000

0   5 km

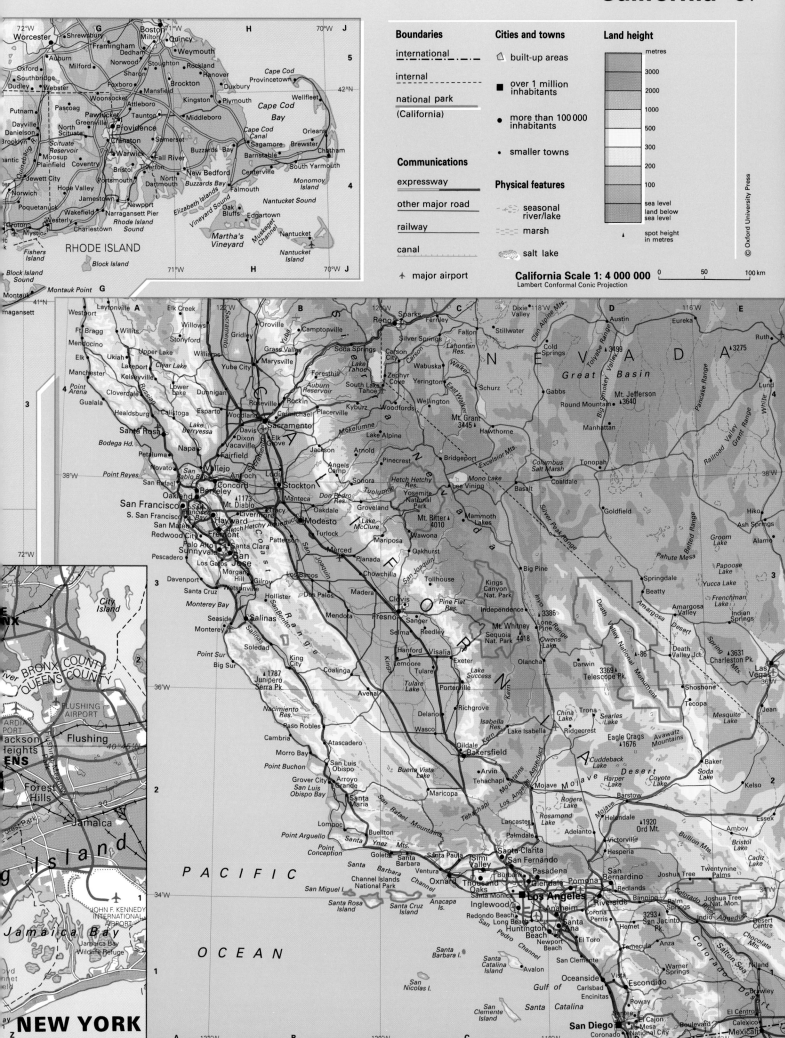

Boundaries
international —·—·—
internal — — —
national park (California)

Communications
expressway
other major road
railway
canal
✈ major airport

Cities and towns
⬠ built-up areas
■ over 1 million inhabitants
● more than 100 000 inhabitants
• smaller towns

Physical features
~~~ seasonal river/lake
≈≈≈ marsh
⬭ salt lake

Land height
metres
3000
2000
1000
500
300
200
100
sea level
land below sea level
▲ spot height in metres

© Oxford University Press

California Scale 1: 4 000 000
Lambert Conformal Conic Projection
0   50   100 km

RHODE ISLAND

NEW YORK

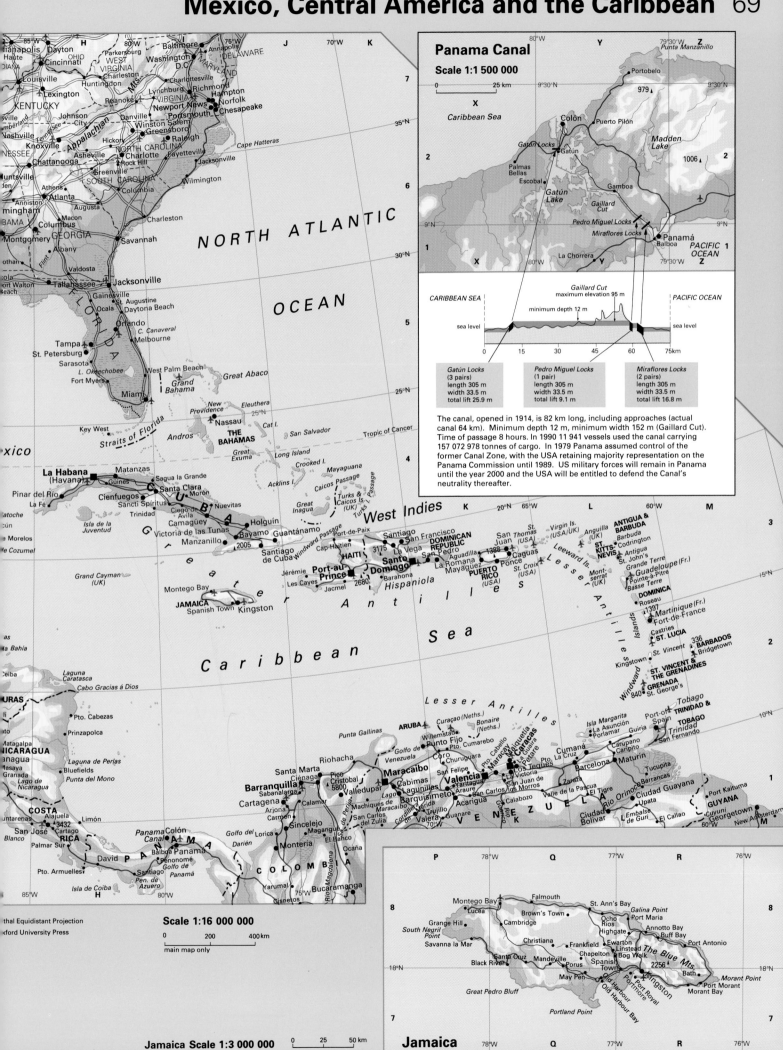

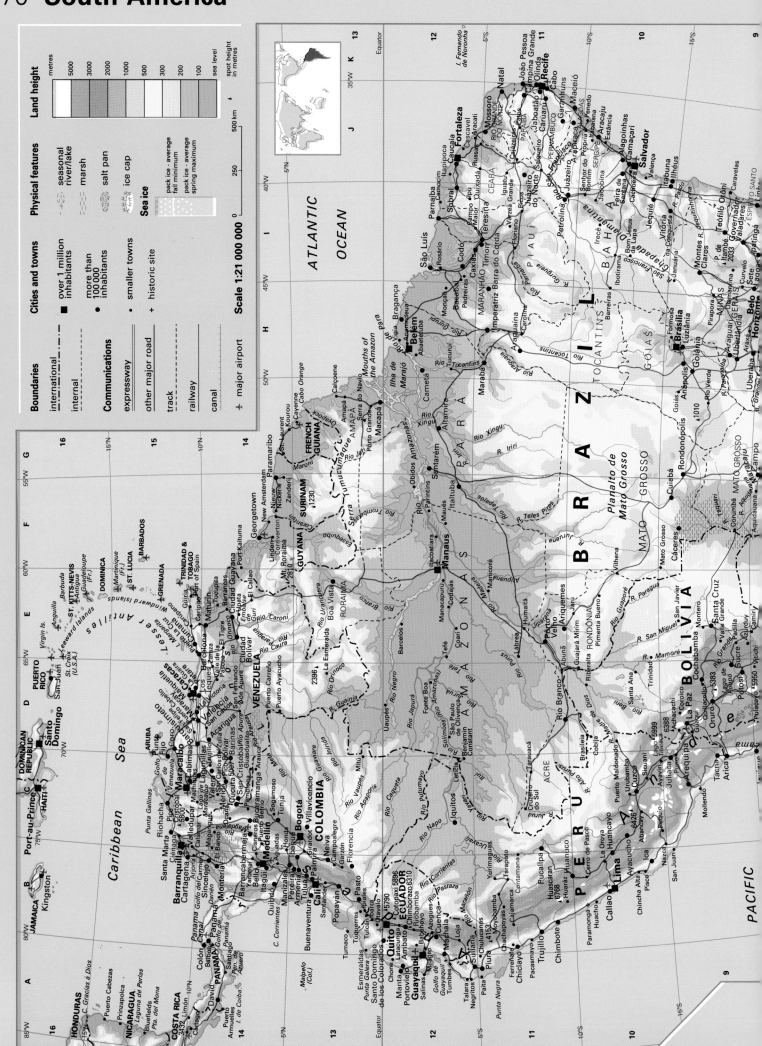

Land height

metres
5000
3000
2000
1000
500
300
200
100
sea level

▲ spot height in metres

Physical features

- seasonal river/lake
- marsh
- salt pan
- ice cap

Sea ice
- pack ice - average fall minimum
- pack ice - average spring maximum

Cities and towns

- ■ over 1 million inhabitants
- ● more than 100 000 inhabitants
- • smaller towns
- + historic site

Boundaries
- international
- internal

Communications
- expressway
- other major road
- track
- railway
- canal
- ✈ major airport

Scale 1:21 000 000

500 km 250 0

ATLANTIC OCEAN

PACIFIC

Caribbean Sea

JAMAICA Kingston
HAITI Port-au-Prince
DOMINICAN REPUBLIC Santo Domingo
PUERTO RICO San Juan

Lesser Antilles
Leeward Islands
Windward Islands
ARUBA
TRINIDAD & TOBAGO Port of Spain
BARBADOS

HONDURAS C. Gracias á Dios
NICARAGUA Bluefields
COSTA RICA Limón
PANAMA Panama Canal

VENEZUELA Caracas
Maracaibo
Valencia
Ciudad Bolívar

COLOMBIA Bogotá
Medellín
Cali
Barranquilla
Cartagena

GUYANA Georgetown
SURINAM Paramaribo
FRENCH GUIANA Cayenne

ECUADOR Quito
Guayaquil

PERU Lima
Callao

BOLIVIA La Paz
Sucre
Santa Cruz
Cochabamba

BRAZIL
Manaus
Belém
São Luís
Fortaleza
Recife
Salvador
Brasília
Belo Horizonte

AMAZONAS
PARÁ
MARANHÃO
CEARÁ
PIAUÍ
BAHIA
MINAS GERAIS
MATO GROSSO
RONDÔNIA
ACRE
RORAIMA
AMAPÁ
GOIÁS
TOCANTINS

Mouths of the Amazon
Rio Amazonas
Planalto de Mato Grosso

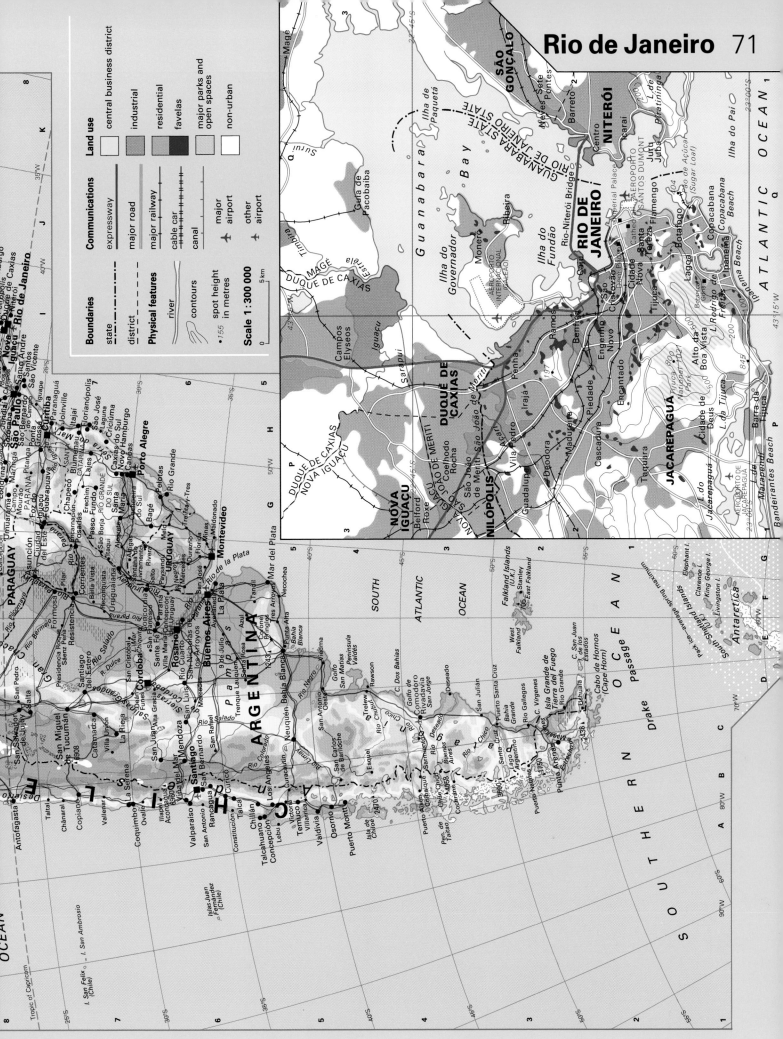

Boundaries

international

disputed
^^^^^^^^^^^^^^^^^^^

internal

Communications

expressway

other major road

railway

canal

✈ major airport

Cities and towns

■ over 1 million inhabitants

● more than 100 000 inhabitants

• smaller towns

Land height

metres
3000
2000
1000
500
300
200
100
sea level
land below sea level
▲ spot height in metres

Conical Orthomorphic Projection

© Oxford University Press

Sea depth

sea level
200
3000
4000
5000

• -86 sea depths shown as minus numbers

Physical features

seasonal river/lake

marsh

ice cap

Scale 1 : 16 000 000

0   160   320 km

ATLANTIC OCEAN

ICELAND
Reykjavík
Akureyri
Ísafjördur
Vatnajökull
Hekla 1491
Höfn

Greenland Sea

Arctic Circle

NORWAY   SWEDEN   FINLAND

Tromsø
Narvik
Bodø
Lofoten Islands
Inarijärvi
Lappland
Murmansk
Kola Peninsula
Kandalaksha
White Sea

Trondheim
Dovrefjell
Jostedalsbreen
Umeå
Skellefteå
Luleå
Oulu
Torne
Kemi

Bergen
Oslo
Stavanger
Hardangervidda

Gulf of Bothnia
Vaasa
Tampere
Sundsvall
Indal
Klar
Dal
Vättern
Vänern
Örebro
Västerås
Uppsala
Stockholm
Mälaren
Norrköping
Linköping
Jönköping
Göteborg
Ålborg
Århus
Gotland
Öland
Åland
Turku
Vantaa
Espoo
Helsinki
Tallinn
Gulf of Finland
St. Petersburg (Leningrad)
Novgorod
Petrozavodsk
Lake Onega
Lake Ladoga
Pskov
Lake Peipus
Lake Ilmen
ESTONIA
Tartu
LATVIA
Riga
G. of Riga
Daugava
Daugavpils
Vitsyebsk

North Sea

DENMARK
Jylland
København (Copenhagen)
Odense
Sjælland
Fyn
Kiel
Esbjerg
Skagerrak
Kattegat
Skåne
Malmö
Bornholm
Baltic Sea
Pomeranian Bay
Rostock
Lübeck
Szczecin
Liepāja
Klaipėda
Kaliningrad (Russia)
Gdynia
Gdańsk
Kaunas
Vilnius
Minsk
Neman
LITHUANIA
Šiauliai
Smolensk
Mahilyow (Mogilev)

UNITED KINGDOM
Shetland Islands
Orkney Islands
Outer Hebrides
The Minch
Cape Wrath
Skye
Inverness
Moray Firth
Ben Nevis 1344 m
Grampians
Aberdeen
Dundee
Edinburgh
Glasgow
Southern Uplands
Malin Head
Newcastle upon Tyne
Middlesbrough
REPUBLIC OF IRELAND
Dublin
Galway
Limerick
Cork
St. George's Channel
Belfast
Central Plain
Isle of Man
Liverpool
Manchester
Leeds
Sheffield
Pennines
Birmingham
Coventry
Cambrian Mts.
Cardiff
Bristol
London
Plymouth
Southampton
Norwich
The Wash
Thames
Scilly Is.
English Channel
Strait of Dover
Channel Islands
Brest
Brittany
Cotentin
Penmarch
le Havre
Caen
Rouen
Amiens
Calais
Lille
Rennes
le Mans
Angers
Nantes
Tours
Orléans
Paris
Paris Basin

NETHERLANDS
Groningen
Frisian Is.
Amsterdam
Den Haag (The Hague)
Utrecht
Rotterdam
Ijsselmeer
Scheldt Est.
Maas
Waal
Antwerpen (Anvers)
Gent
Bruxelles (Brussel)
BELGIUM
Liège
Ardennes
LUXEMBOURG
Luxembourg

GERMANY
Hamburg
Bremen
Weser
Hannover
Bielefeld
Dortmund
Essen
Düsseldorf
Köln (Cologne)
Bonn
Elbe
Magdeburg
Berlin
Leipzig
Halle
Erfurt
Harz Mts.
Dresden
Frankfurt
Chemnitz
Nürnberg (Nuremberg)
Saarbrücken
Stuttgart
Strasbourg
Rhine
Mannheim
Schwäbische Alb
Augsburg
München (Munich)
Bodensee
Donau

POLAND
Warszawa (Warsaw)
Bydgoszcz
Toruń
Poznań
Łódź
Wrocław
Oder
Radom
Lublin
Czestochowa
Katowice
Kraków
Ostrava
Brno
Vistula
Białystok
Brest
Pinsk
Pripet
Pripet Marshes
BELARUS
Hrodna (Grodno)
Babruysk
Dnieper

CZECH REP.
Praha (Prague)
Plzeň
Bohemian Massif
Bohemia
SLOVAKIA
Bratislava
Košice
Tatry Mts.

AUSTRIA
Wien (Vienna)
Linz
Salzburg
Innsbruck
Graz
Tauern
LIECHTENSTEIN
SWITZERLAND
Bern
Zürich
Geneva / Genève
Lausanne
Basel
Jura
Mont Blanc 4807 m

FRANCE
Limoges
Clermont-Ferrand
Lyon
St-Étienne
Dijon
Bordeaux
Bayonne
Garonne
Toulouse
Montpellier
Marseille
Toulon
Nice
Grenoble
Avignon
Rhône
Massif Central
Dordogne
Alpes Maritimes
Golf of Lyons
Perpignan
Pyrénees
ANDORRA
MONACO

Bay of Biscay

PORTUGAL
Porto (Oporto)
Coimbra
Lisboa (Lisbon)
Setúbal
Faro
Algarve
Guadiana
Douro / Duero
Tagus / Tajo

SPAIN
Vigo
A Coruña
Gijón
Oviedo
Santander
Bilbao
San Sebastián
Cantabrian Mts.
León
Burgos
Valladolid
Salamanca
Zaragoza
Ebro
Madrid
Badajoz
Córdoba
Sevilla (Seville)
Jerez de la Frontera
Cádiz
Guadalquivir
Betican Cordilleras
Málaga
Granada
Almería
Murcia
Cartagena
Alicante
Valencia
Albacete
Barcelona
Hospitalet
Lérida
Costa Brava
Palma de Mallorca
Mallorca
Menorca
Ibiza
Balearic Islands
Strait of Gibraltar
Gibraltar (U.K.)

MOROCCO
Rabat-Salé
Casablanca
Meknès
Fès
Kenitra
Tangier (Tanger)
Tétouan
Oujda
Oran

ALGERIA
Alger (Algiers)
Blida
Bejaïa
Skikda
'Annaba
Constantine
Sétif
Atlas Mountains
Sidi Bel-Abbès
Ech Cheliff
Bou Saâda
Djelfa
El Bayadh
Biskra
Gafsa
Touggourt
Hassi Messaoud

TUNISIA
Tunis
Nabeul
Bizerte
Sousse
Tébessa
Sfax
Gabès
Gafsa

LIBYA
Tarābulus (Tripoli)
Mişrātah (Misurata)

ITALY
Torino (Turin)
Milano (Milan)
Genova (Genoa)
Venézia (Venice)
Bologna
Verona
Modena
Ravenna
Firenze (Florence)
Pisa
Ligurian Sea
SAN MARINO
Perúgia
Roma (Rome)
Appenines
Pescara
Napoli (Naples)
Vesuvius 1277
Salerno
Foggia
Bari
Táranto
Gulf of Taranto
Palermo
Messina
Réggio di Calabria
Catánia
Mt Etna 3323
Sicily
Ionian Sea
Cágliari
Sardegna (Sardinia)
Corse (Corsica) (France)
Ajaccio
Bastia
Sássari
Tyrrhenian Sea
MALTA
Valletta

SLOVENIA
Ljubljana
Trieste
Rijeka
Maribor
CROATIA
Zagreb (Agram)
Drava
Osijek
Banja Luka
Split
Dubrovnik
BOSNIA-HERZEGOVINA
Sarajevo
Dinaric Mts.
Adriatic Sea
YUGOSLAVIA
Novi Sad
Beograd (Belgrade)
SERBIA
Kragujevac
Niš
Kosovo
Priština
MONTENEGRO
Podgorica (Titograd)
Shkodër
FYRO MACEDONIA
Skopje
Bitola

HUNGARY
Budapest
Győr
Pécs
Szeged
Arad
Tisza
Hungarian Basin

ROMANIA
Timişoara
Cluj-Napoca
Târgu Mureş
Braşov
Carpathians
Galaţi
Brăila
Ploieşti
Bucureşti (Bucharest)
Craiova
Constanţa
2548 m

MOLDOVA
Chişinău (Kishinev)
Bălti
Iaşi
Odesa

UKRAINE
L'viv (L'vov)
Rivne (Rovno)
Vinnytsya
Zhytomyr
Kyyiv (Kiev)
Chernihiv
Chernivtsi
Dniester

BULGARIA
Sofiya (Sofia)
Plovdiv
Varna
Burgas
Stara Zagora
Pleven
Ruse
Danube (Donau)
Balkan Mts.
Rodopi Planina

GREECE
Thessaloníki (Thessalonica)
Ioánnina
Lárisa
Vólos
Athína (Athens)
Peiraías (Piraeus)
Pátra
Kalámata
Pelopónnisos
Évvoia (Euboea)
Mt. Olympus 2917
Kérkyra (Corfu)
Ionian Sea
Kykládes
Kríti (Crete)
Iráklion
Chaniá (Khaniá)
Rodos (Rhodes)
Aegean Sea
Kríti

TURKEY
İstanbul
Sea of Marmara
İzmir
Edirne
Balıkesir
Dardanelles
Bosporus

Mediterranean Sea

Faeroe Islands

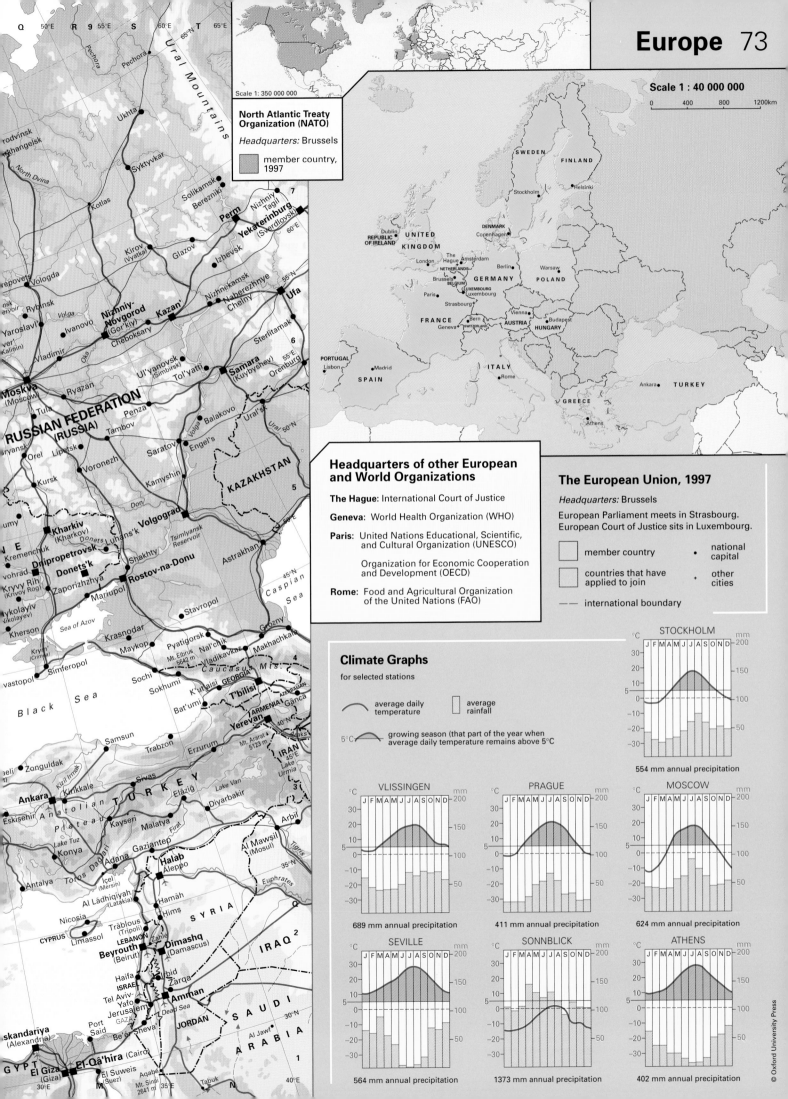

Scale 1 : 350 000 000

North Atlantic Treaty Organization (NATO)

Headquarters: Brussels

member country, 1997

Scale 1 : 40 000 000

0   400   800   1200km

Headquarters of other European and World Organizations

The Hague: International Court of Justice

Geneva: World Health Organization (WHO)

Paris: United Nations Educational, Scientific, and Cultural Organization (UNESCO)

Organization for Economic Cooperation and Development (OECD)

Rome: Food and Agricultural Organization of the United Nations (FAO)

The European Union, 1997

Headquarters: Brussels

European Parliament meets in Strasbourg.
European Court of Justice sits in Luxembourg.

member country

countries that have applied to join

• national capital

+ other cities

– – – international boundary

Climate Graphs

for selected stations

average daily temperature

average rainfall

growing season (that part of the year when average daily temperature remains above 5°C)

STOCKHOLM
554 mm annual precipitation

VLISSINGEN
689 mm annual precipitation

PRAGUE
411 mm annual precipitation

MOSCOW
624 mm annual precipitation

SEVILLE
564 mm annual precipitation

SONNBLICK
1373 mm annual precipitation

ATHENS
402 mm annual precipitation

© Oxford University Press

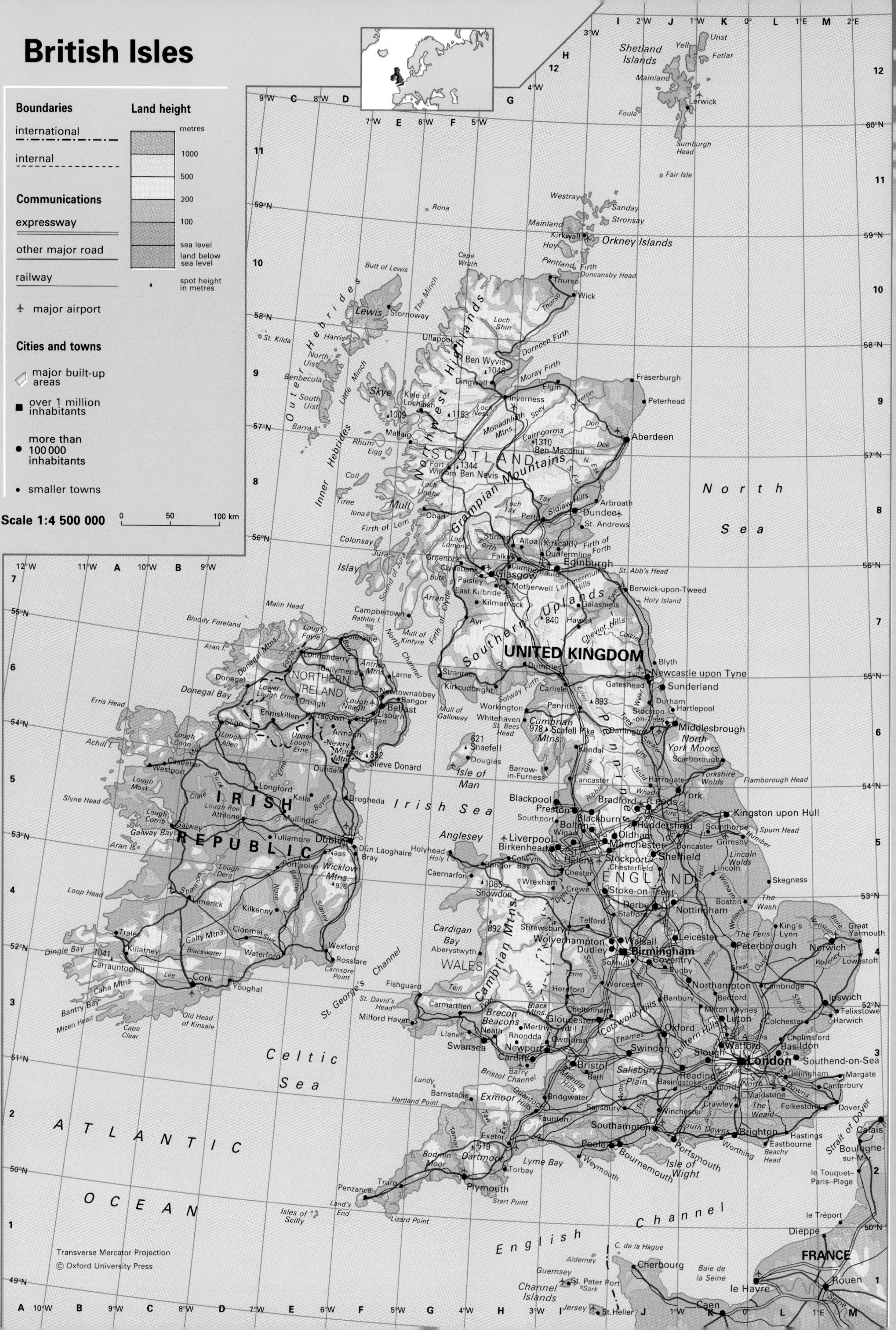

Boundaries
international
internal
Communications
expressway
other major road
railway
major airport
Cities and towns
major built-up areas
over 1 million inhabitants
more than 100 000 inhabitants
smaller towns
Land height
metres
1000
500
200
100
sea level
land below sea level
spot height in metres
Scale 1:4 500 000
0
50
100 km
Transverse Mercator Projection
© Oxford University Press
UNITED KINGDOM
SCOTLAND
ENGLAND
WALES
NORTHERN IRELAND
IRISH REPUBLIC
FRANCE
North Sea
Irish Sea
Celtic Sea
ATLANTIC OCEAN
English Channel
St. George's Channel
Bristol Channel
North Channel
The Minch
Little Minch
Sea of the Hebrides
Strait of Dover
Shetland Islands
Orkney Islands
Outer Hebrides
Inner Hebrides
Isle of Man
Isle of Wight
Isles of Scilly
Channel Islands
Anglesey
Grampian Mountains
Northwest Highlands
Southern Uplands
Pennines
Cambrian Mtns.
Cumbrian Mtns.
North York Moors
Cotswold Hills
Chiltern Hills
Mendip Hills
Brecon Beacons
Exmoor
Dartmoor
Lerwick
Kirkwall
Thurso
Wick
Stornoway
Ullapool
Inverness
Aberdeen
Fraserburgh
Peterhead
Fort William
Ben Nevis
Oban
Perth
Dundee
St. Andrews
Stirling
Edinburgh
Glasgow
Greenock
Paisley
Kilmarnock
Ayr
Dumfries
Stranraer
Campbeltown
Berwick-upon-Tweed
Galashiels
Hawick
Londonderry
Coleraine
Ballymena
Larne
Belfast
Bangor
Lisburn
Omagh
Enniskillen
Armagh
Newry
Slieve Donard
Donegal
Sligo
Dundalk
Drogheda
Dublin
Dún Laoghaire
Bray
Naas
Mullingar
Athlone
Tullamore
Longford
Galway
Castlebar
Westport
Limerick
Kilkenny
Clonmel
Waterford
Wexford
Rosslare
Cork
Youghal
Tralee
Killarney
Carrauntoohill
Newcastle upon Tyne
Sunderland
Gateshead
Durham
Hartlepool
Middlesbrough
Stockton-on-Tees
Darlington
Carlisle
Penrith
Workington
Whitehaven
Kendal
Lancaster
Barrow-in-Furness
Blackpool
Preston
Southport
Blackburn
Bolton
Wigan
Liverpool
Birkenhead
St. Helens
Manchester
Oldham
Stockport
Huddersfield
Bradford
Leeds
Harrogate
York
Scarborough
Kingston upon Hull
Scunthorpe
Grimsby
Doncaster
Sheffield
Chesterfield
Lincoln
Skegness
Chester
Wrexham
Crewe
Stoke-on-Trent
Derby
Nottingham
Stafford
Shrewsbury
Telford
Wolverhampton
Walsall
Dudley
Birmingham
Solihull
Coventry
Leicester
Rugby
Peterborough
Boston
King's Lynn
Norwich
Great Yarmouth
Lowestoft
Northampton
Cambridge
Bedford
Milton Keynes
Luton
Ipswich
Felixstowe
Harwich
Colchester
Chelmsford
Basildon
Southend-on-Sea
Watford
St. Albans
London
Slough
Reading
Oxford
Banbury
Worcester
Hereford
Gloucester
Cheltenham
Swindon
Bristol
Bath
Newport
Cardiff
Barry
Swansea
Neath
Llanelli
Carmarthen
Milford Haven
Fishguard
Aberystwyth
Holyhead
Bangor
Caernarfon
Colwyn Bay
Snowdon
Merthyr Tydfil
Rhondda
Cwmbran
Bridgwater
Taunton
Salisbury
Winchester
Southampton
Portsmouth
Bournemouth
Poole
Weymouth
Exeter
Torbay
Plymouth
Truro
Penzance
Barnstaple
Basingstoke
Guildford
Crawley
Brighton
Worthing
Eastbourne
Hastings
Maidstone
Gillingham
Canterbury
Margate
Folkestone
Dover
Calais
Boulogne-sur-Mer
Le Touquet-Paris-Plage
Le Tréport
Dieppe
Le Havre
Rouen
Caen
Cherbourg
St. Helier
St. Peter Port
Land's End
Lizard Point
Start Point
Hartland Point
Beachy Head
Flamborough Head
Spurn Head
St. Abb's Head
Duncansby Head
Cape Wrath
Butt of Lewis
Malin Head
Bloody Foreland
Erris Head
Slyne Head
Loop Head
Mizen Head
Cape Clear
Old Head of Kinsale
Carnsore Point
St. David's Head
St. Bees Head
Sumburgh Head
The Wash
The Fens
Salisbury Plain
Lyme Bay
Cardigan Bay
Galway Bay
Donegal Bay
Bantry Bay

Population density

people per square kilometre

over 100
10–100
1–9
under 1

Cities

■ over 2 million inhabitants
• 1–2 million inhabitants
○ 0.5–1 million inhabitants

Communications

principal roads
principal railways
navigable rivers
principal canals
✈ principal airports

Boundaries

international

Scale 1: 20 000 000

0   200   400 km

ICELAND

NORWAY
SWEDEN
FINLAND

RUSSIAN FEDERATION (RUSSIA)

Moscow
St. Petersburg (Leningrad)

ESTONIA
LATVIA
LITHUANIA

BELARUS (BYELORUSSIA)

Baltic Sea

North Sea

DENMARK

UNITED KINGDOM

London

REPUBLIC OF IRELAND

NETHERLANDS
BELGIUM
LUX.

GERMANY
Berlin

Paris
FRANCE

POLAND

CZECH REPUBLIC
SLOVAKIA
AUSTRIA
SWITZERLAND
HUNGARY
Budapest
SLOVENIA
CROATIA
BOSNIA HERZEGOVINA

UKRAINE
Kiev

MOLDOVA

ROMANIA
Bucharest

BULGARIA

YUGOSLAVIA
FYROM
MACEDONIA
ALBANIA

GREECE
Athens

Black Sea

Ankara

Istanbul

ITALY
Rome

SPAIN
Madrid

PORTUGAL
Lisbon

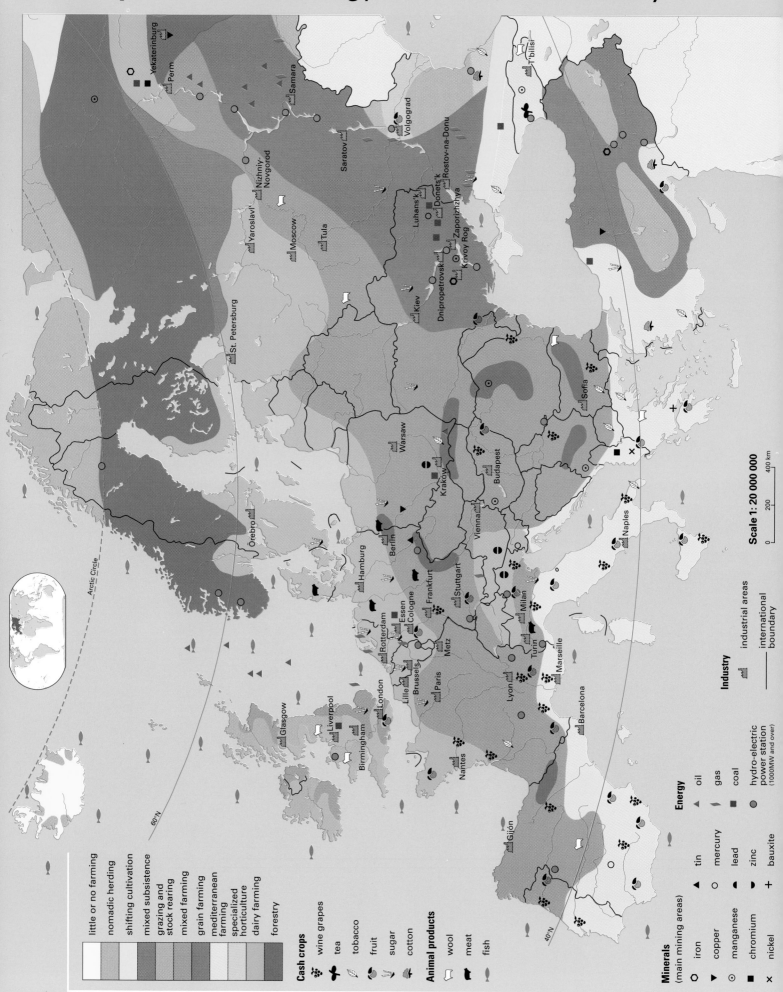

Yekaterinburg
Perm
Samara
Volgograd
Nizhniy Novgorod
Saratov
Rostov-na-Donu
T'bilisi
Yaroslavl'
Moscow
Tula
Donets'k
Luhans'k
Zaporizhzhya
Krivoy Rog
Dnipropetrovs'k
Kiev
St. Petersburg
Warsaw
Sofia
Kraków
Budapest
Vienna
Örebro
Berlin
Hamburg
Frankfurt
Stuttgart
Milan
Naples
Rotterdam
Essen
Cologne
Metz
Turin
Marseille
Glasgow
London
Lyon
Liverpool
Brussels
Lille
Paris
Barcelona
Birmingham
Nantes
Gijón

Arctic Circle
60°N
40°N

Scale 1: 20 000 000
0   200   400 km

Industry
industrial areas
international boundary

Energy
◀ oil
▬ gas
◆ coal
⊙ hydro-electric power station (1000MW and over)

Minerals (main mining areas)
⬡ iron
◀ tin
▶ copper
○ mercury
⊙ manganese
◖ lead
■ chromium
◗ zinc
✕ nickel
+ bauxite

Cash crops
wine grapes
tea
tobacco
fruit
sugar
cotton

Animal products
wool
meat
fish

little or no farming
nomadic herding
shifting cultivation
mixed subsistence
grazing and stock rearing
mixed farming
grain farming
mediterranean farming
specialized horticulture
dairy farming
forestry

Conical Orthomorphic Projection
© Oxford University Press

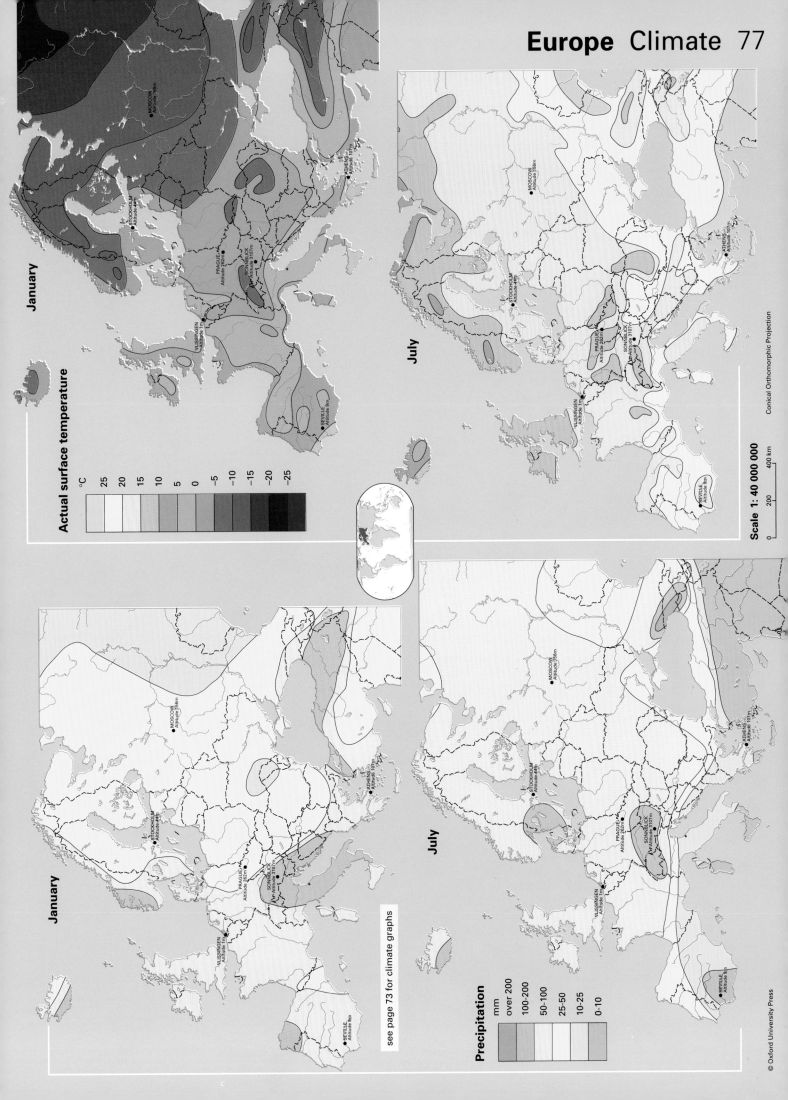

January

Actual surface temperature

°C
25
20
15
10
5
0
−5
−10
−15
−20
−25

July

Conical Orthomorphic Projection

Scale 1: 40 000 000

0   200   400 km

see page 73 for climate graphs

January

July

Precipitation

mm
over 200
100–200
50–100
25–50
10–25
0–10

© Oxford University Press

Boundaries

county

Communications

expressway

other major road

major railway

canal

✈ major airport

✈ other airport

Physical features

river

contours

·155 spot height in metres

Land use

central business district

other major commercial areas

industrial

residential

major parks and open spaces

non-urban

This image of London, United Kingdom was produced by a Landsat satellite orbiting the earth at an altitude of approximately 900 km.

Scale 1:600 000

Scale 1:300 000

0   5km

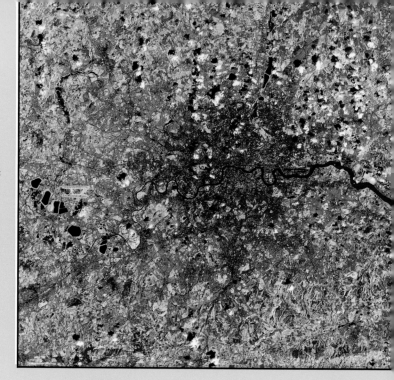

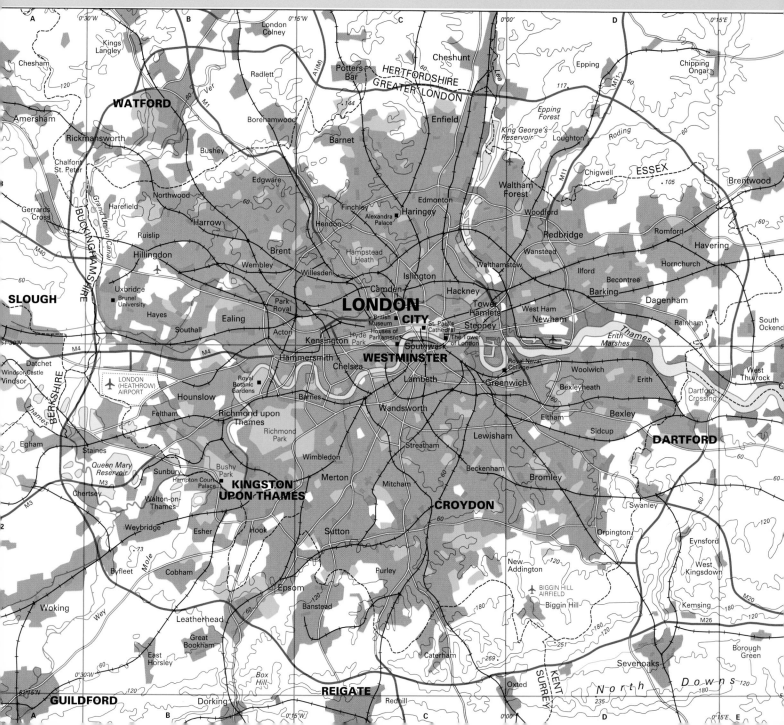

Chesham
Kings Langley
Amersham
Rickmansworth
Chalfont St. Peter
Gerrards Cross
WATFORD
Radlett
London Colney
Cheshunt
Epping
Chipping Ongar
HERTFORDSHIRE
GREATER LONDON
Potters Bar
Borehamwood
Barnet
Bushey
Edgware
Enfield
Epping Forest
Loughton
King George's Reservoir
Roding
Chigwell
ESSEX
Brentwood
Northwood
Harefield
Ruislip
Harrow
Finchley
Alexandra Palace
Hendon
Edmonton
Haringey
Waltham Forest
Woodford
Redbridge
Romford
SLOUGH
Hillingdon
Wembley
Brent
Hampstead Heath
Willesden
Islington
Walthamstow
Ilford
Becontree
Havering
Hornchurch
Uxbridge
Brunel University
Park Royal
Camden
Hackney
West Ham
Barking
Dagenham
Hayes
Ealing
LONDON
British Museum
CITY
St. Paul's Cathedral
Tower Hamlets
Newham
Southall
Acton
Kensington
Houses of Parliament
Stepney
Erith Marshes
Rainham
Datchet
Windsor Castle
Vindsor
Hammersmith
Hyde Park
The Tower of London
WESTMINSTER
Southwark
Royal Naval College
Woolwich
Erith
South Ockenden
Chelsea
Lambeth
Greenwich
Bexleyheath
West Thurrock
Hounslow
Royal Botanic Gardens
Barnes
Wandsworth
Eltham
Bexley
DARTFORD
Feltham
Richmond upon Thames
Richmond Park
Streatham
Lewisham
Sidcup
Egham
Staines
Queen Mary Reservoir
Sunbury
Bushy Park
Wimbledon
Merton
Beckenham
Bromley
Swanley
Chertsey
Hampton Court Palace
KINGSTON UPON THAMES
Mitcham
CROYDON
Orpington
Eynsford
Walton-on-Thames
Esher
Hook
Sutton
Purley
West Kingsdown
Weybridge
Byfleet
Cobham
Epsom
Banstead
New Addington
BIGGIN HILL AIRFIELD
Biggin Hill
Kemsing
Woking
Leatherhead
Great Bookham
East Horsley
Caterham
Sevenoaks
Borough Green
GUILDFORD
Box Hill
REIGATE
Dorking
Redhill
Oxted
KENT
SURREY
North Downs

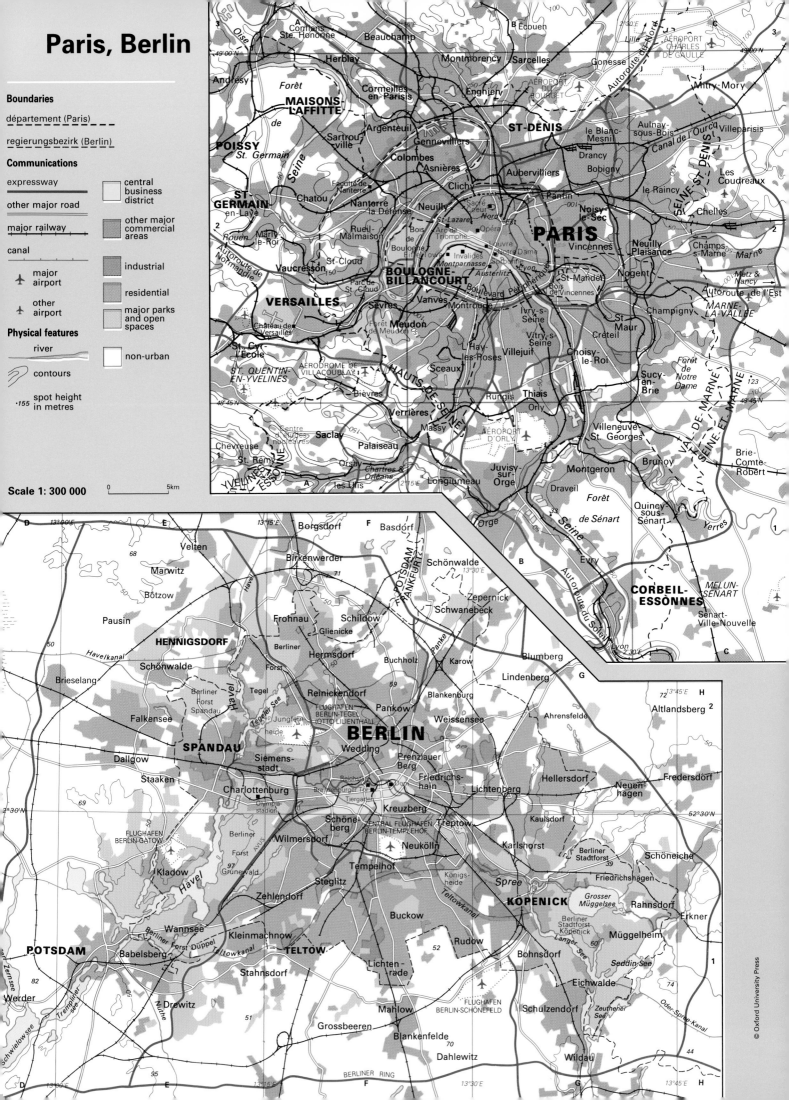

Paris, Berlin

Boundaries

département (Paris)

regierungsbezirk (Berlin)

Communications

expressway

other major road

major railway

canal

✈ major airport

✈ other airport

Physical features

river

contours

·155 spot height in metres

central business district

other major commercial areas

industrial

residential

major parks and open spaces

non-urban

Scale 1: 300 000

0   5km

© Oxford University Press

Land height

metres
| 5000 |
| 3000 |
| 2000 |
| 1000 |
| 500 |
| 300 |
| 200 |
| 100 |
| sea level |

land below
sea level

. spot height
in metres

Sea depth

sea level
| 200 |
| 3000 |
| 4000 |
| 5000 |
| 6000 |

maximum extent
of glaciation

ice cap

sand desert

Land below sea level and sea depths
shown as minus numbers

–·–·– international boundary

Scale 1 : 44 000 000

0   500   1000 km

Zenithal Equal Area Pro
© Oxford University Pres

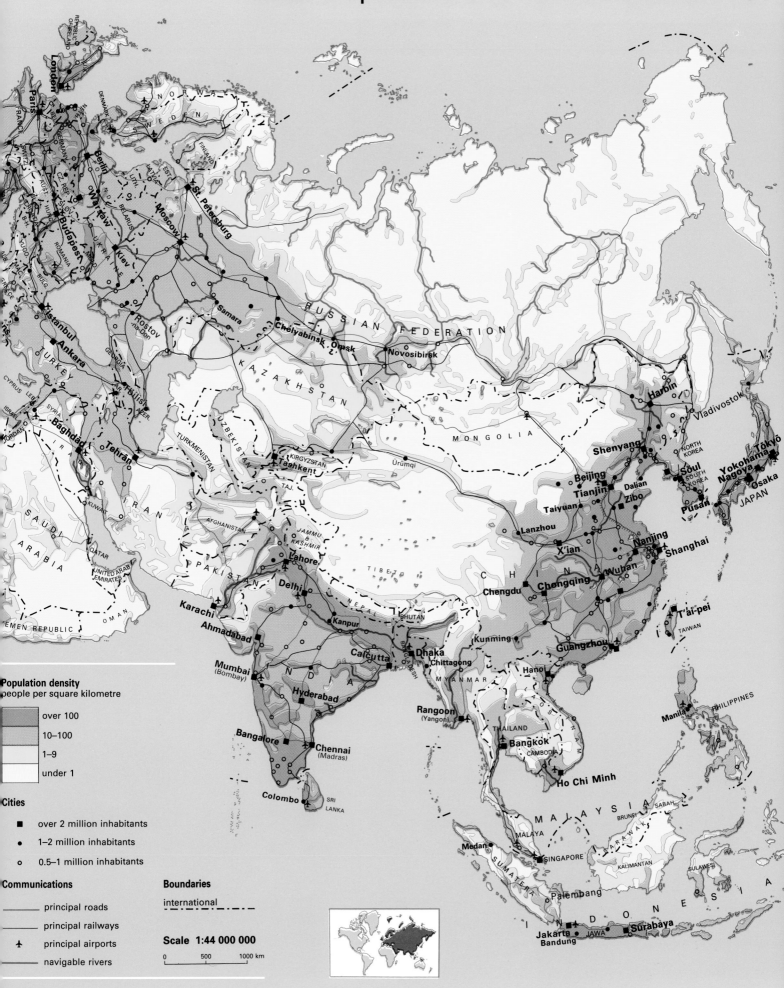

Population density
people per square kilometre

	over 100
	10–100
	1–9
	under 1

Cities

■ over 2 million inhabitants

● 1–2 million inhabitants

○ 0.5–1 million inhabitants

Communications

— principal roads

— principal railways

✈ principal airports

— navigable rivers

Boundaries

international

Scale 1:44 000 000

0   500   1000 km

Mathal Equal Area Projection

Oxford University Press

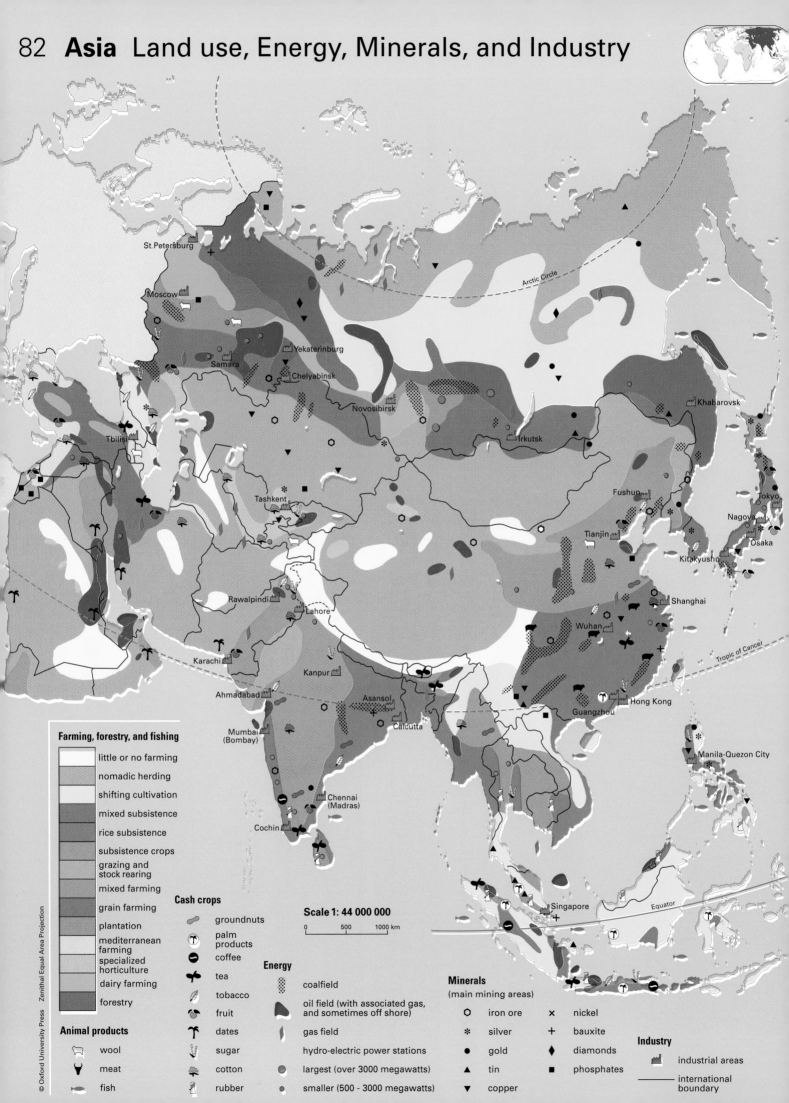

St.Petersburg

Moscow

Yekaterinburg

Samara

Chelyabinsk

Novosibirsk

Tbilisi

Irkutsk

Khabarovsk

Tashkent

Fushun

Tianjin

Tokyo

Nagoya

Osaka

Kitakyushu

Rawalpindi

Lahore

Shanghai

Wuhan

Karachi

Kanpur

Ahmadabad

Asansol

Guangzhou

Hong Kong

Mumbai
(Bombay)

Calcutta

Chennai
(Madras)

Cochin

Manila-Quezon City

Singapore

Arctic Circle

Tropic of Cancer

Equator

© Oxford University Press   Zenithal Equal Area Projection

Farming, forestry, and fishing

- little or no farming
- nomadic herding
- shifting cultivation
- mixed subsistence
- rice subsistence
- subsistence crops
- grazing and stock rearing
- mixed farming
- grain farming
- plantation
- mediterranean farming
- specialized horticulture
- dairy farming
- forestry

Cash crops

- groundnuts
- palm products
- coffee
- tea
- tobacco
- fruit
- dates
- sugar
- cotton
- rubber

Animal products

- wool
- meat
- fish

Energy

- coalfield
- oil field (with associated gas, and sometimes off shore)
- gas field
- hydro-electric power stations
- largest (over 3000 megawatts)
- smaller (500 - 3000 megawatts)

Scale 1: 44 000 000

0   500   1000 km

Minerals
(main mining areas)

- iron ore
- silver
- gold
- tin
- copper
- nickel
- bauxite
- diamonds
- phosphates

Industry

- industrial areas
- international boundary

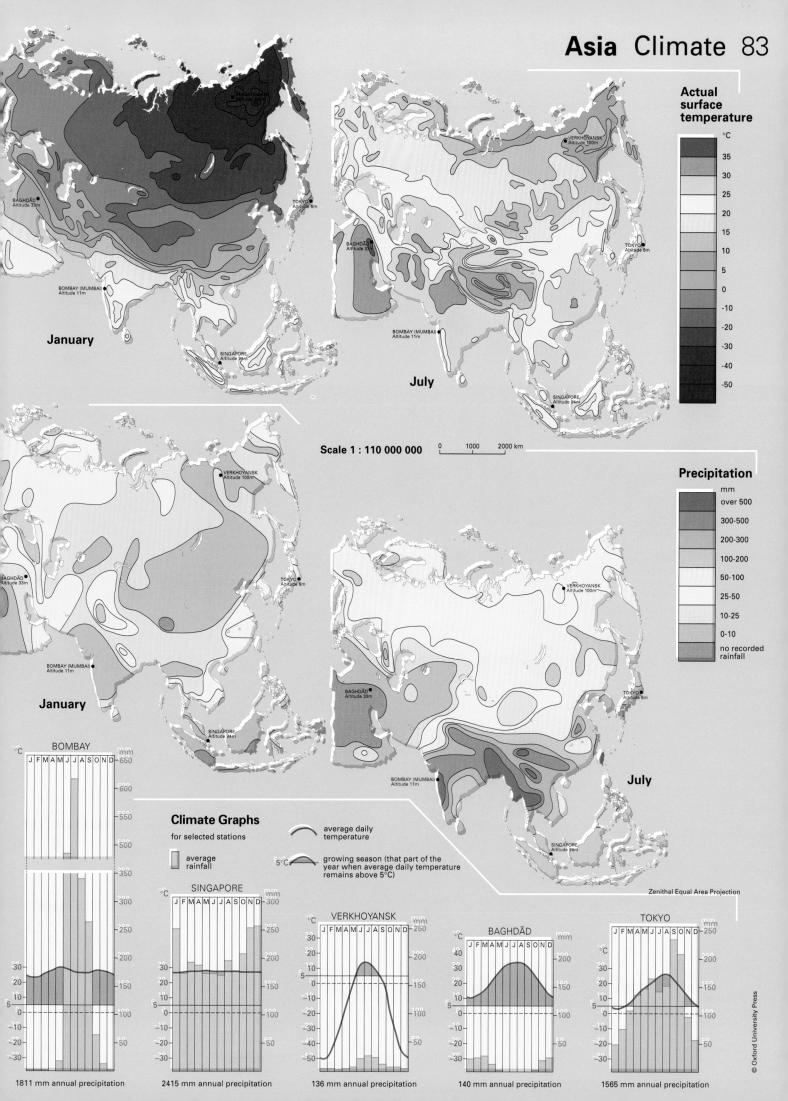

Asia Climate 83

Actual surface temperature

°C
- 35
- 30
- 25
- 20
- 15
- 10
- 5
- 0
- -10
- -20
- -30
- -40
- -50

January

July

VERKHOYANSK Altitude 100m
BAGHDĀD Altitude 33m
TOKYO Altitude 6m
BOMBAY (MUMBAI) Altitude 11m
SINGAPORE Altitude 94m

Scale 1 : 110 000 000

0 1000 2000 km

Precipitation

mm
- over 500
- 300-500
- 200-300
- 100-200
- 50-100
- 25-50
- 10-25
- 0-10
- no recorded rainfall

January

July

Zenithal Equal Area Projection

Climate Graphs

for selected stations

average rainfall

average daily temperature

growing season (that part of the year when average daily temperature remains above 5°C)

BOMBAY

SINGAPORE

VERKHOYANSK

BAGHDĀD

TOKYO

1811 mm annual precipitation

2415 mm annual precipitation

136 mm annual precipitation

140 mm annual precipitation

1565 mm annual precipitation

© Oxford University Press

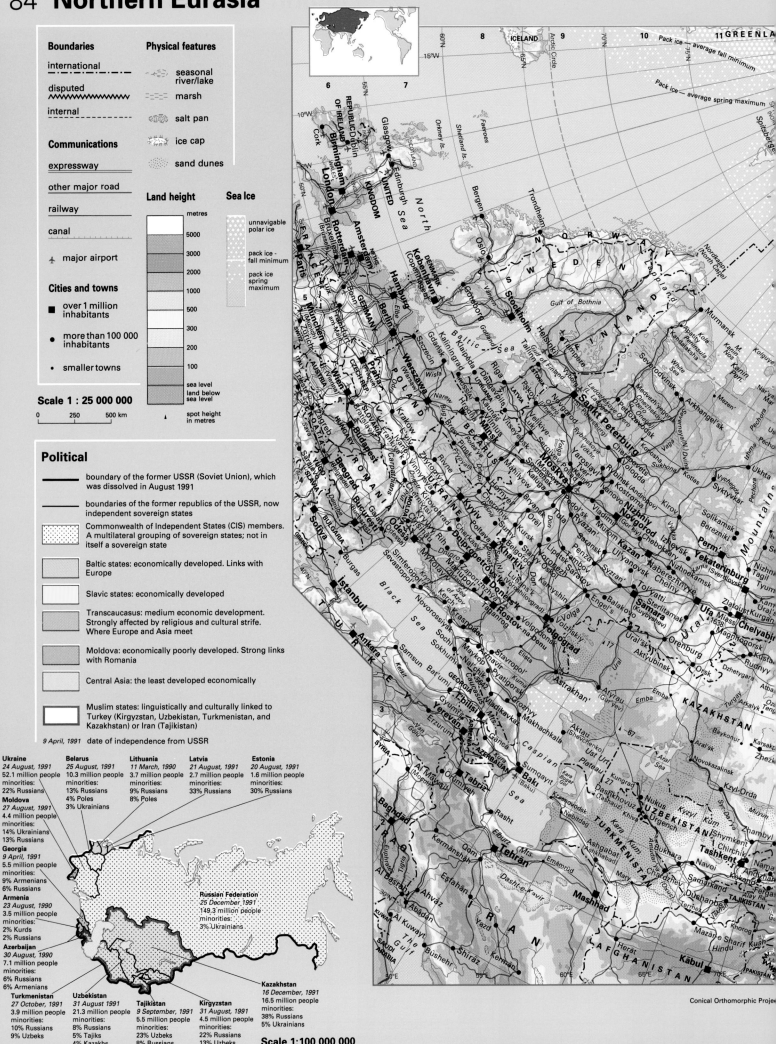

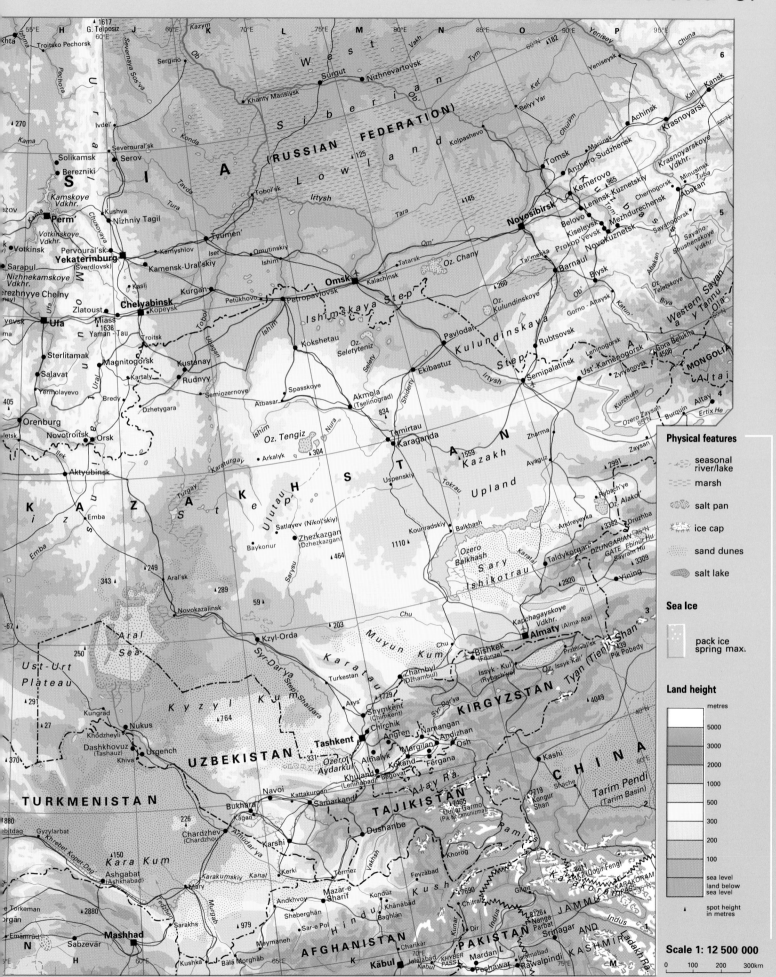

Physical features

- seasonal river/lake
- marsh
- salt pan
- ice cap
- sand dunes
- salt lake

Sea Ice

- pack ice spring max.

Land height

metres
5000
3000
2000
1000
300
200
100
sea level
land below sea level

▲ spot height in metres

Scale 1: 12 500 000

0   100   200   300km

Oxford University Press

Israel & Lebanon

Scale 1:4 000 000

0   50   100 km

Conical Orthomorphic Projection

Scale 1: 12 500 000

0   125   250 km

© Oxford University Press

Boundaries

international

disputed

internal

Communications

expressway

other major road

railway

canal

✈ major airport

Physical features

🌊 seasonal river/lake

marsh

salt pan

ice cap

sand dunes

Land height

	metres
	5000
	3000
	2000
	1000
	500
	300
	200
	100
	sea level
	land below sea level

▲ spot height in metres

Cities and towns

■ over 1 million inhabitants

● more than 100 000 inhabitants

• smaller towns

+ historic sites

India: Population, 1993

males Age females

70+
65-69
60-64
55-59
50-54
45-49
40-44
35-39
30-34
25-29
20-24
15-19
10-14
5-9
0-4

7 6 5 4 3 2 1 0   0 1 2 3 4 5 6 7
percent of total population

Total population: 883.9 million

Crude Birth Rate per thousand: 31

Crude Death Rate per thousand: 10

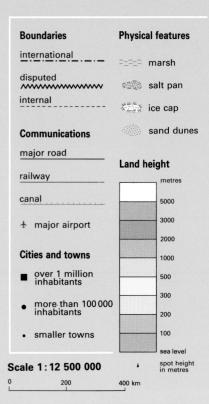

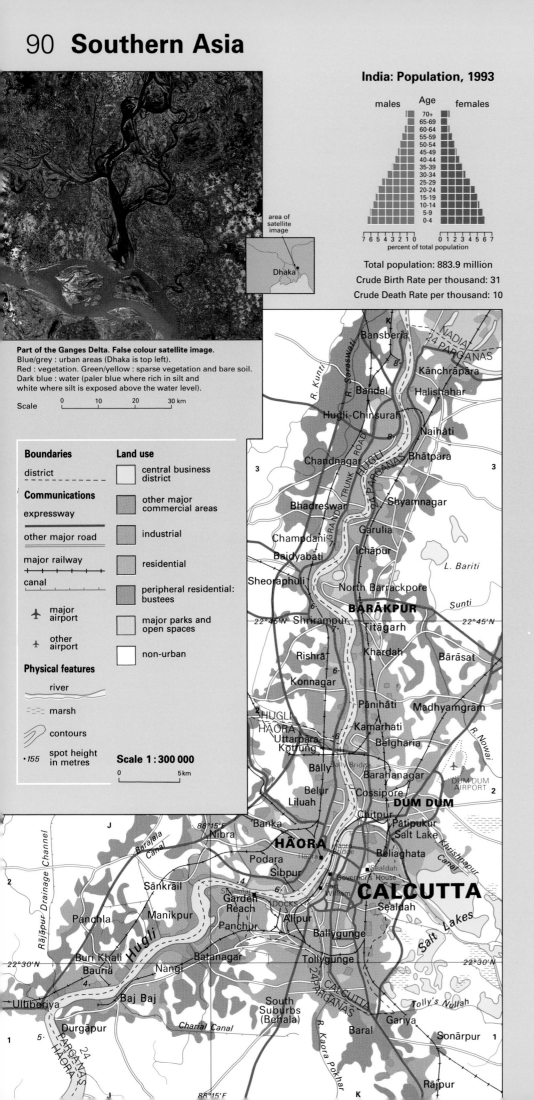

Part of the Ganges Delta. False colour satellite image.
Blue/grey : urban areas (Dhaka is top left).
Red : vegetation. Green/yellow : sparse vegetation and bare soil.
Dark blue : water (paler blue where rich in silt and
white where silt is exposed above the water level).

Scale 0   10   20   30 km

area of
satellite
image

Dhaka

Boundaries
district

Communications
expressway

other major road

major railway

canal

✈ major airport

✈ other airport

Physical features
river

marsh

contours

•155 spot height in metres

Land use
central business district

other major commercial areas

industrial

residential

peripheral residential: bustees

major parks and open spaces

non-urban

Scale 1 : 300 000

0   5km

Boundaries
international

disputed

internal

Communications
major road

railway

canal

✈ major airport

Cities and towns
■ over 1 million inhabitants

● more than 100 000 inhabitants

• smaller towns

Physical features
marsh

salt pan

ice cap

sand dunes

Land height

metres
5000
3000
2000
1000
500
300
200
100
sea level

▲ spot height in metres

Scale 1 : 12 500 000

0   200   400 km

Southern Asia

China
Xizang Zizhiqu (Tibet)

Kun Lun Shan
Tanggula Shan
Nyainqentanglha Shan

K2 (Godwin Austen) 8611
Gasherbrum 8126
Karakoram Pass
Mt. Everest 8848

Jammu and Kashmir
Srinagar
Leh
Gilgit
Chitral
Dir
Khyber Pass
Mardan
Peshawar
Kohat
Islamabad
Rawalpindi
Jhelum
Sialkot
Gujrat
Gujranwala
Lahore
Amritsar
Faisalabad
Jhang
Maghiana
Multan

Himachal Pradesh
Simla
Manali
Chandigarh
Ludhiana
Punjab
Patiala
Ambala
Bhatinda
Ferozpur

Haryana
Hisar
Karnal
Panipat
Meerut
Delhi
New Delhi
Faridabad
Ghaziabad

Rajasthan
Bikaner
Jodhpur
Jaipur
Ajmer
Bhilwara
Udaipur
Kota

Nepal
Kathmandu
Pokhara
Annapurna 8091

Bhutan
Thimphu

Uttar Pradesh
Bareilly
Lucknow
Kanpur
Agra
Gwalior
Allahabad
Varanasi

Bihar
Patna
Gaya
Munger
Bhagalpur

Bangla Desh
Dhaka
Rajshahi
Khulna
Barisal
Chittagong
Comilla

Assam
Guwahati
Shillong
Dibrugarh

Myanmar (Burma)
Mandalay
Monywa
Sittwe
Bassein

India

Madhya Pradesh
Bhopal
Indore
Jabalpur
Raipur
Bilaspur

Gujarat
Ahmadabad
Vadodara
Surat

Maharashtra
Mumbai (Bombay)
Pune
Nagpur
Nasik
Aurangabad

Orissa
Bhubaneshwar
Cuttack
Puri

West Bengal
Calcutta
Haora
Kharagpur

Andhra Pradesh
Hyderabad
Vijayawada
Guntur
Vishakhapatnam

Karnataka
Bangalore
Mysore
Mangalore
Belgaum
Hubli-Dharwad

Tamil Nadu
Chennai (Madras)
Coimbatore
Madurai
Tiruchchirāppalli
Salem

Kerala
Cochin
Trivandrum
Calicut
Quilon

Maldives

Sri Lanka
Colombo
Kandy
Jaffna
Galle
Trincomalee

Bay of Bengal

Andaman Is. (India)
North Andaman
Middle Andaman
South Andaman
Port Blair
Little Andaman

Nicobar Is. (India)
Car Nicobar
Little Nicobar
Great Nicobar

Ten Degree Channel

Lakshadweep (India)
Minicoy I.
Kavaratti I.

Orthomorphic Projection
Oxford University Press

Boundaries

international
disputed
internal

Communications

expressway
expressway under construction
other major road
railway
railway tunnel
canal
✈ major airport

Cities and towns

⬡ built-up areas
■ over 1 million inhabitants
● more than 100 000 inhabitants
• smaller towns

Physical features

seasonal river/lake
marsh
salt pan
ice cap
sand dunes

Land height

metres
5000
3000
2000
1000
500
300
200
100
sea level
land below sea level
▲ spot height in metres

China scale 1 : 19 000 000

0   200   400 km

Conical Orthomorphic Projection

Hong Kong scale 1 : 500 000

0   5 km

Gauss Conformal Projection

© Oxford University

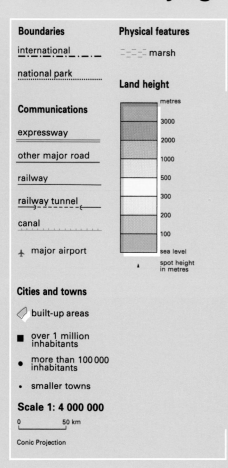

Boundaries

international

national park

Communications

expressway

other major road

railway

railway tunnel

canal

✈ major airport

Physical features

marsh

Land height

metres
3000
2000
1000
500
300
200
100
sea level
▲ spot height in metres

Cities and towns

built-up areas

■ over 1 million inhabitants

● more than 100 000 inhabitants

• smaller towns

Scale 1: 4 000 000

0   50 km

Conic Projection

CHINA

Dazhang Xi

E 119°E Fuqing F 120°E G 121°E H 122°E I 123°E J

8 • Yongchun

Xianyou

Putian

Pingtan Dao

Nanri Dao

P'eng-chia Hsü
Mien Hsü
Hua-p'ing Hsü

Shanyao

Tan-shui

25°N • Anxi

Quanzhou

Chi-lung

San-chung

Panch'iao

T'ai-pei

Tong'an

T'ao-yüan

Chung-li

Chung-ho

Hsin-tien

Xiamen

Chinmen

Chimen Tao (Quemoy)

Hsin-chu

Pingchen

I-lan

Tucheng

25°N

Ho-lung

Miao-li

Lo-tung

Su-ao

Yonaguni

Taiwan Strait

Yüan-li

Ta-chia

3884

Peng-hu Shuitao

Tan-shui Ho

Shanmo

24°N

Ch'ing-shui

Feng-Yüan

Taroko National Park

24°N

Chang-hua

T'ai-chung

Lu-kang

Yüan-lin

Hua-lien

PACIFIC OCEAN

Erh-lin

Nan-t'ou

Chi-pei Tao

Pai-sha Tao

Yü-weng Tao

Pei-kang

Tou-liu

Yü Shan National Park

Kuangfu

Makung (Penghu)

P'eng-hu Tao

Chia-i

Yü Shan 3997

Yü-li

6 Tropic of Cancer

P'eng-hu Lieh-tao (Pescadores Is.)

Pu-tai

Hsin-ying

Ch'eng-kung

23°N

Ch'imei Hsü

Chia-li

Chung

23°N

TAIWAN

T'ai-nan

Yung-kang

Kang-shan

Ch'i-shan

T'ai-tung

Kao-hsiung

Fengshan

P'ing-tung

Ta-ma-li

Lü Tao

5 South China Sea

Tung-chiang

Fang-liao

T'a-wu

22°N

Heng-ch'un

Kenting National Park

Lan Hsü

22°N

120°E

O'luan-pi

4 G 121°E H 122°E I 123°E

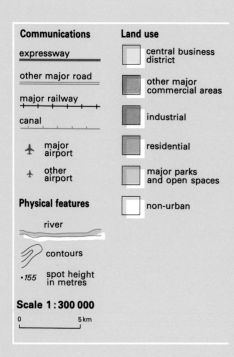

Communications

expressway

other major road

major railway

canal

✈ major airport

✈ other airport

Physical features

river

contours

•155 spot height in metres

Scale 1: 300 000

0   5km

Land use

central business district

other major commercial areas

industrial

residential

major parks and open spaces

non-urban

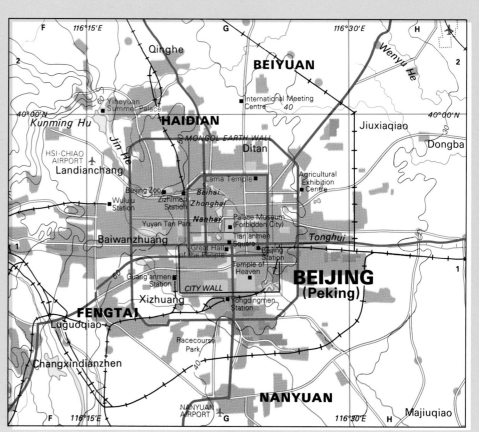

F 116°15'E G 116°30'E H

Qinghe

BEIYUAN

Wenyu He

2

International Meeting Centre

40

40°00'N

Yiheyuan Summer Palace

HAIDIAN

Jiuxiaqiao

Kunming Hu

Jin He

MONGOL EARTH WALL

Ditan

Dongba

HSI-CHIAO AIRPORT

Landianchang

Lama Temple

Agricultural Exhibition Centre

Beijing Zoo

Wulu Station

Zizhimen Station

Baihai Zhonghai

Nanhai

Yuyan Tan Park

Palace Museum (Forbidden City)

1 Baiwanzhuang

Tian'anmen Square

Tonghui

1

Great Hall of the People

Beijing Station

Guang'anmen Station

Temple of Heaven

BEIJING (Peking)

Xizhuang

CITY WALL

Yongdingmen Station

FENGTAI

Luguoqiao

Racecourse Park

Changxindianzhen

40

NANYUAN

NANYUAN AIRPORT

Majiuqiao

F 116°15'E G 116°30'E H

© Oxford University

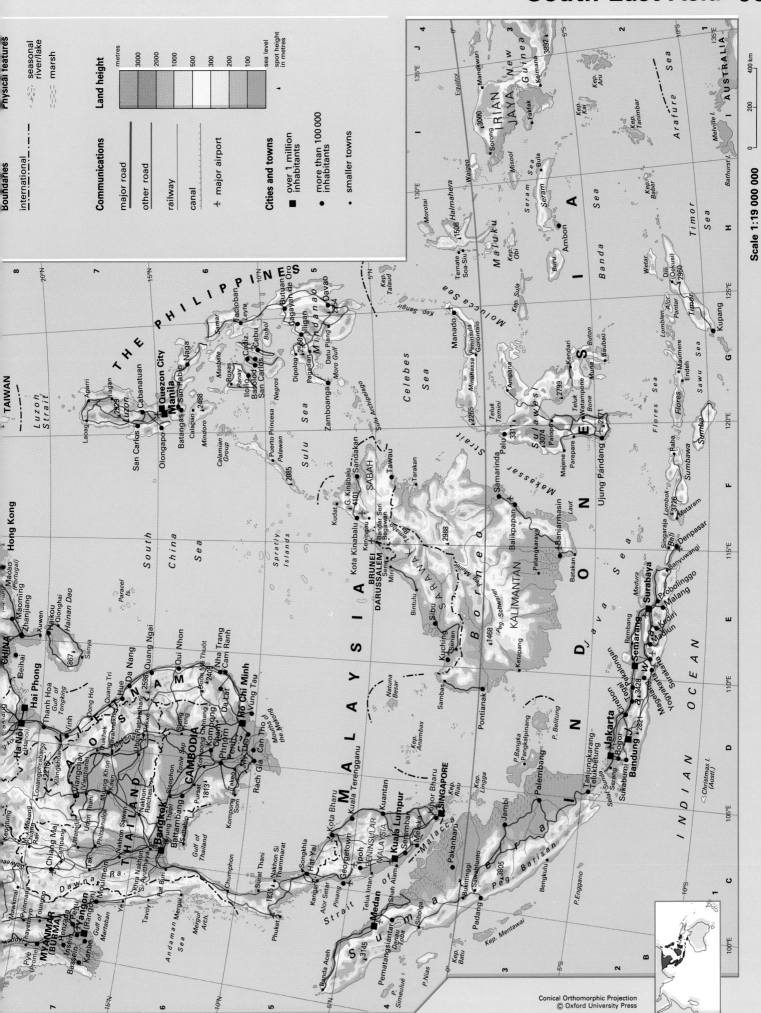

Scale 1:19 000 000

Conical Orthomorphic Projection
© Oxford University Press

Population

Population density
people per square kilometre

- over 700
- 100–700
- 10–100
- 1–10
- under 1

Cities
- ■ over 2 million inhabitants
- ● 1–2 million inhabitants
- ○ 0.5–1 million inhabitants
- · 0.1–0.5 million inhabitants

Japan: Population, 1992

males | Age | females
85+
80-84
75-79
70-74
65-69
60-64
55-59
50-54
45-49
40-44
35-39
30-34
25-29
20-24
15-19
10-14
5-9
0-4

5 4 3 2 1 0 | 0 1 2 3 4 5
percent of total population

Total population: 124.5 million

Crude Birth Rate per thousand: 10

Crude Death Rate per thousand: 7

Scale 1:10 000 000
0   100   200 km

Boundaries
international

Communications
expressway
other major road
railway
✈ major airport

Cities and towns
◁ built-up areas
■ over 1 million inhabitants
● more than 100 000 inhabitants
· smaller towns

Land height
metres
3000
2000
1000
500
300
200
100
sea level
▲ spot height in metres

Scale 1:6 250 000
0   50   100 km

International comparison of aged populations

Percentage of total population aged 65 or over

Japan
Sweden
Germany (West)
France
USA

1900 1920 1940 1960 1980 2000 2020
Year
Projection from 1980

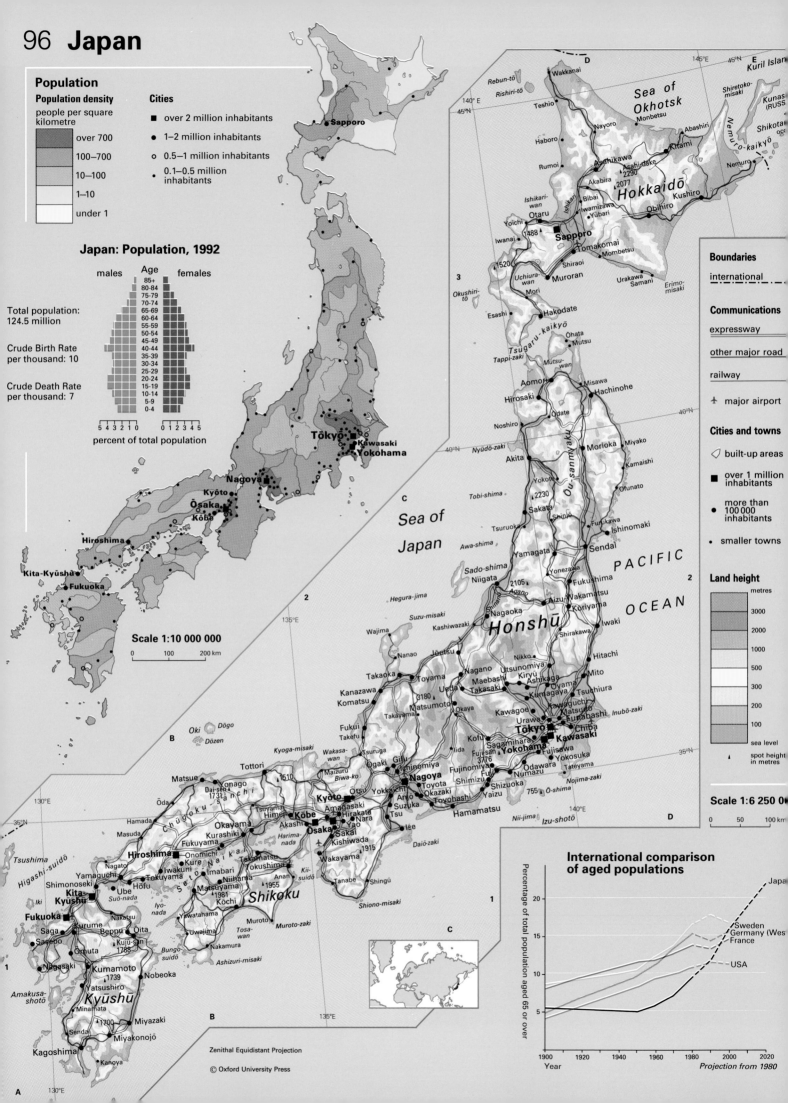

Zenithal Equidistant Projection

© Oxford University Press

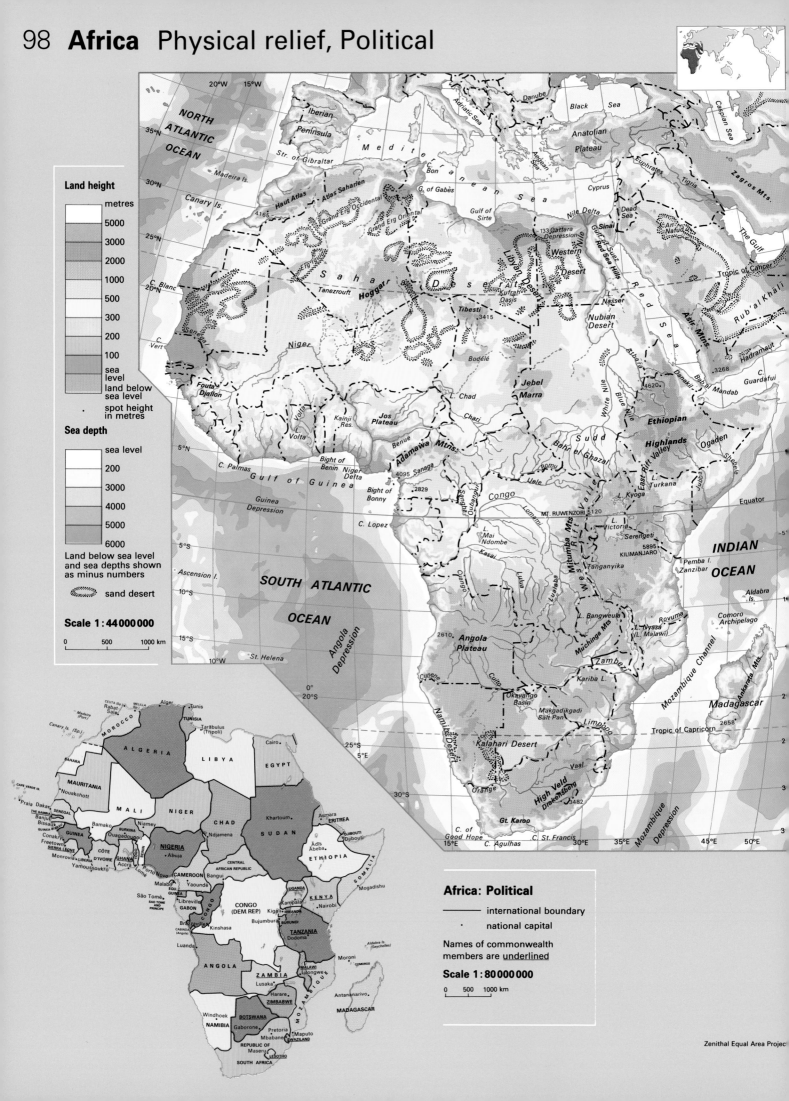

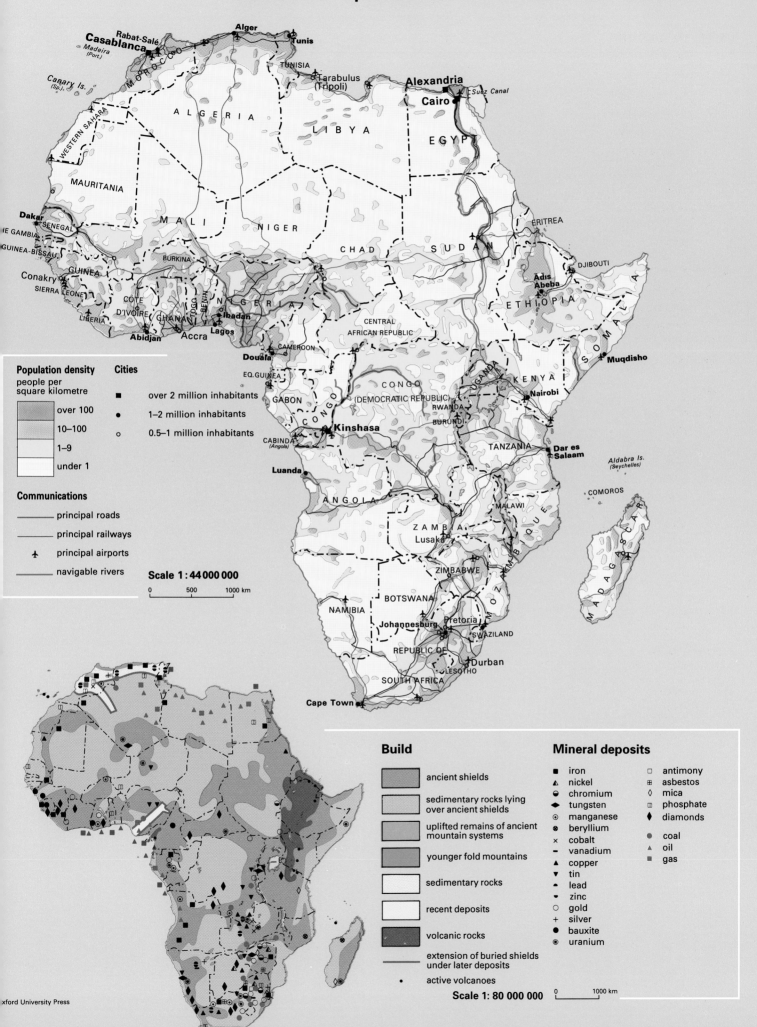

Population density
people per square kilometre

- over 100
- 10–100
- 1–9
- under 1

Cities

- ■ over 2 million inhabitants
- ● 1–2 million inhabitants
- ○ 0.5–1 million inhabitants

Communications

- principal roads
- principal railways
- ✈ principal airports
- navigable rivers

Scale 1 : 44 000 000

0   500   1000 km

Build

- ancient shields
- sedimentary rocks lying over ancient shields
- uplifted remains of ancient mountain systems
- younger fold mountains
- sedimentary rocks
- recent deposits
- volcanic rocks
- extension of buried shields under later deposits
- ● active volcanoes

Mineral deposits

- ■ iron
- ▲ nickel
- ◖ chromium
- ◆ tungsten
- ▲ manganese
- ⊛ beryllium
- × cobalt
- – vanadium
- ▲ copper
- ▼ tin
- ▾ lead
- ▾ zinc
- ○ gold
- + silver
- ● bauxite
- ⊛ uranium
- □ antimony
- ⊞ asbestos
- ◇ mica
- ⊟ phosphate
- ◆ diamonds
- ● coal
- ▲ oil
- ■ gas

Scale 1 : 80 000 000

0   1000 km

Oxford University Press

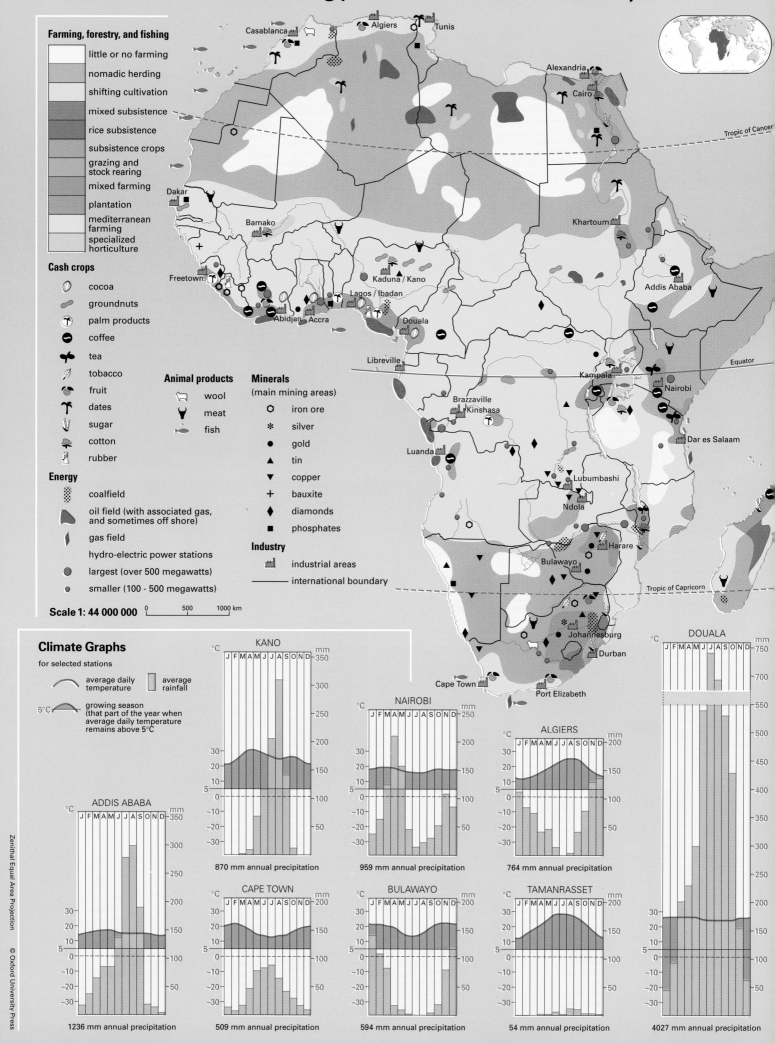

Farming, forestry, and fishing

- little or no farming
- nomadic herding
- shifting cultivation
- mixed subsistence
- rice subsistence
- subsistence crops
- grazing and stock rearing
- mixed farming
- plantation
- mediterranean farming
- specialized horticulture

Cash crops

- cocoa
- groundnuts
- palm products
- coffee
- tea
- tobacco
- fruit
- dates
- sugar
- cotton
- rubber

Energy

- coalfield
- oil field (with associated gas, and sometimes off shore)
- gas field
- hydro-electric power stations
- largest (over 500 megawatts)
- smaller (100 - 500 megawatts)

Animal products

- wool
- meat
- fish

Minerals (main mining areas)

- iron ore
- silver
- gold
- tin
- copper
- bauxite
- diamonds
- phosphates

Industry

- industrial areas
- international boundary

Scale 1: 44 000 000

0   500   1000 km

Casablanca Algiers Tunis
Alexandria
Cairo
Tropic of Cancer
Dakar
Bamako
Khartoum
Freetown
Kaduna / Kano
Addis Ababa
Abidjan Accra Lagos / Ibadan
Douala
Libreville
Kampala
Nairobi
Brazzaville
Kinshasa
Dar es Salaam
Luanda
Lubumbashi
Ndola
Harare
Bulawayo
Johannesburg
Durban
Cape Town Port Elizabeth
Tropic of Capricorn
Equator

Climate Graphs

for selected stations

- average daily temperature
- average rainfall
- growing season (that part of the year when average daily temperature remains above 5°C)

KANO
870 mm annual precipitation

NAIROBI
959 mm annual precipitation

ALGIERS
764 mm annual precipitation

DOUALA
4027 mm annual precipitation

ADDIS ABABA
1236 mm annual precipitation

CAPE TOWN
509 mm annual precipitation

BULAWAYO
594 mm annual precipitation

TAMANRASSET
54 mm annual precipitation

Zenithal Equal Area Projection

© Oxford University Press

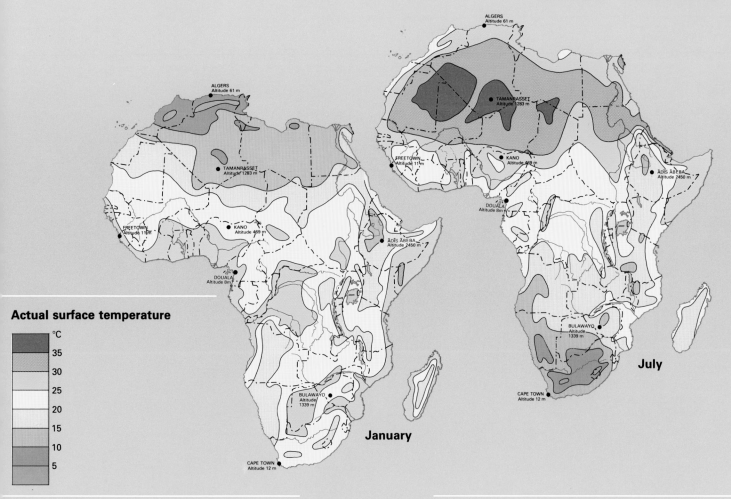

Actual surface temperature

°C
35
30
25
20
15
10
5

July

January

Scale 1 : 80 000 000

0   500   1000 km

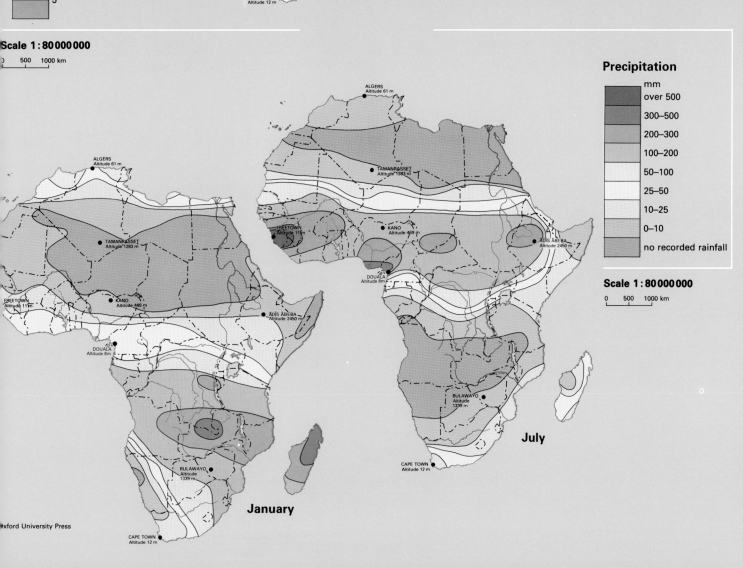

Precipitation

mm
over 500
300–500
200–300
100–200
50–100
25–50
10–25
0–10
no recorded rainfall

Scale 1 : 80 000 000

0   500   1000 km

July

January

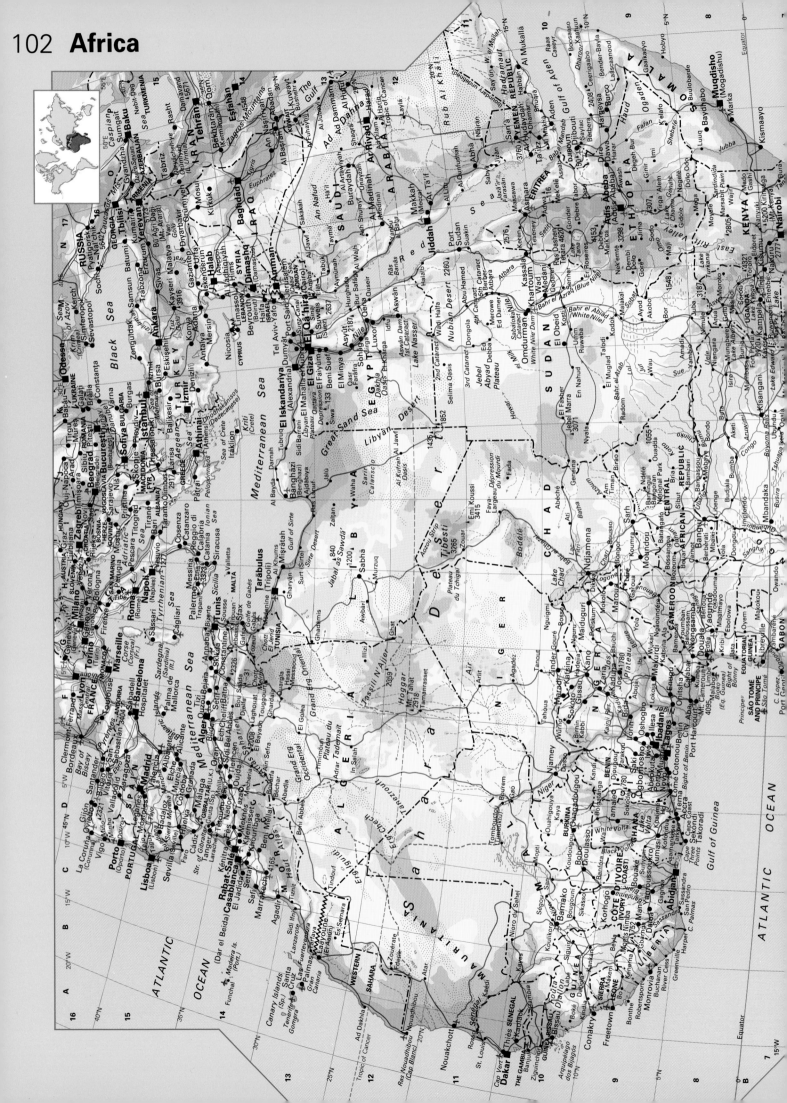

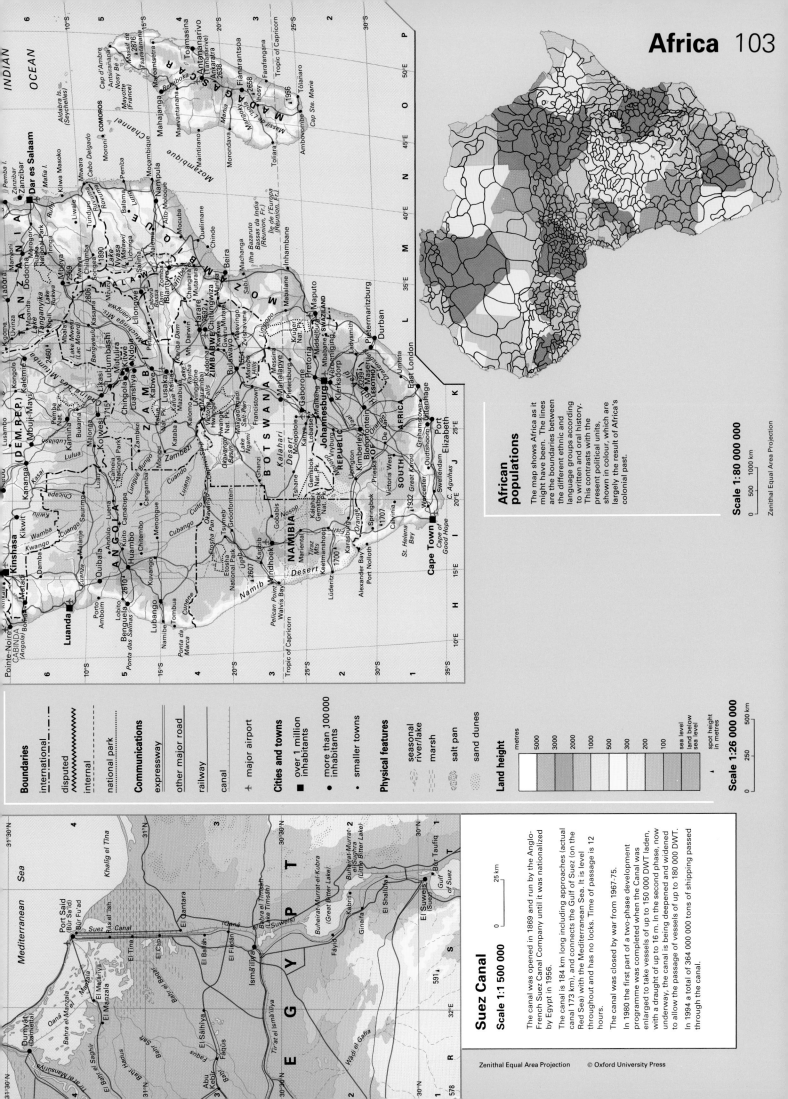

Boundaries

international
disputed
internal
national park

Communications

expressway
other major road
railway
canal
✈ major airport

Cities and towns

■ over 1 million inhabitants
● more than 100 000 inhabitants
• smaller towns

Physical features

seasonal river/lake
marsh
salt pan
sand dunes

Land height

metres
5000
3000
2000
1000
500
300
200
100
sea level
land below sea level
▲ spot height in metres

Scale 1:26 000 000

0 250 500 km

African populations

The map shows Africa as it might have been. The lines are the boundaries between the different ethnic and language groups according to written and oral history. This contrasts with the present political units, shown in colour, which are largely the result of Africa's colonial past.

Scale 1:80 000 000

0 500 1000 km

Zenithal Equal Area Projection

Suez Canal

Scale 1:1 500 000

0 25 km

The canal was opened in 1869 and run by the Anglo-French Suez Canal Company until it was nationalized by Egypt in 1956.

The canal is 184 km long including approaches (actual canal 173 km), and connects the Gulf of Suez (on the Red Sea) with the Mediterranean Sea. It is level throughout and has no locks. Time of passage is 12 hours.

The canal was closed by war from 1967-75.

In 1980 the first part of a two-phase development programme was completed when the Canal was enlarged to take vessels of up to 150 000 DWT laden, with a draught of up to 16 m. In the second phase, now underway, the canal is being deepened and widened to allow the passage of vessels of up to 180 000 DWT.

In 1994 a total of 364 000 000 tons of shipping passed through the canal.

Zenithal Equal Area Projection   © Oxford University Press

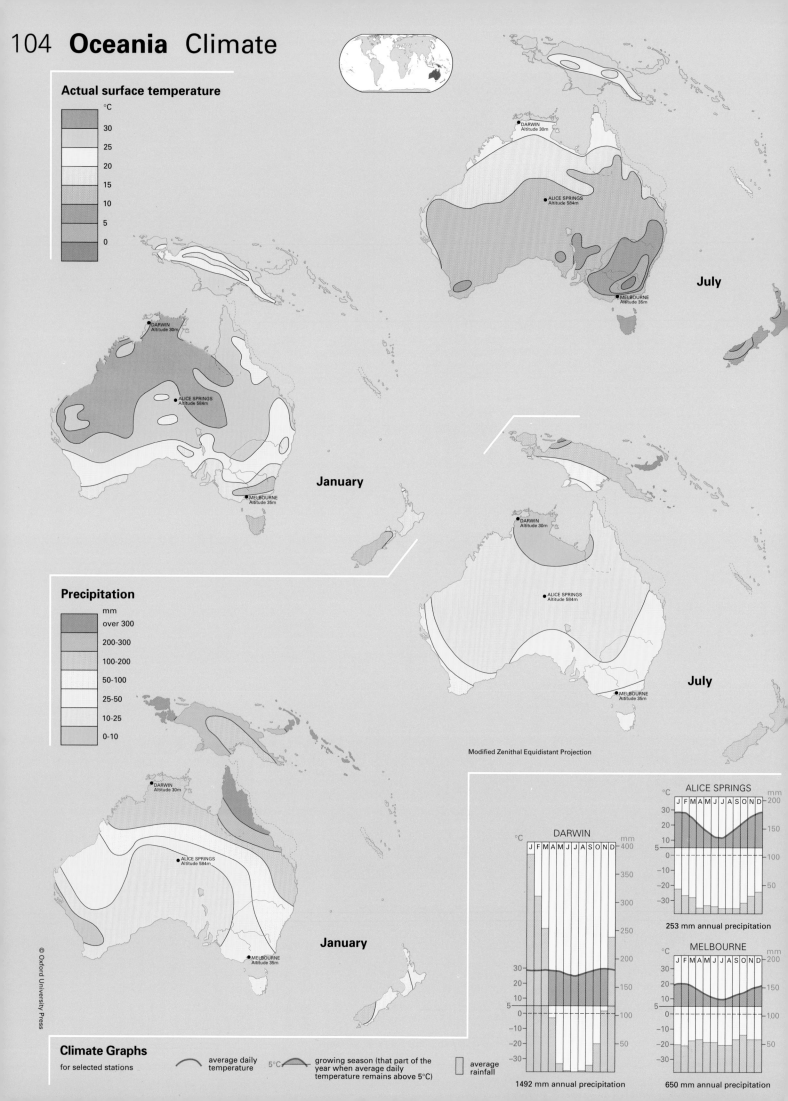

Actual surface temperature

°C
30
25
20
15
10
5
0

July

January

Precipitation

mm
over 300
200-300
100-200
50-100
25-50
10-25
0-10

July

Modified Zenithal Equidistant Projection

January

© Oxford University Press

Climate Graphs
for selected stations

average daily temperature

5°C growing season (that part of the year when average daily temperature remains above 5°C)

average rainfall

DARWIN

ALICE SPRINGS

253 mm annual precipitation

MELBOURNE

1492 mm annual precipitation

650 mm annual precipitation

DARWIN
Altitude 30m

ALICE SPRINGS
Altitude 584m

MELBOURNE
Altitude 35m

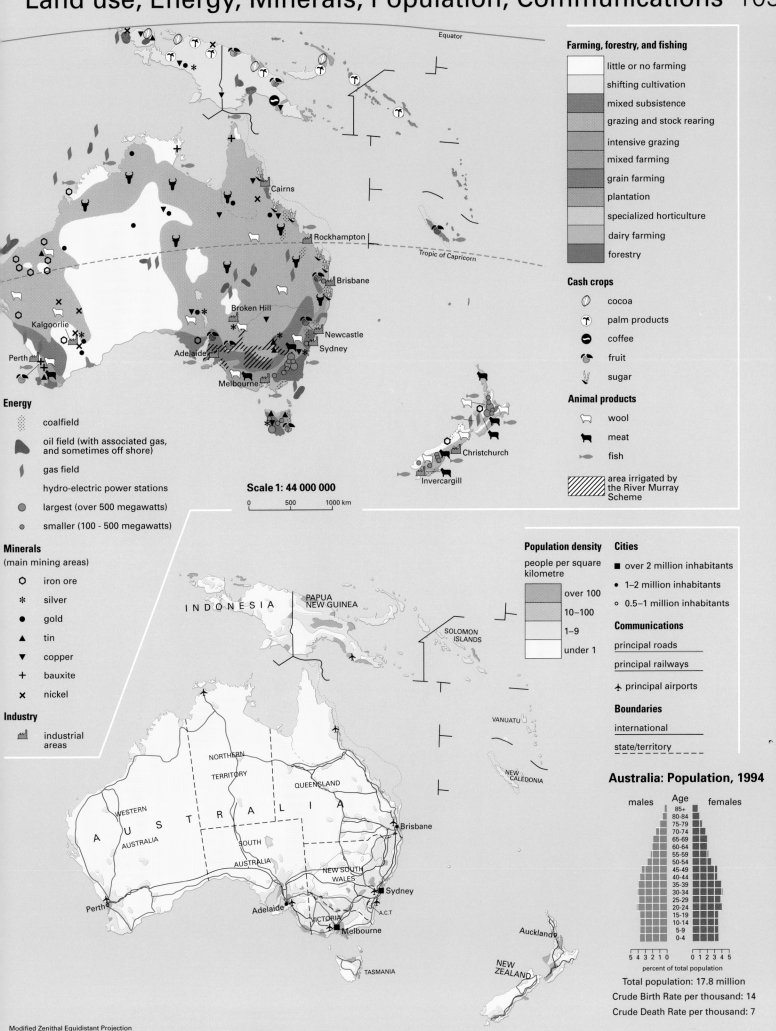

Farming, forestry, and fishing

- little or no farming
- shifting cultivation
- mixed subsistence
- grazing and stock rearing
- intensive grazing
- mixed farming
- grain farming
- plantation
- specialized horticulture
- dairy farming
- forestry

Cash crops

- cocoa
- palm products
- coffee
- fruit
- sugar

Animal products

- wool
- meat
- fish

area irrigated by the River Murray Scheme

Energy

- coalfield
- oil field (with associated gas, and sometimes off shore)
- gas field
- hydro-electric power stations
- largest (over 500 megawatts)
- smaller (100 - 500 megawatts)

Minerals
(main mining areas)

- iron ore
- silver
- gold
- tin
- copper
- bauxite
- nickel

Industry

- industrial areas

Scale 1: 44 000 000

0   500   1000 km

Population density

people per square kilometre

- over 100
- 10–100
- 1–9
- under 1

Cities

- over 2 million inhabitants
- 1–2 million inhabitants
- 0.5–1 million inhabitants

Communications

- principal roads
- principal railways
- principal airports

Boundaries

- international
- state/territory

Australia: Population, 1994

males   Age   females

85+
80-84
75-79
70-74
65-69
60-64
55-59
50-54
45-49
40-44
35-39
30-34
25-29
20-24
15-19
10-14
5-9
0-4

5 4 3 2 1 0   0 1 2 3 4 5

percent of total population

Total population: 17.8 million

Crude Birth Rate per thousand: 14

Crude Death Rate per thousand: 7

Equator

Cairns

Rockhampton

Tropic of Capricorn

Brisbane

Broken Hill

Newcastle

Sydney

Adelaide

Melbourne

Kalgoorlie

Perth

Christchurch

Invercargill

INDONESIA

PAPUA NEW GUINEA

SOLOMON ISLANDS

VANUATU

NEW CALEDONIA

NORTHERN TERRITORY

QUEENSLAND

WESTERN AUSTRALIA

SOUTH AUSTRALIA

NEW SOUTH WALES

A U S T R A L I A

VICTORIA

A.C.T

Perth

Adelaide

Sydney

Melbourne

Auckland

NEW ZEALAND

TASMANIA

Brisbane

Modified Zenithal Equidistant Projection

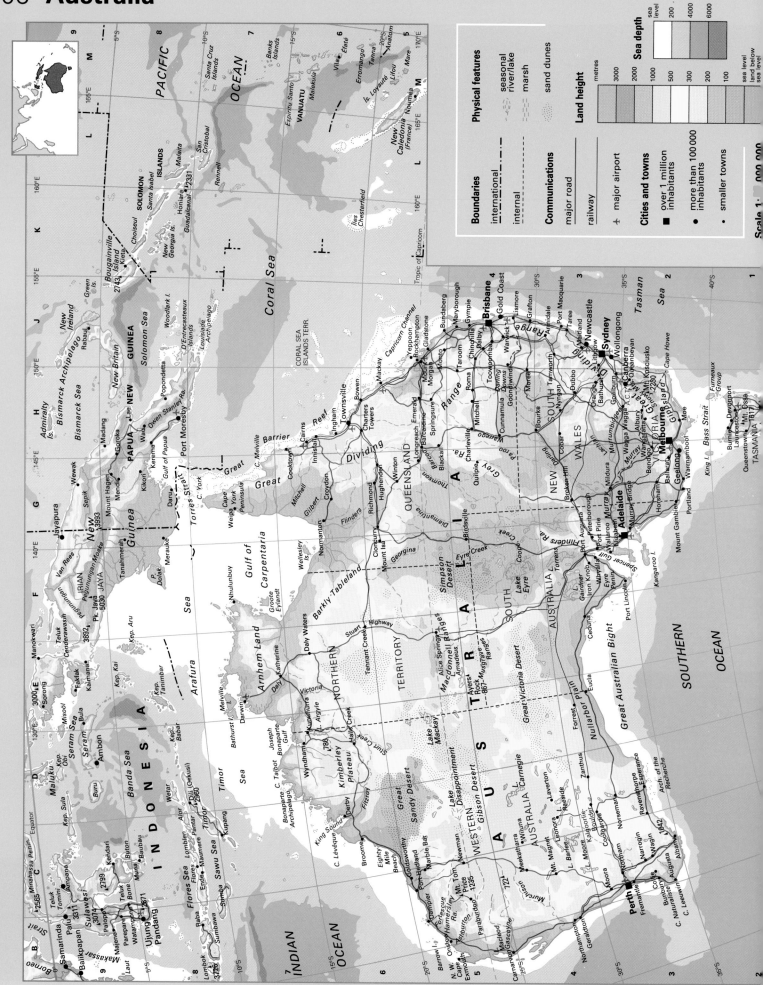

Physical features

- seasonal river/lake
- marsh
- sand dunes

Boundaries

- international
- internal

Communications

- major road
- railway
- ✈ major airport

Cities and towns

- ■ over 1 million inhabitants
- ● more than 100 000 inhabitants
- • smaller towns

Sea depth

sea level | 200 | 4000 | 6000

Land height

metres | 3000 | 2000 | 1000 | 500 | 300 | 200 | 100 | sea level / land below sea level

Scale 1 : 000 000

Zenithal Equidistant Proj
© Oxford University

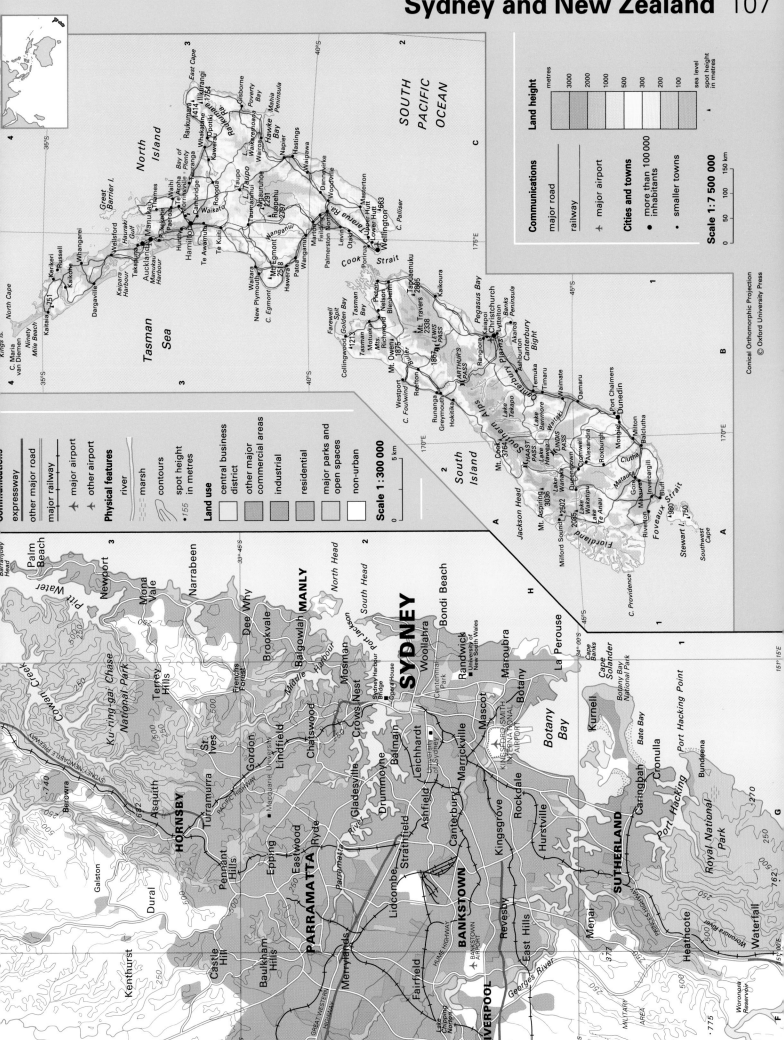

Land height

metres	
3000	
2000	
1000	
500	
300	
200	
100	
sea level	

▲ spot height in metres

Communications

major road

railway

✈ major airport

Cities and towns

● more than 100 000 inhabitants

• smaller towns

Scale 1:7 500 000

0 50 100 150 km

Conical Orthomorphic Projection

© Oxford University Press

Scale 1:300 000

0 5 km

Communications

expressway

other major road

major railway

✈ major airport

✈ other airport

Physical features

river

marsh

contours

•155 spot height in metres

Land use

central business district

other major commercial areas

industrial

residential

major parks and open spaces

non-urban

North Island

North Cape
Kings Is.
C. Maria van Diemen
Ninety Mile Beach
Kaitaia · 751
Kaikohe
Kerikeri
Russell
Whangarei
Dargaville
Kaipara Harbour
Wellsford
Great Barrier I.
Hauraki Gulf
Takapuna
AUCKLAND
Manukau
Manukau Harbour
Waiuku
Thames
Paeroa
Waihi
Te Aroha
Morrinsville
Tauranga
Bay of Plenty
Te Kaha
Opotiki 1754
East Cape
Raukumara 1414
Whakatane
Waikaremoana
Gisborne
Poverty Bay
Mahia Peninsula
Wairoa
Napier
Hastings
Hawke Bay
Waipawa
Dannevirke
Woodville
Masterton
1663
C. Palliser
Upper Hutt
Lower Hutt
WELLINGTON
Cook Strait
Levin
Otaki
Porirua
Palmerston North
Feilding
Marton
Wanganui
Patea
Hawera
C. Egmont
Mt Egmont 2518
New Plymouth
Waitara
Taumarunui
Ruapehu 2797
Ngauruhoe 2291
L. Taupo
Taupo
Rotorua
Tokoroa
Putaruru
Te Awamutu
Te Kuiti
Cambridge
HAMILTON
Huntly
Ngaruawahia
Waikato
Tasman Sea

South Island

Farewell Spit
Collingwood
Golden Bay
Tasman Bay
Motueka
1213
Takaka
Nelson
Richmond
Tasman Mts.
Mt Owen 1875
Westport
C. Foulwind
Buller
Reefton
Runanga
Greymouth
Hokitika
Mt Cook 3764
Mt Aspiring 3036
Jackson Head
Milford Sound
Fiordland
Lake Te Anau 2085
Lake Wakatipu
Lake Manapouri 2502
Mt Aspiring
Southwest Cape
Stewart I. ·750
·980
Foveaux Strait
Bluff
Riverton
Invercargill
Mataura
Gore
Mataura
Balclutha
Clutha
Milton
Port Chalmers
DUNEDIN
Mosgiel
Roxburgh
Alexandra
Cromwell
Queenstown
Lake Wakatipu
Lake Wanaka
Lake Hawea
LINDIS PASS
HAAST PASS
Lake Pukaki
Lake Tekapo
Lake Benmore
Lake Waitaki
Waimate
Oamaru
Timaru
Temuka
Ashburton
Rangiora
Kaiapoi
CHRISTCHURCH
Lyttelton
Banks Peninsula
Akaroa
Canterbury Bight
Pegasus Bay
Kaikoura
Tapuaenuku 2885
Mt Travers 2338
LEWIS PASS
ARTHUR'S PASS
Southern Alps
Canterbury Plains
Blenheim
Picton
South Pacific Ocean

Sydney

Barrenjoey Head
Palm Beach
Pittwater
Newport
Mona Vale
Narrabeen
Dee Why
Brookvale
Terrey Hills
Frenchs Forest
Balgowlah
MANLY
North Head
Mosman
Middle Harbour
Port Jackson
Crows Nest
Chatswood
Lindfield
Gordon
St Ives
Ku-ring-gai Chase National Park
Cowan Creek
Berowra
Asquith
·622
Hornsby
Turramurra
Macquarie University
Eastwood
Ryde
Gladesville
Drummoyne
Balmain
Leichhardt
Ashfield
University of Sydney
SYDNEY
Sydney Harbour Bridge
Opera House
Woollahra
Bondi Beach
South Head
Randwick
University of New South Wales
Centennial Park
Maroubra
La Perouse
Cape Banks
Botany
Mascot
KINGSFORD SMITH INTERNATIONAL AIRPORT
Botany Bay
Kurnell
Cape Solander
Botany Bay National Park
Bate Bay
Cronulla
Bundeena
Port Hacking Point
Port Hacking
Caringbah
SUTHERLAND
Menai
Royal National Park
·270
·762
Heathcote
Waterfall
Woronora River
Woronora Reservoir
·775
Marrickville
Canterbury
Rockdale
Hurstville
Kingsgrove
Revesby
East Hills
BANKSTOWN
BANKSTOWN AIRPORT
·370
Lidcombe
Strathfield
Merrylands
PARRAMATTA
Parramatta River
Baulkham Hills
Castle Hill
Kenthurst
Dural
Galston
Pennant Hills
Epping
Castle Hill
·740
·250
Hume Highway
Great Western Highway
LIVERPOOL
Fairfield
Lake Chipping Norton
Georges River
SYDNEY-NEWCASTLE FREEWAY
PACIFIC HIGHWAY
PRINCES HIGHWAY
MILITARY AREA
·250
·500

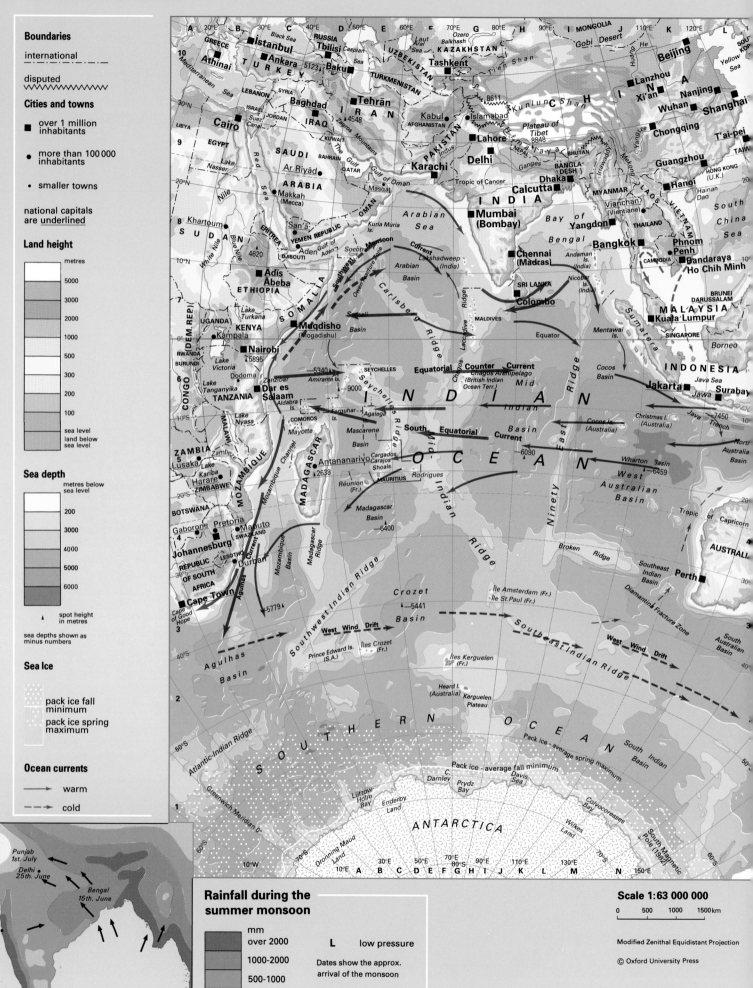

Boundaries

international

disputed

Cities and towns

■ over 1 million inhabitants

● more than 100 000 inhabitants

• smaller towns

national capitals are underlined

Land height

metres
5000
3000
2000
1000
500
300
200
100
sea level
land below sea level

Sea depth

metres below sea level
200
3000
4000
5000
6000

▲ spot height in metres

sea depths shown as minus numbers

Sea Ice

pack ice fall minimum

pack ice spring maximum

Ocean currents

→ warm

⇢ cold

Rainfall during the summer monsoon

mm
over 2000
1000-2000
500-1000
250-500
under 250

L low pressure

Dates show the approx. arrival of the monsoon

Scale 1:56 250 000
0   500   1000 km

Scale 1:63 000 000
0   500   1000   1500km

Modified Zenithal Equidistant Projection

© Oxford University Press

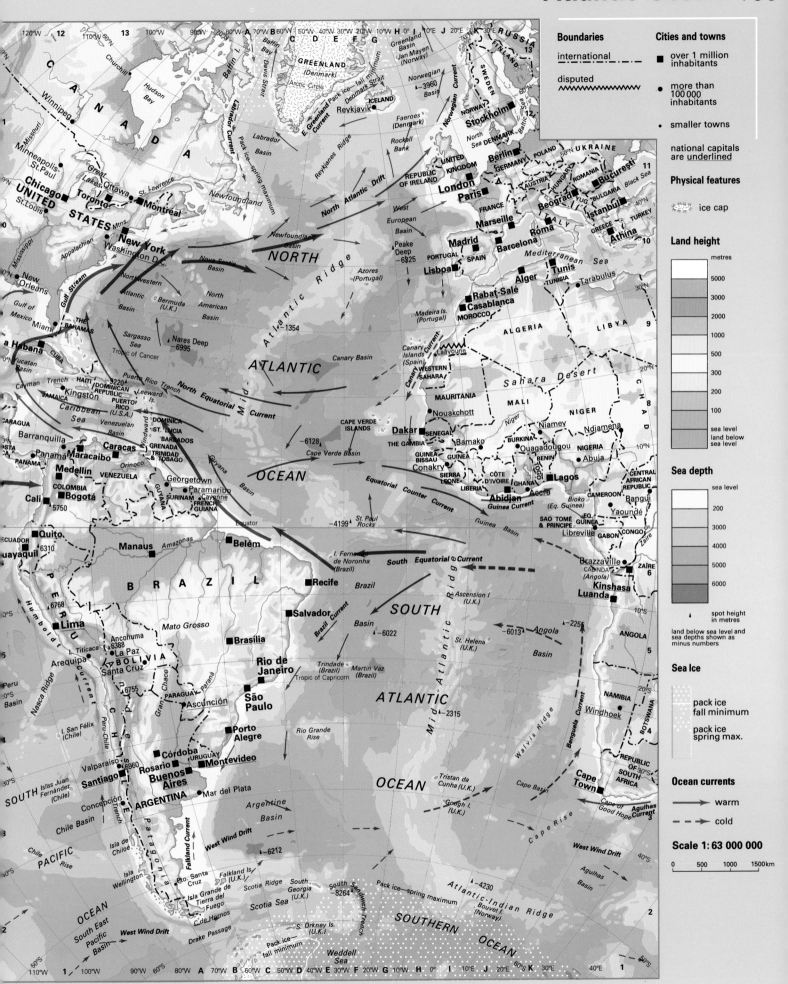

Boundaries

international — — —

disputed ~~~~~

Cities and towns

■ over 1 million inhabitants

● more than 100 000 inhabitants

• smaller towns

national capitals are underlined

Physical features

ice cap

Land height

metres

5000
3000
2000
1000
500
300
200
100
sea level
land below sea level

Sea depth

sea level
200
3000
4000
5000
6000

▲ spot height in metres

land below sea level and sea depths shown as minus numbers

Sea Ice

pack ice fall minimum

pack ice spring max.

Ocean currents

→ warm

⇢ cold

Scale 1: 63 000 000

0   500   1000   1500km

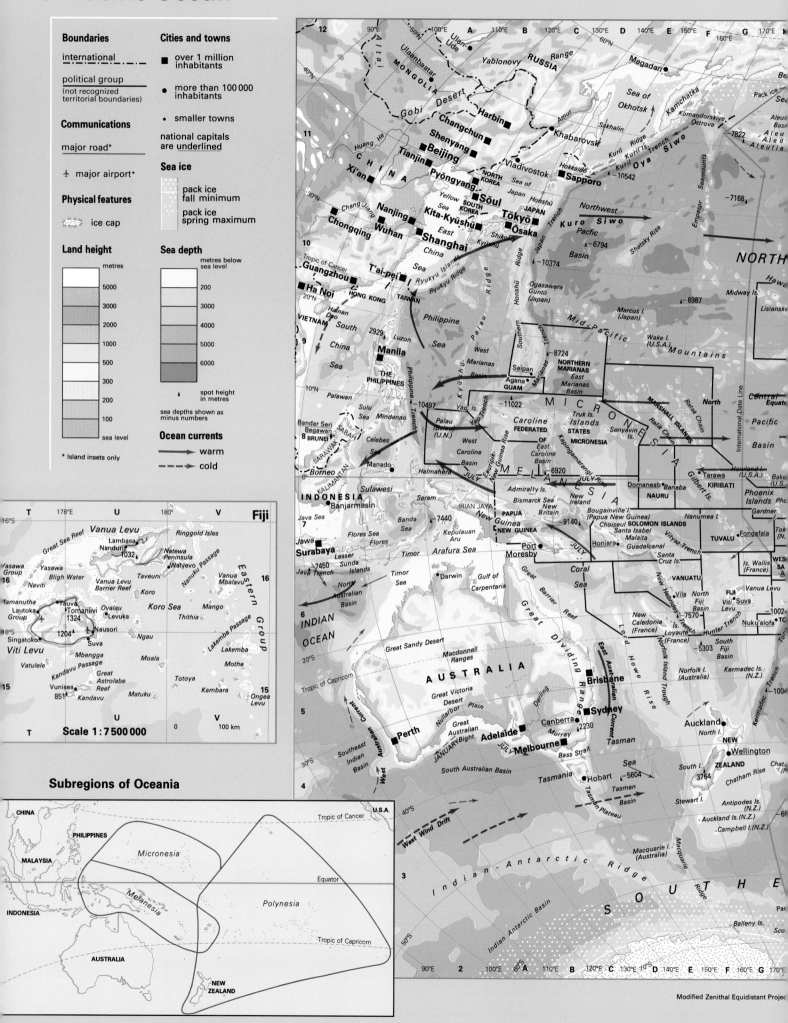

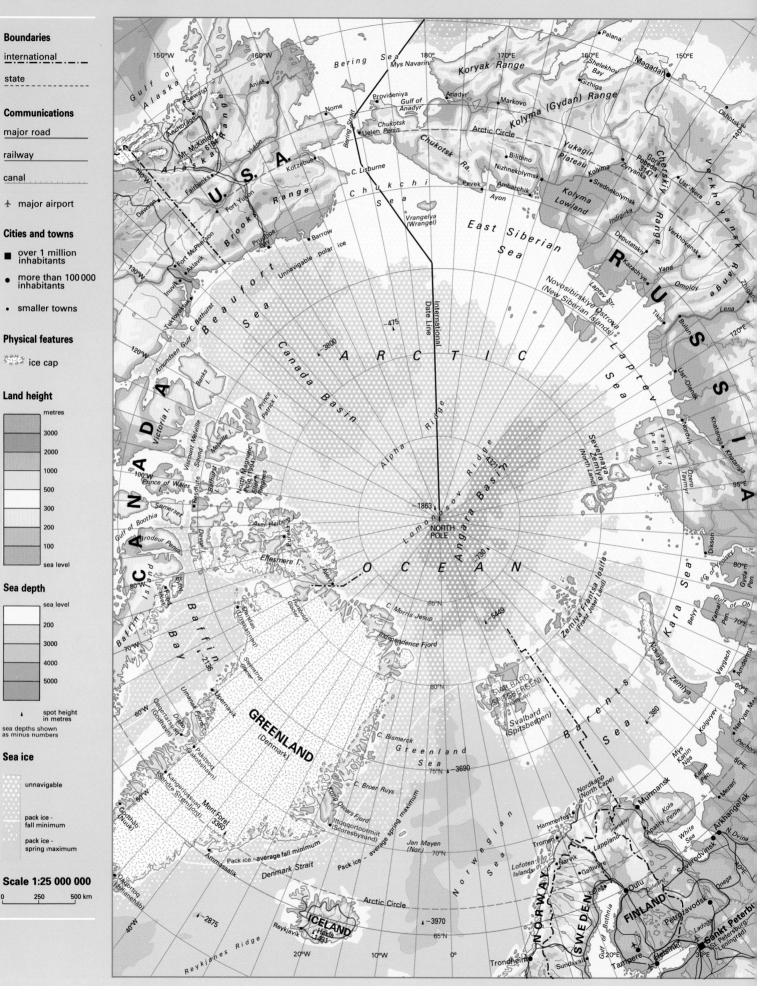

Boundaries

international

state

Communications

major road

railway

canal

✈ major airport

Cities and towns

■ over 1 million inhabitants

● more than 100 000 inhabitants

• smaller towns

Physical features

ice cap

Land height

metres

3000
2000
1000
500
300
200
100
sea level

Sea depth

sea level
200
3000
4000
5000

▲ spot height in metres

sea depths shown as minus numbers

Sea ice

unnavigable

pack ice - fall minimum

pack ice - spring maximum

Scale 1:25 000 000

0   250   500 km

Zenithal Equidistant Projection

© Oxford University Press

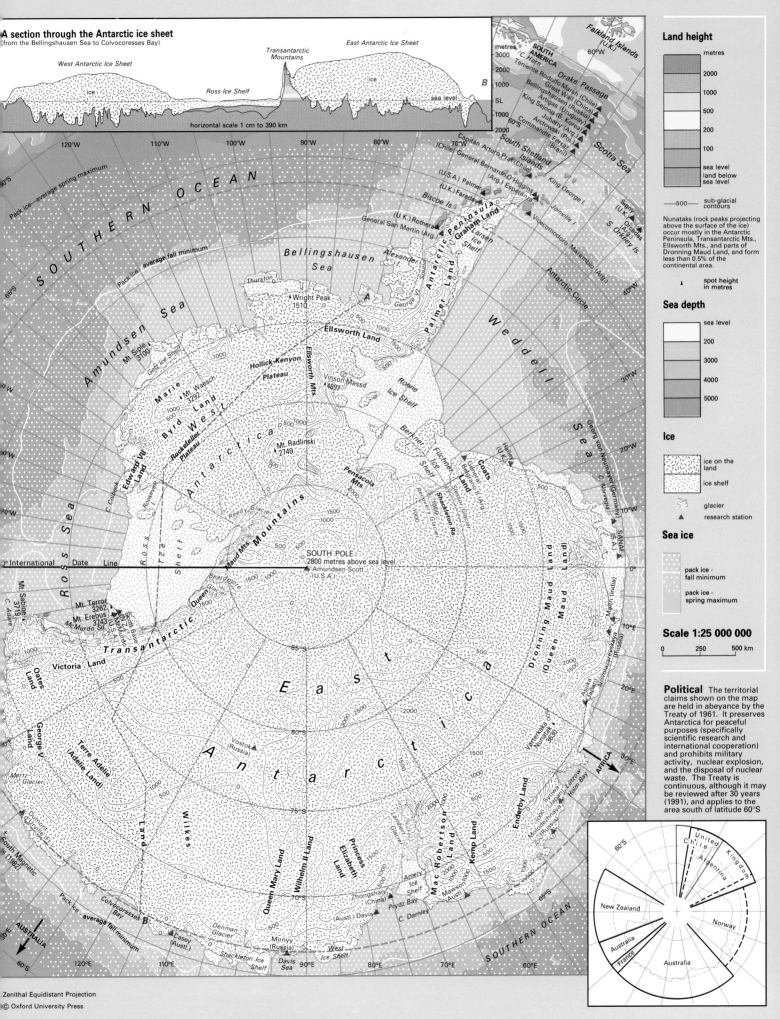

A section through the Antarctic ice sheet (from the Bellingshausen Sea to Colvocoresses Bay)

horizontal scale 1 cm to 390 km

Land height

metres
2000
1000
500
200
100
sea level
land below sea level
—500— sub-glacial contours

Nunataks (rock peaks projecting above the surface of the ice) occur mostly in the Antarctic Peninsula, Transantarctic Mts., Ellsworth Mts., and parts of Dronning Maud Land, and form less than 0.5% of the continental area.

▲ spot height in metres

Sea depth

sea level
200
3000
4000
5000

Ice

ice on the land
ice shelf
glacier
▲ research station

Sea ice

pack ice - fall minimum
pack ice - spring maximum

Scale 1:25 000 000

0   250   500 km

Political The territorial claims shown on the map are held in abeyance by the Treaty of 1961. It preserves Antarctica for peaceful purposes (specifically scientific research and international cooperation) and prohibits military activity, nuclear explosion, and the disposal of nuclear waste. The Treaty is continuous, although it may be reviewed after 30 years (1991), and applies to the area south of latitude 60°S

Zenithal Equidistant Projection
© Oxford University Press

The Earth is part of the **solar system**.
This system consists of a group of planets
and moons that orbit the Sun.
The Solar System is part of the **galaxy** know as the **Milky Way**. This is a
huge group of more than 100 billion stars that orbits around a galactic
centre. Tens of billions of galaxies like the Milky Way make up the
Universe, which is so vast that its outer limits are unknown.

All parts of the Universe are in **constant motion**.
The Milky Way rushes through space at a speed of 600 km/s,
or 2 160 000 km/h. Our Sun is actually a medium-sized star.
It moves around a common galactic centre at a speed of
800 000 km/h. The Earth revolves around the Sun at 106 300 km/h.

Light travels at 299 460 km/s or 10 million kilometres in one year.
This distance is known as a light year. It takes 8 min 17 s for light
to travel from the Sun to the Earth, and about 24 h for light to travel from
the Sun to the farthest extent of our Solar System. The closest star to the
earth, Proxima Centauri, is 4.22 light years away. The Milky Way is
approximately 100 000 light years in diameter. The farthest known galaxy
from the Earth, called Quasar PKS 2000-330, is 15 000 million light years away.

The spiral galaxy M81, part of Ursa Major (Great Bear)
a constellation in the Northern Hemisphere.

Sun

	Pluto	Neptune	Uranus	Saturn	Jupiter	Mars	Earth	Venus	Mercury
mean distance from the Sun, in million km	5 900	4 497	2 870	1 427	778	228	150	108	58
time to orbit the Sun, in days	90 502	60 275	30 660	10 767	4 343	687	365	225	88
diameter, in km	3 000	48 400	52 000	120 000	142 800	6 794	12 756	12 104	4 878
period of rotation, in day	6.38	0.67	0.45	0.42	0.41	1.02	0.99	243.0	58.67

Human use of Earth space
Satellites can be placed in
different orbits around the Earth.
For each satellite purpose
there is a preferred orbit.

low orbits: at 300 km from the Earth, these
are the easiest to reach. Space Shuttle and
the Mir Space Station use these orbits.

polar orbits: these cover the whole globe as it turns on
its axis, and are the chosen orbits for survey satellites.

eliptical or **eccentric orbits:** often used for satellites
designed to study particular areas of the Earth and
needing to spend long periods over a chosen area.

geostationary orbits: at 35 880 km above the Equator,
these are the highest orbits. They enable satellites to
view a large area of the Earth. Each orbit takes 24 h, the
same time that it takes the Earth to rotate on its axis.
So they remain in the same position relative to the Earth.
Communications and weather satellites use these orbits.

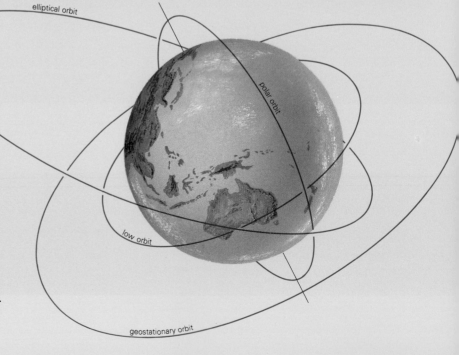

elliptical orbit

polar orbit

low orbit

geostationary orbit

The diagram shows how the Earth **revolves** around the Sun every 365.25 days, while **rotating** on a **tilted axis** of 23.5° every 24h. The Earth's revolution on its tilted axis causes the four seasons, while its rotation causes day and night. The seasons on this diagram apply to the Northern Hemisphere.

The Earth completes one revolution of the Sun every 365.25 days. It follows an elliptical, or slightly egg-shaped, orbit. Thus the distance between the Earth and the Sun varies, from a maximum of 152 million kilometres on July 4th to a minimum of 147 million kilometres on January 3rd. However, this variation has little effect on temperatures on Earth.

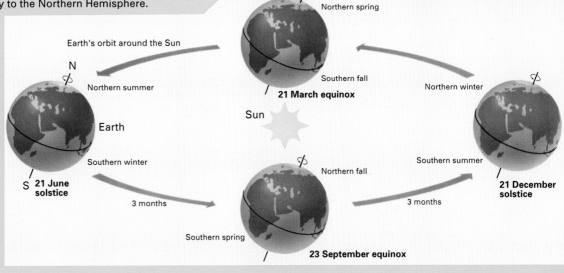

Earth's orbit around the Sun

Northern spring
Southern fall
21 March equinox

N
Northern summer
Earth
Sun
Southern winter
21 June solstice
S

Southern spring
3 months

Northern fall
23 September equinox
3 months

Northern winter
Southern summer
21 December solstice

The diagram of the Earth in June and December shows the variations in the length of day and night. In June, the Northern Hemisphere is tilted at 23.5° towards the Sun, as a result it receives more hours of sunshine. The Sun's rays strike the Earth's atmosphere more directly than at other times of the year, resulting in summer, with its warm temperatures.

Six months later the Earth has rotated halfway around the Sun. Now the Southern Hemisphere is tilted at 23.5° towards the Sun. Thus in December it is summer in the Southern Hemisphere, while it is winter in the Northern Hemisphere.

— Earth's axis

area of the Earth in sunlight

area of the Earth in darkness

— length of day
— length of night } along each line of latitude

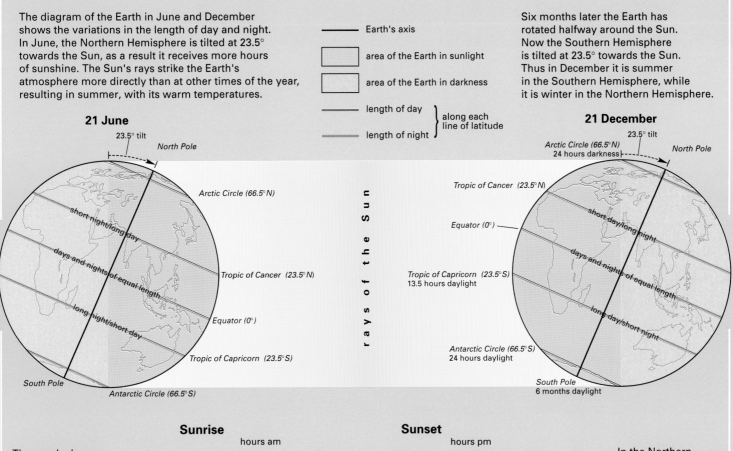

21 June

23.5° tilt
North Pole
Arctic Circle (66.5°N)
short night/long day
days and nights of equal length
long night/short day
Tropic of Cancer (23.5°N)
Equator (0°)
Tropic of Capricorn (23.5°S)
South Pole
Antarctic Circle (66.5°S)

rays of the Sun

21 December

23.5° tilt
Arctic Circle (66.5°N)
24 hours darkness
North Pole
Tropic of Cancer (23.5°N)
short day/long night
Equator (0°)
days and nights of equal length
Tropic of Capricorn (23.5°S)
13.5 hours daylight
long day/short night
Antarctic Circle (66.5°S)
24 hours daylight
South Pole
6 months daylight

The graph shows the time of sunrise and sunset for selected latitudes over the year. It illustrates that changes in the number of hours of daylight are greatest the further the distance travelled from the Equator.

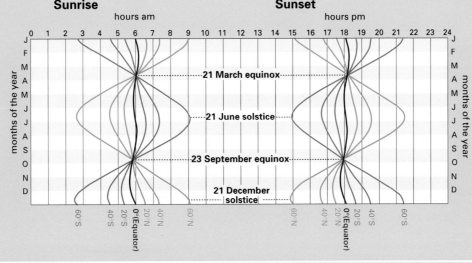

Sunrise
hours am

Sunset
hours pm

months of the year

21 March equinox
21 June solstice
23 September equinox
21 December solstice

60°S 40°S 20°S 0°(Equator) 20°N 40°N 60°N
60°N 40°N 20°N 0°(Equator) 20°S 40°S 60°S

In the Northern Hemisphere at the summer solstice, the Sun never sets at a latitude north of the Arctic Circle. At the same time, south of the Antarctic Circle, the Sun never rises. The opposite occurs at the winter solstice. Places near the Equator experience little variation in the length of day and night.

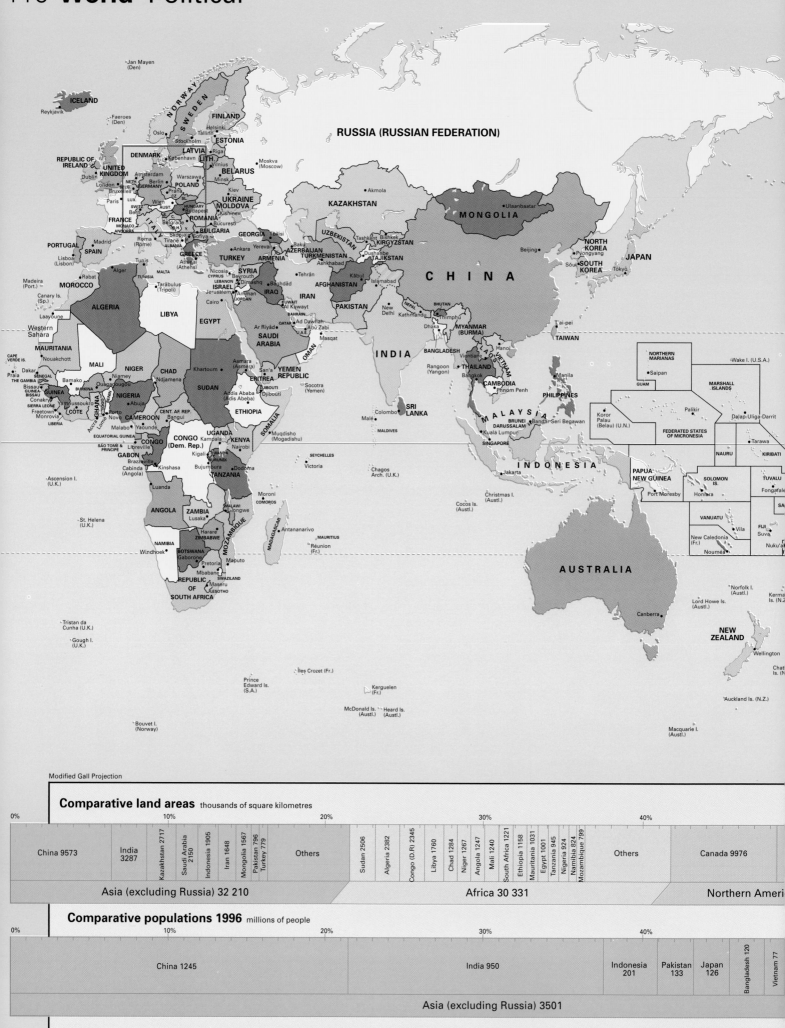

Modified Gall Projection

Comparative land areas thousands of square kilometres

0%		10%							20%															30%										40%		

| China 9573 | India 3287 | Kazakhstan 2717 | Saudi Arabia 2150 | Indonesia 1905 | Iran 1648 | Mongolia 1567 | Pakistan 796 | Turkey 779 | Others | Sudan 2506 | Algeria 2382 | Congo (D.R) 2345 | Libya 1760 | Chad 1284 | Niger 1267 | Angola 1247 | Mali 1240 | South Africa 1221 | Ethiopia 1158 | Mauritania 1031 | Egypt 1001 | Tanzania 945 | Nigeria 924 | Namibia 824 | Mozambique 799 | Others | Canada 9976 |

| Asia (excluding Russia) 32 210 | Africa 30 331 | Northern Ameri |

Comparative populations 1996 millions of people

0%		10%		20%		30%		40%	

| China 1245 | India 950 | Indonesia 201 | Pakistan 133 | Japan 126 | Bangladesh 120 | Vietnam 77 |

| Asia (excluding Russia) 3501 |

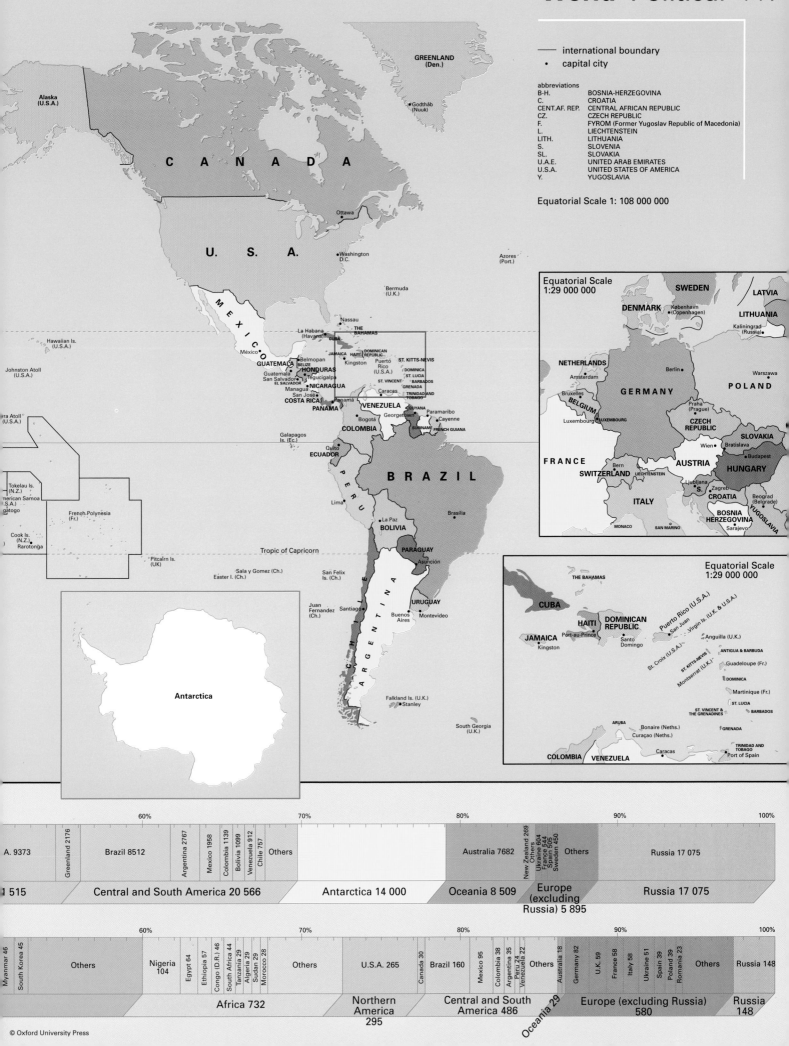

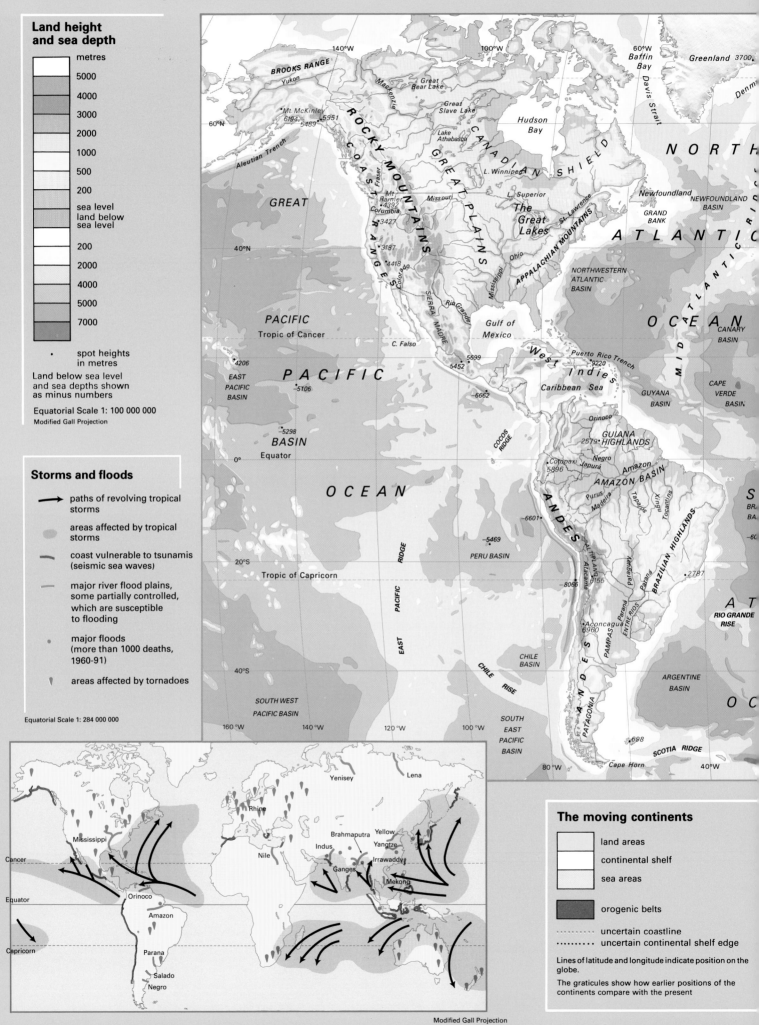

Land height and sea depth

metres

	5000
	4000
	3000
	2000
	1000
	500
	200
	sea level
	land below sea level
	200
	2000
	4000
	5000
	7000

• spot heights in metres

Land below sea level and sea depths shown as minus numbers

Equatorial Scale 1: 100 000 000
Modified Gall Projection

Storms and floods

→ paths of revolving tropical storms

areas affected by tropical storms

coast vulnerable to tsunamis (seismic sea waves)

major river flood plains, some partially controlled, which are susceptible to flooding

• major floods (more than 1000 deaths, 1960-91)

areas affected by tornadoes

Equatorial Scale 1: 284 000 000

The moving continents

	land areas
	continental shelf
	sea areas

orogenic belts

.... uncertain coastline

·········· uncertain continental shelf edge

Lines of latitude and longitude indicate position on the globe.

The graticules show how earlier positions of the continents compare with the present

Modified Gall Projection

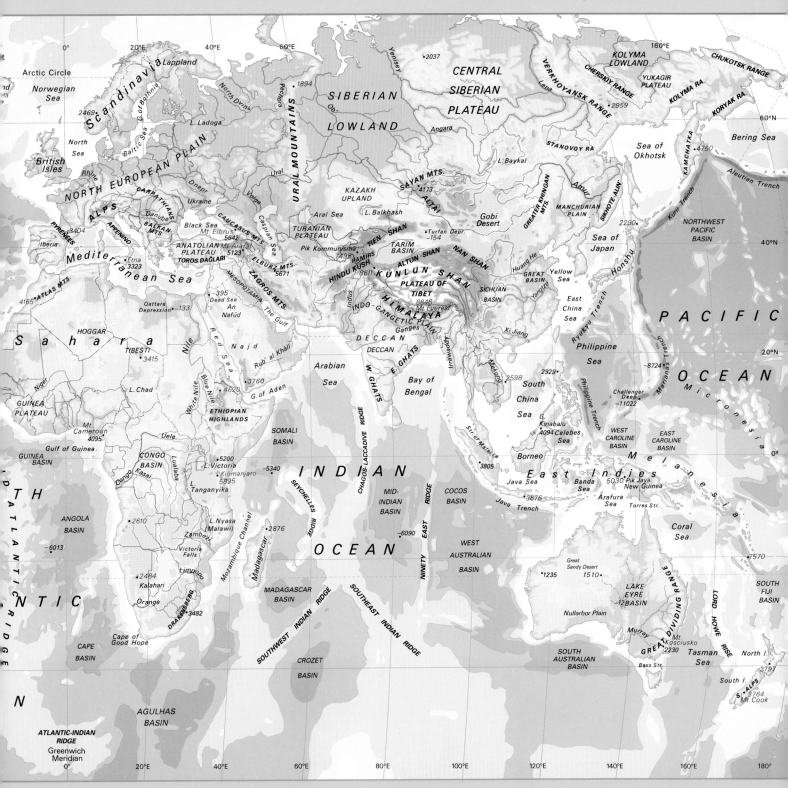

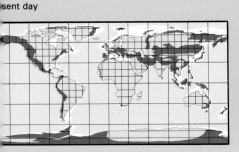

sent day

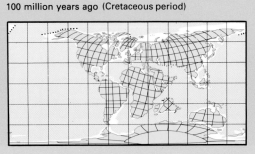

100 million years ago (Cretaceous period)

200 million years ago (Triassic period)

xford University Press

A map showing the earth's plates is located on page 124.

Precipitation

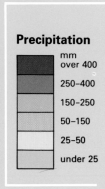

mm
over 400
250–400
150–250
50–150
25–50
under 25

Temperature, ocean currents

actual temperature °C
32
24
16
8
0
−8
−16
−24

Ocean currents

cold
→

warm
→

Pressure and winds
Pressure reduced to sea level

103.5 kilopascals
103.0
102.5
102.0
101.5
101.0
100.5
100.0
 99.5

H high pressure cell

L low pressure cell

Prevailing winds
Arrows fly with the wind:
the heavier the arrow, the
more regular ('constant')
the direction of the wind

Equatorial Scale 1: 248 000 000

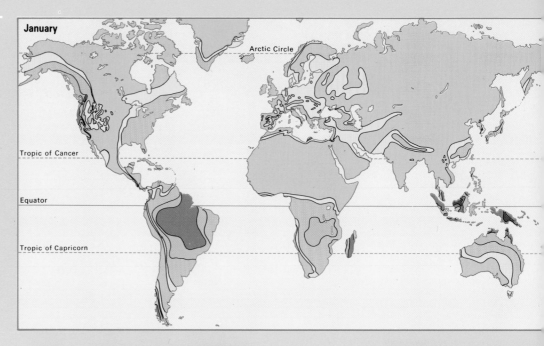

January

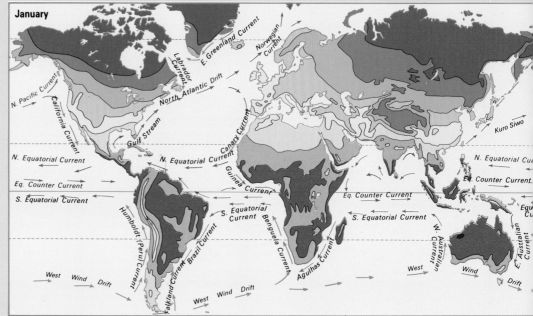

January

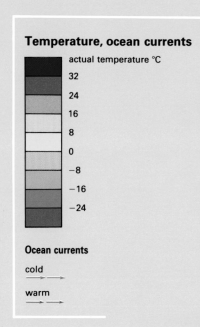

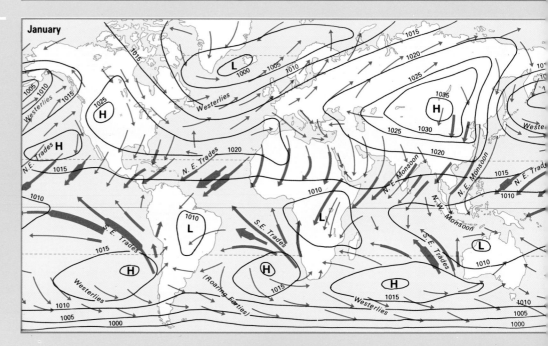

January

Modified Gall Projection
© Oxford University Press

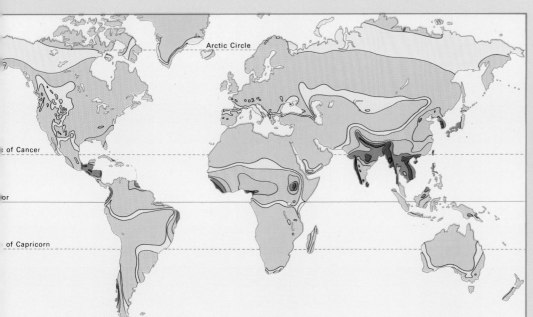

Tropical revolving storms

Tropical revolving storms originate over water in the tropics. They are known as hurricanes in the Atlantic and Pacific, and as typhoons in the western Pacific and Indian Oceans.

temperature 27°C and over at mean sea level

August - September
Maximum frequency in northern hemisphere

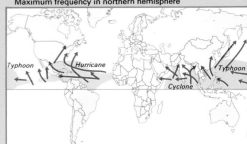

January - March
Maximum frequency in southern hemisphere

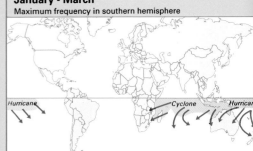

Air masses

fronts

Arctic
Polar
Temperate
Equatorial

January

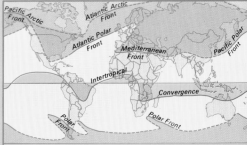

July

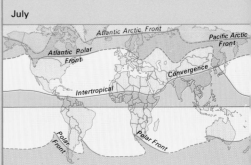

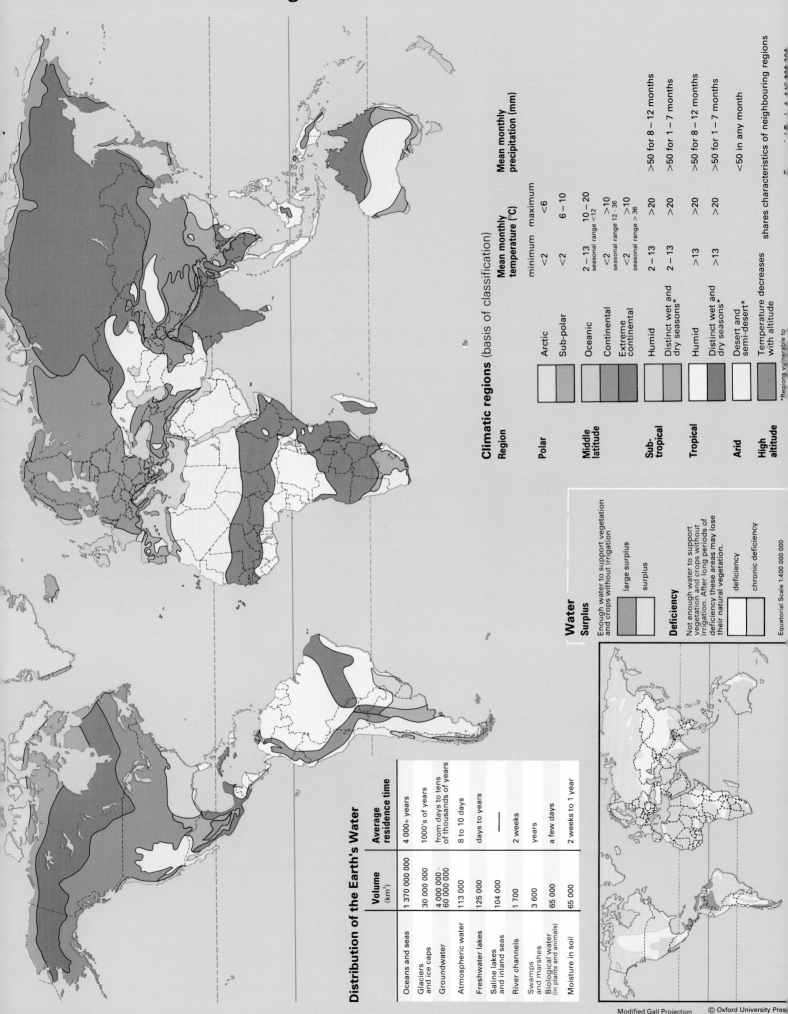

Climatic regions (basis of classification)

Region		Mean monthly temperature (°C) minimum maximum	Mean monthly precipitation (mm)
Polar	Arctic	<2	<6	
	Sub-polar	<2	6 – 10	
Middle latitude	Oceanic	2 – 13	10 – 20 seasonal range <12	
	Continental	<2	>10 seasonal range 12 - 36	
	Extreme continental	<2	>10 seasonal range > 36	
Sub-tropical	Humid	2 – 13	>20	>50 for 8 – 12 months
	Distinct wet and dry seasons*	2 – 13	>20	>50 for 1 – 7 months
Tropical	Humid	>13	>20	>50 for 8 – 12 months
	Distinct wet and dry seasons*	>13	>20	>50 for 1 – 7 months
Arid	Desert and semi-desert*			<50 in any month
High altitude	Temperature decreases with altitude			shares characteristics of neighbouring regions

*Regions vulnerable to

*Regions vulnerable to ...

Water

Surplus

Enough water to support vegetation and crops without irrigation

large surplus

surplus

Deficiency

Not enough water to support vegetation and crops without irrigation. After long periods of deficiency these areas may lose their natural vegetation.

deficiency

chronic deficiency

Equatorial Scale 1:400 000 000

Distribution of the Earth's Water

	Volume (km³)	Average residence time
Oceans and seas	1 370 000 000	4 000+ years
Glaciers and ice caps	30 000 000	1000's of years
Groundwater	4 000 000 - 60 000 000	from days to tens of thousands of years
Atmospheric water	113 000	8 to 10 days
Freshwater lakes	125 000	days to years
Saline lakes and inland seas	104 000	—
River channels	1 700	2 weeks
Swamps and marshes	3 600	years
Biological water (in plants and animals)	65 000	a few days
Moisture in soil	65 000	2 weeks to 1 year

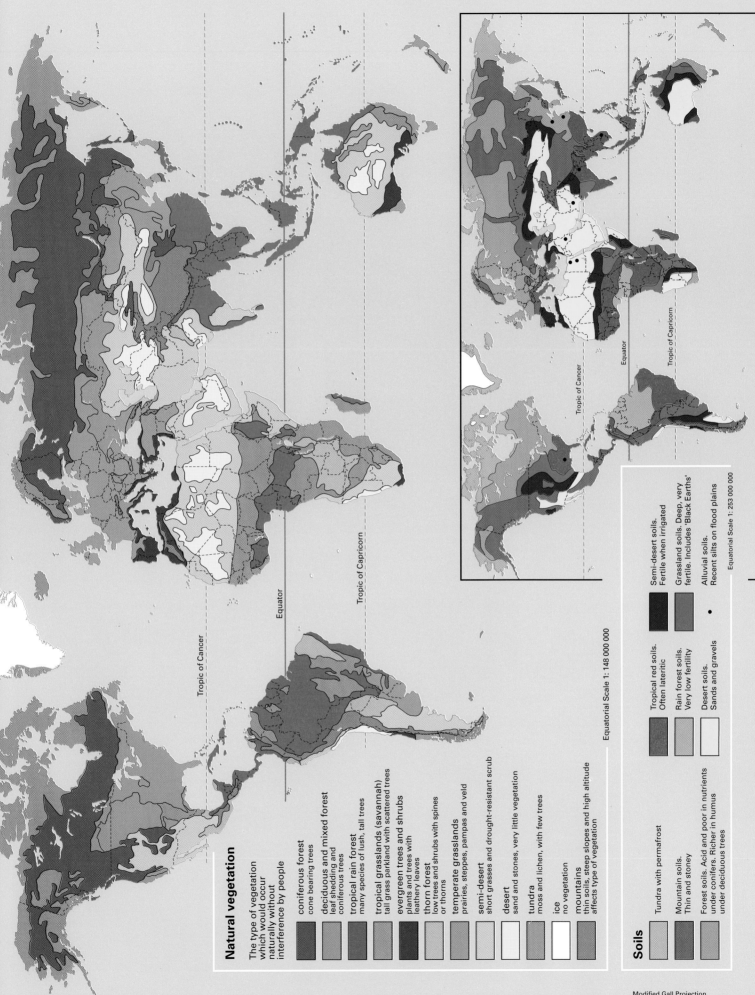

Natural vegetation

The type of vegetation which would occur naturally without interference by people

- coniferous forest
  cone bearing trees
- deciduous and mixed forest
  leaf shedding and coniferous trees
- tropical rain forest
  many species of lush, tall trees
- tropical grasslands (savannah)
  tall grass parkland with scattered trees
- evergreen trees and shrubs
  plants and trees with leathery leaves
- thorn forest
  low trees and shrubs with spines or thorns
- temperate grasslands
  prairies, steppes, pampas and veld
- semi-desert
  short grasses and drought-resistant scrub
- desert
  sand and stones, very little vegetation
- tundra
  moss and lichen, with few trees
- ice
  no vegetation
- mountains
  thin soils, steep slopes and high altitude affects type of vegetation

Soils

- Tundra with permafrost
- Mountain soils.
  Thin and stoney
- Forest soils. Acid and poor in nutrients under conifers. Richer in humus under deciduous trees
- Tropical red soils.
  Often lateritic
- Rain forest soils.
  Very low fertility
- Desert soils.
  Sands and gravels
- Semi-desert soils.
  Fertile when irrigated
- Grassland soils. Deep, very fertile. Includes 'Black Earths'
- Alluvial soils.
  Recent silts on flood plains

Equatorial Scale 1: 148 000 000

Equatorial Scale 1: 253 000 000

Modified Gall Projection
© Oxford University Press

Plate tectonics
Plate boundaries

ridge zones	
trench zones	
passive	
transform faults	
direction of plate movement	
volcano	
areas of deep focus earthquakes	

Equatorial scale 1 : 210 000 000

Gall Projection

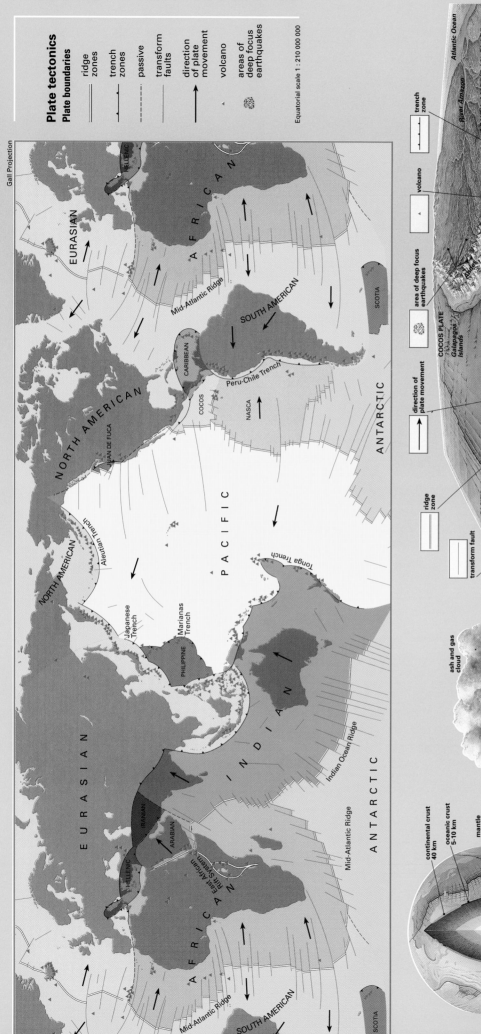

EURASIAN

AFRICAN

NORTH AMERICAN

SOUTH AMERICAN

Mid-Atlantic Ridge

CARIBBEAN

Peru-Chile Trench

COCOS

NASCA

JUAN DE FUCA

Aleutian Trench

NORTH AMERICAN

Japanese Trench

Marianas Trench

PHILIPPINE

PACIFIC

Tonga Trench

ANTARCTIC

SCOTIA

HELLENIC

EURASIAN

IRANIAN

ARABIAN

HELLENIC

East African Rift System

AFRICAN

Indian Ocean Ridge

INDIAN

Mid-Atlantic Ridge

ANTARCTIC

SOUTH AMERICAN

Mid-Atlantic Ridge

SCOTIA

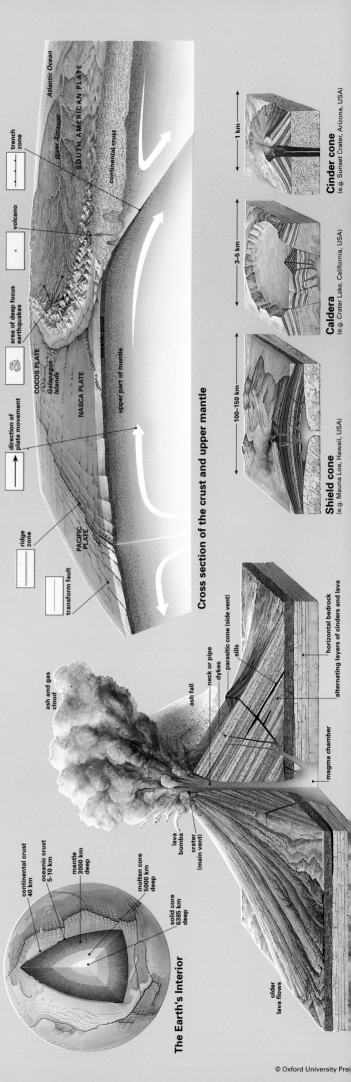

Cross section of the crust and upper mantle

trench zone

volcano

area of deep focus earthquakes

direction of plate movement

ridge zone

transform fault

Atlantic Ocean

River Amazon

SOUTH AMERICAN PLATE

continental crust

COCOS PLATE

Galapagos Islands

NASCA PLATE

Andes

upper part of mantle

PACIFIC PLATE

Cinder cone
(e.g. Sunset Crater, Arizona, USA)

1 km

Caldera
(e.g. Crater Lake, California, USA)

3–5 km

Shield cone
(e.g. Mauna Loa, Hawaii, USA)

100–150 km

ash and gas cloud

ash fall

lava bombs

crater (main vent)

neck or pipe

dykes

parasitic cone (side vent)

sills

horizontal bedrock

alternating layers of cinders and lava

magma chamber

older lava flows

The Earth's Interior

continental crust 40 km

oceanic crust 5–10 km

mantle 3000 km deep

molten core 5000 km deep

solid core 6385 km deep

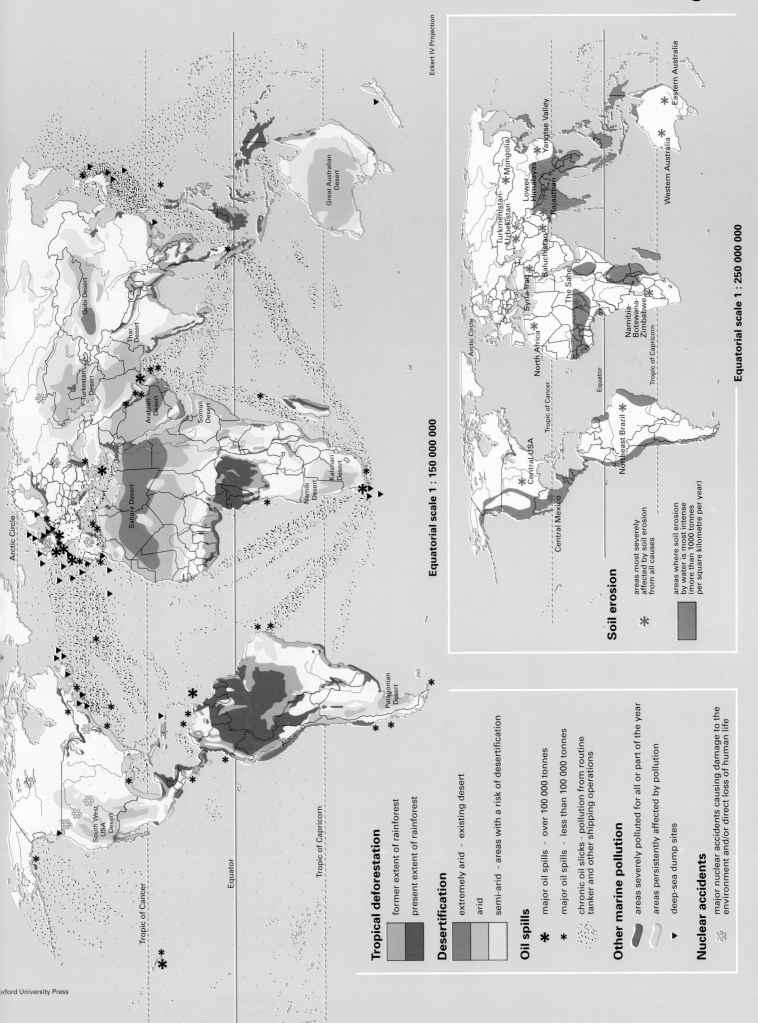

Eckert IV Projection

Gobi Desert

Thar Desert

Turkestan Desert

Arabian Desert

Somali Desert

Sahara Desert

Kalahari Desert

Namib Desert

Great Australian Desert

Tropic of Capricorn

Equator

Tropic of Cancer

Arctic Circle

South West USA Desert

Atacama

Patagonian Desert

Equatorial scale 1 : 150 000 000

Arctic Circle

Turkmenistan-Uzbekistan

Lower Himalayas

Rajasthan

Baluchistan

Syria-Iraq

The Sahel

North Africa

Namibia-Botswana-Zimbabwe

Mongolia

Yangtse Valley

Western Australia

Eastern Australia

Tropic of Cancer

Equator

Tropic of Capricorn

Central USA

Central Mexico

Northeast Brazil

Equatorial scale 1 : 250 000 000

Soil erosion

✳ areas most severely
affected by soil erosion
from all causes

▨ areas where soil erosion
by water is most intense
(more than 1000 tonnes
per square kilometre per year)

Tropical deforestation

▨ former extent of rainforest

▨ present extent of rainforest

Desertification

▨ extremely arid - existing desert

▨ arid

□ semi-arid - areas with a risk of desertification

Oil spills

✲ major oil spills - over 100 000 tonnes

✲ major oil spills - less than 100 000 tonnes

⸪ chronic oil slicks - pollution from routine
tanker and other shipping operations

Other marine pollution

▬ areas severely polluted for all or part of the year

▭ areas persistently affected by pollution

▶ deep-sea dump sites

Nuclear accidents

✳ major nuclear accidents causing damage to the
environment and/or direct loss of human life

Oxford University Press

Eckert IV Projection

Countries with the highest net emissions of greenhouse gases

Total emissions
thousand tonnes of carbon

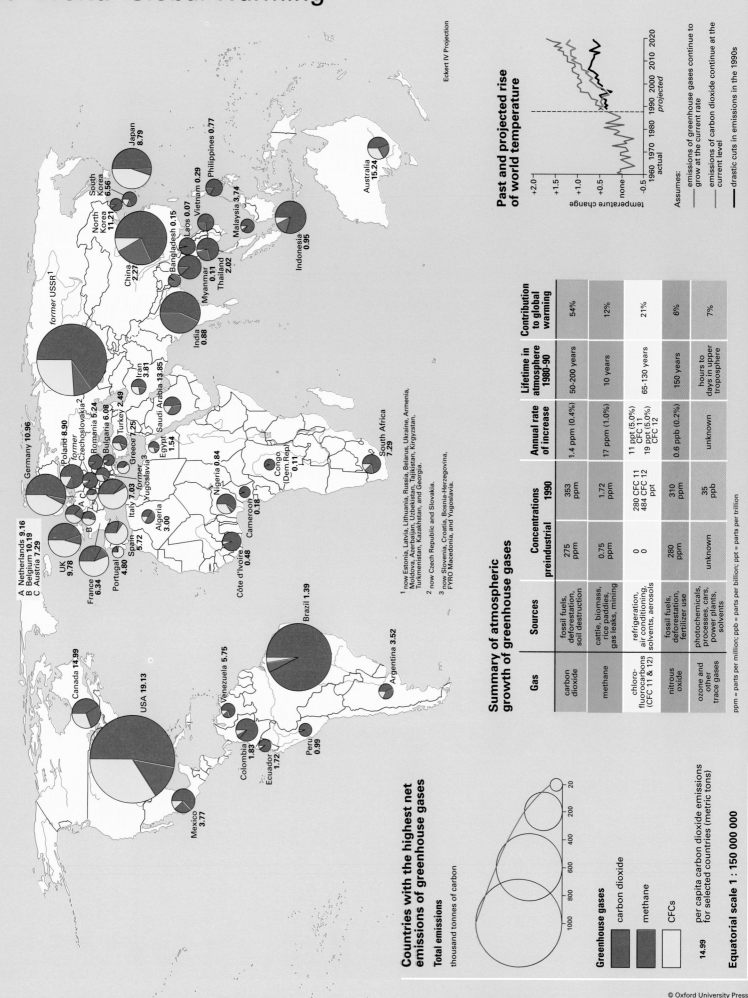

Japan 8.79
South Korea 6.56
North Korea 11.21
China 2.27
Bangladesh 0.15
Laos 0.07
Vietnam 0.29
Philippines 0.77
Myanmar 0.11
Thailand 2.02
Malaysia 3.74
Indonesia 0.95
India 0.88
former USSR[1]
Iran 3.81
Saudi Arabia 13.85
Germany 10.96
Poland 8.90
former Czechoslovakia[2]
Romania 5.24
Bulgaria 6.08
Turkey 2.49
Greece 7.25
Egypt 1.54
A Netherlands 9.16
B Belgium 10.19
C Austria 7.29
UK 9.78
France 6.34
Italy 7.03
former Yugoslavia[3]
Spain 5.72
Portugal 4.80
Algeria 3.00
Côte d'Ivoire 0.48
Cameroon 0.18
Nigeria 0.84
Congo (Dem.Rep.) 0.11
South Africa 7.29
Canada 14.99
USA 19.13
Mexico 3.77
Venezuela 5.75
Colombia 1.83
Ecuador 1.72
Peru 0.99
Brazil 1.39
Argentina 3.52
Australia 15.24

1 now Estonia, Latvia, Lithuania, Russia, Belarus, Ukraine, Armenia, Moldova, Azerbaijan, Uzbekistan, Tajikistan, Kirgyzstan, Turkmenistan, Kazakhstan, and Georgia.

2 now Czech Republic and Slovakia.

3 now Slovenia, Croatia, Bosnia-Herzegovina, FYRO Macedonia, and Yugoslavia.

Greenhouse gases

- carbon dioxide
- methane
- CFCs

14.99 per capita carbon dioxide emissions for selected countries (metric tons)

Equatorial scale 1 : 150 000 000

20
200
400
600
800
1000

Past and projected rise of world temperature

temperature change
+2.0
+1.5
+1.0
+0.5
none
–0.5

1960 1970 1980 1990 2000 2010 2020
actual   projected

Assumes:

— emissions of greenhouse gases continue to grow at the current rate

— emissions of carbon dioxide continue at the current level

— drastic cuts in emissions in the 1990s

Summary of atmospheric growth of greenhouse gases

Gas	Sources	Concentrations preindustrial	Concentrations 1990	Annual rate of increase	Lifetime in atmosphere 1980–90	Contribution to global warming
carbon dioxide	fossil fuels, deforestation, soil destruction	275 ppm	353 ppm	1.4 ppm (0.4%)	50-200 years	54%
methane	cattle, biomass, rice paddies, gas leaks, mining	0.75 ppm	1.72 ppm	17 ppm (1.0%)	10 years	12%
chloro-fluorocarbons (CFC 11 & 12)	refrigeration, air conditioning, solvents, aerosols	0 0	280 CFC 11 484 CFC 12 ppt	11 ppt (5.0%) CFC 11 19 ppt (5.0%) CFC 12	65-130 years	21%
nitrous oxide	fossil fuels, deforestation, fertilizer use	280 ppm	310 ppm	0.6 ppb (0.2%)	150 years	6%
ozone and other trace gases	photochemicals, processes, cars, power plants, solvents	unknown	35 ppb	unknown	hours to days in upper troposphere	7%

ppm = parts per million; ppb = parts per billion; ppt = parts per trillion

© Oxford University Press

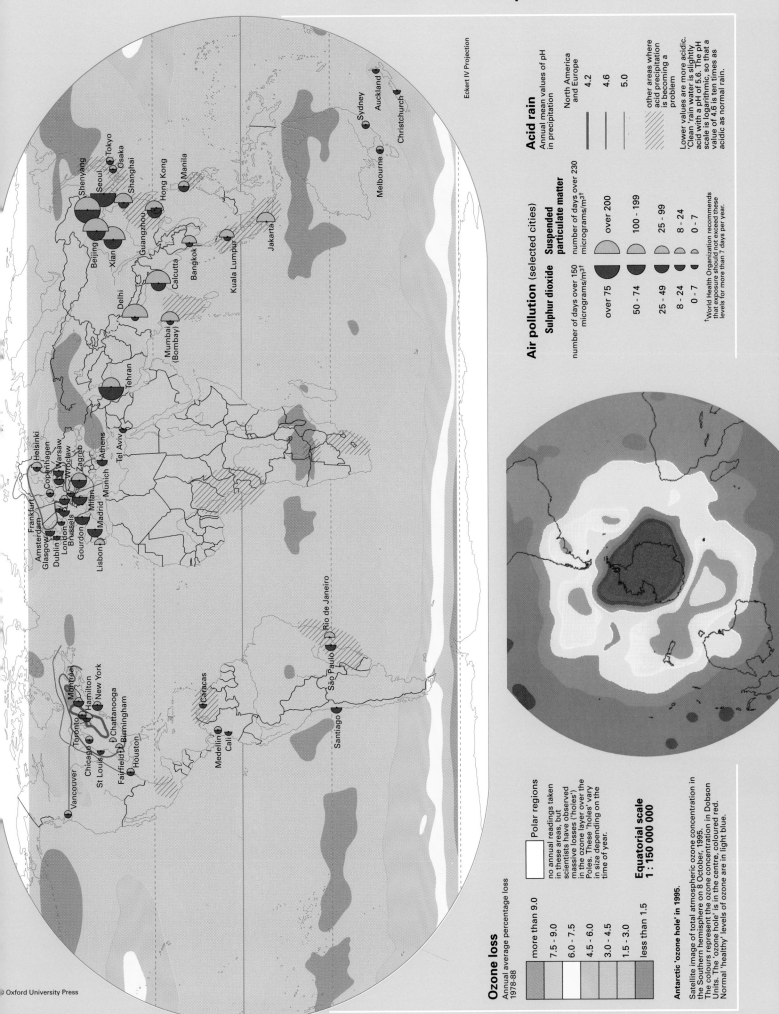

Eckert IV Projection

Acid rain

Annual mean values of pH in precipitation

North America and Europe

	4.2
	4.6
	5.0

other areas where acid precipitation is becoming a problem

Lower values are more acidic. 'Clean' rain water is slightly acid with a pH of 5.6. The pH scale is logarithmic, so that a value of 4.6 is ten times as acidic as normal rain.

Air pollution (selected cities)

Sulphur dioxide
number of days over 150 micrograms/m³

Suspended particulate matter
number of days over 230 micrograms/m³

Sulphur dioxide	Suspended particulate matter
over 75	over 200
50 - 74	100 - 199
25 - 49	25 - 99
8 - 24	8 - 24
0 - 7	0 - 7

†World Health Organization recommends that exposure should not exceed these levels for more than 7 days per year.

Ozone loss

Annual average percentage loss 1978-88

	more than 9.0
	7.5 - 9.0
	6.0 - 7.5
	4.5 - 6.0
	3.0 - 4.5
	1.5 - 3.0
	less than 1.5

Polar regions

no annual readings taken in these areas, but scientists have observed massive losses ('holes') in the ozone layer over the Poles. These 'holes' vary in size depending on the time of year.

Equatorial scale
1 : 150 000 000

Antarctic 'ozone hole' in 1995.

Satellite image of total atmospheric ozone concentration in the Southern hemisphere on 8 October, 1995. The colours represent the ozone concentration in Dobson Units. The 'ozone hole' is in the centre, coloured red. Normal 'healthy' levels of ozone are in light blue.

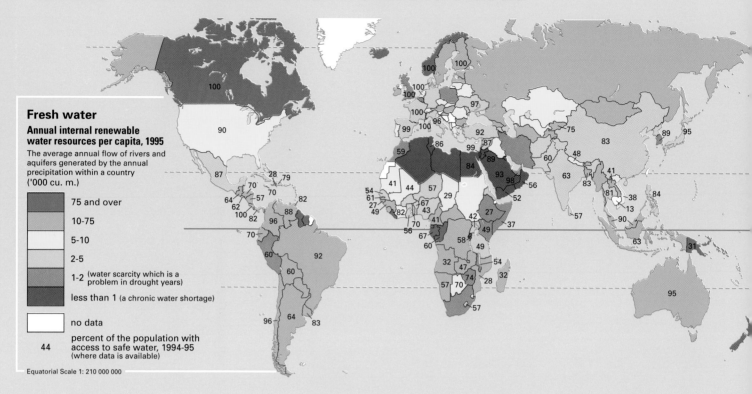

Fresh water

Annual internal renewable water resources per capita, 1995

The average annual flow of rivers and aquifers generated by the annual precipitation within a country ('000 cu. m.)

- 75 and over
- 10-75
- 5-10
- 2-5
- 1-2 (water scarcity which is a problem in drought years)
- less than 1 (a chronic water shortage)
- no data

44   percent of the population with access to safe water, 1994-95 (where data is available)

Equatorial Scale 1: 210 000 000

Protected areas

Percent of national land area protected by national protection systems, 1994

Areas of at least 1000 hectares and with partially restricted access, including scientific reserves, strict nature reserves, national parks, provincial parks, natural monuments, natural land marks, managed nature reserves, wildlife sanctuaries, and protected landscapes or seascapes (natural or cultural).

- 20 and over
- 8-20
- 4-8
- 1-4
- less than 1
- no data

Estimated number of species worldwide

	Those species already identified	Estimated percentage yet to be identified
invertebrates	1 020 561	73-97
micro-organisms	5760	73-97
plants	322 311	0-33
fish	19 056	0-17
reptiles and amphibians	10 484	5-10
mammals	4 000	5-10
birds	9 040	0-6

Endangered species

Selected animal species

- ▼ invertebrates
- ◆ fish
- ▲ reptiles and amphibians
- ● mammals
- ■ birds

Equatorial Scale 1: 210 000 000
Modified Gall Projection

© Oxford University Press

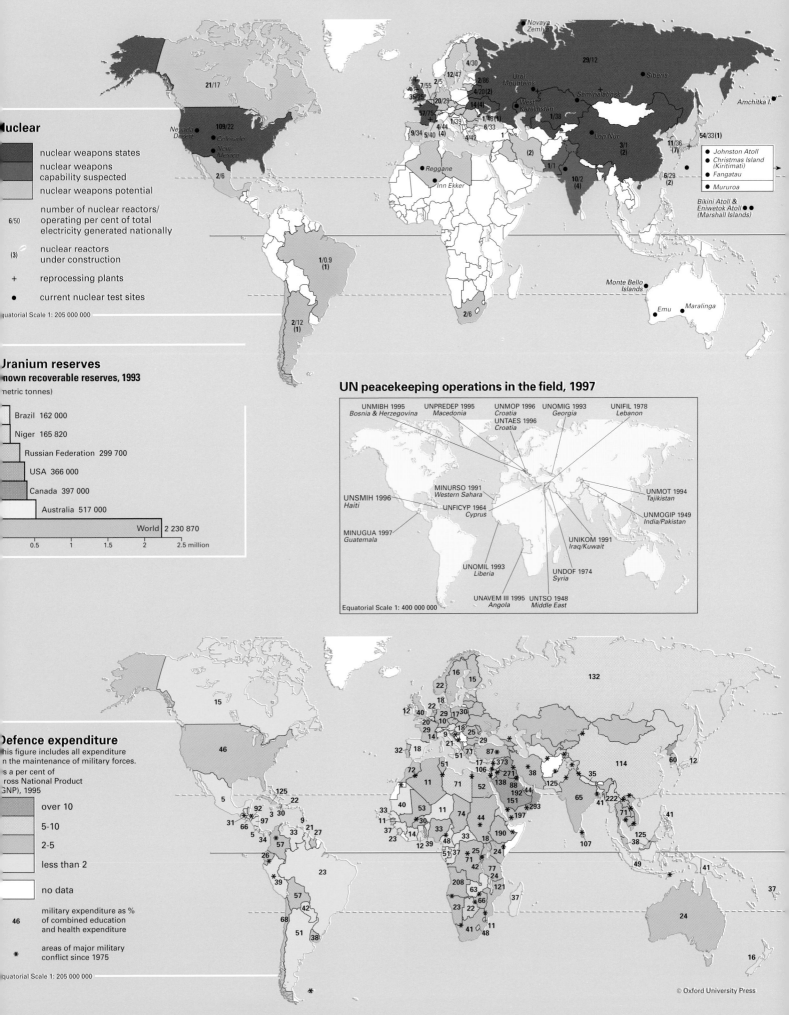

Nuclear

- nuclear weapons states
- nuclear weapons capability suspected
- nuclear weapons potential

6/50   number of nuclear reactors/ operating per cent of total electricity generated nationally

(3)   nuclear reactors under construction

+   reprocessing plants

●   current nuclear test sites

Equatorial Scale 1: 205 000 000

Map labels (Nuclear)

21/17
109/22
Nevada Desert
Colorado
New Mexico
2/6
1/0.9 (1)
2/12 (1)
2/6

12/47
4/30
2/5
7/55
35/29
20/29
57/75
9/34
4/44 (4)
5/40
4/42
14/4
2/86
4/20 (2)
1/39
1/46 (1)
6/33
1
(2)
1/1
Ural Mountains
West Kazakhstan
Semipalatinsk
29/12
Siberia
1/38
Lop Nur
3/1 (2)
10/2 (4)
11/36 (7)
54/33 (1)
6/29 (2)
Novaya Zemlya
Amchitka I.
Reggane
Inn Ekker

● Johnston Atoll
● Christmas Island (Kiritimati)
● Fangatau
● Mururoa
Bikini Atoll & Eniwetok Atoll ● ●
(Marshall Islands)

Monte Bello Islands
Emu   Maralinga

Uranium reserves

Known recoverable reserves, 1993

(metric tonnes)

Country	Reserves
Brazil	162 000
Niger	165 820
Russian Federation	299 700
USA	366 000
Canada	397 000
Australia	517 000
World	2 230 870

Scale: 0.5   1   1.5   2   2.5 million

UN peacekeeping operations in the field, 1997

UNMIBH 1995 Bosnia & Herzegovina
UNPREDEP 1995 Macedonia
UNMOP 1996 Croatia
UNTAES 1996 Croatia
UNOMIG 1993 Georgia
UNIFIL 1978 Lebanon
UNSMIH 1996 Haiti
MINURSO 1991 Western Sahara
UNFICYP 1964 Cyprus
UNMOT 1994 Tajikistan
UNMOGIP 1949 India/Pakistan
MINUGUA 1997 Guatemala
UNIKOM 1991 Iraq/Kuwait
UNOMIL 1993 Liberia
UNDOF 1974 Syria
UNAVEM III 1995 Angola
UNTSO 1948 Middle East

Equatorial Scale 1: 400 000 000

Defence expenditure

This figure includes all expenditure on the maintenance of military forces.

As a per cent of Gross National Product (GNP), 1995

- over 10
- 5-10
- 2-5
- less than 2
- no data

46   military expenditure as % of combined education and health expenditure

*   areas of major military conflict since 1975

Equatorial Scale 1: 205 000 000

Defence map labels

15
46
5
125
22
92 3 30
31 66
97
5 34
57
26
39
57
42
68
51 38
23
16
15
132
22
18
12 40
29 17 30
10
29 18 25
14 9
21
32 18
51
87
17 373
106 271
11 71 52 138 88
72 40 53 11 44 192 44
33 11 74 151 293
37 33 48 33 197
23 14 18 190
12 39 51 37 24
42 25
77
24
208 63 121
66 37
23 22
41 11
48
87
38
125
35
65
41
114
60 12
222
71
41
125
38
49
41
37
24
16
107

© Oxford University Press

Population density

- high : more than 50 persons/km²
- moderate : 6–49 persons/km²
- sparse : 1–5 persons/km²
- isolated settlements only : less than 1 person/km²

Population change

Average annual change

- very high increase : 3 per cent and over
- increase above world average : 1.5 to 3 per cent
- increase below the world average : less than 1.5 per cent
- decrease (by less than 1 per cent)

○ population clusters of continuous built-up area with a population of at least 7 000 000

○ population clusters of continuous built-up area with a population of at least 3 000 000

Equatorial scale 1 : 105 000 000

Tropic of Cancer

Equator

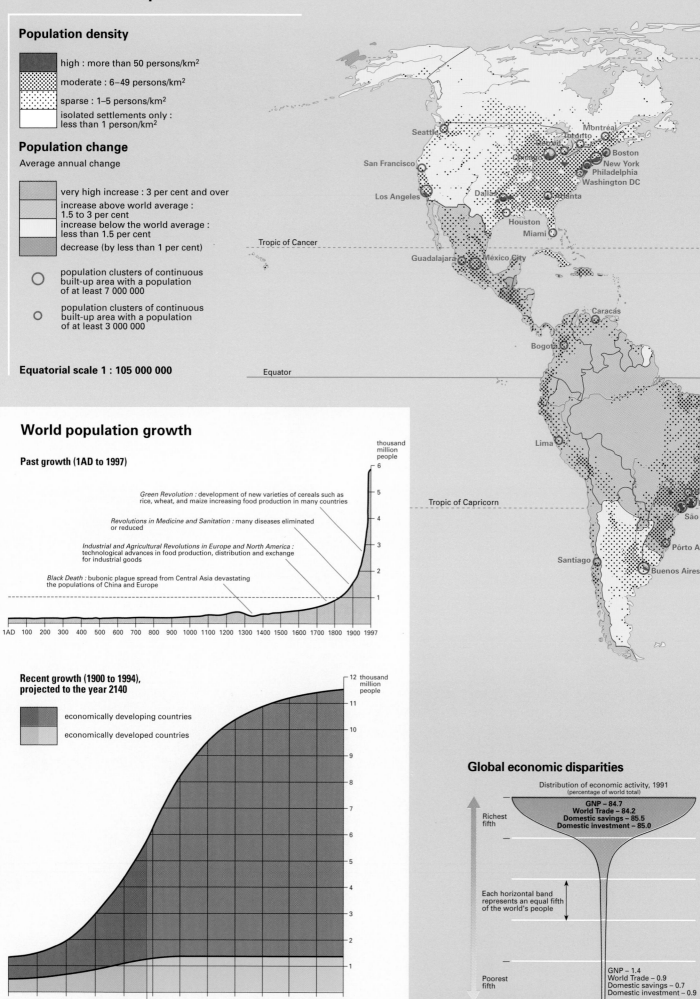

Seattle
San Francisco
Los Angeles
Montréal
Toronto
Detroit
Boston
Chicago
New York
Philadelphia
Washington DC
Dallas
Atlanta
Houston
Miami
Guadalajara
México City
Caracás
Bogotá
Lima
Belo Horizonte
Rio de Janeiro
São Paulo
Pôrto Alegre
Santiago
Buenos Aires

Tropic of Capricorn

World population growth

Past growth (1AD to 1997)

thousand million people

Green Revolution : development of new varieties of cereals such as rice, wheat, and maize increasing food production in many countries

Revolutions in Medicine and Sanitation : many diseases eliminated or reduced

Industrial and Agricultural Revolutions in Europe and North America : technological advances in food production, distribution and exchange for industrial goods

Black Death : bubonic plague spread from Central Asia devastating the populations of China and Europe

1AD 100 200 300 400 500 600 700 800 900 1000 1100 1200 1300 1400 1500 1600 1700 1800 1900 1997

Recent growth (1900 to 1994), projected to the year 2140

thousand million people

- economically developing countries
- economically developed countries

1900 1920 1940 1960 1980 2000 2020 2040 2060 2080 2100 2120 2140

projected

Global economic disparities

Distribution of economic activity, 1991
(percentage of world total)

Richest fifth

GNP – 84.7
World Trade – 84.2
Domestic savings – 85.5
Domestic investment – 85.0

Each horizontal band represents an equal fifth of the world's people

Poorest fifth

GNP – 1.4
World Trade – 0.9
Domestic savings – 0.7
Domestic investment – 0.9

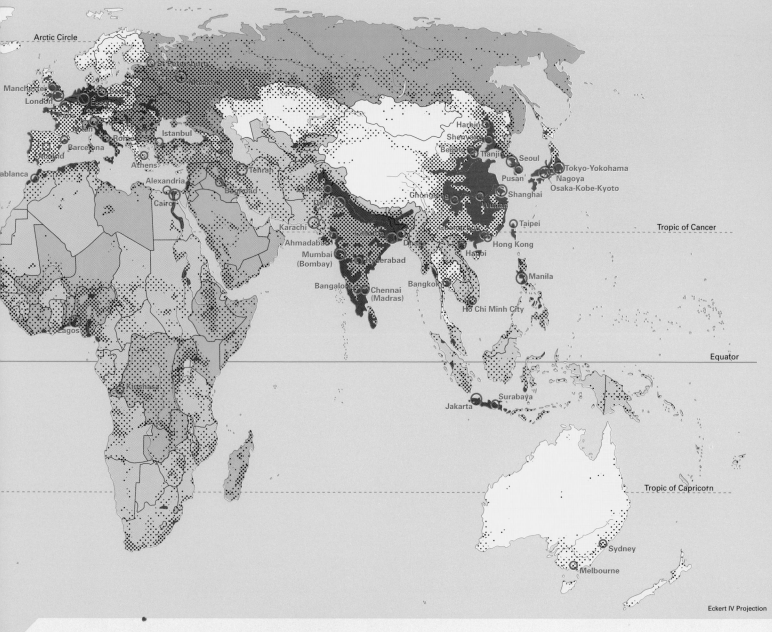

Arctic Circle

Manchester
London
St Petersburg
Barcelona
Madrid
Rome
Istanbul
Athens
Casablanca
Alexandria
Cairo
Baghdad
Tehran
Karachi
Ahmadabad
Mumbai
(Bombay)
Bangalore
Chennai
(Madras)
Hyderabad
Delhi
Dhaka
Harbin
Shenyang
Beijing
Tianjin
Seoul
Pusan
Shanghai
Chongqing
Wuhan
Taipei
Hong Kong
Hanoi
Bangkok
Ho Chi Minh City
Manila
Tokyo-Yokohama
Nagoya
Osaka-Kobe-Kyoto

Lagos
Kinshasa

Jakarta
Surabaya

Sydney
Melbourne

Tropic of Cancer

Equator

Tropic of Capricorn

Eckert IV Projection

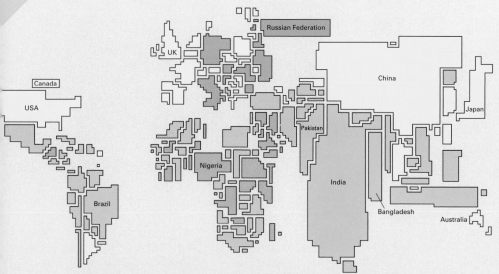

Canada
USA
Brazil

UK
Russian Federation
China
Japan
Pakistan
India
Bangladesh
Nigeria
Australia

Total population

On this map the size of each country represents the number of people living there, rather than the area of land that the country occupies.

Only those countries with at least 1 million people living in them are shown.
One small square represents 1 million people.

This represents Guatemala where eleven million people live.

Population change

The colours on this map represent the same rates of population increase or decrease shown in the legend to the main map above.

Very high increase - over 3 per cent

Increase above the world average - 1.5 to 3 per cent

Increase below the world average - less than 1.5 per cent

Decreasing (by less than 1 per cent)

Further information on this topic is located in the statistical section which begins on page 185.

ford University Press

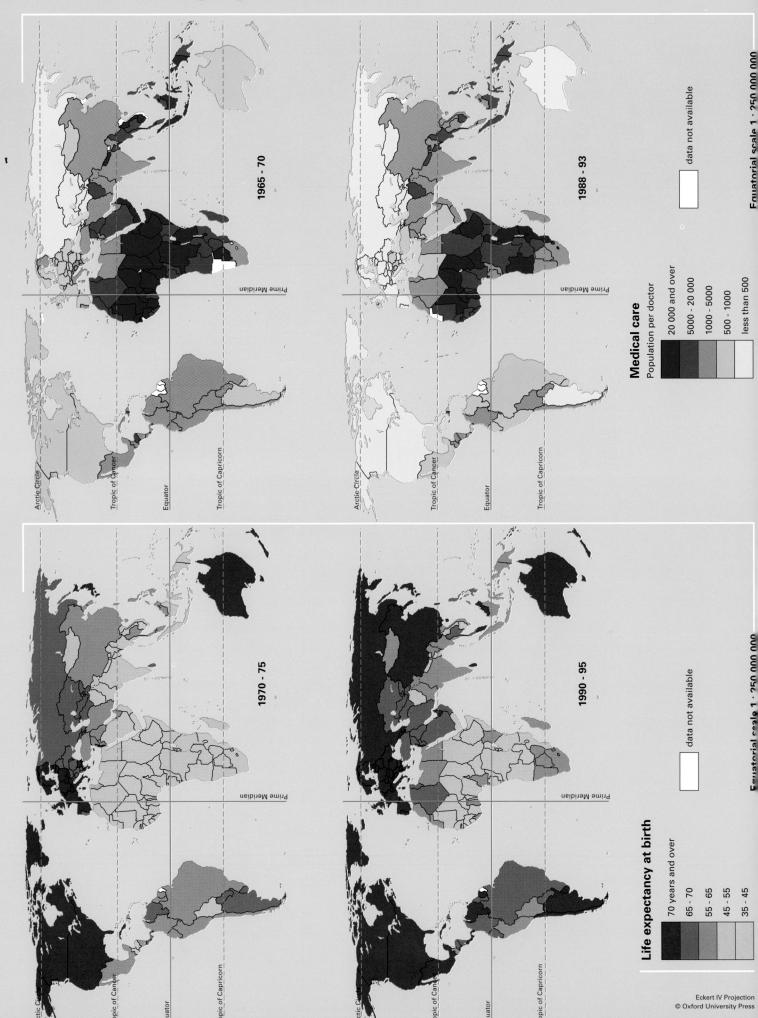

1965 - 70

1988 - 93

1970 - 75

1990 - 95

Medical care

Population per doctor

- 20 000 and over
- 5000 - 20 000
- 1000 - 5000
- 500 - 1000
- less than 500

data not available

Equatorial scale 1 : 250 000 000

Life expectancy at birth

- 70 years and over
- 65 - 70
- 55 - 65
- 45 - 55
- 35 - 45

data not available

Equatorial scale 1 : 250 000 000

Eckert IV Projection
© Oxford University Press

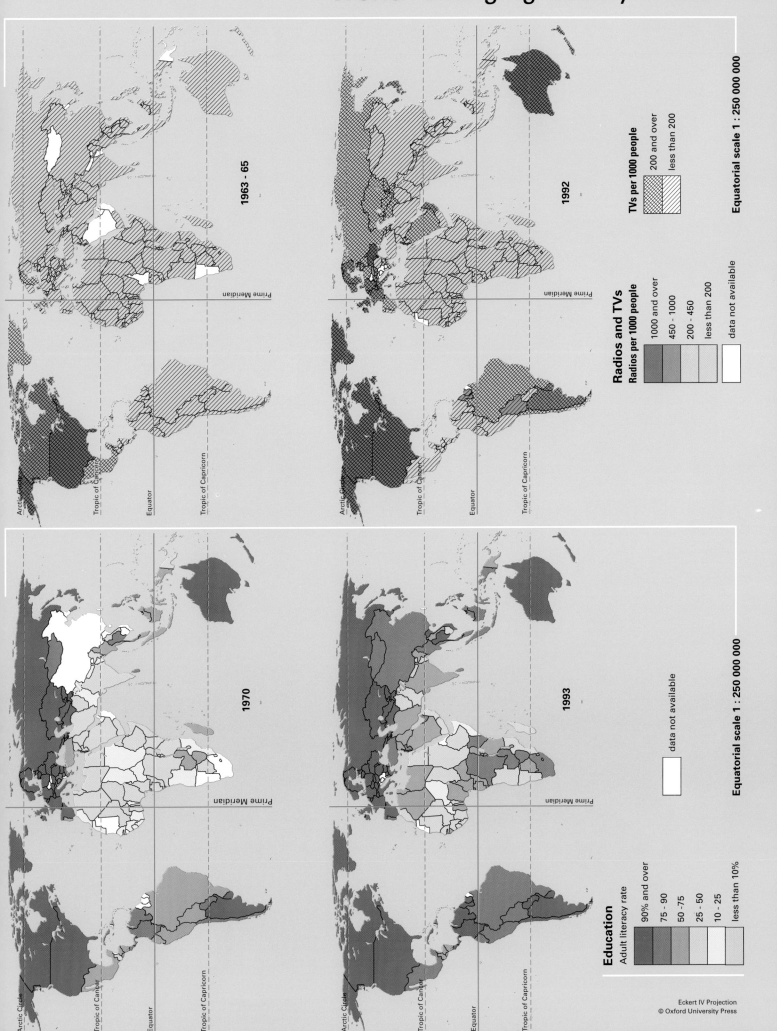

Education

Adult literacy rate

- 90% and over
- 75 - 90
- 50 - 75
- 25 - 50
- 10 - 25
- less than 10%

1970

1993

data not available

Equatorial scale 1 : 250 000 000

Radios and TVs

Radios per 1000 people

- 1000 and over
- 450 - 1000
- 200 - 450
- less than 200
- data not available

TVs per 1000 people

- 200 and over
- less than 200

1963 - 65

1992

Equatorial scale 1 : 250 000 000

Eckert IV Projection
© Oxford University Press

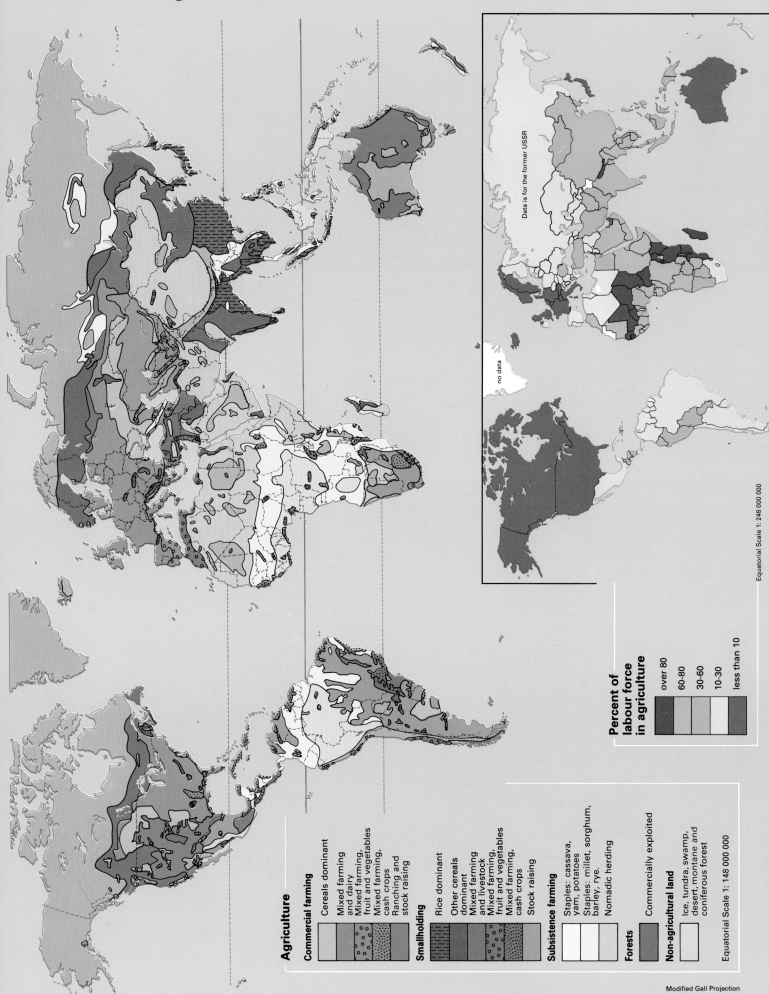

Agriculture

Commercial farming

- Cereals dominant
- Mixed farming and dairy
- Mixed farming, fruit and vegetables
- Mixed farming, cash crops
- Ranching and stock raising

Smallholding

- Rice dominant
- Other cereals dominant
- Mixed farming and livestock
- Mixed farming, fruit and vegetables
- Mixed farming, cash crops
- Stock raising

Subsistence farming

- Staples: cassava, yam, potatoes
- Staples: millet, sorghum, barley, rye.
- Nomadic herding

Forests

- Commercially exploited

Non-agricultural land

- Ice, tundra, swamp, desert, montane and coniferous forest

Equatorial Scale 1: 148 000 000

Percent of labour force in agriculture

- over 80
- 60-80
- 30-60
- 10-30
- less than 10

no data

Data is for the former USSR

Equatorial Scale 1: 248 000 000

Modified Gall Projection

© Oxford University Press

Fertilizer use -selected countries

Europe
Ireland 769
Netherlands 560
United Kingdom
Spain

Oceania
New Zealand
Australia

North America
USA
Canada

Central and South America
Costa Rica
Colombia
Nicaragua
Bolivia

Asia
Rep. of Korea
China
Malaysia
Pakistan
Cambodia

Africa
Eygpt
South Africa
Libya
Kenya
The Gambia

Kilograms per hectare of cropland per year
0 100 200 300 400 500

Nutrition

Average consumption
Megajoules per capita per day

- over 12.5
- 10.8-12.6
- 8-10.7
- under 8
- no data

average consumption per head declining

index of agricultural production per capita
1992-94 (1979-81=100)
(where data is available)

112

Agriculture's contribution to Gross Domestic Product (GDP)

Selected countries

GDP is the annual total value of all goods and services in a country, excluding transactions with other countries

Georgia
Tanzania
Albania
Uganda
Ghana
Côte d'Ivoire
India
Madagascar
Paraguay
Brazil
Ireland
Canada

Per cent of GDP
80 70 60 50 40 30 20 10 0

Cropland

Hectares per capita, 1993

Cropland includes land under temporary and permanent crops, temporary meadows, market gardens, and temporarily fallow land

- over 1.0
- 0.5-1.0
- 0.3-0.5
- 0.1-0.3
- less than 0.1

no data

Irrigated land

Areas permanently provided with water
As a percentage of cropland

- 75 and over
- 45-75
- 30-45
- 5-30
- 1-5
- less than 1

Equatorial Scale 1:248 000 000

Modified Gall Projection
© Oxford University Press

Gross Domestic Product (GDP)

The total value of all the goods and services produced within a country in one year.

GDP per capita ($US), 1992

- 15 000 and over
- 10 000 - 15 000
- 5000 - 10 000
- 3000 - 5000
- 1000 - 3000
- 500 - 1000
- 0 - 500

Equatorial scale 1 : 235 000 000

Industrialization

Industrialized high-income economies

The majority live in cities and enjoy high living standards based on manufacturing services, resource development, and high levels of energy consumption.

Industrializing upper-middle income economies

Manufacturing and other forms of industrial development are growing alongside traditional economies. The majority of the population have rising incomes.

Industrializing lower-middle income economies

Manufacturing and other forms of industrial development are growing alongside traditional economies. The majority of the population remain still relatively poor and rural.

Agricultural low income economies

These predominantly rural countries have made less economic progress in terms of industrializing than others, resulting in lower incomes for the majority and a greater dependence on agriculture.

- • Major oil exporters

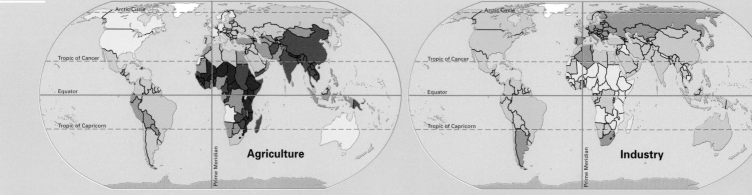

Agriculture

Industry

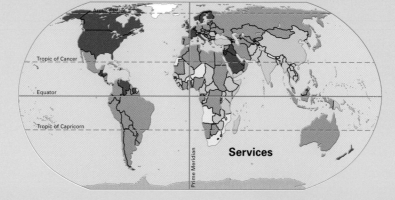

Services

Employment, 1990

Percent of the labour force

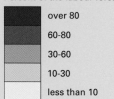

- over 80
- 60-80
- 30-60
- 10-30
- less than 10

Equatorial scale 1 : 405 000 000

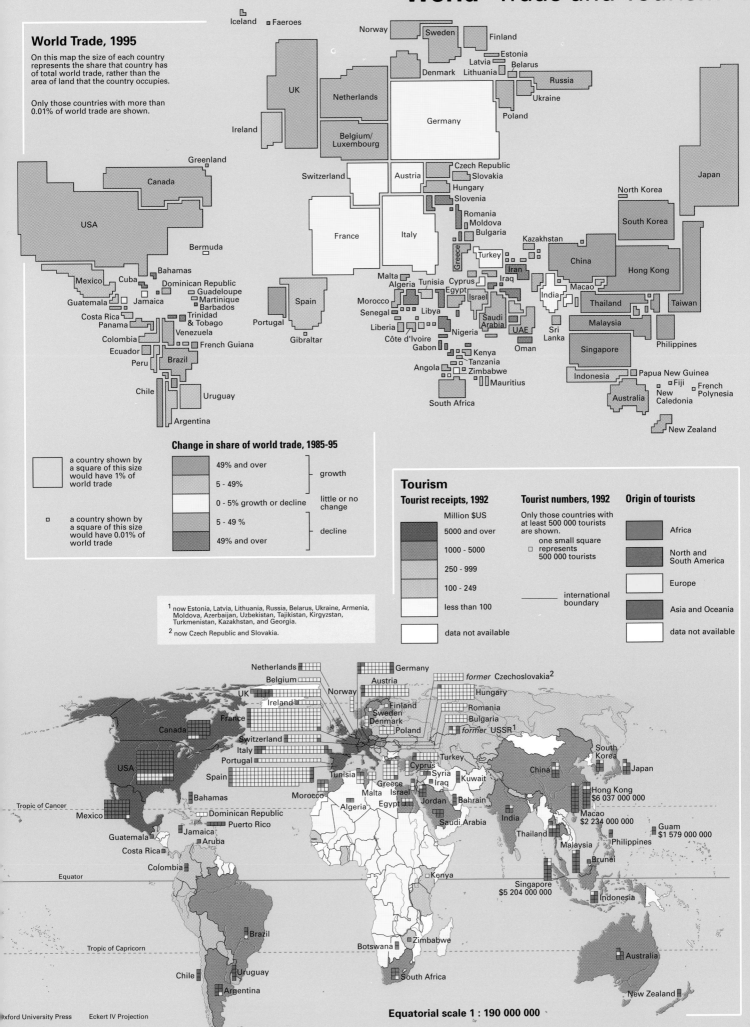

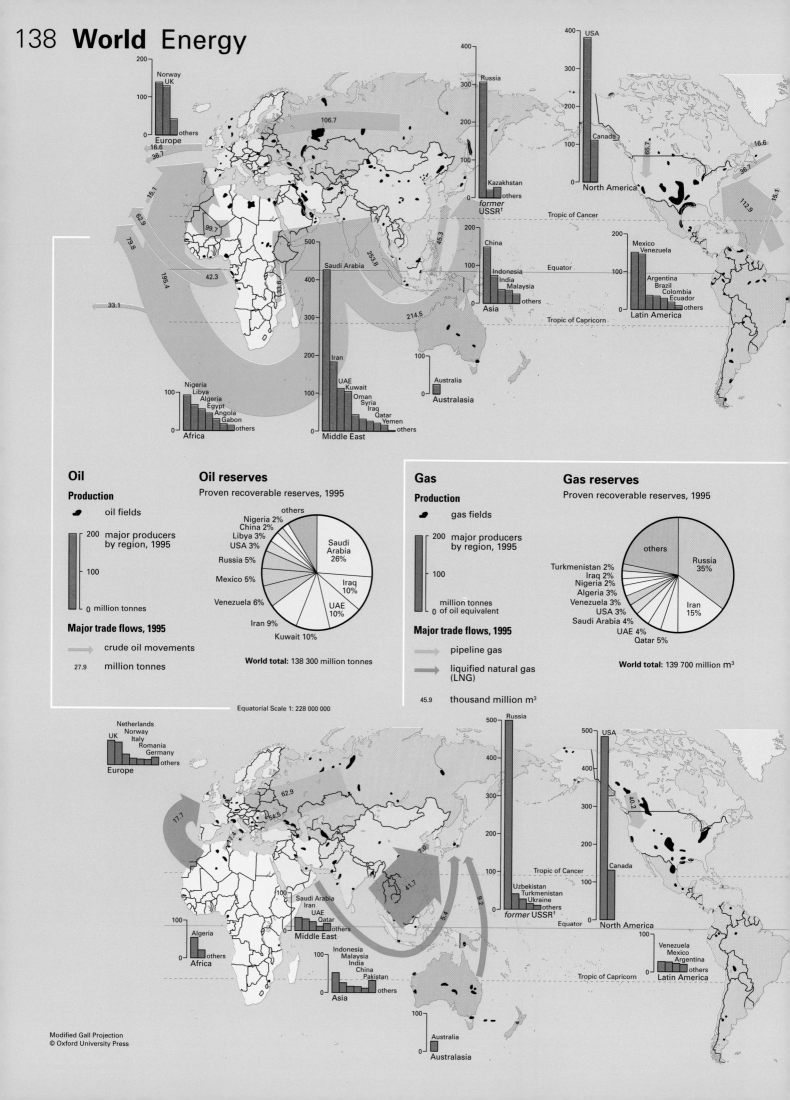

Oil

Production

- 🪨 oil fields

major producers
by region, 1995
200 / 100 / 0 million tonnes

Major trade flows, 1995

➡ crude oil movements

27.9 million tonnes

Oil reserves

Proven recoverable reserves, 1995

others
Nigeria 2%
China 2%
Libya 3%
USA 3%
Russia 5%
Mexico 5%
Venezuela 6%
Iran 9%
Kuwait 10%
UAE 10%
Iraq 10%
Saudi Arabia 26%

World total: 138 300 million tonnes

Gas

Production

- 🪨 gas fields

major producers
by region, 1995
200 / 100 / 0 million tonnes of oil equivalent

Major trade flows, 1995

➡ pipeline gas

➡ liquified natural gas (LNG)

45.9 thousand million m³

Gas reserves

Proven recoverable reserves, 1995

others
Turkmenistan 2%
Iraq 2%
Nigeria 2%
Algeria 3%
Venezuela 3%
USA 3%
Saudi Arabia 4%
UAE 4%
Qatar 5%
Russia 35%
Iran 15%

World total: 139 700 million m³

Equatorial Scale 1: 228 000 000

Modified Gall Projection
© Oxford University Press

Poland
Germany
UK
Czech Republic
Turkey
Spain
others
Europe

27

10

19

27

700

China

8

200

Russia

100

Kazakhstan

Ukraine

17

9

former USSR†

600

500

79

400

200

100

USA

500

400

300

200

100

Canada

North America

Tropic of Cancer

Equator

100

Colombia
others
Latin America

Tropic of Capricorn

8

200

100

South Africa

others

Africa

26

13

21

400

300

200

100

India

others

Asia

200

100

Australia

others

Australasia

9

10

5

Coal

Production

producing areas

200 major producers
by region, 1995

100

million tonnes
of oil equivalent
0

Major trade flows, 1994

coal movements

77 million tonnes

Coal reserves

Proven recoverable reserves, 1995

others

Poland 4%

South Africa 5%

Germany 7%

India 7%

Australia 9%

China 11%

USA 23%

former
USSR†
23%

World total: 1 031 610 million tonnes

Equatorial Scale 1:228 000 000

Electricity

Production, 1994

MW per capita

12 and over

5-12

2-5

1-2

0.5-1

0.1-0.5

less than 0.1

16 hydro-electric energy production
as a percent of total electricity production

* those countries using geothermal energy sources

Nuclear energy

Further information is to be found on page 129.

94

99 42 18

<1

74

7 2 <1

3 19

61 26 <1

17 65 <1

60 20 4 24 14

34 18 97 13 69

8 1 39 62 69 96 0

19 46 15 <1 64

1 9 <1 96 100 2

18 0 34 18 8

18 78 0 0 71 18 45 95

0 0 0 88 6 99 79 24

34 4 41 79 93

0 57 97 79 0 14

37 99 5 10 99 98 99 87 20

77 98 99 69

74 99 87 26 29 79

0 32 58

10 29 79

<1 10

72

20

59

9

18

1 30

92 2 46 2

65 62 19 84

75 68 70

74

78

93

77 48

100

41 98

67

Tropic of Cancer

Equator

Tropic of Capricorn

Modified Gall Projection
Oxford University Press

†Now the independent republics of Armenia, Azerbaijan, Belarus, Estonia,
Georgia, Kazakhstan, Kirgyzstan, Latvia, Lithuania, Moldova, Russia,
Tajikistan, Turkmenistan, Ukraine and Uzbekistan.

Tropic of Cancer

Equator

Tropic of Capricorn

Energy consumption

gigajoules per capita

200 and over

100-200

60-100

30-60 ——— world average

10-30

2-10

less than 2

Equatorial Scale 1: 228 000 000

Fuels such as wood, peat, and animal waste which, though important in many developing countries, are unreliably documented and therefore excluded from the map data.

Energy production

gigajoules per capita

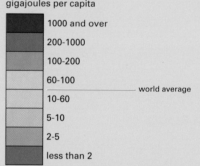

1000 and over

200-1000

100-200

60-100

10-60 ——— world average

5-10

2-5

less than 2

Nuclear energy

*   countries which produce energy from nuclear reactors

Tropic of Cancer

Equator

Tropic of Capricorn

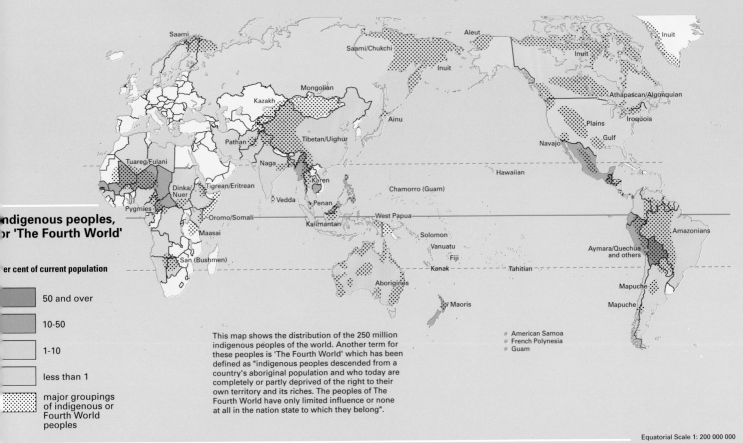

Indigenous peoples, or 'The Fourth World'

per cent of current population

- 50 and over
- 10-50
- 1-10
- less than 1
- major groupings of indigenous or Fourth World peoples

This map shows the distribution of the 250 million indigenous peoples of the world. Another term for these peoples is 'The Fourth World' which has been defined as "indigenous peoples descended from a country's aboriginal population and who today are completely or partly deprived of the right to their own territory and its riches. The peoples of The Fourth World have only limited influence or none at all in the nation state to which they belong".

Labels on map: Saami, Saami/Chukchi, Aleut, Inuit, Inuit, Inuit, Mongolian, Kazakh, Athapascan/Algonquian, Ainu, Pathan, Tibetan/Uighur, Plains, Iroquois, Naga, Navajo, Gulf, Tuareg/Fulani, Karen, Dinka/Nuer, Tigrean/Eritrean, Vedda, Penan, Hawaiian, Pygmies, Oromo/Somali, Chamorro (Guam), West Papua, Kalimantan, Amazonians, Maasai, Solomon, Aymara/Quechua and others, San (Bushmen), Vanuatu, Fiji, Kanak, Tahitian, Mapuche, Aborigines, Mapuche, Maoris

- American Samoa
- French Polynesia
- Guam

Equatorial Scale 1: 200 000 000

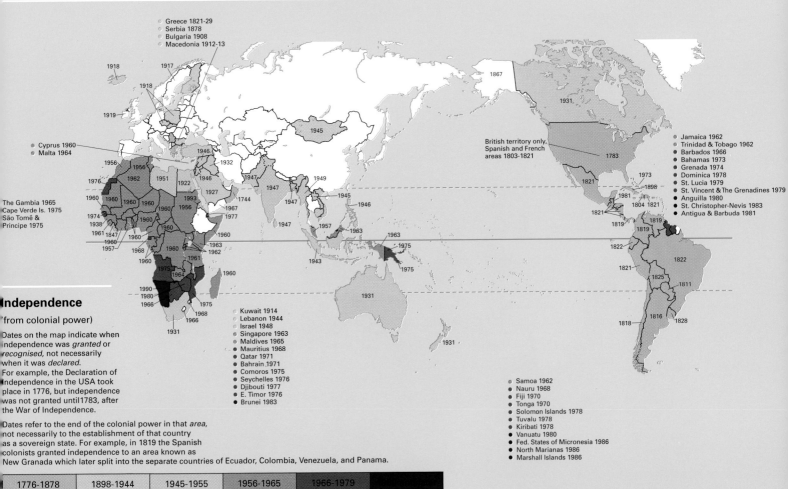

Greece 1821-29
Serbia 1878
Bulgaria 1908
Macedonia 1912-13

British territory only, Spanish and French areas 1803-1821

- Jamaica 1962
- Trinidad & Tobago 1962
- Barbados 1966
- Bahamas 1973
- Grenada 1974
- Dominica 1978
- St. Lucia 1979
- St. Vincent & The Grenadines 1979
- Anguilla 1980
- St. Christopher-Nevis 1983
- Antigua & Barbuda 1981

The Gambia 1965
Cape Verde Is. 1975
São Tomé & Principe 1975

- Kuwait 1914
- Lebanon 1944
- Israel 1948
- Singapore 1963
- Maldives 1965
- Mauritius 1968
- Qatar 1971
- Bahrain 1971
- Comoros 1975
- Seychelles 1976
- Djibouti 1977
- E. Timor 1976
- Brunei 1983

Independence

(from colonial power)

Dates on the map indicate when independence was *granted* or *recognised*, not necessarily when it was *declared*. For example, the Declaration of Independence in the USA took place in 1776, but independence was not granted until 1783, after the War of Independence.

Dates refer to the end of the colonial power in that *area*, not necessarily to the establishment of that country as a sovereign state. For example, in 1819 the Spanish colonists granted independence to an area known as New Granada which later split into the separate countries of Ecuador, Colombia, Venezuela, and Panama.

- Samoa 1962
- Nauru 1968
- Fiji 1970
- Tonga 1970
- Solomon Islands 1978
- Tuvalu 1978
- Kiribati 1978
- Vanuatu 1980
- Fed. States of Micronesia 1986
- North Marianas 1986
- Marshall Islands 1986

| 1776-1878 | 1898-1944 | 1945-1955 | 1956-1965 | 1966-1979 | |

——— international boundaries, 1997

Cyprus 1960
Malta 1964

Equatorial Scale 1: 200 000 000

Modified Gall Projection
Oxford University Press

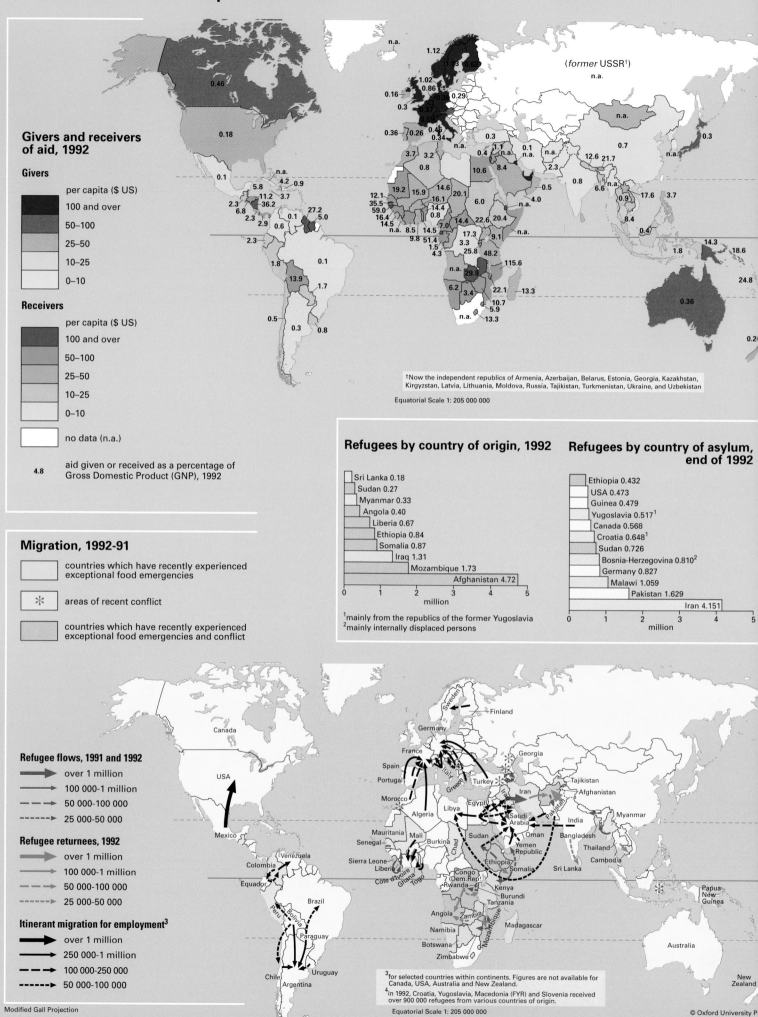

Givers and receivers of aid, 1992

Givers

per capita ($ US)

	100 and over
	50–100
	25–50
	10–25
	0–10

Receivers

per capita ($ US)

	100 and over
	50–100
	25–50
	10–25
	0–10
	no data (n.a.)

4.8   aid given or received as a percentage of Gross Domestic Product (GNP), 1992

†Now the independent republics of Armenia, Azerbaijan, Belarus, Estonia, Georgia, Kazakhstan, Kirgyzstan, Latvia, Lithuania, Moldova, Russia, Tajikistan, Turkmenistan, Ukraine, and Uzbekistan

Equatorial Scale 1: 205 000 000

Migration, 1992-91

	countries which have recently experienced exceptional food emergencies
✳	areas of recent conflict
	countries which have recently experienced exceptional food emergencies and conflict

Refugees by country of origin, 1992

Country	million
Sri Lanka	0.18
Sudan	0.27
Myanmar	0.33
Angola	0.40
Liberia	0.67
Ethiopia	0.84
Somalia	0.87
Iraq	1.31
Mozambique	1.73
Afghanistan	4.72

[1]mainly from the republics of the former Yugoslavia
[2]mainly internally displaced persons

Refugees by country of asylum, end of 1992

Country	million
Ethiopia	0.432
USA	0.473
Guinea	0.479
Yugoslavia	0.517[1]
Canada	0.568
Croatia	0.648[1]
Sudan	0.726
Bosnia-Herzegovina	0.810[2]
Germany	0.827
Malawi	1.059
Pakistan	1.629
Iran	4.151

Refugee flows, 1991 and 1992

→	over 1 million
→	100 000-1 million
⇢	50 000-100 000
⇢	25 000-50 000

Refugee returnees, 1992

→	over 1 million
→	100 000-1 million
⇢	50 000-100 000
⇢	25 000-50 000

Itinerant migration for employment[3]

→	over 1 million
→	250 000-1 million
⇢	100 000-250 000
⇢	50 000-100 000

[3]for selected countries within continents. Figures are not available for Canada, USA, Australia and New Zealand.
[4]in 1992, Croatia, Yugoslavia, Macedonia (FYR) and Slovenia received over 900 000 refugees from various countries of origin.

Equatorial Scale 1: 205 000 000

Modified Gall Projection

© Oxford University P

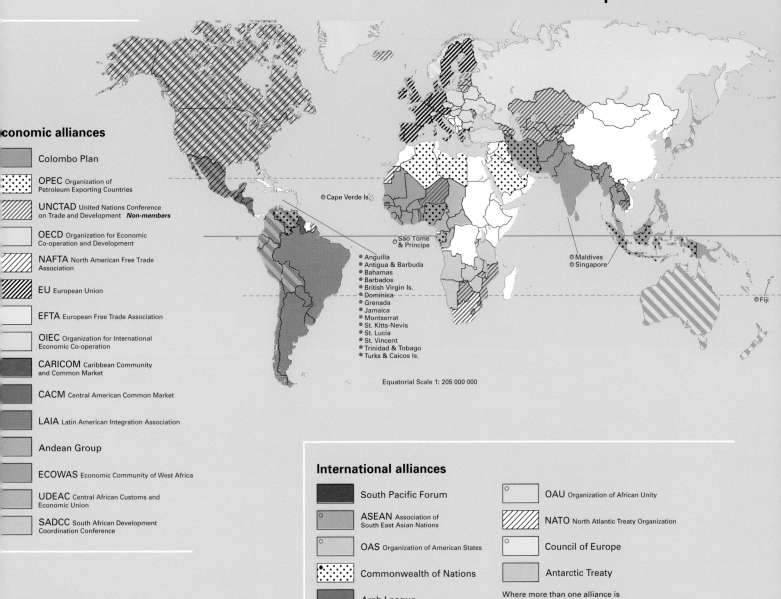

Economic alliances

- Colombo Plan
- **OPEC** Organization of Petroleum Exporting Countries
- **UNCTAD** United Nations Conference on Trade and Development *Non-members*
- **OECD** Organization for Economic Co-operation and Development
- **NAFTA** North American Free Trade Association
- **EU** European Union
- **EFTA** European Free Trade Association
- **OIEC** Organization for International Economic Co-operation
- **CARICOM** Caribbean Community and Common Market
- **CACM** Central American Common Market
- **LAIA** Latin American Integration Association
- Andean Group
- **ECOWAS** Economic Community of West Africa
- **UDEAC** Central African Customs and Economic Union
- **SADCC** South African Development Coordination Conference

Anguilla
Antigua & Barbuda
Bahamas
Barbados
British Virgin Is.
Dominica
Grenada
Jamaica
Montserrat
St. Kitts-Nevis
St. Lucia
St. Vincent
Trinidad & Tobago
Turks & Caicos Is.

○ Cape Verde Is.
○ São Tomé & Príncipe
○ Maldives
○ Singapore
○ Fiji

Equatorial Scale 1: 205 000 000

International alliances

- South Pacific Forum
- **ASEAN** Association of South East Asian Nations
- **OAS** Organization of American States
- Commonwealth of Nations
- Arab League
- **OAU** Organization of African Unity
- **NATO** North Atlantic Treaty Organization
- Council of Europe
- Antarctic Treaty

Where more than one alliance is involved, the country is shown divided by interlocking shading.

United Nations

The following countries are **non-members**

Kiribati
Nauru
Northern Marianas
Switzerland†
Taiwan
Tonga
Tuvalu
Vatican City†
Western Sahara

Information correct as of Feb 1997
† observer status

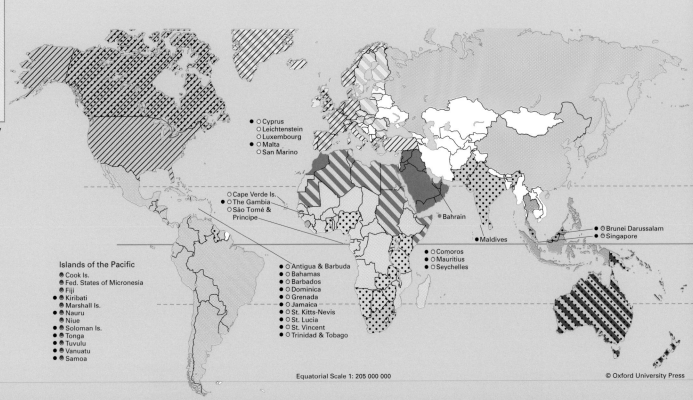

○ Cyprus
○ Leichtenstein
○ Luxembourg
○ Malta
○ San Marino

○ Cape Verde Is.
● The Gambia
○ São Tomé & Príncipe
● Bahrain

● Brunei Darussalam
○ Singapore
○ Maldives

● Comoros
● Mauritius
● Seychelles

Islands of the Pacific

○ Cook Is.
○ Fed. States of Micronesia
○ Fiji
● Kiribati
○ Marshall Is.
● Nauru
○ Niue
○ Soloman Is.
● Tonga
● Tuvulu
○ Vanuatu
○ Samoa

○ Antigua & Barbuda
○ Bahamas
○ Barbados
○ Dominica
○ Grenada
○ Jamaica
○ St. Kitts-Nevis
○ St. Lucia
○ St. Vincent
○ Trinidad & Tobago

Equatorial Scale 1: 205 000 000

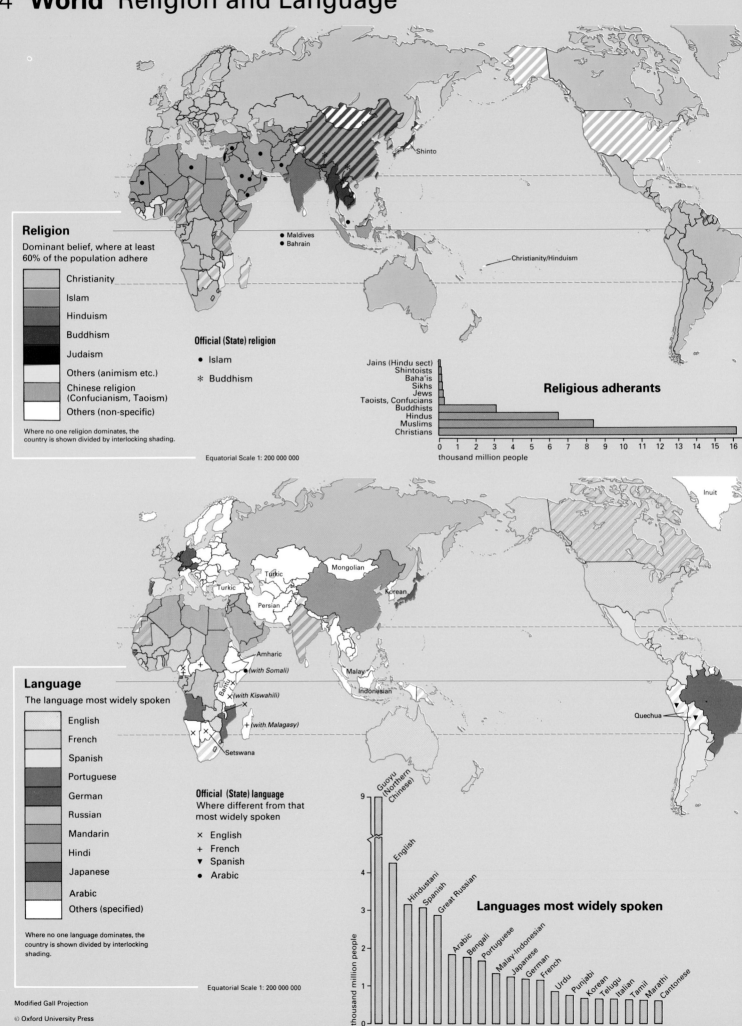

Religion

Dominant belief, where at least 60% of the population adhere

- Christianity
- Islam
- Hinduism
- Buddhism
- Judaism
- Others (animism etc.)
- Chinese religion (Confucianism, Taoism)
- Others (non-specific)

Where no one religion dominates, the country is shown divided by interlocking shading.

Official (State) religion

- ● Islam
- ✳ Buddhism

Equatorial Scale 1: 200 000 000

Shinto

● Maldives
● Bahrain

Christianity/Hinduism

Religious adherants

Jains (Hindu sect)
Shintoists
Baha'is
Sikhs
Jews
Taoists, Confucians
Buddhists
Hindus
Muslims
Christians

thousand million people
0 1 2 3 4 5 6 7 8 9 10 11 12 13 14 15 16

Language

The language most widely spoken

- English
- French
- Spanish
- Portuguese
- German
- Russian
- Mandarin
- Hindi
- Japanese
- Arabic
- Others (specified)

Where no one language dominates, the country is shown divided by interlocking shading.

Official (State) language
Where different from that most widely spoken

- ✕ English
- ✛ French
- ▼ Spanish
- ● Arabic

Amharic
(with Somali)
Bantu
(with Kiswahili)
(with Malagasy)
Setswana
Malay
Indonesian
Turkic
Persian
Turkic
Mongolian
Korean
Inuit
Quechua

Equatorial Scale 1: 200 000 000

Modified Gall Projection

© Oxford University Press

Languages most widely spoken

thousand million people

Guoyu (Northern Chinese)
English
Hindustani
Spanish
Great Russian
Arabic
Bengali
Portuguese
Malay-Indonesian
Japanese
German
French
Urdu
Punjabi
Korean
Telugu
Italian
Tamil
Marathi
Cantonese

9
4
3
0

How to use the index

To find a place on an atlas map use either the grid code or latitude and longitude.

For more information on latitude and longitude look at page 6.

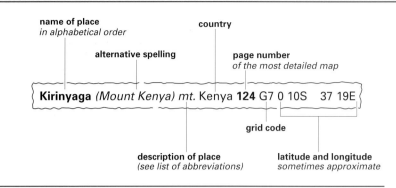

name of place
in alphabetical order

country

alternative spelling

page number
of the most detailed map

Kirinyaga *(Mount Kenya) mt.* Kenya **124** G7 0 10S 37 19E

grid code

description of place
(see list of abbreviations)

latitude and longitude
sometimes approximate

Grid code

Kirinyaga is in grid square G7

Kirinyaga *(Mount Kenya) mt.* Kenya **124** G7 0 10S 37 19E

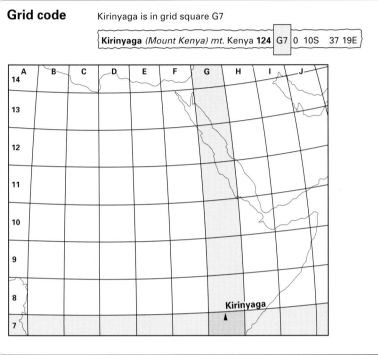

Latitude and Longitude

Kirinyaga is at latitude 0 10S longitude 37 19E

Kirinyaga *(Mount Kenya) mt.* Kenya **124** G7 0 10S 37 19E

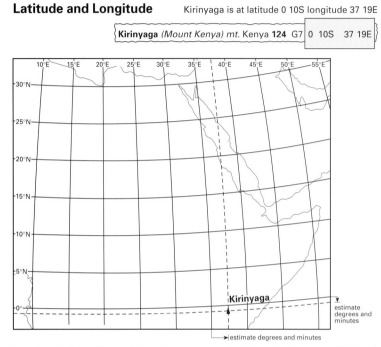

Abbreviations used in the index

admin	administrative area
A.C.T.	Australian Capital Territory
b.	bay or harbour
bor.	borough
c.	cape, point, or headland
can.	canal
co.	county
d.	desert
dep.	depression
est.	estuary
fj.	fjord
g.	gulf
geog. reg.	geographical region
N.H.S	national historic site
i.	island
in.	inlet
I.R.	Indian Reservation
is.	islands
ist.	isthmus
l.	lake, lakes, lagoon
m.	marsh
m.s.	manned meteorological station
mt.	mountain
mts.	mountains
p.	peninsula
pk.	park
plat.	plateau
pn.	plain
pref.	prefecture
prov.	province
r.	river
rd.	road
r.s.	research station
reg.	region
rep.	republic
res.	reservoir
salt l.	salt lake
sd.	sound, strait, or channel
sum.	summit
tn.	town
U.A.E.	United Arab Emirates
U.K.	United Kingdom
U.S.A.	United States of America
v.	valley
vol.	volcano

Abbreviations used on the maps

A.C.T.	Australian Capital Territory
Ákr.	Ákra
App.	Appennino
Arch.	Archipelago
Arg.	Argentina
Arq.	Arquípelago
Austl.	Australia
C.	Cape; Cabo; Cap
Col.	Colombia
D.C.	District of Columbia
Den.	Denmark
D.R.	Democratic Republic
E.	East
Ec.	Ecuador
Eq.	Equatorial
Fj	Fjord
Fr.	France
G.	Gunung; Gebel
Hwy.	Highway
I.	Island; Île; Isla; Ilha
Is.	Islands; Îles; Islas; Ilhas
J.	Jezioro
Jez.	Jezero
Kep.	Kepulauan
M.	Muang
Mt.	Mount; Mountain; Mont
Mte.	Monte
Mts.	Mountains; Monts
N.	North
Nat.Pk.	National Park
Neths.	Netherlands
N.P.	National Park
N.Z.	New Zealand
Pa.	Passage

Peg.	Pegunungan
Pen; Penin.	Peninsula
Pl.	Planina
Port.	Portugal
P.P	Provincial Park
proj.	projected
Prov. Park	Provincial Park
Pt.	Point
Pta.	Punta
Pte.	Pointe
Pto.	Porto; Puerto
R.	River; Rio
Ra.	Range
R.A.	Recreation Area
Res.	Reservoir
R.M.	Regional Municipality
RÉS. FAUN.	Réserve Faunique
Résr.	Réservoir
S.	South; San
S.A.	South Africa
Sa.	Sierra
Sd.	Sound
Sev.	Severnaya
Sp.	Spain
St.	Saint
Ste.	Sainte
Str.	Strait
Terr.	Territory
U.A.E.	United Arab Emirates
u/c.	under construction
U.K.	United Kingdom
U.N.	United Nations
U.S.A.	United States of America
U.S.S.R.	Union of Soviet Socialist Republics
W.	West

A

Abbotsford British Columbia 34 F4 49 02N 122 18W
Aberdeen Saskatchewan 38 B2 52 20N 106 16W
Aberdeen Lake Northwest Territories 51 M3 64 30N 99 00W
Abitibi, Lake Ontario/Québec 41 E2 48 42N 79 45W
Abitibi River Ontario 41 D2 49 40N 81 20W
Abloviak Fiord Québec 46 C4 59 30N 65 25W
Acadia Alberta 54 A1 50 56N 114 00W
Acadia, Cape Northwest Territories 46 A5 61 38N 79 55W
Acton Ontario 44 B2 43 38N 80 04W
Adair, Cape Northwest Territories 51 S5 71 32N 71 24W
Adams Lake British Columbia 35 E2 51 10N 119 30W
Adams River British Columbia 35 E2 51 23N 119 23W
Adelaide Peninsula Northwest Territories 51 M4 68 15N 97 30W
Adlatok River Newfoundland 48 B4 55 40N 62 50W
Adlavik Islands Newfoundland 48 C3 54 55N 58 40W
Admiralty Inlet Northwest Territories 51 P5 72 30N 86 00W
Admiralty Island Northwest Territories 51 L4 69 25N 100 30W
Advocate Harbour Nova Scotia 49 F7 45 20N 64 45W
Agassiz British Columbia 34 H4 49 14N 121 52W
Agassiz Ice Cap Northwest Territories 51 R7 80 15N 76 00W
Agassiz Provincial Forest Manitoba 39 B1 49 50N 96 20W
Agawa Ontario 65 J6 47 22N 84 37W
Aguasabon River Ontario 41 C2 48 50N 87 00W
Ailsa Craig Ontario 44 A2 43 08N 81 34W
Ainslie, Lake Nova Scotia 49 F7 46 10N 61 10W
Airdrie Alberta 37 C2 51 20N 114 00W
Air Force Island Northwest Territories 51 S4 63 30N 71 40W
Air Ronge Saskatchewan 38 B3 55 05N 105 18W
Aishihik Yukon Territory 50 D3 61 34N 137 31W
Aishihik Lake Yukon Territory 50 D3 61 00N 135 05W
Ajax Ontario 41 E1 43 48N 79 00W
Akimiski Island Northwest Territories 51 Q1 52 30N 81 00W
Akimiski Island Bird Sanctuary Northwest Territories 51 Q1 53 00N 81 00W
Akimiski Strait Northwest Territories/Ontario 40 D3 52 40N 82 00W
Aktarvik (Aklavik) Northwest Territories 50 D4 68 15N 135 02W
Aklavik (Aktarvik) Northwest Territories 50 D4 68 15N 135 02W
Akpatok Island Northwest Territories 51 T3 60 30N 68 00W
Akulivik Québec 46 A5 60 53N 78 15W
Albany Island Ontario 40 D3 52 15N 81 34W
Albany River Ontario 40 D3 51 40N 83 20W
Albany River Provincial Park Ontario 40 C3 51 20N 89 10W
Alberni Inlet admin. British Columbia 34 H4 49 05N 124 52W
Albert admin. New Brunswick 49 F7 45 40N 64 55W
Alberta province 8 M3 54 00N 117 30W
Alberton Prince Edward Island 49 F7 46 50N 64 08W
Albiti admin. Québec 43 K9 48 11N 76 00W
Aldershot Ontario 44 C2 43 17N 79 51W
Aldersyde Alberta 37 C2 50 44N 113 53W
Alert Northwest Territories 51 U7 82 30N 62 00W
Alert m.s. Northwest Territories 112 80 31N 60 05W
Alert Bay British Columbia 35 C2 50 34N 126 58W
Alexandria Ontario 41 F1 45 19N 74 38W
Alexis Creek tn. British Columbia 35 D2 52 05N 123 12W
Alexis River Newfoundland 48 C3 52 35N 57 05W
Alfred Ontario 43 M6 45 34N 74 53W
Alfred, Mount British Columbia 34 H5 50 13N 124 07W
Algonquin Provincial Park Ontario 41 E2 45 50N 78 30W
Alix Alberta 37 C2 52 25N 113 11W
Allan Saskatchewan 38 B2 51 54N 106 02W
Allan Water tn. Ontario 40 B3 50 14N 90 12W
Alliston Ontario 44 C3 44 09N 79 51W
Alma New Brunswick 49 F7 45 36N 64 58W
Alma Québec 47 B2 48 32N 71 41W
Almonte Ontario 41 E2 45 14N 76 12W
Alouette Lake British Columbia 34 H4 49 22N 121 22W
Alsask Saskatchewan 38 B2 51 22N 110 00W
Alsek Ranges mts. British Columbia 34 A3 59 30N 137 30W
Alsek River British Columbia/Yukon Territory 34 A3 59 30N 138 00W
Altona Manitoba 39 B1 49 06N 97 35W
Alvin British Columbia 34 H4 49 25N 122 34W
Amadjuak Lake Northwest Territories 51 S3 64 55N 71 00W
Amaranth Manitoba 39 B2 50 36N 98 43W
Amery Manitoba 39 C3 56 45N 94 00W
Amherst Nova Scotia 49 F7 45 50N 64 14W
Amherstburg Ontario 41 D1 42 06N 83 07W
Amherst Island Ontario 43 K5 44 08N 76 43W
Amisk Lake Saskatchewan 38 C2 54 30N 102 15W
Amos Québec 47 A2 48 34N 78 08W
Amqui Québec 47 C2 48 30N 67 30W
Amund Ringnes Island Northwest Territories 51 M6 78 00N 96 00W
Amundsen Gulf Northwest Territories 50 F5/G5 70 30N 125 00W
Anahim Lake tn. British Columbia 35 C2 52 25N 125 18W
Ancaster Ontario 44 C2 43 13N 79 58W
Anderson Lake British Columbia 34 H5 50 38N 122 24W
Anderson River Northwest Territories 50 F4 69 00N 128 10W
Anderson River Delta Bird Sanctuary Northwest Territories 50 F4 69 50N 128 30W
Andrew Alberta 37 C2 53 52N 112 14W
Andrew Gordon Bay Northwest Territories 51 R3 64 27N 75 30W

Ane, Cape Newfoundland 49 D2 46 50N 53 50W
Angers Québec 53 L3 45 32N 75 29W
Angikuni Lake Northwest Territories 51 M3 62 00N 99 45W
Angling Lake I.R. Ontario 40 C3 53 50N 89 30W
Anguille, Cape Newfoundland 49 C2 47 55N 59 24W
Angus Ontario 44 C3 44 19N 79 53W
Anjou Québec 41 B2 45 37N 73 35W
Annacis Island British Columbia 52 G3 49 09N 122 59W
Annapolis admin. Nova Scotia 49 E6 44 40N 65 20W
Annapolis Royal Nova Scotia 49 E6 44 44N 65 32W
Annieville British Columbia 52 G3 49 10N 122 54W
Anthony Island British Columbia 34 B2 52 05N 131 14W
Antigonish admin. Nova Scotia 49 F7 45 30N 62 10W
Antigonish Nova Scotia 49 F7 45 39N 61 55W
Anvil Range mts. Yukon Territory 50 E3 62 25N 133 15W
Apsley Ontario 42 H5 44 45N 78 06W
Arborfield Saskatchewan 38 C2 53 06N 103 39W
Arborg Manitoba 39 B2 50 55N 97 12W
Arcola Saskatchewan 38 C1 49 38N 102 26W
Arctic Bay (Ikpiarjuk) tn. Northwest Territories 51 P5 73 05N 85 20W
Arctic Red River Northwest Territories 50 E4 65 50N 131 20W
Ardrossan Alberta 54 H5 53 33N 113 11W
Argenteuil admin. Québec 43 M6 45 50N 74 30W
Arichat Nova Scotia 49 F7 45 31N 61 00W
Aristazabal Island British Columbia 34 C2 52 40N 129 05W
Armstrong British Columbia 35 E2 50 27N 119 14W
Armstrong Ontario 40 C3 50 18N 89 02W
Arnold's Cove tn. Newfoundland 49 D2 47 45N 54 00W
Arnot Manitoba 39 B3 55 46N 96 42W
Arnprior Ontario 41 E2 45 26N 76 21W
Aroland Ontario 40 C3 50 17N 86 59W
Aroostook New Brunswick 49 A2 46 50N 67 43W
Arran Lake Ontario 44 A3 44 29N 81 16W
Arrowsmith, Mount British Columbia 34 H4 49 00N 124 00W
Arthabaska admin. Québec 43 P6 45 58N 72 11W
Arthur Ontario 41 D1 43 50N 80 32W
Artillery Lake Northwest Territories 50 K3 63 09N 107 52W
Arviat (Eskimo Point) Northwest Territories 51 N3 61 10N 94 05W
Ariliqjuat (Pelly Bay) tn. Northwest Territories 51 P4 68 32N 89 48W
Asbestos Québec 47 B2 45 46N 71 56W
Ashcroft British Columbia 35 D2 50 41N 121 17W
Ashern Manitoba 39 B2 51 10N 98 20W
Asheweig River Ontario 40 C3 53 50N 87 50W
Ashnola River British Columbia 34 H4 49 13N 119 58W
Ashuanipi Newfoundland 48 A3 52 46N 66 05W
Ashuanipi Lake Newfoundland 48 A3 52 45N 66 15W
Ashuanipi River Newfoundland 48 A3 53 30N 66 30W
Aspy Bay Nova Scotia 49 F7 46 58N 60 26W
Assiniboia Saskatchewan 38 B1 49 39N 105 59W
Assiniboine Forest Manitoba 52 D2 49 51N 97 15W
Assiniboine, Mount British Columbia/Alberta 35 E2 50 51N 115 39W
Assiniboine River Manitoba/Saskatchewan 39 B1 49 40N 98 50W
Aston, Cape Northwest Territories 51 T5 70 00N 67 30W
Astray Newfoundland 48 A3 54 36N 66 42W
Astray Lake Newfoundland 48 A3 54 36N 66 42W
Athabasca Alberta 37 C2 54 44N 113 15W
Athabasca, Lake Alberta/Saskatchewan 38 B3 59 10N 109 30W
Athabasca River Alberta 37 C3 57 30N 111 40W
Athabasca Sand Dunes Wilderness Park Saskatchewan 38 B3 59 10N 108 30W
Athens Ontario 43 L5 44 38N 75 57W
Atherley Ontario 44 C3 44 36N 79 21W
Athol Nova Scotia 49 F7 45 40N 64 10W
Atikaki Provincial Park Manitoba 39 B2 51 30N 95 30W
Atik Lake Manitoba 39 B3 55 20N 96 10W
Atikokan Ontario 40 B2 48 45N 91 38W
Atikonak Lake Newfoundland 48 B3 52 40N 64 32W
Atikonak River Newfoundland 48 B3 53 20N 64 50W
Atkinson, Point British Columbia 52 E4 49 20N 123 16W
Atlin British Columbia 34 B3 59 31N 133 41W
Atlin Lake British Columbia 34 B3 59 31N 133 41W
Atlin Provincial Park British Columbia 34 B3 59 10N 133 50W
Atna Peak British Columbia 35 C2 53 53N 128 07W
Attawapiskat Ontario 40 D3 53 00N 82 30W
Attawapiskat Lake Ontario 40 C3 52 18N 87 54W
Attawapiskat River Ontario 40 D3 53 00N 84 00W
Attikamagen Lake Newfoundland 48 A4 55 00N 66 30W
Aubry, Lake Northwest Territories 50 F4 67 30N 127 30W
Auden Ontario 40 C3 50 14N 87 54W
Aujuittuq (Grise Fiord) tn. Northwest Territories 51 Q6 76 25N 82 57W
Aulac New Brunswick 49 F7 45 50N 64 20W
Aulneau Peninsula Ontario 40 B2 49 23N 94 29W
Aupaluk Québec 46 C4 59 12N 69 35W
Aurora Ontario 44 C3 44 00N 79 28W
Ausable River Ontario 44 A2 43 06N 81 36W
Austin Channel Northwest Territories 51 L6 75 35N 103 25W
Auyuittuq National Park Northwest Territories 51 T4 67 00N 67 00W
Avalon Peninsula Newfoundland 49 D2 47 30N 53 30W
Avalon Wilderness Reserve Newfoundland 49 D2 47 00N 53 10W
Avola British Columbia 35 E2 51 47N 119 19W
Avon River Ontario 44 A2 43 20N 81 10W
Awenda Provincial Park Ontario 44 B3/C3 44 50N 80 00W
Axel Heiberg Island Northwest Territories 51 N7 80 00N 90 00W

Aylmer Ontario 44 B1 42 47N 80 58W
Aylmer Québec 53 J2 45 23N 75 51W
Aylmer Lake Northwest Territories 50 K3 64 05N 108 30W
Ayr Ontario 44 B2 43 17N 80 26W
Azure Lake British Columbia 35 D2 52 22N 120 07W

B

Babine Lake British Columbia 35 C2 54 45N 126 05W
Babine Mountains Recreational Area British Columbia 35 C2 54 55N 127 00W
Babine River British Columbia 35 C3 55 44N 127 29W
Bache Peninsula Northwest Territories 51 R6 79 08N 76 00W
Backbone Ranges mts. Northwest Territories 50 F3 63 00N 129 00W
Back River Northwest Territories 50 L4 65 05N 104 55W
Baddeck Nova Scotia 49 F7 46 06N 60 45W
Badger Newfoundland 49 C2 49 00N 56 04W
Baffin reg. Northwest Territories 51 Q5 71 30N 80 00W
Baffin Bay Northwest Territories 51 T5 73 00N 65 00W
Baffin Island Northwest Territories 51 R5 70 00N 75 00W
Baie-Comeau tn. Québec 47 C2 49 12N 68 10W
Baie des Chaleurs b. Québec/New Brunswick 47 C2 47 59N 65 50W
Baie de Valois b. Québec 53 M4 45 27N 73 17W
Baie d'Hudson (Hudson Bay) b. Canada 46 A4 58 00N 79 00W
Baie d'Ungava (Ungava Bay) b. Québec/Northwest Territories 46 C4 59 00N 67 30W
Baie d'Urfé tn. Québec 53 M4 45 26N 73 54W
Baie James (James Bay) b. Canada 47 A3 52 30N 79 30W
Baie la Fontaine Québec 53 L3 45 32N 75 18W
Baie-Saint-Paul tn. Québec 47 B2 47 27N 70 30W
Baie-Trinité tn. Québec 47 C2 49 25N 67 20W
Baie Verte tn. Newfoundland 49 C2 49 55N 56 12W
Baie Verte Nova Scotia 49 F7 46 00N 64 00W
Baie Verte Peninsula Newfoundland 49 C2 49 45N 56 15W
Bailey Creek Ontario 44 C3 44 01N 79 56W
Baillie Islands Northwest Territories 50 F5 70 35N 128 10W
Baillie River Northwest Territories 50 K3 64 40N 105 50W
Baird Peninsula Northwest Territories 51 Q4 69 00N 76 15W
Baker Lake Northwest Territories 51 M3 64 00N 95 10W
Baker Lake (Qamanittuaq) tn. Northwest Territories 51 M3 64 10N 95 30W
Bakers Dozen Islands Northwest Territories 51 R2 56 36N 79 12W
Balcarres Saskatchewan 38 C2 50 49N 103 32W
Baldock Lake Manitoba 39 B3 56 30N 98 25W
Baldy Mountain Manitoba 39 A2 51 27N 100 45W
Balgonie Saskatchewan 38 C2 50 31N 104 15W
Ballantyre Strait Northwest Territories 50 H6 77 30N 115 00W
Ball Lake Alberta 54 G5 53 31N 113 16W
Balmertown Ontario 40 B3 51 04N 93 41W
Balsam Lake Ontario 44 D3 44 37N 78 51W
Balsam Lake Provincial Park Ontario 44 D3 44 30N 78 50W
Bamaji Lake Ontario 40 B3 51 09N 91 25W
Bancroft Ontario 41 E2 45 03N 77 51W
Banff Alberta 37 B2 51 10N 115 34W
Banff National Park Alberta 37 B2 51 00N 116 00W
Banks Island British Columbia 34 B3 53 25N 130 05W
Banks Island Northwest Territories 50 G5 73 15N 121 30W
Banks Island No 1 Bird Sanctuary Northwest Territories 50 G5 73 00N 124 50W
Banks Island No 2 Bird Sanctuary Northwest Territories 50 H4 73 15N 119 00W
Barachois Pont Provincial Park Newfoundland 49 C2 48 28N 58 20W
Baring, Cape Northwest Territories 50 H5 70 02N 117 30W
Barkerville British Columbia 35 D2 53 06N 121 35W
Barkley Sound British Columbia 34 G4 48 58N 125 11W
Barmfield British Columbia 34 G4 48 50N 125 07W
Barnes Ice Cap Northwest Territories 51 R5 70 00N 73 30W
Barnston Island British Columbia 52 H3 49 11N 122 42W
Barrhaven Ontario 53 J2 45 16N 75 47W
Barrhead Alberta 37 C2 54 10N 114 22W
Barrie Ontario 41 E1 44 22N 79 42W
Barrie Island Ontario 42 D6 45 56N 82 39W
Barrière British Columbia 35 D2 51 10N 120 07W
Barrington Nova Scotia 49 E6 43 34N 65 35W
Barrington Lake Manitoba 39 A3 57 00N 100 18W
Barrow Bay Ontario 44 A3 44 58N 81 11W
Barrows Manitoba 39 A2 52 50N 101 26W
Barrow Strait Northwest Territories 51 N5 74 24N 94 10W
Barrys Bay tn. Ontario 41 E2 45 27N 77 41W
Bashaw Alberta 37 C2 52 35N 112 58W
Basin Lake Saskatchewan 38 B2 52 40N 105 10W
Bassano Alberta 37 C2 50 47N 112 28W
Bass Lake Ontario 44 C3 44 36N 79 31W
Bass Lake Provincial Park Ontario 44 C3 44 30N 79 40W
Bataga River British Columbia 35 C3 58 30N 126 40W
Batchawana Bay tn. Ontario 41 D2 46 53N 84 36W
Batchawana Mountain Ontario 41 D2 47 04N 84 34W
Bath New Brunswick 49 A2 46 30N 67 36W
Bath Ontario 43 K5 44 11N 76 47W
Bathurst New Brunswick 49 A2 47 37N 65 40W
Bathurst, Cape Northwest Territories 50 F5 70 31N 127 53W
Bathurst Inlet Northwest Territories 50 K4 66 49N 108 00W

Bathurst Inlet (Kinggauk) tn. Northwest Territories 50 K4 66 50N 108 01W
Bathurst Island Northwest Territories 51 M6 76 00N 99 40W
Batoche National Historic Site Saskatchewan 38 B2 52 45N 107 00W
Batteau Newfoundland 48 C3 53 24N 55 47W
Battle Creek Saskatchewan 38 B1 49 20N 109 30W
Battleford Saskatchewan 38 B2 52 45N 108 20W
Battle Harbour tn. Newfoundland 48 C3 52 16N 55 35W
Battle River Alberta/Saskatchewan 38 C2 52 30N 112 20W
Bauld, Cape Newfoundland 48 C3 51 40N 55 25W
Bay Bulls Newfoundland 49 D2 47 19N 52 50W
Bay de Verde tn. Newfoundland 49 D2 48 03N 52 54W
Bay du Nord Wilderness Reserve Newfoundland 49 D2 48 10N 54 55W
Bayers Lake Nova Scotia 53 P6 44 38N 63 39W
Bayfield Ontario 44 A2 43 33N 81 41W
Bayfield River Ontario 44 A2 43 34N 81 38W
Bay Roberts tn. Newfoundland 49 D2 47 36N 53 16W
Beachburg Ontario 43 K6 45 44N 76 51W
Beacon Hill British Columbia 35 K2 45 28N 75 35W
Beaconsfield Québec 53 M4 45 26N 73 52W
Beale, Cape British Columbia 34 G4 48 46N 125 10W
Beamsville Ontario 44 C2 43 10N 79 31W
Beardmore Ontario 40 C2 49 36N 87 59W
Bear Island Northwest Territories 40 E3 64 01N 83 13W
Bear Lake Manitoba 39 B3 55 10N 96 30W
Bear River Nova Scotia 49 E6 44 34N 65 40W
Bear River Ontario 53 L2 45 22N 75 29W
Bearskin Lake I.R. Ontario 40 B3 53 50N 90 55W
Beatton River British Columbia 35 D3 57 18N 121 15W
Beatty Saugeen River Ontario 44 B3 44 08N 80 54W
Beattyville Québec 47 A2 48 53N 77 10W
Beauce admin. Québec 43 R7 46 15N 70 55W
Beauceville Québec 47 B2 46 12N 70 45W
Beauharnois admin. Québec 43 N6 45 18N 73 52W
Beaumaris Lake Alberta 54 F5 53 38N 113 32W
Beaumont Alberta 54 G4 53 20N 113 28W
Beauport Québec 47 B2 46 52N 71 12W
Beaupré Québec 47 B2 47 03N 70 56W
Beauséjour Manitoba 39 B2 50 04N 96 30W
Beauval Saskatchewan 38 B3 55 09N 107 35W
Beaverbank Nova Scotia 53 P7 44 48N 63 39W
Beaver Creek Ontario 52 C2 43 51N 79 23W
Beaver Creek tn. Yukon Territory 50 C3 62 20N 140 45W
Beaverdell British Columbia 35 E1 49 25N 119 09W
Beaverhill Lake Alberta 37 C2 53 27N 112 32W
Beaver Hill Lake Manitoba 39 B2 54 50N 95 20W
Beaverlodge Alberta 37 B3 55 13N 119 26W
Beaver River Alberta/Saskatchewan 38 B2 52 10N 108 40W
Beaver River Ontario 40 C4 55 15N 89 00W
Beaver River Ontario 44 B3 44 21N 80 33W
Beaverton Ontario 44 C3 44 25N 79 10W
Beaverton River Ontario 44 C3 44 08N 79 06W
Bécancour Québec 47 B2 46 20N 72 30W
Beckwith Island Ontario 44 C3 44 53N 80 06W
Beddington Creek Alberta 54 A2 51 15N 114 11W
Bedford Nova Scotia 49 F6 44 44N 64 40W
Bedford Basin Nova Scotia 53 P6 44 41N 63 37W
Beechey Head c. British Columbia 34 H4 48 19N 123 39W
Beechville Nova Scotia 53 P6 44 37N 63 42W
Beeton Ontario 44 C3 44 04N 79 46W
Beiseker Alberta 37 C2 51 23N 113 32W
Belair Provincial Forest Manitoba 39 B2 50 38N 96 40W
Belcher Islands Northwest Territories 51 R2 56 00N 79 30W
Bella Coola British Columbia 35 C2 52 30N 126 50W
Bella Coola River British Columbia 35 C2 52 22N 126 35W
Bellcarra British Columbia 52 G4 49 19N 122 56W
Belle Bay Newfoundland 49 C2 47 37N 55 18W
Bellechasse admin. Québec 43 R6 46 40N 70 50W
Belledune New Brunswick 49 A2 47 50N 65 45W
Belle Isle i. Newfoundland 48 C3 51 57N 55 21W
Belleoram Newfoundland 49 C2 47 31N 55 25W
Belle Plaine Saskatchewan 38 B2 50 25N 105 09W
Belle River tn. Ontario 41 D1 42 18N 82 43W
Belleville Ontario 41 E1 44 10N 77 23W
Bell-Irving River British Columbia 34 C3 56 42N 129 40W
Bell Island Newfoundland 49 C3 50 50N 55 35W
Bell Peninsula Northwest Territories 51 Q3 64 00N 81 30W
Bells Corners tn. Ontario 53 J2 45 19N 75 49W
Belly River Alberta 37 C1 49 10N 113 40W
Belmont Ontario 44 A1 42 52N 81 06W
Beloeil Québec 43 N6 45 34N 73 15W
Belwood, Lake Ontario 44 B2 43 46N 80 20W
Benedict Mountains Newfoundland 48 C4 54 35N 58 35W
Bengough Saskatchewan 38 B1 49 25N 105 10W
Benito Manitoba 39 A2 51 55N 101 30W
Bentley Alberta 37 C2 52 28N 114 04W
Berens River Manitoba/Ontario 39 B2 52 10N 96 40W
Berens River tn. Manitoba 39 B2 52 22N 97 00W
Beresford New Brunswick 49 A2 47 40N 65 40W
Bergland Ontario 40 B2 48 57N 94 23W
Bernier Bay Northwest Territories 51 P5 71 05N 88 15W
Berthier Québec 43 M8 47 15N 74 40W
Bertrand New Brunswick 49 A2 47 45N 65 05W
Berwick Nova Scotia 49 F7 45 03N 64 44W
Berwyn Alberta 37 B3 56 09N 117 44W
Besnard Lake Saskatchewan 38 B3 55 30N 106 10W
Bethany Ontario 44 D3 44 11N 78 34W
Betsiamites Québec 47 C2 48 56N 68 40W
Bible Hill tn. Nova Scotia 49 F7 45 25N 63 17W
Bienfait Saskatchewan 38 C1 49 09N 102 48W
Big Bay tn. British Columbia 34 G5 50 24N 125 08W
Big Creek Ontario 44 B1 42 43N 80 33W
Biggar Saskatchewan 38 B2 52 03N 107 59W

Bighead River Ontario 44 B3 44 30N 80 47W
Big Indian Lake Nova Scotia 53 P6 44 35N 63 42W
Big Island Northwest Territories 51 S3 62 43N 70 43W
Big Island Ontario 40 B2 49 10N 94 30W
Big Island Lake Alberta 54 H4 53 28N 113 12W
Big Lake Alberta 54 F5 53 37N 113 40W
Big Muddy Lake Saskatchewan 38 C1 49 10N 104 50W
Big Otter Creek Ontario 44 B1 42 46N 80 51W
Big River Newfoundland 48 C3 54 50N 59 10W
Big River tn. Saskatchewan 38 B2 53 50N 107 01W
Big Salmon Range mts. Yukon Territory 50 E3 62 00N 134 30W
Big Sand Lake Manitoba 39 B3 57 50N 99 30W
Big Silver Creek British Columbia 34 H4 49 50N 121 50W
Bigstick Lake Saskatchewan 38 B2 50 20N 109 50W
Bigstone Lake Manitoba 39 B2 53 30N 95 50W
Big Trout Lake tn. Ontario 40 C3 53 45N 89 50W
Big Trout Lake Ontario 40 C3 53 40N 90 00W
Birch Cove Nova Scotia 53 P6 44 40N 63 39W
Birch Hills Saskatchewan 38 B2 53 00N 105 10W
Birch Island Manitoba 39 B2 52 20N 99 50W
Birch Lake Alberta 37 C2 53 19N 111 35W
Birch Lake Ontario 40 B3 51 20N 92 20W
Birch Mountains Alberta 37 C3 57 20N 113 55W
Birch River Alberta 37 B3 59 00N 113 20W
Birds Hill Manitoba 54 E2 49 58N 97 59W
Birken British Columbia 34 H5 50 29N 122 36W
Birkenhead Lake Provincial Park British Columbia 34 H5 50 35N 122 42W
Birtle Manitoba 39 A2 50 26N 101 04W
Biscotasing Ontario 41 D2 47 17N 82 06W
Bishop's Falls tn. Newfoundland 49 C2 49 01N 55 30W
Bistcho Lake Alberta 37 B3 59 45N 118 50W
Bjorne Peninsula Northwest Territories 51 P6 77 37N 87 00W
Black Bay Ontario 40 C2 48 42N 88 26W
Black Bear Island Lake Saskatchewan 38 B3 55 45N 105 50W
Black Birch Lake Saskatchewan 38 B3 56 55N 107 25W
Blackburn Ontario 53 K2 45 26N 75 33W
Black Diamond Alberta 37 C2 50 45N 114 12W
Blackfalds Alberta 37 C2 52 23N 113 47W
Black Island Manitoba 39 B2 51 10N 96 20W
Black Island tn. Newfoundland 48 C3 54 20N 57 50W
Black Lake tn. Québec 43 Q7 46 03N 71 21W
Black Lake Saskatchewan 38 C3 59 10N 104 30W
Black Lake tn. Saskatchewan 38 B3 59 05N 105 35W
Blackmud Creek Alberta 54 F4 53 25N 113 33W
Black River Ontario 44 C3 44 48N 79 08W
Blacks Harbour tn. New Brunswick 49 A2 45 03N 66 49W
Blackville New Brunswick 49 A2 46 44N 65 51W
Blackwater Lake Northwest Territories 50 G3 63 55N 123 05W
Blaine Lake tn. Saskatchewan 38 B2 52 50N 106 54W
Blainville Québec 53 M5 45 39N 73 52W
Blair Ontario 44 B2 43 23N 80 23W
Blanc-Sablon Québec 46 E3 51 26N 57 08W
Blenheim Ontario 41 D1 42 20N 82 00W
Blind River tn. Ontario 41 D2 46 10N 82 58W
Bloodvein River Manitoba 39 B2 51 50N 96 40W
Bloomfield Ontario 43 J4 43 59N 77 14W
Blubber Bay tn. British Columbia 34 H4 49 48N 124 37W
Bluenose Lake Northwest Territories 50 H4 68 30N 119 35W
Blue Ridge tn. Alberta 37 B2 54 08N 115 22W
Blue River tn. British Columbia 35 E2 52 05N 119 09W
Blyth Ontario 44 A2 43 43N 81 26W
Blyth Brook Ontario 44 A2 43 45N 81 31W
Boag Lake Alberta 54 H5 53 31N 113 09W
Bobcaygeon Ontario 41 D1 44 32N 78 33W
Boisbriand Québec 53 M5 45 35N 73 51W
Boissevain Manitoba 39 A1 49 14N 100 02W
Bolton Ontario 44 C2 43 53N 79 44W
Bonavista Newfoundland 49 D2 48 39N 53 07W
Bonavista Bay Newfoundland 49 D2 48 45N 53 30W
Bonavista Peninsula Newfoundland 49 D2 48 50N 53 30W
Bon Echo Provincial Park Ontario 43 J5 44 55N 77 15W
Bonnet Plume River Yukon Territory 50 E4 65 00N 134 15W
Bonnyville Alberta 37 C2 54 16N 110 44W
Boothia, Gulf of Northwest Territories 51 P4 69 00N 88 00W
Boothia Peninsula Northwest Territories 51 N5 70 30N 94 30W
Borden Prince Edward Island 49 F7 46 20N 63 40W
Borden Island Northwest Territories 50 J6 78 30N 110 30W
Borden Peninsula Northwest Territories 51 Q5 73 00N 82 30W
Boston Bar British Columbia 34 H4 49 52N 121 25W
Botwood Newfoundland 49 C2 49 09N 55 21W
Boucherville Québec 53 O5 45 35N 73 30W
Bouctouche New Brunswick 49 F7 46 30N 64 48W
Boundary Range mts. British Columbia 34 B3 58 00N 133 00W
Bourne, Cape Northwest Territories 51 N7 81 35N 91 50W
Bowden Alberta 37 C2 51 55N 114 02W
Bowen Island British Columbia 34 H4 49 23N 123 26W
Bow Island tn. Alberta 37 C1 49 52N 111 22W
Bowman Bay Wildlife Sanctuary Northwest Territories 51 S4 66 00N 74 00W
Bowmanville Ontario 44 D2 43 55N 78 40W
Bowmanville Creek Ontario 44 D3 44 02N 78 47W
Bowness Alberta 54 A2 51 05N 114 14W
Bow River Alberta 37 C2 50 47N 111 55W
Bowron Lake Provincial Park British Columbia 35 D2 53 00N 121 00W
Bowron River British Columbia 35 D2 53 38N 121 40W
Bowser British Columbia 34 H4 49 26N 124 41W

Boyle Alberta 37 C2 54 35N 112 49W
Boyne River Ontario 44 B3 44 07N 80 07W
Bracebridge Ontario 41 E2 45 02N 79 19W
Bradford West Gwillimbury Ontario 41 E1 44 07N 79 34W
Bralorne British Columbia 34 H5 50 46N 122 51W
Bramalea Ontario 52 B1 43 44N 79 44W
Brampton Ontario 52 A1 43 42N 79 46W
Brant admin. Ontario 44 B2 43 03N 80 29W
Brantford Ontario 41 D1 43 09N 80 17W
Bras d'Or Lake Nova Scotia 49 F7 45 50N 60 50W
Brazeau, Mount Alberta 37 B2 52 33N 117 21W
Brazeau River Alberta 37 B2 52 50N 116 20W
Brechin Ontario 44 C3 44 32N 79 11W
Bremner Alberta 54 H5 53 53N 113 13W
Brent Ontario 42 H7 46 02N 78 29W
Breton, Cape Nova Scotia 49 G7 45 50N 59 50W
Breton Cove tn. Nova Scotia 49 F7 46 30N 60 30W
Bretona Alberta 54 G4 53 26N 113 19W
Brevoort Island Northwest Territories 51 U3 63 19N 64 08W
Bridgenorth Ontario 44 D3 44 23N 78 23W
Bridge River British Columbia 34 H5 50 55N 123 25W
Bridgetown Nova Scotia 49 E6 44 50N 65 20W
Bridgewater Nova Scotia 49 F6 44 23N 64 32W
Brier Island Nova Scotia 49 F6 44 15N 66 20W
Brighouse British Columbia 52 F3 49 09N 123 11W
Brighton Ontario 41 E1 44 07N 77 45W
Bristol New Brunswick 49 A2 46 28N 67 34W
Britannia Beach tn. British Columbia 34 H4 49 38N 123 10W
British Columbia prov. 8 K4 56 50N 125 30W
British Empire Range mts. Northwest Territories 51 R7 82 30N 78 10W
British Mountains Yukon Territory/Alaska U.S.A. 50 C4 69 00N 141 00W
Britt Ontario 41 D2 45 46N 80 33W
Broadview Saskatchewan 38 C2 50 22N 102 31W
Brochet Manitoba 39 A3 57 55N 101 40W
Brodeur Peninsula Northwest Territories 51 P5 72 30N 87 30W
Brome admin. Québec 43 P6 45 10N 72 30W
Bromont Québec 43 P6 45 19N 72 38W
Bronte Ontario 44 C2 43 23N 79 43W
Brookfield Nova Scotia 49 F7 45 15N 63 18W
Brooklyn Nova Scotia 49 F6 44 04N 64 42W
Brooks Alberta 37 C2 50 35N 111 54W
Brooks Peninsula British Columbia 35 C2 50 05N 127 45W
Brooks Peninsula Recreational Area British Columbia 35 C2 50 08N 127 45W
Brossard Québec 47 B2 45 28N 73 30W
Broughton Island (Qikiqtarjuaq) tn. Northwest Territories 51 U4 67 30N 63 50W
Brown Lake Northwest Territories 51 N4 65 54N 91 15W
Bruce admin. Ontario 44 A3 44 15N 81 24W
Bruce Creek Ontario 52 C4 43 55N 79 20W
Bruce Mines tn. Ontario 41 D2 46 18N 83 48W
Bruce Peninsula Ontario 44 A4 45 00N 81 20W
Bruce Peninsula National Park Ontario 44 A4 45 00N 81 20W
Bruderheim Alberta 37 C2 53 47N 112 56W
Brunette Island Newfoundland 49 C2 47 16N 55 55W
Bruno Saskatchewan 38 B2 52 17N 105 31W
Brussels Ontario 44 A2 43 44N 81 15W
Buchan Gulf Northwest Territories 51 S5 71 47N 74 16W
Buchans Newfoundland 49 C2 48 49N 56 53W
Buckhorn Ontario 44 D3 44 33N 78 20W
Buckhorn Lake Ontario 44 D3 44 29N 78 25W
Buckingham Québec 47 A2 45 35N 75 25W
Buckinghorse River tn. British Columbia 35 D3 57 25N 122 50W
Buffalo Head Hills Alberta 37 B3 57 25N 115 55W
Buffalo Lake Alberta 37 C2 52 27N 112 54W
Buffalo Narrows tn. Saskatchewan 38 B3 55 52N 108 28W
Buffalo River Alberta 37 C3 59 25N 114 35W
Buffalo Trail Alberta 37 C2 51 45N 110 35W
Bulkley River British Columbia 35 C2 55 00N 127 10W
Buntzen Lake British Columbia 52 G4 49 20N 124 51W
Burden, Mount British Columbia 35 D3 56 10N 123 09W
Burford Ontario 44 B2 43 46N 80 25W
Burgeo Newfoundland 49 C2 47 37N 57 37W
Burin Newfoundland 49 C2 47 02N 55 10W
Burin Peninsula Newfoundland 49 C2 47 00N 55 40W
Burk's Falls tn. Ontario 41 E2 45 37N 79 25W
Burlington Ontario 44 C2 43 19N 79 48W
Burnaby British Columbia 34 H4 49 16N 122 58W
Burnaby Lake British Columbia 52 G3 49 14N 122 57W
Burns British Columbia 54 A1 50 59N 114 02W
Burnside Nova Scotia 53 P6 44 41N 63 35W
Burnside River Northwest Territories 50 K4 66 20N 109 30W
Burns Lake tn. British Columbia 35 C2 54 14N 125 45W
Burnt Islands tn. Newfoundland 49 C2 47 36N 58 50W
Burnt Lake Québec 47 D3 52 15N 63 50W
Burnt River Ontario 44 D3 44 41N 78 43W
Burntwood Lake Manitoba 39 A3 55 20N 100 10W
Burntwood River Manitoba 39 B3 55 50N 97 40W
Burquitlam British Columbia 52 G4 49 15N 122 56W
Burrard Inlet British Columbia 52 F4 49 19N 123 14W
Burstall Saskatchewan 38 B2 50 40N 109 56W
Burwash Landing Yukon Territory 40 D3 61 21N 139 01W
Bushell Park Saskatchewan 38 B2 50 25N 105 30W
Butedale British Columbia 34 C2 53 12N 128 45W
Bute Inlet British Columbia 34 H5 50 31N 124 59W
Buttle Lake British Columbia 34 G4 49 47N 125 30W
Button Bay Manitoba 39 C3 58 50N 94 30W
Button Islands Northwest Territories 46 D5 60 35N 64 45W

Buttonville Ontario 52 C2 43 51N 79 22W
Byam Channel Northwest Territories 51 K6 75 10N 105 00W
Byam Martin Island Northwest Territories 51 L6 75 15N 104 15W
Bylot Island Northwest Territories 51 R5 73 30N 79 00W
Bylot Island Bird Sanctuary Northwest Territories 51 R5 73 30N 79 00W
Byron Bay Newfoundland 48 C3 54 40N 57 50W

C

Cabano Québec 47 C2 47 40N 68 56W
Cabot Head Ontario 44 A4 45 15N 81 17W
Cabot Lake Newfoundland 48 B4 56 09N 62 37W
Cabot Strait Nova Scotia/Newfoundland 49 C2 47 10N 59 30W
Cabri Saskatchewan 38 B2 50 38N 108 28W
Cache Creek tn. British Columbia 35 D2 50 46N 121 17W
Calabogie Ontario 43 K6 45 18N 76 43W
Calais New Brunswick 49 A2 45 10N 67 15W
Caledon East Ontario 44 C2 43 52N 79 53W
Caledonia Nova Scotia 49 E6 44 24N 65 02W
Caledonia Ontario 44 C2 43 05N 79 57W
Caledon Village Ontario 44 C2 43 51N 79 59W
Calgary Alberta 37 C2 51 05N 114 05W
Calgary City admin. Alberta 54 A2 51 10N 114 09W
Calgary Trail hwy. Alberta 54 F4 53 21N 113 32W
Callander Ontario 42 G7 46 13N 79 24W
Calling Lake Alberta 37 C3 55 15N 113 20W
Calmar Alberta 37 C2 53 16N 113 49W
Calvert Island British Columbia 35 C2 51 30N 128 00W
Camanah Pacific Provincial Park British Columbia 34 H4 48 40N 124 35W
Cambridge Ontario 44 C2 43 22N 80 20W
Cambridge Bay (Ikaluktutiak) tn. Northwest Territories 50 K4 69 09N 105 00W
Cambridge-Narrows New Brunswick 49 A2 45 50N 65 55W
Cameron Hills Alberta 37 B3 59 48N 118 00W
Campbell Dam Saskatchewan 38 B2 50 40N 103 20W
Campbellford Ontario 41 E1 44 18N 77 48W
Campbell Lake British Columbia 34 G5 50 02N 125 30W
Campbell, Mount Yukon Territory 50 D3 64 23N 138 43W
Campbell River tn. British Columbia 34 G5 50 00N 125 18W
Campbells Cove tn. Prince Edward Island 49 F7 46 30N 62 15W
Campbellton New Brunswick 49 A2 48 00N 66 41W
Campbellton Newfoundland 49 D2 49 17N 54 56W
Campbellville Ontario 44 C2 43 29N 79 59W
Camperville Manitoba 39 A2 51 00N 100 08W
Campobello Island New Brunswick 49 A1 44 50N 66 50W
Camp Robinson Ontario 40 B3 50 08N 93 12W
Camrose Alberta 37 C2 53 01N 112 50W
Camsell Portage Saskatchewan 38 B3 59 39N 109 12W
CANADA 8/9
Canadian Pacific Irrigational Canal Alberta 53 B1 50 56N 113 57W
Canadian Shield mts. Canada 111 Q13/S12 50 00N 90 00W
Canal Flats tn. British Columbia 35 E2 50 09N 115 50W
Canal Lake Ontario 44 C3 44 34N 79 02W
Candiac Québec 53 N4 45 24N 73 31W
Candle Lake Saskatchewan 38 B2 53 55N 105 10W
Candle Lake tn. Saskatchewan 38 B2 53 50N 105 10W
Canmore Alberta 37 B2 51 07N 115 18W
Canning Nova Scotia 49 F7 45 12N 64 26W
Canoe Lake Saskatchewan 38 B3 55 10N 108 30W
Canora Saskatchewan 38 C2 51 38N 102 28W
Canso Saskatchewan 49 F7 45 20N 61 00W
Canso, Cape Nova Scotia 49 F7 45 19N 60 59W
Cap-aux-Meules tn. Québec 47 D2 47 25N 62 00W
Cap-Chat tn. Québec 47 C2 49 06N 66 42W
Cap-de-la-Madeleine tn. Québec 47 B2 46 22N 72 32W
Cap de Nouvelle-France c. Québec 46 B5 62 30N 73 45W
Cap Dufferin c. Québec 46 A4 58 35N 78 32W
Cape Breton admin. Nova Scotia 49 F7 45 50N 60 30W
Cape Breton Highlands National Park Nova Scotia 49 F7 46 45N 60 40W
Cape Breton Island Nova Scotia 49 F7 46 10N 61 00W
Cape Charles tn. Newfoundland 49 D3 52 13N 55 38W
Cape Croker c. Ontario 44 B3 44 56N 81 01W
Cape Croker Ontario 44 A3 44 56N 81 01W
Cape Dorset (Kingnait) tn. Northwest Territories 51 R3 64 10N 76 40W
Cape Dorset Sanctuaries Northwest Territories 51 R3 64 05N 76 40W
Cape Dyer m.s. Northwest Territories 51 U4 66 37N 61 16W
Cape Le Havre Island Nova Scotia 49 F6 44 10N 64 20W
Cape North tn. Nova Scotia 49 F5 46 50N 60 30W
Cape Sable Island Nova Scotia 49 E6 43 30N 65 37W
Cape St. George tn. Newfoundland 49 C2 48 28N 59 15W
Cape Scott Provincial Park British Columbia 35 C2 50 42N 128 20W
Cape Smith tn. Northwest Territories 46 A5 60 44N 78 29W
Cape Tormentine tn. New Brunswick 49 F7 46 08N 63 47W
Cap Gaspé c. Québec 47 D2 48 46N 64 10W
Cap Hopes Advance c. Québec 46 C5 61 02N 69 38W
Capilano Lake British Columbia 52 F4 49 22N 123 06W
Cap Pelé tn. New Brunswick 49 F7 46 10N 64 10W
Cap Prince-de-Galles c. Québec 46 B5 61 42N 71 30W
Capreol Ontario 41 D2 46 43N 80 56W
Cap-Rouge c. Québec 47 B2 46 45N 71 32W
Cap-Saint-Ignace tn. Québec 43 R8 47 02N 70 29W
Capstick Nova Scotia 49 F7 47 02N 60 31W
Caramat Ontario 41 C2 49 37N 86 09W
Caraquet New Brunswick 49 B2 47 48N 64 59W

Carberry Manitoba 39 B1 49 52N 99 20W
Carbonear Newfoundland 49 D2 47 44N 53 13W
Carcross Yukon Territory 50 E3 60 11N 134 41W
Cardigan Prince Edward Island 49 F7 46 14N 62 37W
Cardinal Ontario 43 L5 44 47N 75 23W
Cardston Alberta 37 C1 49 12N 113 18W
Cariboo Mountains British Columbia 35 D2 53 20N 120 50W
Caribou Manitoba 39 B3 59 20N 97 50W
Caribou Mountains Alberta 37 B3 59 00N 115 30W
Caribou River Manitoba 39 B3 59 30N 95 50W
Carleton admin. New Brunswick 49 A2 46 20N 67 30W
Carleton Ontario 43 L2 48 08N 66 10W
Carleton, Mount New Brunswick 49 A2 47 24N 66 52W
Carleton Place Ontario 41 E2 45 08N 76 09W
Carling Ontario 44 B4 45 24N 80 09W
Carlsbad Springs Ontario 53 L2 45 22N 75 29W
Carlson Landing Alberta 37 C3 58 59N 111 45W
Carlyle Saskatchewan 38 C1 49 39N 102 18W
Carmacks Yukon Territory 50 D3 62 04N 136 21W
Carman Manitoba 39 B1 49 32N 97 59W
Carmanville Newfoundland 49 D2 49 24N 54 18W
Carnduff Saskatchewan 38 C1 49 11N 101 50W
Carp Lake British Columbia 35 D2 54 48N 123 20W
Carp Lake Provincial Park British Columbia 35 D2 54 08N 123 30W
Carp River Ontario 53 J2 45 18N 75 55W
Carrot River Manitoba 39 B2 54 50N 96 40W
Carrot River Saskatchewan 38 C2 53 05N 104 15W
Carrot River tn. Saskatchewan 38 C2 53 18N 103 32W
Carstairs Alberta 37 C2 51 34N 114 06W
Cartierville Québec 53 N5 45 31N 73 43W
Cartmel, Mount British Columbia 34 C3 57 45N 129 12W
Cartwright Newfoundland 48 C3 53 42N 57 01W
Cascade Range mts. British Columbia 34 H4 50 48N 121 15W
Cascade Recreation Area British Columbia 34 H4 49 16N 120 56W
Cascumpec Bay Prince Edward Island 49 F7 46 45N 64 00W
Casselman Ontario 43 L6 45 19N 75 07W
Cassia Mountains British Columbia 34/35 B3 59 50N 131 50W
Cassiar British Columbia 34 C3 59 15N 129 49W
Cassiar Highway British Columbia 34 B3 57 30N 130 10W
Castlegar British Columbia 35 E1 49 18N 117 41W
Castor Alberta 37 C2 52 13N 111 53W
Catalina Newfoundland 49 D2 48 31N 53 05W
Cat Arm Reservoir Newfoundland 49 C3 50 06N 56 50W
Cathacoma Lake Ontario 44 D3 44 46N 78 16W
Cathedral Provincial Park British Columbia 34 H4 49 05N 120 11W
Cat Lake Ontario 40 B3 51 30N 91 50W
Cat Lake I.R. Ontario 40 B3 51 40N 91 50W
Caubvick, Mount (Mont D'Iberville) Newfoundland/Québec 48 B4 58 50N 63 50W
Causapscal Québec 47 C2 48 22N 67 14W
Cavendish Prince Edward Island 49 F7 46 30N 63 20W
Cawes Lake Alberta 54 G4 53 22N 113 28W
Cayoosh Creek British Columbia 34 H5 50 20N 122 20W
Cayuga Ontario 44 C1 42 57N 79 50W
Cecil Lake tn. British Columbia 35 D3 56 19N 120 40W
Cedar Lake Manitoba 39 A2 53 40N 100 30W
Central Butte Saskatchewan 38 B2 50 50N 106 30W
Central Patricia Ontario 40 B3 51 30N 90 09W
Centreville Newfoundland 49 D2 49 01N 53 53W
Centreville Nova Scotia 49 F7 45 10N 64 30W
C. F. B. Boden Ontario 44 C3 44 18N 79 54W
Chalk River Ontario 41 E2 46 01N 77 28W
Chalk River tn. Ontario 43 J7 46 01N 77 27W
Chambly Québec 47 B2 45 27N 73 19W
Champlain admin. Québec 43 N8 47 40N 73 30W
Champlain, Lake Lac Champlain Québec/U.S.A. 43 N5 44 50N 73 10W
Chandler Québec 47 D2 48 21N 64 41W
Channel-Port aux Basques Newfoundland 49 C2 47 34N 59 09W
Chantrey Inlet Northwest Territories 51 M4 67 48N 95 50W
Chapais Québec 47 B2 49 47N 74 54W
Chapleau Ontario 41 D2 47 50N 83 24W
Chapleau Crown Game Reserve Ontario 41 D2 48 30N 83 30W
Chaplin Saskatchewan 38 B2 50 29N 106 40W
Chaplin Lake Saskatchewan 38 B2 50 25N 106 30W
Charlesbourg Québec 47 B2 46 53N 71 16W
Charles Island Northwest Territories 51 S3 39 24N 74 15W
Charles Lake Alberta 37 C3 59 50N 110 33W
Charles, Lake Nova Scotia 53 P6 44 43N 63 32W
Charlevoix-Est admin. Québec 43 R8 47 57N 70 10W
Charlevoix-Ouest admin. Québec 43 R8 47 50N 70 55W
Charlo New Brunswick 49 A2 47 55N 66 20W
Charlotte admin. New Brunswick 49 A2 45 20N 67 20W
Charlotte Lake British Columbia 35 C2 52 11N 125 19W
Charlottetown Newfoundland 48 C3 52 45N 56 07W
Charlottetown Prince Edward Island 49 F7 46 14N 63 09W
Charlton Island Northwest Territories 40 E3 52 00N 79 30W
Charron Lake Manitoba 39 B2 52 40N 95 40W
Chase British Columbia 35 E2 50 49N 119 41W
Châteauguay Québec 47 B2 45 20N 73 42W
Chatham New Brunswick 65 J5 47 02N 65 30W
Chatham Ontario 41 D1 42 24N 82 11W
Chatham Sound British Columbia 34 B2 54 30N 130 30W
Chatsworth Ontario 44 B3 44 27N 80 54W
Chedabucto Bay Nova Scotia 49 F7 45 20N 61 10W
Cheepay River Ontario 40 D3 50 50N 83 40W

Chelsea Québec 53 J2 45 29N 75 48W
Chelsea Brook Québec 53 J3 45 31N 75 51W
Chemainus British Columbia 34 H4 48 54N 123 42W
Chemainus River British Columbia 34 H4 48 58N 124 09W
Chemong Lake Ontario 44 D3 44 26N 78 22W
Cheslatta Lake British Columbia 35 C2 53 44N 125 20W
Chesley Ontario 44 A3 44 18N 81 07W
Chester Nova Scotia 49 F6 44 33N 64 16W
Chesterfield Inlet Northwest Territories 51 N3 63 21N 90 42W
Chesterfield Inlet (Igluligaarjuk) tn. Northwest Territories 51 N3 63 21N 90 42W
Chesterville Ontario 43 L6 45 06N 75 14W
Cheticamp Nova Scotia 49 F7 46 37N 60 59W
Cheticamp Island Nova Scotia 49 F7 46 40N 61 05W
Chetwynd British Columbia 35 D3 55 38N 121 40W
Chibougamau Québec 47 B2 49 56N 72 24W
Chicoutimi admin. Québec 43 Q9 48 10N 71 00W
Chicoutimi Québec 47 B2 48 26N 71 06W
Chidley, Cape Northwest Territories 51 U3 60 23N 64 26W
Chignecto Bay Nova Scotia 49 F7 45 40N 64 40W
Chignecto Game Sanctuary Nova Scotia 49 F7 45 30N 64 35W
Chignetto, Cape Nova Scotia 49 F7 45 20N 64 55W
Chilanko Forks British Columbia 35 D2 52 04N 124 00W
Chilcotin River British Columbia 35 D2 51 54N 123 20W
Chilko Lake British Columbia 35 D2 51 15N 124 59W
Chilkoot Trail N.H.S. British Columbia 34 A3 59 48N 135 00W
Chilko River British Columbia 35 D2 51 59N 124 05W
Chilliwack British Columbia 34 H4 49 06N 121 56W
Chilliwack Lake British Columbia 34 H4 49 04N 121 22W
Chilliwack River British Columbia 34 H4 49 04N 121 52W
Chin, Cape Ontario 44 A4 45 05N 81 17W
Chinchaga River British Columbia 37 B3 57 30N 119 00W
Chip Lake Alberta 37 B2 53 40N 115 23W
Chipman New Brunswick 49 A2 46 11N 65 54W
Chippawa Ontario 44 C2 43 03N 79 04W
Chiputneticook Lakes New Brunswick/U.S.A. 47 C1 45 40N 67 45W
Chisasibi (Fort George) Québec 46 A3 53 50N 79 01W
Choiceland Saskatchewan 38 C2 53 30N 104 33W
Chomedey Québec 53 M5 45 32N 73 46W
Chorkbak Inlet Northwest Territories 51 S3 64 30N 74 25W
Chown, Mount Alberta 37 B2 53 24N 119 25W
Christian Island Ontario 44 B3 44 50N 80 14W
Christian Island tn. Ontario 44 B3 44 49N 80 10W
Christie Bay Northwest Territories 50 J3 62 32N 110 44W
Christina River Alberta 37 C3 55 50N 111 59W
Churchbridge Saskatchewan 38 C2 50 55N 101 58W
Churchill Manitoba 39 C3 58 45N 94 00W
Churchill, Cape Manitoba 39 C3 59 00N 93 00W
Churchill Falls tn. Newfoundland 48 B3 53 35N 64 00W
Churchill Lake Saskatchewan 38 B3 56 05N 108 15W
Churchill Peak British Columbia 35 C3 58 20N 125 02W
Churchill River Manitoba/Saskatchewan 38 B3 57 30N 96 00W
Churchill River Newfoundland 48 B3 53 20N 63 40W
Chute-aux-Outardes Québec 47 C2 49 07N 68 25W
Cirque Mountain Newfoundland 48 B4 58 56N 63 33W
City of Edmonton admin. Alberta 54 F4 53 23N 113 30W
City of Winnipeg admin. Manitoba 54 C2 49 55N 97 23W
City View Ontario 53 K2 45 21N 75 44W
Claire Lake Alberta 37 C3 58 40N 112 00W
Clarence Head c. Northwest Territories 51 R6 76 47N 77 47W
Clarenville Newfoundland 49 D2 48 10N 54 00W
Claresholm Alberta 37 C2 50 02N 113 30W
Clarington Ontario 44 D2 43 55N 78 35W
Clarke City Québec 47 C3 50 11N 66 39W
Clark's Harbour tn. Nova Scotia 49 E6 43 25N 65 38W
Clarkson Ontario 44 C2 43 30N 79 38W
Clayoquot Sound British Columbia 35 C1 49 12N 126 05W
Clear Hills British Columbia 37 B3 56 40N 119 30W
Clearwater British Columbia 35 D2 51 37N 120 03W
Clearwater Bay tn. Ontario 40 B2 49 39N 94 48W
Clearwater Lake British Columbia 35 D2 52 13N 120 20W
Clearwater Lake Manitoba 39 A2 53 50N 101 40W
Clearwater Lake Provincial Park Manitoba 39 A2 54 00N 101 00W
Clearwater River Alberta 37 B2 51 59N 115 20W
Clearwater River Alberta/Saskatchewan 37 C3/D3 56 45N 110 59W
Clearwater River Provincial Park Saskatchewan 38 B3 57 10N 108 10W
Clifford Ontario 44 B2 43 58N 80 00W
Climax Saskatchewan 38 B1 49 12N 108 22W
Clinton British Columbia 35 D2 51 05N 121 38W
Clinton Ontario 44 A2 43 36N 81 33W
Clinton-Colden Lake Northwest Territories 50 K3 63 55N 107 27W
Clinton Creek (Fortymile) Yukon Territory 50 C3 64 25N 140 32W
Cloance Alberta 54 G5 53 35N 113 19W
Clover Bar Alberta 54 G5 53 35N 113 19W
Cloverdale British Columbia 52 G3 49 05N 122 46W
Cluff Lake tn. Saskatchewan 38 B3 58 20N 109 35W
Clyde River (Kangiqtugaapik) tn. Northwest Territories 51 T5 70 30N 68 30W
Coaldale Alberta 37 C1 49 43N 112 37W
Coalhurst Alberta 37 C1 49 45N 112 56W
Coal River British Columbia 35 C3 59 56N 127 11W
Coast Mountains British Columbia 34/5 B3-D1 54 30N 128 00W
Coates Creek Ontario 44 B3 44 22N 80 07W

Coaticook Québec 47 B2 45 08N 71 40W
Coats Island Northwest Territories 51 Q3 62 30N 83 00W
Cobalt Ontario 41 E2 47 24N 79 41W
Cobequid Bay Nova Scotia 49 F7 45 20N 63 40W
Cobequid Mountains Nova Scotia 49 F7 45 30N 64 00W
Cobourg Ontario 41 E1 43 58N 78 11W
Cochrane Alberta 37 C2 51 11N 114 28W
Cochrane Ontario 41 D2 49 04N 81 02W
Cochrane River Manitoba/Saskatchewan 38 C3 58 50N 102 20W
Cockburn Island Ontario 42 C6 45 55N 83 22W
Codette Lake Saskatchewan 38 C2 53 15N 104 10W
Cod Island Newfoundland 48 B3 57 47N 61 47W
Colborne Ontario 41 E1 44 00N 77 53W
Colchester admin. Nova Scotia 49 F7 45 30N 63 30W
Cold Lake Alberta 37 C3 54 46N 61 05W
Cold Lake tn. Alberta 37 C2 54 28N 110 15W
Cold Lake Air Weapons Range Alberta 37 C3 55 10N 110 25W
Coldspring Head Nova Scotia 49 F7 45 55N 63 50W
Coldstream British Columbia 35 E2 50 10N 119 12W
Coldwater Ontario 44 C3 44 43N 79 39W
Cole Harbour Nova Scotia 53 Q6 44 40N 63 27W
Cole Harbour tn. Nova Scotia 53 Q6 44 40N 63 30W
Coleman Alberta 64 D6 49 38N 114 28W
Collingwood Ontario 41 D1 44 30N 80 14W
Collins Ontario 40 C3 50 19N 89 27W
Colonsay Saskatchewan 38 B2 51 59N 105 52W
Colpoys Bay Ontario 44 A3 44 48N 81 04W
Columbia, Mount British Columbia/Alberta 37 B2 52 09N 117 25W
Columbia Mountains British Columbia 35 D2 53 12N 120 49W
Columbia River British Columbia 35 E2 51 15N 116 58W
Colville Lake (K'áhbamitué) tn. Northwest Territories 50 F4 67 02N 126 07W
Colville Lake Northwest Territories 50 F4 67 10N 126 30W
Colwood British Columbia 34 H4 48 27N 123 28W
Combermere Ontario 42 J6 45 22N 77 37W
Come by Chance tn. Newfoundland 49 D2 47 48N 53 58W
Comfort Bight tn. Newfoundland 48 C3 53 09N 55 48W
Comma Island Newfoundland 48 B4 55 20N 60 20W
Committee Bay Northwest Territories 51 P4 68 30N 86 30W
Comox British Columbia 34 H4 49 41N 124 56W
Comox Lake British Columbia 34 G4 49 37N 125 10W
Compton admin. Québec 43 Q6 45 20N 71 35W
Conception Bay Newfoundland 49 D2 47 45N 53 00W
Conception Bay South tn. Newfoundland 49 D2 47 30N 53 00W
Conche Newfoundland 49 C3 50 53N 55 54W
Conestogo Lake Ontario 44 B2 43 47N 80 44W
Conestogo River Ontario 44 B2 43 41N 80 42W
Conklin Alberta 37 C3 55 38N 111 05W
Conne River tn. Newfoundland 49 C2 47 50N 55 46W
Consort Alberta 37 C2 52 01N 110 46W
Contrecoeur Québec 43 N6 45 51N 73 15W
Contwoyto Lake Northwest Territories 50 J4 65 42N 110 50W
Cook's Bay Ontario 44 C3 44 53N 79 31W
Cookstown Ontario 44 C3 44 12N 79 42W
Coppermine (Kugluktuk) Northwest Territories 50 H4 67 49N 115 12W
Coppermine River Northwest Territories 50 J4 66 30N 114 40W
Coquihalla Highway British Columbia 34 H4 49 25N 121 20W
Coquitlam British Columbia 52 G4 49 15N 122 52W
Coquitlam Lake British Columbia 52 G4 49 21N 122 46W
Coquitlam River British Columbia 52 G4 49 17N 122 45W
Coral Harbour 65 J7 50 13N 81 41W
Coral Harbour (Salliq) tn. Northwest Territories 51 Q3 64 10N 83 15W
Cormorant Manitoba 39 A2 54 14N 100 35W
Cormorant Lake Manitoba 39 A2 54 10N 101 30W
Cormorant Provincial Forest Manitoba 39 A2 54 10N 100 50W
Corner Brook tn. Newfoundland 49 C2 48 58N 57 58W
Cornwall Ontario 43 M6 45 02N 74 45W
Cornwall Prince Edward Island 49 F7 46 10N 63 10W
Cornwallis Island Northwest Territories 51 M6 75 15N 95 00W
Cornwall Island Northwest Territories 51 M6 77 30N 95 00W
Coronation Alberta 37 C2 52 05N 111 27W
Coronation Gulf Northwest Territories 50 J4 68 15N 112 30W
Cortes Island British Columbia 34 H5 50 07N 125 01W
Côte-St-Luc Québec 53 N4 45 28N 73 39W
Couchiching, Lake Ontario 44 C3 44 39N 79 22W
Courtenay British Columbia 34 H4 49 40N 124 58W
Courtice Ontario 44 D2 43 57N 78 43W
Courtright Ontario 42 D3 42 49N 82 28W
Coutts Alberta 37 C1 49 01N 111 59W
Cove Island Ontario 44 A4 45 19N 81 44W
Cowansville Québec 47 B2 45 13N 72 44W
Cow Bay Nova Scotia 53 Q6 44 36N 63 26W
Cow Head tn. Newfoundland 49 C2 49 55N 57 48W
Cowichan Lake British Columbia 34 H4 48 50N 124 04W
Cowichan River British Columbia 34 H4 48 48N 123 58W
Cox's Cove tn. Newfoundland 49 C2 49 07N 58 04W
Craigallachie British Columbia 35 E2 50 59N 118 38W
Craigleith Provincial Park Ontario 44 B3 44 30N 80 15W
Craik Saskatchewan 38 B2 51 03N 105 50W
Cranberry Portage Manitoba 39 A2 54 36N 101 22W
Cranbrook British Columbia 35 E1 49 29N 115 48W
Crane Lake Saskatchewan 38 B2 50 10N 109 20W
Crane River tn. Manitoba 39 B2 51 30N 99 18W

Crane River Ontario 44 A4 45 53N 81 31W
Credit River Ontario 52 B1 43 35N 79 43W
Cree Lake Saskatchewan 38 B3 57 30N 106 30W
Cree Lake tn. Saskatchewan 38 B3 57 24N 106 45W
Creemore Ontario 44 B3 44 20N 80 07W
Cree River Saskatchewan 38 B3 58 00N 106 30W
Creighton Saskatchewan 38 C2 54 46N 101 54W
Creston British Columbia 35 E1 49 05N 116 32W
Creswell Bay Northwest Territories 51 N5 72 40N 93 30W
Crofton British Columbia 34 H4 48 52N 123 38W
Croker, Cape Ontario 44 B4 44 58N 80 59W
Crossfield Alberta 37 C2 51 26N 114 02W
Cross Lake Manitoba 39 B2 54 50N 97 20W
Cross Lake tn. Manitoba 39 B2 54 38N 97 45W
Crow Lake Ontario 40 B2 49 10N 93 56W
Crowsnest Highway Alberta 37 C1 49 50N 111 55W
Crowsnest Pass Alberta/British Columbia 35 F1 49 40N 114 41W
Crumlin Ontario 44 A2 43 01N 81 08W
Crystal Bay Ontario 53 J2 45 21N 75 51W
Crystal Beach tn. Ontario 44 C1 42 52N 79 03W
Crystal Lake Ontario 44 C3 44 43N 78 30W
Cub Hills, The Saskatchewan 38 C2 54 20N 104 40W
Cudworth Saskatchewan 38 B2 52 31N 105 44W
Cumberland British Columbia 34 H4 49 37N 124 59W
Cumberland admin. Nova Scotia 49 F7 45 30N 64 10W
Cumberland Ontario 53 L3 45 31N 75 23W
Cumberland House tn. Saskatchewan 38 C2 53 57N 102 20W
Cumberland Lake Saskatchewan 38 C2 54 10N 102 30W
Cumberland Peninsula Northwest Territories 51 U4 66 30N 63 00W
Cumberland Sound Northwest Territories 51 T4 65 30N 66 00W
Cupar Saskatchewan 38 C2 50 57N 104 12W
Cushing, Mount British Columbia 35 C3 57 36N 126 51W
Cut Knife Saskatchewan 38 B2 52 45N 109 01W
Cypress Hills Alberta/Saskatchewan 38 B1 49 32N 109 45W
Cypress Hills Provincial Park Saskatchewan/Alberta 37 C1/D1 49 40N 110 00W

D

Dalhousie Alberta 54 A2 51 06N 114 10W
Dalhousie New Brunswick 49 A2 48 03N 66 22W
Dalhousie, Cape Northwest Territories 50 F5 70 14N 129 42W
Dalmeny Saskatchewan 38 B2 52 22N 106 46W
Dalrymple Lake Ontario 44 C3 44 41N 79 07W
Daniel's Harbour tn. Newfoundland 49 C3 50 14N 57 35W
Danville Québec 43 P6 45 48N 72 01W
D'Arcy British Columbia 34 H5 50 33N 122 28W
Darlington Provincial Park Ontario 44 D2 43 46N 78 46W
Darnley Bay Northwest Territories 50 G4 69 30N 123 30W
Dartmouth Nova Scotia 49 F6 44 40N 63 35W
Dauphin Manitoba 39 A2 51 09N 100 05W
Dauphin, Cape Nova Scotia 49 F7 46 20N 60 25W
Dauphin Lake Manitoba 39 B2 51 10N 99 30W
Dauphin River Manitoba 39 B2 51 50N 98 20W
Dauphin River tn. Manitoba 39 B2 51 50N 98 00W
Davidson Saskatchewan 38 B2 51 15N 105 59W
David Thompson Highway Alberta 37 B2 52 15N 116 35W
Davin Lake Saskatchewan 38 C3 56 45N 103 40W
Davis Inlet tn. Newfoundland 48 B4 55 51N 60 52W
Davy Lake Saskatchewan 38 B3 58 50N 108 10W
Dawson Yukon Territory 50 D3 64 04N 139 24W
Dawson Bay Manitoba 39 A2 52 50N 100 50W
Dawson Creek tn. British Columbia 35 D3 55 44N 120 15W
Dawson, Mount British Columbia 35 E2 51 08N 117 26W
Dawson Range mts. Yukon Territory 50 D3 63 00N 139 30W
Dawsons Landing British Columbia 35 C2 51 28N 127 33W
Daysland Alberta 37 C2 52 52N 112 15W
Dean Channel British Columbia 35 C2 52 18N 127 35W
Dean River British Columbia 35 C2 52 45N 122 30W
Dease Arm b. Northwest Territories 50 G4 66 52N 120 00W
Dease Lake British Columbia 34 B3 58 05N 130 04W
Dease Lake tn. British Columbia 34 B3 58 28N 130 00W
Dease River British Columbia 34 C3 59 05N 129 40W
Dease Strait Northwest Territories 50 K4 68 40N 108 00W
Deas Island British Columbia 52 F3 49 07N 123 04W
Decelles, Réservoir res. Québec 47 A2 47 40N 78 05W
Déception Québec 46 B5 62 10N 74 45W
Dee Lake British Columbia 52 G3 49 14N 122 59W
Deep Cove British Columbia 52 G4 49 19N 122 58W
Deep Inlet Newfoundland 48 B4 55 22N 60 14W
Deep River tn. Ontario 41 E2 46 06N 77 30W
Deerfoot Trail Alberta 54 A2 51 08N 114 01W
Deer Island New Brunswick 49 A1 45 09N 67 00W
Deer Lake tn. Newfoundland 49 C2 49 11N 57 27W
Deer Lake Ontario 40 B2 52 38N 94 25W
Dégelis Québec 47 C2 47 34N 68 40W
Delhi Ontario 44 B1 42 51N 80 30W
Déline (Fort Franklin) Northwest Territories 50 G4 65 11N 123 26W
Delisle Saskatchewan 38 B2 51 56N 107 10W
Deloraine Manitoba 39 A1 49 11N 100 30W
Delta British Columbia 34 H4 49 06N 123 01W
Dempster Highway Yukon Territory/Northwest Territories 50 D4 65 40N 138 10W
Denbigh Ontario 43 J6 45 08N 77 15W
Deninue Kué (Fort Resolution) Northwest Territories 50 J3 61 10N 113 39W
Denman Island British Columbia 34 H4 49 32N 124 49W
Deschambault Lake Saskatchewan 38 C2 54 50N 103 50W

Deseronto Ontario 41 E1 44 12N 77 03W
Desmaraisville Québec 47 A2 49 31N 76 11W
Desolation Sound Marine Park British Columbia 34 H5 50 08N 124 45W
Détroit de Jacques-Cartier sd. Québec 47 D3 50 10N 64 10W
Détroit de Juan de Fuca sd. British Columbia 34 H4 48 18N 123 51W
Détroit d'Honguedo sd. Québec 47 D2 49 30N 64 20W
Détroit d'Hudson (Hudson Strait) Québec/Northwest Territories 46 B5 62 00N 70 00W
Detroit River Ontario/U.S.A. 42 C3 42 15N 83 05W
Deux-Montagnes Québec 53 M5 45 32N 73 56W
Deux Rivières Ontario 42 H7 46 15N 78 17W
Devil's Glen Provincial Park Ontario 44 B3 44 20N 80 30W
Devon Alberta 37 C2 53 22N 113 44W
Devon Island Northwest Territories 51 P6 75 20N 87 30W
Dewar Lakes Northwest Territories 51 S4 68 30N 71 20W
Dewey Soper Game Sanctuary Northwest Territories 51 S4 66 20N 73 50W
Diamond Jenness Peninsula Northwest Territories 50 H5 71 20N 117 00W
Dickson Peak British Columbia 34 H5 50 54N 122 59W
Didsbury Alberta 37 C2 51 40N 114 08W
Diefenbaker, Lake Saskatchewan 38 B2 51 10N 107 30W
Dieppe New Brunswick 49 F7 46 07N 64 49W
Digby admin. Nova Scotia 49 E6 44 20N 65 40W
Digby Nova Scotia 49 E6 44 37N 65 47W
Digby Neck p. Nova Scotia 49 E6 44 30N 66 00W
Dillon Saskatchewan 38 B3 55 56N 108 54W
Dingwall Nova Scotia 49 F7 46 55N 60 29W
Dinorwic Ontario 40 B2 49 41N 92 30W
Disappointment Lake Newfoundland 48 B3 53 49N 62 31W
Dismal Lakes Northwest Territories 50 H4 67 26N 117 07W
Disraeli Québec 43 Q6 45 54N 71 22W
Dixon Entrance sd. British Columbia/Alaska U.S.A. 34 B2 54 28N 132 50W
Doaktown New Brunswick 49 A2 46 34N 66 06W
Dobie River Ontario 40 B3 51 30N 90 05W
Dodge Lake Saskatchewan 38 B3 59 50N 105 25W
Dodsland Saskatchewan 38 B2 51 48N 108 51W
Dog Creek tn. British Columbia 35 D2 51 35N 122 18W
Dog (High) Island Newfoundland 48 B4 56 38N 61 10W
Dog Lake Manitoba 39 B2 51 00N 98 20W
Dog Lake Ontario 41 C2 48 50N 89 30W
Dolbeau Québec 47 B2 48 52N 72 15W
Dollard-des-Ormeaux Québec 53 M4 45 29N 73 50W
Dollarton British Columbia 52 G4 49 18N 122 58W
Dolphin and Union Strait Northwest Territories 50 H4 69 05N 116 00W
Dominion Nova Scotia 49 F7 46 12N 60 01W
Dominion Lake Newfoundland 48 B3 52 35N 61 43W
Don Mills Ontario 52 C1 43 44N 79 22W
Donnacona Québec 47 B2 46 41N 71 45W
Don River Ontario 52 C2 43 48N 79 24W
D'Or, Cape Nova Scotia 49 F7 45 20N 64 50W
Dorcas Bay Ontario 44 A4 45 10N 81 38W
Dorchester New Brunswick 49 F7 45 54N 64 32W
Dorchester admin. Québec 43 R7 46 20N 70 30W
Dorchester, Cape Northwest Territories 51 R4 65 27N 77 27W
Dore Lake Saskatchewan 38 B2 54 50N 107 20W
Dorion Ontario 41 C2 48 49N 88 33W
Dorset Ontario 41 E2 45 14N 78 54W
Dorval Québec 53 N4 45 27N 73 44W
Double Mer in. Newfoundland 48 C3 54 04N 59 10W
Douglas Island British Columbia 52 G4 49 13N 122 46W
Dowling Ontario 41 D2 46 32N 81 21W
Dowling Lake British Columbia 37 C2 51 44N 112 00W
Downton Lake British Columbia 34 H5 50 48N 123 10W
Downton, Mount British Columbia 35 D2 52 45N 124 53W
Dows Lake Ontario 53 K2 45 24N 75 42W
Drayton Ontario 44 B2 43 45N 80 40W
Drayton Valley tn. Alberta 37 C2 53 13N 114 59W
Dresden Ontario 42 D3 42 34N 82 11W
Drowning River Ontario 40 C3 50 30N 86 10W
Drumheller Alberta 37 C2 51 28N 112 40W
Drummond admin. Québec 43 P6 45 50N 72 30W
Drummondville Québec 47 B2 45 52N 72 30W
Dryden Ontario 40 B2 49 48N 92 48W
Drylake tn. Newfoundland 48 A3 52 38N 65 59W
Dubawnt Lake Northwest Territories 51 L3 63 08N 101 30W
Dubreuilville Ontario 41 D2 48 21N 84 32W
Duck Bay tn. Manitoba 39 A2 52 10N 100 10W
Duck Lake tn. Saskatchewan 38 B2 52 52N 106 12W
Duck Mountain Provincial Forest Manitoba 39 A2 51 20N 100 50W
Duck Mountain Provincial Park Manitoba 39 A2 51 40N 101 00W
Duck Mountain Provincial Park Saskatchewan 38 C2 51 40N 101 40W
Dufferin admin. Ontario 44 B3 44 00N 80 20W
Duffey Lake British Columbia 34 H5 50 24N 122 23W
Duncan British Columbia 34 H4 48 46N 123 40W
Duncan, Cape Northwest Territories 40 D3 52 40N 80 50W
Duncan Lake British Columbia 35 E2 50 23N 116 57W
Dundalk Ontario 44 B3 44 10N 80 24W
Dundas Ontario 41 E1 43 16N 79 57W
Dundas Island British Columbia 34 B4 54 33N 131 20W
Dundas Peninsula Northwest Territories 50 J5 74 50N 112 30W
Dundurn Saskatchewan 38 B2 51 49N 106 30W
Dunkirk Saskatchewan 38 B2 50 04N 105 41W
Dunnville Ontario 41 E1 42 54N 79 36W
Dunville Newfoundland 49 D2 47 16N 53 54W

Duparquet Québec 47 A2 48 32N 79 14W
Durham admin. Ontario 44 C3/D3 44 04N 79 11W
Durham Ontario 41 D1 44 11N 80 49W
Durrell Newfoundland 49 D2 49 40N 54 44W
Dutton Ontario 44 A1 42 39N 81 30W
Duvernay Québec 53 N5 45 34N 73 41W
Dyer's Bay Ontario 44 A4 45 10N 81 18W
Dyer's Bay tn. Ontario 44 A4 45 09N 81 20W
Dyke Lake Newfoundland 48 A3 54 30N 66 18W

E

Eabamet Lake Ontario 40 C3 51 32N 87 46W
Eagle Lake Ontario 40 B2 49 35N 93 00W
Eagle Plains tn. Yukon Territory 50 D4 66 30N 136 50W
Eagle River Newfoundland 48 C3 53 00N 58 30W
Eagle River tn. Ontario 40 B2 49 50N 93 12W
Eagle River Saskatchewan 38 B2 51 35N 107 40W
Ear Falls tn. Ontario 40 B3 50 38N 93 13W
Earl Rowe Provincial Park Ontario 44 C3 44 15N 79 45W
East Angus Québec 43 Q6 45 30N 71 40W
East Bay Bird Sanctuary Northwest Territories
    51 Q3 64 20N 82 00W
East Chezzetcook Nova Scotia 49 F6 44 43N 63 14W
Eastend Saskatchewan 38 B1 49 32N 108 50W
Eastern Passage tn. Nova Scotia 53 Q6 44 36N 63 29W
Easterville Manitoba 39 B2 53 00N 99 40W
East Lake Nova Scotia 53 Q7 44 46N 63 29W
Eastmain Québec 47 A3 52 10N 78 30W
East Point Prince Edward Island 49 F7 46 27N 61 59W
Eastport Newfoundland 49 D2 48 39N 53 45W
East St. Paul admin. Manitoba 54 D2 49 59N 97 04W
East Thurlow Island British Columbia 34 G5
    50 24N 125 26W
East York bor. Metropolitan Toronto Ontario 52 C1
    43 43N 79 20W
Eatonia Saskatchewan 38 B2 51 13N 109 22W
Echaot'ine Kúé (Fort Liard) Northwest Territories 50 G3
    60 14N 123 28W
Echoing River Ontario 40 B3 54 30N 92 00W
Echo, Lake Nova Scotia 53 Q6 44 44N 63 24W
Eclipse Sound Northwest Territories 51 R5 72 38N 79 00W
Ecum Secum Nova Scotia 49 F6 44 58N 62 08W
Eddies Cove tn. Newfoundland 48 C3 51 25N 56 27W
Edehon Lake Northwest Territories 51 M3
    60 25N 97 15W
Edgell Island Northwest Territories 46 C5
    61 50N 65 00W
Edgewood British Columbia 35 E1 49 47N 118 08W
Edmonton Alberta 37 C2 53 34N 113 25W
Edmund Lake Manitoba 39 C2 54 50N 93 20W
Edmundston New Brunswick 49 A2 47 22N 68 20W
Edson Alberta 37 B2 53 35N 116 26W
Eduni, Mount Northwest Territories 50 F3 64 13N 128 10W
Edwards Ontario 53 L2 45 19N 75 48W
Edziza, Mount British Columbia 34 B3 57 43N 130 42W
Edzo (Edzoò) Northwest Territories 50 H3
    63 46N 116 03W
Edzoò (Edzo) Northwest Territories 50 H3 63 46N 116 03W
Eganville Ontario 41 E2 45 32N 77 06W
Eglinton Island Northwest Territories 50 H6
    75 48N 118 30W
Egmont British Columbia 34 H4 49 45N 123 55W
Egmont Bay Prince Edward Island 49 F7 46 30N 64 20W
Egmont, Cape Nova Scotia 49 F7 46 50N 60 50W
Eileen Lake Northwest Territories 50 K3 62 16N 107 37W
Ekwan Point Ontario 40 D3 53 20N 82 10W
Elaho River British Columbia 34 H5 50 14N 123 33W
Elbow Saskatchewan 38 B2 51 08N 106 36W
Elbow River Alberta 54 A1 50 59N 114 13W
Elgin admin. Ontario 44 A1 42 38N 81 36W
Elkford British Columbia 35 E2 50 02N 114 55W
Elkhorn Manitoba 39 A1 49 58N 101 14W
Elk Island Manitoba 39 B2 50 50N 96 40W
Elk Island National Park Alberta 37 C2 53 36N 112 53W
Elk Lake tn. Ontario 41 D2 47 44N 80 20W
Elk Lakes Provincial Park British Columbia 35 E2
    50 00N 115 00W
Elk Point tn. Alberta 37 C2 53 54N 110 54W
Ellef Ringnes Island Northwest Territories 51 L6
    78 30N 102 00W
Ellerslie Alberta 54 G4 53 24N 113 28W
Ellesmere Island Northwest Territories 51 Q6
    77 30N 82 30W
Ellesmere Island National Park Reserve
    Northwest Territories 51 S7 82 00N 72 30W
Ellice River Northwest Territories 50 L4 66 20N 104 55W
Elliot Lake tn. Ontario 41 D2 46 25N 82 40W
Elmcreek tn. Manitoba 39 A2 49 41N 97 59W
Elmira Ontario 44 B2 43 36N 80 34W
Elmira Prince Edward Island 49 F7 46 26N 62 05W
Elmvale Ontario 44 C3 44 35N 79 52W
Elora Ontario 44 B2 43 42N 80 26W
Elrose Saskatchewan 38 B2 51 12N 108 01W
Elsa Yukon Territory 50 D3 63 55N 135 29W
Elvira, Cape Northwest Territories 50 K5
    73 20N 108 00W
Embree Newfoundland 49 C2 49 18N 55 02W
Emerald Island Northwest Territories 50 J6 76 48N 114 10W
Emerson Manitoba 39 B1 49 00N 97 11W
Emily Provincial Park Ontario 44 D3 44 20N 78 28W
Endako British Columbia 35 C2 54 10N 125 21W
Enderby British Columbia 35 D2 50 32N 119 10W
Enfield Nova Scotia 49 F6 44 56N 63 34W
Englee Newfoundland 49 C3 50 44N 56 06W
Englehart Ontario 41 E2 47 50N 79 52W
English Bay British Columbia 52 F4 49 17N 123 12W
English River Ontario 40 B3 50 20N 94 50W

Ennadai Lake Northwest Territories 51 L3
    60 58N 101 20W
Enterprise Northwest Territories 50 H3 60 34N 116 15W
Eramosa River Ontario 44 B2 43 33N 80 11W
Erieau Ontario 42 E3 42 16N 81 56W
Erie Beach tn. Ontario 44 D1 42 53N 78 56W
Erie, Lake Ontario/U.S.A. 42 E3 42 15N 81 00W
Eriksdale Manitoba 39 B2 50 52N 98 07W
Erin Ontario 44 B2 43 48N 80 04W
Escuminac, Point New Brunswick 49 B2 47 04N 64 49W
Esker Newfoundland 48 A3 53 53N 66 25W
Eskimo Lakes Northwest Territories 50 E4
    68 30N 132 30W
Eskimo Point (Arviat) Northwest Territories 51 N3
    61 10N 94 05W
Espanola Ontario 41 D2 46 15N 81 46W
Esquimalt British Columbia 34 H4 48 25N 123 29W
Essex admin. Ontario 42 D3 42 10N 82 45W
Essex Ontario 42 D3 42 10N 82 49W
Esterhazy Saskatchewan 38 C2 50 40N 102 02W
Estevan Saskatchewan 38 C1 49 09N 103 00W
Eston Saskatchewan 38 B2 51 09N 108 42W
Etawney Lake Manitoba 39 B3 57 50N 96 40W
Ethelbert Manitoba 39 A2 51 32N 100 25W
Etobicoke bor. Metropolitan Toronto Ontario 52 B1
    43 38N 79 30W
Etobicoke Creek Ontario 52 A1 43 43N 79 47W
Eugenia Lake Ontario 44 B3 44 20N 80 30W
Eureka m.s. Northwest Territories 51 P7 80 00N 85 40W
Eureka River tn. Alberta 37 B3 56 25N 118 48W
Eutsuk Lake British Columbia 35 C2 53 12N 126 32W
Evansburg Alberta 37 B2 53 36N 115 01W
Evans, Mount Alberta 37 B2 52 26N 118 07W
Evans Strait Northwest Territories 51 Q3 63 15N 82 30W
Exeter Ontario 44 A2 43 21N 81 30W
Exploits River Newfoundland 49 C2 48 40N 56 30W
Eyehill River Saskatchewan 38 B2 52 25N 109 50W

F

Faber Lake Northwest Territories 50 H3 63 56N 117 15W
Fairchild Creek Ontario 44 B2 43 13N 80 11W
Fairview Alberta 37 B3 56 03N 118 28W
Fairweather, Mount British Columbia/Alaska U.S.A.
    34 A3 58 50N 137 55W
Falcon Lake tn. Manitoba 39 B1 49 44N 95 18W
Falher Alberta 37 B3 55 44N 117 12W
Fallowfield Ontario 53 J2 45 17N 75 51W
Fall River Nova Scotia 53 P7 44 49N 63 36W
False Bay tn. British Columbia 34 H4 49 29N 124 22W
False Creek British Columbia 52 F4 49 16N 123 08W
Family Lake Manitoba 39 B2 51 50N 95 40W
Fanny Bay tn. British Columbia 34 H4 49 30N 124 50W
Farnham Québec 43 P6 45 17N 72 59W
Farnham, Mount British Columbia 35 E2 50 27N 116 37W
Faro Yukon Territory 50 E3 62 15N 133 30W
Fathom Five National Marine Park Ontario 44 A4
    45 20N 81 35W
Fauquier Ontario 41 D2 49 19N 82 02W
Fawn River Ontario 40 C3 54 20N 89 10W
Felix, Cape Northwest Territories 51 M4 69 54N 97 58W
Fenelon Falls tn. Ontario 44 D3 44 32N 78 45W
Fergus Ontario 44 B2 43 43N 80 24W
Ferland Ontario 40 C3 50 19N 88 30W
Ferme-Neuve Québec 43 L7 46 42N 75 28W
Fermont Québec 47 C3 52 45N 67 00W
Fernie British Columbia 35 E1 49 30N 115 00W
Ferryland Newfoundland 49 D2 47 01N 52 53W
Fife Lake Saskatchewan 38 B1 49 10N 105 45W
Finch Ontario 43 L6 45 08N 75 05W
Finlay Ranges mts. British Columbia 35 C3
    57 00N 125 45W
Finlay River British Columbia 35 C3 57 20N 125 40W
Fiordland Recreation Area British Columbia 35 C2
    52 45N 128 00W
Firebag Hills Saskatchewan 38 B3 57 15N 109 50W
Firebag River Alberta 37 C3 57 30N 110 40W
First Narrows British Columbia 52 F4 49 19N 123 08W
Fish Creek Alberta 54 A1 50 55N 114 10W
Fish Creek Provincial Park Alberta 54 A2 50 55N 114 04W
Fisher Bay Manitoba 39 B2 51 30N 97 30W
Fisher Branch tn. Manitoba 39 B2 51 04N 97 38W
Fisher, Mount British Columbia 35 E1 49 35N 115 20W
Fisher Strait Northwest Territories 51 Q3 63 30N 84 00W
Fishing Branch Game Reserve Yukon Territory 50 D4
    66 30N 139 30W
Fishing Lake Manitoba 39 B2 52 10N 95 40W
Fishing Ships Harbour tn. Newfoundland 48 C3
    52 36N 55 47W
Fitzgerald Alberta 37 C3 59 51N 111 36W
Fitzwilliam Island Ontario 42 E6 45 35N 81 45W
Flamborough Ontario 44 C2 43 20N 79 57W
Flesherton Ontario 44 B3 44 16N 80 32W
Fletchers Lake Nova Scotia 53 P7 44 51N 63 35W
Fleur de Lys Newfoundland Canada 49 C3 50 07N 56 08W
Fleuve Saint-Laurent (St. Lawrence River) Québec
    47 C2 48 20N 69 20W
Flin Flon Manitoba 39 A2 54 50N 102 00W
Florenceville New Brunswick 49 A2 46 26N 67 36W
Flores Island British Columbia 35 C1 49 20N 126 10W
Flour Lake Newfoundland 48 B3 53 44N 64 50W
Foam Lake tn. Saskatchewan 38 C2 51 38N 103 31W
Foch British Columbia 34 H5 50 07N 124 31W
Fogo Newfoundland 49 D2 49 43N 54 12W
Fogo Island Newfoundland 49 D2 49 40N 54 10W
Foleyet Ontario 41 D2 48 05N 82 26W
Foley Lake Alberta 54 H3 53 24N 113 13W
Fond-du-Lac Saskatchewan 38 B3 59 20N 107 09W

Fond du Lac River Saskatchewan 38 C3 59 05N 104 40W
Fontas River British Columbia 35 D3 58 20N 121 25W
Fonthill Ontario 44 C2 43 02N 79 17W
Foothills Municipal District Alberta 54 A1
    50 53N 114 08W
Forbes, Mount Alberta 37 B2 51 52N 116 55W
Ford Alluviaq tn. Québec 46 C4 59 30N 65 20W
Foremost Alberta 37 C1 49 29N 111 25W
Forest Ontario 42 D4 43 06N 82 00W
Forestburg Alberta 37 C2 52 35N 112 04W
Forest Hill Ontario 52 C1 43 42N 79 25W
Forest Lawn Alberta 54 A2 51 02N 113 58W
Forestville Québec 47 C2 48 45N 69 04W
Forrest Lake Saskatchewan 38 B3 57 35N 109 10W
Fort Albany Ontario 40 D3 52 12N 81 40W
Fort Babine British Columbia 35 C3 55 20N 126 35W
Fort Chipewyan Alberta 37 C3 58 46N 111 09W
Fort Coulonge Québec 43 K6 45 51N 76 46W
Forteau Newfoundland 48 C3 51 28N 56 58W
Fort Erie Ontario 41 D1 42 55N 78 56W
Fort Frances Ontario 40 B2 48 37N 93 23W
Fort Franklin (Déline) Northwest Territories 50 G4
    65 11N 123 26W
Fort Fraser British Columbia 35 D2 54 03N 124 30W
Fort Garry Manitoba 54 D2 49 49N 97 10W
Fort Good Hope (Rádeyilikóé) Northwest Territories 50 F4
    66 16N 128 37W
Fort Hope I.R. Ontario 40 C3 51 37N 87 55W
Fort Langley British Columbia 34 H4 49 11N 122 38W
Fort Liard (Echaot'ine Kúé) Northwest Territories 50 G3
    60 14N 123 28W
Fort MacKay Alberta 37 C3 57 11N 111 37W
Fort Macleod Alberta 37 C1 49 44N 113 24W
Fort McMurray Alberta 37 C3 56 45N 111 27W
Fort McPherson (Teetł'it Zheh) Northwest Territories 50 E4
    67 29N 134 50W
Fort Nelson British Columbia 35 D3 58 48N 122 44W
Fort Nelson River British Columbia 35 D3 59 20N 124 05W
Fort Providence (Zhahti Kóé) Northwest Territories
    50 H3 61 03N 117 40W
Fort Qu'Appelle Saskatchewan 38 C2 50 46N 103 54W
Fort Resolution (Denínue Kúé) Northwest Territories
    50 J3 61 10N 113 39W
Fort Rouge Manitoba 54 D2 49 52N 97 07W
Fort St. James British Columbia 35 D2 54 26N 124 15W
Fort St. John British Columbia 35 D3 56 14N 120 55W
Fort Saskatchewan Alberta 54 H5 53 42N 113 12W
Fort Severn Ontario 40 C4 56 00N 87 40W
Fort Simpson (Liídli Kúé) Northwest Territories 50 G3
    61 46N 121 15W
Fort Smith Alberta 37 C3 60 00N 111 51W
Fort Smith reg. Northwest Territories 50 H3
    63 00N 116 00W
Fort Smith (Tthebacha) Northwest Territories 50 J3
    60 01N 111 55W
Fortune Newfoundland 49 C2 47 04N 55 50W
Fortune Bay Newfoundland 49 C2 47 15N 55 30W
Fort Vermilion Alberta 37 B3 58 22N 115 59W
Fort Ware British Columbia 35 C3 57 30N 125 43W
Fort Whyte Manitoba 54 D2 49 49N 97 12W
Fosheim Peninsula Northwest Territories 51 Q6
    79 58N 84 58W
Foster, Mount British Columbia 34 A3 59 49N 135 35W
Foster River Saskatchewan 38 B3 56 20N 105 45W
Fourchu Nova Scotia 49 F7 45 43N 60 17W
Four Mile Lake Ontario 44 D3 44 42N 78 44W
Fox Creek tn. Alberta 37 B2 54 24N 116 48W
Foxe Basin b. Northwest Territories 51 R4 66 20N 79 00W
Foxe Channel Northwest Territories 51 R3 64 15N 79 55W
Foxe Peninsula Northwest Territories 51 R4 64 50N 77 00W
Fox Mine tn. Manitoba 39 A3 56 39N 101 38W
Fox River Manitoba 39 C3 55 50N 94 10W
Fox Valley tn. Saskatchewan 38 B2 50 29N 109 29W
Frances Lake Yukon Territory 50 F3 61 20N 129 30W
François Lake British Columbia 35 C2 54 00N 125 47W
Frankford Ontario 42 J5 44 12N 77 36W
Franklin Bay Northwest Territories 50 F4 69 45N 126 00W
Franklin Island Ontario 44 B4 45 25N 80 20W
Franklin Lake Northwest Territories 51 M4 66 56N 96 03W
Franklin Mountains Northwest Territories 50 G3
    64 25N 124 00W
Fraserdale Ontario 41 D2 49 51N 81 37W
Fraser Lake British Columbia 35 D2 54 00N 124 50W
Fraser Lake Newfoundland 48 B3 54 24N 63 40W
Fraser Plateau British Columbia 35 C2 52 25N 123 50W
Fraser River British Columbia 35 D2 51 36N 122 25W
Fraser River Newfoundland 48 B4 56 50N 63 50W
Fredericton New Brunswick 49 A2 45 57N 66 40W
Fredericton Junction New Brunswick 49 A2
    45 40N 66 38W
Freels, Cape Newfoundland 49 D2 49 15N 53 29W
Freeport Nova Scotia 49 E6 44 17N 66 19W
Frenchman River Saskatchewan 38 B1 49 30N 108 00W
Frenchman's Cove tn. Newfoundland 49 C2 49 04N 58 10W
French River tn. Ontario 42 D2 46 01N 80 40W
French River tn. Ontario 42 F7 46 03N 80 34W
Freshwater Newfoundland 49 D2 47 15N 53 59W
Frobisher Bay (Iqaluit) Northwest Territories 51 T3
    63 00N 67 30W
Frobisher Lake Saskatchewan 38 B3 57 00N 108 00W
Frog Lake Alberta 37 C2 53 55N 110 20W
Frontenac admin. Ontario 43 K5 44 40N 76 45W
Frontenac Québec 43 R6 45 40N 70 50W
Frontenac Provincial Park Ontario 43 K5 44 32N 76 29W
Frozen Strait Northwest Territories 51 Q4 65 40N 84 40W
Fruitvale British Columbia 35 E1 49 08N 117 28W
Fundy, Bay of New Brunswick/Nova Scotia 49 E7
    45 00N 66 00W

Fundy National Park New Brunswick 49 E7
    45 40N 65 10W
Fury and Hecla Strait Northwest Territories 51 Q4
    69 56N 84 00W

G

Gabarus, Bay Nova Scotia 49 F7 45 50N 60 10W
Gabriola Island British Columbia 34 H4 49 10N 123 51W
Gage, Cape Prince Edward Island 49 F7 46 50N 64 20W
Gagetown New Brunswick 49 A2 45 46N 66 29W
Gagnon Québec 47 C3 51 56N 68 16W
Gahmiti (Rae Lakes) tn. Northwest Territories 50 H3
    64 10N 117 20W
Galiano Island British Columbia 34 H4 48 57N 123 25W
Galt Ontario 44 B2 43 21N 80 19W
Gambier Island British Columbia 34 H4 49 30N 123 25W
Gambo Newfoundland 49 D2 48 46N 54 14W
Gananoque Ontario 43 K5 44 20N 76 10W
Ganaraska River Ontario 44 D3 44 02N 78 34W
Gander Newfoundland 49 D2 48 57N 54 34W
Gander Lake Newfoundland 49 D2 48 55N 54 35W
Ganges British Columbia 34 H4 48 51N 123 31W
Gardiner Dam Saskatchewan 38 B2 51 15N 106 40W
Gardner Canal British Columbia 34 C2 53 30N 128 50W
Garibaldi Lake British Columbia 34 H4 49 55N 122 57W
Garibaldi, Mount British Columbia 34 H4 49 53N 123 00W
Garibaldi Provincial Park British Columbia 34 H4
    49 58N 122 45W
Garnish Newfoundland 49 C2 47 14N 55 22W
Garry Lake Northwest Territories 51 L4 66 00N 100 00W
Garry Point British Columbia 52 F3 49 07N 123 14W
Garson Ontario 41 D2 46 32N 80 57W
Gaspé Québec 47 D2 48 50N 64 30W
Gaspereau Lake Nova Scotia 49 F6 44 55N 64 40W
Gataga River British Columbia 35 C3 58 25N 126 40W
Gateshead Island Northwest Territories 51 L5
    70 36N 100 26W
Gatineau admin. Québec 43 K7 46 30N 76 00W
Gatineau Québec 43 L6 45 29N 75 40W
Gauer Lake Manitoba 39 B3 57 10N 97 30W
Gaultois Newfoundland 49 C2 47 36N 55 54W
Geikie River Saskatchewan 38 C3 57 20N 104 40W
George, Cape Nova Scotia 49 F7 45 50N 61 50W
George Island Newfoundland 48 C3 54 16N 57 20W
Georgetown Ontario 44 C2 43 39N 79 56W
Georgetown Prince Edward Island 49 F7 46 12N 62 32W
Georgian Bay Ontario 42 E6 45 30N 81 00W
Georgian Bay Islands National Park Ontario 44 C3
    44 53N 79 53W
Georgia, Strait of British Columbia 34 H4 49 39N 124 34W
Georgina Island British Columbia 44 C3 44 22N 79 17W
Geraldton Ontario 40 C2 49 44N 86 59W
Germansen Landing British Columbia 35 D3
    55 47N 124 42W
Giants Causeway Northwest Territories 50 G6
    5 46N 121 11W
Giants Tomb Island Ontario 44 B3 44 55N 80 00W
Gibsons tn. British Columbia 34 H4 49 24N 123 30W
Gilbert, Mount British Columbia 34 H5 50 50N 124 15W
Gilbert Plains tn. Manitoba 39 A2 51 09N 100 28W
Gilford Island British Columbia 34 C2 50 45N 126 20W
Gil Island British Columbia 34 C2 53 10N 129 15W
Gillam Manitoba 39 C3 56 25N 94 45W
Gillies Bay tn. British Columbia 34 H4 49 42N 124 28W
Gilmour Island Northwest Territories 51 Q2 59 35N 80 01W
Gimli Manitoba 39 B2 50 39N 97 00W
Gitnadoix River Recreational Area British Columbia
    34 C2 54 15N 129 05W
Gjoa Haven (Uqsuqtuq) tn. Northwest Territories 51 M4
    68 39N 96 09W
Glace Bay tn. Nova Scotia 49 G7 46 11N 59 58W
Glacial Mountain British Columbia 34 C2 58 15N 129 25W
Glacier National Park British Columbia 35 E2
    51 00N 117 00W
Gladstone Manitoba 39 B2 50 14N 98 56W
Gladys Lake British Columbia 34 B3 59 50N 132 52W
Glaslyn Saskatchewan 38 B2 53 23N 108 22W
Glenboro Manitoba 39 B2 49 35N 99 20W
Glen Cairn tn. Ontario 53 J2 45 15N 75 45W
Glencoe Ontario 44 A1 42 45N 81 44W
Glenmore Reservoir Alberta 54 A1 50 58N 114 08W
Glenwood Newfoundland 49 D2 49 02N 54 53W
Gloucester admin. New Brunswick 49 A2 47 30N 65 50W
Gloucester Ontario 43 L6 45 21N 75 39W
Gloucester Glen Ontario 53 K2 45 17N 75 41W
Glover Island Newfoundland 49 C2 48 46N 57 43W
Glovertown Newfoundland 49 D2 48 41N 54 02W
Goat Island British Columbia 34 H5 50 03N 124 28W
Goderich Ontario 41 D1 43 43N 81 43W
Gods Lake Manitoba 39 C2 54 40N 94 20W
Gods Lake Narrows tn. Manitoba 39 C2 54 45N 94 09W
Gods Mercy, Bay of Northwest Territories 51 P3
    63 30N 86 00W
Gods River Manitoba 39 C3 56 20N 92 50W
Gogama Ontario 41 D2 47 40N 81 43W
Go Home Lake Ontario 44 C4 45 01N 79 51W
Gold Bridge British Columbia 34 H5 50 51N 122 51W
Golden British Columbia 35 E2 51 19N 116 55W
Golden Ears Provincial Park British Columbia 34 H4
    49 28N 122 25W
Golden Hinde mt. British Columbia 35 C1 49 35N 125 40W
Gold River tn. British Columbia 35 C1 49 41N 125 59W
Goldsmith Channel Northwest Territories 50 K5
    73 00N 106 00W
Golfe du Saint-Laurent (Gulf of Saint Lawrence) Québec
    47 D2 48 40N 62 40W
Goodeve Saskatchewan 38 C2 51 03N 103 11W

Good Hope British Columbia **35** C2 50 59N 127 50W
Good Hope Lake *tn.* British Columbia **34** C3
59 15N 129 20W
Good Hope Mountain British Columbia **35** D2
51 08N 124 10W
Goodsoil Saskatchewan **38** B2 54 24N 109 12W
Goose Bay Newfoundland **48** B3 53 16N 60 10W
Goose River Newfoundland **48** B3 53 30N 61 50W
Gordon Horne Peak British Columbia **35** E2
51 47N 118 50W
Gordon Lake Alberta **37** C3 56 30N 110 25W
Gordon Pittock Reservoir Ontario **44** B2 43 11N 80 43W
Gordon River British Columbia **34** H4 48 38N 124 25W
Gore Bay *tn.* Ontario **41** D2 45 55N 82 28W
Goshen Nova Scotia **49** F7 45 20N 62 55W
Gott Peak British Columbia **34** H5 50 18N 122 16W
Goulbourne Ontario **53** J2 46 15N 75 54W
Gowganda Ontario **41** D2 47 39N 80 46W
Gracefield Québec **43** K7 46 05N 76 05W
Grady Harbour Newfoundland **48** C3 53 48N 56 25W
Graham Island British Columbia **34** B2 53 50N 132 40W
Graham Lake Northwest Territories **51** N6
77 25N 90 30W
Granby Québec **47** B2 45 22N 72 43W
Granby River British Columbia **35** E1 49 27N 118 25W
Grand Bank Newfoundland **49** C2 47 06N 55 46W
Grand Bay *tn.* New Brunswick **49** A2 45 19N 66 14W
Grand Bend Ontario **41** D1 43 21N 81 45W
Grand Centre Alberta **37** C2 54 25N 110 13W
Grande-Anse New Brunswick **49** A2 47 50N 65 10W
Grande-Anse Québec **43** P8 47 05N 72 55W
Grande Cache Alberta **37** B2 53 50N 119 08W
Grande Pointe Manitoba **54** D2 49 45N 97 03W
Grande Prairie *tn.* Alberta **37** B3 55 10N 118 52W
Grande-Rivière *tn.* Québec **47** D2 48 23N 64 31W
Grande rivière de la Baleine *r.* Québec **46** A4
55 05N 75 45W
Grand Étang Nova Scotia **49** F7 46 30N 61 05W
Grande-Vallée *tn.* Québec **47** C2 49 15N 65 10W
Grand Falls *tn.* New Brunswick **65** M6 47 02N 67 46W
Grand Falls-Windsor Newfoundland **49** C2
48 57N 55 40W
Grand Falls/Grand-Sault New Brunswick **49** A2
47 02N 67 46W
Grand Forks British Columbia **35** E1 49 02N 118 30W
Grand Harbour *tn.* New Brunswick **49** E6 44 41N 66 46W
Grandin, Lake Northwest Territories **50** H3
63 50N 119 50W
Grand Jardin Newfoundland **49** C2 48 28N 59 13W
Grand Lake New Brunswick **49** A2 45 55N 66 05W
Grand Lake Newfoundland **48** B3 53 40N 60 30W
Grand Lake Newfoundland **49** C2 49 00N 57 20W
Grand Manan Island New Brunswick **49** E6 44 45N 66 50W
Grand Marais *tn.* Manitoba **39** B2 50 30N 96 35W
Grand-Mère Québec **43** M4 46 36N 72 41W
Grand Narrows *tn.* Nova Scotia **49** F7 45 55N 60 50W
Grand Rapids *tn.* Manitoba **39** B2 53 12N 99 19W
Grand River Ontario **44** C2 43 15N 79 34W
Grand Valley *tn.* Ontario **41** D1 43 54N 80 10W
Grandview Manitoba **39** A2 51 11N 100 51W
Granisle British Columbia **35** C2 54 56N 126 18W
Granite Bay *tn.* British Columbia **34** G5 50 00N 125 00W
Granite Lake Newfoundland **49** C2 48 11N 57 01W
Granville Falls Manitoba **39** A3 56 10N 100 20W
Granville Lake Manitoba **39** A3 56 00N 101 00W
Grasslands National Park Saskatchewan **38** B1
49 10N 107 30W
Grass River Manitoba **39** B2 54 50N 99 20W
Grass River Provincial Park Manitoba **39** A2
54 40N 101 40W
Grassy Narrows *I.R.* Ontario **40** B3 50 10N 93 55W
Gravelbourg Saskatchewan **38** B1 49 53N 106 33W
Gravenhurst Ontario **41** E1 44 55N 79 22W
Grayling River British Columbia **35** C3 59 43N 125 55W
Gray Strait *sd.* Northwest Territories/Québec **46** D5
60 30N 64 50W
Greasy Lake Northwest Territories **50** G3 62 55N 122 15W
Great Bear Lake Northwest Territories **51** G4
66 00N 120 00W
Great Central Lake British Columbia **34** G4
49 22N 125 10W
Great La Cloche Island Ontario **42** E7 46 01N 81 53W
Great Plain of the Koukdjuak Northwest Territories
51 S4 66 25N 72 50W
Great Pubnico Lake Nova Scotia **49** E6 43 45N 65 38W
Great Sand Hills Saskatchewan **38** B2 50 35N 109 20W
Great Slave Lake Northwest Territories **50** J3
62 00N 114 00W
Great Village Nova Scotia **49** F7 45 25N 63 36W
Greely Ontario **53** K2 45 16N 75 33W
Greely Fiord Northwest Territories **51** Q7 80 30N 82 30W
Green Creek Ontario **53** K2 45 25N 75 35W
Green Lake British Columbia **35** D2 51 26N 121 12W
Green Lake *tn.* Saskatchewan **38** B2 54 18N 107 49W
Greenville British Columbia **34** C3 55 05N 129 35W
Greenwater Provincial Park Saskatchewan **38** C2
52 35N 103 25W
Greenwood British Columbia **35** E1 49 08N 118 41W
Greenwood Nova Scotia **49** F7 45 00N 64 50W
Grenfell Saskatchewan **38** C2 50 24N 102 56W
Grenville Québec **43** M6 45 40N 74 38W
Grenville, Mount British Columbia **34** H5 50 59N 124 31W
Gretna Manitoba **39** B1 49 01N 97 34W
Grey *admin.* Ontario **44** B3 44 22N 80 33W
Grey Islands Newfoundland **49** C3 50 50N 55 35W
Grey, Point British Columbia **52** E4 49 16N 123 17W
Grey River Newfoundland **49** C2 47 50N 56 50W
Griffith Island Ontario **44** B3 44 50N 80 54W

Grimsby Ontario **44** C2 43 12N 79 35W
Grimshaw Alberta **37** B3 56 11N 117 36W
Grindstone Provincial Recreation Park Manitoba **39** B2
51 10N 96 50W
Grinnell Peninsula Northwest Territories **51** M6
76 40N 95 00W
Grise Fiord (*Aujuittuq*) *tn.* Northwest Territories **51** Q6
76 25N 82 57W
Grizzly Bear Hills Saskatchewan **38** B3 55 50N 109 30W
Groais Island Newfoundland **49** C3 50 59N 55 36W
Gros Morne *mt.* Newfoundland **49** C2 49 36N 57 47W
Gros Morne National Park Newfoundland **49** C2
49 40N 58 40W
Groswater Bay Newfoundland **48** C3 54 20N 57 40W
Grouard Mission Alberta **37** B3 55 30N 116 10W
Groundhog River Ontario **41** D2 49 00N 82 00W
Guelph Ontario **41** D1 43 34N 80 16W
Gull Bay *I.R.* Ontario **40** C2 49 50N 89 00W
Gull Lake Alberta **37** C2 52 34N 114 00W
Gull Lake Ontario **44** D3 44 48N 78 48W
Gull Lake *tn.* Saskatchewan **38** B2 50 05N 108 30W
Gunisao Lake Manitoba **39** B2 53 30N 96 40W
Gunisao River Manitoba **39** B2 53 30N 96 50W
Guysborough *admin.* Nova Scotia **49** F7 45 20N 61 40W
Guysborough Nova Scotia **49** F7 45 23N 61 30W
Gwaii Haanas National Park Reserve British Columbia
34 B2 52 30N 130 40W
Gwillim Lake Provincial Park British Columbia **35** D3
55 00N 121 00W
Gypsumville Manitoba **39** B2 51 47N 98 38W
Gyrfalcon Islands Northwest Territories **46** C4
59 00N 69 05W

H

Habay Alberta **37** B3 58 50N 118 44W
Hadley British Columbia **35** D1 49 21N 120 02W
Hadley Bay Northwest Territories **50** K5 72 22N 108 30W
Haileybury Ontario **41** E2 47 27N 79 38W
Haines Junction *tn.* Yukon Territory **50** D3 60 45N 137 21W
Hakai Recreational Area British Columbia **35** C2
51 40N 128 00W
Haldimand-Norfolk *admin.* Ontario **44** B1/C1 42
37N 80 39W
Halfway Point *tn.* Newfoundland **49** C2 48 59N 58 06W
Halfway River British Columbia **35** D3 56 42N 122 30W
Haliburton *admin.* Ontario **42** H6 45 10N 78 30W
Haliburton Ontario **41** E2 45 03N 78 30W
Halifax *admin.* Nova Scotia **49** F7 45 00N 63 00W
Halifax Nova Scotia **49** F6 44 40N 63 41W
Halifax Harbour Nova Scotia **53** P6 44 39N 63 33W
Hall Beach (*Sanirajak*) *tn.* Northwest Territories **51** Q4
68 46N 81 12W
Hall Peninsula Northwest Territories **51** T3 63 40N 66 00W
Halls Harbour *tn.* Nova Scotia **49** F7 45 12N 64 37W
Halton *admin.* Ontario **44** C2 43 26N 79 57W
Hamilton Ontario **41** E1 43 15N 79 50W
Hamilton Harbour Ontario **44** C2 43 16N 81 50W
Hamilton Inlet Newfoundland **48** C3 54 08N 58 20W
Hamilton Sound Newfoundland **49** D2 49 30N 54 15W
Hamilton-Wentworth *admin.* Ontario **44** B2/C2 43
14N 80 09W
Hamiota Manitoba **39** A2 50 11N 100 38W
Hampden Newfoundland **49** C2 49 33N 56 51W
Hampton New Brunswick **49** E7 45 30N 65 50W
Hampton Ontario **44** D2 43 48N 78 W
Hanna Alberta **37** C2 51 38N 111 56W
Hannah Bay Ontario **40** D3 51 20N 80 00W
Hanover Ontario **44** A3 44 10N 81 03W
Hanson Lake Road Saskatchewan **38** C2 54 20N 104 35W
Hants *admin.* Nova Scotia **49** F7 45 10N 63 40W
Hantsport Nova Scotia **49** F7 45 04N 64 12W
Happy Valley-Goose Bay *tn.* Newfoundland **48** B3
53 15N 60 20W
Harbour Breton *tn.* Newfoundland **49** C2 47 29N 55 50W
Harbour Deep *tn.* Newfoundland **49** C3 50 22N 56 31W
Harbour Grace *tn.* Newfoundland **49** D2 47 42N 53 13W
Harcourt New Brunswick **49** A2 46 29N 65 18W
Hardisty Alberta **37** C2 52 40N 111 18W
Hardisty Lake Northwest Territories **50** H3
64 30N 117 45W
Hare Bay Newfoundland **49** C3 51 15N 56 00W
Hare Bay *tn.* Newfoundland **49** D2 48 51N 54 00W
Hare Indian River Northwest Territories **50** F4
66 25N 128 00W
Haro Strait British Columbia **34** H4 48 36N 123 17W
Harp Lake Newfoundland **48** B4 55 05N 61 50W
Harrietsfield Nova Scotia **53** P6 44 34N 63 39W
Harrington Harbour *tn.* Québec **47** D3 50 31N 59 30W
Harrison, Cape Newfoundland **48** C3 54 57N 57 57W
Harrison Hot Springs *tn.* British Columbia **34** H4
49 17N 121 47W
Harrison Lake British Columbia **34** H4 49 30N 122 10W
Harriston Ontario **44** B2 43 54N 80 52W
Harrow Ontario **42** D3 42 02N 82 55W
Harrowby Manitoba **39** A2 50 45N 101 28W
Harry Gibbons Bird Sanctuary Northwest Territory **51** P3
63 50N 86 00W
Hartland New Brunswick **49** A2 46 18N 67 31W
Hartney Manitoba **39** A1 49 29N 100 31W
Hart River Yukon Territory **50** D4 65 40N 137 10W
Hastings *admin.* Ontario **42** J5 44 45N 77 40W
Hastings Ontario **42** J5 44 18N 77 57W
Hatchet Lake Saskatchewan **38** C3 58 50N 103 30W
Haultain River Saskatchewan **38** B3 56 20N 106 20W
Havelock Ontario **42** J5 44 26N 77 53W
Havre-Aubert Québec **47** D2 47 15N 61 51W
Havre-Saint-Pierre Québec **47** D3 50 20N 63 38W

Hawke Harbour *tn.* Newfoundland **48** C3 53 03N 55 49W
Hawkes Bay *tn.* Newfoundland **49** C3 50 36N 57 10W
Hawkesbury Ontario **41** F1 45 36N 74 37W
Hay, Cape Northwest Territories **51** N4 72 25N 113 00W
Hayes River Manitoba **39** C3 55 20N 94 10W
Hay Lake Alberta **37** B3 58 52N 119 20W
Hay River Alberta/Northwest Territories **37** B3
58 00N 118 00W
Hay River (*Katloedeeche*) *tn.* Northwest Territories **50** H3
60 51N 115 42W
Hazeldean Ontario **53** J2 45 18N 75 55W
Hazelton British Columbia **35** C3 55 17N 127 42W
Hazen Strait Northwest Territories **50** J6 77 00N 110 00W
Headingley *admin.* Manitoba **54** C2 49 48N 97 23W
Head Lake Ontario **44** D3 44 45N 78 54W
Head of Bay d'Espoir Newfoundland **49** C2 47 56N 55 45W
Hearst Ontario **41** D2 49 42N 83 40W
Heart's Content Newfoundland **49** D2 47 53N 53 22W
Hebron Newfoundland **48** B4 58 12N 62 38W
Hebron Nova Scotia **49** E6 43 57N 66 03W
Hebron Fiord *in.* Newfoundland **48** B4 58 09N 63 00W
Hecate Strait British Columbia **34** B3 54 40N 131 10W
Hecla and Griper Bay Northwest Territories **50** J6
76 25N 112 00W
Hecla Island Manitoba **39** B2 51 00N 96 30W
Hecla Provincial Park Manitoba **39** B2 51 10N 96 30W
Hells Gate *N.H.S.* British Columbia **34** H4 49 52N 121 26E
Henderson Lake British Columbia **34** G4 49 05N 125 03W
Henley Harbour *tn.* Newfoundland **48** C3 51 59N 55 51W
Henrietta Island Newfoundland **48** C3 54 05N 58 28W
Henrietta Maria, Cape Ontario **40** D4 55 10N 82 30W
Henry Kater Peninsula Northwest Territories **51** T4
69 20N 67 20W
Hensall Ontario **44** A2 43 26N 81 31W
Hepworth Ontario **44** A3 44 37N 81 09W
Herbert Saskatchewan **38** B2 50 26N 107 12W
Heriot Bay *tn.* British Columbia **34** G5 50 06N 125 12W
Hermitage-Sandyville Newfoundland **49** C2
47 33N 55 56W
Heron Bay *I.R.* Ontario **41** C2 48 40N 86 17W
Herring Cove Nova Scotia **49** F6 44 35N 63 35W
Herschel Yukon Territory **50** D4 69 34N 139 00W
Herschel Island Yukon Territory **50** D4 69 34N 139 00W
Hespeler Ontario **44** B2 43 26N 80 20W
Hess River Yukon Territory **50** E3 63 25N 133 50W
Hibbard Québec **43** M8 47 53N 74 03W
Hickman, Mount British Columbia **34** B3 57 15N 131 07W
High Level *tn.* Alberta **37** B3 58 10N 117 20W
High Prairie *tn.* Alberta **37** B3 55 26N 116 29W
High River *tn.* Alberta **37** C2 50 35N 113 52W
Highrock Manitoba **39** A3 55 50N 100 22W
Highrock Lake Manitoba **39** A3 55 46N 100 20W
Highrock Lake Saskatchewan **38** B3 57 00N 105 20W
Hillsborough New Brunswick **49** F7 45 56N 64 40W
Hillsborough Bay Prince Edward Island **49** F7
46 10N 63 20W
Hillsburgh Ontario **44** B2 43 46N 80 10W
Hilton Beach *tn.* Ontario **42** C7 46 16N 83 56W
Hinds Lake Reservoir Newfoundland **49** C2 49 00N 57 00W
Hines Creek *tn.* Alberta **37** B3 56 15N 118 36W
Hinton Alberta **37** B2 53 25N 117 34W
Hoare Bay Northwest Territories **51** U4 65 17N 62 55W
Hodgeville Saskatchewan **38** B2 50 07N 106 58W
Hog Island Prince Edward Island **49** F7 46 41N 63 50W
Holden Alberta **37** C2 53 14N 112 14W
Holdfast Saskatchewan **38** B2 50 58N 105 28W
Holland Landing Ontario **44** C2 44 05N 79 29W
Holland River Ontario **44** C3 44 01N 79 39W
Holman (*Uluqsautuuq*) Northwest Territories **50** H5
70 44N 117 44W
Holton Newfoundland **48** C3 54 35N 57 16W
Holyrood Newfoundland **49** D2 47 23N 53 08W
Homathko River British Columbia **35** C2
51 10N 125 05W
Home Bay Northwest Territories **51** T4 69 00N 67 00W
Home Island Newfoundland **48** B5 60 10N 64 14W
Honey Harbour Ontario **44** C2 44 52N 79 48W
Hood River Northwest Territories **50** K4 67 00N 109 20W
Hope British Columbia **34** H4 49 21N 121 28W
Hope Bay Ontario **44** A3 44 54N 81 14W
Hopedale Newfoundland **48** B4 55 28N 60 13W
Hope Island Ontario **44** B3 44 54N 80 11W
Hope Island British Columbia **35** C2 50 55N 127 55W
Hopes Advance Bay Québec **46** C4 59 20N 69 40W
Hopewell Nova Scotia **49** F7 45 29N 62 41W
Hopewell Islands Northwest Territories **46** A4
58 20N 78 10W
Hornaday River Northwest Territories **50** G4
69 00N 123 00W
Hornby Island British Columbia **34** H4 49 31N 124 40W
Hornepayne Ontario **41** D2 49 13N 84 47W
Horner Creek Ontario **44** B2 43 12N 80 35W
Horn Mountains Northwest Territories **50** H3
62 15N 119 15W
Horsefly Lake British Columbia **35** D2 52 25N 121 00W
Horsehills Creek Alberta **54** G5 53 45N 113 23W
Horse Islands Newfoundland **49** C3 50 13N 55 48W
Horseshoe Bay *tn.* British Columbia **34** H4 49 22N 123 17W
Horton River Northwest Territories **50** G4 68 30N 123 50W
Horwood Lake Ontario **41** D2 48 00N 82 20W
Hotsprings Cove *tn.* British Columbia **35** C1
49 20N 126 20W
Hottah Lake Northwest Territories **50** H4 65 04N 118 30W
Houston British Columbia **35** C2 54 24N 126 39W
Houston Point Northwest Territories **40** D3
58 20N 81 00W
Howe Sound British Columbia **34** H4 49 30N 123 25W
Howley Newfoundland **49** C2 49 10N 57 07W

Hubbards Nova Scotia **49** F6 44 38N 64 03W
Hubbart Point Manitoba **39** C3 59 21N 94 41W
Hudson Bay (*Baie d'Hudson*) *b.* Canada **46** A4
58 00N 79 00W
Hudson Bay *tn.* Saskatchewan **38** C2 52 45N 102 45W
Hudson's Hope British Columbia **35** D3 56 00N 121 59W
Hudson Strait (*Détroit d'Hudson*) Northwest Territories
51 S3 62 00N 70 00W
Hugh Keenleyside Dam British Columbia **35** E1
49 33N 118 00W
Hull *admin.* Québec **43** L6 45 40N 75 40W
Hull Québec **47** A2 45 26N 75 45W
Humber Bay Ontario **52** C1 43 36N 79 27W
Humber River Ontario **52** B2 43 48N 79 37W
Humboldt Saskatchewan **38** B2 52 12N 105 07W
100 Mile House British Columbia **35** D2 51 36N 121 18W
Hunter Island British Columbia **35** C2 51 57N 128 05W
Hunter River *tn.* Prince Edward Island **49** F7 46 20N 63 20W
Huntingdon *admin.* Québec **43** M6 45 00N 74 20W
Huntingdon Québec **47** B2 45 05N 74 11W
Huntingdon Island Newfoundland **48** C3 53 47N 56 55W
Hunt River Newfoundland **48** B4 56 20N 61 10W
Huntsville Ontario **41** E2 45 20N 79 13W
Hurd, Cape Ontario **44** A4 45 14N 81 44W
Huron *admin.* Ontario **44** A2 43 38N 79 27W
Huron, Lake Ontario/U.S.A. **42** D5 45 00N 82 30W
Hyde Park Ontario **44** A2 43 00N 81 20W
Hythe Alberta **37** B3 55 18N 119 33W

I

Igloolik (*Iglulik*) Northwest Territories **51** Q4
69 23N 81 46W
Igluisuaktalialuk Island Newfoundland **48** B4
57 20N 61 40W
Igluligaarjuk (*Chesterfield Inlet*) *tn.* Northwest Territories
51 N3 63 21N 90 42W
Iglulik (*Igloolik*) Northwest Territories **51** Q4 69 23N 81 46W
Ignace Ontario **40** B2 49 26N 91 40W
Ikaahuk (*Sachs Harbour*) *tn.* Northwest Territories **50** F5
71 59N 125 13W
Ikaluktutiak (*Cambridge Bay*) *tn.* Northwest Territories
50 K4 69 09N 105 00W
Ikpiarjuk (*Arctic Bay*) *tn.* Northwest Territories **51** P5
73 05N 85 20W
Île-à-la-Crosse *tn.* Saskatchewan **38** B3 55 28N 107 53W
Île aux Coudres *i.* Québec **43** R8 47 23N 70 20W
Île aux Herons *i.* Québec **53** N4 45 26N 73 35W
Île d'Anticosti *i.* Québec **47** D2 49 20N 62 30W
Île de Montréal *i.* Québec **53** M4 45 30N 73 43W
Île des Allumettes *i.* Québec **43** J6 45 53N 77 08W
Ile des Chenes *i.* Manitoba **54** E1 49 41N 96 58W
Île des Soeurs (*Île des Soeurs ou St. Paul*) *i.* Québec **53** N4
45 28N 73 33W
Île des Soeurs ou St. Paul (*Île des Soeurs*) *i.* Québec **53** N4
45 28N 73 33W
Île de Varennes *i.* Québec **53** O5 45 39N73 28W
Île d'Orléans *i.* Québec **47** B2 46 55N 70 59W
Île du Grand Calumet *i.* Québec **43** K6 45 44N 76 40W
Île Jésus *i.* Québec **53** N5 45 35N 73 45W
Île Kettle *i.* Québec **53** K2 45 28N 75 39W
Île Lamèque New Brunswick **49** B2 47 50N 64 40W
Île Lynch *i.* Québec **53** M4 45 25N 73 54W
Île Ste. Hélène *i.* Québec **53** N5 45 31N 73 32W
Îles-de-Boucherville *is.* Québec **53** N5 45 36N73 28W
Îles de la Madeleine *is.* Québec **47** D2 47 30N 61 50W
Ilford Manitoba **39** B3 56 04N 95 40W
Indian Arm *b.* British Columbia **52** G4 49 19N 122 55W
Indian Cabins Alberta **37** B3 59 52N 117 02W
Indian Harbour *tn.* Newfoundland **48** C3 54 27N 57 13W
Indian Head *tn.* Saskatchewan **38** C2 50 35N 103 37W
Indian Tickle Newfoundland **48** C3 53 34N 56 02W
Ingenika River British Columbia **35** C3 56 48N 126 11W
Ingersoll Ontario **44** B2 43 00N 80 53W
Ingonish Nova Scotia **49** F7 46 42N 60 22W
Inklin River British Columbia **34** B3 58 54N 132 50W
Inner Bay Ontario **44** B1 42 35N 80 26W
Innisfail Alberta **37** C2 52 01N 113 59W
Inside Passage British Columbia **34** C2 53 38N 129 40W
Inukjuak Québec **46** A4 58 28N 78 15W
Inuuvik (*Inuvik*) Northwest Territories **50** E4 68 16N 130 40W
Inuvik (*Inuuvik*) Northwest Territories **50** E4 68 16N 133 40W
Inuuvik (*Inuvik*) *reg.* Northwest Territories **50** E4
68 21N 133 43W
Inuvik (*Inuuvik*) *reg.* Northwest Territories **50** E4
68 21N 133 43W
Inverhuron Provincial Park Ontario **44** A3 44 20N 81 30W
Invermere British Columbia **35** E2 50 30N 116 00W
Inverness *admin.* Nova Scotia **49** F7 46 00N 61 30W
Inverness Nova Scotia **49** F7 46 14N 61 19W
Ioco *tn.* British Columbia **52** G4 49 18N 122 51W
Iqaluit (*Frobisher Bay*) Northwest Territories **51** T3
63 44N 68 28W
Irma Alberta **37** C2 52 55N 111 14W
Iron Bridge *tn.* Ontario **41** C2 46 17N 83 14W
Irondale Ontario **44** D3 44 53N 78 30W
Ironside Québec **53** J2 45 27N 75 46W
Iroquois Ontario **43** L5 44 51N 75 19W
Iroquois Falls *tn.* Ontario **41** D2 48 47N 80 41W
Irvine Creek Alberta **54** G4 53 20N 113 29W
Irvines Landing British Columbia **34** H4 49 37N 124 02W
Isaac Creek *tn.* Yukon Territory **50** D3 62 57N 138 34W
Isaac Lake Ontario **44** A3 44 46N 81 13W
Isachsen Northwest Territories **51** L6 78 47N 103 30W
Ishpatina Ridge Ontario **41** D2 47 19N 80 44W
Iskut River British Columbia **34** B3 56 45N 131 10W
Island Falls Dam Saskatchewan **38** C3 55 30N 102 20W

Island Lake Manitoba **39** C2 53 47N 94 30W
Island Lake tn. Manitoba **39** C2 53 50N 94 35W
Islands, Bay of Newfoundland **48** C4 55 09N 59 49W
Isle aux Morts tn. Newfoundland **49** C2 47 35N 58 59W
Isle Madame i. Nova Scotia **49** F7 45 30N 60 58W
Isle Royale i. Ontario **41** C2 48 10N 88 30W
Isle Royale National Park Ontario **41** C2 48 10N 88 30W
Islington Ontario **52** B1 43 38N 79 32W
Ituna Saskatchewan **38** C2 51 09N 103 24W
Ivujivik Québec **46** A5 62 25N 77 54W
Ivvavik National Park Yukon Territory **50** D4
 69 20N 139 30W

J

Jackfish Lake Manitoba **39** B2 50 30N 99 20W
Jackson's Arm tn. Newfoundland **49** C2 49 53N 56 47W
Jacksons Point tn. Ontario **44** C3 44 18N 79 22W
Jaffray Melick Ontario **40** B2 49 49N 94 25W
Jakes Corner Yukon Territory **50** E3 60 20N 133 58W
James Bay (Baie James) Ontario/Québec **40** D3
 53 15N 81 00W
James Bay Preserve Northwest Territories **51** Q1
 53 30N 81 00W
James Ross, Cape Northwest Territories **50** J5
 74 40N 114 25W
James Ross Strait Northwest Territories **51** M4
 69 40N 96 00W
Jarvis Ontario **44** B1 42 52N 80 08W
Jasper Alberta **37** B2 52 55N 118 05W
Jasper National Park Alberta **37** B2 53 00N 118 00W
Jean Marie River (Tthets'éhk'édéli) tn. Northwest Territories
 50 G3 61 32N 120 38W
Jellicoe Ontario **40** C2 49 41N 87 31W
Jennings River British Columbia **34** B3 59 33N 131 40W
Jenpeg Manitoba **39** B2 54 30N 98 00W
Jervis Inlet British Columbia **34** H4 49 47N 124 04W
Jo Batt's Arm tn. Newfoundland **49** D2 49 44N 54 10W
Jock River Ontario **53** J2 45 15N 75 46W
Joggins Nova Scotia **49** F7 45 42N 64 27W
John D'Or Prairie tn. Alberta **37** B3 58 30N 115 08W
John Hart Highway British Columbia **35** D3 55 40N 121 38W
Johnsons Crossing Yukon Territory **60** 29N 133 17W
Johnstone Strait British Columbia **35** C2 50 23N 126 30W
Joliette admin. Québec **43** M8 47 10N 74 55W
Joliette Québec **47** B7 46 02N 73 27W
Jones Ontario **40** B2 49 59N 94 05W
Jones Sound Northwest Territories **51** P6 76 00N 85 00W
Jonquière Québec **47** B2 48 25N 71 16W
Jordan Lake Nova Scotia **49** E6 44 05N 65 20W
Jordan River tn. Ontario **44** H4 48 26N 123 59W
Joseph, Lake Ontario **44** C4 45 11N 79 44W
Joutel Québec **47** A2 49 32N 78 20W
Juan De Fuca Strait (Strait of Juan de Fuca) British Columbia
 34 H4 48 30N 124 31W
Judique Nova Scotia **49** F7 45 55N 61 30W

K

Kabania Lake Ontario **40** C3 52 12N 88 20W
Kabinakagami, Lake Ontario **41** D2 48 54N 84 25W
Kabinakagami River Ontario **41** D2 49 10N 84 10W
Kagawong Ontario **42** D6 45 54N 82 15W
K'ágee (Kakisa) Northwest Territories **50** H3
 60 58N 117 30W
K'áhbamitué (Colville Lake) tn. Northwest Territories **50** F4
 67 02N 126 07W
Kahnawake Québec **53** N4 45 25N 73 42W
Kahshe Lake Ontario **44** C3 44 59N 79 17W
Kaipokok Bay Newfoundland **48** C3 54 55N 59 43W
Kakabeka Falls tn. Ontario **41** C2 48 24N 89 40W
Kakisa (K'ágee) Northwest Territories **50** H3
 60 58N 117 30W
Kakkiviak, Cape Newfoundland **48** B5 60 05N 64 15W
Kakwa Recreation Area British Columbia **35** D2
 54 05N 120 20W
Kakwa River Alberta **37** B2 54 15N 119 45W
Kaladar Ontario **43** J5 44 39N 77 07W
Kamilukuak Lake Northwest Territories **51** L3
 62 22N 101 40W
Kaminak Lake Northwest Territories **51** M3 62 10N 95 00W
Kamloops British Columbia **35** D2 50 39N 120 24W
Kamloops Lake British Columbia **35** D2 50 45N 120 40W
Kamouraska admin. Québec **43** S8 47 20N 69 45W
Kamouraska **43** S8 47 34N 69 51W
Kamsack Saskatchewan **38** C2 51 34N 101 51W
Kamuchawie Lake Saskatchewan/Manitoba **38** C3
 56 20N 102 00W
Kanaaupscow Québec **46** A3 54 00N 76 40W
Kanata Ontario **53** J2 45 20N 75 53W
Kangiqsualujjuaq Québec **46** C4 58 48N 66 08W
Kangiqsujuaq Québec **46** B5 61 40N 71 59W
Kangiqtinq (Rankin Inlet) tn. Northwest Territories **51** N3
 62 49N 92 05W
Kangiqtugaapik (Clyde River) tn. Northwest Territories
 51 T5 70 30N 68 30W
Kangirsuk Québec **46** B5 60 00N 70 00W
Kapiskau River Ontario **40** D3 52 00N 84 50W
Kapuskasing Ontario **41** D2 49 25N 82 26W
Kapuskasing River Ontario **41** D2 48 40N 82 50W
Kasabonika I.R. Ontario **40** C3 53 32N 88 37W
Kasabonika Lake Ontario **40** C3 53 35N 88 35W
Kasba Lake Northwest Territories **51** L3 60 18N 102 07W
Kashechewan I.R. Ontario **40** D3 52 18N 81 37W
Kashottama River Manitoba **39** C3 54 25N 91 10W
Kaslo British Columbia **35** E1 49 54N 116 57W
Kasmere Lake Manitoba **39** A3 59 30N 101 10W

Kates Needle mt. British Columbia **34** B3 57 02N 132 05W
Katłodeeche (Hay River) tn. Northwest Territories
 50 H3 60 51N 115 42W
Kaumajet Mountains Newfoundland **48** B4 57 48N 62 15W
Kazabazua Québec **43** K6 45 56N 76 01W
Kearney Ontario **42** G6 45 35N 79 17W
Kechika River British Columbia **35** C3 58 44N 127 25W
Kedgwick New Brunswick **49** A2 47 38N 67 21W
Keefers British Columbia **34** H5 50 03N 121 32W
Keele Peak Yukon Territory **50** E3 63 25N 130 17W
Keele River Northwest Territories **50** F3 64 10N 128 00W
Keewatin Ontario **40** B2 49 47N 94 30W
Keewatin River Manitoba **39** A3 56 09N 100 59W
Keewatin reg. Northwest Territories **51** M3 63 30N 98 00W
Keith Arm b. Northwest Territories **50** G4 65 05N 122 20W
Kejimkujik National Park Nova Scotia **49** E6 44 20N 65 20W
Keller Lake Northwest Territories **50** G3 63 55N 121 30W
Kellett, Cape Northwest Territories **50** F5 71 59N 126 00W
Kellett Strait Northwest Territories **50** H6 75 45N 117 30W
Kelliher Saskatchewan **38** C2 51 15N 103 41W
Kelowna British Columbia **35** E1 49 50N 119 29W
Kelsey Manitoba **39** B3 56 04N 96 30W
Kelsey Bay tn. British Columbia **35** C2 50 22N 125 29W
Kelvington Saskatchewan **38** C2 52 10N 103 30W
Kemano British Columbia **35** C2 53 39N 127 58W
Kempenfelt Bay Ontario **44** C3 44 22N 79 39W
Kemptville Ontario **41** E2 45 01N 75 38W
Kenamu River Newfoundland **48** B3 52 50N 60 20W
Kenaston Saskatchewan **38** B2 51 30N 106 15W
Kendall Island Bird Sanctuary Northwest Territories **50** D4
 69 30N 135 00W
Kennebecasis River New Brunswick **49** E7 45 30N 65 40W
Kennedy Saskatchewan **38** C2 50 01N 102 21W
Kennedy Lake British Columbia **34** G4 49 12N 125 32W
Kennetcook Nova Scotia **49** F7 45 10N 63 43W
Kenney Dam British Columbia **35** D2 53 38N 124 59W
Kenogami River Ontario **40** D3 50 50N 84 30W
Kenogamissi Lake Ontario **41** D2 48 15N 81 33W
Kenora Ontario **40** B2 49 47N 94 26W
Kensington Prince Edward Island **49** F7 46 26N 63 39W
Kent admin. New Brunswick **49** F7 46 30N 64 50W
Kent admin. Ontario **42** D3 42 25N 82 10W
Kent Peninsula Northwest Territories **50** K4 68 30N 106 00W
Kentville Nova Scotia **49** F7 45 04N 64 29W
Keremeos British Columbia **35** E1 49 12N 119 50W
Kerrobert Saskatchewan **38** B2 51 56N 109 09W
Kesagami Lake Ontario **41** D3 50 30N 80 15W
Kesagami Lake Provincial Park Ontario **41** D3 50 30N 80 15W
Kesagami River Ontario **41** D3 50 30N 80 10W
Keswick Ontario **44** C3 44 15N 79 28W
Kettle Creek Ontario **44** A1 42 47N 81 13W
Kettle Rapids tn. Manitoba **39** C3 56 25N 94 30W
Kettle River British Columbia **35** E1 49 10N 119 02W
Kettle River Manitoba **39** C3 56 40N 89 50W
Kettlestone Bay Québec **46** A5 61 20N 77 54W
Keyano Québec **46** B3 53 52N 73 30W
Key Lake Mine tn. Saskatchewan **38** B3 57 10N 105 30W
Khutzeymateen Provincial Park British Columbia **35** C2
 54 30N 129 50W
Kicking Horse Pass Alberta/British Columbia **35** E2
 51 28N 116 23W
Kiglapait, Cape Newfoundland **48** B4 57 06N 61 22W
Kiglapait Mountains Newfoundland **48** B4
 57 00N 61 35W
Kikkertarjote Island Newfoundland **48** B4
 57 30N 61 58W
Kikkertavak Island Newfoundland **48** B4 56 22N 61 35W
Kilcona Park Manitoba **54** D2 49 56N 97 03W
Kildonan Park Manitoba **54** D2 49 57N 97 07W
Killaloe Ontario **43** J6 45 33N 77 26W
Killam Alberta **37** C2 52 47N 111 51W
Killarney Manitoba **39** B1 49 12N 99 40W
Killarney Ontario **42** E6 45 59N 81 30W
Killarney Provincial Park Ontario **42** D3 46 05N 81 30W
Killear Provincial Park Ontario **44** B4 45 21N 80 13W
Killiniq Northwest Territories **46** D5 60 30N 64 50W
Killiniq Northwest Territories **48** B5
 60 24N 64 31W
Kimberley British Columbia **35** E1 49 40N
 115 58W
Kimmirut (Lake Harbour) tn. Northwest Territories **51** T3
 62 50N 69 50W
Kinbasket Lake British Columbia **35** E2 51 57N 118 02W
Kincardine Ontario **41** D1 44 11N 81 38W
Kincolith British Columbia **34** C3 55 00N 129 57W
Kincora Prince Edward Island **49** F7 46 20N 63 40W
Kindersley Saskatchewan **38** B2 51 27N 109 08W
King Christian Island Northwest Territories **51** L6
 77 45N 102 00W
King City Ontario **41** C2 43 54N 79 31W
Kingcome Inlet tn. British Columbia **35** C2 50 58N 125 15W
Kingfisher Lake I.R. Ontario **40** C3 53 02N 89 50W
Kingfisher Lake Ontario **40** C3 53 05N 89 49W
Kinggauk (Bathurst Inlet) tn. Northwest Territories **50** K4
 66 50N 108 01W
King George Islands Northwest Territories **51** R2
 57 15N 78 30W
King George, Mount British Columbia **35** E2
 50 36N 115 26W
King Island British Columbia **35** C2 52 10N 127 35W
Kingnait (Cape Dorset) tn. Northwest Territories
 51 R3 64 10N 76 40W
Kings admin. New Brunswick **49** E7 45 30N 65 40W
Kings admin. Nova Scotia **49** F6 44 50N 64 50W
Kings admin. Prince Edward Island **49** F7 46 20N 62 40W
Kingsburg Nova Scotia **49** F6 44 20N 64 15W
Kings Landing New Brunswick **49** A2 45 50N 67 00W

Kingsmere Québec **53** J2 45 29N 75 50W
Kingston Ontario **41** E1 44 14N 76 30W
Kingsville Ontario **41** D1 42 02N 82 45W
Kingurutik Lake Newfoundland **48** B4 56 49N 62 20W
King William Island Northwest Territories **51** M4
 69 00N 97 30W
Kinistino Saskatchewan **38** B2 52 28N 105 01W
Kinoje River Ontario **40** D3 51 40N 81 50W
Kinoosao Saskatchewan **38** C3 57 07N 102 02W
Kinsac Nova Scotia **53** P7 44 51N 63 39W
Kinsac Lake Nova Scotia **53** P7 44 50N 63 38W
Kinusheseo River Ontario **40** D3 54 30N 83 50W
Kiosk Ontario **42** H7 46 05N 78 53W
Kipahigan Lake Manitoba **39** A3 55 20N 101 50W
Kipawa Québec **42** G7 46 47N 79 00W
Kipling Saskatchewan **38** C2 50 08N 102 40W
Kirkfield Lift Lock National Park Ontario **44** D3
 44 30N 79 00W
Kirkland Québec **53** M4 45 27N 73 53W
Kirkland Lake Ontario **41** D2 48 10N 80 02W
Kirkland Lake tn. Ontario **65** J6 48 10N 80 02W
Kirkpatrick Lake Alberta **37** C2 51 52N 111 18W
Kirriemuir Alberta **37** C2 51 56N 110 18W
Kiskittogisa Lake Manitoba **39** B2 54 10N 98 50W
Kiskitto Lake Manitoba **39** B2 54 20N 98 50W
Kispiox British Columbia **35** C3 55 21N 127 41W
Kississing Lake Manitoba **39** A3 55 10N 101 30W
Kistigan Lake Manitoba **39** C2 54 42N 92 30W
Kitchener Ontario **41** D1 43 27N 80 03W
Kitikmeot reg. Northwest Territories **50** K4 69 50N 107 30W
Kitimat British Columbia **34** C2 54 05N 128 38W
Kitlope Protected Area British Columbia **35** C2
 53 00N 127 30W
Klappan River British Columbia **34** C3 57 50N 129 40W
Kleinburg Ontario **52** B2 43 50N 79 36W
Klemtu British Columbia **34** C2 52 35N 128 32W
Klinaklini River British Columbia **35** C2 51 18N 125 45W
Klondike Highway Yukon Territory **50** D3 62 55N 136 10W
Klondike River Yukon Territory **50** D3 64 04N 138 50W
Kluane Lake Yukon Territory **50** D3 62 20N 139 00W
Kluane National Park Yukon Territory **50** D3
 60 30N 139 00W
Kluane Wildlife Sanctuary Yukon Territory **50** D3
 61 30N 139 50W
Knee Lake Manitoba **39** C3 55 10N 94 40W
Knight Inlet British Columbia **35** C2 50 45N 125 36W
Knox, Cape British Columbia **34** B2 54 09N 133 05W
Koch Island Northwest Territories **51** R4 69 38N 78 15W
Kogaluc Bay Québec **46** A4 59 20N 77 50W
Kogaluk River Newfoundland **48** B4 56 10N 63 00W
Koidern Yukon Territory **50** C3 61 58N 140 29W
Kokanee Glacier Park British Columbia **35** E1
 49 45N 117 10W
Komoka Ontario **44** A1 42 56N 81 26W
Kootenay Lake British Columbia **35** E1 49 35N 116 30W
Kootenay National Park British Columbia **35** E2
 51 15N 116 25W
Kopka River Ontario **40** C3 50 00N 90 00W
Kotcho Lake British Columbia **35** D3 59 05N 121 10W
Kouchibouguac National Park New Brunswick **49** F7
 46 50N 64 50W
Koukdjuak River Northwest Territories **51** S4
 66 50N 72 50W
Kovik Bay Québec **46** A5 61 35N 77 54W
Kugluktuk (Coppermine) Northwest Territories **50** H4
 67 49N 115 12W
Kunghit Island British Columbia **34** B2 52 02N 131 02W
Kuujjuaq Québec **46** C4 58 25N 68 55W
Kuujjuarapik (Poste-de-la-Baleine, Wapmagoostui)
 Québec **46** A4 55 15N 77 41W
Kwadacha Wilderness Park British Columbia **35** C3
 57 50N 125 00W
Kwataboahegan River Ontario **40** D3 51 10N 82 30W
Kyle Saskatchewan **38** B2 50 50N 108 02W
Kyuquot Sound British Columbia **35** C1 49 59N 127 22W

L

La Baie Québec **47** B2 48 20N 70 55W
La Barrière Park Manitoba **54** D1 49 43N 97 09W
Labelle admin. Québec **43** L7 44 30N 75 20W
Labelle Québec **43** M7 46 17N 74 45W
Laberge, Lake Yukon Territory **50** D3 61 11N 135 12W
Labrador geog. reg. Newfoundland **48** A3 54 00N 64 00W
Labrador City Newfoundland **48** A3 52 57N 66 55W
Lac Abitibi I. Ontario/Québec **47** A2 48 40N 79 40W
Lac Albanel I. Québec **47** B3 51 00N 73 00W
Lac à l'Eau Claire I. Québec **46** B4 56 20N 74 30W
Lac Anuc I. Québec **46** A4 59 15N 75 10W
Lac Assinica I. Québec **47** A3 50 00N 75 20W
Lac au Goéland I. Québec **47** A2 49 45N 76 55W
Lac Aylmer I. Québec **43** Q6 45 50N 71 20W
Lac Bacqueville I. Québec **46** B4 58 50N 74 00W
Lac Batiscan I. Québec **43** Q8 47 23N 71 53W
Lac Bécard I. Québec **46** B5 60 05N 73 45W
Lac Belot I. Northwest Territories **50** F4 66 53N 127 00W
Lac Bérard I. Québec **46** B4 58 25N 70 05W
Lac Bermen I. Québec **46** C3 53 40N 69 00W
Lac Berté I. Québec **47** B2 49 20N 71 10W
Lac Bienville I. Québec **46** B4 55 10N 72 50W
Lac Bourdel I. Québec **46** B4 56 42N 74 15W
Lac Boyd I. Québec **47** A3 52 20N 76 50W
Lac Brochet I. Manitoba **39** A3 58 40N 101 25W
Lac Brochet tn. Manitoba **39** A3 58 45N 101 30W
Lac Brome I. Québec **43** P6 45 15N 72 30W
Lac Brome tn. Québec **43** P6 45 13N 72 30W
Lac Burton I. Québec **46** A3 54 45N 78 25W
Lac Cambrien I. Québec **46** C4 56 20N 69 12W

Lac Cananée I. Québec **46** D4 56 05N 64 05W
Lac Chaconipau I. Québec **46** C4 56 20N 68 45W
Lac Chambeaux I. Québec **46** C3 53 50N 68 30W
Lac Champdoré I. Québec **46** D4 55 50N 65 58W
Lac Champlain (Lake Champlain) I. Québec/U.S.A. **43** N6
 45 08N 73 08W
Lac Châtelain I. Québec **46** B5 60 20N 74 00W
Lac Chavigny I. Québec **46** A4 58 10N 75 10W
Lac Chibougamau I. Québec **47** B2 49 55N 74 20W
Lac Couture I. Québec **46** A5 60 00N 75 20W
Lac de Gras I. Northwest Territories **50** J3 64 10N 110 10W
Lac de la Hutte Sauvage I. Québec **46** D4 56 18N 64 55W
Lac des Bois I. Northwest Territories **50** F4 67 00N 126 00W
Lac Deschênes (Lake Ontario) I. Ontario/Québec **53** J2
 45 22N 75 50W
Lac des Commissaires I. Québec **43** P9 48 09N 72 13W
Lac des Deux Montagnes I. Québec **53** M4 45 30N 73 58W
Lac des Loups Marins I. Québec **46** B4 56 30N 73 30W
Lac des Mille Lacs I. Ontario **40** B3 48 53N 90 22W
Lac des Quinze I. Québec **47** A2 47 45N 79 15W
Lac des Trente et Un Milles I. Québec **43** L7
 46 18N 75 43W
Lac D'Iberville I. Québec **46** B4 55 55N 73 15W
Lac du Bonnet I. Manitoba **39** B2 50 30N 95 50W
Lac du Bonnet tn. Manitoba **39** B2 50 16N 96 03W
Lac Dumoine I. Québec **42** J7 46 55N 77 58W
Lac Duncan I. Québec **47** A3 53 25N 78 00W
Lac du Sable I. Québec **46** C3 54 25N 67 59W
Lac Édouard I. Québec **43** P8 47 40N 72 16W
Lac-Etchemin tn. Québec Canada **47** B2 46 23N 70 32W
Lac Faribault I. Québec **46** B4 59 10N 72 00W
Lac Fleur-de-May I. Newfoundland **48** A3 52 00N 65 02W
Lac Goatanaga I. Québec **43** J8 47 42N 77 23W
Lac Guillaume-Delisle I. Québec **46** A4 56 15N 76 20W
Lachine Québec Canada **53** N4 45 26N 73 42W
Lachute Québec Canada **47** B2 45 39N 74 21W
Lac Ile-à-la Crosse I. Saskatchewan **38** B3 55 40N 107 30W
Lac Jeannin I. Québec **46** C4 56 25N 66 30W
Lac Joseph I. Newfoundland **48** A3 52 45N 65 18W
Lac Kempt I. Québec **47** B2 47 28N 74 08W
Lac Kénogami I. Québec **47** B2 48 20N 71 20W
Lac Kipawa I. Québec **42** G7 46 55N 79 06W
Lac Klotz I. Québec **46** B5 60 30N 73 30W
Lac la Biche I. Alberta **37** C2 54 55N 112 58W
Lac la Biche tn. Alberta **37** C2 54 46N 111 58W
Lac la Croix I. Ontario **41** B2 48 21N 92 09W
Lac la Loche I. Saskatchewan **38** B3 56 30N 109 40W
Lac la Martre I. Northwest Territories **50** H3
 63 20N 118 30W
Lac la Martre (Wha Ti) tn. Northwest Territories **50** H3
 63 00N 117 30W
Lac la Plonge I. Saskatchewan **38** B3 55 05N 107 00W
Lac la Ronge I. Saskatchewan **38** B3/C3 55 10N 105 00W
Lac la Ronge Provincial Park Saskatchewan **38** C3
 55 20N 104 45W
Lac le Moyne I. Québec **46** C4 56 40N 68 45W
Lac le Roy I. Québec **46** A4 58 35N 75 25W
Lac Lesdiguières I. Québec **46** B5 60 40N 74 50W
Lac Magpie I. Québec **47** D3 51 00N 64 40W
Lac Maicasagi I. Québec **47** A2 49 55N 76 45W
Lac Manitou I. Québec **47** C3 50 50N 65 20W
Lac Manouane I. Québec **47** B3 50 45N 70 45W
Lac Matagami I. Québec **47** A2 49 55N 77 30W
Lac Maunoir I. Northwest Territories **50** F4 67 40N 125 50W
Lac-Mégantic tn. Québec Canada **47** B2 45 34N 70 53W
Lac Memphrémagog I. Québec **47** B2 45 05N 72 13W
Lac Mesgouez I. Québec **47** A3 51 25N 75 00W
Lac Minto I. Québec **46** B4 57 15N 74 55W
Lac Mistassini I. Québec **43** B3 51 00N 73 20W
Lac Mistinibi I. Québec **46** D4 55 50N 64 20W
Lac Mitchinamécus I. Québec **43** L8 47 20N 75 02W
Lac Musquaro I. Québec **47** D3 50 50N 60 50W
Lac Nantais I. Québec **46** B5 60 58N 74 00W
Lac Naococane I. Québec **47** B3 52 53N 70 40W
Lac Nichicapau I. Québec **46** C4 54 42N 68 28W
Lac Nichicun I. Québec **47** B3 53 05N 71 05W
Lacombe Alberta Canada **37** C2 52 28N 113 44W
Lac Opiscotéo I. Québec **47** C3 53 15N 68 20W
Lac Otelnuk I. Québec **46** C4 56 10N 68 20W
Lac Parent I. Québec **47** A2 48 30N 77 08W
Lac Payne I. Québec **46** B4 59 25N 74 00W
Lac Péribonka I. Québec **47** B3 50 10N 71 23W
Lac Plétipi I. Québec **47** B3 51 05N 70 10W
Lac Poncheville I. Québec **47** A3 50 12N 76 55W
Lac Potherie I. Québec **46** B4 58 50N 72 25W
Lac Qilalugalik I. Québec **46** A4 58 35N 76 00W
Lac Ramusio I. Québec **46** D4 55 05N 63 50W
Lac Résolution I. Québec **46** C4 55 55N 64 40W
La Crete Alberta **37** B3 58 11N 116 30W
Lac Roberts I. Québec **46** B5 60 25N 70 25W
Lac Saindon I. Québec **46** D4 55 55N 64 30W
Lac Sainte-Anne I. Québec **47** C3 50 15N 67 58W
Lac Saint-Jean I. Québec **47** B2 48 35N 72 00W
Lac-St.-Jean-Est admin. Québec Canada **43** Q9
 48 20N 71 40W
Lac-St.-Jean-Ouest admin. Québec Canada **43** N9
 48 20N 73 00W
Lac St. Joseph I. Ontario **40** B3 51 30N 91 40W
Lac Saint-Louis I. Québec **53** M4 45 25N 73 49W
Lac Saint-Patrice I. Québec **43** J7 46 20N 77 25W
Lac Saint-Pierre I. Québec **47** B2 46 12N 72 49W
Lac Sakami I. Québec **47** A3 53 15N 76 50W
Lac Seul I.R. Ontario **40** B3 50 15N 92 15W
Lac Seul I. Ontario **40** B3 50 20N 92 00W
Lac Simard I. Québec **47** A2 47 40N 78 50W

Lac Simon *l.* Québec **43** L6 45 55N 75 05W
Lac Soscumica *l.* Québec **47** A3 50 15N 77 35W
Lac Tasiaalujjuak *l.* Québec **46** B4 59 35N 71 59W
Lac Tasiat *l.* Québec **46** A4 59 05N 75 25W
Lac Tasiataq *l.* Québec **46** B4 58 50N 71 20W
Lac Tassialouc *l.* Québec **46** B4 59 00N 73 59W
Lac Témiscamingue (*Lake Timiskaming*) *l.* Québec/
   Ontario **47** A2 47 28N 79 30W
Lac Tiblemont *l.* Québec **43** J9 48 17N 77 18W
Lac Tudor *l.* Québec **46** C4 55 50N 65 30W
Lac Wakuach *l.* Québec **46** C4 55 35N 67 40W
Lac Waswanipi *l.* Québec **47** A2 49 35N 76 36W
Lac Wayagamac *l.* Québec **43** P8 47 23N 72 35W
Lac Whitegull *l.* Québec **46** D4 55 25N 64 15W
Ladner British Columbia **34** H4 49 06N 123 05W
La Doré Québec **47** B2 48 40N 72 45W
Lady Evelyn-Smoothwater Provincial Park
   Ontario **41** D2 47 20N 80 30W
Ladysmith British Columbia **34** H4 48 57N 123 50W
Laflèche Saskatchewan **38** B1 49 44N 106 32W
Lagoon City Ontario **44** C3 44 31N 79 11W
La Grande 2 *dam* Québec **46** A3 53 51N 77 38W
La Grande 3 *dam* Québec **46** A3 53 50N 76 09W
La Grande 4 *dam* Québec **46** B3 53 59N 73 40W
La Grande Rivière Québec **46** B3 53 50N 73 59W
La Guadeloupe Québec **43** R6 45 58N 70 57W
Lake Cowichan *tn.* British Columbia **34** H4
   8 50N 124 04W
Lakefield Ontario **41** E1 44 26N 78 16W
Lake Harbour (*Kimmirut*) *tn.* Northwest Territories **51** T3
   62 50N 69 50W
Lakeland Provincial Park Alberta **37** C2 54 45N 112 25W
Lakeland Provincial Recreation Area Alberta **37** C2
   54 45N 111 15W
Lake Louise *tn.* Alberta **37** B2 51 25N 116 14W
Lake of Bays Ontario **42** G6 45 16N 79 01W
Lake of the Rivers Saskatchewan **38** B1 49 50N 105 30W
Lakeside Nova Scotia **53** P6 44 38N 63 42W
Lake Superior Provincial Park Ontario **41** D2
   47 35N 84 40W
Lakeview Newfoundland **49** D2 47 24N 53 10W
Lakeview Ontario **53** J2 45 20N 75 48W
La Loche Saskatchewan **38** B3 56 31N 109 27W
La Malbaie Québec **47** B2 47 39N 70 11W
Lamaline Newfoundland **49** C2 46 52N 55 49W
Lambeth Ontario **44** A1 42 54N 81 20W
Lambton *admin.* Ontario **42** D3 42 45N 82 05W
Lambton, Cape Northwest Territories **50** G5
   71 05N 123 09W
Lamèque New Brunswick **49** B2 47 49N 64 40W
Lampman Saskatchewan **38** C1 49 23N 102 48W
Lanark *admin.* Ontario **43** K6 45 05N 76 20W
Lanark Ontario **43** K6 45 01N 76 30W
Lancaster Ontario **43** M6 45 08N 74 30W
Lancaster Park Alberta **54** F5 53 41N 113 33W
Lancaster Sound Northwest Territories **51** P5
   74 00N 85 00W
L'Ancienne-Lorette Québec **43** Q7 46 48N 71 20W
Lands End Northwest Territories **50** G6 76 22N 122 33W
Langenburg Saskatchewan **38** C2 50 50N 101 42W
Langham Saskatchewan **38** B2 52 22N 106 55W
Langley British Columbia **34** H4 49 06N 122 38W
Lanigan Saskatchewan **38** B2 51 50N 105 01W
L'Annonciation Québec **47** B2 46 24N 74 52W
Lansdowne House *tn.* Ontario **40** C3 52 05N 88 00W
L'Anse-au-Loup Newfoundland **48** C3 51 31N 56 45W
L'Anse aux Meadows Newfoundland **48** C3
   51 36N 55 32W
L'Anse-Pleureuse Québec **47** C2 49 15N 65 40W
Lantzville British Columbia **34** H4 49 15N 124 05W
La Pocatière Québec **47** B2 47 22N 70 03W
La Poile Newfoundland **49** C2 47 41N 58 25W
La Prairie Québec **53** O4 45 25N 73 29W
Larder Lake Ontario **41** E2 48 05N 79 38W
L'Ardoise Nova Scotia **49** F7 45 37N 60 46W
Lark Harbour *tn.* Newfoundland **49** C2 49 06N 58 23W
La Ronge Saskatchewan **38** B3 55 07N 105 18W
Larrys River *tn.* Nova Scotia **49** F7 45 15N 61 25W
La Salle Manitoba **54** C1 49 41N 97 04W
La Salle Ontario **42** C2 42 15N 83 05W
La Salle Québec **53** N4 45 26N 73 40W
La Salle River Manitoba **54** C1 49 42N 97 16W
La Sarre Québec **47** A2 48 49N 79 12W
La Scie Newfoundland **49** C2 49 57N 55 36W
Lashburn Saskatchewan **38** B2 53 06N 109 36W
Lasqueti Island British Columbia **34** H4 49 28N 124 20W
Last Mountain Lake Saskatchewan **38** B2
   51 40N 106 55W
La Tabatière Québec **47** E3 50 50N 58 57W
Latchford Ontario **41** E2 47 20N 79 49W
La Tuque Québec **47** B2 47 26N 72 47W
Laurie River Manitoba **39** A3 56 30N 101 30W
Lauzon Québec **43** Q7 46 49N 71 10W
Laval Québec **43** N5 45 33N 73 45W
Laval-des-Rapides Québec **53** N5 45 33N 73 42W
Laval-Ouest Québec **53** M5 45 33N 73 50W
Lawn Newfoundland **49** C2 46 57N 55 32W
Lawrencetown Nova Scotia **49** E6 44 54N 65 10W
Leader Saskatchewan **38** B2 50 55N 109 31W
Leading Tickles Newfoundland **49** C2 49 29N 55 25W
Leaf Rapids *tn.* Manitoba **39** A3 56 30N 100 00W
Leamington Ontario **41** D1 42 03N 83 36W
Leaside Ontario **53** C1 43 44N 79 15W
Lebel-sur-Quévillon Québec **47** A2 49 05N 77 08W
Leduc Alberta **37** C2 53 17N 113 30W
Leduc County Alberta **54** F4 53 19N 113 32W
Leeds and Grenville *admin.* Ontario **43** K5
   44 35N 76 00W

Le Havre River Nova Scotia **49** F6 44 30N 64 40W
Leitrim Ontario **53** K2 45 20N 75 35W
Lemieux Islands Northwest Territories **51** U3
   64 00N 64 20W
Lennox and Addington *admin.* Ontario **43** J5 44 30N 77 00W
Lenore Lake Saskatchewan **38** C2 52 50N 104 40W
Leoville Saskatchewan **38** B2 53 39N 107 33W
Les Escoumins Québec **47** C2 48 25N 69 29W
Leslie Spit Ontario **52** C1 43 38N 79 19W
Lesser Slave Lake Alberta **37** B3 55 25N 115 25W
Lethbridge Alberta **37** C1 49 43N 112 48W
Level Mountain British Columbia **34** B3 58 33N 131 25W
Lévis Québec **43** Q7 46 47N 71 12W
Lewis Hill *mt.* Newfoundland **49** C2 48 49N 58 30W
Lewisporte Newfoundland **49** C2 49 15N 55 03W
Liard River *tn.* British Columbia **35** C3 59 28N 126 18W
Liard River Northwest Territories **50** G3 61 25N 122 30 W
Liddon Gulf Northwest Territories **50** J6 75 03N 113 00W
Líídlį Kúé (*Fort Simpson*) Northwest Territories **50** G3
   61 46N 121 15W
L'Île Dorval *i.* Québec **53** N4 45 26N 73 44W
L'Île-Perrot *i.* Québec **53** N4 45 26N 73 55W
Lillooet British Columbia **35** D2 50 41N 121 59W
Lillooet Lake British Columbia **34** H5 50 15N 122 38W
Lillooet River British Columbia **34** H4 49 59N 122 25W
Limbour Québec **53** K2 45 29N 75 44W
Lindsay Ontario **41** D1 44 21N 78 44W
Linzee, Cape Nova Scotia **49** F7 46 00N 61 32W
Lions Bay British Columbia **34** H4 49 28N 123 13W
Lions Head *tn.* Ontario **44** A3 44 59N 81 16W
Lipton Saskatchewan **38** C2 50 55N 103 49W
Liscomb Game Sanctuary Nova Scotia **49** F7 45 10N 62 40W
L'Islet *admin.* Québec **43** R8 47 10N 70 10W
L'Isle-Verte Québec **43** S9 48 00N 69 21W
Lismore Nova Scotia **49** F7 45 42N 62 16W
Listowel Ontario **41** D1 43 44N 80 57W
Little Bow River Alberta **37** C2 50 20N 113 40W
Little Buffalo Alberta **37** B3 56 25N 116 15W
Little Buffalo River Alberta **37** C3 59 45N 113 30W
Little Churchill River Manitoba **39** B3 56 40N 96 10W
Little Current *tn.* Ontario **41** D2 45 58N 81 56W
Little Dover Nova Scotia **49** F7 45 20N 61 05W
Little Grand Rapids *tn.* Manitoba **39** B2 52 10N 95 30W
Little Maitland River Ontario **44** A2 43 48N 81 10W
Little Mecatina River Newfoundland **48** B3 52 25N 61 30W
Little Narrows *tn.* Nova Scotia **49** F7 45 59N 61 00W
Little River *tn.* British Columbia **34** H4 49 45N 124 56W
Little Rouge Creek Ontario **52** C2 43 54N 79 15W
Little Sachigo Lake Ontario **40** B3 54 04N 92 11W
Little Smoky River Alberta **37** B2 54 05N 117 45W
Little White River Ontario **42** C7 46 23N 83 20W
Lively Ontario **41** D2 46 25N 81 10W
Liverpool Nova Scotia **49** F6 44 03N 64 43W
Liverpool Bay Northwest Territories **50** E4 69 45N 130 00W
Livingston Yukon Territory **50** E3 61 16N 134 26W
Livingstone Cove *tn.* Nova Scotia **49** F7 45 52N 61 58W
Lloyd George, Mount British Columbia **35** D3
   57 50N 124 58W
Lloyd Lake Alberta **54** A1 50 52N 114 10W
Lloyd Lake Saskatchewan **38** B3 57 20N 108 40W
Lloydminster Saskatchewan **38** B2 53 18N 110 00W
Lobstick Lake Newfoundland **48** A3 54 00N 65 05W
Lockeport Nova Scotia **49** E6 43 43N 65 10W
Lockport Ontario **42** B2 43 10N 97 00W
Lodge Creek Canada/U.S.A. **37** C1 49 15N 110 05W
Logan Lake *tn.* British Columbia **35** D2 50 28N 120 50W
Logan Lake Ontario **44** D3 44 57N 78 59W
Logan, Mount Yukon Territory **50** C3 60 34N 140 25W
Logan Mountains Yukon Territory **50** F3 61 30N 128 30W
London Ontario **41** D1 42 58N 81 15W
Long Beach *tn.* British Columbia **34** G4 49 06N 125 48W
Long Cove *tn.* Newfoundland **49** D2 47 34N 53 40W
Long Creek Saskatchewan **38** C2 49 20N 103 55W
Longford Ontario **44** C3 44 41N 79 21W
Long Harbour *tn.* Newfoundland **49** D2 47 26N 53 48W
Long Island Northwest Territories **51** N4 54 58N 79 20W
Long Island Nova Scotia **49** E6 44 20N 66 15W
Longlac Ontario **40** C2 49 47N 86 34W
Long Lake New Brunswick **49** A2 47 00N 66 50W
Long Lake Nova Scotia **53** P6 44 37N 63 37W
Long Lake Ontario **40** C2 49 00N 87 00W
Long Lake *I.R.* Ontario **40** C2 49 45N 86 32W
Long Point Manitoba **39** B2 52 50N 98 20W
Long Point Ontario **41** D1 42 33N 80 04W
Long Point *tn.* Ontario **44** B1 42 34N 80 15W
Long Point Bay Ontario **44** B2 42 40N 80 14W
Long Point Provincial Park Ontario **44** B1 42 40N 80 15W
Long Pond Newfoundland **49** C2 48 00N 55 52W
Long Range Mountains Newfoundland **49** C3 50 00N 57 20W
Long Sault Ontario **43** M6 45 02N 74 53W
Longueuil Québec **43** N5 45 32N 73 31W
Looking Back Lake Alberta **54** H4 53 18N 113 10W
Lookout, Cape Ontario **40** D4 55 18N 83 56W
Looma Alberta **54** H4 53 20N 113 14W
Loon Lake Nova Scotia **53** P6 44 42N 63 30W
Loon Lake *tn.* Saskatchewan **38** B2 54 00N 109 10W
Loon River Alberta **37** B3 56 40N 115 20W
L'Original Ontario **43** M6 45 37N 74 42W
Loring Ontario **42** G6 45 56N 79 59W
Lorne Park *tn.* Ontario **44** C2 43 31N 79 36W
Lorraine Québec **53** M5 45 38N 73 47W
Lotbinière *admin.* Québec **43** Q7 46 30N 71 35W
Loughborough Inlet British Columbia **34** G5
   50 35N 125 32W
Lougheed Island Northwest Territories **51** K6
   77 26N 105 06W
Louisbourg *N.H.S.* Nova Scotia **49** F7 45 54N 60 02W
Louisbourg Nova Scotia **49** G7 45 56N 59 58W

Louise Island British Columbia **34** B2 52 59N 131 50W
Louiseville Québec **43** P7 46 16N 72 56W
Lourdes Newfoundland **49** C2 48 39N 59 00W
Low, Cape Northwest Territories **51** P3 63 07N 85 18W
Lower Arrow Lake British Columbia **35** E1
   49 40N 118 09W
Lower Foster Lake Saskatchewan **38** B3 56 30N 105 10W
Lower Manitou Lake Ontario **40** B2 49 15N 93 00W
Lower Post British Columbia **35** C3 59 56N 128 09W
Lower Sackville Nova Scotia **49** F6 44 45N 63 40W
Lubicon Lake Alberta **37** B3 56 23N 115 56W
Lucan Ontario **44** A2 43 11N 81 24W
Lucknow Ontario **41** D1 43 58N 81 31W
Lucky Lake *tn.* Saskatchewan **38** B2 50 59N 107 10W
Lulu Island British Columbia **52** F3 49 09N 123 09W
Lumby British Columbia **35** E2 50 15N 118 59W
Lumsden Saskatchewan **38** C2 50 39N 104 52W
Lund British Columbia **34** H4 49 59N 124 46W
Lundar Manitoba **39** B2 50 41N 98 01W
Lunenburg *admin.* Nova Scotia **49** F6 44 35N 64 30W
Lunenburg Nova Scotia **49** F6 44 23N 64 21W
Luseland Saskatchewan **38** B2 52 06N 109 24W
Luther Lake Ontario **44** B2 43 52N 80 26W
Lyall, Mount Alberta/British Columbia **37** C2
   50 05N 114 42W
Lyell Islands British Columbia **34** B2 52 00N 131 00W
Lynn Lake *tn.* Manitoba **39** A3 56 51N 101 01W
Lynx Lake Northwest Territories **50** K3 62 25N 106 15W
Lytton British Columbia **35** D2 50 12N 121 34W

M

Mabel Lake British Columbia **35** E2 50 35N 118 40W
Mabou Nova Scotia **49** F7 46 04N 61 22W
MacAlpine Lake Northwest Territories **51** L4
   66 45N 102 50W
Macamic Québec **47** A2 48 46N 79 02W
Maccan Nova Scotia **49** F7 45 43N 64 16W
Macdiarmid *tn.* Ontario **40** C2 49 23N 88 08W
Macdonald *admin.* Manitoba **54** C2 49 47N 97 23W
MacDowell Ontario **40** B3 52 10N 92 40W
MacDowell Lake Ontario **40** B3 52 15N 92 42W
MacGregor Manitoba **39** B1 49 57N 98 48W
MacGregor Point Provincial Park Ontario **44** A3
   44 24N 81 26W
Mackay Lake Northwest Territories **50** J3 63 55N 110 25W
Mackenzie British Columbia **35** D3 55 18N 123 10W
Mackenzie Bay Yukon Territory **50** D4 69 00N 137 30W
Mackenzie Bison Sanctuary Northwest Territories **50** H3
   61 30N 116 30W
Mackenzie Highway Alberta **37** B3 57 55N 117 40W
Mackenzie King Island Northwest Territories **50** J6
   77 45N 111 00W
Mackenzie Mountains Yukon/Northwest Territories
   50 F3 64 00N 130 00W
Mackenzie River Northwest Territories **50** F4
   65 40N 128 00W
Mackey Ontario **42** J7 46 10N 77 49W
Macklin Saskatchewan **38** B2 52 20N 109 58W
Maclean Strait Northwest Territories **51** L6 77 30N 102 30W
Macmillan Pass Yukon/Northwest Territories
   50 E3 63 23N 130 00W
Macmillan River Yukon Territory **50** E3 63 00N 134 00W
Macoun Lake Saskatchewan **38** C3 56 30N 103 40W
Macrae Point Provincial Park Ontario **44** C3 44 30N 79 10W
MacTier Ontario **44** C4 45 08N 79 47W
Madawaska *admin.* New Brunswick **49** A2 47 30N 68 00W
Madawaska Ontario **41** E2 45 30N 77 59W
Madawaska River Ontario **41** E2 45 10N 77 30W
Madoc Ontario **41** E1 44 30N 77 29W
Mad River Ontario **44** B3 44 18N 80 02W
Madsen Ontario **40** B3 50 58N 93 55W
Maelpeg Reservoir Newfoundland **49** C2 48 20N 56 40W
Magnetawan Ontario **41** E2 45 40N 79 39W
Magnetawan River Ontario **42** F6 45 46N 80 37W
Magog Québec **47** B2 45 16N 72 09W
Magpie River Ontario **41** D2 48 00N 84 50W
Magrath Alberta **37** C1 49 27N 112 52W
Maguse Lake Northwest Territories **51** M3 61 40N 95 10W
Mahone Bay Nova Scotia **49** F6 44 25N 64 15W
Mahone Bay *tn.* Nova Scotia **49** F6 44 27N 64 24W
Mahood Creek British Columbia **52** G3 49 09N 122 50W
Maidstone Saskatchewan **38** B2 53 06N 109 18W
Main Brook *tn.* Newfoundland **49** C3 51 11N 56 01W
Main Channel Ontario **42** E6 45 20N 81 45W
Maitland River Ontario **44** A2 43 50N 81 28W
Major, Lake Nova Scotia **53** Q6 44 45N 63 30W
Makkovik Newfoundland **48** C4 55 05N 59 11W
Makkovik, Cape Newfoundland **48** C4 55 14N 59 09W
Makoop Lake Ontario **40** B3 53 24N 90 50W
Malartic Québec **47** A2 48 09N 78 09W
Malaspina Strait British Columbia **34** H4 49 47N 124 30W
Mallet River Ontario **44** B2 43 51N 80 42W
Malpeque Bay Prince Edward Island **49** F7 46 35N 63 50W
Malton Ontario **44** C2 43 42N 79 38W
Manicouagan Québec **47** C3 50 40N 68 46W
Manigotagan Manitoba **39** B2 51 00N 96 10W
Manigotagan River Manitoba **39** B2 51 00N 96 10W
Manistique Lake Michigan **42** A7 46 15N 85 50W
Manitoba *prov.* **9** R4 55 10N 100 00W
Manito Lake Saskatchewan **38** B2 52 40N 109 20W
Manitou Manitoba **39** B1 49 15N 98 32W
Manitou Lake Ontario **42** D6 45 48N 82 00W
Manitoulin *admin.* Ontario **42** C6 45 45N 83 00W
Manitoulin Island Ontario **41** D2 45 50N 82 20W
Manitouwadge Ontario **41** D2 48 59N 85 55W
Maniwaki Québec **47** A2 46 22N 75 58W
Manning Alberta **37** B3 56 55N 117 37W

Manning Park *tn.* British Columbia **34** H4 49 09N 120 50W
Manning Provincial Park British Columbia **34** H4
   49 09N 120 50W
Manotick Ontario **53** K1 45 14N 75 43W
Mansel Island Northwest Territories **51** R3 62 00N 79 55W
Manson Creek *tn.* British Columbia **35** D3 55 40N 124 32W
Manyberries Alberta **37** C1 49 24N 110 42W
Maple Ontario **41** C2 43 51N 79 29W
Maple Creek *tn.* Saskatchewan **38** B1 49 55N 109 28W
Maple Grove Park Manitoba **54** D2 49 47N 97 06W
Maple Ridge British Columbia **34** H4 49 13N 122 36W
Mara Provincial Park Ontario **44** C3 44 30N 79 15W
Marathon Ontario **41** D2 48 44N 86 23W
Margaree Forks Nova Scotia **49** F7 46 20N 61 10W
Margaree Harbour *tn.* Nova Scotia **49** F7 46 26N 61 08W
Margaret Lake Alberta **37** B3 58 56N 115 25W
Margaretville Nova Scotia **49** E6 45 05N 65 05W
Marieville Québec **43** N6 45 27N 73 08W
Markdale Ontario **41** D1 44 19N 80 39W
Markham Ontario **52** C3 43 54N 79 16W
Markham Bay Northwest Territories **51** R3 63 02N 72 00W
Marmora Ontario **41** E1 44 29N 77 41W
Marten Falls *I.R.* Ontario **40** C3 51 40N 85 55W
Martensville Saskatchewan **38** B2 52 10N 106 30W
Maryfield Saskatchewan **38** C1 49 50N 101 30W
Mary's Harbour *tn.* Newfoundland **48** C3 52 19N 55 50W
Marystown Newfoundland **49** C2 47 10N 55 09W
Marysville New Brunswick **49** A2 45 58N 66 35W
Mascouche Québec **47** B2 45 47N 73 49W
Maskinongé *admin.* Québec **43** M8 47 20N 74 30W
Masset British Columbia **34** B2 54 00N 132 01W
Massey Ontario **41** D1 46 12N 82 05W
Massey Sound Northwest Territories **51** N6 78 30N 94 59W
Masson Québec **53** L3 45 33N 75 24W
Matachewan Ontario **41** D2 47 56N 80 39W
Matagami Québec **65** K6 49 45N 77 45W
Matane Québec **47** C2 48 50N 67 31W
Matapédia Québec **47** C2 47 59N 66 58W
Matheson Ontario **41** D2 48 32N 80 28W
Matsqui British Columbia **34** H4 49 05N 122 22W
Mattagami Lake Ontario **41** D2 47 54N 81 35W
Mattagami River Ontario **41** D2 49 50N 81 50W
Mattawa Ontario **41** E2 46 19N 78 42W
Mattice Ontario **41** D2 49 36N 83 16W
Maurelle Island British Columbia **34** G5 50 16N 125 11W
Maxwell Ontario **44** B3 44 18N 80 23W
Mayerthorpe Alberta **37** B2 53 57N 115 08W
Mayne Island British Columbia **34** H4 48 50N 123 18W
Maynooth Ontario **42** J6 45 14N 77 57W
Mayo Yukon Territory **50** D3 63 34N 135 52W
Mayo Lake Yukon Territory **50** D3 63 50N 135 00W
Mayson Lake Saskatchewan **38** B3 57 50N 107 30W
Mbehchokó (*Rae*) Northwest Territories **50** H3
   62 50N 116 03W
McAdam New Brunswick **49** A2 45 34N 67 20W
McArthur Wildlife Sanctuary Yukon Territory **50** D3
   63 16N 135 50W
McBride British Columbia **35** D2 53 21N 120 19W
McCabe Lake Nova Scotia **53** P7 44 47N 63 43W
McClintock Manitoba **39** C3 57 50N 94 10W
McConnell River Bird Sanctuary Northwest Territories
   51 N3 60 30N 94 00W
McCreary Manitoba **39** B2 50 45N 99 30W
McFarlane River Saskatchewan **38** B3 57 50N 107 55W
McGivney New Brunswick **49** A2 46 22N 66 34W
McGregor Lake Alberta **37** C2 50 25N 112 52W
McGregor River British Columbia **35** D3 54 10N 121 20W
Mckay Lake Newfoundland **48** A3 53 44N 65 37W
McKellar Ontario **42** G6 45 30N 79 55W
McKenzie Creek Ontario **44** B2 43 02N 80 17W
McLeese Lake British Columbia **35** D2 52 25N 122 20W
McLennan Alberta **37** B3 55 42N 116 54W
McLeod Lake British Columbia **35** D2 55 00N 123 00W
McLeod River Alberta **37** B2 53 40N 116 20W
M'Clintock Channel Northwest Territories **51** L5
   72 00N 102 00W
M'Clure, Cape Northwest Territories **50** G5 74 32N 121 19W
M'Clure Strait Northwest Territories **50** H5 74 40N 117 30W
McNabs Island Nova Scotia **53** P6 44 37N 63 31W
McNutt Island Nova Scotia **49** E6 43 40N 65 20W
McQuesten Yukon Territory **50** D3 63 35N 137 20W
McTavish Arm *b.* Northwest Territories **50** H4
   66 30N 118 04W
McVicar Arm *b.* Northwest Territories **50** G4
   65 05N 120 10W
Meadow Lake *tn.* Saskatchewan **38** B2 54 09N 108 26W
Meadow Lake Provincial Park Saskatchewan **38** B2
   54 30N 108 00W
Meadowvale West Ontario **44** C2 43 35N 79 45W
Meaford Ontario **41** D1 44 36N 80 35W
Meaghers Grant Nova Scotia **49** F6 44 56N 63 15W
Mealy Mountains Newfoundland **48** C3 53 30N 59 10W
Meander River *tn.* Alberta **37** B3 59 02N 117 42W
Meares Island British Columbia **35** C1 49 10N 126 00W
Meath Park *tn.* Saskatchewan **38** B3 53 27N 105 22W
Medicine Hat Alberta **37** C2 50 03N 110 41W
Medley Alberta **37** C2 54 25N 110 16W
Meductic New Brunswick **49** A2 45 55N 67 30W
Medway Creek Ontario **44** A2 43 07N 81 18W
Medway River Nova Scotia **49** F6 44 15N 64 50W
Mégantic *admin.* Québec **43** Q7 46 15N 71 30W
Meighen Island Northwest Territories **51** M6
   79 55N 99 00W
Melbourne Island Northwest Territories **50** L4
   68 30N 104 45W
Meldrum Bay *tn.* Ontario **42** C6 45 56N 83 06W
Melfort Saskatchewan **38** C2 52 52N 104 38W
Melita Manitoba **39** A1 49 16N 101 00W

Melville Saskatchewan **38** C2 50 57N 102 49W
Melville Hills Northwest Territories **50** G4
69 00N 121 00W
Melville Island Northwest Territories **50** J6
75 30N 112 00W
Melville, Lake Newfoundland **48** C3 53 45N 59 40W
Melville Peninsula Northwest Territories **51** Q4
68 00N 84 00W
Melville Sound Northwest Territories **50** K4
68 05N 107 30W
Melville Sound Ontario **44** A3 44 58N 81 04W
Menihek Newfoundland **48** A3 54 28N 66 36W
Menihek Lakes Newfoundland **48** A3 53 50N 66 28W
Mer Bleu Conservation Area m. Ontario **53** K2
45 24N 75 31W
Mercy Bay Northwest Territories **50** H5 74 05N 119 00W
Merigomish Nova Scotia **49** F7 45 37N 62 25W
Merivale Ontario **53** K2 45 19N 75 44W
Merrickville Ontario **43** L5 44 55N 75 50W
Merritt British Columbia **35** D2 50 09N 120 49W
Mersey River Nova Scotia **49** F6 44 10N 64 58W
Métabetchouane Québec **43** Q9 48 26N 71 52W
Meta Incognita Peninsula Northwest Territories **51** T3
63 00N 69 00W
Metcalfe Ontario **53** K1 45 14N 75 29W
Metchosin British Columbia **34** H4 48 22N 123 32W
Meteghan Nova Scotia **49** E6 44 12N 66 10W
Metropolitan Toronto admin. Ontario **52** C2 43 44N 79 16W
Meziadin Junction tn. British Columbia **34** C3
56 10N 129 15W
Mica Creek tn. British Columbia **35** E2 52 00N 118 28W
Mica Dam British Columbia **35** E2 52 04N 118 28W
Michaud Point Nova Scotia **49** F7 45 35N 60 40W
Michel Peak British Columbia **35** C2 53 30N 126 25W
Michikamats Lake Newfoundland **48** B3 54 38N 64 19W
Michikamau Lake Newfoundland **48** B3
53 58N 64 00W
Michipicoten Ontario **65** J6 47 57N 84 55W
Michipicoten Island Ontario **41** C2 47 45N 85 45W
Micmac, Lake Nova Scotia **53** P6 44 41N 63 32W
Midale Saskatchewan **38** C1 49 23N 103 21W
Middle Arm tn. Newfoundland **49** C2 49 42N 56 06W
Middle Maitland River Ontario **44** A2 43 48N 81 11W
Middle Ridge Newfoundland **49** C2 48 20N 55 15W
Middle Ridge Wildlife Reserve Newfoundland **49** C2
48 30N 55 15W
Middle Sackville Nova Scotia **53** P7 44 47N 63 41W
Middlesex admin. Ontario **44** A1 42 46N 81 46W
Middleton Nova Scotia **49** E6 44 56N 65 04W
Midhurst Ontario **44** C4 44 26N 79 45W
Midland Ontario **41** E1 44 45N 79 53W
Midnapore Alberta **37** C2 50 55N 114 05W
Midway British Columbia **35** E1 49 02N 118 45W
Midway Mountains British Columbia **35** E1
49 25N 118 45W
Mikkwa River Alberta **37** C3 57 40N 114 08W
Mildmay Ontario **44** A3 44 03N 81 08W
Milestone Saskatchewan **38** C1 49 59N 104 31W
Milk River Alberta **37** C1 49 10N 110 05W
Milk River tn. Alberta **37** C1 49 09N 112 05W
Millbrook Ontario **44** D4 44 09N 78 28W
Mill Creek Alberta **54** G4 53 27N 113 23W
Miller Lake Nova Scotia **53** P7 44 49N 63 35W
Millet Alberta **37** C2 53 06N 113 28W
Mill Island Northwest Territories **51** R3 64 00N 78 00W
Milltown Newfoundland **49** C2 47 54N 55 46W
Mill Village Newfoundland **49** F6 44 10N 64 40W
Millville New Brunswick **49** A2 46 08N 67 12W
Milo Alberta **37** C2 50 34N 112 53W
Milton Nova Scotia **49** F6 44 04N 64 44W
Milton Ontario **41** E1 43 31N 79 53W
Milton Prince Edward Island **49** F7 46 20N 63 10W
Milverton Ontario **44** A2 43 34N 80 55W
Miminegash Prince Edward Island **49** F7
46 54N 64 15W
Minaki Ontario **40** B2 50 00N 94 40W
Minas Basin Nova Scotia **49** F7 45 15N 64 15W
Minas Channel Nova Scotia **49** F7 45 10N 64 50W
Minden Ontario **42** H5 44 56N 78 44W
Minipi Lake Newfoundland **48** B3 52 25N 60 50W
Miniss Lake Ontario **40** B3 50 48N 90 50W
Minitonas Manitoba **39** A2 52 04N 101 02W
Minnedosa Manitoba **39** B2 50 14N 99 50W
Minnitaki Lake Ontario **40** B3 50 02N 91 45W
Minonipi Lake Newfoundland **48** B3 52 50N 60 45W
Minto New Brunswick **49** A2 46 05N 66 05W
Minto Yukon Territory **50** D3 62 34N 136 50W
Minto Inlet Northwest Territories **50** H5 71 20N 117 00W
Mirabel Québec **47** B2 45 41N 74 02W
Miramichi New Brunswick **49** A2 47 02N 65 30W
Miramichi Bay New Brunswick **49** A2 47 05N 65 00W
Mira River Nova Scotia **49** F7 46 00N 60 10W
Miscouche Prince Edward Island **49** F7 46 26N 63 52W
Miscou Island New Brunswick **49** B2 47 55N 64 30W
Misery Point Newfoundland **48** C3 52 01N 55 18W
Missanabie Ontario **41** D2 48 19N 84 05W
Missinaibi Lake Ontario **41** D2 48 23N 83 40W
Missinaibi River Ontario **41** D2 49 30N 83 20W
Mission British Columbia **34** H4 49 08N 122 20W
Missisa Lake Ontario **40** C3 52 18N 85 12W
Mississagi River Ontario **41** D2 46 23N 83 30W
Mississauga Ontario **52** B1 43 38N 79 36W
Mississauga Lake Ontario **44** D3 44 43N 78 17W
Missouri Coteau hills Saskatchewan **38** B2
50 00N 106 30W
Mistassini Québec **47** B2 48 54N 72 13W
Mistassini Québec **47** B3 50 25N 73 50W

Mistastin Lake Newfoundland **48** B4 55 50N 63 15W
Mitchell Ontario **41** D1 43 27N 81 13W
Mitchells Brook tn. Newfoundland **49** D2
47 08N 53 31W
Mittimatalik (Pond Inlet) tn. Northwest Territories **51** R5
72 40N 77 59W
Mobert I.R. Ontario **41** C2 48 40N 85 40W
Moisie Québec **47** C3 50 12N 66 06W
Molson Lake Manitoba **39** B2 54 20N 96 50W
Monarch Mountains British Columbia **35** C2
51 55N 125 57W
Monashee Mountains British Columbia **35** E2
51 30N 118 50W
Moncton New Brunswick **49** F7 46 07N 64 51W
Monkman Pass British Columbia **35** D2 54 30N 121 10W
Monkman Provincial Park British Columbia **35** D2
54 00N 121 10W
Mono Mills Ontario **44** C2 43 55N 79 57W
Montague Prince Edward Island **49** F7 46 10N 62 39W
Montcalm admin. Québec **43** L8 47 10N 75 15W
Mont D'Iberville (Mount Caubvick) mt.
Québec/Newfoundland **46** D4 58 50N 63 40W
Mont Jacques-Cartier mt. Québec **47** C2 49 00N 66 00W
Mont-Joli mt. Québec **47** C2 48 36N 68 14W
Mont-Laurier tn. Québec **47** A2 46 33N 75 30W
Montmagny admin. Québec **43** R7 46 50N 70 20W
Montmagny Québec **47** B2 46 58N 70 34W
Montmartre Saskatchewan **38** C1 54 14N 103 24W
Montmorency admin. Québec **43** Q8 47 34N 71 20W
Montréal Québec **53** N5 45 32N 73 36W
Montréal Est Québec **53** N5 45 37N 73 32W
Montreal Lake Saskatchewan **38** B2 54 15N 105 30W
Montreal Lake tn. Saskatchewan **38** B2 54 03N 105 49W
Montréal Nord Québec **53** N5 45 35N 73 36W
Montreal River Ontario **41** D2 47 20N 84 20W
Montreal River tn. Ontario **41** D2 47 14N 84 39W
Montreal River Saskatchewan **38** B2 54 58N 62 18W
Montrose British Columbia **35** E1 49 06N 117 30W
Mont Royal mt. Québec **53** N5 45 31N 73 40W
Monts Chic-Chocs mts. Québec **47** C2 49 00N 66 40W
Monts Notre Dame mts. Québec **47** C2 47 59N 69 00W
Monts Otish mts. Québec **47** B3 52 30N 70 20W
Monts Povungnituk mts. Québec **46** A5 61 30N 75 00W
Monts Torngat (Torngat Mountains) mts.
Québec/Newfoundland **46** D4 59 30N 64 30W
Moon River Ontario **44** C4 45 05N 79 51W
Moose Creek Provincial Forest Manitoba **39** B2
51 30N 96 45W
Moose Factory Ontario **40** D3 51 16N 80 37W
Moose Jaw Saskatchewan **38** B2 50 23N 105 35W
Moose Jaw River Saskatchewan **38** B2 50 15N 105 10W
Moose Lake tn. Manitoba **39** A2 53 43N 100 20W
Moose Mountain Creek Saskatchewan **38** C2
50 15N 103 25W
Moose Mountain Provincial Park Saskatchewan **38** C1
49 50N 102 20W
Moose River tn. Ontario **40** D3 50 48N 81 18W
Moosomin Saskatchewan **38** C2 50 09N 101 41W
Moosonee Ontario **40** D3 51 18N 80 39W
Morden Manitoba **39** B1 49 12N 98 05W
Morell Prince Edward Island **49** F7 46 25N 62 42W
Moresby Island British Columbia **34** B2 53 00N 132 00W
Morice Lake British Columbia **35** C2 53 55N 127 30W
Moricetown British Columbia **35** C2 55 02N 127 20W
Morinville Alberta **37** C2 53 48N 113 39W
Morris Manitoba **39** B1 49 22N 97 21W
Morrisburg Ontario **41** E1 44 54N 75 11W
Morse Saskatchewan **38** B2 50 24N 107 00W
Morson Ontario **40** B2 49 03N 94 19W
Moser River tn. Nova Scotia **49** F6 44 58N 62 18W
Mostoos Hills Saskatchewan **38** B3 55 20N 109 30W
Mould Bay m.s. Northwest Territories **50** H6
76 14N 119 20W
Mountain Lake Ontario **44** A3 44 42N 81 02W
Mount Albert tn. Ontario **44** C4 44 07N 79 18W
Mount Assiniboine Provincial Park British Columbia **37** E2
50 58N 115 45W
Mount Brydges tn. Ontario **44** A1 42 54N 81 30W
Mount Burke British Columbia **52** P4 49 18N 122 42W
Mount Carleton Provincial Park New Brunswick **49** A2
47 25N 66 50W
Mount Caubvick (Mont D'Iberville) mt.
Québec/Newfoundland **48** B4 58 50N 63 40W
Mount Edziza Provincial Park British Columbia **34** B3
57 40N 131 40W
Mount Forest tn. Ontario **44** B2 43 58N 80 44W
Mount Hope tn. Ontario **44** C2 43 09N 79 54W
Mount Pearl tn. Newfoundland **49** D2 47 31N 52 47W
Mount Revelstoke National Park British Columbia **35** E2
50 40N 118 00W
Mount Robson Provincial Park British Columbia **35** E2
52 50N 118 40W
Mount Seymour Provincial Park British Columbia **52** G4
49 22N 122 56W
Mount Stewart tn. Prince Edward Island **49** F7
46 22N 62 52W
Mount Uniacke tn. Nova Scotia **49** F6 44 54N 63 50W
Mud Bay British Columbia **52** G3 49 04N 122 53W
Mudjatik River Saskatchewan **38** B3 56 40N 107 10W
Mud Lake tn. Newfoundland **48** B3 53 30N 60 10W
Mukutawa River Manitoba **39** B2 53 10N 97 10W
Mulgrave Nova Scotia **49** F7 45 36N 61 25W
Muncho Lake British Columbia **35** C3 59 05N 125 47W
Muncho Lake tn. British Columbia **35** C3 59 00N 125 46W
Muncho Lake Provincial Park British Columbia **35** C3
58 50N 125 40W
Mundare Alberta **37** C2 53 36N 112 20W
Murdochville Québec **47** C2 48 57N 65 30W

Murray Harbour tn. Prince Edward Island **49** F7
46 00N 62 32W
Murray River tn. Prince Edward Island **49** F7
46 00N 62 38W
Murtle Lake British Columbia **35** E2 52 09N 119 40W
Musgrave Harbour tn. Newfoundland **49** D2
49 27N 53 58W
Musgravetown Newfoundland **49** D2 48 24N 53 53W
Muskawa River British Columbia **35** D3 58 30N 123 20W
Muskoka admin. Ontario **42** G6 45 02N 79 30W
Muskoka Falls tn. Ontario **42** G5 44 59N 79 16W
Muskrat Dam Lake Ontario **40** B3 53 25N 91 40W
Musquodoboit Harbour tn. Nova Scotia **49** F6
44 48N 63 10W
Muzon, Cape British Columbia **34** B2 54 41N 132 40W
Myles Bay Ontario **44** A3 44 56N 81 23W
Myrnam Alberta **37** C2 53 40N 111 14W

N

Nachvak Fiord in. Newfoundland **48** B4 59 03N 63 45W
Nackawic New Brunswick **49** A2 46 00N 67 15W
Nagagami Lake Ontario **41** C2 49 25N 85 01W
Nagagami River Ontario **41** D2 49 30N 84 50W
Nahanni Butte (Tthenáágóo) tn. Northwest Territories **50** G3
61 30N 123 20W
Nahanni National Park Reserve Northwest Territories
50 F3 61 30N 126 00W
Nahatlatch River British Columbia **34** H4 49 55N 121 59W
Nahlin River British Columbia **34** B3 58 58N 131 30W
Naicam Saskatchewan **38** C2 52 26N 104 31W
Naikoon Provincial Park British Columbia **34** B2
53 59N 131 35W
Nain Newfoundland **48** B4 56 32N 61 41W
Nakina Ontario **40** C3 50 11N 86 43W
Nakina River British Columbia **34** B3 59 07N 132 59W
Nakusp British Columbia **35** E2 50 15N 117 48W
Namao Alberta **54** G5 53 41N 113 28W
Nanaimo British Columbia **34** H4 49 08N 123 58W
Nanaimo River British Columbia **34** H4 49 08N 123 54W
Nanisivik Northwest Territories **51** Q5 73 00N 79 58W
Nansen Sound Northwest Territories **51** N7 81 00N 90 35W
Nanticoke Ontario **44** B1 42 48N 80 04W
Nanticoke Creek Ontario **44** B1 42 56N 80 16W
Nanton Alberta **37** C2 50 21N 113 46W
Napaktulik Lake Northwest Territories **50** J4 66 30N 112 50W
Napanee Ontario **41** E1 44 15N 76 57W
Napartokh (Black Duck) Bay Newfoundland **48** B4
58 01N 62 19W
Narrow Hills Provincial Park Saskatchewan **38** C2
54 10N 103 30W
Narrows, The sd. Nova Scotia **53** P6 44 40N 63 35W
Naskaupi River Newfoundland **48** B3 54 28N 62 00W
Nass River British Columbia **34** C3 55 10N 129 20W
Nastapoka Islands Northwest Territories **46** A4
56 50N 76 50W
Natashquan Québec **47** D3 50 10N 61 50W
Natashquan Newfoundland **48** B3 52 30N 62 50W
Nation Lakes British Columbia **35** C3 55 08N 125 15W
Nation River British Columbia **35** D3 55 11N 124 25W
Naujat (Repulse Bay) tn. Northwest Territories **51** P4
66 32N 86 15W
Nauwigewauk New Brunswick **49** E7 45 28W 65 53W
Nazko British Columbia **35** D2 53 00N 123 37W
Nechako Plateau British Columbia **35** D2 54 30N 124 15W
Nechako River British Columbia **35** D2 53 35N 124 50W
Neeb Saskatchewan **38** C2 50 09N 107 50W
Neepawa Manitoba **39** B2 50 14N 99 29W
Neguac New Brunswick **49** A2 47 14N 65 03W
Nejanilini Lake Manitoba **39** B3 59 34N 98 51W
Nelson British Columbia **35** E1 49 29N 117 17W
Nelson Forks British Columbia **35** D3 59 30N 124 00W
Nelson House tn. Manitoba **39** B3 55 49N 98 51W
Nelson Island British Columbia **34** H4 49 43N 124 03W
Nelson River Manitoba **39** C3 56 50N 93 40W
Némiscau Québec **47** A3 51 20N 77 01W
Nepean Ontario **41** E2 45 16N 75 48W
Nepewassi Lake Ontario **42** F6 46 22N 80 38W
Nepisiguit River New Brunswick **49** A2 47 25N 66 30W
Nesselrode, Mount British Columbia **34** B3 58 55N 134 20W
Nestor Falls tn. Ontario **40** B2 49 05N 93 55W
Nettilling Lake Northwest Territories **51** S4 66 30N 71 10W
Neudorf Saskatchewan **38** C2 50 43N 103 00W
Neustadt Ontario **44** A3 44 04N 81 00W
New Aiyansh British Columbia **34** C3 55 15N 129 02W
Newboro Ontario **43** K5 44 39N 76 19W
New Brunswick prov. **9** X2 47 30N 66 00W
Newburgh Ontario **43** K5 44 19N 76 52W
New Carlisle Québec **47** C2 48 00N 65 22W
New Denver British Columbia **35** E1 49 59N 117 22W
Newell, Lake Alberta **37** C2 50 26N 111 55W
Newfoundland i. Newfoundland **49** C3 48 30N 56 56W
Newfoundland province **9** Y4/AA2 52 30N 62 30W
New Germany Nova Scotia **49** F6 44 33N 64 44W
New Glasgow Nova Scotia **49** F6 45 36N 62 38W
New Hazelton British Columbia **35** C3 55 15N 127 30W
New Liskeard Ontario **41** E2 47 31N 79 41W
Newmarket Ontario **44** C3 44 03N 79 27W
New Minas Nova Scotia **49** F7 45 03N 64 28W
New Osnaburgh Ontario **40** B3 51 16N 90 15W
New Richmond Québec **47** C2 48 12N 65 52W
New Ross Nova Scotia **49** F6 44 44N 64 27W
Newton British Columbia **52** G3 49 07N 122 50W
Newtown Newfoundland **49** D2 49 12N 53 31W
New Waterford Nova Scotia **49** F7 46 17N 60 05W
New Westminster British Columbia **34** H4 49 10N 122 58W
Niagara admin. Ontario **44** C2 43 02N 79 34W
Niagara Escarpment Ontario **44** C2 43 00N 79 00W

Niagara Falls tn. Ontario **41** E1 43 05N 79 06W
Niagara-on-the-Lake Ontario **41** E1 43 14N 79 16W
Niagara River Ontario/U.S.A. **44** C2 43 15N 79 04W
Nicolet admin. Québec **43** P7 46 18N 72 20W
Nicolet Québec **47** B2 46 14N 72 36W
Nicomeki River British Columbia **52** H3 49 05N 122 43W
Nictau New Brunswick **49** A2 47 16N 67 11W
Night Hawk Lake Ontario **41** D2 48 28N 80 58W
Nipawin Saskatchewan **38** C2 53 23N 104 01W
Nipigon Ontario **41** C2 49 02N 88 26W
Nipigon Bay Ontario **41** C2 48 50N 88 10W
Nipigon, Lake Ontario **40** C2 49 50N 88 30W
Nipishish Lake Newfoundland **48** B3 54 10N 60 30W
Nipissing admin. Ontario **42** G7 46 00N 79 00W
Nipissing Ontario **42** G7 46 05N 79 31W
Nipissing, Lake Ontario **41** E2 46 17N 79 50W
Nisga'a Memorial Lava Bed British Columbia **34** C2
55 10N 129 00W
Nisku Alberta **54** F4 53 18N 113 32W
Nisling Range mts. Yukon Territory **50** D3
62 00N 138 40W
Nitchequon Québec **47** B3 53 10N 70 58W
Nith River Ontario **44** B2 43 12N 80 22W
Nitinat Lake British Columbia **34** H4 48 45N 124 42W
Nitinat River British Columbia **34** H4 49 06N 124 35W
Niverville Manitoba **39** B1 49 39N 97 03W
Nobleton Ontario **44** C2 43 53N 79 39W
Nogies Creek Ontario **44** D3 44 43N 78 31W
Nogies Creek tn. Ontario **44** D3 44 19N 78 30W
Nokomis Saskatchewan **38** B2 51 30N 105 00W
Nokomis Lake Saskatchewan **38** C3 56 55N 103 00W
Nootka Island British Columbia **35** C1 49 45N 126 50W
Nootka Sound British Columbia **35** C1 49 34N 126 39W
Nopiming Provincial Park Manitoba **39** B2
50 40N 95 10W
Noralee British Columbia **35** C2 53 59N 126 26W
Norman Bay tn. Newfoundland **49** C3 52 55N 56 10W
Norman, Cape Newfoundland **48** C3 51 38N 55 54W
Normandale Ontario **44** B1 42 41N 80 19W
Normansland Point Ontario **40** D3 52 00N 81 00W
Norman Wells (Tlegóhti) tn. Northwest Territories **50** F4
65 19N 126 46W
Normétal Québec **47** A2 48 59N 79 23W
Norquay Saskatchewan **38** C2 51 52N 102 05W
Norris Arm tn. Newfoundland **49** C2 49 05N 55 15W
Norris Point tn. Newfoundland **49** C2 49 31N 57 53W
North Arm r. British Columbia **52** F3 49 12N 123 05W
North Arm b. Northwest Territories **50** H3
62 30N 115 30W
North Aulatsivik Island Newfoundland **48** B4
59 46N 64 05W
North Battleford Saskatchewan **38** B2 52 47N 108 19W
North Bay tn. Ontario **41** E2 46 20N 79 28W
North Belcher Islands Northwest Territories **46** A4
56 45N 79 45W
North Bend British Columbia **34** H4 49 54N 121 28W
North, Cape Nova Scotia **49** F7 47 10N 60 25W
North Cape Prince Edward Island **49** F7 47 04N 64 00W
North Caribou Lake Ontario **40** B3 52 50N 90 40W
North Castor River Ontario **53** K2 45 18N 75 31W
North Channel Ontario **41** D2 46 05N 83 00W
Northern Indian Lake Manitoba **39** B3 57 30N 97 30W
Northern Peninsula Newfoundland **49** C3
50 30N 57 00W
Northern Woods and Water Route Canada **38** B2
54 10N 107 20W
North French River Ontario **41** D3 50 20N 81 00W
North Head tn. New Brunswick **49** E6 44 46N 66 45W
North Kent Island Northwest Territories **51** N6
76 40N 90 14W
North Knife Lake Manitoba **39** B3 58 10N 96 40W
North Knife River Manitoba **39** B3 58 40N 95 50W
North Moose Lake Manitoba **39** A2 54 10N 100 10W
North Pender Island British Columbia **34** H4
48 49N 123 17W
North River tn. Manitoba **39** C3 58 55N 94 30W
North River Newfoundland **48** B4 57 30N 63 20W
North River tn. Newfoundland **49** C3 53 49N 57 01W
North River Ontario **53** K2 45 37N 74 35W
North River Bridge tn. Nova Scotia **49** F7
46 16N 60 40W
North Rustico Prince Edward Island **49** F7
46 26N 63 20W
North Saskatchewan River Alberta/Saskatchewan **38** B2
52 40N 106 40W
North Saugeen River Ontario **44** A3 44 18N 81 10W
North Seal River Manitoba **39** B3 59 00N 100 30W
North Spirit Lake Manitoba **39** B3 52 31N 92 55W
North Spirit Lake tn. Ontario **40** B3 52 31N 93 01W
North Sydney Nova Scotia **49** F7 46 13N 60 15W
North Thames River Ontario **44** A2 43 02N 81 14W
North Thompson River British Columbia **35** E2
51 32N 120 00W
North Twin Islands Northwest Territories **40** E3
53 20N 80 00W
Northumberland admin. New Brunswick **49** A2
47 10N 66 30W
Northumberland admin. Ontario **42** H5 44 05N 78 20W
Northumberland Strait Atlantic Provinces **49** F7
46 30N 64 30W
North Vancouver British Columbia **34** H4 49 21N 123 05W
North Wabasca Lake Alberta **37** C3 56 10N 114 40W
Northwest Angle Provincial Park Manitoba **39** B1
49 20N 95 30W
Northwest Arm Nova Scotia **53** P6 44 37N 63 35W
Northwest Bay tn. Ontario **40** B2 48 50N 93 38W
Northwest Gander River Newfoundland **49** C2
48 30N 55 40W

North West River tn. Newfoundland **48** B3
53 32N 60 08W
Northwest Territories terr. **8/9** J6/Y5 65 15N 115 00W
North York bor. Metropolitan Toronto Ontario **52** C2
43 44N 79 26W
Norton New Brunswick **49** E7 45 38N 65 43W
Norway House tn. Manitoba **39** B2 53 59N 97 50W
Norwich Ontario **44** B1 42 59N 80 36W
Nose Creek Alberta **54** A2 51 08N 114 02W
Nose Hill Alberta **54** A2 51 06N 114 07W
Notekwin River Alberta **37** B3 56 55N 118 20W
Notre Dame Bay Newfoundland **49** C2 49 45N 55 30W
Notre-Dame-des-Champs Ontario **53** L2 45 25N 75 28W
Notre-Dame-du-Lac Québec **47** C2 47 38N 68 49W
Nottawasaga Bay Ontario **41** D1 44 40N 80 30W
Nottawasaga River Ontario **44** C3 44 27N 79 53W
Nottingham Island Northwest Territories **51** R3
63 30N 78 00W
Nova Scotia prov. **9** Y1 44 30N 65 00W
Nueltin Lake Manitoba/Northwest Territories **51** M3
60 30N 99 00W
Nunaksaluk Island Newfoundland **48** B4 55 49N 60 20W
Nutak Newfoundland **48** B4 57 28N 61 52W
Nut Mountain Saskatchewan **38** C2 52 20N 102 50W
Nut Mountain tn. Saskatchewan **38** C2 52 08N 103 21W

O

Oakbank Manitoba **39** B1 49 57N 96 54W
Oak Bay British Columbia **34** H4 48 27N 123 18W
Oak Bluff Manitoba **54** C2 49 46N 97 18W
Oak Island Nova Scotia **49** F6 44 30N 63 55W
Oak Lake tn. Manitoba **39** A1 49 40N 100 45W
Oak Ridges tn. Ontario **44** C2 44 55N 79 27W
Oakville Manitoba **39** B1 49 56N 98 00W
Oakville Ontario **44** C2 43 27N 79 41W
Oakwood Ontario **44** D3 44 20N 78 52W
Oba Ontario **65** J6 48 38N 84 17W
Obaska Ontario **53** J9 48 12N 77 20W
Observatory Inlet British Columbia **34** C3
55 05N 129 59W
Ocean Falls British Columbia **35** C2 52 24N 127 42W
Odei River Manitoba **39** B3 55 50N 98 00W
Ogden Alberta **54** A1 50 59N 114 00W
Ogidaki Mountain Ontario **41** D2 46 57N 83 59W
Ogilvie Mountains Yukon Territory **50** D4
65 05N 139 00W
Ogoki Ontario **40** C3 51 38N 85 57W
Ogoki Lake Ontario **40** C3 50 50N 87 10W
Ogoki Reservoir Ontario **40** C3 50 48N 88 18W
Ogoki River Ontario **40** C3 50 50N 88 50W
Oil Springs tn. Ontario **42** D3 42 47N 82 07W
Okak Bay Newfoundland **48** B4 57 28N 62 20W
Okak Islands Newfoundland **48** B4 57 30N 61 50W
Okanagan Lake British Columbia **35** E1 49 45N 119 32W
Okotoks Alberta **37** C2 50 44N 113 59W
Old Crow Yukon Territory **50** D4 67 34N 139 43W
Old Crow River Yukon Territory **50** C4 68 00N 140 00W
Oldman River Alberta **37** C1 49 50N 112 05W
Old Perlican Newfoundland **49** D2 48 05N 53 01W
Olds Alberta **37** C2 51 50N 114 06W
Old Wives Lake Saskatchewan **38** B2 50 15N 106 40W
O'Leary Prince Edward Island **49** F7 46 43N 64 15W
Oliphant Ontario **44** A3 44 44N 81 16W
Oliver British Columbia **35** E1 49 10N 119 37W
Omand's Creek Manitoba **54** C2 49 58N 97 17W
Omemee Ontario **44** D3 44 19N 78 33W
Omineca Mountains British Columbia **35** C3
56 30N 126 30W
Omineca River British Columbia **35** C3 56 02N 126 00W
Onaman Lake Ontario **40** C3 50 00N 87 26W
Onaping Lake Ontario **41** D2 46 57N 81 30W
Ontario prov. **9** S3 51 00N 91 00W
Ootsa Lake British Columbia **35** C2 53 40N 126 30W
Ootsa Lake tn. British Columbia **35** C2 53 42N 125 56W
Opasatika Ontario **41** D2 49 32N 82 52W
Opasquia Provincial Park Ontario **40** B3 53 30N 93 10W
Opeongo Lake Ontario **41** E2 45 42N 78 23W
Opinnagau River Ontario **40** D3 53 30N 83 50W
Orangeville Ontario **41** D1 43 55N 80 06W
Orillia Ontario **41** E1 44 36N 79 26W
Orleans Ontario **53** K2 45 28N 75 34W
Ormstown Québec **47** B2 45 08N 73 59W
Oromocto New Brunswick **49** A2 45 50N 66 28W
Orono Ontario **44** D2 43 59N 78 36W
Oshawa Ontario **41** E1 43 53N 78 51W
Oskélanéo Québec **47** A2 48 07N 75 14W
Osoyoos British Columbia **35** E1 49 00N 119 29W
Ospika River British Columbia **35** D3 56 55N 124 10W
Ossokmanuan Lake Newfoundland **48** A3 53 25N 65 00W
Otoskwin-Attawapiskat Provincial Park Ontario **40** C3
51 50N 89 20W
Otoskwin River Ontario **40** C3 51 50N 89 40W
Ottawa Ontario **53** K2 45 24N 75 38W
Ottawa-Carleton admin. Ontario **43** L6 45 13N 75 50W
Ottawa Islands Northwest Territories **51** Q2
59 10N 80 25W
Ottawa River (Rivière des Outaouais) Ontario/Québec
43 K6 45 34N 76 30W
Otter Lake Saskatchewan **38** C3 55 35N 104 30W
Otter Rapids tn. Ontario **41** D3 50 12N 81 40W
Outlook Saskatchewan **38** B2 51 30N 107 03W
Outremont Québec **53** N5 45 31N 73 36W
Owen Sound tn. Ontario **44** B3 44 34N 80 56W
Owl River Manitoba **39** C3 57 50N 93 20W
Oxbow Saskatchewan **38** C1 49 16N 102 12W
Oxford Nova Scotia **49** F7 45 43N 63 52W

Oxford admin. Ontario **44** B2 43 06N 80 59W
Oxford House tn. Manitoba **39** B2 54 58N 95 17W
Oxford Lake Manitoba **39** B2 54 40N 95 50W
Oyen Alberta **37** C2 51 22N 110 28W
Oyster River British Columbia **34** G4 49 50N 125 42W
Ozhiski Lake Ontario **40** C3 52 01N 88 30W

P

Pacific Rim National Park British Columbia **34** G4
48 52N 125 35W
Packs Harbour tn. Newfoundland **48** C3 53 51N 56 59W
Pacquet Newfoundland **49** C2 49 59N 55 53W
Paddle Prairie tn. Alberta **37** B3 57 57N 117 29W
Paint Lake Provincial Recreation Park Manitoba **39** B3
55 30N 97 00W
Paisley Ontario **44** A3 44 17N 81 16W
Pakashkan Lake Ontario **40** B2 49 21N 90 15W
Pakowki Lake Alberta **37** C1 49 20N 111 55W
Pakwash Lake Ontario **40** B3 50 45N 93 30W
Palmerston Ontario **44** B2 43 50N 80 50W
Panache Lake Ontario **41** D2 46 15N 81 20W
Pangnirtung (Panniqtuuq) Northwest Territories **51** T4
66 05N 65 45W
Panmure Island Prince Edward Island **49** F7
46 10N 62 30W
Panniqtuuq (Pangnirtung) Northwest Territories **51** T4
66 05N 65 45W
Papineau admin. Québec **43** L6 45 40N 75 30W
Paradise Hill tn. Saskatchewan **38** B2 53 32N 109 26W
Paradise River Newfoundland **48** C3 52 50N 57 50W
Paradise River tn. Newfoundland **48** C3 53 27N 57 17W
Parc Cap-Saint Jacques Québec **53** M4 45 57N 73 55W
Parc de Conservation d'Aiguebelle Québec **47** A2
48 30N 78 50W
Parc de Conservation de la Gaspésie Québec **47** C2
48 52N 65 07W
Parc de Conservation de la Jacques-Cartier Québec
47 B2 47 23N 71 25W
Parc de Conservation des Grands-Jardins Québec **47** B2
47 47N 70 59W
Parc de Conservation du Saguenay Québec **47** B2
48 15N 70 15W
Parc de la Gatineau Québec **47** A2 45 36N 76 00W
Parc de Récréation de Frontenac Québec **47** B2
45 52N 71 17W
Parc de Récréation des Îles-de-Boucherville Québec
53 05 45 36N 73 27W
Parc de Récréation d'Oka Québec **53** M4 45 24N 73 58W
Parc de Récréation du Mont-Tremblant Québec **47** B2
46 20N 74 43W
Parc National de Forillon Québec **47** D2 48 58N 64 30W
Parc National de la Mauricie Québec **47** B2
46 50N 73 05W
Parc Paul-Sauvé Québec **53** M4 45 24N 73 58W
Parent Québec **47** B2 47 55N 74 36W
Paris Ontario **44** B2 43 12N 80 25W
Parke Lake Newfoundland **48** C3 53 10N 59 00W
Parkhill Ontario **44** D1 43 10N 81 41W
Parkland County Alberta **54** F4 53 40N 114 02W
Parksville British Columbia **34** H4 49 20N 124 19W
Parrsboro Nova Scotia **49** F7 45 25N 64 21W
Parry, Cape m.s. Northwest Territories **50** G5
70 08N 124 34W
Parry Island Ontario **44** B4 45 17N 80 11W
Parry Islands Northwest Territories **50** K6
75 30N 109 00W
Parry Sound admin. Ontario **42** F6 45 40N 80 08W
Parry Sound Ontario **44** B4 45 21N 80 08W
Parry Sound tn. Ontario **41** D2 45 21N 80 03W
Parson's Pond tn. Newfoundland **49** C3 50 02N 57 43W
Pasadena Newfoundland **49** C2 49 01N 57 36W
Pasfield Lake Saskatchewan **38** B3 58 20N 105 45W
Paspébiac Québec **47** C2 48 03N 65 17W
Pasqui Hills Saskatchewan **38** C2 53 10N 103 00W
Pass Lake Ontario **40** C2 48 34N 88 44W
Paudash Ontario **42** J5 44 56N 77 58W
Paulatuk (Paulatuuq) Northwest Territories **50** G4
69 23N 123 59W
Paulatuuq (Paulatuk) Northwest Territories **50** G4
69 23N 123 59W
Paul Island Newfoundland **48** B4 56 30N 61 25W
Payne Bay Québec **46** C4 59 50N 70 00W
Peace Point tn. Alberta **37** C3 59 07N 112 27W
Peace River Alberta **37** B3 58 40N 114 30W
Peace River tn. Alberta **37** B3 56 14N 117 17W
Peachland British Columbia **35** E1 49 49N 119 48W
Peary Channel Northwest Territories **51** L6
79 40N 101 30W
Peawanuck Ontario **40** C4 55 00N 85 30W
Pedzéh Ki (Wrigley) Northwest Territories **50** G3
63 16N 123 39W
Peel admin. Ontario **44** C2 43 49N 79 57W
Peel County Ontario **52** B2 43 48N 79 41W
Peel River Yukon Territory **50** D4 66 00N 136 00W
Peel River Game Reserve Yukon/Northwest Territories
50 E4 66 30N 133 30W
Peel Sound Northwest Territories **51** M5 73 15N 96 30W
Peerless Lake Alberta **37** C3 56 40N 114 35W
Pefferlaw Ontario **44** C3 44 18N 79 14W
Pefferlaw Brook Ontario **44** C3 44 16N 79 15W
Peggys Cove tn. Nova Scotia **49** F6 44 30N 63 55W
Pelee Island Ontario **42** D2 41 47N 82 40W
Pelee Island tn. Ontario **42** D2 41 45N 82 40W
Pelee Point Ontario **42** D2 41 45N 82 39W
Pelham Ontario **44** C2 43 02N 79 19W
Pelican Bay Manitoba **39** A2 52 40N 100 30W

Pelican Lake Manitoba **39** A2 52 30N 100 30W
Pelican Mountains Alberta **37** C3 55 35N 114 00W
Pelican Narrows tn. Saskatchewan **38** C3
55 12N 102 55W
Pelly Bay (Arviligjuat) tn. Northwest Territories **51** P4
68 32N 89 48W
Pelly Bay Northwest Territories **51** O4 68 53N 89 51W
Pelly Crossing Yukon Territory **50** D3 62 48N 136 30W
Pelly Mountains Yukon Territory **50** E3 61 30N 132 30W
Pelly Point British Columbia **52** F3 49 06N 123 13W
Pelly River Yukon Territory **50** E3 62 50N 134 50W
Pemberton British Columbia **34** H5 50 19N 122 49W
Pembina Alberta **37** B2 53 08N 115 09W
Pembina River Alberta **37** B2 53 15N 116 05W
Pembina River Manitoba **39** B1 49 10N 99 10W
Pembroke Ontario **41** E2 45 49N 77 07W
Penetanguishene Ontario **44** C3 44 47N 79 56W
Penhold Alberta **37** C2 52 08N 113 52W
Péninsule de la Gaspésie p. Québec **47** C2 48 30N 65 30W
Péninsule d'Ungava p. Québec **46** A5-B5 60 50N 76 00W
Penticton British Columbia **35** E1 49 49N 119 38W
Percé Québec **47** D2 48 32N 64 14W
Percé, Cape Nova Scotia **49** G7 46 08N 59 50W
Perdue Saskatchewan **38** B2 52 05N 107 33W
Perkinsfield Ontario **44** C3 44 41N 79 58W
Perrault Falls tn. Ontario **40** B3 50 20N 93 08W
Perry Island tn. Northwest Territories **51** L4 67 48N 102 33W
Perth admin. Ontario **44** A2 43 22N 81 10W
Perth Ontario **41** E1 44 54N 76 15W
Perth-Andover New Brunswick **49** A2 46 45N 67 42W
Petawawa Ontario **41** E2 45 54N 77 17W
Peterborough admin. Ontario **42** H5 44 40N 78 20W
Peterborough Ontario **41** D1 44 19N 78 20W
Peter Pond Lake Saskatchewan **38** B3 55 50N 108 50W
Petite Rivière tn. Nova Scotia **49** F6 44 15N 64 25W
Petite rivière de la Baleine r. Québec **46** A5 56 00N 75 55W
Petit Étang Nova Scotia **49** F7 46 39N 60 59W
Petit lac des Loups Marins l. Québec **46** B4 56 00N 73 15W
Petit lac Manicouagan l. Québec **47** C3 57 55N 67 40W
Petitot River British Columbia **35** D3 59 55N 122 15W
Petitsikapau Lake Newfoundland **48** A3 54 37N 66 25W
Petre, Point Ontario **43** J4 43 50N 77 09W
Petrolia Ontario **42** D3 42 52N 82 09W
Phelps Lake Saskatchewan **38** C3 59 20N 102 55W
Philpots Island Northwest Territories **51** R5 74 57N 79 58W
Pickerel Lake Ontario **41** B2 48 37N 91 19W
Pickering Ontario **52** D2 43 48N 79 11W
Pickering Village Ontario **52** E2 43 51N 79 02W
Pickle Lake tn. Ontario **40** B3 51 28N 90 12W
Pic River Ontario **41** C2 48 50N 86 20W
Picton Ontario **41** E1 44 00N 77 07W
Pictou admin. Nova Scotia **49** F7 45 30N 62 40W
Pictou Nova Scotia **49** F7 45 41N 62 42W
Pictou Island Nova Scotia **49** F7 45 48N 62 35W
Picture Butte tn. Alberta **37** C1 49 53N 112 47W
Pie Island Ontario **41** C2 48 15N 89 06W
Pierceland Saskatchewan **38** B2 54 20N 109 40W
Pierrefonds Québec **53** M4 45 28N 73 50W
Pigeon Lake Alberta **37** C2 53 01N 114 02W
Pigeon Lake Ontario **44** D3 44 27N 78 30W
Pigeon River Manitoba **39** B2 52 10N 96 50W
Pigeon River Ontario **44** D3 44 13N 78 42W
Pikangikum I.R. Ontario **40** B3 51 48N 93 59W
Pikangikum Lake Ontario **40** B3 51 48N 94 00W
Pikwitonei Manitoba **39** B3 55 35N 97 11W
Pilot Butte tn. Saskatchewan **38** C2 50 29N 104 29W
Pilot Mound tn. Manitoba **39** B1 49 13N 98 52W
Pinawa Manitoba **39** B2 50 13N 95 56W
Pincher Creek tn. Alberta **37** C1 49 29N 113 57W
Pinchi Lake British Columbia **35** D2 54 36N 124 25W
Pine, Cape Newfoundland **49** D2 46 38N 53 35W
Pine Falls tn. Manitoba **39** B2 50 33N 96 14W
Pinehouse Lake Saskatchewan **38** B3 55 35N 106 50W
Pineimuta River Ontario **40** B3 52 10N 90 40W
Pine Pass British Columbia **35** D3 55 30N 122 25W
Pine River British Columbia **35** D3 55 50N 121 50W
Pine River Manitoba **39** A2 51 45N 100 30W
Pinery Provincial Park Ontario **42** E4 43 16N 81 50W
Pinto Butte mt. Saskatchewan **38** B1 49 21N 107 25W
Pinware Newfoundland **48** C3 51 37N 56 42W
Pipestone River Ontario **40** B3 52 20N 90 40W
Pistolet Bay Newfoundland **48** C3 51 35N 55 45W
Pitman River British Columbia **35** C3 58 00N 128 15W
Pitt Island British Columbia **34** C3 53 38N 129 59W
Pitt Lake British Columbia **34** H4 49 25N 122 33W
Pitt Meadows tn. British Columbia **34** H4 49 13N 122 42W
Pitt River British Columbia **34** H4 49 42N 122 40W
Placentia Newfoundland **49** D2 47 14N 53 58W
Placentia Bay Newfoundland **49** D2 47 00N 54 30W
Plantagenet Ontario **43** L6 45 32N 75 00W
Plaster Rock tn. New Brunswick **49** A2 46 55N 67 24W
Playgreen Lake Manitoba **39** B2 53 50N 98 00W
Pleasant Bay tn. Nova Scotia **49** F7 46 50N 60 48W
Pledger Lake Ontario **40** D3 50 53N 83 42W
Plessisville Québec **47** B2 46 14N 71 46W
Plum Coulee Manitoba **39** B1 49 12N 97 45W
Plum Point tn. Newfoundland **49** C3 51 04N 56 53W
Pohénégamook Québec **47** C2 28N 69 17W
Pointe au Baril tn. Ontario **44** B4 45 36N 80 23W
Pointe au Baril Station tn. Ontario **42** F6 45 36N 80 22W
Pointe aux Pins c. Ontario **42** 46 31N 55 00W
Pointe-aux-Pins Creek Alberta **54** G5 53 39N 113 16W
Pointe-Claire Québec **43** N6 45 27N 73 50W
Pointe-Claire Québec **53** M4 45 27N 73 50W
Pointe de l'Est c. Québec **47** D2 49 02N 61 40W
Pointe-Gatineau tn. Québec **53** K2 45 27N 75 42W
Pointe Louis-XIV c. Québec **46** A3 54 30N 79 45W

Point Farm Provincial Park Ontario **44** A2 43 49N 81 42W
Point Lake Northwest Territories **50** J4 65 15N 113 04W
Point Pelee National Park Ontario **42** D2 41 57N 82 31W
Point Petre c. Ontario **41** E1 43 50N 77 10W
Point Pleasant Park Nova Scotia **53** P6 44 37N 63 33W
Points North Landing Saskatchewan **38** C3
58 14N 104 05W
Polar Bear Provincial Park Ontario **40** D3 54 50N 83 40W
Pomquet Nova Scotia **49** F7 45 34N 61 52W
Pond Inlet (Mittimatalik) tn. Northwest Territories **51** R5
72 40N 77 59W
Pond Inlet Northwest Territories **51** R5 72 41N 78 00W
Ponds, Island of tn. Newfoundland **48** C3 53 27N 55 52W
Ponhook Lake Nova Scotia **49** F6 44 50N 64 10W
Ponoka Alberta **37** C2 52 42N 113 33W
Ponteix Saskatchewan **38** B1 49 45N 107 20W
Pontiac admin. Québec **42** J7 46 28N 77 00W
Pont-Rouge Québec **43** Q7 46 45N 71 43W
Pont-Viau Québec **53** N5 45 33N 73 41W
Poplar Hill tn. Ontario **40** B3 52 05N 94 18W
Poplar River Manitoba **39** B2 52 50N 97 00W
Porcher Island British Columbia **34** C3 54 00N 130 30W
Porcupine, Cape Newfoundland **48** C3 53 56N 57 08W
Porcupine Hills Manitoba/Saskatchewan **39** A2
52 30N 101 40W
Porcupine Plain tn. Saskatchewan **38** C2 52 36N 103 15W
Porcupine Provincial Forest Manitoba **39** A2
52 30N 101 20W
Portabello Nova Scotia **53** P6 44 44N 63 32W
Portage la Prairie Manitoba **39** B1 49 58N 98 20W
Port Alberni British Columbia **34** H4 49 11N 124 49W
Port Alice British Columbia **35** C2 50 23N 127 24W
Port au Choix Newfoundland **49** C3 50 43N 57 22W
Port au Port Peninsula Newfoundland **49** C2
48 35N 59 00W
Port Bickerton Nova Scotia **49** F7 45 10N 61 40W
Port Blandford Newfoundland **49** D2 48 21N 54 10W
Port Bruce Ontario **41** D1 42 40N 81 00W
Port Bruce Provincial Park Ontario **44** B1 42 40N 81 02W
Port Burwell Northwest Territories **51** U3 60 30N 64 50W
Port Burwell Ontario **44** B1 42 39N 80 47W
Port Burwell Provincial Park Ontario **44** A1 42 40N 80 45W
Port Carling Ontario **42** G6 45 07N 79 35W
Port-Cartier Québec **47** C3 50 02N 66 58W
Port Clements British Columbia **34** B2 53 41N 132 11W
Port Colborne Ontario **44** C1 42 53N 79 16W
Port Coquitlam British Columbia **34** H4 49 16N 122 45W
Port Credit Ontario **52** B1 43 33N 79 36W
Port Dover Ontario **44** B1 42 47N 80 12W
Port Edward British Columbia **34** B2 54 11N 130 16W
Port Elgin New Brunswick **49** F7 46 03N 64 08W
Port Elgin Ontario **41** D1 44 25N 81 23W
Porter Lake Saskatchewan **38** B3 56 20N 107 10W
Port Essington British Columbia **34** C2 54 08N 130 54W
Port Hammond British Columbia **52** H3 49 12N 122 40W
Port Hardy British Columbia **35** C2 50 37N 127 15W
Port Hawkesbury Nova Scotia **49** F7 45 36N 61 22W
Port Hood Nova Scotia **49** F7 46 00N 61 32W
Port Hope Ontario **42** H4 43 58N 78 18W
Port Hope Simpson Newfoundland **48** C3 52 33N 56 18W
Port Kells British Columbia **52** H3 49 09N 122 43W
Portland Inlet British Columbia **34** B2 54 40N 130 30W
Port Lorne Nova Scotia **49** E6 44 56N 65 20W
Port Maitland Nova Scotia **49** E6 43 59N 66 04W
Port Maitland Ontario **44** C1 42 51N 79 33W
Port McNeill British Columbia **35** C2 50 30N 127 01W
Port McNicoll Ontario **44** C3 44 44N 79 49W
Port Mellon British Columbia **34** H4 49 31N 123 30W
Port-Menier Québec **47** D2 49 50N 64 20W
Port Moody British Columbia **34** H4 49 13N 122 57W
Port Mouton Nova Scotia **49** F6 43 58N 64 50W
Port Nelson Manitoba **39** C3 57 03N 92 36W
Portneuf admin. Québec **43** P8 47 02N 72 20W
Port Perry Ontario **44** D3 44 06N 78 58W
Port Renfrew British Columbia **34** H4 48 00N 124 00W
Port Rowan Ontario **44** B1 42 38N 80 27W
Port Royal Nova Scotia **49** E6 44 45N 65 40W
Port Saunders Newfoundland **49** C3 50 39N 57 18W
Port Simpson British Columbia **34** B2 54 33N 130 25W
Port Stanley Ontario **41** D1 42 40N 81 14W
Postville Newfoundland **48** C3 54 54N 59 47W
Pouce Coupé British Columbia **35** D3 55 40N 120 08W
Pouch Cove tn. Newfoundland **49** D2 47 46N 52 46W
Powassan Ontario **41** E2 46 05N 79 22W
Powell Lake British Columbia **34** H5 50 08N 124 26W
Powell River tn. British Columbia **34** H4 49 54N 124 34W
Powerview Manitoba **39** B2 50 30N 96 00W
Preeceville Saskatchewan **38** C2 51 58N 102 40W
Prelate Saskatchewan **38** B2 50 52N 109 22W
Prescott Ontario **41** E1 44 43N 75 33W
Prescott and Russell admin. Ontario **43** M6 45 30N 74 55W
Preston Nova Scotia **53** Q6 44 41N 63 26W
Preston Ontario **44** B2 43 20N 80 21W
Price Island British Columbia **34** C2 52 25N 128 40W
Prim, Point Prince Edward Island **49** F6 46 10N 63 00W
Primrose Lake Saskatchewan **38** B3
55 00N 109 00W
Prince admin. Prince Edward Island **49** F7 46 30N 64 00W
Prince Albert Saskatchewan **38** B2 53 13N 105 45W
Prince Albert National Park Saskatchewan **38** B2
54 00N 106 00W
Prince Albert Peninsula Northwest Territories **50** H5
72 30N 117 00W
Prince Albert Sound Northwest Territories **50** H5
70 15N 115 00W
Prince Alfred, Cape Northwest Territories **50** G5
74 30N 124 50W

Prince Charles Island Northwest Territories **51** R4
67 40N 77 00W
Prince Edward Island prov. **9** Y2 46 30N 63 00W
Prince Edward Island National Park Prince Edward Island
49 F7 46 20N 63 10W
Prince George British Columbia **35** D2 53 55N 122 49W
Prince Gustaf Adolf Sea Northwest Territories **51** K6
78 30N 105 00W
Prince of Wales Island Northwest Territories **51** M5
73 00N 98 00W
Prince of Wales Strait Northwest Territories **50** H5
72 50N 118 00W
Prince Patrick Island Northwest Territories **50** H6
77 00N 120 00W
Prince Regent Inlet Northwest Territories **50** N5
72 40N 90 30W
Prince Rupert British Columbia **34** B2 54 09N 130 20W
Princess Margaret Range mts. Northwest Territories
51 N7 80 00N 92 30W
Princess Royal Island British Columbia **34** C2
53 04N 129 00W
Princeton British Columbia **35** D1 49 25N 120 35W
Princeville Québec **43** Q7 46 10N 71 52W
Prophet River British Columbia **35** D3 58 35N 122 50W
Prophet River tn. British Columbia **35** D3
58 05N 122 42W
Provost Alberta **37** C2 52 21N 110 16W
Pubnico Nova Scotia **49** E6 43 42N 65 48W
Pugwash Nova Scotia **49** F7 45 52N 63 40W
Pukaskwa Provincial Park Ontario **41** C2 48 20N 85 40W
Pukatawagan Manitoba **39** A3 55 46N 101 14W
Pukeashun Mountain British Columbia **35** E2
51 12N 119 14W
Purcell Mountains British Columbia **35** E2
50 58N 116 59W
Purcell's Cove tn. Nova Scotia **53** P6 44 35N 63 33W
Purcell Wilderness Conservancy British Columbia **35** E2
50 00N 116 00W
Purtuniq Québec **46** B5 61 52N 74 00W
Puvirnituq (Povungnituk) Québec **46** A5 60 03N 77 16W

Q

Qamanittuaq (Baker Lake) tn. Northwest Territories
51 M3 64 10N 95 30W
Qausuittuq (Resolute) Northwest Territories **51** N5
74 40N 94 54W
Qikiqtarjuaq (Broughton Island) tn. Northwest Territories
51 U4 67 30N 63 50W
Quadra Island British Columbia **34** G5 50 11N 125 20W
Qualicum Beach tn. British Columbia **34** H4
49 21N 124 27W
Qu'Appelle Saskatchewan **38** C2 50 33N 103 54W
Qu'Appelle Dam Saskatchewan **38** B2 50 55N 106 20W
Qu'Appelle River Saskatchewan **38** C2 50 30N 102 20W
Quaqtaq Québec **46** C5 61 00N 69 40W
Quathiaski Cove tn. British Columbia **34** G5
50 03N 125 11W
Quatsino Sound British Columbia **35** C2 50 25N 128 55W
Québec prov. **9** V3 50 00N 75 00W
Queen Bess, Mount British Columbia **35** D2
51 13N 124 35W
Queen Charlotte British Columbia **34** B2 53 18N 132 04W
Queen Charlotte Islands British Columbia **34** B2
53 30N 131 50W
Queen Charlotte Sound British Columbia **34** C2
51 48N 129 25W
Queen Charlotte Strait British Columbia **35** C2
51 00N 127 55W
Queen Elizabeth Foreland Northwest Territories **51** U3
62 23N 64 28W
Queen Elizabeth Islands Northwest Territories **50** K6
79 00N 105 00W
Queen Maud Bird Sanctuary Northwest Territories **51** L4
67 30N 103 20W
Queen Maud Gulf Northwest Territories **51** L4
68 00N 101 00W
Queens admin. New Brunswick **49** A2 46 00N 65 50W
Queens admin. Nova Scotia **49** E6 44 10N 65 10W
Queens admin. Prince Edward Island **49** F7
46 20N 63 10W
Queenston Ontario **44** C2 43 09N 79 03W
Queenswood Heights Ontario **53** L2 45 28N 75 29W
Quesnel British Columbia **35** D2 53 03N 122 31W
Quesnel Lake British Columbia **35** D2 52 30N 121 20W
Quesnel River British Columbia **35** D2 52 58N 122 29W
Quetico Provincial Park Ontario **41** B2 48 30N 91 30W
Quill Lake tn. Saskatchewan **38** C2 52 03N 104 12W
Quill Lakes Saskatchewan **38** C2 52 03N 104 12W
Quinte, Bay of Ontario **43** J5 44 07N 77 32W
Quirke Lake Ontario **42** D4 46 28N 82 33W
Quispamsis New Brunswick **49** E7 45 25N 65 55W
Quoich River Northwest Territories **51** N3
64 50N 94 40W

R

Raanes Peninsula Northwest Territories **51** P6
78 30N 85 45W
Rabbit Lake Mine tn. Saskatchewan **38** C3
58 10N 103 42W
Rabbit River British Columbia **35** C3 59 20N 127 20W
Rádeyilíkóé (Fort Good Hope) Northwest Territories
50 F4 66 16N 128 37W
Radisson Québec **46** A3 53 50N 77 46W
Radisson Saskatchewan **38** B2 52 27N 107 24W
Radium Hot Springs tn. British Columbia **35** E2
50 39N 116 09W

Radville Saskatchewan **38** C1 49 28N 104 19W
Rae (Mbehchokó) Northwest Territories **50** H3
62 50N 116 03W
Rae River Northwest Territories **50** H4 68 10N 116 50W
Rae Strait sd. Northwest Territories **51** M4
68 50N 95 00W
Ragged Lake Nova Scotia **53** P6 44 37N 63 39W
Rainbow Lake Alberta **37** B3 58 17N 119 16W
Rainbow Lake tn. Alberta **37** B3 58 30N 119 23W
Rainy Lake Ontario **40** B2 48 00N 93 00W
Rainy River Ontario **40** B2 48 40N 94 10W
Rainy River tn. Ontario **40** B2 48 44N 94 33W
Ralston Alberta **37** C2 50 15N 111 10W
Ramea Newfoundland **49** C2 47 31N 57 23W
Ramea Islands Newfoundland **49** C2 47 31N 57 22W
Ramsey Lake Ontario **41** D2 47 13N 82 15W
Rankin Inlet (Kangiqtiniq) tn. Northwest Territories
51 N3 62 49N 92 05W
Rankin Inlet Northwest Territories **51** N3 62 45N 92 05W
Rapide-Blanc-Station Québec **43** N8 47 43N 73 03W
Rapide-des-Cèdres tn. Québec **47** A2 49 00N 77 09W
Rapides de Lachine Québec **53** N4 45 26N 73 39W
Rat Lake Manitoba **39** B3 56 10N 99 40W
Rat River Manitoba **39** B3 56 10N 99 20W
Ratz, Mount British Columbia **34** B3 57 24N 132 19W
Ravenscrag Saskatchewan **38** B1 49 30N 109 08W
Ray, Cape Newfoundland **49** C2 47 37N 59 19W
Raymond Alberta **37** C1 49 27N 112 39W
Raymore Saskatchewan **38** C2 51 24N 104 32W
Razorback mt. British Columbia **35** D2 51 28N 124 35W
Read Island British Columbia **34** G5 50 11N 125 05W
Red Bay tn. Newfoundland **48** C3 51 44N 56 25W
Red Bay tn. Ontario **44** A3 44 47N 81 19W
Redberry Lake Saskatchewan **38** B2 52 45N 107 20W
Redcliff Alberta **37** C2 50 05N 110 47W
Red Deer Alberta **37** C2 52 15N 113 48W
Red Deer Lake Manitoba **39** A2 52 50N 101 30W
Red Deer River Alberta **37** C2 51 20N 112 35W
Red Deer River Saskatchewan **38** C2 52 50N 103 05W
Red Indian Lake Newfoundland **48** C2 48 40N 57 00W
Red Lake Ontario **40** B3 51 50N 93 40W
Red Lake tn. Ontario **40** B3 51 01N 93 50W
Red Lake Road tn. Ontario **40** B2 49 58N 93 22W
Redonda Island British Columbia **34** H5 50 15N 124 50W
Red River British Columbia **35** C3 59 23N 128 14W
Red River Manitoba **39** B1 49 30N 97 20W
Red Rock Ontario **41** C2 48 55N 88 15W
Redstone River Northwest Territories **50** F3
63 47N 126 30W
Red Sucker Lake Manitoba **39** C2 54 13N 94 35W
Redvers Saskatchewan **38** C1 49 34N 101 42W
Redwater Alberta **37** C2 53 57N 113 06W
Red Wine River Newfoundland **48** B3 54 10N 62 10W
Reed Lake Manitoba **39** A2 54 30N 100 10W
Refuge Cove tn. British Columbia **34** H5 50 07N 124 51W
Regina Saskatchewan **38** C2 50 30N 104 38W
Reindeer Grazing Reserve Northwest Territories **50** E4
69 00N 132 00W
Reindeer Island Manitoba **39** B2 52 30N 97 20W
Reindeer Lake Saskatchewan/Manitoba **38** C3
57 30N 102 30W
Reindeer River Saskatchewan **38** C3 56 10N 103 10W
Reliance Northwest Territories **50** K3 62 42N 109 08W
Renews Newfoundland **49** D2 46 56N 52 56W
Renfrew admin. Ontario **43** J6 45 28N 77 10W
Renfrew Ontario **41** E2 45 28N 76 44W
Rennie Lake Northwest Territories **50** K3
61 32N 105 35W
Repentigny Québec **43** N6 45 47N 73 28W
Repulse Bay (Naujat) tn. Northwest Territories **51** P4
66 32N 86 15W
Réserve de la Rivière-Matamec Québec **47** C3
50 30N 66 00W
Réserve Duchénier Québec **47** C2 48 08N 68 40W
Réserve du Parc National de l'Archipel de Mingan Québec
47 D3 50 10N 63 40W
Réserve Faunique Ashuapmushuan Québec **47** B2
49 00N 73 30W
Réserve Faunique Assinica Québec **47** A3 50 48N 75 00W
Réserve Faunique de Baldwin Québec **47** C2 48 40N 66 10W
Réserve Faunique de Cap-Chat Québec **47** C2
48 50N 66 50W
Réserve Faunique de Dunière Québec **47** C2 48 30N 66 50W
Réserve Faunique de l'Île d'Anticosti Québec **47** D2
49 25N 62 58W
Réserve Faunique de Matane Québec **47** C2 48 45N 67 00W
Réserve Faunique de Papineau-Labelle Québec **47** A2
46 20N 75 21W
Réserve Faunique de Port-Daniel Québec **47** D2
48 13N 64 59W
Réserve Faunique de Portneuf Québec **47** B2
47 10N 72 20W
Réserve Faunique de Rimouski Québec **47** C2
48 00N 68 20W
Réserve Faunique des Chic-Chocs Québec **47** C2
49 00N 65 50W
Réserve Faunique de Sept-Îles-Port-Cartier Québec
47 C3 50 30N 67 30W
Réserve Faunique des Lacs-Albanel-Mistassini-et-Waconichi Québec **47** B3 50 10N 74 20W
Réserve Faunique des Laurentides Québec **47** B2
47 50N 71 47W
Réserve Faunique du Saint-Maurice Québec **47** B2
47 08N 73 18W
Réserve Faunique la Vérendrye Québec **41** A2
47 20N 77 10W
Réserve Faunique Mastigouche Québec **47** B2
46 35N 73 47W

Réserve Faunique Rouge-Matawin Québec **47** B2
46 52N 74 35W
Réservoir Baskatong res. Québec **47** A2 46 50N 75 50W
Réservoir Blanc res. Québec **43** N8 47 49N 73 06W
Réservoir Cabonga res. Québec **47** A2 47 31N 76 45W
Réservoir de Caniapiscau res. Québec **46** C3
54 10N 69 10W
Réservoir de La Grande 2 res. Québec **47** A3
53 38N 77 00W
Réservoir de La Grande 3 res. Québec **46** A3
53 54N 75 10W
Réservoir de La Grande 4 res. Québec **46** B3
53 59N 73 10W
Réservoir Dozois res. Québec **47** A2 47 30N 77 26W
Réservoir du Poisson Blanc res. Québec **43** L7
46 05N 75 45W
Réservoir Evans res. Québec **47** A3 50 45N 76 50W
Réservoir Gouin res. Québec **47** B2 48 30N 74 30W
Réservoir Laforge 1 res. Québec **46** B3 54 20N 71 50W
Réservoir Laforge 2 res. Québec **46** B3 54 30N 70 50W
Réservoir Manic 2 res. Québec **47** C2 49 30N 68 25W
Réservoir Manic 3 res. Québec **47** C3 50 05N 67 50W
Réservoir Manicouagan res. Québec **47** C3
51 30N 68 20W
Réservoir Opinaca res. Québec **47** A3 52 30N 76 30W
Réservoir Outardes 4 res. Québec **47** C3 50 20N 69 20W
Réservoir Pipmuacan res. Québec **47** B2 49 30N 70 10W
Réservoir Soscumica-Matagami res. Québec **47** A3
50 10N 77 32W
Réservoir Taureau res. Québec **47** B2 46 47N 73 47W
Resolute (Qausuittuq) Northwest Territories **51** N5
74 40N 94 54W
Resolution Island Northwest Territories **51** U3
61 35N 64 53W
Restigouche admin. New Brunswick **49** A2 47 40N 67 10W
Restigouche River New Brunswick **49** A2 47 35N 67 30W
Reston Manitoba **39** A1 49 33N 101 05W
Revelstoke British Columbia **35** E2 51 02N 118 12W
Revelstoke, Lake British Columbia **35** E2 51 32N 118 40W
Rexton New Brunswick **49** F7 46 41N 64 54W
Ribstone Creek Alberta **37** C2 52 10N 111 55W
Rice Lake Ontario **41** E1 44 12N 78 10W
Richard Collinson Inlet Northwest Territories **50** J5
72 45N 113 55W
Richards Island Northwest Territories **50** E4
69 20N 134 30W
Richardson Mountains Yukon/Northwest Territories
50 D4 67 50N 137 00W
Richardson River Alberta **37** C3 58 15N 110 55W
Rich, Cape Ontario **44** B3 44 43N 80 39W
Richibucto New Brunswick **49** F7 46 42N 64 55W
Richmond British Columbia **34** H4 49 09N 123 09W
Richmond admin Nova Scotia **49** F7 45 40N 60 40W
Richmond admin. Québec **43** P6 45 30N 72 10W
Richmond Québec **43** P6 45 40N 72 10W
Richmond Hill tn. Ontario **52** C2 43 53N 79 26W
Rideau River Ontario **41** E1 44 50N 76 10W
Rideau River and Canal Ontario **53** K2 45 16N 75 43W
Ridgetown Ontario **41** D1 42 26N 81 54W
Riding Mountain Manitoba **39** A2 50 40N 100 40W
Riding Mountain National Park Manitoba **39** A2
50 50N 100 30W
Rigolet Newfoundland **48** C3 54 11N 58 26W
Rimbey Alberta **37** C2 52 38N 114 41W
Rimouski Québec **47** C2 48 27N 68 32W
Riondel British Columbia **35** E1 49 46N 116 51W
Riou Lake Saskatchewan **38** B3 59 00N 106 30W
Ripley Ontario **44** A3 44 04N 81 34W
Ritchtot admin. Manitoba **54** D1 49 44N 97 07W
River Herbert tn. Nova Scotia **49** F7 45 42N 64 25W
River John tn. Nova Scotia **49** F7 45 44N 63 03W
Rivers tn. Manitoba **39** A2 50 02N 100 14W
Riverside-Albert New Brunswick **49** F7 45 40N 64 40W
Rivers Inlet British Columbia **35** C2 51 30N 127 30W
Riverton Manitoba **39** B2 51 00N 97 00W
Riverview New Brunswick **49** F7 46 06N 64 51W
Rivière à la Baleine Québec **46** C4 57 00N 67 30W
Rivière à l'Argent Québec **47** C3 50 30N 69 40W
Rivière Aguanus Québec **47** D3 50 05N 62 02W
Rivière Arnaud Québec **46** B4 59 37N 72 55W
Rivière Ashuapmushuan r. Québec **47** B2 49 22N 73 25W
Rivière aux Feuilles r. Québec **46** B4 58 00N 72 30W
Rivière aux Mélèzes r. Québec **46** B4 57 15N 71 25W
Rivière aux Outardes r. Québec **47** C3 51 38N 69 55W
Rivière-aux-Rats tn. Québec **43** P8 47 11N 72 52W
Rivière Bécancour r. Québec **43** P7 46 15N 72 20W
Rivière Bell r. Québec **47** A2 49 30N 77 30W
Rivière Betsiamites r. Québec **47** C2 48 57N 69 30W
Rivière Blanche r. Québec **53** K3 45 32N 75 38W
Rivière-Bleue tn. Québec **47** C2 47 26N 69 02W
Rivière Broadback r. Québec **47** A3 51 15N 77 42W
Rivière Caniapiscau r. Québec **46** C4 56 38N 69 15W
Rivière Capitachouane r. Québec **43** K8 47 42N 76 49W
Rivière Cascapédia r. Québec **47** C2 48 45N 66 20W
Rivière Chaudière r. Québec **47** B2 46 30N 71 10W
Rivière Chicoutimi r. Québec **43** Q9 48 11N 71 29W
Rivière Chukotat r. Québec **46** A5 61 02N 77 15W
Rivière Coats r. Québec **46** A4 55 30N 76 55W
Rivière Coulonge r. Québec **47** A2 46 44N 77 10W
Rivière d'Argent r. Québec **43** L8 47 00N 75 25W
Rivière Delay r. Québec **46** B4 56 50N 71 40W
Rivière De Pas r. Québec **46** C4 55 12N 65 35W
Rivière de Povungnituk r. Québec **46** A5 61 20N 75 20W
Rivière des Mille Îles r. Québec **53** M5 45 37N 73 47W
Rivière des Outaouais (Ottawa River) r. Ontario/Québec
42 K6 45 34N 76 30W
Rivière des Prairies r. Québec **53** N5 45 36N 73 37W
Rivière du Chêne r. Québec **54** M5 45 34N 73 59W

Rivière du Gué r. Québec **46** B4 56 48N 72 05W
Rivière du Lièvre r. Québec **47** A2 45 50N 75 39W
Rivière-du-Loup admin. Québec **43** S8 47 55N 69 20W
Rivière-du-Loup Québec **47** C2 47 49N 69 32W
Rivière Dumoine r. Québec **47** A2 46 20N 77 52W
Rivière du Petit Mécatina r. Québec **47** E3 56 20N 59 55W
Rivière du Sable r. Québec **46** C4 55 28N 68 20W
Rivière du Vieux Comptoir r. Québec **47** A3 52 33N 78 30W
Rivière Eastmain r. Québec **47** B3 52 20N 72 52W
Rivière False r. Québec **46** C4 57 40N 68 30W
Rivière Ford r. Québec **46** C4 58 10N 65 30W
Rivière Gatineau r. Québec **47** A2 45 48N 75 52W
Rivière George r. Québec **46** C4 57 00N 65 00W
Rivière Harricana r. Québec **47** A4 50 40N 79 20W
Rivière Innuksuac r. Québec **46** A4 58 30N 76 30W
Rivière Kanaaupscow r. Québec **46** A3 54 00N 75 40W
Rivière Kitchigama r. Québec **47** A3 50 35N 78 10W
Rivière Kogaluc r. Québec **46** A4 59 15N 76 05W
Rivière Koksoak r. Québec **46** C4 58 50N 69 10W
Rivière Koroc r. Québec **46** C4 58 40N 65 20W
Rivière Kovik r. Québec **46** A5 61 40N 77 20W
Rivière Magpie r. Québec **47** D3 50 40N 64 25W
Rivière Malbaie r. Québec **43** R8 47 50N 70 25W
Rivière Manicouagan r. Québec **47** C3 50 51N 68 55W
Rivière Manitou r. Québec **47** C3 51 08N 65 30W
Rivière Manouane r. Québec **47** B3 50 05N 70 45W
Rivière Maquatua r. Québec **47** A3 53 05N 78 30W
Rivière Mariet r. Québec **46** A4 59 05N 77 30W
Rivière Matapédia r. Québec **47** C2 48 30N 67 30W
Rivière Matawin r. Québec **47** B2 46 55N 73 39W
Rivière-Matawin tn. Québec **43** P7 46 54N 72 55W
Rivière Mégiscane r. Québec **47** A2 48 17N 76 50W
Rivière Métabetchouane r. Québec **43** P8 47 59N 72 05W
Rivière Mistanipiscou r. Québec **47** E3 51 50N 62 25W
Rivière Mistassibi r. Québec **47** B3 50 20N 72 15W
Rivière Mistassibi Nord-Est r. Québec **47** B3
50 01N 71 59W
Rivière Mistassini r. Québec **47** B2 49 50N 72 40W
Rivière Moisie r. Québec **47** C3 50 52N 66 33W
Rivière Montmorency r. Québec **43** Q8 47 19N 71 12W
Rivière Mucaliq r. Québec **46** C4 58 00N 67 10W
Rivière Nabisipi r. Québec **47** D3 50 59N 62 32W
Rivière Nastapoca r. Québec **46** A4 56 52N 75 10W
Rivière Natashquan r. Québec **47** D3 50 40N 61 35W
Rivière Nicolet r. Québec **43** P7 46 14N 72 35W
Rivière Nipissis r. Québec **47** C3 50 30N 66 05W
Rivière Noire r. Québec **47** A2 46 40N 77 23W
Rivière Nottaway r. Québec **47** A3 50 55N 78 20W
Rivière Olomane r. Québec **47** D3 50 50N 60 05W
Rivière Opinaca r. Québec **47** A3 52 20N 77 50W
Rivière Pentecôte r. Québec **47** C3 50 18N 67 35W
Rivière Peribonka r. Québec **47** B2 48 58N 71 30W
Rivière Pons r. Québec **46** C4 55 50N 69 20W
Rivière Pontax r. Québec **47** A3 51 35N 77 30W
Rivière Racine de Bouleau r. Québec **47** C3 52 00N 68 40W
Rivière Richelieu r. Québec **43** P6 45 08N 72 55W
Rivière Romaine r. Québec **47** D3 51 30N 63 40W
Rivière Rupert r. Québec **47** A3 51 22N 78 00W
Rivière Saguenay r. Québec **47** B2 48 20N 70 43W
Rivière Saint-Augustin r. Québec **47** E3 51 58N 60 10W
Rivière Sainte-Anne r. Québec **47** B2 46 40N 72 11W
Rivière Sainte-Marguerite r. Québec **47** C3
51 20N 67 00W
Rivière Saint-François r. Québec **47** B2 45 40N 71 30W
Rivière Saint-Jean r. Québec **47** D3 51 08N 64 08W
Rivière Saint-Maurice r. Québec **47** B2 47 55N 73 46W
Rivière Saint-Paul r. Québec **47** E3 51 55N 57 59W
Rivière Sakami r. Québec **47** B3 53 05N 74 05W
Rivière Sérigny r. Québec **46** C4 55 30N 69 30W
Rivière Témiscamie r. Québec **47** B3 51 15N 72 40W
Rivière Vachon r. Québec **46** B5 60 40N 72 35W
Rivière Vermillon r. Québec **43** N8 47 19N 73 22W
Rivière-Verte tn. New Brunswick **49** A2 47 19N 68 09W
Rivière Wacouna r. Québec **47** C3 50 57N 66 05W
Rivière Wheeler r. Québec **46** C4 56 25N 67 35W
Rivière Yamaska r. Québec **43** N6 45 40N 73 00W
Robert's Arm tn. Newfoundland **49** C2 49 29N 55 49W
Roberts Bank British Columbia **52** F3 49 06N 123 14W
Roberts Creek tn. British Columbia **34** H4 49 25N 123 37W
Roberval Québec **47** B2 48 31N 72 16W
Roblin Manitoba **39** A2 51 15N 101 20W
Robson, Mount British Columbia **35** E2 53 08N 118 18W
Rock Bay tn. British Columbia **34** G5 50 18N 125 31W
Rockcliffe Park Ontario **53** K2 45 27N 75 39W
Rock Forest tn. Québec **43** P6 45 22N 72 00W
Rockglen Saskatchewan **38** B1 49 11N 105 57W
Rockland Ontario **41** E2 45 33N 75 18W
Rock Point Provincial Park Ontario **44** C1 42 50N 79 30W
Rockwood Ontario **41** D1 43 37N 80 10W
Rocky Bay I.R. Ontario **40** C2 49 26N 88 08W
Rocky Harbour tn. Newfoundland **49** C2 49 39N 57 55W
Rocky Island Lake Ontario **41** D2 46 55N 83 04W
Rocky Lake Nova Scotia **53** P7 44 45N 63 36W
Rocky Mountain House Alberta **37** C2 52 22N 114 55W
Rocky Mountains Forest Reserve Alberta **37** B2
52 30N 116 30W
Rocky Mountain Trench British Columbia **35** C3
57 25N 125 30W
Rocky Saugeen River Ontario **44** B3 44 13N 80 52W
Rocky View Municipal District Alberta **54** A2
51 11N 114 08W
Roddickton Newfoundland **49** C2 50 52N 56 08W
Rodney Ontario **42** E3 42 34N 81 41W
Roes Welcome Sound Northwest Territories **51** P3
64 30N 87 30W
Rogers Pass British Columbia **35** E2 51 23N 117 23W
Rogersville New Brunswick **49** A2 46 44N 65 28W
Romaine River Newfoundland **48** B3 52 30N 64 30W

Rondeau Provincial Park Ontario 42 E3 42 17N 81 51W
Root River Ontario 40 B3 50 50N 91 40W
Rorketon Manitoba 39 B2 51 24N 99 35W
Roseau River Manitoba 39 B1 49 10N 96 50W
Rose Blanche Newfoundland 49 C2 47 37N 58 41W
Rosedale Ontario 44 D3 44 34N 78 47W
Rosemere Québec 53 M5 45 38N 73 49W
Rose Point British Columbia 34 B2 54 11N 131 39W
Rosetown Saskatchewan 38 B2 51 34N 107 59W
Rose Valley tn. Saskatchewan 38 C2 52 19N 103 49W
Ross Bay Junction tn. Newfoundland 48 A3
53 03N 66 12W
Rossburn Manitoba 39 A2 50 40N 100 49W
Rosseau Ontario 41 E2 45 16N 79 39W
Rosseau, Lake Ontario 42 G6 45 10N 79 35W
Rosser admin. Manitoba 54 C2 49 56N 97 23W
Rossignol, Lake Nova Scotia 49 E6 44 10N 65 10W
Ross Island Manitoba 39 B2 54 20N 97 50W
Rossland British Columbia 35 E1 49 05N 117 48W
Rossport Ontario 41 C2 48 50N 87 31W
Ross River tn. Yukon Territory 50 E3 62 02N 132 28W
Ross River Yukon Territory 50 E3 62 30N 131 50W
Rosswood British Columbia 34 C2 54 49N 128 42W
Rosthern Saskatchewan 38 B2 52 40N 106 20W
Rothesay New Brunswick 49 E7 45 23N 66 00W
Rouge River Ontario 52 D2 43 52N 79 15W
Rouge Valley Park Ontario 52 D2 43 50N 79 13W
Rouleau Saskatchewan 38 C2 50 12N 104 56W
Round Pond l. Newfoundland 49 C2 48 10N 56 00W
Route Jacques-Cartier hwy. Québec 47 C3
50 20N 66 00W
Rouyn-Noranda Québec 47 A2 48 15N 79 00W
Rowley Island Northwest Territories 51 R4
69 06N 78 52W
Roxboro Québec 53 M5 45 31N 73 48W
Russell Manitoba 39 A2 50 47N 101 17W
Russell, Cape Northwest Territories 50 H6 75 15N 117 35W
Russell Point c. Northwest Territories 50 J5
73 30N 114 30W

S

Saamba Tu (Trout Lake) tn. Northwest Territories
50 G3 61 00N 121 30W
Saanich British Columbia 34 H4 48 28N 123 22W
Sabine Peninsula Northwest Territories 50 K6
76 20N 109 30W
Sable, Cape Nova Scotia 49 A1 43 23N 65 37W
Sable River tn. Nova Scotia 49 E6 43 50N 65 05W
Sachigo I.R. Ontario 40 B3 53 50N 92 10W
Sachigo Lake Ontario 40 B3 53 49N 92 08W
Sachigo River Ontario 40 B3 54 50N 90 50W
Sachs Harbour (Ikaahuk) tn. Northwest Territories
50 F5 71 59N 125 13W
Sackville New Brunswick 49 F7 45 54N 64 23W
Sacré-Coeur Québec 43 S9 48 13N 69 50W
Saglek Bay Newfoundland 48 B4 58 30N 63 00W
Saglek Fiord Newfoundland 48 B4 58 29N 63 15W
Saguenay admin. Québec 43 S9 48 20N 69 50W
Saint-Agapit Québec 43 Q7 46 34N 71 26W
St. Albans Québec 43 Q7 47 52N 55 51W
St. Albert Alberta 54 F5 53 38N 113 38W
Saint-Ambroise Québec 47 B2 48 33N 71 20W
St. Andrews New Brunswick 49 A2 45 05N 67 04W
St. Anthony Newfoundland 48 C3 51 22N 55 35W
Saint-Antoine New Brunswick 49 F7 46 220N 64 50W
St.-Antoine Québec 43 N6 45 47N 73 59W
St. Barbe Newfoundland 49 C3 51 13N 56 45W
St. Bernard's Newfoundland 49 D2 47 32N 54 57W
St. Boniface Manitoba 54 D2 49 53N 97 06W
St. Bride's Newfoundland 49 D2 46 55N 54 10W
St. Catharines Ontario 41 E1 43 10N 79 15W
St. Charles Manitoba 54 C2 49 53N 97 17W
St. Clair, Lake Ontario/U.S.A. 42 D3 42 30N 82 40W
Saint-Donat Québec 47 B2 46 19N 74 15W
Sainte Anne de Beaupré Québe 43 R8 47 02N 70 58W
Ste. Anne Manitoba 39 B1 49 40N 96 50W
Sainte-Agathe-des-Monts Québec 47 B2 46 03N 74 19W
Sainte-Anne-de-Bellevue Québec 53 M4 45 25N 73 56W
Sainte-Anne-des-Monts Québec 47 C2 49 07N 66 29W
Sainte-Anne-du-Lac Québec 43 L7 46 54N 75 20W
Sainte-Catherine Québec 53 N4 45 25N 73 35W
Sainte-Claire Québec 43 Q7 46 37N 70 51W
Sainte-Croix Québec 43 Q7 46 38N 71 43W
Sainte-Dorothée Québec 53 M5 45 32N 73 49W
Sainte-Eustache Québec 53 M5 45 33N 73 54W
Sainte-Foy Québec 43 R7 46 47N 71 18W
Sainte-Geneviève Québec 53 M4 45 28N 73 54W
St. Eleanors Prince Edward Island 49 F7 46 30N 63 50W
Saint Elias, Mount Yukon Territory/Alaska U.S.A. 50 C3
60 12N 140 57W
Saint Elias Mountains Yukon Territory/Alaska U.S.A.
50 D3 60 30N 139 30W
Sainte-Marie Québec 47 B2 46 26N 71 00W
Sainte-Marthe-sur-le-Lac Québec 53 M5 45 31N 73 55W
Sainte-Rose Québec 53 M5 45 36N 73 47W
Ste. Rose du Lac Manitoba 39 B2 51 04N 99 31W
Sainte-Thérèse Québec 53 M5 45 38N 73 50W
Saint-Félicien Québec 43 M8 48 38N 72 29W
St. Francis Harbour tn. Nova Scotia 49 F7
45 30N 61 20W
St. Francis, Lake Québec 43 M6 45 05N 74 30W
St-François Québec 53 N5 45 38N 73 35W
St. George New Brunswick 49 A2 45 08N 66 50W
St. George's Newfoundland 49 C2 48 26N 58 29W
St.-Georges Québec 47 B2 46 08N 70 40W
St. Georges Bay Newfoundland 49 C3 48 28N 59 00W

St. Georges Bay Nova Scotia 49 F7 45 40N 61 50W
St. Germain Manitoba 54 D2 49 46N 97 08W
Saint-Hubert Québec 53 O7 45 31N 73 25W
Saint-Hubert Québec 53 O7 45 31N 73 25W
Saint-Hyacinthe Québec 47 B2 45 38N 72 57W
St. Ignace Island Ontario 41 C2 48 45N 87 55W
St. Jacobs Ontario 44 B2 43 32N 80 33W
Saint-Jacques New Brunswick 49 A2 47 25N 68 24W
St. James, Cape British Columbia 34 B2 51 58N 131 00W
St. Jean Baptiste Manitoba 39 B1 49 15N 97 20W
Saint-Jean-Port-Joli Québec 47 B2 47 13N 70 16W
Saint-Jean-sur-Richelieu Québec 47 B2 45 18N 73 18W
Saint-Jérôme Québec 47 B2 45 47N 74 01W
Saint John admin. New Brunswick 49 E7 45 20N 65 50W
Saint John New Brunswick 49 E7 45 16N 66 03W
St. John Bay Newfoundland 49 C3 50 50N 57 00W
St. John, Cape Newfoundland 49 C3 50 00N 55 32W
St. John, Lake Ontario 44 C3 44 38N 79 19W
St. John's Newfoundland 49 D2 47 34N 52 43W
Saint Joseph New Brunswick 49 F7 45 59N 64 30W
St. Joseph Island Ontario 41 C2 46 13N 83 57W
St. Joseph, Lake Ontario 40 B3 51 05N 90 35W
Saint-Lambert Québec 53 O5 45 30N 73 29W
Saint-Laurent Québec 53 N5 45 30N 73 43W
St. Lawrence Newfoundland 49 C2 46 55N 55 24W
St. Lawrence, Cape Nova Scotia 49 F7 47 10N 60 40W
St. Lawrence, Gulf of (Golfe dul Saint-Laurent)
Atlantic Provinces 49 B2 48 40N 62 40W
St. Lawrence River (Fleuve Saint-Laurent)
Québec 49 C2 46 55N 55 24W
St. Lawrence Seaway Ontario/Québec/U.S.A. 43 L5/M5
44 38N 75 34W
Saint-Léonard New Brunswick 49 A2 47 10N 67 55W
Saint-Leonard Québec 53 N5 45 34N 73 36W
St. Lewis Newfoundland 48 C3 52 22N 55 41W
St. Lewis River Newfoundland 48 C3 52 20N 56 50W
Saint-Louis-de-Kent New Brunswick 49 F7
46 50N 64 59W
St. Lunaire Newfoundland 48 C3 51 30N 55 29W
St. Malo Manitoba 39 B1 49 20N 96 55W
St. Margarets Bay Nova Scotia 49 F6 44 30N 64 00W
St. Martin, Lake Manitoba 39 B2 51 40N 98 20W
St. Martins New Brunswick 49 E7 45 22N 65 30W
St. Mary, Cape Nova Scotia 49 E6 44 10N 66 10W
St. Mary's Newfoundland 49 D2 46 50N 53 34W
St. Mary's Bay Newfoundland 49 D2 46 50N 53 45W
St. Mary's Bay Nova Scotia 49 E6 44 20N 66 10W
St. Mary's River Nova Scotia 49 F7 45 20N 62 30W
St. Marys Ontario 41 D1 43 15N 81 09W
St. Maurice admin. Québec 43 M8 47 30N 74 10W
Saint-Michel-des-Saints Québec 47 B2 46 40N 73 55W
St. Norbert Manitoba 54 D2 49 46N 97 12W
Saint-Pacôme Québec 47 C2 47 24N 69 58W
St.-Pamphile Québec 47 C2 46 58N 69 48W
Saint-Pascal Québec 47 C2 47 32N 69 48W
St. Paul Alberta 37 C2 53 59N 111 17W
St. Paul Junction Alberta 54 G5 53 37N 113 20W
St. Peters Nova Scotia 49 F7 45 40N 60 53W
St. Peters Prince Edward Island 49 F7 46 26N 62 35W
Saint-Pierre-Jolys Manitoba 39 B1 49 28N 96 58W
Saint-Prosper Québec 43 R7 46 12N 70 29W
Saint-Quentin New Brunswick 49 A2 47 30N 67 20W
Saint-Raymond Québec 43 Q7 46 54N 71 50W
Saint Romauld Québec 43 Q7 46 40N 71 14W
Saint-Siméon Québec 43 S8 47 50N 69 55W
St. Stephen New Brunswick 49 A2 45 12N 67 18W
St. Stephens Newfoundland 49 D2 46 47N 53 46W
St. Theresa Point tn. Manitoba 39 C2 53 45N 94 50W
St. Thomas Ontario 41 D1 42 46N 81 12W
Saint-Tite Québec 43 P7 46 44N 72 34W
Saint-Vincent-de-Paul Québec 53 N5 45 38N 73 39W
St. Walburg Saskatchewan 38 B2 53 38N 109 12W
Sakami Québec 46 D3 53 50N 76 10W
Salaberry-de-Valleyfield Québec 47 B2 45 16N 74 11W
Salisbury New Brunswick 49 E7 46 02N 65 03W
Salisbury Island Northwest Territories 51 R3
63 35N 77 20W
Salliq (Coral Harbour) tn. Northwest Territories 51 Q3
64 10N 83 15W
Salluit Québec 46 A5 62 20N 75 40W
Salmo British Columbia 35 E1 49 11N 117 16W
Salmon River British Columbia 35 D2 54 21N 123 34W
Salmon Arm tn. British Columbia 35 E2 50 41N 119 18W
Salmon Inlet British Columbia 34 H4 49 39N 123 47W
Salmon River New Brunswick 49 A2 46 20N 65 40W
Salmon River tn. Nova Scotia 49 E6 44 10N 66 10W
Saltcoats Saskatchewan 38 C2 51 03N 102 12W
Saltery Bay tn. British Columbia 34 H4 49 47N 124 10W
Saltspring Island British Columbia 34 H4 48 50N 123 30W
Sandilands Provincial Forest Manitoba 39 B1
49 30N 96 00W
Sandspit British Columbia 34 B2 53 14N 131 50W
Sandy Bay tn. Saskatchewan 38 C3 55 30N 102 10W
Sandy Lake Manitoba 39 A2 50 42N 99 50 700W
Sandy Lake Nova Scotia 53 P6 44 44N 63 40W
Sandy Lake Ontario 40 B3 53 02N 93 00W
Sandy Lake I.R. Ontario 40 B3 53 04N 93 20W
Sanikiluaq (Sannikiluaq) Northwest Territories 51 R2
56 32N 79 14W
Sanirajak (Hall Beach) tn. Northwest Territories 51 Q4
68 46N 81 12W
San Juan River British Columbia 34 H4 48 37N 124 20W
Sapawe Ontario 41 B2 48 45N 91 20W
Sardis British Columbia 34 H4 49 07N 121 57W
Sarnia Ontario 41 D1 42 58N 82 23W
Sasaginnigak Lake Manitoba 39 B2 51 30N 95 30W
Sasamat Lake British Columbia 52 G4 49 19N 122 52W
Saskatchewan prov. 8 P3 53 50N 109 00W

Saskatchewan River Saskatchewan/Manitoba 38 C2
53 50N 103 10W
Saskatoon Saskatchewan 38 B2 52 10N 106 40W
Saturna Island British Columbia 34 H4 48 47N 123 07W
Sauble Beach tn. Ontario 44 A3 44 38N 81 17W
Sauble Falls Provincial Park Ontario 44 A3 44 40N 81 15W
Sauble River Ontario 44 A3 44 36N 81 18W
Saugeen River Ontario 44 A3 44 23N 81 18W
Sault Ste. Marie Ontario 43 D2 46 31N 84 20W
Saunders Lake Alberta 54 G4 53 18N 113 29W
Savant Lake Ontario 40 B3 50 30N 90 25W
Savant Lake tn. Ontario 40 B3 50 14N 90 43W
Sawbill Newfoundland 48 A3 53 37N 66 21W
Sayabec Québec 47 C2 48 35 67 41W
Sayward British Columbia 35 C2 50 19N 125 58W
Scarborough bor. Metropolitan Toronto Ontario 52 D2
43 44N 79 16W
Scaterie Island Nova Scotia 49 G7 46 00N 59 45W
Schefferville (Kawawachikamach) Québec 46 C3
54 50N 67 00W
Schreiber Ontario 41 C2 48 48N 87 17W
Schultz Lake Northwest Territories 51 M3 64 45N 97 30W
Scotsburn Nova Scotia 49 F7 45 40N 62 51W
Scott Islands British Columbia 34 C2 50 48N 128 38W
Scott Lake Saskatchewan 38 B3 59 50N 106 30W
Scudder tn. Ontario 42 D1 41 47N 82 39W
Scugog Island Ontario 44 D3 44 10N 78 52W
Scugog, Lake Ontario 44 D3 44 10N 78 51W
Scugog River Ontario 44 D3 44 16N 78 46W
Seaforth Ontario 44 A2 43 03N 81 24W
Sea Island British Columbia 52 F3 49 11N 123 11W
Seal Cove tn. Newfoundland 49 C2 47 27N 55 50W
Seal Cove tn. Nova Scotia 49 E6 44 38N 66 52W
Seal Harbour tn. Nova Scotia 49 F7 45 10N 61 30W
Seal Lake Newfoundland 48 B3 54 20N 61 40W
Seal River Manitoba 39 B3 58 50N 97 00W
Seaside Adjunct Kejimkujik National Park Nova Scotia
49 F6 43 54N 64 48W
Sechelt British Columbia 34 H4 49 28N 123 46W
Sechelt Peninsula British Columbia 34 H4 49 40N 123 55W
Second Narrows British Columbia 52 F4 49 18N 123 03W
Seine River Manitoba 54 D2 49 46N 97 02W
Selkirk Manitoba 39 B3 50 10N 96 52W
Selkirk Ontario 44 C1 42 50N 79 55W
Selkirk Mountains British Columbia 35 E2 51 40N 118 20W
Selkirk Provincial Park Ontario 44 C1 42 50N 79 56W
Selwyn Lake Northwest Territories 50 L3 60 05N 104 25W
Selwyn Mountains Yukon Territory 50 E3 61 30N 130 20W
Semchuk Trail Saskatchewan 38 B3 57 35N 109 20W
Senneterre Québec 47 A2 48 24N 77 16W
Sentinel Peak British Columbia 35 D2 54 56N 121 59W
Sept-Îles Québec 47 C3 50 10N 66 25W
Serpentine British Columbia 52 G3 49 06N 122 46W
Serpentine River British Columbia 52 G3
49 06N 122 46W
Seseganaga Lake Ontario 40 B3 50 00N 90 28W
Setting Lake Manitoba 39 B3 55 10N 98 50W
Seven Islands Bay Newfoundland 48 B4 59 25N 63 50W
70 Mile House British Columbia 35 D2 51 21N 121 25W
Severn Bridge tn. Ontario 44 C3 44 46N 79 20W
Severn Lake Ontario 40 B3 53 54N 90 48W
Severn River Ontario 40 C4 55 30N 88 30W
Severn Sound Ontario 44 C3 44 47N 79 51W
Sexsmith Alberta 37 B3 55 21N 118 47W
Seymour Creek British Columbia 52 F4 49 18N 123 01W
Seymour Inlet British Columbia 35 C2 51 03N 127 05W
Shabaqua Ontario 41 C2 48 35N 89 54W
Shabo Newfoundland 48 A3 53 19N 66 12W
Shabogamo Lake Newfoundland 48 A3 53 15N 66 30W
Shag Harbour tn. Nova Scotia 49 E6 43 32N 65 40W
Shakespeare Ontario 44 B2 43 22N 80 50W
Shaler Mountains Northwest Territories 50 J5
72 10N 111 00W
Shallow Lake tn. Ontario 44 A3 44 38N 81 06W
Shamattawa Manitoba 39 C3 55 51N 92 05W
Shamattawa River Manitoba 40 C3 54 05N 85 50W
Shapio Lake Newfoundland 48 B3 54 58N 61 18W
Sharon Ontario 44 C3 44 06N 79 26W
Shaunavon Saskatchewan 38 B1 49 40N 108 25W
Shawanaga Ontario 44 B4 45 32N 80 16W
Shawanaga Inlet Ontario 44 B4 45 26N 80 24W
Shawanaga Island Ontario 44 B4 45 16N 80 33W
Shawinigan Québec 47 B2 46 33N 72 44W
Shawinigan Sud Québec 43 P7 46 32N 72 44W
Shawnigan Lake tn. British Columbia 34 H4 48 38N 123 39W
Shawville Québec 43 K6 45 36N 76 30W
Shebandowan Ontario 41 B2 48 38N 90 04W
Shediac New Brunswick 49 F7 46 13N 64 35W
Sheet Harbour tn. Nova Scotia 49 F6 44 56N 62 31W
Shefford admin. Québec 43 P6 45 30N 72 45W
Shelburne tn. Ontario 44 B3 44 05N 80 13W
Shelburne admin. Nova Scotia 49 E6 43 50N 65 30W
Shelburne Nova Scotia 49 E6 43 47N 65 20W
Sheldon Creek Ontario 44 C3 44 05N 80 06W
Shellbrook Saskatchewan 38 B2 53 14N 106 24W
Shelsay River British Columbia 34 B3 58 33N 132 02W
Shelter Bay tn. Newfoundland 48 C3 51 09N 117 59W
Shepherd Bay Northwest Territories 51 N4 68 40N 94 00W
Sherbrooke Nova Scotia 49 F7 45 10N 61 58W
Sherbrooke admin. Québec 43 P6 45 20N 72 10W
Sherbrooke Québec 43 P6 45 24N 71 54W
Sherbrooke Lake Nova Scotia 49 F6 44 40N 64 40W
Sherridon Saskatchewan 38 B3 55 07N 101 05W
Sherwood Park tn. Alberta 54 F5 53 31N 113 19W
Sheshatsheits Newfoundland 48 B3 53 30N 60 10W
Shibogama Lake Ontario 40 C3 53 35N 88 15W
Shipiskan Lake Newfoundland 48 B3 54 39N 62 19W
Shippagan New Brunswick 49 B2 47 45N 64 44W

Shirleys Bay Ontario 53 J2 45 22N 75 54W
Shoal Bay tn. Newfoundland 49 D2 49 41N 54 12W
Shoal Harbour tn. Newfoundland 49 D2 48 11N 54 01W
Shoal Lake Ontario/Manitoba 40 B2 49 35N 95 01W
Shoal Lake tn. Manitoba 39 A2 50 28N 100 35W
Shoal Lakes Manitoba 39 B2 50 25N 97 35W
Shubenacadie Nova Scotia 49 F7 45 05N 63 25W
Shubenacadie River Nova Scotia 49 F7 45 10N 63 30W
Shubenacadie Grand Lake Nova Scotia 53 P7
44 53N 63 37W
Shunacadie Nova Scotia 49 F7 46 00N 60 40W
Shuswap Lake British Columbia 35 E2 51 00N 119 00W
Sibbald Point Provincial Park Ontario 44 C3 44 15N 79 20W
Sibley Provincial Park Ontario 41 C2 48 10N 88 50W
Sicamous British Columbia 35 E2 50 50N 119 00W
Sidney British Columbia 34 H4 48 39N 123 25W
Sidney Bay Ontario 44 A3 44 55N 81 04W
Sifton Manitoba 39 A2 51 21N 100 09W
Sifton Pass British Columbia 35 C3 57 51N 126 17W
Sikanni Chief British Columbia 35 D3 57 11N 122 43W
Sikanni Chief River British Columbia 35 D3 57 16N 125 25W
Sillery Québec 43 Q7 46 46N 71 15W
Silver City Yukon Territory 50 D3 60 57N 138 25W
Silver Dollar Ontario 40 B2 49 50N 91 15W
Silverthrone Mountain British Columbia 35 C2
51 30N 126 03W
Silvertip Mountain British Columbia 34 H4 49 09N 121 12W
Simcoe admin. Ontario 44 C3 44 32N 79 54W
Simcoe Ontario 41 D1 42 50N 80 19W
Simcoe, Lake Ontario 41 D1 44 23N 79 18W
Similkameen River British Columbia 34 H4 48 55N 119 25W
Simonette River Alberta 37 B2 54 25N 118 20W
Simpson Bay Northwest Territories 50 J4 69 00N 113 40W
Simpson Peninsula Northwest Territories 51 P4
68 34N 88 45W
Simpson Strait Northwest Territories 51 M4 68 27N 97 45W
Sioux Lookout Ontario 40 B3 50 07N 91 54W
Sioux Narrows Ontario 40 B2 49 23N 94 08W
Sipiwesk Manitoba 39 B3 55 27N 97 24W
Sipiwesk Lake Manitoba 39 B3 55 10N 98 50W
Sir Alexander, Mount British Columbia 35 D2 53 52N 120 25W
Sir James McBrien, Mount Northwest Territories 50 F3
62 15N 128 01W
Sir Wilfred Laurier, Mount British Columbia 35 E2
52 45N 119 40W
Sisipuk Lake Manitoba 39 A3 55 30N 101 40W
Sistonens Corners tn. Ontario 41 C2 48 35N 89 40W
Six Mile Lake Provincial Park Ontario 44 C3 44 50N 79 50W
Skagit Valley Recreation Park British Columbia 34 H4
49 06N 121 09W
Skeena Mountains British Columbia 34/35 C3
56 35N 129 00W
Skeena River British Columbia 34 C2 54 15N 129 15W
Skidegate British Columbia 34 B2 53 13N 132 02W
Skihist Mountain British Columbia 34 H5 50 12N 122 53W
Skownan Manitoba 39 B2 51 58N 99 35W
Slave Lake tn. Alberta 37 C3 55 17N 114 43W
Slave River Alberta/Northwest Territories 50 J3
60 30N 112 50W
Sleeper Islands Northwest Territories 51 R2 57 25N 79 50W
Slocan British Columbia 35 E1 49 46N 117 28W
Slocan Lake British Columbia 35 E1 49 50N 117 20W
Smallwood Reservoir Newfoundland 48 B3 54 10N 64 20W
Smeaton Saskatchewan 38 C2 53 30N 104 50W
Smith Alberta 37 C3 55 10N 114 02W
Smith Arm b. Northwest Territories 50 G4 66 15N 124 00W
Smith Bay Northwest Territories 51 R6 77 12N 78 50W
Smithers British Columbia 34 C2 54 45N 127 10W
Smith Island Northwest Territories 46 A5 60 44N 78 30W
Smith Point Nova Scotia 49 F7 45 05N 63 25W
Smith River British Columbia 35 C3 59 56N 126 28W
Smiths Falls tn. Ontario 41 E1 44 45N 76 01W
Smith Sound Newfoundland 49 R6 77 40N 75 00W
Smithville Ontario 44 C2 43 06N 79 32W
Smokey Newfoundland 48 C3 54 28N 57 14W
Smoky, Cape Nova Scotia 49 F7 46 40N 60 20W
Smoky Lake tn. Alberta 37 C2 54 07N 112 28W
Smoky River Alberta 37 B3 55 30N 117 59W
Smooth Rock Falls tn. Ontario 41 D2 49 17N 81 38W
Smoothrock Lake Ontario 40 C3 50 30N 89 30W
Smoothstone Lake Saskatchewan 38 B2 54 40N 106 30W
Snake Creek Ontario 44 A3 44 23N 81 16W
Snake River Yukon Territory 50 E4 65 20N 133 30W
Snare Lakes (Wekweti) Northwest Territories 50 J3
64 10N 114 20W
Snegamook Lake Newfoundland 48 B3 54 33N 61 27W
Snowbird Lake Northwest Territories 51 L3
60 41N 102 56W
Snowdrift Northwest Territories 50 J3 62 24N 110 44W
Snow Lake tn. Manitoba 39 A2 54 56N 100 00W
Snug Harbour tn. Newfoundland 48 C3 52 53N 55 52W
Snug Harbour tn. Ontario 44 B4 45 22N 80 17W
Soldier Lake Nova Scotia 53 P7 44 49N 63 33W
Sòmbak'e (Yellowknife) Northwest Territories 50 J3
62 30N 114 29W
Somerset Manitoba 39 B1 49 26N 98 39W
Somerset Island Northwest Territories 51 N5
73 15N 93 30W
Sonora Island British Columbia 34 G5 50 21N 125 13W
Sooke British Columbia 34 H4 48 20N 123 42W
Sorel Québec 47 B2 46 03N 73 06W
Soulanges admin. Québec 43 M6 45 15N 74 10W
Sounding Creek Alberta 37 C2 51 40N 111 05W
Sounding Lake Alberta 37 C2 52 08N 110 29W
Souris Manitoba 39 A1 49 38N 100 17W
Souris Prince Edward Island 49 F7 46 22N 62 16W
Souris River Manitoba/U.S.A. 39 A1 49 30N 100 50W
Southampton Ontario 44 A3 44 29N 81 22W

Southampton Island Northwest Territories **51** Q3
64 50N 84 30W
South Aulatsivik Island Newfoundland **48** B4
56 46N 61 30W
South Bay tn. Ontario **40** B3 51 03N 92 45W
South Baymouth Ontario **42** D6 45 34N 82 02W
South Brookfield Nova Scotia **49** E6 44 23N 64 58W
Southend Saskatchewan **38** C3 56 20N 103 14W
Southern Indian Lake Manitoba **39** B3 57 00N 98 00W
Southey Saskatchewan **38** C2 50 57N 104 33W
Southgate River British Columbia **34** H5 50 54N 124 42W
South Gloucester Ontario **53** K2 45 17N 75 34W
South Henik Lake Northwest Territories **51** M3
61 30N 97 30W
South Indian Lake tn. Manitoba **39** B3 56 48N 98 55W
South Knife River Manitoba **39** B3 58 20N 96 10W
South Maitland River Ontario **44** A2 43 39N 81 27W
South Moose Lake Manitoba **39** A2 53 40N 100 10W
South Nahanni River Northwest Territories **50** F3
61 30N 125 00W
South Porcupine Ontario **41** D2 48 28N 81 13W
Southport Prince Edward Island **49** F7 46 10N 63 05W
South River tn. Ontario **41** E2 45 50N 79 23W
South Saskatchewan River Saskatchewan **38** A2
50 50N 110 00W
South Saugeen River Ontario **44** B3 44 00N 80 45W
South Seal River Manitoba **39** B3 58 00N 99 10W
South Twin Lake Northwest Territories **40** E3
53 10N 79 50W
Southwest Miramichi River New Brunswick **49** A2
46 30N 66 50W
Spanish Ontario **42** D7 46 12N 82 12W
Spanish Bank British Columbia **52** F4 49 17N 123 14W
Spanish River Ontario **41** D2 46 33N 81 57W
Sparrow Lake Ontario **44** C3 44 47N 79 23W
Sparwood British Columbia **35** F1 49 55N 114 53W
Spatsizi Plateau Wilderness Park British Columbia **35** C3
57 30N 128 30W
Spear Harbour tn. Newfoundland **48** C3 52 25N 55 42W
Speed River Ontario **44** B2 43 29N 80 17W
Speers Saskatchewan **38** B2 52 43N 107 32W
Spence Bay (Taloyoak) Northwest Territories **51** N4
69 30N 93 20W
Spicer Islands Northwest Territories **51** R4 68 19N 78 52W
Spirit River tn. Alberta **37** B3 55 46N 118 51W
Spiritwood Saskatchewan **38** B2 53 20N 107 33W
Split, Cape Nova Scotia **49** F7 45 20N 64 30W
Split Lake Manitoba **39** B3 56 10N 95 50W
Split Lake tn. Manitoba **39** B3 56 16N 96 08W
Spotted Island Newfoundland **48** C3 53 31N 55 47W
Sprague Manitoba **39** B1 49 02N 95 36W
Spring Water Provincial Park Ontario **44** C3 44 30N 79 45W
Springdale Newfoundland **49** C2 49 30N 56 04W
Springfield admin. Manitoba **54** E2 49 48N 96 57W
Springfield Nova Scotia **49** F6 44 37N 64 52W
Springfield Ontario **44** B1 42 49N 80 57W
Springhill Nova Scotia **49** F7 45 40N 64 04W
Sproat Lake British Columbia **34** C5 49 16N 125 05W
Spruce Grove Alberta **37** C2 53 32N 113 55W
Spruce Woods Provincial Forest Manitoba **39** B1
49 40N 99 40W
Spruce Woods Provincial Park Manitoba **39** B1
49 40N 99 10W
Spry Harbour tn. Nova Scotia **49** F6 44 50N 62 45W
Spuzzum British Columbia **34** H4 49 40N 121 25W
Squamish British Columbia **34** H4 49 41N 123 11W
Squamish River British Columbia **34** H4 49 42N 123 11W
Square Island Newfoundland **48** C3 52 45N 55 52W
Stabuck Manitoba **49** 47N 97 38W
Stanley New Brunswick **49** A2 46 17N 66 45W
Stanley Park British Columbia **52** F4 49 18N 123 08W
Stanstead admin. Québec **43** P6 45 10N 72 10W
Star City Saskatchewan **38** C2 52 52N 104 20W
Stave Lake British Columbia **34** H4 49 21N 122 19W
Stayner Ontario **44** B3 44 25N 80 06W
Stefansson Island Northwest Territories **50** K5
73 20N 105 45W
Steinbach Manitoba **39** B1 49 32N 96 40W
Stellarton Nova Scotia **49** F7 45 34N 62 40W
Stephens Lake Manitoba **39** B3 56 30N 95 00W
Stephenville Newfoundland **49** C2 48 33N 58 32W
Stephenville Crossing Newfoundland **49** C2
48 30N 58 26W
Stettler Alberta **37** C2 52 19N 112 43W
Stevenson Lake Manitoba **39** B2 53 50N 95 50W
Steveston British Columbia **52** F3 49 07N 123 10W
Stewart British Columbia **34** C3 55 07N 129 59W
Stewart Yukon Territory **50** D3 63 19N 139 26W
Stewart Crossing Yukon Territory **50** D3 63 22N 136 41W
Stewart River Yukon Territory **50** D3 63 40N 138 20W
Stewiacke Nova Scotia **49** F7 45 09N 63 22W
Stikine British Columbia **34** B3 56 42N 131 45W
Stikine Ranges mts. British Columbia **34** B3
59 55N 130 55W
Stikine River Recreation Area British Columbia **34** C3
58 07N 129 35W
Stirling Alberta **37** C1 49 34N 112 30W
Stirling Ontario **43** J5 44 18N 77 33W
Stittsville Ontario **53** J2 45 16N 75 54W
Stokes Bay Ontario **44** A3 44 59N 81 23W
Stone Mountain Provincial Park British Columbia **35** D3
58 35N 124 40W
Stonewall Manitoba **39** B2 50 08N 97 20W
Stoney Creek tn. Ontario **44** C2 43 13N 79 46W
Stony Lake Manitoba **39** B3 58 50N 98 30W
Stony Lake Ontario **42** H5 44 33N 78 06W
Stony Mountain tn. Manitoba **39** B2 50 04N 97 17W
Stony Plain tn. Alberta **37** C2 53 32N 114 00W

Stony Rapids tn. Saskatchewan **38** B3 59 14N 105 48W
Storkerson Peninsula Northwest Territories **50** K5
72 30N 106 30W
Stormont, Dundas and Glengarry admin. Ontario **43** L6
45 10N 75 00W
Stormy Lake Ontario **40** B2 49 23N 92 18W
Stouffville Ontario **44** C2 43 59N 79 14W
Stoughton Saskatchewan **38** C1 49 40N 103 00W
Strasbourg Saskatchewan **38** C2 51 05N 104 58W
Stratford Ontario **41** D1 43 07N 80 59
Strathcona Alberta **54** G5 53 31N 113 29W
Strathcona County Alberta **54** G5 53 33N 113 16W
Strathcona Provincial Park British Columbia **34** G4
49 40N 125 30W
Strathmore Alberta **37** C2 51 03N 113 23W
Strathnaver British Columbia **35** D2 53 21N 112 32W
Strathroy Ontario **41** D1 42 57N 81 40W
Streetsville Ontario **44** C2 43 25N 79 44W
Stuart Island tn. British Columbia **34** G5 50 22N 125 09W
Stuart Lake British Columbia **35** D2 54 35N 124 40W
Stuart River British Columbia **35** D2 54 10N 124 05W
Stupart River Manitoba **39** C3 55 30N 94 30W
Sturgeon Bank British Columbia **52** F3 49 10N 123 14W
Sturgeon Bay Manitoba **39** B2 51 50N 98 00W
Sturgeon Creek Manitoba **54** C2 49 56N 97 25W
Sturgeon Falls tn. Ontario **41** E2 46 22N 79 57W
Sturgeon Lake Alberta **37** B3 55 06N 117 32W
Sturgeon Lake Ontario **44** D3 50 00N 91 00W
Sturgeon Landing Saskatchewan **38** C2 54 18N 101 49W
Sturgeon Municipal District Alberta **54** F5
53 38N 113 30W
Sturgeon Point tn. Ontario **44** D3 44 28N 78 42W
Sturgeon River Alberta **54** F5 53 38N 113 38W
Sturgeon River Ontario **44** C3 44 36N 79 46W
Sturgeon River Saskatchewan **38** B2 53 30N 106 20W
Sturgeon River Provincial Park Ontario **41** D2
47 10N 80 40W
Sturgis Saskatchewan **38** C2 51 58N 102 32W
Styx Ontario **44** B3 44 15N 80 58W
Sudbury admin. Ontario **42** E7 46 10N 81 20W
Sudbury Ontario **41** D2 46 30N 81 01W
Sudbury, Regional Municipality of Ontario **42** E7
46 32N 81 00W
Suggi Lake Saskatchewan **38** C2 54 20N 103 10W
Sullivan Bay tn. British Columbia **34** C5 50 55N 126 52W
Sullivan Lake Alberta **37** C2 52 00N 112 00W
Sultan Ontario **41** D2 47 36N 82 45W
Summer Beaver Ontario **40** C2 52 50N 88 30W
Summerford Newfoundland **49** D2 49 29N 54 50W
Summerland British Columbia **35** E1 49 35N 119 41W
Summerside Prince Edward Island **49** F7 46 24N 63 46W
Summerville Newfoundland **49** D2 48 27N 53 33W
Sunbury admin. New Brunswick **49** A2 45 50N 66 40W
Sundre Alberta **37** C2 51 48N 114 38W
Sundridge Ontario **42** G6 45 46N 79 24W
Sunnyside Newfoundland **49** D2 47 51N 53 55W
Superb Mountains British Columbia **34** H5 50 48N 124 41W
Superior, Lake Ontario/U.S.A. **65** I6 48 00N 88 00W
Surrey British Columbia **34** H4 49 08N 122 50W
Sussex New Brunswick **49** E7 45 43N 65 32W
Sussex Corner New Brunswick **49** E7 45 40N 65 30W
Sutherland Saskatchewan **38** B2 52 10N 106 35W
Sutton Ontario **44** C3 44 18N 79 22W
Sutton Québec **43** P6 45 05N 72 36W
Sutton Lake Ontario **40** D3 54 15N 84 44W
Sutton River Ontario **40** D3 54 50N 84 30W
Svendsen Peninsula Northwest Territories **51** Q6
77 45N 84 00W
Sverdrup Islands Northwest Territories **51** M6
78 00N 97 30W
Swan Hills Alberta **37** B2 54 45N 115 45W
Swan Hills tn. Alberta **37** B2 54 43N 115 24W
Swan Lake Manitoba **39** A2 52 20N 100 50W
Swan Lake Provincial Forest Manitoba **39** A2
52 30N 100 30W
Swannell Range British Columbia **35** C3 56 20N 125 30W
Swan River tn. Manitoba **39** A2 52 06N 101 17W
Swift Current tn. Saskatchewan **38** B2 50 17N 107 49W
Swiftcurrent Creek Saskatchewan **38** B1 49 40N 108 30W
Swift River tn. Yukon Territory **50** E3 60 02N 131 10W
Swinburne, Cape Northwest Territories **51** M5
71 13N 98 33W
Swindle Island British Columbia **35** C2 52 33N 128 25W
Sydenham River Ontario **42** D3 42 34N 82 15W
Sydney Nova Scotia **49** F7 46 10N 60 10W
Sydney Mines tn. Nova Scotia **49** F7 46 16N 60 15W
Sylvan Lake tn. Alberta **37** C2 52 19N 114 05W

T

Taber Alberta **37** C1 49 48N 112 09W
Table Bay Newfoundland **48** C3 53 40N 56 25W
Tache admin. Manitoba **54** E2 49 47N 96 43W
Tadoule Lake Manitoba **39** B3 58 35N 98 25W
Tadoule Lake tn. Manitoba **39** B3 58 45N 98 30W
Tadoussac Québec **47** C2 48 09N 69 43W
Tagish Lake British Columbia **34** B3 59 50N 134 33W
Taglish Yukon Territory **40** E3 60 18N 134 16W
Tahiruyak Lake Northwest Territories **50** J5
70 56N 112 30W
Tahoe Lake Northwest Territories **50** K5
70 00N 108 45W
Tahsis British Columbia **35** C1 49 50N 126 39W
Tahtsa Lake British Columbia **35** C2 53 41N 127 30W
Takla Lake British Columbia **35** C3 55 12N 125 45W
Takla Landing British Columbia **35** C3 55 27N 125 59W
Taku Arm l. British Columbia **34** B3 60 10N 134 05W

Taku River British Columbia **34** B3 58 43N 133 20W
Talbot Lake Manitoba **39** B2 54 00N 99 40W
Taloyoak (Spence Bay) Northwest Territories **51** N4
69 30N 93 20W
Taltson River Northwest Territories **50** J3
60 40N 111 30W
Tara Ontario **44** A3 44 29N 81 09W
Taseko Mountain British Columbia **35** D2 51 12N 123 07W
Taseko River British Columbia **35** D2 51 35N 123 40W
Tasisuak Lake Newfoundland **48** B4 56 45N 62 46W
Tasiujaq Québec **46** B4 58 40N 70 00W
Tatamagouche Nova Scotia **49** F7 45 43N 63 19W
Tatamagouche Bay Nova Scotia **49** F7 45 45N 63 15W
Tathlina Lake Northwest Territories **50** H3
60 33N 117 39W
Tatla Lake British Columbia **35** D2 51 59N 124 25W
Tatlatui Provincial Park British Columbia **35** C3
57 00N 127 20W
Tatlayoko Lake British Columbia **35** D2 51 39N 124 23W
Tatnam, Cape Manitoba **39** C3 57 25N 91 00W
Tatshenshini-Alsek Wilderness Park British Columbia
34 A3 59 55N 137 30N
Tatshenshini River British Columbia **34** A3
59 30N 137 30W
Tavistock Ontario **44** B2 43 19N 80 50W
Taylor British Columbia **35** D3 56 09N 120 40W
Taylor Head p. Nova Scotia **49** F6 44 40N 62 30W
Tazin Lake Saskatchewan **38** B3 59 50N 109 10W
Tazin River Saskatchewan **38** B3 59 50N 109 30W
Tecumseh Ontario **42** D3 42 18N 82 49W
Teeswater Ontario **44** A3 43 59N 81 18W
Teeswater River Ontario **44** A3 44 07N 81 22W
Teetł'it Zheh (Fort McPherson) Northwest Territories
50 E4 67 29N 134 50W
Tehek Lake Northwest Territories **51** M3 64 58N 95 38W
Telegraph Creek tn. British Columbia **34** B3
57 56N 131 11W
Telkwa British Columbia **35** C2 54 44N 127 05W
Temagami Ontario **41** E2 47 04N 79 47W
Temagami, Lake Ontario **42** F7 46 58N 80 05W
Témiscaming Québec **47** A2 46 44N 79 05W
Témiscamingue admin. Québec **42** H6 47 35N 78 30W
Templeton Québec **53** K2 45 29N 75 36W
Terence Bay tn. Nova Scotia **49** F6 44 25N 63 45W
Terrace British Columbia **35** C2 54 31N 128 32W
Terrace Bay tn. Ontario **41** C2 48 47N 87 06W
Terra Cotta Ontario **44** C2 43 42N 79 55W
Terra Nova National Park Newfoundland **49** D2
48 40N 54 00W
Terrebonne admin. Québec **43** M7 46 10N 74 30W
Terrebonne Québec **43** N6 45 42N 73 37W
Terrenceville Newfoundland **49** D2 47 40N 54 44W
Teslin Yukon Territory **50** E3 60 10N 132 42W
Teslin Lake British Columbia/Yukon Territory **50** E3
60 00N 132 25W
Teslin River British Columbia **34** B3 59 20N 131 50W
Tetachuk Lake British Columbia Canada **35** C2
53 38N 127 40W
Teulon Manitoba **39** B2 50 26N 97 18W
Texada Island British Columbia **34** H4 49 30N 124 30W
Thamesford Ontario **44** A2 43 03N 81 00W
Thames River Ontario **41** D1 42 40N 82 40W
Thelon Game Sanctuary Northwest Territories **51** L3
64 30N 103 00W
Thelon River Northwest Territories **50** L3 64 40N 104 00W
The Pas Manitoba **39** A2 53 49N 101 14W
Thesiger Bay Northwest Territories **50** G5 71 30N 124 05W
Thessalon Ontario **41** D2 46 15N 83 34W
Thetford Mines tn. Québec **47** B2 46 06N 71 18W
Thicket Portage Manitoba **39** B3 55 20N 97 42W
Thirty Thousand Islands Ontario **42** F6 45 30N 80 30W
Thlewiaza River Northwest Territories **51** M3
60 50N 98 00W
Thomlinson, Mount British Columbia **35** C3
55 30N 127 30W
Thompson Manitoba **39** B3 55 45N 97 54W
Thompson River British Columbia **35** D2 50 12N 121 30W
Thomsen River Northwest Territories **50** H5
73 00N 119 50W
Thorah Island Ontario **44** C3 44 27N 79 13W
Thorhild Alberta **37** C2 54 10N 113 07W
Thornbury Ontario **44** B3 44 34N 80 27W
Thornhill tn. Ontario **52** C2 43 49N 79 26W
Thorold Ontario **44** C2 43 08N 79 14W
Thorsby Alberta **37** C2 53 14N 114 03W
Thousand Islands Ontario/U.S.A. **43** L5 44 22N 75 55W
Three Hills tn. Alberta **37** C2 51 42N 113 16W
Three Mile Plains tn. Nova Scotia **49** F6 44 58N 64 08W
Thunder Bay tn. Ontario **41** C2 48 27N 89 12W
Thurso Québec **47** A2 45 38N 75 19W
Thutade Lake British Columbia **35** C3 56 59N 126 40W
Tide Head tn. New Brunswick **49** A2 47 58N 66 49W
Tignish Prince Edward Island **49** F7 46 58N 64 03W
Tikirarjuaq (Whale Cove) tn. Northwest Territories
51 N3 62 10N 92 36W
Tilbury Ontario **41** D1 42 16N 82 26W
Tilbury Island British Columbia **52** F3 49 08N 123 02W
Tilden Lake tn. Ontario **42** G7 46 37N 79 39W
Tillsonburg Ontario **41** D1 42 53N 80 44W
Timberlea Nova Scotia **49** F6 44 40N 63 45W
Timiskaming, Lake (Lac Témiscamingue) Ontario **41** E2
46 52N 79 15W
Timmins Ontario **41** D2 48 30N 81 20W
Tinnisukutak, Mount British Columbia **34** H5
50 19N 123 47W
Tip Top Mountain Ontario **41** C2 48 16N 85 59W
Tisdale Saskatchewan **38** C2 52 51N 104 01W

Tiverton Ontario **44** A3 44 15N 81 33W
Tłegǫ́hłi (Norman Wells) tn. Northwest Territories **50** F4
65 19N 126 46W
Toad River British Columbia **35** C3 58 50N 125 12W
Toba Inlet British Columbia **34** H5 50 25N 124 30W
Toba River British Columbia **34** H5 50 31N 124 18W
Tobeatic Wildlife Management Area Nova Scotia
44 12N 65 25W
Tobermory Ontario **41** D2 45 15N 81 39W
Tobin Lake Saskatchewan **38** C2 53 30N 103 30W
Tofield Saskatchewan **37** C2 53 22N 112 40W
Tofino British Columbia **35** C1 49 05N 125 51W
Torbay Newfoundland **49** D2 47 40N 52 44W
Tor Bay Nova Scotia **49** F7 45 15N 61 15W
Torch River Saskatchewan **38** C2 53 40N 103 50W
Tornado Mountain Alberta/British Columbia **35** F1
49 57N 114 35W
Torngat Mountains (Monts Torngat) Newfoundland/
Québec **48** B4 59 30N 64 30W
Toronto Ontario **52** C1 43 42N 79 46W
Toronto Islands Ontario **52** C1 43 42N 79 25W
Tottenham Ontario **44** C3 44 02N 79 48W
Touraine Québec **53** K2 45 29N 75 42W
Tracadie Nova Scotia **49** F7 45 38N 61 40W
Tracadie-Sheila New Brunswick **49** B2 47 32N 64 57W
Tracy New Brunswick **49** A2 45 41N 66 42W
Tracy Québec **47** B2 45 59N 73 06W
Trail British Columbia **35** E1 49 04N 117 39W
Tramping Lake Saskatchewan **38** B2 52 10N 109 10W
Trans-Canada Highway Canada **32** M3/N3
Transcona Manitoba **52** D2 49 54N 97 00W
Treherne Manitoba **39** B1 49 39N 98 41W
Trembleur Lake British Columbia **35** D2 54 50N 124 55W
Trenton Ontario **41** E1 44 07N 77 34W
Trenton Nova Scotia **49** F7 45 37N 62 38W
Trent-Severn Waterway Ontario **44** C3 44 13N 79 23W
Trepassey Newfoundland **49** D2 46 45N 53 20W
Trinity Bay Newfoundland **49** D2 47 50N 53 40W
Trinity East Newfoundland **49** D2 48 23N 53 20W
Triton Newfoundland **49** C2 49 30N 55 30W
Trochu Alberta **37** C2 51 50N 113 13W
Trois-Pistoles Québec **47** C2 48 08N 69 10W
Trois-Rivières tn. Québec **47** B2 46 21N 72 34W
Trout Creek tn. Ontario **41** E2 45 59N 79 22W
Trout Lake British Columbia **35** D2 54 30N 114 32W
Trout Lake Ontario **40** B3 51 20N 93 20W
Trout Lake (Saamba Tu) tn. Northwest Territories **50** G3
61 00N 121 30W
Trout River tn. Newfoundland **49** C2 49 29N 58 08W
Troy Nova Scotia **49** F7 45 40N 61 30W
Truro Nova Scotia **49** F7 45 24N 63 18W
Tsawwassen British Columbia **34** H4 49 03N 123 06W
Tsiigehtchic (Arctic Red River) tn. Northwest Territories
50 E4 67 27N 133 46W
Ts'yl-os Provincial Park British Columbia **34** D2
51 10N 123 50W
Tthebacha (Fort Smith) Northwest Territories **50** J3
60 01N 111 55W
Tthenáágóo (Nahanni Butte) tn. Northwest Territories
50 G3 61 30N 123 00W
Tthets'éhk'édéli (Jean Marie River) tn. Northwest Territories
50 G3 62 30N 120 38W
Tuchitua Yukon Territory **50** F3 60 58N 129 03W
Tuktoyaktuk (Tuktuujaqrtuuq) Northwest Territories
50 E4 69 24N 133 01W
Tuktut Nogait National Park Northwest Territories **50** G4
69 00N 121 50W
Tuktuujaqrtuuq (Tuktoyaktuk) Northwest Territories **50** E4
69 24N 133 01W
Tulameen River British Columbia **34** H4 49 30N 120 58W
Tulemalu Lake Northwest Territories **51** M3 62 58N 99 25W
Tulita (Fort Norman) Northwest Territories **50** F3
64 55N 125 29W
Tumbler Ridge tn. British Columbia **35** D3 55 10N 121 01W
Tungsten Northwest Territories **50** F3 61 59N 128 09W
Tunungayualok Island Newfoundland **48** B4 56 05N 61 05W
Turkey Point Ontario **44** B1 42 37N 80 20W
Turkey Point tn. Ontario **44** B1 43 41N 80 20W
Turkey Point Provincial Park Ontario **44** B1 42 45N 80 20W
Turnagain River British Columbia **34** C3 58 25N 129 08W
Turnavik Island Newfoundland **48** C4 55 18N 59 21W
Turner Valley tn. Alberta **37** C2 50 40N 114 17W
Turnor Lake Saskatchewan **38** B3 56 25N 108 40W
Turtle Lake Saskatchewan **38** B3 53 25N 108 58W
Turtleford Saskatchewan **38** B2 53 25N 108 58W
Turtle Mountain Provincial Park Manitoba **39** A1
49 04N 100 10W
Tusket Nova Scotia **49** E6 43 53N 65 58W
Tuxedo Manitoba **54** D2 49 51N 97 13W
Tuya River British Columbia **34** B3 58 45N 130 50W
Tweed Ontario **43** J5 44 29N 77 19W
Tweedsmuir Provincial Park British Columbia **35** C2
52 50N 126 20W
Twelve Mile Bay Ontario **44** B4 45 05N 80 00W
Twenty Mile Creek Ontario **44** C2 43 09N 79 48W
Twillingate Newfoundland **49** D2 49 39N 54 46W
Twin Falls tn. Newfoundland **48** B3 53 30N 64 32W
Twin Islands Northwest Territories **40** E3 53 20N 80 10W
Twin Islands Game Sanctuary Northwest Territories **51** R1
53 20N 79 59W
Two Hills tn. Alberta **37** C2 53 43N 111 42W
Tyne Valley tn. Prince Edward Island **49** F7 46 36N 63 57W

U

Ucluelet British Columbia **35** G4 48 55N 125 34W
Ugjoktok Bay Newfoundland **48** B4 55 08N 60 30W
Uivak, Cape Newfoundland **48** B4 58 29N 62 34W

Ukasiksalik Island Newfoundland **48** B4 55 55N 60 47W
Uluqsatuuq (Holman) Northwest Territories **50** H5 70 44N 117 44W
Umingmaktok (Umingmaktuuq) Northwest Territories **50** K4 67 48N 108 00W
Umingmaktuuq (Umingmaktok) Northwest Territories **50** K4 67 48N 108 00W
Umiujaq Québec **46** A4 56 00N 76 44W
Ungava Bay (Baie d'Ungava) Northwest Territories/ Québec **51** T2 58 00N 72 30W
Unionville Ontario **52** C2 43 51N 79 19W
United States Range mts. Northwest Territories **51** T7 82 25N 68 00W
Unity Saskatchewan **38** B2 52 27N 109 10W
Upper Arrow Lake British Columbia **35** E2 50 25N 117 56W
Upper Campbell Lake British Columbia **34** G4 49 57N 125 36W
Upper Foster Lake Saskatchewan **38** B3 56 40N 105 35W
Upper Liard Yukon Territory **50** F3 60 01N 129 02W
Upper Musquodoboit Nova Scotia **49** F7 45 10N 62 58W
Upper Sackville Nova Scotia **53** P7 44 48N 63 42W
Upper Salmon Reservoir Newfoundland **49** C2 48 20N 56 10W
Upper Windigo Lake Ontario **40** B3 52 30N 91 35W
Uqsuqtuq (Gjoa Haven) tn. Northwest Territories **51** M4 68 39N 96 09W
Uranium City Saskatchewan **38** B3 59 32N 108 43W
Utikuma Lake Alberta **37** B3 55 50N 115 25W
Uxbridge Ontario **44** C3 44 07N 79 09W

V

Valdes Island British Columbia **34** H4 49 05N 123 40W
Val-d'Or Québec **47** A2 48 07N 77 47W
Valemount British Columbia **35** E2 52 50N 119 15W
Valhalla Provincial Park British Columbia **35** E1 49 00N 118 00W
Vallée Jonction Québec **65** L6 46 22N 70 58W
Valleyview Alberta **37** B3 55 04N 117 17W
Val Marie Saskatchewan **38** B1 49 15N 107 44W
Val-Paradis Québec **47** A2 49 10N 79 17W
Vancouver British Columbia **34** H4 49 13N 123 06W
Vancouver-Blaine Freeway British Columbia **52** F3 49 06N 123 03W
Vancouver Harbour British Columbia **52** F4 49 18N 123 06W
Vancouver Island British Columbia **34** G4 48 55N 124 33W
Vanderhoof British Columbia **35** D2 54 00N 124 00W
Vanier Ontario **53** K2 45 27N 75 40W
Vankleek Hill Ontario **43** M6 45 31N 74 39W
Vanscoy Saskatchewan **38** B2 52 01N 106 59W
Vansittart Island Northwest Territories **51** Q4 65 50N 84 00W
Varennes Québec **53** O6 45 39N 73 26W
Vaudreil admin. Québec **43** M6 45 20N 74 20W
Vaughan Ontario **44** C2 43 39N 79 25W
Vauxhall Alberta **37** C2 50 04N 112 07W
Vegreville Alberta **37** C3 53 30N 112 03W
Verdun Québec **53** N4 45 28N 73 34W
Vermilion Alberta **37** C2 53 22N 110 51W
Vermilion Bay Ontario **40** B2 49 51N 93 21W
Vermilion Pass Alberta/British Columbia **37** B2 51 14N 116 03W
Vermilion River Alberta **37** C2 53 40N 111 25W
Vernon British Columbia **35** E2 50 17N 119 19W
Victoria admin. New Brunswick **49** A2 47 10N 67 30W
Victoria admin. Nova Scotia **49** F7 46 30N 60 30W
Victoria admin. Ontario **44** C3/D3 44 45N 79 03W
Victoria British Columbia **34** H4 48 26N 123 20W
Victoria Newfoundland **49** D2 47 46N 53 14W
Victoria Prince Edward Island **49** F7 46 10N 63 30W
Victoria Bridge Nova Scotia **49** F7 45 50N 60 20W
Victoria Harbour Ontario **44** C3 44 45N 79 45W
Victoria Island Northwest Territories **50** J5 70 45N 110 00W
Victoria Lake Newfoundland **49** C2 48 18N 57 20W
Victoria River Newfoundland **49** C2 48 30N 57 50W
Victoriaville Québec **47** B2 46 04N 71 57W
Vienna Ontario Canada **44** B1 42 39N 80 47W
Vieux Fort Québec **47** E3 51 29N 57 59W
Viking Alberta **37** C2 53 07N 111 50W
Ville de Laval Québec **53** N5 45 37N 73 45W
Ville-Marie Québec **47** A2 47 21N 79 26W
Virden Manitoba **39** A1 49 50N 100 57W
Virgil Ontario **44** C2 43 13N 79 07W
Virginiatown Ontario **41** E2 48 08N 79 35W
Viscount Melville Sound Northwest Territories **50** K5 74 10N 107 30W
Voisey Bay Newfoundland **48** B4 56 15N 61 50W
Vulcan Alberta **37** C2 50 24N 113 15W
Vuntut National Park Yukon Territory **50** D4 69 30N 139 30W

W

Wabakimi Lake Ontario **40** C3 50 38N 89 45W
Wabakimi Provincial Park Ontario **40** B3 50 30N 90 50W

Wabana Newfoundland **49** D2 47 38N 52 57W
Wabasca-Desmarais Alberta **37** C3 55 59N 113 50W
Wabasca River Alberta **37** B3 57 30N 115 15W
Wabowden Manitoba **39** B2 54 57N 98 38W
Wabuk Point Ontario **40** C4 55 20N 85 05W
Wabush Newfoundland **48** A3 52 55N 66 52W
Wabush Lake Newfoundland **48** A3 53 05N 66 52W
Wabuskasing Ontario **40** B3 50 20N 93 10W
W.A.C. Bennet Dam British Columbia **35** D3 55 00N 122 11W
Waddington, Mount British Columbia **35** C2 51 22N 125 14W
Wade Lake Newfoundland **48** A3 54 20N 65 38W
Wadena Saskatchewan **38** C2 51 57N 103 58W
Wager Bay Northwest Territories **51** P4 65 20N 89 00W
Waglisla British Columbia **35** C2 52 05N 128 10W
Wainfleet Ontario **44** C1 42 52N 79 22W
Wainwright Alberta **37** C2 52 49N 110 52W
Wakaw Saskatchewan **38** B2 52 40N 105 45W
Wakefield Québec **43** L6 45 38N 75 56W
Wakusp British Columbia **35** E2 50 15N 117 45W
Waldheim Saskatchewan **38** B2 52 39N 106 40W
Wales Island Northwest Territories **51** P4 68 01N 86 40W
Walker Lake Manitoba **39** B2 54 40N 96 40W
Walkerton Ontario **44** A3 44 08N 81 10W
Wallace Nova Scotia **49** F7 45 48N 63 26W
Wallaceburg Ontario **41** D1 42 34N 82 22W
Walton Nova Scotia **49** F7 45 14N 64 00W
Wanapitei Lake Ontario **41** D2 46 45N 80 45W
Wanham Alberta **37** B3 55 44N 118 24W
Wanless Manitoba **39** A2 54 11N 101 21W
Wapawekka Hills Saskatchewan **38** C2 54 50N 104 30W
Wapawekka Lake Saskatchewan **38** C2 54 58N 104 30W
Wapella Saskatchewan **38** C2 50 16N 101 59W
Wapikopa Lake Ontario Canada **40** C4 52 54N 87 50W
Wapiti River Alberta **37** B2 54 40N 119 50W
Wapusk National Park Manitoba **39** C3 57 40N 94 30W
Wardlow Alberta **37** C2 50 54N 111 33W
Wardsville Ontario **42** E3 42 39N 81 45W
Warman Saskatchewan **38** B2 52 19N 106 37W
Warner Alberta **37** C1 49 17N 112 12W
Warrender, Cape Northwest Territories **51** Q5 74 28N 81 46W
Warren Landing tn. Manitoba **39** B2 53 42N 97 54W
Wasaga Beach tn. Ontario **44** C1 44 31N 80 02W
Wasaga Beach Provincial Park Ontario **44** B3 44 30N 80 05W
Wascana Creek Saskatchewan **38** C2 50 20N 104 20W
Wasekamio Lake Saskatchewan **38** B3 56 50N 108 30W
Wasekiu Lake tn. Saskatchewan **38** B2 53 55N 106 00W
Washago Ontario **44** C3 44 45N 79 20W
Waskaganish Québec **47** A3 51 30N 78 45W
Waskaiowaka Lake Manitoba **39** B3 56 40N 96 40W
Waterbury Lake Saskatchewan **38** C3 58 10N 104 55W
Waterdown Ontario **44** C2 43 20N 79 54W
Waterhen Manitoba **39** B2 51 50N 99 30W
Waterhen Lake Manitoba **39** B2 52 00N 99 20W
Waterhen River Saskatchewan **38** B2 54 25N 108 50W
Waterloo admin. Ontario **44** B2 43 30N 80 46W
Waterloo Ontario **41** D1 43 28N 80 32W
Waterton Lakes National Park Alberta **37** C1 49 00N 114 45W
Watford Ontario **42** E3 42 57N 81 53W
Watham Lake Saskatchewan **38** C3 57 00N 104 10W
Wathaman River Saskatchewan **38** C3 56 50N 104 50W
Watrous Saskatchewan **38** B2 51 40N 105 29W
Watson Saskatchewan **38** C2 52 09N 104 31W
Watson Lake tn. Yukon Territory **50** F3 60 02N 128 47W
Waubuno Channel Ontario **44** B4 45 11N 80 16W
Waverley Nova Scotia **49** F6 44 48N 63 35W
Waverley Game Sanctuary Nova Scotia **53** P7 44 49N 63 31W
Wawa Ontario **41** D2 48 04N 84 49W
Wawota Saskatchewan **38** C1 49 56N 102 00W
Weagamow Lake tn. Ontario **40** B3 52 53N 91 22W
Weaver Lake Manitoba **39** B2 52 40N 96 40W
Webbwood Ontario **42** E7 46 16N 81 53W
Webequie Ontario **40** C3 52 59N 87 21W
Wedge Mountain British Columbia **34** H5 50 07N 122 49W
Wedgeport Nova Scotia **49** E6 43 44N 65 59W
Wekusko Manitoba **39** B2 54 31N 99 45W
Wekusko Lake Manitoba **39** B2 54 30N 99 40W
Wekweti (Snare Lakes) Northwest Territories **50** J3 64 10N 114 20W
Weldon Saskatchewan **38** B2 53 00N 105 08W
Welland Ontario **44** C1 42 59N 79 14W
Welland Canal Ontario **44** C2 43 14N 79 13W
Welland River Ontario **44** C2 43 05N 79 46W
Wellesley Ontario **44** B2 43 27N 80 46W
Wellington admin. Ontario **44** B2 43 46N 80 41W
Wellington Nova Scotia **49** F6 44 50N 63 38W
Wellington Ontario **43** J4 43 57N 77 21W
Wellington Prince Edward Island **46** 26N 64 03W
Wellington Channel Northwest Territories **51** N6 75 00N 93 00W
Wells British Columbia **35** D2 53 00N 121 30W
Wells Gray Provincial Park British Columbia **35** D2 52 20N 120 00W
Wells Lake Manitoba **39** A3 57 10N 100 30W

Wembley Alberta **37** B3 55 09N 119 08W
Wemindji (Nouveau Comptoir) Québec **47** A3 52 59N 78 50W
Wenebegon Lake Ontario **41** D2 47 23N 83 06W
Wentworth Nova Scotia **49** F7 45 39N 63 35W
Werner Lake Ontario **40** B3 50 27N 94 54W
Wesleyville Newfoundland **49** D2 49 09N 53 34W
West Bay tn. Newfoundland **48** C3 54 08N 57 26W
West Bay tn. Nova Scotia **49** F7 45 40N 61 10W
West Don River Ontario **52** B2 43 49N 79 31W
West Duffins Creek Ontario **52** C2 43 53N 79 10W
Western Cordillera Canada **8** K4/M3 52 30N 120 00W
Western River Northwest Territories **50** K4 66 40N 107 00W
Westham Island British Columbia **52** F3 49 05N 123 10W
West Highland Creek Ontario **52** C2 43 46N 79 15W
West Humber River Ontario **52** B2 43 48N 79 43W
Westlock Alberta **37** C2 54 09N 113 52W
West Lorne Ontario **44** A1 42 36N 81 35W
Westmorland admin. New Brunswick **49** F7 46 10N 64 50W
Westmount Nova Scotia **49** F7 46 10N 60 10W
Westmount Québec **53** N4 45 29N 73 37W
West Point Prince Edward Island **49** F7 46 38N 64 26W
Westport Newfoundland **49** E6 44 16N 66 20W
Westport Ontario **43** K5 44 41N 76 24W
West Road River British Columbia **35** D2 53 12N 123 50W
West St. Modeste Newfoundland **48** C3 51 36N 56 42W
West St. Paul admin. Manitoba **54** D2 49 59N 97 08W
West Thurlow Island British Columbia **34** G5 50 27N 125 35W
West Vancouver British Columbia **34** H4 49 22N 123 11W
Westville Nova Scotia **49** F7 45 34N 62 44W
Wetaskiwin Alberta **37** C2 52 57N 113 20W
Weyburn Saskatchewan **38** C1 49 39N 103 51W
Weymouth Nova Scotia **49** E6 44 26N 66 00W
Whale Cove (Tikirarjuaq) tn. Northwest Territories **51** N3 62 10N 92 36W
Whaletown British Columbia **34** G5 50 06N 125 02W
Wha Ti (Lac la Martre) tn. Northwest Territories **50** H3 63 00N 117 30W
Wheatley Ontario **42** D3 42 06N 82 27W
Wheeler River Saskatchewan **38** B3 57 30N 105 10W
Whippoorwill Bay Ontario **44** C4 45 01N 81 15W
Whirl Creek Ontario **44** A2 43 29N 81 07W
Whistler British Columbia **34** H5 50 08N 122 58W
Whitby Ontario **44** D2 43 52N 78 56W
White Bay Newfoundland **49** C3 50 00N 56 32W
White Bear Island Newfoundland **48** B4 57 54N 61 42W
White Bear Lake Newfoundland **48** C3 54 32N 59 30W
Whitecap Mountain British Columbia **34** H5 50 44N 122 30W
White City Saskatchewan **38** C2 50 35N 104 20W
Whitecourt Alberta **37** B2 54 10N 115 41W
Whitefish Ontario **42** E7 46 23N 81 22W
Whitefish Bay Ontario **41** D2 46 38N 84 33W
Whitefish Bay Ontario/U.S.A. **42** B7 46 30N 84 45W
Whitefish Lake Ontario **41** D2 48 05N 84 10W
Whitefish Lake Northwest Territories **50** K3 62 30N 106 40W
Whitefox River Saskatchewan **38** C2 53 25N 104 55W
White Handkerchief, Cape Newfoundland **48** B4 59 17N 63 23W
Whitehorse Yukon Territory **50** D3 60 41N 135 08W
White Lake Ontario **41** C2 48 50N 85 30W
Whitemouth Manitoba **39** B1 49 58N 95 59W
Whitemouth Lake Manitoba **39** B1 49 10N 96 00W
Whitemouth River Manitoba **39** B1 49 50N 97 10W
Whitemud Creek Alberta **54** F4 53 18N 113 38W
White Otter Lake Ontario **40** B2 49 07N 91 52W
White Pass British Columbia **34** A3 59 37N 135 07W
White River Ontario **41** C2 48 30N 86 20W
White River tn. Ontario **41** C2 48 35N 85 16W
White River Yukon Territory **50** C2 62 25N 140 05W
White Rock British Columbia **34** H4 49 02N 122 50W
Whitesail Lake British Columbia **35** C2 53 25N 127 10W
Whitesand River Alberta **37** B3 59 00N 115 00W
Whiteshell Provincial Forest Manitoba **39** B1 49 50N 95 40W
Whiteshell Provincial Park Manitoba **39** B2 50 00N 95 20W
Whitewater Creek Saskatchewan/U.S.A. **38** B1 48 50N 107 40W
Whitewater Lake Ontario **40** C3 50 40N 89 30W
Whitewood Saskatchewan **38** C2 50 19N 102 16W
Whitney Ontario **42** H6 45 29N 78 15W
Whitworth Québec **43** S8 47 42N 69 17W
Wholdaia Lake Northwest Territories **50** L3 60 43N 104 10W
Whycocomagh Nova Scotia **49** F7 45 58N 61 08W
Wiarton Ontario **41** D1 44 44N 81 19W
Wildcat Hill Wilderness Area Saskatchewan **38** C2 53 20N 102 20W
Wildwood Alberta **37** B2 53 37N 115 14W
Wilkie Saskatchewan **38** B2 52 27N 108 42W
William, Lake Nova Scotia **53** P7 44 46N 63 34W
William River Saskatchewan **38** B3 58 50N 108 55W
Williams Lake tn. British Columbia **35** D2 52 08N 122 07W
Williston Lake British Columbia **35** D3 56 00N 124 00W
Willmore Wilderness Park Alberta **37** B2 53 40N 119 30W

Will, Mount British Columbia **34** C3 57 30N 128 44W
Willowbunch Lake Saskatchewan **38** B1 49 20N 105 50W
Willow Lake Northwest Territories **50** H3 62 10N 119 08W
Winchester Ontario **47** E2 45 05N 75 21W
Windermere Lake Ontario **41** D2 47 58N 83 47W
Windigo Québec **43** N8 47 45N 73 22W
Windigo Lake Ontario **40** B3 52 35N 91 32W
Windsor Nova Scotia **49** F7 45 00N 64 09W
Windsor Ontario **41** D1 42 18N 83 00W
Windsor Québec **47** B2 45 35N 72 01W
Windsor Junction Nova Scotia **53** P7 44 48N 63 38W
Winefred Lake Alberta **37** C3 55 30N 110 31W
Wingham Ontario **41** D1 43 54N 81 19W
Winisk Lake Ontario **40** C3 52 55N 87 22W
Winisk River Ontario **40** C3 54 50N 87 00W
Winisk River Provincial Park Ontario **40** C3 52 50N 87 30W
Winkler Manitoba **39** B1 49 12N 97 55W
Winnipeg Manitoba **39** B1 49 53N 97 10W
Winnipeg Beach tn. Manitoba **39** B2 50 30N 97 00W
Winnipeg, Lake Manitoba **39** B2 53 00N 97 00W
Winnipegosis Manitoba **39** B2 51 40N 99 59W
Winnipegosis, Lake Manitoba **39** A2/B2 52 10N 100 00W
Winnipeg River Manitoba **39** B2 50 20N 95 30W
Winokapau Lake Newfoundland **48** B3 53 10N 62 52W
Winona Ontario **44** C2 43 12N 79 38W
Winterburn Alberta **54** F5 53 33N 113 41W
Witless Bay tn. Newfoundland **49** D2 47 16N 52 50W
Wolfe admin. Québec **43** Q6 45 40N 71 40W
Wolfe Island Ontario **41** E1 44 11N 76 25W
Wolfville Nova Scotia **49** F7 45 06N 64 22W
Wollaston, Cape Northwest Territories **50** H5 71 06N 118 04W
Wollaston Lake Saskatchewan **38** C3 58 20N 103 00W
Wollaston Lake tn. Saskatchewan **38** C3 58 05N 103 38W
Wollaston Peninsula Northwest Territories **50** H4 69 30N 115 00W
Wolseley Saskatchewan **38** C2 50 25N 103 15W
Woodbridge Ontario **52** B2 43 47N 79 36W
Wood Buffalo National Park Alberta/ Northwest Territories **37** C3 59 00N 112 30W
Woodfibre British Columbia **34** H4 49 36N 123 08W
Wood Islands tn. Prince Edward Island **49** F7 45 50N 62 40W
Woodland Caribou Provincial Park Ontario **40** B3 51 10N 94 20W
Wood Mountain Saskatchewan **38** B1 49 15N 106 20W
Woodside Nova Scotia **53** P6 44 39N 63 31W
Woods Lake Newfoundland **48** A3 54 30N 65 13W
Woods, Lake of the Ontario **40** B2 49 15N 94 45W
Woodstock Ontario Canada **41** D1 43 07N 80 46W
Woodstock New Brunswick **49** A2 46 10N 67 36W
Woodville Ontario **44** D3 44 24N 78 44W
Wrigley (Pedzéh Ki) Northwest Territories **50** G3 63 16N 123 39W
Wrong Lake Manitoba **39** B2 52 40N 96 10W
Wunnummin Lake Ontario **40** C3 52 55N 89 10W
Wyebridge Ontario **44** C3 44 41N 79 53W
Wynniatt Bay Northwest Territories **50** J5 72 45N 110 30W
Wynyard Saskatchewan **38** C2 51 50N 104 10W

Y

Yale British Columbia **34** H4 49 31N 121 29W
Yamaska admin. Québec **43** P7 46 00N 72 50W
Yarmouth admin. Nova Scotia **49** E6 43 50N 65 40W
Yarmouth Nova Scotia **49** E6 43 53N 66 02W
Yates River Alberta **37** B3 59 40N 116 25W
Yathkyed Lake Northwest Territories **51** M3 62 40N 98 00W
Yellow Grass Saskatchewan **38** C1 49 49N 104 11W
Yellowhead Highway Canada **32** M3/N3
Yellowhead Pass Alberta/British Columbia **37** B2 52 53N 118 28W
Yellowknife (Sômbak'è) Northwest Territories **50** J3 62 30N 114 29W
Yellowknife River Northwest Territories **50** J3 62 35N 114 10W
Yoho National Park British Columbia **35** E2 51 00N 116 00W
York admin. Ontario **44** C2 43 57N 79 39W
York bor. Metropolitan Toronto Ontario **52** C2 43 41N 79 28W
York New Brunswick **49** A2 46 10N 66 50W
York, Cape Northwest Territories **51** P5 73 48N 87 00W
York Factory Historic Site N.H.S. Manitoba **39** C3 57 08N 92 25W
York Landing tn. Manitoba **39** B3 56 00N 96 01W
Yorkton Saskatchewan **38** C2 51 12N 102 29W
Youbou British Columbia **34** H4 48 52N 124 12W
Young Saskatchewan **38** B2 51 45N 105 45W
Yukon River Yukon Territory/Alaska U.S.A. **50** D3 63 00N 138 50W
Yukon Territory territory **8** H5/J5 64 15N 135 00W

Z

Zeballos British Columbia **35** C1 49 57N 126 10W
Zhahti Kóe (Fort Providence) Northwest Territories **50** H3 61 03N 117 40W
Zürich Ontario **44** A2 43 25N 81 37W

A

Aba Nigeria 102 G9 5 06N 7 21E
Ābādān Iran 89 G5 30 20N 48 15E
Abadla Algeria 102 E14 31 01N 2 45W
Abaetetuba Brazil 70 H12 1 45S 48 54W
Abakan *r.* Russian Federation 87 O5 52 00N 88 00E
Abakan Russian Federation 87 P5 53 43N 91 25E
Abancay Peru 70 C10 13 37S 72 52W
Abashiri Japan 96 D3 44 02N 114 17E
Ābd al Kūrī *i.* Socotra 89 H1 11 55N 52 20E
Abéché Chad 102 J10 13 49N 20 49E
Abeokuta Nigeria 102 F9 7 10N 3 26E
Aberdeen Hong Kong China 92 B1 22 14N 114 09E
Aberdeen Maryland U.S.A. 66 B2 39 31N 76 10W
Aberdeen South Dakota U.S.A. 65 G6 45 28N 98 30W
Aberdeen United Kingdom 74 I9 57 10N 2 04W
Aberdeen Washington U.S.A. 64 B6 46 58N 123 49W
Aberystwyth U.K. 74 G4 52 25N 4 05W
Abhā Saudi Arabia 102 N11 18 14N 42 31E
Abidjan Côte d'Ivoire 102 E9 5 19N 4 01W
Abilene Texas U.S.A. 64 G3 32 27N 99 45W
Abottstown Pennsylvania U.S.A. 66 A2 39 54N 77 00W
Absaroka Range *mts.* U.S.A. 64 D6/E5 45 00N 110 00W
Abu Dhabi *see* Abū Zabī
Abu Durba Egypt 88 N9 28 29N 33 20E
Abu Hamed Sudan 102 L11 19 32N 33 20E
Abu Kamāl Syria 88 F5 34 29N 40 56E
Abu Tig Egypt 88 D4 27 06N 31 17E
Abuja Nigeria 102 G9 9 10N 7 11E
Abunā Brazil 70 D11 9 41S 65 20W
Abū Zabī *(Abu Dhabi)* U.A.E. 89 H3 24 28N 54 25E
Acambaro Mexico 68 D4 20 01N 100 42W
Acaponeta Mexico 68 C4 22 30N 102 25W
Acapulco Mexico 68 E3 16 51N 99 56W
Açari *r.* Brazil 71 P2 22 50S 43 22W
Acarigua Venezuela 70 D14 9 35N 69 12W
Acatlán Mexico 68 E3 18 12N 98 02W
Acayucán Mexico 68 E3 17 59N 94 58W
Accra Ghana 102 E9 5 33N 0 15W
Achacachi Bolivia 70 D9 16 01S 68 44W
Achill Island Republic of Ireland 74 A5 53 55N 10 05W
Achinsk Russian Federation 85 L7 56 20N 90 33E
Acklins Island The Bahamas 69 J4 22 30N 74 30W
Aconcagua *mt.* Argentina 71 C6 32 40S 70 02W
Acre *admin.* Brazil 70 C11 8 30S 71 30W
Acton United Kingdom 78 B3 51 31N 0 17W
A.C.T. *see* Australian Capital Territory
Ada Oklahoma U.S.A. 65 G3 34 47N 96 41W
Adachi Japan 97 C4 35 46N 139 48E
Adams New York U.S.A. 43 K4 43 50N 76 02W
Adam's Bridge India/Sri Lanka 91 D1 9 10N 79 30E
Adana Turkey 88 E6 37 00N 35 19E
Adapazari Turkey 88 D7 40 45N 30 23E
Adare, Cape Antarctica 113 71 30S 170 24E
Ad Dahna *geog. reg.* Saudi Arabia 102 O13 6 00N 47 00E
Ad Dakhla Western Sahara 102 B12 23 50N 15 58W
Ad Dammām Saudi Arabia 89 H4 26 25N 50 06E
Ad Dawḥah *(Doha)* Qatar 89 H4 25 15N 51 36E
Ad Dilam Saudi Arabia 89 G3 23 59N 47 06E
Ad Dir'īyah Saudi Arabia 89 G3 24 45N 46 32E
Addis Ababa *see* Ādīs Ābeba
Addison New York U.S.A. 66 A5 42 07N 77 16W
Ad Dīwānīyah Iraq 88 F5 32 00N 44 57E
Adelaide Australia 106 F3 34 56S 138 36E
Adelanto California U.S.A. 67 D2 34 35N 117 24W
Adélie Land *see* Terre d'Adélie
Aden Yemen Republic 89 G1 12 50N 45 03E
Aden, Gulf of Indian Ocean 89 G1 12 30N 47 30E
Adirondack Mountains New York U.S.A. 65 L5 43 15N 74 40W
Ādīs Ābeba *(Addis Ababa)* Ethiopia 102 M9 9 03N 38 42E
Admiralty Island Alaska U.S.A. 34 B3 57 45N 134 30W
Admiralty Islands Papua New Guinea 106 H9 2 30S 147 00E
Adoni India 91 D3 15 38N 77 16E
Adrar Algeria 102 E13 27 51N 0 19W
Adrian Michigan U.S.A. 42 B2 41 55N 84 01W
Adriatic Sea Mediterranean Sea 72 J4 43 00N 15 00E
Ādwa Ethiopia 102 M10 14 12N 38 56E
Aegean Sea Mediterranean Sea 72 K3 39 00N 24 00E
AFGHANISTAN 90 A6/B6
Afognak Island Alaska U.S.A. 8 E4 58 10N 152 50W
Afyon Turkey 88 D6 38 46N 30 32E
Agadès Niger 102 G11 17 00N 7 56E
Agadir Morocco 102 D14 30 30N 9 40W
Agalega Islands Seychelles 108 E5 10 00S 56 00E
Agana Guam 110 E9 13 28N 144 45E
Agano *r.* Japan 96 C2 37 50N 139 30E
Agartala India 91 G4 23 49N 91 15E
Agra India 91 D5 27 09N 78 00E
Agram *see* Zagreb
Agua Prieta Mexico 68 C6 31 20N 109 32W
Aguadas Colombia 70 B14 5 36N 75 30W
Aguadilla Puerto Rico 69 K3 18 27N 67 08W
Aguascalientes Mexico 68 D4 21 51N 102 18W
Agulhas Basin Indian Ocean 108 A2 45 00S 20 00E
Agulhas, Cape Republic of South Africa 103 J1 34 50S 20 00E
Ahklun Mountains *mts.* Alaska U.S.A. 8 C4/5 60 00N 161 00W
Ahmadabad India 91 C4 23 03N 72 40E
Ahmadnagar India 91 C3 19 08N 74 48E
Ahrensfelde Germany 79 G2 52 35N 13 35E
Ahuachapán El Salvador 68 G2 13 57N 89 49W
Ahvāz Iran 89 G5 31 17N 48 43E
Aïn Sefra Algeria 102 E14 32 45N 0 35W
Aïr *mts.* Niger 102 G11 19 10N 8 20E
Aire *r.* United Kingdom 74 J5 53 40N 1 00W
Aizu-Wakamatsu Japan 96 C2 37 30N 139 58E
Ajaccio Corsica 72 G4 41 55N 8 43E
Ajdābiyā Libya 102 J14 30 46N 20 14E
Ajlūn Jordan 88 O11 32 20N 35 35E
Ajmer India 91 C5 26 29N 74 40E
Ajo Arizona U.S.A. 64 D3 32 24N 112 51W
Akabira Japan 96 D3 43 40N 141 55E
Akaroa N.Z. 107 B2 43 49S 172 58E
Akashi Japan 96 B1 34 39N 135 00E
Aketi Congo (D.R.) 102 J8 2 42N 23 51E
Akhtubinsk Russian Federation 86 F4 48 20N 46 10E
Akita Japan 96 D2 39 44N 140 05E
'Akko Israel 88 O11 32 55N 35 04E
Akmola *(Tselinograd)* Kazakhstan 87 L5 51 10N 71 28E
Akobo Sudan 102 L9 7 50N 33 05E
Akola India 91 D4 20 49N 77 05E
Ak'ordat Eritrea 88 E2 15 26N 3745E
Akron Ohio U.S.A. 65 J5 41 04N 81 31W
Akron Pennsylvania U.S.A. 66 B3 40 09N 76 12W
Āksum Ethiopia 88 E1 14 10N 38 45E
Aktau *(Shevchenko)* Kazakhstan 86 G3 43 37N 51 11E
Aktyubinsk Kazakhstan 87 H5 50 16N 57 13E
Akureyri Iceland 72 B9 65 41N 18 04W
Akyab *see* Sittwe
Alabama *r.* Alabama U.S.A. 65 I3 31 00N 88 00W
Alabama *state* U.S.A. 65 I3 32 00N 87 00W
Alagoas *admin.* Brazil 70 J11 9 30S 37 00W
Alagoinhas Brazil 70 J10 12 09S 38 21W
Alajuela Costa Rica 69 H2 10 00N 84 12W
Alakanuk Alaska U.S.A. 8 C5 62 39N 164 48W
Al 'Amārah Iraq 89 G5 31 51N 47 10E
Alamo California U.S.A. 67 E3 37 23N 115 10W
Alamosa Colorado U.S.A. 64 E4 37 28N 105 54W
Åland *is.* Finland 72 J8 60 15N 20 00E
Alanya Turkey 88 D6 36 32N 32 02E
Al Artāwīyah Saudi Arabia 89 G4 26 31N 45 21E
Ala Shan *mts.* China 93 K6/7 40 00N 102 30E
Alaska *state* U.S.A. 8 D5/F5 63 10N 157 30W
Alaska, Gulf of *g.* U.S.A. 8 F4/G4 58 00N 147 00W
Alaska Highway Alaska U.S.A. 50 B3 64 30N 147 00W
Alaska Peninsula Alaska U.S.A. 8 D4 56 30N 159 00W
Alaska Range *mts.* Alaska U.S.A. 50 B3/C3 62 30N 145 00W
Alatna Alaska U.S.A. 8 E6 66 33N 152 49W
Al 'Ayn U.A.E. 89 I3 24 10N 55 43E
Alay Range *mts.* Asia 87 L2 39 00N 70 00E
Albacete Spain 72 E3 39 00N 1 52W
ALBANIA 72 K4
Albany Australia 106 B3 34 57S 117 54E
Albany Georgia U.S.A. 65 J3 31 37N 84 10W
Albany New York U.S.A. 65 L5 42 40N 73 49W
Albany Oregon U.S.A. 64 B5 44 38N 123 07W
Al Başrah Iraq 89 G5 30 30N 47 50E
Al Bayḍā' *see* Beida
Albert, Lake Uganda/Congo (D.R.) 102 L8 2 00N 31 00E
Albert Lea Minnesota U.S.A. 65 H5 43 38N 93 16W
Albion Michigan U.S.A. 42 B3 42 14N 84 45W
Al Bi'r Saudi Arabia 88 E4 28 50N 36 16E
Ålborg Denmark 72 G 7 57 05N 9 50E
Al Bū Kamāl Syria 86 E1 34 29N 40 56E
Albuquerque New Mexico U.S.A. 64 E4 35 05N 106 38W
Al Buraymī Oman 89 I3 24 16N 55 48E
Alchevs'k *(Kommunarsk)* Ukraine 86 D4 48 30N 38 47E
Aldabra Islands Indian Ocean 103 O6 9 00S 46 00E
Aldama Mexico 68 E4 22 54N 98 05W
Aldan *r.* Russian Federation 85 P7 59 00N 132 30E
Aldan Russian Federation 85 O7 58 44N 124 22E
Alderney *i.* Channel Islands British Isles 74 I1 49 43N 2 12W
Alegrete Brazil 71 G7 29 45S 55 40W
Aleksandrovsk-Sakhalinskiy Russian Federation 85 Q6 50 55N 142 12E
Alenuihaha Channel *sd.* Hawaiian Islands 111 Y18 20 20N 156 20W
Aleppo *see* Halab
Aleutian Basin Pacific Ocean 110 I13 54 00N 178 00W
Aleutian Range *mts.* Alaska U.S.A. 8 D4 56 30N 159 00W
Aleutian Ridge Pacific Ocean 110 I13 53 55N 178 00W
Aleutian Trench Pacific Ocean 110 I13 50 55N 178 00W
Alexander Archipelago *is.* Alaska U.S.A. 8 H4 57 00N 137 00W
Alexander Bay *tn.* Republic of South Africa 103 I2 28 40S 16 30E
Alexander Island Antarctica 113 71 00S 70 00W
Alexandra N.Z. 107 A1 45 15S 169 23E
Alexandria Egypt *see* El Iskandarîya
Alexandria Louisiana U.S.A. 65 H3 31 19N 92 29W
Alexandria Bay *tn.* New York U.S.A. 43 L5 44 20N 75 55W
Al Fuḥayḥīl Kuwait 89 G4 29 07N 47 02E
Algarve *geog. reg.* Portugal 72 D3 37 30N 8 00W
Alger *(Algiers)* Algeria 102 F15 36 50N 3 00E
ALGERIA 102 E13
Algiers *see* Alger
Al Hadīthah Iraq 88 F5 34 06N 42 25E
Al Harīq Saudi Arabia 89 G3 23 34N 46 35E
Al Ḥasakah Syria 88 F6 36 32N 40 44E
Al Hillah Iraq 88 F5 32 28N 44 29E
Al Ḥudaydah Yemen Republic 88 F1 14 50N 42 58E
Al Hufūf Saudi Arabia 89 G4 25 20N 49 34E
Alicante Spain 72 E3 38 21N 0 29W
Alice Texas U.S.A. 65 G2 27 45N 98 06W
Alice Springs *tn.* Australia 106 E5 23 42S 133 52E
Aligarh India 91 D5 27 54N 78 04E
Aling Kangri *mt.* China 92 F5 32 51N 81 03E
Alipur India 90 K2 22 32N 88 19E
Al Jahrah Kuwait 89 G4 29 22N 47 40E
Al Jawf Libya 102 J12 24 12N 23 18E
Al Jawf Saudi Arabia 88 E4 29 49N 39 52E
Al Jubayl Saudi Arabia 89 G4 26 59N 49 40E
Al Kūt Iraq 89 G5 32 30N 45 51E
Al Khums Libya 102 H14 32 39N 14 16E
Al Kufrah Oasis Libya 102 J12 24 10N 23 15E
Al Kuwayt Kuwait 89 G4 29 20N 48 00E
Al Lādhiqīyah *(Latakia)* Syria 88 E6 35 31N 35 47E
Allagash River Maine U.S.A. 43 S7 46 45N 69 20W
Allahabad India 91 E5 25 27N 81 50E
Allende Mexico 68 D5 28 22N 100 50W
Allentown Pennsylvania U.S.A. 65 K5 40 37N 75 30W
Alleppey India 91 D1 9 30N 76 22E
Alliance Ohio U.S.A. 42 E1 40 56N 81 06W
Alliance Nebraska U.S.A. 64 F5 42 08N 102 54W
Al Līth Saudi Arabia 88 F3 20 10N 40 20E
Alloa United Kingdom 74 H8 56 07N 3 49W
Alma Michigan U.S.A. 42 B4 43 23N 84 40W
Alma-Ata *see* Almaty
Al Madīnah *(Medina)* Saudi Arabia 88 E3 24 30N 39 35E
Almalyk Uzbekistan 87 K3 40 50N 69 40E
Al Manāmah Bahrain 89 H4 26 12N 50 38E
Almaty *(Alma-Ata)* Kazakhstan 87 M3 43 19N 76 55E
Al Mawşil *(Mosul)* Iraq 86 E2 36 21N 43 08E
Al Mayādīn Syria 88 F6 35 01N 40 28E
Amazon *see* Rio Amazonas
Almería Spain 72 E3 36 50N 2 26W
Al'met'yevsk Russian Federation 87 G5 54 50N 52 22E
Al Miqdādiyah Iraq 88 F5 33 58N 44 58E
Al Mubarraz Saudi Arabia 89 G4 25 26N 49 37E
Al Mukallā Yemen Republic 89 G1 14 34N 49 09E
Al Mukhā Yemen Republic 88 F1 13 20N 43 16E
Alor *i.* Indonesia 95 G2 8 15S 124 30E
Alor Setar Malaysia 95 C5 6 07N 100 21E
Alpena Michigan U.S.A. 42 C6 45 04N 83 27W
Alpes Maritimes *mts.* France/Italy 72 G4 44 15N 6 45E
Alpha New Jersey U.S.A. 66 C3 40 40N 75 11W
Alpha Ridge Arctic Ocean 112 85 00N 120 00W
Alpine Texas U.S.A. 64 F3 30 22N 103 40W
Alps *mts.* Europe 72 G5 46 00N 7 30E
Al Qāmishlī Syria 88 F6 37 03N 41 15E
Al Qunfudhah Saudi Arabia 88 F2 19 09N 41 07E
Alsek River Alaska U.S.A. 34 A3 59 15N 138 40W
Alta Gracia Argentina 71 E6 31 42S 64 25W
Altai *mts.* Mongolia 92 H8 47 00N 92 30E
Altamaha *r.* Georgia U.S.A. 65 J3 32 00N 82 00W
Altamira Brazil 70 G12 3 13S 52 15W
Altay China 92 G8 47 48N 88 07E
Altay *mts.* Russian Federation 85 K6 51 00N 89 00E
Altlandsberg Germany 79 G2 52 34N 1345E
Alto da Boa Vista Brazil 71 P2 22 58S 43 17W
Alto Molocue Mozambique 103 M4 15 38S 37 42E
Altoona Pennsylvania U.S.A. 65 K5 40 32N 78 32W
Altun Shan *mts.* China 92 G6 37 30N 86 00E
Altus Oklahoma U.S.A. 64 G3 34 39N 99 21W
Alva Oklahoma U.S.A. 64 G4 36 48N 98 40W
Al Wajh Saudi Arabia 88 E4 26 16N 36 28E
Alwar India 91 D5 27 32N 76 35E
Alyat Azerbaijan 86 F2 39 57N 49 25E
Amadeus, Lake Australia 106 E5 24 00S 132 30E
Amadi Sudan 102 L9 5 32N 30 20E
Amagasaki Japan 96 C1 34 42N 135 23E
Amakusa-shotō *is.* Japan 96 B1 32 50N 130 05E
Amapá *admin.* Brazil 70 G13 2 00N 52 30W
Amapá Brazil 70 G13 2 00N 50 50W
Amargosa Desert California U.S.A. 67 D3 36 45N 116 37W
Amargosa Valley *tn.* California U.S.A. 67 D3 36 40N 116 22W
Amarillo Texas U.S.A. 64 F4 35 14N 101 50W
Amazon, Mouths of the *est.* Brazil 70 G13 1 00N 51 00W
Amazonas *admin.* Brazil 70 D12/F12 4 30S 65 00W
Ambala India 91 D6 30 19N 76 49E
Ambarchik Russian Federation 85 S9 69 39N 162 37E
Ambato Ecuador 70 B12 1 18S 78 39W
Ambon Indonesia 95 H3 3 41S 128 10E
Ambovombe Madagascar 103 O2 25 10S 46 06E
Amboy California U.S.A. 67 E2 34 33N 115 44W
Amderma Russian Federation 85 I9 66 44N 61 35E
Amdo China 92 H5 32 22N 91 07E
Ameca Mexico 68 D4 20 34N 104 03W
American Falls *tn.* Idaho U.S.A. 64 D5 42 47N 112 50W
American Samoa Pacific Ocean 111 J6 15 00S 170 00W
Amersham United Kingdom 78 A3 51 40N 0 38W
Amery Ice Shelf Antarctica 113 70 00S 70 00E
Amga *r.* Russian Federation 85 P8 60 30N 130 00E
Amga Russian Federation 85 P8 61 51N 131 59E
Amgun' *r.* Russian Federation 85 P6 52 00N 137 00E
Amiens France 72 F5 49 54N 2 18E
Amirante Islands Seychelles 108 E6 5 00S 55 00E
Amman Jordan 88 E5 31 04N 46 17E
Ammassalik *see* Tasiilaq
Ampana Indonesia 95 G3 0 54S 121 35E
Amravati India 91 D4 20 58N 77 50E
Amritsar India 91 C6 31 35N 74 56E
Amroha India 91 D5 28 54N 78 29E
Amsterdam Netherlands 72 F6 52 22N 4 54E
Am Timan Chad 102 J10 10 59N 20 18E
Amudar'ya *(Oxus) r.* Asia 87 J2 39 00N 64 00E
Amundsen Sea Southern Ocean 113 72 00S 130 00W
Amundsen-Scott *r.s.* South Pole Antarctica 113 90 00S
Amur *(Heliong Jiang) r.* Asia 93 P9 52 30N 126 30E
Amursk Russian Federation 85 P6 50 16N 136 55E
Anabar *r.* Russian Federation 85 N10 71 30N 113 00E
Anacapa Islands California U.S.A. 67 C2 34 01N 119 23W
Anaconda Montana U.S.A. 64 D6 46 09N 112 56W
Anacortes Washington U.S.A. 34 H4 48 30N 122 42W
Anadolu Dağlari *mts.* Turkey 86 C3/E3 40 30 38 30E
Anadyr' *r.* Russian Federation 85 T9 65 00N 175 00E
Anadyr' Russian Federation 85 T8 64 50N 178 00E
Anadyr', Gulf of Russian Federation 85 U8 65 00N 178 00W
Anaheim California U.S.A. 67 D1 33 50N 117 54W
Anai Mudi *mt.* India 91 D2 10 20N 77 15E
Anan Japan 96 B1 33 54N 134 40E
Ananindeua Brazil 70 H12 1 22S 48 20W
Anantapur India 91 D2 14 42N 77 05E
Anápolis Brazil 70 H9 16 19S 48 58W
Anatolian Plateau Turkey 73 M3 39 00N 39 00E
Anatom *i.* Vanuatu 106 L5 20 10S 169 50E
Anchorage Alaska U.S.A. 8 F5 61 10N 150 00W
Anda China 93 P8 46 25N 125 20E
Andaman Islands India 91 G2 12 00N 94 00E
Andaman Sea Indian Ocean 95 B6 13 00N 95 00E
Anderson Indiana U.S.A. 65 I5 40 05N 85 41W
Anderson South Carolina U.S.A. 65 J3 34 30N 82 39W
Andes *mts.* South America 70 B13/C5 10 00S 77 00W
Andhra Pradesh *admin.* India 91 D3 16 00N 79 00E
Andizhan Uzbekistan 87 L3 40 40N 72 12E
Andkhvoy Afghanistan 89 K6 36 58N 65 00E
ANDORRA 72 F4
Andrésy France 79 A2 48 59N 2 03E
Andreyevka Kazakhstan 87 N4 45 50N 80 34E
Andreyevka Ukraine 86 D4 49 34N 36 38E
Andropov *see* Rybinsk
Andros *i.* The Bahamas 69 I4 24 00N 78 00W
Androscoggin River Maine U.S.A. 47 B1 44 27N 70 50W
Andros Town The Bahamas 65 K1 24 45N 77 50W
Androth Island India 91 C2 10 51N 73 41E
Andulo Angola 103 I5 11 29S 16 43E
Angara *r.* Russian Federation 85 L7 58 00N 97 30E
Angara Basin Arctic Ocean 112
Angarsk Russian Federation 85 M6 52 31N 103 55E
Angel de la Guarda *i.* Mexico 68 B5 29 00N 113 30W
Angels Camp California U.S.A. 67 B4 38 04N 120 34W
Angers France 72 E5 47 29N 0 32W
Anglesey *i.* United Kingdom 74 G5 53 20N 4 25W
Angola Indiana U.S.A. 42 A2 41 38N 85 01W
Angola New York U.S.A. 42 G3 42 39N 79 02W
ANGOLA 103 I5
Angola Basin Atlantic Ocean 109 I5 15 00S 3 00E
Angoon Alaska U.S.A. 34 B3 57 30N 133 35W
Angren Uzbekistan 87 L3 41 01N 70 10E
Anguilla *i.* Leeward Islands 69 L3 18 14N 63 05W
Anjō Japan 96 C1 34 56N 137 05E
Ankara *r.* Turkey 86 C2 39 50N 32 10E
Ankara Turkey 88 D6 39 55N 32 50E
Ankaratra *mt.* Madagascar 103 O4 19 25S 47 12E
'Annaba Algeria 102 G15 36 55N 7 47E
An Nabk Saudi Arabia 88 E5 31 21N 37 20E
An Nabk Syria 88 E5 34 02N 36 43E
An Nafud *d.* Saudi Arabia 88 F4 28 20N 40 30E
An Najaf Iraq 88 F5 31 59N 44 19E
Annapolis Maryland U.S.A. 65 K4 38 59N 76 30W
Annapurna *mt.* Nepal 91 E5 28 34N 83 50E
Ann Arbor Michigan U.S.A. 42 C3 42 18N 83 43W
An Nāşirīyah Iraq 89 G5 31 04N 46 17E
Annette Island Alaska U.S.A. 34 B3 55 10N 131 30W
Anniston Alabama U.S.A. 65 I3 33 38N 85 50W
Annotto Bay *tn.* Jamaica 69 R8 18 16N 76 47W
Anqing China 93 N5 30 46N 119 40E
Ansari Nagar India 108 L4 28 33N 77 12E
Anshan China 93 O7 41 05N 122 58E
Anshun China 93 L4 26 15N 105 51E
Antakya *see* Hatay
Antalya Turkey 88 D6 36 53N 30 42E
Antananarivo *(Tananarive)* Madagascar 103 O4 18 52S 47 30E
Antarctica 113
Antarctic Peninsula Antarctica 113 68 00S 65 00W
Antigua Guatemala 68 F2 14 33N 90 42W
Antigua *i.* Antigua & Barbuda 69 L3 17 09N 61 49W
ANTIGUA & BARBUDA 69 L3
Antioch California U.S.A. 67 B4 38 01N 121 49W
Antipodes Islands Southern Ocean 110 H3 49 42S 178 50E
Antofagasta Chile 71 C8 23 40S 70 23W
Antrim Mountains United Kingdom 74 E6 55 00N 6 10W
Antseranana Madagascar 103 O5 12 19S 49 17E
An Tuc *see* An Khe
Antwerp New York U.S.A. 43 L5 44 13N 75 38W
Antwerp Ohio U.S.A. 42 B2 41 10N 84 44W
Antwerpen *(Anvers)* Belgium 72 F6 51 13N 4 25E
Anuradhapura Sri Lanka 91 E1 8 20N 80 25E
Anvers *see* Antwerpen
Anxi China 94 E8 25 03N 118 13E
Anyang China 93 M6 36 04N 114 20E
Anza California U.S.A. 67 D1 33 33N 116 41W
Anzhero-Sudzhensk Russian Federation 85 K7 56 10N 86 01E
Aomori Japan 96 D3 40 50N 140 43E
Aozou Strip Chad 102 I12 23 00N 17 00E
Aparri The Philippines 95 G7 18 22N 121 40E
Apatity Russian Federation 84 F9 67 32N 33 21E
Apatzingán Mexico 68 D3 19 05N 102 20W
Apia Samoa 110 I6 13 48S 171 45W
Ap Lei Chau *i.* Hong Kong China 92 B1 22 10N 114 00E
Appalachian Mountains U.S.A. 65 J4 37 00N 82 00W
Appennini *mts.* Italy 72 H4 43 00N 12 30E
Appleton Wisconsin U.S.A. 65 I5 44 17N 88 24W
'Aqaba Jordan 88 D4 29 32N 35 00E
'Aqaba, Gulf of Middle East 88 D4 28 40N 34 40E
Aquidauana Brazil 70 F8 20 27S 55 45W
Aquiles Sedan Mexico 64 E2 28 37N 105 54W
Ara India 91 E5 25 34N 84 40E
Ara *r.* Japan 97 C3 35 39N 139 51E
Arabian Basin Indian Ocean 108 F7/8 10 00N 65 00E

Arabian Sea Indian Ocean **108** F8 17 00N 60 00E
Aracaju Brazil **70** J10 10 54S 37 07W
Aracati Brazil **70** J12 4 32S 37 45W
Arad Romania **72** K5 46 10N 21 19E
Arafura Sea Australia/Indonesia **106** E8/F8 8 00S 132 00E
Aragats mt. Armenia **86** E3 40 32N 44 11E
Araguaina Brazil **70** H11 7 16S 48 18W
Araguari Brazil **70** H9 18 38S 48 13W
Arãk Iran **89** G5 34 05N 49 42E
Araks r. Asia **73** Q3 39 30N 46 00E
Aral Sea Asia **87** H3/J4 45 00N 60 00E
Aral'sk Kazakhstan **87** J4 46 56N 61 43E
Aran Island Republic of Ireland **74** C6 55 00N 8 30W
Aran Islands Republic of Ireland **74** B5 53 10N 9 50W
Arapiraca Brazil **70** J11 9 45S 36 40W
Ar'ar Saudi Arabia **88** F5 30 58N 41 03E
Araraquara Brazil **71** H8 21 46S 48 08W
Ararat, Mount Turkey **73** P3 39 44N 44 15E
Aras (Araks, Araxes) r. Turkey **88** F7 40 00N 43 30E
Arauca Colombia **70** C14 7 04N 70 41W
Araure Venezuela **69** K1 9 36N 69 15W
Araxá Brazil **70** H9 19 37S 46 50W
Araxes (Araks, Aras) r. Iran **89** G6 38 40N 46 30E
Arbil Iraq **88** F6 36 12N 44 01E
Arbroath United Kingdom **74** I8 56 34N 2 35W
Archipelago Dehalak is. Ethiopia **88** F2 15 45N 40 12E
Arctic National Wildlife Refuge Alaska U.S.A. **50** C4
  68 30N 144 30W
Arctic Ocean 112
Arctowski r.s. Antarctica **113** 62 09S 58 28W
Ardabil Iran **88** G6 38 15N 48 18E
Ardennes mts. Belgium **72** G6 50 10N 5 45E
Ardmore Oklahoma U.S.A. **65** G3 34 11N 97 08W
Arequipa Peru **70** C9 16 25S 71 32W
Argenteuil France **79** A2 48 57N 2 14E
ARGENTINA 71 D5
Argentine Basin Atlantic Ocean **109** D2 42 00S 45 00W
Argun (Ergun He) r. Asia **93** N9 51 30N 120 00E
Argyle, Lake Australia **106** D6 17 00S 128 30E
Århus Denmark **72** H7 56 15N 10 10E
Arica Chile **70** C9 18 30S 70 20W
Arima Trinidad and Tobago **69** T10 10 38N 61 17W
Aripuaná r. Brazil **70** E11 7 00S 60 30W
Ariquemes Brazil **70** E11 9 55S 63 06W
Arizona state U.S.A. **64** D3 34 00N 112 00W
Arizpe Mexico **68** B6 30 20N 110 11W
Arjona Colombia **70** B15 10 14N 75 22W
Arkalyk Kazakhstan **87** K5 50 17N 66 51E
Arkansas r. U.S.A. **65** G4 36 00N 97 00W
Arkansas state U.S.A. **68** F7 34 00N 93 00W
Arkansas City Kansas U.S.A. **65** G4 37 03N 97 02W
Arkhangel'sk Russian Federation **84** G8 64 32N 40 40E
Arlit Niger **102** G11 18 50N 7 00E
Armagh United Kingdom **74** E6 54 21N 6 39W
Armavir Russian Federation **84** G4 44 59N 41 40E
ARMENIA 86 E3/F2
Armenia Colombia **70** B13 4 32N 75 40W
Armenia Mountain mt. Pennsylvania U.S.A. **43** K2
  41 45N 76 55W
Armidale Australia **106** I3 30 32S 151 40E
Arnhem Land geog. reg. Australia **106** E7 13 00S 133 00E
Arnold California U.S.A. **67** B4 38 15N 120 20W
Arquípélago dos Bijagós is. Guinea-Bissau **102** B10
  11 20N 16 40W
Ar Ramâdî Iraq **88** F5 33 27N 43 19E
Ar Ramlah Jordan **88** O9 29 28N 25 58E
Arran i. United Kingdom **74** F7 55 35N 5 15W
Ar Raqqah Syria **88** E6 35 57N 39 03E
Ar Riyâd Saudi Arabia **89** G3 24 39N 46 46E
Arthur's Pass N.Z. **107** B2 42 55S 171 34E
Artigas r.s. Antarctica **113** 62 11S 58 51W
Artigas Uruguay **71** F6 30 25S 56 28W
Arua Uganda **102** L8 3 02N 30 56E
ARUBA 70 D15
Arun r. United Kingdom **74** K2 51 00N 0 30W
Arunachal Pradesh admin. India **91** G5/H5 28 00N 95 00E
Arusha Tanzania **102** M7 3 23S 36 40E
Aruwimi r. Congo (D.R.) **102** J8 2 00N 25 00E
Arvin California U.S.A. **67** C2 35 11N 118 50W
Arys' Kazakhstan **87** K3 42 26N 68 49E
Arzamas Russian Federation **86** E6 55 24N 43 48E
Asahi-dake mt. Japan **96** D3 43 42N 142 54E
Asahikawa mt. Japan **96** D3 43 46N 142 23E
Asaka Japan **97** B4 35 47N 139 37E
Asamankese Ghana **102** E9 5 45N 0 45W
Asansol India **91** F4 23 40N 86 59E
Ascension Island Atlantic Ocean **109** G6 7 57S 14 22W
Âseb Eritrea **102** N10 13 01N 42 47E
Ashburton N.Z. **107** B2 43 54S 171 45E
Ashburton r. Australia **106** B5 22 30S 116 00E
Ashdod Israel **88** O10 31 48N 34 48E
Asheville North Carolina U.S.A. **65** J4 35 35N 82 35W
Ashfield Australia **107** G2 33 53S 151 07E
Ashfork Arizona U.S.A. **64** D4 35 13N 112 29W
Ashgabat (Ashkhabad) Turkmenistan **87** H2
  37 58N 58 24E
Ashikaga Japan **96** C2 36 21N 139 26E
Ashina Japan **97** B1 35 13N 139 36E
Ashizuri-misaki c. Japan **96** B1 32 42N 133 00E
Ashkhabad see Ashgabat
Ashland Kentucky U.S.A. **65** J4 38 28N 82 40W
Ashland Ohio U.S.A. **42** D1 40 52N 82 19W
Ashland Oregon U.S.A. **64** B5 42 14N 122 44W
Ashok Nagar India **108** L4 28 38N 77 07E
Ashqelon Israel **88** I2 23N 13 05E
Ash Shäriqah U.A.E. **89** I4 25 20N 55 20E
Ash Shuraÿf Saudi Arabia **88** E4 25 50N 39 00E
Ash Springs California U.S.A. **67** E3 37 32N 115 12W

Ashtabula Ohio U.S.A. **42** F2 41 53N 80 47W
Asmara Eritrea **88** E2 15 20N 38 58E
Asnières France **79** B2 48 55N 2 17E
Aspiring, Mount N.Z. **107** A2 44 22S 168 44E
Asquith Australia **107** G3 33 41S 151 07E
Assam admin. India **91** G5 26 20N 92 00E
As Samâwah Iraq **89** G5 31 18N 45 18E
Assis Brazil **71** G8 22 37S 50 25W
As Suq Saudi Arabia **88** F3 21 55N 42 02E
As Suwaydâ' Syria **88** P11 32 43N 36 33E
Astârã Azerbaijan **86** F2 38 27N 48 53E
Astoria Oregon U.S.A. **64** B6 46 12N 123 50W
Astrakhan' Russian Federation **84** G5 46 22N 48 04E
Asuka r.s. Antarctica **113** 71 32S 24 08E
Asunción Paraguay **71** F7 25 15S 57 40W
Aswa r. Uganda **102** L8 3 30N 32 30E
Aswân Egypt **102** L12 24 05N 32 56E
Aswân Dam Egypt **102** L12 23 40N 31 50E
Asyût Egypt **102** L13 27 14N 31 07E
Atacama Desert see Desierto de Atacama
Atar Mauritania **102** C12 20 32N 13 08W
Atbara r. Sudan **102** L11 17 28N 34 30E
Atbara Sudan **102** L11 17 42N 34 00E
Atbasar Kazakhstan **87** K5 51 49N 68 18E
Atchison Kansas U.S.A. **65** H4 39 33N 95 09W
Athens Georgia U.S.A. **65** J3 33 57N 83 24W
Athens Pennsylvania U.S.A. **66** B4 41 57N 76 31W
Athínai (Athens) Greece **72** N2 38 00N 23 44E
Athlone Republic of Ireland **74** D5 53 25N 7 56W
Ati Chad **102** I10 13 11N 18 20E
Atlanta Georgia U.S.A. **65** J3 33 45N 84 23W
Atlantic City New Jersey U.S.A. **65** L4 39 23N 74 27W
Atlantic-Indian Ridge Atlantic Ocean **109** H1/J1
  53 00S 3 00E
Atlantic Ocean 109
Atlas Mountains Morocco **72** F2 32 00N 2 00W
Atlas Saharien mts. Algeria **102** E14 33 30N 1 00E
Atrek r. Iran/Turkmenistan **87** G2 37 00N 54 50E
At Tä'if Saudi Arabia **88** F3 21 15N 40 21E
Atyrau (Gur'yev) Kazakhstan **86** G4 47 08N 51 59E
Aubervilliers France **79** B2 48 55N 2 22E
Auburn Indiana U.S.A. **42** A2 41 22N 85 02W
Auburn Maine U.S.A. **65** L5 44 04N 70 27W
Auburn Reservoir California U.S.A. **67** B4
  39 05N 120 55W
Auckland N.Z. **107** B3 36 51S 174 46E
Auckland Islands Southern Ocean **110** G2
  50 35S 116 00E
Au Gres Michigan U.S.A. **42** C5 44 03N 83 40W
Augsburg Germany **72** H5 48 21N 10 54E
Augusta Australia **106** B3 34 19S 115 09E
Augusta Georgia U.S.A. **65** J3 33 29N 82 00W
Augusta Maine U.S.A. **65** M5 44 17N 69 50W
Aulnay-sous-Bois France **79** C2 48 57N 2 31E
Aurangâbâd India **91** D3 19 52N 75 22E
Au Sable Michigan U.S.A. **42** C5 44 25N 83 20W
Au Sable River Michigan U.S.A. **42** B5 44 40N 84 10W
Austin California U.S.A. **67** D4 39 30N 117 05W
Austin Texas U.S.A. **65** G3 30 18N 97 47W
AUSTRALIA 106
Australian Capital Territory (A.C.T.) admin. Australia
  106 H2 35 00S 144 00E
Austral Ridge Pacific Ocean **111** K5 24 00S 155 30W
AUSTRIA 72 H5
Autlán Mexico **68** D3 19 48N 104 20W
Avalon California U.S.A. **67** C1 33 21N 118 19W
Avawatz Mountains mts. California U.S.A. **67** D2
  35 32N 116 30W
Avellaneda Argentina **71** F6 34 40S 58 20W
Avenal California U.S.A. **67** B3 36 00N 120 10W
Avignon France **72** G4 43 56N 4 48E
Avon r. United Kingdom **74** J3 51 27N 1 40W
Avon Lake tn. Ohio U.S.A. **42** D2 41 31N 82 01W
Awali r. Lebanon **88** O11 33 35N 35 32E
Awash Ethiopia **102** N9 9 01N 41 10E
Awa-shima i. Japan **96** C2 38 40N 139 15E
Awbäri Libya **102** H13 26 35N 12 46E
Ayacucho Peru **70** C10 13 10S 74 15W
Ayaguz Kazakhstan **87** N4 47 59N 80 27E
Ayaviri Peru **70** C10 14 53S 70 35W
Ayers Rock mt. Australia **106** E4 25 18S 131 18E
Ayod Sudan **102** L9 8 08N 31 24E
Ayon r. Russian Federation **85** S9 69 55N 169 10E
Ayr United Kingdom **74** G7 55 28N 4 38W
'Aÿûnah Saudi Arabia **88** E4 28 06N 35 08E
AZERBAIJAN 86 F3
Aziscohos Lake Maine U.S.A. **43** R6 45 08N 70 59W
Azogues Ecuador **70** B12 2 46S 78 56W
Azores is. Atlantic Ocean **109** F10 38 30N 28 00W
Azoum r. Chad **102** J10 12 00N 21 00E
Azov, Sea of Asia **86** D4 46 00N 36 00E
Azuero, Peninsula de Panama **69** H1 7 40N 81 00W
Azul Argentina **71** F5 36 46S 59 50W
Azurduy Bolivia **71** E9 20 00S 64 29W
Az Zabadâni Syria **88** P11 33 42N 36 03E
Az Zahrân (Dhahran) Saudi Arabia **89** H4 26 13N 50 02E

B

Ba'albek Lebanon **88** P12 34 00N 36 12E
Babadag mt. Azerbaijan **86** F3 41 02N 48 07E
Babahoyo Ecuador **70** B12 1 53S 79 31W
Bab el Mandab sd. Red Sea **102** N10 12 30N 47 00E
Babelsberg Germany **79** E1 52 23N 13 05E
Babruysk Belarus **72** L6 53 08N 29 10E
Babushkin Russian Federation **86** M2/N2 55 55N 37 44E
Babylon hist. site Iraq **88** F5 32 33N 44 25E

Bacabal Brazil **70** I12 4 15S 44 45W
Bacäu Romania **86** B4 46 33N 26 58E
Bacolod The Philippines **95** G6 10 38N 122 58E
Badajoz Spain **72** D3 38 53N 6 58W
Bad Axe Michigan U.S.A. **42** D4 43 49N 82 59W
Badli India **90** L4 28 44N 77 09E
Badulla Sri Lanka **91** E1 6 59N 81 03E
Bafoussam Cameroon **102** H9 5 31N 10 25E
Bäfq Iran **89** I5 31 35N 55 21E
Bagé Brazil **71** G6 31 22S 54 06W
Baghdâd Iraq **88** F5 33 20N 44 26E
Baghlän Afghanistan **89** K6 36 11N 68 44E
BAHAMAS, THE 69 H4
Baharampur India **91** F4 24 00N 88 30E
Bahawalpur Pakistan **91** C5 29 24N 71 47E
Bahia admin. Brazil **70** I10 12 00S 42 30W
Bahía Blanca Argentina **71** E5 38 45S 62 15W
Bahía Blanca b. Argentina **71** E5 39 00S 61 00W
Bahia de Campeche b. Mexico **68** E4/F4 20 00N 95 00W
Bahia Grande b. Argentina **71** D2 51 30S 68 00W
Bahraich India **91** E5 27 35N 81 36E
BAHRAIN 89 H4
Bahrain, Gulf of The Gulf **89** H4 25 55N 50 30E
Bahr el Abiad (White Nile) r. Sudan **102** L10
  14 00N 32 20E
Bahr el Arab r. Sudan **102** K10 10 00N 27 30E
Bahr el Azraq (Blue Nile) r. Sudan **102** L10 13 00N 33 45E
Bahr el Ghazal r. Chad **102** I10 14 00N 16 00E
Baicheng China **93** O8 45 37N 122 48E
Baidyabati India **90** K3 22 48N 88 20E
Baile Atha Cliath see Dublin
Baiwanzhuang China **94** B3 39 55N 116 18E
Baja California p. Mexico **68** B5 27 30N 113 00W
Baja California Norte admin. Mexico **64** C3
  27 30N 113 00W
Baja California Sur admin. Mexico **64** D2
  26 00N 112 00W
Baj Baj India **90** J1 22 28N 88 10E
Baker California U.S.A. **67** D2 35 16N 116 06W
Baker Oregon U.S.A. **64** C5 44 46N 117 50W
Baker Island Alaska U.S.A. **34** B3 55 30N 133 30W
Baker, Mount Washington U.S.A. **34** H4
  48 48N 121 50W
Bakersfield California U.S.A. **67** C2 35 25N 119 00W
Bakı (Baku) Azerbaijan **86** F3 40 22N 49 53E
Baku see Bakı
Balaghat India **91** E4 21 48N 80 16E
Balaghat Range mts. India **91** D3 18 45N 77 00E
Balakovo Russian Federation **86** G6 52 04N 47 46E
Balama Mozambique **103** M5 13 19S 38 35E
Bälä Morghäb Afghanistan **89** J6 35 34N 63 20E
Balashikha Russian Federation **86** D6 55 47N 37 59E
Balashov Russian Federation **86** E6 51 33N 43 10E
Balboa Panama **69** I2 8 57N 79 33W
Balclutha N.Z. **107** A1 46 14S 169 44E
Bald Mountain California U.S.A. **67** E3
  37 27N 115 45W
Balearic Islands Spain **72** F3 40 00N 2 00E
Balgowlah Australia **107** H2 33 48S 151 16E
Bali i. Indonesia **95** F2 8 30S 115 00E
Balikesir Turkey **72** L3 39 37N 27 51E
Balikpapan Indonesia **95** F3 1 15S 116 50E
Balkan Mountains Europe **72** K4 43 00N 25 00E
Balkhash Kazakhstan **87** L4 46 50N 74 57E
Balkhash, Lake see Ozero Balkhash
Ballarat Australia **106** G2 37 36S 143 58E
Balleny Islands Southern Ocean **110** G1 66 30S 1 64E
Bälly India **90** K2 22 38N 88 20E
Ballygunge India **90** K2 22 31N 88 20E
Ballymena United Kingdom **74** E6 54 52N 6 17W
Balmain Australia **107** G2 33 51S 151 11E
Balsas Mexico **68** E3 18 00N 99 44W
Bälti (Bel'tsy) Moldova **72** L5 47 44N 28 41E
Baltic Sea Europe **72** J7 55 15N 17 00E
Baltimore Maryland U.S.A. **65** K4 39 18N 76 38W
Baluchistan geog. reg. Pakistan **90** A5/B5
  27 30N 65 00E
Bam Iran **89** I4 29 07N 58 07E
Bamako Mali **102** D10 12 40N 7 59W
Bambari Central African Republic **102** J9 5 40N 20 37E
Bamenda Cameroon **102** H9 5 55N 10 09E
Bamingui Bangoran National Park
  Central African Republic **102** I9 8 00N 20 00E
Banaba i. Nauru **110** G7 1 00S 167 00E
Banas r. India **91** D5 26 00N 75 00E
Banbury United Kingdom **74** J4 52 04N 1 20W
Banda India **91** E5 25 28N 80 20E
Banda Aceh Indonesia **95** B5 5 30N 95 20E
Bandama Blanc r. Côte d'Ivoire **102** D9 8 00N 5 45W
Bandar Abbäs Iran **89** I4 27 12N 56 15E
Bandarbeyla Somalia **102** P9 9 30N 50 50E
Bandar-e Lengeh Iran **89** H4 26 34N 54 52E
Bandar-e Torkeman Iran **89** H6 36 55N 54 01E
Bandar Khomeynï Iran **89** G5 30 40N 49 08E
Bandar Seri Begawan Brunei Darussalam **95** F4
  4 53N 114 57E
Banda Sea Indonesia **95** H2 5 50S 126 00E
Bandeirantes Beach Brazil **71** B1 23 01S 43 23W
Bandel India **90** K3 22 55N 88 20E
Bandirma Turkey **88** C7 40 21N 27 58E
Bandundu Congo (D.R.) **103** I7 3 20S 17 24E
Bandung Indonesia **95** D2 6 57S 107 34E
Banfora Burkina **102** E10 10 36N 4 45W
Bangalore India **91** D2 12 58N 77 35E
Bangassou Central African Republic **102** J8
  4 41N 22 48E
Banghäzï (Benghazi) Libya **102** J14 32 07N 20 04E
Bangkok (Krung Thep) Thailand **95** C6 13 44N 100 30E

BANGLADESH 91 F4/G4
Bangor Maine U.S.A. **65** M5 44 49N 68 47W
Bangor Northern Ireland U.K. **74** F6 54 40N 5 40W
Bangor Wales U.K. **74** G5 53 13N 4 08W
Bangui Central African Republic **102** I8 4 23N 18 37E
Bangweulu, Lake Zambia **103** K5 11 15S 29 45E
Banja Luka Bosnia-Herzegovina **72** J4 44 47N 17 11E
Banjarmasin Indonesia **95** E3 3 22S 114 33E
Banjul The Gambia **102** B10 13 28N 16 39W
Banka India **90** K2 22 36N 88 17E
Banks Islands Vanuatu **106** L7 13 40S 167 30E
Banks Peninsula N.Z. **107** B2 43 44S 173 00E
Bankstown Australia **107** G2 33 55S 151 02E
Bann r. United Kingdom **74** E7 54 20N 6 10W
Bansberia India **90** K3 22 57N 88 23E
Banstead United Kingdom **78** C2 51 19N 0 12W
Bantry Bay Republic of Ireland **74** B3 51 35N 9 40W
Banyuwangi Indonesia **95** E2 8 12S 114 22E
Baoding China **93** N6 38 54N 115 26E
Baoji China **93** L5 34 23N 107 16E
Baotou China **93** L7 40 38N 109 59E
Ba'qübah Iraq **88** F5 33 45N 44 40E
Barahanagar India **90** K2 22 38N 88 23E
Barajala Canal India **90** J2 22 35N 88 12E
Bäräkpur India **91** F4 22 45N 88 22E
Baral India **90** K1 22 27N 88 22E
Baranavichy Belarus **86** B5 53 09N 26 00E
Baranof Alaska U.S.A. **34** B3 57 05N 134 50W
Baranof Island Alaska U.S.A. **34** A3 57 30N 135 00W
Bäräsat India **90** K2 22 43N 88 30E
Barbacena Brazil **71** I8 21 13S 43 47W
BARBADOS 69 M2
Barbuda i. Antigua & Barbuda **69** L3 17 41N 61 48W
Barcaldine Australia **106** H5 23 31S 145 15E
Barcelona Spain **72** F4 41 25N 2 10E
Barcelona Venezuela **70** D15 10 08N 64 43W
Barcelos Brazil **70** E12 0 59S 62 58W
Barcoo r. Australia **106** G5 24 00S 144 00E
Barddhamän India **91** F4 23 14N 87 52E
Bareilly India **91** D5 28 20N 79 24E
Barents Sea Arctic Ocean **112** 75 00N 40 00E
Barga China **91** I6 30 51N 81 20E
Bari Italy **72** J4 41 07N 16 52E
Barinas Venezuela **70** C14 8 36N 70 15W
Barisal Bangladesh **91** G4 22 41N 90 20E
Bariti, Lake India **90** K3 22 48N 88 26E
Barking bor. United Kingdom **78** D3 51 33N 0 06E
Barkly-Tableland geog. reg. Australia **106** F6
  17 30S 137 00E
Barlee, Lake Australia **106** B4 28 30S 120 00E
Barnaul Russian Federation **85** K6 53 21N 83 45E
Barnes United Kingdom **78** C2 51 28N 0 15W
Barnet United Kingdom **78** C3 51 39N 0 12W
Barnstaple r. United Kingdom **74** G3 51 05N 4 04W
Barquisimeto Venezuela **70** D15 10 03N 69 18W
Barra i. United Kingdom **74** D9 57 00N 7 25W
Barra da Tijuca Brazil **71** P1 23 00S 43 20W
Barra do Corba Brazil **70** H11 5 30S 45 12W
Barrancabermeja Colombia **70** C14 7 06N 73 54W
Barrancas Venezuela **70** E14 8 45N 62 13W
Barrancones Point Trinidad and Tobago **69** T10
  10 30N 61 28W
Barranjoey Head c. Australia **107** H3 33 35S 151 20E
Barranquilla Colombia **70** C15 11 10N 74 50W
Barre Vermont U.S.A. **65** L5 44 13N 72 31W
Barreiras Brazil **70** I10 12 09S 44 58W
Barreto Brazil **71** Q2 22 53S 43 07W
Barretos Brazil **71** H8 20 33S 48 34W
Barrow Alaska U.S.A. **8** D7 71 16N 156 50W
Barrow r. Republic of Ireland **74** D5 52 55N 7 00W
Barrow-in-Furness U.K. **74** H6 54 07N 3 14W
Barrow Island Australia **106** B5 21 00S 115 00E
Barrow, Point Alaska U.S.A. **8** D7 71 05N 156 00W
Barry United Kingdom **74** H3 51 24N 3 18W
Bartlesville Oklahoma U.S.A. **65** G4 36 44N 95 59W
Bartolome, Cape Alaska U.S.A. **34** B3 55 15N 133 39W
Barysaw Belarus **86** B5 54 09N 28 30E
Basalt California U.S.A. **67** C4 38 02N 118 18W
Basalt Island Hong Kong China **92** L2 22 19N 114 21E
Basdorf Germany **79** E2 52 44N 13 27E
Basel Switzerland **72** G5 47 33N 7 36E
Basildon United Kingdom **74** L3 51 34N 0 25W
Basingstoke U.K. **74** J3 51 16N 1 05W
Baskunchak Russian Federation **86** F4 48 14N 46 44E
Bassas da India i. Mozambique Channel **103** M3
  22 00S 40 00E
Bassein Myanmar **91** G3 16 46N 94 45E
Basse Terre i. Lesser Antilles **69** L3 16 00N 61 20W
Basse Terre Trinidad and Tobago **69** T9 10 07N 61 17W
Bass Strait Australia **106** H1/2 40 00S 145 00E
Bastia Corsica France **72** G4 42 14N 9 26E
Bastrop Louisiana U.S.A. **65** H3 32 49N 91 54W
Bata Equatorial Guinea **102** G8 1 51N 9 49E
Batakan Indonesia **95** E3 4 04S 114 39E
Batala India **91** D6 31 48N 75 17E
Batanagar India **90** K2 22 30N 88 14E
Batang China **93** J5 30 02N 99 01E
Batangafo Central African Republic **102** I9 7 27N 18 11E
Batangas The Philippines **95** G6 13 46N 121 01E
Bate Bay Australia **107** G1 34 03S 151 11E
Bath Jamaica **69** R7 17 57N 76 22W
Bath United Kingdom **74** I3 51 23N 2 22W
Batha r. Chad **102** I10 13 00N 18 00E
Bathsheba Barbados **69** V12 13 12N 59 32W
Bathurst Australia **106** H3 33 27S 149 35E
Bathurst Island Australia **106** E7 12 00S 130 00E
Batna Algeria **102** G15 35 34N 6 10E
Baton Rouge Louisiana U.S.A. **65** H3 30 30N 91 10W

Batroûn Lebanon **88** O12 36 16N 35 40E
Battambang Cambodia **95** C6 13 06N 103 13E
Batticaloa Sri Lanka **91** E1 7 43N 81 42E
Battle Creek Michigan U.S.A. **65** I5 42 20N 85 21W
Bat'umi Georgia **86** E3 41 37N 41 36E
Bat Yam Israel **88** O10 32 01N 34 45E
Baubau Indonesia **95** G2 5 30S 122 37E
Bauchi Nigeria **102** G10 10 16N 9 50E
Baulkham Hills Australia **107** F2/G2 33 46S 151 00E
Bauru Brazil **71** H8 22 19S 49 07W
Bayamo Cuba **69** I4 20 23N 76 39W
Bay City Michigan U.S.A. **65** J5 43 35N 83 52W
Bay City Texas U.S.A. **65** G2 28 59N 96 00W
Baydhabo Somalia **102** N8 3 08N 43 34E
Bayfield Barbados **69** W12 13 10N 59 25W
Baykal, Lake see Ozero Baykal
Baykonur Kazakhstan **87** K4 47 50N 66 03E
Bay of Plenty N.Z. **107** C3 37 48S 177 12E
Bayonne France **72** E4 43 30N 1 28W
Bayonne New Jersey U.S.A. **66** Y1 40 39N 74 07W
Bay Ridge tn. New York U.S.A. **66** Y1 40 37N 74 02W
Baytown Texas U.S.A. **65** H2 29 43N 94 59W
Bazar-Dyuzi mt. Azerbaijan **86** F3 41 14N 47 50E
Bcharre Lebanon **88** P12 34 15N 36 00E
Beachy Head c. United Kingdom **74** L2 50 44N 0 16E
Beardmore Glacier Antarctica **113** 84 00S 170 00E
Bear Lake U.S.A. **64** D5 42 00N 111 20W
Beatrice Nebraska U.S.A. **65** G5 40 17N 96 45W
Beatty California U.S.A. **67** D3 36 54N 116 45W
Beauchamp France **79** A3 49 00N 2 12E
Beaufort South Carolina U.S.A. **65** J3 32 26N 80 40W
Beaufort Island Hong Kong China **92** C1 22 11N 114 15E
Beaufort Sea Arctic Ocean **112** 72 00N 135 00W
Beaumont Texas U.S.A. **65** H3 30 04N 94 06W
Beaver Alaska U.S.A. **8** F6 66 22N 147 30W
Beaver Island Michigan U.S.A. **42** B6 45 40N 85 30W
Béchar Algeria **102** E14 31 35N 2 17W
Becharof Lake Alaska U.S.A. **8** D4 58 00N 156 30W
Beckenham United Kingdom **78** C2 51 24N 0 02W
Beckley West Virginia U.S.A. **65** J4 37 46N 81 12W
Becontree United Kingdom **78** D3 51 34N 0 10E
Bedford United Kingdom **74** K4 52 08N 0 29W
Be'ér Sheva' Israel **88** O10 31 15N 34 47E
Beeville Texas U.S.A. **65** G2 28 25N 97 47W
Begovat Uzbekistan **87** K4 40 14N 69 14E
Behala see South Suburbs
Behbehân Iran **89** H5 30 34N 5018E
Behm Canal U.S.A. **34** B3 56 00N 131 00W
Bei'an China **93** P8 48 16N 126 36E
Beida (Al Bayda') Libya **72** K2 32 00N 21 30E
Beihai China **93** M3 21 29N 109 10E
Beihai i. China **94** B1 39 57N 116 22E
Beijing (Peking) China **94** B1 39 55N 116 26E
Beira Mozambique **103** L4 19 49S 34 52E
Beirut see Beyrouth
Beiyuan China **94** B2 40 02N 116 25E
Bejaïa Algeria **102** G15 36 49N 5 03E
Bela Pakistan **90** B5 26 12N 66 20E
BELARUS 72 L6
Belau see Palau
Belém Brazil **70** H12 1 27S 48 29W
Belfast Maine U.S.A. **47** C1 44 26N 69 01W
Belfast United Kingdom **74** F5 54 35N 5 55W
Belford Roxe Brazil **71** P2 22 45S 43 24W
Belgaum India **91** C3 15 54N 74 36E
Belgharia India **90** K2 22 39N 88 23E
BELGIUM 72 F6
Belgorod Russian Federation **84** F6 50 38N 36 36E
Belgrade see Beograd
Beliaghata India **90** K2 22 34N 88 23E
BELIZE 68 G3
Belize tn. Belize **68** G3 17 29N 88 10W
Bellaire Michigan U.S.A. **42** A5 44 59N 85 12W
Bellary India **91** D3 15 11N 76 54E
Bella Vista Argentina **71** F7 28 31S 59 00W
Belleplaine Barbados **69** V12 13 14N 59 35W
Bellevue Ohio U.S.A. **42** D2 41 16N 82 51W
Bellingham Washington U.S.A. **64** B6 48 45N 122 29W
Bellingshausen r.s. Antarctica **113** 62 12S 58 58W
Bellingshausen Sea Southern Ocean **113** 71 00S 85 00W
Bello Colombia **70** B14 6 20N 75 41W
Belmopan Belize **68** G3 17 13N 88 48W
Belogorsk Russian Federation **85** O6 50 55N 128 26E
Belo Horizonte Brazil **70** I9 19 54S 43 54W
Belovo Russian Federation **87** O5 54 27N 86 19E
Belted Range mts. California U.S.A. **67** D3 37 28N 116 05W
Bel'tsy see Bălţi
Belur India **90** K2 22 37N 88 20E
Belvidere New Jersey U.S.A. **66** C3 40 50N 75 05W
Belyy Russian Federation **85** J10 73 00N 70 00E
Belyy Yar Russian Federation **85** K7 58 28N 85 03E
Bemidji Minnesota U.S.A. **65** H6 47 29N 94 52W
Benbecula i. United Kingdom **74** D9 57 25N 7 20W
Bend Oregon U.S.A. **64** B5 44 04N 121 20W
Bendigo Australia **106** G2 36 48S 144 21E
Benfica Brazil **71** P2 22 52S 43 16W
Bengal, Bay of Indian Ocean **91** F3/G3 17 00N 88 00E
Bengbu China **93** N5 32 56N 117 27E
Benghazi see Banghâzi
Bengkulu Indonesia **95** C3 3 46S 102 16E
Benguela Angola **103** H5 12 34S 13 24E
Beni Abbès Algeria **102** E14 30 11N 2 14W
Beni Mellal Morocco **102** D14 32 22N 6 29W
BENIN 102 F10
Benin, Bight of b. West Africa **102** F9 5 50N 2 30E
Benin City Nigeria **102** G9 6 19N 5 41E
Beni Suef Egypt **102** L13 29 05N 31 05E

Benjamin Constant Brazil **70** C12 4 23S 69 59W
Ben Macdui mt. United Kingdom **74** H9 57 04N 3 40W
Benmore, Lake N.Z. **107** B2 44 30S 170 10E
Ben Nevis mt. United Kingdom **74** G8 56 40N 5 00W
Bénoué see Benue
Benson Arizona U.S.A. **64** D3 31 58N 110 19W
Bentham's Barbados **69** V13 13 18N 59 40W
Benton California U.S.A. **67** C3 37 49N 118 30W
Benton Harbor tn. Michigan U.S.A. **65** I5 42 07N 86 27W
Benue (Bénoué) r. Nigeria/Cameroon **102** H9 8 00N 7 40E
Ben Wyvis mt. United Kingdom **74** G9 57 40N 4 35W
Benxi China **93** O7 41 21N 123 45E
Beograd (Belgrade) Yugoslavia **72** K4 44 50N 20 30E
Beppu Japan **96** B1 33 18N 131 30E
Berber Sudan **102** L11 18 01N 34 00E
Berbera Somalia **102** O10 10 28N 45 02E
Berbérati Central African Republic **102** I8 4 19N 15 51E
Berdyans'k Ukraine **86** D4 46 45N 36 47E
Berdychiv Ukraine **86** B4 49 54N 28 39E
Berezniki Russian Federation **84** H7 59 26N 56 49E
Berezovo Russian Federation **85** I8 63 58N 65 00E
Bergen Norway **72** G8 60 23N 5 20E
Ber Harbor tn. Maine U.S.A. **47** C1 44 24N 68 10W
Bering Strait Russian Federation/U.S.A. **8** B6 69 00N 169 00W
Berkakit Russian Federation **85** O7 56 36N 124 49E
Berkeley California U.S.A. **67** A3 37 53N 122 17W
Berkner Island Antarctica **113** 80 00S 45 00W
Berkshire co. United Kingdom **74** J3 51 28N 1 00W
Berlin Germany **72** H6 52 32N 13 25E
Berlin New Hampshire U.S.A. **65** L5 44 27N 71 13W
Berlin Lake res. Ohio U.S.A. **42** D3 41 01N 81 06W
Bermuda i. Atlantic Ocean **109** B10 32 50N 64 20W
Bern Switzerland **72** G5 46 57N 7 26E
Berowra Australia **107** G3 33 37S 151 09E
Bertoua Cameroon **102** H8 4 34N 13 42E
Berwick Pennsylvania U.S.A. **66** B4 41 04N 76 13W
Berwick-upon-Tweed U.K. **74** I7 55 46N 2 00W
Beskudnikovo Russian Federation **86** M2 55 54N 37 38E
Bethel Alaska U.S.A. **8** C5 60 49N 161 49W
Bethesda Maryland U.S.A. **66** A1 39 00N 77 05W
Bethlehem Middle East **88** E5 31 42N 35 12E
Bethlehem Pennsylvania U.S.A. **66** C3 40 36N 75 22W
Betican Cordilleras mts. Spain **72** E3 37 00N 3 00W
Betsiboka r. Madagascar **103** O4 17 00S 46 30E
Bexley bor. United Kingdom **78** D2 51 27N 0 09E
Bexleyheath United Kingdom **78** D2 51 28N 0 05E
Beyla Guinea **102** D9 8 42N 8 39W
Beyrouth (Beirut) Lebanon **88** E5 33 52N 35 30E
Beyşehir Gölü l. Turkey **88** D3 37 40N 31 43E
Bhâtpâra India **90** K3 22 52N 88 25E
Bhadgaon Nepal **91** F5 27 41N 85 26E
Bhadravati India **91** D2 13 54N 75 38E
Bhadreswar India **90** K3 22 50N 88 20E
Bhagalpur India **91** F5 25 14N 86 59E
Bhandara India **91** D4 21 10N 79 41E
Bharatpur India **91** D5 27 14N 77 29E
Bharuch India **91** C4 21 40N 73 02E
Bhatinda India **91** C6 30 10N 74 58E
Bhavnagar India **91** C4 21 46N 72 14E
Bhilwara India **91** C5 25 23N 74 39E
Bhima r. India **91** D3 17 00N 77 00E
Bhiwandi India **91** C3 19 21N 73 08E
Bhopal India **91** D4 23 17N 77 28E
Bhubaneshwar India **91** F4 20 13N 85 50E
Bhuj India **90** B4 23 12N 69 54E
Bhusawal India **91** D4 21 01N 75 50E
BHUTAN 91 F5/G5
Białystok Poland **72** K6 53 09N 23 10E
Bibai Japan **96** D3 43 21N 141 53E
Biche Trinidad and Tobago **69** T9 10 26N 61 07W
Bida Nigeria **102** G9 9 06N 5 59E
Bidar India **91** D3 17 56N 77 35E
Biddeford Maine U.S.A. **65** L5 43 29N 70 27W
Bielefeld Germany **72** G6 52 02N 8 32E
Bièvres France **79** A2 48 45N 2 11E
Big Black r. Mississippi U.S.A. **65** H3 33 00N 90 00W
Bigelow Mountain mt. Maine U.S.A. **43** R6 45 10N 70 18W
Big Flats tn. New York U.S.A. **66** B5 42 08N 76 57W
Biggin Hill tn. United Kingdom **78** D2 51 18N 0 04E
Bighorn r. U.S.A. **64** E6 45 00N 108 00W
Bighorn Mountains U.S.A. **64** E6 44 00N 108 00W
Big Lake Maine U.S.A. **47** C2 45 10N 67 45W
Big Pine California U.S.A. **67** C3 37 10N 118 18W
Big Rapids tn. Michigan U.S.A. **42** A4 43 42N 85 31N
Big Sioux r. Minnesota/South Dakota U.S.A. **65** G5 44 00N 96 00W
Big Smokey Valley California U.S.A. **67** D4 38 52N 117 08W
Big Spring tn. Texas U.S.A. **64** F3 32 15N 101 30W
Big Sur California U.S.A. **67** B3 36 15N 121 47W
Bihar admin. India **91** F4 24 40N 86 00E
Bijapur India **91** D3 16 47N 75 48E
Bijar Iran **89** G6 35 52N 47 39E
Bikaner India **91** C5 28 01N 73 22E
Bilaspur India **91** E4 27 51N 82 00E
Bila Tserkva Ukraine **86** C4 49 49N 30 10E
Bilbao Spain **72** E4 43 15N 7 58W
Bilhorod-Dnistrovs'kyy Ukraine **86** C4 46 10N 30 19E
Bilibino Russian Federation **85** S9 68 00N 166 15E
Billings Montana U.S.A. **64** E6 45 47N 108 30W
Biloxi Mississippi U.S.A. **65** I3 30 24N 88 55W
Binghamton New York U.S.A. **66** C5 42 06N 75 55W
Bintulu Malaysia **95** F4 3 10N 113 02E
Bioko i. Equatorial Guinea **102** G8 3 00N 8 20E
Birao Central African Republic **102** J10 10 11N 22 49E

Biratnagar Nepal **91** F5 26 27N 87 17E
Birdsville Australia **106** F4 25 50S 139 20E
Birjand Iran **89** I5 32 55N 59 10E
Birkenhead United Kingdom **74** H5 53 24N 3 02W
Birkenwerder Germany **79** F2 52 42N 13 17E
Birmingham Alabama U.S.A. **65** I3 33 30N 86 55W
Birmingham United Kingdom **74** J4 52 30N 1 50W
Birnin Kebbi Nigeria **102** F10 12 30N 4 11E
Birobidzhan Russian Federation **85** P5 48 49N 132 54E
Biscay, Bay of Atlantic Ocean **72** E5 45 30N 2 50W
Biscoe Islands Antarctica **113** 66 00S 67 00W
Bishkek (Frunze) Kirgyzstan **87** L4 42 53N 74 46E
Bishop California U.S.A. **67** C3 37 22N 118 24W
Biskra Algeria **72** G2 34 50N 5 41E
Bismarck North Dakota U.S.A. **64** F6 46 50N 100 48W
Bismarck Archipelago is. Papua New Guinea **106** H9/I9 2 00S 146 00E
Bismarck, Cape Greenland **112** 77 00N 18 00W
Bismarck Sea Papua New Guinea **106** H9 3 30S 148 00E
Bissau Guinea-Bissau **102** B10 11 52N 15 39W
Bitola FYROM **72** K4 41 01N 21 21E
Bitterroot Range mts. U.S.A. **64** D6 46 00N 114 00W
Biwa-ko l. Japan **96** C2 35 20N 135 20E
Biya r. Russian Federation **87** O5 51 00N 88 00E
Biysk Russian Federation **85** K6 52 35N 85 16E
Bizerte Tunisia **102** G15 37 18N 9 52E
Blackall Australia **106** H5 24 23S 145 27E
Blackburn United Kingdom **74** I5 53 45N 2 29W
Black Lake Michigan U.S.A. **42** B6 45 30N 84 20W
Black Lake New York U.S.A. **43** L5 44 30N 75 30W
Black Mountains United Kingdom **74** H3 51 55N 3 10W
Black Point Hong Kong China **92** A2 22 24N 113 54E
Blackpool United Kingdom **74** H5 53 50N 3 03W
Black River Michigan U.S.A. **42** D4 43 25N 82 35W
Black River New York U.S.A. **43** L4 43 50N 75 35W
Black River tn. Jamaica **69** Q8 18 02N 77 52W
Black Sea Europe **86** C3/D3 43 00N 35 00E
Black Volta r. Ghana **102** E10 9 00N 2 40W
Blackwater r. Republic of Ireland **74** C4 52 10N 9 05W
Blackwell Oklahoma U.S.A. **65** G4 36 47N 97 18W
Blagoveshchensk Russian Federation **85** O6 50 19N 127 30E
Blaine Washington U.S.A. **34** H4 49 00N 122 44W
Blanchisseuse Trinidad and Tobago **69** T10 10 47N 61 20W
Blankenburg Germany **79** F2 52 35N 13 26E
Blankenfelde Germany **79** F1 52 19N 13 24E
Blantyre Malawi **103** L4 15 46S 35 00E
Blenheim N.Z. **107** B2 41 31S 173 57E
Blida Algeria **102** F15 36 30N 2 50E
Bligh Water sd. Fiji **110** T16-U16 17 00S 178 00E
Bloemfontein Republic of South Africa **103** K2 29 07S 26 14E
Bloody Foreland c. Republic of Ireland **74** C7 55 10N 8 15W
Bloomington Illinois U.S.A. **65** I5 40 29N 89 00W
Bloomington Indiana U.S.A. **65** I4 39 10N 86 31W
Bloomsburg Pennsylvania U.S.A. **66** B4 41 01N 76 27W
Bluefield West Virginia U.S.A. **65** J4 37 14N 81 17W
Bluefields Nicaragua **69** H2 12 00N 83 49W
Blue Mountains, The Jamaica **69** R8 18 00N 76 30W
Blue Nile see Bahr el Azraq
Bluff N.Z. **107** A1 46 36S 168 20E
Bluff Island Hong Kong China **92** C1 22 19N 114 21E
Blumberg Germany **79** G2 52 37N 13 28E
Blumenau Brazil **71** H7 26 55N 49 07W
Blyth United Kingdom **74** J7 55 07N 1 30W
Blythe California U.S.A. **64** D3 33 38N 114 35W
Bo Sierra Leone **102** C9 7 58N 11 45W
Boa Vista Brazil **70** E13 3 23S 55 30W
Bobigny France **79** B2 48 55N 2 28E
Bobo Dioulasso Burkina **102** E10 11 11N 4 18W
Bocas del Dragons (The Dragon's Mouths) sd. Venezuela **69** S10 10 47N 61 18W
Bodega Head c. California U.S.A. **67** A4 38 18N 123 06W
Bodélé dep. Chad **102** I11 17 00N 17 50E
Bodensee l. Switzerland **72** G5 47 40N 9 30E
Bodmin Moor United Kingdom **74** G2 50 35N 4 40W
Bodø Norway **72** H9 67 18N 14 26E
Bogalusa Louisiana U.S.A. **65** I3 30 56N 89 53W
Bogor Indonesia **95** D2 6 34S 106 45E
Bogotá Colombia **70** C13 4 38N 74 05W
Bog Walk tn. Jamaica **69** Q8 18 06N 77 01W
Bo Hai b. China **93** N6 38 30N 118 30E
Bohemian Massif hills Europe **72** H5 50 00N 15 00E
Bohnsdorf Germany **79** G1 52 23N 13 33E
Bohol i. The Philippines **95** G5 10 00N 124 00E
Bois Blanc Island Michigan U.S.A. **42** B6 45 45N 84 30W
Boise Idaho U.S.A. **64** C5 43 38N 116 12W
Boise City Oklahoma U.S.A. **64** F4 36 44N 102 31W
Bokaro Bihar India **91** F4 23 46N 85 55E
Boké Guinea **102** C10 10 57N 14 13W
Bolgatanga Ghana **102** E10 10 44N 0 53W
Bolhrad Ukraine **86** B4 45 42N 28 35E
BOLIVIA 70 E9
Bologna Italy **72** H4 44 30N 11 20E
Bolton United Kingdom **74** I5 53 35N 2 26W
Bolzano Italy **72** H5 46 30N 11 22E
Boma Congo (D.R.) **103** H6 5 50S 13 03E
Bombay see Mumbai
Bom Jesus da Lapa Brazil **70** I10 13 16S 43 23W
Bomu r. Central Africa **102** J8 4 50N 24 00E
Bonaire i. Lesser Antilles **69** K2 12 15N 68 27W
Bonaparte Archipela. is. Australia **106** D7 19 00S 126 00E
Bonasse Trinidad and Tobago **69** S9 10 05N 61 52W

Bondi Beach Australia **107** H2 33 45S 151 17E
Bondo Congo (D.R.) **102** J8 1 22N 23 54E
Bongor Chad **102** I10 10 18N 15 20E
Bonn Germany **72** G6 50 44N 7 06E
Bonners Ferry tn. Idaho U.S.A. **35** E1 48 41N 116 20W
Bonny, Bight of b. West Africa **102** G8 2 10N 7 30E
Bonthe Sierra Leone **102** C9 7 32N 12 30W
Boosaaso Somalia **102** O10 11 18N 49 10E
Bor Sudan **102** L9 6 18N 31 34E
Bordeaux France **72** E4 44 50N 0 34W
Borehamwood tn. United Kingdom **78** B3 51 40N 0 16W
Borgsdorf Germany **79** F2 52 44N 13 17E
Borisoglebsk Russian Federation **86** E5 51 23N 42 02E
Borneo i. Indonesia/Malaysia **95** D3/F5 1 00N 113 00E
Bornholm i. Denmark **72** J7 55 02N 15 00E
Borüjerd Iran **89** G5 33 55N 48 48E
Borzya Russian Federation **85** N6 50 24N 116 35E
BOSNIA-HERZEGOVINA 72 J4
Bosphorous strait Europe/Asia **72** L4 41 00N 29 00E
Bossangoa Central African Republic **102** I9 6 27N 17 21E
Bosso Niger **102** H10 13 43N 13 19E
Boston Massachusetts U.S.A. **65** L5 42 20N 71 05W
Boston United Kingdom **74** K4 52 29N 0 01W
Boston Mountains Arkansas U.S.A. **65** H4 36 00N 94 00W
Botafogo Brazil **71** Q2 22 57S 43 11W
Botanical Gardens Brazil **71** Q2 22 58S 43 14W
Botany Australia **107** G2 33 58S 151 12E
Botany Bay Australia **107** G2 34 04S 151 08E
Botany Bay National Park Australia **107** G1 34 02S 151 10E
Bothnia, Gulf of Finland/Sweden **72** K8 61 00N 19 10E
Botoşani Romania **86** B4 47 44N 26 41E
BOTSWANA 103 J3
Bötzow Germany **79** E2 52 40N 13 07E
Bouaké Côte d'Ivoire **102** D9 7 42N 5 00W
Bouar Central African Republic **102** I9 5 58N 15 35E
Bouârfa Morocco **102** E14 32 30N 1 59W
Bougainville Island Papua New Guinea **106** I8/J8 6 15S 155 00E
Bougouni Mali **102** D10 11 25N 7 28W
Boulder Colorado U.S.A. **64** E5 40 02N 105 16W
Boulevard California U.S.A. **67** D1 32 39N 116 15W
Boulogne-Billancourt France **79** A2 48 50N 2 15E
Boundary Bald Mountain Maine U.S.A. **43** R6 45 45N 70 14W
Bourem Mali **102** E11 16 59N 0 20W
Bourke Australia **106** H3 30 09S 145 59E
Bournemouth United Kingdom **74** J2 50 43N 1 54W
Bou Saâda Algeria **102** F15 35 10N 4 09E
Bousso Chad **102** I10 10 32N 16 45E
Bouvet Island Southern Ocean **109** I1 54 26S 3 24E
Bowen Australia **106** H5 20 00S 148 10E
Bowling Green Kentucky U.S.A. **65** I4 37 00N 86 29W
Bowling Green Missouri U.S.A. **65** H4 39 21N 91 11W
Bowling Green Ohio U.S.A. **42** C2 41 22N 83 40W
Bowman North Dakota U.S.A. **64** F6 46 11N 103 26W
Box Hill United Kingdom **78** B2 51 16N 0 13W
Boyne r. Republic of Ireland **74** E5 53 40N 6 35W
Boyne City Michigan U.S.A. **42** A6 45 13N 85 00W
Boyoma Falls Congo (D.R.) **102** J2 27 29N 83 28E
Bozeman Montana U.S.A. **64** D6 45 40N 111 00W
Bozoum Central African Republic **102** I9 6 16N 16 22E
Bradenton Florida U.S.A. **65** J2 27 29N 82 33W
Bradford United Kingdom **74** J5 53 48N 1 45W
Brady Texas U.S.A. **64** G3 31 08N 99 22W
Bragança Brazil **70** H12 1 02S 46 46W
Brahmapur India **91** E3 19 21N 84 51E
Brahmaputra r. India/Bangladesh **91** G5 26 40N 93 00E
Brăila Romania **72** L5 45 17N 27 58E
Brainerd Minnesota U.S.A. **65** H6 46 20N 94 10W
Brandenburgen Tor sight Germany **79** F2 52 31N 13 23E
Brasileia Brazil **70** D10 10 59S 68 45W
Brasília Brazil **70** I9 15 45S 47 57W
Braşov Romania **72** L5 45 39N 25 35E
Bratislava Slovakia **72** J5 48 10N 17 10E
Bratsk Russian Federation **85** M7 56 20N 101 50E
Bratsk Vodokhrahnilishche res. Russian Federation **85** M7 56 00N 102 00E
Bray Republic of Ireland **74** E5 53 12N 6 06W
BRAZIL 70 G10
Brazil Basin Atlantic Ocean **109** F5/6 10 00S 26 00W
Brazos r. Texas U.S.A. **65** G3 32 00N 97 00W
Brazzaville Congo **103** I4 4 14S 15 14E
Brecon Beacons mts. United Kingdom **74** H3 51 53N 3 30W
Bredy Russian Federation **87** J5 52 23N 60 16E
Bremen Germany **72** G6 53 05N 8 48E
Bremerton Washington U.S.A. **64** B6 47 34N 122 40W
Brenham Texas U.S.A. **65** G3 30 09N 96 24W
Brent United Kingdom **78** B3 51 33N 0 17W
Brentwood United Kingdom **78** E3 51 38N 0 18E
Brest Belarus **72** K6 52 08N 23 40E
Brest France **72** E5 48 23N 4 30W
Brewer Maine U.S.A. **47** C1 44 52N 68 01W
Brewerton New York U.S.A. **43** K4 43 15N 76 09W
Brewster Washington U.S.A. **34** J4 48 05N 119 50W
Brezhnev see Naberezhnyye Chelny
Bria Central African Republic **102** J9 67 32N 22 00E
Brickfield Trinidad and Tobago **69** T9 10 20N 61 18W
Bridgefield California U.S.A. **67** C4 38 14N 119 15W
Bridgeport Connecticut U.S.A. **65** L5 41 12N 73 12W
Bridgeton New Jersey U.S.A. **66** C2 39 26N 75 14W
Bridgetown Barbados **69** V12 13 06N 59 37W
Bridgwater U.K. **74** H3 51 08N 3 00W
Brie-Comte-Robert France **79** C1 48 41N 2 37E

Brieselang Germany 79 E2 52 36N 13 00E
Brigham City Utah U.S.A. 64 D5 41 30N 112 02W
Brighton United Kingdom 74 K2 50 50N 0 10W
Brighton Beach tn. New York U.S.A. 66 Z1
40 34N 73 58W
Brisbane Australia 106 I4 27 30S 153 00E
Bristol United Kingdom 74 I3 51 27N 2 35W
Bristol Bay Alaska U.S.A. 8 D4 57 30N 159 00W
Bristol Channel United Kingdom 74 H3 51 20N 3 50W
Bristol Lake California U.S.A. 67 E2 34 30N 115 40W
British Indian Ocean Territory see Chagos Archipelago
British Isles United Kingdom Europe 74
Brittany Peninsula France 72 E5 48 00N 4 00W
Brno Czech Republic 72 J5 49 13N 16 40E
Brockton Massachusetts U.S.A. 65 L5 42 06N 71 01W
Brody Ukraine 86 B5 50 05N 25 08E
Broer Ruys, Cape Greenland 112 73 30N 20 20W
Broken Hill tn. Australia 106 G3 31 57S 141 30E
Broken Ridge Indian Ocean 108 I3 30 00S 93 00E
Bromley bor. U.K. 78 D2 51 31N 0 01W
Bronx County admin. New York U.S.A. 67 Z2
40 48N 73 50W
Brookings South Dakota U.S.A. 65 G5 44 19N 96 47W
Brooklyn Maryland U.S.A. 66 B2 39 14N 76 38W
Brooklyn New York U.S.A. 66 Z1 40 41N 73 57W
Brooklyn Marine Park New York U.S.A. 66 Z1
40 35N 73 53W
Brooks Range mts. Alaska U.S.A. 8 E6/G6
67 55N 155 00W
Brookvale Australia 107 H2 33 46S 151 16E
Broome Australia 106 C6 17 58S 122 15E
Browning Montana U.S.A. 64 D6 48 33N 113 00W
Brownsville Texas U.S.A. 65 G2 25 54N 97 30W
Brownwood Texas U.S.A. 64 G3 31 42N 98 59W
BRUNEI DARUSSALAM 95 F4
Brunoy France 79 C1 48 40N 2 31E
Brunswick Georgia U.S.A. 65 J3 31 09N 81 30W
Brussels see Bruxelles
Bruxelles (Brussels) Belgium 72 F6 50 50N 4 21E
Bryan Ohio U.S.A. 42 B2 41 30N 84 34W
Bryan Texas U.S.A. 65 G3 30 41N 96 24W
Bryansk Russian Federation 84 F6 53 15N 34 09E
Bucaramanga Colombia 70 C14 7 08N 73 10W
București (Bucharest) Romania 72 L4 44 25N 26 07E
Buchanan Liberia 102 C9 5 57N 10 02W
Bucharest see București
Bucholz Germany 79 F2 51 25N 6 45E
Buckinghamshire co. U.K. 78 A3 51 50N 0 50W
Buckow Germany 79 F1 52 24N 1324E
Budapest Hungary 72 J5 47 30N 19 03E
Budjala Congo (D.R.) 102 I8 2 38N 19 48E
Buellton California U.S.A. 67 B2 34 36N 120 12W
Buenaventura Colombia 70 B13 3 54N 77 02W
Buenaventura Mexico 68 C5 29 50N 107 30W
Buena Vista Lake California U.S.A. 67 C2
35 13N 119 18W
Buenos Aires Argentina 71 F6 34 40S 58 30W
Buenos Aires, Lake Argentina/Chile 71 C3
47 00S 72 00W
Buff Bay tn. Jamaica 69 R8 18 18N 76 40W
Buffalo Wyoming U.S.A. 64 E5 44 21N 106 40W
Bug r. Ukraine 72 M5 48 00N 31 00E
Bugul'ma Russian Federation 87 G5 54 32N 52 46E
Bujumbura Burundi 103 K7 3 22S 29 19E
Bukachacha Russian Federation 85 N6 53 00N 116 58E
Bukama Congo (D.R.) 103 K6 9 13S 25 52E
Bukavu Congo (D.R.) 102 K7 2 30S 28 50E
Bukhara Uzbekistan 87 J2 39 47N 64 26E
Bukittinggi Indonesia 95 C7 0 18S 100 20E
Bukoba Tanzania 102 L7 1 19S 31 49E
Bula Indonesia 106 E9 3 07S 130 27E
Bulandshahr India 91 D5 28 30N 77 49E
Bulawayo Zimbabwe 103 K3 20 10S 28 43E
BULGARIA 72 L4
Buller r. N.Z. 107 B2 41 50S 171 35E
Bullion Mountains mts. California U.S.A. 67 D2
34 30N 116 15W
Bull Shoals Lake U.S.A. 65 H4 36 00N 93 00W
Bulun Russian Federation 85 O10 70 45N 127 20E
Bumba Congo (D.R.) 102 J8 2 10N 22 30E
Bunbury Australia 106 B3 33 20S 115 34E
Bundaberg Australia 106 I5 24 50S 152 21E
Bundeena Australia 107 G1 34 06S 151 07E
Bungo-suidō sd. Japan 98 B13 33 00N 132 30E
Bunia Congo (D.R.) 102 L8 1 33N 30 13E
Buôn Mê Thuôt Vietnam 95 D6 12 41N 108 02E
Bura Kenya 102 N7 1 06S 39 58E
Buraydah Saudi Arabia 88 F4 26 20N 43 59E
Burbank California U.S.A. 67 C2 34 10N 118 17W
Burco Somalia 102 O9 9 31N 45 33E
Burdur Turkey 88 D6 37 44N 30 17E
Bure r. United Kingdom 74 M4 52 47N 1 20E
Bureya r. Russian Federation 85 P6
52 00N 133 00E
Burgas Bulgaria 72 L4 42 30N 27 29E
Burgos Spain 72 E4 42 21N 3 41W
Burhanpur India 91 D4 21 18N 76 08E
Buri Khali India 90 J1 22 30N 88 10E
BURKINA 102 E10
Burlington Colorado U.S.A. 64 F4 39 17N 102 17W
Burlington Iowa U.S.A. 65 H5 40 50N 91 07W
Burlington New Jersey U.S.A. 66 C3 40 05N 74 51W
Burlington Vermont U.S.A. 65 L5 44 28N 73 14W
BURMA see MYANMAR
Burnie Australia 106 H1 41 03S 145 55E
Burquin China 87 O4 47 44N 86 55E
Bursa Turkey 72 L4 40 12N 29 04E

Bûr Safâga Egypt 102 L13 25 43N 33 55E
Bûr Sa'id see Port Said
Burt Lake Michigan U.S.A. 42 B6 45 30N 84 40W
Buru i. Indonesia 95 H3 3 30S 126 30E
BURUNDI 103 L7
Burwell Nebraska U.S.A. 64 G5 41 48N 99 09W
Büshehr Iran 73 R2 28 57N 50 52E
Bushey United Kingdom 78 B3 51 39N 0 22W
Busira r. Congo (D.R.) 102 I7 1 00S 20 00E
Buta Congo (D.R.) 102 K8 2 49N 24 50E
Bute i. United Kingdom 74 F5 55 50N 5 05W
Buton i. Indonesia 95 G3 5 00S 122 45E
Butovo Russian Federation 86 M1 55 30N 37 32E
Butte Montana U.S.A. 64 D6 46 00N 112 31W
Butt of Lewis c. United Kingdom 74 E10 58 30N 6 20W
Butuan The Philippines 95 G6 8 56N 125 31E
Buulobarde Somalia 102 O8 3 50N 45 33E
Büyük Ağrı Daği (Mt. Ararat) mt. Turkey 88 F6
39 44N 44 15E
Buzău Romania 86 B4 45 09N 26 49E
Byarezina r. Belarus 86 B5 54 00N 29 00E
Bydgoszcz Poland 72 J6 53 16N 18 00E
Byfleet United Kingdom 78 B2 51 21N 0 29W
Byrranga Mountains Russian Federation 85 L10
75 00N 100 00E

C

Cabanatuan The Philippines 95 G7 15 30N 120 58E
Cabimas Venezuela 70 C15 10 26N 71 27W
Cabinda admin. Angola 103 H6 5 30S 12 20E
Cabinet Mountains Montana U.S.A. 35 E1
48 15N 115 45W
Cabo Brazil 70 J11 8 16S 35 00W
Cabo Blanco c. Costa Rica 69 G1 9 36N 85 06W
Cabo Catoche c. Mexico 69 G4 21 38N 87 08W
Cabo Corrientes c. Colombia 70 B14 5 29N 77 36W
Cabo Corrientes c. Mexico 68 C4 20 25N 105 42W
Cabo de Hornos (Cape Horn) c. Chile 71 D1
56 00S 67 15W
Cabo Delgado c. Mozambique 103 N5 10 45S 40 45E
Cabo Dos Bahías c. Argentina 71 D4 45 00S 65 30W
Cabo Falso c. Mexico 68 B4 22 50N 109 55W
Cabo Gracias à Dios c. Nicaragua 69 H3 15 00N 83 10W
Cabo Guardafui see Raas Caseyr
Cabo Orange c. Brazil 70 G13 4 25N 51 32W
Cabo San Juan c. Argentina 71 E2 54 45S 63 46W
Cabo Santa Elena c. Costa Rica 69 G2 10 54N 85 56W
Cabo Virgenes c. Argentina 71 D2 52 20S 68 00W
Cáceres Brazil 70 F9 16 05S 57 40W
Cáceres Spain 72 D3 39 29N 6 18W
Cachoeira Brazil 71 Q2 22 55S 43 05W
Cachoeira do Sul Brazil 71 G7 30 03S 52 52W
Cachoeiro de Itapemirim Brazil 71 I8 20 51N 41 07W
Cadillac Michigan U.S.A. 42 A5 44 15N 85 23W
Cádiz Spain 72 D3 36 32N 6 18W
Cadiz The Philippines 95 G6 10 57N 123 18E
Cadiz Lake California U.S.A. 67 E2 34 17N 115 23W
Caen France 72 E5 49 11N 0 22W
Caernarfon United Kingdom 74 G5 53 08N 4 16W
Cagayan de Oro The Philippines 95 G5 8 29N 124 40E
Cágliari Italy 72 G3 39 13N 9 08E
Caguas Puerto Rico 69 K3 18 14N 66 04W
Caha Mountains Republic of Ireland 74 B3 51 40N 9 40W
Caicos Passage sd. West Indies 69 J4 22 20N 72 30W
Cairngorms mts. United Kingdom 74 H9 57 10N 3 30W
Cairns Australia 106 H6 16 51S 145 43E
Cairo Egypt see El Qâ'hira
Cairo Illinois U.S.A. 65 I4 37 01N 89 09W
Cajamarca Peru 70 B11 7 09S 78 32W
Cajàzeiras Brazil 70 J11 6 52S 38 31W
Caju Brazil 71 Q2 22 55S 43 13W
Calabar Nigeria 102 G8 4 56N 8 22E
Calabozo Venezuela 69 K1 8 58N 67 28W
Calais France 72 F6 50 57N 1 52E
Calais Maine U.S.A. 47 C2 45 11N 67 16W
Calama Chile 71 D8 22 30S 68 55W
Calamar Colombia 70 C15 10 16N 74 55W
Calamian Group is. The Philippines 95 G6
12 00N 120 00E
Calapan The Philippines 95 G6 13 23N 121 10E
Calçoene Brazil 70 G13 2 30N 50 55W
Calcutta India 91 F4 22 30N 88 20E
Caldwell Idaho U.S.A. 64 C5 43 39N 116 40W
Caledonia New York U.S.A. 42 J3 42 59N 77 52W
Cali Colombia 70 B13 3 24N 76 30W
Calicut India 91 D2 11 15N 75 45E
Caliente Nevada U.S.A. 64 D4 37 36N 114 31W
California state U.S.A. 67 38 30N 121 45W
California Trinidad and Tobago 69 T9 10 24N 61 28W
Calistoga California U.S.A. 67 A4 38 36N 122 35W
Callao Peru 70 B10 12 05S 77 08W
Callicoon Pennsylvania U.S.A. 66 C4 41 46N 75 03W
Calvinia Republic of South Africa 103 I1 31 25S 19 47E
Camaçari Brazil 70 J10 12 44S 38 16W
Camacupa Angola 103 I5 12 03S 17 50E
Camagüey Cuba 69 I4 21 25N 77 55W
Camanche Reservoir res. California U.S.A. 67 B4
38 15N 120 57W
CAMBODIA 95 C6/D6
Cambria California U.S.A. 67 B2 35 34N 121 05W
Cambrian Mountains United Kingdom 74 H4
52 15N 3 45W
Cambridge Jamaica 69 Q8 18 18N 77 54W
Cambridge Maryland U.S.A. 65 K4 38 34N 76 04W
Cambridge N.Z. 107 C3 37 53S 175 28E

Cambridge United Kingdom 74 L4 52 12N 0 07E
Camden New Jersey U.S.A. 66 C2 39 57N 75 06W
Cameia National Park Angola 103 J5 12 00S 22 00E
CAMEROON 102 H9
Cametá Brazil 70 H12 2 12S 49 30W
Camiri Bolivia 70 E8 20 08S 63 33W
Camocin Brazil 70 J12 2 55S 40 50W
Camorta i. Nicobar Islands 91 G1 7 30N 93 30E
Campbell New York U.S.A. 66 A5 42 14N 77 11W
Campbell Island Southern Ocean 110 G2 52 30S 169 10E
Campbeltown United Kingdom 74 F5 55 26N 5 36W
Campeche Mexico 68 F3 19 50N 90 30W
Camp Hill tn. Pennsylvania U.S.A. 66 B3 40 14N 76 56W
Campina Grande Brazil 70 J11 7 15S 35 50W
Campinas Brazil 71 H8 22 54S 47 06W
Campoalegre Colombia 70 B13 2 49N 75 19W
Campo Grande Brazil 70 G8 20 24S 54 35W
Campo Maior Brazil 70 J12 4 50S 42 12W
Campo Mourão Brazil 71 G8 24 01S 52 24W
Campos Brazil 71 I8 21 46S 41 21W
Campos Elyseos Brazil 71 P3 22 42S 43 16W
Camptonville California U.S.A. 67 B4 39 28N 121 01W
Cam Rahn Vietnam 95 D6 11 54N 109 14E
Canada Basin Arctic Ocean 112 80 00N 140 00W
Canadian r. U.S.A. 64 F4 35 00N 104 00W
Canakkale Turkey 88 C7 40 09N 26 25E
Cananea Mexico 68 B6 30 59N 110 20W
Canary Basin Atlantic Ocean 109 E9/F9 26 20N 30 00W
Canary Islands Spain 102 B13 28 30N 15 10W
Canaveral, Cape Florida U.S.A. 65 J2 28 28N 80 28W
Canberra Australia 106 H2 35 18S 149 08E
Cancún Mexico 69 G4 21 09N 86 45W
Canfield Ohio U.S.A. 42 D2 41 02N 80 47W
Cangamba Angola 103 I5 13 40S 19 47E
Cangrejos Point Trinidad and Tobago 69 T9
10 25N 61 29W
Cangzhou China 93 N6 38 19N 116 54E
Canisteo New York U.S.A. 42 J3 42 16N 77 36W
Cannanore India 91 D2 11 53N 75 23E
Cannonsville Reservoir New York U.S.A. 66 C5
42 05N 75 20W
Canôas Brazil 71 G7 28 55S 51 10W
Cantabrian Mountains Spain 72 D4 43 00N 5 30W
Cantaro Trinidad and Tobago 69 T10 10 42N 61 28W
Canterbury Australia 107 G2 33 55S 151 07E
Canterbury United Kingdom 74 M3 51 17N 1 05E
Canterbury Bight N.Z. 107 B2 44 00S 172 00E
Canterbury Plains N.Z. 107 B2 43 45S 171 56E
Can Tho Vietnam 95 D5 10 03N 105 46E
Canton New York U.S.A. 43 L5 44 35N 75 11W
Canton Ohio U.S.A. 65 J5 40 48N 81 23W
Canton see Guangzhou
Canton East Pennsylvania U.S.A. 43 K2 41 38N 76 50W
Caparo Trinidad and Tobago 69 T10 10 31N 61 25W
Caparo r. Trinidad and Tobago 69 T9 10 31N 61 25W
Cap Blanc see Ras Nouadhibou
Cap d'Ambre c. Madagascar 103 O5 12 00S 49 15E
Cape Basin Atlantic Ocean 109 I3 36 00S 6 00E
Cape Coast tn. Ghana 102 E9 5 10N 1 13W
Cape Cod Bay U.S.A. 66 K4 41 00N 70 00W
Cape Girardeau tn. Missouri U.S.A. 65 I4 37 19N 89 31W
Cape May tn. New Jersey U.S.A. 66 D1 38 56N 74 54W
Cape May Court House tn. New Jersey U.S.A. 66 D2
39 05N 74 50W
Cape Rise Atlantic Ocean 109 J2 42 00S 11 00E
Cape Town Republic of South Africa 103 I1
33 56S 18 28E
Cape Verde Basin Atlantic Ocean 109 E8 11 00N 35 00W
Cape Verde Islands Atlantic Ocean 109 F8
16 00N 24 00W
Cape York Peninsula Australia 106 G7 12 30S 142 30E
Cap-Haïtien Haiti 69 J3 19 47N 72 17W
Capitán Arturo Prat r.s. Antarctica 113 62 30S 59 41W
Capricorn Channel Australia 106 I5 23 00S 152 30E
Caprivi Strip Namibia 103 J4 17 30S 27 50E
Cap Ste. Marie c. Madagascar 103 O2 25 34S 45 10E
Cap Vert c. Senegal 102 B10 14 43N 17 33W
Caracas Venezuela 70 D15 10 35N 66 56W
Caratinga Brazil 70 I9 19 50S 42 06W
Caravelas Brazil 70 J9 17 45S 39 15W
Carbondale Pennsylvania U.S.A. 43 L2 41 35N 75 31W
Cardamom Hills India 91 D1 9 50N 77 00E
Cárdenas Mexico 68 E4 22 00N 99 41W
Cardiff United Kingdom 74 H3 51 30N 3 13W
Cardigan Bay United Kingdom 74 G4 52 30N 4 30W
Cargados Carajos Shoals Indian Ocean 108 E5
16 00S 60 00E
Cariacica Brazil 70 I9 20 15S 40 23W
Caribbean Sea Central America 69 I3 15 00N 75 00W
Caribou Maine U.S.A. 47 C2 46 52N 68 01W
Caringbah Australia 107 G1 34 03S 151 07E
Caripito Venezuela 70 E15 10 07N 63 07W
Carlisle Pennsylvania U.S.A. 66 A3 40 12N 77 12W
Carlisle United Kingdom 74 I6 54 54N 2 55W
Carlisle Bay Barbados 69 V12 13 05N 59 37W
Carlsbad California U.S.A. 67 D1 33 09N 117 20W
Carlsbad New Mexico U.S.A. 64 F3 32 25N 104 14W
Carlsberg Ridge Indian Ocean 108 E7/F6 5 00N 65 00E
Carmarthen United Kingdom 74 G3 51 51N 4 20W
Carmen Colombia 70 B14 9 46N 75 06W
Carnegie, Lake Australia 106 C4 27 00S 124 00E
Carnegie Ridge Pacific Ocean 111 R7 1 30S 95 00W
Car Nicobar i. Nicobar Islands 91 G1 9 00N 93 00E
Carnot Central African Republic 102 I8 4 59N 15 56E
Carnsore Point Republic of Ireland 74 E3 52 10N 6 22W
Caro Michigan U.S.A. 36 C4 43 29N 83 24W

Carolina Brazil 70 H11 7 20S 47 25W
Caroline Island Pacific Ocean 111 L7 10 00S 150 00W
Caroline Islands Pacific Ocean 110 E8/F8 8 00N 148 00E
Carona Arena Dam Trinidad and Tobago 69 T10 10 30N 61 15W
Caroni Trinidad and Tobago 69 T10 10 36N 61 22W
Caroni r. Trinidad and Tobago 69 T10 10 35N 61 20W
Carpathians mts. Europe 72 K5/L5 49 00N 22 00E
Carpentaria, Gulf of Australia 106 F7/G7 13 30S 138 00E
Carrauntoohill mt. Republic of Ireland 74 B3 52 00N 9 45W
Carson r. California U.S.A. 67 C4 39 15N 119 36W
Carson City Nevada U.S.A. 64 C4 39 10N 119 46W
Carson Sink dep. California U.S.A. 67 C4 39 45N 118 33W
Cartagena Colombia 70 B15 10 24N 75 33W
Cartagena Spain 72 E3 37 36N 0 59W
Caruarú Brazil 70 J11 8 15S 35 55W
Carúpano Venezuela 70 E15 10 39N 63 14W
Carvers California U.S.A. 67 D4 38 49N 117 12W
Casablanca (Dar el Beida) Morocco 102 D1 33 39N 7 35W
Casa Grande Arizona U.S.A. 64 D3 32 52N 111 46W
Cascade Range mts. North America 64 B5/6
48 00N 121 00W
Cascadura Brazil 71 P2 22 53S 43 21W
Cascavel Brazil 70 J12 4 10S 38 15W
Casey r.s. Antarctica 113 66 18S 110 32E
Casper Wyoming U.S.A. 64 E5 42 50N 106 20W
Caspian Lowlands Kirgyzstan 86 F4/G4 48 00N 50 00E
Caspian Sea Asia 86 G3 41 00N 50 00E
Cass River Michigan U.S.A. 42 C4 43 30N 83 30W
Castlebar Republic of Ireland 74 B5 53 52N 9 17W
Castle Hill tn. Australia 107 F3 33 44S 150 59E
Castle Mountain mt. California U.S.A. 67 B2
35 57N 120 20W
Castle Peak mt. Hong Kong China 92 A2 22 23N 113 57E
Castries St. Lucia 69 L2 14 02N 60 59W
Catamarca Argentina 71 D7 28 28S 65 46W
Catánia Italy 72 J3 37 31N 15 06E
Catanzaro Italy 88 A6 38 54N 16 36E
Cataract, 1st (R. Nile) Egypt 102 L12 24 00N 32 45E
Cataract, 2nd (R. Nile) Sudan 102 L12 21 40N 31 12E
Cataract, 3rd (R. Nile) Sudan 102 L11 19 45N 30 25E
Cataract, 4th (R. Nile) Sudan 102 L11 18 40N 32 10E
Cataract, 5th (R. Nile) Sudan 102 L11 18 25N 33 52E
Caterham United Kingdom 78 C2 51 17N 0 04W
Cathedral sight Brazil 71 Q2 22 55S 43 11W
Cat Island The Bahamas 69 I4 24 30N 75 30W
Catskill Mountains New York U.S.A. 65 K5 42 10N 74 20W
Cattaraugus New York U.S.A. 42 H3 42 20N 78 54W
Caucaia Brazil 70 J12 3 44S 38 45W
Caucasus Mountains Eurasia 86 E3 43 00N 43 00E
Caxias Brazil 70 I12 4 53N 43 20W
Caxias do Sul Brazil 71 G7 29 14S 51 10W
Cayenne French Guiana 70 G13 4 55N 52 18W
Cayman Trench Caribbean Sea 111 R9 15 00N 80 00W
Ceará admin. Brazil 70 I11/J11 5 30S 40 00W
Cebu The Philippines 95 G6 10 17N 123 56E
Cedar r. Iowa U.S.A. 65 H5 42 00N 92 00W
Cedar City Utah U.S.A. 64 D4 37 40N 113 04W
Cedar Creek r. North Dakota U.S.A. 64 F6 46 00N 102 00W
Cedar Rapids tn. Iowa U.S.A. 65 H5 41 59N 91 39W
Cedros i. Mexico 68 A5 28 00N 115 00W
Cedros Bay Trinidad and Tobago 69 S9 10 08N 61 50W
Cedros Point Trinidad and Tobago 69 S9 10 07N 61 49W
Ceduna Australia 106 E3 32 07S 133 42E
Ceerigaabo Somalia 102 O10 10 40N 47 20E
Celaya Mexico 68 D4 20 32N 100 48W
Celebes Sea Indonesia 95 G4 3 00N 122 00E
Celtic Sea British Isles 74 E3 51 00N 7 00W
CENTRAL AFRICAN REPUBLIC 102 I9
Central Cordilleras hills Spain 72 D4 41 00N 5 00W
Central Pacific Basin Pacific Ocean 110 I9 10 00N 177 00W
Central Park New York U.S.A. 66 Z2 40 47N 73 58W
Central Plain Ireland 72 D6 53 30N 8 00W
Central Siberian Plateau Russian Federation 85 M9/N8
65 00N 110 00E
Centreville Maryland U.S.A. 66 B2 39 02N 76 05W
Centro Brazil 71 Q2 22 53S 43 07W
Ceram see Seram
Cerro de Pasco Peru 70 B10 10 43S 76 15W
Ceyhan r. Turkey 88 E6 37 45N 36 45E
Chacachacaré i. Trinidad and Tobago 69 S10
10 41N 61 45W
Chachapoyas Peru 70 B11 6 13S 77 54W
CHAD 102 I10
Chad, Lake West Africa 102 H10 13 50N 14 00E
Chagai Hills Afghanistan/Pakistan 89 J4 29 30N 63 00E
Chaghcharān Afghanistan 89 K5 34 31N 65 15E
Chagos Archipelago (British Indian Ocean Territory)
Indian Ocean 108 G6 6 00S 73 00E
Chagos-Laccadive Ridge Indian Ocean 108 G6/G7
0 00 75 00E
Chaguanas Trinidad and Tobago 69 T10 10 31N 61 25W
Chaguaramas Trinidad and Tobago 69 S10
10 41N 61 38W
Châh Bahâr Iran 89 J4 25 16N 60 41E
Chaine des Mitumba (Mitumba Mountains) mts.
Congo (D.R.) 103 K5 7 30S 27 30E
Chai Wan Hong Kong China 92 C1 22 15N 114 14E
Chai Wan Kok Hong Kong China 92 B2 22 23N 114 06E
Chalfont St. Peter United Kingdom 78 A3 51 37N 0 33W
Chalkyitsik Alaska U.S.A. 50 C4 66 38N 143 49W
Challenger Fracture Zone Pacific Ocean 111 P4/R4
33 30S 100 00W
Chaman Pakistan 90 B6 30 55N 66 27E
Chambal r. India 91 D5 26 00N 77 00E
Chamberlain Lake Maine U.S.A. 47 B4 46 15N 69 20W
Chamo, Lake Ethiopia 102 M9 5 55N 37 35E
Champaign Illinois U.S.A. 65 I4 40 07N 88 14W

Champdani India 108 K3 22 48N 88 21E
Champigny France 79 C2 48 49N 2 32E
Champlain New York U.S.A. 43 N5 44 59N 73 29W
Champotón Mexico 68 F3 19 20N 90 43W
Champs-sur-Marne France 79 C2 48 51N 2 35E
Chañaral Chile 71 C7 26 23S 70 40W
Chandalar River Alaska U.S.A. 50 B4 66 40N 148 30W
Chandigarh India 91 D6 30 44N 76 54E
Chandnagar India 108 K3 22 52N 88 22E
Chandrapur India 91 D3 19 58N 79 21E
Changara Mozambique 103 L4 16 50S 33 17E
Chang Cheng see Great Wall
Changde China 93 M4 29 03N 111 35E
Chang-hua Taiwan 94 G7 24 06N 120 31E
Chang Jiang (Yangtze) r. China 93 L5 31 00N 110 00E
Changsha China 93 M4 28 10N 113 00E
Changxindian China 94 A1 39 50N 116 12E
Changzhi China 93 M6 36 05N 113 12E
Changzhou China 93 O5 31 39N 120 45E
Chaniá (Khaniá) Greece 72 K3 35 31N 24 01E
Channel Islands British Isles 74 I1 49 30N 2 30W
Channel Islands California U.S.A. 67 C1 33 15N 119 45W
Channel Islands National Park California U.S.A. 67 B2
34 04N 120 00W
Chao'an China 93 N3 23 42N 116 36E
Chaoyang China 93 O7 41 36N 120 25E
Chapada Diamantina mts. Brazil 70 I10 12 30S 42 30W
Chapecó Brazil 71 G7 27 14S 52 41W
Chapelton Jamaica 69 Q8 18 05N 77 16W
Chardzhev (Chardzhou) Turkmenistan 87 J2
39 09N 63 34E
Chardzhou see Chardzhev
Chari r. Chad/Sudan 102 I10 11 00N 16 00E
Chärikär Afghanistan 89 K5 35 01N 69 11E
Charleston South Carolina U.S.A. 65 K3 32 48N 79 58W
Charleston West Virginia U.S.A. 65 J4 38 23N 81 40W
Charleston Peak mt. California U.S.A. 67 E3 36 16N 115 41W
Charleville Australia 106 H4 26 25S 146 13E
Charlevoix Michigan U.S.A. 42 A6 45 19N 85 16W
Charlotte Michigan U.S.A. 42 B3 42 33N 84 50W
Charlotte North Carolina U.S.A. 65 J4 35 03N 80 50W
Charlottenburg Germany 79 E2 52 32N 13 18E
Charlottesville Virginia U.S.A. 65 K4 38 02N 78 29W
Charters Towers Australia 106 H5 20 02S 146 20E
Chateaugay New York U.S.A. 43 M5 44 55N 74 06W
Chatham Alaska U.S.A. 34 B3 57 30N 135 00W
Chatham Islands Pacific Ocean 110 I3 44 00S 176 30W
Chatham Rise Pacific Ocean 110 H3 45 00S 175 00E
Chatham Strait sd. Alaska U.S.A. 34 B3 57 45N 134 50W
Chatou France 79 A2 48 54N 2 10E
Chatswood Australia 107 G2 33 48S 151 11E
Chattanooga Tennessee U.S.A. 65 I4 35 02N 85 18W
Chautauqua Lake New York U.S.A. 42 G3 42 12N 79 30W
Chazy New York U.S.A. 43 N5 44 53N 73 29W
Cheboksary Russian Federation 84 G7 56 08N 47 12E
Cheboygan Michigan U.S.A. 42 B6 45 40N 84 28W
Cheju do (Quelpart) i. South Korea 93 P5 33 00N 126 30E
Chek Chue (Stanley) Hong Kong China 92 C1 22 12N 114 12E
Chek Keng Hong Kong China 92 D2 22 25N 114 21E
Chek Lap Kok i. Hong Kong China 92 A1 22 18N 113 56E
Chelles France 79 C2 48 53N 2 53E
Chelmsford United Kingdom 74 L3 51 44N 0 28E
Chelsea Michigan U.S.A. 42 B3 42 19N 84 01W
Chelsea United Kingdom 78 C2 51 29N 0 10W
Cheltenham United Kingdom 74 I3 51 54N 2 04W
Chelyabinsk Russian Federation 84 I5 55 12N 61 25E
Chemnitz Germany 72 H6 50 50N 12 55E
Chemung River New York U.S.A. 43 K3 42 05N 76 55W
Chenab r. Pakistan 91 D7 30 30N 71 30E
Chengde China 93 N7 40 59N 117 52E
Chengdu China 93 K5 30 37N 104 06E
Ch'eng-kung Taiwan 94 H6 23 06N 121 22E
Chennai (Madras) India 91 E2 13 05N 80 18E
Cheremkhovo Russian Federation 85 M6 53 08N 103 01E
Cheremuski Russian Federation 86 M1 55 38N 37 38E
Cherepovets Russian Federation 84 F7 59 09N 37 50E
Cherkasy Ukraine 72 M5 49 27N 32 04E
Cherkessk Russian Federation 86 E3 44 14N 42 05E
Cherkizovsky Russian Federation 86 M2 55 50N 37 44E
Chernihiv Ukraine 72 M6 51 30N 31 18E
Chernivtsi Ukraine 72 L5 48 19N 25 52E
Chernobyl' see Chornobyl'
Chernogorsk Russian Federation 87 P5 53 48N 91 16E
Cherokee Iowa U.S.A. 65 G5 42 45N 95 32W
Cherrapunji Meghalaya India 91 G5 25 16N 91 42E
Cherry Creek California U.S.A. 67 E4 39 54N 114 53W
Cherskiy Range mts. Russian Federation 85 P9/Q8
66 30N 140 00E
Chertanovo Russian Federation 86 M1 55 34N 37 35E
Chertsey United Kingdom 78 A2 51 23N 0 30W
Chesaning Michigan U.S.A. 42 B4 43 12N 84 08W
Chesapeake Virginia U.S.A. 65 K4 36 45N 76 15W
Chesapeake Bay U.S.A. 65 K4 39 00N 76 20W
Chesham United Kingdom 78 A3 51 43N 0 02W
Chester Maryland U.S.A. 66 B1 38 59N 76 16W
Chester Pennsylvania U.S.A. 66 C2 39 50N 75 23W
Chester United Kingdom 74 I5 53 12N 2 54W
Chester River Maryland U.S.A. 66 C2 39 25N 76 00W
Chesterfield United Kingdom 74 J5 53 15N 1 25W
Chestertown Maryland U.S.A. 66 B1 39 13N 76 04W
Chesuncook Lake Maine U.S.A. 43 S7 46 00N 69 22W
Chetlat Island India 91 C2 11 46N 72 50E
Chetumal Mexico 68 G3 18 30N 88 17W
Cheung Chau i. Hong Kong China 92 B1 22 10N 114 00E
Cheung Sha Hong Kong China 92 A1 22 14N 113 57E
Cheung Sha Wan Hong Kong China 92 B2 22 20N 114 08E
Chevak Alaska U.S.A. 8 B5 63 33N 165 36W
Cheviot Hills United Kingdom 74 I7 55 25N 2 20W

Chevreuse France 79 A1 48 43N 2 05E
Chewelan Washington U.S.A. 35 E1 48 17N 117 44W
Cheyenne r. U.S.A. 64 F5 44 00N 102 00W
Cheyenne Wyoming U.S.A. 64 F5 41 08N 104 50W
Chhapra India 91 E5 25 46N 84 44E
Chia-i Taiwan 94 G6 23 09N 120 11E
Chiang Mai Thailand 93 J2 18 48N 98 59E
Chiang Rai Thailand 93 J2 19 56N 99 51E
Chiba pref. Japan 97 C4 35 30N 140 15E
Chiba Japan 96 D2 35 38N 140 07E
Chicago Illinois U.S.A. 65 I5 41 50N 87 45W
Chicapa r. Angola/Congo (D.R.) 103 J6 8 00S 20 30E
Chichagof Island Alaska U.S.A. 8 H4 57 40N 136 00W
Chickasha Oklahoma U.S.A. 65 G4 35 03N 97 57W
Chicken Alaska U.S.A. 50 C3 64 04N 142 00W
Chiclayo Peru 70 B11 6 47S 79 47W
Chignik Alaska U.S.A. 8 D4 56 18N 158 27W
Chigwell United Kingdom 78 D3 51 37N 0 05E
Chihuahua Mexico 68 C5 28 40N 106 06W
CHILE 71 C5/C8
Chile Basin Pacific Ocean 111 R4 36 00S 84 00W
Chile Chico Chile 71 C3 46 34S 71 44W
Chile Rise Pacific Ocean 111 Q4 40 00S 92 00W
Chillán Chile 71 C5 36 37S 72 10W
Chilpancingo Mexico 68 E3 17 33N 99 30W
Chiltern Hills United Kingdom 74 K3 51 40N 1 00W
Chilumba Malawi 103 L5 10 25S 34 18E
Chi-lung Taiwan 94 H8 25 10N 121 43E
Chi Ma Wan Peninsula Hong Kong China 92 A1 22 14N 113 58E
Chimborazo mt. Ecuador 70 B12 1 29S 78 52W
Chimbote Peru 70 B11 9 04S 78 34W
Chi'mei Hsü i. Taiwan 94 F6 23 11N 119 25E
Chimen Tao (Quemoy) i. China 94 E7 24 26N 118 24E
Chimkent see Shymkent
CHINA 92
China Lake California U.S.A. 67 D2 35 45N 117 36W
Chinandega Nicaragua 68 G2 12 35N 87 10W
Chincha Alta Peru 70 B10 13 25S 76 07W
Chinchilla Australia 106 I4 26 42S 150 35E
Chinde Mozambique 103 M4 18 35S 36 28E
Chindwin r. Myanmar 91 H5 25 00N 95 00E
Chinese Turkestan geog. reg. China 92 E6/F7
40 00N 80 00E
Chingola Zambia 103 K5 12 31S 27 53E
Ch'ing-shui Taiwan 94 G7 24 12N 120 33E
Chinju South Korea 93 P6 35 10N 128 06E
Chinko r. Central African Republic 102 J9 5 00N 24 00E
Chinmen Taiwan 94 E7 24 30N 118 20E
Chi-pei Tao i. Taiwan 94 F6 23 44N 119 36E
Chippewa River Michigan U.S.A. 42 B4 43 36N 84 45W
Chipping Norton, Lake Australia 107 F2 33 54S 150 56E
Chiquimula Guatemala 68 G2 14 48N 89 32W
Chirchik Uzbekistan 87 K3 41 28N 69 31E
Ch'i-shan Taiwan 94 G5 22 44N 120 31E
Chisinău (Kishinev) Moldova 72 L5 47 00N 28 50E
Chita Russian Federation 85 N6 52 03N 113 35E
Chitembo Angola 103 I5 13 33S 16 47E
Chitpur India 108 K2 22 36N 88 23E
Chitral Pakistan 91 C7 35 52N 71 58E
Chittagong Bangladesh 91 G4 22 20N 91 48E
Chittoor India 91 D2 13 13N 79 06E
Chitungwiza Zimbabwe 103 L4 18 00S 31 06E
Chocolate Mountains California U.S.A. 67 E1 33 30N 115 30W
Choiseul i. Solomon Islands 106 J8 7 00S 157 00E
Choisy-le-Roi France 79 B2 48 49N 2 29E
Cholame California U.S.A. 67 B2 35 44N 120 17W
Choluteca Honduras 68 G2 13 15N 87 10W
Chone Ecuador 70 A12 0 44S 80 04W
Ch'ŏngjin North Korea 93 P7 41 50N 129 55E
Ch'ŏngju South Korea 93 P6 36 39N 127 27E
Chongqing China 93 L4 29 30N 106 35E
Chŏnju South Korea 93 P6 35 50N 127 09E
Chornobyl' (Chernobyl') Ukraine 86 C5 51 17N 30 15E
Chott El Jerid salt l. Tunisia 102 G14 30 00N 9 00E
Chott Melrhir salt l. Algeria 102 F14 34 00N 6 10E
Chowchilla California U.S.A. 67 B3 37 07N 120 14W
Choybalsan Mongolia 93 M8 48 02N 114 32E
Christchurch N.Z. 107 B2 43 32S 172 38E
Christiana Jamaica 69 Q8 18 13N 77 29
Christianshåb see Qasigiannguit
Christmas Island Indian Ocean 95 D1 10 28S 105 35E
Chu Kazakhstan 87 L3 43 34N 73 44E
Chu r. Asia 87 L3 44 30N 70 30E
Chudskoye Ozero (Peipsi Järve, Lake Peipus) l.
Russian Federation 86 B4 58 40N 27 30E
Chugach Mountains mts. Alaska U.S.A. 8 G5 61 40N 145 00W
Chūgoku-sanchi mts. Japan 96 B2 35 00N 133 00E
Chukchi Sea Arctic Ocean 112 70 00N 170 00W
Chukotsk Peninsula Russian Federation 85 U9
66 00N 175 00W
Chukotsk Range mts. Russian Federation 85 T9
68 00N 175 00E
Chula Vista California U.S.A. 67 D1 32 36N 117 05W
Chulucanas Peru 70 A11 5 08S 80 10W
Chulym r. Russian Federation 85 K7 57 30N 87 30E
Chumphon Thailand 95 B6 10 30N 99 11E
Chuna r. Russian Federation 85 L7 57 30N 98 00E
Ch'unch'ŏn South Korea 93 P6 37 56N 127 40E
Chung-ho Taiwan 94 H7 25 00N 121 00E
Chung Hom Kok Hong Kong China 92 C1 22 13N 114 12E
Chung-li Taiwan 94 H7 24 55N 121 08E
Chung Yang Shanmo mts. Taiwan 94 G5-H7
23 00N 120 00E
Chunya r. Russian Federation 85 M8 62 00N 101 00E
Chupara Point Trinidad and Tobago 69 T10 10 48N 61 22W
Churu India 91 C5 28 18N 75 00E
Churuguara Venezuela 69 K2 10 52N 69 35W

Chusovaya r. Russian Federation 87 H6 58 00N 59 00E
Cicilian Gates pass Turkey 88 D6 37 17N 34 46E
Cidade de Deus Brazil 71 P2 22 58S 43 20W
Cidade Nova Brazil 71 Q2 22 55S 43 12W
Ciego de Avila Cuba 69 I4 21 51N 78 47W
Ciénaga Colombia 70 C15 11 01N 74 15W
Cienfuegos Cuba 69 H4 22 10N 80 27W
Cilo Dağı mt. Turkey 86 E2 37 30N 44 00E
Cima California U.S.A. 67 E2 35 14N 115 30W
Cimarron r. U.S.A. 65 G4 36 00N 98 00W
Cincinnati Ohio U.S.A. 65 J4 39 10N 83 30W
Circle Alaska U.S.A. 50 C4 65 49N 144 11W
Cirebon Indonesia 95 D2 6 46S 108 33E
Cisco Texas U.S.A. 64 G3 32 23N 98 59W
Cisneros Colombia 70 B14 6 32N 75 04W
City Island New York U.S.A. 67 Z2 40 50N 73 46W
Ciudad Acuña Mexico 68 D5 29 20N 100 58W
Ciudad Bolívar Venezuela 70 E14 8 06N 63 36W
Ciudad Camargo Mexico 68 C5 27 41N 105 10W
Ciudad del Carmen Mexico 68 F3 18 38N 91 50W
Ciudad del Este (Presidente Stroessner) Paraguay 71 G7
25 32N 54 34W
Ciudad Guayana Venezuela 70 E14 8 22N 62 37W
Ciudad Juárez Mexico 68 C6 31 42N 106 29W
Ciudad Lerdo Mexico 68 D5 25 34N 103 30W
Ciudad Madero Mexico 68 E4 22 19N 97 50W
Ciudad Manté Mexico 68 E4 22 44N 98 59W
Ciudad Obregón Mexico 68 C5 27 28N 109 59W
Ciudad Victoria Mexico 68 E4 23 43N 99 10W
Civil Lines India 108 L4 28 40N 77 13E
Cizre Turkey 88 F6 37 21N 42 11E
Clan Alpine Mountains California U.S.A. 67 D4
39 34N 117 53W
Clare Michigan U.S.A. 42 B4 43 49N 84 47W
Clare r. Republic of Ireland 74 C5 53 26N 8 55W
Clarence Island British Isles South Shetland Islands
71 G0 61 10S 54 00W
Clarence Strait sd. Alaska U.S.A. 34 B3 56 00N 133 30W
Clarendon Pennsylvania U.S.A. 42 G2 41 46N 79 06W
Clarion Fracture Zone Pacific Ocean 111 M9/N9
18 00N 130 00W
Clark Fork r. Montana U.S.A. 35 E1 43 00N 115 55W
Clark Hill Lake U.S.A. 65 J3 33 00N 82 00W
Clarksburg West Virginia U.S.A. 65 J4 39 16N 80 22W
Clarks Ferry Pennsylvania U.S.A. 66 B3 40 23N 77 00W
Clarksville Tennessee U.S.A. 65 I4 36 31N 87 21W
Clayton New York U.S.A. 43 K5 44 15N 76 06W
Clear, Cape Republic of Ireland 74 B3 51 30N 9 30W
Clear Lake California U.S.A. 67 A4 39 04N 122 48W
Clearwater Florida U.S.A. 65 J2 27 57N 82 48W
Clearwater r. Idaho U.S.A. 64 C6 46 00N 116 00W
Clermont-Ferrand France 72 F5 45 47N 3 05E
Cleveland New York U.S.A. 45 J5 43 15N 75 50W
Cleveland Ohio U.S.A. 42 E2 41 30N 81 41W
Cleveland Peninsula Alaska U.S.A. 34 B3 55 30N 132 00W
Clichy France 79 B2 48 54N 2 19E
Clinton Iowa U.S.A. 65 H5 41 51N 90 12W
Clinton Oklahoma U.S.A. 64 G4 35 32N 98 59W
Clipperton Fracture Zone Pacific Ocean 111 N8/O8
10 00N 120 00W
Clipperton Island Pacific Ocean 111 P9 10 20N 109 13W
Cloncurry Australia 106 G5 20 41S 140 30E
Clonmel Republic of Ireland 74 D4 52 21N 7 42W
Cloverdale California U.S.A. 67 A4 38 47N 123 01W
Clovis California U.S.A. 67 C3 36 47N 119 43W
Clovis New Mexico U.S.A. 64 F3 34 14N 103 13W
Cluj-Napoca Romania 72 K5 46 47N 23 37E
Clutha r. N.Z. 107 A1 46 00S 169 30E
Clyde Ohio U.S.A. 42 D2 41 17N 82 58W
Clyde r. United Kingdom 74 G7 55 50N 4 25W
Clydebank United Kingdom 74 G7 55 54N 4 24W
Coahuila admin. Mexico 64 F2 26 00N 103 00W
Coaldale California U.S.A. 67 D4 38 02N 117 52W
Coalinga California U.S.A. 67 B3 36 08N 120 22W
Coari Brazil 70 E12 4 08S 63 07W
Coast Range mts. California U.S.A. 67 B3 37 00N 121 20W
Coatepec Mexico 68 E3 19 29N 96 59W
Coatesville Pennsylvania U.S.A. 66 C2 39 59N 75 50W
Coats Land geog. reg. Antarctica 113 77 00S 25 00W
Coatzacoalcos (Puerto Mexico) Mexico 68 F3
18 10N 94 25W
Cobán Guatemala 68 F3 15 28N 90 20W
Cobar Australia 106 H3 31 32S 145 51E
Cobham United Kingdom 78 B2 51 20N 0 24W
Cobija Bolivia 70 D10 11 01S 68 45W
Cochabamba Bolivia 70 D9 17 26S 66 10W
Cochin India 91 D1 9 56N 76 15E
Cochrane Chile 71 C3 47 16S 72 33W
Cochranton Pennsylvania U.S.A. 42 F2 41 32N 80 03W
Cocos Basin Indian Ocean 108 I6 5 00S 96 00E
Cocos Bay Trinidad and Tobago 69 T9/U9 10 25N 61 05W
Cocos Islands see Isla del Coco
Cocos Ridge Pacific Ocean 111 R8 4 00N 90 00W
Cod, Cape Massachusetts U.S.A. 65 M5 42 05N 70 12W
Codajás Brazil 70 E12 3 55S 62 00W
Codó Brazil 70 I12 4 28S 43 51W
Codrington Antigua and Barbuda 69 L3 17 43N 61 49W
Coelhoto Rocha Brazil 71 P2 22 46S 43 05W
Coeur d'Alene Idaho U.S.A. 64 C6 47 40N 116 46W
Cohocton River New York U.S.A. 66 A5 42 20N 77 20W
Coihaique Chile 71 C3 45 35S 72 08W
Coimbatore India 91 D2 11 00N 76 57E
Coimbra Portugal 72 D4 40 12N 8 25W
Colbeck, Cape Antarctica 113 77 00S 158 00W
Colchester United Kingdom 74 L3 51 54N 0 54E
Cold Springs California U.S.A. 67 D4 39 22N 117 53W
Coldwater Michigan U.S.A. 42 A2 41 57N 85 01W

Coleen River Alaska U.S.A. 50 C4 67 30N 142 30W
Coleraine United Kingdom 74 E7 55 08N 6 40W
Colima Mexico 68 D3 19 14N 103 41W
Coll i. United Kingdom 74 E8 56 40N 6 35W
College Alaska U.S.A. 8 F5 64 54N 147 55W
Collie Australia 106 B3 33 20S 116 06E
Collingwood N.Z. 107 B2 40 41S 172 41E
Cologne see Köln
Colombes France 79 B2 48 55N 2 15E
COLOMBIA 70 C13
Colombo Sri Lanka 91 D1 6 55N 79 52E
Colón Panama 69 I1 9 21N 79 54W
Colonsay i. United Kingdom 74 E8 56 05N 6 15W
Colorado r. Texas U.S.A. 65 G2 29 00N 96 00W
Colorado state U.S.A. 64 E4 39 00N 106 00W
Colorado Desert California U.S.A. 67 D1 33 18N 116 00W
Colorado Plateau Arizona U.S.A. 64 D4 36 00N 111 00W
Colorado River Aqueduct California U.S.A. 67 D1
Colorado Springs tn. Colorado U.S.A. 64 F4 38 50N 104 50W
Columbia Missouri U.S.A. 65 H4 38 58N 92 20W
Columbia Pennsylvania U.S.A. 66 B3 40 02N 76 30W
Columbia r. North America 64 B6 46 00N 120 00W
Columbia South Carolina U.S.A. 65 J3 34 00N 81 00W
Columbus Georgia U.S.A. 65 J3 32 28N 84 59W
Columbus Indiana U.S.A. 65 I4 39 12N 85 57W
Columbus Mississippi U.S.A. 65 I3 33 30N 88 27W
Columbus Nebraska U.S.A. 65 G5 41 27N 97 21W
Columbus Ohio U.S.A. 65 J5 39 59N 83 03W
Columbus Channel Trinidad and Tobago/Venezuela
69 S9/T9 10 00N 61 45W
Columbus Salt Marsh California U.S.A. 67 D4
38 06N 117 57W
Colville r. Alaska U.S.A. 8 D6 69 00N 158 00W
Colville Washington U.S.A. 35 E1 48 33N 117 55W
Colvocoresses Bay Antarctica 113 66 00S 120 00E
Colwyn Bay tn. United Kingdom 74 H5 53 18N 3 43W
Comilla Bangladesh 91 G4 23 28N 91 10E
Comitán Mexico 68 F3 16 18N 92 09W
Commandante Ferraz r.s. Antarctica 113 62 05S 58 24W
Comodoro Rivadavia Argentina 71 D3 45 50S 67 30W
Comorin, Cape India 91 D1 8 04N 77 35E
COMOROS 103 N5
Conakry Guinea 102 C9 9 30N 13 43W
Concepción Chile 71 C5 36 50S 73 03W
Concepción Paraguay 71 F8 23 22S 57 26W
Concepción del Uruguay Argentina 71 F6 32 30S 58 15W
Conchos r. Mexico 68 C5 27 30N 107 00W
Concord California U.S.A. 67 A3 37 59N 122 03W
Concord New Hampshire U.S.A. 65 L5 43 13N 71 34W
Concordia Argentina 71 F6 31 25S 58 00W
Concordia Kansas U.S.A. 65 G5 39 35N 97 39W
Concrete Washington U.S.A. 34 H4 48 32N 121 46W
Conduit r. Israel 88 O11 32 25N 35 00E
Conecuh r. Alabama U.S.A. 65 I3 31 00N 87 00W
Coney Island New York U.S.A. 66 Z1 40 34N 74 00W
Conflans-Ste. Honorine France 79 A3 49 01N 2 09E
CONGO 102 I7
Congo r. Congo/Congo (D.R.) 102 I7 2 00S 17 00E
CONGO, THE DEMOCRATIC REPUBLIC OF THE 102 J7
Conneaut Ohio U.S.A. 42 F2 41 58N 80 34W
Connecticut r. U.S.A. 65 L5 43 00N 72 00W
Connecticut state U.S.A. 65 L5 41 00N 73 00W
Conset Bay Barbados 69 W12 13 10N 59 25W
Constanţa Romania 72 L4 44 12N 28 40E
Constantine Algeria 102 G15 36 22N 6 40E
Constitución Chile 71 C5 35 20S 72 25W
Contamana Peru 70 B11 7 19S 75 04W
Conyngham Pennsylvania U.S.A. 66 B3 40 59N 76 04W
Cook Inlet Alaska U.S.A. 8 E5 60 00N 152 30W
Cook Islands Pacific Ocean 111 K6 19 30S 159 50W
Cook, Mount N.Z. 107 B2 43 36S 170 09E
Cook Strait N.Z. 107 B2 41 24S 174 36E
Cooktown Australia 106 H6 15 29S 145 15E
Coolgardie Australia 106 C3 31 01S 121 12E
Cooper Creek Australia 106 F4 28 00S 138 00E
Coosa r. U.S.A. 65 I3 33 00N 86 00W
Coos Bay tn. Oregon U.S.A. 64 B5 43 23N 124 12W
Copacabana Brazil 71 Q2 22 58S 43 11W
Copacabana Beach Brazil 71 Q2 22 59S 43 11W
Copenhagen see København
Copiapó Chile 71 C7 27 20S 70 23W
Copper r. Alaska U.S.A. 8 F5 60 30N 144 50W
Copper Harbor Michigan U.S.A. 65 I6 47 28N 87 54W
Coquet r. United Kingdom 74 J7 55 20N 1 50W
Coquimbo Chile 71 C7 29 57S 71 25W
Coral Sea Pacific Ocean 106 I6/J7 15 00S 154 00E
Coral Sea Islands Territory admin. Australia 106 I6
17 00S 150 00E
Corantijn (Courantyne) r. Suriname 70 F13 4 30N 57 30W
Corbeil-Essonnes France 79 C1 48 36N 2 29E
Cordillera de Mérida mts. Venezuela 69 J1 8 00N 72 00W
Córdoba Argentina 71 E6 31 25S 64 11W
Córdoba Mexico 68 E3 18 55N 96 55W
Córdoba Spain 72 E3 37 53N 4 46W
Cordova Alaska U.S.A. 8 F5 60 29N 145 52W
Corfu see Kérkyra
Corinth Mississippi U.S.A. 65 I3 34 58N 88 30W
Cork Republic of Ireland 74 C3 51 54N 8 28W
Cormeilles-en-Paris France 79 A2 48 58N 2 11E
Corning New York U.S.A. 66 A5 42 10N 77 04W
Coro Venezuela 70 D15 11 20N 70 00W
Coroico Bolivia 70 D9 16 19S 67 45W
Coromandel Coast India 91 E2 12 30N 81 30E
Coromandel Peninsula N.Z. 107 C3 37 00S 175 42E
Corona California U.S.A. 8 F5 60 29N 145 52W
Coronado California U.S.A. 67 D1 32 40N 117 07W
Coronation Island Alaska U.S.A. 34 B3 55 50N 134 15N

Coronel Pringles Argentina **71** E5 37 56S 61 25W
Corpus Christi Texas U.S.A. **65** G2 27 47N 97 26W
Corrientes Argentina **71** F7 27 30S 58 48W
Corriverton Guyana **70** F14 5 53N 57 10W
Corry Pennsylvania U.S.A. **42** G2 41 56N 79 39W
Corse (Corsica) i. France **72** G4 42 00N 9 00E
Corsica see Corse
Çoruh r. Turkey **88** F7 40 45N 40 45E
Corumbá Brazil **70** F9 19 00S 57 35W
Corunna Michigan U.S.A. **42** B3 42 58N 84 05W
Corvallis Oregon U.S.A. **64** B5 44 34N 123 16W
Cosenza Italy **88** A6 39 17N 16 16E
Cossipore India **108** K2 22 37N 88 23E
Costa Blanca geog. reg. Spain **72** E3 38 15N 0 20W
Costa Brava geog. reg. Spain **72** F4 38 15N 0 20W
COSTA RICA **69** H1/2
Cotagaita Bolivia **70** D8 20 47S 65 40W
CÔTE D'IVOIRE (IVORY COAST) **102** D9
Cotentin p. France **72** E5 49 30N 1 30W
Cotonou Benin **102** F9 6 24N 2 31E
Cotopaxi mt. Ecuador **70** B12 0 40S 78 28W
Cotswold Hills United Kingdom **74** I3 51 40N 2 10W
Council Bluffs Iowa U.S.A. **65** G5 41 14N 95 54W
Courantyne see Corantijn
Couva r. Trinidad and Tobago **69** T9 10 25N 61 24W
Couva Trinidad and Tobago **69** T9 10 25N 61 27W
Coventry United Kingdom **74** J4 52 25N 1 30W
Covington Kentucky U.S.A. **65** J4 39 04N 84 30W
Cowan Creek Australia **107** G3 33 36S 151 13E
Cox's Bazar Bangladesh **91** G4 21 25N 91 59E
Coyote Lake California U.S.A. **67** D2 35 05N 116 45W
Craig Alaska U.S.A. **34** B3 55 29N 133 06W
Craiova Romania **72** K4 44 18N 23 47E
Cranberry Lake New York U.S.A. **43** N5 44 10N 74 50W
Crawley United Kingdom **74** K3 51 07N 0 12W
Crescent City California U.S.A. **64** B5 41 46N 124 13W
Crescent Island Hong Kong China **92** C3 22 32N 114 19E
Creston Iowa U.S.A. **65** H5 41 04N 94 20W
Crestview Florida U.S.A. **65** I3 30 44N 86 34W
Créteil France **79** B2 48 47N 2 28E
Crete, Sea of Mediterranean Sea **88** B6/C6 35 00N 20 00E
Crete see Kríti
Crewe United Kingdom **74** I5 53 05N 2 27W
Criciúma Brazil **71** H7 28 45S 49 25W
Crimea see Krym
CROATIA **72** J5
Cromwell N.Z. **107** A1 45 03S 169 12E
Cronulla Australia **107** G1 34 04S 151 09E
Crooked Island Hong Kong China **92** C3 22 33N 114 18E
Crooked Island The Bahamas **69** J4 22 45N 74 10W
Crookston Minnesota U.S.A. **65** G6 47 47N 96 36W
Cross Sound sd. Alaska U.S.A. **34** A3 58 00N 137 00W
Crow Peak mt. Montana U.S.A. **64** D6 46 19N 111 56W
Crows Nest Australia **107** G2 33 50S 151 12E
Croydon Australia **106** I4 27 11S 142 15E
Croydon bor. United Kingdom **78** C2 51 23N 0 06W
Crozet Basin Indian Ocean **108** E3/F3 40 00S 55 00E
Cruzeiro do Sul Brazil **70** C11 7 40S 72 39W
Cuando r. Southern Africa **103** J4 16 00S 21 30E
Cuango r. Angola **103** I6 9 00S 18 30E
Cuanza r. Angola **103** H6 9 40S 15 00E
CUBA **69** I4
Cubango r. Southern Africa **103** I4 17 00S 18 00E
Cúcuta Colombia **70** C14 7 55N 73 31W
Cuddalore India **91** D2 11 43N 79 46E
Cuddapah India **91** D2 14 30N 78 50E
Cuddeback Lake California U.S.A. **67** D2 35 17N 117 29W
Cuenca Ecuador **70** B12 2 54S 79 00W
Cuernavaca Mexico **68** E3 18 57N 99 15W
Cuiabá Brazil **70** F9 15 32S 56 05W
Cuito r. Angola **103** I4 17 30S 19 30E
Culiacán Mexico **68** C4 24 50N 107 23W
Cumaná Venezuela **70** E15 10 29N 64 12W
Cumberland r. U.S.A. **65** I4 37 00N 86 00W
Cumberland Plateau U.S.A. **65** I4 36 00N 85 00W
Cumbernauld United Kingdom **74** H7 55 57N 4 00W
Cumbrian Mountains United Kingdom **74** H6 54 30N 3 00W
Cumuto Trinidad and Tobago **69** S10 10 25N 61 12W
Cunene r. Angola/Namibia **103** H4 17 00S 13 30E
Cunnamulla Australia **106** H4 28 04S 145 40E
Cunningham Park New York U.S.A. **67** Z1 40 45N 73 45W
Cunupia Trinidad and Tobago **69** T10 10 32N 61 22W
Curaçao i. Lesser Antilles **69** K2 12 20N 68 20W
Curacautin Chile **71** C5 38 28S 71 52W
Curicó Chile **71** C5 35 00S 71 15W
Curitiba Brazil **71** H7 25 25S 49 25W
Currant California U.S.A. **67** E4 38 44N 115 30W
Curvelo Brazil **70** I9 18 45S 44 27W
Cuttack India **91** F4 20 26N 85 56E
Cuyahoga Falls tn. Ohio U.S.A. **42** E2 41 08N 81 27W
Cuyahoga River Ohio U.S.A. **42** E2 41 20N 81 35W
Cuyuni r. Guyana **69** M1 7 00N 59 00W
Cuzco Peru **70** C10 13 32S 1 57W
Cwmbran United Kingdom **74** H3 51 39N 3 00W
CYPRUS **88** D5
CZECH REPUBLIC **72** J5
Częstochowa Poland **72** J6 50 49N 19 07E

D

Dabola Guinea **102** C10 10 48N 11 02W
Dadra & Nagar Haveli admin. India **91** C4 20 00N 73 00E
Dagenham United Kingdom **78** D3 51 33N 0 08E
Da Hinggan Ling (Greater Khingan Range) mts. China **93** N8/O9 50 00N 122 00E
Dahlewitz Germany **79** F1 52 19N 13 27E
Dāhod India **91** C4 22 48N 74 18E
Dahongliutan Kashmir **91** D7 35 55N 79 10E

Dahūk Iraq **88** F6 36 52N 43 00E
Daiō-zaki c. Japan **96** C1 34 16N 136 55E
Dairût Egypt **88** D4 27 34N 30 48E
Dai-sen mt. Japan **96** B2 35 23N 133 34E
Dakar Senegal **102** B10 14 38N 17 27W
Dakhla Oasis Egypt **102** K13 26 00N 28 00E
Dalälven r. Sweden **72** J8 60 30N 15 30E
Da Lat Vietnam **95** D6 11 56N 108 25E
Dalbandin Pakistan **90** A5 28 56N 64 30E
Dalby Australia **106** I4 27 11S 151 12E
Dalhart Texas U.S.A. **64** F4 36 05N 102 32W
Dali (Xiaguan) China **93** K4 25 33N 100 09E
Dalian China **93** O6 38 53N 121 37E
Dall Island Alaska U.S.A. **34** B2 55 00N 133 00W
Dallas Texas U.S.A. **65** G3 32 47N 96 48W
Dallgow Germany **79** E2 52 32N 13 03E
Dalton Georgia U.S.A. **65** J3 34 46N 84 59W
Daly r. Australia **106** E7 14 00S 132 00E
Daly Waters tn. Australia **106** E6 16 13S 133 20E
Daman India **91** C4 20 15N 72 58E
Damanhûr Egypt **88** D3 31 03N 30 28E
Damascus see Dimashq
Dāmāvand Iran **89** H6 35 47N 52 04E
Dāmāvand mt. Iran **86** G2 35 56N 52 08E
Damba Angola **103** I6 6 44S 15 20E
Damoh India **91** D4 23 50N 79 30E
Dampier Australia **106** B5 20 45S 116 48E
Danau Toba l. Indonesia **95** B4 2 30N 98 30E
Da Nang Vietnam **95** D7 16 04N 108 14E
Danbury Connecticut U.S.A. **65** L5 41 24N 73 26W
Dandong China **93** O7 40 08N 124 24E
Dangori India **91** H5 27 40N 95 35E
Danli Honduras **69** G2 14 02N 86 30W
Dannemora New York U.S.A. **43** N5 44 44N 73 45W
Dannevirke N.Z. **107** C2 40 12S 176 06E
Danube (Donau) r. Europe **72** K4 44 00N 25 00E
Danville Illinois U.S.A. **65** I5 40 09N 87 37W
Danville Pennsylvania U.S.A. **43** M4 58 58N 76 37W
Danville Virginia U.S.A. **65** K4 36 34N 79 25W
Daqing Kazakhstan **92** D8 46 37N 129 10E
Dar'ā Syria **88** P11 32 37N 36 06E
Darbhanga India **91** F5 26 10N 85 54E
Dardanelles strait Turkey **72** L4 40 08N 26 10E
Dar el Beida see Casablanca
Dar es Salaam Tanzania **103** M6 6 51S 39 18E
Dargaville N.Z. **107** B3 35 56S 173 52E
Darhan Mongolia **93** L8 48 30N 105 58E
Darjiling India **91** F5 27 02N 88 20E
Darling r. Australia **106** G3 30 30S 144 00E
Darling Downs mts. Australia **106** H4 28 00S 148 30E
Darlington United Kingdom **74** J6 54 31N 1 34W
Darnah Libya **102** J14 32 46N 22 39E
Darnley, Cape Antarctica **113** F67 16S 69 53E
Darrington Washington U.S.A. **34** H4 48 15N 121 37W
Dartford United Kingdom **78** D2 51 27N 0 13E
Dartmoor United Kingdom **74** H2 50 35N 3 50W
Daru Papua New Guinea **106** G8 9 05S 143 10E
Darwin Australia **106** E7 12 23S 130 44E
Darwin United Kingdom **74** I7 36 36N 117 36W
Daryācheh-ye Orūmiyeh (Lake Urmia) l. Iran **89** G6 37 20N 45 55E
Dashkhovuz (Tashauz) Turkmenistan **87** H3 41 49N 59 58E
Dasht-e-Kavir geog. reg. Iran **89** H5/I5 34 30N 54 30E
Dasht-i-Margo d. Afghanistan **89** J5 30 30N 62 30E
Datchet United Kingdom **78** A2 51 30N 0 35W
Datong China **93** M7 40 02N 113 33E
Datong He r. China **93** K6 37 30N 102 00E
Datong Shan mts. China **93** J6/K6 38 00N 99 00E
Datu Piang The Philippines **95** G5 7 02N 124 30E
Daugava r. Belarus **72** L7 55 00N 29 00E
Daugavpils Latvia **72** L7 55 52N 26 31E
Dauphin Pennsylvania U.S.A. **66** B3 40 23N 76 56W
Davangere India **91** D2 14 30N 75 52E
Davao The Philippines **95** H5 7 05N 125 38E
Davenport California U.S.A. **67** A3 37 02N 122 14W
Davenport Iowa U.S.A. **65** H5 41 32N 90 36W
David Panama **69** H1 8 26N 82 26W
Davidson Mountains mts. Alaska U.S.A. **50** C4 68 30N 143 30W
Davis r.s Antarctica **113** 68 36S 77 58E
Davis Sea Antarctica **113** 65 00S 90 00E
Davison Michigan U.S.A. **42** C4 43 02N 83 30W
Dawna Range mts. Myanmar **95** B7 17 10N 98 00E
Daylight Pass California U.S.A. **67** D3 36 45N 116 58W
Dayr az Zawr Syria **88** F6 35 20N 40 02E
Dayton Ohio U.S.A. **65** J4 39 45N 84 10W
Daytona Beach tn. Florida U.S.A. **65** J2 29 11N 81 01W
Dazhang Xi r. China **94** E8 25 00N 118 00E
D & D see Daman and Diu
De Aar Republic of South Africa **103** J1 30 40S 24 01E
Dead Sea Israel/Jordan **88** E5 31 35N 35 30E
Deán Funes Argentina **71** E4 30 25S 64 22W
Dearborn Michigan U.S.A. **42** C3 42 18N 83 14W
Death Valley California U.S.A. **67** D3 36 40N 117 09W
Death Valley Junction California U.S.A. **67** D3 36 18N 116 25W
Death Valley National Monument California U.S.A. **67** D3 36 30N 117 00W
Débé Trinidad and Tobago **69** T9 10 12N 61 27W
Debrecen Hungary **72** K5 47 30N 21 37E
Debre Mark'os Ethiopia **102** M10 10 19N 37 41E
Debre Tabor Ethiopia **102** M10 11 50N 38 06E
Decatur Alabama U.S.A. **65** I3 34 36N 87 00W
Decatur Illinois U.S.A. **65** I5 39 51N 88 57W
Decatur Indiana U.S.A. **42** B1 40 50N 84 57W
Deccan plat. India **91** D3 18 00N 78 00E

Dee r. Dumfries & Galloway Scotland U.K. **74** G7 54 55N 4 00W
Dee r. Aberdeenshire Scotland U.K. **74** I9 57 05N 2 10W
Dee r. England United Kingdom **74** I5 53 16N 3 10W
Deep Bay Hong Kong China **92** A3 22 30N 113 55E
Dee Why Australia **107** H2 33 45S 151 17E
Defiance Ohio U.S.A. **42** B1 41 17N 84 21W
Degeh Bur Ethiopia **102** N9 8 11N 43 31E
Dehra Dun India **91** D6 30 19N 78 03E
Dekese Congo (D.R.) **103** J7 3 28S 21 24E
Delaware state U.S.A. **66** C2 39 00N 75 00W
Delaware Bay U.S.A. **66** C2 39 10N 75 10W
Delaware River U.S.A. **66** C2 39 40N 75 30W
Delhi India **91** D5 28 40N 77 14E
Delhi New York U.S.A. **66** D5 42 18N 74 55W
Delhi Cantonment India **108** L4 28 35N 77 08E
Delicias Mexico **64** E2 28 10N 105 30W
De Long Mountains Alaska U.S.A. **8** C6 68 30N 162 00W
Delphos Phio U.S.A. **42** B1 40 50N 84 21W
Del Rio Texas U.S.A. **64** F2 29 23N 100 56W
Delta Colorado U.S.A. **64** E4 38 42N 108 04W
Delta Junction Alaska U.S.A. **50** B3 63 30N 146 00W
Dembī Dolo Ethiopia **102** L9 8 34N 34 50E
Deming New Mexico U.S.A. **68** C2 32 17N 107 46W
Den Haag (The Hague) Netherlands **72** F6 52 05N 4 16E
Denison Texas U.S.A. **65** G3 33 47N 96 34W
Denizli Turkey **72** L3 37 46N 29 05E
Denman Glacier Antarctica **113** 67 00S 100 00E
DENMARK **72** G 7
Denpasar Indonesia **95** F2 8 40S 115 14E
Denton Texas U.S.A. **65** G3 33 14N 97 18W
D'Entrecasteaux Islands Papua New Guinea **106** I7/I8 9 15S 150 45E
Denver Colorado U.S.A. **64** E4 39 45N 105 00W
Deodora Brazil **71** P2 22 51S 43 22W
Dépression du Mourdi dep. Chad **102** J11 17 00N 22 41E
Deputatskiy Russian Federation **85** P9 69 15N 139 59E
Dera Ghazi Khan Pakistan **91** C6 30 05N 70 44E
Dera Ismail Khan Pakistan **91** C6 31 51N 70 56E
Derbent Russian Federation **86** F3 42 03N 48 18E
Derby Australia **106** C6 17 19S 123 38E
Derby United Kingdom **74** J4 52 55N 1 30W
Descanso California U.S.A. **67** D2 32 51N 116 35W
Desé Ethiopia **102** M10 11 05N 39 40E
Deseado Argentina **71** D3 47 44S 65 56W
Desert Center California U.S.A. **67** E1 33 44N 115 23W
Desierto de Atacama (Atacama Desert) d. Chile **70** C8 22 30S 70 00W
Des Moines Iowa U.S.A. **65** H5 41 35N 93 35W
Des Moines r. Iowa U.S.A. **65** H5 41 00N 92 00W
Desna r. Russian Federation **84** F6 52 00N 32 30E
Detroit Michigan U.S.A. **65** J5 42 23N 83 05W
Deveron r. United Kingdom **74** I9 57 25N 3 03W
Devil's Lake tn. North Dakota U.S.A. **64** G6 48 03N 98 57W
Devonport Australia **106** H1 41 09S 146 16E
Dexter Maine U.S.A. **47** C2 45 01N 69 19W
Dezfūl Iran **89** G5 32 23N 48 28E
Dezhou China **93** N6 37 29N 116 11E
Dhahran see Az Zahrān
Dhaka Bangladesh **91** G4 23 42N 90 22E
Dhamār Yemen Republic **88** F1 14 33N 44 30E
Dhanbad India **91** F4 23 47N 86 32E
Dharoor r. Somalia **102** O10 10 00N 54 00E
Dhārwād India **91** D3 15 30N 75 04E
Dhoraji India **90** C4 21 42N 70 32E
Dhule India **91** C4 20 52N 74 50E
Diablo Range mts. California U.S.A. **67** B3 36 30N 120 38W
Diamantina Brazil **70** I9 18 17S 43 37W
Diamantina r. Australia **106** G5 24 00S 143 00E
Diamantina Fracture Zone Indian Ocean **108** J3/K3
Dibrugarh India **91** G5 27 29N 94 56E
Dickinson North Dakota U.S.A. **64** F6 46 54N 102 48W
Diego Martin Trinidad and Tobago **69** S10 10 48N 61 34W
Dijon France **72** G5 47 20N 5 02E
Dikson Russian Federation **85** K10 73 32N 80 39E
Dikwa Nigeria **102** H10 12 01N 13 55E
Dili (Oekusi) Indonesia **95** H2 8 33S 125 34E
Dillingham Alaska U.S.A. **8** D4 59 03N 158 30W
Dimashq (Damascus) Syria **88** E5 33 30N 36 19E
Dimitrovgrad Russian Federation **86** F5 54 14N 49 37E
Dinajpur Bangladesh **91** F5 25 38N 88 44E
Dinaric Alps mts. Europe **72** J4 44 00N 17 00E
Dindigul India **91** D2 10 23N 78 00E
Dingle Bay Republic of Ireland **74** A4 52 05N 10 15W
Dingwall United Kingdom **74** G9 57 35N 4 29W
Dipolog The Philippines **95** G5 8 34N 123 23E
Dir Pakistan **91** C7 35 12N 71 54E
Dire Dawa Ethiopia **102** N9 9 35N 41 50E
Disappointment, Lake Australia **106** C5 23 00S 123 00E
Discovery Bay tn. Hong Kong China **92** B1 22 18N 114 01E
Discovery Bay Hong Kong China **92** B1 22 18N 114 02E
Disko (Qeqertarsuaq Disko) i. Greenland **9** AA6 70 00N 54 00W
Disko Bugt (Qeqertarsuup Tunua) b. Greenland **9** AA6 69 00N 54 00W
Ditan China **94** B1 39 58N 116 24E
Diu Daman and Diu India **90** C4 20 41N 71 03E
Divinópolis Brazil **70** I8 20 08S 44 53W
Divriği Turkey **88** E6 39 23N 38 06E
Dixie Valley California U.S.A. **67** C4 39 41N 118 04W
Diyarbakir Turkey **88** F6 37 55N 40 14E
Djambala Congo **102** H7 2 32S 14 43E
Djelfa Algeria **102** F14 34 43N 3 14E

DJIBOUTI **102** N10
Djibouti Djibouti **102** N10 11 35N 43 11E
Djougou Benin **102** F9 9 40N 1 47E
Dnieper r. Ukraine/Belarus **72** M6 52 30N 30 30E
Dniestr r. Europe **72** L5 48 00N 27 00E
Dnipro r. Europe **86** C4 47 30N 33 00E
Dniprodzerzhyns'k Ukraine **86** C4 48 30N 34 37E
Dnipropetrovs'k Ukraine **86** C4 48 29N 35 00E
Dodge City Kansas U.S.A. **64** F4 37 45N 100 02W
Dodoma Tanzania **103** M6 6 10S 35 40E
Dogai Coring l. China **91** F6 34 30N 89 00E
Dōgo i. Japan **96** B2 36 20N 133 15E
Doha see Ad Dawhah
Dolo Ethiopia **102** N8 4 11N 42 03E
DOMINICA **69** L3
DOMINICAN REPUBLIC **69** K3
Don r. England U.K. **74** J5 53 37N 1 02W
Don r. Russian Federation **86** E4 50 00N 41 00E
Don r. Scotland U.K. **74** I9 57 15N 2 55W
Donau see Danube
Doncaster United Kingdom **74** J5 53 32N 1 07W
Donegal Republic of Ireland **74** C6 54 39N 8 07W
Donegal Bay Republic of Ireland **74** C6 54 30N 8 30W
Donegal Mountains Republic of Ireland **74** C6/D7 55 00N 8 05W
Donets r. Asia **73** N5 49 00N 39 00E
Donets'k Ukraine **86** D4 48 00N 37 50E
Dongba China **94** C1 39 58N 116 38E
Dongchuan China **93** K4 26 07N 103 05E
Dong Hoi Vietnam **95** D7 17 32N 106 35E
Dongola Sudan **102** L11 19 10N 30 27E
Dongou Congo **102** I8 2 02N 18 02E
Don Pedro Reservoir res. California U.S.A. **67** B3 37 45N 120 23W
Donting Hu l. China **93** M4 29 00N 112 30E
Dordogne r. France **72** F4 44 50N 1 30E
Dori r. Afghanistan **89** K5 31 20N 65 30E
Dorking United Kingdom **78** B1 51 14N 0 20W
Dornoch Firth est. U.K. **74** H9 57 55N 3 55W
Dortmund Germany **72** G5 51 32N 7 27E
Dos Palos California U.S.A. **67** B3 36 59N 120 39W
Dosso Niger **102** F10 13 03N 3 10E
Dothan Alabama U.S.A. **65** I3 31 12N 85 25W
Double Island Hong Kong China **92** C3 22 31N 114 08E
Douglas Alaska U.S.A. **34** B3 58 15N 134 24W
Douglas Arizona U.S.A. **64** E3 31 21N 109 34W
Douglas British Isles **74** G6 54 09N 4 29W
Dourados Brazil **71** G8 22 09S 54 52W
Douro r. Spain/Portugal **72** D4 41 00N 7 30W
Dover United Kingdom **74** M3 51 08N 1 19E
Dover Delaware U.S.A. **65** K4 39 10N 75 32W
Dover, Strait of English Channel **72** F6 51 00N 1 20W
Dovrefjell mts. Norway **72** H8 62 15N 9 10E
Doylestown Pennsylvania U.S.A. **66** C3 40 18N 75 08W
Dōzen is. Japan **96** B2 36 05N 133 00E
Dragon's Mouths, The (Bocas del Dragons) Trinidad and Tobago **69** S10 10 37N 61 50W
Drakensberg mts. Republic of South Africa **103** K1 30 00S 28 00E
Drake Passage sd. Southern Ocean **71** C1/E1 58 00S 66 00W
Drancy France **79** B2 48 55N 2 28E
Drava r. Europe **72** J5 46 00N 18 00E
Draveil France **79** B1 48 40N 2 25E
Dresden Germany **72** H6 51 03N 13 45E
Drewitz Germany **79** E1 52 20N 13 08E
Drogheda Republic of Ireland **74** E5 53 43N 6 21W
Dronning Maud Land (Queen Maud Land) geog. reg. Antarctica **113** 73 00S 10 00E
Drummond Island Michigan U.S.A. **42** C7 46 00N 83 40W
Drummoyne Australia **107** G2 33 51S 151 09E
Druzhba Kazakhstan **87** N4 45 18N 82 29E
Dubayy United Arab Emirates **89** I4 25 14N 55 17E
Dubbo Australia **106** H3 32 16S 148 41E
Dublin (Baile Átha Cliath) Republic of Ireland **74** E5 53 20N 6 15W
Dublin Georgia U.S.A. **65** J3 32 31N 82 54W
Dubno Ukraine **86** B5 50 28N 25 40E
Dubrovnik Croatia **72** J4 42 40N 18 07E
Dubuque Iowa U.S.A. **65** H5 42 31N 90 41W
Ducie Island Pitcairn Islands **111** N5 24 40S 124 48W
Duckwater California U.S.A. **67** E4 38 53N 115 41W
Duckwater Peak mt. California U.S.A. **67** E4 38 54N 115 27W
Dudinka Russian Federation **85** K9 69 27N 86 13E
Dudley United Kingdom **74** I4 52 30N 2 05W
Duke Island Alaska U.S.A. **34** B2 54 50N 131 30W
Duluth Minnesota U.S.A. **65** H6 46 45N 92 10W
Dum Dum India **90** K2 22 37N 88 24E
Dumfries United Kingdom **74** H7 55 04N 3 37W
Dumont d'Urville r.s. Antarctica **113** 66 40S 140 01E
Dumyāt (Damietta) Egypt **102** L14 31 26N 31 48E
Duncan Oklahoma U.S.A. **65** G3 34 30N 97 57W
Duncannon Pennsylvania U.S.A. **66** A3 40 24N 77 03W
Duncan Passage sd. Andaman Islands **91** G2 11 00N 93 00E
Duncansby Head c. United Kingdom **74** H10 58 39N 3 02W
Dundalk Republic of Ireland **74** E6 54 01N 6 25W
Dundalk Maryland U.S.A. **66** B2 39 15N 76 31W
Dundas see Pituffik
Dundee New York U.S.A. **66** B5 42 32N 76 59W
Dundee United Kingdom **74** I8 56 28N 3 00W
Dunedin N.Z. **107** B1 45 53S 170 30E
Dunfermline United Kingdom **74** H8 56 04N 3 29W
Dunkirk New York U.S.A. **65** K5 42 29N 79 21W

Dún Laoghiare Republic of Ireland 74 E5 53 17N 6 08W
Dunmore Pennsylvania U.S.A. 66 C4 41 25N 75 38W
Dunnigan California U.S.A. 67 B4 38 53N 121 57W
Duque de Caxias admin. Brazil 71 P2 22 42S 43 14W
Duque de Caxias Brazil 71 P2 22 46S 43 18W
Dural Australia 107 G3 33 41S 151 02E
Durand Michigan U.S.A. 42 C3 42 55N 83 58W
Durango admin. Mexico 64 E2 25 00N 105 00W
Durango Colorado U.S.A. 64 E4 37 16N 107 53W
Durango Mexico 68 D4 24 01N 104 40W
Durant Oklahoma U.S.A. 65 G3 33 59N 96 24W
Durazno Uruguay 71 F6 33 22S 56 31W
Durban Republic of South Africa 103 L2 29 53S 31 00E
Durgāpur India 91 F4 24 47N 87 44E
Durg-Bhilai India 91 E4 21 12N 81 20E
Durham North Carolina U.S.A. 65 K4 36 00N 78 54W
Durham United Kingdom 74 J6 54 47N 1 34W
Dushanbe Tajikistan 87 K2 38 38N 68 51E
Düsseldorf Germany 72 G6 51 13N 6 47E
Duyun China 93 L4 26 16N 107 29E
Dyer California U.S.A. 67 C3 37 39N 118 01W
Dzhzmbul see Zhambyl
Dzhetygara Kazakhstan 87 J5 52 14N 61 10E
Dzhezkazgan see Zhezkazgan
Dzhugdzhur Range mts. Russian Federation 85 P7
57 00N 137 00E
Dzungarian Basin see Junggar Pendi
Dzungarian Gate pass Kazakhstan/China 87 N4
45 00N 83 00E
Dzyarzhynsk Belarus 86 B5 55 40N 27 01E

E

Eagle Alaska U.S.A. 8 G5 64 46N 141 20W
Eagle Crags mt. California U.S.A. 67 D2 35 25N 117 04W
Eagle Lake Maine U.S.A. 43 S7 46 25N 69 20W
Eagle Pass tn. Texas U.S.A. 64 F2 28 44N 100 31W
Ealing bor. United Kingdom 78 B3 51 31N 0 18W
East Antarctica geog. reg. Antarctica 113
East Berlin Pennsylvania U.S.A. 66 A2 39 58N 77 00W
Eastbourne United Kingdom 74 L2 50 46N 0 17E
East Cape N.Z. 107 C3 37 41S 178 33E
East Caroline Basin Pacific Ocean 110 E8 4 00N 148 00E
Easter Island Pacific Ocean 111 P5 27 05S 109 20W
Easter Island Fracture Zone Pacific Ocean 111 Q5/R5
24 00S 100 00W
Eastern Ghats mts. India 91 D2/E3 15 00N 80 00E
Eastern Group is. Fiji 110 V15-16 17 40S 178 30W
Eastern Sayan mts. Russian Federation 85 L6 53 00N 97 30E
East Falkland i. Falkland Islands 71 F2 52 00S 58 50W
East Fork Chandalar River r. Alaska U.S.A. 50 B4
66 50N 147 00W
East Hills tn. Australia 107 G2 33 58S 150 59E
East Horsley United Kingdom 78 B2 51 16N 0 26W
East Kilbride United Kingdom 74 G7 55 46N 4 10W
East Lamma Channel Hong Kong China 92 B1
22 14N 114 08E
East London Republic of South Africa 103 K1
33 00S 27 54E
East Marianas Basin Pacific Ocean 110 F9 13 00N 153 00E
Easton Pennsylvania U.S.A. 66 C3 40 41N 75 13W
East Pacific Basin Pacific Ocean 111 K9 16 00N 153 00E
East Pacific Ridge Pacific Ocean 111 O5 20 00S 113 00W
East Pacific Rise Pacific Ocean 111 P9 13 00N 103 00W
Eastport Maine U.S.A. 49 A1 44 55N 67 01W
East Rift Valley East Africa 102 M8 6 00N 37 00E
East River New York U.S.A. 67 Z2 40 43N 74 00W
East Siberian Sea Arctic Ocean 112 72 00N 165 00E
East Stroudsburg Pennsylvania U.S.A. 66 C4
41 00N 75 00W
East Walker r. California U.S.A. 67 C4 38 48N 1119 03W
Eastwood Australia 107 G2 33 48S 151 05E
Eaton Rapids tn. Michigan U.S.A. 42 B3 42 30N 84 40W
Eau Claire tn. Wisconsin U.S.A. 65 H5 44 50N 91 30W
Eauripik-New Guinea Rise Pacific Ocean 110 E8
2 00N 142 00E
Ebinur Hu l. China 92 F7 45 00N 83 00E
Ebolowa Cameroon 102 H8 2 56N 11 11E
Ebro r. Spain 72 E4 42 00N 2 00W
Ech Cheliff Algeria 102 F15 36 05N 1 15E
Écouen France 79 B3 49 01N 2 22E
ECUADOR 70 B12
Ed Damer Sudan 102 L11 17 37N 33 59E
Ed Debba Sudan 102 L11 18 02N 30 56E
Edéa Cameroon 102 H8 3 47N 10 13E
Eden r. United Kingdom 74 I6 54 50N 2 45W
Eden North Carolina U.S.A. 65 K4 36 30N 79 46W
Edgecombe, Cape c. Alaska U.S.A. 34 A3 57 00N 135 45W
Edgewood Maryland U.S.A. 66 B2 39 25N 76 18W
Edgware United Kingdom 78 B3 51 36N 0 16W
Edinboro Pennsylvania U.S.A. 42 F2 41 53N 80 08W
Edinburgh United Kingdom 74 H7 55 57N 3 13W
Edirne Turkey 72 L4 41 40N 26 34E
Edmonton United Kingdom 78 C3 51 37N 0 04W
Edogawa Japan 97 C3 35 41N 139 51E
Edward, Lake Congo (D.R.) 102 K7 0 30S 29 00E
Edward VII Land geog. reg. Antarctica 113
75 00S 150 00W
Edwards Plateau Texas U.S.A. 64 F3 31 00N 100 00W
Éfaté (Vaté) i. Vanuatu 106 L6 17 30S 168 00E
Eğirdir Gölü l. Turkey 88 D6 37 52N 30 51E
Egham United Kingdom 78 A2 51 26N 0 34W
Egmont, Cape N.Z. 107 B3 39 17S 173 45E
Egmont, Mount (Mount Taranaki) N.Z. 107 B3
39 18S 174 04E
EGYPT 73 M1
Eichwalde Germany 79 G1 52 23N 13 37E

Eigg i. United Kingdom 74 E8 56 55N 6 10W
Eight Degree Channel Indian Ocean 91 C1 8 00N 73 30E
Eighty Mile Beach Australia 106 C6 19 00S 121 00E
Ekibastuz Kazakhstan 87 M5 51 50N 75 10E
El Aaiún see Laayoune
El Arco Mexico 68 B5 28 00N 113 25W
Elat Israel 88 D4 29 33N 34 57E
El Banco Colombia 70 C14 9 04N 73 59W
El Bayadh Algeria 102 F14 33 40N 1 00E
Elbe r. Europe 72 H6 53 00N 11 30E
Elbert, Mount Colorado U.S.A. 64 E4 39 05N 106 27W
El'brus mt. Russian Federation 86 E3 43 21N 42 29E
Elburz Mountains Iran 89 H6 36 15N 51 00E
El Cajon California U.S.A. 67 D1 32 48N 116 58W
El Callao Venezuela 70 E14 7 18N 61 50W
El Centro California U.S.A. 64 C3 32 47N 115 33W
El Cerro del Aripo mt. Trinidad and Tobago 69 T10
10 49N 61 14W
El Descanso California U.S.A. 67 D1 32 13N 116 52W
El Dorado Arkansas U.S.A. 68 F6 33 12N 92 40W
El Dorado Kansas U.S.A. 65 G4 37 51N 96 52W
Eldoret Kenya 102 M8 0 31N 35 17E
Elektrostal' Russian Federation 86 D6 55 46N 38 30E
Elephant Island British Isles South Shetland Island
71 F0 62 00S 55 00W
Eleuthera i. The Bahamas 69 I5 25 05N 76 30W
El Faiyûm Egypt 102 L13 29 19N 30 50E
El Fasher Sudan 102 K10 13 37N 25 22E
El Fuerte Mexico 68 C5 26 28N 108 35W
Elgin United Kingdom 74 H9 57 39N 3 20W
El Giza Egypt 102 L14 30 01N 31 12E
El Golea Algeria 102 F14 30 35N 2 51E
Elido Insurgentes Mexico 64 D2 25 00N 110 45W
El Iskandrîya (Alexandria) Egypt 73 L2 31 13N 29 55E
Elista Russian Federation 84 G5 46 18N 44 14E
Elizabeth Australia 106 F3 34 45S 138 39E
Elizabeth New Jersey U.S.A. 66 Y1 40 39N 74 13W
Elizabeth City North Carolina U.S.A. 65 K4
36 18N 76 16W
Elizabethtown Pennsylvania U.S.A. 66 B3 40 10N 76 38W
El Jadida Morocco 102 D14 33 19N 8 35W
El Jafr Jordan 88 P10 30 16N 36 11E
Elk California U.S.A. 67 A4 39 08N 123 43W
Elk City Oklahoma U.S.A. 64 G4 34 25N 99 26W
Elk Creek California U.S.A. 67 A4 39 36N 122 34W
El Khârga Egypt 102 L13 25 27N 30 32E
Elkhart Indiana U.S.A. 65 I5 41 52N 85 56W
Elkhorn r. Nebraska U.S.A. 65 G3 42 00N 98 00W
Elkland Pennsylvania U.S.A. 66 A4 42 00N 77 20W
Elko Nevada U.S.A. 64 C5 40 50N 115 46W
Ellis Island New Jersey U.S.A. 66 Y1 40 42N 74 02W
Ellsworth Maine U.S.A. 47 C1 44 34N 68 24W
Ellsworth Land geog. reg. Antarctica 113 75 00S 80 00W
Ellsworth Mountains Antarctica 113 80 00S 90 00W
El Mahalla El Kubra Egypt 102 L14 30 59N 31 10E
El Médano Mexico 68 B4 24 35N 111 29W
Elmhurst Pennsylvania U.S.A. 66 C4 41 20N 75 32W
el Milk r. Sudan 102 K11 17 00N 29 00E
El Minya Egypt 102 L13 28 06N 30 45E
Elmira New York U.S.A. 65 K5 42 06N 76 50W
El Muglad Sudan 102 K10 11 01N 27 50E
El Obeid Sudan 102 L10 13 11N 30 10E
El Paso Texas U.S.A. 64 E3 31 45N 106 30W
El Porvenir Mexico 68 C6 31 15N 105 48W
El Progreso Honduras 68 G3 15 20N 87 50W
El Qâ'hira (Cairo) Egypt 73 M1 30 03N 31 15E
El Qunaytirah Syria 88 O11 33 08N 35 49E
El Reno Oklahoma U.S.A. 65 G4 35 32N 97 57W
El Salto Mexico 68 C4 23 47N 105 22W
EL SALVADOR 68 G2
El Sueco Mexico 68 C5 29 54N 106 22W
El Suweis (Suez) Egypt 73 M1 29 59N 32 33E
Eltanin Fracture Zone Pacific Ocean 111 L2/N2
52 00S 135 00W
Eltham United Kingdom 78 D2 51 27N 0 03E
El Tigre Venezuela 70 E14 8 44N 64 18W
El Toro California U.S.A. 67 D1 33 36N 117 40W
El Tucuche mt. Trinidad and Tobago 69 T10
10 44N 61 25W
Eluru India 91 E3 16 45N 81 10E
Ely California U.S.A. 67 E4 39 16N 114 53W
Ely Nevada U.S.A. 64 D4 39 15N 114 53W
Elyria Ohio U.S.A. 65 J5 41 22N 82 06W
Emämrüd Iran 89 H6 36 15N 54 59E
Emba Kazakhstan 84 H5 48 47N 58 05E
Emba r. Kazakhstan 87 H4 47 30N 56 00E
Embalse de Guri l. Venezuela 70 E14 7 30N 62 30W
Emerald Australia 106 H5 23 30S 148 08E
Emi Koussi mt. Chad 102 I11 19 52N 18 31E
Emmaus Pennsylvania U.S.A. 66 C3 40 00N 75 00W
Empalme Mexico 68 B5 28 00N 110 49W
Emperor Seamounts Pacific Ocean 110 G12
42 00N 170 00E
Emporia Kansas U.S.A. 65 G4 38 24N 96 10W
Emporium Pennsylvania U.S.A. 42 H2 41 31N 78 14W
Encantado Brazil 71 P2 22 54S 43 18W
Encarnación Paraguay 71 F7 27 20S 55 50W
Encinitas California U.S.A. 67 D1 33 04N 117 17W
Ende Indonesia 106 C8 8 51S 121 40E
Endeh Indonesia 95 G2 8 51S 121 40E
Enderby Land geog. reg. Antarctica 113 65 00S 45 00E
Endicott New York U.S.A. 66 B5 42 06N 76 03W
Endicott Mountains Alaska U.S.A. 50 A4
67 35N 152 30W
Enfield bor. United Kingdom 78 C3 51 39N 0 05W
Engel's Russian Federation 84 G6 51 30N 46 07E

Engenho Novo Brazil 71 P2 22 54S 43 16W
Enghien France 79 B2 48 58N 2 19E
England country United Kingdom 74 I5 53 00N 2 00W
English Channel U.K./France 72 E6 50 00N 2 00W
Enid Oklahoma U.S.A. 65 G4 36 24N 97 54W
En Nahud Sudan 102 K10 12 41N 28 28E
Enniskillen United Kingdom 74 D6 54 21N 7 38W
Enosburg Falls tn. Vermont U.S.A. 43 P5 44 55N 72 49W
Ensenada Mexico 68 A6 31 53N 116 38W
Entebbe Uganda 102 L8 0 04N 32 27E
Enugu Nigeria 102 G9 6 20N 7 29E
Epping Australia 107 G2 33 46S 151 05E
Epping United Kingdom 78 D3 51 42N 0 08E
Epping Forest United Kingdom 78 D3 51 40N 0 04E
Epsom United Kingdom 78 B2 51 20N 0 16W
EQUATORIAL GUINEA 102 G8/H8
Erciyas Daği mt. Turkey 86 D2 38 32N 35 27E
Erdenet Mongolia 93 K8 49 12N 104 05E
Erebus, Mount Antarctica 113 77 40S 167 20E
Erechim Brazil 71 G7 27 35S 52 15W
Erenhot China 93 M7 43 50N 112 00E
Erfurt Germany 72 H6 50 58N 11 02E
Erg Chech geog. reg. Algeria 102 E12 24 30N 3 00W
Erg Iguidi geog. reg. Algeria 102 D13 26 00N 6 00W
Ergun He see Argun
Erh-lin Taiwan 94 B3 23 52N 120 18E
Erie Pennsylvania U.S.A. 65 J5 42 07N 80 05W
Erimo-misaki c. Japan 96 D3 41 55N 143 13E
Erin Point Trinidad and Tobago 69 S9 10 03N 61 39W
Erith United Kingdom 78 D2 51 29N 0 11E
Erith Marshes United Kingdom 78 D3 51 30N 0 08E
ERITREA 102 N10 14 40N 40 15E
Erkner Germany 79 H1 52 25N 13 46E
Erne r. Republic of Ireland 74 D5 53 50N 7 30W
Erode India 91 D2 11 21N 77 43E
Erris Head c. Republic of Ireland 74 A6 54 20N 10 00W
Erromango i. Vanuatu 106 L6 19 00S 169 00E
Er Roseires Sudan 102 L10 11 52N 34 23E
Ertix He r. China 87 O4 47 30N 88 00E
Erzgebirge mts. Europe 72 H6 50 58N 13 00E
Erzincan Turkey 88 E6 39 44N 39 30E
Erzurum Turkey 73 P3 39 57N 41 17E
Esashi Japan 96 D3 41 50N 140 10E
Esbjerg Denmark 72 G 55 20N 8 20E
Escanaba Michigan U.S.A. 65 I6 45 47N 87 04W
Escobal Panama 69 Y2 9 11N 79 59W
Escondido California U.S.A. 64 C3 33 07N 117 05W
Eşfahān Iran 89 H5 32 41N 51 41E
Esher United Kingdom 78 B2 51 22N 0 22W
Eskişehir Turkey 88 D6 39 46N 30 30E
Esmeraldas Ecuador 70 B13 0 56N 79 40W
Esparto California U.S.A. 67 A4 38 42N 122 00W
Esperance Australia 106 C3 33 49S 121 52E
Esperanza r.s. Antarctica 113 63 24S 57 00W
Espírito Santo admin. Brazil 70 J9 18 40S 40 00W
Espíritu Santo i. Vanuatu 106 L6 15 10S 167 00E
Espoo Finland 72 K8 60 10N 24 40E
Esquel Argentina 71 C4 42 55S 71 20W
Es Semara Western Sahara 102 C13 26 25N 11 30W
Essen Germany 72 G6 51 27N 6 57E
Essequibo r. Guyana 70 F13 2 30N 58 00W
Essex California U.S.A. 67 E2 34 45N 115 15W
Essex Maryland U.S.A. 66 B2 39 00N 76 00W
Essex co. United Kingdom 78 D3 51 46N 0 30E
Essonne admin. France 79 A1 48 42N 2 05E
Estância Brazil 70 J10 11 15S 37 28W
ESTONIA 72 L7
Estrecho de Magallanes sd. Chile 71 C2 53 00S 71 00W
Estrela r. Brazil 71 Q3 22 42S 43 14W
Etawah India 91 D5 26 46N 79 01E
ETHIOPIA 102 M9
Etna, Mount Italy 72 H3 37 45N 15 00E
Etolin Island Alaska U.S.A. 34 B3 56 10N 132 30W
Etosha National Park Namibia 103 I4 18 30S 16 00E
Etosha Pan salt l. Namibia 103 I4 18 30S 16 30E
Euboea see Evvoia
Eucla Australia 106 D3 31 40S 128 51E
Euclid Ohio U.S.A. 42 E2 41 34N 81 33W
Eugene Oregon U.S.A. 64 B5 44 03N 123 04W
Euphrates (Firat) r. Iraq/Syria/Turkey 88 F5
34 40N 42 00E
Eureka California U.S.A. 64 B5 40 49N 124 10W
Evansville Indiana U.S.A. 65 I4 38 00N 87 33W
Everest, Mount China/Nepal 91 F5 27 59N 86 56E
Everett Washington U.S.A. 64 B6 47 59N 122 14W
Evry France 79 B1 48 38N 2 27E
Évvoia (Euboea) i. Greece 72 K3 38 00N 24 00E
Ewarton Jamaica 69 Q8 18 11N 77 06W
Excelsior Mountain California U.S.A. 67 C4
38 02N 119 19W
Excelsior Mountains mts. California U.S.A. 67 C4
38 15N 118 30W
Exe r. United Kingdom 74 H2 50 55N 3 32W
Exeter California U.S.A. 67 C3 36 17N 119 09W
Exeter United Kingdom 74 H2 50 43N 3 31W
Exmoor United Kingdom 74 H3 51 08N 3 40W
Exmouth Australia 106 A5 21 54S 114 10E
Eyasi, Lake Tanzania 103 L7 4 00S 35 00E
Eynsford United Kingdom 78 D2 51 22N 0 13E
Eyre Creek Australia 106 F4 26 00S 138 00E
Eyre, Lake Australia 106 F4 28 00S 136 00E
Eyre Peninsula Australia 106 F3 34 00S 136 00E

F

Fada Chad 102 J11 17 14N 21 32E
Faeroe Islands Atlantic Ocean 72 D8 62 00N 7 00W
Fafan r. Ethiopia 102 N9 7 30N 44 00E

Fairbanks Alaska U.S.A. 8 F5 64 50N 147 50W
Fairfield Australia 107 F2 33 52S 150 57E
Fairfield California U.S.A. 67 A4 38 14N 122 03W
Fair Isle i. United Kingdom 74 J11 59 32N 1 38W
Fairmont West Virginia U.S.A. 65 J4 39 28N 80 08W
Fairview Park tn. Hong Kong China 92 B2
22 29N 114 03E
Faisalabad Pakistan 91 C6 31 25N 73 09E
Faizabad India 91 E5 26 46N 82 08E
Fakfak Indonesia 95 I3 2 55S 132 17E
Falam Myanmar 92 H3 22 58N 93 45E
Falfurrias Texas U.S.A. 65 G2 27 17N 98 10W
Falkensee 1. Germany 79 E2 52 35N 13 08E
Falkirk United Kingdom 74 H8 55 59N 3 48W
Falkland Islands South Atlantic Ocean 71 E2/F2
52 30S 60 00W
Fallon Nevada U.S.A. 67 C4 39 29N 118 46W
Fall River tn. Massachusetts U.S.A. 65 L5
41 41N 71 08W
Falmouth Jamaica 69 Q8 18 29N 77 39W
Famagusta Cyprus 88 D6 35 07N 33 57E
Fang-liao Taiwan 94 C2 22 22N 120 36E
Fan Lau Hong Kong China 92 A1 22 12N 113 51E
Fanling Hong Kong China 92 B2 22 29N 114 07E
Faraday r.s. Antarctica 113 65 15S 64 16W
Farafangana Madagascar 103 L3 22 50S 47 50E
Faräh Afghanistan 89 J5 32 22N 62 07E
Farah Rud r. Afghanistan 89 J5 32 00N 62 00E
Farewell Spit N.Z. 107 B2 40 30S 172 50E
Fargo North Dakota U.S.A. 65 G6 46 52N 96 49W
Faridabad India 91 D5 28 24N 77 18E
Farmington Maine U.S.A. 43 R5 44 41N 70 11W
Farmington New Mexico U.S.A. 64 E4 36 43N 108 12W
Farmington Falls tn. Maine U.S.A. 43 R5 44 36N 70 05W
Faro Portugal 72 D3 37 01N 7 56W
Fatehgarh India 91 D5 27 22N 79 38E
Faya-Largeau Chad 102 I11 17 58N 19 06E
Fayetteville Arkansas U.S.A. 65 H4 36 03N 94 10W
Fayetteville North Carolina U.S.A. 65 K4 35 03N 78 53W
Fderik Mauritania 102 C12 22 30N 12 30W
FEDERATED STATES OF MICRONESIA 110 E8/F8
Feilding N.Z. 107 C2 40 14S 175 34E
Feira de Santana Brazil 70 J10 12 17S 38 53W
Felixstowe United Kingdom 74 M3 51 58N 1 20E
Feltham United Kingdom 78 B2 51 27N 0 25W
Fengshan Taiwan 94 G5 22 38N 120 21E
Fengtai China 94 B1 39 51N 116 17E
Feng-Yüan Taiwan 94 G7 24 15N 120 43E
Fens, The geog. reg. U.K. 74 K4/L4 52 45N 0 05E
Fenton Michigan U.S.A. 42 C3 42 48N 83 42W
Fergana Uzbekistan 87 L3 40 23N 71 19E
Fergus Falls tn. Minnesota U.S.A. 65 G6 46 18N 96 07W
Fernley California U.S.A. 67 C4 39 36N 119 17W
Ferreñafe Peru 70 B11 6 42S 79 45W
Fès Morocco 102 D14 34 05N 5 00W
Fethiye Turkey 88 C6 36 37N 29 06E
Fetlar i. United Kingdom 74 K12 60 37N 0 52W
Feyzäbad Afghanistan 89 L6 37 06N 70 34E
Fianarantsoa Madagascar 103 I3 21 27S 47 05E
FIJI 110 H6
Filchner Ice Shelf Antarctica 113 80 00S 37 00W
Finchley United Kingdom 78 C3 51 36N 0 10W
Findlay Ohio U.S.A. 42 C2 41 02N 83 40W
Finisterre, Cape Spain 72 D4 42 52N 9 16W
FINLAND 72 L8
Finland, Gulf of Finland/Russian Federation 72 K7
59 40N 23 30E
Fiordland N.Z. 107 A1 45 09S 167 18E
Firat (Euphrates) r. Turkey/Syria/Iraq 88 E6
37 30N 38 00E
Firenze (Florence) Italy 72 H4 43 47N 11 15E
Firozabad India 91 D5 27 09N 78 24E
Firozpur India 91 C6 30 55N 74 38E
Firth of Clyde est. United Kingdom 74 F5 55 45N 5 00W
Firth of Forth est. United Kingdom 74 I8 56 05N 3 00W
Firth of Lorn est. United Kingdom 74 E8 56 15N 6 00W
Fish r. Namibia 103 I2 26 30S 17 30E
Fishguard United Kingdom 74 G3 51 59N 4 59W
Fitzroy r. Australia 106 C6 18 00S 124 00E
Five Points California U.S.A. 67 B3 36 26N 120 06W
Flagstaff Arizona U.S.A. 64 D4 35 12N 111 38W
Flagstaff Lake Maine U.S.A. 43 R6 45 14N 70 20W
Flamborough Head c. U.K. 74 K6 54 06N 0 04W
Flamengo Brazil 71 Q2 22 56S 43 10W
Flatbush New York U.S.A. 66 Z1 40 38N 73 56W
Flathead Lake Montana U.S.A. 64 D6 47 55N 114 05W
Flathead River Montana U.S.A. 35 T1 48 55N 114 30W
Flatlands New York U.S.A. 66 Z1 40 37N 73 54W
Flattery, Cape Washington U.S.A. 64 B6
48 24N 124 43W
Flemington New Jersey U.S.A. 66 D3 40 31N 74 52W
Fletcher Pond l. Michigan U.S.A. 42 C5 44 59N 83 53W
Flinders r. Australia 106 G6 19 00S 141 30E
Flinders Range mts. Australia 106 G4 30 00S 138 00E
Flint r. Georgia U.S.A. 65 J3 31 00N 84 00W
Flint Michigan U.S.A. 65 J5 43 03N 83 40W
Flint River Michigan U.S.A. 42 C4 43 12N 83 50W
Florence Alabama U.S.A. 65 I3 34 48N 87 40W
Florence Italy see Firenze
Florence South Carolina U.S.A. 65 K3 34 12N 79 44W
Florencia Colombia 70 B13 1 37N 75 37W
Flores Guatemala 68 G3 16 58N 89 50W
Flores i. Indonesia 95 G2 8 30S 121 00E
Flores Sea Indonesia 106 C8 7 00S 119 00E
Floriano Brazil 70 I11 6 45S 43 00W
Florianópolis Brazil 71 H7 27 35S 48 31W
Florida state U.S.A. 65 J2 28 00N 82 00W
Florida Uruguay 71 F6 34 04S 56 14W

Florida Bay Florida U.S.A. **65** J2 25 00N 81 00W
Florida Keys is. Florida U.S.A. **65** J1 25 00N 80 00W
Florida, Straits of Cuba/U.S.A. **69** H4 24 00N 81 00W
Florissant Missouri U.S.A. **65** H4 38 49N 90 24W
Floyd Bennet Field New York U.S.A. **67** Z1 40 35N 73 52W
Flushing New York U.S.A. **67** Z2 40 45N 73 49W
Fóggia Italy **72** J4 41 28N 15 33E
Folkestone United Kingdom **74** M3 51 05N 1 11E
Folsom Lake California U.S.A. **67** B4 38 43N 121 08W
Fond du Lac Wisconsin U.S.A. **65** I5 43 48N 88 27W
Fongafala Tuvalu **110** H7 8 00S 178 30E
Fonte Boa Brazil **70** D12 2 33S 65 59W
Foresthill California U.S.A. **67** B4 39 02N 120 49W
Forest Hills tn. New York U.S.A. **67** Z1 40 43N 73 51W
Formosa Argentina **71** F7 26 07S 58 14W
Formosa Brazil **70** H9 15 30S 47 22W
Forrest Australia **106** D3 30 49S 128 03E
Fortaleza Brazil **70** J12 3 45S 38 35W
Fort Bragg California U.S.A. **64** B4 39 29N 123 48W
Fort Collins Colorado U.S.A. **64** F4 40 35N 105 05W
Fort-de-France Lesser Antilles **69** L2 14 36N 61 05W
Fort Dodge Iowa U.S.A. **65** H5 42 31N 94 10W
Fortescue r. Australia **106** B5 21 30S 117 30E
Forth r. United Kingdom **74** G8 56 00N 3 30W
Fort Kent Maine U.S.A. **47** C2 47 15N 68 35W
Fort Lauderdale Florida U.S.A. **65** J2 26 08N 80 08W
Fort Myers Florida U.S.A. **65** J2 26 39N 81 51W
Fort Peck Lake Montana U.S.A. **64** E6 48 01N 106 28W
Fort Pierce Florida U.S.A. **65** J2 27 28N 80 20W
Fort Portal Uganda **102** L8 0 40N 30 17E
Fort Randall Alaska U.S.A. **8** C4 55 10N 162 47W
Fort Scott Kansas U.S.A. **65** H4 37 52N 94 43W
Fort Smith Arkansas U.S.A. **65** H4 35 22N 94 27W
Fort Stockton Texas U.S.A. **64** F3 30 54N 102 54W
Fort Sumner New Mexico U.S.A. **64** F3 34 27N 104 16W
Fort Walton Beach Florida U.S.A. **65** I3 30 25N 86 38W
Fort Wayne Indiana U.S.A. **65** I5 41 05N 85 08W
Fort William United Kingdom **74** F8 56 49N 5 07W
Fort Worth Texas U.S.A. **65** G3 32 45N 97 20W
Fort Yukon Alaska U.S.A. **8** F6 66 35N 145 20W
Foshan China **93** M3 23 03N 113 08E
Foula i. United Kingdom **74** I12 60 08N 2 05W
Foulwind, Cape N.Z. **107** B2 41 45S 171 28E
Foumban Cameroon **102** H9 5 43N 10 50E
Four Corners tn. California U.S.A. **67** D2 35 01N 117 32W
Four Roads tn. Trinidad and Tobago **69** T10 10 42N 61 33W
Fouta Djallon geog. reg. Guinea **102** C10 12 00N 13 10W
Foveaux Strait N.Z. **107** A1 46 42S 167 59E
Foyle United Kingdom **74** D6 54 40N 7 30W
Foz do Iguaçu Argentina **71** G7 25 33S 54 31W
Franca Brazil **70** H8 20 33S 47 27W
FRANCE **72** F5
Francis Case, Lake South Dakota U.S.A. **64** G5
43 00N 99 00W
Francistown Botswana **103** K3 21 11S 27 32E
Frankenmuth Michigan U.S.A. **42** C4 43 19N 83 44W
Frankfield Jamaica **69** Q8 18 08N 77 22W
Frankfort Kentucky U.S.A. **65** J4 38 11N 84 53W
Frankfurt Germany **72** G6 50 06N 8 41E
Frankfurt admin. Germany **79** F2 52 40N 13 25E
Franklin Pennsylvania U.S.A. **42** G2 41 24N 79 49W
Franklin D. Roosevelt Lake Washington U.S.A. **64** C6
48 05N 118 15W
Franklinville New York U.S.A. **42** H3 42 20N 78 28W
Franz Josef Land see Zemlya Frantsa-Iosifa
Fraserburgh United Kingdom **74** I9 57 42N 2 00W
Fredericksburg Pennsylvania U.S.A. **66** B3
40 27N 76 26W
Fredericksburg Virginia U.S.A. **65** K4 38 18N 77 30W
Frederick Sound Alaska U.S.A. **34** B3 57 00N 134 00W
Frederikshab see Paamiut
Fredersdorf Germany **79** G2 52 31N 13 44E
Fredonia New York U.S.A. **42** G3 42 27N 79 22W
Freeport Texas U.S.A. **65** G2 28 56N 95 20W
Freeport The Bahamas **65** K2 26 30N 78 42W
Freetown Sierra Leone **102** C9 8 30N 13 17W
Fremantle Australia **106** B3 32 07S 115 44E
Fremont California U.S.A. **67** B3 37 32N 121 59W
Fremont Ohio U.S.A. **42** C2 41 21N 83 08W
French Creek Pennsylvania U.S.A. **42** F2 41 40N 80 10W
French Guiana territory France **70** G13 5 00N 53 00W
Frenchman Fork r. U.S.A. **64** F5 40 00N 103 00W
Frenchman Lake California U.S.A. **67** E3
36 50N 115 58W
French Polynesia Pacific Ocean **111** L5 21 00S 150 00W
French's Forest tn. Australia **107** G2/G3 33 45S 151 14E
Fresnillo Mexico **68** D4 23 10N 102 54W
Fresno California U.S.A. **64** C4 36 44N 119 47W
Fresno r. California U.S.A. **67** C3 37 09N 119 52W
Friant California U.S.A. **67** C3 36 59N 119 44W
Friedrichshagen Germany **79** G1 52 27N 13 38E
Friedrichshain Germany **79** F2 52 32N 13 26E
Frisian Islands is. Germany **72** G6 53 00N 7 00E
Frohnau Germany **79** F2 52 38N 13 19E
Frontera Mexico **68** F3 18 32N 92 39W
Frunze see Bishkek
Fuerteventura i. Canary Islands **102** C13 28 25N 14 00W
Fuerte r. Mexico **64** E2 26 00N 109 00W
Fuji Japan **96** C2 35 10N 138 37E
Fujinomiya Japan **96** C2 35 16N 138 33E
Fuji-san mt. Japan **96** C2 35 23N 138 42E
Fujisawa Japan **96** C2 35 20N 139 29E
Fukui Japan **96** C2 36 04N 136 12E
Fukuoka Japan **96** B1 33 39N 130 21E
Fukushima Japan **96** D2 37 44N 140 28E
Fukuyama Japan **96** B1 34 29N 133 21E
Fullerton Trinidad and Tobago **69** S9 10 05N 61 54W
Funabashi Japan **96** D2 35 42N 139 59E

Funakoshi Japan **97** B2 35 18N 139 34E
Funchal Madeira **102** B14 32 40N 16 55W
Fuquing China **94** F8 25 43N 119 21E
Furnace Creek California U.S.A. **67** D3 36 28N 116 52W
Furneaux Group is. Australia **106** H1 45 00S 148 00E
Furukawa Japan **96** D2 38 34N 140 56E
Fushun China **93** O7 41 50N 123 54E
Fustic Barbados **69** V13 13 18N 59 43W
Fuxin China **93** O7 42 04N 121 39E
Fuzhou China **93** N4 26 09N 119 17E
Fyn i. Denmark **72** G7 55 30N 10 00E

G

Gaalkacyo Somalia **102** O9 6 47N 47 12E
Gabbs California U.S.A. **67** D4 38 53N 117 57W
Gabès Tunisia **102** H14 33 52N 10 06E
GABON **102** H7
Gaborone Botswana **103** K3 24 45S 25 55E
Gadag India **91** D3 15 26N 75 42E
Gadsden Alabama U.S.A. **65** I3 34 00N 86 00W
Gafsa Tunisia **102** H14 34 28N 8 43E
Gagarin Russian Federation **86** L1 55 40N 37 27E
Gagnoa Côte d'Ivoire **102** D9 6 04N 5 55W
Gaillard Cut Panama Canal **69** Y2 9 05N 79 40W
Gainesville Florida U.S.A. **65** J2 29 37N 82 21W
Gainesville Texas U.S.A. **65** G3 33 09N 97 38W
Gairdner, Lake Australia **106** F3 32 50S 136 00E
Galana r. Kenya **102** M7 3 30S 34 30E
Galapagos Rise Pacific Ocean **111** R6 12 00S 97 00W
Galashiels United Kingdom **74** I7 55 37N 2 49W
Galeão Brazil **71** Q2 22 49S 43 14W
Galeota Point Trinidad and Tobago **69** U9 10 09N 60 00W
Galera Point Trinidad and Tobago **69** U10 10 49N 60 54W
Galesburg Illinois U.S.A. **65** H5 40 58N 90 22W
Galilee, Sea of see Lake Tiberias
Galina Point Jamaica **69** R8 18 24N 76 58W
Galle Sri Lanka **91** E1 6 01N 80 13E
Gallivare Sweden **112** 67 10N 20 40E
Gallup New Mexico U.S.A. **64** E4 32 32N 108 46W
Galston Australia **107** G3 33 39S 151 03E
Galty Mountains Republic of Ireland **74** C4 52 20N 8 10W
Galveston Texas U.S.A. **65** H2 29 17N 94 48W
Galway Republic of Ireland **74** B5 53 16N 9 03W
Galway Bay Republic of Ireland **74** B5 53 15N 9 15W
Gambell Alaska U.S.A. **8** A5 63 46N 171 45W
Gambia r. Senegal/The Gambia **102** C10 13 45N 13 15W
GAMBIA, THE **102** B10
Gambier Islands Pitcairn Islands **111** M5 23 10S 135 00W
Gamboa Panama **69** Y2 9 08N 79 42W
Gananoque r. India **91** E5 26 30N 85 00E
Ganga (Ganges) r. India **91** F4 25 00N 87 30E
Ganga, Mouths of the est. Bangladesh/India **91** F4
21 30N 89 00E
Ganganagar India **91** C5 29 54N 73 56E
Gangdisê Shan mts. China **93** F5 31 00N 82 30E
Ganges see Ganga
Gangtok India **91** F5 27 20N 88 39E
Ganzhou China **93** M4 25 45N 114 51E
Gao Mali **102** E11 16 19N 0 09W
Garden City Kansas U.S.A. **64** F4 37 57N 100 54W
Gardēz Afghanistan **89** K5 33 37N 69 07E
Gardner Island Pacific Ocean **110** I4 4 40S 174 32W
Gariya India **90** K1 22 27N 88 23E
Garland Texas U.S.A. **65** G3 32 55N 96 37W
Garonne r. France **72** F4 44 45N 0 30E
Garoua Cameroon **102** H9 9 17N 13 22E
Garulia India **90** K3 22 49N 88 23E
Gary Indiana U.S.A. **65** I5 41 34N 87 20W
Garyarsa China **91** E6 31 46N 80 21E
Garzón Colombia **70** B13 2 14N 75 37W
Gascoyne r. Australia **106** A5 25 00S 114 00E
Gasherbrum mts. Kashmir **91** D7 35 46N 76 38E
Gaspar Grande i. Trinidad and Tobago **69** S10
10 40N 61 39W
Gastonia North Carolina U.S.A. **65** J4 35 14N 81 12W
Gata, Cape Cyprus **88** N12 34 40N 33 01E
Gateshead United Kingdom **74** J6 54 58N 1 35W
Gates of the Arctic National Park and Preserve
Alaska U.S.A. **34** A4 67 00N 153 00W
Gatún Panama **69** Y2 9 16N 79 55W
Gatún Lake Panama **69** Y2 9 15N 79 50W
Gatun Locks Panama **69** Y2 9 16N 79 55W
Gaya India **91** F4 24 48N 85 00E
Gaylord Michigan U.S.A. **42** B2 45 02N 84 41W
Gaza Middle East **88** O10 31 30N 34 28E
Gaza Strip territory Middle East **88** O10 31 28N 34 05E
Gaziantep Turkey **73** N3 37 04N 37 21E
Gbarnga Liberia **102** D9 7 02N 9 26W
Gdańsk Poland **72** J6 54 22N 18 41E
Gdynia Poland **72** J6 54 31N 18 30E
Gebel el Tih p. Egypt **88** N9/O9 29 30N 33 45E
Gebel Katherina hill Egypt **88** N9 28 30N 33 57E
Gebel Mûsa (Mount Sinai) Egypt **88** N9 28 32N 33 59E
Gedaref Sudan **102** M10 14 01N 35 24E
Gediz r. Turkey **88** C6 38 40N 27 30E
Geelong Australia **106** G2 38 10S 144 26E
Gejiu China **93** K3 23 25N 103 05E
Gemsbok National Park Botswana **103** J2 26 00S 21 00E
Genalē r. Ethiopia **102** M9 6 00N 40 00E
Geneina Sudan **102** J10 13 27N 22 30E
General Belgrano II r.s. Antarctica **113** T7 77 52S 34 37W
General Bernardo O'Higgins r.s. Antarctica **113** 63
19S 57 54W
General San Martin r.s. Antarctica **113** 68 08S 67 06W

Geneseo New York U.S.A. **42** J3 42 46N 77 49W
Geneva New York U.S.A. **43** K3 42 53N 76 59W
Geneva Ohio U.S.A. **42** F2 41 48N 80 57W
Genève (Geneva) Switzerland **72** G5 46 13N 6 09E
Gennevilliers France **79** B2 48 56N 2 17E
Genova (Genoa) Italy **72** G4 44 24N 8 56E
Gent Belgium **72** F6 51 02N 3 42E
Georges River Australia **107** F2 33 57S 150 57E
Georgetown Guyana **70** F14 6 46N 58 10W
Georgetown Malaysia **95** C5 5 25N 100 20E
Georgetown South Carolina U.S.A. **65** K3
33 23N 79 18W
George V Land geog. reg. Antarctica **113** 70 00S 150 00E
George VI Sound Antarctica **113** 72 00S 67 00W
GEORGIA **73** P4
Georgia state U.S.A. **65** J3 33 00N 83 00W
Georgina r. Australia **106** F5 22 30S 138 00E
Georg von Neumayer r.s. Antarctica **113** 70 37S 8 22W
Geraldton Australia **106** A4 28 49S 144 36E
GERMANY **72** G6
Gerrards Cross United Kingdom **78** A3 51 35N 0 34W
Gettysburg National Military Park Pennsylvania U.S.A.
66 A2 39 57N 77 15W
Getz Ice Shelf Antarctica **113** 75 00S 120 00W
Ghadāmis Libya **102** H12 24 58N 10 11E
Ghadāmis Libya **102** G14 30 08N 9 30E
Ghaghara r. India **91** E5 26 20N 83 30E
GHANA **102** E9
Ghanzi Botswana **103** J3 21 42S 21 39E
Ghardaïa Algeria **102** F14 32 20N 3 40E
Gharyān Libya **102** H14 32 10N 13 01E
Ghaziabad India **91** D5 28 39N 77 26E
Ghazni Afghanistan **89** K5 33 33N 68 26E
Gibraltar territory U.K. **72** D3 36 09N 5 21W
Gibraltar, Strait of Spain/Morocco **72** D3 35 58N 5 30W
Gibson Desert Australia **106** C5 25 00S 123 00E
Gidolē Ethiopia **102** M9 5 38N 37 28E
Gifu Japan **96** C2 35 27N 136 46E
Gijón Spain **72** D4 43 32N 5 40W
Gila r. U.S.A. **64** D3 33 00N 114 00W
Gila Bend Arizona U.S.A. **64** D3 32 56N 112 42W
Gilbert r. Australia **106** G6 17 00S 142 30E
Gilbert Islands Pacific Ocean **110** H7 0 00 173 00E
Gilgit Kashmir **91** C7 35 54N 74 20E
Gillette Wyoming U.S.A. **64** E5 44 18N 105 30W
Gillingham United Kingdom **74** L3 51 24N 0 33E
Ginir Ethiopia **102** N9 7 06N 40 40E
Gippsland geog. reg. Australia **106** H2 37 30S 147 00E
Girard Pennsylvania U.S.A. **42** F2 42 01N 80 20W
Girardot Colombia **70** C13 4 19N 74 47W
Girga Egypt **102** L13 26 17N 31 58E
Gisborne N.Z. **107** C3 38 40S 178 01E
Gizhiga Russian Federation **85** S8 62 00N 160 34E
Glacier Bay Alaska U.S.A. **34** A3 58 50N 136 30W
Glacier Bay National Park Alaska U.S.A. **50** D2
58 45N 136 30W
Glacier National Park Montana U.S.A. **64** D6
48 50N 114 00W
Gladesville Australia **107** G2 33 50S 151 08E
Gladstone Australia **106** I5 23 52S 151 16E
Glasgow United Kingdom **74** G7 55 53N 4 15W
Glassboro New Jersey U.S.A. **66** C2 39 42N 75 07W
Glazov Russian Federation **87** G6 58 09N 52 42E
Glen Burnie Maryland U.S.A. **66** B2 39 10N 76 37W
Glendale California U.S.A. **67** C2 34 09N 118 16W
Glens Falls tn. New York U.S.A. **65** L5 43 17N 73 41W
Glienicke Germany **79** F2 52 39N 13 19E
Globe Arizona U.S.A. **64** D3 33 23N 110 48W
Gloucester United Kingdom **74** I3 51 53N 2 14W
Goa admin. India **91** C3 15 00N 74 00E
Goalpara Assam India **91** G5 26 10N 90 38E
Gobabis Namibia **103** I3 22 30S 18 58E
Gobi Desert Mongolia **93** J7/L7 48 30N 100 00E
Godāvari r. India **91** E3 18 00N 80 30E
Godhavn see Qeqertarsuaq
Godhra India **91** C4 22 49N 73 40E
Godthåb see Nuuk
Godwin Austen see K2
Goiânia Brazil **70** H9 16 43S 49 18W
Goiás admin. Brazil **70** H10 14 00S 48 00W
Goiás Brazil **70** G9 15 57S 50 07W
Golan Heights territory Israel **88** O11 33 00N 35 50E
Gold Coast tn. Australia **106** I4 27 59S 153 22E
Golden Bay N.Z. **107** B2 40 40S 172 49E
Goldfield California U.S.A. **67** D3 37 42N 117 15W
Goldsboro North Carolina U.S.A. **65** K4 35 23N 78 00W
Goldsworthy Australia **106** B5 20 20S 119 31E
Goleta California U.S.A. **67** C2 34 26N 119 50W
Golfe de Gabès g. Tunisia **102** H14 34 20N 10 30E
Golfe de California g. Mexico **64** D2 27 00N 111 00W
Golfo de Guayaquil g. Ecuador **70** A12 3 00S 81 30W
Golfo de Honduras g. Caribbean Sea **68** G3
17 00N 87 30W
Golfo del Darién g. Colombia/Panama **69** I1
9 00N 77 00W
Golfo de Panamá g. Panama **69** I1 8 00N 79 00W
Golfo de San Jorge g. Argentina **71** E4 47 00S 66 00W
Golfo de Tehuantepec g. Mexico **68** E3/F3
15 30N 95 00W
Golfo de Venezuela g. Venezuela **70** C15 12 00N 71 30W
Golfo di Taranto g. Italy **88** A6 40 00N 17 00E
Golfo San Matías g. Argentina **71** E4 42 00S 64 00W
Golmud China **92** H6 36 22N 94 55E
Gomel' see Homyel'
Gomera i. Canary Islands **102** B13 28 08N 17 14W
Gómez Palacio Mexico **68** D5 25 39N 103 30W
Gonder Ethiopia **102** M10 12 39N 37 29E
Gondia India **91** E4 21 23N 80 14E

Gonesse France **79** B2 48 59N 2 27E
Gongzhuling China **93** O7 43 30N 124 48E
Good Hope, Cape of Republic of South Africa **103** I1
34 30S 19 00E
Goodland Kansas U.S.A. **64** F4 39 20N 101 43W
Goondiwindi Australia **106** I4 28 30S 150 17E
Gora Belukha mt. Russian Federation **87** O4
49 50N 86 44E
Gora Kamen' mt. Russian Federation **85** L9
69 06N 94 59E
Gorakhpur India **91** E5 26 45N 83 23E
Gora Narodnaya mt. Russian Federation **85** I9
65 02N 60 01E
Gora Pobeda mt. Russian Federation **85** Q9
65 10N 146 00E
Gora Tebulos-mta mt. Georgia/Russian Federation
86 F3 42 32N 45 28E
Gora Telposiz mt. Russian Federation **87** H7 63 59N 59 02E
Gorda Rise Pacific Ocean **111** M12/N12 43 00N 130 00W
Gordon Australia **107** G2 33 46S 151 09E
Gore Ethiopia **102** M9 8 10N 35 29E
Gore N.Z. **107** A1 46 06S 168 56E
Gorgān Iran **89** H6 36 50N 54 29E
Gor'kiy see Nizhniy Novgorod
Gorkiy Park Russian Federation **86** M1 55 44N 37 37E
Gorman California U.S.A. **67** C2 34 48N 118 50W
Gorno-Altaysk Russian Federation **87** O5 51 59N 85 56E
Goroka Papua New Guinea **106** H8 6 02S 145 22E
Gorontalo Indonesia **95** G4 0 33N 123 05E
Göteborg Sweden **72** H7 57 45N 12 00E
Gotland i. Sweden **72** J7 57 30N 18 40E
Gough Island Atlantic Ocean **109** H2 40 20S 10 00W
Goulburn Australia **106** H3 34 47S 149 43E
Gourde, Point Trinidad and Tobago **69** S10 10 40N 61 36W
Gouré Niger **102** G10 13 59N 10 15E
Governador Valadares Brazil **70** I9 18 51S 41 57W
Governor's Harbour The Bahamas **65** K2 25 20N 76 20W
Govind Ballash Pant Sagar l India **91** E4 24 30N 82 30E
Gowanda New York U.S.A. **42** H3 42 28N 78 57W
Grafton Australia **106** I4 29 40S 152 56E
Graham Texas U.S.A. **64** G3 33 07N 98 36W
Graham Land geog. reg. Antarctica **113** 67 00S 64 00W
Grahamstown Republic of South Africa **103** K1
33 18S 26 32E
Grampian Mountains U.K. **74** G8/H8 56 45N 4 00W
Granada Spain **72** E3 37 10N 3 35W
Granada Nicaragua **69** G2 11 58N 85 59W
Gran Canaria i. Canary Islands **102** B13 28 00N 15 35W
Gran Chaco geog. reg. Argentina **71** F5 23 00S 62 30W
Gran Couva Trinidad and Tobago **69** T9 10 24N 61 23W
Grand r. South Dakota U.S.A. **64** F6 46 00N 102 00W
Grand Bahama i. The Bahamas **69** I5 27 00N 78 00W
Grand Canal see Yun
Grand Canyon U.S.A. **64** D4 36 04N 112 07W
Grand Canyon National Park Arizona/Nevada U.S.A.
64 D4 34 00N 114 00W
Grand Canyon Village Arizona U.S.A. **64** D4 36 02N 112 09W
Grand Cayman i. Caribbean Sea **69** H4 19 20N 81 15W
Grand Coulee Washington U.S.A. **35** E1 47 58N 119 00W
Grand Coulee Dam Washington U.S.A. **64** C6 47 59N 118 58W
Grand Erg Occidental d. Algeria **102** F13/G13 30 30N 0 30E
Grand Erg Oriental geog. reg. Algeria **102** F13 30 15N 6 45E
Grande Rivière tn. Trinidad and Tobago **69** T10
10 50N 61 03W
Grande Terre i. Lesser Antilles **69** L3 17 00N 61 40W
Grand Forks North Dakota U.S.A. **65** G6 47 57N 97 05W
Grand Island tn. Nebraska U.S.A. **65** G5 40 56N 98 21W
Grand Junction tn. Colorado U.S.A. **64** E4 39 04N 108 33W
Grand Ledge Michigan U.S.A. **42** B3 42 45N 84 44W
Grand Rapids tn. Michigan U.S.A. **65** I5 42 57N 86 40W
Grand Rapids tn. Minnesota U.S.A. **65** H6 47 13N 93 31W
Grand Rapids tn. Ohio U.S.A. **42** C2 41 23N 83 52W
Grand River Michigan U.S.A. **42** A3 42 55N 85 15W
Grand River Ohio U.S.A. **42** F2 41 25N 80 57W
Grand Traverse Bay Michigan U.S.A. **42** A6 45 00N 85 30W
Grand Union Canal U.K. **78** B3 51 37N 0 29W
Grange Hill tn. Jamaica **69** P8 18 19N 78 11W
Granite Peak Montana U.S.A. **64** E6 45 10N 109 50W
Grant Range mts. California U.S.A. **67** E4
38 24N 115 27W
Grants Pass tn. Oregon U.S.A. **64** B5 42 26N 123 20W
Grasonville Maryland U.S.A. **66** B2 38 58N 76 12W
Grass Island China **92** D2 22 29N 114 22E
Grass Valley California U.S.A. **67** B4 39 13N 121 04W
Grassy Hill mt. China **92** B2 22 25N 114 01E
Gravesend United Kingdom **78** E2 51 27N 0 22E
Gravina Island Alaska U.S.A. **34** B3 55 25N 131 45W
Grayling Michigan U.S.A. **42** B5 44 40N 84 43W
Grays United Kingdom **78** E2 51 29N 0 20E
Graz Austria **72** J5 47 05N 15 22E
Great Abaco i. The Bahamas **69** I5 26 40N 77 00W
Great Astrolabe Reef Fiji **110** U15 18 45S 178 50E
Great Australian Bight b. Australia **106** D3/E3
33 00S 130 00E
Great Barrier Island N.Z. **107** C3 36 13S 175 24E
Great Barrier Reef Australia **106** G7/I5 15 00S 146 00E
Great Basin dep. California U.S.A. **67** D4 40 22N 116 00W
Great Basin Nevada U.S.A. **64** C4 40 00N 117 00W
Great Bend Pennsylvania U.S.A. **66** C4 41 58N 75 45W
Great Bend Kansas U.S.A. **64** G4 38 22N 98 47W
Great Bookham United Kingdom **78** B2 51 16N 0 21W
Great Dividing Range mts. Australia **106** G7/H2
35 00N 148 00E
Great Egg Harbour River New Jersey U.S.A.
66 D2 39 35N 74 55W
Greater Antilles is. West Indies **69** H4/K3 19 00N 78 00W
Greater Khingan Range see Da Hinggan Ling
Greater London co. U.K. **78** C3 51 30N 0 10W

Great Exuma *i.* The Bahamas **69** I4 23 30N 76 00W
Great Falls *tn.* Montana U.S.A. **64** D6 47 30N 111 16W
Great Inagua *i.* The Bahamas **69** J4 21 40N 73 00W
Great Karoo *mts.* Republic of South Africa **103** J1
   32 30S 22 30E
Great Kills Park New York U.S.A. **66** Y1 40 33N 74 11W
Great Miquelon St.-Pierre et Miquelon **49** C2
   46 55N 56 13W
Great Nicobar *i.* Nicobar Islands **91** G1 6 30N 94 00E
Great Oasis, The *geog. reg.* Egypt **88** D3 25 00N 30 30E
Great Ouse *r.* United Kingdom **74** K4 52 30N 0 20E
Great Pedro Bluff *c.* Jamaica **69** Q7 17 51N 77 45W
Great Salt Lake Utah U.S.A. **64** D5 41 10N 112 40W
Great Sand Sea Sahara Desert **102** J13 27 00N 25 00E
Great Sandy Desert Australia **106** C5/D5 21 00S 124 00E
Great Sea Reef Fiji **110** T16-U16 16 30S 178 00E
Great Victoria Desert Australia **106** D4/E4
   28 00S 130 00E
Great Wall China **93** M6 40 00N 111 00E
Great Wall (Chang Cheng) *r.s.* Antarctica **113** G2 13S 58 58W
Great Yarmouth United Kingdom **74** M4 52 37N 1 44E
Great Zab *r.* Iraq **88** F6 36 00N 44 00E
GREECE **72** K3
Greeley Colorado U.S.A. **64** F5 40 26N 104 43W
Green *r.* U.S.A. **64** D5 42 00N 110 00W
Green Bay *tn.* Wisconsin U.S.A. **65** I5 44 32N 88 00W
Green Bay Wisconsin U.S.A. **65** I6 45 00N 87 00W
Green Creek *tn.* New Jersey U.S.A. **66** D2 39 03N 74 54W
Greene New York U.S.A. **66** C5 42 20N 75 45W
Green Island China **93** B1 22 17N 114 06E
Green Islands Papua New Guinea **106** I9 4 30S 154 15E
GREENLAND (Kalaalit Nunaat) **9** BB7
Greenland Basin Atlantic Ocean **109** H13 72 00N 0 00
Greenland Sea Arctic Ocean **112** 76 00N 5 00W
Green Mountains Vermont U.S.A. **65** L5 43 00N 73 00W
Greenock United Kingdom **74** G7 55 57N 4 45W
Greensboro Maryland U.S.A. **66** C1 38 58N 75 49W
Greensboro North Carolina U.S.A. **65** K4 36 03N 79 50W
Greenville Liberia **102** D9 5 01N 9 03W
Greenville Maine U.S.A. **43** S6 45 28N 69 36W
Greenville Mississippi U.S.A. **65** H3 33 23N 91 03W
Greenville South Carolina U.S.A. **65** J4 52N 82 25W
Greenville Texas U.S.A. **65** G3 33 09N 97 06W
Greenwich *bor.* United Kingdom **78** C2 51 29N 0 00
Greenwood Mississippi U.S.A. **65** H3 33 31N 90 10W
GRENADA **69** L2
Grenoble France **72** G5 45 11N 5 43E
Grey Range *mts.* Australia **106** G4 27 00S 144 00E
Greymouth N.Z. **107** B2 42 27S 171 12E
Gridley California U.S.A. **67** B4 39 24N 121 42W
Griffin Georgia U.S.A. **65** J3 33 15N 84 17W
Grimsby United Kingdom **74** K5 53 35N 0 05W
Grodno *see* Hrodna
Groningen Netherlands **72** G6 53 13N 6 35E
Grønnedal (Kangilinnguit) Greenland **9** BB5
   61 20N 48 00W
Groom Lake California U.S.A. **67** E3 37 18N 115 49W
Groote Eylandt *i.* Australia **106** F7 14 00S 137 00E
Grootfontein Namibia **103** I4 19 32S 18 05E
Grossbeeren Germany **79** F1 52 20N 13 19E
Grosser Müggelsee *l.* Germany **79** G1 52 26N 13 39E
Grosser Zernsee *l.* Germany **79** D1 52 22N 12 57E
Groveland California U.S.A. **67** B3 37 43N 120 56W
Groznyy Russian Federation **84** G4 43 21N 45 42E
Guadalajara Mexico **68** D4 20 40N 103 20W
Guadalcanal *i.* Solomon Islands **106** J8/K8 9 30S 160 00E
Guadalquivir *r.* Spain **72** E3 37 30N 4 00W
Guadalupe Brazil **71** P2 22 50S 43 23W
Guadalupe *i.* Mexico **68** A2 29 00N 118 24W
Guadeloupe *i.* Lesser Antilles **69** L3 16 30N 61 30W
Guadiana *r.* Spain/Portugal **72** D3 39 00N 5 30W
Guaico Trinidad and Tobago **69** T10 10 35N 61 09W
Guajará Mirim Brazil **70** D10 10 50S 65 21W
Gualala California U.S.A. **67** A4 38 45N 123 31W
GUAM **110** E9
Guamúchil Mexico **68** C5 25 28N 108 10W
Guanabara Bay Brazil **71** Q2/3 22 45S 43 10W
Guanabara State *admin.* Brazil **71** Q2/3 22 45S 43 10W
Guanare Venezuela **69** K1 9 04N 69 45W
Guang'anmen China **94** B1 39 40N 116 20E
Guangzhou (Canton) China **93** M4 23 08N 113 20E
Guantánamo Cuba **69** I4 20 09N 75 14W
Guapo Bay Trinidad and Tobago **69** S9 10 12N 61 40W
Guaqui Bolivia **70** D9 16 38S 68 50W
Guarapuava Brazil **71** G2 25 22S 51 28W
Guasave Mexico **64** E2 25 33N 108 30W
Guasdualito Venezuela **70** C14 7 15N 70 40W
GUATEMALA **68** F3
Guatemala Guatemala **68** F2 14 38N 90 22W
Guatemala Basin Pacific Ocean **111** U9/J9 12 00N 95 00W
Guatuaro Point Trinidad and Tobago **69** U9
   10 20N 60 58W
Guayaguayare Trinidad and Tobago **69** T9
   10 09N 61 01W
Guayaguayare Bay Trinidad and Tobago **69** T9
   10 07N 61 03W
Guayaquil Ecuador **70** A12 2 13S 79 54W
Guaymas Mexico **68** B5 27 59N 110 54W
Gudri *r.* Pakistan **90** A5 26 00N 67 00E
Guernsey *i.* British Isles **74** I1 46 27N 2 35W
Guia de Pacobaiba Brazil **71** Q3 22 42S 43 10W
Guildford United Kingdom **74** K3 51 14N 0 35W
Guilin China **93** M4 25 21N 110 11E
GUINEA **102** C10
Guinea Basin Atlantic Ocean **109** H6/7 1 00N 8 00W
GUINEA-BISSAU **102** B10
Guinea, Gulf of Atlantic Ocean **102** E8 3 50N 3 00W
Güines Cuba **69** H4 22 50N 82 02W

Güiria Venezuela **70** E15 10 37N 62 21W
Guiyang China **93** L4 26 35N 106 40E
Gujarat *admin.* India **91** C4 23 20N 72 00E
Gujranwala Pakistan **91** C6 32 06N 74 11E
Gujrat Pakistan **91** C6 32 35N 74 06E
Gulbarga India **91** D3 17 22N 76 47E
Gulf of Santa Catalina California U.S.A. **67** D1
   33 07N 117 52W
Gulfport Mississippi U.S.A. **65** I3 30 21N 80 08W
Gulf, The Middle East **89** H4 27 20N 51 00E
Gulu Uganda **102** L8 2 46N 32 21E
Gunnison *r.* Colorado U.S.A. **64** E4 38 00N 107 00W
Guntersville, Lake Alabama U.S.A. **65** I3 34 00N 86 00W
Guntur India **91** E3 16 20N 80 27E
Gunung Kinabalu *mt.* Malaysia **95** F5 6 03N 116 32E
Gur'yev *see* Atyrau
Gusau Nigeria **102** G10 12 12N 6 40E
Guthrie Oklahoma U.S.A. **65** G4 35 53N 97 26W
Guwahati India **91** G5 26 10N 91 45E
GUYANA **70** F13
Guyana Basin Atlantic Ocean **109** D7 8 00N 50 00W
Gwalior India **91** D5 26 12N 78 09E
Gweru Zimbabwe **103** K4 19 27S 29 49E
Gyangze China **91** F5 28 53N 89 35E
Gyaring Co *l.* China **91** F6 31 05N 88 00E
Gyda Peninsula Russian Federation **85** J10 70 00N 77 30E
Gympie Australia **106** I4 26 10S 152 35E
Györ Hungary **72** J5 47 41N 17 40E
Gyumri (Leninakan) Armenia **86** E3 40 47N 43 49E
Gyzylarbat Turkmenistan **87** H2 39 00N 56 23E

H

Haast Pass New Zealand **107** A2 44 06S 169 21E
Hab *r.* Pakistan **90** B5 25 20N 67 00E
Habbān Yemen Republic **89** G1 14 21N 47 04E
Haboro Japan **96** D3 44 23N 141 43E
Hachinohe Japan **96** D3 40 30N 141 30E
Hackensack River New Jersey U.S.A. **66** Y2 40 47N 74 06W
Hackettstown New Jersey U.S.A. **66** D3 40 52N 74 50W
Hackney *bor.* United Kingdom **78** C3 51 33N 0 03W
Hadano Japan **96** C2 35 25N 139 10E
Haddonfield New Jersey U.S.A. **66** C2 39 53N 75 01W
Hadejia Nigeria **102** G10 12 30N 10 03E
Hadera Israel **88** O11 32 26N 34 55E
Hadhramaut *geog. reg.* Yemen Republic **89** G2
   15 40N 47 30E
Hadiboh Yemen Republic **89** H1 12 36N 53 59E
Haeju North Korea **93** P6 38 04N 125 40E
Hagerstown Maryland U.S.A. **65** K4 39 39N 77 44W
Ha Giang Vietnam **93** L3 22 50N 104 58E
Haidian China **94** B1 39 59N 116 21E
Haifa Israel **88** D5 32 49N 34 59E
Haikou China **93** M3 20 05N 110 25E
Hā'il Saudi Arabia **88** F4 27 31N 41 45E
Hailar China **93** N8 49 15N 119 41E
Hainan Dao *i.* China **93** L2/M2 18 50N 109 50E
Haines Alaska U.S.A. **50** D2 59 11N 135 23W
Hai Phong (Haiphong) Vietnam **93** L3 20 50N 106 41E
HAITI **69** J3
Hakodate Japan **93** S7 41 46N 140 44E
Halab (Aleppo) Syria **88** E6 36 14N 37 10E
Halaib Sudan **102** M12 22 12N 36 30E
Halawa, Cape Hawaiian Islands **111** Y18 21 09N 157 15W
Halba Lebanon **88** P12 34 33N 36 04E
Halishahar India **108** K3 22 55N 88 25E
Hall Basin Greenland **51** U7 80 20N 62 30W
Halle Germany **72** H6 51 28N 11 58E
Halley *r.s.* Antarctica **113** 75 35S 26 15W
Halls Creek *tn.* Australia **106** D6 18 17S 127 38E
Hallstead Pennsylvania U.S.A. **66** C4 41 57N 75 45W
Halmahera *i.* Indonesia **95** H4 0 30S 127 00E
Halvø *p.* Greenland **9** X8 76 00N 67 30W
Hamāh Syria **88** E6 35 10N 36 45E
Hamada Japan **96** B1 34 52 10N 124 04E
Hamadān Iran **89** G5 34 46N 48 35E
Hamamatsu Japan **96** C1 34 42N 137 42E
Hambantota Sri Lanka **91** E1 6 07N 81 07E
Hamburg Germany **72** H6 53 33N 10 00E
Hamburg New York U.S.A. **42** H3 42 44N 78 50W
Hamburg Pennsylvania U.S.A. **66** C4 40 33N 75 59W
Hamersley Range *mts.* Australia **106** B5 22 00S 117 00E
Hamhŭng North Korea **93** P6 39 54N 127 35E
Hami (Kumul) China **92** H7 42 37N 93 32E
Hamilton New Zealand **107** C3 37 47S 175 17E
Hamilton Ohio U.S.A. **65** J4 39 23N 84 33W
Hammersmith *bor.* United Kingdom **78** C2 51 30N 0 14W
Hammond Indiana U.S.A. **65** I5 41 36N 87 30W
Hammonton New Jersey U.S.A. **66** D2 39 38N 74 49W
Hampton Virginia U.S.A. **65** K4 37 02N 76 23W
Hancock New York U.S.A. **66** C4 41 58N 75 17W
Handan China **93** M6 36 35N 114 31E
Hangzhou China **93** O5 30 18N 120 07E
Hannibal Missouri U.S.A. **65** H4 39 41N 91 20W
Ha Nôi (Hanoi) Vietnam **93** L3 21 01N 105 52E
Hanover Pennsylvania U.S.A. **66** B2 39 47N 76 59W
Haora *admin.* India **90** K2 22 40N 88 18E
Haora India **91** F4 22 35N 88 20E
Happy Valley Hong Kong China **92** C1 22 16N 114 11E
Haql Saudi Arabia **88** D4 29 14N 34 56E
Harad Saudi Arabia **89** G3 24 12N 49 08E
Harare Zimbabwe **103** L4 17 50S 31 03E
Harbin China **93** P8 45 45N 126 41E
Harbor Beach *tn.* Michigan U.S.A. **42** D4 43 51N 82 40W
Harbor Springs *tn.* Michigan U.S.A. **42** B5 45 25N 84 59W
Hardangervidda *mts.* Norway **72** G8 60 10N 7 00E
Harefield United Kingdom **78** B3 51 36N 0 28W

Härer Ethiopia **102** N9 9 20N 42 10E
Hargeysa Somalia **102** N9 9 31N 44 02E
Haridwar India **91** D5 29 58N 78 09E
Harima-nada *sea* Japan **96** B1 34 30N 134 30E
Haringey *bor.* United Kingdom **78** C3 51 35N 0 07W
Harlem New York U.S.A. **66** Y2 40 48N 73 56W
Harlingen Texas U.S.A. **65** G2 26 12N 97 43W
Harper Liberia **102** D8 4 25N 7 43W
Harper Lake California U.S.A. **67** D2 35 03N 117 15W
Harrington Delaware U.S.A. **66** C1 38 55N 75 35W
Harris *i.* United Kingdom **74** D9 57 50N 6 55W
Harrisburg Pennsylvania U.S.A. **65** K5 40 17N 76 54W
Harrisonburg Virginia U.S.A. **65** K4 38 27N 78 54W
Harrisville Michigan U.S.A. **42** C5 44 41N 83 19W
Harrisville New York U.S.A. **43** L4 44 09N 75 20W
Harrogate United Kingdom **74** J6 54 00N 1 33W
Harrow *bor.* United Kingdom **78** B3 51 34N 0 20W
Hartford Connecticut U.S.A. **65** L5 41 00N 72 00W
Hartland Point United Kingdom **74** G3 51 02N 4 31W
Hartlepool United Kingdom **74** J6 54 41N 1 13W
Harveys Lake *tn.* Pennsylvania U.S.A. **66** B4 41 22N 76 04W
Harwich United Kingdom **74** M3 51 57N 1 17E
Haryana *admin.* India **91** D5 29 20N 75 30E
Harz Mountains Europe **72** H6 52 00N 10 00E
Hassan India **91** D2 13 01N 76 03E
Hassi Messaoud Algeria **102** G14 31 52N 5 43E
Hastings Barbados **69** V12 13 05N 59 36W
Hastings United Kingdom **74** L2 50 51N 0 36E
Hastings Michigan U.S.A. **42** A3 42 38N 85 17W
Hastings Nebraska U.S.A. **65** G5 40 37N 98 22W
Hatay (Antakya) Turkey **86** D2 36 12N 36 10E
Ha Tsuen Hong Kong China **92** A2 22 26N 113 59E
Hatteras, Cape North Carolina U.S.A. **65** K4 35 14N 75 31W
Hattiesburg Mississippi U.S.A. **65** I3 31 20N 89 19W
Hat Yai Thailand **95** C5 7 00N 100 25E
Haud *geog. reg.* Africa **102** N9 8 00N 50 00E
Hauraki Gulf New Zealand **107** C3 36 38S 175 04E
Haut Atlas *mts.* Morocco **102** D14 30 45N 6 50W
Hauts-de-Seine *admin.* France **79** A2 81 48 45N 2 16E
Hauz Khas India **108** L4 28 34N 77 11E
Havana *see* La Habana
Havel *r.* Germany **79** E2 52 35N 13 13E
Havelkanal *can.* Germany **79** E2 52 38N 13 02E
Havering United Kingdom **78** D3 51 34N 0 14E
Havre Montana U.S.A. **64** E6 48 34N 109 40W
Havre de Grace Maryland U.S.A. **66** B2 39 33N 76 06W
Hawaii *i.* Hawaiian Islands **111** Z17 19 50N 157 50W
Hawaiian Islands Pacific Ocean **110** I10/K10
   25 00N 166 00W
Hawaiian Ridge Pacific Ocean **111** J10 23 00N 166 00W
Hawea, Lake New Zealand **107** A2 44 28S 169 17E
Hawera New Zealand **107** B3 39 35S 174 17E
Hawick United Kingdom **74** I7 55 25N 2 47W
Hawke Bay New Zealand **107** C3 39 23S 177 12E
Hawley Pennsylvania U.S.A. **66** C4 41 28N 75 11W
Hawthorne California U.S.A. **67** C4 38 33N 118 37W
Hayama Japan **97** B2 35 16N 139 35E
Hayes United Kingdom **78** B3 51 31N 0 25W
Hayes Halvø *p.* Greenland **51** T6 76 00N 67 30W
Hayward California U.S.A. **67** A3 37 40N 122 07W
Hazelton Pennsylvania U.S.A. **66** C3 40 58N 75 59W
Healdsburg California U.S.A. **67** A4 38 36N 122 53W
Heard Island Indian Ocean **108** G1 53 07S 73 20E
Heart *r.* North Dakota U.S.A. **64** F6 47 00N 102 00W
Heathcote Australia **107** G1 34 05S 151 00E
Hebi China **93** M6 35 57N 114 08E
Hebron Middle East **88** O10 31 32N 35 06E
Heceta Island Alaska U.S.A. **34** B3 55 45N 134 40W
Hechuan China **93** L5 30 02N 106 5E
Hefei China **93** N5 31 55N 117 18E
Hegang China **93** Q8 47 36N 130 30E
Hegura-jima *i.* Japan **96** C2 37 52N 136 56E
Hei Ling Chau *i.* Hong Kong China **92** B1 22 15N 114 02E
Hekla *mt.* Iceland **72** B8 64 00N 19 41W
Hekou China **93** K3 22 30N 104 00E
Helan Shan *mts.* China **93** L6 38 00N 106 00E
Helena Montana U.S.A. **64** D6 46 35N 112 00W
Helendale California U.S.A. **67** D2 34 45N 117 19W
Heliong Jiang (Amur) *r.* Asia **93** P9 52 30N 126 30E
Hellersdorf Germany **79** G2 52 32N 13 35E
Helmand *r.* Afghanistan **89** J5 34 00N 62 30E
Helsinki Finland **72** K8 60 08N 25 00E
Hemet California U.S.A. **67** D1 33 45N 116 58W
Henderson Nevada U.S.A. **64** D4 36 00N 114 00W
Hendon United Kingdom **78** C3 51 35N 0 14W
Heng-ch'un Taiwan **94** G5 22 03N 120 45E
Hengyang China **93** M4 26 58N 112 31E
Hennigsdorf *admin.* Germany **79** E2 52 39N 13 08E
Henryetta Oklahoma U.S.A. **65** G4 35 27N 96 00W
Henzada Myanmar **95** B7 17 36N 95 26E
Herāt Afghanistan **89** J5 34 20N 62 12E
Herblay France **79** A2 48 59N 2 10E
Hereford United Kingdom **74** I4 52 04N 2 43W
Hermel Lebanon **88** P12 34 25N 36 23E
Hermon New York U.S.A. **43** L5 44 28N 75 12W
Hermon, Mount Lebanon/Syria **88** O11 33 24N 35 50E
Hermosillo Mexico **68** B5 29 15N 110 59W
Hernodorf Germany **79** F2 52 38N 13 18E
Hesperia California U.S.A. **67** D2 34 25N 117 19W
Hertfordshire *co.* United Kingdom **78** C3 51 50N 0 05W
Hetch Hetchy Aqueduct California U.S.A. **67** B3
   37 35N 121 45W
Hetch Hetchy Reservoir California U.S.A. **67** C3
   37 57N 119 45W
Hickory North Carolina U.S.A. **65** J4 35 44N 81 23W
Hicksville Ohio U.S.A. **42** B2 41 18N 84 45W
Hidalgo Mexico **68** E4 24 16N 99 28W
Hidalgo del Parral Mexico **68** C5 26 58N 105 40W

Higashi-suidō *sd.* Japan **96** A1 34 10N 130 00E
High Bridge New Jersey U.S.A. **66** D3 40 42N 74 53W
Highgate Jamaica **69** R8 18 16N 76 53W
High Island Hong Kong China **92** D2 22 21N 114 21E
High Island Reservoir Hong Kong China **92** D2
   22 22N 114 20E
High Point *tn.* North Carolina U.S.A. **65** K4
   35 58N 80 00W
High Veld *mts.* Republic of South Africa **103** K2
   28 00S 28 00E
Hiiumaa *i.* Estonia **86** A6 58 55N 22 30E
Hiko California U.S.A. **67** E3 37 36N 115 14W
Hillaby, Mount Barbados **69** V12 13 12N 59 35W
Hillingdon *bor.* United Kingdom **78** B3 51 32N 0 27W
Hillsdale U.S.A. **67** A4 38 34N 137 W
Hilo Hawaiian Islands **111** Z17 19 42N 155 04W
Hilton New York U.S.A. **42** J4 43 16N 77 46W
Himachal Pradesh *admin.* India **91** D6 32 00N 77 30E
Himalaya *mts.* Asia **91** D6-G5 28 00N 85 00E
Himeji Japan **96** B1 34 50N 134 40E
Hinckley Lake *res.* New York U.S.A. **43** L4
   43 20N 75 05W
Hindu Kush *mts.* Afghanistan **89** K6 35 00N 70 00E
Hirakata Japan **96** C1 34 45N 135 38E
Hirakud Reservoir India **91** E4 21 40N 83 40E
Hirosaki Japan **96** D3 40 34N 140 28E
Hiroshima Japan **96** B1 34 23N 132 27E
Hisar India **91** D5 29 10N 75 45E
Hispaniola *i.* West Indies **69** J3 18 00N 70 00W
Hitachi Japan **96** D2 36 35N 140 40E
Ho Ghana **102** F9 6 38N 0 38E
Hobart Australia **106** H1 42 54S 147 18E
Hoboken New Jersey U.S.A. **66** Y1 40 44N 74 02W
Hobyo Somalia **102** O9 5 20N 48 30E
Ho Chi Minh (Saigon) Vietnam **95** D6 10 46N 106 43E
Ho Chung Hong Kong China **92** C2 22 22N 114 14E
Hodogaya Japan **97** B2 35 26N 139 36E
Höfn Iceland **72** C8 64 16N 15 10W
Hofu Japan **96** B1 34 02N 131 34E
Hoggar *mts.* Algeria **102** G12 23 45N 6 00E
Hohhot China **93** M7 40 49N 117 37E
Hoi Ha Hong Kong China **92** C2 22 28N 114 20E
Hokitika New Zealand **107** B2 42 43S 170 58E
Hokkaidō *i.* Japan **96** D3 43 30N 143 00E
Holetown Barbados **69** V12 13 11N 59 38W
Holguín Cuba **69** I4 20 54N 76 15W
Hollick-Kenyon Plateau Antarctica **113** 77 00S 100 00W
Hollis Reservoir Trinidad and Tobago **69** T10
   10 42N 61 11W
Holly Michigan U.S.A. **42** C3 42 48N 83 37W
Holsteinsborg *see* Sisimiut
Holston *r.* U.S.A. **65** J4 37 00N 82 00W
Ho-lung Taiwan **94** G7 24 37N 120 46E
Holy Cross Alaska U.S.A. **8** D5 62 10N 159 53W
Holyhead United Kingdom **74** G5 53 19N 4 38W
Holy Island *i.* Wales United Kingdom **74** G5
   53 16N 4 39W
Holy Island (Lindisfarne) *i.* England United Kingdom
   74 J7 55 41N 1 48W
Ho Man Tin Hong Kong China **92** B1 22 19N 114 10E
Homer Alaska U.S.A. **8** E4 59 40N 151 37W
Homestead Florida U.S.A. **65** J2 25 29N 80 29W
Homyel' (Gomel') Belarus **72** M6 52 25N 31 00E
Honda Colombia **70** C14 5 15N 74 50W
HONDURAS **68** G2
Honesdale Pennsylvania U.S.A. **66** C4 41 34N 75 15W
Hong *see* Song-koi
Hong Kong *admin.* China **93** M3 23 00N 114 00E
Hong Kong *i.* China **92** B1/C1 22 10N 114 10E
Hong Lok Yuen Hong Kong China **92** B2 22 27N 114 09E
Honiara Solomon Islands **106** J8 9 28S 159 57E
Honokaa Hawaiian Islands **111** Z18 20 04N 155 27W
Honolulu Hawaiian Islands **111** Y18 21 19N 157 50W
Honshū *i.* Japan **96** C2 37 15N 139 00E
Hood, Mount Oregon U.S.A. **64** B6 45 24N 121 41W
Hook United Kingdom **78** B2 51 17N 0 58W
Hoolehua Hawaiian Islands **111** Y18 21 11N 157 06W
Hoonah Alaska U.S.A. **34** A3 58 06N 135 25W
Hooper Bay *tn.* Alaska U.S.A. **8** B5 61 29N 166 10W
Hope Barbados **69** V13 13 20N 59 36W
Hopkinsville Kentucky U.S.A. **65** I4 36 50N 87 30W
Ho Pui Hong Kong China **92** B2 22 24N 114 04E
Horki Belarus **86** C5 54 17N 30 59E
Horlivka Ukraine **86** D4 48 17N 38 05E
Hormuz, Strait of The Gulf **89** I4 26 35N 56 30E
Horn, Cape *see* Cabo de Hornos
Hornchurch United Kingdom **78** D3 51 34N 0 13E
Hornell New York U.S.A. **42** J3 42 19N 77 39W
Hornsby Australia **107** G3 33 42S 151 06E
Horseheads New York U.S.A. **42** K3 42 11N 76 51W
Horsham Australia **106** G2 36 45S 142 15E
Horsham United Kingdom **74** K3 51 04N 0 21W
Hospet India **91** D3 15 16N 76 20E
Hospitalet Spain **72** F4 41 21N 2 06E
Hotan China **92** E6 37 07N 79 57E
Hotan *r.* China **92** F6 39 00N 80 30E
Hot Springs Arkansas U.S.A. **65** H3 34 30N 93 02W
Houghton Lake Michigan U.S.A. **42** B5 44 20N 84 45W
Houghton Lake *tn.* Michigan U.S.A. **42** B5 44 17N 84 45W
Houlton Maine U.S.A. **47** C2 46 09N 67 50W
Houma China **93** M5 35 36N 111 15E
Houma Louisiana U.S.A. **65** H2 29 35N 90 44W
Hounslow *bor.* United Kingdom **78** B2 51 28N 0 21W
Houston Texas U.S.A. **65** G2 29 45N 95 25W
Hovd Mongolia **92** H8 48 00N 91 43E
Hövsgöl Nuur *l.* Mongolia **93** K9 51 00N 100 30E
Howar *r.* Sudan **102** K11 17 00N 25 00E
Howe, Cape Australia **106** H2 37 20S 149 59E
Hoy *i.* United Kingdom **74** H10 58 48N 3 20W

Hrodna (Grodno) Belarus 72 K6 53 40N 23 50E
Hsin-chu Taiwan 94 G7 24 48N 120 59E
Hsin-tien Taiwan 94 H7 24 57N 121 32E
Hsin-ying Taiwan 94 G6 23 18N 120 18E
Huacho Peru 70 B10 11 05S 77 36W
Huainan China 93 N5 32 41N 117 06E
Huajuápan de León Mexico 68 E3 17 50N 97 48W
Hua-lien Taiwan 94 H6 23 58N 121 35E
Huambo Angola 103 I5 12 44S 15 47E
Huancayo Peru 70 B10 12 05S 75 12W
Huang Hai see Yellow Sea
Huang He r. China 93 M6 38 00N 111 00E
Huangshi China 93 N5 30 13N 115 05E
Huanuco Peru 70 B11 9 55S 76 11W
Hua-p'ing Hsü i. Taiwan 94 H8 25 26N 121 57E
Huaráz Peru 70 B11 9 33S 77 31W
Huascaran mt. Peru 70 B11 9 08S 77 36W
Huashixia China 93 J6 35 13N 99 12E
Huatabampo Mexico 64 C2 26 49N 109 40W
Hubbard Lake Michigan U.S.A. 42 C5 44 50N 83 30W
Huddersfield United Kingdom 74 J5 53 39N 1 47W
Hudson County admin. New Jersey U.S.A. 66 Y2
45 47N 74 04W
Hudson River New York U.S.A. 65 L5 42 00N 73 55W
Huê Vietnam 93 L2 16 28N 107 35E
Huevos i. Trinidad and Tobago 69 S10 10 47N 61 11W
Hughenden Australia 106 G5 20 50S 144 10E
Hugli admin. India 90 J2 22 40N 88 18E
Hugli r. India 90 J2 22 30N 88 14E
Hugli-Chinsurah India 90 K3 22 54N 88 23E
Hugo Oklahoma U.S.A. 65 G3 34 01N 95 31W
Huixtla Mexico 68 F3 15 09N 92 30W
Huizhou China 93 M3 23 08N 114 28E
Humaitá Brazil 70 E11 7 33S 63 01W
Humber r. United Kingdom 74 K5 53 40N 0 10W
Humboldt r. Nevada U.S.A. 64 C5 41 00N 118 00W
Humboldt Glacier Greenland 112 79 46N 64 00W
Humboldt Salt Marsh California U.S.A. 67 D4
39 49N 117 58W
Hungarian Basin Europe 72 J5/K5 47 00N 20 00E
HUNGARY 72 J5
Hung Hom Hong Kong China 92 C1 22 18N 114 11E
Hüngnam North Korea 93 P6 39 49N 127 40E
Hunjiang China 93 P7 41 54N 126 23E
Hunter Trench Pacific Ocean 110 H5 23 00S 175 00E
Huntington West Virginia U.S.A. 65 J4 38 24N 82 26W
Huntington Mexico 69 H7 40 54N 85 30W
Huntington Beach California U.S.A. 67 C1 33 40N 118 00W
Huntly New Zealand 107 C3 37 34S 175 10E
Huntsville Alabama U.S.A. 65 I3 34 44N 86 35W
Huntsville Texas U.S.A. 65 G3 30 43N 95 34W
Hurghada Egypt 88 D4 27 17N 33 47E
Huron River Michigan U.S.A. 42 C3 42 10N 83 15W
Hurstville Australia 107 G2 33 58S 151 06E
Husn Jordan 88 O11 32 29N 35 53E
Hutchinson Kansas U.S.A. 65 G4 38 03N 97 56W
Huzhou China 93 O5 30 56N 120 04E
Hwange Zimbabwe 103 K4 18 22S 26 29E
Hwange National Park Zimbabwe 103 K4 19 00S 26 00E
Hyder Alaska U.S.A. 34 B3 55 45N 130 10W
Hyderabad India 91 D3 17 22N 78 26E

I

Iaşi Romania 72 L5 47 09N 27 38E
Ibadan Nigeria 102 F9 7 23N 3 56E
Ibagué Colombia 70 B13 4 25N 75 20W
Ibarra Ecuador 70 B13 0 23N 78 05W
Ibb Yemen Republic 88 F1 14 03N 44 10E
Ibi Nigeria 102 G9 8 11N 9 44E
Ibiza i. Balearic Islands Spain 72 F3 38 54N 1 26E
Ibotirama Brazil 70 I10 12 13S 43 12W
Ibri Oman 89 I3 23 15N 56 35E
Ica Peru 70 B10 14 02S 75 48W
Icacos Trinidad and Tobago 69 S9 10 04N 61 55W
Icacos Point Trinidad and Tobago 69 S9 10 41N 61 42W
Icaraí Brazil 71 Q2 22 55S 43 07W
Içel (Mersin) Turkey 73 M3 36 47N 34 37E
ICELAND 72 B9
Ichalkaranji India 91 C3 16 40N 74 33E
Ichāpur India 90 K3 22 48N 88 22E
Ichikawa Japan 97 C3 35 45N 139 55E
Ichinomiya Japan 96 C2 35 18N 136 48E
Icy Strait sd. Alaska U.S.A. 34 A3 58 20N 135 45W
Idaho state U.S.A. 64 D5 44 00N 115 00W
Idaho Falls tn. Idaho U.S.A. 64 D5 43 30N 112 01W
Idfu Egypt 102 L12 24 58N 32 50E
Igarka Russian Federation 85 K9 67 31N 86 33E
Iguaçu r. Brazil 71 P3 22 44S 43 16W
Iguala Mexico 68 E3 18 21N 99 31W
Iguape Brazil 71 H8 24 37S 47 30W
Iguatu Brazil 70 J11 6 22S 39 20W
Ihosy Madagascar 103 O3 22 23S 46 09E
Iida Japan 96 C2 35 32N 137 48E
IJsselmeer l. Netherlands 72 G6 52 50N 5 15E
Ikela Congo (D.R.) 102 J7 1 06S 23 06E
Iki i. Japan 96 A1 33 50N 129 40E
Ikuta Japan 97 B3 35 36N 139 34E
Ilagan The Philippines 95 G7 17 07N 121 53E
I-lan Taiwan 94 H7 24 45N 121 44E
Île Amsterdam i. Indian Ocean 108 G3 37 56S 77 40E
Ilebo Congo (D.R.) 103 J7 4 20S 20 35E
Île de l'Europa i. Mozambique Channel 103 H3
22 20S 40 20E
Ilek r. Kazakhstan/Russian Federation 87 H5
51 00N 57 00E
Île St. Paul i. Indian Ocean 108 G3 38 44S 77 30E
Îles Chesterfield is. Pacific Ocean 106 J6 19 00S 153 30E

Îles Crozet is. Indian Ocean 108 E2 46 27S 52 00E
Ilesha Nigeria 102 F9 7 39N 4 38E
Îles Kerguelen is. Indian Ocean 108 F2 49 30S 69 30E
Îles Loyauté is. Pacific Ocean 106 L5/6 21 00S 167 00E
Îles Wallis is. Pacific Ocean 110 I6 13 16S 176 15W
Ilford United Kingdom 78 D3 51 33N 0 06E
Ilha Bazaruto i. Mozambique 103 M3 21 40S 35 30E
Ilha de Marajó i. Brazil 70 G12 1 30S 50 00W
Ilha de Paquetá i. Brazil 71 Q2 22 46S 43 07W
Ilha do Fundão i. Brazil 71 Q2 22 52S 43 13W
Ilha do Governador i. Brazil 71 Q2 22 47S 43 13W
Ilha do Pai i. Brazil 71 Q2 22 59S 43 05W
Ilha Fernando de Noronha i. Brazil 70 K12 3 50S 32 25W
Ilhéus Brazil 70 J10 14 50S 39 06W
Ili r. Asia 87 M3 44 00N 80 00E
Iliamna Lake Alaska U.S.A. 8 D4 59 30N 155 30W
Iligan The Philippines 95 G5 8 12N 124 13W
Ilikurangi N.Z. 107 C3 37 30S 177 40E
Illapel Chile 71 B7 31 40S 71 13W
Illinois state U.S.A. 65 I5 40 00N 89 00W
Illizi Algeria 102 G13 26 45N 8 30E
Illoqqortoormiut (Scoresbysund) tn. Greenland 112
70 30N 22 45W
Ilmen, Lake Russian Federation 72 M7 58 00N 31 30E
Iloilo The Philippines 95 G6 10 41N 122 33E
Ilorin Nigeria 102 F9 8 32N 4 34E
Ilulissat (Jakobshavn) Greenland 9 AA6 69 10N 51 05W
Imabari Japan 96 B3 34 04N 133 00E
Imatra Finland 86 B7 61 14N 28 50E
Imi Ethiopia 102 N9 6 28N 42 10E
Imperatriz Brazil 70 H11 5 32S 47 28W
Impfondo Congo 102 I8 1 36N 18 00E
Imphal India 91 G4 24 47N 93 55E
Inarijärvi l. Finland 72 L9 69 15N 27 30E
Ince Burun c. Turkey 86 C3 42 05N 34 55E
Inch'ŏn South Korea 93 P6 37 30N 126 38E
Indalsälven r. Sweden 72 J8 63 00N 15 30E
Independence California U.S.A. 67 C3 36 48N 118 14W
Independence Kansas U.S.A. 65 G4 37 13N 95 43W
Independence Fjord Greenland 112 82 00N 30 00W
INDIA 90 B4/F4
Indiana state U.S.A. 65 I5 40 00N 86 00W
Indian-Antarctic Basin Southern Ocean 110 A2/C2
57 00S 113 00E
Indian-Antarctic Ridge Southern Ocean 110 C2
51 00S 124 00E
Indianapolis Indiana U.S.A. 65 I4 39 45N 86 10W
Indian Ocean 108
Indian Springs California U.S.A. 67 E3 36 33N 115 40W
Indigirka r. Russian Federation 85 Q9 70 00N 147 30E
Indio California U.S.A. 67 D1 33 44N 116 14W
INDONESIA 95 C3/J6
Indravati r. India 91 E3 19 00N 81 30E
Indus r. Pakistan 90 B5/C6 26 00N 68 00E
Indus, Mouths of the est. Pakistan 90 B4 24 00N 67 00E
Inebolu Turkey 86 C3 41 57N 33 45E
Ingham Australia 106 H6 18 35S 146 12E
Inglefield Bay sd. Greenland 112 78 30N 68 55W
Inglewood California U.S.A. 67 C1 33 58N 118 22W
Inhambane Mozambique 103 M3 23 51S 35 29E
Inn r. Europe 72 H5 48 00N 12 00E
Inner Hebrides is. United Kingdom 74 E8 56 45N 6 45W
Inner Mongolia Autonomous Region see Nei Mongol
Zizhiqu
Innisfail Australia 106 H6 17 30S 146 00E
Innsbruck Austria 72 H5 47 17N 11 25E
Inongo Congo (D.R.) 102 I7 1 55S 18 20E
In Salah Algeria 102 F13 27 20N 2 03E
Insein Myanmar 95 B7 16 54N 96 08E
Inta Russian Federation 85 I9 66 04N 60 01E
Inubō-zaki c. Japan 96 D3 35 41N 140 52E
Invercargill New Zealand 107 A1 46 25S 168 22E
Inverness United Kingdom 74 G9 57 27N 4 15W
Inyo Range mts. California U.S.A. 67 D3 36 37N 117 52W
Ioánnina Greece 72 K3 39 40N 20 51E
Iona i. United Kingdom 74 E8 56 19N 6 25W
Ione Washington U.S.A. 35 E1 48 45N 117 25W
Ionia Michigan U.S.A. 42 A3 42 58N 85 06W
Ionian Islands Greece 72 K3 39 00N 20 00E
Ionian Sea Mediterranean Sea 72 J3 38 00N 17 00E
Iowa state U.S.A. 65 H5 42 00N 94 00W
Iowa City Iowa U.S.A. 65 H5 41 39N 91 31W
Ipanema Brazil 71 Q2 22 59S 43 13W
Ipanema Beach Brazil 71 Q2 23 00S 43 14W
Ipatinga Brazil 70 I9 19 32S 42 30W
Ipiales Colombia 70 B13 0 52N 77 38W
Ipoh Malaysia 95 C4 4 36N 101 05E
Ipswich England United Kingdom 74 M4 52 04N 1 10E
Ipu Brazil 70 I12 4 32S 40 44W
Iquique Chile 70 C8 20 15S 70 08W
Iquitos Peru 70 C12 3 51S 73 13W
Irajá Brazil 71 P2 22 50S 43 19W
Irákleio (Iraklion) Greece 72 L3 35 20N 25 08E
IRAN 89 H5
Irānshahr Iran 89 J4 27 15N 60 41E
Irapuato Mexico 68 D4 20 40N 101 30W
IRAQ 88 F5
Irbid Jordan 88 E5 32 33N 35 51E
Irecê Brazil 70 I10 11 22S 41 51W
Irian Jaya admin. Indonesia 95 I3 3 00S 133 00E
Iringa Tanzania 103 M6 7 49S 35 39E
Irish Sea British Isles 74 F5 53 30N 5 30W
Irkutsk Russian Federation 85 N8 52 18N 104 15E
Irois Bay Trinidad and Tobago 69 S9 10 09N 61 45W
Iron Knob tn. Australia 106 F3 32 44S 137 08E
Ironwood Michigan U.S.A. 65 H6 46 25N 90 08W
Irrawaddy r. Myanmar 91 G3 20 00N 95 00E
Irtysh r. Asia 87 L6 57 30N 72 30E

Irving Texas U.S.A. 65 G3 32 49N 96 57W
Isabella Reservoir California U.S.A. 67 C2 35 41N 118 28W
Ísafjördour Iceland 72 A9 66 05N 23 08W
Ise Japan 96 C1 34 29N 136 41E
Iset' r. Russian Federation 87 K6 56 30N 65 30E
Ishikari r. Japan 96 D3 43 20N 141 45E
Ishikari-wan b. Japan 96 D3 43 30N 141 00E
Ishim r. Russian Federation 87 K5 56 00N 69 00E
Ishim Russian Federation 87 K6 56 21N 69 30E
Ishimskaya Step geog. reg. Kazakhstan/Russian
Federation 87 L5 54 00N 71 00E
Ishinomaki Japan 96 D2 38 25N 141 18E
Isiro Congo (D.R.) 102 K8 2 50N 27 40E
Iskenderun Turkey 88 E6 36 37N 36 08E
Isla de Coiba i. Panama 69 H7 7 40N 82 00W
Isla de Cozumel i. Mexico 69 G3 20 30N 87 00W
Isla de la Juventud i. Cuba 69 H4 22 00N 82 30W
Isla del Coco (Cocos Islands) i. Costa Rica 111 R8
5 33N 87 00W
Isla de los Estados i. Argentina 71 E2 55 00S 64 00W
Isla de Patos i. Venezuela 69 S10 10 38N 61 51W
Isla Grande de Tierra del Fuego i. Chile/Argentina 71 D2
54 00S 67 30W
Islamabad Pakistan 91 C6 33 40N 73 08E
Isla Margarita i. Venezuela 69 L2 11 30N 64 00W
Islands, Bay of New Zealand 107 B3 35 13S 174 12E
Isla San Ambrosio i. Chile 71 B7 26 28S 79 53W
Isla San Felix i. Chile 70 A7 26 23S 80 00W
Islas de la Bahia i. Honduras 69 G3 16 40N 86 00W
Islas Galapagos is. Pacific Ocean 111 Q7 0 05S 90 00W
Islas Juan Fernández i. Chile 71 B6 33 30S 80 00W
Islas Marias i. Mexico 68 C4 22 00N 107 00W
Islas Revillagigedo is. Pacific Ocean 68 B3
19 00N 112 30W
Isla Wellington i. Chile 111 S3 48 50S 79 00W
Islay i. United Kingdom 74 E7 55 48N 6 12W
Isle of Man British Isles 74 G6 54 15N 4 30W
Isle of Wight United Kingdom 74 J2 50 40N 1 20W
Islington bor. United Kingdom 78 C3 51 33N 0 06W
Ismâ'iliya Egypt 88 D5 30 36N 32 16E
Isna Egypt 88 D4 25 16N 32 30E
Isogo Japan 97 B2 35 23N 139 37E
ISRAEL 88 E5
Issyk-Kul' (Rybach'ye) Kirgyzstan 87 M3 42 28N 76 09E
Istanbul Turkey 72 L4 41 02N 28 57E
Istmo de Tehuantepec ist. Mexico 68 F3 17 20N 93 10W
Itabaiana Brazil 70 J10 10 42S 37 37W
Itabashi Japan 97 B4 35 46N 139 39E
Itabuna Brazil 70 J10 14 48S 39 18W
Itacoatiara Brazil 70 F12 3 06S 58 22W
Itagüi Colombia 70 B14 6 13N 75 40W
Itaituba Brazil 70 F12 4 15S 55 56W
Itajaí Brazil 71 H7 26 50S 48 39W
ITALY 72 H4
Itapipoca Brazil 70 J12 3 29S 39 35W
Itaqui Brazil 71 F29 10S 56 30W
Itarsi India 91 D4 22 39N 77 48E
Itui r. Brazil 70 C11 5 30S 71 00W
Ivano-Frankivs'k Ukraine 86 A4 48 40N 24 40E
Ivanovo Russian Federation 84 G7 57 00N 41 00E
Ivanpah Lake California U.S.A. 67 E2 35 31N 115 22W
Ivdel' Russian Federation 84 I8 60 45N 60 30E
IVORY COAST see CÔTE D'IVOIRE
Ivry-sur-Seine France 79 B2 48 48N 2 24E
Iwaki Japan 96 D2 37 03N 140 58E
Iwakuni Japan 96 B1 34 10N 132 09E
Iwamizawa Japan 96 D3 43 12N 141 47E
Iwanai Japan 96 D3 43 01N 140 32E
Iwo Nigeria 102 F9 7 38N 4 11E
Ixtaccihuatl mt. Mexico 68 E3 19 11N 98 38W
Ixtapec Mexico 68 E3 16 32N 95 10W
Iyo-nada b. Japan 96 B1 33 50N 132 00E
Izhevsk (Ustinov) Russian Federation 84 H7 56 49N 53 11E
Izhma r. Russian Federation 84 H8 64 00N 54 00E
Izmaylovskiy Park Russian Federation 86 N2
55 46N 37 46E
Izmir Turkey 72 L3 38 25N 27 10E
Izmit see Kocaeli
Izmit Russian Federation 88 C4 40 47N 29 55E
Izra' Syria 88 P11 32 52N 36 15E
Izu-shotō is. Japan 96 C1 34 20N 139 20E

J

Jabal Akhdar mt. Oman 89 I3 24 00N 56 30E
Jabal as Sawdā' mts. Libya 102 H13 29 00N 15 00E
Jabalpur India 91 D4 23 10N 79 59E
Jaboatão Brazil 70 J11 8 05S 35 00W
Jacarepagua Brazil 71 P2 22 57S 43 21W
Jackman Maine U.S.A. 43 R6 45 37N 70 16W
Jackson Barbados 69 V12 13 09N 59 40W
Jackson California U.S.A. 67 B4 38 19N 120 47W
Jackson Michigan U.S.A. 35 J5 42 15N 84 24W
Jackson Mississippi U.S.A. 65 H3 32 20N 90 11W
Jackson Tennessee U.S.A. 65 I4 35 37N 88 50W
Jackson Wyoming U.S.A. 64 D5 43 28N 110 45W
Jackson Head New Zealand 107 A2 43 58S 168 37E
Jackson Heights tn. New York U.S.A. 67 Z2
40 45N 73 52W
Jacksonville Florida U.S.A. 65 J3 30 20N 81 40W
Jacksonville North Carolina U.S.A. 65 K3 34 45N 77 26W
Jacksonville Beach tn. Florida U.S.A. 65 J3 30 18N 81 24W
Jack Wade Alaska U.S.A. 8 C4 64 05N 141 35W
Jacmel Haiti 69 J3 18 18N 72 32W
Jacobabad Pakistan 90 B5 28 16N 68 30E
Jacobina Brazil 70 I10 11 13S 40 30W
Jaffna Sri Lanka 91 D1 9 40N 80 01E
Jagdalpur India 91 E3 19 04N 82 05E

Jahrom Iran 89 H4 28 29N 53 32E
Jaipur India 91 D5 26 53N 75 50E
Jakarta Indonesia 95 D2 6 08S 106 45E
Jakobshavn see Ilulissat
Jalālābād Afghanistan 89 L5 34 26N 70 25E
Jalapa Enriquez Mexico 68 E3 19 32N 96 56W
Jalgaon India 91 D4 21 01N 75 39E
Jalna India 91 D3 19 50N 75 58E
Jālū Libya 102 J13 29 02N 21 33E
JAMAICA 69 I3
Jamaica New York U.S.A. 67 Z1 40 42N 73 48W
Jamaica Bay New York U.S.A. 67 Z1 40 37N 73 50W
Jamaica Bay Wildlife Refuge New York U.S.A. 67 Z1
40 37N 73 50W
Jambi Indonesia 95 C3 1 34S 103 37E
James r. South Dakota U.S.A. 65 G5 44 00N 98 00W
James r. Virginia U.S.A. 65 K4 37 00N 77 00W
Jamestown New York U.S.A. 65 K5 42 05N 79 15W
Jamestown North Dakota U.S.A. 65 G6 46 54N 98 42W
Jamiltepec Mexico 68 E3 16 18N 97 51W
Jammu India 91 D6 32 43N 74 54E
Jammu & Kashmir state Southern Asia 91 D6
29 40N 76 30E
Jamnagar India 90 C4 22 28N 70 06E
Jamshedpur India 91 F4 22 47N 86 12E
Janesville Wisconsin U.S.A. 65 I5 42 42N 89 02W
Jan Mayen i. Arctic Ocean 112 71 00N 9 00W
Januária Brazil 70 I9 15 28S 44 23W
JAPAN 96
Japan, Sea of Pacific Ocean 96 C2 39 00N 137 00E
Japan Trench Pacific Ocean 110 E11 35 00N 143 00E
Jarú Brazil 70 E10 10 24S 62 45W
Jāsk Iran 89 I4 25 40N 57 46E
Jaunpur India 91 E5 25 44N 82 41E
Java Sea Indonesia 95 D2/E2 7 00S 112 00E
Java Trench Indian Ocean 108 J6 10 00S 110 00E
Jawa i. Indonesia 95 D2/E2 7 00S 110 00E
Jayapura Indonesia 95 J3 2 37S 140 39E
Jaza'ir Farasān is. Saudi Arabia 88 F2 16 45N 42 10E
Jean California U.S.A. 67 E2 35 46N 115 20W
Jebel Abyad Plateau Sudan 102 K11 18 00N 28 00E
Jebel Marra mts. Sudan 102 J10 13 00N 24 00E
Jefferson r. Russian Federation 42 F2 41 44N 80 46W
Jefferson City Missouri U.S.A. 65 H4 38 33N 92 10W
Jenin Jordan 88 O11 32 28N 35 18E
Jenner California U.S.A. 67 A4 38 27N 123 08W
Jequié Brazil 70 I10 13 52S 40 06W
Jérémie Haiti 69 J3 18 40N 74 09W
Jerez de la Frontera Spain 72 D3 36 41N 6 08W
Jericho Middle East 88 O10 31 51N 35 27E
Jersey i. British Isles 74 I4 49 13N 2 07W
Jersey City New Jersey U.S.A. 66 Y2 40 44N 74 06W
Jerusalem Israel/Jordan 88 E5 31 47N 35 13E
Jessore Bangladesh 91 F4 23 10N 89 12E
Jhang Pakistan 91 C6 31 19N 72 22E
Jhansi India 91 D5 25 27N 78 34E
Jhelum Pakistan 91 C6 32 58N 73 45E
Jhelum r. Pakistan 91 C6 32 30N 72 30E
Jiamusi China 93 Q8 46 59N 130 29E
Ji'an China 93 N4 27 08N 115 00E
Jiangmen China 93 M3 22 40N 113 05E
Jiaxing China 93 O5 30 15N 120 52E
Jiayuguan China 93 J6 39 47N 98 14E
Jiddah Saudi Arabia 88 E3 21 30N 39 10E
Jilin China 93 P7 43 53N 126 35E
Jima Ethiopia 102 M9 7 39N 36 47E
Jiménez Mexico 64 F2 29 05N 100 40W
Jim Thorpe Pennsylvania U.S.A. 66 C3 40 52N 75 43W
Jinan China 93 N6 36 41N 117 00E
Jingdezhen China 93 N4 29 17N 117 12E
Jin He r. China 94 B1 39 58N 116 16E
Jinhua China 93 N4 29 06N 119 40E
Jining China 93 N5 35 24N 116 34E
Jining Nei Mongol Zizhiqu China 93 M7 40 58N 113 01E
Jinja Uganda 102 L8 0 27N 33 14E
Jinsha Jiang (Yangtze) r. China 93 K4 27 30N 103 00E
Jinxi China 93 O7 40 46N 120 47E
Jiparaná r. Brazil 70 E10 8 25S 62 30W
Jiujiang China 93 N4 29 41N 116 03E
Jixi China 93 Q8 45 17N 131 00E
Jīzān Saudi Arabia 88 F2 16 56N 42 33E
João Pessoa Brazil 70 J11 7 06S 34 53W
Jodhpur India 91 C5 26 18N 73 08E
Jōetsu Japan 96 C2 37 06N 138 15E
Johannesburg Republic of South Africa 103 K2
26 10S 28 02E
John Day r. Oregon U.S.A. 64 B5 45 00N 120 00W
John H. Kerr Reservoir U.S.A. 65 K4 37 00N 78 00W
Johnson City New York U.S.A. 66 C5 42 06N 75 57W
Johnson City Tennessee U.S.A. 65 J4 36 20N 82 21W
Johnstown Pennsylvania U.S.A. 65 K5 40 20N 78 56W
Johor Bharu Malaysia 95 C4 1 27N 103 45E
Joinville Brazil 71 H7 26 20S 48 55W
Joinville Island Antarctica 113 63 00S 56 00W
Jonesboro Arkansas U.S.A. 65 H4 35 50N 90 41W
Jonesville Michigan U.S.A. 42 B3 41 59N 84 39W
Jönköping Sweden 72 H7 57 45N 14 10E
Joplin Missouri U.S.A. 65 H4 37 04N 94 31W
JORDAN 88 E5
Jordan r. Middle East 88 O11 32 15N 32 10E
Jordan Valley tn. Hong Kong China 92 C1 22 19N 114 13E
Jos Nigeria 102 G9 9 54N 8 53E
Joseph Bonaparte Gulf Australia 106 D7 14 00S 128 30E
Joshua Tree tn. California U.S.A. 67 D2 34 09N 116 20W
Joshua Tree National Monument California U.S.A. 67 D1
33 54N 116 00W
Jos Plateau Nigeria 102 G10 9 30N 8 55E

Jostedalsbreen *glacier* Norway 72 G8 61 40N 7 00E
Joûnié Lebanon 88 O11 33 58N 35 38E
Juàzeiro Brazil 70 I11 9 25S 40 30W
Juàzeiro do Norte Brazil 70 J11 7 10S 39 18W
Juba Sudan 102 L8 4 50N 31 35E
Jubany *r.s.* Antarctica 113 62 14S 58 40W
Jubba *r.* Somalia 102 N8 3 00N 42 30E
Jubilee Reservoir Hong Kong China 92 B2 22 24N 114 08E
Juchitán Mexico 68 E3 16 27N 95 05W
Juiz de Fora Brazil 71 I8 21 47S 43 23W
Juliaca Peru 70 C9 15 29S 70 09W
Julianháb *see* Qaqortoq
Jullundur India 91 D6 31 18N 75 40E
Junagadh India 90 C4 21 32N 70 32E
Junction City Kansas U.S.A. 65 G4 39 02N 96 51W
Jundiaí Brazil 71 H8 23 10S 46 54W
Juneau Alaska U.S.A. 8 J4 58 20N 134 20W
Jungfernheide Germany 79 F2 52 35N 13 15E
Junggar Pendi *(Dzungarian Basin)* China 92 G7
44 00N 87 30E
Junipero Serra Peak *mt.* California U.S.A. 67 B3
36 09N 121 26W
Junk Bay Hong Kong China 92 C1 22 18N 114 15E
Jur *r.* Sudan 102 K9 8 00N 28 00E
Jura *mts.* France/Switzerland 72 G5 46 30N 6 00E
Jura, Sound of United Kingdom 74 F7 56 00N 5 45W
Juru Juba *pt.* Brazil 71 Q2 22 56S 43 08W
Juvisy-sur-Orge France 79 B1 48 42N 2 22E
Jylland *p.* Denmark 72 G 7 55 00N 9 00E

K

K2 *(Qogir Feng, Godwin Austen) mt.* China/India 92 E6
35 47N 76 30E
Kābul Afghanistan 89 K5 34 30N 69 10E
Kābul *r.* Afghanistan 89 K5 34 40N 69 30E
Kabwe Zambia 103 K5 14 29S 28 25E
Kaçkar Daği *mt.* Turkey 86 E3 40 50N 41 09E
Kadmat Island India 91 C2 11 08N 72 46E
Kadoma Zimbabwe 103 K4 18 21N 29 55E
Kaduna Nigeria 102 G10 10 28N 7 25E
Kaduna *r.* Nigeria 102 G10 9 00N 6 30E
Kaédi Mauritania 102 C11 16 12N 13 32W
Kaesŏng South Korea 93 P6 37 59N 126 30E
Kafue *r.* Zambia 103 K4 16 00S 27 00E
Kafue Zambia 103 K4 15 44S 28 10E
Kafue National Park Zambia 103 K5 15 00S 25 30E
Kagan Uzbekistan 87 J2 39 45N 64 32E
Kagoshima Japan 96 B1 31 37N 130 32E
Kahoolawe *i.* Hawaiian Islands 111 Y18 20 30N 156 40W
Kahuku Point Hawaiian Islands 111 Y18 21 42N 158 00W
Kaiapoi New Zealand 107 B2 43 23S 172 39E
Kaikohe N.Z. 107 B3 35 25S 173 48E
Kaikoura N.Z. 107 B2 42 24S 173 41E
Kailash India 108 M4 28 33N 77 15E
Kailua Hawaiian Islands 111 Z17 19 43N 155 59W
Kaimana Indonesia 95 I3 3 39S 133 44E
Kainji Reservoir Nigeria 102 F10 10 25N 4 56E
Kaipara Harbour N.Z. 107 B3 36 12S 174 06E
Kairouan Tunisia 102 H15 35 42N 10 01E
Kaitaia N.Z. 107 B3 35 07S 173 16E
Kaiwi Channel *sd.* Hawaiian Islands 111 Y18
21 20N 157 30W
Kakhovs'ke Vodoskhovyshche *res.* Ukraine 86 C4
47 30N 35 00E
Kākināda India 91 E3 16 59N 82 20E
Kalachinsk Russian Federation 87 L6 55 02N 74 40E
Kalae *(South Cape)* Hawaiian Islands 111 Z17
18 58N 155 24W
Kalahari Desert Southern Africa 103 J3 23 30S 23 00E
Kalahari Gemsbok National Park Republic of South Africa
103 I2 26 00S 20 30E
Kalámai Greece 88 E6 37 02N 22 07E
Kalamáta Greece 72 K3 37 02N 22 07E
Kalamazoo Michigan U.S.A. 65 I5 42 17N 85 36W
Kalat Pakistan 90 B5 29 01N 66 38E
Kalémié Congo (D.R.) 103 K6 5 57S 29 10E
Kalgoorlie-Boulder Australia 106 C3 30 49S 121 29E
Kalimantan *admin.* Indonesia 95 E3 2 30S 115 00E
Kalinin *see* Tver'
Kaliningrad *admin.* Russian Federation 86 A5
54 40N 20 30E
Kaliningrad Russian Federation 86 D6 55 56N 37 55E
Kalinkavichy Belarus 86 B5 52 10N 29 13E
Kalispell Montana U.S.A. 64 D6 48 12N 114 19W
Kalkaji India 108 M4 28 32N 77 16E
Kalmeny Island India 91 C2 10 05N 73 15E
Kalomo Zambia 103 K4 17 02S 26 29E
Kalpeni Island India 91 C2 10 05N 73 15E
Kaluga Russian Federation 84 F6 54 31N 36 16E
Kalutara Sri Lanka 91 D1 6 35N 79 59E
Kama *r.* Russian Federation 87 H6 58 00N 55 30E
Kamaishi Japan 96 D2 39 18N 141 52E
Kamakura Japan 97 B2 35 19N 139 33E
Kamarán *i.* Yemen Republic 88 F2 15 21N 42 40E
Kamarhati India 91 G4 22 40N 88 22E
Kambara *i.* Fiji 110 V15 18 57S 178 58W
Kamchatka *p.* Russian Federation 85 R7 57 30N 160 00E
Kamchatka Bay Russian Federation 85 S7 55 00N 164 00E
Kamensk-Ural'skiy Russian Federation 84 I7
56 29N 61 49E
Kamet *mt.* India 91 D6 30 55N 79 36E
Kamina Congo (D.R.) 103 K6 8 46S 25 00E
Kampala Uganda 102 L8 0 10N 32 40E
Kamskoye Vodokranilishche *res.* Russian Federation
87 H6 58 30N 56 00E

Kam"yanets'-Podil's'kiyy Ukraine 86 B4 48 40N 26 36E
Kamyshin Russian Federation 84 G6 50 05N 45 24E
Kamyshlov Russian Federation 87 J6 56 55N 62 41E
Kan *r.* Russian Federation 87 P6 56 30N 95 00E
Kanagawa Japan 97 B2 35 29N 139 38E
Kanagawa *pref.* Japan 97 B3 35 29N 139 38E
Kananga Congo (D.R.) 103 J6 5 53S 22 26E
Kanazawa Japan 96 C2 36 35N 136 38E
Kanbe Myanmar 95 B7 16 45N 96 04E
Kanchipuram India 91 D2 12 50N 79 44E
Kānchrāpāra India 90 K3 22 56N 88 26E
Kandahār Afghanistan 89 K5 31 35N 65 45E
Kandalaksha Russian Federation 84 F9 67 09N 32 31E
Kandavu *i.* Fiji 110 U15 19 10S 178 30E
Kandavu Passage *sd.* Fiji 110 T15–U15 18 50S 178 00E
Kandi Benin 102 F10 11 05N 2 59E
Kandla India 90 C4 23 03N 70 11E
Kandy Sri Lanka 91 E1 7 17N 80 40E
Kane Basin Greenland 51 S6 79 30N 70 00W
Kaneohe Hawaiian Islands 111 Y18 21 25N 157 48W
Kangān Iran 89 H4 27 51N 52 07E
Kangar Malaysia 95 C6 6 28N 100 11E
Kangaroo Island Australia 106 F2 35 50S 137 50E
Kangerlussuaq *fj.* Greenland 9 AA6 67 00N 50 59W
Kangerttittivaq *sd.* Greenland 9 EE7 70 20N 22 30W
Kangilinnguit *(Grønnedal)* Greenland 9 BB5
61 20N 48 00W
Kangnŭng South Korea 93 P6 37 48N 127 52E
Kang-shan Taiwan 94 G5 22 45N 120 18E
Kanin, Cape Russian Federation 72 P9 68 38N 43 20E
Kanin Peninsula Russian Federation 84 G9
68 00N 45 00E
Kankakee Illinois U.S.A. 65 I5 41 08N 87 52W
Kankan Guinea 102 D10 10 22N 9 11W
Kanker India 91 E4 20 17N 81 30E
Kannapolis North Carolina U.S.A. 65 J4 35 30N 80 36W
Kano Nigeria 102 G10 12 00N 8 31E
Kanoya Japan 96 B1 31 22N 130 50E
Kanpur India 91 E5 26 27N 80 14E
Kansas *state* U.S.A. 64 G4 38 00N 98 00W
Kansas City Missouri U.S.A. 65 H4 39 02N 94 33W
Kansk Russian Federation 85 L7 56 11N 95 48E
Kanye Botswana 103 K3 24 59S 25 19E
Kao-hsiung Taiwan 94 G5 22 36N 120 17E
Kaolack Senegal 102 B10 14 09N 16 08W
Kapaa Hawaiian Islands 111 X19 22 04N 159 20W
Kapchagayskoye Vodokhranilishche *res.* Kazakhstan
87 M3 44 00N 78 00E
Kap Farvel *see* Nunap Isura
Kapingamarangi Rise Pacific Ocean 110 F8 3 00N 154 00E
Kapsukas *see* Mariampolé
Kara Bogaz Gol, Zaliv *b.* Turkmenistan 86 G3
42 00N 53 00E
Karabük Turkey 88 D7 41 12N 32 36E
Karachi Pakistan 90 B4 24 51N 67 02E
Karaganda Kazakhstan 87 L4 49 53N 73 07E
Karaginskiy *i.* Russian Federation 85 S7 58 00N 164 00E
Karaj Iran 89 H6 35 48N 50 58E
Karaikkudi India 91 D2 10 04N 78 46E
Karak Jordan 88 O10 31 11N 35 42E
Karakoram Pass China/Kashmir 91 D7 35 33N 77 51E
Kara Kum *geog. reg.* Turkmenistan 87 H2/J2
40 00N 60 00E
Karakumskiy Kanal *can.* Turkmenistan 87 J2
37 30N 62 30E
Karama Jordan 88 O10 31 58N 35 34E
Karaman Turkey 86 C2 37 11N 33 13E
Karasburg Namibia 103 I2 28 00S 18 43E
Kara Sea Russian Federation 85 I11/J10 75 00N 70 00E
Karatal *r.* Kazakhstan 87 M4 45 00N 78 00E
Karatau *mts.* Kazakhstan 87 K3 43 00N 70 00E
Karaturgay *r.* Kazakhstan 87 J5/K5 50 00N 65 00E
Karbalā' Iraq 88 F5 32 37N 44 03E
Kariba Dam Zambia/Zimbabwe 103 K4 16 31S 28 50E
Kariba, Lake Zambia/Zimbabwe 103 K4 17 00S 28 00E
Karibib Namibia 103 I3 21 59S 15 51E
Karisimbi, Mount Rwanda/Congo (D.R.) 102 K7
1 32S 29 27E
Karkinitskiy Zaliv *g.* Ukraine 86 C4 46 00N 32 50E
Karlshorst Germany 79 G1 52 28N 13 32E
Karnafuli Reservoir Bangladesh 91 G4 22 30N 92 20E
Karnal India 91 D5 29 41N 76 58E
Karnataka *admin.* India 91 D2 14 40N 75 30E
Karol Bagh India 108 L4 28 39N 77 11E
Karow Germany 79 F2 52 38N 13 28E
Kars Turkey 88 F7 40 35N 43 05E
Karsakpay Kazakhstan 84 I5 47 47N 66 43E
Karshi Uzbekistan 87 K2 38 53N 65 45E
Kartaly Russian Federation 87 J5 53 06N 60 37E
Karwar India 91 C2 14 50N 74 09E
Kasai *r.* Angola/Congo (D.R.) 103 I7 4 00S 19 00E
Kasama Zambia 103 L5 10 10S 31 11E
Kasaragod India 91 C2 12 30N 74 59E
Kasese Uganda 102 L8 0 10N 30 06E
Kāshān Iran 89 H5 33 59N 51 35E
Kashi China 92 E6 39 29N 76 02E
Kashiwazaki Japan 96 C2 37 22N 138 33E
Kasli Russian Federation 87 J6 55 54N 60 45E
Kassala Sudan 102 M11 15 24N 36 30E
Kastamonu Turkey 88 D7 41 22N 33 47E
Kasur Pakistan 91 C6 31 07N 74 30E
Kataba Zambia 103 K4 16 02S 25 03E
Katase Japan 97 A2 35 18N 139 30E
Katha Myanmar 91 H4 24 11N 96 20E
Katherine Australia 106 E7 14 29S 132 20E
Kathiawar *p.* India 90 C4 21 10N 71 00E
Kathmandu Nepal 91 F5 27 42N 85 19E
Katihar India 91 F5 25 33N 87 34E

Katowice Poland 72 J6 50 15N 18 59E
Katsina Ala Nigeria 102 G9 7 10N 9 30E
Kattakurgan Uzbekistan 87 K2 39 54N 66 13E
Kattegat *sd.* Denmark/Sweden 72 H7 57 00N 11 00E
Katun' *r.* Russian Federation 87 O5 51 30N 86 00E
Kauai *i.* Hawaiian Islands 111 X18–19 22 00N 159 30W
Kauai Channel *sd.* Hawaiian Islands 111 X18
21 45N 158 50W
Kaula *i.* Hawaiian Islands 111 W18 21 35N 160 40W
Kaulakahi Channel *sd.* Hawaiian Islands 111 X18
21 58N 159 50W
Kaulsdorf Germany 79 G1 52 29N 13 34E
Kaunas Lithuania 72 K6 54 52N 23 55E
Kau Sai Chau *i.* Hong Kong China 92 C2 22 22N 114 19E
Kau Yi Chau Hong Kong China 92 B1 22 17N 114 04E
Kavaratti India 91 C2 10 32N 72 43E
Kawagoe Japan 96 C2 35 55N 139 30E
Kawaguchi Japan 96 C2 35 47N 139 44E
Kawaihae Hawaiian Islands 111 Z18 20 02N 155 05W
Kawasaki Japan 96 C2 35 30N 139 45E
Kawawa Japan 97 B3 35 31N 139 33E
Kawerau N.Z. 107 C3 38 05S 176 42E
Kaya Burkina 102 E10 13 04N 1 09W
Kayes Mali 102 C10 14 26N 11 28W
Kayseri Turkey 86 E3 38 42N 35 28E
Kazach'ye Russian Federation 85 P10 70 46N 136 15E
KAZAKHSTAN 87 H4/O4
Kazakh Upland Kazakhstan 87 L5 47 00N 75 00E
Kazan' Russian Federation 84 G7 55 45N 49 10E
Kazbek *mt.* Georgia 86 E3 42 42N 44 30E
Kāzerūn Iran 89 H4 29 35N 51 40E
Kazym *r.* Russian Federation 85 I8 63 00N 67 30E
Kearney Nebraska U.S.A. 64 G5 40 42N 99 04W
Kearny New Jersey U.S.A. 66 Y2 40 45N 74 07W
Kediri Indonesia 95 E2 7 45S 112 01E
Keetmanshoop Namibia 103 I2 26 36S 18 08E
Kefallonía *i.* Greece 88 E6 38 00N 20 00E
Kei Ling Ha Lo Wai Hong Kong China 92 C2
22 25N 114 16E
Kei Lun Wai Hong Kong China 92 A2 22 24N 113 58E
K'elafo Ethiopia 102 N9 5 37N 44 10E
Kelkit *r.* Turkey 88 E7 40 20N 37 40E
Kells Republic of Ireland 74 E5 53 44N 6 53W
Kelseyville California U.S.A. 67 A4 38 58N 122 50W
Kelso California U.S.A. 67 E2 35 01N 115 39W
Kemerovo Russian Federation 85 K7 55 25N 86 05E
Kemi *r.* Finland 72 L9 67 00N 27 00E
Kemp Land *geog. reg.* Antarctica 113 65 00S 60 00E
Kemsing United Kingdom 78 D2 51 18N 0 14E
Kenai Alaska U.S.A. 8 E5 60 35N 151 19W
Kendal United Kingdom 74 I6 54 20N 2 45W
Kendari Indonesia 95 G3 3 57S 122 36E
Kenema Sierra Leone 102 C9 7 57N 11 11W
Kengtung Myanmar 95 B8 21 15N 99 40E
Keningau Malaysia 95 F5 5 21N 116 11E
Kénitra Morocco 102 D14 34 20N 6 34W
Kennebec *r.* Maine U.S.A. 47 C1 44 40N 69 42W
Kenosha Wisconsin U.S.A. 65 I5 42 34N 87 50W
Kensington *bor.* United Kingdom 78 C3 51 29N 0 10W
Kenthurst Australia 107 F3 33 40S 151 01E
Kenting National Park Taiwan 94 G5 22 00N 120 50E
Kentucky *state* U.S.A. 65 I4 37 00N 85 00W
KENYA 102 M8
Kenya, Mount *see* Kirinyaga
Kepulauan Anambas *is.* Indonesia 95 D4 3 00N 106 20E
Kepulauan Aru *is.* Indonesia 95 I2 6 00S 134 30E
Kepulauan Babar *is.* Indonesia 95 H2 7 50S 129 30E
Kepulauan Batu *is.* Indonesia 95 B3 0 18S 98 29E
Kepulauan Kai *is.* Indonesia 95 I2 5 30S 132 30E
Kepulauan Lingga *is.* Indonesia 95 C3 0 10S 104 30E
Kepulauan Mentawai *is.* Indonesia 95 B3 2 00S 99 00E
Kepulauan Obi *is.* Indonesia 95 H3 1 30S 127 30E
Kepulauan Riau *is.* Indonesia 95 C4 0 30N 14 30E
Kepulauan Sangir *is.* Indonesia 95 H4 3 00N 125 30E
Kepulauan Sula *is.* Indonesia 95 G3/H3 1 50S 124 50E
Kepulauan Talaud *is.* Indonesia 95 H4 4 00N 127 00E
Kepulauan Tanimbar *is.* Indonesia 95 I2 7 30S 131 30E
Kerala *admin.* India 91 D2 10 10N 76 30E
Kerch' Ukraine 86 D4 45 22N 36 27E
Kerema Papua New Guinea 106 H8 7 59S 145 46E
Keren Eritrea 102 M11 15 46N 38 30E
Kerguelen Plateau Indian Ocean 108 G1/H1
55 00S 80 00E
Kerikeri N.Z. 107 B3 35 14S 173 57E
Kerki Turkmenistan 87 K2 37 53N 65 10E
Kérkyra *(Corfu)* Greece 72 J3 39 00N 19 00E
Kermadec Islands Pacific Ocean 110 I5 30 00S 178 30W
Kermadec Trench Pacific Ocean 110 I4 33 00S 177 00W
Kermān Iran 89 I5 30 18N 57 05E
Kern *r.* California U.S.A. 67 C3 36 00N 118 28W
Kerrville Texas U.S.A. 64 G3 30 03N 99 09W
Kerulen *r.* Mongolia 93 M8 47 30N 112 30E
Ket' *r.* Russian Federation 85 K6 58 00N 87 00E
Ketapang Indonesia 95 E3 1 50S 109 59E
Ketchikan Alaska U.S.A. 8 J4 55 25N 131 40W
Kettle Creek Pennsylvania U.S.A. 42 41 30N 77 45W
Keuka Lake New York U.S.A. 43 J3 42 30N 77 10W
Keweenaw Peninsula Michigan U.S.A. 65 I6
47 00N 88 00W
Key West Florida U.S.A. 65 J1 24 34N 81 48W
Khabarovsk Russian Federation 85 P5 48 32N 135 08E
Khambhat India 91 C4 22 19N 72 39E
Khambhat, Gulf of India 91 C4 20 30N 72 00E
Khammam India 91 E3 17 16N 80 13E
Khānābād Afghanistan 89 K6 36 42N 69 08E
Khānaqin Iraq 89 G5 34 22N 45 22E
Khandwa India 91 D4 21 49N 76 23E

Khaniá *see* Chaniá
Khanty-Mansiysk Russian Federation 85 I8
61 01N 69 00E
Khān Yūnis Middle East 88 O10 31 21N 34 18E
Kharan Pakistan 90 B5 28 32N 65 26E
Kharagpur India 91 F4 22 23N 87 22E
Khardah India 90 K2 22 43N 88 20E
Khärg Island Iran 89 H4 29 14N 50 20E
Kharkiv *(Khar'kov)* Ukraine 86 D4 50 00N 36 15E
Khartoum Sudan 102 L11 15 33N 32 35E
Khāsh Iran 89 J4 28 14N 61 15E
Khash *r.* Afghanistan 89 J6 31 30N 62 30E
Khashm el Girba Sudan 88 E1 14 59N 35 48E
Khatanga Russian Federation 85 M10 71 59N 102 31E
Khemisset Morocco 102 D14 33 50N 6 03W
Kherson Ukraine 86 C4 46 39N 32 38E
Kheta *r.* Russian Federation 85 L10 71 30N 95 00E
Khilok *r.* Russian Federation 85 M6 51 00N 107 30E
Khimki Russian Federation 86 L2 55 51N 37 28E
Khimki-Khovrino Russian Federation 86 L2
55 51N 37 30E
Khimki Reservoir Russian Federation 86 L2 55 49N 37 29E
Khíos *i.* Greece 88 C6 38 00N 26 00E
Khiva Uzbekistan 87 J3 41 25N 60 49E
Khmel'nyts'kyy Ukraine 86 B4 49 25N 26 59E
Khodzheyli Uzbekistan 87 H3 42 25N 59 25E
Kholmsk Russian Federation 85 Q5 47 02N 142 03E
Khon Kaen Thailand 93 K2 16 25N 102 50E
Khoper *r.* Russian Federation 86 E5 50 20N 42 00E
Khorat *see* Nakhon Ratchasima
Khorochevo Russian Federation 86 L2 55 46N 37 30E
Khorog Tajikistan 87 L3 37 22N 71 32E
Khorramābād Iran 89 G5 33 29N 48 21E
Khorramshahr Iran 89 G5 30 25N 48 09E
Khouribga Morocco 102 D14 32 54N 6 57W
Khrebet Kopet Dag' *mts.* Turkmenistan 87 H2
39 50N 56 00E
Khrishnapur Canal India 90 K2 22 34N 88 23E
Khujand *(Leninabad)* Kirgyzstan 87 K3 40 20N 69 55E
Khulna Bangladesh 91 F4 22 49N 89 34E
Khyber Pass Afghanistan/Pakistan 91 L5 34 06N 71 05E
Kiatak *(Northumberland Island) i.* Greenland 51 S6
77 30N 72 30W
Kibombo Congo (D.R.) 103 K7 3 58S 25 54E
Kiel Germany 72 H6 54 20N 10 08E
Kiev *see* Kyyiv
Kieta Papua New Guinea 106 J8 6 15S 155 37E
Kigali Rwanda 102 L7 1 56S 30 04E
Kigoma Tanzania 103 K7 4 52S 29 36E
Kii-suidō *sd.* Japan 96 B1 34 00N 134 45E
Kikládhes *is.* Greece 88 B6 37 00N 25 00E
Kikori Papua New Guinea 95 K2 7 25S 144 13E
Kikwit Congo (D.R.) 103 I6 5 02S 18 51E
Kilanea Hawaiian Islands 111 W19 22 05N 159 35W
Kilimanjaro *mt.* Tanzania 102 M7 3 04S 37 22E
Kilkenny Republic of Ireland 74 D4 52 39N 7 15W
Killarney Republic of Ireland 74 B4 52 03N 9 30W
Killeen Texas U.S.A. 65 G3 31 08N 97 44W
Kilmarnock United Kingdom 74 F5 55 36N 4 30W
Kiltan Island India 91 C2 11 30N 73 00E
Kilwa Masoko Tanzania 103 M6 8 55S 39 31E
Kimberley Republic of South Africa 103 J2 28 45S 24 46E
Kimberley Plateau Australia 106 D6 17 30S 126 00E
Kimch'aek North Korea 93 P7 40 41N 129 12E
Kindia Guinea 102 C10 10 03N 12 49W
Kindu Congo (D.R.) 103 K7 3 00S 25 56E
Kineshma Russian Federation 86 E6 57 28N 42 08E
King City California U.S.A. 67 B3 36 13N 121 09W
King George Island South Shetland Islands 71 F0
62 00S 58 00W
King George's Reservoir United Kingdom 78 C3
51 41N 0 05W
King Island Australia 106 G2 40 00S 144 00E
Kingman Arizona U.S.A. 64 D4 35 12N 114 02W
Kings *r.* California U.S.A. 67 C3 36 32N 119 30W
Kings Canyon National Park California U.S.A. 67 C3
36 45N 118 30W
Kings County *admin.* New York U.S.A. 66 Y1
40 37N 74 02W
King Sejong *r.s.* Antarctica 113 62 13S 58 47W
Kingsgrove Australia 107 G2 33 58S 151 09E
King's Lynn United Kingdom 74 L4 52 45N 0 24E
King Sound Australia 106 C6 16 00S 123 00E
Kings Point *tn.* New York U.S.A. 67 Z40 49N 73 45W
Kingsport Tennessee U.S.A. 65 J4 36 33N 82 34W
Kingston Jamaica 69 R7 17 58N 76 48W
Kingston upon Hull United Kingdom 74 K5 53 45N 0 20W
Kingston-upon-Thames United Kingdom 78 B2
51 25N 0 18W
Kingstown St. Vincent and The Grenadines 69 L2
13 12N 61 14W
Kingsville Texas U.S.A. 65 G2 27 32N 97 53W
Kinkala Congo 103 H7 4 18S 14 49E
Kinshasa Congo (D.R.) 103 I7 4 18S 15 18E
Kipili Tanzania 103 L6 7 30S 30 39E
Kirensk Russian Federation 85 M7 57 45N 108 02E
KIRGHIZIA *see* Kirgyzstan
Kirghiz Step *geog. reg.* Kazakhstan 86 F4/K4
48 00N 58 00E
KIRGYZSTAN *(KIRGHIZIA)* 87 L3/M3
KIRIBATI Pacific Ocean 110 H8
Kirikkale Turkey 73 M3 39 51N 33 32E
Kirinyaga *(Mount Kenya) mt.* Kenya 102 M7 0 10S 37 19E
Kiritimati Island Kiribati 111 K8 2 10N 157 00W
Kirkcaldy United Kingdom 74 H8 56 07N 3 10W
Kirkcudbright United Kingdom 74 G6 54 50N 4 03W
Kirksville Missouri U.S.A. 65 H5 40 12N 92 35W
Kirkūk Iraq 88 F6 35 28N 44 26E

Kirkwall United Kingdom 74 I10 58 59N 2 58W
Kirov (Vyatka) Russian Federation 84 G7 58 00N 49 38E
Kirovabad see Gäncä
Kirovakan see Vanadzor
Kirovohrad Ukraine 84 E5 48 31N 32 15E
Kirti Nagar India 108 L4 28 39N 77 09E
Kiryū Japan 96 C2 36 26N 139 18E
Kisangani Congo (D.R.) 102 K8 0 33N 25 14E
Kiselevsk' Russian Federation 87 O5 54 01N 86 41E
Kishinev see Chisinău
Kishiwada Japan 96 C1 34 28N 135 22E
Kislovodsk Russian Federation 86 E3 43 56N 42 44E
Kismaayo Somalia 102 N7 0 25S 42 31E
Kisumu Kenya 102 L7 0 08S 34 47E
Kita Japan 97 B4 35 46N 139 43E
Kita-Kyūshū Japan 96 B1 33 52N 130 49E
Kitami Japan 96 D3 43 51N 143 54E
Kitridge Point Barbados 69 W12 13 08N 59 22W
Kitwe Zambia 103 K5 0 08S 30 30E
Kızıl Irmak r. Turkey 88 D7 40 30N 34 00E
Kizlyar Russian Federation 86 F3 43 51N 46 43E
Kladow Germany 79 E1 52 27N 13 08E
Klaipėda Lithuania 72 K7 55 43N 21 07E
Klamath r. U.S.A. 64 B5 42 00N 123 00W
Klamath Falls tn. Oregon U.S.A. 64 B5 42 14N 121 47W
Klarälven r. Sweden 72 H8 61 00N 13 00E
Kleinmachnow Germany 79 E1/F1 52 24N 13 13E
Klerksdorp Republic of South Africa 103 K2 26 52S 26 39E
Klukwan Alaska U.S.A. 50 D2 59 25N 135 55W
Klyazma r. Russian Federation 86 E6 56 00N 42 00E
Klyuchevskaya Sopka mt. Russian Federation 85 S7 56 03N 160 38E
Knossós hist. site Greece 88 C6 35 18N 25 10E
Knoxville Tennessee U.S.A. 65 J4 36 00N 83 57W
Košice Slovakia 72 K5 48 44N 21 15E
Kōbe Japan 96 C1 34 40N 135 12E
København (Copenhagen) Denmark 72 H4 55 43N 12 34E
Kobryn Belarus 86 A5 52 16N 24 22E
Kobuk r. Alaska U.S.A. 8 D7 67 00N 157 30W
Kocaeli (Izmit) Turkey 73 L4 40 47N 29 55E
Koch Bihär India 91 F5 26 18N 89 32E
Kōchi Japan 96 B1 33 33N 133 32E
Kochubey Russian Federation 86 F3 44 25N 46 33E
Kodiak Alaska U.S.A. 8 E4 57 49N 152 30W
Kodiak Island Alaska U.S.A. 8 E4 57 20N 153 40W
Kodok Sudan 102 L9 9 51N 32 07E
Koforidua Ghana 102 E9 6 01N 0 12W
Kofu Japan 96 C2 35 42N 138 34E
Kohat Pakistan 91 C6 33 37N 71 30E
Kohima India 91 G5 25 40N 94 08E
Koh-i-Mazar mt. Afghanistan 89 K5 32 3ON 66 23E
Kohoku Japan 97 B3 35 30N 139 39E
Kohtla-Järve Estonia 86 B6 59 28N 27 20E
Kokand Uzbekistan 87 L3 40 33N 70 55E
Kokomo Indiana U.S.A. 65 I5 40 30N 86 09W
Kokshetau Kazakhstan 87 K5 53 18N 69 25E
Kola Peninsula Russian Federation 84 F9 67 30N 37 30E
Kolguyev r. Russian Federation 84 G9 69 00N 49 30E
Kolhapur India 91 C3 16 40N 74 20E
Köln (Cologne) Germany 72 G6 50 56N 6 57E
Kolomna Russian Federation 86 D6 55 05N 38 45E
Kolomyya Ukraine 86 A4 48 31N 25 00E
Kolpashevo Russian Federation 85 K7 58 21N 82 59E
Kolpino Russian Federation 86 C6 59 44N 30 39E
Kolwezi Congo (D.R.) 103 K5 10 45S 25 25E
Kolyma r. Russian Federation 85 R9 66 30N 152 00E
Kolyma (Gydan) Range mts. Russian Federation 85 R8 63 00N 160 00E
Kolyma Lowland Russian Federation 85 R9 69 00N 155 00E
Komae Japan 97 B3 35 38N 139 34E
Komandorskiye Ostrova is. Russia 110 G13 55 00N 166 30E
Komatsu Japan 96 C2 36 25N 136 27E
Kommunarsk see Alchevs'k
Komotiní Greece 88 C7 41 06N 25 25E
Kompong Cham Cambodia 95 D6 11 59N 105 26E
Kompong Chhnang Cambodia 95 C6 12 16N 104 39E
Kompong Som Cambodia 95 C6 10 38N 103 28E
Komsomol'sk-na-Amure Russian Federation 85 P6 50 32N 136 59E
Konda r. Russian Federation 87 K7 60 00N 65 00E
Kondūz Afghanistan 89 K6 36 45N 68 51E
Kong Christian X Land geog. reg. Greenland 9 FF8 75 00N 27 30W
Kongolo Congo (D.R.) 103 K6 5 20S 27 00E
Kong Oscar Fjord Greenland 133 EE7 72 30N 23 00W
Kongur Shan mt. China 87 M2 39 00N 75 10E
Konnagar India 90 K2 22 42N 88 20E
Konosha Russian Federation 84 G8 60 58N 40 08E
Konotop Ukraine 86 C6 51 15N 33 14E
Konya Turkey 73 M3 37 51N 32 30E
Koocanusa, Lake Montana U.S.A. 35 E1 48 55N 115 10W
Köpenick Germany 79 G1 52 27N 13 36E
Kopeysk Russian Federation 86 J5 55 08N 61 39E
Korea Bay China/North Korea 93 O6 39 00N 124 00E
Korea Strait Japan/South Korea 93 P7/Q7 33 00N 129 00E
Korhogo Côte d'Ivoire 102 D9 9 22N 5 31W
Kórinthos Greece 88 B6 37 56N 22 55E
Kōriyama Japan 96 D2 37 23N 140 22E
Korla China 92 G7 41 48N 86 10E
Koro i. Fiji 110 U16 17 20S 179 25E
Koro Sea Fiji 110 U16-V16 17 35S 180 00
Korosten' Ukraine 86 B5 51 00N 28 30E
Korsakov Russian Federation 85 Q5 46 36N 142 50E

Koryak Range mts. Russian Federation 85 T8 62 00N 170 00E
Kosciusko Island Alaska U.S.A. 34 B3 56 00N 133 45W
Kosciusko, Mount South Australia 106 H2 36 28S 148 17E
Kosti Sudan 102 L10 13 11N 32 28E
Kostroma Russian Federation 84 G7 57 46N 40 59E
Kostyantynivka Ukraine 86 D4 48 33N 37 45E
Kota India 91 D5 25 11N 75 58E
Kota Bharu Malaysia 95 C5 6 08N 102 14E
Kota Kinabalu Malaysia 95 F5 5 59N 116 04E
Kotlas Russian Federation 84 G8 61 15N 46 35E
Kōtō Japan 97 C3 35 40N 139 49E
Kotri Pakistan 90 B5 25 22N 68 18E
Kotto r. Central African Republic 102 J9 7 00N 22 30E
Kotuy r. Russian Federation 85 M9 67 30N 102 00E
Kotzebue Alaska U.S.A. 8 C6 66 51N 162 40W
Kotzebue Sound Alaska U.S.A. 8 C6 66 40N 162 20W
Koudougou Burkina 102 E10 12 15N 2 23W
Koulamoutou Gabon 102 H7 1 12S 12 29E
Koulikoro Mali 102 D10 12 55N 7 31W
Koumra Chad 102 I9 8 56N 17 32E
Kounradskiy Kazakhstan 87 L4 46 58N 74 59E
Kourou French Guiana 70 G14 5 08N 52 37W
Kovel' Ukraine 86 A5 51 12N 24 48E
Kovrov Russian Federation 86 E6 56 23N 41 21E
Kovzha r. Russian Federation 86 D7 61 00N 37 00E
Kowloon Hong Kong China 92 B1 22 19N 114 11E
Kowloon Tong Hong Kong China 92 C2 22 20N 114 11E
Koyukuk r. Alaska U.S.A. 8 E6 66 00N 154 00W
Kpalimé Togo 102 E9 6 55N 0 44E
Kragujevac Serbia Yugoslavia 72 K4 44 01N 20 55E
Kramators'k Ukraine 86 D4 48 43N 37 33E
Krasnodar Russian Federation 84 F5 45 02N 39 00E
Krasnovodsk Turkmenistan 86 G3 40 01N 53 00E
Krasnoyarsk Russian Federation 85 L7 56 05N 92 46E
Krasnoyarskoye Vodokhranilishche res. Russian Federation 87 P5/6 55 00N 91 00E
Krasny Stroitel Russian Federation 86 M1 55 31N 37 08E
Krasnyy Kut Russian Federation 86 F5 50 58N 47 00E
Krasnyy Luch Ukraine 86 D4 48 10N 39 00E
Kremenchuk Ukraine 86 C4 49 03N 33 25E
Kremenchuts'ke Vodokranilishche res Ukraine 86 C4 49 30N 32 30E
Kreuzberg Germany 79 F2 52 30N 13 24E
Kribi Cameroon 102 H8 2 56N 9 56E
Krishna r. India 91 D6 16 00N 79 00E
Kríti (Crete) i. Greece 72 L3 35 00N 25 00E
Krivoy Rog see Kryvy Rih
Kruger National Park Republic of South Africa 103 L3 24 00S 32 00E
KKrung Thep see Bangkok
Kruzof Island Alaska U.S.A. 50 D2 57 15N 135 40W
Krym' (Crimea) p. Ukraine 86 C3/4 46 00N 34 00E
Kryvyy Rih (Krivoy Rog) Ukraine 84 F5 47 55N 33 24E
Kuala Lumpur Malaysia 95 C4 3 09N 101 42E
Kuala Terengganu Malaysia 95 C5 5 20N 103 09E
Kuangfu Taiwan 94 H6 23 40N 121 25E
Kuantan Malaysia 95 C4 3 48N 103 19E
Kuban' r. Russian Federation 86 E4 45 05N 38 00E
Kuching Malaysia 95 F4 1 35N 110 21E
Kudat Malaysia 95 F5 6 54N 116 50E
Kuito Angola 103 I5 12 25S 16 56E
Kuiu Island Alaska U.S.A. 34 B3 56 45N 134 00W
Kujū-san mt. Japan 96 B1 33 07N 131 14E
Kulundinskaya Step' geog. reg. Kazakhstan/Russian Federation 87 M5/N5 52 00N 80 00E
Kuma r. Russian Federation 84 G4 45 00N 45 00E
Kumagaya Japan 96 C2 36 09N 139 22E
Kumamoto Japan 96 D4 48 33N 130 42E
Kumasi Ghana 102 E9 6 45N 1 35W
Kumba Cameroon 102 G8 4 39N 9 26E
Kumbakonam India 91 D2 10 59N 79 24E
Kumkahi, Cape Hawaiian Islands 111 Z17 19 30N 154 50W
Kumul see Hami
Kunar r. Asia 91 C6 35 30N 71 20E
Kunashir i. Russia 96 E3 44 30N 146 20E
Kungrad Uzbekistan 87 H3 43 06N 58 54E
Kunlun Shan mts. China 92 F6/G6 36 30N 85 00E
Kunming China 93 K4 25 04N 102 41E
Kunming Hu l. China 94 A1 40 00N 116 15E
Kunsan South Korea 93 P6 35 57N 126 42E
Kunti India 90 K3 22 55N 88 20E
Kuntsevo Russian Federation 86 L1 55 43N 37 25E
Kununurra Australia 106 D6 15 42S 128 50E
Kupang Indonesia 95 G1 10 13S 123 38E
Kupreanof Island Alaska U.S.A. 50 E2 56 50N 133 30W
Kura r. Azerbaijan 86 G3 43 00N 48 00E
Kurashiki Japan 96 B1 34 36N 133 43E
Kurchum r. Kazakhstan 87 N4 49 00N 85 00E
Kure Japan 96 B1 34 14N 132 32E
Kureyka r. Russian Federation 85 L9 67 30N 91 00E
Kurgan Russian Federation 84 I7 55 30N 65 20E
Kuria Muria Islands Oman 89 I2 17 30N 56 00E
Kurihama Japan 97 B3 35 12N 139 41E
Kuril Islands Russian Federation 85 R5/R6 50 00N 150 00E
Kuril Ridge Pacific Ocean 110 F12 47 50N 152 00E
Kuril Trench Pacific Ocean 110 F12 45 40N 154 00E
Ku-ring-gai Chase National Park Australia 107 G3 33 40S 151 00E
Kurnell Australia 107 G1 34 01S 151 12E
Kurnool India 91 D3 15 51N 78 01E
Kursk Russian Federation 84 F6 51 45N 36 14E
Kurtalan Turkey 88 F6 37 58N 41 36E
Kurume Japan 96 B1 33 20N 130 29E
Kushiro Japan 96 D3 42 58N 144 24E
Kushka Turkmenistan 87 J1 35 14N 62 15E

Kushva Russian Federation 87 H6 58 20N 59 48E
Kuskokwim r. Alaska U.S.A. 8 C5 61 30N 160 45W
Kuskokwim Bay Alaska U.S.A. 8 C4 58 50N 164 00W
Kuskokwim Mountains Alaska U.S.A. 8 D5 62 00N 158 00W
Kustanay Kazakhstan 87 J5 53 15N 63 40E
Kütahya Turkey 88 C6 39 25N 29 56E
Kuvango Angola 103 I5 14 27S 16 20E
KUWAIT 89 G4
Kuybyshev see Samara
Kuybyshev Forest Russian Federation 86 M2 55 50N 37 45E
Kuytun China 92 F7 44 30N 85 00E
Kuzbass geog. reg. Russian Federation 87 O5/6 55 00N 87 00E
Kuzey Anadolu Dağları mts. Turkey 88 E7 41 15N 36 20E
Kuz'minki Russian Federation 86 M1/N1 55 41N 37 45E
Kwai Chung Hong Kong China 92 B2 22 22N 114 07E
Kwangju South Korea 93 P6 35 07N 126 52E
Kwango r. Congo (D.R.) 103 I6 6 00S 17 00E
Kwekwe (Que Que) Zimbabwe 103 K4 18 55S 29 49E
Kwethluk Alaska U.S.A. 8 C5 60 46N 161 34W
Kwigillingok Alaska U.S.A. 8 C4 59 50N 163 10W
Kwilu r. Congo (D.R.) 103 I6 6 00S 19 00E
Kwun Tong Hong Kong China 92 C1 22 18N 114 13E
Kwu Tung Hong Kong China 92 B3 22 30N 114 06E
Kyburz California U.S.A. 67 B4 38 47N 120 19W
Kyklades is. Greece 72 K3/L3 37 00N 25 00E
Kyle of Lochalsh United Kingdom 74 F9 57 17N 5 43W
Kyoga, Lake Uganda 102 L8 2 00N 34 00E
Kyoga-misaki c. Japan 96 C2 35 48N 135 12E
Kyōto Japan 96 C2 35 02N 135 45E
Kyūshū i. Japan 96 B1 32 20N 131 00E
Kyūshū-Palau Ridge Pacific Ocean 110 D9/D10 15 00N 135 00E
Kyyiv (Kiev) Ukraine 86 C5 50 25N 30 30E
Kyzyl Russian Federation 85 L6 51 45N 94 28E
Kyzyl Kum d. Asia 87 I3/K3 43 00N 65 00E
Kzyl-Orda Kazakhstan 87 K3 44 25N 65 28E

L

Laascaanood Somalia 102 O9 8 35N 46 55E
La Asunción Venezuela 70 L2 11 06N 63 53W
Laayoune (El Aaiún) Western Sahara 102 C13 27 10N 13 11W
Labé Guinea 102 C10 11 17N 12 11W
Labrador Basin Atlantic Ocean 109 B12/C12 58 00N 50 00W
Lábrea Brazil 70 E11 7 20S 64 46W
La Brea Trinidad and Tobago 69 S9 10 14N 61 37W
Labytnangi Russian Federation 85 I9 66 43N 66 28E
La Ceiba Honduras 69 G3 15 45N 86 45W
Lac Fitri r. Chad 102 I10 13 00N 17 30E
Lachlan r. Australia 106 G3 34 00S 145 00E
La Chorrera Panama 69 I1 8 51N 79 46W
Lac Léman l. Switzerland 72 G5 46 20N 6 20E
Lac Mai-Ndombe l. Congo (D.R.) 102 I7 2 00S 18 20E
Lac Moero see Mweru, Lake
La Coruña Spain 72 D4 43 22N 8 24W
La Crosse Wisconsin U.S.A. 65 H5 43 48N 91 04W
Ladakh Range mts. Kashmir 91 D6 34 30N 78 30E
la Défense France 79 A2 48 53N 2 14E
Ladozhskoye Ozero (Lake Ladoga) Russian Federation 84 F8 61 00N 30 00E
Ladysmith Republic of South Africa 103 K2 28 34S 29 47E
La Esmeralda Venezuela 70 D13 3 11N 65 33W
Lafayette Indiana U.S.A. 65 I5 40 25N 86 54W
Lafayette Louisiana U.S.A. 65 H3 30 12N 92 18W
La Fé Cuba 69 H4 22 02N 84 15W
Laghouat Algeria 102 F14 33 49N 2 55E
Lagoa Brazil 71 Q2 22 58S 43 13W
Lago Argentino l. Argentina 71 C2 50 10S 72 30W
Lago da Tijuca l. Brazil 71 P2 22 59S 43 22W
Lago de Chapala l. Mexico 68 D4 20 05N 103 00W
Lago de Maracaibo l. Venezuela 70 C14 9 50N 71 30W
Lago de Marapendi l. Brazil 71 Q2 23 00S 43 20W
Lago de Nicaragua l. Nicaragua 69 G2 11 50N 86 00W
Lago de Piratininga l. Brazil 71 Q2 22 57S 43 05W
Lago de Poopó l. Bolivia 70 D9 18 30S 67 00W
Lago do Jacarepaguá l. Brazil 71 P2 22 58S 43 23W
Lagos Nigeria 102 F9 6 27N 3 28E
Lago Rodrigo de Freitas l. Brazil 71 Q2 22 58S 43 13W
Lago Titicaca l. Peru/Bolivia 70 C9/D9 16 00S 69 30W
La Grande Oregon U.S.A. 64 C6 45 21N 118 05W
La Grange Georgia U.S.A. 65 I3 33 02N 85 02W
La Guaira Venezuela 70 D15 10 38N 66 55W
Laguna Brazil 71 H7 28 29S 48 45W
Laguna Caratasca l. Honduras 69 H3 15 05N 84 00W
Laguna de Perlas l. Nicaragua 69 H2 12 30N 83 30W
Laguna Madre l. Mexico 68 E4 25 00N 98 00W
Laguna Mar Chiquita l. Argentina 71 E6 30 30S 62 30W
Lagunillas Venezuela 70 C15 10 07N 71 16W
La Habana (Havana) Cuba 69 H4 23 07N 82 25W
Lahaina Hawaiian Islands 111 Y18 20 50N 156 40W
Lahontan Reservoir res. California U.S.A. 67 C4 39 22N 119 08W
Lahore Pakistan 91 C6 31 34N 74 22E
Lai Chi Chong Hong Kong China 92 C2 22 27N 114 17E
Lai Chi Wo Hong Kong China 92 C3 22 32N 114 15E
Lajes Brazil 71 G7 27 48S 50 20W
Lajpat Nagar India 108 M4 28 34N 77 15E
La Junta Colorado U.S.A. 64 F4 37 59N 103 34W
Lake Alpine California U.S.A. 67 B4 38 30N 120 00W
Lake Berryessa California U.S.A. 67 A4 38 37N 122 15W
Lake Charles tn. Louisiana U.S.A. 65 H3 30 13N 93 13W

Lake City Michigan U.S.A. 42 A5 44 22N 85 12W
Lake Crowley California U.S.A. 67 C3 37 38N 118 45W
Lake Isabella tn. California U.S.A. 67 C2 35 37N 118 28W
Lakeland Florida U.S.A. 65 J2 28 02N 81 59W
Lakemba i. Fiji 110 V15 18 10S 178 49W
Lakemba Passage sd. Fiji 110 V15-16 18 10S 179 00W
Lake McClure California U.S.A. 67 B3 37 38N 120 16W
Lake Orion tn. Michigan U.S.A. 42 C3 42 47N 83 13W
Lake Oroville California U.S.A. 67 B4 39 37N 121 30W
Lake Success California U.S.A. 67 C3 36 07N 118 55W
Lake Tahoe California U.S.A. 67 B4 39 07N 120 03W
Lakeport California U.S.A. 64 B4 39 04N 122 56W
Lakeview Oregon U.S.A. 64 B5 42 13N 120 21W
Lakshadweep admin. India 91 C1 9 30N 73 00E
Lalitpur India 91 D4 24 42N 78 24E
Lamar Colorado U.S.A. 64 F4 38 04N 102 37W
Lambaréné Gabon 102 H7 0 41S 10 13E
Lambasa Fiji 110 U16 16 25S 179 24E
Lambert Glacier Antarctica 113 73 00S 70 00E
Lambertville New Jersey U.S.A. 66 C3 40 22N 74 57W
Lambeth bor. United Kingdom 78 C2 51 30N 0 07W
La Mesa California U.S.A. 67 D1 32 45N 117 00W
Lamma Island Hong Kong China 92 B1 22 12N 114 08E
Lammermuir Hills United Kingdom 74 I7 55 50N 2 45W
Lampang Thailand 95 B7 18 16N 99 30E
Lampazos Mexico 68 D5 27 00N 100 30W
Lam Tei Hong Kong China 92 A2 22 25N 113 59E
Lamu Kenya 102 N7 2 17S 40 54E
Lanai i. Hawaiian Islands 111 Y18 20 50N 156 55W
Lanai City Hawaiian Islands 111 Y18 20 50N 156 56W
Lancang Jiang (Mekong) r. China 93 K3 27 30N 99 10E
Lancaster California U.S.A. 64 C3 34 42N 118 09W
Lancaster Ohio U.S.A. 65 J4 39 43N 82 37W
Lancaster Pennsylvania U.S.A. 66 C3 40 01N 76 19W
Lancaster United Kingdom 74 I6 54 03N 2 48W
Landianchang China 94 A1 39 58N 116 17E
Land's End c. United Kingdom 74 F5 50 03N 5 44W
Langer See l. Germany 79 G1 52 24N 13 36E
Lan Hsü i. Taiwan 94 H5 22 04N 121 32E
Lansdale Pennsylvania U.S.A. 66 C3 40 14N 75 17W
Lansing Michigan U.S.A. 65 J5 42 44N 85 34W
Lantau Channel Hong Kong China 92 A1 22 11N 113 52E
Lantau Island Hong Kong China 92 A1 22 15N 113 56E
Lantau Peak Hong Kong China 92 A1 22 15N 113 55E
Lanzarote i. Canary Islands 102 C13 29 00N 13 38W
Lanzhou China 93 K6 36 01N 103 45E
Laoag The Philippines 95 G7 18 14N 120 36E
Lao Cai Vietnam 93 K3 22 30N 103 57E
La Oroya Peru 70 B10 11 36S 75 54W
LAOS 95 C7/D7
La Paz Bolivia 70 D9 16 30S 68 10W
La Paz Mexico 68 B4 24 10N 110 17W
Lapeer Michigan U.S.A. 42 C4 43 03N 83 09W
La Perouse Australia 107 G2/H2 33 59S 151 14E
La Pesca Mexico 68 E3 23 46N 97 47W
La Plata Argentina 71 F5 34 52S 57 55W
Laporte Pennsylvania U.S.A. 66 B4 41 25N 76 29W
Lappland geog. reg. Finland/Sweden 72 K9/L9 67 30N 20 05E
Laptev Sea Arctic Ocean 112 76 00N 125 00E
Laptev Strait Russian Federation 85 Q10 73 00N 141 00E
Lär Iran 89 H4 27 42N 54 19E
Larache Morocco 102 D15 35 12N 6 10W
Laramie Wyoming U.S.A. 64 E5 41 20N 105 38W
Laredo Texas U.S.A. 64 G2 27 32N 99 22W
La Rioja Argentina 71 D7 29 26S 66 50W
Lárisa Greece 72 K3 39 38N 22 25E
Larkana Pakistan 90 B5 27 32N 68 18E
Larnaca Cyprus 88 D5 34 54N 33 29E
Larne United Kingdom 74 F6 54 51N 5 49W
La Romana Dominican Republic 69 K3 18 27N 68 57W
Larsen Ice Shelf Antarctica 113 67 00S 62 00W
La Rumorosa California U.S.A. 67 D1 32 35N 116 02W
Las Cruces New Mexico U.S.A. 64 E3 32 18N 106 47W
La Serena Chile 71 C7 29 54S 71 18W
Lashio Myanmar 93 J3 22 58N 97 48E
Las Palmas Canary Islands 102 B13 28 08N 15 27W
Las Vegas Nevada U.S.A. 64 C4 36 10N 115 10W
Las Vegas New Mexico U.S.A. 64 E4 35 36N 105 15W
Latacunga Ecuador 70 B12 0 58S 78 36W
Latakia see Al Lādhiqiyah
Latur India 91 D3 18 24N 76 34E
LATVIA 72 L7
Lau Fau Shan Hong Kong China 92 A2 22 28N 113 59E
Launceston Australia 106 H1 41 25S 147 07E
Laurel Maryland U.S.A. 66 B2 39 06N 76 51W
Laurel Mississippi U.S.A. 65 I3 31 41N 89 09W
Lausanne Switzerland 72 G5 46 32N 6 39E
Laut i. Indonesia 106 B9 4 40N 107 50E
Lautoka Fiji 110 T16 17 36S 177 28E
La Vega Dominican Republic 69 J3 19 15N 70 33W
Laverton Australia 106 C4 28 49S 122 25E
La Victoria Venezuela 70 D15 10 16N 67 21W
Lawrence Kansas U.S.A. 64 G4 38 58N 95 15W
Lawrence Park tn. Pennsylvania U.S.A. 42 F3 42 08N 80 02W
Lawrenceville New York U.S.A. 43 M5 44 46N 74 40W
Lawton Oklahoma U.S.A. 64 G3 34 36N 98 25W
Laylá Saudi Arabia 89 G3 22 16N 46 45E
Laysan i. Hawaiian Islands 110 I10 25 46N 171 44W
Laytonville California U.S.A. 67 A4 39 41N 123 29W
Lea r. United Kingdom 78 D3 51 40N 0 05W
Leatherhead United Kingdom 78 B2 51 18N 0 20W
LEBANON 88 D5
Lebanon Pennsylvania U.S.A. 66 B3 40 21N 76 25W
Lebanon Missouri U.S.A. 65 H3 37 40N 92 40W
le Blanc-Mesnil France 79 B2 48 56N 2 28E
Lebu Chile 71 C5 37 38S 73 43W
Lee r. Republic of Ireland 74 C3 51 50N 8 50W

Leeds United Kingdom 74 J5 53 50N 1 35W
Leeuwin, Cape Australia 106 A3 34 24S 115 09E
Lee Vining California U.S.A. 67 C3 37 58N 119 09W
Leeward Islands Lesser Antilles 69 L3 17 30N 64 00W
le Havre France 72 F5 49 30N 0 06E
Lehighton Pennsylvania U.S.A. 66 C3 40 50N 75 42W
Leicester United Kingdom 74 J4 52 38N 1 05W
Leichhardt Australia 107 G2 33 53S 151 09E
Leipzig Germany 72 H6 51 20N 12 25E
Leizhou Bandao p. China 93 M3 21 00N 110 00E
le Mans France 72 F5 48 00N 0 12E
Lena r. Russian Federation 85 O9 70 00N 125 00E
Leninabad see Khujand
Leninakan see Gyumri
Leningrad see Sankt-Peterburg
Lenino Russian Federation 86 M1 55 35N 37 10E
Leninogorsk Kazakhstan 87 N5 50 23N 83 32E
Leninsk-Kuznetskiy Russian Federation 85 K6 54 44N 86 13E
Lenkoran' Azerbaijan 86 F2 38 45N 48 50E
Lensk Russian Federation 85 N8 60 48N 114 55E
León Mexico 68 D4 21 10N 101 42W
León Nicaragua 68 G2 12 24N 86 52W
León r. Texas U.S.A. 65 G3 32 00N 98 00W
León Spain 72 D4 42 35N 5 34W
Leonora Australia 106 C4 28 54S 121 20E
Léré Chad 102 H9 9 41N 14 17E
Lérida Spain 72 F4 41 37N 0 38E
Le Roy New York U.S.A. 42 H3 42 59N 78 01W
Lerwick United Kingdom 74 J12 60 09N 1 09W
Les Cayes Haiti 69 J3 18 15N 73 46W
Les Coudreaux France 79 C2 48 54N 2 36E
LESOTHO 103 K2
Lesser Antilles is. West Indies 69 K2/L3 18 00N 65 00W
les Ulis France 79 A1 48 41N 2 11E
Lésvos i. Greece 88 C6 39 00N 26 00E
Leticia Colombia 70 C12 4 09S 69 57W
Lévêque, Cape Australia 106 C6 16 25S 122 55E
Levin New Zealand 107 C2 40 37S 175 17E
Levuka Fiji 110 U16 17 42N 178 50E
Lewis i. United Kingdom 74 E10 58 15N 6 30W
Lewisburg Pennsylvania U.S.A. 66 B3 40 58N 76 55W
Lewisham bor. United Kingdom 78 C2 51 27N 0 00
Lewis Pass New Zealand 107 B2 42 23S 172 24E
Lewiston Idaho U.S.A. 64 C6 46 25N 117 00W
Lewiston Maine U.S.A. 65 L5 44 00N 70 14W
Lewistown Montana U.S.A. 64 E6 47 04N 109 26W
Lexington Kentucky U.S.A. 65 J4 38 03N 84 30W
Lexington Heights tn. Michigan U.S.A. 42 D4 43 15N 82 32W
Leyte i. The Philippines 95 G6 11 00N 125 00E
Lhasa China 92 H4 29 41N 91 10E
L'Hay-les-Roses France 79 B2 48 47N 2 19E
Lhazê China 92 G4 29 08N 87 43E
Lianyungang China 93 N5 34 37N 119 10E
Liaoyang China 93 O7 41 16N 123 12E
Liaoyuan China 93 P7 42 53N 125 10E
Libby Montana U.S.A. 35 E1 48 25N 115 33W
Libenge Congo (D.R.) 102 I8 3 39N 18 39E
Liberal Kansas U.S.A. 64 F4 37 03N 100 56W
LIBERIA 102 D9
Liberty Reservoir Maryland U.S.A. 66 B2 39 25N 76 55W
Libreville Gabon 102 G8 0 30N 9 25E
LIBYA 102 H13
Libyan Desert North Africa 102 J13 25 00N 25 00E
Libyan Plateau Egypt 102 J14 31 00N 26 00E
Lichinga Mozambique 103 M5 13 19S 35 13E
Lichtenberg Germany 79 G2 52 32N 13 30E
Lichtenrade Germany 79 F2 52 23N 13 22E
Lida Belarus 86 B5 53 50N 25 19E
Lida California U.S.A. 67 D3 37 29N 117 29W
Lidcombe Australia 107 G2 33 52S 151 03E
LIECHTENSTEIN 72 G5
Liège Belgium 72 G6 50 38N 5 35E
Liepāja Latvia 72 K7 56 30N 21 00E
Lifou i. Îles Loyauté Pacific Ocean 106 L5 21 00S 167 00E
Lihue Hawaiian Islands 110 X18 21 59N 159 23W
Ligurian Sea Mediterranean Sea 72 G4 44 00N 9 00E
Likasi Congo (D.R.) 103 K5 10 58S 26 47E
Liku Indonesia 95 D4 1 47N 109 19E
Lille France 72 F6 50 39N 3 05E
Lilongwe Malawi 103 L5 13 58S 33 49E
Liluah India 90 K2 22 37N 88 20E
Lima Ohio U.S.A. 65 J4 40 43N 84 06W
Lima Peru 70 B10 12 06S 8 40W
Limassol Cyprus 73 M2 34 04N 33 03E
Limbe Cameroon 102 G8 3 58N 9 10E
Limeira Brazil 71 H8 22 34S 47 25W
Limerick Republic of Ireland 74 C4 52 04N 8 38W
Limnos i. Greece 88 C6 39 00N 25 00E
Limoges France 72 F5 45 50N 1 15E
Limón Costa Rica 69 H2 10 00N 83 01W
Limpopo r. Southern Africa 103 L3 22 30S
Linares Mexico 68 E4 24 54N 99 38W
Lincoln Nebraska U.S.A. 65 G5 40 49N 96 41W
Lincoln United Kingdom 74 K5 53 14N 0 33W
Lincoln Wolds hills United Kingdom 74 K5 53 25N 0 05W
Linden Guyana 70 F14 5 59N 58 19W
Lindenberg Germany 79 G2 52 37N 13 31E
Lindfield Australia 107 G2 33 47S 151 10E
Lindis Pass New Zealand 107 A2 44 35S 169 39E
Line Islands Kiribati 111 J8/K7 0 00 160 00W
Linglestown Pennsylvania U.S.A. 66 B3 40 20N 76 50W
Linhares Brazil 70 J9 19 22S 40 04W
Linköping Sweden 72 J7 58 25N 15 35E
Linstead Jamaica 69 Q8 18 08N 77 02W
Linton North Dakota U.S.A. 64 F6 46 17N 100 14W

Lin Tong Mei Hong Kong China 92 B2 22 29N 114 06E
Linxia China 93 K6 35 31N 103 08E
Linz Austria 72 H5 48 19N 14 18E
Lipetsk Russian Federation 84 F6 52 37N 39 36E
Lisas, Point Trinidad and Tobago 69 T9 10 22N 61 37W
Lisboa (Lisbon) Portugal 72 D3 38 44N 9 08W
Lisburn United Kingdom 74 E6 54 31N 6 03W
Lisburne, Cape Alaska U.S.A. 8 B6 68 54N 166 18W
Lisianski i. Hawaiian Islands 110 I10 26 04N 173 58W
Lismore Australia 106 I4 28 48S 153 17E
Litani r. Lebanon 88 O11 33 35N 35 40E
Lithgow Australia 106 I3 33 30S 150 09E
LITHUANIA 72 K7
Little Aden Yemen Republic 89 F1 12 47N 44 55E
Little Andaman i. Andaman Islands 91 G2 10 30N 92 40E
Little Colorado r. Arizona U.S.A. 64 D4 36 00N 111 00W
Little Falls tn. Minnesota U.S.A. 65 H6 45 58N 94 20W
Little Lake tn. California U.S.A. 67 D2 35 56N 117 54W
Little Minch sd. United Kingdom 74 E9 57 45N 6 30W
Little Miquelon St.-Pierre et Miquelon 49 C2 46 50N 56 13W
Little Missouri r. U.S.A. 64 F6 46 00N 104 00W
Little Nicobar i. Nicobar Islands 91 G1 7 00N 94 00E
Little Rock Kansas U.S.A. 65 H3 34 42N 92 17W
Little Sioux r. U.S.A. 65 G5 42 00N 96 00W
Little Snake r. U.S.A. 65 E4 41 00N 108 00W
Little Traverse Bay b. Michigan U.S.A. 42 A6 45 25N 85 00W
Liuzhou China 93 L3 24 17N 109 15E
Livermore California U.S.A. 67 B3 37 40N 121 46W
Liverpool Australia 107 F2 33 56S 150 56E
Liverpool Pennsylvania U.S.A. 66 A3 40 34N 77 01W
Liverpool United Kingdom 74 I5 53 25N 2 55W
Livingston Montana U.S.A. 64 D6 45 40N 110 33W
Livingston South Shetland Islands 71 E0 62 38S 60 30W
Livingston see Maramba
Liwale Tanzania 103 M6 9 47S 38 00E
Lizard Point United Kingdom 74 F1 49 56N 5 13W
Ljubljana Slovenia 72 H5 46 04N 14 30E
Llanelli United Kingdom 74 G3 51 42N 4 10W
Llanos geog. reg. Venezuela 70 D14/E14 7 30N 67 30W
Lobatse Botswana 103 K2 25 11S 25 40E
Lobito Angola 103 H5 12 20S 13 34E
Loch Linnhe b. United Kingdom 74 F8 56 35N 5 25W
Loch Lomond l. United Kingdom 74 G8 56 10N 4 35W
Loch Ness l. United Kingdom 74 G9 57 02N 4 30W
Loch Shin l. United Kingdom 74 G10 58 05N 4 30W
Loch Tay l. United Kingdom 74 G8 56 31N 4 10W
Lockhart Texas U.S.A. 65 G2 29 54N 97 14W
Lockport New York U.S.A. H4 43 11N 78 39W
Lod Israel 88 O10 31 57N 34 54E
Lodeynoye Pole Russian Federation 86 C7 60 43N 33 30E
Lodi California U.S.A. 67 B4 38 07N 121 18W
Lodi India 108 L4 28 35N 77 13E
Łódź Poland 72 J6 51 49N 19 28E
Lofoten Islands Norway 72 H9/J9 68 30N 15 00E
Logan Utah U.S.A. 64 D5 41 45N 111 50W
Logone r. Chad 102 H10 11 00N 15 00E
Loire r. France 72 F5 47 00N 2 30E
Loja Ecuador 70 B12 3 59S 79 16W
Lok Ma Chau Hong Kong China 92 B3 22 31N 114 05E
Lokoja Nigeria 102 G9 7 49N 6 44E
Lol r. Sudan 102 K9 9 00N 28 00E
Loloda Indonesia 95 H4 1 39N 127 37E
Lomblen i. Indonesia 95 G2 8 30S 123 30E
Lombok i. Indonesia 95 F2 8 30S 116 30E
Lomé Togo 102 F9 6 10N 1 21E
Lomela Congo (D.R.) 102 J7 2 19S 23 15E
Lomela r. Congo (D.R.) 102 J7 3 00S 23 00E
Lomonosov Ridge Arctic Ocean 112 87 00N 60 00W
Lompoc California U.S.A. 67 B2 35 38N 120 27W
London United Kingdom 74 K3 51 30N 0 10W
Londonderry United Kingdom 74 D6 54 59N 7 19W
Londrina Brazil 71 G8 23 18S 51 13W
Lone Pine California U.S.A. 67 C3 36 35N 118 04
Long Bay Barbados 69 W12 13 05N 59 30W
Long Beach California U.S.A. 67 C1 33 47N 118 11W
Long Beach tn. California U.S.A. 64 C3 33 47N 118 15W
Long Branch New Jersey U.S.A. 65 L5 40 17N 73 59W
Long Island The Bahamas 69 I4/J4 23 20N 75 00W
Long Island City New York U.S.A. 66 Z2 40 46N 73 55W
Longjumeau France 79 B1 48 41N 2 18E
Longford Republic of Ireland 74 D5 53 44N 7 47W
Long Island The Bahamas 69 I4/J4 23 20N 75 00W
Longreach Australia 106 G5 23 30S 144 15E
Longview Texas U.S.A. 65 H3 32 20N 94 45W
Longview Washington U.S.A. 64 B6 46 08N 122 56W
Loop Head c. Republic of Ireland 74 B4 52 30N 9 55W
Lopez, Cape Gabon 02 F7 0 36S 8 45E
Lop Nur l. China 92 H7 40 15N 90 20E
Lorain Ohio U.S.A. 65 J5 41 28N 82 11W
Lord Howe Rise Pacific Ocean 110 G5 27 30S 162 00E
Loreto Mexico 64 D2 26 00N 111 20W
Lorica Colombia 69 I1 9 14N 75 50W
Los Alamos New Mexico U.S.A. 64 E3 35 52N 106 19W
Los Angeles California U.S.A. 64 C3 34 00N 118 15W
Los Angeles Chile 71 C5 37 28S 72 23W
Los Angeles Aqueduct California U.S.A. 67 C2 35 12N 118 08W
Los Mochis Mexico 68 C5 25 48N 109 00W
Los Teques Venezuela 70 D15 10 25N 67 01W
Lost Hills California U.S.A. 67 C2 35 37N 119 41W
Lo-tung Taiwan 94 H7 24 00N 121 00E
Louangphabang (Luang Prabang) Laos 95 C7 19 53N 102 10E
Loubomo Congo 103 H7 4 09S 12 47E

Lough Allen l. Republic of Ireland 74 C6 54 15N 8 00W
Lough Conn l. Republic of Ireland 74 B6 54 05N 9 10W
Lough Corrib l. Republic of Ireland 74 B5 53 10N 9 10W
Lough Derg l. Republic of Ireland 74 C4 52 55N 8 10W
Lough Foyle l. United Kingdom 74 D7 55 10N 7 10W
Lough Mask l. Republic of Ireland 74 B5 53 40N 9 30W
Lough Neagh l. United Kingdom 74 E6 54 35N 6 30W
Lough Ree l. Republic of Ireland 74 D5 53 35N 8 00W
Louisade Archipelago is. Papua New Guinea 106 I7 12 00S 153 00E
Louisiana state U.S.A. 65 H3 32 00N 92 00W
Louisville Kentucky U.S.A. 65 I4 38 13N 85 48W
Lowell Massachusetts U.S.A. 65 L5 42 38N 71 19W
Lower Bay New York U.S.A. 66 Y1 40 32N 74 04W
Lower Hutt New Zealand 107 C2 41 13S 174 55E
Lower Lake California U.S.A. 67 A4 38 55N 122 37W
Lower Lough Erne l. United Kingdom 74 D6 54 25N 7 45W
Lower Red Lake Minnesota U.S.A. 65 H6 48 00N 95 00W
Lowestoft United Kingdom 74 M4 52 29N 1 45E
Lo Wu Hong Kong China 92 B3 22 32N 114 06E
Lowville New York U.S.A. 43 L4 43 47N 75 30W
Loyalsock Creek Pennsylvania U.S.A. 66 B4 41 25N 76 50W
Lualaba r. Congo (D.R.) 103 K7 4 00S 26 30E
Luanda Angola 103 H6 8 50S 13 15E
Luang Prabang see Louangphrabang
Luangwa r. Zambia 103 L5 12 00S 32 30E
Luanshya Zambia 103 K5 13 09S 28 24E
Luau Angola 103 J5 10 42S 22 12E
Lubango Angola 103 H5 14 55S 13 30E
Lubbock Texas U.S.A. 64 F3 33 35N 101 53W
Lübeck Germany 72 H6 53 52N 10 40E
Lubilash r. Congo (D.R.) 103 J6 4 00S 24 00E
Lublin Poland 72 K6 51 18N 22 31E
Lubumbashi Congo (D.R.) 103 K5 11 41S 27 29E
Lucea Jamaica 69 P8 18 26N 78 11W
Lucknow India 91 E5 26 50N 80 54E
Lüderitz Namibia 103 I2 26 38S 15 10E
Ludhiana India 91 D6 30 56N 75 52E
Ludlow California U.S.A. 67 D2 34 43N 116 11W
Ludwigsburg Germany 72 G5 48 54N 9 11E
Luena Angola 103 I5 11 47S 19 52E
Lufkin Texas U.S.A. 65 H3 31 21N 94 47W
Luguoqiao China 94 A1 39 51N 116 13E
Luiana r. Angola 103 J4 17 00S 21 00E
Lu-kang Taiwan 94 G7 24 04N 120 22E
Luk Keng Hong Kong China 92 C3 22 32N 114 13E
Luleå Sweden 72 K9 65 35N 22 10E
Lulua r. Congo (D.R.) 103 J6 9 00S 22 00E
Lumberton North Carolina U.S.A. 65 K3 34 37N 79 03W
Lund California U.S.A. 67 E4 38 53N 115 01W
Lundy i. United Kingdom 74 G3 51 11N 4 40W
Lune r. United Kingdom 74 I6 54 07N 2 40W
Lung Kwu Chau i. Hong Kong China 92 A2 22 23N 113 53E
Lungue Bungo r. Angola/Zambia 103 J5 13 00S 22 00E
Luni r. India 91 C5 26 00N 73 00E
Luning California U.S.A. 67 C4 38 30N 118 10W
Luoshan China 93 M4 32 29N 114 40W
Luoyang China 93 M5 34 47N 112 26E
Lurgan United Kingdom 74 E6 54 28N 6 20W
Lurio r. Mozambique 103 M5 14 00S 39 00E
Lusaka Zambia 103 K4 15 26S 28 20E
Lusambo Congo (D.R.) 103 J7 4 59S 23 26E
Lüshun China 93 O6 38 46N 121 15E
Lü-Tao i. Taiwan 94 H5 22 48N 121 35E
Luton United Kingdom 74 K3 51 53N 0 25W
Luts'k Ukraine 86 B5 50 42N 25 16E
Lützow-Holm Bay Antarctica 113 69 00S 38 00E
Luuq Somalia 102 N8 2 52N 42 34E
Luxembourg Luxembourg 72 G5 49 37N 6 08E
LUXEMBOURG 72 G5
Luxor Egypt 102 L13 25 41N 32 24E
Luzhou China 93 L4 28 55N 105 25E
Luziânia Brazil 70 H9 16 16S 47 57W
Luzon i. The Philippines 95 G7 15 00N 122 00E
Luzon Strait China/The Philippines 95 G8 20 00N 121 30E
L'viv (L'vov) Ukraine 86 A4 49 50N 24 00E
Lyme Bay United Kingdom 74 H2 50 40N 2 55W
Lynchburg Virginia U.S.A. 65 K4 37 24N 79 09W
Lynden Washington U.S.A. 34 H4 48 56N 122 28W
Lyndonville New York U.S.A. 44 D2 43 30N 78 45W
Lynn Canal sd. Alaska U.S.A. 34 A3 58 50N 135 05W
Lyon France 72 F5 45 46N 4 50E
Lyons, Gulf of France 72 F5 43 00N 6 00E
Lysychans'k Ukraine 86 D4 48 53N 38 25E
Lyttelton New Zealand 107 B2 43 36S 172 42E
Lyubertsy Russian Federation 86 D6 55 38N 37 58E
Lyublino Russian Federation 86 M1/N1 55 38N 37 44E

M

Ma'ān Jordan 88 E5 30 11N 35 43E
Ma'anshan China 93 N5 31 49N 118 32E
Maas r. Netherlands 72 G6 51 40N 5 00E
Mabalane Mozambique 103 L3 23 51S 32 38E
Mabashi Japan 97 C4 35 48N 139 55E
Macao territory Portugal 93 M3 22 10N 113 40E
Macapá Brazil 70 G13 0 04N 51 04W
Macdonnell Ranges mts. Australia 106 E5 24 00S 132 30E
MACEDONIA, FORMER YUGOSLAV REPUBLIC OF (FYROM) 72 K4
Maceió Brazil 70 J11 9 40S 35 44W
Machala Ecuador 70 B12 3 20S 79 57W
Machanga Mozambique 103 L3 20 58N 35 01E
Machias Maine U.S.A. 47 C1 44 50N 67 20W
Machilapatnam India 91 E3 16 12N 81 11E
Machiques Venezuela 70 C15 10 04N 72 37W

Mackay Australia 106 H5 21 10S 149 10E
Mackay, Lake Australia 106 D5 22 30S 128 00E
Mackinac, Straits of sd. Michigan U.S.A. 42 B6 45 48N 84 43W
Mackinaw City Michigan U.S.A. 65 J6 45 47N 84 43W
Macleod, Lake Australia 106 A5 24 00S 113 30E
Macon Georgia U.S.A. 65 J3 32 49N 83 37W
Macquarie Island Southern Ocean 110 F2 54 29S 158 58E
Macquarie Ridge Southern Ocean 110 F2 55 00S 160 00E
Mac Robertson Land geog. reg. Antarctica 113 70 00S 60 00E
Macuro Venezuela 69 S10 10 38N 61 55W
Mādaba Jordan 88 O10 31 44N 35 48E
MADAGASCAR 103 O3
Madagascar Basin Indian Ocean 108 E4 25 00S 55 00E
Madagascar Ridge Indian Ocean 108 D3/4 30 00S 45 00E
Madang Papua New Guinea 106 H8 5 14S 145 45E
Madeira Islands Atlantic Ocean 102 B14 32 45N 17 00W
Madinat ash Sha'b Yemen Republic 89 F1 12 50N 44 56E
Madhya admin. India 91 D4 23 00N 78 30E
Madhyamgram India 90 L4 22 41N 88 27E
Madison Maine U.S.A. 43 S5 44 48N 69 53W
Madison Wisconsin U.S.A. 65 I5 43 04N 89 22W
Madiun Indonesia 95 E2 7 37S 111 33E
Mado Gashi Kenya 102 M8 0 45N 39 11E
Madras see Chennai
Madrid Spain 72 E4 40 25N 3 43W
Madura i. Indonesia 95 E2 7 00S 113 00E
Madurai India 91 D1 9 55N 78 07E
Madureira Brazil 71 P2 22 52S 43 21W
Maebashi Japan 96 C2 36 24N 139 04E
Mae Nam Mun r. Thailand 93 K2 15 00N 102 00E
Mae Nam Ping r. Thailand 93 J2 16 20N 99 40E
Mae Sot Thailand 93 J2 16 44N 98 32E
Maevantanana Madagascar 103 O4 16 57S 46 50E
Mafia Island Tanzania 103 M6 7 00S 39 00E
Mafikeng Republic of South Africa 103 K2 25 53S 25 39E
Mafraq Jordan 88 E5 32 20N 36 12E
Magadan Russian Federation 85 R7 59 38N 150 50E
Magangué Colombia 70 C14 9 14N 4 46W
Magdeburg Germany 72 H6 52 08N 11 37E
Magé Brazil 71 Q3 22 43S 43 04W
Magelang Indonesia 95 E2 7 28S 110 11E
Maghâgha Egypt 88 D4 28 39N 30 50E
Magnitogorsk Russian Federation 84 H6 53 28N 59 06E
Maha Sarakham Thailand 93 K2 16 08N 103 21E
Mahadeo Hills India 91 D4 22 30N 78 00E
Mahajanga Madagascar 103 O4 15 40S 46 20E
Mahalapye Botswana 103 K3 23 05S 26 52E
Mahanadi r. India 91 E4 21 00N 84 00E
Maharashtra admin. India 91 C3/D3 19 30N 75 00E
Mahia Peninsula New Zealand 107 C3 39 10S 177 53E
Mahilyow (Mogilev) Belarus 72 M6 53 54N 30 20E
Mahlow Germany 79 F1 52 22N 13 24E
Mahoning River r. Ohio U.S.A. 42 F2 41 05N 80 40W
Mahrauli India 108 L4 28 30N 77 11E
Maidstone United Kingdom 74 L3 51 17N 0 32E
Maiduguri Nigeria 102 H10 11 53N 13 16E
Maikala Range mts. India 91 E4 22 30N 81 30E
Maine state U.S.A. 65 M6 45 00N 70 00W
Mainland i. Orkney Islands United Kingdom 74 H11 59 00N 3 15W
Mainland i. Shetland Islands United Kingdom 74 J12 60 15N 1 20W
Maintirano Madagascar 103 N4 18 01S 44 03E
Mai Po Hong Kong China 92 B2 22 29N 114 03E
Maiquetía Venezuela 70 D15 10 38N 66 59W
Maisons-Lafitte France 79 A2 48 57N 2 09E
Maitland Australia 106 I3 32 33S 151 33E
Maitri r.s. Antarctica 113 70 37S 8 22E
Maizuru Japan 96 C2 35 30N 135 20E
Majene Indonesia 95 F3 3 33S 118 59E
Maji Ethiopia 102 M9 6 12N 35 32E
Majiuqiao China 94 C1 39 45N 116 33E
Makassar Strait sd. Indonesia 95 F3/4 0 00 119 00E
Makat Kazakhstan 87 G4 47 38N 53 16E
Makeni Sierra Leone 102 C9 8 57N 12 02W
Makgadikgadi Salt Pan Botswana 103 K3 21 00S 26 00E
Makhachkala Russian Federation 84 G4 42 59N 47 30E
Makiyivka Ukraine 86 D4 48 01N 38 00E
Makkah (Mecca) Saudi Arabia 88 E3 21 26N 39 49E
Makoku Gabon 102 H8 0 38N 12 47E
Makran geog. reg. Iran/Pakistan 89 J4 25 55N 61 30E
Makung (Penghu) Taiwan 94 F6 23 35N 119 33E
Makurdi Nigeria 102 G9 7 44N 8 35E
Malabar Coast India 91 C2/D1 12 00N 74 00E
Malabo Equatorial Guinea 102 G8 3 45N 8 48E
Malacca, Strait of (Selat Melaka) Indonesia 95 C4/B5 4 00N 100 00E
Malaga New Jersey U.S.A. 66 C2 39 34N 75 03W
Málaga Spain 72 E3 36 43N 4 25W
Malaita i. Solomon Islands 106 K8 9 00S 161 00E
Malakal Sudan 102 L9 9 31N 31 40E
Malang Indonesia 95 E2 7 59S 112 45E
Malanje Angola 103 I6 9 32S 16 20E
Mälaren l. Sweden 72 J7 59 30N 17 00E
MALAWI 103 L5
Malawi, Lake see Nyasa, Lake
Malaya see Peninsular Malaysia
MALAYSIA 95 C5/E5
Malden Island Pacific Ocean 111 K7 4 03S 154 59W
MALDIVES 108 G7
Maldonado Uruguay 71 G6 34 57S 54 59W
Malegaon India 91 C4 20 32N 74 38E
Malekula i. Vanuatu 106 L6 16 30S 167 20E

Malema Mozambique **103** M5 14 57S 37 25E
MALI 102 D10
Malin Head c. Republic of Ireland **74** D7 55 30N 7 20W
Mallaig United Kingdom **74** F9 57 00N 5 50W
Mallawi Egypt **88** D4 27 44N 30 50E
Mallorca i. Balearic Islands **72** F3 39 50N 2 30E
Malmö Sweden **72** H7 55 35N 13 00E
Malone New York U.S.A. **43** M5 44 52N 74 19W
Malonga Congo (D.R.) **103** J5 10 26S 23 10E
Malpelo i. Colombia **70** A13 4 00N 81 35W
MALTA 72 H3
Malta Montana U.S.A. **64** E6 48 22N 107 51W
Ma Lui Shui Hong Kong China **92** C2 22 25N 114 12E
Maluku (Moluccas) Indonesia **95** H3 4 00S 127 00E
Malviya Nagar India **108** L4 28 32N 77 12E
Mamanutha Group is. Fiji **110** T16 17 40S 177 00E
Mambasa Congo (D.R.) **102** K8 1 20N 29 05E
Mammoth Lakes tn. California U.S.A. **67** C3 37 38N 118 58W
Mamonovo Russian Federation **86** A5 54 30N 19 59E
Man Côte d'Ivoire **102** D9 7 31N 7 37W
Manacapuru Brazil **70** E12 3 16S 60 37W
Manado Indonesia **95** G4 1 32N 124 55E
Managua Nicaragua **69** G2 12 06N 86 18W
Manali India **91** D6 32 12N 77 06E
Manaus Brazil **70** F12 3 06S 60 00W
Manchester California U.S.A. **67** A4 38 58N 123 42W
Manchester Michigan U.S.A. **42** B3 42 10N 84 01W
Manchester New Hampshire U.S.A. **65** L5 42 59N 71 28W
Manchester Tennessee U.S.A. **65** I4 35 29N 86 04W
Manchester United Kingdom **74** I5 53 30N 2 15W
Mandalay Myanmar **91** H4 21 57N 96 04E
Mandeville Jamaica **69** Q8 18 02N 77 31W
Mandvi India **90** B4 22 50N 69 25E
Mandya India **91** D2 12 34N 76 55E
Mangalore India **91** C2 12 54N 74 51E
Mango i. Fiji **110** V16 17 20S 179 20W
Mangoky r. Madagascar **103** N3 22 00S 45 00E
Mangui China **93** O9 52 05N 122 17E
Manhattan California U.S.A. **67** D4 38 31N 117 05W
Manhattan Kansas U.S.A. **65** G4 39 11N 96 35W
Manhattan New York U.S.A. **66** Z2 40 48N 73 58W
Mania r. Madagascar **103** N4 19 30S 50 30E
Manica Mozambique **103** L4 18 56S 32 52E
Manicoré Brazil **70** E11 5 48S 61 16W
Maniitsoq (Sukkertoppen) Greenland **9** AA6 65 25N 53 00W
Manikpur India **90** J2 22 32N 88 12E
Manila The Philippines **95** G6 14 37N 120 58E
Manipur admin. India **91** G4 24 30N 94 00E
Manipur r. India/Myanmar **91** G4 23 30N 93 00E
Manitowoc Wisconsin U.S.A. **65** I5 44 04N 87 40W
Manizales Colombia **70** B14 5 03N 75 32W
Manjra r. India **91** D3 18 30N 76 00E
Man Kam To Hong Kong China **92** B3 22 32N 114 07E
Mankato Minnesota U.S.A. **65** H5 44 10N 94 00W
Manly Australia **107** H2 33 48S 151 17E
Mannar Sri Lanka **91** D1 8 58N 79 54E
Mannar, Gulf of India/Sri Lanka **91** D1 8 30N 79 00E
Manokwari Indonesia **95** I3 0 53S 134 05E
Mansfield Ohio U.S.A. **42** D1 40 46N 82 31W
Mansfield Pennsylvania U.S.A. **43** J2 41 47N 77 05W
Manta Ecuador **70** A12 0 59S 80 44W
Manukau New Zealand **107** B3 37 00S 174 52E
Manukau Harbour New Zealand **107** B3 37 02S 174 43E
Manyoni Tanzania **103** L6 5 46S 34 50E
Manzanilla Bay Trinidad and Tobago **69** T9/10 10 40N 61 55W
Manzanilla Point Trinidad and Tobago **69** T10 10 31N 61 01W
Manzanillo Cuba **69** I4 20 21N 77 21W
Manzanillo Mexico **68** D3 19 00N 104 20W
Manzhouli China **93** N8 46 36N 117 28E
Maoming China **93** M3 21 50N 110 56E
Ma On Shan Hong Kong China **92** C2 22 26N 114 13E
Ma On Shan mt. Hong Kong China **92** C2 22 24N 114 16E
Maple Heights tn. Ohio U.S.A. **42** E2 41 24N 81 35W
Maputo Mozambique **103** L2 26 58S 32 35E
Marabá Brazil **70** H11 5 23S 49 10W
Maracaibo Venezuela **70** C15 10 44N 71 37W
Maracay Venezuela **70** D15 10 20N 67 28W
Maradi Niger **102** G10 13 29N 7 10E
Maramba (Livingstone) Zambia **103** K4 17 50S 25 53E
Maranhão admin. Brazil **70** H11 5 20S 46 00W
Maraval Trinidad and Tobago **69** T10 10 42N 61 31W
Marble Bar tn. Australia **106** B5 21 16S 119 45E
Marble Canyon tn. Arizona U.S.A. **64** D4 36 50N 111 38W
Marchfield Barbados **69** W12 13 07N 59 29W
Marcus Island Pacific Ocean **110** F10 24 30N 157 30E
Mardan Pakistan **91** C6 34 14N 72 05E
Mar del Plata Argentina **71** F5 38 00S 57 32W
Mardin Turkey **88** F6 37 19N 40 43E
Mare i. Îles Loyauté **111** Q9 21 00S 167 30E
Margai Caka l. China **91** F7 35 00N 87 00E
Margate United Kingdom **74** M3 51 24N 1 24E
Margilan Uzbekistan **87** J4 40 41N 71 45E
Maria Elena Chile **71** D8 22 18S 69 40W
Marianas Trench Pacific Ocean **110** E9 16 00N 147 30E
Maria van Diemen, Cape New Zealand **107** B4 34 29S 172 39E
Maricopa California U.S.A. **67** C2 35 04N 119 25W
Marie Byrd Land geog. reg. Antarctica **113** 77 00S 130 00W
Mariental Namibia **103** I3 24 36S 17 59E
Marietta Pennsylvania U.S.A. **66** B3 40 04N 76 33W
Mariinsk Russian Federation **87** O6 56 14N 87 45E
Marijampolė (Kapsukas) Lithuania **86** A5 54 31N 23 20E

Marília Brazil **71** G8 22 13S 49 58W
Mariners Harbor New York U.S.A. **66** Y1 40 38N 74 10W
Maringá Brazil **71** G8 23 26S 52 02W
Marion Ohio U.S.A. **65** J5 40 35N 83 08W
Marion, Lake South Carolina U.S.A. **65** J3 33 00N 80 00W
Mariposa California U.S.A. **67** C3 37 30N 119 59W
Mariscal Estigarribia Paraguay **71** E8 22 03S 60 35W
Mariupol Ukraine **73** N5 47 05N 37 34E
Marjayoun Lebanon **88** O11 33 22N 35 34E
Marka Somalia **102** N8 1 42N 44 47E
Markha r. Russian Federation **85** N6 64 00N 12 30E
Markovo Russian Federation **85** T8 64 40N 170 24E
Marlette Michigan U.S.A. **42** C4 43 20N 83 04W
Marlton New Jersey U.S.A. **66** D2 39 55N 74 55W
Marly-le-Roi France **79** A2 48 52N 2 05E
Marmara, Sea of Turkey **72** F5 41 15N 28 10E
Marne r. France **72** F5 49 00N 4 00E
Marne-la-Vallée France **79** C2 48 50 2 37E
Maroantsetra Madagascar **103** O4 15 23S 49 44E
Maroni r. Suriname **70** G13 4 00N 54 30W
Maroua Cameroon **102** H10 10 35N 14 20E
Maroubra Australia **107** G2/H2 33 57S 151 15E
Marquesas Islands Pacific Ocean **111** M7 10 00S 137 00W
Marquette Michigan U.S.A. **65** I4 46 33N 87 23W
Marrakech Morocco **102** D14 31 49N 8 00W
Marrickville Australia **107** G2 33 55S 151 09E
Marsabit Kenya **102** M8 2 20N 37 59E
Marseille France **72** G4 43 18N 5 22E
MARSHALL ISLANDS 110 G8
Marsh Harbour The Bahamas **65** K2 26 31N 77 05W
Martaban, Gulf of Myanmar **95** B7 15 30N 92 30E
Martinique i. Lesser Antilles **69** L2 14 30N 61 00W
Martin Lake Alabama U.S.A. **65** I3 33 00N 86 00W
Martinsville Virginia U.S.A. **65** K4 36 43N 79 53W
Martin Vaz i. Atlantic Ocean **109** F4 21 00S 27 30W
Marton New Zealand **107** C2 40 05S 175 23E
Marwitz Germany **79** E2 52 44N 13 08E
Mary Turkmenistan **87** J2 37 42N 61 54E
Maryborough Australia **106** I4 25 32S 152 36E
Maryland state U.S.A. **65** K4 39 00N 77 00W
Marysville California U.S.A. **64** B4 39 10N 121 34W
Marysville Pennsylvania U.S.A. **66** B3 40 00N 76 00W
Masada see Mezada
Masan South Korea **93** P6 35 10N 128 35E
Masaya Nicaragua **69** G2 11 59N 86 03W
Masbate The Philippines **95** G6 12 21N 123 36E
Mascarene Basin Indian Ocean **108** E5 15 00S 55 00E
Mascot Australia **107** G2 33 56S 151 12E
Maseru Lesotho **103** K2 29 19S 27 29E
Mashhad Iran **89** I6 36 16N 59 34E
Masindi Uganda **102** L8 1 41N 31 45E
Masirah i. Oman **89** I3 20 25N 58 40E
Mason Michigan U.S.A. **42** B3 42 34N 84 27W
Mason City Iowa U.S.A. **65** H5 43 10N 93 10W
Masqat Oman **89** I3 23 37N 58 38E
Massachusetts state U.S.A. **65** L5 42 00N 72 00W
Massachusetts Bay U.S.A. **65** K5 42 00N 70 00W
Massawa Eritrea **88** E2 15 42N 39 25E
Massena New York U.S.A. **65** L5 44 56N 74 57W
Massif Central France **72** F4 45 00N 3 30E
Massif de l'Isola mts. Madagascar **103** N3 23 00S 45 00E
Massif de Tsaratanana mts. Madagascar **103** N5 14 00S 49 00E
Massillon Ohio U.S.A. **42** E1 40 48N 81 32W
Massy France **79** B1 48 44N 2 17E
Masterton New Zealand **107** C2 40 57S 175 39E
Masuda Japan **96** B1 34 42N 131 51E
Masuku Gabon **102** H7 1 40S 13 31E
Masvingo Zimbabwe **103** L3 20 05S 30 50E
Matadi Congo (D.R.) **103** H6 5 50S 13 32E
Matagalpa Nicaragua **69** G2 12 52N 85 58W
Matale Sri Lanka **91** E1 7 28N 80 37E
Matamoros Mexico **68** D5 25 33N 103 51W
Matamoros Mexico **68** E5 25 50N 97 31W
Matanzas Cuba **69** H4 23 04N 81 35W
Matara Sri Lanka **91** E1 5 57N 80 32E
Mataram Indonesia **95** F2 8 36S 116 07E
Mataura New Zealand **107** A1 46 12S 168 52E
Mataura r. New Zealand **107** A1 45 45S 168 50E
Matehuala Mexico **68** D4 23 40N 100 40W
Matelot Trinidad and Tobago **69** T10 10 49N 61 07W
Mathura India **91** D5 27 30N 77 42E
Mato Grosso admin. Brazil **70** F10 14 00S 56 00W
Mato Grosso r. Brazil **70** F9 15 05S 59 57W
Mato Grosso do Sul admin. Brazil **70** F8/9 20 00S 55 00W
Matopo Hills Zimbabwe **103** K3 21 00S 28 30E
Matrah Oman **89** I3 23 31N 58 18E
Matsudo Japan **96** C2 35 46N 139 54E
Matsue Japan **96** B2 35 29N 133 04E
Matsumoto Japan **96** C2 36 18N 137 58E
Matsuyama Japan **96** B1 33 50N 132 47E
Matuku i. Fiji **110** U15 19 11S 179 45E
Matura Trinidad and Tobago **69** T10 10 40N 61 04W
Matura Bay Trinidad and Tobago **69** T10 10 40N 61 04W
Maturín Venezuela **70** E14 9 45N 63 10W
Maués Brazil **70** F12 3 22S 57 38W
Maui i. Hawaiian Islands **111** Y18 21 00N 156 30W
Maumee River r. Ohio U.S.A. **42** C2 41 30N 83 50W
Maumere Indonesia **95** G2 8 35S 122 13E
Mauna Kea mt. Hawaiian Islands **111** Z17 19 50N 155 25W
Mauna Loa vol. Hawaiian Islands **111** Z17 19 28N 155 35W
MAURITANIA 102 C11
MAURITIUS 108 E4
Ma Wan i. Hong Kong China **92** B2 22 21N 114 03E

Ma Wan Chung Hong Kong China **92** A1 22 17N 113 56E
Mawkmai Myanmar **95** B8 20 12N 97 37E
Mawlaik Myanmar **91** G4 23 40N 94 26E
Mawson r.s. Antarctica **113** 67 36S 62 52E
Mayaguana i. The Bahamas **69** J4 22 30N 72 40W
Mayagüez Puerto Rico **69** K3 18 13N 67 09W
Mayaro Bay Trinidad and Tobago **69** U9 10 07N 61 00W
Maykop Russian Federation **89** G7 44 37N 40 48E
Mayotte i. Indian Ocean **103** N5 13 00S 45 00E
May Pen Jamaica **69** Q7 17 58N 77 15W
Mayumba Gabon **103** H7 3 23S 10 38E
Mayville New York U.S.A. **42** G3 42 15N 79 32W
Mazabuka Zambia **103** K4 15 50S 27 47E
Mazār-e Sharif Afghanistan **89** K6 36 42N 67 06E
Mazatenango Guatemala **68** F2 14 31N 91 30W
Mazatlán Mexico **68** C4 23 11N 106 25W
Mbabane Swaziland **103** L2 26 20S 31 08E
Mbaiki Central African Republic **102** I8 3 53N 18 01E
Mbala Zambia **103** L6 8 50S 31 24E
Mbalmayo Cameroon **102** H8 3 30N 11 31E
Mbandaka Congo (D.R.) **102** I7 0 03N 18 28E
Mbengga i. Fiji **110** U15 18 24S 178 09E
Mbeya Tanzania **103** L6 8 54S 33 29E
Mbuji-Mayi Congo (D.R.) **103** J6 6 10S 23 39E
McAlester Oklahoma U.S.A. **65** G3 34 56N 95 46W
McAllen Texas U.S.A. **65** G2 26 13N 98 15W
McComb Mississippi U.S.A. **65** H3 31 13N 90 29W
McCook Nebraska U.S.A. **64** F5 40 13N 100 35W
McGrath Alaska U.S.A. **8** D5 62 58N 155 40W
McKinley Alaska U.S.A. **8** E5 62 02N 151 01W
McKinney Texas U.S.A. **65** G3 33 14N 96 37W
McMurdo r.s. Antarctica **113** T7 51S 166 40E
McMurdo Sound Antarctica **113** 55 00S 165 00E
McPherson Kansas U.S.A. **65** G4 38 22N 97 41W
Mead, Lake U.S.A. **64** D4 36 10N 114 25W
Meadville Pennsylvania U.S.A. **65** J5 41 38N 80 10W
Mecca see Makkah
Mecheria Algeria **102** E14 33 31N 0 20W
Medan Indonesia **95** B4 3 35N 98 39E
Medellín Colombia **70** B14 6 15N 75 36W
Medenine Tunisia **102** H14 33 24N 10 25E
Medford Oregon U.S.A. **64** B5 42 20N 122 52W
Media Pennsylvania U.S.A. **66** C2 39 56N 75 23W
Medina see Al Madīnah
Medina Ohio U.S.A. **42** E2 41 07N 81 51W
Medinipur West Bengal India **91** F4 22 25N 87 24E
Mediterranean Sea Africa/Europe **72** F3/K3 35 00N 18 00E
Medvedkovo Russian Federation **86** M2 55 55N 37 08E
Medvezh'yegorsk Russian Federation **84** F8 62 56N 34 28E
Medway r. United Kingdom **74** L3 51 24N 0 40E
Meekatharra Australia **106** B4 26 30S 118 30E
Meerut India **91** D5 29 00N 77 45E
Mēga Ethiopia **102** M8 4 02N 38 19E
Meghalaya admin. India **91** G5 25 30N 91 00E
Meguro Japan **97** B3 35 36N 139 43E
Mei Xian China **93** N3 24 19N 116 13E
Mek'ele Ethiopia **102** M10 13 32N 39 33E
Meknès Morocco **102** D14 33 53N 5 37W
Mekong see Lancang Jiang
Mekong, Mouths of the est. Vietnam **95** D5 9 30N 106 45E
Melaka Malaysia **95** C4 2 11N 102 16E
Melbourne Australia **106** H2 37 45S 144 58E
Melbourne Florida U.S.A. **65** J2 28 04N 80 38W
Melitopol' Ukraine **86** D4 43 46N 35 22E
Melo Uruguay **71** G6 32 22S 54 10W
Melun-Senart admin. France **79** C1 48 35N 20 35E
Melville Bugt b. Qimusseriarsuaq
Melville, Cape Australia **106** G7 14 08S 144 31E
Melville Island Australia **106** E7 11 30S 131 00E
Memphis N.H.S. Egypt **88** D4 29 52N 31 12E
Memphis Tennessee U.S.A. **65** I4 35 10N 90 00W
Menai Australia **107** G1 34 01S 151 01E
Menderes r. Turkey **88** C6 37 50N 28 10E
Mendi Papua New Guinea **106** G6 6 13S 143 39E
Mendip Hills United Kingdom **74** I3 51 18N 2 45W
Mendocino California U.S.A. **67** A4 39 20N 123 47W
Mendocino Seascarp Pacific Ocean **111** L12 41 00N 145 00W
Mendota California U.S.A. **67** B3 36 44N 120 24W
Mendoza Argentina **71** D6 32 48S 68 52W
Mengdingjie China **93** J3 23 03N 99 03E
Menongue Angola **103** I5 14 36S 17 48E
Menorca i. Balearic Islands **72** F3 39 45N 4 15E
Mentor Ohio U.S.A. **65** J5 41 42N 81 22W
Meoqui Mexico **64** E2 28 18N 105 30W
Merah see Song-koi
Merauke Indonesia **106** G8 8 30S 140 22E
Merced California U.S.A. **64** B4 37 17N 120 29W
Mercedes Argentina **71** D6 33 41S 65 28W
Mercedes Uruguay **71** F6 34 15S 58 02W
Mergui Myanmar **95** B6 12 26N 98 34E
Mergui Archipelago Myanmar **95** B6 11 00N 97 40E
Mérida Mexico **68** G4 20 59N 89 39W
Mérida Venezuela **70** C14 8 24N 71 08W
Meridian Mississippi U.S.A. **65** I3 32 21N 88 42W
Merowe Sudan **102** L11 18 30N 31 49E
Merrylands Australia **107** F2/G2 33 50S 150 59E
Mersey r. United Kingdom **74** I5 53 20N 2 53W
Mersin see İçel
Merthyr Tydfil United Kingdom **74** H3 51 46N 3 23W
Merton bor. United Kingdom **78** C2 51 25N 0 12W
Mertz Glacier Antarctica **113** 68 00S 145 00E
Mesa Arizona U.S.A. **64** D3 33 25N 111 50W
Mesopotamia geog. reg. Middle East **88** F5/F6 35 00N 42 00E
Mesquite Lake California U.S.A. **67** E2 35 43N 115 36W
Messina Italy **72** J3 38 13N 15 33E

Messina Republic of South Africa **103** K3 22 23S 30 00E
Metlakatla Alaska U.S.A. **34** B3 55 09N 131 35W
Mettler California U.S.A. **67** C2 35 03N 119 00W
Metz France **72** G5 49 07N 6 11E
Meudon France **79** A2 48 48N 2 15E
Meuse r. Belgium/France **72** F5 50 00N 5 00E
Mexicali Mexico **68** A6 32 36N 115 30W
MEXICO 68 D4
Mexico New York U.S.A. **43** K4 43 26N 76 15W
México City Mexico **68** E3 19 25N 99 10W
Mexico, Gulf of Mexico **68** F4/G4 25 00N 90 00W
Meymaneh Afghanistan **89** J6 35 55N 64 47E
Mezada (Masada) hist. site Israel **88** O10 31 17N 35 20E
Mezen' Russian Federation **84** G9 65 50N 44 20E
Mezhdurechensk Russian Federation **87** O5 53 43N 88 11E
Miami Florida U.S.A. **65** J2 25 45N 80 15W
Miami Oklahoma U.S.A. **65** H4 36 53N 94 54W
Miāneh Iran **89** G6 37 23N 47 45E
Mianwali Pakistan **91** C6 32 32N 71 33E
Miao-li Taiwan **94** G7 24 37N 120 49E
Miass Russian Federation **84** I6 55 00N 60 08E
Michelson, Mount Alaska U.S.A. **50** C4 69 19N 144 20W
Michigan state U.S.A. **65** I6 45 00N 85 00W
Michigan, Lake U.S.A. **65** I5 45 00N 87 00W
Michurinsk Russian Federation **86** E5 52 54N 40 30E
Micronesia geog. reg. Pacific Ocean **110** G8 10 00N 160 00E
Mid-Atlantic Ridge Atlantic Ocean **109** D8/F11 15 00S 13 00W
Middle America Trench Pacific Ocean **111** P9/Q9 16 30N 99 00W
Middle Andaman i. Andaman Islands **91** G2 12 30N 93 00E
Middleburg Pennsylvania U.S.A. **66** A3 40 47N 77 03W
Middleburg Republic of South Africa **103** K2 31 28S 25 01E
Middleburg Heights tn. Ohio U.S.A. **42** E2 41 20N 81 49W
Middle Harbour Australia **107** G2 33 48S 151 14E
Middle Loup r. Nebraska U.S.A. **64** F5 42 00N 101 00W
Middlesbrough United Kingdom **74** J6 54 35N 1 14W
Middletown Delaware U.S.A. **66** C2 39 27N 75 44W
Middletown Pennsylvania U.S.A. **66** B3 40 12N 76 44W
Mid-Indian Basin Indian Ocean **108** H6 10 00S 80 00E
Mid-Indian Ridge Indian Ocean **108** F3/G3
Midland Michigan U.S.A. **65** J5 43 38N 84 14W
Midland Texas U.S.A. **64** F3 32 00N 102 09W
Midland Beach New York U.S.A. **66** Y1 40 33N 74 07W
Midori Japan **97** B3 35 33N 139 39E
Mid-Pacific Mountains Pacific Ocean **110** F10/H10 21 00N 160 00E
Midway Islands Pacific Ocean **110** I10 28 15N 177 25W
Mien Hsü i. Taiwan **94** I8 25 31N 122 07E
Milagro Ecuador **70** B12 2 11S 79 36W
Milano (Milan) Italy **72** G5 45 28N 9 12E
Mildura Australia **106** G3 34 14S 142 13E
Miles City Montana U.S.A. **64** E6 46 24N 105 48W
Milford Delaware U.S.A. **66** C1 38 54N 75 25W
Milford New Jersey U.S.A. **66** C3 40 34N 75 06W
Milford Pennsylvania U.S.A. **66** D4 41 19N 74 48W
Milford Utah U.S.A. **64** D4 38 22N 113 00W
Milford Haven United Kingdom **74** F3 51 44N 5 02W
Milford Sound tn. New Zealand **107** A2 44 36S 167 49E
Mill Creek Michigan U.S.A. **42** C4 43 10N 83 00W
Millersburg Pennsylvania U.S.A. **66** B3 40 32N 76 57W
Millerstown Pennsylvania U.S.A. **66** A3 40 32N 77 08W
Millinocket Maine U.S.A. **47** C2 45 42N 68 43W
Millville New Jersey U.S.A. **66** C2 39 24N 75 02W
Milton New Zealand **107** A1 46 07S 169 58E
Milton Keynes United Kingdom **74** K4 52 02N 0 42W
Milton, Lake Ohio U.S.A. **42** F2 41 05N 80 59W
Milwaukee Wisconsin U.S.A. **65** I5 43 03N 87 56W
Minahassa Peninsula Indonesia **95** G4 0 30N 123 00E
Minamata Japan **96** B1 32 13N 130 23E
Minas Uruguay **71** F6 34 20S 55 15W
Minas Gerais admin. Brazil **70** I9 17 30S 45 00W
Minatitlán Mexico **68** F3 17 59N 94 32W
Minch, The sd. United Kingdom **74** F10 58 00N 6 00W
Mindanao i. The Philippines **95** G5/H5 8 00N 125 00E
Minden Louisiana U.S.A. **65** H3 32 36N 93 17W
Mindoro i. The Philippines **95** G6 13 00N 121 00E
Mingäçevir Azerbaijan **86** F3 40 45N 47 03E
Minicoy Island India **91** C1 8 29N 73 01E
Minneapolis Minnesota U.S.A. **65** H5 45 00N 93 15W
Minnesota r. U.S.A. **65** G5 44 00N 95 00W
Minnesota state U.S.A. **65** H6 47 00N 95 00W
Minot North Dakota U.S.A. **64** F6 48 16N 101 19W
Minsk Belarus **72** L6 53 51N 27 30E
Minusinsk Russian Federation **85** L6 53 43N 91 45E
Miraflores Locks Panama **69** Y1 8 59N 79 36W
Miraj India **91** C3 16 51N 74 42E
Miri Malaysia **95** F4 4 23N 114 00E
Mirnyy r.s. Antarctica **113** 66 33S 93 01E
Mirnyy Russian Federation **85** N8 62 30N 113 58E
Mirpur Khas Pakistan **90** B5 25 33N 69 05E
Mirs Bay Hong Kong China **92** D3 22 33N 114 24E
Mirzapur India **91** E5 25 09N 82 34E
Misawa Japan **96** D3 40 42N 141 26E
Misfaq Egypt **88** N10 31 01N 33 11E
Miskolc Hungary **72** J4 48 07N 20 47E
Misoöl i. Indonesia **95** I3 1 50S 129 55E
Miṣrātah (Misurata) Libya **72** J2 32 23N 15 06E
Mississippi r. U.S.A. **65** H3/H5 35 00N 90 00W
Mississippi state U.S.A. **65** H3 32 00N 90 00W
Mississippi Delta Louisiana U.S.A. **65** I2 30 00N 90 00W
Missoula Montana U.S.A. **64** D6 46 52N 114 00W
Missouri r. U.S.A. **65** H4 39 00N 93 00W

Missouri *state* U.S.A. **65** H4 38 00N 93 00W
Misurata *see* Miṣrātah
Mitcham United Kingdom **78** C2 51 24N 0 09W
Mitchell Australia **106** H4 26 30S 147 56E
Mitchell *r.* Australia **106** G6 16 00S 142 30E
Mitchell South Dakota U.S.A. **65** G5 43 40N 98 01W
Mitilini Greece **88** C6 39 06N 26 34E
Mitino Russian Federation **86** L2 55 53N 37 24E
Mitkof Island Alaska U.S.A. **34** B3 56 40N 132 45W
Mito Japan **96** D2 36 22N 140 29E
Mitry-Mory France **79** C2 48 58N 2 38E
Mits'iwa Eritrea **102** M11 15 42N 39 25E
Mitú Colombia **70** C13 1 07N 70 05W
Mitumba Mountains *see* Chaine des Mitumba
Miyako Japan **96** D2 39 38N 141 59E
Miyakonojō Japan **96** B1 31 43N 131 02E
Miyazaki Japan **96** B1 31 56N 131 27E
Mizen Head *c.* Republic of Ireland **74** B3 51 30N 9 50W
Mizoram *admin.* India **91** G4 23 40N 93 30E
Mnevniki Russian Federation **86** L2 55 46N 37 29E
Moala *i.* Fiji **110** U15 18 34S 179 56E
Mobaye Central African Republic **102** J8 4 19N 21 11E
Mobile Alabama U.S.A. **65** I3 30 40N 88 05W
Moçambique Mozambique **103** N5 15 03S 40 45E
Mocuba Mozambique **103** M4 16 52S 36 57E
Módena Italy **72** H4 44 39N 10 55E
Modesto California U.S.A. **64** B4 37 37N 121 00W
Moe Australia **106** H2 38 09S 146 22E
Mogadishu *see* Muqdisho
Mogilev *see* Mahilyow
Mogocha Russian Federation **85** N6 53 44N 119 45E
Mogollon Rim *plat.* Arizona U.S.A. **64** D3 34 00N 111 00W
Mohe China **93** O9 52 55N 122 20E
Mohyliv-Podil's'kyy Ukraine **86** B4 48 29N 27 49E
Mojave California U.S.A. **64** C4 35 02N 118 11W
Mojave *r.* California U.S.A. **67** D2 34 47N 117 15W
Mojave Desert California U.S.A. **67** D2 35 08N 117 21W
Mokelumne *r.* California U.S.A. **67** B4 38 13N 121 05W
Mokolo Cameroon **102** H10 10 49N 13 54E
Mokp'o South Korea **93** P5 34 50N 126 25E
Moksha *r.* Russian Federation **86** E5 54 30N 43 00E
Molango Mexico **68** E4 20 48N 98 44W
MOLDOVA 72 L5
Mole *r.* United Kingdom **78** B2 51 15N 0 20W
Molepolole Botswana **103** K3 24 25S 25 30E
Mollendo Peru **70** C9 17 00S 72 00W
Molodezhnaya *r.s.* Antarctica **113** 67 40S 45 51E
Molokai *i.* Hawaiian Islands **111** Y18 21 40N 155 55W
Molopo *r.* Southern Africa **103** J2 26 30S 22 30E
Moluccas *see* Maluku
Molucca Sea Indonesia **95** G3/H4 0 30S 125 30E
Mombasa Kenya **103** L7 4 04S 39 40E
Mombetsu Japan **96** D3 42 28N 142 10E
MONACO 72 G4
Monadhliath Mountains United Kingdom **74** G9
57 10N 4 00W
Monahans Texas U.S.A. **64** F3 31 35N 102 54W
Mona Vale Australia **107** H3 33 41S 151 18E
Monbetsu Japan **96** D3 44 23N 143 22E
Monção Brazil **70** H12 3 30S 45 10W
Monclova Mexico **68** D5 26 55N 101 25W
Moneró Brazil **71** Q2 22 48S 43 11W
Mong Kok Hong Kong China **92** B1 22 09N 114 09E
MONGOLIA 92 H8/M8
Mongu Zambia **103** J4 15 13S 23 09E
Monitor Range *mts.* California U.S.A. **67** D4
38 23N 116 52W
Mono Lake California U.S.A. **67** C4 38 00N 119 00W
Monos *i.* Trinidad and Tobago **69** S10 10 42N 61 42W
Monroe Louisiana U.S.A. **65** H3 32 31N 92 06W
Monroe Michigan U.S.A. **42** C2 41 56N 83 21W
Monrovia Liberia **102** C9 6 20N 10 46W
Montana *state* U.S.A. **64** E6 47 00N 111 00W
Mont Blanc *mt.* France/Italy **72** G5 45 50N 6 52E
Mont Cameroun *mt.* Cameroon **102** G8 4 13N 9 10E
Montego Bay *tn.* Jamaica **69** Q8 18 27N 77 56W
Montenegro *admin.* Yugoslavia **72** J4 42 30N 19 00E
Monterey California U.S.A. **64** B4 36 35N 121 55W
Monterey Bay California U.S.A. **67** B3 36 46N 121 51W
Montería Colombia **70** B14 8 45N 75 54W
Montero Bolivia **70** E9 17 20S 63 15W
Monterrey Mexico **68** D5 25 40N 100 20W
Montes Claros *tn.* Brazil **70** I9 16 45S 43 52W
Montevideo Uruguay **71** F6 34 55S 56 10W
Montgeron France **79** B1 48 42N 2 27E
Montgomery Alabama U.S.A. **65** I3 32 22N 86 20W
Montgomery Pennsylvania U.S.A. **66** B4 41 09N 76 54W
Montmorency France **79** B2 48 59N 2 19E
Monto Australia **106** I5 24 53S 151 06E
Montpelier Ohio U.S.A. **42** B2 41 35N 84 35W
Montpellier France **72** F4 43 36N 3 53E
Montrose Colorado U.S.A. **64** E4 38 29N 107 53W
Montrose Pennsylvania U.S.A. **66** C4 41 49N 75 53W
Montrouge France **79** B2 48 49N 2 19E
Montserrat *i.* Lesser Antilles **69** L3 16 45N 62 14W
Monts Nimba *mts.* Guinea/Liberia **102** D9 7 39N 8 30W
Monywa Myanmar **92** J3 22 05N 95 12E
Moora Australia **106** B3 30 40S 116 01E
Moore, Lake Australia **106** B4 30 00S 117 30E
Moorestown New Jersey U.S.A. **66** D2 39 58N 74 54W
Moorhead Minnesota U.S.A. **65** G6 46 51N 96 44W
Moosehead Lake Maine U.S.A. **43** S6 45 40N 69 40W
Mooselookmeguntic Lake Maine U.S.A. **47** B1
44 56N 71 00W
Mopti Mali **102** E10 14 29N 4 10W
Moradabad India **91** D5 28 50N 78 45E
Morant Bay *tn.* Jamaica **69** R7 17 53N 76 25W

Morant Point Jamaica **69** R7 17 55N 76 12W
Moratuwa Sri Lanka **91** D1 6 47N 79 53E
Moray Firth *est.* United Kingdom **74** H9 57 45N 3 45W
Moreau *r.* South Dakota U.S.A. **64** F6 45 00N 102 00W
Moree Australia **106** H4 29 29S 149 53E
Morelia Mexico **68** D3 19 40N 101 11W
Morenci Arizona U.S.A. **64** E3 33 05N 109 22W
Morgantown West Virginia U.S.A. **65** K4 39 38N 79 57W
Mori Japan **96** D3 42 07N 140 33E
Morioka Japan **96** D2 39 43N 141 08E
MOROCCO 102 D14
Morogoro Tanzania **103** M6 6 49S 37 40E
Moro Gulf The Philippines **95** G5 7 00N 123 00E
Morón Cuba **69** I4 22 08N 78 39W
Morondava Madagascar **103** N3 20 19S 44 17E
Moroni Comoros **103** N5 11 40S 43 16E
Morotai *i.* Indonesia **95** H4 2 30N 128 30E
Moroto Uganda **102** L8 2 32N 34 41E
Morrinsville New Zealand **107** C3 37 39S 175 32E
Morris Jesup, Cape Greenland **112** 83 20N 33 00W
Morrisville New Jersey U.S.A. **66** D3 40 05N 74 58W
Morro Bay *tn.* California U.S.A. **67** B2 35 24N 120 53W
Moruga *r.* Trinidad and Tobago **69** T9 10 06N 61 15W
Moruga Trinidad and Tobago **69** T9 10 06N 61 17W
Moscow Idaho U.S.A. **64** C6 46 44N 117 00W
Moscow City *admin.* Russian Federation **86** M1/2
55 50N 37 45E
Moscow Oblast *admin.* Russian Federation **86** N2
55 50N 37 45E
Moscow *see* Moskva
Moses Lake *tn.* Washington U.S.A. **64** C6 47 09N 119 20W
Mosgiel New Zealand **107** B1 45 53S 170 21E
Moshi Tanzania **102** M7 3 21S 37 19E
Moskva Russian Federation **84** F7
55 45N 37 42E
Moskva (*Moscow*) Russian Federation **84** F7
55 45N 37 42E
Moskva *r.* Russian Federation **86** M1/N1 55 36N 37 45E
Mosman Australia **107** G2 33 50S 151 14E
Mosquito Creek Lake *res.* Ohio U.S.A. **42** F2
41 20N 80 45W
Mossoró Brazil **70** J11 5 10S 37 18W
Mosul *see* Al Mawsil
Mothe *i.* Fiji **110** V15 18 39S 178 32W
Motherwell United Kingdom **74** G7 55 48N 3 59W
Motueka New Zealand **107** B2 41 07S 173 01E
Mouila Gabon **102** H7 1 50S 11 02E
Moulmein Myanmar **95** B7 16 30N 97 39E
Moundou Chad **102** I9 8 35N 16 01E
Mount Carmel *tn.* Pennsylvania U.S.A. **66** B3
40 48N 76 25W
Mount Cobb *tn.* Pennsylvania U.S.A. **66** C4
41 24N 75 32W
Mount Darwin *tn.* Zimbabwe **103** L4 16 45S 31 39E
Mount Desert Island Maine U.S.A. **47** C1 44 22N 68 15W
Mount Diablo California U.S.A. **67** B3 37 54N 121 55W
Mount Gambier *tn.* Australia **106** G2 37 51S 140 50E
Mount Grant California U.S.A. **67** C4 38 34N 118 48W
Mount Hagen *tn.* Papua New Guinea **106** G8 5 54S 144 13E
Mount Holly *tn.* New Jersey U.S.A. **66** D3 40 00N 74 47W
Mount Isa *tn.* Australia **106** F5 20 50S 139 29E
Mount Jefferson California U.S.A. **67** D4 38 47N 116 58W
Mount Magnet *tn.* Australia **106** B4 28 06S 117 50E
Mount Morgan *tn.* Australia **106** I5 23 40S 150 25E
Mount Pleasant *tn.* Michigan U.S.A. **42** B4
43 36N 84 46W
Mount Ritter California U.S.A. **67** C3 37 40N 119 15W
Mount Vernon *tn.* Illinois U.S.A. **65** I4 38 19N 88 52W
Mount Vernon *tn.* Washington U.S.A. **34** H4
48 25N 122 20W
Mount Whitney California U.S.A. **67** C3 36 35N 118 17W
Mount Whitney National Park California U.S.A. **64** C4
36 30N 118 30W
Mountain Village Alaska U.S.A. **8** C5 62 09N 163 49W
Mourne Mountains United Kingdom **74** E6 54 05N 6 05W
Moy *r.* Republic of Ireland **74** C5 53 55N 8 55W
Moyale Kenya **102** M8 3 31N 39 04E
Moyobamba Peru **70** B11 6 04S 76 56W
MOZAMBIQUE 103 L4
Mozambique Basin Indian Ocean **108** C3 35 00S 40 00E
Mozambique Channel Mozambique/Madagascar **103** N4
18 00S 42 00E
Mpanda Tanzania **103** L6 6 21S 31 01E
Mtwara Tanzania **103** N5 10 17S 40 11E
Muang Khon Kaen Thailand **95** C7 16 25N 102 50E
Muang Lampang Thailand **93** J2 18 16N 99 30E
Muang Nan Thailand **93** K2 18 47N 100 50E
Muang Phrae Thailand **93** K2 18 07N 100 09E
Muchinga Mountains Zambia **103** L5 12 30S 32 30E
Mudanjiang China **93** P7 44 36N 129 42E
Mufulira Zambia **103** K5 12 30S 28 12E
Müggelheim Germany **79** G2 52 24N 13 40E
Muǧla Turkey **88** C6 37 13N 28 22E
Muhammad Qol Sudan **88** E3 20 53N 37 09E
Mui Wo Hong Kong China **92** A1 22 16N 113 59E
Mulegé Mexico **68** B5 26 54N 112 00W
Mull *i.* United Kingdom **74** F8 56 25N 6 00W
Mullett Lake Michigan U.S.A. **42** B6 45 30N 84 30W
Mullingar Republic of Ireland **74** D5 53 32N 7 20W
Mull of Galloway *c.* United Kingdom **74** G6
54 38N 4 50W
Mull of Kintyre *p.* United Kingdom **74** F7 55 17N 5 55W
Multan Pakistan **91** C6 30 10N 71 36E
Mumbai (*Bombay*) India **91** C3 18 56N 72 51E
Muna *i.* Indonesia **95** G3 5 00S 122 00E
München (*Munich*) Germany **72** H5 48 08N 11 35E
Muncie Indiana U.S.A. **65** I5 40 11N 85 22W
Muncy Pennsylvania U.S.A. **66** B4 41 12N 76 47W
Mungbere Congo (D.R.) **102** K8 2 40N 28 25E
Munger India **91** F5 25 24N 86 29E

Munich *see* München
Municipal Colony India **108** L4 28 42N 77 12E
Muqdisho (*Mogadishu*) Somalia **102** O8 2 02N 45 21E
Murat *r.* Turkey **88** F6 38 50N 40 20E
Murchison *r.* Australia **106** B4 26 00S 117 00E
Murcia Spain **72** E3 37 59N 1 08W
Murfreesboro Tennessee U.S.A. **65** I4 35 50N 86 25W
Murgab *r.* Asia **87** J2 37 00N 62 30E
Murmansk Russian Federation **84** F7 68 59N 33 08E
Murom Russian Federation **86** F5 55 34N 42 04E
Muroran Japan **96** D3 42 21N 140 59E
Muroto Japan **96** B1 33 13N 134 11E
Muroto-zaki *c.* Japan **96** B1 33 13N 134 11E
Murray *r.* Australia **106** G3 34 00S 142 00E
Murray Bridge Australia **106** F2 35 10S 139 17E
Murray Seascarp Pacific Ocean **111** M11 32 00N 138 00W
Murrumbidgee *r.* Australia **106** H3 34 30S 146 30E
Murwara India **91** E4 23 49N 80 28E
Murzuq Libya **102** H13 25 55N 13 55E
Muş Turkey **88** F6 38 45N 41 30E
Musgrave Ranges Australia **106** E4 26 00S 132 00E
Musin Nigeria **102** F9 6 30N 3 15E
Muskegon Michigan U.S.A. **65** I5 43 13N 86 15W
Muskegon River Michigan U.S.A. **42** A5 44 00N 85 05W
Muskogee Oklahoma U.S.A. **65** G4 35 50N 95 21W
Musquiz Mexico **64** F2 27 50N 101 00W
Musselshell *r.* Montana U.S.A. **64** E6 47 00N 108 00W
Mutarara Mozambique **103** M4 17 30S 35 06E
Mutare Zimbabwe **103** L4 18 58N 32 40E
Mutsu Japan **96** D3 41 18N 141 15E
Mutsu-wan *b.* Japan **96** D3 41 05N 140 40E
Muyun Kum *d.* Kazakhstan **87** L3 44 00N 70 00E
Muzaffarnagar India **91** D5 29 28N 77 42E
Muzaffarpur India **91** F5 26 07N 85 23E
Muzon, Cape *c.* Alaska U.S.A. **34** B2 54 41N 132 40W
Mwanza Tanzania **102** L7 2 31S 32 56E
Mwaya Tanzania **103** L6 9 33S 33 56E
Mweru, Lake (*Lac Moero*) Congo (D.R.) **103** K6
8 30S 28 30E
My Tho Vietnam **95** D6 10 21N 106 21E
MYANMAR (*BURMA*) **91** G4
Myerstown Pennsylvania U.S.A. **66** B3 40 23N 76 18W
Myingyan Myanmar **92** J3 21 25N 95 20E
Myitkyina Myanmar **93** J4 25 24N 97 25E
Mykolayiv Ukraine **86** C4 46 57N 32 00E
Mymensingh Bangladesh **91** G4 24 45N 90 23E
Mys Chelyuskin *c.* Russian Federation **85** M11
77 44N 103 55E
Mys Kanin Nos *c.* Russian Federation **84** G9
68 38N 43 20E
Mys Navarin *c.* Russian Federation **85** T8 62 17N 179 13E
Mys Olyutorskiy *c.* Russian Federation **85** T7
59 58N 170 25E
Mysore India **91** D2 12 18N 76 37E
Mys Tolstoy *c.* Russian Federation **85** R7 59 00N 155 00E
Mytishchi Russian Federation **86** D6 55 54N 37 47E
Mzuzu Malawi **103** L5 11 31S 34 00E

N

Naas Republic of Ireland **74** E5 53 13N 6 39W
Naberezhnyye Chelny (*Brezhnev*) Russian Federation
84 H7 55 42N 52 19E
Nabeul Tunisia **72** G3 36 30N 10 44E
Nablus Jordan **88** O11 32 13N 35 16E
Nabq Egypt **88** O9 28 04N 34 26E
Nacimiento Reservoir *res.* California U.S.A. **67** B2
35 45N 120 57W
Nacogdoches Texas U.S.A. **65** H3 31 36N 94 40W
Nadia *admin.* India **90** K3 22 58N 88 18E
Nadiad India **91** C4 22 42N 72 55E
Nador Morocco **102** E14 35 10N 3 00W
Nadym Russian Federation **85** J9 65 25N 72 40E
Naga The Philippines **95** G6 13 36N 123 12E
Naga Hills India **91** G5 26 00N 95 00E
Nagai Japan **97** B1 35 11N 139 37E
Nagaland *admin.* India **91** G5 26 00N 94 30E
Nagano Japan **96** C2 36 39N 138 10E
Nagaoka Japan **96** C2 37 27N 138 50E
Nagasaki Japan **96** A1 32 45N 129 52E
Nagato Japan **96** B1 34 22N 131 11E
Nagercoil India **91** D1 8 11N 77 30E
Nagornyy Russian Federation **85** O7 55 57N 124 54E
Nagoya Japan **96** C2 35 08N 136 53E
Nagpur India **91** D4 21 10N 79 12E
Nagqu China **91** G6 31 30N 91 57E
Nahariyya Israel **88** O11 33 01N 35 05E
Naihāti India **90** K3 22 53N 88 27E
Nairobi Kenya **102** L7 1 17S 36 50E
Najd *geog. reg.* Saudi Arabia **88** F4 25 40N 42 30E
Najrān Saudi Arabia **88** F2 17 37N 44 40E
Naka Japan **97** B2 35 25N 139 38E
Nakahara Japan **97** B3 35 34N 139 39E
Nakamura Japan **96** B1 33 02N 132 58E
Nakano Japan **97** B3 35 42N 139 40E
Nakatsu Japan **96** B1 33 37N 131 11E
Nakhichevan *see* Naxicivan
Nakhodka Russian Federation **85** P4 42 53N 132 54E
Nakhon Ratchasima (*Khorat*) Thailand **95** C6
14 59N 102 06E
Nakhon Sawan Thailand **95** B7 15 42N 100 10E
Nakhon Si Thammarat Thailand **95** B5 8 24N 99 58E
Nakuru Kenya **102** M7 0 16S 36 05E
Nal *r.* Pakistan **90** B5 26 10N 65 30E
Nal'chik Russian Federation **84** G4 43 31N 43 38E
Namangan Uzbekistan **87** L3 40 59N 71 41E
Nam Chung Hong Kong China **92** C3 22 31N 114 12E
Nam Co *l.* China **91** G6 30 50N 90 30E

Nam Dinh Vietnam **93** L3 20 25N 106 12E
Namib Desert Namibia **103** H3 22 00S 14 00E
Namibe Angola **103** H4 15 10S 12 09E
NAMIBIA 103 I3
Nam Ngum Reservoir Laos **93** K2 18 35N 102 40E
Nampa Idaho U.S.A. **64** C5 43 35N 116 34W
Namp'o North Korea **93** P6 38 51N 125 10E
Nampula Mozambique **103** M4 15 09S 39 14E
Namtu Myanmar **93** J3 23 04N 97 26E
Nanao Japan **96** C2 37 03N 136 58E
Nanchang China **93** N4 28 33N 115 58E
Nanchong China **93** L5 30 54N 106 06E
Nancy France **72** G5 48 42N 6 12E
Nanda Devi *mt.* India **91** D6 30 21N 79 58E
Nänded India **91** D3 19 11N 77 21E
Nanduri Fiji **110** U16 16 26S 179 08E
Nangi India **90** J1 22 30N 88 13E
Nanhai *i.* China **94** B1 39 55N 116 22E
Nanjing China **93** N5 32 03N 118 47E
Nan Ling *mts.* China **93** M2/M3 25 00N 112 00E
Nanning China **93** L3 22 50N 108 19E
Nanortalik Greenland **9** BB5 60 10N 45 05W
Nanpan Jiang *r.* China **93** L3 25 00N 106 00E
Nanping China **93** N4 26 40N 118 07E
Nanri Dao *i.* China **94** F8 25 13N 119 29E
Nansei-shoto *see* Ryukyu Islands
Nanterre France **79** A2 48 53N 2 12E
Nantes France **72** E5 47 14N 1 35W
Nanticoke Pennsylvania U.S.A. **66** B4 41 13N 76 00W
Nantong China **93** O5 32 06N 121 04E
Nan-t'ou Taiwan **94** G6 23 54N 120 42E
Nantucket Island Massachusetts U.S.A. **65** L5
41 15N 70 05W
Nanuku Passage *sd.* Fiji **110** V16 16 40S 179 25W
Nanumea Island Pacific Ocean **110** H7 5 30S 175 40E
Nanyang China **93** M5 33 06N 112 31E
Nanyuan China **94** B1 39 48N 116 23E
Nanyuki Kenya **102** M8 0 01N 37 05E
Napa California U.S.A. **67** A4 38 18N 122 17W
Napier New Zealand **107** C3 39 30S 176 54E
Naples Florida U.S.A. **65** J2 26 09N 81 48W
Naples Italy *see* Napoli
Napoleon Ohio U.S.A. **42** B2 41 24N 84 09W
Napoopoo Hawaiian Islands **111** Z17 19 29N 155 55W
Napoli (*Naples*) Italy **72** H4 40 50N 14 15E
Nara Japan **96** C1 34 41N 135 49E
Narayanganj Bangladesh **91** G4 23 36N 90 28E
Nares Deep Atlantic Ocean **109** B9 26 00N 61 10W
Narew *r.* Europe **86** A5 53 00N 21 00E
Narmada *r.* India **91** C4/D4 22 00N 75 00E
Narrabeen Australia **107** H3 33 43S 151 18E
Narrogin Australia **106** B3 32 57S 117 07E
Narsaq Greenland **9** BB5 61 00N 46 00W
Narva Estonia **86** B6 59 22N 28 17E
Narvik Norway **72** J9 68 26N 17 25E
Nar'yan Mar Russian Federation **84** H9 67 37N 53 02E
Nasca Ridge Pacific Ocean **111** R5/S6 20 00S 81 00W
Nashua New Hampshire U.S.A. **65** L5 42 44N 71 28W
Nashville Tennessee U.S.A. **65** I3 20 00N 73 28E
Nasik India **91** C3 20 00N 73 48E
Nassau The Bahamas **69** I5 25 05N 77 20W
Nasser, Lake Egypt **88** D3 22 35N 31 40E
Natal Brazil **70** J11 5 46S 35 15W
Natchez Mississippi U.S.A. **65** H3 31 32N 91 24W
Natewa Peninsula Fiji **110** V16 16 40S 180 00
National City California U.S.A. **67** D1 32 39N 117 05W
Natron, Lake Tanzania **102** M7 2 00S 36 00E
Natuna Besar *i.* Indonesia **95** D4 3 40N 108 00E
Naturaliste, Cape Australia **106** B3 33 32S 115 01E
NAURU 110 G7
Nausori Fiji **110** U16 18 01S 178 31E
Navadwip India **91** F4 23 24N 88 23E
Navet *r.* Trinidad and Tobago **69** T9 10 16N 61 10W
Navet Trinidad and Tobago **69** T9 10 15N 61 10W
Navet Dam Trinidad and Tobago **69** T9 10 26N 61 12W
Naviti *i.* Fiji **110** T16 17 08S 177 15E
Navoi Uzbekistan **87** K3 40 04N 65 02E
Navojoa Mexico **68** C5 7 04N 109 28W
Navsari India **91** C4 20 58N 73 01E
Naxcivan (*Nakhchevan'*) Azerbaijan **86** F2 39 12N 45 24E
Nayoro Japan **96** D4 44 21N 142 30E
Nazareth Israel **88** O11 32 41N 35 16E
Nazareth Pennsylvania U.S.A. **66** C3 40 44N 75 18W
Nazca Peru **70** C10 14 53N 74 54W
Nazwá Oman **89** I3 22 56N 57 33E
Ndélé Central African Republic **102** J9 8 25N 20 38E
Ndjamena Chad **102** I10 12 10N 14 59E
Ndola Zambia **103** K5 13 00S 28 39E
Neath United Kingdom **74** H3 51 40N 3 48W
Nebitdag Turkmenistan **87** H3 39 31N 54 24E
Nebraska *state* U.S.A. **64** F5 42 00N 102 00W
Neckei *i.* Hawaiian Islands **111** J10 23 25N 164 42W
Necochea Argentina **71** F5 38 31S 58 46W
Needles California U.S.A. **64** D3 34 51N 114 36W
Negelē Ethiopia **102** M9 5 20N 39 35E
Negev *d.* Israel **88** O10 30 10N 35 00E
Negombo Sri Lanka **91** D1 7 13N 79 51E
Negritos Peru **70** A12 4 42S 81 18W
Negros *i.* The Philippines **95** G5 10 00N 123 00E
Neijiang China **93** L4 29 32N 105 03E
Nei Mongol Zizhiqu (*Inner Mongolia Autonomous Region*)
admin. China **93** M7 42 30N 112 00E
Neiva Colombia **70** B13 2 58N 75 15W
Nek'emtē Ethiopia **102** M9 9 04N 36 30E
Nellore India **91** D2 14 29N 80 00E
Nelson *admin.* New Zealand **107** B2 41 30S 172 30E
Nemuro Japan **96** E3 43 22N 145 36E
Nemuro-Kaikyō *sd.* Japan **96** E3 44 00N 146 00E

Nenana Alaska U.S.A. **8** F5 61 35N 149 10W
Nene r. United Kingdom **74** K4 52 25N 0 05E
Nenjiang China **93** O8 49 10N 125 15E
Nen Jiang r. China **93** P9 50 00N 125 00E
NEPAL 91 E5
Nerchinsk Russian Federation **85** N6 52 02N 116 38E
Neryungri Russian Federation **85** O7 56 39N 124 38E
Nestor Trinidad and Tobago **69** T10 10 31N 61 09W
Netanya Israel **88** O11 32 20N 34 51E
NETHERLANDS 72 G6
Netzahualcóyotl Mexico **68** E3 19 24N 99 02W
Neuenhagen Germany **79** G2 52 32N 13 41E
Neuilly France **79** B2 48 53N 2 17E
Neuilly Plaisance France **79** C2 48 51N 2 31E
Neukölln Germany **79** F1 52 29N 13 28E
Neuquén Argentina **71** D5 38 55N 68 05W
Nevada state U.S.A. **64** C4 39 00N 118 00W
Neves Brazil **71** Q2 22 51S 43 05W
Nevinnomyssk Russian Federation **86** E3 44 38N 41 59E
Neviot Egypt **88** O9 28 58N 34 38E
New r. U.S.A. **65** J4 37 00N 81 00W
New Addington United Kingdom **78** D2 51 21N 0 01E
New Albany Indiana U.S.A. **65** I4 38 17N 85 50W
New Amsterdam Guyana **70** F14 6 18N 57 30W
Newark Delaware U.S.A. **65** K4 39 42N 75 45W
Newark New Jersey U.S.A. **66** Y1 40 43N 74 11W
Newark New York U.S.A. **43** J4 43 03N 77 06W
Newark Ohio U.S.A. **65** J5 40 03N 82 25W
Newark Bay New Jersey U.S.A. **66** Y1 40 40N 74 08W
Newark Lake California U.S.A. **67** E4 39 44N 115 44W
New Bedford Massachusetts U.S.A. **65** L4 41 38N 70 55W
New Bern North Carolina U.S.A. **65** K4 35 05N 77 04W
Newberry Michigan U.S.A. **42** A7 46 22N 85 30W
New Bloomfield Pennsylvania U.S.A. **66** A3
  40 25N 76 13W
New Braunfels Texas U.S.A. **65** G2 29 43N 98 09W
New Britain i. Papua New Guinea **106** H8/I8
  4 45S 150 30E
Newburgh New York U.S.A. **65** L5 41 30N 74 00W
New Caledonia i. Pacific Ocean **106** K5/L5
  22 00S 165 00E
Newcastle Australia **106** I3 32 55S 151 46E
New Castle Delaware U.S.A. **66** C2 39 40N 75 34W
Newcastle Wyoming U.S.A. **64** F5 43 52N 104 14W
Newcastle upon Tyne United Kingdom **74** J7
  54 59N 1 35W
New Delhi India **91** D5 28 37N 77 14E
New Dorp New York U.S.A. **66** Y1 40 34N 74 06W
Newfane New York U.S.A. **42** H4 43 17N 78 42W
Newfoundland Basin Atlantic Ocean **109** D11/E11
  44 00N 40 00W
New Georgia Islands Solomon Islands **106** J8
  8 00S 157 30E
New Grant Trinidad and Tobago **69** T9 10 17N 61 19W
New Guinea i. Pacific Ocean **106** E9/H8 5 00S 141 00E
Newham bor. United Kingdom **78** D3 51 30N 0 02E
New Hampshire state U.S.A. **65** L5 43 00N 72 00W
New Haven Connecticut U.S.A. **65** L5 41 18N 72 55W
New Hebrides Trench Pacific Ocean **110** G6
  15 00S 169 00E
New Hope Pennsylvania U.S.A. **66** C3 40 22N 74 56W
New Iberia Louisiana U.S.A. **65** H2 30 00N 91 51W
New Ireland i. Papua New Guinea **106** I9 3 15S 152 30E
New Jersey state U.S.A. **65** L4 40 00N 75 00W
New Jersey Turnpike road New Jersey U.S.A. **66** Y2
  40 50N 74 05W
New London Connecticut U.S.A. **65** L5 41 21N 72 06W
New London Ohio U.S.A. **42** D2 41 05N 82 24W
Newman Australia **106** B5 23 20S 119 34E
New Mexico state U.S.A. **64** E3 35 00N 107 00W
New Milford Pennsylvania U.S.A. **66** C4 41 52N 75 44W
New Orleans Louisiana U.S.A. **65** H2 30 00N 90 03W
Newport Australia **107** H3 33 39S 151 19E
Newport United Kingdom **74** H3 51 35N 3 00W
Newport Vermont U.S.A. **43** P5 44 56N 72 13W
Newport Beach California U.S.A. **67** D1 33 38N 117 55W
Newport News Virginia U.S.A. **65** K4 36 59N 76 26W
New Providence i. The Bahamas **69** I5 25 00N 77 30W
Newry United Kingdom **74** E6 54 11N 6 20W
New Siberian Islands Russian Federation **85** Q10
  75 00N 145 00E
New South Wales state Australia **106** G3/I3
  32 00S 145 00E
New Springville New York U.S.A. **66** Y1 40 35N 74 10W
New Territories admin. Hong Kong China **92** B2
  22 20N 114 00E
Newton Falls tn. New York U.S.A. **43** M5 44 13N 74 58W
Newtownabbey United Kingdom **74** F6 54 40N 5 54W
New Ulm Minnesota U.S.A. **65** H5 44 19N 94 28W
New York New York U.S.A. **65** L5 40 40N 73 50W
New York state U.S.A. **65** K5 43 00N 76 00W
Neyriz Iran **89** H4 29 14N 54 18E
Neyshābūr Iran **89** I6 36 13N 58 49E
Ngami, Lake Botswana **103** I3 20 00S 23 00E
Ngangla Ringco r. China **91** E6 31 40N 83 00E
Nganze Co l. China **91** F6 31 00N 87 00E
Ngaoundére Cameroon **102** H9 7 20N 13 35E
Ngau i. Fiji **110** U15/16 18 00S 179 16E
Ngau Chi Wan Hong Kong China **92** C2 22 25N 114 10E
Ngau Kwu Long Hong Kong China **92** A1 22 18N 113 58E
Ngauruhoe, Mount New Zealand **107** C3 39 10S 175 38E
Ngau Tam Mei Hong Kong China **92** B2 22 28N 114 04E
Ngong Ping Hong Kong China **92** A2 22 15N 113 56E
Nguigmi Niger **102** H10 14 19N 13 06E
Nguru Nigeria **102** H10 12 53N 10 30E
Nha Trang Vietnam **95** D6 12 15N 109 10E
Nhulunbuy Australia **106** F7 12 30S 136 56E
Niagara Falls tn. New York U.S.A. **65** K5 43 06N 79 04W

Niamey Niger **102** F10 13 32N 2 05E
Niangara Congo (D.R.) **102** K8 3 45N 27 54E
Nibra India **90** K2 22 35N 88 15E
NICARAGUA 69 G2
Nice France **72** G4 43 42N 7 16E
Nicobar Islands India **91** G1 8 30N 94 00E
Nicosia Cyprus **73** M3 35 11N 33 23E
Nidd r. United Kingdom **74** J6 54 02N 1 30W
Nieuw Nickerie Suriname **70** F14 5 52N 57 00W
NIGER 102 G11
Niger r. Nigeria **102** G9 5 30N 6 15E
NIGERIA 102 G10
Nihoa i. Hawaiian Islands **111** J10 23 03N 161 55W
Niigata Japan **96** C2 37 58N 139 02E
Niihama Japan **96** B1 33 57N 133 15E
Niihau i. Hawaiian Islands **111** H8 21 50N 160 11W
Nii-jima i. Japan **96** C1 34 20N 139 15E
Nikko Japan **96** C2 36 45N 139 37E
Nikolayevsk-na-Amure Russian Federation **85** Q6
  53 10N 140 44E
Nikol'skiy see Satlayev
Nikopol' Ukraine **86** C4 45 34N 34 25E
Niland California U.S.A. **67** E1 33 14N 115 30W
Nile r. Sudan/Egypt **88** D4 28 30N 30 40E
Nilgiri Hills India **91** D2 11 30N 76 30E
Nimule Sudan **102** L8 3 35N 32 03E
Nim Wan Hong Kong China **92** A2 22 25N 113 56E
9 de Julio (Nueve de Julio) tn. Argentina **71** E5
  35 28S 60 58W
Ninepin Group Hong Kong China **92** C1 22 15N 114 20E
Ninety East Ridge Indian Ocean **108** H4/H6
Ninety Mile Beach New Zealand **107** B4
  34 45S 172 58E
Nineveh hist. site Iraq **88** F6 36 24N 43 08E
Ningbo China **93** O4 29 54N 121 33E
Ninh Binh Vietnam **93** L3 20 14N 106 00E
Niobrara r. U.S.A. **64** E5 42 00N 102 00W
Nioro du Sahel Mali **102** D11 15 12N 9 35W
Niš Serbia Yugoslavia **72** K4 43 20N 21 54E
Nishi Japan **97** B2 35 26N 139 37E
Niterói Brazil **71** I8 22 54S 43 06W
Niue i. Pacific Ocean **111** J6 19 02S 169 55W
Nizamabad India **91** D3 18 40N 78 05E
Nizhneangarsk Russian Federation **85** M7
  55 48N 109 35E
Nizhnekamsk Russian Federation **84** H7 55 38N 51 49E
Nizhnekamskoye Vodokhranilishche res.
  Russian Federation **87** G6 56 00N 53 30E
Nizhnekolymsk Russian Federation **85** S9 68 34N 160 58E
Nizhnevartovsk Russian Federation **87** M7 60 57N 76 40E
Nizhniy Novgorod (Gor'kiy) Russian Federation **84** G7
  56 20N 44 00E
Nizhniy Novgorod Vodokhranilishche (Gor'kovskoye) res.
  Russian Federation **86** E6 57 00N 43 00E
Nizhniy Tagil Russian Federation **84** H7 58 00N 59 58E
Nizhnocartovsk Russian Federation **85** J8 60 57N 76 40E
Nizhnyaya (Lower) Tunguska r. Russian Federation
  85 L8/M8 64 00N 95 00E
Nkongsamba Cameroon **102** G9 4 59N 9 53E
Noatak Alaska U.S.A. **8** C6 67 33N 163 10W
Noatak r. Alaska U.S.A. **8** C6 67 33N 163 10W
Nobeoka Japan **96** B1 32 36N 131 40E
Nobi Japan **97** B1 35 11N 139 41E
Nogales Arizona U.S.A. **64** D3 31 20N 110 56W
Nogales Mexico **68** B6 31 20N 111 00W
Nogent France **79** C2 48 50N 2 30E
Noisy-le-Sec France **79** B2 48 53N 2 27E
Nojima-zaki c. Japan **96** C1 34 54N 139 54E
Nola Central African Republic **102** I8 3 28N 16 08E
Nome Alaska U.S.A. **8** B5 64 30N 165 30W
Nong Khai Thailand **93** K2 17 52N 102 44E
Noorvik Alaska U.S.A. **8** C6 66 50N 161 14W
Nordkapp (North Cape) c. Norway **84** E10 71 11N 25 40E
Nordvik Russian Federation **85** N10 74 01N 111 30E
Nore r. Republic of Ireland **74** D4 52 25N 7 02W
Norfolk Nebraska U.S.A. **65** G5 42 01N 97 25W
Norfolk Virginia U.S.A. **65** K4 36 54N 76 18W
Norfolk Island Pacific Ocean **110** G5 29 05S 167 59E
Norfolk Island Trough Pacific Ocean **110** G5
  27 30S 166 00E
Norfolk Lake Arkansas U.S.A. **65** H4 36 00N 92 00W
Noril'sk Russian Federation **85** K9 69 21N 88 02E
Normanton Australia **106** G6 17 40S 141 05E
Norridgewook Maine U.S.A. **43** S5 44 43N 69 48W
Norris Lake Tennessee U.S.A. **65** J4 36 00N 84 00W
Norristown Pennsylvania U.S.A. **66** C3 40 07N 75 20W
Norrköping Sweden **72** J7 58 35N 16 10E
Norseman Australia **106** C3 32 15S 121 47E
Northam Australia **106** B3 31 40S 116 40E
North American Basin Atlantic Ocean **109** C10
  34 00N 55 00W
Northampton Australia **106** A4 28 27S 114 37E
Northampton United Kingdom **74** K4 52 14N 0 54W
North Andaman i. Andaman Islands **91** G2 13 00N 93 00E
North Atlantic Ocean **109** D7/D11
North Australian Basin Indian Ocean **108** K5
  14 00S 115 00E
North Baltimore Ohio U.S.A. **42** C2 41 12N 83 43W
North Barrackpore India **90** K3 22 46N 88 21E
North Bergen New Jersey U.S.A. **66** Y2 40 46N 74 02W
North Canadian r. U.S.A. **64** F4 36 00N 100 00W
North Cape New Zealand **107** B4 34 25S 173 03E
North Cape Norway see Nordkapp
North Carolina state U.S.A. **65** K4 36 00N 80 00W
North Cascades National Park Washington U.S.A. **34** H4
  48 45N 121 20W
North Channel British Isles **74** F7 55 20N 5 50W
North Dakota state U.S.A. **64** F6 47 00N 102 00W

North Downs hills United Kingdom **74** L3 51 13N 0 30W
North Dvina r. Russian Federation **73** P8 63 00N 43 00E
North East Pennsylvania U.S.A. **42** G3 42 13N 79 51W
Northern Ireland United Kingdom **74** D6
NORTHERN MARIANAS 110 E9
Northern Range mts. Trinidad and Tobago **69** T10
  10 47N 61 27W
Northern Territory territory Australia **106** E6/F5
  19 00S 132 00E
North Esk r. United Kingdom **74** I8 56 50N 2 50W
North European Plain Europe **72** J6/K6 54 00N 20 00E
North Fiji Basin Pacific Ocean **110** H6 18 00S 173 00E
North Fork American r. California U.S.A. **67** B4
  39 24N 120 43W
North Fork Koyukuk River Alaska U.S.A. **50** A4
  67 30N 151 30W
North Head Australia **107** H2 33 49S 151 18E
North Island New Zealand **107** B3/C3 39 00N 176 00E
NORTH KOREA 93 P6/7
North Land see Severnaya Zemlya
North Las Vegas California U.S.A. **67** E3 36 11N 115 09W
North Little Rock Arkansas U.S.A. **65** H3 34 46N 92 16W
North Loup r. Nebraska U.S.A. **64** F5 42 00N 100 00W
North Palisade mt. California U.S.A. **67** C3
  37 06N 118 33W
North Platte Nebraska U.S.A. **64** F5 41 09N 100 45W
North Platte r. U.S.A. **64** E5 42 00N 107 00W
North Point tn. Barbados **69** V13 13 20N 59 37W
North Point tn. Hong Kong China **92** C1 22 18N 114 12E
North Pole Arctic Ocean **112** 90 00N
North Port Russian Federation **86** L2 55 50N 37 30E
North Sea Atlantic Ocean **72** F7 57 00N 4 00E
North Stratford New Hampshire U.S.A. **43** Q5
  44 46N 71 36W
North Uist i. United Kingdom **74** D9 57 04N 7 15W
Northumberland Pennsylvania U.S.A. **66** B3
  40 54N 76 49W
Northumberland Island see Kiatak
North West Cape Australia **106** A5 21 48S 114 10E
North West Christmas Island Ridge Pacific Ocean
  111 J8 9 30N 170 00W
Northwestern Atlantic Basin Atlantic Ocean **109** B10
  33 00N 70 00W
Northwest Highlands United Kingdom **74** F8/G10
  58 00N 5 00W
Northwest Pacific Basin Pacific Ocean **110** F11
  35 00N 150 00E
Northwood United Kingdom **78** B3 51 36N 0 25W
North York Moors United Kingdom **74** K6 55 22N 0 45W
Norton Kansas U.S.A. **64** G4 39 51N 99 53W
Norton Sound Alaska U.S.A. **8** C5 64 00N 162 30W
Norvegia, Cape Antarctica **113** 71 28S 12 25W
Norwalk Ohio U.S.A. **42** D2 41 14N 82 37W
NORWAY 72 G7/L9
Norwegian Basin Arctic Ocean **109** H13 67 00N 0 00
Norwegian Sea Arctic Ocean **112** 70 00N 5 00E
Norwich New York U.S.A. **43** L3 42 32N 75 32W
Norwich United Kingdom **74** M4 52 38N 1 18E
Noshiro Japan **96** D3 40 13N 140 00E
Nosop r. Southern Africa **103** I3 25 00S 20 30E
Nosy Bé i. Madagascar **103** N5 13 00S 47 00E
Nottingham United Kingdom **74** J4 52 58N 1 10W
Nouadhibou Mauritania **102** B12 20 54N 17 01W
Nouakchott Mauritania **102** A11 18 09N 15 58W
Nouméa New Caledonia **106** L5 22 16S 166 26E
Nova Friburgo Brazil **71** I8 22 16S 42 34W
Nova Iguaçu Brazil **71** I8 22 46S 43 23W
Nova Iguaçu admin. Brazil **71** P3 33 48S 43 20W
Nova Scotia Basin Atlantic Ocean **109** C10 39 00N 55 00W
Novaya Zemlya is. Russian Federation **85** H10
  74 00N 55 00E
Novgorod Russian Federation **84** F7 58 30N 31 20E
Novi Sad Yugoslavia **72** J5 45 15N 19 51E
Novo Hamburgo Brazil **71** G7 29 37S 51 07W
Novocheboksarsk Russian Federation **86** F6
  56 05N 47 27E
Novocherkassk Russian Federation **86** E4 47 25N 40 05E
Novokazalinsk Kazakhstan **87** J4 45 48N 62 06E
Novokuybyshevsk Russian Federation **86** G5
  53 05N 49 59E
Novokuznetsk Russian Federation **85** K6 53 45N 87 12E
Novolazarevskaya r.s. Antarctica **113** 70 46S 11 50E
Novomoskovsk Russian Federation **86** D5 54 06N 38 15E
Novorossiysk Russian Federation **84** F4 44 44N 37 46E
Novoshakhtinsk Russian Federation **86** D4 47 46N 39 55E
Novosibirsk Russian Federation **85** K7 55 04N 83 05E
Novosibirskiye Ostrova (New Siberian Islands) is.
  Russia **112** 75 00N 145 00E
Novotroitsk Russian Federation **87** H5 51 11N 58 16E
Novvy Port Russian Federation **85** J9 67 38N 72 33E
Novvy Urengoy Russian Federation **85** J9 66 00N 77 20E
Nowai r. India **90** K2 22 39N 88 28E
Nowgong India **91** G5 26 20N 92 41E
Noyes Island Alaska U.S.A. **34** B6 56 30N 133 45W
Nubian Desert Sudan **102** L12 21 00N 33 00E
Nueces r. Texas U.S.A. **64** G2 28 00N 99 00W
Nueva Rosita Mexico **68** D5 27 58N 101 11W
Nueva San Salvador El Salvador **68** G2 13 40N 89 18W
Nueve de Julio see 9 de Julio
Nuevitas Cuba **69** I4 21 34N 77 18W
Nuevo Casas Grandes Mexico **68** C6 30 22N 107 53W
Nuevo Laredo Mexico **68** E5 27 39N 99 30W
Nuevo Leon admin. Mexico **64** D2 25 30N 100 00W
Nu Jiang (Salween) r. China/Myanmar **93** J4
  25 00N 99 00E
Nuku'alofa Tonga **110** I5 21 09S 175 14W
Nukus Uzbekistan **87** H3 42 28N 59 07E
Nullarbor Plain Australia **106** D3 32 00S 128 00E

Numazu Japan **96** C2 35 08N 138 50E
Nunap Isura (Kap Farvel) c. Greenland **9** CC4
  60 00N 44 00W
Nunivak Island Alaska U.S.A. **8** B5 60 00N 166 00W
Nura r. Kazakhstan **87** L5 51 00N 71 00E
Nuremberg (Nürnberg) Germany **72** H5 49 27N 11 05E
Nusaybin Turkey **88** F6 37 05N 41 11E
Nushki Pakistan **90** B5 29 33N 66 01E
Nuthe r. Germany **79** E1 52 21N 13 07E
Nuuk (Godthåb) Greenland **9** AA5 64 10N 51 40W
Nuussuaq p. Greenland **9** AA7 70 50N 53 00W
Nyâêntênglha Shan mts. China **92** G4/H5
  30 00N 90 00E
Nyala Sudan **102** J10 12 01N 24 50E
Nyasa, Lake (Lake Malawi) Southern Africa **103** L5
  12 00S 35 00E
Nyngan Australia **106** H3 31 34S 147 14E
Nyoman r. Lithuania/Russian Federation **86** A5
  55 00N 22 00E

O

Oahe, Lake U.S.A. **64** F6 45 00N 100 00W
Oahu i. Hawaiian Islands **111** X18/Y18 21 30N 158 10W
Oak Harbor tn. Ohio U.S.A. **42** C2 41 31N 83 10W
Oak Harbour tn. Washington U.S.A. **34** H4
  48 17N 122 38W
Oakhurst California U.S.A. **67** C3 37 20N 119 39W
Oakland California U.S.A. **64** B4 37 50N 122 15W
Oak Ridge tn. Tennessee U.S.A. **65** J4 36 02N 84 12W
Oamaru New Zealand **107** B1 45 06S 170 58E
Oano Islands Pitcairn Islands **111** N5 23 32S 125 00W
Oasis California U.S.A. **67** D3 33 29N 117 56W
Oates Land geog. reg. Antarctica **113** 70 00S 150 00E
Oaxaca Mexico **68** E3 17 05N 96 41W
Ob' r. Russian Federation **85** I9 65 30N 66 00E
Ob', Gulf of Russian Federation **85** J9 68 00N 74 00E
Oban United Kingdom **74** F8 56 25N 5 29W
Oberlin Ohio U.S.A. **42** D2 41 17N 82 14W
Obidos Brazil **70** F12 1 52S 55 30W
Obihiro Japan **96** D3 42 56N 143 10E
Ocala Florida U.S.A. **65** J2 29 11N 82 09W
Ocaña Colombia **70** C14 8 16N 73 21W
Ocatlán Mexico **68** D4 20 21N 102 42W
Oceanside California U.S.A. **67** D1 33 12N 117 23W
Ochokovo Russian Federation **86** L1 55 39N 37 30E
Ocho Rios Jamaica **69** Q8 18 24N 77 06W
Ōda Japan **96** B2 35 10N 132 29E
Odate Japan **96** D3 40 18N 140 32E
Odawara Japan **96** C2 35 15N 139 08E
Odense Denmark **72** H7 55 24N 10 25E
Oder r. Europe **72** J6 52 30N 16 00E
Oder-Spree Kanal can. Germany **79** G1 52 21N 13 43E
Odesa (Odessa) Ukraine **72** M5 46 30N 30 46E
Odessa Delaware U.S.A. **66** C2 39 27N 75 40W
Odessa Texas U.S.A. **64** F3 31 50N 102 23W
Oekusi see Dili
Ofuna Japan **97** B2 53 21N 139 32E
Ofunato Japan **96** D2 39 04N 141 43E
Ogaden geog. reg. Africa **102** O9 7 00N 51 00E
Ōgaki Japan **96** C2 35 22N 136 36E
Ogasawara Guntō i. Pacific Ocean **110** E10 27 30N 43 00E
Ogbomosho Nigeria **102** G9 8 05N 4 11E
Ogden Utah U.S.A. **64** D5 41 14N 111 59W
Ogdensburg New York U.S.A. **43** L5 44 42N 75 31W
Ogooué r. Gabon **102** G7 0 50S 9 50E
Ōhata Japan **96** D3 41 22N 141 11E
Ohio state U.S.A. **65** J5 40 00N 83 00W
Ohio River Pennsylvania U.S.A. **65** I4 40 30N 80 05W
Oil River Pennsylvania U.S.A. **42** G2 41 26N 79 44W
Oildale California U.S.A. **67** C2 35 25N 119 00W
Oise r. France **79** A3 49 00N 2 05E
Oistins Barbados **69** V12 13 04N 59 35W
Oistins Bay Barbados **69** V12 13 03N 59 34W
Ōita Japan **96** B1 33 15N 131 36E
Ojinaga Mexico **68** D5 29 35N 104 26W
Oka r. Russian Federation **86** E5/6 55 00N 42 00E
Okanagan r. North America **64** C6 49 00N 119 00W
Okanogan Washington U.S.A. **34** J4 48 22N 119 35W
Okara Pakistan **91** C6 30 49N 73 31E
Okavango r. Southern Africa **103** I4 17 50S 20 00E
Okavango Basin Botswana **103** J4 19 00S 23 00E
Okaya Japan **96** C2 36 03N 138 00E
Okayama Japan **96** B1 34 40N 133 54E
Okazaki Japan **96** C1 34 58N 137 10E
Okeechobee, Lake Florida U.S.A. **65** J2 27 00N 81 00W
Okha Russian Federation **85** Q6 53 35N 143 01E
Okhotsk Russian Federation **85** Q7 59 20N 143 15E
Okhotsk, Sea of Russian Federation **85** Q7
  55 00N 148 00E
Oki is. Japan **96** B2 36 05N 133 00E
Okinawa i. Japan **93** P4 26 30N 128 00E
Oklahoma state U.S.A. **64** G4 36 00N 98 00W
Oklahoma City Oklahoma U.S.A. **65** G4 35 28N 97 33W
Oktyabr'skiy Russian Federation **86** G5 54 52 43N 156 14E
Okushiri-tō i. Japan **96** C3 42 15N 139 30E
Olancha California U.S.A. **67** C3 36 18N 118 00W
Öland i. Sweden **72** J7 56 45N 51 50E
Olcott New York U.S.A. **44** D2 43 20N 78 40W
Oldham United Kingdom **74** I5 53 33N 2 07W
Old Harbor Alaska U.S.A. **50** D2 57 12N 153 20W
Old Harbour tn. Jamaica **69** Q7 17 56N 77 07W
Old Harbour Bay tn. Jamaica **69** Q7 17 54N 77 06W
Old Head of Kinsale c. Republic of Ireland **74** C3
  51 40N 8 30W
Old Town Maine U.S.A. **47** C1 44 55N 68 41W
Olean New York U.S.A. **42** H3 42 05N 78 26W
Olekma r. Russian Federation **85** O7 59 00N 121 00E

Olekminsk Russian Federation **85** O8 60 25N 120 25E
Olenëk r. Russian Federation **85** O10 72 00N 122 00E
Olenëk Russian Federation **85** N9 68 28N 112 18E
Olinda Brazil **70** J11 8 00S 34 51W
Olongapo The Philippines **95** G6 14 49N 120 17E
Olsztyn Poland **86** A5 53 48N 20 29E
O'luan-pi c. Taiwan **94** G5 21 54N 120 53E
Olympia Washington U.S.A. **64** B6 47 03N 122 53W
Olympus mt. Cyprus **88** D5 34 55N 32 52E
Olympus mt. Greece **72** K4 40 05N 22 21E
Olympus, Mount Washington U.S.A. **64** B6 47 49N 123 42W
Om' r. Russian Federation **85** J7 55 30N 79 00E
Omagh United Kingdom **74** D6 54 36N 7 18W
Omaha Nebraska U.S.A. **65** G5 41 15N 96 00W
Omak Washington U.S.A. **35** E1 48 25N 119 30W
OMAN 89 I2
Oman, Gulf of Iran/Oman **89** I3 24 30N 58 30E
Omboué Gabon **102** G7 1 38S 9 20E
Omdurman Sudan **102** L11 15 37N 32 29E
Ommaney, Cape Alaska U.S.A. **34** B3 56 10N 134 40W
Omo r. Ethiopia **102** M9 7 00N 37 00E
Omolon r. Russian Federation **85** R9/S9 65 00N 160 00E
Omoloy r. Russian Federation **85** P9 70 00N 132 00E
Omsk Russian Federation **85** J7 55 00N 73 22E
Omutinskiy Russian Federation **87** K6 56 30N 67 40E
Ōmuta Japan **96** B1 33 02N 130 26E
Onaway Michigan U.S.A. **42** B6 45 23N 84 14W
Onega, Lake see Ozero Onezhskoy
Oneida New York U.S.A. **43** L4 43 04N 75 40W
Oneida Lake New York U.S.A. **43** L4 43 10N 75 55W
Oneonta New York U.S.A. **43** L3 42 56N 75 04W
Onezhskoye Ozero (Lake Onega) l. Russian Federation **84** F8 62 00N 40 00E
Ongea Levu i. Fiji **110** V15 19 11S 178 28W
Onitsha Nigeria **102** G9 6 10N 6 47E
Onomichi Japan **96** B1 34 25N 133 11E
Onon r. Russian Federation/Mongolia **93** M9 51 00N 114 00E
Onslow Australia **106** B5 21 41S 115 12E
Ontonagon Michigan U.S.A. **65** I6 46 52N 89 18W
Opala Congo (D.R.) **102** J7 0 40S 24 20E
Oporto see Porto
Opotiki New Zealand **107** C3 38 01S 177 17E
Orai India **91** D5 26 00N 79 26E
Oran Algeria **102** E15 35 45N 0 38W
Orán Argentina **71** E8 23 07S 64 16W
Orange Australia **106** H3 33 19S 149 10E
Orange r. Southern Africa **103** H3 28 35S 17 30E
Orange Texas U.S.A. **65** H3 30 05N 93 43W
Orangeburg South Carolina U.S.A. **65** J3 33 28N 80 53W
Orcadas i.s. Antarctica **113** 60 44S 44 44W
Orchard Park tn. New York U.S.A. **42** H3 42 46N 78 45W
Ord Mountain California U.S.A. **67** D2 34 42N 116 50W
Ordu Turkey **88** E7 41 00N 37 52E
Ordzhonikidze see Vladikavkaz
Örebro Sweden **72** J7 59 17N 15 13E
Oregon state U.S.A. **64** B5/C5 44 00N 120 00W
Oregon City Oregon U.S.A. **64** B6 45 21N 122 36W
Orekhovo-Zuyevo Russian Federation **86** D6 55 47N 39 00E
Orël Russian Federation **84** F6 52 58N 36 04E
Orem Utah U.S.A. **64** D5 40 20N 111 45W
Orenburg Russian Federation **84** H6 51 50N 55 00E
Orge r. France **79** B1 48 40N 2 22E
Orissa admin. India **91** E4 20 20N 83 00E
Orizaba Mexico **68** E3 18 51N 97 08W
Orkney Islands u.a. United Kingdom **74** H11 59 00N 3 00W
Orland California U.S.A. **67** A4 39 45N 122 13W
Orlando Florida U.S.A. **65** J2 28 33N 81 21W
Orléans France **72** F5 47 54N 1 54E
Orly France **79** B1 48 44N 2 24E
Oropucha r. Trinidad and Tobago **69** T10 10 36N 61 05W
Oroville Washington U.S.A. **35** E1 48 57N 119 27W
Orpington United Kingdom **78** D2 51 23N 0 05E
Orsay France **79** A1 48 42N 2 11E
Orsha Belarus **86** C5 54 30N 30 23E
Orsk Russian Federation **84** H6 51 13N 58 35E
Ortoire r. Trinidad and Tobago **69** T9 10 16N 61 15W
Orümiyeh Iran **88** F6 37 40N 45 00E
Oruro Bolivia **70** D9 17 59S 67 08W
Ōsaka Japan **96** C1 34 40N 135 30E
Osh Kirgizstan **87** L3 40 37N 72 49E
Oshkosh Wisconsin U.S.A. **65** I5 44 01N 88 32W
Oshogbo Nigeria **102** F9 7 50N 4 35E
Osijek Croatia **72** J5 45 33N 18 41E
Oslo Norway **72** H7 59 56N 10 45E
Osmaniye Turkey **88** E6 37 04N 36 15E
Osorno Chile **71** C4 40 35S 73 14W
Ossa, Mount Australia **106** H1 41 52S 146 04E
Ostankino Russian Federation **86** M2 55 50N 37 37E
Ostrava Czech Republic **72** J5 49 50N 18 15E
Oswego New York U.S.A. **43** K4 43 27N 76 31W
Otaheite Bay Trinidad and Tobago **69** S9 10 15N 61 30W
Otaki New Zealand **107** C2 40 46S 175 09E
Otaru Japan **96** D3 43 14N 140 59E
Otavalo Ecuador **70** B13 0 13N 78 15W
Otsego Lake New York U.S.A. **66** D5 42 45N 74 55W
Ottawa Canada **42** B2 45 24N 75 40W
Ottumwa Iowa U.S.A. **65** H5 41 02N 92 26W
Ouachita Mountains U.S.A. **65** G3/H3 34 00N 95 00W
Ouadda Central African Republic **102** J8 8 09N 22 20E
Ouagadougou Burkina **102** E10 12 20N 1 40W
Ouahigouya Burkina **102** E10 13 31N 2 20W
Ouargla Algeria **102** G14 32 00N 5 16E
Oudtshoorn Republic of South Africa **103** J1 33 35S 22 12E
Ouham r. Central African Republic **102** I9 7 00N 17 30E

Ouichita r. U.S.A. **65** H3 34 00N 93 00W
Oujda Morocco **102** E14 34 41N 1 45W
Oulu Finland **72** L9 65 02N 25 27E
Ouse r. United Kingdom **74** J5 53 40N 1 00W
Outer Hebrides is. United Kingdom **74** D9 58 00N 7 00W
Ovalau i. Fiji **110** U16 17 40S 178 47E
Ovalle Chile **71** C6 30 33S 71 16W
Oviedo Spain **72** D4 43 21N 7 18W
Owando Congo **102** I7 0 27S 15 44E
Owego New York U.S.A. **66** B5 42 06N 76 16W
Owen Fracture Zone Indian Ocean **108** E7/8 10 00N 55 00E
Owen, Mount New Zealand **107** B2 41 33S 172 33E
Owensboro Kentucky U.S.A. **65** I4 37 45N 87 05W
Owens Lake California U.S.A. **64** C4 36 27N 117 57W
Owen Stanley Range Papua New Guinea **106** H8 9 15S 148 30E
Owosso Michigan U.S.A. **42** B4 43 00N 84 11W
Owyhee r. U.S.A. **64** C5 43 00N 117 00W
Oxford United Kingdom **74** J3 51 46N 1 15W
Oxnard California U.S.A. **64** C3 34 11N 119 10W
Oxted United Kingdom **78** C1 51 15N 0 01W
Oxus see Amudar'ya
Oyama Japan **96** C2 36 18N 139 48E
Oyapock r. Brazil **70** G13 3 00N 52 30W
Oyem Gabon **102** H8 1 34N 11 31E
Ōmuta Japan
Ozark Plateau Missouri U.S.A. **65** H4 37 00N 93 00W
Ozarks, Lake of the Missouri U.S.A. **65** H4 38 00N 93 00W
Ozero Alakol' salt l. Kazakhstan **87** N4 46 00N 82 00E
Ozero Aydarkul' l. Kazakhstan **87** K3 41 00N 68 00E
Ozero Balkhash (Lake Balkhash) l. Kazakhstan **87** L4/M4 46 00N 75 00E
Ozero Baykal (Lake Baykal) l. Russian Federation **85** M6 54 00N 109 00E
Ozero Chany salt l. Russian Federation **85** J6 55 00N 77 30E
Ozero Il'men' l. Russian Federation **84** F7 58 00N 31 30E
Ozero Issyk-Kul' salt l. Kirgyzstan **87** M3 42 30N 77 30E
Ozero Khanka l. Asia **85** P5 45 00N 132 30E
Ozero Kulundinskoye l. Russian Federation **87** M5 53 00N 80 00E
Ozero Manych Gudilo l. Russian Federation **86** E4 46 30N 43 00E
Ozero Seletyteniz l. Kazakhstan **87** L5 53 30N 73 00E
Ozero Sevan l. Armenia **86** F3 40 00N 45 00E
Ozero Taymyr l. Russian Federation **85** M10 74 00N 102 30E
Ozero Teletskoye l. Russian Federation **87** O5 52 00N 88 00E
Ozero Tengiz salt l. Kazakhstan **87** K5 51 00N 69 00E
Ozero Zaysan l. Kazakhstan **87** N4 48 00N 84 00E

P

Paamiut (Frederikshåb) Greenland **9** BB5 62 05N 49 30W
Pabna Bangladesh **91** F4 24 00N 89 15E
Pacasmayo Peru **70** B11 7 27S 79 33W
Pachuca Mexico **68** E4 20 10N 98 44W
Pacific-Antarctic Ridge Pacific Ocean **111** L2/O2 55 00S 135 00W
Pacific Grove California U.S.A. **64** B4 36 36N 121 56W
Pacific Ocean 110
Padang Indonesia **95** C3 1 00S 100 21E
Padilla Bolivia **70** E9 19 18S 64 20W
Paducah Kentucky U.S.A. **65** I4 37 03N 88 36W
Paeroa New Zealand **107** C3 37 23S 175 40E
Pagadian The Philippines **95** G5 7 50N 123 30E
Pahala Hawaiian Islands **111** Z17 19 12N 155 28W
Paharganj India **108** L4 28 38N 77 12E
Pahute Mesa California U.S.A. **67** D3 37 15N 116 20W
Painesville Ohio U.S.A. **42** E2 41 43N 81 15W
Pai-sha Tao i. Taiwan **94** F6 23 40N 119 33E
Paisley United Kingdom **74** F5 55 50N 4 26W
Paita Peru **70** A11 5 11S 81 09W
Pakanbaru Indonesia **95** C4 0 33N 101 30E
PAKISTAN 90 A5/C5
Pakokku Myanmar **92** H3 21 20N 95 05E
Pak Sha Tsuen Hong Kong China **92** B2 22 25N 114 01E
Pak Tam Chung Hong Kong China **92** C2 22 24N 114 19E
Pakxé Laos **95** D7 15 05N 105 55E
Palaiseau France **79** A1 48 43N 2 15E
Palana Russian Federation **85** R7 59 05N 159 59E
Palangkaraya Indonesia **95** E3 2 16S 113 55E
Palau (Belau) i. Pacific Ocean **110** D8 7 30N 134 30E
Palawan i. The Philippines **95** F5 10 00N 119 00E
Palayankottai India **91** D1 8 42N 77 46E
Palembang Indonesia **95** C3 2 59S 104 45E
Palermo Italy **72** H3 38 08N 13 23E
Palestine Texas U.S.A. **65** G3 31 45N 95 39W
Palghat India **91** D2 10 46N 76 42E
Palk Strait India **91** D2 10 00N 80 00E
Palliser, Cape New Zealand **107** C2 41 37S 175 15E
Palma de Mallorca Balearic Islands **72** F3 39 35N 2 39E
Palmar Sur Costa Rica **69** H1 8 57N 83 28W
Palmas Bellas Panama **69** X2 9 16N 80 05W
Palmas, Cape Liberia **102** D9 4 25N 7 50W
Palm Beach Australia **107** H3 33 36S 151 19E
Palmdale California U.S.A. **67** C2 34 35N 118 07W
Palmer Alaska U.S.A. **8** F5 61 35N 149 10W
Palmer r.s. Antarctica **113** 64 46S 64 03W
Palmer Land geog. reg. Antarctica **113** 72 00S 62 00W
Palmerston Atoll i. Pacific Ocean **111** J6 18 04S 163 10W
Palmerston Pennsylvania U.S.A. **66** C3 40 46N 75 32W
Palmerston North New Zealand **107** C2 40 22S 175 37E
Palmira Colombia **70** B13 3 33N 76 17W
Palm Springs California U.S.A. **67** D1 33 49N 116 33W
Palmyra New Jersey U.S.A. **66** C3 40 00N 75 01W

Palmyra New York U.S.A. **43** J4 43 03N 77 14W
Palmyra Atoll i. Pacific Ocean **111** K8 5 52N 162 05W
Palo Alto California U.S.A. **67** A3 37 26N 122 10W
Palomares Mexico **68** E3 17 10N 95 04W
Palopo Indonesia **95** G3 3 01S 120 12E
Palo Seco Trinidad and Tobago **69** S9 10 06N 61 36W
Palu Indonesia **95** F3 0 54S 119 52E
Pamirs mts. Asia **87** L2/M2 38 00N 74 00E
Pamlico Sound North Carolina U.S.A. **65** K4 35 00N 76 00W
Pampas geog. reg. Argentina **71** E5 36 00S 63 00W
Pamplona Colombia **70** C14 7 24N 72 38W
PANAMA 69 H1
Panamá Panama **69** I1 8 57N 19 30W
Panama Canal Panama **69** I1 9 00N 80 00W
Panama City Florida U.S.A. **65** I3 30 10N 85 41W
Panamint Mountains California U.S.A. **67** D3 36 24N 117 15W
Panay i. The Philippines **95** G6 11 00N 122 00E
Pancake Range mts. California U.S.A. **67** E4 38 45N 115 55W
Panch'iao Taiwan **94** H8 25 01N 121 27E
Panchla India **90** J2 22 32N 88 08E
Panchur India **90** K2 22 31N 88 15E
Panevėžys Lithuania **86** A5 55 44N 24 24E
Pangkalpinang Indonesia **95** D3 2 05S 106 09E
Pānihāti India **90** K2 22 41N 88 23E
Panipat India **91** D5 29 24N 76 58E
Panke r. Germany **79** F2 52 38N 13 27E
Pankow Germany **79** F2 52 35N 13 25E
Pantar i. Indonesia **95** G2 8 30S 124 00E
Pantin France **79** B2 48 54N 2 25E
Pão de Açúcar (Sugar Loaf) mt. Brazil **71** Q2 22 57S 43 09W
Papa Hawaiian Islands **111** Z17 19 12N 155 53W
Papantla Mexico **68** E4 20 30N 97 21W
Papoose Lake California U.S.A. **67** E3 37 08N 115 52W
Papua, Gulf of Papua New Guinea **106** G8/H8 8 15S 144 45E
PAPUA NEW GUINEA 106 G8/I8
Pará admin. Brazil **70** G12 4 30S 52 30W
Paraburdoo Australia **106** B5 23 15S 117 45E
Paracel Islands South China Sea **95** E7 16 00N 113 30E
PARAGUAY 71 F8
Paraiba admin. Brazil **70** J11 7 20S 37 10W
Parakou Benin **102** F9 9 23N 2 40E
Paramaribo Suriname **70** F14 5 52N 55 14W
Paramonga Peru **70** B10 10 42S 77 50W
Paraná admin. Brazil **71** G8 24 30S 53 00W
Paraná r. Argentina **71** E6 31 45S 60 30W
Paranguá Brazil **71** H7 25 32S 48 36W
Parbhani India **91** D3 19 16N 76 51E
Parepare Indonesia **95** F3 4 00S 119 40E
Paria, Gulf of Trinidad and Tobago **69** S9 10 30N 61 45W
Parintins Brazil **70** F12 2 38S 56 45W
Paris France **72** F5 48 52N 2 20E
Paris Texas U.S.A. **65** G3 33 41N 95 33W
Paris Basin France **72** F5 48 00N 2 30E
Parkersburg West Virginia U.S.A. **65** J4 39 17N 81 33W
Park Royal United Kingdom **78** B3 51 32N 0 17W
Parma Ohio U.S.A. **42** E2 41 24N 81 44W
Parnaiba Brazil **70** I12 2 58S 41 46W
Pärnu Estonia **86** A6 58 28N 24 30E
Paroo r. Australia **106** G4 29 00S 144 30E
Parramatta Australia **107** G2 33 49S 151 00E
Parramatta River Australia **107** G2 33 49S 151 05E
Parras Mexico **68** D5 25 30N 102 11W
Pasadena California U.S.A. **67** C2 34 10N 118 08W
Pasadena Texas U.S.A. **65** G2 29 42N 95 14W
Pascagoula Mississippi U.S.A. **65** I3 30 21N 88 32W
Pasco Washington U.S.A. **64** C6 46 15N 119 07W
Passaic New Jersey U.S.A. **66** Y2 40 50N 74 08W
Passaic River New Jersey U.S.A. **66** Y2 40 46N 74 09W
Passo Fundo Brazil **71** G7 28 16S 52 20W
Pasto Colombia **70** B13 1 12N 77 17W
Patagonia geog. reg. Argentina **71** C2/D4 48 00S 70 00W
Patan India **91** C4 23 51N 72 11E
Patan Nepal **91** F5 27 40N 85 20E
Patea New Zealand **107** B3 39 45S 174 28E
Pate Island Kenya **102** N7 2 05S 41 05E
Paterson New Jersey U.S.A. **65** L5 40 55N 74 08W
Pathankot India **91** D6 32 16N 75 43E
Patiala India **91** D6 30 21N 76 27E
Pātipukur India **90** K2 22 36N 88 24E
Patna India **91** F5 25 37N 85 12E
Patos Brazil **70** J11 6 55S 37 15W
Pátra Greece **72** J5 38 14N 21 44E
Pátrai Greece **102** J15 38 14N 21 44E
Patterson California U.S.A. **67** B3 37 29N 121 09W
Paulding Ohio U.S.A. **42** B2 41 00N 84 37W
Paungde Myanmar **91** H3 18 30N 95 30E
Pausin Germany **79** E2 52 39N 13 04E
Pavlodar Kazakhstan **87** M5 52 21N 76 59E
Pavlohrad Ukraine **86** D4 48 34N 35 50E
Paysandú Uruguay **71** F6 32 21S 58 05W
Peake Deep Atlantic Ocean **109** F11 43 00N 20 05W
Pearl r. Mississippi U.S.A. **65** H3 32 00N 90 00W
Pearl Harbor Hawaiian Islands **111** Y18 21 22N 158 00W
Pechora r. Russian Federation **84** H9 67 00N 52 00E
Pechora Russian Federation **84** H9 65 14N 57 18E
Pecos r. U.S.A. **64** F3 30 00N 102 00W
Pecos Texas U.S.A. **64** F3 31 25N 103 30W
Pécs Hungary **72** J5 46 04N 18 15E
Pedreiras Brazil **70** I12 4 32S 44 40W
Pedro Juan Caballero Brazil **71** F8 22 30S 55 44W
Pedro Miguel Locks Panama **69** Y2 9 01N 79 36W
Pedro, Point c. Sri Lanka **91** E1 9 49N 80 14E
Pegasus Bay New Zealand **107** B2 43 22S 172 55E

Pegu Myanmar **95** B7 17 18N 96 31E
Pegunungan Barisan mts. Indonesia **95** C3 2 30S 102 30E
Pegunungan Muller mts. Indonesia **95** F4 0 00 113 00E
Pegunungan Schwaner mts. Indonesia **95** E3 1 00S 111 00E
Pegunungan Van Rees mts. Indonesia **106** F9 2 45S 138 30E
Pei-kang Taiwan **94** G6 23 38N 120 18E
Peipsi Järve (Lake Peipus, Chudskoye Ozero) l. Estonia/Russian Federation **72** L7 58 40N 27 30E
Peiraias (Piraeus) Greece **72** K3 37 57N 23 42E
Pekalongan Indonesia **95** D2 6 54S 109 37E
Peking see Beijing
Pelham Bay Park New York U.S.A. **67** Z2 40 50N 73 48W
Pelican Point Namibia **103** H3 22 54S 14 25E
Pelopónnisos geog. reg. Greece **72** K3 37 00N 22 00E
Pelotas Brazil **71** G6 31 45S 52 20W
Pematangsiantar Indonesia **95** B4 2 59N 99 01E
Pemba Mozambique **103** N5 13 00S 40 30E
Pemba Island Tanzania **103** M6 5 30S 39 50E
Pemba National Park Congo (D.R.) **103** K6 9 00S 26 30E
Pembroke New York U.S.A. **42** D2 45 49N 77 08W
Penal Trinidad and Tobago **69** T9 10 10N 61 28W
Pen Argyl Pennsylvania U.S.A. **66** C3 40 52N 75 25W
Pendleton Oregon U.S.A. **64** C6 45 40N 118 46W
Pend Oreille Lake Idaho U.S.A. **35** E1 48 10N 116 20W
Pend Oreille River Washington U.S.A. **35** E1 48 50N 117 25W
Penedo Brazil **70** J10 10 16S 36 33W
Peng Chau i. Hong Kong China **92** B1 22 17N 114 02E
P'eng-chia Hsü i. Taiwan **94** I8 24 38N 122 02E
Penghu see Makung
P'eng-hu Lieh-tao (Pescadores Islands) i. Taiwan **94** F 23 30N 119 30E
Peng-hu Shuitao sd. Taiwan **94** F6 23 30N 119 30E
P'eng-hu Tao i. Taiwan **94** F6 23 34N 119 35E
Penha Brazil **71** P2 22 49S 43 17W
Peninsula de Paria Venezuela **69** S10 10 44N 61 52W
Peninsula de Taitao Chile **71** C3 46 30S 75 00W
Peninsular Malaysia (Malaya) admin. Malaysia **95** C4 5 00N 102 00E
Pennant Hills Australia **107** G3 33 44S 151 04E
Penner r. India **91** D2 14 30N 77 30E
Pennines hills United Kingdom **74** I6
Pennsauken New Jersey U.S.A. **66** C2 39 58N 75 03W
Pennsylvania state U.S.A. **65** K5 41 00N 78 00W
Penn Yan New York U.S.A. **43** J3 42 41N 77 03W
Penobscot River Maine U.S.A. **47** C2 45 15N 68 30W
Penonomé Panama **69** H1 8 30N 80 20W
Penrith United Kingdom **74** I6 54 40N 2 44W
Pensacola Florida U.S.A. **65** I3 30 26N 87 12W
Pensacola Mountains Antarctica **113** 84 00S 60 00W
Penza Russian Federation **84** G6 53 11N 45 00E
Penzance United Kingdom **74** F2 50 07N 5 33W
Peoria Illinois U.S.A. **65** I5 40 43N 89 38W
Pepacton Reservoir New York U.S.A. **66** D5 42 05N 74 55W
Pereira Colombia **70** B13 4 47N 75 46W
Pergunungan Maoke mts. Indonesia **106** F9 4 00S 137 00E
Perm' Russian Federation **87** H6 58 01N 56 10E
Pernambuco admin. Brazil **70** J11 8 00S 37 30W
Perovo Russian Federation **86** M1 55 44N 37 46E
Perpignan France **72** F4 42 42N 2 54E
Perrysburg Ohio U.S.A. **42** C2 41 33N 83 39W
Perth Australia **106** B3 31 58S 115 49E
Perth United Kingdom **74** H8 56 42N 3 28W
PERU 70 B10
Peru Basin Pacific Ocean **111** Q6 18 00S 95 00W
Peru-Chile Trench Pacific Ocean **111** S6 13 00S 87 00W
Perúgia Italy **72** H4 43 07N 12 23E
Pervoural'sk Russian Federation **87** H6 56 59N 59 58E
Pescadero California U.S.A. **67** A3 37 15N 122 24W
Pescadores Islands see P'eng-hu Lieh-tao
Pescara Italy **72** H4 42 27N 14 13E
Peshawar Pakistan **91** C6 34 01N 71 40E
Petah Tiqwa Israel **88** O11 32 05N 34 53E
Petaluma California U.S.A. **67** A4 38 13N 122 39W
Petare Venezuela **70** D15 10 31N 66 50W
Petauke Zambia **103** L5 14 15S 31 20E
Peterborough Australia **106** F3 33 00S 138 51E
Peterborough United Kingdom **74** K4 52 35N 0 15W
Peterhead United Kingdom **74** J9 57 30N 1 46E
Petersburg Alaska U.S.A. **8** 52 56 49N 132 58W
Petersburg Virginia U.S.A. **65** K4 37 14N 77 24W
Petoskey Michigan U.S.A. **42** B6 45 22N 84 59W
Petra hist. site Jordan **88** O10 30 19N 35 26E
Petrolina Brazil **70** I11 9 22S 40 30W
Petropavlovsk Kazakhstan **87** K5 54 53N 69 13E
Petropavlovsk-Kamchatskiy Russian Federation **85** R6 53 03N 158 43E
Petrópolis Brazil **71** I8 22 30S 43 06W
Petrozavodsk Russian Federation **84** F8 61 46N 34 19E
Petukhovo Russian Federation **87** K6 55 05N 67 55E
Pevek Russian Federation **85** U8 69 41N 170 19E
Phenix City Alabama U.S.A. **65** I3 32 28N 85 01W
Philadelphia Pennsylvania U.S.A. **65** K4 40 00N 75 10W
Philip Smith Mountains Alaska U.S.A. **50** B4 67 30N 147 30W
Philippine Sea Pacific Ocean **110** C9/10 21 00N 130 00E
Philippine Trench Pacific Ocean **110** C9 12 00N 127 00E
PHILIPPINES, THE 95 G7/H5
Phillipsburg New Jersey U.S.A. **66** C3 40 41N 75 12W
Phitsanulok Thailand **95** C7 16 49N 100 18E
Phnom Penh Cambodia **95** C6 11 35N 104 55E
Phoenix Arizona U.S.A. **64** D3 33 30N 112 03W
Phoenix Island Pacific Ocean **110** I3 3 30S 174 30W

Phoenix Islands Kiribati **110** I7 4 40S 177 30W
Phoenixville Pennsylvania U.S.A. **66** C3 40 07N 75 31W
Phôngsali Laos **93** K3 21 40N 102 06E
Phra Nakhon Sri Ayutthaya Thailand **95** C6
14 20N 100 35E
Phuket Thailand **95** B5 7 52N 98 22E
Píatra Neamţ Romania **86** B4 46 53N 26 23E
Piauí admin. Brazil **70** I11 7 30S 43 00W
Pico Bolivar mt. Venezuela **70** C14 8 33N 1 03W
Pico Cristóbal mt. Colombia **70** C15 10 53N 73 48W
Pico de Itambé mt. Brazil **70** I9 18 23S 43 21W
Picos Brazil **70** I11 7 05S 41 24W
Picton New Zealand **107** B2 41 18S 174 00E
Picture Rocks tn. Pennsylvania U.S.A. **66** B4
41 17N 76 40W
Pidurutalagala mt. Sri Lanka **91** E1 7 01N 80 45E
Piedade Brazil **71** P2 22 53N 43 19W
Piedras Negras Mexico **68** D5 28 40N 100 32W
Pierre South Dakota U.S.A. **64** F5 44 23N 100 20W
Pierreville Trinidad and Tobago **69** T9 10 17N 61 01W
Pietermaritzburg Republic of South Africa **103** L2
29 36S 30 24E
Pietersburg Republic of South Africa **103** K3
23 54N 29 23E
Pigeon Michigan U.S.A. **42** C4 43 50N 83 15W
Pijijiapan Mexico **68** F3 15 42N 93 12W
Pikes Peak Colorado U.S.A. **64** E4 38 50N 105 03W
Pikesville Maryland U.S.A. **66** B2 39 23N 76 44W
Pik Kommunizma see Qullai Garmo
Pik Pobedy mt. Kirgyzstan **87** N3 42 25N 80 15E
Pilar Paraguay **71** F7 26 51S 58 20W
Pimenta Bueno Brazil **70** E10 11 40S 61 14W
Pinar del Rio Cuba **69** H4 22 24N 83 42W
Pindhos Mountains Greece **72** K3/4 40 00N 21 00E
Pine Bluff Arkansas U.S.A. **65** H3 34 13B 92 00W
Pinecrest California U.S.A. **66** B2 39 23N 76 44W
Pine Flat Reservoir California U.S.A. **67** C3
36 52N 119 17W
Pine River Michigan U.S.A. **42** B4 43 23N 84 40W
Ping Chau Hong Kong China **92** C2 22 33N 114 26E
Pingchen Taiwan **94** H7 24 57N 121 12E
Pingdingshan China **93** M5 33 50N 113 20E
Ping Shan Hong Kong China **92** B2 22 27N 114 00E
Pingtan Dao i. China **94** F8 25 00N 119 00E
P'ing-tung Taiwan **94** G5 22 40N 120 30E
Pingxiang China **95** D8 22 06N 106 44E
Pingxiang China **95** L3 27 35N 113 46E
Ping Yeung Hong Kong China **92** B3 22 32N 114 09E
Pinsk Belarus **72** L6 52 08N 26 01E
Pioneer Ohio U.S.A. **42** B2 41 42N 84 33W
Piraeus see Peiraiás
Pirapora Brazil **70** I9 17 20S 44 54W
Pirgos Greece **88** B6 37 40N 21 27E
Pisa Italy **72** H4 43 43N 10 24E
Pisco Peru **70** B10 13 46S 76 12W
Pitanga Brazil **71** G8 24 45S 51 43W
Pitcairn Islands Pacific Ocean **111** N5 25 04S 130 06W
Pitch Point Trinidad and Tobago **69** S9 10 15N 61 37W
Pitti Island India **91** C2 11 00N 73 00E
Pittsburgh Pennsylvania U.S.A. **65** K5 40 26N 80 00W
Pittsfield Massachusetts U.S.A. **65** L5 42 27N 73 15W
Pitt Water inlet Australia **107** H3 33 37S 151 19E
Pitufik (Dundas) Greenland **9** X8 76 30N 68 58W
Piura Peru **70** A11 5 15S 80 38W
Pivdennyy Bun r. Ukraine **86** C4 48 00N 30 00E
Placerville California U.S.A. **67** B4 38 43N 120 50W
Plainview Texas U.S.A. **64** F3 34 12N 101 43W
Planada California U.S.A. **67** B3 37 18N 120 19W
Planalto de Mato Grosso geog. reg. Brazil **70** F10
13 00S 56 00W
Plateau de Tchigaï plat. Chad/Niger **102** H12
21 30N 15 00E
Plateau du Tademaït plat. Algeria **102** F13 8 45N 2 00E
Platte r. U.S.A. **64** F5 41 00N 100 00W
Plattsburgh New York U.S.A. **65** L5 44 42N 73 29W
Playa Azul Mexico **68** D3 18 00N 102 24W
Pleven Bulgaria **72** K4 43 25N 24 04E
Ploieşti Romania **72** L4 44 57N 26 01E
Plovdiv Bulgaria **72** K4 42 08N 24 45E
Plover Cove Reservoir Hong Kong China **92** C2
22 28N 114 15E
Plymouth United Kingdom **74** G2 50 23N 4 10W
Plzeň Czech Republic **72** H5 49 45N 13 25E
Po r. Italy **72** H5 45 00N 10 00E
Pocatello Idaho U.S.A. **64** D5 42 35N 112 26W
Pochutla Mexico **68** E3 15 45N 96 30W
Pocono Summit tn. Pennsylvania U.S.A. **66** C4
41 06N 75 25W
Podara India **90** K2 22 34N 88 17E
Podgorica (Titograd) Yugoslavia **72** J4 42 28N 19 17E
Podkamennaya (Stony) Tunguska r. Russian Federation
85 L8/M8 62 00N 97 30E
Podol'sk Russian Federation **84** F7 55 23N 37 32E
Point-à-Pitre Guadeloupe **69** L3 16 14N 61 32W
Point Arena c. California U.S.A. **67** A4 39 57N 123 45W
Point Arguello c. California U.S.A. **67** B2 34 34N 120 39W
Point Buchon c. California U.S.A. **67** B2 35 15N 120 55W
Point Conception c. California U.S.A. **67** B2
34 27N 120 28W
Pointe-à-Pierre tn. Trinidad and Tobago **69** T9
10 20N 61 26W
Point Fortin tn. Trinidad and Tobago **69** S9 10 21N 61 41W
Point Hope tn. Alaska U.S.A. **8** B6 68 20N 166 50W
Point-Noire Congo **103** H7 4 46S 11 53E
Point Reyes c. California U.S.A. **67** A3 37 59N 123 01W
Point Sur c. California U.S.A. **67** B3 36 19N 121 53W
Poissy France **79** A2 48 56N 2 03E

Pok Fu Lam Hong Kong China **92** B1 22 15N 114 08E
Pokhara Nepal **91** E5 28 14N 83 58E
POLAND **72** J6
Poles'ye Pripyats' marsh Belarus **84** E6 52 00N 27 00E
Pollachi India **91** D2 10 38N 77 00E
Poltava Ukraine **86** C4 49 35N 34 35E
Polynesia geog. reg. Pacific Ocean **111** J4/L9
30 00S 166 00W
Pomeranian Bay Baltic Sea **72** H6/J6 54 00N 14 00E
Pomona California U.S.A. **67** D2 34 04N 117 45W
Ponca City Oklahoma U.S.A. **65** G4 36 41N 97 04W
Ponce Puerto Rico **69** K3 18 01N 66 36W
Pondicherry India **91** D2 11 59N 79 50E
Ponta da Marca c. Angola **103** H4 16 33S 11 43E
Ponta das Salinas c. Angola **103** H5 12 50S 12 54E
Ponta Grossa Brazil **71** G7 25 07S 50 09W
Ponta Porã Brazil **71** F8 22 27S 55 39W
Pontchartrain, Lake Louisiana U.S.A. **65** H3
30 00N 90 00W
Pontiac Michigan U.S.A. **42** C3 42 39N 83 18W
Pontianak Indonesia **95** D3 0 05S 109 16E
Poole r. Trinidad and Tobago **69** T9 10 02N 61 11W
Poole United Kingdom **74** I2 50 43N 1 59W
Pool Malebo l. Congo (D.R.) **103** I7 5 00S 17 00E
Popacatepetl mt. Mexico **68** E3 19 02N 98 38W
Popayán Colombia **70** B13 2 27N 76 32W
Poplar Bluff tn. Missouri U.S.A. **65** H4 36 16N 90 25W
Popondetta Papua New Guinea **106** H8 8 45S 148 15E
Porbandar India **90** B4 21 04N 69 40E
Porcupine r. Alaska U.S.A. **8** G6 67 15N 144 00W
Porirua New Zealand **107** B2 41 08S 174 50E
Porlamar Venezuela **69** L2 11 01N 63 54W
Poronaysk Russian Federation **85** Q5 49 13N 143 05E
Portadown United Kingdom **74** E6 54 26N 6 27W
Portales New Mexico U.S.A. **64** F3 34 12N 103 20W
Port Alexander Alaska U.S.A. **34** B3 56 13N 134 40W
Port Allegany Pennsylvania U.S.A. **42** H2
41 48N 78 18W
Port Angeles Washington U.S.A. **64** B6 48 06N 123 26W
Port Antonio Jamaica **69** R8 18 10N 76 27W
Port Arthur Texas U.S.A. **65** H2 29 55N 93 56W
Port Augusta Australia **106** F3 32 30S 137 27E
Port-au-Prince Haiti **69** J3 18 33N 72 20W
Port Austin Michigan U.S.A. **42** D5 44 04N 82 59W
Port Blair Andaman Islands **91** G2 11 40N 92 44E
Port Chalmers New Zealand **107** B1 45 49S 170 37E
Port Clinton Ohio U.S.A. **42** D2 41 30N 82 58W
Port-de-Paix Haiti **69** J3 19 56N 72 52W
Port Elizabeth New Jersey U.S.A. **66** D2 39 19N 74 59W
Port Elizabeth Republic of South Africa **103** K1
33 58S 25 36E
Porterville California U.S.A. **67** C3 36 05N 119 01W
Port Gentil Gabon **102** G7 0 40S 8 50E
Port Hacking b. Australia **107** G1 34 04S 151 07E
Port Hacking Point Australia **107** G1 34 05S 151 10E
Port Harcourt Nigeria **102** G8 4 43N 7 05E
Port Hedland Australia **106** B5 20 24S 118 36E
Port Huron Michigan U.S.A. **42** D3 42 59N 82 28W
Port Island Hong Kong China **92** D3 22 30N 114 21E
Port Jackson b. Australia **107** H2 33 51S 151 15E
Port Kaituma Guyana **70** F14 7 44N 59 53W
Portland Australia **106** G2 38 21S 141 38E
Portland Maine U.S.A. **65** L5 43 41N 70 18W
Portland Michigan U.S.A. **42** B2 42 52N 84 53W
Portland Oregon U.S.A. **64** B6 45 32N 122 40W
Portland Canal sd. Alaska U.S.A. **34** B3 55 00N 130 10W
Portland Point Jamaica **69** Q7 17 42N 77 11W
Portlaoise Republic of Ireland **74** D5 53 02N 7 17W
Port Lincoln Australia **106** F3 34 43S 135 49E
Port Macquarie Australia **106** I3 31 28S 152 25E
Port Maria Jamaica **69** R8 18 22N 76 54W
Port Morant Jamaica **69** R7 17 53N 76 20W
Portmore Jamaica **69** R7 17 53N 77 33W
Port Moresby Papua New Guinea **106** H8 9 30S 147 07E
Port Nolloth Republic of South Africa **103** I2
29 17S 16 51E
Port Norris New Jersey U.S.A. **66** C2 39 15N 75 02W
Porto (Oporto) Portugal **72** D4 41 09N 8 37W
Pôrto Alegre Brazil **71** G6 30 03S 51 10W
Porto Amboim Angola **103** H5 10 47S 13 43E
Portobelo Panama **69** Y3 9 33N 79 37W
Port-of-Spain Trinidad and Tobago **69** S10
10 38N 61 31W
Pôrto Grande Brazil **70** G13 0 43N 51 23W
Porto Novo Benin **102** F9 6 30N 2 47E
Pôrto Velho Brazil **70** E11 8 45S 63 54W
Portoviejo Ecuador **70** A12 1 07S 80 28W
Port Pirie Australia **106** F3 33 11S 138 01E
Port Royal Jamaica **69** R7 17 55N 76 52W
Port Said (Bûr Sa'îd) Egypt **102** L14 31 17N 32 18E
Portsmouth United Kingdom **74** J2 50 48N 1 05W
Portsmouth New Hampshire U.S.A. **65** L5
43 03N 70 47W
Portsmouth Virginia U.S.A. **65** K4 36 50N 76 20W
Port Sudan Sudan **102** M11 19 38N 37 07E
PORTUGAL **72** D3
Porus Jamaica **69** Q8 18 02N 77 25W
Posadas Argentina **71** F7 27 27S 55 50W
P'ot'i Georgia **86** E3 42 11N 41 41E
Potiskum Nigeria **102** H10 11 40N 11 03E
Po Toi Island Hong Kong China **92** C1 22 10N 114 10E
Potomac River Maryland U.S.A. **66** A3 39 10N 77 30W
Potosi Bolivia **70** D9 19 34S 65 45W
Potsdam admin. Germany **79** F2 52 40N 13 25E
Potsdam Germany **79** D1 52 24N 13 04E
Potsdam New York U.S.A. **43** L5 44 40N 75 01W
Potter's Bar United Kingdom **78** C3 51 42N 0 11W
Pottstown Pennsylvania U.S.A. **66** C3 40 15N 75 38W

Pottsville Pennsylvania U.S.A. **66** B3 40 41N 76 10W
Poughkeepsie New York U.S.A. **65** L5 41 43N 73 56W
Poverty Bay New Zealand **107** C3 38 43S 177 59E
Poway California U.S.A. **67** D2 32 57N 117 01W
Powell, Lake U.S.A. **64** D4 37 00N 110 00W
Poyang Hu l. China **93** N4 29 00N 116 30E
Poza Rica Mexico **68** E4 20 34N 97 26W
Poznań Poland **72** J6 52 25N 16 53E
Pradesh admin. India **91** E4 26 00N 81 00E
Praha (Prague) Czech Republic **72** H6 50 06N 14 26E
Prairie Dog Town Fork r. U.S.A. **64** F3 34 00N 101 00W
Pratt Kansas U.S.A. **64** G4 37 40N 98 45W
Preau Trinidad and Tobago **69** T9 10 12N 61 19W
Prenzlauer Berg Germany **79** F2 52 33N 13 25E
Prescott Arizona U.S.A. **64** D3 34 34N 112 28W
Presidencia Roque Sáenz Peña Argentina **71** E7
6 45S 60 30W
Presidente Prudente Brazil **71** G8 22 09S 51 24W
Presidente Stroessner see Ciudad del Este
Presque Isle Maine U.S.A. **47** C2 46 42N 68 01W
Presque Isle tn. Maine U.S.A. **65** M6 46 42N 68 01W
Preston United Kingdom **74** I5 53 46N 2 42W
Pretoria Republic of South Africa **103** K2 25 45S 28 12E
Prettyboy Reservoir Maryland U.S.A. **66** B2
39 38N 76 45W
Price r. Utah U.S.A. **64** D4 39 00N 110 00W
Price Utah U.S.A. **64** D4 39 35N 110 49W
Prieska Republic of South Africa **103** J2 29 40S 22 45E
Priest Lake Idaho U.S.A. **35** E1 49 45N 116 50W
Priestly Mountain Maine U.S.A. **43** S7 46 34N 69 23W
Priest River tn. Idaho U.S.A. **35** E1 48 11N 116 55W
Prince Edward Island Indian Ocean **108** C2
46 30S 37 20E
Prince of Wales Island Alaska U.S.A. **8** J4
56 00N 132 00W
Princess Elizabeth Land geog. reg. Antarctica **113**
72 00S 80 00E
Princes Town Trinidad and Tobago **69** T9 10 16N 61 23W
Prince William Sound Alaska U.S.A. **8** F5
61 00N 147 30W
Principe i. Gulf of Guinea **102** G8 1 37N 7 27E
Prinzapolca Nicaragua **69** H2 13 19N 83 35W
Pripet r. Ukraine **72** L6 52 00N 28 00E
Pripet Marshes Belarus **72** L6 52 00N 28 00E
Pripyats' r. Belarus **86** B5/C5 52 30N 27 00E
Priština Yugoslavia **72** K4 42 39N 21 20E
Probolinggo Indonesia **95** E2 7 45S 113 12E
Proddatur India **91** D2 14 45N 78 34E
Progreso Mexico **68** G4 21 20N 89 40W
Prokhladnyy Russian Federation **86** E3 43 46N 44 03E
Prokop'yevsk Russian Federation **85** K6 53 55N 86 45E
Propriá Brazil **70** J10 10 15S 36 51W
Prospect Park New York U.S.A. **66** Z1 40 40N 73 57W
Providence Rhode Island U.S.A. **65** L5 41 50N 71 28W
Providence, Cape New Zealand **107** A1 46 01S 166 28E
Providenlya Russian Federation **85** U8 64 30N 73 11E
Provo Utah U.S.A. **64** D5 40 15N 111 40W
Prudhoe Bay Alaska U.S.A. **8** F7 70 05N 148 20W
Prudhoe Bay tn. Alaska U.S.A. **50** B5 70 05N 148 20W
Prydz Bay Antarctica **113** 68 00S 75 00E
Przhevaľsk Kirgyzstan **85** J4 42 31N 78 22E
Pskov Russian Federation **84** E7 57 48N 28 26E
Ptsich r. Belarus **86** B5 53 00N 28 00E
Ptsich tn. Belarus **86** B5 52 15N 28 49E
Pucallpa Peru **70** C11 8 21S 74 33W
Puebla Mexico **68** E3 19 03N 98 10W
Pueblo Colorado U.S.A. **64** F4 38 17N 104 38W
Puerto Aisén Chile **71** C3 45 27S 72 58W
Puerto Armuelles Panama **69** H1 8 19N 82 51W
Puerto Ayacucho Venezuela **70** D14 5 39N 67 32W
Puerto Barrios Guatemala **68** G3 15 41N 88 32W
Puerto Berrio Colombia **70** C14 6 28N 74 28W
Puerto Cabello Venezuela **70** D15 10 29N 68 02W
Puerto Cabezas Nicaragua **69** H2 14 02N 83 24W
Puerto Carreño Colombia **70** D14 6 08N 69 27W
Puerto Cortés Honduras **68** G3 15 50N 87 55W
Puerto Cumarebo Venezuela **69** K2 11 31N 69 30W
Puerto de Morelos Mexico **69** G4 20 49N 86 52W
Puerto La Cruz Venezuela **70** E15 10 14N 64 40W
Puerto Maldonado Peru **70** D10 12 37S 69 11W
Puerto Mexico see Coatzacoalcos
Puerto Montt Chile **71** C4 41 28S 73 00W
Puerto Natales Chile **71** C2 51 41S 72 15W
Puerto Peñasco Mexico **68** B6 31 20N 113 35W
Puerto Pilón Panama **69** Y2 9 21N 79 48W
Puerto Princesa The Philippines **95** F5 9 46N 118 45E
PUERTO RICO **69** K3
Puerto Rico Trench Atlantic Ocean **109** B8
21 00N 65 00W
Puerto Santa Cruz Argentina **71** D2 50 03S 68 35W
Puerto Vallarta Mexico **68** C4 20 36N 105 15W
Pui O Hong Kong China **92** A1 22 15N 113 58E
Pukekohe New Zealand **107** B3 37 12S 174 54E
Pulacuyo Bolivia **70** D8 20 25S 66 41W
Pulau Bangka i. Indonesia **95** C2 2 30S 107 00E
Pulau Dolak (Pulau Yos Sudarso) i. Indonesia **106** F8
7 45S 138 15E
Pulau Nias i. Indonesia **95** B4 1 00N 97 30E
Pulau Simeulue i. Indonesia **95** B4 2 30N 96 00E
Pulau Yos Sudarso see Pulau Dolak
Pu-li Taiwan **94** G6 23 58N 120 55E
Pullman Washington U.S.A. **64** C6 46 46N 117 09W
Pune India **91** C3 18 34N 73 58E
Punjab admin. India **90** D3 30 40N 75 30E
Puno Peru **70** C9 15 53S 70 03W
Punta Alta Argentina **71** E5 38 50S 62 00W

Punta Arenas Chile **71** C2 53 10S 70 56W
Punta del Mona c. Nicaragua **69** H2 11 36N 83 37W
Punta Eugenia c. Mexico **68** A5 27 50N 115 05W
Punta Galera c. Ecuador **70** A13 0 49N 80 03W
Punta Gallinas c. Colombia **70** C15 12 27N 1 44W
Punta Gorda Belize **68** G3 16 10N 88 45W
Punta Manzanillo c. Panama **69** Y3 9 37N 79 36W
Punta Negra c. Peru **70** A11 6 06S 81 09W
Puntarenas Costa Rica **69** H2 10 00N 84 50W
Puntcak Jaya mt. Indonesia **106** F9 4 05S 137 09E
Punto Fijo Venezuela **70** C15 11 50N 70 16W
Puquio Peru **70** C10 14 44S 74 07W
Pur r. Russian Federation **85** J9 67 00N 77 30E
Puri India **91** F3 19 49N 85 54E
Purley United Kingdom **78** C2 51 21N 0 07W
Purnia India **91** F5 25 47N 87 28E
Pursat Cambodia **95** C6 12 27N 103 40E
Purt r. Romania/Moldova **84** B4 46 00N 28 00E
Pusa India **108** L4 28 38N 77 10E
Pusan South Korea **93** P6 35 05N 129 02E
Pu-tai Taiwan **94** G6 23 21N 120 11E
Putian China **94** F8 25 32N 119 02E
Putoran Mountains Russian Federation **85** L9
68 00N 95 00E
Puttalam Sri Lanka **91** D1 8 02N 79 50E
Pyasina r. Russian Federation **85** K10 71 00N 90 00E
Pyatigorsk Russian Federation **86** E3 44 04N 43 06E
Pyè Myanmar **91** H3 18 50N 95 14E
Pyinmana Myanmar **95** B7 19 45N 96 12E
Pymatuning Lake res. Ohio/Pennsylvania U.S.A. **42** F2
41 35N 80 30W
Pyŏngyang North Korea **93** P6 39 00N 125 47E
Pyramid Lake Nevada U.S.A. **64** C5 40 00N 119 00W
Pyramids hist. site Egypt **88** D4 29 50N 30 50E
Pyrénées mts. France/Spain **72** F4 42 50N 0 30E

Q

Qaanaaq (Thule) Greenland **9** X8 77 30N 69 00W
Qaidam Pendi (Qaidam Basin) China **92** H6 37 30N 94 00E
Qamdo China **91** H6 31 11N 97 18E
Qanâ el Suweis see Suez Canal
Qaqortoq (Julianehåb) Greenland **9** BB5 60 45N 46 00W
Qasigiannguit (Christianshåb) Greenland **51** W4
68 50N 51 10W
Qasr-e-Shirin Iraq **89** G5 34 32N 45 35E
Qasr Farâfra Egypt **102** K13 27 03N 28 00E
QATAR **89** H4
Qaţrâna Jordan **88** P10 31 14N 36 03E
Qazvin Iran **89** G6 36 16N 50 00E
Qena Egypt **102** L13 26 08N 32 42E
Qeqertarsuaq (Godhavn) Greenland **9** AA6
69 18N 53 40W
Qeqertarsuaq Disko (Disko) i. Greenland **9** Y6
70 00N 54 00W
Qeqertarsuup Tunua (Disko Bugt) b. Greenland **9** AA6
69 00N 54 00W
Qezi'ot Israel **88** O10 30 53N 34 28E
Qiemo China **92** G8 38 08N 85 33E
Qila Saifullah Pakistan **90** B6 30 42N 68 30E
Qilian Shan mts. China **93** J6 39 00N 98 00E
Qimusseriarsuaq (Melville Bugt) b. Greenland **9** Y8
75 30N 62 30W
Qingdao China **93** O6 36 04N 120 22E
Qinghai Hu l. China **93** K6 37 00N 100 00E
Qinghe China **94** B2 40 01N 116 20E
Qingjiang China **93** N4 33 35N 119 02E
Qinhuangdao China **93** N6 39 55N 119 37E
Qin Ling mts. China **93** L5 34 00N 107 30E
Qionghai China **93** M2 19 17N 110 30E
Qiqihar China **93** O8 47 23N 124 00E
Qogir Feng see K2
Qom Iran **89** H5 34 39N 50 57E
Qomishëh Iran **89** H5 32 01N 51 55E
Quakertown Pennsylvania U.S.A. **66** C3 40 27N 75 20W
Quang Ngai Vietnam **95** D7 15 09N 108 50E
Quang Tri Vietnam **95** D7 16 45N 107 11E
Quantock Hills United Kingdom **74** H3 51 05N 3 15W
Quanzhou China **93** N3 24 53N 118 36E
Quarry Bay tn. Hong Kong China **92** C1 22 17N 114 13E
Quartzite Mountain California U.S.A. **67** D3
37 31N 116 21W
Queanbeyan Australia **106** H2 35 24S 149 17E
Queen Mary Land geog. reg. Antarctica **113**
70 00S 90 00E
Queen Mary Reservoir United Kingdom **78** B2
51 25N 0 27W
Queen Maud Land see Dronning Maud Land
Queen Maud Mountains Antarctica **113** 85 00S 180 00
Queens New York U.S.A. **66** Z1 40 44N 73 54W
Queens County admin. New York U.S.A. **67** Z2
40 47N 73 50W
Queensland state Australia **106** F6/I4 23 00S 143 00E
Queenstown Australia **106** H1 42 07S 145 33E
Queenstown New Zealand **107** A1 45 02S 168 40E
Quelimane Mozambique **103** M4 17 53S 36 51E
Quelpart see Cheju do
Quemoy see Chinmen Tao
Que Que see Kwekwe
Querétaro Mexico **68** D4 20 38N 100 23W
Quetta Pakistan **90** B6 30 15N 67 00E
Quezaltenango Guatemala **68** F2 14 50N 91 30W
Quezon City The Philippines **95** G6 14 39N 121 02E
Quibala Angola **103** H5 10 48S 14 59E
Quibdó Colombia **70** B14 5 40N 76 38W
Quilá Mexico **68** C4 24 26N 107 11W

Quillacollo Bolivia **70** D9 17 26S 66 16W
Quilon India **91** D1 8 53N 76 38E
Quilpie Australia **106** G4 26 35S 144 14E
Quincy Illinois U.S.A. **65** H4 39 55N 91 22W
Quincy-sous-Sénart France **79** C1 48 40N 2 33E
Qui Nhon Vietnam **95** D6 13 47N 109 11E
Quito Ecuador **70** B12 0 14S 78 30W
Quixadá Brazil **70** J12 4 57S 39 04W
Qullai Garmo (Pik Kommunizma) mt. Tajikistan
 87 L2 38 59N 72 01E
Qus Egypt **88** D4 25 53N 32 48E
Quseir Egypt **102** L13 26 04N 34 15E

R

Raas Caseyr (Cabo Guardafui) c. Somalia **102** P10
 11 50N 51 16E
Raba Indonesia **95** F2 8 27S 118 45E
Rabat-Salé Morocco **102** D14 34 02N 6 51W
Rabaul Papua New Guinea **106** I9 4 13S 152 11E
Rachel California U.S.A. **67** E3 37 41N 115 47W
Radford Virginia U.S.A. **65** J4 37 07N 80 34W
Radlett United Kingdom **78** B3 51 41N 0 19W
Radlinski, Mount Antarctica **113** 82 30S 105 00W
Radom Poland **72** K6 51 26N 21 10E
Radom Sudan **102** J9 9 58N 24 53E
Raeside, Lake Australia **106** C4 29 00S 122 00E
Rafah Egypt **88** O10 31 18N 34 15E
Rafsanjān Iran **89** I5 30 25N 56 00E
Rahimyar Khan Pakistan **90** C5 28 22N 70 20E
Rahnsdorf Germany **79** G1 52 26N 13 42E
Raichur India **91** D3 16 15N 77 20E
Raigarh India **91** E4 21 53N 83 28E
Railroad Valley California U.S.A. **67** E4 38 18N 115 38W
Rainham United Kingdom **78** D3 51 31N 0 12E
Rainier, Mount Washington U.S.A. **64** B6 46 25N 121 45W
Raipur India **91** E4 21 16N 81 42E
Raisin River r. Michigan U.S.A. **42** C2 41 55N 83 40W
Rajahmundry India **91** E3 17 01N 81 52E
Rajapalaiyam India **91** D1 9 26N 77 36E
Rajasthan admin. India **91** C5 26 30N 73 00E
Rajkot India **91** C4 21 18N 70 53E
Rājpur India **90** K1 22 25N 88 25E
Rajshahi Bangladesh **91** F4 24 24N 88 40E
Raleigh North Carolina U.S.A. **65** K4 35 46N 78 39W
Ralik Chain is. Pacific Ocean **110** G8 7 30N 167 30E
Ramat Gan Israel **88** O10 32 04N 34 48E
Ramos Brazil **71** P2 22 51S 43 16W
Rampur Himachal Pradesh India **91** D6 31 26N 77 37E
Rampur Uttar Pradesh India **91** D5 28 50N 79 05E
Ramtha Jordan **88** O11 32 34N 36 00E
Rancagua Chile **71** C6 34 10S 70 45W
Ranchi India **91** F4 23 22N 85 20E
Randwick Australia **107** G2/H2 33 50S 151 14E
Rangeley Maine U.S.A. **43** R5 44 58N 70 39W
Rangiora New Zealand **107** B2 43 19S 172 36E
Rangoon see Yangon
Rangpur Bangladesh **91** F5 25 45N 89 21E
Rani Bagh India **108** L4 28 41N 77 06E
Raniganj West Bengal India **91** F4 23 35N 87 07E
Rann of Kachchh geog. reg. India/Pakistan **90** B4/C4
 24 00N 69 00E
Rapid City South Dakota U.S.A. **64** F5 44 06N 103 14W
Raquette River r. New York U.S.A. **43** M5 44 35N 74 58W
Ras al Hadd c. Oman **89** I3 22 31N 59 45E
Râs Banâs c. Egypt **102** M12 23 58N 35 50E
Ras Dashen Terara mt. Ethiopia **102** M13 13 15N 38 27E
Ras Fartak c. Yemen Republic **89** H2 15 20N 52 12E
Râs Ghârib Egypt **88** D4 28 22N 33 04E
Rasht Iran **89** G6 37 18N 49 38E
Râs Kasar c. Sudan **88** E2 18 02N 38 22E
Ras Lanuf Libya **102** I14 30 31N 18 34E
Ra's Madrakah c. Oman **89** I2 18 58N 57 50E
Râs Muhammad c. Egypt **88** O8 27 44N 34 15E
Ras Nouadhibou (Cap Blanc) c. Mauritania **102** B12
 20 53N 17 01W
Ratak Chain is. Pacific Ocean **110** H9 10 00N 172 30E
Rat Buri Thailand **95** B6 13 30N 99 50E
Rathlin Island United Kingdom **74** E7 55 20N 6 10W
Ratlam India **91** D4 23 18N 75 06E
Ratnapura Sri Lanka **91** E1 6 41N 80 25E
Raton New Mexico U.S.A. **64** F4 36 45N 104 27W
Raukumara mt. New Zealand **107** C3 37 45S 178 09E
Raukumara Range New Zealand **107** C3 38 00S 177 55E
Raurkela India **91** E4 22 16N 85 01E
Ravenna Italy **72** H4 44 25N 12 12E
Ravensthorpe Australia **106** C3 33 34S 120 01E
Ravi r. Pakistan **91** C6 31 00N 73 00E
Rawalpindi Pakistan **91** C6 33 40N 73 08E
Rawlins Wyoming U.S.A. **64** E5 41 46N 107 16W
Rawson Argentina **71** E4 43 15S 65 06W
Raymondville Texas U.S.A. **65** G2 26 30N 97 48W
Reading Pennsylvania U.S.A. **65** K5 40 20N 75 55W
Reading United Kingdom **74** K3 51 28N 0 59W
Rebun-tõ i. Japan **96** D4 45 25N 141 04E
Recherche, Archipelago of the is. Australia **106** C3
 35 00S 122 50E
Recife Brazil **70** J11 8 06S 34 53W
Reconquista Argentina **71** F7 29 08S 59 38W
Recovery Glacier Antarctica **113** 81 00S 25 00W
Red Bluff California U.S.A. **64** B5 40 11N 122 16W
Redbridge bor. United Kingdom **78** D3 51 34N 0 05E
Redding California U.S.A. **64** B5 40 35N 122 24W
Redhead Trinidad and Tobago **69** U10 10 44N 60 58W
Redhill tn. United Kingdom **78** C1 51 14N 0 11W
Redondo Beach California U.S.A. **67** C1 33 51N 118 24W

Red River Dakota U.S.A. **65** G6 46 00N 97 00W
Red River Texas/Oklahoma/Louisiana U.S.A. **65** H3
 32 00N 93 00W
Red Sea Middle East **102** M12 27 00N 35 00E
Red Wing Minnesota U.S.A. **65** H5 44 33N 92 31W
Redwood City California U.S.A. **67** A3 37 28N 122 15W
Reed City Michigan U.S.A. **42** A4 43 54N 85 31N
Reedsport Oregon U.S.A. **64** B5 43 42N 124 05W
Reedy Glacier Antarctica **113** 85 00S 140 00W
Reefton New Zealand **107** B2 42 07S 171 52E
Reggio di Calabria Italy **72** J3 38 06N 15 39E
Registan geog. reg. Afghanistan **89** J5 30 30N 65 00E
Rehovot Israel **88** O10 31 54N 34 46E
Reigate United Kingdom **78** C2 51 14N 0 13W
Reims France **72** F5 49 15N 4 02E
Reinickendorf Germany **79** F2 52 35N 13 22E
Reisterstown Maryland U.S.A. **66** B2 39 27N 76 51W
Rembang Indonesia **95** E2 6 45S 111 22E
Rennell i. Solomon Islands **106** K7 11 45S 160 15E
Rennes France **72** E5 48 06N 1 40W
Reno California U.S.A. **67** C4 39 32N 119 49W
Reno Nevada U.S.A. **64** C4 39 32N 119 49W
Republic Washington U.S.A. **35** E1 48 39N 118 45W
REPUBLIC OF IRELAND **74** C5
REPUBLIC OF SOUTH AFRICA **103** J2
Resistencia Argentina **71** F7 27 28S 59 00W
Réunion i. Indian Ocean **108** E4 21 00S 55 30E
Reutov Russian Federation **86** N2 55 46N 37 47E
Revesby Australia **107** G2 33 57S 151 01E
Revillagigedo Island Alaska U.S.A. **34** B3 55 30N 131 30W
Rewa India **91** E4 24 32N 81 18E
Reyes Peak mt. California U.S.A. **67** C2 34 38N 119 17W
Reykjanes Ridge Atlantic Ocean **109** E12 57 00N 33 00W
Reykjavik Iceland **72** A8 64 09N 21 58W
Reynosa Mexico **68** E5 26 05N 98 18W
Rēzekne Latvia **86** B6 56 30N 27 22E
Rhine r. Europe **72** G5 48 00N 7 30E
Rhode Island state U.S.A. **65** L5 41 00N 71 00W
Rhodes see Ródos
Rhondda United Kingdom **74** H3 51 40N 3 30W
Rhône r. Switzerland/France **72** F4 44 50N 4 50E
Rhum i. United Kingdom **74** E9 57 00N 6 20W
Ribble r. United Kingdom **74** I3 53 44N 2 56W
Ribeira Brazil **71** Q2 22 50S 43 10W
Ribeirão Prêto Brazil **70** H8 21 09S 47 48W
Riberalta Bolivia **70** D10 10 59S 66 06W
Richgrove California U.S.A. **67** C2 35 46N 119 04W
Richland Washington U.S.A. **64** C6 46 17N 119 17W
Richmond Australia **106** G5 20 45S 143 05E
Richmond California U.S.A. **64** B4 37 46N 122 20W
Richmond Indiana U.S.A. **65** J4 39 50N 84 51W
Richmond New York U.S.A. **66** Y1 40 36N 74 10W
Richmond New Zealand **107** B2 41 31S 173 39E
Richmond Virginia U.S.A. **65** K4 37 34N 77 27W
Richmond County admin. New York U.S.A. **66** Y1
 40 37N 74 02W
Richmond upon Thames United Kingdom **78** B2
 51 28N 0 19W
Rickmansworth United Kingdom **78** A3 51 38N 0 29W
Ridgecrest California U.S.A. **67** D2 35 37N 117 43W
Ridgeway Pennsylvania U.S.A. **42** H2 41 25N 78 45W
Riga Latvia **72** K7 56 53N 24 08E
Riga, Gulf of Estonia/Latvia **72** K7 57 30N 23 30E
Rijeka Croatia **72** H5 45 20N 14 27E
Ringgold Isles Fiji **110** V16 16 10S 179 50W
Rio Alto Purus r. Peru **70** C10 10 30S 72 00W
Rio Amazonas (Amazon) r. Brazil **70** G12 2 00S 53 00W
Rio Apaporis r. Colombia **70** C13 1 00N 72 30W
Rio Apure r. Venezuela **70** D14 7 40N 68 00W
Rio Aquidauana r. Brazil **70** F9 20 00S 56 00W
Rio Araguaia r. Brazil **70** H17 20S 49 00W
Rio Arauca r. Venezuela **70** D14 7 10N 68 30W
Riobamba Ecuador **70** B12 1 44S 78 40W
Rio Beni r. Bolivia **70** D10 13 00S 67 30W
Rio Bermejo r. Argentina **71** E7 25 00S 61 00W
Rio Branco r. Brazil **70** E13 0 00 62 00W
Rio Branco tn. Brazil **70** D11 9 59S 67 49W
Rio Caquetá r. Colombia **70** C12 0 05S 72 30W
Rio Caroni r. Venezuela **70** E14 7 00N 62 30W
Rio Caura r. Venezuela **70** E14 6 00N 64 00W
Rio Chico r. Argentina **71** D4 45 00S 67 30W
Rio Chubut r. Argentina **71** D4 43 30S 67 30W
Rio Claro tn. Trinidad and Tobago **69** T9 10 33N 61 11W
Rio Colorado r. Argentina **71** D5 37 30S 69 00W
Rio Corrientes r. Peru **70** B12 2 30S 76 30W
Rio Cuarto Argentina **71** E6 33 08S 64 20W
Rio de Janeiro admin. Brazil **71** I8 22 00S 42 30W
Rio de Janeiro tn. Brazil **71** I8 22 50S 43 17W
Rio de Janeiro State admin. Brazil **71** Q2 22 50S 43 05W
Rio de la Plata est. Uruquay/Argentina **71** F5
 35 00S 57 00W
Rio de Para r. Brazil **70** H12 1 00S 48 00W
Rio Deseado r. Argentina **71** D3 47 00S 68 00W
Rio Dulce r. Argentina **71** E7 29 00S 63 00W
Rio Gallegos r. Argentina **71** D2 51 35S 68 10W
Rio Grande r. Bolivia **70** E9 18 00S 65 00W
Rio Grande r. Brazil **70** G8 20 00S 50 00W
Rio Grande r. Mexico/U.S.A. **64** G2 26 00N 99 00W
Rio Grande tn. Argentina **71** D2 53 45N 67 46W
Rio Grande tn. Brazil **71** G6 32 03S 52 08W
Rio Grande tn. Mexico **68** D4 23 50N 103 02W
Rio Grande do Norte admin. Brazil **70** J11 6 00S 37 00W
Rio Grande do Sul admin. Brazil **70** G7 30 00S 54 00W
Rio Guainia r. Colombia/Venezuela **70** D13 2 30N 67 30W
Rio Guaporé r. Brazil/Bolivia **70** E10 13 00S 62 00W
Rio Guarico r. Venezuela **69** K1 8 00N 67 30W
Rio Guaviare r. Colombia **70** C13 3 00N 70 00W

Rio Gurgueia r. Brazil **70** I11 9 00S 44 00W
Rio Gurupi r. Brazil **70** H12 4 00S 47 00W
Riohacha Colombia **70** C15 11 34N 72 58W
Rio Iguaçu r. Brazil **71** G7 26 00S 51 00W
Rio Inírida r. Colombia **70** C13 2 30N 70 00W
Rio Iriri r. Brazil **70** G12 5 00S 54 50W
Rio Japurá r. Brazil **70** D12 2 00S 67 30W
Rio Jari r. Brazil **70** G13 2 00N 54 00W
Rio Jequitinhonha r. Brazil **70** I9 16 00S 41 00W
Rio Juruá r. Brazil **70** D12 4 30S 67 00W
Rio Juruena r. Brazil **70** F10 10 00S 57 40W
Rio Limay r. Argentina **71** D5 39 30S 69 30W
Rio Madeira r. Brazil **70** E11 6 00S 61 30W
Rio Madre de Dios r. Bolivia **70** D10 12 00S 68 00W
Rio Magdalena r. Colombia **70** C14 8 00N 73 30W
Rio Mamoré r. Bolivia **70** E9/10 15 00S 65 00W
Rio Marañon r. Peru **70** B12 4 50S 77 30W
Rio Meta r. Colombia **70** C14 6 00N 71 00W
Rio Napo r. Peru **70** C12 2 30S 73 30W
Rio Negro r. Argentina **71** E5 40 00S 65 00W
Rio Negro r. Brazil **70** D12 0 05S 67 00W
Rio Negro r. Uruguay **71** F6 33 00S 57 30W
Río Orinoco r. Venezuela **70** D13 3 00N 67 00W
Rio Paraguá r. Bolivia **70** E10 14 00S 61 30W
Rio Paragua r. Venezuela **70** E14 6 00N 63 30W
Río Paraguay r. Paraguay/Argentina **71** F7
 26 30S 58 00W
Río Paraná r. Paraguay/Argentina **71** F7 27 00S 56 00W
Río Paranaíba r. Brazil **70** H9 18 00S 49 00W
Rio Pardo r. Brazil **70** J9 15 10S 40 00W
Rio Parana Panema r. Brazil **71** G8 22 30S 52 00W
Río Parnaíba r. Brazil **70** I11 7 30S 45 00W
Rio Pastaza r. Peru **70** B12 2 30S 77 00W
Río Pilcomayo r. Paraguay/Argentina **71** F8
 24 00S 60 00W
Rio Purus r. Brazil **70** D11/E11 7 00S 65 00W
Rio Putumayo r. Colombia/Peru **70** C12 2 30S 72 30W
Río Salado r. Argentina **71** D5/6 35 00S 66 30W
Rio San Miguel r. Bolivia **70** E9/10 15 00S 63 30W
Rio São Francisco r. Brazil **70** J11 8 30S 39 00W
Rio Solimões r. Brazil **70** D12 3 30S 69 00W
Rio Tapajós r. Brazil **70** F11 6 30S 57 00W
Rio Taquari r. Brazil **70** F9 18 00S 57 30W
Rio Tefé r. Brazil **70** D12 4 30S 65 30W
Rio Teles Pires r. Brazil **70** F11 8 00S 57 00W
Rio Tocantins r. Brazil **70** H10 10 00S 49 00W
Rio Trombetas r. Brazil **70** F13 1 30N 57 00W
Rio Ucayali r. Peru **70** C11 6 00S 74 00W
Río Uraricuera r. Brazil **70** E13 3 00N 62 30W
Rio Uruguay r. Uruguay/Argentina **71** F6 32 00S 57 40W
Río Vaupés r. Colombia **70** C13 1 30N 72 00W
Rio Verde r. Paraguay **71** F8 23 00S 58 00W
Rio Verde tn. Brazil **70** G9 17 50S 50 55W
Rio Verde tn. Mexico **68** D4 21 58N 100 00W
Rio Xingu r. Brazil **70** G12 2 30S 52 30W
Río Yavari r. Peru/Brazil **70** C12 5 00S 72 30W
Rishiri-to i. Japan **96** D4 45 10N 141 20E
Rishrã India **90** K2 22 43N 88 19E
Ritter, Mount California U.S.A. **64** C4 37 40N 119 15W
Rivera Uruguay **71** F6 30 52S 55 30W
River Cess tn. Liberia **102** D9 5 28N 9 32W
Riverside California U.S.A. **64** C3 33 59N 117 22W
Riverside New Jersey U.S.A. **66** D3 40 02N 74 58W
Riverton New Zealand **107** A1 46 22S 168 01E
Rivne (Rovno) Ukraine **86** B5 50 39N 26 10E
Roanoke Virginia U.S.A. **65** K4 37 15N 79 58W
Robertsport Liberia **102** C9 6 45N 11 22W
Robin's Nest mt. Hong Kong China **92** C3 22 33N 114 11E
Robinson Summit sum. California U.S.A. **67** E4
 39 27N 115 06W
Roca Alijos is. Mexico **111** O10 24 59N 115 49W
Rochester Minnesota U.S.A. **65** H5 84 01N 92 27W
Rochester New York U.S.A. **65** K5 43 12N 77 37W
Rockall Bank Atlantic Ocean **109** G12 58 00N 15 00W
Rockaway Beach New York U.S.A. **66** Z1 40 33N 73 55W
Rockaway Inlet New York U.S.A. **66** Z1 40 34N 73 56W
Rockdale Australia **107** G2 33 57S 151 08E
Rockefeller Plateau Antarctica **113** 79 00S 140 00W
Rockford Illinois U.S.A. **65** I5 42 16N 89 06W
Rockford Ohio U.S.A. **42** B1 40 42N 84 40W
Rock Hall tn. Maryland U.S.A. **66** B2 39 08N 76 14W
Rockhampton Australia **106** I5 23 22S 150 32E
Rock Hill tn. South Carolina U.S.A. **65** J3 34 55N 81 01W
Rock Island tn. Illinois U.S.A. **65** H5 41 30N 90 34W
Rock Springs tn. Wyoming U.S.A. **64** E5 41 35N 109 13W
Rockville Maryland U.S.A. **66** A2 39 05N 77 10W
Rocky Mount tn. North Carolina U.S.A. **65** K4
 35 46N 77 48W
Roding r. United Kingdom **78** D3 51 45N 0 15E
Rodopi Planina mts. Bulgaria **72** K4 41 00N 25 00E
Rodos (Rhodes) i. Greece **72** L3 36 00N 28 00E
Rodrigues i. Indian Ocean **108** F5 19 43S 63 26E
Rogers City Michigan U.S.A. **42** C6 45 24N 83 50W
Rogers Lake California U.S.A. **67** D2 34 55N 117 48W
Rokugo r. Japan **97** C3 35 31N 139 46E
Rolla Missouri U.S.A. **65** H4 37 56N 91 55W
Roma Australia **106** H4 26 32S 148 46E
ROMANIA **72** K5
Roma (Rome) Italy **72** H4 41 53N 12 30E
Rome Georgia U.S.A. **65** I3 34 01N 85 02W
Rome New York U.S.A. **65** K5 43 13N 75 28W
Romford United Kingdom **78** D3 51 35N 0 11E
Rona r. United Kingdom **74** F11 59 10N 5 50W
Rondônia admin. Brazil **70** E10 11 30S 63 00W
Rondonópolis Brazil **70** G9 16 29S 54 37W
Ronne Ice Shelf Antarctica **113** 77 00S 60 00W
Roosevelt Island Antarctica **113** 79 00S 160 00W
Roraima admin. Brazil **70** E13 2 30N 62 30W

Rosamond Lake California U.S.A. **67** C2 34 50N 118 05W
Rosario Argentina **71** E6 33 00S 60 40W
Rosário Brazil **70** I12 3 0SS 44 15W
Rosario Baja California Mexico **68** A6 30 02N 115 46W
Rosario Sinaloa Mexico **68** C4 23 00N 105 51W
Rosarito Mexico **68** B5 28 38N 114 02W
Roscommon Michigan U.S.A. **42** B4 44 31N 84 37W
Roseau Dominica **69** L3 15 18N 61 23W
Roseburg Oregon U.S.A. **64** B5 43 13N 123 21W
Roseville Michigan U.S.A. **42** D2 42 29N 82 52W
Ross Ice Shelf Antarctica **113** 80 00S 180 00
Ross Lake Washington U.S.A. **34** H4 48 50N 121 05W
Rosslare Republic of Ireland **74** E5 52 16N 6 22W
Rosso Mauritania **102** B11 16 29N 15 53W
Ross Sea Antarctica **113** 75 00S 180 00
Rostock Germany **72** H6 54 06N 12 09E
Rostov Russian Federation **86** D6 57 11N 39 23E
Rostov-na-Donu Russian Federation **84** F5
 47 15N 39 45E
Roswell New Mexico U.S.A. **64** F3 33 24N 104 33W
Rothera r.s. Antarctica **113** 67 34S 68 07W
Rotorua New Zealand **107** C3 38 08S 176 14E
Rotterdam Netherlands **72** F6 51 54N 4 28E
Rouen France **72** F5 49 26N 1 05E
Rouge, Point Trinidad and Tobago **69** S9 10 09N 61 47W
Round Island Hong Kong China **92** C1 22 12N 114 10E
Round Mountain tn. California U.S.A. **67** D4
 38 43N 117 03W
Rovno see Rivne
Rovuma (Ruvuma) r. Mozambique **103** M5 11 30S 38 00E
Roxas The Philippines **95** G6 11 36N 122 45E
Roxburgh New Zealand **107** A1 45 33S 169 19E
Royal National Park Australia **107** G1 34 06S 151 06E
Royal Oak Michigan U.S.A. **42** C3 42 31N 83 08W
Rtishchevo Russian Federation **86** E5 52 16N 43 45E
Ruaha National Park Tanzania **103** M6 7 00S 35 00E
Ruapehu mt. New Zealand **107** C3 39 18S 175 34E
Rub Al Khālī d. Saudi Arabia **89** G2 19 30N 48 00E
Rubtsovsk Russian Federation **85** K6 51 43N 81 11E
Ruby Alaska U.S.A. **8** D5 64 41N 155 35W
Rudnya Russian Federation **86** E5 50 49N 44 35E
Rudnyy Kazakhstan **87** J5 53 00N 63 05E
Rudow Germany **79** F1 52 24N 13 29E
Rueil-Malmaison France **79** A2 48 52N 2 12E
Rufiji r. Tanzania **103** M6 7 30S 38 40E
Rugao China **93** O5 32 27N 120 35E
Rugby United Kingdom **74** J4 52 23N 1 15W
Ruislip United Kingdom **78** B3 51 35N 0 25W
Rukwa, Lake Tanzania **103** L6 8 00S 32 30E
Rumford Maine U.S.A. **47** B1 44 33N 70 34W
Runanga New Zealand **107** B2 42 24S 171 15E
Rungis France **79** B2 48 45N 2 22E
Ruse Bulgaria **72** L4 43 50N 25 59E
Rusk Texas U.S.A. **65** G3 31 49N 95 11W
Russas Brazil **70** J12 4 56N 38 02W
Russell Kansas U.S.A. **64** G4 38 54N 98 51W
Russian r. California U.S.A. **64** B4 38 30N 123 03W
RUSSIAN FEDERATION (RUSSIA) **85** J8/M8
Rust'avi Georgia **86** F3 41 34N 45 03E
Ruston Louisiana U.S.A. **65** H3 32 32N 92 39W
Ruth California U.S.A. **67** E4 39 16N 114 59W
Ruth Nevada U.S.A. **64** D4 39 16N 114 59W
Rutland Vermont U.S.A. **65** L5 43 37N 72 59W
Rutog China **92** E5 33 27N 79 43E
Ruvuma (Rovuma) r. Tanzania/Mozambique **103** M5
 11 30S 38 00E
Ruwenzori National Park Rwanda **102** L7 0 30S 29 30E
RWANDA **102** L7
Ryazan' Russian Federation **84** F6 54 37N 39 43E
Rybach'ye see Issyk-Kul
Rybinsk (Andropov) Russian Federation **84** F7 58 03N 38 50E
Rybinskoye Vodokhranilische res. Russian Federation
 84 F7 59 00N 38 00E
Rybinsk Reservoir Russian Federation **73** N7 59 00N 38 00E
Ryde Australia **107** G2 33 49S 151 06E
Ryde United Kingdom **74** J2 50 44N 1 10W
Ryukyu Islands (Nansei-shoto) Japan **93** P4
 27 30N 127 30E
Ryukyu Ridge Pacific Ocean **110** C10 25 50N 128 00E
Rzhev Russian Federation **86** C6 56 15N 34 18E

S

Saarbrücken Germany **72** G5 49 15N 6 58E
Saaremaa i. Estonia **86** A6 58 20N 22 00E
Sabah admin. Malaysia **95** F5 5 00N 115 00E
Sabaloka Cataract (River Nile) Sudan **102** L11
 16 19N 32 40E
Sabanalarga Colombia **69** J2 10 38N 74 55W
Sabhā Libya **102** H13 27 02N 14 26E
Sabi r. Zimbabwe/Mozambique **103** L3 20 30S 33 00E
Sabinas r. Mexico **64** F2 26 30N 100 00W
Sabinas Mexico **68** D5 27 50N 101 09W
Sabinas Hidalgo Mexico **68** D5 26 33N 100 10W
Sabine r. U.S.A. **65** H3 30 00N 94 00W
Sabine, Mount Antarctica **113** 72 00S 169 00W
Sabkhet el Bardawīl l. Egypt **88** N10 31 10N 33 35E
Sable, Cape Florida U.S.A. **65** J2 25 08N 80 07W
Sabyã Saudi Arabia **88** F2 17 07N 42 39E
Sabzevar Iran **89** I6 36 15N 57 38E
Saclay France **79** A1 48 43N 2 09E
Sacramento California U.S.A. **67** B4 38 33N 121 30W
Sacramento Mountains U.S.A. **64** F3 33 00N 105 00W
Sadar Bazar India **108** L4 28 39N 77 12E
Sadiya India **91** H5 27 49N 95 38E
Sado-shima i. Japan **96** C2 38 20N 138 30E
Safi Morocco **102** D14 32 20N 9 17W
Saga Japan **96** B1 33 16N 130 18E

Sagamihara Japan **96** C2 35 34N 139 22E
Sagami-wan Japan **97** B2 35 00N 139 30E
Sagar India **91** D4 23 50N 78 44E
Sagavanirktok River r. Alaska U.S.A. **50** B4
68 00N 149 00W
Saginaw Michigan U.S.A. **65** J5 43 25N 83 54W
Saginaw Bay Michigan U.S.A. **65** J5 44 00N 84 00W
Sagua la Grande Cuba **69** H4 22 48N 80 06W
Sahara Desert North Africa **102** D12/J12
Saharanpur India **91** D5 29 58N 77 33E
Sahiwal Pakistan **91** C6 30 41N 73 11E
Sahuaripa Mexico **68** C5 29 00N 109 13W
Sahuayo Mexico **68** D4 20 05N 102 42W
Saïda (Sidon) Lebanon **88** O11 33 32N 35 22E
Saidpur Bangladesh **91** F5 25 48N 89 00E
Saigon see Ho Chi Minh City
Sai Kung Hong Kong China **92** C2 22 23N 114 16E
St. Abb's Head c. United Kingdom **74** I7 55 55N 2 09W
St. Albans United Kingdom **74** K3 51 46N 0 21W
St. Albans New York U.S.A. **67** Z1 40 42N 73 46W
St. Albans Vermont U.S.A. **47** B1 44 49N 73 07W
St. Andrews United Kingdom **74** I8 56 20N 2 48W
St. Ann's Bay tn. Jamaica **69** Q8 18 26N 77 12W
St. Augustine Florida U.S.A. **65** J2 29 54N 81 19W
St. Bees Head c. United Kingdom **74** H6 54 31N 3 39W
St-Cloud France **79** A2 48 51N 2 11E
St. Cloud Minnesota U.S.A. **65** H6 45 34N 94 10W
St. Croix r. North America **65** H6 46 00N 93 00W
St. Croix i. West Indies **69** L3 22 45N 65 00W
St. Cyr-l'École France **79** A2 48 47N 2 03E
St. David's Head c. United Kingdom **74** F3 51 55N 5 19W
St-Denis France **79** B2 48 57N 2 22E
St. Elias, Mount Alaska U.S.A. **8** G5 60 12N 140 57W
St-Étienne France **72** F5 45 26N 4 23E
St. Francis r. U.S.A. **65** H4 35 00N 90 00W
St. George's Grenada **69** L2 12 04N 61 44W
St. George's Channel British Isles **74** E3 52 00N 6 00W
St -Germain-en-Laye France **79** A2 48 54N 2 04E
St. Helena i. Atlantic Ocean **109** H5 15 58S 5 43W
St. Helena Bay Republic of South Africa **103** I1 32 00S 17 30E
St. Helens United Kingdom **74** I5 53 28N 2 44W
St. Helier Channel Islands **74** I1 49 12N 2 07W
St. Ignace Michigan U.S.A. **65** J6 45 53N 84 44W
St. Ives Australia **107** G3 33 44S 151 10E
Saint John r. North America **65** M6 46 00N 69 00W
St. John's Antigua and Barbuda **69** L3 17 08N 61 50W
St. Johns Michigan U.S.A. **42** B4 43 01N 84 31W
St. Joseph Missouri U.S.A. **65** H4 39 45N 94 51W
St. Joseph Trinidad and Tobago **69** T10 10 39N 61 25W
St. Joseph River Indiana/Ohio U.S.A. **42** B2
41 12N 84 55W
St. Kilda i. United Kingdom **74** C9 57 49N 8 34W
ST. KITTS-NEVIS **69** L3
St. Laurent French Guiana **70** G14 5 29N 54 03W
St. Lawrence Island Alaska U.S.A. **8** A5/B5
63 15N 169 50W
St. Louis Missouri U.S.A. **65** H4 38 40N 90 15W
St. Louis Senegal **102** B11 16 01N 16 30W
ST. LUCIA **69** L2
St-Mandé France **79** B2 48 50N 2 26E
St. Mary's River Indiana/Ohio U.S.A. **42** B1
40 50N 84 55W
St. Maur France **79** B2 48 48N 2 30E
St. Paul Minnesota U.S.A. **65** H5 45 00N 93 10W
St. Paul Rocks Atlantic Ocean **109** F7 0 23N 29 23W
St. Peter Port Channel Islands **74** I1 49 27N 3 32W
St. Petersburg Florida U.S.A. **65** J2 27 45N 82 40W
St. Petersburg Russian Federation see Sankt-Peterburg
Saint-Pierre i. St.-Pierre et Miquelon **49** C2
46 46N 56 12W
Saint-Pierre tn. St.-Pierre et Miquelon **49** C2
46 46N 56 12W
Saint-Pierre et Miquelon admin. France **49** C2
46 55N 56 12W
St. Quentin-en-Yvelines France **79** A2 48 46N 2 06E
St. Remy France **79** A1 48 42N 2 04E
St. Thomas i. West Indies **69** K3 18 00N 65 30W
St. Vincent i. St. Vincent and The Grenadines **69** L2
13 15N 61 12W
ST. VINCENT AND THE GRENADINES **69** L2
Saipan Northern Marianas **110** E9 15 12N 145 43E
Saitama pref. Japan **97** B4 36 00N 139 30E
Sai Wan Hong Kong China **92** B1 22 17N 114 07E
Sakai Japan **96** C1 34 35N 135 28E
Sākākah Saudi Arabia **88** F4 29 59N 40 12E
Sakakawea, Lake North Dakota U.S.A. **64** F6
48 00N 103 00W
Sakarya r. Turkey **88** D7 40 05N 30 15E
Sakata Japan **96** C2 38 55N 139 51E
Sakhalin i. Russian Federation **85** Q6 50 00N 143 00E
Sakhalin Bay Russian Federation **85** Q6 54 00N 141 00E
Salalah Oman **89** H2 17 00N 54 04E
Salamanca Mexico **68** D4 20 34N 101 12W
Salamanca Spain **72** D4 40 58N 5 40W
Salavat Russian Federation **87** H5 53 22N 55 50E
Salay Gomez i. Pacific Ocean **111** P5 26 28S 105 28W
Salekhard Russian Federation **85** I9 66 33N 66 35E
Salem India **91** D2 11 38N 78 08E
Salem Massachusetts U.S.A. **65** L5 42 32N 70 53W
Salem New Jersey U.S.A. **66** C2 39 35N 75 28W
Salem Oregon U.S.A. **64** B5 44 57N 123 01W
Salerno Italy **72** H4 40 40N 14 46E
Salgueiro Brazil **70** J11 8 04S 39 05W
Salibea Trinidad and Tobago **69** T10 10 42N 61 02W
Salima Malawi **103** L5 13 45S 34 29E
Salina Kansas U.S.A. **65** G4 38 50N 97 36W
Salinas California U.S.A. **64** B4 36 39N 121 40W
Salinas Ecuador **70** A12 2 15S 80 58W

Salinas r. California U.S.A. **67** B3 36 31N 121 30W
Salinas Grandes l. Argentina **71** D6/E7 30 00S 65 00W
Saline Michigan U.S.A. **42** C3 42 12N 83 46W
Salisbury Maryland U.S.A. **65** K4 38 22N 75 37W
Salisbury North Carolina U.S.A. **65** J4 35 20N 80 30W
Salisbury United Kingdom **74** J3 51 05N 1 48W
Salisbury Plain United Kingdom **74** J3 51 10N 1 55W
Salmon Idaho U.S.A. **64** D6 45 11N 113 55W
Salmon r. Idaho U.S.A. **64** C6 45 00N 116 00W
Salmon Reservoir res. New York U.S.A. **43** L4
43 30N 75 50W
Salmon River Mountains Idaho U.S.A. **64** C5/D6
45 00N 115 00W
Salpausselka geog. reg. Finland **72** L8 61 40N 26 00E
Salt Jordan **88** O11 32 03N 35 44E
Salt r. Arizona U.S.A. **64** D3 34 00N 110 00W
Salta Argentina **71** D8 24 46S 65 28W
Salt Fork r. Texas/Oklahoma U.S.A. **64** F3
35 00N 100 00W
Saltillo Mexico **68** D5 25 30N 101 00W
Salt Lake tn. India **90** K2 22 35N 88 23E
Salt Lake City Utah U.S.A. **64** D5 40 45N 111 55W
Salt Lakes India **90** K2 22 30N 88 20E
Salto Uruguay **71** F6 31 27S 57 50W
Salton Sea l. California U.S.A. **64** C3 33 00N 116 00W
Salvador Brazil **70** J10 12 58S 38 29W
Salween (Nu Jiang) r. China/Myanmar **95** B8
20 00N 103 00E
Salzburg Austria **72** H5 47 48N 13 03E
Samani Japan **96** D3 42 07N 142 57E
Samar i. The Philippines **95** G6/H6 12 00N 125 00E
Samara (Kuybyshev) Russian Federation **84** H6
53 10N 50 10E
Samara r. Russian Federation **87** G5 52 30N 53 00E
Samara (Kuybyshevskoye) Vodokhranilishche res.
Russian Federation **86** F5/G5 55 00N 45 00E
Samarinda Indonesia **95** F3 0 30S 117 09E
Samarkand Uzbekistan **87** K2 39 40N 66 57E
Sämarrä' Iraq **88** F5 34 13N 43 52E
Sambalpur India **91** E4 21 28N 84 04E
Sambas Indonesia **95** D4 1 22N 109 15E
SAMOA **110** I6/J6
Sámos i. Greece **88** C6 37 00N 26 00E
Samsun Turkey **73** N4 41 17N 36 22E
San Mali **102** D10 13 21N 4 57W
San'a Yemen Republic **88** F2 15 23N 44 14E
SANAE (South African National Expedition) r.s. Antarctica
113 70 18S 2 25W
Sanaga r. Cameroon **102** H8 4 30N 12 20E
Sanak Islands Alaska U.S.A. **8** C3 54 26N 162 40W
Sanandaj Iran **89** G6 35 18N 47 01E
San Andrés Tuxtla Mexico **68** E3 18 28N 95 15W
San Angelo Texas U.S.A. **64** F3 31 28N 100 28W
San Antonio Chile **71** C6 33 35S 71 39W
San Antonio Texas U.S.A. **64** G2 29 25N 98 30W
San Antonio r. Texas U.S.A. **65** G2 29 00N 97 00W
San Antonio Oeste Argentina **71** E4 40 45S 64 58W
San Benito r. California U.S.A. **67** B3 36 45N 121 18W
San Benito Mountain California U.S.A. **67** B3
36 23N 120 38W
San Bernardino California U.S.A. **64** C3 34 07N 117 18W
San Bernardo Chile **71** C6 33 37S 70 45W
San Carlos Luzon The Philippines **95** G7 15 59N 120 22E
San Carlos Negros The Philippines **95** G6
10 30N 123 29E
San Carlos Venezuela **70** D14 9 39N 68 35W
San Carlos de Bariloche Argentina **71** C4 41 11S 71 23W
San Carlos del Zulia Venezuela **70** C14 9 01N 71 58W
San Clemente California U.S.A. **67** D1 33 26N 117 36W
San Clemente Island California U.S.A. **64** C3
33 26N 117 36W
San Cristóbal Argentina **71** E6 30 20S 61 14W
San Cristóbal Mexico **68** F3 16 45N 92 40W
San Cristóbal Venezuela **70** C14 7 46N 72 15W
San Cristobal i. Solomon Islands **106** K7 11 00S 162 00E
Sancti Spíritus Cuba **69** I4 21 55N 79 28W
Sandakan Malaysia **95** F5 5 52N 118 04E
Sanday i. United Kingdom **74** I11 59 15N 2 30W
San Diego California U.S.A. **64** C3 32 45N 117 10W
Sandpoint Idaho U.S.A. **35** E1 48 17N 116 34W
Sandpoint tn. Idaho U.S.A. **64** C6 48 17N 116 34W
Sandusky Michigan U.S.A. **42** D4 43 56N 82 50W
Sandusky Ohio U.S.A. **42** D2 41 27N 82 42W
Sandusky Bay Ohio U.S.A. **42** D2 41 30N 82 50W
Sandusky River r. Ohio U.S.A. **42** C2 41 00N 83 15W
Sandy River r. Maine U.S.A. **43** R5 44 45N 70 12W
San Felipe Mexico **68** B6 31 03N 114 52W
San Felipe Venezuela **70** D15 10 25N 68 40W
San Fernando California U.S.A. **67** C2 34 17N 118 27W
San Fernando Mexico **68** A5 29 59N 115 10W
San Fernando Trinidad and Tobago **69** T9 10 16N 61 28W
San Fernando de Apure Venezuela **70** D14 7 53N 67 15W
Sanford Florida U.S.A. **65** J2 28 49N 81 17W
San Francique Trinidad and Tobago **69** S9 10 05N 61 39W
San Francisco Argentina **71** E6 31 29S 62 06W
San Francisco California U.S.A. **67** A3 37 30N 122 25W
San Francisco Dominican Republic **69** J3 19 19N 70 15W
San Francisco del Oro Mexico **68** C5 26 52N 105 50W
Sangar Russian Federation **85** N8 64 02N 127 30E
Sangha r. Africa **102** I8 2 00N 17 00E
Sangli India **91** C3 16 55N 74 37E
Sangre de Cristo Mountains New Mexico U.S.A. **64** E4
37 00N 105 00W
Sangre Grande Trinidad and Tobago **69** T10
10 35N 61 08W
San Jacinto Peak California U.S.A. **67** D1 33 48N 116 40W
San Javier Bolivia **70** E9 16 22S 62 38W

San Joaquin r. California U.S.A. **67** B3 37 15N 120 49W
San Joaquin Valley California U.S.A. **67** B3
37 00N 120 22W
San José California U.S.A. **64** B4 37 20N 121 55W
San José Costa Rica **69** H1 9 59N 84 04W
San José Uruguay **71** F6 34 27S 56 40W
San José del Cabo Mexico **68** C4 23 01N 109 40W
San Juan Argentina **71** D6 31 33S 68 31W
San Juán Peru **70** B9 15 22S 75 07W
San Juan Puerto Rico **69** K3 18 29N 66 08W
San Juan Trinidad and Tobago **69** T10 10 39N 61 27W
San Juan r. U.S.A. **64** D4 37 00N 110 00W
San Juan de los Morros Venezuela **69** K1
9 53N 67 23W
San Juan Islands Washington U.S.A. **34** H4
48 30N 123 00W
San Juan Mountains Colorado U.S.A. **64** E4
37 50N 107 50W
San Julián Argentina **71** D3 49 17S 67 45W
Sänkräil India **90** J2 22 33N 88 14E
Sankt-Peterburg (Leningrad, St. Petersburg)
Russian Federation **84** F7 59 55N 30 25E
Sankuru r. Congo (D.R.) **103** J7 4 00S 23 30E
Sanliurfa (Urfa) Turkey **86** D7 37 08N 38 45E
San Lucas Mexico **68** C4 22 50N 109 52W
San Luis Argentina **71** D6 33 20S 66 23W
San Luis Obispo California U.S.A. **64** B4
35 16N 120 40W
San Luis Obispo Bay California U.S.A. **67** B2
35 03N 120 39W
San Luis Potosí Mexico **68** D4 22 10N 101 00W
San Luis Reservoir California U.S.A. **67** B3
37 04N 121 08W
San Marcos Texas U.S.A. **65** G2 29 54N 97 57W
SAN MARINO **72** H4 44 00N 12 00E
San Mateo California U.S.A. **67** A3 37 33N 122 22W
Sanmenxia China **93** M5 34 46N 111 17E
San Miguel El Salvador **68** G2 13 28N 88 10W
San Miguel de Tucumán Argentina **71** D7
26 47S 65 15W
San Miguel Island California U.S.A. **67** B2
34 03N 120 22W
Sanming China **93** N4 26 16N 117 35E
San Nicolas de los Arroyos Argentina **71** E6
33 25S 60 15W
San Nicolas Island California U.S.A. **67** C1
33 15N 119 30W
San Pablo The Philippines **95** G6 14 03N 121 19E
San Pablo Bay California U.S.A. **67** A3 37 38N 122 15W
San Pedro Argentina **71** E8 24 12S 64 55W
San Pedro Côte d'Ivoire **102** D9 4 45N 6 37W
San Pedro Dominican Republic **69** K3 18 30N 69 18W
San Pedro Channel California U.S.A. **67** C1
33 37N 118 30W
San Pedro de las Colonias Mexico **68** D5
25 50N 102 59W
San Pedro Sula Honduras **68** G3 15 26N 88 01W
San Rafael Argentina **71** D6 34 35S 68 24W
San Rafael California U.S.A. **64** B4 37 58N 122 30W
San Salvador El Salvador **68** G2 13 40N 89 10W
San Salvador i. The Bahamas **69** J4 24 00N 74 32W
San Salvador de Jujuy Argentina **71** D8 24 10S 65 48W
San Sebastián Spain **72** E4 43 19N 1 59W
Santa Ana Bolivia **70** D10 13 46S 65 37W
Santa Ana California U.S.A. **64** C3 33 44N 117 54W
Santa Ana El Salvador **68** G2 14 00N 89 31W
Santa Ana Mexico **64** D3 30 31N 111 08W
Santa Barbara California U.S.A. **64** C3 33 29N 119 01W
Santa Barbara Mexico **68** C5 26 48N 105 50W
Santa Barbara Channel California U.S.A. **67** B2
34 15N 120 00W
Santa Barbara Island California U.S.A. **67** C1
33 29N 119 02W
Santa Catalina Island California U.S.A. **64** C3
33 25N 118 25W
Santa Catarina admin. Brazil **71** G7 27 00S 51 00W
Santa Clara California U.S.A. **67** B3 37 21N 121 57W
Santa Clara Cuba **69** I4 22 25N 79 58W
Santa Clarita California U.S.A. **67** C2 34 23N 118 33W
Santa Cruz Bolivia **70** E9 17 50S 63 10W
Santa Cruz California U.S.A. **64** B4 36 58N 122 03W
Santa Cruz Canary Islands **102** B13 28 28N 16 15W
Santa Cruz Jamaica **69** Q8 18 03N 77 43W
Santa Cruz r. Argentina **71** D2 50 00S 70 00W
Santa Cruz Island California U.S.A. **64** C3
34 00N 119 40W
Santa Cruz Islands Solomon Islands **106** L7
11 00S 167 00E
Santa Fé Argentina **71** E6 31 35S 60 50W
Santa Fe New Mexico U.S.A. **64** E4 35 41N 105 57W
Santa Isabel i. Solomon Islands **106** J8 7 30S 158 30E
Santa Maria Brazil **71** G7 29 45S 53 40W
Santa Maria California U.S.A. **64** B3 34 56N 120 25W
Santa Marta Colombia **70** C15 11 18N 74 10W
Santa Monica California U.S.A. **67** C2 34 00N 118 28W
Santa Paula California U.S.A. **67** C2 34 20N 119 04W
Santa Rosa Argentina **71** E5 36 37S 64 17W
Santa Rosa California U.S.A. **64** B4 38 26N 122 43W
Santa Rosa Honduras **68** G2 14 48N 88 43W
Santa Rosa New Mexico U.S.A. **64** E4 34 56N 104 42W
Santa Rosa Island California U.S.A. **64** B3
34 00N 120 05W
Santa Rosalia Mexico **68** B5 27 20N 112 20W
Santa Teresa Brazil **71** Q2 22 57S 43 12W
Santa Ynez Mountains California U.S.A. **67** B2
34 31N 120 00W
Santana do Livramento Brazil **71** F6 30 52S 55 30W
Santander Colombia **70** B13 3 00N 76 25W

Santander Spain **72** E4 43 28N 3 48W
Santarém Brazil **70** G12 2 26S 54 41W
Santee California U.S.A. **67** D1 32 51N 116 59W
San Tin Hong Kong China **92** B3 22 30N 114 04E
Santi Nagar India **108** L4 28 40N 77 10E
Santiago Chile **71** C6 33 30S 70 40W
Santiago Panama **69** H2 8 08N 80 59W
Santiago de Cuba Cuba **69** I4 20 00N 75 49W
Santiago del Estero Argentina **71** E7 27 47S 64 15W
Santiago Ixcuintla Mexico **68** C4 21 50N 105 11W
Santo Andre Brazil **71** H8 23 39S 46 29W
Santo Domingo Dominican Republic **69** K3
18 30N 69 57W
Santo Domingo de los Colorados Ecuador **70** B12
0 13S 79 09W
Santos Brazil **71** H8 23 56S 46 22W
San Uk Ha Hong Kong China **92** C3 22 30N 114 14E
San Vicente El Salvador **68** G2 13 38N 88 42W
Sanya (Ya Xian) China **93** L2 18 25N 109 27E
São Bernardo do Campo Brazil **71** H8 23 45S 46 34W
São Borja Brazil **71** F7 28 35S 56 01W
São Cristovão Brazil **70** J2 22 52S 43 15S
São Gonçalo Brazil **71** Q2 22 48S 43 08W
São João de Meriti Brazil **71** P2 22 47S 43 22W
São Joao de Meriti admin. Brazil **71** P2 22 46S 43 23W
São José Brazil **71** H7 27 35S 48 40W
São José do Rio Prêto Brazil **70** H8 20 50S 49 20W
São José dos Campos Brazil **71** H8 23 07S 45 52W
São Luís Brazil **70** I12 2 34S 44 16W
Saône r. France **72** F5 46 30N 5 00E
São Paulo Brazil **71** H8 23 33S 46 39W
São Paulo admin. Brazil **70** G8/H8 21 30S 50 00W
São Tomé i. Gulf of Guinea **102** G8 0 25N 6 35E
SÃO TOMÉ AND PRINCIPE **102** G8
São Vicente Brazil **71** H8 23 57S 46 23W
Sapporo Japan **96** D3 43 05N 141 21E
Saqqez Iran **89** G6 36 14N 46 15E
Sarajevo Bosnia-Herzegovina **72** J4 43 52N 18 26E
Sarakhs Iran **89** J6 36 32N 61 07E
Saransk Russian Federation **84** G6 54 12N 45 10E
Sarapui r. Brazil **71** P3 22 44S 43 17W
Sarapul Russian Federation **87** H6 56 30N 53 49E
Sarasota Florida U.S.A. **65** J2 27 20N 82 32W
Saratov Russian Federation **84** G6 51 30N 45 55E
Saravan Iran **89** J4 27 25N 62 17E
Sarawak admin. Malaysia **95** F4 1 00N 111 00E
Sarcelles France **79** B2 48 59N 2 22E
Sardegna (Sardinia) i. Italy **72** G4 40 00N 9 00E
Sardindida Plain Kenya **102** M8/N8 2 00N 40 00E
Sar-e Pol Afghanistan **89** K6 36 13N 65 55E
Sargasso Sea Atlantic Ocean **109** B9 27 00N 66 00W
Sargeant Barbados **69** V12 13 05N 59 35W
Sargodha Pakistan **91** C6 32 01N 72 40E
Sarh Chad **102** I9 9 08N 18 22E
Sarir Calanscio d. Libya **102** J13 26 00N 22 00E
Sark i. British Isles **74** I1 49 26N 2 22W
Sarmiento Argentina **71** D3 45 38S 69 08W
Sartrou-ville France **79** A2 48 56N 2 11E
Sary Ishikotrau d. Kazakhstan **87** M3/4 45 00N 77 00E
Sarysu r. Kazakhstan **87** K4 47 00N 67 30E
Sasebo Japan **96** A1 33 10N 129 42E
Sassandra Côte d'Ivoire **102** D5 58N 6 08W
Sassandra r. Côte d'Ivoire **102** D9 5 50N 6 55W
Sassari Italy **72** G4 40 43N 8 34E
Satlayev (Nikol'skiy) Kazakhstan **87** K4 47 54N 67 25E
Satna India **91** E4 24 33N 80 50E
Satpura Range mts. India **91** C4/D4 21 40N 75 00E
Sattahip Thailand **95** C6 12 36N 100 56E
SAUDI ARABIA **88** F3
Sault Ste. Marie Michigan U.S.A. **42** B7 46 29N 84 22W
Saurimo Angola **103** J6 9 39S 20 24E
Sava r. Europe **72** J5 45 00N 16 00E
Savannah Georgia U.S.A. **65** J3 32 04N 81 07W
Savannah r. U.S.A. **65** J3 33 00N 82 00W
Savannakhet Laos **95** C7 16 34N 104 45E
Savanna la Mar Jamaica **69** P8 18 13N 78 08W
Sawahlunto Indonesia **95** C3 0 41S 100 52E
Sawankhalok Thailand **93** J2 17 19N 99 50E
Sawu Sea Indonesia **95** G2 9 00S 122 00E
Sayano-Shushenskoya Vodokhranilicheo res.
Russian Federation **85** P5 52 00N 92 00E
Sayanogorsk Russian Federation **85** L6 53 00N 91 26E
Saylac Somalia **102** N9 11 21N 43 30E
Saynshand Mongolia **93** M7 44 58N 111 10E
Sayram Hu r. China **87** N3 44 45N 80 30E
Sayre Pennsylvania U.S.A. **66** B4 41 58N 76 03W
Say'ün Yemen Republic **89** G2 15 59N 48 44E
Scafell Pike mt. United Kingdom **74** H6 54 27N 3 14W
Scandinavia geog. reg. Europe **72** H8/J9 64 00N 15 00E
Scarborough United Kingdom **74** K6 54 17N 0 24W
Sceaux France **79** B2 48 46N 218E
Scheldt Estuary Europe **72** F6 51 30N 3 30E
Schenectady New York U.S.A. **65** L5 42 48N 73 57W
Schildow Germany **79** F2 52 40N 13 21E
Schöneberg Germany **79** F2 52 29N 13 21E
Schöneiche Germany **79** G1 52 28N 13 43E
Schönwalde Frankfurt Germany **79** F2 52 43N 13 26E
Schönwalde Potsdam Germany **79** E2 52 41N 13 27E
Schulzendorf Germany **79** G1 52 20N 13 34E
Schurz California U.S.A. **67** C4 38 57N 118 48W
Schuyikili River Pennsylvania U.S.A. **66** B3 40 40N 76 00W
Schwäbische Alb mts. Germany **72** G5 48 00N 9 00E
Schwanebeck Germany **79** F2 52 40N 13 27E
Schwielowsee l. Germany **79** D1 52 19N 13 58E
Scilly, Isles of United Kingdom **74** E1 49 56N 6 20W
Scoresbysund tn. see Illoqqortoormiut

Scotia Ridge Atlantic Ocean **109** C1 53 00S 50 00W
Scotland admin. United Kingdom **74** F8 56 00N 4 00W
Scott Base r.s. Antarctica **113** 77 51S 166 45E
Scott Island Southern Ocean **110** H1 66 35S 180 00
Scottsbluff Nebraska U.S.A. **64** F5 41 52N 103 40W
Scottys Junction California U.S.A. **67** D3 37 21N 117 08W
Scranton Pennsylvania U.S.A. **65** K5 41 25N 75 40W
Scunthorpe United Kingdom **74** K5 53 35N 0 39W
Sealdah India **90** K2 22 32N 88 22E
Searles Lake California U.S.A. **67** D2 35 42N 117 17W
Seattle Washington U.S.A. **64** B6 47 35N 122 20W
Sebewaing Michigan U.S.A. **42** C4 43 44N 83 26W
Seboomcook Lake Maine U.S.A. **43** S6 45 55N 69 50W
Sedalia Missouri U.S.A. **65** H4 38 42N 93 15W
Seddinsee l. Germany **79** G1 52 23N 13 42E
Ségou Mali **102** D10 13 28N 6 18W
Seine r. France **72** F5 48 00N 4 30E
Seine-et-Marne admin. France **79** C1 48 44N 2 38E
Seine-St-Denis admin. France **79** C2 48 55N 2 35E
Sekondi Takoradi Ghana **102** E9 4 59N 1 43W
Selat Melaka see Malacca, Strait of
Selat Sunda sd. Indonesia **95** D2 5 50S 105 30E
Seldovia Alaska U.S.A. **8** E4 59 29N 151 40W
Selemdzha r. Russian Federation **85** P6 53 00N 132 00E
Selenge r. Mongolia **93** K8 49 00N 102 00E
Selety r. Kazakhstan **87** L5 52 50N 73 00E
Selima Oasis Sudan **102** K12 21 22N 29 19E
Selma Alabama U.S.A. **65** I3 32 24N 87 01W
Selsingrove Pennsylvania U.S.A. **66** B3 40 48N 76 53W
Semarang Indonesia **95** E2 6 58S 110 29E
Semenovskoye Russian Federation **86** M1 55 39N 37 32E
Seminoe Reservoir Wyoming U.S.A. **64** E5 42 00N 106 00W
Seminole Oklahoma U.S.A. **65** G4 35 15N 96 40W
Semiozernoye Kazakhstan **87** J5 52 22N 64 06E
Semipalatinsk Kazakhstan **87** N5 50 26N 80 16E
Semnān Iran **89** H6 35 30N 53 25E
Senart-Ville-Nouvelle France **79** C1 48 36N 2 35E
Sendai Honshu Japan **96** D2 38 16N 140 52E
Sendai Kyūshū Japan **96** B1 31 50N 130 17E
SENEGAL 102 C10
Sénégal r. Senegal/Mauritania **102** B11 16 45N 14 45W
Senhor do Bonfim Brazil **70** I10 10 28S 40 11W
Sennar Sudan **102** L10 13 31N 33 38E
Sennar Dam Sudan **88** D1 13 20N 33 45E
Senyavin Islands Pacific Ocean **110** G8 7 00N 161 30E
Seoul see Soŭl
Sepik r. Papua New Guinea **106** G9 4 15S 143 00E
Sequoia National Park California U.S.A. **67** C3
   36 23N 118 38W
Seram (Ceram) i. Indonesia **95** H3 3 30S 129 30E
Seram Sea Indonesia **95** H3 2 30S 130 00E
Serang Indonesia **95** D2 6 07S 106 09E
Serbia admin. Yugoslavia **72** K4 44 50N 21 00E
Serdan Mexico **68** C5 28 40N 105 57W
Seremban Malaysia **95** C4 2 43N 102 57E
Serengeti National Park Tanzania **102** L7 2 30S 35 00E
Sergino Russian Federation **85** I8 62 30N 65 40E
Sergipe admin. Brazil **70** J10 11 00S 38 00W
Sergiyev Posad (Zagorsk) Russian Federation **84** F7
   56 20N 38 10E
Seria Brunei Darussalam **95** E4 4 39N 114 23E
Serian Malaysia **95** F4 1 10N 110 35E
Serov Russian Federation **84** I7 59 42N 60 32E
Serpukhov Russian Federation **86** D5 54 53N 37 25E
Serra Brazil **71** I9 20 06S 40 16W
Serra do Mar mts. Brazil **71** H7 27 30S 49 00W
Serra do Navio Brazil **70** G13 1 00N 52 05W
Serra Grande mts. Brazil **71** Q2 22 55S 43 02W
Serra Tumucumaque mts. Brazil **70** F13/G13
   2 00N 55 00W
Setagaya Japan **97** B3 35 37N 139 38E
Sete Lagoas Brazil **70** I9 19 29S 44 15W
Sete Pontes Brazil **71** Q2 22 51S 43 04W
Sétif Algeria **102** G15 36 11N 5 24E
Setit r. Sudan **102** M10 14 20N 36 15E
Seto-Naikai sd. Japan **96** B1 34 00N 132 30E
Settat Morocco **102** D14 33 04N 7 37W
Sevastopol' Ukraine **86** C3 44 36N 33 31E
Sevenoaks United Kingdom **78** D2 51 16N 0 12E
Severn r. United Kingdom **74** I4 52 30N 2 30W
Severna Park tn. Maryland U.S.A. **66** B2 39 00N 76 00W
Severnaya (North) Donets r. Asia **84** F5 49 00N 37 00E
Severnaya (North) Dvina r. Russian Federation **84** G8
   63 00N 43 00E
Severnaya Sos'va r. Russian Federation **84** I8
   62 30N 62 00E
Severnaya Zemlya (North Land) is. Russian Federation
   85 L12 80 00N 95 00E
Severodvinsk Russian Federation **84** F8 64 35N 39 50E
Severoural'sk Russian Federation **87** J7 60 10N 59 56E
Sevier r. Utah U.S.A. **64** D4 39 00N 113 00W
Sevilla (Seville) Spain **72** D3 37 24N 5 59W
Sèvres France **79** A2 48 49N 2 13E
Seward Alaska U.S.A. **8** F5 60 05N 149 34W
Seward Peninsula Alaska U.S.A. **8** B6/C6
   65 20N 165 00W
SEYCHELLES 108 E6
Seychelles Ridge Indian Ocean **108** E6/F5
Seym r. Russian Federation **86** C5 51 00N 34 00E
Seymchan Russian Federation **85** R8 62 54N 152 26E
Sfax Tunisia **102** H14 34 45N 10 43E
Sha Chau i. Hong Kong China **92** A2 22 21N 113 53E
Shache China **93** D4 38 27N 77 16E
Shackleton Ice Shelf Antarctica **113** 66 00S 100 00E
Shackleton Range Antarctica **113** 81 00S 20 00W
Shah Alam Malaysia **95** C4 3 02N 101 31E
Shahdara India **108** M4 28 40N 77 17E
Shahdol India **91** E4 23 19N 81 26E

Shahjahanpur India **91** D5 27 53N 79 55E
Shakhty Russian Federation **86** E4 47 43N 40 16E
Shaki Nigeria **102** F9 8 39N 3 25E
Sha Lo Wan Hong Kong China **92** A1 22 17N 113 54E
Sham Chung Hong Kong China **92** C2 22 26N 114 17E
Sham Chun River Hong Kong China **92** B3
   22 30N 114 00E
Shamokin Pennsylvania U.S.A. **66** B3 40 45N 76 34W
Sham Shek Tsuen Hong Kong China **92** A1
   22 17N 113 53E
Sham Shui Po Hong Kong China **92** B1 22 20N 114 09E
Sham Tseng Hong Kong China **92** B2 22 22N 114 03E
Shanghai China **93** O5 31 06N 121 22E
Shangqui China **93** N5 34 27N 115 07E
Shangrao China **93** N4 28 28N 117 54E
Shantou China **93** N3 23 23N 116 39E
Shanyao China **94** E8 25 07N 118 44E
Shaoguan China **93** M3 24 54N 113 33E
Shaoxing China **93** O8 30 02N 120 35E
Shaoyang China **93** M4 27 10N 111 25E
Shaqrā' Saudi Arabia **89** G4 25 18N 45 15E
Sharon Pennsylvania U.S.A. **65** J5 41 46N 80 30W
Sharp Island Hong Kong China **92** C2 22 22N 114 17E
Sharp Peak Hong Kong China **92** D2 22 26N 114 22E
Shashi China **93** M5 30 16N 112 20E
Shasta Lake California U.S.A. **64** B5 40 45N 122 20W
Shasta, Mount California U.S.A. **64** B5 41 25N 122 12W
Sha Tau Kok Hong Kong China **92** C3 22 33N 114 13E
Sha Tin Hong Kong China **92** C2 22 22N 114 10E
Shatsky Rise Pacific Ocean **110** G11 34 00N 160 00E
Shau Kei Wan Hong Kong China **92** C1 22 16N 114 13E
Shebelé r. Ethiopia/Somalia **102** N9 6 00N 44 00E
Sheberghān Afghanistan **89** K6 36 41N 65 45E
Sheboygan Wisconsin U.S.A. **65** I5 43 46N 87 44W
Sheenjek River r. Alaska U.S.A. **50** C4 67 30N 144 30W
Sheffield United Kingdom **74** J5 53 23N 1 30W
Shek Kip Mei Hong Kong China **92** C2 22 20N 114 10E
Shek Kong Hong Kong China **92** B2 22 26N 114 06E
Shek Kwu Chau i. Hong Kong China **92** A1
   22 12N 113 59E
Shek O Hong Kong China **92** C1 22 14N 114 15E
Shek Pik Hong Kong China **92** A1 22 13N 113 53E
Shek Pik Reservoir Hong Kong China **92** A1
   22 14N 113 54E
Shek Uk Shan mt. Hong Kong China **92** C2
   22 26N 114 18E
Shek Wu Hui Hong Kong China **92** B3 22 30N 114 07E
Shelby Montana U.S.A. **64** D6 48 30N 111 52W
Shelekhov Bay Russian Federation **85** R8
   60 00N 157 00E
Shelikof Strait sd. Alaska U.S.A. **8** D4/E4
   57 30N 155 00W
Shelter Island Hong Kong China **92** C1 22 19N 114 19E
Shenandoah Iowa U.S.A. **65** G5 40 48N 95 22W
Shenandoah Pennsylvania U.S.A. **66** B3 40 49N 76 11W
Shenyang China **93** O7 41 50N 123 26E
Shenzhen China **93** M3 22 31N 114 08E
Shenzhen Special Economic Zone China **92** B3
   22 35N 114 05E
Sheoraphuli India **90** K3 22 46N 88 20E
Sheridan Wyoming U.S.A. **64** E5 44 48N 106 57W
Shetland Islands u.a. United Kingdom **74** J12
   60 00N 1 15W
Sheung Shui Hong Kong China **92** B3 22 31N 114 07E
Shevchenko see Aktau
Shiawassee River Michigan U.S.A. **42** B4 43 05N 84 12W
Shibuya Japan **97** B3 35 39N 139 42E
Shickshinny Pennsylvania U.S.A. **66** B4 41 30N 76 00W
Shiderty r. Kazakhstan **87** L5 51 30N 74 30E
Shihezi China **92** G7 44 19N 86 10E
Shijiazhuang China **93** M6 38 04N 114 28E
Shikarpor Pakistan **90** B5 27 58N 68 42E
Shikoku i. Japan **96** B1 33 40N 134 00E
Shikotan i. Japan **96** E3 43 47N 148 45E
Shiliguri India **91** F5 26 42N 88 30E
Shilka r. Russian Federation **85** N6 52 30N 117 30E
Shillong India **91** G5 25 34N 91 53E
Shiloh New Jersey U.S.A. **66** C2 39 28N 75 18W
Shimizu Japan **96** C2 35 01N 138 29E
Shimoga India **91** D2 13 56N 75 31E
Shimonoseki Japan **96** B1 33 59N 130 58E
Shinagawa Japan **97** B3 35 37N 139 44E
Shinagawa Bay b. Japan **97** C3 35 56N 139 50E
Shinano r. Japan **96** C2 37 40N 138 00E
Shindand Afghanistan **89** J5 33 16N 62 05E
Shingū Japan **96** C1 33 42N 136 00E
Shinjō Japan **96** D2 38 45N 140 18E
Shinjuku Japan **97** B3 35 41N 139 42E
Shinyanga Tanzania **103** L7 3 40S 33 25E
Shiono-misaki c. Japan **96** C1 33 28N 135 47E
Shipki Pass India **91** D6 31 50N 78 50E
Shirakawa Japan **96** D2 37 07N 140 11E
Shiraoi Japan **96** D3 42 34N 141 19E
Shīrāz Iran **89** H4 29 38N 52 34E
Shiretoko-misaki c. Japan **96** E3 44 24N 145 20E
Shishmaref Alaska U.S.A. **8** B6 66 15N 166 11W
Shivaji Park tn. India **108** L4 28 40N 77 07E
Shizuishan China **93** L6 39 04N 106 22E
Shizuoka Japan **96** C1 34 59N 138 24E
Shkodër Albania **72** J4 42 03N 19 01E
Shoshone California U.S.A. **67** D2 35 58N 116 17W
Shreveport Louisiana U.S.A. **65** H3 32 30N 93 46W
Shrewsbury United Kingdom **74** I4 52 43N 2 45W
Shrirampur India **90** K3 22 45N 88 21E
Shuangliao China **93** O7 43 30N 123 29E
Shuangyashan China **93** Q8 46 42N 131 20E
Shuen Wan Hong Kong China **92** C2 22 28N 114 12E

Shumagin Islands is. Alaska U.S.A. **8** D4
   55 00N 159 00W
Shumen Bulgaria **86** B3 43 17N 26 55E
Shunde China **93** M3 22 50N 113 16E
Shuqrah Yemen Republic **89** G1 13 23N 45 44E
Shwebo Myanmar **91** H4 22 35N 95 42E
Shyamnagar India **90** K3 22 50N 88 24E
Shymkent (Chimkent) Kazakhstan **87** K3 42 16N 69 05E
Sialkot Pakistan **91** C6 32 29N 74 35E
Sibi Pakistan **90** B5 29 31N 67 54E
Sibiti Congo **103** H7 3 40S 13 24E
Sibolga Indonesia **95** B4 1 42N 98 48E
Sibpur India **90** K2 22 34N 88 19E
Sibu Malaysia **95** F4 2 19N 111 50E
Sibut Central African Republic **102** I9 5 46N 19 06E
Sichuan Pendi (Sichuan Basin) China **93** K5/L5
   32 00N 107 00E
Sicily i. Italy **72** H3 37 00N 14 00E
Sicuani Peru **70** C10 14 21S 71 13W
Sidcup United Kingdom **78** D2 51 26N 0 07E
Sidi Barrani Egypt **102** K14 31 38N 25 58E
Sidi Bel Abbès Algeria **102** E15 35 15N 0 39W
Sidi Ifni Morocco **102** C13 29 24N 10 12W
Sidlaw Hills United Kingdom **74** H8 56 30N 3 10W
Sidney New York U.S.A. **66** C5 42 19N 75 24W
Sidney Lanier, Lake Georgia U.S.A. **65** J3
   34 00N 84 00W
Sidon see Saïda
Siemensstadt Germany **79** F2 52 33N 13 14E
Sierra Blanca tn. Texas U.S.A. **64** E3 31 10N 105 22W
Sierra de Maracaju mts. Brazil **70** F8/G9 20 00S 55 00W
Sierra de Perija mts. Colombia/
   Venezuela **69** J1 10 00N 73 00W
SIERRA LEONE 102 C9
Sierra Madre mts. Mexico **64** E2 26 00N 108 00W
Sierra Madre del Sur mts. Mexico **68** D3/E3
   17 30N 100 00W
Sierra Madre Occidental mts. Mexico **68** C5/D4
   26 00N 107 00W
Sierra Madre Oriental mts. Mexico **68** D5/E4
   23 30N 100 00W
Sierra Nevada mts. U.S.A. **64** C4 37 00N 119 00W
Sierras de Córdoba mts. Argentina **71** D6/E6
   32 30S 65 00W
Sierraville California U.S.A. **67** B4 39 37N 120 21W
Signy r.s. South Orkney Islands **113** 60 43S 45 36W
Siguiri Guinea **102** D10 11 28N 9 07W
Sikar India **91** D5 27 33N 75 12E
Sikasso Mali **102** D10 11 18N 5 38W
Sikhote-Alin' mts. Russian Federation **85** P5
   45 00N 137 00E
Sikkim admin. India **91** F5 27 30N 88 30E
Silchar India **91** G4 24 49N 92 47E
Silifke Turkey **88** D6 36 22N 33 57E
Siling Co l. China **91** F6 31 45N 88 50E
Silver City New Mexico U.S.A. **64** E3 32 47N 108 16W
Silver Creek tn. New York U.S.A. **42** G3 42 32N 79 10W
Silver Peak Range mts. California U.S.A. **67** D3
   37 30N 117 45W
Silver Spring tn. Maryland U.S.A. **66** A1 39 00N 77 01W
Silver Springs California U.S.A. **67** C4 39 25N 119 14W
Simanggang Malaysia **95** E4 1 10N 111 32E
Simferopol' Ukraine **86** C3 44 57N 34 05E
Simi Valley California U.S.A. **67** C2 34 16N 118 47W
Simla India **91** D6 31 07N 77 09E
Simpson Desert Australia **106** F4/5 24 30S 137 30E
Sinai p. Egypt **102** L13 29 15N 34 00E
Sinai, Mount see Gebel Mûsa
Sinaloa admin. Mexico **64** E2 25 30N 109 00W
Sincelejo Colombia **70** B14 9 17N 75 23W
Sind geog. reg. Pakistan **90** B5 26 20N 68 40E
SINGAPORE 95 C4
Singaraja Indonesia **95** F2 8 06S 115 04E
Singatoko Fiji **110** T15 18 10S 177 30E
Sing Buri Thailand **93** K1 14 56N 100 21E
Singkiang Ughur Autonomous Region
   see Xinjiang Uygur Zizhiqu
Sinŭiju North Korea **93** O7 40 04N 124 25E
Sioux City Iowa U.S.A. **65** G5 42 30N 96 28W
Sioux Falls tn. South Dakota U.S.A. **65** G5 43 34N 96 42W
Siparia Trinidad and Tobago **69** S9 10 08N 61 31W
Siping China **93** O7 43 15N 124 25E
Siple, Mount Antarctica **113** 73 25S 122 50W
Siret r. Romania **86** B4 47 00N 26 00E
Sirretta Peak mt. California U.S.A. **67** C2 35 56N 118 20W
Sirte see Surt
Sirte Desert Libya **102** I14 30 00N 16 00E
Sirte, Gulf of Libya **102** I14 31 00N 17 00E
Sisimiut (Holsteinsborg) Greenland **9** AA6 66 55N 53 30W
Sisophon Cambodia **95** C6 13 37N 102 58E
Sisquoc r. California U.S.A. **67** B2 34 50N 120 05W
Sitka Alaska U.S.A. **8** J4 57 05N 135 20W
Sitka Sound U.S.A. **8** J4 57 05N 135 50W
Sittwe (Akyab) Myanmar **91** G4 20 09N 92 55E
Sivas Turkey **73** N3 39 44N 37 01E
Siwa Egypt **102** K13 29 11N 25 31E
Sjaelland i. Denmark **72** H5 55 15N 11 30E
Skagit River r. Washington U.S.A. **34** H4 48 40N 121 15W
Skagway Alaska U.S.A. **50** D2 59 23N 135 20W
Skåne geog. reg. Sweden **72** H7 56 00N 14 00E
Skegness United Kingdom **74** L5 53 10N 0 21E
Skellefteälven r. Sweden **72** J8 65 00N 19 00E
Skerriegard geog. reg. Norway **72** G8/F8 62 00N 5 00E
Skidka Algeria **102** G15 36 53N 6 54E
Skopje FYROM **72** K4 42 00N 21 28E
Skovorodino Russian Federation **85** O6 54 00N 123 53E
Skowhegan Maine U.S.A. **43** S5 44 46N 69 44W

Skye i. United Kingdom **74** E9 57 20N 6 15W
Slaney r. Republic of Ireland **74** E4 52 30N 6 35W
Slessor Glacier Antarctica **113** 79 00S 22 00W
Slieve Donard mt. United Kingdom **74** E6 54 11N 5 55W
Sligo Republic of Ireland **74** C6 54 17N 8 28W
Slough United Kingdom **74** K3 51 31N 0 36W
SLOVAKIA 72 J5
SLOVENIA 72 H5
Slov''yans'k Ukraine **86** D4 48 51N 37 36E
Sluch' r. Ukraine **86** B5 51 00N 27 00E
Slyne Head c. Republic of Ireland **74** A5 53 25N 10 10W
Smoky Hills Kansas U.S.A. **64** G4 39 00N 100 00W
Smolensk Russian Federation **84** F6 54 49N 32 04E
Smyrna Delaware U.S.A. **66** C2 39 18N 75 37W
Snaefell mt. British Isles **74** G6 54 16N 4 28E
Snake r. U.S.A. **64** C5 44 00N 118 00W
Snake River Plain U.S.A. **64** D5 43 00N 114 00W
Snowdon mt. United Kingdom **74** G5 53 04N 4 05W
Snowy Mountains Australia **106** H2 36 50S 147 00E
Snyder Texas U.S.A. **64** F3 32 43N 100 54W
Soar r. United Kingdom **74** J4 52 40N 1 20W
Soa-Siu Indonesia **95** H4 0 40N 127 30E
Sobat r. Sudan **102** L9 8 00N 33 00E
Sobral Brazil **70** I12 3 45S 40 20W
Sochi Russian Federation **84** F4 43 35N 39 46E
Society Islands Pacific Ocean **111** K6 16 30S 153 00W
Socotra i. Yemen Republic **89** H1 12 05N 54 10E
Soda Lake California U.S.A. **67** D2 35 09N 116 04W
Soda Springs California U.S.A. **67** B4 3919N 120 23W
Sodo Ethiopia **102** M9 6 49N 37 41E
Sofiya (Sofia) Bulgaria **72** K4 42 40N 23 18E
Sogamoso Colombia **70** C14 5 43N 72 56W
Sohâg Egypt **102** L13 26 33N 31 42E
Sokhumi Georgia **73** P4 43 01N 41 01E
Sok Kwu Wan Hong Kong China **92** B1 22 13N 114 08E
Sokodé Togo **102** F9 8 59N 1 11E
Soko Islands Hong Kong China **92** A1 22 10N 113 54E
Sokolniki Park Russian Federation **86** M2 55 50N 37 40E
Sokoto Nigeria **102** G10 13 02N 5 15E
So Kwun Wat Hong Kong China **92** B2 22 23N 114 00E
Solāpur India **91** D3 17 43N 75 56E
Solander, Cape Australia **107** G14 34 01S 151 14E
Soledad California U.S.A. **67** B3 36 25N 121 20W
Solihull United Kingdom **74** J4 52 25N 1 45W
Solikamsk Russian Federation **84** H7 59 40N 56 45E
Sol'-Iletsk Russian Federation **87** G5 51 09N 55 00E
Solntsevo Russian Federation **86** L1 55 36N 37 25E
SOLOMON ISLANDS 106 J8
Solomon Sea Papua New Guinea **106** I8 7 00S 150 00E
Solway Firth est. United Kingdom **74** H6 54 40N 3 40W
SOMALIA 102 O8/9
Somali Basin Indian Ocean **108** E7 5 00N 55 00E
Sombrerete Mexico **68** D4 23 38N 103 40W
Somoto Nicaragua **69** G2 13 29N 86 36W
Son r. India **91** E4 24 00N 81 00E
Sonārpur India **90** K2 22 26N 88 26E
Songea Tanzania **103** M5 10 42S 35 59E
Songhua Jiang r. China **93** P8 46 00N 128 00E
Songkhla Thailand **95** C5 7 12N 100 35E
Song-koi (Hong, Merah, Yuan Jiang) r. China/Vietnam
   93 K3 22 00N 104 00E
Sonoita Mexico **64** D3 31 53N 112 52W
Sonora California U.S.A. **67** B4 38 00N 120 21W
Sonora admin. Mexico **64** D2 29 00N 110 00W
Sonora r. Mexico **64** D3 30 00N 110 00W
Sonoyta Mexico **68** B6 31 53N 112 52W
Sonsonate El Salvador **68** G2 13 43N 89 44W
Sorocaba Brazil **71** H8 23 30S 47 32W
Sorong Indonesia **95** I3 0 50S 131 17E
Soroti Uganda **102** L8 1 42N 33 37E
Soŭl (Seoul) South Korea **93** P6 37 32N 127 00E
Soûr (Tyre) Lebanon **88** O11 33 16N 35 12E
Sousse Tunisia **102** H15 35 50N 10 38E
South African National Expedition see SANAE
Southall United Kingdom **78** B3 51 31N 0 23W
Southampton United Kingdom **74** J2 50 55N 1 25W
South Andaman i. Andaman Islands **91** G2
   11 30N 93 00E
South Atlantic Ocean Atlantic Ocean **109** G5
South Australia state Australia **106** E3/F4
   27 00S 135 00E
South Australian Basin Indian Ocean **108** L3
   38 00S 125 00E
South Bend Indiana U.S.A. **65** I5 41 40N 86 15W
South Carolina state U.S.A. **65** J3 34 00N 81 00W
South Cape see Kalae
South China Sea Pacific Ocean **95** E6/F7
   15 00N 110 00E
South Colton New York U.S.A. **43** M5 44 31N 74 54W
South Dakota state U.S.A. **64** F5 45 00N 102 00W
South Downs hills United Kingdom **74** K2 50 50N 0 30W
South East Cape Australia **106** H1 43 38S 146 48E
Southeast Indian Basin Indian Ocean **108** J3
   32 00S 108 00E
Southeast Indian Ridge Indian Ocean **108** H2/J2
Southend-on-Sea United Kingdom **74** L3 51 33N 0 43E
Southern Alps mts. South Island New Zealand
   107 A2/B2 43 07S 171 13E
Southern Honshu Ridge Pacific Ocean **110** E10
   25 50N 142 30E
Southern Uplands mts. United Kingdom **74** G7/I7
   2 30W 55 00N
South East Pacific Basin Pacific Ocean **111** Q2/Q3
   53 00S 95 00W
South Esk r. United Kingdom **74** I8 56 40N 2 55W
South Fiji Basin Pacific Ocean **110** H5 25 00S 176 50E
South Fork American r. California U.S.A. **67** B4
   38 48N 120 40W

South Georgia *i.* South Atlantic Ocean **109** E1
54 00S 36 30W
South Head Australia **107** H2 33 50S 151 17E
South Indian Basin Indian Ocean **108** L3 55 00S 130 00E
South Island New Zealand **107** A1/B2 42 30S 172 00E
SOUTH KOREA **93** P6
South Loup *r.* Nebraska U.S.A. **64** G5 42 00N 99 00W
South Magnetic Pole **113**
South Negril Point *c.* Jamaica **69** P8 18 16N 78 22W
South Ockendon United Kingdom **78** E3 51 32N 0 18E
South Platte *r.* U.S.A. **64** F5 41 00N 103 00W
South Point Barbados **69** V12 13 02N 59 32W
South Pole Antarctica **113** 90 00S
Southport United Kingdom **74** H5 53 39N 3 01W
South Sandwich Trench Atlantic Ocean **109** E1/F1
55 00S 30 00W
South Shetland Islands Southern Ocean **71** E0
62 00S 60 00W
South Sioux City Nebraska U.S.A. **65** G5 42 28N 96 24W
South Suburbs (Behala) India **90** K1 22 28N 88 18E
South Uist *i.* United Kingdom **74** D9 57 20N 7 15W
Southwark United Kingdom **78** C3 51 30N 0 06W
Southwest Cape New Zealand **107** A1 48 00S 168 00E
Southwest Indian Ridge Indian Ocean **108** D2/E3
40 00S 50 00E
South West Pacific Basin Pacific Ocean **111** K4
35 00S 155 00W
Sovetsk Russian Federation **86** A6 55 02N 21 50E
Sovetskaya Gavan' Russian Federation **85** Q5
48 57N 140 16E
Sozh *r.* Belarus **86** C5 53 30N 31 00E
SPAIN **72** E3
Spandau Germany **79** E2 52 32N 13 13E
Spanish Town Jamaica **69** R7 17 59N 79 58W
Sparks California U.S.A. **67** C4 39 34N 119 46W
Sparks Nevada U.S.A. **64** C4 39 34N 119 46W
Spartanburg South Carolina U.S.A. **65** J3
34 56N 81 57W
Spassk-Dal'niy Russian Federation **85** P4
44 37N 132 37E
Spasskoye Kazakhstan **87** K5 52 07N 68 32E
Speightstown Barbados **69** V12 13 15N 59 39W
Spencer Iowa U.S.A. **65** G5 43 08N 95 08W
Spencer Gulf Australia **106** F3 34 00S 137 00E
Spey *r.* United Kingdom **74** H9 57 00N 4 30W
Spitsbergen *i.* Arctic Ocean **84** D11 79 00N 15 00E
Split Croatia **72** J4 43 31N 16 28E
Spokane Washington U.S.A. **64** C6 47 40N 117 25W
Spratly Islands South China Sea **95** E5/F5 8 45N 111 54E
Spree *r.* Germany **79** G1 52 27N 13 32E
Springbok Republic of South Africa **103** I2 29 44S 17 56E
Springdale California U.S.A. **67** D3 37 02N 116 46W
Springdale Illinois U.S.A. **65** I4 39 49N 89 39W
Springfield Massachusetts U.S.A. **65** L5 42 07N 72 35W
Springfield Missouri U.S.A. **68** F7 37 11N 93 19W
Springfield Ohio U.S.A. **65** J4 39 55N 83 48W
Springfield Oregon U.S.A. **64** B5 44 03N 123 01W
Springsure Australia **106** H5 24 09S 148 04E
Sprint Mountains California U.S.A. **67** E3
36 22N 115 52W
Spurn Head *c.* United Kingdom **74** L5 53 36N 0 07E
Sredinnyy Range *mts.* Russian Federation **85** R7
57 00N 158 00E
Srednekolymsk Russian Federation **85** R9
67 27N 153 35E
Sretensk Russian Federation **85** N6 52 15N 117 52E
Srikakulam India **91** E3 18 19N 84 00E
SRI LANKA **91** E1
Srinagar Kashmir **91** C6 34 08N 74 50E
Staaken Germany **79** E2 52 32N 13 06E
Stafford United Kingdom **74** I4 52 48N 2 07W
Stahnsdorf Germany **79** E1/F1 52 23N 13 13E
Staines United Kingdom **78** B2 51 26N 0 30W
Stakhanov Ukraine **86** D4 48 34N 38 40E
Standish Michigan U.S.A. **42** C4 43 59N 83 58W
Stanley Falkland Islands **71** F2 51 45S 57 56W
Stanley Hong Kong *see* Chek Chue
Stanovoy Range *mts.* Russian Federation **85** O7
56 00N 122 30E
Stara Zagora Bulgaria **72** L4 42 25N 25 37E
Start Point *c.* United Kingdom **74** H2 50 13N 3 38W
Staryy Oskol Russian Federation **84** F6 51 20N 37 50E
State College Pennsylvania U.S.A. **65** K5 40 48N 77 52W
Staten Island New York U.S.A. **66** Y1 40 35N 74 10W
Staunton Virginia U.S.A. **65** K4 38 10N 79 05W
Stavanger Norway **72** G7 58 58N 5 45E
Stavropol' Russian Federation **84** G5 45 03N 41 59E
Stebbins Alaska U.S.A. **8** C5 63 32N 162 20W
Steenstrup Glacier Greenland **9** Z8 75 00N 56 00W
Steep Island Hong Kong China **92** C1 22 16N 114 18E
Steglitz Germany **79** F1 52 27N 13 19E
Stephens Passage *sd.* Alaska U.S.A. **34** B3
58 00N 134 00W
Stepney United Kingdom **78** C3 51 31N 0 04W
Step' Shaidara *geog. reg.* Kazakhstan **87** K3
40 00N 65 00E
Sterling Colorado U.S.A. **64** F5 40 37N 103 13W
Sterlitamak Russian Federation **84** H6 53 40N 55 59E
Steubenville Ohio U.S.A. **65** J5 40 22N 80 39W
Stewart Island New Zealand **107** A1 46 55S 167 55E
Stillwater California U.S.A. **67** C4 39 31N 118 33W
Stillwater Reservoir New York U.S.A. **43** L4 43 55N 75 00W
Stirling United Kingdom **74** H8 56 07N 3 57W
Stockholm Sweden **72** J7 59 20N 18 05E
Stockport United Kingdom **74** I5 53 25N 2 10W
Stockton California U.S.A. **64** B4 37 59N 121 20W
Stockton-on-Tees United Kingdom **74** J6 54 34N 1 19W
Stoke-on-Trent United Kingdom **74** I5 53 00N 2 10W

Stokhod *r.* Ukraine **86** B5 51 30N 25 20E
Stonecutters Island Hong Kong China **92** B1
22 18N 114 08E
Stonyford California U.S.A. **67** A4 39 23N 122 34W
Stornoway United Kingdom **74** E10 58 12N 6 23W
Stour *r.* United Kingdom **74** L4 51 10N 1 10E
Stranraer United Kingdom **74** F6 54 55N 5 02W
Strasbourg France **72** G5 48 35N 7 45E
Strathfield Australia **107** G2 33 52S 151 06E
Streatham United Kingdom **78** C2 51 26N 0 07W
Strogino Russian Federation **86** L2 55 49N 37 46E
Stronsay *i.* United Kingdom **74** I11 59 07N 2 37W
Stroudsburg Pennsylvania U.S.A. **66** C4 41 00N 75 12W
Stuart Creek *r.* Australia **106** D6 19 00S 127 30E
Stuart Highway *rd.* Australia **106** E6 20 00S 135 00E
Stung Treng Cambodia **95** D6 13 31N 105 59E
Sturt Creek *r.* Australia **106** D6 19 00S 127 30E
Stuttgart Germany **72** G5 48 47N 9 12E
Suō-nada *b.* Japan **96** B1 33 50N 131 30E
Su-ao Taiwan **94** H7 24 33N 121 48E
Suakin Sudan **102** M11 19 08N 37 17E
Suck *r.* Republic of Ireland **74** C5 53 40N 8 30W
Sucre Bolivia **70** D9 19 05S 65 15W
Sucy-en-Brie France **72** C2 48 49N 231E
SUDAN **102** K10
Sudr Egypt **88** D4 29 40N 32 42E
Sue *r.* Sudan **102** K9 7 00N 28 00E
Suez (El Suweis) Egypt **88** D4 29 59N 32 33E
Suez Canal (Qanā el Suweis) Egypt **88** D5 31 30N 32 20E
Suez, Gulf of Egypt **88** D4 29 56N 32 32E
Sugar Island *i.* Michigan U.S.A. **42** B7 46 29N 84 11W
Sugar Notch Pennsylvania U.S.A. **66** C4 41 12N 75 55W
Sugarloaf *see* Pão de Açúcar
Sugarloaf Mountain *mt.* Maine U.S.A. **43** R6
45 02N 70 18W
Suginami Japan **97** B3 35 41N 139 40E
Sühbaatar Mongolia **93** L9 50 10N 106 14E
Suir *r.* Republic of Ireland **74** D4 52 15N 7 05W
Sukabumi Indonesia **95** D2 6 55S 106 50E
Sukhona *r.* Russian Federation **84** G8 60 00N 45 00E
Sukkertoppen *see* Maniitsoq
Sukkur Pakistan **90** B5 27 42N 68 54E
Sulaiman Range *mts.* Pakistan **90** B5/C6 30 00N 70 00E
Sulawesi *i.* Indonesia **95** F3/G3 2 00S 120 00E
Sulaymānīyah Iraq **89** G6 35 32N 45 27E
Sullana Peru **70** A12 4 52S 80 39W
Sultanpur India **91** E5 26 15N 82 04E
Sulu Archipelago The Philippines **95** G5 6 00N 121 00E
Sulu Sea The Philippines/Malaysia **95** F5/G5
8 00N 120 00E
Sumatera *i.* Indonesia **95** B4/C3 0 00 100 00E
Sumba *i.* Indonesia **95** F2 10 00S 120 00E
Sumbawa *i.* Indonesia **95** F2 8 00S 118 00E
Sumburgh Head *c.* United Kingdom **74** J12
59 51N 1 16W
Sumgait Azerbaijan **102** O16 40 35N 49 38E
Sumida Japan **97** C3 35 42N 139 49E
Summer Strait *sd.* Alaska U.S.A. **34** B3 56 30N 133 30W
Sumqayıt Azerbaijan **86** F3 40 35N 49 38E
Sumy Ukraine **86** C5 50 55N 34 49E
Sunbury Pennsylvania U.S.A. **66** B3 40 52N 76 47W
Sunbury United Kingdom **78** B2 51 24N 0 25W
Sunch'ŏn South Korea **93** P5 34 56N 127 28E
Sunderland United Kingdom **74** J6 54 55N 1 23W
Sundsvall Sweden **72** J8 62 22N 17 20E
Sung Kong *i.* Hong Kong China **92** C1 22 11N 114 17E
Sunnyvale California U.S.A. **67** A3 37 23N 122 01W
Sunset Peak Hong Kong China **92** A1 22 15N 113 57E
Sunshine Island Hong Kong China **92** B2 22 16N 114 03E
Suntar Russian Federation **85** N8 62 10N 117 35E
Sunti *r.* India **90** K3 22 46N 88 00E
Sunyani Ghana **102** E9 7 22N 2 18W
Superior Wisconsin U.S.A. **65** H6 46 42N 92 05W
Şūr Oman **89** I3 22 34N 59 32E
Sura *r.* Russian Federation **86** F6 55 00N 46 30E
Surabaya Indonesia **95** E2 7 14S 112 45E
Surakarta Indonesia **95** E2 7 32S 110 50E
Surat India **91** C4 21 10N 72 54E
Surat Thani Thailand **95** B5 9 09N 99 20E
Surendranagar India **91** C4 22 44N 71 43E
Surgut Russian Federation **85** J8 61 13N 73 20E
SURINAME **70** F13
Surt (Sirte) Libya **102** I14 31 13N 16 35E
Surui *r.* Brazil **71** Q3 22 40S 43 08W
Susitna *r.* Alaska U.S.A. **8** E5 62 10N 150 15W
Susquehanna River Pennsylvania U.S.A. **43** K2
41 45N 76 25W
Susuman Russian Federation **85** Q8 62 46N 148 08E
Sutherland Australia **107** G1 34 02S 151 03E
Sutlej *r.* Pakistan **91** C6 30 30N 73 00E
Sutton United Kingdom **78** C2 51 22N 0 12W
Suva Fiji **110** U15 18 08S 178 25E
Suzhou Anhui China **93** N5 33 38N 117 02E
Suzhou Jiangsu China **93** O5 31 21N 120 40E
Suzu-misaki *c.* Japan **96** C2 37 30N 137 21E
Suzuka Japan **96** C1 34 52N 136 37E
Svalbard (Spitsbergen) *i.* Arctic Ocean **112**
79 00N 15 00E
Sverdlovsk *see* Yekaterinburg
Svobodnyy Russian Federation **85** O6 51 24N 128 05E
Swale *r.* United Kingdom **74** J6 54 15N 1 30W
Swanley United Kingdom **78** D2 51 24N 0 12E
Swansea United Kingdom **74** H3 51 38N 3 57W
Swanton Ohio U.S.A. **42** C2 41 36N 83 54W
Swanton Vermont U.S.A. **43** N5 44 56N 73 08W
SWAZILAND **103** L2
SWEDEN **72** H7/K9
Swedesboro New Jersey U.S.A. **66** C2 39 45N 75 18W
Sweetwater Texas U.S.A. **64** F3 32 27N 100 25W

Swellendam Republic of South Africa **103** J1
34 01S 20 26E
Swindon United Kingdom **74** J3 51 34N 1 47W
SWITZERLAND **72** G5
Sydney Australia **106** I3 33 55S 151 10E
Syeverodonets'k Ukraine **86** D4 48 58N 38 29E
Syktyvkar Russian Federation **84** H8 61 42N 50 45E
Sylhet Bangladesh **91** G4 24 53N 91 51E
Syowa *r.s.* Antarctica **113** 69 00S 39 35E
Syracuse New York U.S.A. **65** K5 43 03N 76 10W
Syr-Dar'ya *r.* Asia **87** K3 42 00N 73 30E
SYRIA **102** M14
Syrian Desert Middle East **88** E5 32 30N 39 20E
Syzran' Russian Federation **84** G6 53 10N 48 29E
Szczecin Poland **72** H6 53 25N 14 32E
Szeged Hungary **72** K5 46 15N 20 09E

T
Tabaquite Trinidad and Tobago **69** T9 10 23N 61 18W
Tabas Iran **89** I5 33 37N 56 54E
Table Rock Lake Missouri U.S.A. **65** H4 36 38N 93 17W
Tabora Tanzania **103** L7 5 01S 32 48E
Tabriz Iran **89** G6 38 05N 46 18E
Tabuaeran Island Kiribati **111** K8 4 00N 158 10W
Tabūk Saudi Arabia **88** E4 28 33N 36 36E
Ta-chia Taiwan **94** G7 24 20N 120 34E
Tacloban The Philippines **95** G6 11 15N 125 01E
Tacna Peru **70** C9 18 00S 70 15W
Tacoma Washington U.S.A. **64** B6 47 16N 122 30W
Tadmur Syria **88** E5 34 40N 38 10E
Taegu South Korea **93** P6 35 52N 128 36E
Taejŏn South Korea **93** P6 36 20N 127 26E
Tafila Jordan **88** O10 30 52N 35 36E
Taganrog Russian Federation **84** F5 47 14N 38 55E
Tagus *r.* Spain **72** E3 39 45N 4 45W
Tahat, Mount Algeria **102** G12 23 18N 5 33E
Tahiti *i.* French Polynesia **111** L6 17 30S 148 30W
Tahoe, Lake U.S.A. **64** C4 39 00N 120 00W
Tahoua Niger **102** G10 14 57N 5 19E
Tahta Egypt **88** D4 26 47N 31 31E
Tai'an China **93** N6 36 15N 117 10E
T'ai-chung Taiwan **94** O3 24 09N 124 40E
Tai Lam Chung Hong Kong China **92** B2 22 22N 114 01E
Tai Lam Chung Reservoir Hong Kong China **92** B2
22 23N 114 01E
Tai Long Hong Kong China **92** D2 22 25N 114 22E
Tai Long Wan *b.* Hong Kong China **92** D2
22 20N 114 20E
Tai Mei Tuk Hong Kong China **92** C2 22 28N 114 14E
Tai Mong Tsai Hong Kong China **92** C2 22 23N 114 18E
Tai Mo Shan *mt.* Hong Kong China **92** B2
22 25N 114 07E
T'ai-nan Taiwan **94** O3 23 01N 120 14E
Tai O Hong Kong China **92** A1 22 15N 113 52E
T'ai-pei Taiwan **94** O4 25 05N 121 32E
Tai Po Hong Kong China **92** C2 22 27N 114 10E
Tai Shui Hang Hong Kong China **92** B1 22 17N 114 01E
Tai Tam Reservoir Hong Kong China **92** C1
22 15N 114 12E
Tai Tam Wan *b.* Hong Kong China **92** C1 22 13N 114 13E
Tai Tan Hong Kong China **92** C2 22 26N 114 19E
Taitō Japan **97** C3 35 43N 139 48E
T'ai-tung Taiwan **94** H5 22 43N 121 10E
Tai Wai Hong Kong China **92** C2 22 23N 114 10E
TAIWAN **94**
Taiwan Strait China/Taiwan **94** F7 24 00N 119 30E
Tai Wan Tau Hong Kong China **92** C1 22 17N 114 17E
Taiyuan China **93** M6 37 50N 112 30E
Ta'izz Yemen Republic **88** F1 13 35N 44 02E
TAJIKISTAN **87** K2/L2
Tak Thailand **95** B7 16 51N 99 08E
Takamatsu Japan **96** B2 34 20N 134 01E
Takaoka Japan **96** C2 36 47N 137 00E
Takapuna New Zealand **107** B3 36 48S 174 46E
Takasaki Japan **96** C2 36 20N 139 00E
Takatsu Japan **97** B3 35 35N 139 37E
Takayama Japan **96** C2 36 09N 137 16E
Takefu Japan **96** C2 35 54N 136 10E
Takeo Cambodia **95** C6 11 00N 104 46E
Taku Inlet Alaska U.S.A. **34** B3 58 30N 134 00W
Talara Peru **70** A12 4 38S 81 18W
Talbot, Cape Australia **106** D7 13 49S 126 42E
Talca Chile **71** C5 35 28S 71 40W
Talcahuano Chile **71** C5 36 40S 73 10W
Taldykorgan Kazakhstan **87** M4 45 02N 78 23E
Tallahassee Florida U.S.A. **65** J3 30 26N 84 16W
Tallinn Estonia **86** A6 59 22N 24 48E
Tall Kalakh Syria **88** P12 34 45N 36 17E
Tal'menka Russian Federation **87** N5 53 50N 83 36E
Talodi Sudan **102** L10 10 40N 30 25E
Talparo Trinidad and Tobago **69** T9 10 30N 61 16W
Taltal Chile **71** C7 25 26S 70 33W
Tama *r.* Japan **97** B3 35 44N 139 50E
Tamabo Range Malaysia **95** F4 4 00N 115 30E
Tamale Ghana **102** E9 9 26N 0 49W
Ta-ma-li Taiwan **94** H5 22 37N 121 00E
Tamana, Mount Trinidad and Tobago **69** T9
10 27N 61 14W
Tamanrasset Algeria **102** G12 22 50N 5 28E
Tamaqua Pennsylvania U.S.A. **66** C3 40 04N 75 58W
Tamar *r.* United Kingdom **74** G2 50 35N 4 15W
Tamazunchale Mexico **68** E4 21 18N 98 46W
Tambov Russian Federation **84** G6 52 44N 41 28E
Tamil Nadu *admin.* India **91** D2 12 00N 78 30E
Tampa Florida U.S.A. **65** J2 27 58N 82 38W
Tampere Finland **72** K8 61 32N 23 45E
Tampico Mexico **68** E4 22 18N 97 52W

Tamworth Australia **106** I3 31 07S 150 57E
Tana *r.* Kenya **102** M7 1 00S 39 50E
Tana, Lake Ethiopia **102** M10 12 20N 37 20E
Tanabe Japan **96** C1 33 43N 135 22E
Tanahmerah Indonesia **106** G8 6 08S 140 18E
Tanana Alaska U.S.A. **8** E6 65 11N 152 10W
Tanana *r.* Alaska U.S.A. **8** G5 63 00N 143 00W
Tananarive *see* Antananarivo
Tandil Argentina **71** F5 37 18S 59 10W
Tanezrouft *geog. reg.* Algeria **102** E12 24 00N 0 30W
Tanga Tanzania **103** M6 5 07S 39 05E
Tanganyika, Lake East Africa **103** L6 7 00S 30 00E
Tanger (Tangiers) Morocco **102** D15 35 48N 5 45W
Tanggula Shan *mts.* China **92** H5 32 30N 92 30E
Tangiers *see* Tanger
Tangra Yumco *l.* China **91** F6 31 00N 86 15E
Tangshan China **93** N6 39 37N 118 05E
Tanjungkarang-Telukbetung Indonesia **95** D2
5 28S 105 16E
Tan Kwai Tsuen Hong Kong China **92** A2
22 25N 113 59E
Tanna *i.* Vanuatu **106** L6 19 30S 169 00E
Tannu Ola *mts.* Russian Federation **85** L6
51 00N 92 30E
Tanout Niger **102** G10 15 05N 8 50E
Tan-shui Taiwan **94** H8 25 13N 121 29E
Tan-shui Ho *r.* Taiwan **94** H7 24 40N 121 20E
Tanta Egypt **88** D5 30 48N 31 00E
TANZANIA **103** L6
Taolānaro Madagascar **103** O2 25 01S 47 00E
T'ao-yüan Taiwan **94** H7 25 00N 121 15E
Tapachula Mexico **68** F2 14 54N 92 15W
Tāpi *r.* India **91** D4 21 30N 76 30E
Tappi-zaki *c.* Japan **96** D3 41 14N 140 21E
Tapti *r.* India **91** C4 21 30N 74 30E
Tapuaenuku *mt.* New Zealand **107** B2 42 00S 173 40E
Taquara Brazil **71** P2 22 55S 43 22W
Tara *r.* Russian Federation **87** M6 56 30N 77 00E
Tarābulus (Tripoli) Libya **102** H14 32 54N 13 11E
Tarakan Indonesia **95** F4 3 20N 117 38E
Taranaki, Mount *see* Egmont, Mount
Táranto Italy **72** J4 40 28N 17 15E
Taranto, Gulf of *g.* Italy **72** J3 40 00N 17 00E
Tarapoto Peru **70** B11 6 31S 76 23W
Tararua Range New Zealand **107** C2 40 44S 175 25E
Tarauacá Brazil **70** C11 8 06S 70 45W
Tarawa Kiribati **110** H8 1 30N 173 00E
Taree Australia **106** I3 31 54S 152 26E
Tarfaya Morocco **102** C13 27 58N 12 55W
Târgu Mureş Romania **72** K5 46 33N 24 34E
Tarija Bolivia **70** E8 21 33S 64 45W
Tarim He *r.* China **92** F7 41 00N 82 00E
Tarim Pendi (Tarim Basin) China **92** F6/G6
39 00N 84 00E
Tarko-Sale Russian Federation **85** J8 64 55N 77 50E
Tarkwa Ghana **102** E9 5 16N 1 59W
Taroko National Park Taiwan **94** H7 24 15N 121 30E
Taroom Australia **106** H4 25 39S 149 50E
Tarsus Turkey **88** D6 26 25N 34 52E
Tartary, Gulf of Russian Federation **85** Q5/6
50 00N 141 00E
Tartu Estonia **72** L7 58 20N 26 44E
Tartūs Syria **88** E5 34 55N 35 52E
Tashauz *see* Dashkhovuz
Tashkent Uzbekistan **87** K3 41 16N 69 13E
Tasiilaq (Ammassalik) Greenland **133** BB6
65 45N 37 45W
Tasman Basin Pacific Ocean **110** F3 46 00S 154 00E
Tasman Bay New Zealand **107** B2 41 00S 173 14E
Tasmania *state* Australia **106** H1 43 00S 147 00E
Tasman Mountains New Zealand **107** B2
41 01S 172 22E
Tasman Plateau Southern Ocean **110** E3
48 00S 147 00E
Tasman Sea Pacific Ocean **110** F4 40 00S 155 00E
Tassili N'Ajjer *mts.* Algeria **102** G13 26 00N 6 20E
Tatarsk Russian Federation **86** C5 54 15N 31 34E
Tatarsk Russian Federation **87** M6 55 14N 76 00E
Tateyama Japan **96** C1 34 59N 139 50E
Tatry Mountains Europe **72** J5 49 00N 20 00E
Tauern *mts.* Austria **72** H5 47 00N 14 00E
Taumarunui New Zealand **107** C3 38 53S 175 16E
Taung-gyi Myanmar **93** J4 20 55N 97 02E
Taunton United Kingdom **74** H3 51 01N 3 06W
Taupo New Zealand **107** C3 38 42S 176 05E
Taupo, Lake New Zealand **107** C3 38 55S 175 49E
Tauranga New Zealand **107** C3 37 41S 176 10E
Tauva Fiji **110** T16 17 31S 177 53E
Tavda *r.* Russian Federation **84** I7 58 00N 64 00E
Taveuni *i.* Fiji **110** U16/V16 16 40S 180 00
Tavoy Myanmar **95** B6 14 02N 98 12E
Taw *r.* United Kingdom **74** H2 50 58N 3 55W
Taymā' Saudi Arabia **88** E4 27 37N 38 30E
Taymyr Peninsula Russian Federation **85** M11/L10
75 00N 100 00E
Tayshet Russian Federation **85** L7 55 56N 98 01E
Taz *r.* Russian Federation **85** K9 67 00N 82 00E
Taza Morocco **102** E14 34 16N 4 01W
T'bilisi (Tiflis) Georgia **86** E3 41 43N 44 48E
Tchibanga Gabon **102** H7 2 49S 11 00E
Te Anau, Lake New Zealand **107** A1 45 13S 167 45E
Te Aroha New Zealand **107** C3 37 32S 175 43E
Te Awamutu New Zealand **107** C3 38 01S 175 20E
Tébessa Algeria **102** G15 35 21N 8 06E

Tecate Mexico **64** C3 32 33N 116 38W
Tecopa California U.S.A. **67** D2 35 51N 116 13W
Tecumseh Michigan U.S.A. **42** C3 42 01N 83 56W
Tedzhen r. Turkmenistan/Iran **87** J2 37 00N 61 00E
Tees r. United Kingdom **74** J6 54 30N 1 25W
Tefé Brazil **70** E12 3 24S 64 45W
Tegal Indonesia **95** D2 6 52S 109 07E
Tegeler See l. Germany **79** F2 52 35N 13 00E
Tegucigalpa Honduras **68** G2 14 05N 87 14W
Tehachapi California U.S.A. **67** C2 35 08N 118 27W
Tehachapi Mountains mts. California U.S.A. **67** C2 34 52N 118 45W
Tehrān Iran **89** H6 35 40N 51 26E
Tehuacán Mexico **68** E3 18 30N 97 26W
Tehuantepec Mexico **68** E3 16 21N 95 13W
Teifi r. United Kingdom **74** G4 52 03N 4 30W
Tekapo, Lake New Zealand **107** A2/B2 43 53S 170 32E
Tekezē r. Ethiopia **88** E1 13 48N 38 05E
Te Kuiti New Zealand **107** C3 38 20S 175 10E
Tel r. India **91** E4 20 30N 83 30E
Tela Honduras **68** G3 15 46N 87 25W
Tel Aviv-Yafo Israel **88** D5 32 05N 34 46E
Telescope Peak mt. California U.S.A. **67** D3 36 11N 117 05W
Telford United Kingdom **74** I4 52 42N 2 28W
Teller Alaska U.S.A. **8** B6 65 12N 166 23W
Teltow Germany **79** F1 52 24N 13 16E
Teltowkanal can. Germany **79** E1 52 23N 13 10E
Teluk Bone b. Indonesia **95** G3 4 00S 121 00E
Teluk Cenderawasih b. Indonesia **106** F9 2 15S 135 30E
Teluk Intan Malaysia **95** C4 4 02N 101 01E
Teluk Tomini b. Indonesia **95** G3 0 20S 121 00E
Tema Ghana **102** E9 5 41N 0 00
Temblor Range mts. California U.S.A. **67** C2 35 23N 119 53W
Teme r. United Kingdom **74** I4 52 15N 2 25W
Temecula California U.S.A. **67** D1 33 30N 117 08W
Temirtau Kazakhstan **87** L5 50 05N 72 55E
Tempelhof Germany **79** F1 52 28N 13 23E
Temple Texas U.S.A. **65** G3 31 06N 97 22W
Temuco Chile **71** C5 38 45S 72 40W
Temuka New Zealand **107** B2 44 15S 171 17E
Tenali India **91** E3 16 13N 80 36E
Ten Degree Channel Andaman Islands/Nicobar Islands **91** G1 10 00N 93 00E
Tenerife i. Canary Islands **102** B13 28 15N 16 35W
Teniente Rodolfo Marsh Martin r.s. Antarctica **113** 62 12S 58 55W
Tennant Creek tn. Australia **106** E6 19 31S 134 15E
Tennessee r. U.S.A. **65** I4 35 00N 88 00W
Tennessee state U.S.A. **65** I4 35 00N 87 00W
Teófilo Otôni Brazil **70** I9 17 52S 41 31W
Tepatitlán Mexico **68** D4 20 50N 102 46W
Tépeji Mexico **68** E3 19 55N 99 21W
Tepic Mexico **68** D4 21 30N 104 51W
Teresina Brazil **70** I11 5 09S 42 46W
Termez Uzbekistan **87** K2 37 15N 67 15E
Ternate Indonesia **95** H4 0 48N 127 23E
Ternopil' Ukraine **86** B4 49 35N 25 39E
Terpeniya Bay Russian Federation **85** Q5 48 00N 144 0E
Terre d'Adélie (Adélie Land) geog. reg. Antarctica **113** 70 00S 135 00E
Terre Haute Indiana U.S.A. **65** I4 39 27N 87 24W
Terrey Hills tn. Australia **107** G3 33 41S 151 14E
Terror, Mount Antarctica **113** 77 00S 160 00E
Teseney Eritrea **102** M11 15 10N 36 48E
Teshio Japan **96** D3 44 53N 141 46E
Test r. United Kingdom **74** J3 51 05N 1 30W
Teterboro Airport New Jersey U.S.A. **66** Y2 40 50N 74 03W
Tétouan Morocco **102** D15 35 34N 5 22W
Texarkana Arkansas U.S.A. **65** H3 33 28N 94 02W
Texas state U.S.A. **64** G3 31 00N 100 00W
Texoma, Lake U.S.A. **65** G3 34 00N 97 00W
THAILAND **95** B7/C7
Thailand, Gulf of Southern Asia **95** C6 10 50N 101 00E
Thakhek Laos **95** C7 17 22N 104 50E
Thames New Zealand **107** C3 37 09S 175 33E
Thames r. United Kingdom **74** K3 51 30N 0 20W
Thane India **91** C3 19 14N 73 02E
Thanh Hoa Vietnam **95** D7 19 49N 105 48E
Thanjavur India **91** D2 10 46N 79 09E
Thar Desert India **91** C5 27 30N 72 00E
Thayetmyo Myanmar **95** B7 19 20N 95 10E
Thebes hist. site Egypt **88** D4 25 41N 32 40E
The Bronx New York U.S.A. **66** Z2 40 50N 73 55W
The Brothers is. Hong Kong China **92** A2 22 20N 113 58E
The Crane tn. Barbados **69** W12 13 06N 59 25W
The Dalles tn. Oregon U.S.A. **64** B6 45 36N 121 10W
The Everglades swamp Florida U.S.A. **65** J2 26 00N 81 00W
The Hague see 's-Gravenhage
Thermopolis Wyoming U.S.A. **64** E5 43 39N 108 12W
Thessaloniki (Thessalonica) Greece **72** K4 40 38N 22 58E
Thiais France **79** B2 48 45N 2 24E
Thief River Falls tn. Minnesota U.S.A. **65** G6 48 12N 96 48W
Thiès Senegal **102** B10 14 49N 16 52W
Thimphu Bhutan **91** F5 27 32N 89 43E
Thingangyun Myanmar **93** J2 16 47N 96 12E
Thithia i. Fiji **110** V16 17 45S 179 20W
Thomasville Georgia U.S.A. **65** J3 30 50N 83 59W
Thomson r. Australia **106** G5 24 00S 141 00E
Thornapple Michigan U.S.A. **42** A3 42 38N 85 15W
Thousand Oaks California U.S.A. **67** C2 34 10N 118 50W
Three Kings Islands New Zealand **107** B4 34 10S 172 07E

Three Mile Bay tn. New York U.S.A. **43** K5 44 04N 76 12W
Three Points, Cape Ghana **102** E9 4 43N 2 06W
Thule see Qaanaaq
Thunder Bay b. Michigan U.S.A. **42** C6 45 00N 83 25W
Thurrock United Kingdom **78** E2 51 28N 0 20E
Thurso r. United Kingdom **74** H10 58 15N 3 35W
Thurso United Kingdom **74** H10 58 35N 3 32W
Thurston Island Antarctica **113** 70 00S 100 00W
Tian'anmen China **94** B1 40 50N 116 26E
Tianjin China **93** N6 39 08N 117 12E
Tianshui China **93** L5 34 25N 105 58E
Tiberias Israel **88** O11 32 48N 35 32E
Tiberias, Lake (Sea of Galilee) Israel **88** O11 32 45N 35 30E
Tibesti mts. Chad **102** I12 21 00N 17 00E
Tibet Autonomous Region see Xizang Zizhiqu
Tibooburra Australia **106** G4 29 25S 142 02E
Tiburón i. Mexico **68** B5 28 30N 112 30W
Ticul Mexico **68** G4 20 22N 89 31W
Tiergarten park Germany **79** F2 52 31N 13 23E
Tierra Blanca Mexico **68** E3 18 28N 96 21W
Tiffin Ohio U.S.A. **42** C2 41 07N 83 11W
Tiflis see T'bilisi
Tighina Moldova **86** B4 46 50N 29 29E
Tigris r. Turkey/Iraq **73** P2 34 30N 44 00E
Tijuana California U.S.A. **67** D1 32 30N 117 00W
Tijuana Mexico **68** A6 32 29N 117 10W
Tijuca Brazil **71** P2 22 56S 43 16W
Tijuca National Park Brazil **71** P2 22 58S 43 17W
Tikhoretsk Russian Federation **86** E4 45 52N 40 07E
Tikrit Iraq **88** F5 34 36N 43 42E
Tiksi Russian Federation **85** O10 71 40N 128 45E
Tilak Nagar India **108** L4 28 38N 77 07E
Timaru New Zealand **107** B2 44 24S 171 15E
Timbira r. Brazil **71** Q3 22 40S 43 12W
Timbuktu see Tombouctou
Timişoara Romania **72** K5 45 45N 21 15E
Timimóun Algeria **102** F13 29 15N 0 14E
Timiryazev Park Russian Federation **86** M2 55 50N 37 32E
Timon Brazil **70** I11 5 08S 42 52W
Timor i. Indonesia **95** G1/H2 9 00S 125 00E
Timor Sea Indonesia **95** H1/H2 10 45S 126 00E
Tindouf Algeria **102** D13 27 42N 8 10W
Tionesta Pennsylvania U.S.A. **42** G2 41 31N 79 30W
Tionesta Lake Pennsylvania U.S.A. **42** G2 41 30N 79 29W
Tiranë (Tirana) Albania **72** J4 41 20N 19 49E
Tiraspol' Moldova **72** L5 46 50N 29 38E
Tiraz Mountains Namibia **103** I2 25 30S 16 30E
Tiree i. United Kingdom **74** E8 56 30N 6 55W
Tiruchchirāppalli India **91** D2 10 50N 78 41E
Tirunelveli India **91** D1 8 45N 77 43E
Tirupati India **91** D2 13 39N 79 25E
Tiruppur India **91** D2 11 05N 77 20E
Tisza r. Hungary/Yugoslavia **72** K5 48 00N 20 30E
Titãgarh India **90** K2 22 44N 88 22E
Tititbawassee River r. Michigan U.S.A. **42** B4 43 50N 84 25W
Titograd see Podgorica
Titusville Pennsylvania U.S.A. **42** G2 41 37N 79 42W
Tiu Chung Chau i. Hong Kong China **92** C1/2 22 20N 114 19E
Tizimin Mexico **68** G4 21 10N 88 09W
Tizi Ouzou Algeria **102** F15 36 44N 4 05E
Tiznit Morocco **102** D13 29 43N 9 44W
Tlemcen Algeria **102** E14 34 53N 1 21W
Toamasina Madagascar **103** O4 18 10S 49 23E
Tobago i. Trinidad and Tobago **69** L2 11 15N 60 40W
Tobi-shima i. Japan **96** C2 39 12N 139 32E
Tobol r. Russian Federation **85** I7 57 00N 67 30E
Tobol'sk Russian Federation **85** I7 58 15N 68 12E
Tobyhanna Pennsylvania U.S.A. **66** C4 41 11N 75 25W
Tocantins admin. Brazil **70** H10 12 00S 47 00W
Toco Trinidad and Tobago **69** U10 10 49N 60 57W
Tocopilla Chile **71** C8 22 05S 70 10W
TOGO **102** F9
Tok r. Russian Federation **85** A. 50 C3 63 20N 142 59W
Tokelau Islands Pacific Ocean **110** I9 9 00S 168 00W
Tokrau r. Kazakhstan **87** M4 48 00N 75 00E
Tokushima Japan **96** B1 34 03N 134 34E
Tokuyama Japan **96** B1 34 03N 131 48E
Tōkyō Japan **96** C2 35 40N 139 45E
Tōkyō-bay Japan **97** C2 35 30N 139 50E
Toledo Ohio U.S.A. **65** J5 41 40N 83 35W
Toliara Madagascar **103** N3 23 20S 43 41E
Tollhouse California U.S.A. **67** C3 37 01N 119 25W
Tollygunge India **90** K2 22 30N 88 19E
Tolly's Nullah r. India **90** K1 22 28N 88 05E
Tolo Channel Hong Kong China **92** C2 22 28N 114 17E
Tolo Harbour Hong Kong China **92** C2 22 26N 114 14E
Toluca Mexico **68** E3 19 20N 99 40W
Tol'yatti Russian Federation **84** G6 53 32N 49 24E
Tom' r. Russian Federation **87** O5 54 00N 87 30E
Tomakomai Japan **96** D3 42 39N 141 33E
Tomaniivi mt. Fiji **110** U16 17 37S 178 01E
Tomatlán Mexico **68** C3 19 54N 105 18W
Tombigbee r. U.S.A. **65** I3 32 00N 88 00W
Tombouctou (Timbuktu) Mali **102** E11 16 49N 2 59W
Tombua Angola **103** H4 15 49S 11 53E
Tom Price, Mount Australia **106** B5 22 49S 117 51E
Tomsk Russian Federation **85** K7 56 30N 85 05E
Tonalá Mexico **68** F3 16 08N 93 41W
Tonasket Washington U.S.A. **35** E1 48 42N 119 28W
TONGA **110** I5
Tong'an China **94** E7 24 43N 118 07E
Tonga Trench Pacific Ocean **110** I5 20 00S 173 00W

Tongchuan China **93** L6 35 05N 109 02E
Tong Fuk Hong Kong China **92** A1 22 14N 113 56E
Tonghai China **93** K3 24 07N 104 45E
Tonghua China **93** P7 41 42N 125 45E
Tongking, Gulf of China/Vietnam **95** D7 20 00N 107 30E
Tongling China **93** N5 30 58N 117 48E
Tonle Sap l. Cambodia **95** C6 12 00N 103 50E
Tonopah California U.S.A. **67** D4 38 05N 117 15W
Tonopah Nevada U.S.A. **64** C4 38 05N 117 15W
Tooele Utah U.S.A. **64** D5 40 32N 112 18W
Toowoomba Australia **106** I4 27 35S 151 54E
Topaz California U.S.A. **67** C4 38 37N 119 32W
Topeka Kansas U.S.A. **65** G4 39 02N 95 41W
Torbay United Kingdom **74** H2 50 27N 3 30W
Torino (Turin) Italy **72** G5 45 04N 7 40E
Tornealven (Torniojok) r. Sweden/Finland **72** K9 67 30N 22 00E
Tornionjoki (Torneälven) r. Findland/Sweden **72** K9 67 30N 22 00E
Tororo Uganda **102** L8 0 42N 34 12E
Toros Dağlari Turkey **73** M3 37 10N 33 10E
Torrens, Lake Australia **106** F3 31 00S 137 50E
Torreón Mexico **68** D5 25 34N 103 25W
Torres Strait Australia **106** G7/8 10 00S 142 30E
Toruń Poland **72** J6 53 01N 18 35E
Tosa-wan b. Japan **96** B1 33 20N 133 40E
Toshima Japan **97** B3 35 43N 139 41E
Totoya i. Fiji **110** U15 18 56S 179 50W
Totsuka Japan **97** B3 35 23N 139 32E
Tottori Japan **96** B2 35 32N 134 12E
Touggourt Algeria **102** G14 33 08N 6 04E
Tou-liu Taiwan **94** G6 23 42N 120 32E
Toulon France **72** G4 43 07N 5 55E
Toulouse France **72** F4 43 33N 1 24E
Toungoo Myanmar **95** B7 18 57N 96 26E
Tours France **72** F5 47 23N 0 42E
Towanda Pennsylvania U.S.A. **66** B4 41 46N 76 27W
Tower Hamlets United Kingdom **78** C3 51 30N 0 02W
Town Island Hong Kong China **92** D2 22 20N 114 21E
Towne Pass California U.S.A. **67** D3 36 25N 117 17W
Townsville Australia **106** H6 19 13S 146 48E
Towson Maryland U.S.A. **66** B2 39 25N 76 36W
Toyama Japan **96** C2 36 42N 137 14E
Toyiabe Range mts. California U.S.A. **67** D4 39 18N 117 12W
Toyohashi Japan **96** C1 34 46N 137 22E
Toyota Japan **96** C2 35 05N 137 09E
Tozeur Tunisia **102** G14 33 55N 8 07E
Trâblous (Tripoli) Lebanon **88** E5 34 27N 35 50E
Trabzona Turkey **88** E7 41 00N 39 43E
Tralee Republic of Ireland **74** B4 52 16N 9 42W
Transantarctic Mountains Antarctica **113**
Travers, Mount New Zealand **107** B2 42 01S 172 44E
Traverse City Michigan U.S.A. **65** I5 44 46N 85 38W
Treinta-y-Tres Uruguay **71** F3 33 16S 54 17W
Trelew Chile **71** D4 43 13S 65 15W
Tremplinersee l. Germany **79** E1 52 21N 13 02E
Trenque Lauquen Argentina **71** E3 35 56S 62 43W
Trent r. United Kingdom **74** K5 53 10N 0 50W
Trenton New Jersey U.S.A. **65** L5 40 15N 74 43W
Treptow Germany **79** F1 52 29N 13 27E
Tres Arroyos Argentina **71** E3 38 26S 60 17W
Três Lagoas Brazil **70** G8 20 46S 51 43W
Trichur India **91** D2 10 32N 76 14E
Trieste Italy **72** H5 45 39N 13 47E
Trincomalee Sri Lanka **91** E1 8 34N 81 13E
Trindade i. Atlantic Ocean **109** F4 20 30S 29 20W
Trinidad Bolivia **70** E10 14 46S 64 50W
Trinidad Colorado U.S.A. **64** F4 37 11N 104 31W
Trinidad Cuba **69** H4 21 48N 80 00W
Trinidad i. Trinidad and Tobago **69** L2 11 00N 61 30W
TRINIDAD AND TOBAGO **69** L2
Trinity r. U.S.A. **65** G3 32 00N 96 00W
Trinity Hills Trinidad and Tobago **69** T9 10 07N 61 07W
Trinity Islands is. Alaska U.S.A. **8** E4 56 45N 154 15W
Tripoli Lebanon see Trâblous
Tripoli Libya see Taràbulus
Tripura admin. India **91** G4 23 40N 92 00E
Tristan da Cunha i. Atlantic Ocean **109** G2 37 15S 12 30W
Trivandrum India **91** D1 8 30N 76 57E
Troitsk Russian Federation **87** J5 54 08N 61 33E
Troitsko Pechorsk Russian Federation **87** H7 62 40N 56 08E
Tromsø Norway **72** J9 69 42N 19 00E
Trona California U.S.A. **67** D2 35 46N 117 24W
Trondheim Norway **72** H8 63 36N 10 23E
Troy Alabama U.S.A. **65** I3 31 49N 86 00W
Troy Montana U.S.A. **35** E1 48 28N 115 55W
Troy New York U.S.A. **65** L5 42 43N 73 43W
Troy N.H.S. Turkey **88** C6 39 55N 26 17E
Truckee r. California U.S.A. **67** C4 39 34N 119 35W
Trujillo Peru **70** B11 8 06S 79 00W
Trujillo Venezuela **70** C14 9 20N 70 38W
Truk Islands Caroline Islands **110** F8 7 30N 152 30E
Truro United Kingdom **74** F2 50 16N 5 03W
Tsangpo see Yarlung Zangbo Jiang
Tsarskoye Selo Russian Federation **86** B9 59 43N 30 22E
Tsavo National Park Kenya **102** M7 3 30S 38 00E
Tselinograd see Akmola
Tseung Kwan O Hong Kong China **92** C1 22 19N 114 14E
Tshane Botswana **103** J3 24 05S 21 54E
Tshuapa r. Congo (D.R.) **102** J7 1 00S 23 00E
Tsimlyansk Reservoir Russian Federation **73** P5 47 30N 43 00E
Tsimlyanskoye Vodokhranilishche res. Russian Federation **86** E4 47 30N 42 00E
Tsing Chau Tsai Hong Kong China **92** B2 22 20N 114 02E
Tsing Yi i. Hong Kong China **92** B2 22 20N 114 00E

Tsing Yi Hong Kong China **92** B2 22 21N 114 06E
Tsin Shui Wan Hong Kong China **92** C1 22 14N 114 12E
Tsu Japan **96** C1 34 41N 136 30E
Tsuchiura Japan **96** D2 36 05N 140 11E
Tsuen Wan Hong Kong China **92** B2 22 22N 114 06E
Tsugaru-kaikyō sd. Japan **96** D3 41 30N 140 30E
Tsumeb Namibia **103** I4 19 13S 17 42E
Tsunashima Japan **97** B3 35 13N 139 38E
Tsuruga Japan **96** C2 35 40N 136 05E
Tsuruoka Japan **96** C2 38 42N 139 50E
Tsushima i. Japan **96** A1 34 30N 129 20E
Tsuyama Japan **96** B2 35 04N 134 01E
Tsz Wan Shan Hong Kong China **92** C2 22 21N 114 12E
Tuamotu Archipelago is. Pacific Ocean **111** M6 15 00S 145 00W
Tuamotu Ridge Pacific Ocean **111** L6 19 00S 144 00W
Tuapse Russian Federation **86** D3 44 06N 39 08E
Tuba r. Russian Federation **87** P5 54 00N 93 00E
Tubruq Libya **102** J14 32 05N 23 59E
Tubuai Islands Pacific Ocean **111** L5 23 23S 149 27W
Tucheng Taiwan **94** H7 24 52N 121 49E
Tucson Arizona U.S.A. **64** D3 32 15N 110 57W
Tucumcari New Mexico U.S.A. **64** F4 35 11N 103 44W
Tucupita Venezuela **70** E14 9 02N 62 04W
Tucuruí Brazil **70** H12 3 42S 49 44W
Tuen Mun Hong Kong China **92** A2 22 23N 113 57E
Tula Russian Federation **84** F6 54 11N 37 38E
Tula Hidalgo Mexico **68** E4 20 01N 99 21W
Tula Tamaulipas Mexico **68** E4 23 00N 99 41W
Tulare California U.S.A. **67** C3 36 13N 119 22W
Tulare Lake California U.S.A. **67** C3 36 04N 119 45W
Tulcán Ecuador **70** B13 0 50N 77 48W
Tulkarm Jordan **88** O11 32 19N 35 02E
Tullamore Republic of Ireland **74** D5 53 16N 7 30W
Tulsa Oklahoma U.S.A. **65** G4 36 07N 95 58W
Tulun Russian Federation **85** M6 54 32N 100 35E
Tumaco Colombia **70** B13 1 51N 78 46W
Tumbes Peru **70** A12 3 37S 80 27W
Tumkur India **91** D2 13 20N 77 06E
Tunapuna Trinidad and Tobago **69** T10 10 38N 61 23W
Tunduru Tanzania **103** M5 11 08S 37 21E
Tungabhadra r. India **91** D3 16 00N 77 00E
Tung-chiang Taiwan **94** G5 22 26N 120 30E
Tung Lung Chau i. Hong Kong China **92** C1 22 15N 114 17E
Tunis Tunisia **102** H15 36 50N 10 13E
TUNISIA **102** G14
Tunja Colombia **70** C14 5 33N 73 23W
Tunkhannock Pennsylvania U.S.A. **43** L2 41 32N 75 46W
Tuolumne r. California U.S.A. **67** B3 37 53N 120 09W
Tupelo Mississippi U.S.A. **65** I3 34 15N 88 43W
Tupiza Bolivia **70** D8 21 27S 65 45W
Túquerres Colombia **70** B13 1 06N 77 37W
Tura Russian Federation **85** M8 64 20N 100 17E
Turbotville Pennsylvania U.S.A. **66** B4 41 00N 76 00W
Turfan see Turpan
Turfan Depression China **92** G7 42 40N 89 30E
Turgay r. Kazakhstan **87** J4 49 30N 63 30E
Turkana, Lake Ethiopia/Kenya **102** M8 4 00N 36 00E
Turkestan Kazakhstan **87** K3 43 17N 68 16E
TURKEY **73** M3
TURKMENISTAN **87** H3/J2
Turks and Caicos Islands West Indies **69** J4 21 30N 72 00W
Turks Island Passage sd. West Indies **69** J4 21 30N 71 30W
Turku Finland **72** K8 60 27N 22 15E
Turin see Torino
Turpan (Turfan) China **92** G7 42 55N 89 06E
Turramurra Australia **107** G3 33 44S 151 07E
Turukhansk Russian Federation **85** K9 65 49N 88 00E
Tuscaloosa Alabama U.S.A. **65** I3 33 12N 87 33W
Tushino Russian Federation **86** L2 55 52N 37 26E
Tuticorin India **91** D1 8 48N 78 10E
TUVALU **110** H7
Tuxpan Nayarit Mexico **68** C4 21 58N 105 20W
Tuxpan Veracruz Mexico **68** E4 20 58N 97 23W
Tuxtla Gutierrez Mexico **68** F3 16 45N 93 09W
Tuz Gölü (Lake Tuz) l. Turkey **88** D6 38 40N 33 25E
Tver' (Kalinin) Russian Federation **84** F7 56 49N 35 57E
Tweed r. United Kingdom **74** I7 55 45N 2 10W
24 Parganas admin. India **90** K1 22 69 42N 19 00E
Twin Falls tn. Idaho U.S.A. **64** D5 42 34N 114 30W
Twin Peak mt. California U.S.A. **67** B4 39 06N 120 14W
Twisp Washington U.S.A. **34** H4 48 22N 120 08W
Tyan-Shan' (Tien Shan) **85** J4 41 00N 76 00E
Tyler Texas U.S.A. **65** G3 32 22N 95 18W
Tym r. Russian Federation **85** K7 59 00N 82 30E
Tynda Russian Federation **85** O7 55 10N 124 35E
Tyne r. United Kingdom **74** J7 55 00N 1 50W
Tyre see Soûr
Tyrrhenian Sea Europe **72** H3 40 00N 12 00E
Tyumen' Russian Federation **84** I7 57 11N 65 29E
Tyung r. Russian Federation **85** N8 65 00N 119 00E
Tywi r. United Kingdom **74** H3 51 53N 3 35W

U

U.A.E. see UNITED ARAB EMIRATES
Uaupés Brazil **70** D12 0 07S 67 05W
Ubagan r. Kazakhstan **87** J5/K5 54 00N 65 00E
Ubangi r. Central African Republic **102** I8 4 00N 18 00E
Ube Japan **96** B1 33 57N 131 16E
Uberaba Brazil **70** H9 19 47S 47 57W
Uberlândia Brazil **70** H9 18 57S 48 17W
Ubly Michigan U.S.A. **42** D4 43 44N 82 58W

Ubon Ratchathani Thailand **95** C7 15 15N 104 50E
Ubundu Congo (D.R.) **102** K7 0 24S 25 30E
Uchiura-wan b. Japan **96** D3 42 30N 140 40E
Uda r. Russian Federation **85** P6 54 00N 134 00E
Udaipur India **91** C4 24 36N 73 47E
Udgir India **91** D3 18 26N 77 11E
Udon Thani Thailand **95** C7 17 25N 102 45E
Ueda Japan **96** C2 36 27N 138 13E
Uele r. Congo (D.R.) **102** K8 4 00N 27 00E
Uelen Russian Federation **85** U9 66 13N 169 48W
Ufa Russian Federation **84** H6 54 45N 55 58E
Ugab r. Namibia **103** I3 21 00S 15 00E
UGANDA 102 L8
Ugra r. Russian Federation **86** C5 54 30N 34 00E
Uinta Mountains Utah U.S.A. **64** D5 40 00N 111 00W
Uitenhage Republic of South Africa **103** K1
33 46S 25 25E
Ujjain India **91** D4 23 11N 75 50E
Ujung Pandang Indonesia **95** F2 5 09S 119 28E
U.K. see UNITED KINGDOM
Ukhta Russian Federation **84** H8 63 33N 53 44E
Ukiah California U.S.A. **64** B4 39 09N 123 12W
UKRAINE 86 A4/D4
Ulaanbaatar (Ulan Bator) Mongolia **93** L8
47 54N 106 52E
Ulaangom Mongolia **92** H8 49 59N 92 00E
Ulan Bator see Ulaanbaatar
Ulan-Ude Russian Federation **85** M6 51 55N 107 40E
Ulhasnagar India **91** C3 19 15N 73 08E
Uliastay Mongolia **93** J8 47 42N 96 52E
Ullapool United Kingdom **74** F9 57 54N 5 10W
Ulsan South Korea **93** P6 35 32N 129 21E
Uluberiya India **90** J1 22 28N 88 07E
Ulungur Hu l. China **92** G8 47 10N 87 10E
Ulutau mts. Kazakhstan **87** K4 49 00N 67 00E
Ul'yanovsk Russian Federation **84** G6 54 19N 48 22E
Uman' Ukraine **86** C4 48 45N 30 10E
Umanak Fjord (Uummannaq Fjord) Greenland **9** AA7
71 00N 52 00W
Umbagog Lake New Hampshire/Maine U.S.A. **43** Q5
44 45N 71 00W
Umeå Sweden **72** K8 63 50N 20 15E
Umiat Alaska U.S.A. **8** E6 69 25N 152 20W
Umm as Samim geog. reg. Oman **89** I3 22 10N 56 00E
Umm Ruwaba Sudan **102** L10 12 50N 31 20E
Umtata Republic of South Africa **103** K1 31 35S 28 47E
Umuarama Brazil **71** G8 23 43S 52 57W
Unalakleet Alaska U.S.A. **8** C5 63 52N 160 50W
'Unayzah Saudi Arabia **88** F4 26 06N 43 58E
Union New Jersey U.S.A. **66** Y1 40 42N 74 14W
Union, Cape Greenland **51** V7 80 30N 59 00W
Union City New Jersey U.S.A. **66** Y2 40 45N 74 01W
Union City Pennsylvania U.S.A. **42** G2 41 56N 79 51W
Union City Reservoir res. Pennsylvania U.S.A. **42** G2
41 58N 79 54W
Uniontown Pennsylvania U.S.A. **65** K4 39 54N 79 44W
Unionville Michigan U.S.A. **42** C4 43 41N 83 29W
UNITED ARAB EMIRATES (U.A.E.) **89** H3
UNITED KINGDOM (U.K.) **74**
UNITED STATES OF AMERICA (U.S.A.) **64**
Unst i. United Kingdom **74** K12 60 45N 0 55W
Unuk River r. Alaska U.S.A. **34** B3 56 00N 131 00W
Unzha r. Russian Federation **86** E6 58 00N 44 00E
Upata Venezuela **70** E14 8 02N 62 25W
Upernavik Greenland **9** Z7 72 40N 56 05W
Upington Republic of South Africa **103** J2
28 28S 21 14E
Upolu Point Hawaiian Islands **111** Z18 20 16N 155 52W
Upper Bay U.S.A. **66** Y1 40 40N 74 03W
Upper Hutt New Zealand **107** C2 41 07S 175 04E
Upper Lake California U.S.A. **67** A4 39 10N 122 56W
Upper Lough Erne l. Northern Ireland **74** D6
54 15N 7 30W
Upper Manzanilla Trinidad and Tobago **69** T10
10 32N 61 03W
Upper Red Lake Minnesota U.S.A. **65** H6 48 04N 94 48W
Upper Sandusky Ohio U.S.A. **42** C1 40 48N 83 17W
Uppsala Sweden **72** J7 59 55N 17 38E
Ur hist. site Iraq **89** G5 30 56N 46 08E
Uraga Japan **97** B1 35 15N 139 42E
Uraga-suidō sd. Japan **97** B2/C1 35 10N 139 45E
Urakawa Japan **96** D3 42 10N 142 46E
Ural r. Asia **84** H5 48 00N 52 00E
Ural Mountains Russian Federation **84** H6/H8
57 00N 60 00E
Ural'sk Kazakhstan **86** G5 51 19N 51 20E
Urawa Japan **96** C2 35 52N 139 40E
Urayasu Japan **97** C3 35 40N 139 50E
Ure r. United Kingdom **74** J6 54 20N 1 40W
Urengoy Russian Federation **85** J9 65 59N 78 30E
Urfa Turkey **88** E6 37 08N 38 45E
Urgench Uzbekistan **87** J3 41 35N 60 41E
Urmia, Lake see Daryache-ye
Urmston Road sd. Hong Kong China **92** A2
22 22N 113 54E
Uruapan Mexico **68** D3 19 26N 102 04W
Urubamba Peru **70** C10 13 20S 72 07W
Uruguaiana Brazil **71** F7 29 45S 57 05W
URUGUAY 71 F6
Ürümqi China **92** G7 43 43N 87 38E
Usa r. Russian Federation **85** H9 66 00N 60 00E
U.S.A. see UNITED STATES OF AMERICA
Ushuaia Argentina **71** D2 54 48S 68 19W
Usinsk Russian Federation **84** H9 65 57N 57 27E
Üsküdar Turkey **88** C7 41 02N 29 02E
Usol'ye-Sibirskoye Russian Federation **85** M6
52 48N 103 40E

Ussuri (Wusul Jiang) r. Russian Federation **85** P5
47 00N 134 00E
Ussuriysk Russian Federation **85** P4 43 48N 131 59E
Ust'-Ilimsk Russian Federation **85** M7 58 03N 102 39E
Ustinov see Izhevsk
Ust'-Kamchatsk Russian Federation **85** S7
56 14N 162 28E
Ust'-Kamenogorsk Kazakhstan **87** N4 49 58N 82 36E
Ust'-Kut Russian Federation **85** M7 56 48N 105 42E
Ust'Maya Russian Federation **85** P8 60 25N 134 28E
Ust'-Nera Russian Federation **85** Q8 64 35N 143 14E
Ust'Olenëk Russian Federation **85** N10 72 59N 119 57E
Ust Urt Plateau Asia **87** H3 43 30N 55 00E
Usulután Mexico **68** G2 13 20N 88 25W
Utah state U.S.A. **64** D4 39 00N 112 00W
Utah Lake Utah U.S.A. **64** D5 40 10N 111 50W
Utica New York U.S.A. **65** K5 43 06N 75 15W
Utrecht Netherlands **72** G6 52 05N 5 07E
Utsunomiya Japan **96** C2 36 33N 139 52E
Uttaradit Thailand **95** C7 17 38N 100 05E
Uttarpära-Kotrung India **90** K2 22 39N 88 20E
Uttar Pradesh admin. India **91** E5 27 00N 80 00E
Uummannaq Fjord (Umanak Fjord) Greenland **9** AA7
71 00N 52 00W
Uvalde Texas U.S.A. **64** G2 29 14N 99 49W
Uvinza Tanzania **103** L6 5 08S 30 23E
Uvs Nuur l. Mongolia **92** H9 50 10N 92 30E
Uwajima Japan **96** B1 33 13N 132 32E
Uxbridge United Kingdom **78** B3 51 33N 0 30W
Uyuni Bolivia **70** D8 20 28S 66 47W
Uza r. Russian Federation **86** F5 52 30N 45 30E
UZBEKISTAN 87 J3/K3

V

Vaal r. Republic of South Africa **103** K2 27 30S 25 30E
Vaasa Finland **72** K8 63 06N 21 36E
Vacaville California U.S.A. **67** A4 38 21N 122 00W
Vadodara India **91** C4 22 19N 73 14E
Vaga r. Russian Federation **84** G8 62 00N 43 00E
Vail New Jersey U.S.A. **66** C3 40 59N 75 01W
Vakh r. Russian Federation **85** K6 61 30N 80 30E
Vakhsh r. Asia **87** K2 37 00N 69 00E
Valdai Hills Russian Federation **86** C6 57 00N 32 30E
Val de Marne admin. France **79** C3 48 50N 2 30E
Valdés, Peninsula Argentina **71** E4 42 30S 63 00W
Valdivia Chile **71** C5 39 46S 73 15W
Valdosta Georgia U.S.A. **65** J3 30 51N 83 51W
Valença Brazil **70** J10 13 22S 39 06W
Valença r. Trinidad and Tobago **69** T10 10 39N 61 12W
Valencia Spain **72** E3 39 29N 0 24W
Valencia Trinidad and Tobago **69** T10 10 39N 61 12W
Valencia Venezuela **70** D15 10 14N 67 59W
Valera Venezuela **70** C14 9 21N 70 38W
Valladolid Mexico **68** G3 20 41N 88 11W
Valladolid Spain **72** E4 41 39N 4 45W
Valle de la Pascua Venezuela **70** D14 9 15N 66 00W
Valledupar Colombia **70** C15 10 31N 73 16W
Valle Grande Bolivia **70** E9 18 30S 64 04W
Vallejo California U.S.A. **64** B4 38 05N 122 14W
Vallenar Chile **71** C7 28 36S 70 45W
Valletta Malta **72** H3 35 54N 14 32E
Valley tn. Barbados **69** V12 13 07N 59 35W
Valparai India **91** D2 10 19N 76 58E
Valparaíso Chile **71** C6 33 05S 71 40W
Valsad India **90** C4 20 53N 70 28E
Van Turkey **88** F6 38 28N 43 20E
Vanadzor (Kirovakan) Armenia **86** E3 40 49N 44 30E
Van Buren Maine U.S.A. **47** C2 47 10N 67 59W
Vancouver Washington U.S.A. **64** B6 45 38N 122 40W
Vänern, Lake Sweden **72** H7 59 00N 13 30E
Van Etten New York U.S.A. **66** B5 42 13N 76 33W
Van Gölü (Lake Van) l. Turkey **88** F6 38 33N 42 46E
Vantaa Finland **72** K8 60 20N 24 50E
Vanua Levu i. Fiji **110** U16 16 20S 179 00E
Vanua Levu Barrier Reef Fiji **110** U16 17 10S 179 00E
Vanua Mbalavu i. Fiji **110** V16 17 15S 178 55W
VANUATU 106 L6
Vanves France **79** B2 48 49N 2 17E
Van Wert Ohio U.S.A. **42** B1 40 53N 84 36W
Varanasi India **91** E5 25 20N 83 00E
Varna Bulgaria **72** L4 43 12N 27 57E
Várzea Grande Brazil **70** I11 6 32S 42 05W
Vassar Michigan U.S.A. **42** C4 43 23N 83 33W
Västerås Sweden **72** J7 59 36N 16 32E
Vasyugan r. Russian Federation **85** J7 59 00N 77 30E
Vaté see Éfate
Vatnajökull ice cap Iceland **72** B8 64 30N 17 00W
Vättern l. Sweden **72** H7 58 20N 14 20E
Vatulele i. Fiji **110** T15 18 30S 177 38E
Vaucresson France **79** A2 48 51N 2 08E
Vaygach i. Russian Federation **85** H10 70 00N 59 00E
Velikaya r. Russian Federation **86** B6 57 00N 28 45E
Velikiye-Luki Russian Federation **84** F7 56 19N 30 31E
Vellore India **91** D2 12 56N 79 09E
Velten Germany **79** E2 52 42N 13 12E
Venézia (Venice) Italy **72** H5 45 26N 12 20E
VENEZUELA 70 D14
Venice see Venezia
Ventspils Latvia **86** A6 57 22N 21 31E
Ventura California U.S.A. **64** C3 34 16N 119 18W
Veracruz Mexico **68** E3 19 11N 96 10W
Veraval India **90** C4 20 53N 70 28E
Verde r. Arizona U.S.A. **64** D3 34 00N 112 00W
Vereeniging Republic of South Africa **103** K2
26 41S 27 56E
Verkhoyansk Russian Federation **85** P9 67 35N 133 25E
Verkhoyansk Range mts. Russian Federation **85** O9/P8
65 00N 130 00E
Vermilion Ohio U.S.A. **42** D2 41 24N 82 21W

Vermont state U.S.A. **65** L5 44 00N 73 00W
Vernon Texas U.S.A. **64** G3 34 10N 99 19W
Verona Italy **72** H5 45 26N 11 00E
Verrières France **79** B1 48 44N 2 16E
Versailles France **79** A2 48 48N 2 07E
Vesuvius vol. Italy **72** H4 40 49N 14 26E
Viangchan (Vientiane) Laos **95** C7 17 59N 102 38E
Vicecomodoro Marambio r.s. Antarctica **113**
64 14S 56 38W
Vicente Guerrero Mexico **68** A6 30 48N 116 00W
Vicksburg Mississippi U.S.A. **65** H3 32 21N 90 51W
Victoria r. Australia **106** E6 16 00S 131 00E
Victoria state Australia **106** G2/H2 37 00S 145 00E
Victoria Chile **71** C5 38 20S 72 30W
Victoria Canada **64** B6 48 25N 123 22W
Victoria de las Tunas Cuba **69** I4 20 58N 76 59W
Victoria Falls Zambia/Zimbabwe **103** K4 17 55S 25 51E
Victoria Harbour Hong Kong China **92** B1/C1
22 21N 114 00E
Victoria, Lake East Africa **102** L7 2 00S 33 00E
Victoria Land geog. reg. Antarctica **113** 75 00S 157 00E
Victoria Peak Hong Kong China **92** B1 22 17N 114 10E
Victoria West Republic of South Africa **103** J1
31 25S 23 08E
Victorville California U.S.A. **67** D2 34 31N 117 18W
Viedma Argentina **71** E4 40 45S 63 00W
Vienna see Wien
Vientiane see Viangchan
VIETNAM 95 D6/D7
Vigia Brazil **70** H12 0 50S 48 07W
Vigo Spain **72** D4 42 15N 8 44W
Vijayawada India **91** E3 16 34N 80 40E
Vila Vanuatu **106** L6 17 45S 168 18E
Vila Pedro Brazil **71** P2 22 49S 43 20W
Vila Velha Brazil **70** I8 20 23S 40 18W
Vilhena Brazil **70** E10 12 40S 60 08W
Villa Constitución Mexico **68** B5 25 05N 111 45W
Villahermosa Mexico **68** F3 18 00N 92 53W
Villa María Argentina **71** E6 32 25S 63 15W
Villa Montes Bolivia **70** E8 21 15S 63 30W
Villanueva Mexico **68** D4 22 24N 102 53W
Villarrica Chile **71** C5 39 15S 72 15W
Villa Unión Argentina **71** D7 29 27S 62 46W
Villa Unión Mexico **68** C4 23 10N 106 12W
Villavicencio Colombia **70** C3 4 09N 73 38W
Villejuif France **79** B2 48 47N 2 23E
Villeneuve St. Georges France **79** B1 48 43N 2 27E
Villepreista France **79** C2 48 50N 1 58E
Vilnius Lithuania **72** L6 54 40N 25 19E
Vilyuy r. Russian Federation **85** O8 64 00N 123 00E
Vilyuysk Russian Federation **85** O8 63 46N 121 35E
Viña del Mar Chile **71** C6 33 02S 71 35W
Vincennes France **79** B2 48 51N 2 27E
Vincennes Indiana U.S.A. **65** I4 38 42N 87 30W
Vindhya Range mts. India **91** C4/D4 23 00N 75 00E
Vineland New Jersey U.S.A. **65** K4 39 29N 75 02W
Vinh Vietnam **95** D7 18 42N 105 41E
Vinnytsya Ukraine **72** L5 49 11N 28 30E
Vinson Massif mts. Antarctica **113** 78 02S 22 00W
Vinton California U.S.A. **67** B4 39 48N 120 12W
Virgin r. U.S.A. **64** D4 37 00N 114 00W
Virgin Islands West Indies **69** L3 18 00N 64 30W
Virginia Minnesota U.S.A. **65** H6 47 30N 92 28W
Virginia state U.S.A. **65** K4 38 00N 77 00W
Virginia Beach tn. Virginia U.S.A. **65** K4 36 51N 75 59W
Visalia California U.S.A. **67** C3 36 20N 119 18W
Vista California U.S.A. **67** D1 33 12N 117 15W
Vishakhapatnam India **91** E3 17 42N 83 24E
Vistula r. Poland **72** J6 53 30N 19 00E
Vitichi Bolivia **70** D8 20 14S 65 22W
Viti Levu i. Fiji **110** T15-U16 18 10S 177 55E
Vitim r. Russian Federation **85** N7 59 00N 113 00E
Vitim Russian Federation **85** N7 59 28N 112 35E
Vitória Brazil **70** I8 20 20S 40 18W
Vitória da Conquista Brazil **70** I10 14 53S 40 52W
Vitry-sur-Seine France **79** B2 48 47N 2 24E
Vitsyebsk Belarus **72** M7 55 10N 30 14E
Vityaz Trench Pacific Ocean **110** Q7 9 30S 170 00E
Vivi r. Russian Federation **85** L9 61 00N 96 00E
Vize i. Russian Federation **85** J11 79 30N 77 00E
Vizianagaram India **91** E3 18 07N 83 30E
Vladikavkaz (Ordzhonikidze) Russian Federation **84** G7
43 02N 44 43E
Vladimir Russian Federation **84** G7 56 08N 40 25E
Vladimir Volynskiy Ukraine **73** P7 50 51N 24 19E
Vladivostok Russian Federation **85** P4 43 09N 131 53E
Vlorë Albania **72** J4 40 29N 19 29E
Vohkma Russian Federation **86** F6 58 00N 45 30E
Volga r. Russian Federation **84** G5/6 50 00N 45 00E
Volgodonsk Russian Federation **84** G5 47 35N 42 08E
Volgograd Russian Federation **84** G5 48 45N 44 30E
Volgogradskoye Vodokhranilishche res.
Russian Federation **86** E4 50 00N 45 30E
Volkhov r. Russian Federation **86** C6 59 00N 31 30E
Vologda Russian Federation **84** F7 59 10N 39 55E
Vólos Greece **88** B6 39 22N 22 57E
Vol'sk Russian Federation **86** F5 52 04N 47 22E
Volta, Lake Ghana **102** E9 7 30N 0 30W
Volta Redonda mt. Brazil **71** I8 22 31S 44 05W
Volzhskiy Russian Federation **84** G5 48 48N 44 45E
Vorkuta Russian Federation **85** I9 67 27N 64 00E
Vorna r. Russian Federation **86** E5 52 00N 43 00E
Voronezh Russian Federation **84** F6 51 40N 39 13E
Vørterkaka Nunatak mt. Antarctica **113** 71 45S 32 00E
Vosges France **72** G5 48 10N 6 30E
Vostochnyy Russian Federation **85** P4 42 52N 132 56E
Vostok r.s. Antarctica **113** 78 27S 106 49E
Votkinsk Russian Federation **87** G6 57 00N 54 00E

Votkinskoye Vodokhranilische Russian Federation
87 H6 57 00N 55 30E
Vpadina Karagiye mud flat Kazakhstan **86** G3
43 20N 51 30E
Vrangelya (Wrangel) i. Russian Federation **85**
T10 61 30N 180 00
Vryburg Republic of South Africa **103** J2 26 57S 24 44E
Vung Tau Vietnam **95** D6 10 21N 107 04E
Vunisea Fiji **110** U15 19 04S 178 09E
Vyatka r. Russian Federation **84** G7 58 00N 50 00E
Vyatka see Kirov
Vyaz'ma Russian Federation **86** C6 55 12N 34 17E
Vyborg Russian Federation **84** E8 60 45N 28 41E
Vychegda r. Russian Federation **84** H8 62 00N 52 00E
Vyshniy-Volochek Russian Federation **86** C6
57 34N 34 23E

W

Wa Ghana **102** E10 10 07N 2 28W
Waal r. Netherlands **72** G6 51 50N 6 00E
Wabash r. North America **65** I4 38 00N 87 30W
Wabuska California U.S.A. **67** C4 39 09N 119 13W
Waco Texas U.S.A. **64** G3 31 33N 97 10W
Wadi al Masilah r. Yemen Republic **89** H2
16 00N 50 00E
Wadi Araba r. Israel **88** O10 30 30N 35 10E
Wadi el 'Arish r. Egypt **88** N9/10 30 05N 33 50E
Wadi Halfa Sudan **102** L12 21 55N 31 20E
Wad Medani Sudan **102** L10 14 24N 33 30E
Waesch, Mount Antarctica **113** 77 00S 127 30W
Wagga Wagga Australia **106** H2 35 07S 147 24E
Wagin Australia **106** B3 33 02S 117 20E
Waglan Island Hong Kong China **92** C1 22 10N 114 18E
Wah Pakistan **91** C6 33 50N 72 44E
Waha Libya **102** J13 28 10N 19 57E
Wahiawa Hawaiian Islands **111** X18 21 35N 158 05W
Wahpeton North Dakota U.S.A. **65** G6 46 16N 96 36W
Waialua Hawaiian Islands **111** X18 21 35N 158 08W
Waigeo i. Indonesia **95** I3 0 15S 130 45E
Waihi New Zealand **107** C3 37 57S 175 44E
Waikaremoana, Lake New Zealand **107** C3
38 46S 177 06E
Waikato r. New Zealand **107** C3 37 25S 175 45E
Wailuku Hawaiian Islands **111** Y18 20 54N 156 30W
Waimate New Zealand **107** B2 44 44S 171 03E
Wainwright Alaska U.S.A. **8** D7 70 39N 160 10W
Waipawa New Zealand **107** C3 39 57S 176 35E
Wairoa New Zealand **107** C3 39 03S 177 25E
Waitaki r. New Zealand **107** B2 44 45S 170 30E
Waitara New Zealand **107** B3 39 00S 174 14E
Wajima Japan **96** C2 37 23N 136 53E
Wajir Kenya **102** N8 1 46N 40 05E
Wakasa-wan b. Japan **96** C2 35 40N 135 30E
Wakatipu, Lake New Zealand **107** A1 45 06S 168 31E
Wakayama Japan **96** C1 34 12N 135 10E
Wake Island Pacific Ocean **110** G10 19 18N 166 36E
Wakkanai Japan **96** D4 45 26N 141 43E
Wako Japan **97** B4 35 46N 139 37E
Wales Alaska U.S.A. **8** B6 65 38N 168 09W
Wales admin. United Kingdom **74** G4
Walker r. California U.S.A. **67** C4 39 08N 119 00W
Walker Lake California U.S.A. **67** C4 38 45N 118 44W
Walker Lake Nevada U.S.A. **64** C4 38 40N 118 43W
Wallaroo Australia **106** F3 33 57S 137 36E
Walla Walla Washington U.S.A. **64** C6 46 05N 118 18W
Wallenpaupack, Lake Pennsylvania U.S.A. **66** C4
41 30N 75 20W
Walsall United Kingdom **74** J4 52 35N 1 58W
Walsenburg Colorado U.S.A. **64** F3 37 36N 104 48W
Waltham Forest bor. United Kingdom **78** C3
51 36N 0 00
Walthamstow United Kingdom **78** C3 51 34N 0 01W
Walton-on-Thames United Kingdom **78** B2
51 24N 0 25W
Walvis Bay tn. Namibia **103** H3 22 59S 14 31E
Walvis Ridge Atlantic Ocean **109** I3/4 30 00S 3 00E
Walyevo Fiji **110** V16 17 35S 179 58E
Wamba r. Congo (D.R.) **103** I6 6 30S 17 30E
Wanaka, Lake New Zealand **107** A2 44 28S 169 09E
Wandsworth bor. United Kingdom **78** C2 51 27N 0 11W
Wanganui New Zealand **107** C3 39 56S 175 03E
Wanganui r. New Zealand **107** C3 39 30S 175 00E
Wang Chau i. Hong Kong China **92** C2 22 20N 114 22E
Wang Toi Shan Hong Kong China **92** B2 22 26N 114 05E
Wan Medani Sudan **88** D1 14 24N 33 30E
Wansee Germany **79** E1 52 24N 13 09E
Wanstead United Kingdom **78** D3 51 34N 0 02E
Wanxian China **93** L5 30 54N 108 20E
Warangal India **91** D3 18 00N 79 35E
Wardha r. India **91** D4 20 30N 79 00E
Warm Springs California U.S.A. **67** D4 38 12N 116 24W
Warner Springs tn. California U.S.A. **67** D1
33 19N 116 38W
Warrego r. Australia **106** H4 27 30S 146 00E
Warren Michigan U.S.A. **42** C3 42 30N 83 02W
Warren Ohio U.S.A. **65** J5 41 15N 80 49W
Warren Pennsylvania U.S.A. **42** G2 41 52N 79 09W
Warrnambool Australia **106** G2 38 23S 142 03E
Warszawa (Warsaw) Poland **72** K6 52 15N 21 00E
Warwick Australia **106** I4 28 12S 152 00E
Warwick Rhode Island U.S.A. **65** L5 41 42N 71 23W
Wash, The b. United Kingdom **74** L4 52 55N 0 10E
Washington state U.S.A. **64** B6/C6 47 00N 120 00W
Washington Crossing Pennsylvania U.S.A. **66** D3
40 17N 74 53W
Washington D.C. District of Columbia U.S.A. **65** K4
38 55N 77 00W

Watampone Indonesia **95** G3 4 33S 120 20E
Waterfall *tn.* Australia **107** G1 34 08S 151 00E
Waterford Republic of Ireland **74** D4 52 15N 7 06W
Waterloo Iowa U.S.A. **65** H5 42 30N 92 20W
Waterloo New York U.S.A. **43** K3 42 55N 76 53W
Waterloo Trinidad and Tobago **69** T9 10 28N 61 28W
Watertown New York U.S.A. **65** K5 43 57N 75 56W
Watertown South Dakota U.S.A. **65** G5 44 54N 97 08W
Waterville Maine U.S.A. **65** M5 44 34N 69 41W
Waterville New York U.S.A. **43** L3 42 55N 75 24W
Waterville Ohio U.S.A. **42** C2 41 29N 83 44W
Watford United Kingdom **74** K3 51 39N 0 24W
Watkins Glen New York U.S.A. **43** K3 42 23N 76 53W
Wau Papua New Guinea **106** H8 7 22S 146 40E
Wau Sudan **102** K9 7 40N 28 04E
Waukegan Illinois U.S.A. **65** I5 42 21N 87 52W
Waukesha Wisconsin U.S.A. **65** I5 43 01N 88 14W
Wausau Wisconsin U.S.A. **65** I5 44 58N 89 40W
Waveney *r.* United Kingdom **74** M4 52 30N 1 30E
Waverly New York U.S.A. **66** B5 42 01N 76 33W
Wawona California U.S.A. **67** C3 37 32N 119 39W
Waycross Georgia U.S.A. **65** J3 31 12N 82 22W
Weald, The *geog. reg.* United Kingdom **74** L3
51 05N 0 25E
Wear *r.* United Kingdom **74** J6 54 40N 1 50W
Weddell Sea Southern Ocean **113** 71 00S 40 00W
Wedding Germany **79** F2 52 33N 13 21E
Weifang China **93** N6 36 44N 119 10E
Weigelstown Pennsylvania U.S.A. **66** B2
39 59N 79 47W
Wei He *r.* China **93** L5 34 00N 106 00E
Weipa Australia **106** G7 12 35S 141 56E
Weirton West Virginia U.S.A. **65** J5 40 24N 80 37W
Weissensee Germany **79** F2 51 12N 11 05E
Welland *r.* United Kingdom **74** K4 52 50N 0 00
Wellesley Islands Australia **106** F6 16 30S 139 00E
Wellington California U.S.A. **67** C4 38 45N 119 23W
Wellington Kansas U.S.A. **65** G4 37 17N 97 25W
Wellington New Zealand **107** B2 41 17S 174 46E
Wellington Ohio U.S.A. **42** D2 41 11N 82 13W
Wellsboro Pennsylvania U.S.A. **66** A4 41 45N 77 18W
Wellsford New Zealand **107** B3 36 18S 174 31E
Wellsville New York U.S.A. **42** J4 42 07N 77 56W
Wembley United Kingdom **78** B3 51 33N 0 18W
Wensum *r.* United Kingdom **74** M4 52 45N 1 10E
Wenyu He *r.* China **94** C2 40 02N 116 32E
Wenzhou China **93** O4 28 02N 120 40E
Werder Germany **79** D1 52 23N 12 56E
Wernersville Pennsylvania U.S.A. **66** B3 40 19N 76 06W
Weser *r.* Germany **72** G6 53 00N 8 00E
West Antarctica *geog. reg.* Antarctica **113**
80 00S 120 00W
West Australian Basin Indian Ocean **108** I4/J5
20 00S 100 00E
West Bank *territory* Israel **88** O11 32 00N 35 00E
West Bengal *admin.* India **91** F4 22 00N 88 00E
West Branch Michigan U.S.A. **42** B5 44 16N 84 14W
West Caroline Basin Pacific Ocean **110** D8
3 00N 136 00E
West Chester Pennsylvania U.S.A. **66** C2 39 58N 75 37W
Western Australia *state* Australia **106** A5/D3
25 00S 117 00E
Western Ghats *mts.* India **91** C2/3 15 30N 74 00E
WESTERN SAHARA 102 C12
Western Sayan *mts.* Russian Federation **85** L6
52 30N 92 30E
Western Yamuna Canal India **108** L4 28 40N 77 08E
West European Basin Atlantic Ocean **109** G11
47 00N 18 00W
West Falkland *i.* Falkland Islands **71** E2/F2
51 00S 60 40W
Westfield New York U.S.A. **42** G3 42 20N 79 34W
West Grand Lake Maine U.S.A. **47** C2 45 15N 68 00W
West Ham United Kingdom **78** D3 51 32N 0 01E
West Ice Shelf Antarctica **113** 66 00S 85 00E
West Indies *is.* Caribbean Sea **69** J4/K4 22 00N 69 00W
West Kingsdown United Kingdom **78** D2 51 20N 0 16E
Westlake Ohio U.S.A. **42** E2 41 25N 81 54W
West Lamma Channel Hong Kong China **92** B1
22 10N 114 00E
West Marianas Basin Pacific Ocean **110** D9
16 00N 137 30E
West Memphis Arkansas U.S.A. **65** H4 35 09N 90 11W
Westminster *bor.* United Kingdom **78** C2 51 30N 0 09W
Westminster Maryland U.S.A. **66** A2 39 35N 77 00W
West Palm Beach *tn.* Florida U.S.A. **65** J2
26 42N 80 05W
West Plains Missouri U.S.A. **65** H4 36 44N 91 51W
Westport California U.S.A. **67** A4 39 39N 123 47W
Westport Republic of Ireland **74** B5 53 48N 9 32W
West Port Russian Federation **86** L1
Westray *i.* United Kingdom **74** I11 59 18N 3 00W
West Siberian Lowland Russian Federation **85** J7/J8
60 00N 75 00E
West Thurrock United Kingdom **78** E2 51 29N 0 17E
West Virginia *state* U.S.A. **65** J4 39 00N 80 00W
West Walker *r.* California U.S.A. **67** C4 38 44N 119 27W
Wetar *i.* Indonesia **95** H2 7 15S 126 45E
Wewak Papua New Guinea **106** G9 3 35S 143 35E
Wexford Republic of Ireland **74** E4 52 20N 6 27W
Wey *r.* United Kingdom **78** B2 51 18N 0 30W
Weybridge United Kingdom **78** B2 51 22N 0 28W
Weymouth United Kingdom **74** I2 50 37N 2 25W
Whakatane New Zealand **107** C3 37 58S 176 59E
Whangarei New Zealand **107** B3 35 43S 174 19E
Wharton Pennsylvania U.S.A. **43** H2 41 32N 78 02N
Wharton Basin Indian Ocean **108** I5/J5 15 00S 100 00E

Wheeler Lake Alabama U.S.A. **65** I3 34 00N 87 00W
Wheeling West Viriginia U.S.A. **65** J5 40 05N 80 43W
White *r.* Arkansas U.S.A. **65** H4 35 00N 92 00W
White *r.* South Dakota U.S.A. **64** D2 43 00N 103 00W
Whitefish Montana U.S.A. **35** F1 48 25N 114 21W
Whitehaven United Kingdom **74** H6 54 33N 3 35W
White Nile *see* Bahr el Abiad
White Nile Dam Sudan **102** L11 14 18N 32 20E
White Sea Russian Federation **84** F9 66 00N 37 30E
White Volta *r.* Ghana **102** E10 9 30N 1 30W
Whitney, Mount California U.S.A. **64** C4
36 35N 118 17W
Whitney Point *tn.* New York U.S.A. **66** C5
42 20N 75 58W
Whyalla Australia **106** F3 33 04S 137 34E
Wichita Kansas U.S.A. **65** G4 37 43N 97 20W
Wichita *r.* Texas U.S.A. **64** F3 33 00N 100 00W
Wichita Falls *tn.* Texas U.S.A. **64** G3 33 55N 98 30W
Wick United Kingdom **74** H10 58 26N 3 06W
Wickliffe Ohio U.S.A. **42** E2 41 38N 81 25W
Wicklow Mountains Republic of Ireland **74** E5
53 00N 6 20W
Wien *(Vienna)* Austria **72** J5 48 13N 16 22E
Wigan United Kingdom **74** I5 53 33N 2 38W
Wildau Germany **79** G1 52 18N 13 38E
Wildwood *tn.* New Jersey U.S.A. **66** D1 38 59N 74 49W
Wilhelm II Land *geog. reg.* Antarctica **113** 70 00S 90 00E
Wilkes-Barre Pennsylvania U.S.A. **66** C4 41 15N 75 50W
Wilkes Land *geog. reg.* Antarctica **113** 68 00S 105 00E
Willemstad Curaçao **69** K2 12 12N 68 56W
Willesden United Kingdom **78** C3 51 33N 0 14W
Williams California U.S.A. **67** A4 39 09N 122 09W
Williams Bridge New York U.S.A. **67** Z2 40 53N 73 51W
Williamsport Pennsylvania U.S.A. **66** B4 41 16N 77 03W
Williamstown New Jersey U.S.A. **66** D2 39 41N 74 59W
Williston North Dakota U.S.A. **64** F6 48 09N 103 39W
Willits California U.S.A. **67** A4 39 23N 123 22W
Willmar Minnesota U.S.A. **65** G6 45 06N 95 03W
Willoughby Hills *tn.* Ohio U.S.A. **42** E2 41 35N 81 29W
Willow Grove Pennsylvania U.S.A. **66** C3 40 08N 75 07W
Willow River *r.* Michigan U.S.A. **42** D4 43 50N 82 58W
Willows California U.S.A. **67** A4 39 32N 122 10W
Willow Springs *tn.* Missouri U.S.A. **65** H4
36 59N 91 59W
Wilmersdörf Germany **79** F1 52 28N 13 16E
Wilmington Delaware U.S.A. **65** K4 39 46N 75 31W
Wilmington North Carolina U.S.A. **65** K3 34 14N 77 55W
Wilson New York U.S.A. **44** D2 43 15N 78 50W
Wilson North Carolina U.S.A. **65** K4 35 43N 77 56W
Wiluna Australia **106** C4 26 37S 120 12E
Wimbledon United Kingdom **78** C2 51 25N 0 13W
Winchester United Kingdom **74** J3 51 04N 1 19W
Winchester Virginia U.S.A. **65** K4 39 11N 78 12W
Windhoek Namibia **103** I3 22 34S 17 06E
Wind River Range *mts.* Wyoming U.S.A. **64** E5
43 00N 109 00W
Windsor United Kingdom **78** A2 51 29N 0 38W
Windward Islands Lesser Antilles **69** L2 12 30N 62 00W
Windward Passage *sd.* Cuba/Haiti **69** J3/J4
20 00N 73 00W
Winnemucca Nevada U.S.A. **64** C5 40 58N 117 45W
Winona Minnesota U.S.A. **65** H5 44 02N 91 37W
Winslow Arizona U.S.A. **64** D4 35 01N 110 43W
Winston-Salem North Carolina U.S.A. **65** J4
36 05N 80 18W
Winthrop New York U.S.A. **43** M5 44 58N 74 50W
Winton Australia **106** G5 22 22S 143 00E
Wisconsin *r.* Wisconsin U.S.A. **65** H5 45 00N 90 00W
Wisconsin *state* U.S.A. **65** H6 45 00N 90 00W
Wisła *r.* Poland **86** A5 53 00N 19 00E
Witham *r.* United Kingdom **74** K5 53 05N 0 10W
Woking United Kingdom **78** A2 51 20N 0 34W
Wolcott New York U.S.A. **43** K4 43 14N 76 51W
Wollongong Australia **106** I3 34 25S 150 52E
Wolverhampton United Kingdom **74** I4 52 36N 2 08W
Wong Chuk Hang Hong Kong China **92** C1
22 15N 114 10E
Wŏnju South Korea **93** P6 37 24N 127 52E
Wŏnsan North Korea **93** P6 39 07N 127 26E
Woodbine New Jersey U.S.A. **66** D2 39 14N 74 49W
Woodbury New Jersey U.S.A. **66** C2 39 50N 75 09W
Woodford United Kingdom **78** D3 51 37N 0 02E
Woodlark Island Papua New Guinea **106** I8
9 10S 152 50E
Woodstown New Jersey U.S.A. **66** C2 39 39N 75 19W
Woodville New Zealand **107** C2 40 21S 175 52E
Woodward Oklahoma U.S.A. **64** G4 36 26N 99 25W
Woollahra Australia **107** H2 33 53S 151 15E
Woolwich United Kingdom **78** D2 51 29N 0 04E
Wooster Ohio U.S.A. **42** E1 40 46N 81 57W
Worcester Massachusetts U.S.A. **65** L5 42 17N 71 48W
Worcester Republic of South Africa **103** I3 33 39S 19 26E
Worcester United Kingdom **74** I4 52 11N 2 13W
Workington United Kingdom **74** H6 54 39N 3 33W
Worland Wyoming U.S.A. **64** E5 44 01N 107 58W
Woronora Reservoir Australia **107** F1 34 07S 150 56E
Woronora River Australia **107** G1 34 07S 151 00E
Worthing Barbados **69** V12 13 05N 59 37W
Worthing United Kingdom **74** K2 50 48N 0 23W
Worthington Minnesota U.S.A. **65** G5 43 37N 95 36W
Wrangel *see* Vrangelya
Wrangell Alaska U.S.A. **8** J4 56 28N 132 23W
Wrangell Island Alaska U.S.A. **34** B3 56 25N 132 05W
Wrangell Mountains *mts.* Alaska U.S.A. **8** G5
62 00N 143 00W
Wrangell-St. Elias National Park Alaska U.S.A. **50** C3
62 00N 142 30W

Wrath, Cape United Kingdom **74** G10 58 37N 5 01W
Wrexham *tn.* United Kingdom **74** H5 53 03N 3 00W
Wright Corners New York U.S.A. **44** D2 43 10N 78 45W
Wright Peak *mt.* South Dakota U.S.A. **113** 73 15S 94 00W
Wrightsville Pennsylvania U.S.A. **66** B3 40 02N 76 30W
Wrocław Poland **72** J6 51 05N 17 00E
Wuhai China **93** L6 39 40N 106 40E
Wuhan China **93** M5 30 35N 114 19E
Wuhu China **93** N5 31 23N 118 25E
Wukari Nigeria **102** G9 7 49N 9 49E
Wurno Nigeria **102** G10 13 18N 5 29E
Wusul Jiang *(Ussuri)* *r.* China **93** Q8 47 00N 134 00E
Wutongqiao China **93** K4 29 21N 103 48E
Wuxi China **93** O5 31 35N 120 19E
Wuyi Shan *mts.* China **93** N4 26 00N 116 30E
Wuzhou China **93** M3 23 30N 111 21E
Wye *r.* United Kingdom **74** H4 51 58N 2 35W
Wyndham Australia **106** D6 15 30S 128 09E
Wyoming *state* U.S.A. **64** E5 43 00N 108 00W

X

Xaanfuun Somalia **102** P10 10 27N 51 15E
Xaidulla China **91** D7 36 27N 77 46E
Xam Hua Laos **93** K3 20 28N 104 05E
Xiaguan *see* Dali
Xiamen China **93** N3 24 28N 118 05E
Xi'an China **93** L5 34 16N 108 54E
Xiangfan China **93** M5 32 05N 112 03E
Xiangkhoang Laos **95** C7 19 21N 102 23E
Xiangtan China **93** M4 27 48N 112 55E
Xianyang China **93** L5 34 22N 108 42E
Xianyou China **94** E8 25 23N 118 40E
Xigaze China **92** G4 29 18N 88 50E
Xi Jiang *r.* China **93** M3 23 30N 111 00E
Xingtai China **93** M6 37 08N 114 29E
Xining China **93** K6 36 35N 101 55E
Xinjiang Uygur Zizhiqu *(Sinkiang Uighur Autonomous Region) admin.* China **92** F6/G7 41 00N 85 00E
Xinjin China **93** O6 39 25N 121 58E
Xiqing Shan *mts.* China **93** K5 34 00N 102 30E
Xizang Zizhiqu *(Tibet Autonomous Region) admin.*
China **92** F5/H5 33 30N 85 00E
Xizhuang China **94** B1 39 51N 116 20E
Xochimilco Mexico **68** E3 19 08N 99 09W
Xuanhua China **93** M4 40 36N 115 01E
Xuchang China **93** M5 34 03N 113 48E
Xuwen China **93** M3 20 25N 110 08E
Xuzhou China **93** N5 34 17N 117 18E

Y

Yablonovy Range *mts.* Russian Federation **85** M6/N6
51 30N 110 00E
Yabrūd Syria **88** P11 33 58N 36 39E
Yaizu Japan **96** C1 34 54N 138 20E
Yakima Washington U.S.A. **64** B6 46 37N 120 30W
Yakima *r.* Washington U.S.A. **64** B6 47 00N 120 00W
Yakutat Alaska U.S.A. **50** D2 59 50N 139 49W
Yakutat Bay *b.* Alaska U.S.A. **34** A3 59 50N 140 00W
Yakutsk Russian Federation **85** O8 62 10N 129 50E
Yalu *r.* China/North Korea **93** P7 41 00N 127 00E
Yamagata Japan **96** D2 38 16N 140 16E
Yamaguchi Japan **96** B1 34 10N 131 28E
Yamal Peninsula Russian Federation **85** I10/J10
72 00N 70 00E
Yaman-Tau *mt.* Russian Federation **87** H5
54 58N 59 00E
Yamato Japan **97** A2 35 29N 139 27E
Yambio Sudan **102** K8 4 34N 28 21E
Yamburg Russian Federation **85** J9 68 19N 77 09E
Yamoussoukro Côte d'Ivoire **102** D9 6 50N 5 20W
Yamuna *r.* India **91** D5 26 00N 79 30E
Yamunanagar India **91** D6 30 07N 77 17E
Yana *r.* Russian Federation **85** P9 69 00N 135 00E
Yanbu'al Bahr Saudi Arabia **88** E3 24 07N 38 04E
Yangcheng China **93** O5 33 23N 120 10E
Yangon *(Rangoon)* Myanmar **95** B7 16 47N 96 10E
Yangquan China **93** M6 37 52N 113 29E
Yangtze *see* Chang Jiang (lower course)
Yangtze *see* Jinsha Jiang (upper course)
Yanji China **93** P7 42 52N 129 32E
Yanjing China **93** J4 29 01N 98 38E
Yankton South Dakota U.S.A. **65** G5 42 53N 97 24W
Yantai China **93** O6 37 30N 121 22E
Yao Japan **96** C1 34 36N 135 37E
Yaoundé Cameroon **102** H8 3 51N 11 31E
Yap Islands Pacific Ocean **110** D8 9 30N 138 09E
Yap Trench Pacific Ocean **110** D8 10 00N 139 00E
Yaqui *r.* Mexico **68** C5 28 00N 109 50W
Yaritagua Venezuela **69** K2 10 05N 69 07W
Yarkant He *r.* China **85** J3 36 00N 76 00E
Yarlung Zangbo Jiang *(Tsangpo) r.* China **92** H4
29 00N 92 30E
Yaroslavl' Russian Federation **84** F7 57 34N 39 52E
Yarumal Colombia **70** B14 6 59N 75 25W
Yasawa *i.* Fiji **110** T16 16 50S 177 30E
Yasawa Group *is.* Fiji **110** T16 17 00S 177 40E
Yatsushiro Japan **96** B1 32 31N 130 35E
Yau Tong Hong Kong China **92** C1 22 18N 114 14E
Yauza *r.* Russian Federation **86** M2 55 45N 37 43E
Yawatahama Japan **96** B1 33 27N 132 24E
Yazd Iran **89** H5 31 54N 54 22E
Yazoo *r.* Mississippi U.S.A. **65** H3 33 00N 90 00W
Ye Myanmar **95** B7 15 15N 97 50E
Yekaterinburg *(Sverdlovsk)* Russian Federation **84** I7
56 52N 60 35E
Yelets Russian Federation **86** D5 52 35N 38 30E

Yell *i.* United Kingdom **74** J12 60 35N 1 10W
Yellow Sea *(Huang Hai)* China **93** O6 35 30N 122 30E
Yellowstone *r.* U.S.A. **64** E6 46 00N 108 00W
Yellowstone Lake Wyoming U.S.A. **64** D5
44 30N 110 20W
Yellowstone National Park Wyoming U.S.A. **64** D5
44 00N 110 30W
YEMEN REPUBLIC 88 F2
Yenakiyeve Ukraine **86** D4 48 14N 38 15E
Yenisey *r.* Russian Federation **85** K8 64 00N 87 30E
Yenisey, Gulf of Russian Federation **85** J10/K10
72 30N 80 00E
Yeniseysk Russian Federation **85** L7 58 27N 92 13E
Yeppoon Australia **106** I5 23 05S 150 42E
Yerevan Armenia **73** P4 40 10N 44 31E
Yerington California U.S.A. **67** C4 39 00N 119 11W
Yermolayevo Russian Federation **87** H5 52 46N 55 54E
Yerres *r.* France **79** C1 48 40N 2 36E
Yesil *r.* Turkey **88** E7 41 00N 36 25E
Yevpatoriya Ukraine **86** C4 45 12N 33 20E
Ye Xian China **93** N6 37 10N 119 55E
Yibin China **93** K4 28 42N 104 30E
Yichang China **93** M5 30 46N 111 20E
Yichun China **93** P8 47 41N 129 10E
Yinchuan China **93** L6 38 30N 106 19E
Yingkou China **93** O7 40 40N 122 17E
Yining China **92** F7 43 50N 81 28E
Yirga 'Alem Ethiopia **102** M9 6 48N 38 22E
Yiyang China **93** M4 28 39N 112 10E
Yoakum Texas U.S.A. **65** G2 29 18N 97 20W
Yogyakarta Indonesia **95** E2 7 48S 110 24E
Yoichi Japan **96** D3 43 14N 140 47E
Yokadouma Cameroon **102** I8 3 26N 15 06E
Yokkaichi Japan **96** C1 34 58N 136 38E
Yokohama Tōkyō Japan **96** C2 35 27N 139 38E
Yokosuka Japan **96** C2 35 18N 139 38E
Yokote Japan **96** D3 39 20N 140 31E
Yola Nigeria **102** H9 9 14N 12 32E
Yonago Japan **96** B2 35 27N 133 20E
Yonaguni *i.* Japan **94** F2 24 29N 123 00E
Yongchun China **94** E8 25 18N 118 13E
York Pennsylvania U.S.A. **65** K4 39 57N 76 44W
York United Kingdom **74** J5 53 58N 1 05W
York, Cape Australia **106** G7 10 42S 142 32E
Yorkshire Wolds *hills* United Kingdom **74** K6
54 00N 0 45W
Yosemite National Park California U.S.A. **64** C4
37 30N 119 00W
Yoshkar-Ola Russian Federation **86** F6 56 38N 47 52E
Yŏsu South Korea **93** P5 34 50N 127 30E
You Jiang *r.* China **93** L3 23 30N 107 00E
Youghal Republic of Ireland **74** D3 51 51N 7 50W
Youngstown New York U.S.A. **42** G4 43 14N 79 01W
Youngstown Ohio U.S.A. **65** J5 41 05N 80 40W
Youngsville Pennsylvania U.S.A. **42** G2 41 52N 79 22W
Ypsilanti Michigan U.S.A. **42** C3 42 15N 83 36W
Yuan Jiang *see* Song-koi
Yüan-li Taiwan **94** G7 24 29N 120 40E
Yüan-lin Taiwan **94** G6 23 57N 120 33E
Yuba *r.* California U.S.A. **64** B4 39 22N 121 12W
Yūbari Japan **96** D3 43 04N 141 59E
Yucatan *p.* Mexico **68** G3 19 00N 89 00W
Yucatan Basin Caribbean Sea **109** R 20 00N 85 00W
Yucca Lake California U.S.A. **67** D3 37 00N 116 02W
Yuci China **93** M6 37 40N 112 44E
Yuen Long Hong Kong China **92** B2 22 26N 114 02E
Yugakir Plateau Russian Federation **85** R9
66 30N 156 00E
YUGOSLAVIA 72 K4
Yu Jiang *r.* China **93** L3 23 00N 109 00E
Yukon Delta Alaska U.S.A. **8** C5 62 45N 164 00W
Yukon Flats National Wildlife Refuge Alaska U.S.A.
50 B4 66 30N 147 30W
Yü-li Taiwan **94** H6 23 22N 121 20E
Yuma Arizona U.S.A. **64** D3 32 40N 114 39W
Yumen China **93** J6 39 54N 97 43E
Yun *(Grand Canal)* China **94** C1 39 54N 116 33E
Yung-kang Taiwan **94** G5 23 00N 120 15E
Yung Shue Wan Hong Kong China **92** B1
22 13N 114 06E
Yurimaguas Peru **70** B11 5 54S 76 07W
Yü Shan *mt.* Taiwan **94** G6 23 25N 120 52E
Yü Shan National Park Taiwan **94** G6/H6
23 15N 121 00E
Yushu China **91** H6 33 06N 96 48E
Yü-weng Tao *i.* Taiwan **94** F6 23 36N 119 30E
Yuzhno-Sakhalinsk Russian Federation **85** Q5
46 58N 142 45E
Yvelines *admin.* France **79** A1 48 42N 2 03E

Z

Zacapa Guatemala **68** G3 15 00N 89 30E
Zacatecas Mexico **68** D4 22 48N 102 33W
Zacatecoluca El Salvador **68** G2 13 29N 88 51W
Zagazig Egypt **88** D5 30 36N 31 30E
Zagreb *(Agram)* Croatia **72** J5 45 48N 15 58E
Zagros Mountains Iran **89** G5 32 45N 48 50E
Zāhedān Iran **89** J4 29 32N 60 54E
Zahlé Lebanon **88** E5 33 50N 35 55E
ZAÏRE *see* CONGO (D.R.)
Zaltan Libya **102** I13 28 15N 19 52E
Zambeze *(Zambezi) r.* Mozambique **103** L4
16 00S 34 00E
Zambezi *(Zambeze)* Zambia **103** J5 13 33S 23 08E
ZAMBIA 103 K5
Zamboanga The Philippines **95** G5 6 55N 122 05E

Zanderij Suriname **70** F14 5 26N 55 14W
Zanesville Ohio U.S.A. **65** J4 39 55N 82 02W
Zanjän Iran **89** G6 36 40N 48 30E
Zanthus Australia **106** C3 31 01S 123 32E
Zanzibar *i.* Tanzania **103** M6 6 10S 39 13E
Zanzibar Tanzania **103** M6 6 10S 39 12E
Zaozhuang China **93** N5 34 53N 117 38E
Zaporizhzhya Ukraine **86** D4 47 50N 35 10E
Zaragoza Spain **72** E4 41 39N 0 54W
Zarand Iran **89** I5 30 50N 56 35E
Zaraza Venezuela **70** D14 9 23N 65 20W
Zarembo Island Alaska U.S.A. **34** B3 56 30N 132 50W
Zaria Nigeria **102** G10 11 01N 7 44E
Zarqa Jordan **88** E5 32 04N 36 05E
Zaysan Kazakhstan **87** N4 47 30N 84 57E
Zefat Israel **88** O11 32 57N 35 27E
Zehlendorf Germany **79** F1 52 26N 13 15E
Zelenogradsk Russian Federation **86** A5 54 57N 20 28E
Zemlya Frantsa-Iosifa *(Franz Josef Land) is.*
    Russian Federation **85** G12/112 80 00N 50 00E
Zepernick Germany **79** G2 52 41N 13 31E
Zephyr Cove California U.S.A. **67** C4 39 07N 119 57W
Zeuthener See *l.* Germany **79** G1 52 20N 13 40E
Zeya *r.* Russian Federation **85** O6 53 00N 127 30E
Zeya Russian Federation **85** O6 53 48N 127 14E
Zeyskoye Vodokhranilishche *res.* Russia **93** P9
    49 30N 130 00E
Zhambyl *(Dzhambul)* Kazakhstan **87** L3
    42 50N 71 25E
Zhangjiakou China **93** M7 40 51N 114 59E
Zhangzhou China **93** N3 24 31N 117 40E
Zhanjiang China **93** M3 21 10N 110 20E
Zharma Kazakhstan **87** N4 48 50N 80 50E
Zhengzhou China **93** M5 34 45N 113 38E
Zhenjiang China **93** N5 32 08N 119 30E
Zhezkazgan *(Dzhezkazgan)* Kazakhstan **87** K4
    47 44N 67 42E
Zhigansk Russian Federation **85** O9 66 48N 123 27E
Zhitomir *see* Zhytomyr
Zhlobin Belarus **86** C5 52 50N 30 00E
Zhmerynka Ukraine **86** B4 49 00N 28 02E
Zhob Pakistan **90** B6 31 30N 69 30E
Zhonghai *l.* China **94** B1 39 56N 116 22E
Zhongshan Antarctica **113** 69 22S 76 23E
Zhuzhou China **93** M4 27 53N 113 07E
Zhytomyr *(Zhitomir)* Ukraine **86** B5 50 18N 28 40E
Zibo China **93** N6 36 51N 118 01E
Zigong China **93** K4 29 25N 104 47E
Ziguinchor Senegal **102** B10 12 35N 16 20W
ZIMBABWE 103 K4
Zinder Niger **102** G10 13 46N 8 58E
Ziqudukou China **92** J5 33 03N 95 51E
Zlatoust Russian Federation **84** H7 55 10N 59 38E
Zomba Malawi **103** M4 15 22S 35 22E
Zonguldak Turkey **73** M4 41 26N 31 47E
Zouar Chad **102** I12 20 30N 16 30E
Zouérate Mauritania **102** C12 22 44N 12 21W
Zunyi China **93** L4 27 35N 106 48E
Zürich Switzerland **72** G5 47 23N 8 33E
Zushi Japan **97** B2 35 17N 139 39E
Zvishavane Zimbabwe **103** L3 20 20S 30 02E
Zyryanka Russian Federation **85** R9 65 42N 150 49E
Zyryanovsk Kazakhstan **87** N4 49 45N 84 16E

Abbreviation used on the maps

admin	administrative area
A.C.T.	Australian Capital Territory
b.	bay or harbour
bor.	borough
c.	cape, point, or headland
can.	canal
co.	county
d.	desert
dep.	depression
est.	estuary
fj.	fjord
g.	gulf
geog. reg.	geographical region
N.H.S	national historic site
i.	island
in.	inlet
I.R.	Indian Reservation
is.	islands
ist.	isthmus
l.	lake, lakes, lagoon
m.	marsh
m.s.	manned meteorological station
mt.	mountain
mts.	mountains
p.	peninsula
pk.	park
plat.	plateau
pn.	plain
pref.	prefecture
prov.	province
r.	river
rd.	road
r.s.	research station
reg.	region
rep.	republic
res.	reservoir
salt l.	salt lake
sd.	sound, strait, or channel
sum.	summit
tn.	town
U.A.E.	United Arab Emirates
U.K.	United Kingdom
U.S.A.	United States of America
v.	valley
vol.	volcano

Abbreviation used on the maps

A.C.T.	Australian Capital Territory
Ákr.	Ákra
App.	Appennino
Arch.	Archipelago
Arg.	Argentina
Arq.	Arquipelago
Austl.	Australia
C.	Cape; Cabo; Cap
Col.	Colombia
D.C.	District of Columbia
Den.	Denmark
D.R.	Democratic Republic
E.	East
Ec.	Ecuador
Eq.	Equatorial
Fj	Fjord
Fr.	France
G.	Gunung; Gebel
Hwy.	Highway
I.	Island; Île; Isla; Ilha
Is.	Islands; Îles; Islas; Ilhas
J.	Jezioro
Jez.	Jezero
Kep.	Kepulauan
M.	Muang
Mt.	Mount; Mountain; Mont
Mte.	Monte
Mts.	Mountains; Monts
N.	North
Nat.Pk.	National Park
Neths.	Netherlands
N.P.	National Park
N.Z.	New Zealand
Pa.	Passage
Peg.	Pegunungan
Pen; Penin.	Peninsula
Pl.	Planina
Port.	Portugal
P.P	Provincial Park
proj.	projected
Prov. Park	Provincial Park
Pt.	Point
Pta.	Punta
Pte.	Pointe
Pto.	Porto; Puerto
R.	River; Rio
Ra.	Range
R.A.	Recreation Area
Res.	Reservoir
R.M.	Regional Municipality
RÉS. FAUN.	Réserve Faunique
Résr.	Réservoir
S.	South; San
S.A.	South Africa
Sa.	Sierra
Sd.	Sound
Sev.	Severnaya
Sp.	Spain
St.	Saint
Ste.	Sainte
Str.	Strait
Terr.	Territory
U.A.E.	United Arab Emirates
u/c.	under construction
U.K.	United Kingdom
U.N.	United Nations
U.S.A.	United States of America
U.S.S.R.	Union of Soviet Socialist Republics
W.	West

Glossary

Ákra	cape (Greek)
Älv	river (Swedish)
Bahia	bay (Spanish)
Bahr	stream (arabic)
Baie	bay (French)
Bugt	bay (Danish)
Cabo	cape (Portuguese; Spanish)
Cap	cape (French)
Capo	cape (Italian)
Cerro	hill (Spanish)
Chaîne	mountain range (French)
Chapada	hills (Portuguese)
Chott	salt lake (Arabic)
Co	lake (Chinese)
Collines	hills (French)
Cordillera	mountain range (Spanish)
Costa	coast (Spanish)
Côte	coast (French)
-dake	peak (Japanese)
Danau	lake (Indonesian)
Dao	island (Chinese)
Dasht	desert (Persian; Urdu)
Djebel	mountain (Arabic)
Do	island (Korean; Vietnamese)
Embalse	reservoir (Spanish)
Erg	dunes (Arabic)
Estrecho	strait (Spanish)
Estreito	strait (Portuguese)
Gebel	mountain (Arabic)
Golfe	gulf; bay (French)
Golfo	gulf; bay (Italian; Spanish)
Göiü	lake (Turkish)
Gora	mountain (Russian)
Gunto	islands (Japanese)
Gunung	mountain (Indonesian; Malay)
Hafen	harbour (German)
Hai	sea (Chinese)
Ho	river (Chinese)
Hu	lake (Chinese)
Île; Isle	island (French)
Ilha	island (Portuguese)
Inseln	islands (German)
Isla	island (Spanish)
Istmo	isthmus (Spanish)
Jabal;Jebel	mountain (Arabic)
Jezero	lake (Serbo-Croat)
Jezioro	lake (Polish)
Jiang	river (Chinese)
-jima	island (Japanese)
-kaikyō	strait (Japanese)
Kamen'	rock (Russian)
Kap	cape (Danish)
Kepulauan	islands (Indonesian)
-ko	lake (Japanese)
Lac	lake (French)
Lago	lake (Italian; Portuguese; Spanish)
Laguna	lagoon (Spanish)
Ling	mountain range (Chinese)
Llyn	lake (Welsh)
-misaki	cape (Japanese)
Mont	mountain (French)
Montagne	mountain (French)
Monts	mountains (French)
Monti	mountains (Italian)
More	sea (Russian)
Muang	city (Thai)
Mys	cape (Russian)
-nada	gulf;sea (Japanese)
-nama	cape (Japanese)
Ostrova	islands (Russian)
Ozero	lake (Russian)
Pergunungan	mountain range (Indonesia)
Pendi	basin (Chinese)
Pic	summit (French; Spanish)
Pico	summit (Spanish)
Pik	summit (Russian)
Planalto	plateau (Portuguese)
Planina	mountain range (Bulgarian; Serbo-Croat)
Poluostrov	peninsula (Russian)
Puerto	port (Spanish)
Pulau-pulau	islands (Indonesian)
Puncak	mountain (Indonesian)
Punta	cape (Italian; Spanish)
Ras; Rås	cape (Arabic)
Ra's	cape (Persian)
Rio	river (Portuguese; Spanish)
Rivière	river (French)
Rubha	cape (Gaelic)
-saki	cape (Japanese)
Salina	salt pan (Spanish)
-san	mountain (Japanese)
-sanchi	mountains (Japanese)
-sanmyaku	mountain range (Japanese)
Sebkra	salt pan (Arabic)
See	lake (German)
Selat	strait (Indonesian)
Seto	strait (Japanese)
Shan	mountains (Chinese)
-shima	island (Japanese)
-shotō	islands (Japanese)
Sierra	mountain range (Spanish)
Song	river (Vietnamese)
-suidō	strait (Japanese)
Tassili	plateau (Berber)
Tau	mountain (Chinese)
Teluk	bay (Indonesian)
-tō	island (Japanese)
Tonle	lake (Cambodian)
-wan	bay (Japanese)
-zaki	cape (Japanese)
Zaliv	bay (Russian)

Land

1. Land and Fresh Water Area

PROVINCE OR TERRITORY	LAND (KM²)	FRESHWATER (KM²)	TOTAL (KM²)
Newfoundland	371 690	34 030	405 720
Prince Edward Island	5 660	–	5 660
Nova Scotia	52 840	2 650	55 490
New Brunswick	72 090	1 350	73 440
Quebec	1 356 790	183 890	1 540 680
Ontario	891 190	177 390	1 068 580
Manitoba	548 360	101 590	649 950
Saskatchewan	570 700	81 630	652 330
Alberta	644 390	16 800	661 190
British Columbia	929 730	18 070	947 800
Yukon	478 970	4 480	483 450
Northwest Territories	3 293 020	133 300	3 426 320
Canada	**9 215 430**	**755 180**	**9 970 610**

SOURCE: *Canada Year Book 1997.*

2. Primary Land Cover in Canada

LAND COVER CLASS	PREDOMINANT COVER IN THE CLASS	AREA[a] (KM², 000)	% CANADA TOTAL[b]
Forest and taiga	Closed canopy forest and/or open stands of trees with secondary occurrences of wetland, barren land, or others	4 456	45
Tundra/sparse vegetation	Well-vegetated to sparsely vegetated or barren land, mostly in arctic or alpine environments	2 303	23
Wetland	Treed and non-treed fens, bogs, swamps, marshes, shallow open water, and coastal and shore marshes	1 244	12
Fresh water	Lakes, rivers, streams, and reservoirs dogs	755	8
Cropland	Fenced land (including cropland and pasture land), hedge rows, farms, and orchards	658	6
Rangeland	Generally nonfenced pasture land, grazing land; includes natural grassland that is not necessarily used for agriculture	203	2
Ice/snow	Permanent ice and snow fields (glaciers, ice caps)	272	3
Built-up	Urban and industrial land	79	1
Total		**9 970**	**100**

[a]Includes the area of all land and fresh water. [b]Rounded to the nearest percent. NOTE: Data for this table are derived from satellite imagery and may deviate slightly from other sources of data.
SOURCE: Energy, Mines and Resources Canada (1989). From *The State of Canada's Environment*, published by the authority of the Minister of the Environment and the Minister of Supply and Services Canada, 1991.

3. Land Use in Canada

LAND USE CLASS	PREDOMINANT ACTIVITY IN THE CLASS	AREA[a] (KM², 000)	% OF CANADA[b]
Forestry[c]	Active forest harvesting or potential for future harvesting	2 440	24
Recreation and conservation[d]	Recreation and conservation within national, provincial, and territorial parks, wildlife reserves, sanctuaries, etc.	756	8
Agriculture[e]	Agriculture on improved farmland (cropland, improved pasture, summerfallow) and unimproved farmland	680	7
Urban	Built-up urban areas	20	<1
Other activities	Includes hunting and trapping, mining, energy developments, and transportation	6 074	61
Total		**9 970**	**100**

[a] Includes the area of all land and fresh water. [b]Rounded to the nearest percent. [d] National Conservation Areas Database, State of the Environment Directorate, Environment Canada. [e] Statistics Canada (1994c).
SOURCE: *Report on the Demographic Situation in Canada 1996*, Statistics Canada, Cat. No. 91-209-XPE.

Population

4. Total Population Growth, 1851 to 1996

CENSUS YEAR	POPULATION (000)	AVERAGE ANNUAL RATE OF POPULATION GROWTH (%)
1851	2 436.3	—
1861	3 229.6	2.9
1871	3 689.3	1.3
1881	4 324.8	1.6
1891	4 833.2	1.1
1901	5 371.3	1.1
1911	7 206.6	3.0
1921	8 787.9	2.0
1931	10 376.8	1.7
1941	11 506.7	1.0
1951[1]	14 009.4	1.7
1961	18 238.2	2.5
1971	21 568.3	1.5
1981	24 343.2	1.1
1991	27 296.9	1.5
1996[2]	28 846.7	1.1

[1]Newfoundland included for the first time.
[2]1996 Census.
SOURCE: *Canada Year Book 1992*; 1996 Census.

5. Population Growth, 1961 to 1996, and Population Density, 1996

PROVINCE OR TERRITORY	1961	1971	1981	1991	1996	POPULATION DENSITY/KM² 1996
Newfoundland	457 853	522 104	567 181	568 474	551 792	1.4
Prince Edward Island	104 629	111 641	122 506	129 765	134 557	24.0
Nova Scotia	737 007	788 960	847 882	899 942	909 282	16.4
New Brunswick	597 936	634 557	696 403	723 900	738 133	10.1
Quebec	5 259 211	6 027 764	6 438 403	6 895 963	7 138 795	4.6
Ontario	6 236 092	7 703 106	8 625 107	10 084 885	10 753 573	10.1
Manitoba	921 686	988 247	1 026 241	1 091 942	1 113 898	1.7
Saskatchewan	925 181	926 242	968 313	988 928	990 237	1.5
Alberta	1 331 944	1 627 874	2 237 724	2 545 553	2 696 826	4.1
British Columbia	1 629 082	2 184 021	2 744 467	3 282 061	3 724 500	3.9
Yukon	14 628	18 388	23 153	27 797	30 766	0.06
Northwest Territories	22 998	34 807	45 741	57 649	64 402	0.02
Canada	**18 238 247**	**21 568 310**	**24 343 181**	**27 296 859**	**28 846 761**	**2.9**

SOURCE: *Canada Year Book*, various years; 1996 Census, *A National Overview*, Statistics Canada, April 1996.

6. Births, Deaths, Migration, Infant Mortality, and Life Expectancy, 1995

DEMOGRAPHIC CATEGORY		NFLD	PEI	NS	NB	QUE	ONT	MAN	SASK	ALTA	BC	YT	NWT	CANADA
Birth Rate/1000		10.2	12.9	11.4	11.3	11.9	13.2	14.2	13.3	14.1	12.4	15.4	24.5	**12.8**
Death Rate/1000		6.8	8.4	8.2	7.8	7.2	7.1	8.5	8.4	5.8	7.0	5.2	3.5	**7.1**
Number of Immigrants (000)		0.61	0.16	3.8	0.64	26.8	115.5	3.6	1.9	14.6	44.5	0.09	0.1	**212.2**
Number of Emigrants (000)		0.27	0.08	0.83	1.00	6.3	19.7	2.3	1.00	7.8	7.1	0.07	0.8	**46.6**
Interprovincial In-migration		9.5	2.9	18.2	13.4	26.9	78.7	19.1	20.7	60.0	75.8	2.8	3.3	—
Interprovincial Out-migration		16.1	2.4	19.9	14.1	37.6	81.7	21.6	23.1	56.8	51.7	2.0	4.0	—
Infant Mortality/1000 [1994]		8.2	6.4	6.0	5.3	5.7	6.0	7.0	8.9	7.4	6.3	2.3	14.6	6.3
Life Expectancy at Birth (in years) [1994]	M	73.9	n.a.	74.3	74.7	74.4	75.5	74.9	75.3	75.6	75.8	n.a.	n.a.	75.1
	F	80.0	n.a.	80.5	80.7	81.2	81.1	80.9	81.8	81.4	81.5	n.a.	n.a.	81.2

SOURCE: *Report on the Demographic Situation in Canada 1996*, Statistics Canada, Cat. No. 91-209-XPE.

7. Population by First Language, 1991 and 1996[1]

OFFICIAL LANGUAGE	1991	1996	% Change 1981–1996[2]
English	16 169 875	16 890 615	15.0
French	6 502 860	6 636 660	8.3
NON-OFFICIAL LANGUAGE			
Aboriginal	172 610	186 935	24.4
Italian	510 990	484 500	–3.1
Portuguese	212 090	211 290	32.6
Spanish	177 425	212 890	230.6
German	466 245	450 140	–7.3
Croatian	39 660	50 105	(26.2)
Dutch	149 870	143 705	5.3
Ukrainian	187 010	162 695	–33.6
Russian	35 300	57 495	101.8
Polish	189 815	213 410	83.8
Finnish	27 705	24 735	–20.6
Hungarian	79 770	77 235	–0.5
Greek	126 205	121 180	3.8
Arabic	107 750	148 555	234.7
Indo-Iranian	301 335	430 485	(42.9)
Tamil	30 535	66 835	(119.0)
Chinese	498 845	715 640	236.3
Vietnamese	78 570	106 515	276.3
Tagalog (Filipino)	99 715	133 215	268.0
Korean	36 185	54 540	(50.6)
Total Single Response	26 686 850	28 125 560	18.4
Total Multiple Response	307 190	402 560	(31.1)
Canada	**26 994 045**	**28 528 125**	**17.2**

[1]The first language is the language learned at home in childhood and still understood by the individual at the time of the census. [2]Percent change in brackets indicates change from 1991 to 1996.
SOURCE: Census of Canada 1981, 1991, and 1996.

8. Components of Population Growth, 1960 to 1995

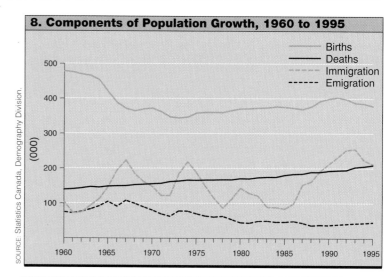

SOURCE: Statistics Canada, Demography Division.

9. Percentage of People Who Are Bilingual (English and French), 1971, 1986, and 1996

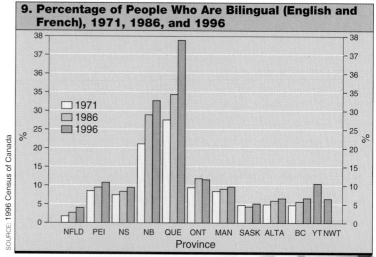

SOURCE: 1996 Census of Canada

10. Population by Ethnic Origin, 1991

PROVINCE OR TERRITORY	BRITISH	FRENCH	DUTCH	GERMAN	ITALIAN	ABORIGINAL	POLISH	SCANDINAVIAN	UKRAINIAN	CARIBBEAN	MULTIPLE ORIGINS	TOTAL
Newfoundland	442 805	9 700	445	1 320	295	5 340	175	510	120	60	98 290	568 474
% Distribution	77.9	1.7	0.08	0.23	0.05	0.9	0.03	0.09	0.02	17.2	17.2	100.0
Prince Edward Island	56 405	11 845	1 250	645	40	395	145	180	65	0	55 165	129 765
% Distribution	43.5	8.6	1.0	0.5	0.03	0.3	0.1	0.1	0.05	0	42.5	100.0
Nova Scotia	391 810	55 310	8 960	24 830	2 715	7 530	2 365	1 525	1 365	190	358 105	899 942
% Distribution	43.5	6.1	1.0	2.8	0.3	0.8	0.3	0.2	0.2	0.02	39.8	100.0
New Brunswick	236 385	235 010	3 045	4 480	1 320	4 270	580	1 475	470	105	212 675	723 900
% Distribution	32.7	32.5	0.4	0.6	0.2	0.6	0.1	0.2	0.06	0.02	29.4	100.0
Quebec	286 080	5 077 830	7 100	31 345	174 530	65 405	23 695	3 195	11 450	26 755	572 395	6 895 963
% Distribution	4.1	73.6	0.1	0.5	2.5	1.0	0.3	0.05	0.2	0.4	8.3	100.0
Ontario	2 536 515	527 580	179 760	289 420	486 765	71 005	154 155	26 415	104 995	59 860	3 278 050	10 084 885
% Distribution	25.2	5.2	1.8	2.9	4.8	0.7	1.5	0.3	1.0	0.6	32.5	100.0
Manitoba	183 485	53 580	24 465	93 995	8 120	74 340	21 600	14 255	74 280	1 745	409 985	1 091 942
% Distribution	16.8	4.9	2.2	8.6	0.7	6.8	2.0	1.3	6.8	0.2	37.5	100.0
Saskatchewan	160 720	30 070	11 285	121 310	1 975	66 270	11 770	23 360	55 955	275	417 360	988 928
% Distribution	16.3	3.0	1.1	12.3	0.2	6.7	1.2	2.4	5.7	0.03	42.2	100.0
Alberta	493 195	74 615	54 750	185 630	24 745	68 445	32 840	45 985	104 350	3 615	1 068 180	2 545 553
% Distribution	19.4	2.9	2.2	7.3	1.0	2.7	1.3	1.8	4.1	0.1	42.0	100.0
British Columbia	812 470	68 790	66 525	156 635	49 265	74 415	25 225	56 715	52 760	1 745	1 294 650	3 282 061
% Distribution	24.8	2.1	2.0	4.8	1.5	2.3	0.8	1.7	1.6	0.05	39.5	100.0
Yukon	5 295	875	295	1060	135	3 775	110	430	385	10	13 495	27 797
% Distribution	19.0	3.1	1.1	3.8	0.5	13.6	0.4	1.6	1.4	—	48.6	100.0
Northwest Territories	5 885	1 390	305	885	160	29 415	150	320	445	30	15 890	57 649
% Distribution	10.2	2.4	0.5	1.5	0.4	51.0	0.4	0.5	0.8	0.05	27.6	100.0
Canada	5 611 050	6 146 600	358 180	911 560	750 055	470 615	272 810	174 370	406 645	94 395	7 794 250	27 296 859
% Distribution	20.6	22.5	1.3	3.3	2.7	1.5	1.0	0.6	1.5	0.4	28.6	100.0

SOURCE: *Ethnic Origin: The Nation.* Cat. No. 93–315. 1991 Census of Canada.

11. Aging of the Canadian Population, 1921-1996 (%)

	AGE 0-64 (%)	65 AND OVER (%)	RATIO OF 65 AND OVER TO 0-64 (%)	AVERAGE ANNUAL CHANGE
1921	95.2	4.8	5.0	—
1931	94.4	5.6	5.9	0.86
1941	93.3	6.7	7.1	1.27
1951	92.2	7.8	8.4	1.26
1956	92.3	7.7	8.4	-0.04
1961	92.4	7.6	8.3	-0.25
1966	92.3	7.7	8.3	0.15
1971	91.9	8.1	8.8	0.93
1976	91.3	8.7	9.5	1.48
1981	90.3	9.7	10.7	2.40
1986	89.3	10.7	11.9	2.38
1991	88.4	11.6	13.1	2.42
1996	87.8	12.2	13.8	2.6

SOURCE: Statistics Canada, Census of Canada 1991, *Age, Sex and Matrimonial Status,* Cat. No. 93-310; calculations by the author of *Report on the Demographic Situation in Canada 1996.* Cat. No. 91-209-XPE, and Census of Canada 1996.

12. Income Groups, 1995

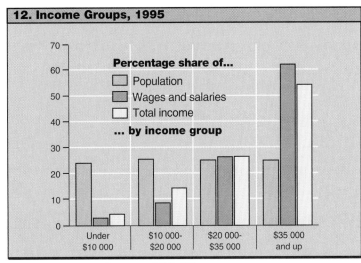

Percentage share of...
- Population
- Wages and salaries
- Total income

... by income group

SOURCE: Statistics Canada, Cat. No. 13-207-XPE, 1995.

13. Canadians Living Below the Poverty Line, 1981-1993

	1981	1983	1985	1987 (000)	1989	1991	1993
Total	**3 737**	**4 485**	**4 287**	**4 035**	**3 603**	**4 360**	**4 894**
Children under 18	1 049	1 264	1 205	1 099	956	1 244	1 447
Adults, 18 to 65	1 952	2 497	2 395	2 271	1 999	2 476	2 758
Adults, 65 and over	737	725	687	665	649	641	690
Family Members, Total	**2 670**	**3 239**	**3 062**	**2 790**	**2 378**	**2 983**	**3 461**
Children under 18	1 049	1 264	1 205	1 099	956	1 244	1 447
Adults, 18 to 65	1 359	1 757	1 629	1 486	1 258	1 586	1 843
Adults, 65 and over	262	218	229	205	165	153	171
Single Individuals, Total	**1 067**	**1 246**	**1 225**	**1 245**	**1 225**	**1 377**	**1 433**
Adults, 18 to 65	592	740	766	785	742	890	915
Adults, 65 and over	474	507	458	459	484	488	519

SOURCE: *The Canadian Global Almanac 1997.* J. R. Colombo, ed. Toronto: Macmillan Canada; © Statistics Canada.

14. Geographic Distribution of the Population[1]

SELECTED PARALLELS OF LATITUDE	POPULATION	%
South of 49°	17 827 382	70.4
Between 49° and 54°	6 898 501	27.3
Between 54° and 60°	505 222	2.0
North of 60°	78 226	0.3
SELECTED DISTANCES NORTH OF CANADA-US BORDER		
0 - 150 km	18 218 596	72.0
151 - 300 km	3 394 247	13.4
301 - 600 km	2 630 864	10.4
Over 600 km	1 065 624	4.2
Total Canadian Population	**25 354 064**	**100.0**

[1]While the population data is dated, it is unlikely the % values have changed very much.
SOURCE: 1986 Census of Canada, *Canada's Population From Ocean to Ocean,* Minister of Supply and Services Canada, 1989.

15. Population, by Sex and Age Group, 1994

SEX AND AGE	CANADA	NFLD	PEI	NS	NB	QUE	ONT (000)	MAN	SASK	ALTA	BC	YT	NWT
Male	**14 482.9**	**292.6**	**66.4**	**462.4**	**376.0**	**3 586.9**	**5 395.1**	**561.0**	**505.9**	**1 365.8**	**1 821.6**	**15.7**	**33.5**
0-4	1 027.6	17.9	4.8	30.9	24.0	246.0	387.4	42.8	38.8	106.7	123.0	1.3	4.0
5-9	1 008.5	20.1	5.2	32.1	25.7	228.6	377.1	41.9	41.1	108.0	123.8	1.2	3.8
10-14	1 015.0	23.0	5.0	31.7	27.0	247.8	365.7	41.1	41.2	105.4	123.0	1.2	3.0
15-19	1 005.0	25.2	5.1	33.2	28.5	251.3	362.6	40.4	38.8	96.2	120.1	1.1	2.6
20-24	1 042.3	26.2	5.2	36.0	30.0	242.4	392.6	42.4	34.7	99.7	129.1	1.1	2.8
25-29	1 163.5	24.4	4.9	36.9	29.9	283.9	446.1	43.1	34.3	111.7	143.8	1.2	3.4
30-34	1 357.7	24.6	5.4	42.0	33.5	338.8	518.5	49.7	41.6	133.5	165.0	1.7	3.4
35-39	1 280.0	24.3	5.3	39.5	32.0	330.5	466.0	46.5	41.9	130.8	158.9	1.5	2.8
40-44	1 127.7	23.4	4.8	35.0	29.5	292.2	408.5	40.7	36.1	107.4	146.4	1.5	2.3
45-49	1 001.6	20.2	4.6	32.4	26.7	262.4	369.6	35.9	29.5	87.2	130.0	1.2	1.8
50-54	764.9	14.6	3.3	24.5	19.8	204.7	282.9	27.3	22.7	64.9	98.2	0.9	1.2
55-59	630.7	11.9	2.8	20.4	15.6	161.7	239.3	22.9	20.7	53.1	80.8	0.4	0.9
60-64	596.1	10.5	2.7	18.3	14.6	152.1	227.2	22.3	20.7	48.3	78.1	0.5	0.6
65-69	518.5	9.0	2.4	15.7	12.9	129.4	199.9	20.3	19.5	40.0	68.8	0.3	0.4
70-74	416.8	7.4	2.0	14.0	11.2	97.9	159.9	17.6	17.2	31.4	57.8	0.2	0.1
75-79	264.0	5.1	1.5	9.9	7.7	60.6	96.3	12.6	12.8	20.4	36.9	0.1	0.1
80-84	163.4	3.1	0.9	6.2	4.6	35.7	60.0	8.3	8.4	12.4	23.6	0.1	0.1
85 +	99.7	1.7	0.7	3.7	2.9	21.0	35.6	5.3	5.9	8.5	14.3	0.0	0.0
Female	**14 765.2**	**289.8**	**68.1**	**474.3**	**383.2**	**3 694.3**	**5 532.7**	**570.0**	**510.2**	**1 350.5**	**1 846.7**	**14.4**	**30.9**
0-4	977.8	17.1	4.6	29.2	23.3	234.1	368.1	41.1	36.9	101.2	117.2	1.3	3.7
5-9	966.4	19.2	4.8	30.7	24.5	218.9	361.7	39.9	39.4	103.4	119.3	1.0	3.6
10-14	969.4	22.3	4.8	31.0	25.7	236.8	348.6	38.5	39.7	99.9	118.1	1.1	2.8
15-19	957.3	23.7	5.0	31.5	27.3	239.7	344.3	39.2	36.4	92.2	114.3	1.0	2.6
20-24	1 015.2	24.5	4.7	34.3	28.9	234.4	384.6	40.0	33.6	97.8	128.7	1.0	2.9
25-29	1 141.3	23.7	4.9	35.4	29.2	273.4	444.4	41.4	33.6	109.4	141.7	1.2	3.1
30-34	1 324.4	24.4	5.8	41.5	32.6	327.8	506.1	47.5	41.4	128.9	163.7	1.7	3.1
35-39	1 268.1	24.5	5.3	40.2	32.2	325.6	466.4	44.9	39.9	124.5	160.4	1.6	2.6
40-44	1 127.9	22.9	4.7	35.5	29.6	291.6	417.1	40.7	34.1	102.8	145.6	1.3	1.9
45-49	990.0	19.6	4.4	32.0	25.7	262.4	370.3	34.8	28.1	84.2	125.8	1.2	1.4
50-54	761.2	13.9	3.3	24.2	19.0	208.1	283.5	27.3	22.8	62.0	95.4	0.6	1.0
55-59	637.8	11.4	2.9	20.3	15.8	169.0	243.3	23.3	20.8	51.2	78.7	0.4	0.7
60-64	618.3	10.3	2.7	19.5	15.4	166.4	235.7	23.1	21.1	47.7	75.5	0.3	0.6
65-69	588.5	9.5	2.6	18.5	15.0	154.9	226.5	23.1	21.1	42.8	74.0	0.2	0.3
70-74	534.5	8.5	2.5	17.8	14.1	133.2	205.0	22.9	20.3	38.4	71.4	0.2	0.2
75-79	382.8	6.6	2.1	14.1	10.6	96.1	139.2	17.7	17.0	27.7	51.4	0.1	0.1
80-84	274.5	4.5	1.6	10.1	7.8	67.3	100.9	13.1	12.8	19.6	36.6	0.1	0.1
85 +	229.7	3.2	1.4	8.6	6.6	54.7	87.0	11.6	11.0	16.6	28.9	0.0	0.1

SOURCE: *Annual Demographic Statistics, 1994.* Cat. No. 91-213.

16. Composition of Canadian Families, 1961-1996

	1961		1971		1981		1991		1996	
	NO. OF FAMILIES	%	NO. OF FAMILIES	%	NO. OF FAMILIES (000)	%	NO. OF FAMILIES	%	NO. OF FAMILIES	%
Total Families[1]	**4 147**	**100.0**	**5 071**	**100.0**	**6 325**	**100.0**	**7 356**	**100.0**	**7 838**	**100.0**
Without Children at Home	**1 217**	**29.3**	**1 545**	**30.5**	**2 013**	**31.8**	**2 580**	**35.1**	**2 730**	**34.8**
With Children at Home	**2 930**	**70.7**	**3 526**	**69.5**	**4 312**	**68.2**	**4 776**	**64.9**	**5 108**	**65.2**
One child	839	20.2	1 045	20.6	1 580	25.0	1 945	26.4	2 106	26.9
Two children	855	20.6	1 077	21.2	1 648	26.1	1 927	26.2	2 047	26.1
Three children	557	13.4	677	13.4	730	11.5	691	9.4	729	9.3
Four children	312	7.5	367	7.2	243	3.8	165	2.2	175	2.2
Five children or more	162	3.9	186	3.7	70	1.1	33	0.4	51	0.7
Lone Parent Families	**385**	**9.3**	**471**	**9.3**	**653**	**10.3**	**955**	**13.0**	**1 138**	**14.5**
Lone female parent	305	7.4	371	7.3	541	8.6	786	10.7	192	2.5
Lone male parent	80	1.9	100	2.0	112	1.8	168	2.3	945	12.1

[1]Based on the census family definition: a husband and wife (without children or with children who never married) or a parent with one or more children who never married, living together in the same home.
(2) Includes six or more children.
SOURCE: *The Canadian Global Almanac 1997.* J. R. Colombo, ed. Toronto: Macmillan Canada; © *Census of Canada,* Statistics Canada; Census of Canada 1996.

17. Population of Census Metropolitan Areas, 1961 to 1996

CENSUS METROPOLITAN AREA	POPULATION DENSITY PEOPLE/KM² 1996	KM²	1961	1971	1981[1,2]	1991	1996[3]
Calgary	161.6	5 083	279 062	403 319	625 966	754 033	821 628
Chicoutimi-Jonquière	93.1	1 723	127 616	133 703	158 229	160 928	160 454
Edmonton	90.5	9 536	359 821	495 702	740 882	839 924	862 597
Halifax	132.8	2 508	193 353	222 637	277 727	320 501	332 518
Hamilton	459.6	1 358	401 071	498 523	542 095	599 760	624 360
Kitchener	464.9	824	154 864	226 846	287 801	356 421	382 940
London	189.4	2 105	226 669	286 011	326 817	381 522	398 616
Montreal	826.6	4 024	2 215 627	2 743 208	2 862 286	3 127 242	3 326 510
Oshawa	300.6	894	—	120 318[1]	186 446	240 104	268 773
Ottawa-Hull	177.7	5 686	457 038	602 510	743 821	920 857	1 010 498
Quebec	213.3	3 150	379 067	480 502	583 820	645 550	671 889
Regina	56.6	3 422	113 749	140 734	173 226	191 692	193 652
Saint John	35.8	3 509	98 083	106 744	121 012	124 981	125 705
St. Catharines-Niagara	266.0	1 400	257 796	303 429	342 645	364 552	372 406
St. John's	220.4	790	106 666	131 814	154 835	171 859	174 051
Saskatoon	41.2	5 322	95 564	126 449	175 058	210 023	219 056
Sherbrooke	150.4	979	—	—	125 183	139 194	147 384
Sudbury	61.4	2 612	127 446	155 424	156 121	157 613	160 488
Thunder Bay	54.7	2 295	102 085	112 093	121 948	124 427	125 562
Toronto	726.6	5 868	1 919 409	2 628 043	3 130 392	3 893 046	4 263 757
Trois-Rivières	160.5	872	—	—	125 343	136 303	139 956
Vancouver	649.4	2 821	826 798	1 082 352	1 268 183	1 602 502	1 831 665
Victoria	480.4	633	155 763	195 800	241 450	287 897	304 287
Windsor	323.4	862	217 215	258 643	250 885	262 075	278 685
Winnipeg	163.6	4 078	476 543	540 262	592 061	652 354	667 209

—not applicable.
[1]Adjusted due to boundary changes.
[2]Based on 1986 Census Metropolitan Area.
[3]1996 Census.
SOURCE: *Canada Year Book* various years.

18. Percentage of Population in Urban Areas, 1851 to 1996

PROVINCE	1851	1871	1891	1911	1931	1951	1971	1991	1996
Newfoundland	—	—	—	—	—	43.3	57.2	53.6	56.9
Prince Edward Island	—	9.4	13.1	16.0	19.5	25.1	38.3	39.9	44.2
Nova Scotia	7.5	8.3	19.4	36.7	46.6	54.5	56.7	53.5	54.8
New Brunswick	14.0	17.6	19.9	26.7	35.4	42.8	56.9	47.7	48.8
Quebec	14.9	19.9	28.6	44.5	59.5	66.8	80.6	77.6	78.4
Ontario	14.0	20.6	35.0	49.5	63.1	72.5	82.4	81.8	83.3
Manitoba	—	—	23.3	39.3	45.2	56.0	69.5	72.1	71.8
Saskatchewan	—	—	—	16.1	20.3	30.4	53.0	63.0	63.3
Alberta	—	—	—	29.4	31.8	47.6	73.5	79.8	79.5
British Columbia	—	9.0	42.6	50.9	62.3	68.6	75.7	80.4	82.1
Canada	**13.1**	**18.3**	**29.8**	**41.8**	**52.5**	**62.4**	**76.1**	**76.6**	**77.9**

SOURCE: *Urban Development in Canada* by Leroy O. Stone, *1961 Census Monograph*; Census of Canada.

19. Total Population by Aboriginal Identity, 1996[1]

PROVINCE OR TERRITORY	POPULATION (000)			
	INDIAN	MÉTIS	INUIT	TOTAL[1]
Newfoundland	4.4	4.6	4.1	13.2
Prince Edward Island	0.8	0.1	.01	0.9
Nova Scotia	10.9	0.8	0.2	12.0
New Brunswick	8.8	1.0	0.1	9.9
Quebec	45.0	15.6	8.2	69.4
Ontario	112.8	21.5	1.2	136.9
Manitoba	80.6	45.4	0.3	127.1
Saskatchewan	72.8	35.9	0.2	109.5
Alberta	69.2	49.5	0.6	120.6
British Columbia	107.4	25.6	0.7	134.9
Yukon	5.3	0.6	1.0	6.0
Northwest Territories	11.1	3.7	24.5	39.5
Canada	**529.0**	**204.1**	**40.2**	**779.8**

[1]Footnote: The totals do not add up because people reported multiple origins.
SOURCE: Census of Canada 1996.

20. Status Indian Population[1], 1995

PROVINCE OR TERRITORY	TOTAL INDIAN POPULATION	ON RESERVE	OFF RESERVE	ON CROWN LAND	NUMBER OF BANDS
Atlantic Provinces	23 225	15 315	7 897	13	31
Quebec	57 223	39 450	16 641	1 132	39
Ontario	134 160	66 522	66 335	2 303	126
Manitoba	91 565	59 311	30 709	1 545	61
Saskatchewan	92 325	46 457	44 272	1 596	70
Alberta	74 123	46 808	24 665	2 650	43
British Columbia	99 720	51 718	47 648	354	197
Yukon	7 088	677	3 376	3 035	16
Northwest Territories	13 621	195	3 588	9 838	25
Canada	**593 050**	**325 453**	**245 131**	**22 466**	**609**

[1]Status Indians are those settled on reserves registered with the Department of Indian and Northern Affairs under the provisions of the Indian Act. Note: Total number of reserves is 2 370 (1993/4), but only 884 are inhabited.
SOURCE: *The Canadian Global Almanac 1997*. J. R. Colombo, ed. Toronto: Macmillan Canada; Indian and Northern Affairs Canada.

21. Distribution of Immigrants by Class and Category, 1995[1]

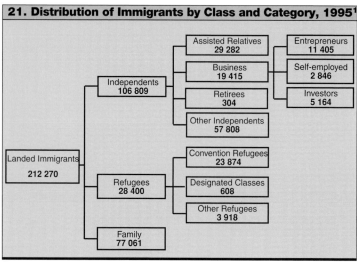

Landed Immigrants 212 270
- Independents 106 809
  - Assisted Relatives 29 282
  - Business 19 415
    - Entrepreneurs 11 405
    - Self-employed 2 846
    - Investors 5 164
  - Retirees 304
  - Other Independents 57 808
- Refugees 28 400
  - Convention Refugees 23 874
  - Designated Classes 608
  - Other Refugees 3 918
- Family 77 061

[1]Preliminary data as of October 15, 1996.
SOURCE: Citizenship and Immigration Canada, unpublished data.
From *Report on The Demographic Situation in Canada 1996*. Statistics Canada Cat. No. 91-209 XPE.

21a. Total Population by Visible Minority, 1996

TOTAL POPULATION	28 528 125
TOTAL VISIBLE MINORITY POPULATION (2)	3 197 480
Chinese	860 150
South Asian	670 590
Black	573 860
Arab/West Asian	244 665
Filipino	234 195
Southeast Asian	172 765
Latin American	176 970
Japanese	68 135
Korean	64 835
Visible minority, n.i.e. (3)	69 745
Multiple visible minority (4)	61 575
All others (5)	25 330 645

SOURCE: Statistics Canada

22. Numbers of Immigrants and Immigration Rates, Canada, 1944-1995

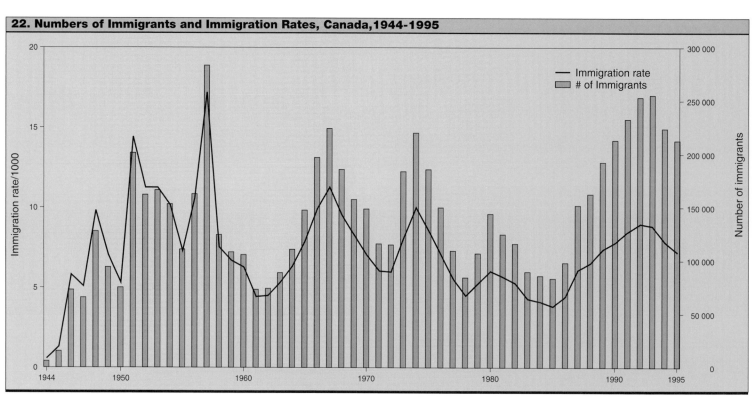

SOURCE: Statistics Canada.

23. Immigrant Population by Place of Birth, 1970 to 1995

COUNTRY OR REGION	1970	1975	1980	1985	1990	1995[1]
Great Britain	23 688	29 454	16 445	3 998	6 701	4 555
Portugal	8 594	9 158	4 222	917	5 396	n.a.
Italy	8 659	4 919	1 873	733	1 058	n.a.
Poland	1 403	1 191	1 395	3 642	16 446	2 436
Total Europe	**75 006**	**68 733**	**40 210**	**18 530**	**50 059**	**41 187**
Philippines	3 305	7 688	6 147	3 183	12 492	15 804
India	7 089	13 401	9 531	4 517	12 513	18 227
Hong Kong	2 250	6 438	3 874	5 121	22 789	24 868
China	3 397	6 235	8 965	5 166	13 971	20 935
Total Asia	**23 682**	**52 024**	**73 026**	**39 438**	**112 854**	**129 001**
United States	20 859	16 729	8 098	5 614	4 995	4 317
Caribbean	13 371	18 790	7 515	6 240	11 721	12 881
Africa	4 017	11 715	5 383	3 912	13 691	14 586
South America	4 506	13 102	5 381	4 273	8 544	7 529
Oceania	—	2 675	944	612	1 671	1 880
Total	**147 713**	**187 881**	**143 117**	**84 302**	**212 166**	**212 270**

[1]In 1995 there were 10 461 immigrants from Yugoslavia, Bosnia-Herzegovina and Croatia.
SOURCE: Statistics Canada, *Report on the Demographic Situation in Canada 1990: Current Demographic Analysis*, Dec. 1991, Cat. No. 91-209E.

24. Employment, Unemployment, and Participation Rates[1], 1995

PROVINCE	POPULATION OVER 15 YEARS (000)	LABOUR FORCE (000)	EMPLOYED (000)	UNEMPLOYED (000)	PARTICIPATION RATE (%)
Newfoundland	455	242	197	44	53.1
Prince Edward Island	105	69	59	10	65.6
Nova Scotia	731	437	384	53	59.8
New Brunswick	598	354	314	41	59.3
Quebec	5 805	3 612	3 204	408	62.2
Ontario	8 720	5 732	5 231	501	65.7
Manitoba	850	563	521	42	66.3
Saskatchewan	749	494	460	34	66.0
Alberta	2 068	1 489	1 373	116	72.0
British Columbia	2 947	1 935	1 762	173	65.7
Canada	**23 027**	**14 928**	**13 506**	**1 422**	**64.8**

[1]The participation rate is the percentage of the population (over 15 years of age) in the labour force and includes both employed and unemployed.
SOURCE: *Canada Year Book 1997*.

25. Employees by Industry, 1997

PROVINCE OR TERRITORY	EMPLOYEES (000)									
	FORESTRY	MINING	MANUFACTURING	TRANSPORTATION AND COMMUNICATION	CONSTRUCTION	TRADE	FINANCE, INSURANCE, AND REAL ESTATE	SERVICES	PUBLIC ADMINISTRATION	TOTAL
Newfoundland	1.9	2.8	12.8	13.4	5.2	28.8	6.9	56.3	15.6	**144.9**
Prince Edward Island	—[1]	—	5.6	3.0	2.8	7.8	2.1	18.5	5.5	**45.8**
Nova Scotia	2.4	3.1	36.9	24.5	14.0	62.2	17.0	126.7	26.7	**314.9**
New Brunswick	4.9	3.2	32.0	22.1	11.9	48.9	12.3	95.0	20.8	**253.1**
Quebec	7.3	15.5	503.9	196.2	100.0	505.3	154.5	1 014.6	169.2	**2 700.0**
Ontario	8.1	21.2	850.4	313.2	162.1	827.1	310.3	1 660.6	237.0	**4 422.8**
Manitoba	0.6	3.9	57.5	42.6	14.3	77.1	26.4	170.6	29.1	**425.0**
Saskatchewan	1.1	10.1	25.2	27.5	14.5	66.3	23.1	138.0	25.1	**335.3**
Alberta	2.3	68.1	109.8	92.7	71.4	221.8	61.1	460.3	63.7	**1 162.2**
British Columbia	28.8	12.7	165.8	112.5	73.9	273.8	89.1	612.5	72.5	**1 454.9**
Yukon	—	—	—	1.5	0.8	1.8	0.5	4.7	3.5	**14.2**
NWT	—	1.9	—	2.4	1.6	3.4	0.9	8.6	5.7	**25.3**
Canada	66.9	143.4	1 800.4	851.4	427.7	2 124.4	704.2	4 366.6	674.3	**11 299.0**

[1] Data unavailable, not applicable or confidential represented by dash (—).
SOURCE: Statistics Canada.

26. Labour Force 15 Years and Over by Detailed Occupation (Based on the 1991 Standard Occupational Classification) and Sex

OCCUPATION	BOTH SEXES	MALES	FEMALES
Total Labour force	**14 812 700**	**8 007 955**	**6 804 750**
Occupation—Not applicable (1)	495 160	239 470	255 690
All occupations (2)	**14 317 545**	**7 768 485**	**6 549 060**
Management occupations	1 289 125	880 240	408 885
Business, finance, and administrative occupations	2 718 250	766 570	1 951 680
Natural and applied sciences and related occupations	712 495	585 420	127 080
Health occupations	719 450	152 825	566 625
Occupations in social science, education, government service, and religion	975 385	393 715	581 670
Occupations in art, culture, recreation, and sport	386 315	179 930	206 390
Sales and service occupations	3 724 430	1 609 510	2 114 920
Trades, transport and equipment operators, and related occupations	2 018 355	1 896 255	122 100
Occupations unique to primary industry	680 685	534 015	146 670
Occupations unique to processing, manufacturing, and utilities	1 093 045	770 010	323 030

SOURCE: Statistics Canada

Agriculture

27. Net Income and Cash Receipts from Farming, 1983, 1989, and 1995

PROVINCE	CASH RECEIPTS ($000 000)			NET INCOME[1] ($000 000)		
	1983	1989	1995	1983	1989	1995
Newfoundland	34.8	57.9	67.2	4.5	11.3	11.8
Prince Edward Island	172.3	256.1	311.3	25.4	77.8	87.4
Nova Scotia	236.0	315.1	328.7	26.4	71.5	52.6
New Brunswick	199.8	272.1	286.9	30.8	65.6	44.7
Quebec	2 710.1	3 648.9	4 378.6	484.9	917.6	1 073.9
Ontario	4 989.9	5 662.5	6 157.5	810.7	941.2	1 001.6
Manitoba	1 797.6	2 101.7	2 461.3	215.2	295.3	360.6
Saskatchewan	4 026.1	4 474.8	5 249.6	702.9	760.1	1 386.1
Alberta	3 750.8	4 509.4	5 846.1	412.4	782.6	1 377.5
British Columbia	914.9	1 163.9	1 527.1	38.1	175.7	205.9
Canada	**18 832.3**	**22 462.4**	**26 614.3**	**2 751.4**	**4 099.0**	**5 602.1**

[1]Income excludes the value of inventory change.
SOURCE: Statistics Canada, *Agriculture Economic Statistics*, Nov. 1996, Cat. No. 21-603 UPE.

28. Agricultural Land Use, 1996

PROVINCE	FARMLAND AREA (000 ha)	% CHANGE 1986–1996	% CLASSED AS CLASS 1, 2, or 3	NUMBER OF FARMS	AVERAGE FARM SIZE (ha) (CHANGE 1986–1996)	CROPLAND AREA (000 ha)	SUMMER FALLOW AREA (000 ha)	TAME OR SEEDED PASTURE (000 ha)
Newfoundland	43.8	+19.7	0.005	731	60 (+7.1 %)	7.2	0.1	2.4
Prince Edward Island	265.2	−2.6	71.2	2 200	120 (+25.0%)	170.4	0.4	11.8
Nova Scotia	427.3	+2.6	20.7	4 021	98 (+1.0 %)	112.4	0.6	25.0
New Brunswick	386.0	−5.6	17.9	3 206	117 (+1.7 %)	135.0	0.4	19.9
Quebec	3 456.2	−5.0	1.4	35 716	96 (+9.1 %)	1 738.8	8.8	197.3
Ontario	5 616.9	−0.5	6.8	67 118	83 (+9.2 %)	3 545.0	19.6	348.4
Manitoba	7 732.1	−0.1	8.0	24 341	318 (+12.4 %)	4 699.2	323.7	356.2
Saskatchewan	26 569.1	−0.1	25.0	56 979	466 (+11.2 %)	14 398.7	4 431.5	1 233.3
Alberta	21 029.2	+1.8	16.2	58 990	357 (0.0 %)	9 546.6	1 436.7	1 914.6
British Columbia	2 529.1	+4.9	1.0	21 653	117 (−7.1 %)	565.7	39.0	240.2
Canada	**68 055.0**	**+0.3**	**4.6**	**274 955**	**243 (+5.2 %)**	**34 918.7**	**6 260.7**	**4 349.1**

NOTE: Information about the territories is excluded because of the small number of farms.   SOURCE: Census of Canada 1996.

29. Number of Farms and Average Size, 1901 to 1996

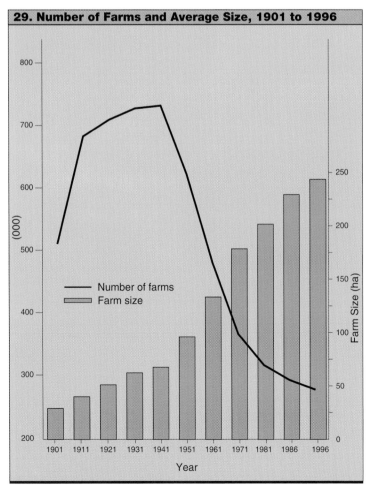

SOURCE: Statistics Canada, Census of Agriculture

30. Farm Cash Receipts, 1995 ($000 000)

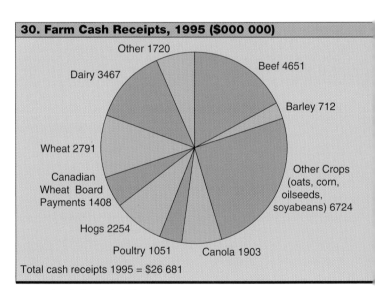

Total cash receipts 1995 = $26 681

SOURCE: *Canada Year Book 1997.*

31. Census Farms by Product Type, 1996

PROVINCE	TOTAL FARMS	CATTLE	SMALL GRAINS (EXCLUDING WHEAT) + OILSEED	WHEAT	DAIRY	MISCELLANEOUS SPECIALTY	FIELD CROPS, OTHER THAN GRAINS	HOGS	FRUITS AND VEGETABLES	MIXED FARMS LIVESTOCK COMBINATION	MIXED FARMS OTHER COMBINATIONS	POULTRY + EGGS
Newfoundland	740	40	—	—	70	215	60	15	190	25	70	60
Prince Edward Island	2 215	640	40	10	340	185	550	105	140	95	50	50
Nova Scotia	4 455	1 050	10	5	520	1 185	260	95	950	95	135	140
New Brunswick	3 405	890	20	5	420	795	525	75	425	70	95	90
Quebec	35 990	6 265	2 695	85	10 770	7 225	2 395	2 325	2 270	420	650	880
Ontario	67 520	15 405	12 645	530	8 460	11 295	6 620	2 730	4 110	2 200	1 585	1 940
Manitoba	24 385	7 555	6 240	3 510	980	1 745	1 705	960	245	530	450	460
Saskatchewan	56 995	9 300	20 260	20 470	535	1 665	1 830	510	160	1 065	980	220
Alberta	59 005	25 850	10 600	5 370	1 500	6 090	4 795	1 190	255	1 585	1 105	675
British Columbia	21 835	4 970	250	130	1 285	6 065	2 135	250	4 170	800	590	1 185
Canada	276 550	71 960	52 760	30 110	24 880	36 470	20 880	8 255	12 935	6 885	5 710	5 700

SOURCE: Statistics Canada, Cat. No. 93-348. *Canada Year Book 1997.*

32. Wheat Statistics, 1984 to 1995

	1984[1]	1985	1986	1987	1988	1989	1990	1991	1992	1993	1994	1995	10-YEAR AVERAGE
Carryover from Previous Crop Year (000 t)	9 190	7 598	8 569	12 731	7 305	5 032	6 442	10 285	9 803	12 193	11 117	5 940	9 198
Production (000 t)	21 199	24 252	31 378	25 992	15 996	24 334	32 709	31 946	28 879	27 232	23 122	24 102*	26 654
Total Supply (000 t)	30 389	31 850	39 947	38 723	23 301	29 366	39 151	42 253	39 967	39 452	34 242	30 042	35 860
Exports (000 t)	17 542	17 683	20 783	23 519	12 413	17 418	21 913	25 376	20 328	19 304	20 761	16 198	19 971
Domestic Use (000 t)	5 250	5 598	6 433	7 899	5 856	5 581	6 766	7 074	7 448	9 054	7 542	7 866	6 860
Carryover at the End of the Crop Year (000 t)	7 598	8 569	12 731	7 305	5 032	6 442	10 285	9 803	12 193	11 117	5 940	6 633	9 032
Final Price ($/t)[2]		186	160	130	134	197	172	135	134	157	164	195	254	166

[1]The crop year begins 1 August and ends 31 July.   n.a.—not available   SOURCE: *Canada Year Book*, various years; Canadian Grains Industry, *Statistical Handbook* and *The Canadian Wheat Board Annual Report.*
[2]Canadian Wheat Board payments to producers for No. 1 Canadian Western Red Spring Wheat. * 1996 production was 30 495 000 t.

33. World Wheat Imports and Exports, Various Years

COUNTRY	IMPORTS (000 000 t) 1981	1990	1995	10-YEAR AVERAGE 1986-1995
Former USSR[1]	19.6	14.5	3.7	13.7
China	13.2	9.6	12.6	11.2
Morocco	n.a.	1.9	2.4	1.8
Pakistan	n.a.	1.1	2.0	1.7
Egypt	6.0	6.0	6.1	6.5
Japan	5.6	5.5	5.9	5.7
Iran	1.4	4.1	3.1	3.5
Brazil	4.6	2.8	5.8	3.9
South Korea	1.9	4.1	2.6	3.8
Algeria	2.3	3.5	3.2	4.3
Iraq	1.6	0.2	0.9	1.8
Indonesia	1.5	2.0	3.6	2.4
World Total	**100.7**	**90.6**	**89.6**	**97.0**

COUNTRY	EXPORTS (000 000 t) 1981	1990	1995	10-YEAR AVERAGE 1986-1995
Argentina	4.3	5.1	4.4	5.2
Australia	11.4	11.9	12.1	11.2
Canada	28.5	21.9	16.2	19.8
European Community	13.9	18.5	12.6	18.5
United States	48.8	28.3	33.6	34.2
World Total	**100.7**	**90.6**	**89.6**	**97.0**

[1]Historical data are not available from the individual republics.
SOURCE: *The Canadian Wheat Board Annual Report, 1990–1991.*

34. Canadian Bulk Wheat Exports (including Durum), 1980, 1985, 1990, and 1995

COUNTRY OR REGION	1980[1] (000 t)	1985	1990	1995
Western Europe	**2 347**	**1 298**	**935**	**1 065**
Great Britain	1 409	633	281	205
Italy	765	240	320	405
Eastern Europe	**5 129**	**6 285**	**7 228**	**38**
Former USSR[2]	3 971	6 019	7 228	n.a.
Africa	**901**	**934**	**2 047**	**1 778**
Iran	96	41	1 419	806
Asia	**4 467**	**4 672**	**7 328**	**9 104**
China	2 879	2 780	2 923	4 787
Indonesia	n.a.	n.a.	285	931
Japan	1 381	1 323	1 393	1 517
South Korea	n.a.	n.a.	1 258	289
North and South America	**2 049**	**2 275**	**2 818**	**3 965**
Brazil	n.a.	n.a.	383	1 120
United States	n.a.	159	660	928
Total	**15 569**	**17 114**	**21 913**	**16 000**

[1]The crop year extends from 1 August to 31 July. [2]The Soviet Union was dissolved in 1991. Data for Russia and the other independent countries that were formed after dissolution are not available for the years prior to 1992. n.a.—not available.
SOURCE: *The Canadian Wheat Board Annual Report.*

35. World Wheat Production, Various Years

COUNTRY	1981	1990	1995	10-YEAR AVERAGE 1986-1995
		(000 000 t)		
Australia	16.4	15.1	17.0	14.2
Canada	24.8	32.7	25.0	26.7
China	59.6	98.2	103.0	95.7
European Community	58.0	84.6	87.8	81.2
India	36.3	49.7	65.4	53.5
Pakistan	n.a.	14.4	17.0	14.6
Russian Federation	81.1	108.0	30.1	40.8
Turkey	17.0	20.0	15.5	17.7
United States	75.8	74.5	59.4	60.2
Ukraine	n.a.	30.4	16.3	21.2
Total	**n.a.**	**592.4**	**541.7**	**540.3**

SOURCE: *The Canadian Wheat Board Annual Reports.*

36. Livestock and Livestock Products, 1995

PROVINCE	CATTLE AND CALVES (000 HEAD)[1]	PIGS (000 HEAD)[2]	SHEEP AND LAMBS (000 HEAD)	POULTRY (TONNES)	EGGS (000 DOZEN)	MILK AND CREAM (000 kL)
Newfoundland	8	5	6	10 081	6 701	31
Prince Edward Island	94	118	5	2 800	2 365	95
Nova Scotia	127	133	26	29 071	17 498	170
New Brunswick	105	84	6	21 816	12 997	122
Quebec	1 477	3 410	127	237 349	82 800	2 768
Ontario	2 226	3 330	227	301 877	182 689	2 383
Manitoba	1 422	1 869	33	39 143	52 332	281
Saskatchewan	2 825	907	83	23 131	22 183	207
Alberta	5 540	2 115	264	75 416	41 782	573
British Columbia	865	213	83	120 013	61 288	573
Canada	**14 689**	**12 183**	**860**	**860 697**	**482 635**	**7 022**

SOURCE: Statistics Canada, CANSIM, matrices 1150, 1166, 9500-9510; Cat. Nos. 23-001 and 23-202. *Canada Year Book 1997.*

37. Farm Cash Receipts from Farming Operations, 1995[1]

	NFLD	PEI	NS	NB	QUE	ONT ($000)	MAN	SASK	ALTA	BC	CANADA
Wheat, excluding durum	—	2 154	1 065	461	16 125	127 858	396 910	1 008 678	627 926	12 923	2 194 100
Wheat, excluding durum, CWB[2] payments	—	—	—	—	—	—	164 781	509 164	264 256	7 747	945 948
Durum wheat	—	—	—	—	—	—	22 549	472 600	105 439	—	600 588
Durum wheat, CWB payments	—	—	—	—	—	—	12 507	304 093	61 984	—	378 584
Oats	—	357	144	422	7 048	6 315	48 124	88 231	70 628	4 012	225 281
Barley	—	7 738	221	2 624	16 744	11 998	60 006	311 679	302 402	4 449	717 861
Barley, CWB payments	—	—	—	—	—	—	5 694	45 641	31 166	896	83 397
Flaxseed	—	—	—	—	—	—	98 906	138 959	9 544	—	247 409
Canola	—	—	—	—	—	21 069	360 976	808 151	702 117	14 692	1 907 005
Soybeans	—	460	—	—	72 049	590 910	—	—	—	—	663 419
Corn	—	—	157	—	221 219	473 146	11 893	—	1 307	—	707 722
Potatoes	1 259	149 598	6 958	64 522	62 151	51 600	68 820	15 645	53 631	29 241	503 425
Vegetables	3 953	6 756	22 274	8 957	228 822	357 328	21 299	1 477	44 709	127 170	822 745
Apples	—	—	8 736	1 716	28 198	70 795	—	—	—	53 619	163 064
Other tree fruits	—	—	244	—	—	53 116	—	—	—	14 158	67 518
Other berries and grapes	62	682	13 198	3 922	14 770	38 035	845	—	499	93 071	165 084
Floriculture and nursery	5 767	1 564	19 197	9 883	125 529	402 515	22 111	10 879	57 853	213 316	868 614
Tobacco	—	5 095	1 360	347	19 543	270 046	—	—	—	—	296 391
Ginseng	—	—	—	—	—	47 300	—	—	—	26 070	73 370
Mustard seed	—	—	—	—	—	—	847	58 935	12 127	—	71 909
Lentils	—	—	—	—	—	—	12 417	119 686	6 858	—	138 961
Dry peas	—	—	—	—	—	—	23 300	131 717	63 115	—	218 132
Hay and clover	—	—	10	122	3 367	5 421	1 656	7 382	57 435	10 703	86 096
Maple products	—	—	910	3 092	77 076	9 897	—	—	—	—	90 975
Forest products	75	750	10 978	7 490	56 141	16 412	844	1 964	3 514	30 617	128 785
Miscellaneous crops	1 054	2 778	4 708	4 672	27 032	29 071	33 118	24 320	34 331	6 560	167 644
Total Crops	**13 107**	**179 311**	**95 233**	**113 470**	**992 477**	**2 671 901**	**1 413 092**	**4 077 882**	**2 575 254**	**662 666**	**12 794 393**
Cattle	1 324	28 368	27 545	26 022	174 578	756 203	261 710	574 790	2 210 190	162 457	4 223 187
Calves	67	66	1 900	1 550	183 920	85 942	51 606	60 466	5 757	32 698	423 972
Hogs	1 227	24 838	26 605	17 868	685 468	588 454	311 129	158 052	391 687	47 193	2 252 521
Dairy	22 880	43 299	88 258	61 744	1 295 689	1 169 532	128 720	96 035	268 448	292 287	3 466 892
Hens and chickens	16 180	4 358	39 738	28 951	305 254	341 455	38 489	26 460	91 697	158 395	1 050 977
Turkeys	—	—	5 937	4 646	52 813	101 082	16 448	8 434	20 707	27 764	237 831
Eggs	8 554	2 758	19 375	10 113	112 845	212 800	56 124	23 768	53 146	83 134	582 617
Miscellaneous livestock	313	695	5 763	8 985	28 996	73 951	16 920	16 185	28 669	19 855	200 332
Total Livestock	**51 047**	**105 449**	**227 202**	**161 621**	**2 858 289**	**3 372 524**	**943 880**	**994 898**	**3 118 563**	**837 927**	**12 671 400**
Total Other Payments (e.g. insurance)	**3 077**	**26 542**	**6 279**	**11 768**	**527 796**	**113 113**	**104 326**	**176 808**	**152 243**	**26 529**	**1 148 481**
Total Receipts	**67 231**	**311 302**	**328 714**	**286 859**	**4 378 562**	**6 157 538**	**2 461 298**	**5 249 588**	**5 846 060**	**1 527 122**	**26 614 274**

[1] Those listed have total production exceeding $60 million.
[2] Canadian Wheat Board.
SOURCE: Statistics Canada Cat. No. 21-603UPE.

Forestry and Fishing

38. Forest Land, Harvests, and Forest Fires

PROVINCE OR TERRITORY	TOTAL AREA (000 HA)	AREA OF FOREST (000 HA)	AREA OF PRODUCTIVE FOREST (000 HA)	TOTAL AREA HARVESTED AND (% CLEARCUT) (000 HA) 1993	TOTAL VOLUME OF WOOD CUT 1994 (000 000 M³)	FOREST FIRE LOSSES AS A % OF PRODUCTIVE FOREST[1] (AVERAGE 1990-1994)
Newfoundland	40 572	22 524	11 271	21 (100)	2.4	0.50
Prince Edward Island	566	294	278	3 (49)	0.5	0.02
Nova Scotia	5 549	3 923	3 767	43 (100)	5.1	0.03
New Brunswick	7 344	6 106	5 954	101 (69)	9.3	0.06
Quebec	154 068	83 895	53 991	312 (86)	38.4	0.30
Ontario	106 858	57 995	42 204	206 (90)	26.0	0.04
Manitoba	64 995	26 277	15 239	11 (100)	1.8	2.70
Saskatchewan	65 233	28 806	12 633	20 (100)	4.9	3.50
Alberta	66 119	38 214	25 705	45 (100)	17.9	0.07
British Columbia	94 780	60 565	51 739	208 (87)	75.1	0.07
Yukon	48 345	27 549	7 470	0.6 (100)	0.4	2.20
Northwest Territories	342 632	61 437	14 321	0.5 (100)	0.2	0.20
Canada	**997 061**	**417 585**	**244 572**	**969 (87)**	**182.0**	**1.00**

[1]In 1994, 54.5% of all forest fires were caused by lightning, 43.7% were from human causes, and 1.8% were from unknown causes.
SOURCES: Compendium of Canadian Forestry Statistics, 1995; *Canada Year Book 1997*.

39a. Trade of Wood Pulp, 1993[1]

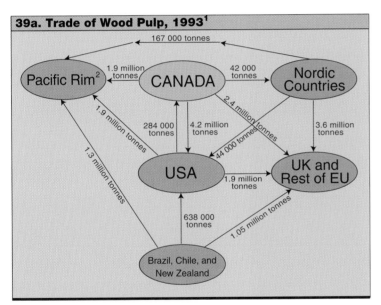

[1]Approximately 43% of Canada's production is exported.
[2]Pacific Rim = Japan, China, and Korea.
SOURCE: Food and Agriculture Organization.

39b. Trade of Softwood Lumber, 1993[1]

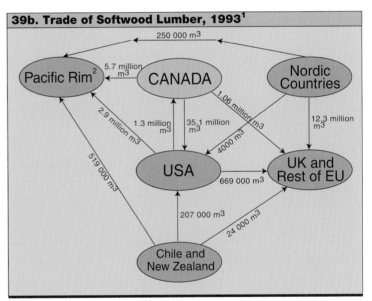

[1]Approximately 75% of Canada's production is exported.
[2]Pacific Rim = Japan, China, and Korea.
SOURCE: Food and Agriculture Organization.

39c. Trade of Newsprint, 1993[1]

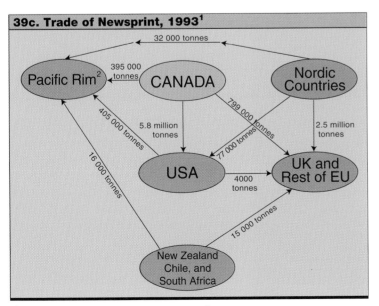

[1]Over 95% of Canada's production is exported.   [2]Pacific Rim = Japan, China, and Korea.
SOURCE: Food and Agriculture Organization.

SOURCE: *The State of Canada's Forests*, 1995–1996, Natural Resources Canada.

40. Fish Catches, 1994

SPECIES	ATLANTIC COAST			PACIFIC COAST		
	QUANTITY (000 t)	% CHANGE 1990-1994	VALUE ($000 000)	QUANTITY (000 t)	% CHANGE 1990-1994	VALUE ($000 000)
Total Groundfish	**144.30**	**−77.30**	**123.50**	**147.40**	**12.50**	**101.00**
Cod	22.70	−94.10	29.60	3.10	−43.60	1.80
Haddock	7.00	−67.10	14.00	—	—	—
Redfish	50.70	−36.90	15.70	14.90	−36.30	12.60
Halibut	1.30	−83.60	8.00	5.30	−12.80	33.60
Flatfishes	15.20	−15.60	18.00	6.30	6.80	4.40
Turbot	11.00	−23.60	14.40	2.10	7.70	0.40
Pollock	15.60	43.10	10.90	3.60	500.00	1.20
Hake	14.70	63.30	9.00	103.80	29.90	14.80
Cusk	1.70	21.40	1.40	—	—	—
Catfish	0.50	150.00	0.20	—	—	—
Other	4.00	66.60	2.40	8.30	−8.80	32.30
Total Pelagic	**250.10**	**−32.50**	**73.70**	**106.70**	**−23.30**	**261.30**
Herring	206.80	−19.00	27.70	39.30	−2.20	63.70
Mackerel	20.60	40.10	7.00	—	—	—
Tuna	0.60	28.80	9.70	0.60	120.60	1.40
Alewife	5.80	−7.90	1.60	—	—	—
Eel	0.80	164.80	3.30	—	—	—
Salmon	0.10	−73.80	0.70	65.40	−31.40	195.20
Skate	6.40	6 391.80	2.20	0.40	203.00	0.20
Smelt	1.40	100.80	1.80	—	—	—
Capelin	2.20	−97.50	0.60	—	—	—
Other	5.30	119.50	19.20	1.00	−68.80	0.80
Total Shellfish	**290.70**	**39.20**	**911.60**	**26.40**	**74.80**	**93.60**
Clams	26.10	39.40	27.00	4.00	−35.50	37.40
Oysters	2.60	−18.80	4.60	5.30	37.10	4.20
Scallops	91.40	14.30	138.70	0.10	57.40	0.50
Squid	5.80	50.60	3.00	0.20	251.00	0.20
Mussels	6.10	—	6.50	—	—	—
Lobster	41.40	−7.90	354.20	—	—	—
Shrimps	48.70	75.20	99.20	4.20	73.40	15.60
Crab	64.90	148.70	272.80	5.60	171.80	24.20
Other	3.70	−7.50	5.50	7.10	1 729.90	11.60
All Fisheries	**717.50**	**−40.90**	**1 123.30**	**280.80**	**−1.50**	**473.10**

Note: The total catch for the inland fisheries in 1994 was 36 000 t with a value of $75 000 000. The main species include smelt yellow pickerel, perch, and whitefish. This was a decline of 20% since 1990.
SOURCE: Department of Fisheries and Oceans, *Canada Year Book 1997*.

41. Fur Production, 1992–1996

	QUANTITY (000)				
	1992	1993	1994	1995	1996
Total pelts	1 812 089	1 883 052	2 238 964	2 078 245	2 416 262
Wildlife pelts	816 474	1 060 662	1 346 964	1 128 245	1 467 452
Ranch raised pelts	995 615	822 390	892 000	950 000	948 810
	VALUE ($)				
	1992	1993	1994	1995	1996
Total pelts	34 981 796	57 307 680	57 166 358	83 403 137	75 806 232
Wildlife pelts	14 485 773	23 115 771	25 944 659	25 429 117	34 540 976
Ranch raised pelts	20 496 023	34 191 909	31 221 699	57 974 020	41 265 256

SOURCE: Statistics Canada

42. Water Withdrawal, by Use, and Consumption, 1981–1991

WATER WITHDRAWALS	1981	1986 (000 000 m^3)	1991
TOTAL WATER WITHDRAWALS	37 254	42 217	45 095
Agriculture	3 125	3 559	3 991
Mining	648	593	363
Manufacturing	9 937	7 984	7 282
Thermal power	19 281	25 364	28 357
Municipal	4 263	4 717	5 102
Water consumption	**3 892**	**4 279**	**5 367**

SOURCE: Environment Canada, Water and Habitat Conversion Branch.

Mining

43. Production of Leading Minerals, 1994

MINERAL	PROVINCE OR TERRITORY												
	CANADA	NFLD	PEI	NS	NB	QUE	ONT ($000 000)	MAN	SASK	ALTA	BC	YT	NWT
Metals													
Cobalt	134.70	—	—	—	—	—	108.60	26.10	—	—	—	—	—
Copper	1 909.60	—	—	—	27.70	223.50	726.60	133.50	—	—	796.60	—	—
Gold	2 468.90	1.80	—	—	6.20	690.20	1 166.00	44.00	—	0.60	205.60	56.40	221.60
Iron Ore	1 214.90	743.10	—	—	—	—	n.a.	—	—	—	1.80	—	—
Lead	125.40	—	—	—	56.90	—	—	0.30	—	—	42.60	—	25.50
Molybdenum	113.40	—	—	—	—	—	—	—	—	—	113.40	—	—
Nickel	1 229.40	—	—	—	—	—	925.20	304.10	—	—	—	—	—
Platinum Group	144.50	—	—	—	—	—	—	—	—	—	—	—	—
Silver	171.80	—	—	—	52.40	52.40	45.60	7.90	—	—	29.40	0.20	4.00
Uranium	616.30	—	—	—	—	—	n.a.	—	—	—	—	—	—
Zinc	1 330.70	—	—	—	397.70	190.70	223.10	127.60	—	—	157.40	—	234.20
Total Metals	9 749.50	796.90	—	—	543.50	1 824.90	3 482.70	664.50	540.20	0.60	1 354.40	56.60	485.30
Non-metals													
Asbestos	232.70	2.10	—	—	—	230.70	—	—	—	—	—	—	—
Peat	133.30	0.78	—	—	40.40	43.80	—	—	—	—	—	—	—
Potash (K20)	1 287.10	—	—	—	—	—	—	—	—	—	—	—	—
Salt	300.70	—	—	—	—	—	174.40	—	26.90	—	—	—	—
Sulphur	165.80	—	—	—	5.30	5.50	28.60	1.20	0.50	113.70	4.20	—	—
Total Non-metals	2 610.20	4.70	—	112.10	252.20	598.70	273.40	14.40	159.20	159.20	47.00	—	—
Fuels													
Coal	1 811.70	—	—	217.20	28.50	—	—	—	130.00	575.10	860.90	—	—
Natural Gas	11 052.10	—	—	—	—	—	46.50	—	509.10	9 351.30	11 123.00	22.20	10.20
Crude Oil	13 345.10	—	—	201.20	—	—	40.30	0.30	1 872.40	10 652.50	321.40	—	173.70
Total Fuels	26 208.90	—	—	418.40	28.50	—	86.80	83.60	2 511.70	20 579.00	2 294.60	22.20	183.90
Structural Materials[1] Total	2 582.40	35.90	1.20	79.20	37.90	532.70	1 078.40	57.70	24.70	346.30	370.20	7.00	11.10
Total, All Minerals	41 151.0	837.50	1.20	609.80	862.00	2 956.30	4 921.40	820.50	4 225.20	21 085.00	4 066.20	85.80	680.30

[1]Structural materials include clay products, lime, cement, sand and gravel, and stone.
[2]—means nil or confidential.
SOURCE: *General Review of the Mineral Industries 1994*, Statistics Canada, Cat. No. 26-202-XPB, 1995.

44. Mineral Reserves, Closing Stocks, 1992–1995

MINERAL	1992	1993	1994	1995
Crude petroleum (000 000 m³)[1]	1 326	1 281	1 252	1 259
Natural gas (000 000 000 m³)[1]	2 711	2 672	2 232	1 898
Crude bitumen (000 000 m³)[1]	164.3	164.7	158.8	169.6
Coal (megatonnes)[1]	8 623	8 623	8 623	8 623
Copper (000 t)[2]	10 755	9 740	9 533	9 250
Nickel (000 t)[2]	5 605	5 409	5 334	5 832
Lead (000 t)[2]	4 328	4 149	3 861	3 660
Zinc (000 t)[2]	14 584	14 206	14 514	14 712
Molybdenum (000 t)[2]	163	161	148	129
Silver (t)[2]	15 974	15 576	19 146	19 073
Gold (t)[2]	1 345	1 333	1 513	1 540
Uranium (000 t)[3]	397	397	381	369

[1]Proved reserves recoverable with present technology and prices. [2]Proven and probable reserves.
[3]Reserves recoverable from mineable ore.
SOURCE: Canadian Petroleum Association, *Statistical Yearbook*; Alberta Energy Conservation Board, *Alberta's Reserves of Crude Oil, Oil Sands, Gas, Natural Gas Liquids and Sulphur*, Statistics Canada, Catalogue nos. 26–206 and 26–201; Natural Resources Canada, *Canadian Mineral Yearbook*.

45. Canada's World Role as a Producer of Certain Important Minerals, 1995

MINERAL		WORLD	RANK OF FIVE LEADING COUNTRIES				
			1	2	3	4	5
Potash (K$_2$O equivalent)		24 231	Canada	C.I.S.[1]	Germany	United States	Israel
(mine production)	000 t		9 066	5 605	3 278	1 480	1 326
	% of world total		37.4	23.1	13.5	6.1	5.5
Uranium (U concentrates)		33 573	Canada	F.S.U.[2]	Niger	United States	Australia
(mine production)	t		10 426	8 000	2 965	2 324	2 200
	% of world total		31.1	23.8	8.8	6.9	6.6
Zinc		6 983	Canada	China	Australia	Peru	United States
(mine production)	000 t		1 121	930	930	689	678
	% of world total		16.1	13.3	13.3	9.9	9.7
Sulphur, elemental		37 371	United States	Canada	C.I.S.	Poland	Saudi Arabia
(mine production)	000 t		10 400	7 846	3 754	2 349	1 720
	% of world total		27.8	21.0	10.0	6.3	4.6
Asbestos		2 317	C.I.S.	Canada	China	Brazil	Zimbabwe
(mine production)	000 t		1 000	524	250	180	145
	% of world total		43.2	22.6	10.8	7.8	6.3
Nickel		1 014	Russia	Canada	New Caledonia	Australia	Indonesia
(mine production)	000 t		251	182	121	104	87
	% of world total		24.8	17.9	11.9	10.3	8.6
Cadmium		19 297	Japan	Canada	Belgium	China	United States
(refined production)	t		2 652	2 349	1 710	1 296	1 266
	% of world total		13.7	12.2	8.9	6.7	6.6
Aluminum		19 701	United States	Russia	Canada	China	Australia
(primary metal)	000 t		3 375	2 790	2 172	1 658	1 293
	% of world total		17.1	14.2	11.0	8.4	6.6
Copper		10 061	Chile	United States	Canada	Russia	Indonesia
(mine production)	000 t		2 488	1 852	726	536	460
	% of world total		24.7	18.4	7.2	5.3	4.6
Platinum group metals		287 093	South Africa	Russia	Canada	United States	Japan
(mine production)	kg		189 200	69 600	16 963	6 900	2 580
	% of world total		65.9	24.2	5.9	2.4	0.9
Salt		188 982	United States	China	Canada	Germany	India
(mine production)	000 t		42 100	25 000	10 875	10 800	9 500
	% of world total		22.3	13.2	5.8	5.7	5.0
Titanium concentrates (ilmenite, rutile, slag)	000 t	5 932•	Australia	South Africa	Norway	Canada	India
			2 210	1 080	830	815•	300
	% of world total		37.3	18.2	14.0	13.7	5.1
Cobalt		20 608	F.S.U.	Zaire	Zambia	Canada	Cuba
(shipments)	t		5 000	3 981	2 800	2 016	1 561
	% of world total		24.3	19.3	13.6	9.8	7.6
Silver		13 955	Mexico	Peru	United States	Canada	Chile
	t		2 324	1 908	1 450	1 285	1 041
	% of world total		16.7	13.7	10.4	9.2	7.5
Gypsum		98 607	United States	China	Thailand	Canada	Iran
(mine production)	000 t		16 600	11 000	8 533	8 463	8 230
	% of world total		16.8	11.2	8.7	8.6	8.3
Molybdenum (Mo content)		116 922	United States	China	Chile	Canada	Russia
(mine production)	t		59 000	18 000	16 000	9 522	4 500
	% of world total		50.5	15.4	13.7	8.1	3.8
Gold		2 156	South Africa	United States	Australia	Canada	China
(mine production)	t		524	312	253	152	141
	% of world total		24.3	14.5	11.7	7.1	6.5
Lead		2 679	Australia	China	United States	Peru	Canada
(mine production)	000 t		455	420	394	233	210
	% of world total		17.0	15.7	14.7	8.7	7.9

• Estimated
[1] C.I.S.: Commonwealth of Independent States; [2] F.S.U.: former Soviet Union.
SOURCES: Natural Resources Canada, from *World Nonferrous Metal Statistics* and the *Canadian Minerals Yearbook*; U.S. Bureau of Mines.

Energy

46. Coal, Supply and Demand

	1960	1970	1980 (10⁶ t)	1991	1994
Supply					
Production	10.0	15.1	36.7	71.1	72.8
Imports	11.5	18.0	15.6	12.4	9.2
Total Supply	**21.5**	**33.1**	**52.3**	**83.5**	**82.0**
Demand					
Domestic	20.4	25.7	37.3	49.4	52.9
Exports	0.9	4.3	15.3	34.1	31.6
Total Demand	**21.3**	**30.0**	**52.6**	**83.5**	**84.5**

Includes bituminous, sub-bituminous, and lignite.
SOURCE: Statistics Canada, *Coal and Coke Statistics*, Cat. No. 45-002. *Canada Year Book 1997*.

47. Electricity, Supply and Demand

	1960	1970	1980 (10⁹ kW/h)	1991	1994
Supply					
Production	114.0	204.7	367.3	489.2	550.3
Imports	1.0	3.2	2.9	6.2	8.3
Total Supply	**115.0**	**207.9**	**370.2**	**495.4**	**551.2**
Demand					
Domestic	109.0	202.3	239.9	470.8	507.6
Exports	6.0	5.6	30.3	24.6	51.0
Total Demand	**115.0**	**207.9**	**370.2**	**495.4**	**558.6**

SOURCE: Statistics Canada, *Electric Power Statistics*, Cat. No. 57-202. *Canada Year Book 1997*.

48. Marketable Natural Gas, Supply and Demand

	1960	1970	1980 (10⁹ m³)	1991	1994
Supply					
Production	12.5	52.9	69.8	105.2	152.3
Imports	0.2	0.3	5.6	0.3	1.0
Total Supply	**12.7**	**53.2**	**75.4**	**105.5**	**153.4**
Demand					
Domestic	9.4	29.5	43.3	54.8	80.7
Exports	3.1	22.1	22.6	47.6	71.4
Total Demand	**12.5**	**51.6**	**75.4**	**102.4**	**152.1**

SOURCE: Statistics Canada, *Crude Petroleum and Natural Gas Production*, Cat. No. 26-006. *Canada Year Book 1997*.

50. Petroleum, Supply and Demand

	1960	1970	1980 (10⁶ m³)	1991	1994
Supply					
Production	36.5	80.2	89.5	96.7	126.9
Imports	21.2	33.1	32.2	31.5	42.5
Total Supply	**57.7**	**113.3**	**121.7**	**128.2**	**169.4**
Demand					
Domestic	46.8	74.3	109.8	84.4	99.9
Exports	10.7	38.9	11.9	44.2	79.8
Total Demand	**57.5**	**113.2**	**121.7**	**128.6**	**179.7**

SOURCE: Statistics Canada, *Refined Petroleum Products*, Cat. No. 45-004. *Canada Year Book 1997*.

51. Energy Summary, 1994

	(PETAJOULES)
Primary Production	13 941
Net Supply	8 418
Producer's Own Consumption	976
Non-energy Use	745
Energy Use	6 697
Industrial	2 086
Transportation	2 027
Agriculture	195
Residential	1 277
Public Administration	145
Commercial and Institutional	967

SOURCE: *Canada Year Book 1997*.

49. Marketable Natural Gas Remaining Established Reserves in Canada, 1995

	REMAINING RESERVES AT 1994-12-31	1995 GROSS ADDITIONS	1996 NET PRODUCTION*	REMAINING RESERVES AT 1995-12-31	NET CHANGES IN RESERVES DURING 1995
NATURAL GAS			(000 000 M³)		
Conventional Areas					
British Columbia	242 227	29 629	18 316	253 540	11 313
Alberta	1 547 635	144 107	123 957	1 567 785	20 150
Saskatchewan	85 301	8 747	7 439	86 609	1 308
Ontario	13 415	(979)	454	11 982	(1 433)
Quebec	107	—	2	105	(2)
New Brunswick	4	—	—	4	—
Mainland Territories	9 297	109	537	8 869	(428)
TOTAL MARKETABLE NATURAL GAS	**1 897 986**	**181 613**	**150 705**	**1 928 894**	**30 908**

SOURCE: Canadian Association of Petroluem Producers, *Statistical Handbook*, July 1996.

52. Conventional Crude Oil and Equivalent Remaining Established Reserves in Canada, 1995

	REMAINING RESERVES AT 1994-12-31	1995 GROSS ADDITIONS*	1995 NET PRODUCTION*	REMAINING RESERVES AT 1995-12-31	NET CHANGE IN RESERVES DURING 1995
CRUDE OIL			(000 M³)		
Conventional Areas					
British Columbia	19 431	3 816	1 969	21 278	1 847
Alberta	409 543	39 779	54 926	394 396	(15 147)
Saskatchewan	135 283	30 972	18 053	148 202	12 919
Manitoba	6 477	503	635	6 345	(132)
Ontario	2 046	177	285	1 938	(108)
Quebec	0	—	—	0	0
New Brunswick	5	—	—	5	0
Mainland Territories	16 249	1 381	1 698	15 932	(317)
	589 034	**76 628**	**77 566**	**588 096**	**(938)**
Frontier Areas					
Mackenzie/Beaufort	53 950	—	—	53 950	0
Arctic islands	114	75	37	152	38
Eastcoast Offshore	135 695	1 375	1 241	135 829	134
	189 759	**1 450**	**1 278**	**189 931**	**172**
TOTAL CRUDE OIL	**778 793**	**78 078**	**78 844**	**778 027**	**(766)**
PENTANES PLUS					
Conventional Areas					
British Columbia	5 640	454	357	5 737	97
Alberta	104 554	9 929	8 665	105 818	1 264
Saskatchewan	518	(67)	46	405	(113)
Manitoba	19	—	2	17	(2)
Mainland Territories	2 685	218	343	2 560	(125)
TOTAL PENTANES PLUS	**113 416**	**10 534**	**9 413**	**114 537**	**1 121**
TOTAL CRUDE OIL AND EQUIVALENT	**892 209**	**88 612**	**88 257**	**892 564**	**355**
DEVELOPED SYNTHETIC CRUDE OIL					
Alberta	310 333	113 787	16 153	407 967	97 634
DEVELOPED BITUMEN					
Alberta	169 640	36 553	8 743	197 450	27 810
TOTAL CONVENTIONAL AND NONCONVENTIONAL	**1 309 182**	**238 952**	**113 153**	**1 497 981**	

SOURCE: Canadian Association of Petroleum Producers, *Statistical Handbook*, July 1996.

53. Installed Electrical Generating Capacity by Fuel Type and Region, 1960, 1970, 1990, and 1993

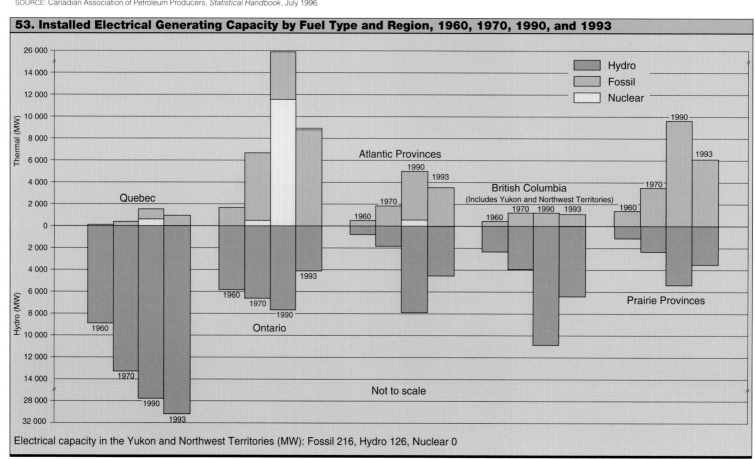

Electrical capacity in the Yukon and Northwest Territories (MW): Fossil 216, Hydro 126, Nuclear 0

SOURCE: Natural Resources Canada, *Electrical Power in Canada*, 1975, 1990, 1993.

54. Electricity Production and Consumption, 1960 to 1993

PROVINCE OR TERRITORY	1960		1970		1980		1993	
	PRODUCTION	CONSUMPTION (GW.h)	PRODUCTION	CONSUMPTION (GW.h)	PRODUCTION	CONSUMPTION (GW.h)	PRODUCTION	CONSUMPTION (GW.h)
Newfoundland	1 512	1 427	4 854	4 770	46 374	8 545	40 846	10 904
Prince Edward Island	79	79	250	250	127	518	59	806
Nova Scotia	1 814	1 733	3 511	3 706	6 868	6 814	9 714	9 919
New Brunswick	1 738	1 684	5 142	4 221	9 323	8 838	15 112	13 873
Quebec	50 433	44 002	75 877	69 730	97 917	118 254	154 443	170 153
Ontario	35 815	37 157	63 857	69 488	110 283	106 509	140 708	137 483
Manitoba	3 742	4 021	8 449	8 601	19 468	13 927	27 121	18 642
Saskatchewan	2 204	2 124	6 011	5 402	9 204	9 827	15 303	15 279
Alberta	3 443	3 472	10 035	9 880	23 451	23 172	48 277	46 960
British Columbia	13 409	13 413	26 209	25 761	43 416	42 789	58 586	58 672
Yukon	89	89	224	220	381	381	335	335
Northwest Territories	100	100	304	308	494	494	584	584
Canada	**114 378**	**109 304**	**204 723**	**202 337**	**367 306**	**340 068**	**511 088**	**483 610**

SOURCE: Statistics Canada, *Electrical Power Statistics, Vol. II*, Cat. No. 57-202.

Manufacturing

55. Summary Statistics, Annual Census of Manufacturers, 1965–1994

YEAR	NUMBER OF ESTABLISHMENTS[1]	PRODUCTION AND RELATED WORKERS		COST OF FUEL AND ELECTRICITY ($000)	COST OF MATERIALS AND SUPPLIES USED ($000)	VALUE OF SHIPMENTS OF GOODS OF OWN MANUFACTURE ($000)	VALUE ADDED ($000)
		NUMBER	WAGES ($000)				
1965	33 310	1 115 892	5 012 345	675 641	18 622 213	33 889 425	14 927 764
1970	31 928	1 167 063	7 232 256	903 264	25 699 999	46 380 935	20 047 801
1975	30 100	1 271 786	12 699 228	1 805 398	51 177 942	88 427 031	36 105 457
1980	35 495	1 346 187	22 162 309	4 448 859	99 897 576	168 058 662	65 851 774
1984	36 464	1 240 816	28 294 553	7 306 383	136 133 629	230 070 091	88 667 660
1990	39 864	1 393 324	40 406 450	7 936 055	168 664 306	298 918 513	122 972 463
1994	31 974	1 243 026	41 405 000	9 151 600	202 655 000	352 834 700	142 858 800

[1]The increase in the number of establishments between 1975 and 1980 was largely a result of the addition of 4 962 small establishments by improved coverage.
SOURCE: Manufacturing Industries of Canada: National and Provincial areas. Statistics Canada Cat. No. 31-203XPD. *Canada Year Book 1976-77, 1992.*

56. Principal Statistics on Manufacturing Industries, by Province, 1994

PROVINCE OR TERRITORY	NUMBER OF ESTABLISHMENTS[1]	NUMBER OF EMPLOYEES[1]	SALARIES AND WAGES	COST OF FUEL AND ELECTRICITY ($000 000)	COST OF MATERIALS, SUPPLIES, AND GOODS FOR RESALE	VALUE OF SHIPMENTS AND OTHER REVENUE	VALUE ADDED
Newfoundland	250	9 042	256.3	77.9	679.6	1 422.6	661.4
Prince Edward Island	133	2 663	54.4	13.5	333.1	538.0	194.5
Nova Scotia	668	25 547	710.1	189.5	3 149.7	5 413.1	2 048.5
New Brunswick	623	24 912	728.1	296.4	4 235.3	7 081.2	2 542.7
Quebec	10 164	326 902	9 871.6	2 763.1	44 302.9	85 133.0	38 435.8
Ontario	12 510	616 048	21 649.3	3 750.8	110 996.1	184 923.1	71 169.0
Manitoba	1 004	39 208	1 077.0	205.8	4 000.7	7 542.7	3 371.8
Saskatchewan	683	15 937	486.6	148.2	2 665.3	4 409.6	1 613.8
Alberta	2 385	69 027	2 265.0	713.1	15 022.9	25 260.1	9 739.7
British Columbia	3 513	113 377	4 296.0	992.1	17 232.8	31 046.5	13 055.1
Yukon and Northwest Territories	41	363	10.4	1.3	37.1	64.9	26.5
Canada	**31 974**	**1 243 026**	**41 405.0**	**9 151.6**	**202 655.5**	**352 834.7**	**142 858.8**

[1]In 1987 for Canada there were 36 790 establishments and 1 864 018 employees.
SOURCE: *Manufacturing Industries of Canada, national and provincial areas, Statistics Canada Cat. No. 31-203, Annual.*

Transportation

57. St. Lawrence Seaway Traffic by Classification and Direction, 1995

MONTREAL-LAKE ONTARIO SECTION

COMMODITIES	UPBOUND (000 t)	SOURCES AND DESTINATIONS OF UPBOUND COMMODITIES (%)	DOWNBOUND (000 t)	SOURCES AND DESTINATIONS OF DOWNBOUND COMMODITIES (%)
Wheat	—	—	8 090.6	Can→Can 62 US→Can 27 US→For 10
Corn	—	—	2 259.2	US→Can 63 US→For 32 Can→Can 5
Barley	—	—	206.2	US→Can 38 Can→Can 16 US→For 46
Soybeans	—	—	2 025.4	US→For 18 Can→Can 15 US→Can 63
Flaxseed	—	—	432.6	Can→For 90 Can→Can 10
Total Agricultural Products	**3.2**		**14 695.5**	
Bituminous Coal	1.9		940.5	US→Can 92 US→For 8
Coke	79.4		806.8	US→Can 75 US→For 14 Can→Can 9
Iron Ore	10 959.4	Can→US 47 Can→Can 51	—	
Aluminium Ore and Concentrates	270.2	For→Can 72 Can→US 16 Can→Can 13	—	
Clay and Bentonite	6.7	For→US 100	224.3	US→Can 58 US→For 42
Stone and Gravel	—	—	807.8	Can→Can 52 US→Can 48
Salt	—	—	1 449.1	Can→Can 70 US→Can 30
Total Mine Products	**12 021.9**		**4 476.9**	
Gasoline	245.8	Can→Can 11 For→Can 72 US→Can 17	—	
Fuel Oil	152.3	Can→Can 72 Can→US 22 For→Can 6	558.9	Can→Can 97 Can→US 3
Chemicals	138.5	For→Can 44 US→Can 11 For→US 35 US→US 10	382.2	Can→For 50 Can→Can 30 Can→US 10
Sodium Products	124.5	US→Can 93 For→Can 7	—	
Iron and Steel Products	3 746.7	For→Can 33 For→US 63 Can→US 4	970.2	Can→For 16 US→For 83
Sugar	260.5	For→Can 82 Can→Can 18	—	—
Scrap Iron and Steel	93.8	Can→US 87 Can→Can 13	56.0	US→For 45 Can→For 55
Total Manufactures[1]	**5 327.1**		**2 158.3**	
Grand Total (000 t)	**17 352.4**		**21 332.4**	
($000)	**26 224.6**		**19 555.3**	

WELLAND CANAL SECTION

COMMODITIES	UPBOUND (000 t)	SOURCES AND DESTINATIONS OF UPBOUND COMMODITIES (%)	DOWNBOUND (000 t)	SOURCES AND DESTINATIONS OF DOWNBOUND COMMODITIES (%)
Wheat	—	—	8 155.7	Can→Can 62 US→Can 27 US→For 10
Corn	—	—	2 432.0	US→Can 67 US→For 29 Can→Can 4
Barley	—	—	206.2	US→Can 38 Can→Can 16 US→For 46
Soybeans	—	—	2 003.3	US→For 18 US→Can 63 Can→Can 14 Can→For 5
Flaxseed	—	—	432.6	Can→For 90 Can→Can 10
Total Agricultural Products	**0.0**		**14 948.3**	
Bituminous Coal	—	—	3 998.1	US→Can 98 US→For 2
Coke	90.1	Can→US 33 For→US 67	869.1	US→Can 82 US→For 13 Can→Can 3
Iron Ore	5 416.3	Can→US 95 Can→Can 2	912.6	US→Can 100
Aluminium Ore and Concentrates	234.1	For→Can 67 Can→US 18 Can→Can 14	—	—
Clay and Bentonite	6.8	For→US 100	224.3	US→Can 58 US→For 42
Stone, Gravel, and Sand	525.5	Can→US 100	1 053.5	Can→Can 42 US→Can 56
Salt	—	—	2 309.7	Can→Can 66 US→Can 31 Can→US 3
Total Mine Products	**6 537.0**		**9 863.0**	
Gasoline	18.0	Can→Can 39 For→Can 61	0.0	
Fuel Oils	53.7	Can→Can 100	551.3	US→Can 4 Can→Can 95
Chemicals	63.1	For→US 27 US→US 23	480.9	Can→For 39 Can→Can 32 Can→For 20
Sodium Products	40.3	US→Can 100	0.0	
Iron and Steel Production	2 691.9	For→US 89 For→Can 7 Can→US 5	807.7	US→For 99
Cement	1 187.3	Can→US 91 Can→Can 9	6.7	US→US 100
Scrap Iron and Steel	118.7	Can→Can 10 Can→US 90	25.5	US→For 100
Total Manufactures[1]	**5 925.1**		**2 037.5**	
Grand Total (000 t)	**12 462.1**		**26 914.2**	
($000)	**14 636.4**		**37 257.3**	

[1]Includes unclassified cargoes.

SOURCE: *The St. Lawrence Seaway Traffic Report—1995 Navigation Season*, St. Lawrence Seaway Authority (Ottawa) and the Saint Lawrence Seaway Development Corporation (Washington).

58. Shipments of Selected Manufacturing Industries, by Major Group, 1990-1994

MAJOR INDUSTRY GROUP	1994 ($000 000)	% CHANGE 1993/1994
Total	**352 835**	**13.9**
Food	42 810	6.2
Beverage	6 713	2.3
Tobacco products	2 472	23.2
Rubber Products	3 412	10.5
Plastic Products	7 102	14.7
Leather and allied products	1 006	8.2
Primary textile	3 073	12.4
Textile products	3 170	10.2
Clothing	6 147	3.6
Wood	22 907	20.0
Furniture and fixture	4 523	13.4
Paper and allied products	25 648	20.8
Printing and publishing	13 496	5.1
Primary metal	23 442	18.3
Fabricated metal products	17 815	15.6
Machinery, except electrical	12 374	22.6
Transportation equipment	76 132	18.7
Aircraft and parts	5 743	−10.1
Motor vehicle	44 558	25.3
Truck, bus body and trailer	1 567	14.8
Motor vehicle parts and accessories	19 996	15.4
Railroad rolling stocks	1 991	23.3
Shipbuilding and repair	976	−2.0
Boatbuilding and repair	304	5.0
Other transportation equipment	998	44.9
Electrical and electronic products	23 862	17.6
Non-metallic mineral products	6 698	2.6
Refined petroleum and coal	17 535	−1.7
Chemical products	25 598	13.2
Other manufacturing	6 899	12.7

SOURCE: *Inventories, Shipments and Orders in Manufacturing Industries*, Statistics Canada Cat. No. 31-203 1994.

59. Principal Seaway Ports[2], 1995

CANADA	INBOUND	OUTBOUND
	Cargo 000 t[1]	
Hamilton	11 043.5	701.50
Port Cartier	4 663.8	2 112.60
Baie Comeau	2 642.7	0.00
Quebec City	2 247.1	1 007.60
Montreal	2 198.1	96.00
Sept Iles	821.1	3 949.70
Trois Rivières	802.9	78.10
Toronto	798.3	18.50
Sorel	404.0	116.30
Pointe Noire	379.6	3 845.20
Thorold	298.7	6.50
Picton	238.9	567.00
Windsor	179.3	1 373.40
Sarnia	105.1	817.30
Thunder Bay	9.3	6 702.10
Goderich	0.0	757.50
Total	**30 289.0**	**26 622.0**
UNITED STATES		
Indiana-Burns Harbor	3 046.9	566.10
Cleveland	2 043.9	400.00
Detroit	1 934.5	471.50
Chicago	1 167.8	1 357.40
Ashtabula	709.6	659.80
Toledo	263.9	3 579.30
Duluth-Superior	230.2	4 510.20
Milwaukee	227.8	768.50
Sandusky	0.0	1 659.80
Conneaut	0.0	725.20
Total	**11 986.2**	**16 374.6**

[1]Tonnage figures are limited to cargo volumes moved through Seaway lock structures.
[2]Area includes all ports or installations within a 20 km radius of the main harbour.
SOURCE: *The St. Lawrence Seaway Traffic Report—1995 Navigation Season.*

60. Cargo Loaded and Unloaded at 20 Leading Canadian Ports, Tonnage by Sector: Domestic and International Shipping, 1995

PORT	DOMESTIC			INTERNATIONAL			TOTAL
	LOADED	UNLOADED	TOTAL	LOADED	UNLOADED	TOTAL	
	('000 t)	('000 t)	('000 t)	('000 t)	('000 t)	('000 t)	('000 t)
Vancouver	1 542	1 116	2 658	61 887	5 049	66 936	69 594
Port-Cartier	2 833	1 789	4 621	17 213	3 077	20 290	24 912
Sept-Îles/Pte-Noire	3 936	572	4 508	17 085	1 549	18 634	23 142
Saint John	1 482	943	2 425	7 725	8 589	16 314	18 739
Montréal/Contrecoeur	738	4 950	5 688	5 546	7 367	12 913	18 601
Québec/Lévis	2 824	1 327	4 151	3 997	9 235	13 232	17 383
Halifax	1 786	784	2 569	5 365	5 310	10 676	13 245
Hamilton	312	6 061	6 373	485	5 071	5 556	11 929
Port Hawkesbury	32	151	183	7 003	4 705	11 708	11 891
Thunder Bay	7 219	224	7 443	4 021	26	4 047	11 490
Prince Rupert	9	28	37	11 259	71	11 330	11 367
Fraser River	4 498	1 342	5 840	1 556	949	2 504	8 345
Baie-Comeau	603	1 755	2 358	2 983	2 211	5 194	7 552
Come-By-Chance	42	7	49	2 684	3 375	6 059	6 108
Nanticoke	534	1 255	1 790	144	3 675	3 819	5 609
Sorel	122	2 997	3 120	1 910	566	2 475	5 595
Howe Sound	1 014	4 257	5 271	1	54	55	5 326
Sault Ste. Marie	110	615	725	272	3 836	4 108	4 833
Windsor Ont.	1 298	1 093	2 391	543	1 704	2 247	4 638
East Coast Vanc Isl	1 268	2 861	4 129	—	—	—	4 129
Subtotal	**32 202**	**34 126**	**66 328**	**151 682**	**66 417**	**218 099**	**284 427**
Other ports	18 168	16 244	34 412	24 925	16 791	41 716	76 127
Grand Total	**50 370**	**50 370**	**100 740**	**176 607**	**83 208**	**259 815**	**360 554**

SOURCE: Statistics Canada Cat. No. 54-205, *Shipping in Canada 1995.*

204

61. Visits and Expenditures of Canadian Residents in Selected Countries, 1995 (excluding USA)

COUNTRY	VISITS (000)	%	SPENDING ($000 000)
Europe			
Austria	106	1.9	60.3
Belgium	95	1.7	41.3
Denmark	34	0.6	19.7
France	449	8.0	467.6
Germany	249	4.4	181.9
Greece	65	1.2	73.1
Ireland (Rep.)	86	1.5	93.3
Italy	169	3.0	153.4
Netherlands	181	3.2	98.4
Portugal	48	0.9	54.0
Spain	90	1.6	88.3
Switzerland	146	2.6	81.6
United Kingdom	735	13.1	769.8
Yugoslavia	3	0.1	3.6
Other	327	5.8	253.3
Total	**2 783**	**49.4**	**2 439.7**
Africa	**124**	**2.2**	**147.2**
Asia			
Hong Kong	123	2.2	137.7
Japan	59	1.0	125.3
Other	393	7.0	517.1
Total	**574**	**10.2**	**780.1**
Central America	**142**	**2.5**	**99.0**
Bermuda and Caribbean			
Bahamas	115	2.0	50.0
Barbados	91	1.6	42.6
Bermuda	95	1.7	96.0
Cuba	184	2.9	118.7
Dominican Republic	136	2.4	86.5
Jamaica	92	1.6	58.8
Other	535	9.5	185.6
Total	**1 247**	**22.1**	**638.1**
South America	**130**	**2.3**	**127.1**
North America			
Mexico	505	9.0	351.3
Other	13	0.2	2.0
Total	**518**	**9.2**	**353.3**
Oceania and Other Ocean Islands	**113**	**2.0**	**206.0**
Grand Total	**5 632**	**100.0**	**4 790.4**

SOURCE: *Touriscope International Travel 1995*. Statistics Canada Cat. No. 66-201-XPB.

62. Visits and Expenditures of Canadian Residents Returning from the United States, by Selected States, 1995

COUNTRY	VISITS (000)	%	SPENDING ($000 000)
Arizona	284	0.9	217.1
California	954	2.9	608.2
Colorado	127	0.4	61.5
Connecticut	185	0.6	30.5
District of Columbia	173	0.5	59.6
Florida	1 870	5.7	1 800.4
Georgia	879	2.7	101.9
Hawaii	299	0.9	350.9
Idaho	495	1.5	33.5
Illinois	653	2.0	163.4
Kentucky	521	1.6	35.0
Louisiana	92	0.3	56.9
Maine	1 068	3.3	170.5
Maryland	526	1.6	37.6
Massachusetts	715	2.2	175.6
Michigan	2 480	7.5	251.2
Minnesota	818	2.5	135.8
Montana	704	2.1	115.4
Nevada	709	2.2	405.2
New Hampshire	915	2.8	80.0
New Jersey	358	1.1	77.7
New York	4 831	14.7	551.7
North Carolina	802	2.4	74.9
North Dakota	680	2.1	85.8
Ohio	1 001	3.0	87.4
Oregon	380	1.2	64.4
Pennsylvania	1 421	4.3	107.5
South Carolina	748	2.3	211.9
Tennessee	534	1.6	54.3
Texas	294	0.9	179.3
Utah	185	0.6	31.7
Vermont	1 604	4.9	121.3
Virginia	866	2.6	79.1
Washington	2 227	6.8	277.8
Wisconsin	307	0.9	43.2
Other States	2 167	6.6	289.6
Total	**32 869**	**100.0**	**7 227.7**

SOURCE: *Touriscope International Travel 1995*. Statistics Canada Cat. No. 66-201-XPB.

63. Trips of One or More Nights between Canada and the United States, 1987-1996

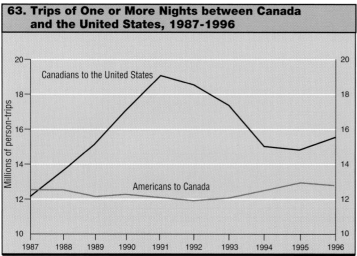

SOURCE: International Travel Statistics Canada Cat. No. 66-201

64. Trips of One or More Nights between Canada and the United States, by Purpose of Trip, 1996

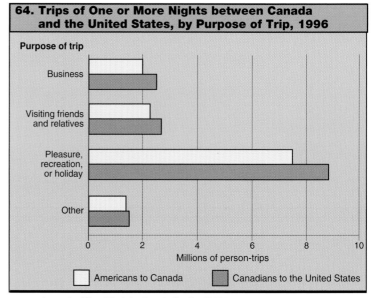

SOURCE: International Travel Statistics Canada Cat. No. 66-201

65. Trip Characteristics of United States Residents Entering Canada, Staying One or More Nights in Province Visited, 1995

TRIP CHARACTERISTICS	ATLANTIC PROVINCES	QUEBEC	ONTARIO	MANITOBA	SASKATCHEWAN	ALBERTA	BRITISH COLUMBIA	CANADA
Number of province-visits (000)	846	1 946	6 895	283	185	925	3 235	14 315
Spending in province ($000 000)	302	762	1 942	86	59	420	1 228	4 799
Average spending per visit ($)	357.10	391.50	281.60	303.60	321.60	454.10	379.60	335.20
Number of visit-nights (000)	3 359	6 572	21 854	1 002	675	3 912	11 704	49 078
Average number of nights	4.0	3.4	3.2	3.5	3.7	4.2	3.6	3.4
Average spending per visit-night ($)	89.90	116.00	88.80	85.60	88.00	107.30	104.90	97.80
Region of Residence (000)								
New England	344	669	351	6	6	37	72	1 486
Middle Atlantic	130	541	2 067	10	9	59	177	2 994
South Atlantic	131	237	501	12	10	69	218	1 179
East North Central	98	222	2 872	49	34	132	207	3 614
West North Central	32	53	433	150	57	76	115	915
East South Central	19	20	114	4	6	21	27	210
West South Central	20	45	138	13	9	79	128	431
Mountain	16	29	111	18	33	193	254	654
Pacific	56	128	303	19	19	234	1 881	2 641
Other states	1	2	5	1	1	26	156	190
Total	**846**	**1 946**	**6 895**	**283**	**185**	**925**	**3 235**	**14 315**
Purpose of Trip (000)								
Business, convention, and employment	57	352	1 095	40	30	141	307	2 022
Visiting friends or relatives	188	309	1 146	61	46	135	565	2 450
Other pleasure, recreation or holiday	556	1 112	4 002	155	84	555	2 022	8 487
Other	44	173	653	26	25	94	341	1 356
Total	**846**	**1 946**	**6 895**	**283**	**185**	**925**	**3 235**	**14 315**
Quarter of Entry (000)								
First	28	275	800	31	13	81	383	1 611
Second	158	495	1 881	81	61	230	888	3 793
Third	580	829	3 084	122	81	499	1 514	6 709
Fourth	80	347	1 130	49	29	115	451	2 201
Total	**846**	**1 946**	**6 895**	**283**	**185**	**925**	**3 235**	**14 315**
Type of Transportation (000)								
Automobile	**518**	**1 156**	**5 057**	**199**	**136**	**485**	**2 054**	**9 605**
Non-automobile								
Plane	151	548	1 216	69	42	355	622	3 002
Bus	57	187	379	12	6	40	167	848
Other methods	120	56	243	2	—	45	393	860
Total	**846**	**1 946**	**6 895**	**283**	**185**	**925**	**3 235**	**14 315**

SOURCE: *Touriscope International Travel 1995*. Statistics Canada Cat. No. 66-201-XPB.

66. Foreign Investment in Canada 1970, 1990, 1995

	1970	1990	1995
United States	22 054	84 311	113 092
United Kingdom	2 641	18 217	16 477
Japan	103	5 203	6 702
France	475	3 859	5 293
Germany	364	5 148	4 974
Netherlands	452	3 162	4 305
Switzerland	353	3 139	3 417
Hond Kong	20	1 370	3 179
Belg./Lux.	194	681	2 754
Bermuda	29	1 278	1 582
Sweden	126	598	1 097

SOURCE: Statistics Canada as presented in *Colombo's 1997 Canadian Global Almanac*.

67. Top 10 Overseas Countries Visited by Canadians for One or More Nights, 1986–1996

RANK	1986	1991	1996
1.	United Kingdom	United Kingdom	United Kingdom
2.	France	Mexico	Mexico
3.	Mexico	France	France
4.	West Germany	Germany	Germany
5.	Netherlands, The	Netherlands, The	Cuba
6.	Switzerland	Cuba	Italy
7.	Italy	Dominican Republic	Netherlands, The
8.	Austria	Italy	Hong Kong
9.	Jamaica	Switzerland	Switzerland
10.	Dominican Republic	Hong Kong	Dominican Republic

68. Trip Characteristics of Residents of Countries Other than the United States Entering Canada, Staying One or More Nights in Province Visited, 1995

TRIP CHARACTERISTICS	ATLANTIC PROVINCES	QUEBEC	ONTARIO	MANITOBA	SASKATCHEWAN	ALBERTA	BRITISH COLUMBIA	CANADA
Number of province-visits (000)	200	1 095	1 928	77	49	713	1 429	5 491
Spending in province ($000 000)	122.8	836.6	1 274.0	42.7	22.3	487.3	1 252.7	4 038.4
Average spending per visit ($)	615.40	763.90	660.90	552.70	453.90	683.20	876.60	735.50
Number of visit-nights (000)	1 512	8 992	15 577	556	275	4 469	11 524	42 904
Average number of nights	7.6	8.2	8.1	7.2	5.6	6.3	8.1	7.8
Average spending per visit-night ($)	81.20	93.00	81.80	76.80	81.30	109.00	108.70	94.10
Area of Residence (000)								
Europe	**141**	**766**	**1 037**	**51**	**28**	**367**	**634**	**3 024**
France	11	367	176	3	1	21	32	611
Germany	34	78	177	12	7	110	208	626
Italy	7	40	57	4	1	10	28	146
Netherlands	7	17	50	5	3	26	35	142
Scandinavia	5	13	30	2	1	10	20	79
United Kingdom	52	114	353	17	9	141	213	898
Other Europe	26	139	195	9	6	49	99	522
Africa	**1**	**18**	**27**	**1**	**1**	**5**	**11**	**64**
Asia	**22**	**175**	**627**	**17**	**15**	**271**	**620**	**1 748**
Japan	13	55	265	7	9	159	296	804
Other Asia	9	120	362	10	6	112	325	944
Central America	—	**5**	**7**	—	—	—	**1**	**13**
Bermuda and Caribbean	**7**	**24**	**67**	—	—	**4**	**7**	**109**
South America	**4**	**52**	**59**	**1**	—	**10**	**23**	**149**
North America	**12**	**28**	**31**	**3**	**2**	**5**	**25**	**107**
Oceania and Other Ocean Islands	**12**	**27**	**72**	**4**	**3**	**50**	**108**	**277**
Australia	10	23	57	3	1	40	85	218
Other	3	4	15	1	1	10	23	58
Total	**200**	**1 095**	**1 928**	**77**	**49**	**713**	**1 429**	**5 491**
Purpose of Trip (000)								
Business, convention and employment	24	184	329	12	4	52	148	752
Visiting friends or relatives	55	243	557	34	19	127	317	1 351
Other pleasure, recreation or holiday	112	634	966	29	26	516	912	3 195
Other	9	34	76	2	1	18	52	193
Total	**200**	**1 095**	**1 928**	**77**	**49**	**713**	**1 429**	**5 491**
Quarter of Entry (000)								
I	13	99	180	3	1	34	162	492
II	42	278	572	20	22	199	337	1 471
III	122	549	844	40	22	417	713	2 706
IV	22	170	331	14	4	64	217	822
Total	**200**	**1 095**	**1 928**	**77**	**49**	**713**	**1 429**	**5 491**

SOURCE: *Touriscope International Travel 1995*. Statistics Canada Cat. No. 66-201-XPB.

Trade

69. Exports From Canada, Principal Nations, 1987, 1989, 1991, and 1995

COUNTRY	1987	1989	1991	1995
			($000 000)	
United States	91 756	98 548	103 449	196 161
Japan	7 036	8 803	7 111	11 857
United Kingdom	2 850	3 441	2 920	3 748
Germany[1]	1 515	1 801	2 125	3 150
South Korea	1 167	1 645	1 861	2 695
Netherlands	1 021	1 534	1 655	1 584
Belgium	1 123	1 398	1 073	1 823
France	1 037	1 268	1 350	1 888
China	1 432	1 120	1 849	3 212
Italy	843	1 099	1 017	1 768
Hong Kong	480	1 050	817	1 377
Australia	689	1 031	628	1 139
Brazil	n.a.	n.a.	n.a.	1 265
Mexico	n.a.	n.a.	n.a.	1 107
Taiwan	n.a.	n.a.	n.a.	1 683
All Countries	**121 462**	**134 511**	**138 079**	**247 703**

[1]Figures for 1987 and 1989 do not include the former East Germany.
SOURCE: Statistics Canada, *Exports by Countries*, Cat. No. 65-003.

70. Imports to Canada, Principal Nations, 1987, 1989, 1991, and 1995

COUNTRY	1987	1989	1991	1995
			($000 000)	
United States	76 716	88 017	86 235	150 705
Japan	8 351	9 571	10 249	12 103
United Kingdom	4 276	4 562	4 182	5 470
Germany[1]	3 649	3 709	3 734	4 801
South Korea	1 912	2 441	2 110	3 204
Taiwan	2 166	2 351	2 212	2 792
France	1 590	2 019	2 670	3 125
Italy	1 793	2 015	1 792	3 270
Mexico	1 165	1 704	2 574	5 341
China	812	1 182	1 852	4 639
Hong Kong	1 097	1 160	1 021	1 305
Brazil	858	1 129	706	1 038
Australia	n.a.	n.a.	n.a.	1 283
Malaysia	n.a.	n.a.	n.a.	1 549
Singapore	n.a.	n.a.	n.a.	1 299
Sweden	n.a.	n.a.	n.a.	1 305
All Countries	**116 238**	**135 033**	**135 284**	**225 493**

[1]Figures for 1987 and 1989 do not include the former East Germany.
SOURCE: Statistics Canada, *Imports by Countries*, Cat. No. 65-006.

71. Principal Commodities, Imported and Exported, 1995

	IMPORTS	EXPORTS
	($000 000)	
Food, Feed, Beverages, and Tobacco	**13 289.4**	**19 747.7**
Fruits and vegetables	2 905.6	1 042.7
Cereals	317.70	4 742.5
Crude Materials, Inedible	**12 266.3**	**29 672.8**
Mineral fuels	8 176.2	22 924.4
Fabricated Materials	**24 240.0**	**17 895.3**
Organic chemicals	3 700.8	3 046.0
Plastics	6 875.5	6 034.3
Forestry Products	**9 494.0**	**42 188.2**
Wood and articles of wood	1 916.3	14 445.9
Paper and paperboard	3 818.1	15 708.3
Wood pulp	844.90	11 703.1
Textiles and Clothing	**9 438.4**	**3 430.8**
Metals, Glass, Ceramics, and Jewellery	**20 179.0**	**25 025.9**
Iron and steel and articles thereof	8 217.6	6 870.0
Aluminum and articles thereof	2 499.7	6 608.0
Machinery and Equipment	**133 680.8**	**106 360.8**
Machinery, boilers, appliances, engines	42 355.9	22 170.1
Vehicles and accessories	41 371.6	58 166.9
Electrical machinery and parts	29 472.2	11 957.4
Optical, photo, etc.	7 136.5	2 226.3
Other	**5 888.7**	**3 381.5**
Total	**225 493.2**	**247 703.4**

SOURCE: *Imports by Country*, Statistics Canada, 1995 Cat. No. 65-006 XPB. *Exports by Country*, Statistics Canada. 1995, Cat. No. 65-003 XPB.

72. Trade Balances by Province, 1994, $ billion

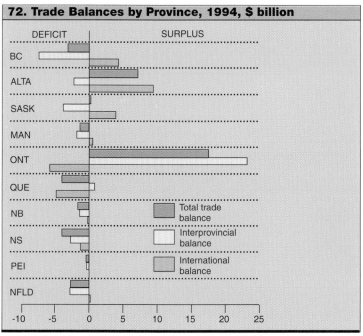

SOURCE: Statistics Canada, *Provincial Economic Accounts*, Cat. No. 13-213.

The Economy

73. Gross Domestic Product by Industry[1], 1970 to 1996

INDUSTRY	1970	1980	1990	1996
Agricultural and Related Services	2.9	2.1	2.2	2.2
Fishing, Trapping, Logging, and Forestry	0.3	0.2	0.8	0.7
Mining	6.4	4.1	4.0	4.4
Manufacturing	19.7	17.7	18.1	18.8
Construction	6.2	5.7	6.4	4.8
Trade	10.5	9.6	11.5	12.2
Finance, Insurance, and Real Estate	12.3	13.4	15.7	16.3
Transportation, Communications, and Utilities	9.1	10.1	11.5	12.4
Community, Business, and Personal Services	20.2	20.2	23.1	22.5
Government Services	7.5	6.7	6.6	5.7

[1]Based on per cent of Canada's GDP. Total GDP in 1996 (based on 1986 prices) was $551 020 000 000.
SOURCE: *Canadian Economic Observer*.

74. Gross Domestic Product by Province[1], 1970 to 1996

PROVINCE OR TERRITORY	1970	1980	1990	1996
			%	
Newfoundland	1.4	1.3	1.3	1.3
Prince Edward Island	0.3	0.3	0.3	0.3
Nova Scotia	2.5	2.0	2.5	2.4
New Brunswick	1.9	1.6	2.0	2.0
Quebec	25.5	23.3	23.1	22.0
Ontario	42.0	37.1	40.8	40.5
Manitoba	4.2	3.6	3.5	3.4
Saskatchewan	3.4	4.0	3.1	3.3
Alberta	8.0	13.9	10.7	11.3
British Columbia	10.6	12.4	12.2	13.0
Yukon and Northwest Territories	0.3	0.4	0.5	0.4

[1]Based on per cent of Canada's GDP.
SOURCE: *Canadian Economic Observer*.

75. Inflation Rates, 1915 to 1996

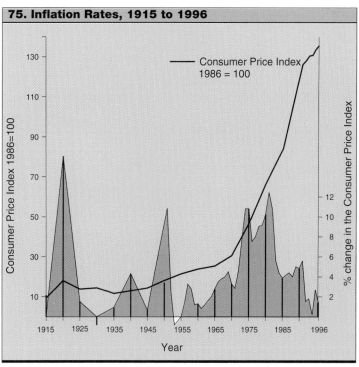

NOTE: Prior to 1950, data was compiled every five years. Since 1950, data has been compiled annually.

Conservation and Pollution

76. Ecozone Biophysical Characteristics[1]

ECOZONE	LANDFORMS	VEGETATION	SOILS AND SURFACE MATERIALS	CLIMATE
Atlantic Maritime	Hills and coastal plains	Mixed broadleaf and conifer stands	Acid and well-weathered soils (podzols) and soils with clay-rich sublayers (luvisols), moraine, marine bottom soils, and rock debris	Cool to cold winters, mild summers, moderate to heavy precipitation
Mixed-Wood Plain	Plains, some interior hills	Mixed broadleaf and conifer stands	Temperate region soils with clay-rich sublayers (luvisols), marine bottom soils, moraine, rock	Cool to cold winters, warm to hot summers, moderate precipitation
Boreal Shield	Plains, uplands, interior hills, many lakes and streams	Conifer and broadleaf boreal stands	Acid and well-weathered soils (podzols), lake bottom soils, moraine, rock	Cold winters, warm to hot summers, moderate precipitation
Prairie	Plains, some foothills	Short and mixed grasslands, aspen parkland	Organically rich, relatively fertile grassland soils (chernozems), moraine, and lake bottom materials	Cold winters, hot summers minimal precipitation
Boreal Plain	Plains, some foothills	Conifer and broadleaf boreal stands	Temperate region soils with clay-rich sublayers (luvisols), moraine and lake bottom materials	Cold winters, warm summers, moderate precipitation
Montane Cordillera	Mountainous highlands, interior plains	Mixed vegetation, conifer stands to sage brush	Temperate region soils with clay-rich sublayers (luvisols), soils with minimal weathering (brunisols), moraine, rock, rock debris	Cool to cold winters, warm to hot summers, and in lee areas, moist in montane areas
Pacific Maritime	Mountainous highlands, some coastal plains	Coastal western and mountain hemlock	Acid and well-weathered soils (podzols), moraine, rock, rock debris	Mild winters, mild summers, heavy precipitation, especially in fall and winter
Boreal Cordillera	Mountainous highlands, some hills and plains	Boreal, some alpine tundra and open woodland	Soils with minimal weathering (brunisols), moraine, rock	Cold winters, mild summers, minimal precipitation in lee areas, moist in montane areas
Tundra Cordillera	Mountainous highlands	Alpine and arctic tundra	Soils with minimal weathering (brunisols), frozen soils (cryosols), moraine, rock	Very cold winters, cool summers, minimal precipitation
Taiga Plain	Plains, some foothills	Open woodland, shrublands, and wetlands	Soils with minimal weathering (brunisols), some frozen soils (cryosols), organic materials, moraine	Cold winters, mild to warm summers, moderate precipitation
Taiga Shield	Plains, uplands, some interior hills, many lakes and streams	Open woodlands, some arctic tundra and lichen heath	Soils with minimal weathering (brunisols), acid and well-weathered soils (podzols), some frozen soils (cryosols), moraine, rock	Cold winters, warm summers, moderate precipitation
Hudson Bay Plain	Plains	Wetland, arctic tundra, and some conifer stands	Organic soils, sea bottom and beach materials	Cold winters, mild summers, minimal precipitation
Southern Arctic	Plains, some interior hills	Shrub/herb/heath arctic tundra	Frozen soils (cryosols), moraine rock, marine bottom sediments	Cold winters, cool summers, minimal precipitation
Northern Arctic	Plains and hills	Herb-lichen arctic tundra	Frozen soils (cryosols), moraine, rock, marine bottom sediments	Very cold winters, cool summers, minimal precipitation
Arctic Cordillera	Mountainous highlands	Largely non-vegetated, some shrub/herb arctic tundra	Frozen soils (cryosols), rock, rock debris, ice	Very cold winters, cool to cold summers, minimal precipitation

[1]This list is meant to be illustrative only and is not a comprehensive presentation of the characteristics of these areas.
SOURCE: Environment Canada, Lands Directorate. *Terrestrial Ecozones of Canada*, by E. Wiken, unpublished working paper, August, 1983.

77. Conservation Lands and Waters, Area and Number of Reserves, 1990

PROVINCE OR TERRITORY	NATIONAL PARKS	NATIONAL WILDLIFE AREAS, MIGRATORY BIRD SANCTUARIES	PROVINCIAL/ TERRITORIAL PARKS	PROVINCIAL/ TERRITORIAL WILDLIFE AREAS	PROVINCIAL/ TERRITORIAL WILDERNESS AREAS	PROVINCIAL/ TERRITORIAL ECOLOGICAL RESERVES	OTHER PROVINCIAL/ TERRITORIAL RESERVES	AREA OF PROVINCE/ TERRITORY	% OF PROVINCE/ TERRITORY RESERVED	TOTAL AREA OF RESERVES WITH NO LOGGING, MINING, OR SPORT HUNTING[1]	% OF PROVINCE/ TERRITORY RESERVED WITH NO LOGGING, MINING, OR SPORT HUNTING
					TOTAL AREA IN KM² / NUMBER OF RESERVES						
British Columbia	6 302 / 6	54 / 15	52 337 / 387	177 / 6	1 315 / 1	1 558 / 120	—	948 596	6.5	22 685	2.4
Alberta	54 085 / 4.8	145 / 7	1 365 / 106	680 / 8	5 607 / 4	185 / 10	309 / 114	661 185	9.4	56 420	8.5[2]
Saskatchewan	4 781 / 2	827 / 23	9 081 / 31	18 848 / 1 662	—	8 / 1	769 / 298	651 900	5.1	6 289	1.0
Manitoba	2 976 / 1	1 / 2	14 314 / 60	30 658 / 74	—	178 / 9	15 666 / 5	650 087	9.8	3 189	0.5
Ontario	2 171 / 5	443 / 23	56 273 / 217	9 240 / 45	618 / 37	—	539 / 323	1 068 582	6.5	24 249	2.2
Quebec	935 / 3	661 / 42	4 000 / 16	67 000 / 16	—	484 / 21	537 / 1	1 540 680	4.8	5 956	0.4
New Brunswick	445 / 2	62 / 7	217 / 49	3 219 / 19	—	—	1 / 3	73 436	5.4	663	0.9
Nova Scotia	1 332 / 2	66 / 15	131 / 107	1 396 / 25	—	1 / 2	3 / 4	55 491	5.3	1 387	2.5
Prince Edward Island	26 / 1	1 / 1	42 / 67	29 / 5	—	—	—	5 657	1.7	97	1.7
Newfoundland	2 338 / 2	9 / 1	235 / 75	—	1 070 / 1	23 / 6	—	404 517	0.9	2 597	0.6

77. Conservation Lands and Waters, Area and Number of Reserves, 1990 (cont'd)

PROVINCE OR TERRITORY	NATIONAL PARKS	NATIONAL WILDLIFE AREAS, MIGRATORY BIRD SANCTUARIES	PROVINCIAL/ TERRITORIAL PARKS	PROVINCIAL/ TERRITORIAL WILDLIFE AREAS	PROVINCIAL/ TERRITORIAL WILDERNESS AREAS	PROVINCIAL/ TERRITORIAL ECOLOGICAL RESERVES	OTHER PROVINCIAL/ TERRITORIAL RESERVES	AREA OF PROVINCE/ TERRITORY	% OF PROVINCE/ TERRITORY RESERVED	TOTAL AREA OF RESERVES WITH NO LOGGING, MINING, OR SPORT HUNTING[1]	% OF PROVINCE/ TERRITORY RESERVED WITH NO LOGGING, MINING, OR SPORT HUNTING
Yukon	32 183 / 2		114 / 1	5 918 / 2	—	—	—	482 515	7.9	32 273	6.7
Northwest Territories	74 698 / 3.2	113 405 / 15	130 / 44	26 464 / 3	—	—	—	3 379 684	6.4	98 658	2.9
Canada	182 272 / 34	115 674 / 151	138 239 / 1 160	163 629 / 1 865	8 680 / 43	2 437 / 169	17 824 / 748	9 922 330	6.3	254 463	2.6

[1]Not including hunting by aboriginal peoples under treaty or land claim settlements.
[2]Two-thirds of this area is accounted for by the Alberta portion of Wood Buffalo National Park.
SOURCE: Reprinted with permission from *Endangered Spaces: The Future for Canada's Wilderness*, Monte Hummel, ed., published by Key Porter Books Limited, Toronto, Ontario. Copyright © 1989 Monte Hummel.

78. Major Air Pollutants for Selected Canadian Cities

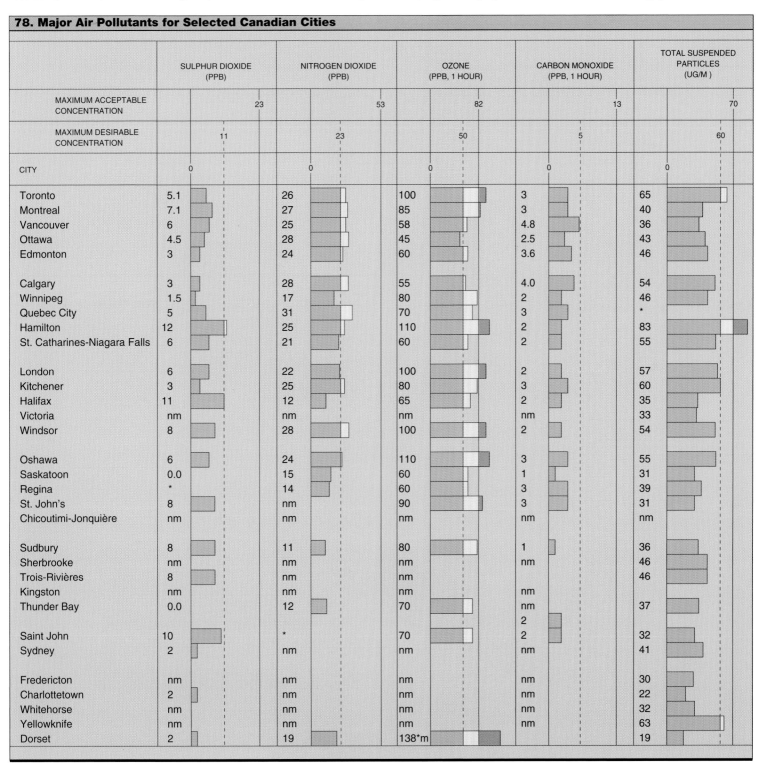

	SULPHUR DIOXIDE (PPB)	NITROGEN DIOXIDE (PPB)	OZONE (PPB, 1 HOUR)	CARBON MONOXIDE (PPB, 1 HOUR)	TOTAL SUSPENDED PARTICLES (UG/M)
MAXIMUM ACCEPTABLE CONCENTRATION	23	53	82	13	70
MAXIMUM DESIRABLE CONCENTRATION	11	23	50	5	60
CITY					
Toronto	5.1	26	100	3	65
Montreal	7.1	27	85	3	40
Vancouver	6	25	58	4.8	36
Ottawa	4.5	28	45	2.5	43
Edmonton	3	24	60	3.6	46
Calgary	3	28	55	4.0	54
Winnipeg	1.5	17	80	2	46
Quebec City	5	31	70	3	*
Hamilton	12	25	110	2	83
St. Catharines-Niagara Falls	6	21	60	2	55
London	6	22	100	2	57
Kitchener	3	25	80	3	60
Halifax	11	12	65	2	35
Victoria	nm	nm	nm	nm	33
Windsor	8	28	100	2	54
Oshawa	6	24	110	3	55
Saskatoon	0.0	15	60	1	31
Regina	*	14	60	3	39
St. John's	8	nm	90	3	31
Chicoutimi-Jonquière	nm	nm	nm	nm	nm
Sudbury	8	11	80	1	36
Sherbrooke	nm	nm	nm	nm	46
Trois-Rivières	8	nm	nm	nm	46
Kingston	nm	nm	nm	nm	
Thunder Bay	0.0	12	70	nm / 2	37
Saint John	10	*	70	2	32
Sydney	2	nm	nm	nm	41
Fredericton	nm	nm	nm	nm	30
Charlottetown	2	nm	nm	nm	22
Whitehorse	nm	nm	nm	nm	32
Yellowknife	nm	nm	nm	nm	63
Dorset	2	19	138*m		19

* insufficient data collected.   nm – not measured.   *M – based on absolute maximum ozone peak (other measurements use 99.9 percentile, but this was not available for Dorset).   *Based on city average.

SOURCE: T. Furmancyk, Environment Canada, Regulatory Affairs and Program Integration Branch, in *The State of Canada's Environment*, published by the Minister of the Environment and the Minister of Supply and Services Canada, 1991.

Climate

79. Average Daily Temperature (°C)

STATION	JAN	FEB	MAR	APR	MAY	JUNE	JULY	AUG	SEPT	OCT	NOV	DEC	ANNUAL
Goose Bay	−17.3	−15.5	−9.2	−1.8	5.1	10.9	15.5	14.2	9.0	2.5	−4.0	−13.4	−0.3
St. John's West	−4.0	−4.6	−2.0	1.8	6.4	11.3	15.8	15.6	11.8	7.3	3.3	−1.4	5.1
Charlottetown	−7.2	−7.5	−3.0	2.7	9.2	14.8	18.8	18.4	14.0	8.6	3.1	−3.6	5.7
Halifax	−5.8	−6.0	−1.7	3.6	9.4	14.7	18.3	18.1	13.8	8.5	3.2	−3.0	6.1
Saint John	−8.2	−7.7	−2.6	3.2	9.1	13.8	16.9	16.7	12.7	7.5	2.1	−5.0	4.9
Kuujjuarapik	−22.8	−23.1	−17.5	−7.1	1.2	6.3	10.2	10.6	7.2	2.1	−5.0	−16.6	−4.5
Quebec	−12.4	−11.0	−4.6	3.3	10.8	16.3	19.1	17.6	12.5	6.5	−0.5	−9.1	4.0
Sept-Îles	−14.6	−13.0	−6.8	0.0	5.9	11.6	15.2	14.2	9.2	3.4	−2.7	−11.0	0.9
Montreal	−10.3	−8.8	−2.4	5.7	12.9	18.0	20.8	19.4	14.5	8.3	1.6	−6.9	6.1
Ottawa	−10.7	−9.2	−2.6	5.9	13.0	18.1	20.8	19.4	14.7	8.3	1.5	−7.2	6.0
Thunder Bay	−15.0	−12.8	−5.6	2.7	9.0	13.9	17.7	16.4	11.2	5.4	−2.6	−11.3	2.4
Toronto	−4.5	−3.8	1.0	7.5	13.8	18.9	22.1	21.1	16.9	10.7	4.9	−1.5	8.9
Windsor	−5.0	−3.9	1.7	8.1	14.4	19.7	22.4	21.3	17.4	10.9	4.7	−1.9	9.1
The Pas	−21.4	−17.5	−10.0	0.5	8.7	14.8	17.7	16.4	9.9	3.5	−7.7	−18.0	−0.3
Winnipeg	−18.3	−15.1	−7.0	3.8	11.6	16.9	19.8	18.3	12.4	5.7	−4.7	−14.6	2.4
Churchill	−26.9	−25.4	−20.2	−10.0	−1.1	6.1	11.8	11.3	5.5	−1.4	−12.5	−22.7	−7.1
Regina	−16.5	−12.9	−6.0	4.1	11.4	16.4	19.1	18.1	11.6	5.1	−5.1	−13.6	2.6
Saskatoon	−17.5	−13.9	−7.0	3.9	11.5	16.2	18.6	17.4	11.2	4.8	−6.0	−14.7	2.0
Calgary	−9.6	−6.3	−2.5	4.1	9.7	14.0	16.4	15.7	10.6	5.7	−3.0	−8.3	3.9
Edmonton	−14.2	−10.8	−5.4	3.7	10.3	14.2	16.0	15.0	9.9	4.6	−5.7	−12.2	2.1
Penticton	−2.0	0.7	4.5	8.7	13.3	17.6	20.3	19.9	14.7	8.7	3.2	−1.1	9.0
Vancouver	3.0	4.7	6.3	8.8	12.1	15.2	17.2	17.4	14.3	10.0	6.0	3.5	9.9
Prince Rupert	0.8	2.5	3.7	5.5	8.4	10.9	12.9	13.3	11.3	8.0	3.8	1.7	6.9
Alert	−31.9	−33.6	−33.1	−25.1	−11.6	−1.0	3.4	1.0	−9.7	−19.5	−27.0	−29.5	−18.1
Inuvik	−28.8	−28.5	−24.1	−14.1	−0.7	10.6	13.8	10.5	3.3	−8.2	−21.5	−26.1	−9.5
Yellowknife	−27.9	−24.5	−18.5	−6.2	5.0	13.1	16.5	14.1	6.7	−1.4	−14.8	−24.1	−5.2
Whitehorse	−18.7	−13.1	−7.2	0.3	6.6	11.6	14.0	12.3	7.3	0.7	−10.0	−15.9	−1.0
Resolute	−32.0	−33.0	−31.2	−23.5	−11.0	−0.6	4.0	1.9	−5.0	−15.2	−24.3	−29.0	−16.6

80. Average Monthly Precipitation (mm)

STATION	JAN	FEB	MAR	APR	MAY	JUNE	JULY	AUG	SEPT	OCT	NOV	DEC	ANNUAL
Goose Bay	64.9	57.0	68.6	57.1	66.4	100.9	119.4	98.3	90.6	78.8	79.9	77.6	959.5
St. John's West	179.4	154.9	146.3	124.5	107.0	93.5	77.8	113.8	117.0	149.0	152.8	163.5	1579.5
Charlottetown	97.1	82.3	83.1	88.3	94.2	87.5	78.5	90.1	91.9	112.4	115.0	116.7	1137.1
Halifax	146.9	119.1	122.6	124.4	110.5	98.4	96.8	109.6	94.9	128.9	154.4	167.0	1473.5
Saint John	128.3	102.6	109.9	109.7	123.1	104.8	103.7	103.0	111.3	122.5	146.2	167.6	1432.8
Kuujjuarapik	28.1	21.1	21.1	25.1	36.4	57.3	72.7	89.0	93.6	73.3	62.1	35.1	614.9
Quebec	90.0	74.4	85.0	75.5	99.9	110.2	118.5	119.6	123.7	96.0	106.1	108.9	1207.7
Sept-Îles	86.8	68.9	80.9	93.4	96.3	92.4	90.8	99.6	111.5	100.8	99.6	107.0	1127.9
Montreal	63.3	56.4	67.6	74.8	68.3	82.5	85.6	100.3	86.5	75.4	93.4	85.6	939.7
Ottawa	50.8	49.7	56.6	64.8	76.8	84.3	86.5	87.8	83.6	74.7	81.0	72.9	869.5
Thunder Bay	32.4	25.6	40.9	47.1	69.3	84.0	79.9	88.5	86.4	60.9	49.4	39.3	703.5
Toronto	55.2	52.6	65.2	65.4	68.0	67.0	71.0	82.5	76.2	63.3	76.1	76.5	818.9
Windsor	50.3	53.7	72.0	80.3	75.7	97.0	85.3	85.7	86.7	57.9	75.4	81.6	901.6
The Pas	16.6	15.1	21.0	26.2	33.6	63.1	69.1	65.0	58.3	37.5	26.6	19.8	451.9
Winnipeg	19.3	14.8	23.1	35.9	59.8	83.8	72.0	75.3	51.3	29.5	21.2	18.6	504.4
Churchill	17.3	12.8	18.3	22.6	30.5	44.5	50.7	60.5	52.6	46.5	35.5	19.7	411.6
Regina	14.7	13.0	16.5	20.4	50.8	67.3	58.9	40.0	34.4	20.3	11.7	15.9	364.0
Saskatoon	15.9	12.9	16.0	19.7	44.2	63.4	58.0	36.8	32.1	16.9	14.1	17.2	347.2
Calgary	12.2	9.9	14.7	25.1	52.9	76.9	69.9	48.7	48.1	15.5	11.6	13.2	398.8
Edmonton	22.9	15.5	15.9	21.8	42.8	76.1	101.0	69.5	47.5	17.7	16.0	19.2	465.8
Penticton	27.3	20.6	20.4	25.8	33.0	34.4	23.3	28.4	23.0	15.7	24.3	32.1	308.5
Vancouver	149.8	123.6	108.8	75.4	61.7	45.7	36.1	38.1	64.4	115.3	169.9	178.5	1167.4
Prince Rupert	250.8	216.5	188.2	181.0	142.0	119.5	112.9	162.8	244.7	378.9	284.4	269.8	2551.6
Alert	7.8	5.2	6.8	9.4	9.9	12.7	25.0	23.8	24.3	13.2	8.8	7.4	154.2
Inuvik	15.6	11.1	10.8	12.6	19.1	22.2	34.1	43.9	24.2	29.6	17.5	16.8	257.4
Yellowknife	14.9	12.6	10.6	10.3	16.6	23.3	35.2	41.7	28.8	34.8	23.9	14.7	267.3
Whitehorse	16.9	11.9	12.1	8.3	14.4	31.2	38.5	39.3	35.2	23.0	18.9	18.9	268.8
Resolute	3.5	3.2	4.7	6.2	8.3	12.7	23.4	31.5	22.8	13.1	5.7	4.6	139.6

SOURCE: Average Daily Temperature and Average Monthly Precipitation statistics are from Environment Canada, Atmospheric Environment Service. These statistics for the 1961-1990 period are from a preliminary draft.

81. Annual Average "Number of Days with" and Hours of Bright Sunshine

STATION	WINDS (>63 km/h)	HAIL[4]	AVERAGE[1] NUMBER OF DAYS WITH[2]: THUNDER[5]	FOG[6]	FREEZING TEMPER- ATURES[7]	FREEZING PRECIP- ITATION[8]	RAIN[9]	SNOW[10]	BRIGHT SUNSHINE[3] (HOURS)
Goose Bay	1	*	9	14	215	13	102	97	1 564.9
St. John's	23	*	3	124	176	38	156	88	1 497.4
Charlottetown	6	*	9	47	169	17	124	68	1 818.4
Halifax	3	*	9	122	163	19	125	64	1 885.0
Saint John	6	*	11	106	173	12	124	59	1 865.3
Kuujjuarapik	3	*	6	45	243	10	83	100	1 497.8
Quebec	*	*	24	35	180	15	115	73	1 851.7
Sept-Îles	9	*	7	51	206	8	93	72	1 990.6
Montreal	1	*	25	20	155	13	114	62	2 054.0
Ottawa	*	*	24	35	165	16	107	62	2 008.5
Thunder Bay	*	*	26	38	204	8	88	61	2 202.8
Toronto	*	*	27	35	155	10	99	47	2 045.4
Windsor	2	*	33	37	136	9	105	45	n/a
The Pas	*	*	23	15	209	12	65	73	2 167.5
Winnipeg	1	3	27	20	195	12	72	57	2 321.4
Churchill	11	*	7	48	258	19	58	100	1 827.9
Regina	9	1	23	29	204	14	59	58	2 331.1
Saskatoon	*	*	19	25	202	9	57	59	2 449.7
Calgary	6	3	25	22	201	5	58	62	2 314.4
Edmonton	*	3	22	17	185	8	70	59	2 263.7
Penticton	*	*	12	1	129	1	78	29	2 032.2
Vancouver	*	*	6	45	55	1	156	15	1 919.6
Prince Rupert	4	8	2	37	107	0	218	35	1 224.1
Alert	10	0	0	46	338	5	10	93	1 767.4
Inuvik	*	*	1	24	267	6	36	99	1 898.8
Yellowknife	*	*	5	21	226	13	46	82	2 276.6
Whitehorse	*	*	6	16	224	1	52	120	1 843.8
Resolute	25	0	*	62	324	13	20	82	1 505.1

*denotes a value less than 0.5 (but not zero).
[1]Average, mean, or normal refer to the value of the particular element averaged over the period from 1951-1980.
[2]A "day with" is counted once per day regardless of the number of individual occurrences of that phenomenon that day.
[3]Bright sunshine is reported in hours and tenths.
[4]Hail is a piece of ice with a diameter of 5 mm or more.
[5]Thunder is reported when thunder is heard or lightning or hail is seen.
[6]Fog is a suspension of small water droplets in air that reduces the horizontal visibility at eye level to less than 1 km.
[7]Freezing temperature is a temperature below 0°C.
[8]Freezing precipitation is rain or drizzle of any quantity that freezes on impact.
[9]Rain is a measurable amount of liquid water (rain, showers, or drizzle) equal to or greater than 0.2 mm.
[10]Snow is a measurable amount of solid precipitation (snow, snow grains, ice crystals, or ice and snow pellets) equal to or greater than 0.2 cm.
SOURCE: Environment Canada. *The Climates of Canada*. David Phillips. Supply and Services Canada. Ottawa, 1990; Environment Canada, Atmospheric Environment Service. *Canadian Climate Normals*; Environment Canada, Atmospheric Environment Service. *Principal Station Data*.

1996 World Population Data Sheet

REGION OR COUNTRY	POPULATION MID-1996 (MILLIONS)	BIRTHS PER 1000 POPULATION	DEATHS PER 1000 POPULATION	NATURAL INCREASE (ANNUAL %)	"DOUBLING TIME" IN YEARS AT CURRENT RATE	PROJECTED POPULATION TO 2025 (MILLIONS)	INFANT MORTALITY RATE[a]	TOTAL FERTILITY RATE[b]	PERCENT AGE <15/65+	LIFE EXPECTANCY AT BIRTH TOTAL/MALE/FEMALE (YEARS)	PERCENT URBAN	ADULT LITERACY 1990-95	HUMAN DEVELOPMENT INDEX (HDI), 1994	SECONDARY SCHOOL ENROLLMENT[c] (%) MALE/FEMALE	PER CAPITA GNP, 1994 (US$)
WORLD	**5 771**	**24**	**9**	**1.5**	**46**	**8 193**	**62**	**3.0**	**32/ 6**	**66/64/68**	**43**	**—**	**—**	**58/50**	**4 740**
MORE DEVELOPED	**1 171**	**12**	**10**	**0.1**	**501**	**1 268**	**9**	**1.6**	**20/14**	**74/70/78**	**75**	**—**	**—**	**92/95**	**18 130**
LESS DEVELOPED	**4 600**	**27**	**9**	**1.9**	**37**	**6 925**	**68**	**3.4**	**35/ 5**	**64/62/65**	**35**	**—**	**—**	**52/42**	**1 090**
LESS DEVELOPED (EXCL. CHINA)	**3 383**	**31**	**10**	**2.2**	**32**	**5 433**	**73**	**4.0**	**38/ 4**	**61/60/63**	**38**	**—**	**—**	**50/39**	**1 320**
AFRICA	**732**	**41**	**13**	**2.8**	**25**	**1 462**	**91**	**5.7**	**44/ 3**	**55/53/56**	**31**	**—**	**—**	**36/30**	**660**
SUB-SAHARAN AFRICA	**597**	**44**	**14**	**2.9**	**24**	**1 248**	**96**	**6.1**	**46/ 3**	**52/51/54**	**27**	**—**	**—**	**26/21**	**550**
NORTHERN AFRICA	**164**	**32**	**8**	**2.4**	**29**	**272**	**64**	**4.3**	**40/ 4**	**64/62/65**	**45**	**—**	**—**	**61/52**	**1 100**
Algeria	29.0	30	6	2.4	29	47.2	55	4.3	40/ 4	67/67/68	50	62	0.737	66/55	1 690
Egypt	63.7	30	7	2.2	31	97.6	62	3.6	40/ 4	64/62/65	44	51	0.614	81/69	710
Libya	5.4	45	8	3.7	19	14.4	63	6.4	45/ 3	64/62/66	85	76	—	95/95	—
Morocco	27.6	29	6	2.2	31	40.7	57	4.0	38/ 5	68/66/70	47	44	0.566	40/29	1 150
Sudan	28.9	42	12	3.0	23	58.4	80	6.1	43/ 3	54/53/55	27	46	0.333	24/19	—
Tunisia	9.2	23	6	1.7	41	13.4	43	3.4	37/ 5	68/67/69	60	67	0.748	55/49	1 800
Western Sahara	0.2	47	19	2.8	25	0.4	152	7.0	—/—	46/45/47	—	n.a.	—	—/—	—
WESTERN AFRICA	**204**	**45**	**14**	**3.1**	**23**	**463**	**92**	**6.1**	**46/ 3**	**53/52/54**	**24**	**—**	**—**	**28/20**	**330**
Benin	5.6	49	18	3.1	22	12.3	86	7.1	47/ 3	48/46/49	36	37	0.368	17/7	370
Burkina Faso	10.6	47	19	2.8	24	20.9	94	6.9	48/ 3	45/44/46	15	19	0.221	11/6	300
Cape Verde	0.4	27	8	1.9	36	0.7	65	4.1	45/ 6	65/64/66	44	99	0.547	21/20	910
Côte d'Ivoire	14.7	50	15	3.5	20	33.4	88	5.7	47/ 2	51/50/52	46	40	0.368	33/17	510
Gambia	1.2	48	21	2.7	26	2.1	90	5.9	45/ 2	50/48/52	26	39	0.281	25/13	360
Ghana	18.0	42	12	3.0	23	38.0	66	5.5	45/ 3	56/54/58	36	65	0.468	44/28	430
Guinea	7.4	44	20	2.4	29	13.1	139	5.9	44/ 3	44/42/46	29	36	0.271	17/6	510
Guinea-Bissau	1.1	43	21	2.1	32	2.0	140	5.8	43/ 3	44/42/45	22	55	0.291	9/4	240
Liberia	2.1	44	12	3.1	22	6.8	113	6.4	44/ 3	58/55/60	44	38	—	—/—	—
Mali	9.7	52	20	3.1	22	23.7	106	7.3	48/ 3	46/44/48	26	31	0.229	12/6	250
Mauritania	2.3	39	14	2.5	28	4.4	101	5.0	45/ 4	52/50/53	39	38	0.355	19/11	480
Niger	9.5	53	19	3.4	21	22.4	123	7.4	49/ 3	47/45/48	15	14	0.206	9/4	230
Nigeria	103.9	43	12	3.1	22	246.0	87	6.0	45/ 3	56/55/58	16	57	0.393	32/27	280
Senegal	8.5	43	16	2.7	26	16.9	68	6.0	45/ 3	49/48/50	43	33	0.326	21/11	610
Sierra Leone	4.6	46	19	2.7	26	8.7	143	6.2	44/ 3	46/44/47	35	31	0.176	22/12	150
Togo	4.6	47	11	3.6	19	11.7	89	6.9	49/ 2	57/55/59	30	52	0.365	34/12	320
EASTERN AFRICA	**227**	**45**	**15**	**2.9**	**24**	**456**	**106**	**6.3**	**47/ 3**	**50/48/51**	**21**	**—**	**—**	**16/12**	**210**
Burundi	5.9	46	16	3.0	23	12.2	102	6.6	46/ 4	50/48/52	6	35	0.247	8/5	150
Comoros	0.6	47	11	3.6	20	1.4	80	6.8	48/ 3	58/56/60	29	57	0.412	21/17	510
Djibouti	0.6	38	16	2.2	32	1.1	115	5.8	41/ 2	48/47/50	77	46	0.319	14/10	780[g]
Eritrea	3.6	43	15	2.8	25	7.0	105	6.1	44/ 3	50/49/52	17	n.a.	0.269	17/13	—
Ethiopia	57.2	46	16	3.1	23	129.7	120	6.8	49/ 3	50/48/52	15	36	0.244	12/11	130
Kenya	28.2	40	13	2.7	25	49.1	62	5.4	48/ 3	51/49/52	27	78	0.463	28/23	260
Madagascar	15.2	44	12	3.2	22	34.4	93	6.1	46/ 3	57/55/58	26	80	0.350	14/14	230
Malawi	9.5	50	20	3.0	23	18.5	134	6.7	48/ 3	46/45/46	17	56	0.320	6/3	140
Mauritius	1.1	20	7	1.3	54	1.5	18.1	2.4	29/ 6	69/65/73	44	83	0.831	58/60	3 180
Mozambique	16.5	45	19	2.7	26	35.1	148	6.5	46/ 2	46/45/48	33	40	0.281	9/6	80
Reunion	0.7	21	6	1.6	44	0.9	8	2.3	31/ 6	73/69/77	73	n.a.	—	—/—	—
Rwanda	6.9	44	17	2.7	25	13.7	110	6.2	48/ 3	47/46/49	5	61	0.187	11/9	210[g]
Seychelles	0.1	23	8	1.5	46	0.1	*12.9*	2.7	31/ 7	70/68/73	50	58	0.845	—/—	6 210
Somalia	9.5	50	19	3.2	22	21.3	122	7.0	48/ 3	47/45/49	24	24	—	9/5	—
Tanzania	29.1	43	14	3.0	23	56.3	92	6.3	47/ 3	49/47/50	21	68	0.357	6/5	90[g]
Uganda	22.0	52	19	3.3	21	37.4	115	7.3	47/ 3	45/44/46	11	62	0.328	14/8	200
Zambia	9.2	45	15	3.0	23	18.5	107	6.5	47/ 3	49/48/50	42	78	0.369	25/14	350
Zimbabwe	11.5	35	9	2.5	28	17.3	53	4.4	45/ 3	62/61/62	31	85	0.513	51/40	490

REGION OR COUNTRY	POPULATION MID-1996 (MILLIONS)	BIRTHS PER 1000 POPULATION	DEATHS PER 1000 POPULATION	NATURAL INCREASE (ANNUAL %)	"DOUBLING TIME" IN YEARS AT CURRENT RATE	PROJECTED POPULATION TO 2025 (MILLIONS)	INFANT MORTALITY RATE[a]	TOTAL FERTILITY RATE[b]	PERCENT AGE <15/65+	LIFE EXPECTANCY AT BIRTH TOTAL/MALE/FEMALE (YEARS)	PERCENT URBAN	ADULT LITERACY 1990-95	HUMAN DEVELOPMENT INDEX (HDI), 1994	SECONDARY SCHOOL ENROLLMENT[c] (%) MALE/FEMALE	PER CAPITA GNP, 1994 (US$)
MIDDLE AFRICA	86	46	16	2.9	24	189	106	6.3	46/ 3	49/47/51	33	—	—	30/15	—
Angola	11.5	47	20	2.7	26	26.6	137	6.5	45/ 3	46/44/48	32	42	0.335	—/—	—
Cameroon	13.6	41	12	2.9	24	29.2	65	5.9	44/ 4	56/55/58	41	63	0.468	32/23	680
Central African Republic	3.3	42	17	2.5	28	5.2	97	5.1	43/ 3	49/47/52	39	60	0.355	17/6	370
Chad	6.5	44	18	2.6	27	12.9	122	5.9	41/ 3	48/46/49	22	48	0.288	13/2	190
Congo	2.5	40	17	2.3	31	4.2	109	5.2	44/ 3	46/44/48	58	75	0.500	—/—	640
Equatorial Guinea	0.4	41	15	2.6	27	0.9	103	5.3	43/ 4	52/50/54	37	79	0.462	—/—	430
Gabon	1.2	29	14	1.5	47	1.8	95	5.0	34/ 5	55/52/58	73	63	0.562	—/—	3 550
Sao Tome and Principe	0.1	35	9	2.6	26	0.2	50.8	4.5	47/ 4	63/62/65	46	57	—	—/—	250
Zaire	46.5	48	16	3.2	22	107.6	108	6.6	48/ 3	48/46/50	29	77	0.381	33/15	—
SOUTHERN AFRICA	51	32	8	2.4	29	82	49	4.3	38/ 4	65/62/67	53	—	—	67/79	2 840
Botswana	1.5	38	11	2.7	26	3.0	41	5.0	43/ 5	66/64/71	46	70	0.673	49/55	2 800
Lesetho	2.1	38	12	2.6	27	3.8	79	5.2	41/ 5	55/54/57	16	71	0.457	22/31	700
Namibia	1.6	37	11	2.7	26	3.0	57	5.4	42/ 5	59/58/60	32	—	0.570	49/61	2 030
South Africa	44.5	31	8	2.3	30	70.1	46	4.1	37/ 5	66/63/68	57	82	0.716	71/84	3 010
Swaziland	1.0	43	11	3.2	22	2.5	93	6.1	46/ 2	56/52/61	30	77	0.582	51/50	1 160
NORTH AMERICA	295	15	9	0.6	114	372	7	2.0	22/13	76/73/79	75	—	—	99/98	25 220
Canada	30.0	13	7	0.6	116	36.6	6.2	1.6	21/12	78/74/81	77	99	0.960	104/103	19 570
United States	265.2	15	9	0.6	114	335.1	7.5	2.0	22/13	76/72/79	75	98	0.942	98/97	25 860
LATIN AMERICA AND THE CARIBBEAN	486	26	7	1.9	36	678	43	3.1	35/ 5	69/66/72	71	—	—	—/—	3 290
CENTRAL AMERICA	127	28	5	2.3	30	197	37	3.4	37/ 4	71/68/74	65	—	—	51/52	3 310
Belize	0.2	38	5	3.3	21	0.4	34	4.5	44/ 4	72/70/74	48	91	0.806	46/48	2 550
Costa Rica	3.6	26	4	2.2	31	5.5	13.0	3.1	34/ 5	76/74/79	44	95	0.889	45/49	2 380
El Salvador	5.9	32	6	2.6	27	9.2	41	3.8	40/ 4	68/65/70	45	72	0.592	27/30	1 480
Guatemala	9.9	36	7	2.9	24	17.0	51	5.1	45/ 3	65/62/67	39	56	0.572	25/23	1 190
Honduras	5.6	34	6	2.8	25	9.7	50	5.2	45/ 3	68/66/71	47	73	0.575	29/37	580
Mexico	94.8	27	5	2.2	32	142.1	34	3.1	36/ 4	73/70/76	71	90	0.853	57/58	4 010
Nicaragua	4.6	33	6	2.7	26	9.1	49	4.6	44/ 3	65/62/68	63	66	0.530	39/44	330
Panama	2.7	22	4	1.8	39	3.8	18	3.0	33/ 5	73/71/75	55	91	0.864	60/65	2 670
CARIBBEAN	36	23	8	1.5	45	47	42	2.8	31/ 7	69/67/72	60	—	—	46/52	—
Antigua and Barbuda	0.1	18	6	1.2	58	0.1	18	1.7	25/ 6	73/71/75	31	89	0.892	—/—	6 970
Bahamas	0.3	18	5	1.3	52	0.4	23.8	1.9	29/ 5	72/68/75	84	98	0.894	95/95	11 790
Barbados	0.3	14	9	0.5	133	0.3	9.1	1.6	24/12	76/73/78	38	97	0.907	90/80	6 530
Cuba	11.0	14	7	0.7	102	12.4	9.4	1.5	22/ 9	75/73/77	74	96	0.723	73/81	—
Dominica	0.1	20	7	1.3	55	0.1	18.4	2.1	32/10	78/74/80	61	94	0.873	—/—	2 830
Dominican Republic	8.1	29	6	2.3	31	11.7	52	3.3	37/ 4	68/66/71	61	82	0.718	30/43	1 320
Grenada	0.1	29	6	2.4	29	0.2	12	3.8	43/ 5	71/68/73	—	98	0.843	—/—	2 620
Guadeloupe	0.4	18	6	1.2	56	0.5	10.3	2.0	26/ 9	75/71/78	48	—	—	—/—	—
Haiti	7.3	35	12	2.3	30	11.2	74	4.8	40/ 4	57/55/58	32	45	0.338	22/21	220
Jamaica	2.6	24	5	1.8	38	3.3	24.0	3.0	34/ 7	74/71/76	53	85	0.736	62/70	1 420
Martinique	0.4	15	6	0.9	75	0.5	6	1.7	24/10	76/73/79	81	n.a.	—	—/—	—
Netherlands Antilles	0.2	20	7	1.3	53	0.3	6.3	2.2	26/ 7	75/72/78	92	n.a.	—	—/—	—
Puerto Rico	3.8	17	8	1.0	71	4.3	11.5	2.1	27/10	74/70/79	73	n.a.	—	—/—	7 000[g]
St. Kitts-Nevis	0.04	22	9	1.3	54	0.1	24	2.4	32/ 9	69/66/71	42	98	0.853	—/—	4 760
Saint Lucia	0.1	26	6	2.0	35	0.2	23.0	3.1	37/ 7	72/69/75	48	67	0.838	—/—	3 450
St. Vincent and the Grenadines	0.1	25	7	1.8	38	0.2	17	3.1	37/ 6	73/71/74	25	96	0.836	—/—	2 120
Trinidad and Tobago	1.3	18	7	1.2	60	1.4	12.2	2.2	31/ 6	71/68/73	65	98	0.880	74/78	3 740
SOUTH AMERICA	323	25	7	1.8	39	434	46	3.0	34/ 5	68/65/71	75	—	—	—/—	3 360
Argentina	34.7	20	8	1.2	58	46.5	22.9	2.7	31/ 9	72/69/76	87	96	0.884	70/75	8 060

REGION OR COUNTRY	POPULATION MID-1996 (MILLIONS)	BIRTHS PER 1000 POPULATION	DEATHS PER 1000 POPULATION	NATURAL INCREASE (ANNUAL %)	"DOUBLING TIME" IN YEARS AT CURRENT RATE	PROJECTED POPULATION TO 2025 (MILLIONS)	INFANT MORTALITY RATE[a]	TOTAL FERTILITY RATE[b]	PERCENT AGE <15/65+	LIFE EXPECTANCY AT BIRTH TOTAL/MALE/FEMALE (YEARS)	PERCENT URBAN	ADULT LITERACY 1990-95	HUMAN DEVELOPMENT INDEX (HDI), 1994	SECONDARY SCHOOL ENROLLMENT[c] (%) MALE/FEMALE	PER CAPITA GNP, 1994 (US$)
Bolivia	7.6	36	10	2.6	27	13.1	71	4.8	41/ 4	60/59/62	58	83	0.589	40/34	770
Brazil	160.5	25	8	1.7	41	202.3	58	2.8	34/ 4	66/64/69	76	83	0.783	—/—	3 370
Chile	14.5	21	6	1.6	45	18.1	13.1	2.5	30/ 7	72/69/76	85	95	0.891	65/70	3 560
Colombia	38.0	27	6	2.1	33	52.7	28	3.0	33/ 4	69/66/72	67	91	0.848	57/68	1 620
Ecuador	11.7	29	6	2.3	31	17.8	40	3.6	36/ 4	69/66/71	59	90	0.775	54/56	1 310
Guyana	0.7	25	7	1.8	39	0.8	48	2.6	38/ 4	65/62/68	33	98	0.649	56/59	530
Paraguay	5.0	34	6	2.8	25	9.4	38	4.5	42/ 4	69/66/71	50	92	0.706	36/38	1 570
Peru	24.0	29	7	2.1	33	33.9	60	3.5	36/ 4	66/64/68	70	89	0.717	60/60	1 890
Suriname	0.4	23	6	1.6	43	0.6	28	2.4	35/ 5	70/68/73	49	93	0.792	—/—	870
Uruguay	3.2	18	10	0.8	84	3.7	20.1	2.3	26/12	73/69/76	90	97	0.883	—/—	4 650
Venezuela	22.3	26	5	2.1	33	34.8	23.5	3.1	38/ 4	72/69/75	84	91	0.861	29/41	2 760
ASIA	**3 501**	**24**	**8**	**1.6**	**43**	**4 898**	**62**	**2.9**	**32/ 5**	**65/64/67**	**33**	**—**	**—**	**57/45**	**2 150**
ASIA (Excluding China)	**2 283**	**28**	**9**	**1.9**	**37**	**3 406**	**68**	**3.5**	**35/ 5**	**63/62/64**	**35**	**—**	**—**	**56/42**	**3 110**
WESTERN ASIA	**176**	**32**	**7**	**2.4**	**29**	**328**	**48**	**4.4**	**39/ 4**	**67/65/69**	**63**	**—**	**—**	**63/46**	**3 840**
Armenia	3.8	14	7	0.7	98	4.1	15	1.7	31/ 7	71/68/74	69	99	0.651	80/90	670
Azerbaijan	7.6	21	7	1.4	50	10.3	25	2.2	33/ 5	71/66/75	53	97	0.636	89/88	500
Bahrain	0.6	29	3	2.6	27	0.9	19	3.7	32/ 2	73/71/76	88	85	0.870	98/101	7 500
Cyprus	0.7	16	8	0.9	81	1.0	9	2.2	25/11	77/75/79	53	94	0.907	94/96	10 380[g]
Gaza	0.9	55	5	5.0	14	3.8	32	8.0	51/ 3	71/70/72	94	n.a.	—	—/—	—
Georgia	5.4	11	9	0.2	330	6.0	18	1.3	24/10	73/69/76	55	99	0.637	—/—	580[g]
Iraq	21.4	44	7	3.7	19	52.6	67	6.7	47/ 3	66/65/67	70	58	0.531	53/34	—
Israel	5.8	21	6	1.5	47	8.0	6.9	2.9	30/ 9	77/75/79	90	92	0.907	84/91	14 410
Jordan	4.2	32	6	2.6	27	8.3	34	4.6	42/ 3	68/66/70	78	87	0.730	52/54	1 390
Kuwait	1.8	26	2	2.3	30	3.4	12	3.6	29/ 1	75/73/77	96	79	0.844	60/60	19 040
Lebanon	3.8	25	5	2.0	34	6.1	28	2.9	33/ 7	75/73/78	86	92	0.794	73/78	—
Oman	2.3	53	4	4.9	14	5.5	24	6.9	36/ 3	71/70/72	12	20	0.718	64/57	5 200
Qatar	0.7	18	2	1.6	43	0.9	11	3.6	30/ 1	73/70/75	91	79	0.840	82/84	14 540
Saudi Arabia	19.4	36	4	3.2	22	50.3	24	5.5	43/ 2	70/69/72	79	63	0.774	54/43	7 240
Syria	15.6	44	6	3.7	19	31.7	44	6.9	49/ 4	66/65/67	51	71	0.755	52/42	—
Turkey	63.9	23	7	1.6	43	91.8	47	2.7	33/ 5	68/65/70	63	82	0.772	74/48	2 450
United Arab Emirates	1.9	23	4	1.9	36	3.0	23	4.1	32/ 1	72/70/74	82	79	0.866	84/94	21 420[g]
West Bank	1.7	45	5	4.0	17	3.4	33	4.3	48/ 4	71/69/72	—	n.a.	—	—/—	—
Yemen	14.7	53	21	3.2	22	36.6	83	7.7	52/ 3	52/51/53	23	39	0.361	38/7	280
SOUTH CENTRAL ASIA	**1 385**	**30**	**10**	**2.1**	**34**	**2 105**	**80**	**3.8**	**37/ 4**	**59/59/60**	**27**	**—**	**—**	**54/36**	**340**
Afghanistan	21.5	50	22	2.8	24	45.3	163	6.9	41/ 3	43/43/44	18	32	—	22/8	—
Bangladesh	119.8	31	11	2.0	35	175.8	88	3.7	40/ 3	57/57/57	16	38	0.368	25/13	230
Bhutan	0.8	39	16	2.3	30	1.5	121	5.4	39/ 4	51/51/50	17	42	0.338	8/2	400
India	949.6	29	10	1.9	37	1 384.6	79	3.4	36/ 4	59/58/59	26	52	0.446	59/38	310
Iran	63.1	36	7	2.9	24	106.8	57	5.1	44/ 3	67/65/68	58	69	0.780	74/58	—
Kazakstan	16.5	18	9	0.9	81	20.5	27	2.3	31/ 6	69/64/73	56	98	0.709	89/91	1 110
Kyrgyzstan	4.6	25	8	1.6	43	7.0	29	3.1	38/ 5	68/64/72	35	97	0.635	—/—	610
Maldives	0.3	43	7	3.6	19	0.6	50	6.2	47/ 3	65/63/66	26	93	0.611	49/49	900
Nepal	23.2	39	12	2.6	26	43.5	98	5.2	42/ 3	55/56/53	10	28	0.347	46/23	200
Pakistan	133.5	39	10	2.9	24	232.9	91	5.6	41/ 3	61/61/61	28	38	0.445	28/13	440
Sri Lanka	18.4	20	5	1.5	47	23.2	18.4	2.3	35/ 4	73/70/75	22	90	0.711	71/78	640
Tajikistan	5.9	28	7	2.1	33	13.1	47	3.7	43/ 4	68/65/71	28	98	0.580	98/101	350
Turkmenistan	4.6	32	8	2.4	29	7.9	46	3.9	41/ 4	66/62/69	45	98	0.723	99/97	—
Uzbekistan	23.2	29	7	2.3	30	42.3	28	3.5	41/ 4	69/66/72	39	97	0.662	96/92	950
SOUTHEAST ASIA	**496**	**27**	**8**	**1.9**	**37**	**727**	**52**	**3.3**	**36/ 4**	**64/62/66**	**30**	**—**	**—**	**48/44**	**1 240**
Brunei	0.3	27	3	2.4	29	0.4	7.4	3.1	35/ 3	74/73/76	67	88	0.882	67/74	14 240

REGION OR COUNTRY	POPULATION MID-1996 (MILLIONS)	BIRTHS PER 1000 POPULATION	DEATHS PER 1000 POPULATION	NATURAL INCREASE (ANNUAL %)	"DOUBLING TIME" IN YEARS AT CURRENT RATE	PROJECTED POPULATION TO 2025 (MILLIONS)	INFANT MORTALITY RATE[a]	TOTAL FERTILITY RATE[b]	PERCENT AGE <15/65+	LIFE EXPECTANCY AT BIRTH TOTAL/MALE/FEMALE (YEARS)	PERCENT URBAN	ADULT LITERACY 1990-95	HUMAN DEVELOPMENT INDEX (HDI), 1994	SECONDARY SCHOOL ENROLLMENT[c] (%) MALE/FEMALE	PER CAPITA GNP, 1994 (US$)
Cambodia	10.9	45	16	2.9	24	22.8	111	5.8	46/ 3	49/48/51	13	35	0.348	—/—	—
Indonesia	201.4	24	8	1.6	43	276.5	66	2.9	35/ 4	63/61/65	31	84	0.668	48/39	880
Laos	5.0	43	15	2.9	24	9.8	102	6.1	45/ 3	52/50/53	19	57	0.459	31/19	320
Malaysia	20.6	28	5	2.4	29	34.5	11	3.3	36/ 4	72/70/75	51	84	0.832	56/61	3 520
Myanmar (Burma)	46.0	31	12	1.9	37	72.2	49	4.0	36/ 4	61/60/62	25	83	0.475	23/23	—
Philippines	72.0	30	9	2.1	33	113.5	34	4.1	38/ 4	65/63/66	49	95	0.672	71/75	960
Singapore	3.0	16	5	1.1	62	3.6	4.0	1.8	23/ 7	76/74/79	100	91	0.900	69/71	23 360
Thailand	60.7	20	6	1.4	48	75.1	35	2.2	30/ 4	70/68/72	19	94	0.833	38/37	2 210
Vietnam	76.6	30	7	2.3	30	118.8	42	3.7	40/ 5	65/63/67	19	94	0.557	—/—	190
EAST ASIA	**1 443**	**16**	**7**	**1.0**	**70**	**1 739**	**40**	**1.8**	**26/ 7**	**71/69/73**	**36**	**—**	**—**	**64/57**	**3 940**
China	1 217.6	17	7	1.1	66	1 492.0	44	1.8	27/ 6	70/68/72	29	82	0.626	60/51	530
Hong Kong	6.4	12	5	0.7	99	8.1	5.0	1.2	19/ 9	78/75/81	—	92	0.914	69/73	21 650
Japan	125.8	10	7	0.2	315	125.8	4.2	1.5	16/15	80/77/83	78	99	0.940	95/97	34 630
Korea, North	23.9	24	6	1.9	38	32.1	28	2.4	29/ 4	70/67/73	61	99	0.765	—/—	—
Korea, South	45.3	15	6	0.9	75	50.8	11	1.7	23/ 6	72/68/76	74	98	0.890	97/96	8 220
Macao	0.4	15	3	1.2	58	0.6	6	1.6	24/ 7	69/67/71	97	—	—	—/—	—
Mongolia	2.3	22	8	1.4	51	3.6	61	3.8	40/ 4	64/62/65	55	83	0.661	—/—	340
Taiwan	21.4	15	5	1.0	70	25.5	5.1	1.8	24/ 7	74/72/78	75	86	—	94/98	—
EUROPE	**728**	**11**	**11**	**−0.1**	**—**	**743**	**11**	**1.5**	**19/14**	**73/68/77**	**74**	**—**	**—**	**89/94**	**12 310**
NORTHERN EUROPE	**94**	**13**	**11**	**0.2**	**445**	**100**	**6**	**1.7**	**20/15**	**76/73/79**	**83**	**—**	**—**	**95/99**	**18 340**
Denmark	5.2	13	12	0.2	462	5.4	5.4	1.8	17/15	75/73/78	85	99	0.927	112/115	28 110
Estonia	1.5	9	15	−0.5	—	1.4	15	1.4	20/13	70/64/75	70	100	0.776	87/96	2 820
Finland	5.1	13	10	0.3	224	5.2	4.7	1.8	19/14	77/73/80	64	100	0.940	110/130	18 850
Iceland	0.3	17	7	1.0	68	0.3	3.4	2.1	25/11	79/77/81	91	100	0.942	105/101	24 590
Ireland	3.6	13	9	0.5	144	3.8	5.9	1.9	25/11	76/74/79	57	98	0.929	101/110	13 630
Latvia	2.5	9	16	−0.7	—	2.3	19	1.3	21/13	67/61/73	69	99	0.711	84/90	2 290
Lithuania	3.7	12	12	−0.1	—	3.9	14	1.5	22/12	69/63/75	68	98	0.762	76/79	1 350
Norway	4.4	14	10	0.4	182	5.0	5.2	1.9	19/16	78/75/81	73	100	0.943	118/114	26 480
Sweden	8.8	12	11	0.1	630	9.6	4.4	1.9	19/17	78/76/81	83	99	0.936	99/100	23 630
United Kingdom	58.8	13	11	0.2	385	62.5	6.2	1.7	19/16	77/74/79	90	99	0.931	91/94	18 410
WESTERN EUROPE	**181**	**11**	**10**	**0.1**	**716**	**187**	**6**	**1.4**	**18/15**	**77/73/80**	**79**	**—**	**—**	**104/104**	**24 900**
Austria	8.1	11	10	0.1	866	8.2	5.5	1.4	18/15	77/73/80	65	99	0.932	109/104	24 950
Belgium	10.2	12	10	0.1	630	10.5	7.6	1.6	18/16	76/73/80	97	99	0.932	103/104	22 920
France	58.4	12	9	0.3	217	63.6	6.1	1.7	20/15	78/74/82	74	99	0.946	104/107	23 470
Germany	81.7	9	11	−0.1	—	79.3	5.5	1.3	16/15	76/72/79	85	99	0.924	101/100	25 580
Liechtenstein	0.03	12	7	0.5	139	0.03	5.6	1.3	19/10	72/68/75	—	98	—	—/—	—
Luxembourg	0.4	14	9	0.4	169	0.4	5.3	1.7	18/14	76/73/79	86	100	0.899	72/73	39 850
Netherlands	15.5	13	9	0.4	173	17.4	5.5	1.6	18/13	77/74/80	61	99	0.940	126/120	21 970
Switzerland	7.1	12	9	0.3	231	7.5	5.1	1.5	18/15	78/75/82	68	99	0.930	93/89	37 180
EASTERN EUROPE	**309**	**10**	**14**	**−0.4**	**—**	**319**	**16**	**1.4**	**21/12**	**68/62/73**	**68**	**—**	**—**	**80/89**	**2 310**
Belarus	10.3	10	13	−0.3	—	11.2	13	1.4	22/12	69/64/74	69	98	0.806	89/96	2 160
Bulgaria	8.4	9	13	−0.4	—	7.9	15.5	1.4	19/15	71/68/75	68	98	0.780	66/70	1 160
Czech Republic	10.3	10	11	−0.1	—	10.6	7.9	1.4	19/13	73/70/77	75	99	0.882	85/88	3 210
Hungary	10.2	11	14	−0.3	—	9.3	11.5	1.6	18/14	70/65/74	64	99	0.857	79/82	3 840
Moldova	4.3	14	12	0.3	277	5.1	23	2.0	27/ 9	68/64/71	47	96	0.612	67/72	870
Poland	38.6	12	10	0.2	462	40.5	13.5	1.7	23/11	72/68/76	62	99	0.834	82/87	2 470
Romania	22.6	10	12	−0.2	—	21.2	23.9	1.3	21/12	70/66/73	55	97	0.748	83/82	1 230
Russia	147.7	9	15	−0.5	—	153.1	18	1.4	21/12	65/57/71	73	98	0.792	84/91	2 650
Slovakia	5.4	12	10	0.3	248	6.1	11.2	1.7	23/11	72/68/77	57	n.a.	0.873	87/90	2 230
Ukraine	51.1	10	15	−0.5	—	54.0	14	1.5	20/14	68/63/73	68	98	0.689	65/95	1 570

REGION OR COUNTRY	POPULATION MID-1996 (MILLIONS)	BIRTHS PER 1000 POPULATION	DEATHS PER 1000 POPULATION	NATURAL INCREASE (ANNUAL %)	"DOUBLING TIME" IN YEARS AT CURRENT RATE	PROJECTED POPULATION TO 2025 (MILLIONS)	INFANT MORTALITY RATE[a]	TOTAL FERTILITY RATE[b]	PERCENT AGE <15/65+	LIFE EXPECTANCY AT BIRTH TOTAL/MALE/FEMALE (YEARS)	PERCENT URBAN	ADULT LITERACY 1990-95	HUMAN DEVELOPMENT INDEX (HDI), 1994	SECONDARY SCHOOL ENROLLMENT[c] (%) MALE/FEMALE	PER CAPITA GNP, 1994 (US$)
SOUTHERN EUROPE	**143**	**10**	**9**	**0.1**	**652**	**137**	**11**	**1.3**	**17/14**	**76/73/79**	**75**	**—**	**—**	**88/93**	**14 180**
Albania	3.3	23	6	1.7	41	4.6	33.2	2.8	33/ 6	72/70/76	37	72	0.655	84/72	360
Bosnia-Herzegovina	3.6	13	7	0.6	122	3.9	—	—	23/ 7	72/70/75	—	n.a.	—	—/—	—
Croatia	4.4	11	11	−0.0	—	4.2	10.2	1.5	20/12	71/66/75	54	97	0.760	80/86	2 530
Greece	10.5	10	9	0.1	1 386	10.0	8.3	1.3	18/13	77/75/80	72	95	0.923	100/98	7 710
Italy	57.3	9	10	−0.0	—	54.4	8.3	1.2	15/16	77/74/80	97	97	0.921	81/82	19 270
Macedonia	2.1	16	8	0.8	86	2.3	24.1	2.1	24/ 8	72/70/74	58	n.a.	0.748	53/55	790
Malta	0.4	13	7	0.6	120	0.4	9.1	1.9	22/11	77/75/79	89	84	0.887	91/84	7 970[e]
Portugal	9.9	11	10	0.1	866	10.0	7.9	1.4	18/14	75/71/78	48	85	0.890	63/74	9 370
San Marino	0.03	11	8	0.3	204	0.03	7.5	1.2	15/15	76/73/79	91	96	—	—/—	—
Slovenia	2.0	10	10	0.0	6 931	2.0	6.5	1.3	19/12	73/69/77	50	n.a.	0.886	88/90	7 140
Spain	39.3	9	9	0.1	1 155	34.6	7.2	1.2	17/15	77/73/81	64	95	0.934	107/120	13 280
Yugoslavia[d]	10.2	13	10	0.3	224	10.6	18.6	1.9	22/11	72/69/74	57	93	—	64/65	—
OCEANIA	**29**	**19**	**7**	**1.1**	**60**	**39**	**24**	**2.5**	**26/10**	**73/71/76**	**70**	**—**	**—**	**70/71**	**13 770**
Australia	18.3	14	7	0.8	92	23.1	5.8	1.8	21/12	78/75/81	85	99	0.931	83/86	17 980
Federated States of Micronesia	0.1	38	8	3.0	23	0.2	52	5.6	43/ 3	64/62/66	26	n.a.	—	—/—	1 890
Fiji	0.8	25	5	2.0	34	1.1	19	3.0	38/ 3	63/61/65	39	79	0.863	64/65	2 320
French Polynesia	0.2	26	5	2.1	34	0.4	13	3.1	36/ 3	70/68/72	57	n.a.	—	68/87	—
Guam	0.2	30	4	2.6	27	0.2	9.7	3.5	30/ 4	74/72/76	38	—	—	—/—	—
Marshall Islands	0.1	26	4	2.2	31	0.2	63	5.9	51/ 3	62/60/63	65	93	—	—/—	1 680
New Caledonia	0.2	26	6	2.0	34	0.3	8	3.0	33/ 5	72/70/75	70	n.a.	—	82/88	—
New Zealand	3.6	16	8	0.9	82	4.3	7.0	2.0	23/12	76/73/79	85	99	0.937	103/103	13 190
Palau	0.02	22	8	1.4	50	0.02	25	3.1	30/ 6	67/—/—	69	n.a.	—	—/—	—
Papua-New Guinea	4.3	34	10	2.3	30	7.5	63	4.7	42/ 2	56/56/57	15	72	0.525	15/10	1 160
Solomon Islands	0.4	39	5	3.4	20	0.8	28	5.7	47/ 3	70/68/73	13	60	0.556	21/13	800
Vanuatu	0.2	38	9	2.9	24	0.3	45	5.3	44/ 4	63/—/—	18	53	0.547	23/18	1 150
Western Samoa	0.2	31	8	2.3	30	0.3	21	4.8	41/ 4	65/—/—	21	97	0.684	—/—	970

(—) indicates data unavailable or inapplicable.
[a] Infant deaths per 1000 live births
[b] Average number of children born to a woman in her lifetime at current birth rate.
[c] Ratio of the total number enrolled in secondary school to the applicable age group (gross enrollment ratio).
[d] On 27 April 1992, Serbia and Montenegro formed a new state, the Federal Republic of Yugoslovia.
[e] 1993.

Countries and Regions of the World Statistical Data and Capital Cities

COUNTRIES AND REGIONS	AREA (000 KM²)	POPULATION 1996 (000 000)	CAPITAL CITY	COUNTRIES AND REGIONS	AREA (000 KM²)	POPULATION 1996 (000 000)	CAPITAL CITY
Afghanistan	647.5	21.5	Kabul	Dominican Republic	48.4	8.1	Santo Domingo
Albania	28.7	3.3	Tirana	Ecuador	283.6	11.7	Quito
Algeria	2 381.7	29.0	Algiers	Egypt	1 001.5	63.7	Cairo
American Samoa	0.2	0.05	Pago Pago	El Salvador	21.0	5.9	San Salvador
Andorra	0.5	0.06	Andorra-la-Vella	Equatorial Guinea	28.1	0.4	Malabo
Angola	1 246.7	11.5	Luanda	Eritrea	12.1	3.6	Asmara
Anguilla	0.155	0.007	Valley	Estonia	45.1	1.5	Tallinn
Antigua and Barbuda	0.44	0.1	St. John's	Ethiopia	1 221.9	57.2	Addis Ababa
Argentina	2 766.9	34.7	Buenos Aires	Falkland Islands	12.0	0.002	Stanley
Armenia	29.8	3.8	Yerevan	Fiji	18.3	0.8	Suva
Aruba	0.193	0.07	Oranjestad	Finland	337.0	5.1	Helsinki
Australia	7 686.9	18.3	Canberra	France	547.0	58.4	Paris
Austria	83.9	8.1	Vienna	French Guiana	91.0	0.1	Cayenne
Azerbaijan	86.6	7.6	Baku	French Polynesia	3.9	0.2	Papeete
Bahamas	13.9	0.3	Nassau	Gabon	267.7	1.2	Libreville
Bahrain	0.6	0.6	Manama	Gambia	11.3	1.2	Banjul
Bangladesh	144.0	119.8	Dhaka	Gaza	0.363	0.9	Gaza
Barbados	0.4	0.3	Bridgetown	Georgia	69.7	5.4	T̃bilisi
Belgium	30.5	10.2	Brussels	Germany	356.9	81.7	Berlin
Belize	22.9	0.2	Belmopan	Ghana	238.5	18.0	Accra
Benin	112.6	5.6	Porto Novo	Greece	131.9	10.5	Athens
Belarus	207.6	10.3	Minsk	Greenland	2 175.6	0.6	Nuuk
Bermuda	0.05	0.06	Hamilton	Grenada	0.3	0.1	St. George's
Bhutan	47.0	0.8	Thimphu	Guadaloupe	1.7	0.4	Basse-Terre
Bolivia	1 098.6	7.6	La Paz	Guam	0.5	0.2	Agaña
Bosnia-Herzegovina	51.1	3.6	Sarajevo	Guatemala	108.9	9.9	Guatemala
Botswana	600.4	1.5	Gaborone	Guinea	245.9	7.4	Conakry
Brazil	8 511.9	160.5	Brasilia	Guinea-Bissau	36.1	1.1	Bissau
Brunei Darussalam	5.8	0.3	Bandar Seri Begawan	Guyana	215.0	0.7	Georgetown
Bulgaria	110.9	8.4	Sofia	Haiti	27.6	7.3	Port-au-Prince
Burkina Faso	273.8	10.6	Ouagadougou	Honduras	111.9	5.6	Tegucigalpa
Burundi	27.8	5.9	Bujumbura	Hungary	93.0	10.2	Budapest
Cambodia	181.0	10.9	Phnom Penh	Iceland	103.0	0.3	Reykjavik
Cameroon	475.4	13.6	Yaoundé	India	3 287.6	949.6	New Delhi
Canada	9 970.6	29.6	Ottawa	Indonesia	1 919.4	201.4	Jakarta
Cape Verde	4.0	0.4	Praia	Iran	1 648.0	63.1	Tehran
Cayman Islands	0.3	0.03	George Town	Iraq	434.9	21.4	Baghdad
Central African Republic	623.0	3.3	Bangui	Ireland	70.3	3.6	Dublin
Chad	1 284.0	6.5	Ndjamena	Israel	20.8	5.8	Jerusalem
Chile	757.0	14.5	Santiago	Italy	301.2	57.3	Rome
China	9 597.0	1 217.6	Beijing	Jamaica	11.0	2.6	Kingston
Hong Kong	1.0	6.4	Victoria	Japan	377.8	125.8	Tokyo
Colombia	1 138.9	38.0	Bogotá	Jordan	91.9	4.2	Amman
Comoros	2.2	0.6	Moroni	Kazakhstan	2 717.3	16.5	Almaty
Congo	341.5	2.5	Brazzaville	Kenya	582.7	28.2	Nairobi
Congo (Dem. Rep.)	2 345.4	46.5	Kinshasha	Kiribati	0.7	0.07	Tarawa
Cook Islands	0.3	0.02	Avarua	Korea, North	120.5	23.9	Pyongyang
Costa Rica	51.1	3.6	San José	Korea, South	98.5	45.3	Seoul
Côte D'Ivoire	322.5	14.7	Yamoussoukro	Kuwait	17.8	1.8	Kuwait
Croatia	56.5	4.4	Zagreb	Kyrgyzstan	198.5	4.6	Bishbek
Cuba	110.8	11.0	Havana	Laos	236.8	5.0	Vientiane
Cyprus	9.3	0.7	Nicosia	Latvia	63.7	2.5	Riga
Czech Republic	78.7	10.3	Prague	Lebanon	10.4	3.8	Beirut
Denmark	43.1	5.2	Copenhagen	Lesotho	30.4	2.1	Maseru
Djibouti	22.0	0.6	Djibouti	Liberia	111.4	2.1	Monrovia
Dominica	0.8	0.1	Roseau	Libya	1 759.5	5.4	Jamahiriya

Countries and Regions of the World Statistical Data and Capital Cities

COUNTRIES AND REGIONS	AREA (000 KM²)	POPULATION 1996 (000 000)	CAPITAL CITY
Liechtenstein	0.2	0.03	Vaduz
Lithuania	65.2	3.7	Vilnius
Luxembourg	2.6	0.4	Luxembourg
Macau	0.016	0.4	Macau
Macedonia	25.3	2.1	Skopje
Madagascar	587.0	15.2	Antananarivo
Malawi	118.5	9.5	Lilongwe
Malaysia	329.8	20.6	Kuala Lumpur
Maldives	0.3	0.3	Malé
Mali	1 240.0	9.7	Bamako
Malta	0.3	0.4	Valletta
Marshall Islands	0.2	0.1	Majuro
Martinique	1.1	0.4	Fort-de-France
Mauritania	1 030.7	2.3	Nouakchott
Mauritius	1.9	1.1	Port Luis
Mayotte (Mahore)	0.4	0.1	Mamoutzou
Mexico	1 972.6	94.8	Mexico City
Micronesia, Federated States of	0.7	0.1	Kolonia
Moldova	33.7	4.3	Kishinev
Monaco	195 ha	0.03	Monaco-Ville
Mongolia	1 565.0	2.3	Ulan Bator
Montserrat	0.1	0.01	Plymouth
Morocco	446.3	27.6	Rabat
Mozambique	784.1	16.5	Maputo
Myanmar (Burma)	678.5	46.0	Rangoon
Namibia	824.3	1.6	Windhoek
Nepal	140.8	23.2	Kathmandu
Netherlands Antilles	0.8	0.2	Willemstad
Netherlands	37.3	15.5	The Hague
New Caledonia	18.6	0.2	Nouméa
New Zealand	268.7	3.6	Wellington
Nicaragua	129.5	4.6	Managua
Niger	1 266.7	9.5	Niamey
Nigeria	923.8	103.9	Lagos
Northern Marianas	0.5	0.04	Saipan
Norway	323.8	4.4	Oslo
Oman	212.5	2.3	Masqat
Pakistan	803.9	133.5	Islamabad
Palau	0.3	0.02	Koror
Panama	78.2	2.7	Panama City
Papua New Guinea	461.7	4.3	Port Moresby
Paraguay	406.8	5.0	Asunciön
Peru	1 285.2	24.0	Lima
Philippines	300.0	72.0	Manila
Poland	312.7	38.6	Warsaw
Portugal	92.1	9.9	Lisbon
Puerto Rico	9.1	3.8	San Juan
Qatar	11.0	0.7	Doha
Reunion	2.5	0.7	Saint-Denis
Romania	237.5	22.6	Bucharest
Russia	17 075.0	147.7	Moscow
Rwanda	26.3	6.9	Kigali
St. Kitts-Nevis	0.4	0.04	Basseterre
St. Lucia	0.6	0.1	Castries
St. Vincent and the Grenadines	0.3	0.1	Kingtown

COUNTRIES AND REGIONS	AREA (000 KM²)	POPULATION 1996 (000 000)	CAPITAL CITY
Saint Helena	0.41	0.006	Jamestown
Saint Pierre and Miquelon	0.24	0.006	Saint-Pierre
San Marino	0.06	0.03	San Marino
São Tomé and Principe	1.0	0.1	São Tomé
Saudi Arabia	2 149.7	19.4	Riyadh & Jeddah
Senegal	196.2	8.5	Dakar
Seychelles	0.5	0.1	Victoria
Sierra Leone	71.6	4.6	Freetown
Singapore	0.6	3.0	Singapore
Slovakia	48.8	5.4	Bratislava
Slovenia	20.3	2.0	Ljubljana
Solomon Islands	28.5	0.4	Honiara
Somalia	637.6	9.5	Mogadishu
South Africa	1 221.0	44.5	Pretoria
Spain	504.8	39.3	Madrid
Sri Lanka	65.6	18.4	Colombo
Sudan	2 505.8	28.9	Khartoum
Suriname	163.3	0.4	Paramaribo
Swaziland	17.4	1.0	Mbabane
Sweden	450.0	8.8	Stockholm
Switzerland	41.3	7.1	Berne
Syria	185.2	15.6	Damascus
Tajikistan	143.1	5.9	Dushanbe
Taiwan	36.0	21.4	Taipei
Tanzania	945.1	29.1	Dar-es-Salaam
Thailand	514.0	60.7	Bangkok
Togo	56.8	4.6	Lomé
Tonga	0.8	0.1	Nuku'alofa
Trinidad and Tobago	5.1	1.3	Port of Spain
Tunisia	163.6	9.2	Tunis
Turkey	780.6	63.9	Ankara
Turks and Caicos Islands	0.4	0.012	Cockburn Town
Turkmenistan	488.1	4.6	Ashkhabad
Uganda	236.0	22.0	Kampala
Ukraine	603.7	51.1	Kiev
United Arab Emirates	83.6	1.9	Abu Dhabi
United Kingdom	244.8	58.8	London
United States	9 372.6	265.2	Washington
Uruguay	176.2	3.2	Montevideo
Uzbekistan	447.4	23.2	Tashkent
Vanuatu	14.8	0.2	Port Vila
Vatican City	44 ha	0.001	Vatican City
Venezuela	912.0	22.3	Caracas
Vietnam	329.7	76.6	Hanoi
Virgin Islands (UK)	0.1	0.02	Road Town
Virgin Islands (US)	0.4	0.1	Charlotte Amalie
Wallis and Futuna	0.3	0.014	Mata-Utu
West Bank	0.59	1.7	Jericho
Western Sahara	252.1	0.2	La'youn
Western Samoa	2.8	0.2	Apia
Yemen	528.0	14.7	Sana
Yugoslavia	102.3	10.2	Belgrade
Zambia	752.6	9.2	Lusaka
Zimbabwe	390.6	11.5	Harare

*On 27 April, 1992, Serbia and Montenegro formed a new State, the Federal Republic of Yugoslavia.
NOTES: Please refer to page 219 for notes to this table.

Definitions

Mid-1996 Population: Estimates are based on a recent census or on official national data or on UN, US Census Bureau, or World Bank projections. The effects of refugee movements, large numbers of foreign workers, and population shifts due to contemporary political events are taken into account to the extent possible.

Birth and Death Rates: These rates are often referred to as "crude rates" since they do not take a population's age structure into account. Thus, crude death rates in more developed countries, with a relatively large proportion of older persons, are often higher than those in less developed countries.

Rate of Natural Increase (RNI): Birth rate minus the death rate, implying the annual rate of population growth without regard for migration. Expressed as a percentage.

Population "Doubling Time": The number of years until the population will double assuming a *constant* rate of natural increase (RNI). Based upon the *unrounded* RNI, this column provides an indication of potential growth associated with a given RNI. It is not intended to forecast the actual doubling of any population.

Population in 2025: Population projections are based on reasonable assumptions on the future course of fertility, mortality, and migration. Projections are based on official country projections, or on series issued by the UN, the US Bureau of the Census, World Bank, or PRB projections.

Infant Mortality Rate: The annual number of deaths of infants under age one year per 1000 live births. Rates shown with decimals are completely registered national statistics, while those without are estimates from sources cited above. Rates shown in italics are based upon less than 50 annual infant deaths and, as a result, are subject to considerable yearly variability.

Total Fertility Rate (TFR): The average number of children a woman will have assuming that current age-specific birth rates will remain constant throughout her childbearing years (usually considered to be ages 15-49).

Population Under Age 15/Age 65+: The percentage of the total population in those age groups, often considered the "dependent ages."

Note

This table lists all geopolitical entities with populations of 150 000 or more and all members of the UN. These include sovereign states, dependencies, overseas departments, and some territories whose status or boundaries may be undetermined or in dispute. *More developed countries*, following the UN classification, comprise all of Europe and North America, plus Australia, Japan, New Zealand, and the former USSR. All other regions are classified as *less developed*.

Sources: The Human Development Index was compiled by the United Nations Development Program, *Human Development Report 1996*, (New York: Oxford University Press, 1996); Adult Literacy data are from the United Nations Development Program, *Human Development Report 1996* (New York: Oxford University Press, 1996); all other data is from the *1996 World Population Data Sheet*, Population Reference Bureau, 1875 Connecticut Avenue NW, Suite 520, Washington, DC 20009.

Notes to Countries and Regions of the World Statistical Data

The table lists most of the geopolitical entities in the world, including all members of the UN, other sovereign states, dependencies, overseas departments, and territories whose status or boundaries may be in dispute.

Populations are estimates based on a recent census or on official national data or on UN, US Census Bureau, or World Bank projections and provided by the Population Reference Bureau in the *1996 World Population Data Sheet*. For some smaller places, estimates are earlier than 1996.

More statistical data on the principal countries of the world can be found on pages 213–217.

SOURCE: *1996 World Population Data Sheet*, Population Reference Bureau, 1875 Connecticut Avenue NW, Suite 520, Washington, DC 20009; http://www.prb.org/prb. *The Oxford Dictionary of the World*, David Munro, Oxford University Press, 1995.

OXFORD
UNIVERSITY PRESS

70 Wynford Drive Don Mills Ontario M3C 1J9
www.oup.can

Oxford New York
Athens Auckland Bangkok Bogotá
Buenos Aires Calcutta Cape Town Chennai
Dar es Salaam Delhi Florence Hong Kong
Istanbul Karachi Kuala Lumpur Madrid
Melbourne Mexico City Mumbai Nairobi
Paris São Paulo Singapore Taipei Tokyo
Toronto Warsaw

and associated companies in

Berlin Ibadan

OXFORD is a trade mark of Oxford University Press

Copyright © Oxford University Press (Canada) 1998. All rights reserved.
No part of this book may be reproduced in any form without written permission of the publisher. Photocopying or reproducing mechanically in any
other way parts of this book without the written permission of the publisher
is an infringement of the copyright law.

© Maps copyright Oxford University Press.

This book is printed on permanent (acid-free) paper ∞

Canadian Cataloguing in Publication Data

Oxford University Press (Canada)
  Canadian Oxford school atlas

7ᵗʰ ed.
ISBN 0-19-541309-1

1. Atlases, Canadian. 2. Canada—Maps. I. Stanford, Quentin H.
II. Title.

G1021.087 1998   912   C98-930035-8

Canadian Cataloguing in Publication Data

Oxford University Press (Canada)
Canadian Oxford world atlas

4th ed.
Previous eds. Published under title: New Canadian Oxford atlas.
ISBN 0-19-541319-9 (bound)   ISBN 0-19-541320-2 (pbk.)

1. Atlases, Canadian. I. Stanford, Quentin H. II. Title. III: Title: New
Canadian Oxford atlas.

G1021.088 1998   912   C98-930092-7

First school edition 1957
Second school edition 1963
Third school edition 1972
Fourth school edition 1977
Fifth school edition 1985
Sixth school edition 1992
Seventh school edition 1998

Cover Design: Brett Miller

Printed and bound in Canada by Friesens

5 6 7 8—03 02 01 00 99

Acknowledgements

The Publisher would like to thank the following for their assistance in the
preparation of this atlas:

James, C. Johnston, Canadian Heritage, Parks Canada; Deborah Russ, Cana-
dian Association of Petroleum Producers; Laurie Morrison, Natural Resources
Canada; Mary-Anne Killeen, National Transportation Agency; Fisheries and
Oceans, Ottawa; Kathleen O'Brien, Geomatics Canada; Bertha Bissonnette,
Energy, Mines and Resources Canada; The City of Calgary Planning and
Building Department; Sharon Budd, Canadian Heritage; Barbara Ballantyne,
Forestry Canada; Terry Huff, Tgit Geomatics Ltd.; Allen Andrew, The City of
Winnipeg Land and Development Services Department; The Canadian Wheat
Board; The St. Lawrence Seaway Authority; Canadian Forest Service, Natural
Resources Canada; Statistics Canada; Eugene Peters, Public Works Canada;
Greenpeace; Hardlines; Gary Hinks; and the Department of Public Information,
United Nations.

Credits

Front cover Canadian Oxford School Atlas, 7th ed.: Lonny Kalfus/Tony Stone
Images
Front cover Canadian Oxford World Atlas, 4th ed.: Ken Davies/Masterfile

Pages 7, 36, 45 and 55. LANDSAT data received by the Canada Centre for
Remote Sensing. Provided courtesy of RADARSAT International; pages 62 and
78 NRSC Ltd./Science Photo Library; page 90 CNES, 1990 Distribution Spot
Image/Science Photo Library; page 114 Dr. Jean Lorre/Science Photo Library;
page 127 Photo Science Library.

Canadian Government statistics and maps are reproduced/adapted with permission of the Minister of Industry, Science, and Technology 1997. Information
provided through the cooperation of Statistics Canada.

Maps pages 10-21 and 26-31 *The National Atlas of Canada, 5th edition*,
Energy, Mines and Resources Canada; page 17 *Human Activity and the Envi-
ronment, 1994*, Statistics Canada; *State of the Environment Report for Canada*,
Environment Canada, 1996; *Conserving Canada's Natural Legacy*, Environ-
ment Canada-CD ROM 1996; page 19 *Canadian Grains Industry, Statistical
Handbook, 1995*, Canadian Grains Council; page 20 *World Conservation
Strategy*, International Union for Conservation of Nature and Natural Resources
(IUCN), 1980; Parks Canada; *Electric Power Statistics, Generating Stations,
1994*, Statistics Canada; *Electric Power in Canada, 1993*, Natural Resources,
Canada, 1994; pages 22-23 National Energy Board; *Oil and Gas Map*, Bank of
Montreal; Natural Resources Canada; Canadian Association of Petroleum Pro-
ducers; the Coal Association of Canada; page 24 *Manufacturing Industries of
Canada: National and Provincial Areas, 1993*, Statistics Canada; page 25
Imports by Country, 1995, Statistics Canada; *Exports by Country*, 1995, Statis-
tics Canada; pages 26-28 *Census by Canada*, 1991 and 1996.